MODIFICATION OF TREATIES BY SUBSEQUENT PRACTICE

Modification of Treaties by Subsequent Practice

IRINA BUGA

OXFORD
UNIVERSITY PRESS

OXFORD
UNIVERSITY PRESS

Great Clarendon Street, Oxford, OX2 6DP,
United Kingdom

Oxford University Press is a department of the University of Oxford. It furthers the University's objective of excellence in research, scholarship, and education by publishing worldwide. Oxford is a registered trade mark of Oxford University Press in the UK and in certain other countries

First Edition published in 2018

Impression: 1

Published in the United States of America by Oxford University Press
198 Madison Avenue, New York, NY 10016, United States of America

British Library Cataloguing in Publication Data
Data available

Library of Congress Control Number: 2017958587

ISBN 978–0–19–878782–2

Printed and bound by
CPI Group (UK) Ltd, Croydon, CR0 4YY

To my parents, grandparents, and Mike

Foreword

If the States Parties to a treaty issue a statement of their common understanding of a treaty provision, how can we know if they are interpreting the treaty or amending it? If they make no statement, but one of them does something in relation to the subject matter of the treaty and the other makes no objection or other comment, does that practice evidence a common understanding of the treaty? If the treaty is amended, is it the same treaty as it was before, or a new treaty which came into existence when the original was amended? What if the treaty is one that, like bilateral investment treaties, appears to create rights for individuals? What if the practice is not that of States Parties but of other States, establishing new rules of customary international law, or consisting of resolutions adopted by majority votes in organs of international organizations? These are the kinds of question that tax even the most astute analytical lawyers. Indeed, some of the questions are more like a Buddhist *koan* than a soluble legal problem. And yet these are questions that are faced day in and day out by practising international lawyers.

Most legal monographs would map out the field of established treaty law and work cautiously towards problems such as these. But this masterly study starts with the problems and tackles them head on. It does so against the background of the work of the International Law Commission on subsequent agreements and subsequent practice in relation to the interpretation of treaties. Combining precise analysis with robust digging into the mass of State practice and international case law, Dr Buga's text makes a major contribution to the analysis of this most subtle and most important set of questions. It both clarifies the problems and, brimming with ideas, stimulates thought.

Sophisticated and immensely accomplished, her study discerns differences in the approaches that are adopted to these problems in different fields, such as international human rights and WTO law. Focusing on the value of interpretation and modification as sources of stability in international relations, which secure the adaptation and organic development of international law, she has produced a lucid and principled framework for handling these crucial questions.

Vaughan Lowe
London, 2017

Acknowledgments

There are so many people to whom I am grateful and indebted for their support, guidance, and friendship throughout the writing of this book. Though it seems impossible to give them the credit they deserve by means of a few, short sentences, I will try nevertheless.

I must begin by thanking my PhD supervisors, Professor Alfred Soons and Professor Alex Oude Elferink, without whom the initial project that led to this book would not have come to fruition. They answered my ceaseless questions with patience and insight, and provided guidance and sparring sessions throughout the endeavour. I am likewise grateful to the members of the Doctoral Thesis Committee, Professor Cedric Ryngaert, Professor Liesbeth Lijnzaad, Professor Ige Dekker, Professor André Nollkaemper, and Dr. Catherine Brölmann.

My deep appreciation goes to the colleagues and legal scholars whose advice and feedback have helped steer this project forward and shaped my ideas, particularly Professor Georg Nolte, whose work on the topic in the context of the International Law Commission has been a source of inspiration and whose advice on my earlier work was highly valuable; Seline Trevisanut and Ingo Venzke, for dealing with my many queries; my former colleagues at the Netherlands Institute for the Law of the Sea, for their enthusiasm and interest; and the Public International Law Department of Utrecht University in general, for the truly enriching experience. Moreover, my gratitude goes out to the members of the Royal Netherlands Society for International Law (KNVIR) for their appreciation of my research with the François Research Prize, and the Netherlands Organization for Scientific Research (NWO) for their generous funding of my doctoral work. I would also like to kindly thank my OUP editors and anonymous reviewers.

The years spent in Utrecht and Oxford, at the International Court of Justice in The Hague, and practicing arbitration in Paris and Amsterdam, have all contributed in important ways to my personal development and the gradual development of this book. I am generally indebted to the inspiring people who have expanded my knowledge and understanding of international law over these years. To name only a few, I would like to express my deep gratitude to Professor Vaughan Lowe, for his supervision and invaluable insight into international dispute settlement during my studies at the University of Oxford, to Mr. Philippe Couvreur, for his words of wisdom and motivation during my time at the International Court of Justice, and to Professor Leonard Besselink and Professor Ewoud Hondius, for their guidance and encouragement during the Legal Research programme. I would also like to thank Professor Kees Roelofsen, whose International Law course during my undergraduate studies first introduced me to this fascinating field.

Now in Amsterdam, I must thank my brilliant colleagues at De Brauw Blackstone Westbroek, who constantly challenge me to sharpen my thinking as well as my writing. In particular, I am grateful to the talented international arbitration group and to Marc Ynzonides for all the encouragement, and to 'Brauwerij XXI' for their support and poking fun when I needed it.

My friends have been amazing during this entire process. Special thanks go out to, in no particular order, Stef, Paulette, Masha, Inge, Romi, Nate, Philip, Sandi, Anna, Sibel, Gala, Andrea, Selma, Mistale, Luke, Marli, Erik, Charlotte, Andrew, Sebastiaan, Micky, Hein-Jan, Eveline, Linda, and many others, for providing much-needed support – and distraction.

As for my parents, Mihaela and Iulian, two of the most amazing people I know, I cannot begin to thank them for their infinite support and pep talks, and for involuntarily becoming 'experts' on subsequent practice over the years. This work is dedicated to them, to my grandmother Maria, for always believing in me and sharing her wisdom and anecdotes, and to my grandparents Constantin, Ernestina, and Jacques, who I wish could still be here today.

Last but certainly not least, I cannot imagine having written this book without the love, support, and unwavering patience of Mike Blommestijn.

Amsterdam, December 2017

Table of Contents

List of Cases

EUROPEAN COURT OF HUMAN RIGHTS

EUROPEAN COURT OF JUSTICE

INTER-AMERICAN COURT OF HUMAN RIGHTS

INTERNATIONAL ARBITRAL TRIBUNALS (GENERAL)

INTERNATIONAL CENTRE FOR THE SETTLEMENT OF INVESTMENT DISPUTES

INTERNATIONAL COURT OF JUSTICE

INTERNATIONAL CRIMINAL TRIBUNAL FOR THE FORMER YUGOSLAVIA

INTERNATIONAL CRIMINAL TRIBUNAL FOR RWANDA

INTERNATIONAL TRIBUNAL FOR THE LAW OF THE SEA

IRAN-UNITED STATES CLAIMS TRIBUNAL

NATIONAL COURTS

Canada

Chile

France

Germany

PERMANENT COURT OF INTERNATIONAL JUSTICE

WORLD TRADE ORGANIZATION

List of Primary Legal Sources

INTERNATIONAL TREATIES

EUROPEAN COUNCIL

INSTITUT DE DROIT INTERNATIONAL

INTERNATIONAL COMMITTEE OF THE RED CROSS

INTERNATIONAL INSTITUTE FOR THE UNIFICATION OF PRIVATE LAW

International Law Commission

International Maritime Organization

International Seabed Authority

Meeting of States Parties to the Law of the Sea Convention

List of Abbreviations

AB	Appellate Body
Add	Addendum
ACHR	American Convention on Human Rights
AIDI	*Annuaire de l'Institut de Droit International*
AJIL	American Journal of International Law
Am Pol Sci Rev	American Political Science Review
Am U Intl L Rev	American University International Law Review
Ankara L Rev	Ankara Law Review
Ann Droit Mar Aér	*Annuaire de Droit Maritime et Aérien*
ARIEL	Austrian Review of International and European Law
ATS	Antarctic Treaty System
ASIL Proc	Proceedings of the Annual Meetings of the American Society of International Law
Aust YBIL	Australian Yearbook of International Law
BC Intl & Comp L Rev	Boston College International and Comparative Law Review
Berkeley JIL	Berkeley Journal of International Law
BFSP	British and Foreign State Papers
BIT	Bilateral investment treaty
BSIS J Intl Stud	BSIS Journal of International Studies
BU Intl LJ	Boston University International Law Journal
BVerfGE	Bundesverfassungsgericht
BWC	Biological Weapons Convention
BYBIL	British Yearbook of International Law
CAB	American Civil Aeronautics Board
Can Council Intl L Proc	Canadian Council on International Law: Proceedings
CARU	Administrative Commission of the River Uruguay
CAT	Committee against Torture
CBD	Convention on Biological Diversity
CBLJ	Canadian Business Law Journal
CERD	International Convention on the Elimination of All Forms of Racial Discrimination
CESCR	Committee on Economic, Social and Cultural Rights
CETS	Council of Europe Treaty Series
Chi J Intl L	Chicago Journal of International Law
Chinese JIL	Chinese Journal of International Law
CITES	Convention on International Trade in Endangered Species of Wild Fauna and Flora
CJICL	Cambridge Journal of International and Comparative Law
CLCS	Commission on the Limits of the Continental Shelf
CLR	California Law Review
CMLR	Common Market Law Review
CMS	Convention on Migratory Species of Wild Animals
Colum J Transnat'l L	Columbia Journal of Transnational Law

Conn JIL	Connecticut Journal of International Law
COP	Conference of the Parties
Cornell ILJ	Cornell International Law Journal
CTS	Consolidated Treaty Series
CUP	Cambridge University Press
CYBIR	Cyprus Yearbook of International Relations
Denver JIL & Policy	Denver Journal of International Law and Policy
DIIS	Danish Institute for International Studies
Doc	Document
DOALOS	Division for Ocean Affairs and the Law of the Sea
DSB	Dispute Settlement Body
DSU	Dispute Settlement Understanding
ECHR	European Convention on Human Rights
ECJ	European Court of Justice
ECOSOC	Economic and Social Council
ECR	European Court Reports
ECtHR	European Court of Human Rights
ECU	European Currency Unit
EEC	European Economic Community
EEZ	Exclusive economic zone
EJIL	European Journal of International Law
EJLS	European Journal of Legal Studies
ELR	European Law Review
Ethics & Intl Aff	Ethics and International Affairs
ETS	European Treaty Series
EU	European Union
EWCA Civ	England and Wales Court of Appeal (Civil Division) Decisions
EWHC Comm	England and Wales High Court (Commercial Court) Decisions
F Supp	(United States) Federal Supplement
FAO	Food and Agriculture Organization of the United Nations
Fordham ILJ	Fordham International Law Journal
Fordham L Rev	Fordham Law Review
FSA	Agreement for the Implementation of the Provisions of the United Nations Convention on the Law of the Sea of 10 December 1982 relating to the Conservation and Management of Straddling Fish Stocks and Highly Migratory Fish Stocks
FTC	Free Trade Commission
Ga J Intl & Comp L	Georgia Journal of International and Comparative Law
GAOR	General Assembly Official Records
GATS	General Agreement on Trade in Services
GATT	General Agreement on Tariffs and Trade
GC	Grand Chamber (ECtHR)
Geo Immigr LJ	Georgetown Immigration Law Journal
Geo LJ	Georgetown Law Journal
Geo Wash L Rev	George Washington Law Review
GoJIL	Göttingen Journal of International Law
GWILR	George Washington International Law Review
GYBIL	German Yearbook of International Law
Hague Yb IL	Hague Yearbook of International Law

Harv ILJ	Harvard International Law Journal
Harv L Rev	Harvard Law Review
HR L Rev	Human Rights Law Review
HRC	(United Nations) Human Rights Committee
HRILD	Human Rights and International Legal Discourse
IACtHR	Inter-American Court of Human Rights
IATA	International Air Transport Association
IBRU	International Boundary Research Unit
ICC	International Criminal Court
ICCPR	International Covenant on Civil and Political Rights
ICESCR	International Covenant on Economic, Social and Cultural Rights
ICJ	International Court of Justice
ICJ Pleadings	International Court of Justice—Pleadings, Oral Arguments, Documents
ICJ Reports	International Court of Justice—Reports of Judgments, Advisory Opinions and Orders
ICLQ	International and Comparative Law Quarterly
ICL Rev	International Community Law Review
ICRC	International Committee of the Red Cross
ICRW	International Convention for the Regulation of Whaling
ICSID	International Centre for Settlement of Investment Disputes
ICSID Rev For Inv LJ	ICSID Review-Foreign Investment Law Journal
ICTR	International Criminal Tribunal for Rwanda
ICTY	International Criminal Tribunal for the Former Yugoslavia
IFRI	Institut Français des Relations Internationales
IJIL	Indian Journal of International Law
IJMCL	International Journal of Marine and Coastal Law
ILA	International Law Association
ILC	International Law Commission
ILDC	International Law in Domestic Courts
ILM	International Legal Materials
ILR	International Law Reports
ILO	International Labour Organization
ILSA JIL	International Law Students Association Journal of International Law
ILT	International Legal Theory
IMF	International Monetary Fund
IMO	International Maritime Organization
INMARSAT	International Maritime Satellite Organization
INTELSAT	International Telecommunications Satellite Organization
Intl L Assn Rep Conf	International Law Association Report of Conferences
Iran-US CTR	Iran-United States of America Claims Tribunal Reports
IRRC	International Review of the Red Cross
ISA	International Seabed Authority
Isr L Rev	Israeli Law Review
Isr Yb HR	Israel Yearbook on Human Rights
ITLOS	International Tribunal for the Law of the Sea
ITO	International Trade Organization
IWC	International Whaling Commission

J Air L & Comm	Journal of Air Law and Commerce
J Envtl L	Journal of Environmental Law
J Intl Econ L	Journal of International Economic Law
J Space L	Journal of Space Law
JCSL	Journal of Conflict and Security Law
JWIT	The Journal of World Investment and Trade
JWT	Journal of World Trade
JWTL	Journal of World Trade Law
JYBIL	Japanese Yearbook of International Law
KB	*Koninklijk Besluit* (Royal Decree)
L & Pol Intl Bus	Law and Policy in International Business
LGDJ	*Librairie générale de droit et de jurisprudence*
LIEI	Legal Issues of European Integration
LJIL	Leiden Journal of International Law
LNTS	League of Nations Treaty Series
LPICT	The Law and Practice of International Courts and Tribunals
LOSC	United Nations Convention on the Law of the Sea
Mar Policy	Marine Policy
Max Plack UNYB	Max Planck United Nations Yearbook
MEA	Multilateral environmental agreement
Mich L Rev	Michigan Law Review
MJIL	Michigan Journal of International Law
MOP	Meeting of the Parties
MoU	Memorandum of Understanding
MPEPIL	Max Planck Encyclopedia of Public International Law
NAFTA	North American Free Trade Agreement
NATO	North Atlantic Treaty Organization
NC JIL & Comm Reg	North Carolina Journal of International Law and Commercial Regulation
NGO	Non-governmental organization
NILR	Netherlands International Law Review
NJIL	Nordic Journal of International Law
Notre Dame L Rev	Notre Dame Law Review
NTIR	*Nederlands Tijdschrift voor Internationaal Recht*
NYBIL	Netherlands Yearbook of International Law
NYU Ann Surv Am L	NYU Annual Survey of American Law
NYU J Intl L & Pol	New York University Journal of International Law and Politics
ODILA	Ocean Development and International Law—The Journal of Marine Affairs
OECD	Organization for Economic Co-operation and Development
OJ	Official Journal of the European Union
OSCE	Organization for Security and Co-operation in Europe
OUP	Oxford University Press
ÖzöR	*Österreichische Zeitschrift für öffentliches Recht*
PCIJ	Permanent Court of International Justice
PCIJ Series A, B & A/B	Permanent Court of International Justice—Reports of Judgments, Advisory Opinions and Orders
PPA	Protocol of Provisional Application
QIL	Questions of International Law

RBDI	*Revue Belge de Droit International*
RC	*Recueil des cours de l'Académie de droit international* (Collected Courses, Hague Academy of International Law)
RECIEL	Review of European Community and International Environmental Law
Res	Resolution
Rev Intl Théorie Droit	*Revue international de la théorie du droit*
Revue Roumaine	*Revue roumaine des sciences sociales*
RGDIP	*Revue générale de droit international public*
RHDI	*Revue hellénique de droit international*
RIDA	*Revue internationale des droits de l'antiquité*
RFMO	Regional fisheries management organization
RIAA	(United Nations) Reports of International Arbitral Awards
RICR	*Revue Internationale de Croix-Rouge*
S Afr LJ	South African Law Journal
San Diego L Rev	San Diego Law Review
SCR	Supreme Court Reports
Sess	Session
SFDI	*Société française pour le droit international*
Sing JICL	Singapore Journal of International and Comparative Law
SRFC	Sub-Regional Fisheries Commission
SPLOS	Meeting of States Parties to the UN Law of the Sea Convention
Stan J Intl L	Stanford Journal of International Law
Stat	(United States) Statutes at Large
Sup Ct Rev	The Supreme Court Review
Supp	Supplement
Syd L Rev	Sydney Law Review
TGS	Transactions of the Grotius Society
TIL	The International Lawyer
TRIPS Agreement	Agreement on Trade-Related Aspects of Intellectual Property Rights
Tul L Rev	Tulane Law Review
U Chi L Rev	University of Chicago Law Review
U Pa J Const L	University of Pennsylvania Journal of Constitutional Law
UCLA L Rev	UCLA Law Review
UDHR	Universal Declaration of Human Rights
UN	United Nations
UNCHR	United Nations Commission on Human Rights
UNCIO	United Nations Conference on International Organization
UNCLOS I	First United Nations Conference on the Law of the Sea, 1958
UNCLOS II	Second United Nations Conference on the Law of the Sea, 1960
UNCLOS III	Third United Nations Conference on the Law of the Sea, 1973–82
UNEP	United Nations Environment Programme
UNESCO	United Nations Educational, Scientific and Cultural Organization
UNFCCC	United Nations Framework Convention on Climate Change
UNGA	United Nations General Assembly
UNSC	United Nations Security Council
UNTS	United Nations Treaty Series
UP	University Press

Utrecht J Intl & Eur L	Utrecht Journal of International and European Law
Vand JIL	Vanderbilt Journal of International Law
Vand J Transn'l L	Vanderbilt Journal of Transnational Law
VCDR	Vienna Convention on Diplomatic Relations
VCLT	Vienna Convention on the Law of Treaties
VCLTIO	Vienna Convention on the Law of Treaties between States and International Organizations and between International Organizations
VJIL	Virginia Journal of International Law
WHA	World Health Assembly
WHO	World Health Organization
Wm & Mary L Rev	William and Mary Law Review
WTO	World Trade Organization
WTO Agreement	Marrakesh Agreement Establishing the World Trade Organization
Yale LJ	Yale Law Journal
Yale JIL	Yale Journal of International Law
Yale HR & Dev LJ	Yale Human Rights and Development Law Journal
Yale LJ	Yale Law Journal
Yale Stud W Pub Ord	Yale Studies in World Public Order
YBILC	Yearbook of the International Law Commission
ZaöRV	*Zeitschrift für ausländisches öffentliches Recht und Völkerrecht*

1
Introduction

> [T]oday's rule reflects in part yesterday's deviance; and (...) the cloth of obligation is partly cut from the pattern of non-conformity.
>
> Sir Elihu Lauterpacht[1]

1.1 Background

International law has an intrinsically living character—it constantly adapts to changes in the international community. Treaties, the principal tool for regulating inter-State relations, undergo transformation and modernization to reflect those developments. Thus, treaties are more than just 'dry parchments'.[2] At their inception, they merely photograph a momentary state of normative relations in flux[3]—'an approximate replica of a living practice, like a picture of a living person'[4]—but, over time, take on a life of their own, embodying a continuous process.[5]

One crucial way in which a treaty evolves is through its application in practice: 'subsequent practice' is a well-established tool for treaty interpretation, a guide to understanding the will of the parties.[6] While its initial aim is to shed light on what the parties originally intended,[7] subsequent practice can develop away from

[1] E Lauterpacht, 'The Development of the Law of International Organization by the Decisions of International Tribunals' (1976-IV) 152 RC 377, 389.

[2] ILC, *Report of the International Law Commission on the work of its 60th session*, UN Doc A/63/10 (2008) Annex A, 'Treaties over Time in Particular: Subsequent Agreement and Practice' (Mr Georg Nolte) 365 [Nolte, Annex A] para 1.

[3] See RR Baxter, 'Multilateral Treaties as Evidence of Customary International Law' (1965–66) 41 BYBIL 275, 299.

[4] K Wolfke, 'Treaties and Custom: Aspects of Interrelation' in J Klabbers and R Lefeber (eds), *Essays on the Law of Treaties: A Collection of Essays in Honour of Bert Vierdag* (Martinus Nijhoff, 1998) 31, 35.

[5] See eg *Reservations to the Convention on the Prevention and Punishment of the Crime of Genocide*, Advisory Opinion of 28 May 1951, Dissenting Opinion of Judge Alvarez, ICJ Reports 49, 53 ('[treaties] can be compared to ships which leave the yards in which they have been built, and sail away independently').

[6] See eg J-P Cot, 'La conduite subséquente des parties à un traité' (1966) 70 RGDIP 632, 663. See also *Husserl v Swiss Air Transport*, 351 F Supp 702, 707 (SDNY 1972) Court of Appeals, Second Circuit.

[7] See eg AD McNair, *The Law of Treaties* (Clarendon Press, 1961) 424, referring to this phenomenon as 'practical construction'. See further Section 2.1, n 12.

that original intention,[8] evidencing the parties' contemporary understanding of the treaty.[9]

In fact, subsequent practice may even diverge from treaty provisions to such an extent that it can no longer be said to constitute an act of treaty interpretation or application,[10] but rather one of *modification*.[11] Such practice can also give rise to new rules of customary international law, which in turn may impact pre-existing treaty provisions.[12]

Determining when the 'switch' from treaty interpretation to treaty modification occurs, however, is itself an act of interpretation. It poses difficulty to legal scholars and dispute settlement bodies alike, especially in light of the silence of the 1969 Vienna Convention on the Law of Treaties (VCLT)[13] on this point, and impacts States' expectations as to their treaty obligations. The difficult exercise of distinguishing between interpretation and modification, and of identifying the operation and potential effects of treaty modifications by subsequent practice, forms the subject of this book.

To stay relevant, treaty provisions must keep pace with new policies, technological developments, changing economic and social interests, the proliferation of international institutions and actors, and evolving moral conceptions. They must likewise allow for the possibility of redressing shortcomings and ineffective compromises by

[8] M Akehurst, *A Modern Introduction to International Law* (6th edn, Harper Collins Academic, 1987) 5. See also FG Jacobs, 'Varieties of Approach to Treaty Interpretation: With Special Reference to the Draft Convention on the Law of Treaties Before the Vienna Diplomatic Conference' (1969) 18 ICLQ 318, 329.

[9] L Crema, 'Subsequent Agreements and Subsequent Practice Within and Outside the Vienna Convention' in G Nolte (ed), *Treaties and Subsequent Practice* (OUP, 2013) 13, 23; J Arato, 'Treaty Interpretation and Constitutional Transformation: Informal Change in International Organizations' (2013) 38 Yale JIL 289, 307. See further Section 2.5.3.

[10] Interpretation could be described as the process of determining the meaning of the text, while application entails determining the consequences that follow from that meaning in a given case. See RK Gardiner, *Treaty Interpretation* (OUP, 2008) 27–8. cf McNair, *Law of Treaties*, 365, fn 1. The act of application of a treaty always presupposes its interpretation. See G Distefano, 'La pratique subséquente des États parties à un traité' (1994) 40 AFDI 41. See also Harvard Research in International Law, 'Draft Convention on the Law of Treaties' (1935) 29 AJIL Supp 653 [1935 Harvard Draft Convention] 938; MK Yasseen, 'L'interprétation des traités d'après la Convention de Vienne sur le droit des traités' (1976-III) 151 RC 1, 47; P Sands and J Commission, 'Treaty, Custom and Time: Interpretation/Application?' in M Fitzmaurice, O Elias, and P Merkouris (eds), *Treaty Interpretation and the Vienna Convention on the Law of Treaties: 30 Years On* (Martinus Nijhoff, 2010) 39, 40. The debate on the nature and interrelation of the notions of interpretation and application goes beyond the scope of the present book. See further Section 2.3.4.

[11] In fact, it has been argued that 'l'application elle-même des traités n'est (...) qu'une révision continue'—G Scelle, *Théorie juridique de la révision des traités* (Librairie du Recueil Sirey, 1936) 11. See further I Buga, 'Subsequent Practice and Treaty Modification' in MJ Bowman and D Kritsiotis (eds), *Conceptual and Contextual Perspectives on the Modern Law of Treaties* (CUP, forthcoming).

[12] This touches upon the complex interaction between treaties and customary law. See eg ILC, *Report of the International Law Commission on the work of its 63rd session*, UN Doc A/66/10 (2011) Annex A, 'Formation and evidence of customary international law' (Mr Michael Wood) 302 [Wood, Annex A] paras 7–9; ILC, 'Formation and evidence of customary international law—Note by Michael Wood, Special Rapporteur', UN Doc A/CN.4/653 (2012) para 21. See further Ch 4.

[13] 1155 UNTS 331.

the drafters,[14] as well as intended ambiguities.[15] At the same time, States often have (highly) divergent interests, making it challenging to reach agreement on specific rules[16] and (further) politicizing the amendment process.[17] Such difficulties can be observed in a wide range of contexts, from the stalemates in trade negotiations encountered in the Doha Round at the World Trade Organization (WTO),[18] impeding further amendments to WTO obligations, to the non-use of formal amendment procedures under the 1982 UN Law of the Sea Convention (LOSC),[19] with States resorting to other mechanisms to bring about treaty change.[20] The same fundamental problem applies in the context of the Charter of the United Nations.[21] Crucially, formal amendment procedures, particularly in large multilateral treaty

[14] See J Brunnée, 'Treaty Amendments' in DB Hollis (ed), *The Oxford Guide to Treaties* (OUP, 2012) 347 ('Some issues may have been too difficult to settle in the original negotiations and may become amenable to agreement only once parties have begun to interact under the treaty's auspices. Other issues may be unforeseen by the original negotiators, or may arise due to changes in other areas of international law. In yet other circumstances the underlying issue, or the parties' understanding of the issue (...) may change, sometimes rapidly so.'). See also eg S Rosenne, *Breach of Treaty* (Grotius Publications, 1985) 121.

[15] See G Gottlieb, 'The Interpretation of Treaties by Tribunals' (1969) 63 ASIL Proc 122, 130 ('Often, parties to a treaty who are unable to agree on a specific provision adopt vague language, thus in effect postponing agreement and delegating to the interpreters the responsibility for reaching an acceptable solution.'). See also *Autopista Concesionada de Venezuela, CA v Bolivarian Republic of Venezuela*, ICSID Case No ARB/00/5, Decision on Jurisdiction, 27 September 2001, para 97 ('The drafters of the Convention deliberately chose not to define the terms "legal dispute", "investment", "nationality" and "foreign control" (...) [but] preferred giving the parties the greatest latitude to define these terms themselves'); *Mihaly International Corp v Sri Lanka*, ICSID Case No ARB/00/2, Award, 15 March 2002, para 33 ('the definition [of investment] was left to be worked out in the subsequent practice of the States, thereby preserving its integrity and flexibility and allowing for future progressive development of international law on the topic of investment'). Note also the relation between evolutionary interpretation and subsequent practice, discussed in Section 2.5.3.

[16] See eg C McLachlan, 'The Evolution of Treaty Obligations in International Law' in G Nolte (ed), *Treaties and Subsequent Practice* (OUP, 2013) 69, 70–1.

[17] See J Kammerhofer, *Uncertainty in International Law: A Kelsenian Perspective* (Routledge, 2011) 132; J-M Sorel and V Boré Eveno, 'Article 31 (1969)' in O Corten and P Klein (eds), *The Vienna Convention on the Law of Treaties: A Commentary*, vol I (OUP, 2011) 804, 807. cf ILC, 'Third Report on the Law of Treaties, by Sir Humphrey Waldock, Special Rapporteur' (1964) II YBILC 5 [Waldock, Third Report on the Law of Treaties] 48 para 3 ('the amendment and revision of treaties is still essentially a political question'); McNair, *Law of Treaties*, 534 ('treaty revision is a matter for politics and diplomacy'); S Sur, *L'interprétation en droit international public* (LGDJ, 1974) 12; R Higgins, *Problems and Process: International Law and How We Use It* (Clarendon Press, 1994) 5.

[18] For recent developments in the context of the Doha Round, see <www.wto.org/english/tratop_e/dda_e/dda_e.htm> accessed 22 June 2016, including the so-called 'Nairobi Package' concluded in December 2015, which may have brought the Doha Round to an end. See eg S Donnan, 'World Trade Organisation Moves on from Stalled Doha Round', *Financial Times* (19 December 2015).

[19] 1833 UNTS 3.

[20] See further I Buga, 'Between Stability and Change in the Law of the Sea Convention: Subsequent Practice, Treaty Modification and Regime Interaction' in DR Rothwell and others (eds), *The Oxford Handbook on the Law of the Sea* (OUP, 2015) 46. See also OR Young, 'Commentary on Shirley V Scott "The LOSC Convention as a Constitutional Regime for the Oceans"' in AG Oude Elferink (ed), *Stability and Change in the Law of the Sea: The Role of the LOS Convention* (Martinus Nijhoff, 2005) 39, 44; DR Rothwell, 'The Impact of State Practice on the Jurisdictional Framework Contained in the LOS Convention: A Commentary' in AG Oude Elferink (ed), *Stability and Change in the Law of the Sea: The Role of the LOS Convention* (Martinus Nijhoff, 2005) 145, 149; Y Tanaka, *The International Law of the Sea* (CUP, 2012) 33.

[21] 59 Stat 1031. See eg H Kelsen, *The Law of the United Nations: A Critical Analysis of Its Fundamental Problems* (Stevens & Sons, 1951) 818–19; J Liang, 'Modifying the UN Charter through Subsequent

regimes, can be extremely cumbersome if not altogether unfeasible.[22] This makes it difficult for treaties to adapt and continue fulfilling their purpose over time.[23] The issue is particularly acute in light of the rise of large multilateral treaties over the past century.[24] Complex treaty regimes are therefore often more prone to subsequent development through mechanisms other than formal amendment.[25] In fact, the more sophisticated the treaty, the more complex the range of amendment procedures called upon.[26]

In light of the difficulties encountered with formal amendment procedures, subsequent practice provides a key tool for treaty change[27]—not only in its capacity as a means of interpretation and as a constitutive element of subsequent customary law, but also as a means of treaty *modification*.[28] Its value as a direct expression of the parties' intention is 'instinctively obvious'.[29] In fact, the difficulty of pinpointing the moment when interpretation transitions into modification by subsequent practice stems from the reason that the two ultimately achieve the same function as part of a continuous process of treaty change: ensuring the prevalence of the parties' intentions.[30]

But the treaty modifying potential of subsequent practice must be examined with caution. This is to be done in accordance with the threshold[31] required for modification in the circumstances of each given case—its occurrence must not be presumed.[32] This ensures that a perceived modification does not go beyond the

Practice: Prospects for the Charter's Revitalisation' (2012) 81 NJIL 1, 2. See further Sections 3.3.4 and 5.3.1(a).

[22] See eg MJ Bowman, 'The Multilateral Treaty Amendment Process—A Case Study' (1995) 44 ICLQ 540; Arato, 'Treaty Interpretation', 355, citing, *inter alia*, AV Dicey, *Introduction to the Law of the Constitution* (8th edn, Macmillan, 1915) 469–70; Liang, 'Modifying the UN Charter', 1; McLachlan, 'Evolution of Treaty Obligations', 71. It should be noted that some treaties do not provide for their own amendment at all—see eg the 1971 Convention on Wetlands of International Importance especially as Waterfowl Habitat, 996 UNTS 245 (Ramsar Convention), a procedure added by means of the Protocol to Amend the Convention on Wetlands of International Importance especially as Waterfowl Habitat 1982 (1983) 22 ILM 698 (Paris Protocol).

[23] Nolte, Annex A, para 1. See also eg MJ Bowman, '"Normalizing" the International Convention for the Regulation of Whaling' (2007–2008) 29 MJIL 293, 333.

[24] R Crootof, 'Change Without Consent: How Customary International Law Modifies Treaties' (2016) 41 Yale JIL 237, 243.

[25] Thus, unsurprisingly, '[g]reat changes in international law stand in stark contrast to relatively little new treaty text.'—I Venzke, *How Interpretation Makes International Law: On Semantic Change and Normative Twists* (OUP, 2012) 197. See also eg J Robinson, 'Metamorphosis of the United Nations' (1958-II) 94 RC 493, 558 (pointing out that the UN Charter has 'undergone great changes, without any formal acts directed towards this purpose').

[26] See eg Bowman, 'The Multilateral Treaty Amendment Process', 542; Brunnée, 'Treaty Amendments', 351.

[27] The rate of development of subsequent practice is also increasing against the backdrop of increasing global interdependence, the rise of overarching international institutions, and leaps in technological and ideological developments, all facilitating communication and cooperation, and exponentially accelerating State (and State-non-State actor) interaction.

[28] This book does not purport to deal exhaustively with the effects of subsequent practice, eg estoppel or acquiescence as such. See eg RR Churchill, 'The Impact of State Practice on the Jurisdictional Framework Contained in the LOS Convention' in AG Oude Elferink (ed), *Stability and Change in the Law of the Sea: The Role of the LOS Convention* (Martinus Nijhoff, 2005) 91, 92–105.

[29] B Simma, 'Miscellaneous Thoughts on Subsequent Agreements and Practice' in G Nolte (ed), *Treaties and Subsequent Practice* (OUP, 2013) 46.

[30] G Haraszti, *Some Fundamental Problems of the Law of Treaties* (Akadémiai Kiadó, 1973) 141.

[31] See eg Section 3.3.3(b).

[32] See Section 3.1.

common intentions of the treaty parties,[33] especially in the context of international organizations.[34] For the informal nature of subsequent practice is both its greatest advantage and its most significant drawback. Subsequent practice can be diffuse, ambiguous, and inconsistent—many instances of practice never even become visible to the public eye or the international community, whether due to the nature of the practice or confidentiality.[35]

These 'difficulties, and the concomitant legal uncertainty, though considerable, are not prohibitive'.[36] On the contrary, they constitute more of a reason to engage in the analysis of subsequent practice. A better methodology is required to evaluate how subsequent practice operates in different contexts and account for its full range of effects. There is, for instance, significant debate as to what type and degree of practice, as well as *whose* practice, should be able to influence a treaty.[37] Reference points are needed in order to distinguish between subsequent practice as a means of treaty interpretation, as a source of modification, and as a component of subsequent customary law with the potential to override pre-existing treaty provisions.

The topic has been receiving increasing attention in recent years. Notably, in recognition of the need to understand subsequent practice more generally, the International Law Commission (ILC) has taken up consideration of its effects: initially, in the context of a broader study on the evolution of treaties over time,[38] and, later, in relation to the topic of subsequent agreements and practice in treaty interpretation.[39] As the former Chairman of the Study Group on 'Treaties over

[33] For instance, the 'active' parties may genuinely not have intended to modify the treaty, or the 'passive' parties may not have intended to acquiesce in the practice through their silence, as explained in Section 2.3.5. See eg AM Feldman, 'Evolving Treaty Obligations: A Proposal for Analyzing Subsequent Practice Derived from WTO Dispute Settlement' (2009) 41 NYU J Intl L & Pol 655, 699; S Kadelbach, 'Domestic Constitutional Concerns with Respect to the Use of Subsequent Agreements and Practice at the International Level' in G Nolte (ed), *Treaties and Subsequent Practice* (OUP, 2013) 145. See also S Bastid, *Les traités dans la vie internationale: conclusion et effets* (Économica, 1985) 179. cf A Guzman, 'Against Consent' (2012) 52 VJIL 747, 753 ('An excessive commitment to consent can cripple efforts to use international law as a tool to help solve the world's largest problems.').

[34] It is debatable whether the practice of international organizations constitutes 'collective' subsequent practice, or whether it is too far removed from the consent of the parties to the constitutive treaty, achieving flexibility 'at the expense of oversight'—Arato, 'Treaty Interpretation', 353, 355. See Section 2.3.1(c).

[35] See eg D Bethlehem, 'The Secret Life of International Law' (2012) 1 CJICL 23, 36: 'The secret life of international law has a tremendous bearing on the visible life of international law. (...) It may not be visible, but it is there, it is weighty, it has effects, and it can, with sufficient scholarship and informed enquiry, be deduced and identified.'

[36] ME Villiger, *Customary International Law and Treaties: A Manual on the Theory and Practice of the Interrelation of Sources* (2nd rev edn, Kluwer International, 1997) para 349.

[37] See in particular Section 2.3.1.

[38] ILC, *Topical summary of the discussion held in the Sixth Committee of the General Assembly during its sixty-first session*, UN Doc A/CN.4/577/Add.1 (23 January 2007) para 31. See eg ILC, *Report of the International Law Commission on the work of its 64th session*, UN Doc A/67/10 (2012) Ch X ('Treaties over Time') [ILC Report on the Work of Its 64th Session].

[39] See most recently ILC, 'Fourth Report on Subsequent Agreements and Subsequent Practice in relation to the Interpretation of Treaties, by Georg Nolte, Special Rapporteur', UN Doc A/CN.4/694 (2016) [Nolte, Fourth Report on Subsequent Practice] and the draft conclusions provisionally adopted by the Commission in ILC, *Report of the International Law Commission on the work of its 68th session*, UN Doc A/71/10 (2016) Ch VI [ILC Draft Conclusions on Subsequent Agreements and Subsequent Practice (2016)]. See also the discussion in Section 3.1 of this book.

Time',[40] now Special Rapporteur on the topic of 'Subsequent Agreements and Subsequent Practice in Relation to Interpretation of Treaties',[41] Georg Nolte, explains, subsequent practice has 'rarely been the subject of extensive empirical, comparative or theoretical research,' and often only surfaces in the context of legal proceedings.[42] Examples of subsequent practice have never been collected in any systematic way. In fact, the question of treaty amendment or modification in general still remains relatively underexplored,[43] despite the fact that it constitutes a fundamental aspect of international law-making.[44] By exploring the process of subsequent practice as a mechanism for treaty adaptation both theoretically and through practice—culminating in a systematic analysis of examples in Chapter 5—that is precisely the issue this book aims to address.

1.2 Relevance of the Topic

Subsequent practice provides a key tool for treaty change, both in its capacity as a means of interpretation and as a means of treaty modification. This book aims to paint a more vivid picture of the 'mechanics' of the latter process—a controversial and until recently neglected topic with potentially far-reaching effects. The distinction between treaty interpretation and modification lies at the heart of this endeavour. While interpretation and modification may at times seem indistinguishable as part of the same continuous process of treaty change, the difficulty of making the distinction is not insurmountable, nor is it immaterial, for the legal effects of interpretation and modification are distinct.[45] For instance, unlike interpretations, the result of a modification will have automatic effect in all situations where the treaty is applied.[46] Under certain circumstances, modification could conceivably even create a basis of obligation outside the underlying treaty.[47] Furthermore, the application of a modification may be limited temporally because it reflects a concrete change in the previous meaning of the affected provision. Thus, unlike interpretation, it may not apply retroactively in legal proceedings in which the provision in question was modified subsequent to the dispute.[48] Distinguishing between interpretation and modification also helps establish when a body entitled to interpret or apply a treaty has gone beyond its competence and veered into the realm of actual treaty change.[49] Moreover, the knowledge that a modification has occurred can prompt confirmation by means of formal treaty amendment.[50] Perhaps most importantly, modification often reaches further than even 'dynamic' interpretation

[40] See eg Nolte, Annex A, 365.

[41] See most recently Nolte, Fourth Report on Subsequent Practice.

[42] Nolte, Annex A, para 13. Note that the same can be said of the process of customary international law formation. See eg Wood, Annex A, para 5.

[43] See eg Bowman, 'The Multilateral Treaty Amendment Process', 541, citing eg McNair, *Law of Treaties*, 534.

[44] ILC, 'Second Report on the Law of Treaties by Mr H Lauterpacht, Special Rapporteur' (1954) II YBILC 123, para 16.

[45] See Section 3.4.1. [46] Ibid. [47] See Sections 3.3.6(a) and 3.4.1.

[48] See Section 3.4.1. [49] Ibid. See also Section 2.5.4 on implied powers.

[50] See further Sections 3.4.1 and 3.4.4, and the examples in eg Section 5.3.2(b).

(the latter, in principle, does not alter the rights and obligations enshrined in the treaty)—sometimes far outside the 'four corners' of the text. It can give rise to entirely new obligations and may even create international organizations, as evidenced by the examples of practice in Chapter 5.[51]

The concomitant difficulty of pinpointing when interpretation becomes modification underscores the ambiguity that currently surrounds the issue of modification of treaties by subsequent practice, as well as the importance of investigating the phenomenon further. Based on theory and international practice, this book aims to provide indicators for distinguishing between the interpretative and modifying potential of subsequent practice—an admittedly complex, open-ended task.

Clarifying the process of how modification by subsequent practice operates—in other words, clarifying part of the process of the formation of international law and the means of identifying it—is not merely of theoretical interest, but of importance to States, dispute settlement bodies, and other international legal actors alike.[52]

For States, subsequent practice can create new rights and obligations, or modify existing ones. To illustrate this point, one could take the often-cited example of the voting practice of the Security Council in relation to Article 27(3) of the UN Charter. While Article 27(3) requires the 'concurring votes' of the permanent members of the Security Council for certain decisions, in practice the Council has taken it to mean 'non-objection', contrary to the drafters' original intention.[53] Although the Security Council's practice has sometimes been characterized as interpretation, the majority of commentators agree that Article 27(3) has been effectively modified, with far-reaching implications for Security Council action.[54]

Modification by subsequent practice can also lead to the emergence of new institutional mechanisms. For instance, the 1947 General Agreement on Tariffs and Trade (GATT)[55] was initially only intended to establish the International Trade Organization (ITO).[56] Since the ITO never came into being, the GATT was applied provisionally on the basis of the 1947 Provisional Protocol of Application (PPA).[57] Through sustained subsequent practice, and despite its provisionally binding nature, it evolved into the *de facto* international organization for world trade.[58]

Given these effects, elucidating the process of subsequent practice could help more accurately define States' expectations in relation to their treaty obligations. States may have to become more vigilant in their actions—or lack of reaction—to

[51] See eg Section 5.3.1(d). See also eg Section 3.3.5.
[52] See Section 2.3.1(c).
[53] See Sections 3.4.2 and 5.2.1.
[54] Ibid.
[55] 55 UNTS 187.
[56] Havana Charter for an International Trade Organization, *United Nations Conference on Trade and Employment—Final Act and Related Documents* (Interim Committee for the ITO, April 1948) (ITO Charter).
[57] 55 UNTS 308.
[58] See eg D Carreau, P Juillard, and T Flory, *Droit international économique* (2nd edn, LGDJ, R Pichon et R Durand-Auzias, 1980) 258; O Long, *Law and Its Limitations in the GATT Multilateral Trade System* (Martinus Nijhoff, 1985) 45; F Roessler, 'The Competence of GATT' (1987) 21 JWTL 73; GM Berrisch, 'The Establishment of New Law through Subsequent Practice in GATT' (1991) 16 NC JIL & Comm Reg 497, 522; JJ Jackson, *The World Trading System: Law and Policy of International Economic Relations* (2nd edn, MIT Press, 1997) 31, 41–2, 58–9; M Matsushita, TJ Schoenbaum, and P Mavroidis, *The World Trade Organization: Law, Practice, and Policy* (2nd edn, OUP, 2006) 2, 106; AH Qureshi and AR Ziegler, *International Economic Law* (2nd edn, Sweet & Maxwell, 2007). See further Section 5.3.1(d).

emerging subsequent practice. International actors engaging in 'lawmaking through interpretative practice' must be aware of the repercussions.[59] Moreover, subsequent practice could clarify the relationships *between* a State's different treaty obligations. Furthermore, through its various legal manifestations[60]—as a tool for treaty interpretation, a means of treaty modification, and the raw material of customary law—subsequent practice can serve as a vehicle for regime interaction, adapting treaty regimes in line with external developments.[61] This bears upon the issue of fragmentation and treaty congestion in international law.[62] In the absence of clear hierarchies or an overarching legislature or judiciary to enact new law and promote consistency, coupled with the constant expansion and diversification of international law, international legal regimes[63] develop in parallel and often without regard to other regimes, producing 'specialized rules and rule-systems that have no clear relationship to each other'.[64] Fragmentation increases the likelihood of conflicting legal norms,[65] and with it, the need for harmonization through interpretation and, increasingly, informal modification. In fact, treaty regimes are shaped more by informal processes, as a result of an increased need for flexibility in international law,[66] than through formal law-making.[67] Of course, modification by subsequent practice—indeed, modification and amendment in general[68]—can also be a source of, rather than a solution for, fragmentation.[69]

[59] Venzke, *How Interpretation Makes International Law*, 262.

[60] See eg L Boisson de Chazournes, 'Subsequent Practice, Practices, and "Family-Resemblance": Towards Embedding Subsequent Practice in its Operative Milieu' in G Nolte (ed), *Treaties and Subsequent Practice* (OUP, 2013) 53, 54.

[61] See eg Buga, 'Between Stability and Change', 46; R Wolfrum and N Matz, *Conflicts in International Environmental Law* (Springer, 2010) 140.

[62] See generally ILC, 'Fragmentation of International Law: Difficulties Arising from the Diversification and Expansion of International Law, Report of the Study Group of the International Law Commission, Finalized by Martti Koskenniemi', UN Doc A/CN.4/L.682 (2006) [Koskenniemi Fragmentation Report]; MA Young, *Trading Fish, Saving Fish: The Interaction between Regimes in International Law* (CUP, 2011).

[63] For a definition of the term 'regime', see Koskenniemi, Fragmentation Report, para 12.

[64] Koskenniemi, Fragmentation Report, para 483.

[65] 'Conflict' may refer not only to a strict incompatibility entailing that two norms cannot be applied simultaneously, but also 'policy conflicts' when one treaty frustrates the operation of another. See eg Koskenniemi, Fragmentation Report, para 24; J Pauwelyn, *Conflict of Norms in Public International Law: How WTO Law Relates to Other Rules of International Law* (CUP, 2003) 50. See further Section 3.3.1. For a discussion of the concept of 'legal norms' stemming from both formal and informal processes, see eg S Toope, 'Formality and Informality' in D Bodansky, J Brunnée, and E Hey (eds), *The Oxford Handbook of International Environmental Law* (OUP, 2007) 107; J Vranken, 'Exciting Times for Legal Scholarship' (2012) 2 *Recht en Methode in Onderzoek en Onderwijs* 42, 43.

[66] N Matz-Lück, 'Norm Interpretation across International Regimes: Competences and Legitimacy' in MA Young (ed), *Regime Interaction in International Law: Facing Fragmentation* (CUP, 2012) 201, 204–5.

[67] M Koskenniemi, 'Hegemonic Regimes' in MA Young (ed), *Regime Interaction in International Law: Facing Fragmentation* (CUP, 2012) 305, 317. See also text to nn 25–6.

[68] I Sinclair, *The Vienna Convention on the Law of Treaties* (2nd edn, Manchester UP, 1984) 106; ME Villiger, *Commentary on the 1969 Vienna Convention on the Law of Treaties* (Martinus Nijhoff, 2009) 513 (comparing the fragmenting effects of modifications to that of reservations).

[69] See further Buga, 'Between Stability and Change', 60–3 (on the role of subsequent practice in regime interaction in the LOSC context).

As for dispute settlement bodies, indicators by means of which to assess subsequent practice could allow them to more easily fulfil their judicial function, providing an additional means of evaluating the scope of disputing parties' obligations.[70] Modification by subsequent practice may also carry significant jurisdictional implications for dispute settlement or even treaty supervisory mechanisms. One can, for instance, imagine a dispute involving a treaty containing a compromissory clause providing for a particular court's jurisdiction over disputes concerning the treaty's 'interpretation and application'. The applicant State is likely to argue that the subsequent practice in question falls under the scope of the treaty's 'interpretation and application' without displacing the treaty as the underlying basis of obligation.[71] The respondent State, on the other hand, may claim that the original treaty no longer constitutes the basis of the dispute, and that the court consequently lacks jurisdiction, since the parties' subsequent practice has modified the treaty and created an *independent* obligation—one that could even constitute new customary law—thereby rendering ineffective the original treaty provisions.[72] The court would have to determine whether the result of the subsequent practice in relation to the treaty still falls under the scope of the original instrument or instead establishes an independent source of title.[73] Depending on the circumstances, it may also have to decide whether it is dealing with supervening subsequent customary law stemming from the parties' practice.

It is also interesting to briefly reflect upon the *domestic* relevance of this topic. It is of course true that in national legal systems, the law can be adapted through parliamentary procedures and national court judgments, leaving less room or need for subsequent practice.[74] In the international legal system, no equivalent legislature or judiciary exists to adapt the law on behalf of the international community:

> In national law, the most important subsequent developments after the enactment of a law, or the conclusion of a contract, are amendments by the legislature or by the parties to the contract, and evolutive interpretations by courts (...) [whereas in] international law, the situation

[70] Nolte, Annex A, para 20.

[71] See eg *Interpretation of the Air Transport Services Agreement between the United States of America and France (United States/France)*, Award of 22 December 1963, 16 RIAA 5, 69 (where the Tribunal held that the agreement constituted a sufficient jurisdictional basis to be able to determine the rights of the parties, as well as any modifications thereto).

[72] See *United States-United Kingdom Arbitration concerning Heathrow Airport User Charges*, Award on the First Question, Decision of 30 November 1992, 24 RIAA 1 [*Heathrow Airport User Charges Arbitration*] para 6.8. The Tribunal regarded the MoU in question as subsequent conduct useful for interpreting the treaty, but stated that if the MoU had modified the original agreement it would not have been able to decide the case, since the Treaty's jurisdictional provision referred only to disputes 'arising under the Treaty'. Note the discussion in Section 2.3.1(a) as to whether MoUs constitute relevant 'practice'. See also G Nolte, 'Introductory Report for the Study Group on Treaties over Time: Jurisprudence of the International Court of Justice and Arbitral Tribunals of Ad Hoc Jurisdiction Relating to Subsequent Agreements and Subsequent Practice' in G Nolte (ed), *Treaties and Subsequent Practice* (OUP, 2013) 169 [Nolte, Introductory Report on Treaties over Time] 207; J Crawford, 'A Consensualist Interpretation of Article 31(3) of the Vienna Convention on the Law of Treaties' in G Nolte (ed), *Treaties and Subsequent Practice* (OUP, 2013) 29, 33. See further Section 3.3.6(a) on the relation between modification by subsequent practice and the underlying treaty.

[73] See *Dispute between Argentina and Chile concerning the Beagle Channel*, Award of 18 February 1977, 21 RIAA 53 [*Beagle Channel Arbitration*] para 169.

[74] See Nolte, Introductory Report on Treaties over Time, 170 ('In domestic law there is less room, if at all, for legally relevant subsequent agreements or subsequent practice with regard to legislation and perhaps even with regard to contracts between private individuals.').

is more complicated. Different sources (...) are subject to different rules and mechanisms; moreover, they interact with each other.[75]

Nevertheless, numerous conceptual parallels exist between domestic law and international law with regard to subsequent practice. For instance, in the sphere of national constitutional law, the rigid amendment procedures prescribed by certain constitutions, such as Article V of the Constitution of the United States, are designed to serve the community interest in providing legal certainty and safeguarding against arbitrary amendments.[76] But too rigid a constitutional amendment process, much like that of a treaty, can hamper necessary development.[77] Thus, inflexible procedures like Article V of the Constitution of the United States can in practice be circumvented by the use of alternative adaptation mechanisms such as informal judicial amendment and statutes, just as treaties are adapted through subsequent practice.[78] Other examples of informal modification through practice in the national legal sphere[79] include the subtle interchange between dynamic interpretation and modification of contractual terms in light of the legitimate expectations and contemporary intentions of the contracting parties,[80] the modification through parties' subsequent practice of agreed terms in employment contracts,[81] and the tacit termination or setting aside of legislation in favour of subsequent custom.[82] Parallels to the question of modification by subsequent practice can also be identified in the context of transnational commercial law.[83] Although its significance on

[75] Nolte, Annex A, para 18. See also Distefano, 'La pratique subséquente', 47; M Kamto, 'La volonté de l'Etat en droit international' (2004) 310 RC 133; Gardiner, *Treaty Interpretation*, 225; Venzke, *How Interpretation Makes International Law*, 7; McLachlan, 'Evolution of Treaty Obligations', 72.

[76] See eg DS Lutz, *Toward a Theory of Constitutional Amendment* (1994) 88 Am Pol Sci Rev 355, 362; Z Elkins, T Ginsburg, and J Melton, *The Endurance of National Constitutions* (CUP, 2009) 101; R Dixon, 'Partial Constitutional Amendments' (2011) 13 U Pa J Const L 643, 645–6.

[77] See eg R Dixon, 'Updating Constitutional Rules' (2011) 1 Sup Ct Rev 319, 321.

[78] See eg Elkins, Ginsburg, and Melton, *The Endurance of National Constitutions*, 163, 177. See also S Levinson, 'How Many Times Has the United States Constitution Been Amended? (A) <26; (B) 26; (C) 27; (D) >27: Accounting for Constitutional Change' in S Levinson (ed), *Responding to Imperfection: The Theory and Practice of Constitutional Amendment* (Princeton UP, 1995) 13, 18–19; L Tribe, 'Taking Text and Structure Seriously: Reflections on Free-Form Method in Constitutional Interpretation' (1995) 108 Harv L Rev 1221, 1225; DA Strauss, 'The Irrelevance of Constitutional Amendments' (2001) 114 Harv L Rev 1457, 1459 (arguing that, due to the use of alternative means for constitutional change in light of the difficulties encountered with Art V, the US constitutional system 'would look the same today if Article V of the Constitution had never been adopted and the Constitution contained no provision for formal amendment').

[79] Examples are taken from the Dutch legal system, as an area of expertise of the author.

[80] J Hijma and others, *Rechtshandeling en Overeenkomst* (7th edn, Kluwer, 2013) 283.

[81] HL Bakels, WHACM Bouwens, MS Houwerzijl, and WL Roozendaal, *Schets van het Nederlandse Arbeidsrecht* (21st edn, Kluwer, 2011) 67.

[82] Hijma and others, *Rechtshandeling en Overeenkomst*, 292.

[83] See eg R Goode, 'Usage and Its Reception in Transnational Commercial Law' (1997) 46 ICLQ 1, 7–18, as cited in R Goode, H Kronke, and E McKendrick (eds), *Transnational Commercial Law: Text, Cases, and Materials* (OUP, 2007) 43–4: 'On the one hand there was a clear rule of the UCP [Uniform Customs and Practice for Documentary Credits] that a credit was to be presumed revocable unless otherwise indicated [a rule that remained in force for 60 years]; on the other a long-settled practice of calling for irrevocable, rather than revocable, credits. Should not the tribunal [called upon to decide whether, in mercantile usage, the credit was to be considered revocable or irrevocable] rely on the practice (if duly proved or capable of judicial notice) rather than treating the rule as evidence of usage or of a general principle of documentary credits law?'

the national plane falls outside the scope of this book, these examples illustrate the wider relevance of subsequent practice for the development of the law at both the international and national level.

A better understanding of subsequent practice could enhance legal certainty in international treaty relations, as States continue to revise their expectations in a dynamic, ever-evolving arena in which legal sources are intricately intertwined. Such insight could also improve the ability of dispute settlement bodies to tackle difficult cases of tacit treaty modification. Ultimately, its recognition as a tool for treaty adaptation will largely depend on the extent to which it can withstand a more systematic examination based on certain conditions and evidentiary standards, in order to ensure that its outcome does not stray from the intention of the parties.[84] This can help strike a more accurate balance between the stability of treaties on the one hand, and the organic evolution of treaty commitments on the other—an insufficiently explored issue of great significance.

1.3 A Word on Terminology

It is important to define what is meant by 'modification' in the context of the present book. 'Modification' is employed in a wide sense to mean the variation of a treaty or individual provisions by means of the implied or informal consent of the treaty parties.[85] It thus represents the counterpart to formal treaty amendment.[86] As discussed later on,[87] 'modification' refers to *altering* treaty provisions, as well as to *supplementing* them with an important 'novel' element or direction[88] (as opposed to mere clarification). It is also taken to include the effect of tacitly *terminating* treaty provisions (desuetude). Furthermore, 'modification' includes subsequent modifications to *previously* established modifications by subsequent practice, which could conceivably even change the respective rule back to its initial meaning.[89]

The choice of the term 'modification'—also preferred by the ILC[90]—is deliberate. The case law and doctrine often refer to treaty modification established by

[84] Venzke, *How Interpretation Makes International Law*, 234.

[85] See eg G Distefano, 'L'accord tacite ou l'univers parallèle du droit des traités' (2015) 18 QIL 17, 30, remarking that subsequent practice evidences the parties' tacit agreement to modify the treaty, or, '[e]n d'autres termes, le comportement des Etats, *dans l'application du traité*, a comme effet de prouver leur "dissentiment mutual" (*mutuus dissensus*), c'est-à-dire l'opposé du "consentement mutual" à l'origine du traité' (emphasis in the original).

[86] ME Villiger, *Customary International Law and Treaties: A Study of Their Interactions and Interrelations, with Special Consideration of the 1969 Vienna Convention on the Law of Treaties* (Brill, 1985) para 292 fn 2.

[87] See in particular Section 3.3.1.

[88] Venzke, *How Interpretation Makes International Law*, 236.

[89] See in particular Section 3.3.3(b).

[90] See eg ILC, 'Draft articles on the law of treaties' (1964) II YBILC 176 [1964 Draft Articles on the Law of Treaties] 198, Art 68; ILC, 'Draft articles on the law of treaties' (1966) II YBILC 177 [1966 Draft Articles on the Law of Treaties] 182, Art 38; ILC, 'Draft articles on the law of treaties with commentaries' (1966) II YBILC 187 [1966 Draft Articles on the Law of Treaties with Commentaries] 236. See further Sections 3.1–3.2.

the agreement of *all* the treaty parties as 'amendment', and to modification *inter se*—between a subset of the parties only—as 'modification'.[91] The same terminology is employed in the Vienna Convention: Article 40 VCLT refers to an 'amendment' requiring unanimity, while Article 41 VCLT refers to 'modification' as an agreement to modify between certain of the parties only. For present purposes, however, the term 'modification' is taken in a broader sense than the definition in Article 41 VCLT to denote the variation of treaty provisions by means of an implied or informal agreement between all or a subset of the treaty parties. By contrast, formal treaty adaptation procedures as set out in Articles 39 to 41 VCLT are referred to as 'amendments'.[92] Moreover, the term 'desuetude' is used to denote the termination of a treaty (provision) by means of the parties' tacit consent, in contrast to 'treaty termination' in the sense of Article 54 VCLT, which takes place by means of formal procedures as prescribed, for instance, by Article 65 VCLT.[93] In addition, in the specific context of treaties constituting international organizations, certain commentators have referred to the process of modification by subsequent practice as 'transformation', denoting a change brought about through the practice of the organization and its organs.[94] Since the practice of international organizations, in addition to State practice *within* international organizations and other 'classical' forms of State practice, forms part of the subject matter of the present book,[95] it is included within the scope of the term 'modification'.

Lastly, as dealt with in Chapter 4, treaty 'modification' by subsequent customary law differs from treaty modification by subsequent practice, *inter alia*, in that the former displaces or substitutes the treaty provision in question without becoming 'part and parcel' of the treaty,[96] whereas the latter actually modifies its substance. Yet the process of customary law is intricately linked to that of subsequent practice. This overlap adds an extra dimension to the discussion on subsequent practice. For the sake of convenience, the outcome of both processes will be included in the term 'modification'.

Thus, the notion of 'modification' is taken here as an overarching concept—covering alterations or extensions of treaty provisions between all or a subset of the treaty parties, as well as the notion of desuetude—referring generally to a situation

[91] See eg *Administrateur des affaires maritimes v Dorca Marina and others* (Joined Cases 50-58/82) [1982] ECR 3949, discussed in Section 5.2.3(d). cf A Rigaux and D Simon, 'Article 41 (1969)' in O Corten and P Klein (eds), *The Vienna Convention on the Law of Treaties: A Commentary* (OUP, 2011) 986, 989 ('international practice often utilizes these terms ['amendment' and 'modification'] as synonyms'); R Kolb, *The Law of Treaties: An Introduction* (Edward Elgar, 2016) 193 fn 488 ('[a]mendment, revision or modification are roughly synonymous').

[92] A possible alternative might be 'revision', but this is often taken to imply large-scale changes to the original text. See eg Villiger, *Commentary*, 511. The term 'amendment' is also sometimes applied in the literature to denote a modification of the treaty as a whole. cf I Brownlie, *Principles of Public International Law* (6th edn, OUP, 2003) 601, arguing that there is no 'distinction of quality' between amendment of a certain treaty provision and revision of the treaty as a whole. See also P Daillier and A Pellet (eds), *Droit International Public (NQ Dinh)* (6th rev edn, LGDJ, 1999) 291; Aust, *Modern Treaty Law*, 220. cf also A Chanaki, *L'adaptation des traités dans le temps* (Bruylant 2013), employing the term 'adaptation' to cover amendment, revision, and modification.

[93] See further Sections 3.3.1 and 3.3.2(b).

[94] See Arato, 'Treaty Interpretation', 289.

[95] See eg Sections 2.3.1(c) and 5.3.1.

[96] See eg Pauwelyn, *Conflict of Norms*, 142.

in which the operation of a treaty or an individual provision is tacitly varied by means of subsequent practice or subsequent customary law.

1.4 The Approach

This book seeks to demonstrate the relevance and dynamism of the process of treaty modification by subsequent practice and to show—theoretically and by means of an array of examples drawn from treaty practice—how this phenomenon can be identified and understood.

Generally, the approach is to cast the net wide, but to sort through the 'catch' cautiously. While giving due regard throughout to the theoretical and practical limitations of subsequent practice, the central concepts—including the very notion of 'modification' already set out—are employed in a broad sense, so as not to limit the exploration of subsequent practice at the expense of the completeness of the analysis. Such an approach also avoids terminological complications and takes into account various forms of relevant practice going beyond formal amendment. For instance, a broader notion of 'practice' is preferred, given the diversity of means by which consent to an international obligation can be expressed.[97] While the practice of States, based on consent, remains the focal point, flexibility will be maintained in applying the notion of practice—a concept that defies strict conceptual compartmentalization[98] and can, depending on the circumstances, also be taken to include 'institutional' practice.[99]

It should be mentioned that, theoretically, there is no limit to the process of modification by subsequent practice: the will of the parties, as masters of their own treaty,[100] is determinative of the direction in which the law develops, such that even *jus cogens* norms could arguably be modified or reversed. In reality, however, such limits, even if theoretically not absolute, play an important role. Thus, the book focuses on how the phenomenon operates in practice given different factors and limitations.

The pragmatic, methodical approach of this book is reflected especially in the systematic analysis of examples of potential modifying practice in its penultimate chapter. As pointed out in the ongoing ILC discussions, compiling a non-exhaustive yet representative 'repertoire' of practice would allow us to identify and draw links among analogous cases.[101] Thus, certain guidelines could be derived to provide

[97] See eg C Tomuschat, 'Obligations Arising for States Without or Against Their Will' (1993-IV) 241 RC 195, 277; L Boisson de Chazournes, 'Qu'est-ce que la pratique en droit international?' in SFDI (ed), Colloque de Geneve, *La pratique et le droit international* (Pédone, 2004) 13, 14 ('la définition de la pratique est juridiquement très volatile').

[98] Boisson de Chazournes, 'Subsequent Practice', 68.

[99] See Sections 1.2 and 2.3.1(c).

[100] Sinclair, *Vienna Convention*, citing McNair, *Law of Treaties*, 169; Villiger, *Commentary*, 429. See also eg the German Federal Constitutional Court's decision in *Lissabon*, Federal Constitutional Court, 123 BVerfGE 267 (Case Nos 2 BvE 2/08, 2 BvE 5/08, 2 BvR 1010/08, 2 BvR 1022/08, 2 BvR 1259/08, 2 BvR 182/09) Judgment of 30 June 2009 para 235 (English excerpts at <www.bverfg.de/entscheidungen/es20090630_2bve000208en.html> accessed 25 June 2016).

[101] Nolte, Annex A, para 20: 'Although such a collection could not aspire to completeness, it would nevertheless provide an exemplary overview. This would be helpful for practitioners who would then

future reference points for analysing modifications by subsequent practice, and contribute to a 'common background of understanding',[102] consistency in approach, and increased legal certainty regarding the process. To this end, the compilation of examples in Chapter 5 brings together, and builds upon, the analysis in the chapters on the interpretation, modification, and customary modification of treaties that precede it, demonstrating the effects of the process by focusing on international practice as such. The wealth of material pertinent to the discussion is also more easily structured and analysed in this way. In this sense, the systematic collection of examples forms the capstone of the analysis in this book. By taking a practice-driven, example-based approach that supplements the more theoretical chapters, patterns and parameters can be identified that inform our understanding of the process of treaty modification by subsequent practice.

Methodologically, this book employs a primarily positivist, empirical approach to exploring the operation of subsequent practice that is more descriptive than prescriptive, as reflected in the analysis of examples of practice in Chapter 5. It adopts an internal, legal perspective rather than an interdisciplinary one precisely due to the controversial nature of the topic in the legal context. The aim is less to engage in a normative inquiry as to what the process of modification by subsequent practice *ought* to be, than to study the legal materials available in order to structure and systematize in a largely inductive fashion. This also constitutes an important limit of the investigation: this book does not distinguish based on the perceived legitimacy of the institution from which the practice in question emanates. Such an approach, it is submitted, is what is principally missing from the existing scholarship on the subject. Moreover, an account of what can and does occur under different conditions when treaties are modified by subsequent practice can inform our understanding of when it *ought* to be invoked and thus contribute to the normative perspective.

The structure of the book reflects the need to explore the modification of treaties by subsequent practice systematically. It begins by setting out the parameters of the concept of subsequent practice as a means of treaty interpretation, then moves on to its capacity for treaty modification, analysing its different implications in turn, including subsequent customary law, and, finally, explores the phenomenon by means of a systematic analysis of examples of potential modifications by subsequent practice.

First, Chapter 2 examines the concept of 'subsequent practice' in light of the drafting history of the Vienna Convention (Section 2.2), and its constitutive elements pursuant to Articles 31(3)(b) (Section 2.3) and 32 VCLT (Section 2.4). The varying role accorded to subsequent practice in the interpretative process is then explained (Section 2.5). This provides the basic reference point for its more controversial application as a source of treaty *modification*—the central focus of Chapter 3. One crucial element is the ILC draft provision on treaty modification by subsequent practice ultimately excluded from the 1969 Vienna Convention (Section 3.2). The

more easily be able to reason from analogy. A repertory should also provide courts and tribunals with illustrative guidance on the relevance of subsequent agreement and practice.'

[102] Ibid. para 22.

conclusions drawn from these ILC discussions prove useful in analysing the validity, evidentiary standards, and results of the process of modification by subsequent practice (Section 3.3). The difficulties involved in identifying modification by subsequent practice, as distinguished from interpretation, are explored next (Section 3.4), and the factors conducive to modification by subsequent practice, and its limitations and alternatives, are considered in turn (Section 3.5). Chapter 4 then focuses on the treaty modifying potential of subsequent customary law. This requires looking into the drafting history of the ultimately deleted ILC provision on modification by customary law (Section 4.2), the complex process of formation and identification of customary law and its parallels to the emergence of subsequent practice (Section 4.3), and the interplay between customary law and treaties as a basis for identifying the former's treaty modifying potential (Section 4.4). The particular requirements for and effects of such customary modification require an in-depth analysis (Section 4.5), which facilitates a fuller comparison between the processes of modification by subsequent customary law and modification by subsequent practice (Section 4.6).

Finally, these processes of treaty modification by subsequent practice and subsequent customary law—to the extent that the two are distinct—are analysed further by means of the collection of examples of practice in Chapter 5, which combines all the elements considered in the preceding chapters. This 'repertoire' of practice spans a wide range of legal fields in order to ensure that it is sufficiently representative, with a focus on major treaty regimes, such as the UN Charter and the LOSC. Examples are drawn from both within (Section 5.2) and outside (Section 5.3) the context of dispute settlement, as well as within (Section 5.3.1) and outside (Section 5.3.2) the context of international organizations.

This approach aims to provide a useable framework through which to elucidate and contextualize the process of treaty modification by subsequent practice, to reveal the bigger picture, highlight its implications, and sketch its limits and alternatives.

2

Subsequent Practice as a Means of Treaty Interpretation

2.1 Introduction

The 1969 Vienna Convention on the Law of Treaties has been referred to as the 'Treaty of Treaties'.[1] Many of its provisions represent customary international law,[2] and deal with the formation and effects of international written agreements between States. In its 'general rule of interpretation' contained in Article 31, widely regarded as a major achievement,[3] the Convention reads:

Article 31—General Rule of Interpretation

1. A treaty shall be interpreted in good faith in accordance with the ordinary meaning to be given to the terms of the treaty in their context and in the light of its object and purpose.
2. The context for the purpose of the interpretation of a treaty shall comprise, in addition to the text, including its preamble and annexes:
   (a) any agreement relating to the treaty which was made between all the parties in connexion with the conclusion of the treaty;
   (b) any instrument which was made by one or more parties in connexion with the conclusion of the treaty and accepted by the other parties as an instrument related to the treaty.
3. There shall be taken into account, together with the context:
   (a) any subsequent agreement between the parties regarding the interpretation of the treaty or the application of its provisions;
   (b) any subsequent practice in the application of the treaty which establishes the agreement of the parties regarding its interpretation;
   (c) any relevant rules of international law applicable in the relations between the parties.

[1] See eg RD Kearney and RE Dalton, 'The Treaty on Treaties' (1970) 64 AJIL 495.

[2] See eg *Legal Consequences for States of the Continued Presence of South Africa in Namibia (South West Africa) Notwithstanding Security Council Resolution 276 (1970)*, Advisory Opinion of 21 June 1971, ICJ Reports 16 [*Namibia Advisory Opinion*] para 94; *Fisheries Jurisdiction (United Kingdom of Great Britain and Northern Ireland v Iceland)*, Jurisdiction of the Court, Judgment of 2 February 1973, ICJ Reports 3 [*Fisheries Jurisdiction (UK v Iceland)*, Jurisdiction] para 24; *Arbitral Award of 31 July 1989 (Guinea-Bissau v Senegal)*, Judgment of 12 November 1991, ICJ Reports 53, para 48; *Gabčíkovo-Nagymaros Project (Hungary/Slovakia)*, Judgment of 25 September 1997, ICJ Reports 7, para 46.

[3] See eg NQ Dinh, P Daillier, and A Pellet, *Droit international public* (7th edn, LGDJ, 2002) 265–6; P Reuter, *Introduction au droit des traités* (Armand Colin, 1972) 103.

4. A special meaning shall be given to a term if it is established that the parties so intended.

Article 32 of the Convention, on supplementary means of interpretation, reads as follows:

Article 32—Supplementary Means of Interpretation

Recourse may be had to supplementary means of interpretation, including the preparatory work of the treaty and the circumstances of its conclusion, in order to confirm the meaning resulting from the application of article 31, or to determine the meaning when the interpretation according to article 31:

(a) leaves the meaning ambiguous or obscure; or
(b) leads to a result which is manifestly absurd or unreasonable.

The International Court of Justice (ICJ) first declared that Article 31 VCLT constitutes customary international law in the *Libya/Chad* case.[4] This has been reaffirmed numerous times in the Court's judgments[5] and in the decisions of other international dispute settlement bodies,[6] although interpretations differ as to the precise application of the structure of Article 31.[7] In principle, the interpretative means contained therein are non-hierarchical and thus applied as part of a

[4] *Territorial Dispute (Libyan Arab Jamahiriya/Chad)*, Judgment of 3 February 1994, ICJ Reports 6 [*Libya/Chad*] para 41.

[5] See notably *Maritime Delimitation and Territorial Questions between Qatar and Bahrain (Qatar v Bahrain)*, Jurisdiction and Admissibility, Judgment of 15 February 1995, ICJ Reports 6 [*Qatar v Bahrain*, Jurisdiction and Admissibility] para 33; *Oil Platforms (Islamic Republic of Iran v United States of America)*, Preliminary Objection, Judgment of 12 December 1996, ICJ Reports 803, para 23; *Kasikili/Sedudu Island (Botswana/Namibia)*, Judgment of 13 December 1999, ICJ Reports 1045, paras 18–20; *LaGrand (Germany v United States of America)*, Judgment of 27 June 2001, ICJ Reports 466, para 99; *Legality of Use of Force (Serbia and Montenegro v Belgium)*, Preliminary Objections, Judgment of 15 December 2004, ICJ Reports 279, para 100; *Sovereignty over Pulau Ligitan and Pulau Sipadan (Indonesia/Malaysia)*, Judgment of 17 December 2002, ICJ Reports 625 [*Indonesia/Malaysia*] paras 37–8; *Avena and Other Mexican Nationals (Mexico v United States of America)*, Judgment of 31 March 2004, ICJ Reports 48, para 83; *Application of the Convention on the Prevention and Punishment of the Crime of Genocide (Bosnia and Herzegovina v Serbia and Montenegro)*, Judgment of 26 February 2007, ICJ Reports 43, para 160; *Legal Consequences of the Construction of a Wall in the Occupied Palestinian Territory*, Advisory Opinion of 9 July 2004, ICJ Reports 136 [*Israeli Wall Advisory Opinion*] para 94; *Arbitral Award of 31 July 1989*, para 48.

[6] See eg *Arbitration Regarding the Iron Rhine ('Ijzeren Rijn') Railway (Belgium v The Netherlands)*, Award of 24 May 2005, 27 RIAA 35 [*Iron Rhine Railway Arbitration*] para 45; *Prosecutor v Dusko Tadić* (Appeals Chamber) Decision on the Defence Motion for Interlocutory Appeal on Jurisdiction, Case No IT-94-1-T (2 October 1995) para 30; *Golder v United Kingdom* App no 4451/70 (ECtHR, 21 February 1975) para 30; *Japan—Taxes on Alcoholic Beverages II*, Report of the Appellate Body (4 October 1996) WT/DS8/AB/R, WT/DS10/AB/R, and WT/DS11/AB/R, 10; *United States–Standards for Reformulated and Conventional Gasoline*, Report of the Appellate Body (29 April 1996) WT/DS2/AB/R, 17; *United States–Countervailing Duties on Certain Corrosion-Resistant Carbon Steel Flat Products from Germany*, Report of the Appellate Body (28 November 2002) WT/DS213/AB/R, para 61. The customary status of Art 31 VCLT has even been recognized in the case law of non-parties to the VCLT, such as the United States. See eg *Haitian Centers Council v McNary*, 969 F.2d 1350, 1361–62 (1992) Court of Appeals, Second Circuit; *Gonzalez v Gutierrez*, 311 F.3d 942, 949 fn 15 (2002) Court of Appeals, Ninth Circuit, as explained in EJ Criddle, 'The Vienna Convention on the Law of Treaties in US Treaty Interpretation' (2004) 44 VJIL 431.

[7] ME Villiger, *Commentary on the 1969 Vienna Convention on the Law of Treaties* (Martinus Nijhoff, 2009) 440; M Sorel and V Boré Eveno, 'Article 31 (1969)' in O Corten and P Klein (eds), *The Vienna Conventions on the Law of Treaties: A Commentary*, vol I (OUP, 2011) 805, 810–11.

simultaneous exercise.[8] They have been compared to 'sacred texts that are often difficult to apply but are constantly invoked'.[9]

Article 31(3)(b) qualifies subsequent practice as a primary means of treaty interpretation. The ICJ has made use of it in a large number of cases.[10] In the *Kasikili/Sedudu Island* judgment, for instance, the Court highlighted that the role of subsequent practice as a means of treaty interpretation is confirmed abundantly not only in its own case law, but also in that of other international tribunals.[11]

It should be noted that subsequent practice was initially intended to shed light on the parties' original intention.[12] However, in recent decades, the emphasis has moved away from the quest for the parties' original intention, to that for their current understanding of the meaning of the treaty.[13] Over time, practice 'acquires a force of its own', and develops away from the parties' original intentions.[14] Thus, subsequent practice can evidence both the parties' original and later intention.[15]

[8] 1966 Draft Articles on the Law of Treaties with Commentaries, 219–20 (Art 27, comment 8).

[9] Sorel and Boré Eveno, 'Article 31', 807.

[10] See eg *Corfu Channel* (*United Kingdom of Great Britain and Northern Ireland v Albania*), Merits, Judgment of 9 April 1949, ICJ Reports 4, 25; *Arbitral Award Made by the King of Spain on 23 December 1906* (*Honduras v Nicaragua*), Judgment of 18 November 1960, ICJ Reports 192, 206–7; *Temple of Préah Vihéar* (*Cambodia v Thailand*), Merits, Judgment of 15 June 1962, ICJ Reports 6, 33–5; *Certain Expenses of the United Nations* (*Article 17, paragraph 2, of the Charter*), Advisory Opinion of 20 July 1962, ICJ Reports 151 [*Certain Expenses Advisory Opinion*] 157, 160–1, 172–5; *Military and Paramilitary Activities in and against Nicaragua* (*Nicaragua v United States of America*), Jurisdiction and Admissibility, Judgment of 26 November 1984, ICJ Reports 392 [*Nicaragua v US*, Jurisdiction and Admissibility] paras 36–47; *Libya/Chad*, paras 66–71; *Legality of the Use by a State of Nuclear Weapons in Armed Conflict*, Advisory Opinion of 8 July 1996, ICJ Reports 66 [*WHO Nuclear Weapons Advisory Opinion*] para 19. These cases were cited by the Court in *Kasikili/Sedudu Island*, para 49.

[11] *Kasiliki/Sedudu Island*, para 49. See further S Torres Bernárdez, 'Interpretation of Treaties by the International Court of Justice' in G Hafner and others (eds), *Liber Amicorum Professor Seidl-Hohenveldern in Honour of his 80th Birthday* (Kluwer Law International, 1998) 721. cf G Fitzmaurice, 'The Law and Procedure of the International Court of Justice 1951–4: Treaty Interpretation and Other Treaty Points' (1957) 33 BYBIL 203, 211. See also Section 2.5.2.

[12] See eg *Interpretation of Article 3, Paragraph 2, of the Treaty of Lausanne*, Advisory Opinion of 21 November 1925, PCIJ Series B, No 12 [*Lausanne Advisory Opinion*] 24; *Jurisdiction of the Courts of Danzig*, Advisory Opinion of 3 March 1928, PCIJ Series B, No 15, 17–18; AD McNair, *The Law of Treaties* (Clarendon Press, 1961) 424. See for the early use of the same term eg *Factor v Laubenheimer*, 290 US 276 (1933) Supreme Court. Similarly, in a landmark case, the Supreme Court of Canada in *R v Sioui* [1990] 1 SCR 1025, unanimously held that a document signed in 1760 constituted a treaty under the Indian Act based, *inter alia*, upon an examination of the parties' subsequent practice. See further *Corfu Channel*, 25; *Anglo-Iranian Oil Co* (*United Kingdom v Iran*), Preliminary Objection, Judgment of 22 July 1952, ICJ Reports 93, 107. cf MJ Bowman, '"Normalizing" the International Convention for the Regulation of Whaling' (2007–2008) 29 MJIL 324.

[13] Nolte, Introductory Report on Treaties over Time, 177, citing W Karl, *Vertrag und spätere Praxis im Völkerrecht: Zum Einfluß der Praxis auf Inhalt und Bestand völkerrechtliche Verträge* (Springer, 1983) 139; J-P Cot, 'La conduite subséquente des parties à un traité' (1966) 70 RGDIP 632; G Distefano, 'La pratique subséquente des États parties à un traité' (1994) 40 AFDI 41. See also FG Jacobs, 'Varieties of Approach to Treaty Interpretation: With Special Reference to the Draft Convention on the Law of Treaties Before the Vienna Diplomatic Conference' (1969) 18 ICLQ 324.

[14] M Akehurst, *A Modern Introduction to International Law* (6th edn, Harper Collins Academic, 1987) 5. See also Jacobs, 'Varieties of Approach to Treaty Interpretation', 329. The extent to which this can lead to treaty modification is the focus of Chapter 3 of this book.

[15] L Crema, 'Subsequent Agreements and Subsequent Practice Within and Outside the Vienna Convention' in G Nolte (ed), *Treaties and Subsequent Practice* (OUP, 2013) 23. See also J Arato, 'Subsequent Practice and Evolutive Interpretation: Techniques of Treaty Interpretation over Time and Their Diverse Consequences' (2010) 9 LPICT 307. See further Section 2.5.3.

To understand the application of subsequent practice as a tool for treaty interpretation, Section 2.2 focuses on the background of Article 31(3)(b) and its drafting history. The main elements of the notion of 'subsequent practice' are then analysed in Section 2.3. These parameters for determining when practice constitutes 'relevant' subsequent practice in the sense of Article 31(3)(b) are also instrumental to understanding the process of *modification* by subsequent practice in the following chapter. Next, Section 2.4 considers the role of subsequent practice as a secondary means of interpretation under Article 32 VCLT. Section 2.5 places subsequent practice in the context of the various interpretative methods employed by different dispute settlement bodies. Particular attention is accorded to the relation between interpretation based on subsequent practice and two special forms of 'dynamic' interpretation: the evolutionary treaty approach and the implied powers doctrine.

The findings in this chapter lay the groundwork for the analysis of subsequent practice as a means of treaty modification in Chapter 3 and subsequent customary law as a source of treaty modification in Chapter 4.

2.2 The Drafting History of Article 31(3)(b) VCLT

It is useful to explore briefly the drafting history and meaning of the 'general rule' on treaty interpretation in Article 31 VCLT, in particular its paragraph (3)(b). It represents the only provision in a general international law treaty dealing exclusively with the role of subsequent practice. Insight into this provision is necessary not only to frame the discussion on subsequent practice in general, but also to provide the basis for understanding subsequent practice as a source of treaty *modification*: applying the rules on interpretation constitutes a requisite first step in determining whether modification has occurred.

The International Law Commission began its work on the drafting of the Vienna Convention in 1949. The preparations lasted twenty years, time in which the Commission proposed several draft versions and released a number of reports by its Special Rapporteurs, including, chronologically, Sir Hersch Lauterpacht, Sir Gerald Fitzmaurice, and Sir Humphrey Waldock. The notions of 'subsequent practice' and 'object and purpose' proved to be among the most difficult to tackle.[16]

A first draft on the interpretation of treaties was only prepared in 1964, influenced significantly by the 1957 Articles on interpretation of the *Institut de Droit International*,[17] which emphasized the primacy of the text.[18] By then, Article 69 of the draft articles already contained the core of present-day Article 31, including its provision on 'subsequent practice'.[19] Article 69(3) of the 1964 draft articles read:

[16] ME Villiger, 'The Rules on Interpretation: Misgivings, Misunderstandings, Miscarriage? The "Crucible" Intended by the International Law Commission' in E Cannizzaro (ed), *The Law of Treaties Beyond the Vienna Convention* (OUP, 2011) 105, 108.

[17] (1956) 46 AIDI 317.

[18] See eg Waldock, Third Report on the Law of Treaties, 54 para 4; ILC, 'Summary record of the 726th meeting', *Summary records of the 16th session* (1964) I YBILC 20.

[19] See also Art 19(a) of the 1935 Harvard Draft Convention, 937.

There shall also be taken into account, together with the context: (...) (b) any subsequent practice in the application of the treaty which clearly establishes the understanding of all the parties regarding its interpretation.

By 1966, the ILC had agreed that the ordinary meaning of treaty terms would only constitute the starting point of the interpretative process.[20] The focus of the ILC was on settling the structure of what had become Article 27 on treaty interpretation.[21] Specifically, Article 27(3) of the 1966 draft articles, identical in wording to the current provision in Article 31(3) VCLT, read:

There shall be taken into account, together with the context: (...) (b) any subsequent practice in the application of the treaty which establishes the understanding of the parties regarding its interpretation.

The express reference to 'all' the parties had been removed, along with the word 'clearly'. It was also subsequently agreed to replace the term 'understanding', which had been meant to emphasize that acceptance of the practice by other parties need not be explicit,[22] with 'agreement'.

The work of Sir Gerald Fitzmaurice during the drafting process that eventually led to the formulation of Article 31 VCLT is also worthy of note. Taking as a reference point the ICJ's case law between 1951 and 1954,[23] Fitzmaurice formulated the major principles of treaty interpretation that formed the basis for the ILC draft provisions on treaty interpretation.[24] He outlined three *subsidiary* principles of interpretation, 'effectiveness', 'subsequent practice', and 'contemporaneity', which he saw as complementary to the three primary ones: 'actuality', the 'natural and ordinary meaning', and 'integration'. With regard to the principle of subsequent practice, Fitzmaurice remarked, as early as then, that:

Where the practice has brought about a change or development in the meaning of the treaty through a *revision* of its terms by conduct, it is permissible to give effect to this change or development as an agreed revision but not as an interpretation of its original terms.[25]

The question of modification by subsequent practice hence arose in the early stages of the drafting process of Article 31 VCLT. As dealt with at length in Chapter 3 of

[20] ILC, 'Summary record of the 884th meeting', *Summary records of the 18th session* (1966) I(2) YBILC 268 [Summary record of 884th meeting] 270.

[21] ILC, 'Summary record of the 869th meeting', *Summary records of the 18th session* (1966) I(2) YBILC 179, 183; ILC, 'Summary record of the 883rd meeting', *Summary records of the 18th session* (1966) I(2) YBILC 261, 267 [Summary record of 883rd meeting]; ILC, 'Summary record of the 893rd meeting', *Summary records of the 18th session* (1966) I(2) YBILC 327 [Summary record of 893rd meeting] 328; ILC, 'Summary record of the 894th meeting', *Summary records of the 18th session* (1966) I(2) YBILC 335 [Summary record of 894th meeting] 346–7.

[22] 'Sixth Report on the Law of Treaties, by Sir Humphrey Waldock, Special Rapporteur' (1966) II YBILC 51 [Waldock, Sixth Report on the Law of Treaties] 98 para 18.

[23] Fitzmaurice, 'The Law and Procedure of the International Court of Justice' (1957), 211–12.

[24] I Tammelo, *Treaty Interpretation and Practical Reason: Towards a General Theory of Legal Interpretation* (Law Book Co, 1967).

[25] Fitzmaurice, 'The Law and Procedure of the International Court of Justice' (1957), 212. See also on 'emergent purpose', G Fitzmaurice, 'The Law and Procedure of the International Court of Justice: Treaty Interpretation and Certain Other Treaty Points' (1951) 28 BYBIL 8.

this book,[26] the rule now codified in Article 31(3)(b) VCLT blurs the distinction between treaty interpretation and modification.[27] It could also be argued that the formulation and context of then draft Article 27(3)(b), identical in wording to current Article 31(3)(b), implicitly allowed for the possibility of establishing the parties' agreement to diverge from the originally intended meaning of treaty provisions, and effectively modify a treaty.[28] Jacobs contrasts this wording to the much more 'specific' formulation in the fourth paragraph of the same article ('a special meaning shall be given to a term if it is established that the parties so intended'), which makes it clear that it refers to the parties' intention at the time of the treaty's conclusion, not the period thereafter.[29]

Initially, subsequent practice had been classified under 'other evidence or indications of the intentions of the parties', similar to what is now Article 32 VCLT.[30] The ILC soon decided to include it as a distinct element in the 'General rule', as an authentic means of interpretation analogous to subsequent agreements.[31] According to the Commentary to the Draft Articles:

> [T]he application of the means of interpretation in the article would be a single combined operation. All the various elements, as they were present in any given case, would be thrown into the crucible, and their interaction would give the legally relevant interpretation.[32]

Thus, subsequent practice is hierarchically equal to the other interpretative means such as 'ordinary meaning' and 'object and purpose'. The structure of the 'general rule on interpretation' was meant to reflect a logical progression, 'not any legal obligatory hierarchy'.[33] The wording 'taken into account' in Article 31(3) VCLT does not detract from the obligatory character of subsequent practice as an element of interpretation—this open formulation[34] was chosen over terms such as 'be subject to' in order to leave the results of the interpretation open[35]—nor does it create enforceable obligations with regard to the application of certain interpretative means in Article 31 VCLT over others:

> [I]t is only logic which suggests that the elements in paragraph 3 [subsequent agreement and subsequent practice] (...) should follow and not precede the elements in the previous paragraphs. The logical consideration which suggests this is that these elements are extrinsic

[26] See in particular Section 3.2.

[27] K Wolfke, 'Treaties and Custom: Aspects of Interrelation' in J Klabbers and R Lefeber (eds), *Essays on the Law of Treaties: A Collection of Essays in Honour of Bert Vierdag* (Martinus Nijhoff, 1998) 31, 34. See also M Akehurst, 'The Hierarchy of the Sources of International Law' (1974–75) 47 BYBIL 273, 278.

[28] Jacobs, 'Varieties of Approach to Treaty Interpretation', 331 (referring eg to the 1966 Draft Articles on the Law of Treaties with Commentaries, 220).

[29] Ibid. 331.

[30] See Waldock, Third Report on the Law of Treaties, 52 (Art 71(2)).

[31] 1964 Draft Articles on the Law of Treaties, 203, para 13. See also Waldock, Sixth Report on the Law of Treaties, 98–9, para 18; 1966 Draft Articles on the Law of Treaties with Commentaries, 221–2, para 15.

[32] 1966 Draft Articles on the Law of Treaties with Commentaries, 219–20.

[33] Ibid. 220, para 9. See also Waldock, Sixth Report on the Law of Treaties, 95, para 4.

[34] See Bowman, '"Normalizing"', 325; J Crawford, 'A Consensualist Interpretation of Article 31(3) of the Vienna Convention on the Law of Treaties' in G Nolte (ed), *Treaties and Subsequent Practice* (OUP, 2013) 29, 29–30.

[35] Waldock, Third Report on the Law of Treaties, 61 para 32.

to the text. But these three elements are all of an obligatory character and by their very nature could not be considered to be norms of interpretation in any way inferior to those which precede them.[36]

As to the element of subsequent practice itself, the ILC emphasized that subsequent practice has to be consistent and occur with a certain frequency,[37] and, crucially, that it must establish the agreement of the parties to the interpretation. This only requires the actual practice of some of the parties to the treaty,[38] coupled with the acquiescence of the parties not actively participating in the practice ('qualified passive conduct'[39]), and the absence of objections.[40] The interpretation achieved must thus reflect the agreement of *all* the parties, despite the deletion of the express reference to 'all' in the draft article:

By omitting the word 'all' the Commission did not intend to change the rule. It considered that the phrase 'the understanding of the parties' necessarily means 'the parties as a whole'. It omitted the word 'all' merely to avoid any possible misconception that every party must individually have engaged in the practice where it suffices that it should have accepted the practice.[41]

The degree to which practice reflects agreement determines its interpretative weight.[42] The Commission in 1964 had observed in this regard that an individual State's practice might be especially relevant in relation to the 'performance of an obligation which particularly concerns that State'.[43] However, it considered that the practice of individual States does not amount to 'concordant' practice demonstrating the common understanding of all the parties as to the meaning of a treaty, and hence should only be taken into account as a 'further' means of interpretation.[44] This latter statement was, however, subsequently omitted from the 1966 Report.

The ILC excluded from the discussion on the draft articles the question of whether the practice of international organizations as such could constitute subsequent practice in relation to treaties constituting international organizations (constitutive treaties)—a question addressed in Section 2.3.1 (c). The Commission remarked:

The problem of the effect of the practice of organs of an international organisation upon the interpretation of its constituent instrument raises the question of how far individual Member States are bound by the practice. Although the practice of the organ as such may be consistent, it may have been opposed by individual Members or by a group of Members which have been outvoted. This special problem appears to relate to the law of international organisations rather than to the general law of treaties and the Commission did not consider that it would be appropriate to deal with it in the present articles.[45]

[36] 1966 Draft Articles on the Law of Treaties with Commentaries, 220.
[37] Waldock, Third Report on the Law of Treaties, 59 para 24.
[38] Villiger, *Commentary*, 431.
[39] Ibid. 432, fn 69 ('qualified passive conduct approximates to customary law').
[40] Waldock, Sixth Report on the Law of Treaties, 99, para 18; 1966 Draft Articles on the Law of Treaties with Commentaries, 222, para 15 (Art 27).
[41] 1966 Draft Articles on the Law of Treaties with Commentaries, 222, para 15.
[42] Ibid. [43] 1964 Draft Articles on the Law of Treaties, 204, para 13. [44] Ibid.
[45] Ibid. para 14.

However, certain ILC members noted that the practice of the parties to an international organization, as separate from that of the organization itself, had often led to interpretations that effectively *modified* the treaties concerned. They stated that '[n]othing said in the draft articles on interpretation should be capable in any way of preventing that progressive development within international organizations.'[46] The distinction between interpretation and modification by subsequent practice, including practice in the context of international organizations, is discussed in detail in Chapter 3.[47]

The ILC draft article on interpretation was considered at the 1968–69 Vienna Conference on the Law of Treaties.[48] The overall reaction to draft Article 27 was positive, although views differed as to whether, for instance, it succeeded in establishing parity between the different means of interpretation, or rather, as was argued by the United States, the article remained dominated by the textual approach.[49] Article 31 was ultimately adopted by 97 votes to none,[50] prompting the Chairman of the Conference to comment that 'the Conference had successfully disposed of the most controversial and difficult subject in the whole field of the law of treaties'.[51] The Convention was adopted and opened for signature the next day.

2.3 Subsequent Practice under Article 31(3)(b): Constitutive Elements

The Vienna Convention may not establish clear evidentiary standards for identifying and applying subsequent practice, but it does set out the main underlying elements of the notion in Article 31(3)(b) VCLT. The present section deals with these elements, which include the scope of the term 'practice' (Section 2.3.1), the boundaries of what can be considered 'subsequent' practice (Section 2.3.2), and the distinction, to the extent possible, between 'subsequent practice' and 'subsequent agreement' (Section 2.3.3). Two basic qualifications to subsequent practice under Article 31(3)(b) VCLT are that the practice must occur 'in the application of the

[46] ILC, 'Summary record of the 766th meeting', *Summary records of the 16th session* (1964) I YBILC 282 [Summary record of 766th meeting] para 39 (De Luna). See also ibid. paras 45–6 (Lachs).

[47] See in particular Section 3.4.

[48] See eg *Documents of the Conference, Official Records of the United Nations Conference on the Law of Treaties—First and Second Session (26 March–24 May 1968 and 9 April–22 May 1969)* UN Doc A/CONF.39/11/Add.2 (1971).

[49] *Summary Records of the Plenary Meetings and of the Meetings of the Committee of the Whole, Official Records of the United Nations Conference on the Law of Treaties—First Session (26 March–24 May 1968)*, UN Doc A/CONF.39/11, 31st Meeting of the Committee of the Whole (19 April 1968) 164, 167, para 44.

[50] *Summary Records of the Plenary Meetings and of the Meetings of the Committee of the Whole, Official Records of the United Nations Conference on the Law of Treaties—Second Session (9 April–22 May 1969)*, UN Doc A/CONF.39/11/Add.1, 13th Plenary Meeting (6 May 1969) 51, 57.

[51] Ibid. para 77 (Ago). cf ILC, *Survey of International Law in Relation to the Work of Codification of the International Law Commission: Preparatory work within the purview of article 18, paragraph 1, of the International Law Commission* (Memorandum submitted by the Secretary General) UN Doc A/CN.4/1/Rev.1 (1949) para 91.

treaty' (Section 2.3.4), and, most importantly, establish the 'agreement of the parties' (Section 2.3.5). When subsequent practice does not satisfy the requirement of establishing the parties' agreement in accordance with the elements set out, it may nevertheless qualify as 'relevant practice'[52] under Article 32 VCLT instead.[53]

2.3.1 The notion of 'practice': What and whose practice?

There are three relevant questions to be dealt with from the outset. The first question is what types of practice can constitute subsequent practice in the sense of Article 31(3)(b) VCLT. This first question cannot be answered exhaustively, given the diversity of practice by means of which parties can express their understanding of rights and obligations flowing from a treaty. The second question, closely related to the first, is the degree of determinacy required for practice to be taken as relevant, and the evidentiary value to be assigned to it depending on the context. The third question, inherently linked to the previous two points, is *whose* practice can constitute subsequent practice in the sense of Article 31(3)(b) VCLT. This requires an exploration of the practice of State organs and that of *non*-State actors. The latter may include the practice of (organs of) international organizations, as well as other institutional arrangements and private actors that impact treaties. These three questions—of direct relevance to Chapter 3 on subsequent practice as a means of modification—are dealt with in turn.

2.3.1a The meaning of 'practice'

'Practice'[54] includes any type of positive action, whether physical or verbal[55]—for instance, the reliance on the provisions of a treaty to support a State's chosen course of action,[56] or the adoption of legislation,[57] or enforcement action[58] based on a treaty—and abstention from action (omission) in the application of a treaty.[59] Put simply, practice covers 'what states do in their relations with one another'.[60] In a more dynamic sense, it represents the 'process of continuous interaction, of continuous demand and response' between States.[61] It also covers more controversial

[52] McNair, *Law of Treaties*, 431. [53] See Section 2.4. [54] See also Section 4.3.2.

[55] ILC, 'Second Report on Identification of Customary International Law, by Michael Wood, Special Rapporteur', UN Doc A/CN.4/672 (2014) [Wood, Second Report] para 48 ('Draft conclusion 7', para 1). See also eg J Crawford, *Brownlie's Principles of Public International Law* (8th edn, OUP, 2012) 24.

[56] *The Chamizal Case* (*Mexico/United States*), Award by the International Boundary Commission, 15 June 1911, 11 RIAA 309, 328; Wolfke, 'Treaties and Custom', 34–5.

[57] *Anglo-Iranian Oil*, 107; *Maritime Dispute* (*Peru v Chile*), Judgment of 27 January 2014, General List No 137 [*Peru v Chile*] paras 119ff.

[58] See eg *Peru v Chile*, paras 126ff.

[59] Wood, Second Report, paras 42, 48 ('Draft conclusion 7', para 3); U Linderfalk, *On the Interpretation of Treaties: The Modern International Law as Expressed in the 1969 Vienna Convention on the Law of Treaties* (Springer, 2007) 165; P Tomka, 'Custom and the International Court of Justice' (2013) 12 LPICT 195, 210.

[60] JL Brierly, *The Law of Nations* (6th edn, OUP, 1963) 59.

[61] MS McDougal, 'The Hydrogen Bomb Tests and the International Law of the Sea' (1955) 49 AJIL 356, 357.

forms of practice, such as a State's argumentation in a legal dispute,[62] subsequent treaties with third States,[63] and patterns of treaties,[64] for instance when considering whether the conclusion of a large number of BITs could collectively amount to subsequent practice.[65] It is not possible, nor desirable, to provide an exhaustive list of what could constitute practice.[66] In any case, the crucial element is, *stricto sensu*, not the practice itself, but the fact that it establishes the 'agreement of the parties regarding its interpretation' as dictated by Article 31(3)(b) VCLT.[67]

Unilateral State declarations are a highly controversial form of practice.[68] Such statements may not qualify as relevant practice within the meaning of Article 31(3)(b) VCLT because they do not reflect the 'common intention' of the parties.[69] However, this should not necessarily affect their validity as evidence of subsequent practice, but rather their probative value. Unilateral declarations do not, in any case, *automatically* amount to relevant subsequent practice establishing the agreement of the parties in the sense of Article 31(3)(b).[70]

There is also a certain degree of controversy as to whether *abstract* statements and votes[71] by State representatives at diplomatic conferences can constitute relevant practice—assuming the latter is sufficiently consistent.[72] As Villiger points out, there are a number of considerations that militate in favour of counting statements by State representatives as relevant practice.[73] One argument is that even

[62] *Certain Expenses Advisory Opinion*, 157. See further Section 2.3.1(b).

[63] See eg *Plama Consortium Limited v Republic of Bulgaria*, ICSID Case No ARB/03/24 (ECT), Decision on Jurisdiction, 8 February 2005, 20 ICSID Rev For Inv LJ 262, para 195. cf T Gazzini, 'Bilateral Investment Treaties' in T Gazzini and E De Brabandere (eds), *International Investment Law: The Sources of Rights and Obligations* (Martinus Nijhoff, 2012) 99, 123, citing *Wintershall Aktiengesellschaft v Argentine Republic*, ICSID Case No ARB/04/14, Award, 8 December 2008, para 128. Treaties with third States can thus also qualify as relevant practice under Art 32 VCLT. See further Sections 2.3.4 and 2.4.

[64] See eg *Report of the International Law Commission covering its 2nd session*, UN Doc A/1316 (1950) II YBILC 364, 368ff; M Akehurst, 'Custom as a Source of International Law' (1974–75) 47 BYBIL 1, 43; ME Villiger, *Customary International Law and Treaties: A Study of Their Interactions and Interrelations, with Special Consideration of the 1969 Vienna Convention on the Law of Treaties* (Brill, 1985) para 19.

[65] Gazzini, 'Bilateral Investment Treaties', 101, arguing that extensive participation in the conclusion of BITs by virtually all States 'may amount to subsequent practice for the purpose of interpreting or even modifying Article II:1 GATS'. This is especially plausible given that the 'content of BITs is to a large extent similar or identical, at least with regard to the main substantive rules', even impacting customary international law—ibid. 104, citing *Mondev International Ltd v United States of America*, ICSID ARB(AF)/99/2 (NAFTA), Award of 11 October 2002 [*Mondev v US*] para 43. See further eg SM Schwebel, 'The Influence of Bilateral Investment Treaties on Customary International Law' (2004) 98 ASIL Proc 27; JE Alvarez, 'A BIT on Custom' (2009) 42 NYU J Intl L & Pol 17.

[66] Wood, Second Report, para 41, citing *Report of the International Law Commission covering its 2nd session* (1950), 368.

[67] See further Section 2.3.5.

[68] See eg *Peru v Chile*, para 112.

[69] C McLachlan, 'The Evolution of Treaty Obligations in International Law' in G Nolte (ed), *Treaties and Subsequent Practice* (OUP, 2013) 69, 78.

[70] See *Kasikili/Sedudu Island*, paras 52–70, 79. See further Section 2.3.5.

[71] See eg H Meijers, 'On International Customary Law in the Netherlands' in IF Dekker and HHG Post (eds), *On the Foundations and Sources of International Law* (Asser Press, 2003) 77, 84.

[72] See Section 2.3.1(b).

[73] Villiger, *Commentary*, 5. See also J Lang, *Le plateau continental de la mer du Nord: Arrêt de la Cour internationale de Justice* (LGDJ, 1970) 93; HWA Thirlway, *International Customary Law and Codification: An Examination of the Continuing Role of Custom in the Present Period of Codification of International Law* (AW Sijthoff, 1972) 57; Akehurst, 'Custom', 8.

'traditional' examples of State practice, such as the opinions of legal advisors and diplomatic notes (so-called 'factual' practice), may contain abstract statements on legal rules. Moreover, as a result of changes in the international community over the past decades, the UN and certain other bodies have now become major fora for expressing State views, a fact enhanced by the increasing accessibility of records of State practice in organizations and bodies like the UN, at diplomatic conferences, and in the context of the ILC.[74] This is also why UN General Assembly resolutions can be considered 'evidences of a recognized source of law in the form of state practice',[75] a matter also relevant to the discussion on practice in the context of international organizations.[76]

Another issue is the value of memoranda of understanding (MoUs).[77] Though their legal force is uncertain, they have been qualified as subsequent practice[78] as well as subsequent agreements[79]—a distinction discussed further in this chapter.[80] For instance, in the relatively recent *Costa Rica v Nicaragua* case before the ICJ, Judge ad hoc Guillaume in his Declaration relied on the 1994 MoU between the two States' Ministers of Tourism as subsequent practice to confirm his conclusion that the freedom of navigation enjoyed by Costa Rica under the treaty could be extended to the conveyance of tourists on the river.[81] MoUs can also fall under 'other relevant rules' in the sense of Article 31(3)(c) VCLT. Ultimately, their interpretative potential under paragraph 3 of Article 31 VCLT will depend on the content of the specific understanding and the context within which it was agreed.

A further illustration of the diversity of practice, and the debate surrounding certain more controversial forms, is the consideration by the WTO Panel in *Japan–Alcoholic Beverages II* that 'panel reports adopted by the GATT Contracting Parties and the WTO Dispute Settlement Body constitute subsequent practice in a specific case'.[82] The Appellate Body rejected this view:

> [T]he essence of subsequent practice in interpreting a treaty has been recognized as a 'concordant, common and consistent' sequence of acts or pronouncements which is sufficient

[74] Villiger, *Commentary*, 6. See also R Higgins, *Themes and Theories: Selected Essays, Speeches and Writings in International Law* (OUP, 2009) 63.

[75] Higgins, *Themes and Theories*, 62. See also M Bos, *A Methodology of International Law* (North-Holland, 1984) 86. cf Section 4.3.1.

[76] See Section 2.3.1(c).

[77] See eg A Aust, *Modern Treaty Law and Practice* (3rd edn, CUP, 2013) 26; G Hafner, 'Subsequent Agreements and Practice: Between Interpretation, Informal Modification, and Formal Amendment' in G Nolte (ed), *Treaties and Subsequent Practice* (OUP, 2013) 105, 113.

[78] *Heathrow Airport User Charges Arbitration*, para 6.7 (qualifying the MoU as 'consensual subsequent practice of the Parties'); *Delimitation of the Abyei Area (The Government of Sudan/The Sudan People's Liberation Movement/Army)*, Final Award of 22 July 2009, 48 ILM 1357, paras 650–5.

[79] See eg A Aust, 'Alternatives to Treaty-Making: MOUs as Political Commitments' in DB Hollis (ed), *The Oxford Guide to Treaties* (OUP, 2012) 46, 62.

[80] See Section 2.3.3.

[81] *Dispute regarding Navigational and Related Rights (Costa Rica v Nicaragua)*, Judgment of 13 July 2009, Declaration of Judge ad hoc Guillaume, ICJ Reports 290, para 16.

[82] *Japan–Taxes on Alcoholic Beverages*, Report of the Panel (11 July 1996) WT/DS8/R, WT/DS10/R and WT/DS11/R, para 6.10. See also E-U Petersmann, 'The Dispute Settlement System of the World Trade Organization and the Evolution of the GATT Dispute Settlement System since 1948' (1994) 31 CMLR 1157, 1175.

to establish a discernable pattern implying the agreement of the parties regarding its interpretation. An isolated act is generally not sufficient to establish subsequent practice; it is a sequence of acts establishing the agreement of the parties that is relevant.[83]

The Appellate Body considered that panel reports do not constitute subsequent practice because they are only binding with respect to the specific dispute between the parties concerned, and thus not constitutive of a 'concordant, common and consistent' sequence of acts establishing the agreement of the parties generally.[84] On the other hand, it considered that panel reports should be taken into account when relevant to the interpretative process as 'an important part of the GATT *aquis*', and as a source of legitimate expectations among the organization's members.[85]

The question of whether WTO panel reports, which are adopted automatically in the absence of a consensus among the parties to oppose the adoption, sufficiently reflect the parties' agreement in order to qualify as subsequent practice in the sense of Article 31(3) VCLT—and indeed whether the practice of (organs of) international organizations in general is capable of constituting subsequent practice—is dealt with further in this chapter.[86] Regardless, the Appellate Body's statement does not exclude the possibility that a series of panel reports containing the same interpretation can constitute a 'sequence of acts' establishing the parties' agreement to that effect.[87]

2.3.1b The determinacy and evidentiary value of practice

For practice to count as relevant, it must be identifiable and accessible. One problem encountered in this respect is that treaty practice often remains undocumented, unpublicized, or confidential, especially at the international level: States may be reluctant to publish their practice in relation to a treaty for fear that it may have unintended consequences or bind them to a certain interpretation, or, for instance, the practice may be that of an executive organ that does not record or publish their activities.[88] In the latter case, the other treaty parties may not be aware of the practice.[89] This may not give them the chance to react or to create a sequence of acts relevant to the interpretation of the treaty, an issue explored further in Section 2.3.5.[90]

[83] *Japan–Alcoholic Beverages II*, 13 (footnotes omitted). See also E Canal-Forgues, 'Sur l'interprétation dans le droit de l'OMC' (2001) 1 RGDIP 21.

[84] The Appellate Body's definition of subsequent practice as 'concordant, common and consistent' has been deemed restrictive—see Section 2.3.5(c).

[85] *Japan–Alcoholic Beverages II*, 14 (arguing that the Ministerial Conference and the General Council have exclusive authority to adopt interpretations of the agreement, and rejecting the panel's characterization of panel reports as 'other decisions of the Contracting Parties of GATT 1947'). See also eg *United States–Tax Treatment for 'Foreign Sales Corporations'*, Report of the Panel (8 October 1999) WT/DS108/R [*US-FSC*] para 7.75.

[86] See Section 2.3.1(c).

[87] ATL Chua, 'Precedent and Principles of WTO Panel Jurisprudence' (1998) 16 Berkeley JIL 171, 185.

[88] G Nolte, 'Third Report for the ILC Study Group on Treaties over Time: Subsequent Agreements and Subsequent Practice of States Outside of Judicial or Quasi-Judicial Proceedings' in G Nolte (ed), *Treaties and Subsequent Practice* (OUP, 2013) 307 [Nolte, Third Report on Treaties over Time] 318.

[89] Nolte, Third Report on Treaties over Time, 318.

[90] See in particular Section 2.3.5(a) on the significance of silence.

Practice must also be sufficiently determinate to count as relevant.[91] The weight accorded to this requirement and the degree of determinacy called for varies per dispute settlement body.[92] The determinacy of the practice carries implications for its evidentiary value in the interpretative process. As pointed out by President Winiarski in the *Certain Expenses Advisory Opinion*, the problem of attributing precise legal significance to the practice of treaty parties lies in the fact that it is oftentimes difficult to assess whether States have acted in a certain way because the law so requires, or for reasons of convenience or expediency.[93] An example is 'parallel conduct' by States in the independent granting of oil concessions. This is sometimes regarded as a factor indicative of a tacit acceptance of a certain boundary, but courts and tribunals are reluctant to accord mere 'parallel activity' sufficient legal value on its own to amount to relevant subsequent practice, rather than in conjunction with other factors.[94]

For one thing, the practice of an *individual* State can be a source of contradictory practice. One interesting example is where a State does not endorse (or even protests against) the legal claim underlying another State's conduct, but at the same time grants it aid or assistance (complicity). For instance, a number of States declared the actions of the United States in Iraq in 2003 illegal, yet still rendered it some form of assistance.[95] Thus, the question arises whether more significance should be attached to a State's actions than to its statements, or whether only 'unequivocal' instances of practice should count towards the development of international law.[96] Can such contradictory simultaneous[97] practice by one and the same State be regarded as relevant subsequent practice? The answer will undoubtedly depend on

[91] See Section 2.3.5. See also eg G Nolte, 'Second Report for the ILC Study Group on Treaties over Time: Jurisprudence Under Special Regimes Relating to Subsequent Agreements and Subsequent Practice' in G Nolte (ed), *Treaties and Subsequent Practice* (OUP, 2013) 210 [Nolte, Second Report on Treaties over Time] 221, 236. See further eg *Philippe Gruslin v Malaysia*, ICSID Case No ARB/99/3 (Belgo-Luxembourg/Malaysia BIT), Award, 27 November 2000 (2002) 5 ICSID Rep 484, para 23.13. Practice does not need to demonstrate uniformity, but rather a degree of conformity—see Nolte, Third Report on Treaties over Time, 310, citing Karl, *Vertrag*, 118.

[92] Nolte, Second Report on Treaties over Time, 304 ('General Conclusion 14') ('Subsequent practice must not necessarily be very determinate or specific'). See also ILC Draft Conclusions on Subsequent Agreements and Subsequent Practice (2016), 122 ('Conclusion 9').

[93] *Certain Expenses Advisory Opinion*, Dissenting Opinion of President Winiarski, ICJ Reports 227, 232.

[94] *Land and Maritime Boundary between Cameroon and Nigeria* (*Cameroon v Nigeria: Equatorial Guinea intervening*), Judgment of 10 October 2002, ICJ Reports 303 [*Cameroon v Nigeria*, Judgment] para 304; *Continental Shelf* (*Tunisia/Libyan Arab Jamahiriya*), Judgment of 24 February 1982, ICJ Reports 18 [*Tunisia/Libya*] para 117; *Territorial and Maritime Dispute between Nicaragua and Honduras in the Caribbean Sea* (*Nicaragua v Honduras*), Judgment of 8 October 2007, ICJ Reports 659 [*Nicaragua v Honduras*] para 258. cf ILC, 'Second Report on Subsequent Agreements and Subsequent Practice in Relation to Treaty Interpretation, by Georg Nolte, Special Rapporteur', UN Doc A/CN.4/671 (2014) [Nolte, Second Report on Subsequent Practice] para 43; *Indonesia/Malaysia*, para 79.

[95] See O Corten, 'Quels droits et quels devoirs pour les États tiers? Les effets juridiques d'une assistance à une acte d'agression' in K Bannelier and others (eds), *L'intervention en Irak et le droit international* (Pédone, 2004) 104.

[96] G Nolte and HP Aust, 'Equivocal Helpers—Complicit States, Mixed Messages and International Law' (2009) 58 ICLQ 1, 20.

[97] The simultaneous practice referred to here should be distinguished from the practice of a State that at a later point in time attempts to change its position to a contradictory stance.

the circumstances of the given case. However, in principle, a simultaneous objection should eliminate the possibility of interpreting the 'complicit' practice as a legal endorsement,[98] precluding the creation of legitimate expectations: 'Protest is the opposite of acquiescence.'[99]

Second, practice emanating from *different* sources may be manifested in contradictory ways. The approach to such practice can vary per tribunal and per treaty regime: in the WTO context, any practice that meets with opposition or is contradicted by the practice of any other party is disregarded, whereas in the context of the European Convention on Human Rights (ECHR), the European Court of Human Rights (ECtHR) has also accepted the practice of a 'vast majority' of States or 'near consensus' as relevant.[100]

Inconsistent practice may prevent the concretization of the meaning of a rule or term.[101] This can be illustrated with an example from the investment treaty context, where subsequent practice has not been particularly helpful in settling the meaning of 'investment'. The numerous instances in which States have argued in favour of a narrow definition of 'investment' to advance short-term interests in the context of legal proceedings do not carry the same weight as the broad definitions adopted at the general policymaking stage,[102] as reflected for instance in the 'dramatically broad' definitions of 'investment' adopted under their BITs.[103] However, the inconsistency of practice in these different contexts in relation to the definition of 'investment' creates ambiguity as to the meaning of the term.

This indicates that some sources of subsequent practice are more reliable than others, depending, among other things, on the context or forum within which the practice occurs.[104] For instance, the positions expressed by States in abstract verbal statements at diplomatic conferences, already discussed,[105] may reflect a 'trading ploy' rather than their actual view as to the law.[106] The same has been

[98] Nolte and Aust, 'Equivocal Helpers', 23.

[99] Akehurst, 'Custom', 39. See further Section 2.3.5(b).

[100] Nolte, Second Report on the Law of Treaties, 305 ('General Conclusion 16').

[101] Nolte, Introductory Report on the Law of Treaties, 178, citing eg *Rights of Nationals of the United States of America in Morocco (France v United States of America)*, Judgment of 27 August 1952, ICJ Reports 176 [*Rights of Nationals*] 211.

[102] JD Mortenson, 'The Meaning of "Investment": ICSID's *Travaux* and the Domain of International Investment Law' (2001) 51 Harvard ILJ 257, 261.

[103] Ibid. 311–12. See also *Biwater Gauff (Tanzania) Ltd v United Republic of Tanzania*, ICSID Case No ARB/05/22, Award, 24 July 2008, paras 313–15 (discussing the BIT practice of defining 'investment' to cover virtually any conceivable economic asset or enterprise, and suggesting that trends in 'very substantial numbers of BITs across the world' could generate an 'international consensus'); D Krishan, 'A Notion of ICSID Investment' in TJ Grierson Weiler (ed), *Investment Treaty Arbitration and International Law* (Juris Publishing, 2008) 61. As to the related view that treaties can be regarded as State practice, see eg Akehurst, 'Custom', 43.

[104] See eg MN Shaw, *International Law* (6th edn, CUP, 2008) 80.

[105] See Section 2.3.1(a).

[106] J Laylin, 'Emerging Customary Law of the Sea' (1976) 10 TIL 610, 670. See also Bowman, '"Normalizing"', 305: 'In relation to statements in particular, one important factor concerns the extent to which they reflect an objective, disinterested, and dispassionate view of the law, as opposed to assertions of a political character, especially those that represent attempts to protect or advance a State's own position in an ongoing dispute.' For similar reasons, the ICJ in *Indonesia/Malaysia*, para 135, considered that it could not 'take into consideration acts having taken place after the date on which the

argued with regard to certain 'political' provisions.[107] Likewise, practice that comes to light in judicial or arbitral proceedings must be treated with caution. Such evidence or statements may have been advanced with a specific, short-term goal in mind, namely, to put forward any arguments deemed effective in defending the State's position in the proceedings, such as jurisdictional objections, rather than as a reflection of the State's long-term position on a legal issue. Thus, for instance, in a case before the Iran-US Claims Tribunal, Iran argued that the filing of official counterclaims did not constitute relevant subsequent practice in the sense of Article 31(3)(b) VCLT because the counterclaims were filed purely as a 'defence strategy'.[108] The Tribunal, however, rejected this argument: first, because it did not consider the subjective intention of the parties relevant when determining the presence of subsequent practice, and, second, because Iran should in that case have preserved its jurisdictional position with respect to the counterclaim in question.[109] The question of the relevance of practice put forward in the course of judicial or arbitral proceedings ties in with the discussion regarding unilateral statements in Section 2.3.1(a). The value of unilateral assertions may be very limited due to their perception as self-serving.[110]

In the specific context of investment arbitration, another problem with taking into account practice that comes to light in the course of legal proceedings is that, pursuant to the investor-State dynamic, usually only the practice of the respondent State will be taken into account in interpreting the applicable law.[111] Moreover, a significant problem is that pleadings in arbitral proceedings are seldom made public, and many arbitral awards remain confidential, making it difficult to assess this particular form of subsequent practice.[112]

dispute between the parties crystallized unless such acts are a normal continuation of prior acts and are not undertaken for the purpose of improving the position of the Party which relies on them'. cf Villiger, *Customary International Law and Treaties* (1985), para 26, citing RR Baxter, 'Treaties and Custom' (1970-I) 129 RC 25, 44, Akehurst, 'Custom', 5, and A Bleckmann, 'Zur Feststellung und Auslegung von Völkergewohnheitsrecht' (1977) 37 ZaöRV 504, 506.

[107] See *Texaco Overseas Petroleum Company and California Asiatic Oil Company v Government of the Libyan Arab Republic* (1979) 53 ILR 389, 492 ('article 2 [of the Charter of Economic Rights and Duties of States, GA Res 3281 (XXIX), UN GAOR, 29th Sess, Supp No 31 (1974) 50] must be analyzed as a political rather than as a legal declaration concerned with the ideological strategy of development'), discussed in Villiger, *Customary International Law and Treaties* (1985), para 22.

[108] *Islamic Republic of Iran and United States of America*, Interlocutory Award No ITL 83-B1-FT (Counterclaim) (9 September 2004) 2004 WL 2210709 (Iran-US CTR) para 129.

[109] Ibid. para 130.

[110] C Schreuer, 'Diversity and Harmonization of Treaty Interpretation in Investment Arbitration' in M Fitzmaurice, O Elias, and P Merkouris (eds), *Treaty Interpretation and the Vienna Convention on the Law of Treaties: 30 Years On* (Martinus Nijhoff, 2010) 129, 146. See also *Aguas del Tunari SA v Republic of Bolivia*, ICSID Case No ARB/02/3, Decision on Respondent's Objections to Jurisdiction, 21 October 2005, paras 260–3.

[111] M Paparinskis, *The International Minimum Standard and Fair and Equitable Treatment* (OUP, 2013) 145.

[112] To identify patterns in subsequent practice, one would be faced with two undesirable options: 'either to proceed on the basis of positions of States contained in all awards (and therefore probably make erroneous assumptions about the nature and content of State practice), or focus on those positions that may be clearly identified through publicly available pleadings (and attribute disproportionate influence to the practice of [the treaty parties]'—ibid.

One follow-up question is whether the position taken by a State in one case could have 'horizontal' effects for the interpretation of the same or similar treaties in other cases. For instance, States are careful when taking a certain position in one investment arbitration, for fear that their actions may adversely affect the position of their investors in future proceedings. As discussed, one should not automatically presume that case-specific arguments advanced by a State constitute unilateral instances of treaty-related 'subsequent practice' capable of binding that State.[113]

The approach of exercising caution in assigning value to (evidence of) practice advanced during judicial proceedings is, for instance, reflected in the ICJ's treatment of affidavits, that is, documents containing testimony given under oath before a notary or other authorized public official. Although the Court has in some cases accepted the submission of affidavits, it has shown 'great reserve'[114] in assessing their evidentiary value,[115] especially with regard to documents prepared in view of a case before the Court.[116]

It is submitted here that the determinacy of the practice and the context in which it occurs should be a matter primarily pertaining to evidentiary weight.[117] Tribunals can attach varying degrees of evidentiary weight to statements made in the context

[113] OK Fauchald, 'The Legal Reasoning of ICSID Tribunals—An Empirical Analysis' (2008) 19 EJIL 301, 348, citing *Sempra Energy International v Argentine Republic*, ICSID Case No ARB/02/16 (Argentina-US BIT), Decision on Objections to Jurisdiction, 11 May 2005, para 146. See also *Enron Corporation and Ponderosa Assets LP v Argentine Republic*, ICSID Case No ARB/01/3, Decision on Jurisdiction, 14 January 2004, para 48; *Enron Corporation and Ponderosa Assets LP v Argentine Republic*, ICSID Case No ARB/01/3, Decision on Jurisdiction (Ancillary Claim), 2 August 2004, para 39; *Gas Natural SDG, SA v Argentine Republic*, ICSID Case No ARB/03/10, Decision of the Tribunal on Preliminary Questions on Jurisdiction, 17 June 2005, para 47 fn 12. See further J Crawford, 'Book Review of *L'Estoppel en droit international public. Précédé d'un apercu de la theorie de l'estoppel en droit anglais*, by Antoine Martin' (1980) 51 BYBIL 290, 291, stating that States before a tribunal 'are, after all, attempting to persuade a tribunal whose decision is only a "subsidiary" source of general international law. It would be odd if argument, which is subordinate to decision, could somehow rise above the latter in its formal status as a law-creating agency.' cf Villiger, *Customary International Law and Treaties* (1985), para 19, responding that 'this view possibly overlooks the fact that one instance of practice, such as would be found in the position taken up before the ICJ, cannot create law, whereas an ICJ judgment has *eo ipso* a function'.

[114] *Armed Activities on the Territory of the Congo (New Application: 2002) (Democratic Republic of the Congo v Rwanda)*, Jurisdiction and Admissibility, Judgment of 3 February 2006, ICJ Reports 6, para 65, citing *Military and Paramilitary Activities in and against Nicaragua (Nicaragua v United States of America)*, Merits, Judgment of 27 June 1986, ICJ Reports 14 [*Nicaragua v US*, Merits] para 70. See also eg *Pulp Mills on the River Uruguay (Argentina v Uruguay)*, Judgment of 20 April 2010, ICJ Reports 14 [*Pulp Mills*] paras 166, 168.

[115] *Armed Activities on the Territory of the Congo*, para 129 ('[w]hile a notarized affidavit is entitled to a certain respect, the Court must observe that it is provided by a party in the case and provides at best indirect "information" that is unverified.'); *Application of the Convention on the Prevention and Punishment of the Crime of Genocide (Croatia v Serbia)*, Merits, Judgment of 3 February 2015, para 196 ('[i]n determining the evidential weight of any statement by an individual, the Court necessarily takes into account its form and circumstances in which it was made.').

[116] *Certain Activities Carried Out by Nicaragua in the Border Area (Costa Rica v Nicaragua)*, Merits, Judgment of 16 December 2015, para 83 ('Affidavits will be treated "with caution", in particular those made by State officials for purposes of litigation.'), citing *Application of the Convention on the Prevention and Punishment of the Crime of Genocide (Croatia v Serbia)*, paras 196–7, in turn citing *Nicaragua v Honduras*, para 244.

[117] cf Fauchald, 'The Legal Reasoning of ICSID Tribunals', 344.

of legal proceedings as compared to other instances of practice, especially by differentiating between highly case-specific statements and statements of a more general nature.[118] The former statements do not automatically represent relevant 'subsequent practice' in relation to the treaty, and, even if they do, may be accorded lower evidentiary weight.

2.3.1c Relevant actors

Since it is difficult to separate the question of *what* constitutes 'practice' from that of *whose* practice counts, the ensuing section addresses issues of attribution and relevant actors.[119]

State practice

In relation to forms of practice *within* a State, it has been noted that whether a given instance of conduct amounts to relevant State practice depends on rules of attribution, such as those formulated in the Articles on State Responsibility for determining when a State incurs international responsibility for the acts of its organs.[120] Overall, however, the approach of attributing to the State the 'conduct of any State organ' in Article 4 of those rules seems too broad for the purpose of identifying *relevant* subsequent practice.[121]

In principle, relevant practice may emanate from all State organs—legislative, executive, or judicial—as long as these are attributable to the State as acts of treaty interpretation.[122] National legislation has already been mentioned as a source of practice.[123] National court judgments have also been recognized as a valid source of State practice by the International Criminal Tribunal for the Former Yugoslavia (ICTY) and International Criminal Tribunal for Rwanda (ICTR),[124] the ICJ,[125]

[118] Ibid. 348. [119] See also Section 4.3.2.

[120] Nolte, Introductory Report on Treaties over Time, 197.

[121] Nolte, Annex A, para 27. See eg Arts 9 and 10 of the ILC, 'Draft articles on responsibility of States for internationally wrongful acts', UN Doc A/56/10 (2001) II(2) YBILC 76 [Articles on State Responsibility].

[122] ILC, 'Statement of the Chairman of the Study Group on Treaties over Time' (8 August 2011) <http://legal.un.org/ilc/sessions/63/pdfs/treaties_over_time_sg_chair_report_28aug2011.pdf> accessed 24 June 2016 [Nolte, Statement 2011] 8; Nolte, Second Report on Treaties over Time, 304 ('General Conclusion 11'). See also ILC, *Topical Summary of the discussion held in the Sixth Committee of the General Assembly during its 66th session*, UN Doc A/CN.4/650 (20 January 2012) Ch II(E); ILC, 'Subsequent agreements and subsequent practice in relation to the interpretation of treaties, Text of the draft conclusions provisionally adopted by the Drafting Committee on first reading' (6 June 2016) UN Doc A/CN.4/L.874, 2 ('Draft conclusion 5', para 1); ILC Draft Conclusions on Subsequent Agreements and Subsequent Practice (2016), 121 ('Conclusion 5', para 1) ('Subsequent practice under articles 31 and 32 may consist of any conduct in the application of a treaty which is attributable to a party to the treaty under international law.').

[123] See Section 2.3.1(a).

[124] See eg *Prosecutor v Kupreškić and others* (TC) Judgment, Case No IT-95-16-T (14 January 2000) para 541; *Prosecutor v Akayesu* (TC) Judgment, Case No ICTR-96-4-T (2 September 1998) paras 503, 542.

[125] *Jurisdictional Immunities of the State (Germany v Italy: Greece Intervening)*, Judgment of 3 February 2012, ICJ Reports 99, para 73. See also I Venzke, *How Interpretation Makes International Law: On Semantic Change and Normative Twists* (OUP, 2012) 238.

and in the literature[126]—with the caveat that a national judgment must be viewed in the context of the structures of the specific State to determine whether the respective court represents the highest authority in relation to that State's interpretative position on the treaty.[127] Moreover, engagement by domestic courts with decisions of other domestic courts in different jurisdictions 'may add to the development of a subsequent practice together with other domestic courts'.[128] On the one hand, the decisions invoked must be representative of practice generally accepted in the case law in other jurisdictions.[129] On the other hand, where practice diverges across different jurisdictions on a particular matter, emphasis may be placed on the jurisdictions of the most relevant States in that context, and, as mentioned, on higher courts.[130]

Furthermore, it is not only high-ranking officials that can impact State practice, but also, depending on the circumstances, lower State authorities charged with applying the treaty,[131] as confirmed in the case law.[132] In the *Rights of Nationals* case, the ICJ took into account the practice of local customs officials.[133] The Court's approach was even more far-reaching in the *Kasikili/Sedudu Island* case,[134] where it considered that the 'long-standing, unopposed' use of the island by members of a local tribe could, under certain circumstances,[135] constitute subsequent practice in the sense of Article 31(3)(b) VCLT. In this case, the Court concluded that the occupation of the island by the tribesmen did not constitute subsequent practice in relation to the treaty within the meaning of Article 31(3)(b), since 'as far as Bechuanaland, and subsequently Botswana, were concerned, the intermittent presence of the Masubia [tribesmen] on the Island did not trouble anyone and was tolerated, not least because it did not appear to be connected with interpretation of the terms of the 1890 Treaty'.[136]

[126] See eg Nolte, Third Report on Treaties over Time, 317. See also Nolte, Fourth Report on Subsequent Practice, para 112 ('Draft conclusion 13').

[127] RK Gardiner, *Treaty Interpretation* (OUP, 2008) 229. On treaty interpretation by domestic courts, see generally HP Aust and G Nolte (eds), *The Interpretation of International Law by Domestic Courts: Uniformity, Diversity, Convergence* (OUP, 2016).

[128] Nolte, Fourth Report on Subsequent Practice, para 108, citing A Tzanakopulos, 'Judicial Dialogue as a Means of Interpretation' in Aust HP and G Nolte (eds), *The Interpretation of International Law by Domestic Courts: Uniformity, Diversity, Convergence* (OUP, 2016) 72, 94.

[129] Nolte, Fourth Report on Subsequent Practice, para 108.

[130] Ibid. para 109.

[131] Nolte, Introductory Report on Treaties over Time, 198.

[132] See eg *Case concerning the Question Whether the Re-evaluation of the German Mark in 1961 and 1969 Constitutes a Case for Application of the Clause in Article 2(e) of Annex I A of the 1953 Agreement on German External Debts between Belgium, France, Switzerland, the United Kingdom of Great Britain and Northern Ireland and the United States of America on the one hand and the Federal Republic of Germany on the other,* Award of 16 May 1980, 19 RIAA 67, para 31; *Question of the Tax Regime Governing Pensions Paid to Retired UNESCO Officials Residing in France,* Award of 14 January 2003, 25 RIAA 231, paras 66, 74, cited in Nolte, Introductory Report on Treaties over Time, 198 fn 209. See also Section 3.3.3(a).

[133] *Rights of Nationals*, 211.

[134] *Kasikili/Sedudu Island*, paras 73–4.

[135] Ibid. para 74, listing two conditions: first, the occupation by the local tribe must be linked to the belief of the Caprivi authorities that the treaty boundary followed a certain route, and, second, it must be shown that the Bechuanaland authorities 'were fully aware of and accepted this as a confirmation of the Treaty boundary'.

[136] Ibid. paras 74–5. By contrast, the ICJ did take into account the practice of private entities such as fishermen as evidence of a tacit agreement between the parties in *Peru v Chile*, paras 103–11.

A number of writers have argued that subsequent practice must stem from the actions of 'properly authorized organs' of the States parties to a treaty.[137] This seems to be implied in the decision of the ICJ in the *Temple of Préah Vihéar* case. Thailand here argued that certain boundary maps did not constitute relevant practice, since they had been approved by lower ranking officials that lacked the authority and necessary expertise in cartography to apply the treaty. The Court rejected this argument, additionally pointing to the awareness of higher officials of those acts at the time:

> The Court cannot accept these contentions either on the facts or the law. If the Siamese authorities did show these maps only to minor officials, they clearly acted at their own risk, and the claim of Thailand could not, on the international plane, derive any assistance from that fact. But the history of the matter (...) shows clearly that the maps were seen by such [highly-ranked] persons.[138]

However, the Court did not consider the practice of local authorities in itself sufficient to establish that Thailand had been in possession of the Temple at all material times, and hence had felt no need to react positively to the maps:

> [T]he Court finds it difficult to regard such local acts as overriding and negativing the consistent and undeviating attitude of the central Siamese authorities to the frontier line as mapped.[139]

The issue of which State organs are entitled to act on behalf of the State at the international level and contribute to relevant practice depends on the context and nature of the treaty provision in question: '[w]hereas the interpretation of certain treaty provisions can only be affected by the conduct of certain high executive state organs (...) other treaty provisions can be influenced by legislative, judicial, and to a certain extent also social practice'.[140]

In principle, the acts of relatively low-ranking officials can contribute to subsequent practice as long as they are conducted with the (tacit) consent of higher authorities.[141] In other words, it is reasonable to conclude that subsequent practice can be attributed to a State if the conduct in question has been carried out—or at least accepted—by the State organs responsible for the application of the treaty.[142] The State practice in question should on the whole be concordant among the different sub-State actors: if multiple national authorities are involved in the making

[137] G Haraszti, *Some Fundamental Problems of the Law of Treaties* (Akadémiai Kiadó, 1973) 145; Thirlway, *International Customary Law*, 56–7; Hafner, 'Subsequent Agreements and Practice', 112.

[138] *Temple of Préah Vihéar*, 25.

[139] Ibid. 30.

[140] Nolte, Second Report on Treaties over Time, 304 ('General Conclusion 12'). See eg *Dudgeon v United Kingdom* App no 7525/76 (ECtHR, 22 October 1981) para 60. cf *United States of America et al and Islamic Republic of Iran et al*, Award No 108-A-16/582/591-FT (25 January 1984) 5 Iran-US CTR 57, 71; *International Schools Services Inc and National Iranian Copper Industries Company*, Interlocutory Award No ITL 37-111-FT (6 April 1984) Dissenting Opinion of President Lagergren, 5 Iran-US CTR 348, 353.

[141] See Nolte, Statement 2011, para 27; Nolte, Introductory Report on Treaties over Time, 199.

[142] See eg Nolte, Introductory Report on Treaties over Time, 197–8.

and implementation of the treaty, their practice must amount to the 'unequivocal expression' of the position of the State with regard to that treaty.[143]

Practice of international organizations

Evidence of subsequent practice is not necessarily limited to the practice of or within States. Such evidence may also be found in the practice of international organizations,[144] in the context of which the subsequent practice of the individual States parties to the constitutive treaty appears, in fact, to 'fade into the background'.[145] The separate legal order of international organizations adds an extra dimension to treaties establishing organizations compared to 'classic' treaty regimes,[146] with inevitable implications for the interpretative practices applicable in that context,[147] and subsequent practice in particular. Although this book does not engage fully with the discussion on the distinct nature of constitutive treaties, it is essential to note that, once established, an organization in a sense takes on a will of its own, separate from that of its original creators, and acquires varying degrees of authority under international law,[148] including the ability to shape the law through its practice.

[143] *Tax Regime Governing Pensions to Retired UNESCO Officials*, para 74.

[144] See eg Karl, *Vertrag*, 114–17, 170–1; G McGinley, 'Practice as a Guide to Treaty Interpretation' (1985) 9 The Fletcher Forum 211, 212–13; HWA Thirlway, 'The Law and Procedure of the International Court of Justice: 1960–1989, Part Three' (1991) 62 BYBIL 1, 49; CF Amerasinghe, 'Interpretation of Texts in Open International Organizations' (1994) 65 BYBIL 175, 198; G Ress, 'The Interpretation of the Charter' in B Simma (ed), *The Charter of the United Nations: A Commentary*, vol I (2nd edn, OUP, 2002) 13, 38–42; Linderfalk, *On the Interpretation of Treaties*, 166; RR Churchill, 'The Impact of State Practice on the Jurisdictional Framework Contained in the LOS Convention' in AG Oude Elferink (ed), *Stability and Change in the Law of the Sea: The Role of the LOS Convention* (Martinus Nijhoff, 2005) 91, 92; Gardiner, *Treaty Interpretation*, 247–8; Sorel and Eveno, 'Article 31', 826; Venzke, *How Interpretation Makes International Law*, 238; S Kadelbach, 'The Interpretation of the Charter' in B Simma and others (eds), *The Charter of the United Nations: A Commentary* (3rd edn, OUP, 2012) 71, 80. It has even been suggested that the practice of one international organization can influence the interpretation of the constituent instrument of another international organization—ILC, 'Third Report on Subsequent Agreements and Subsequent Practice in relation to the Interpretation of Treaties, by Georg Nolte, Special Rapporteur', UN Doc A/CN.4/683 (2015) [Nolte, Third Report on Subsequent Practice] para 50.

[145] C Brölmann, 'Specialized Rules of Treaty Interpretation: International Organizations' in DB Hollis (ed), *The Oxford Guide to Treaties* (OUP, 2012) 507.

[146] Moreover, the interpretation of decisions of organs of international organizations, such as UN Security Council resolutions, amounts to a different kind of interpretative exercise—see ibid. 523.

[147] See generally eg JHH Weiler, 'The Interpretation of Treaties—A Re-examination' (2010) 21 EJIL 507. This is also suggested by the formulation of Art 5 VCLT: 'The present Convention applies to any treaty which is the constituent instrument of an international organization (...) *without prejudice to any relevant rules of the organization*' (emphasis added), which can be taken to include special interpretative rules in the context of the constitutive treaty. See further eg J Klabbers, *An Introduction to International Institutional Law* (2nd edn, CUP, 2009) 88; K Schmalenbach, 'Art. 5 Treaties Constituting International Organizations and Treaties Adopted within an International Organization' in O Dörr and K Schmalenbach (eds), *Vienna Convention on the Law of Treaties: A Commentary* (Springer, 2012) 89, 96 para 15.

[148] See ILC, 'Draft Articles on the Responsibility of International Organizations', UN GAOR, 66th Session, Supp No 10, UN Doc A/66/10 (2011) Ch V [Draft Articles on the Responsibility of International Organizations] Art 2(a) (on the legal personality of international organizations). The General Commentary to the Draft Articles on the Responsibility of International Organizations, 70 para 88, notes the 'very significant differences among international organizations with regard to their powers and functions, size of membership, relations between the organization and its members, procedures for

What does this entail for the identification and analysis of subsequent practice in relation to constitutive treaties? It could be said that the subsequent practice of international organizations occurs not as part of the law of treaties, but as part of international institutional law.[149] This point has generated significant debate, which, true to its focus, this book endeavours to tackle as much as possible from a treaty law perspective.

Two types of practice can be distinguished in the context of international organizations,[150] though the ICJ has yet to (explicitly) make the distinction:[151] first, the practice of the States parties to the constitutive treaty within and under the umbrella of the organization, and second, the practice of the organization 'itself'.[152] This is also indicated by Article 2(1)(j) of the 1986 Vienna Convention on the Law of Treaties between States and International Organizations or between International Organizations (VCLTIO),[153] which refers to the 'established practice of the organization' as part of the 'rules of the organization'.[154] These two types of practice are sometimes difficult to distinguish, such as when individual States act as part of the plenary organ or conference of the parties of the organization.[155] The practice of an

deliberation, structure and facilities, as well as the primary rules including treaty obligations by which they are bound'.

[149] E Lauterpacht, 'The Development of the Law of International Organization by the Decisions of International Tribunals' (1976-IV) 152 RC 379; G Ulfstein, 'Treaty Bodies and Regimes' in DB Hollis (ed), *The Oxford Guide to Treaties* (OUP, 2012) 428, 438.

[150] See ILC, 'Third Report on Identification of Customary International Law, by Michael Wood, Special Rapporteur', UN Doc A/CN.4/682 (2015) [Wood, Third Report] para 71 ('First—and this is fundamental—we need to distinguish the practice of States within international organizations from that of international organizations as such. While this may not always be easy to do (...) and while there is often a lack of clarity in the literature, in principle the practice of international organizations (...) should not be assimilated to that of the States themselves'). cf Nolte, Third Report on Subsequent Practice, para 56 (arguing that this distinction does not exclude the possibility of assessing both forms of subsequent practice in combination.').

[151] See eg *WHO Nuclear Weapons Advisory Opinion*, paras 19, 27 (equating WHO practice with subsequent practice in the sense of Art 31(3)(b) VCLT); *Applicability of Article VI, Section 22, of the Convention on the Privileges and Immunities of the United Nations*, Advisory Opinion of 15 December 1989, ICJ Reports 177 [*Privileges and Immunities Advisory Opinion*] para 48 (conflating the acts of organs of the organization with general UN practice); DW Greig, *Intertemporality and the Law of Treaties* (British Institute of International and Comparative Law 2003) 88–9.

[152] See eg ILC, 'Fourth Report on Relations between States and International Organizations (Second Part of the Topic) by Mr. Leonardo Díaz-González, Special Rapporteur' (1989) II(1) YBILC 153; ILC, 'Summary record of the 2133rd meeting', *Summary records of the 41st session* (1989) I YBILC 281, para 3, 11; O Elias, 'Who Can Make Treaties? International Organizations' in DB Hollis (ed), *The Oxford Guide to Treaties* (OUP, 2012) 73, 90; Brölmann, 'Specialized Rules', 515; Ulfstein, 'Treaty Bodies', 438. cf CF Amerasinghe, *Principles of the Institutional Law of International Organizations* (2nd edn, CUP, 2005) 53.

[153] (1986) 25 ILM 543.

[154] See also Art 2(b) of the ILC Draft Articles on the Responsibility of International Organizations—see UNGA, 'Responsibility of International Organizations: Texts and Titles of Draft Articles 1 to 67 Adopted by the Draft Committee on Second Reading in 2011', UN Doc A/CN.4/L.778 (2011) 1.

[155] It is difficult enough to distinguish between States acting in their capacity as members of an organ or in their capacity as States parties to the constitutive treaty—Nolte, Third Report on Subsequent Practice, para 60, citing *Parliament v Council and Commission* (Joined Cases C-181/91 and C-248/91) [1993] ECR I-3685, para 12. See eg Meijers, 'On International Customary Law in the Netherlands', 84: 'Does a state, when voting on the acceptance of a resolution, for instance in the General Assembly of the United Nations, act as a state, or as part of an organ of the United Nations, a separate subject

international organization can, of course, influence the subsequent practice of its member States, triggering their agreement through subsequent practice as to a certain interpretation of the constitutive treaty.[156]

Both types of practice—that of international organizations as such, and that of the member States of an organization—have generated interpretations, as well as tacit modifications,[157] of constitutive treaties.[158] The question is how close such 'organizational' practice, which seems to have attracted a significant amount of attention compared to the practice of States parties themselves,[159] comes to (collective) State practice, and whether it does not stray too much from the intended meaning of 'subsequent practice' under Article 31(3)(b) VCLT.

There is a 'constant oscillation between the position of the organization as a party in its own right, and the position of the organization as a vehicle for its own member States'.[160] International organizations may be autonomous, but they are also the product of sovereign States whose individual practice—and individual *consent*—counts even from 'behind the institutional veil'.[161] According to the traditional reliance on the doctrine of State consent,[162] classifying organizational practice as 'subsequent practice' may pose legitimacy problems and 'strain the bonds of state consent from which these bodies derive their treaty-based authority in the first place'.[163] One could argue that an organization's application of its own treaty is an act independent of the will of the individual members and cannot be attributed to them.[164] This leads to the consent-based problem and potential legitimacy deficit associated with regarding the interpretative practice of an organization as capable of establishing an agreement between the States parties to the constitutive treaty.

One author argues, for instance, that such 'informal tracks of constitutional change take the development of the organization out of the hands of the parties, and thereby supplant a form of international law making'.[165] The practice

of international law? The answer seems evident: as part of the UN organ (...) [only when] it states its reasons for voting in the way it did, or gives its point of view vis-à-vis that resolution, we may identify an act of state'.

156 See eg R Higgins, 'The Development of International Law by the Political Organs of the United Nations' (1965) 59 ASIL Proc 116, 119.

157 See eg Sections 3.5.1(a), 5.2.1, and 5.3.1.

158 For different views on the significance of institutional practice in the specific context of the UN Charter, see eg JE Alvarez, *International Organizations as Law-Makers* (OUP, 2005) 88–9; J Klabbers, 'Checks and Balances in the Law of International Organizations' in M Sellers (ed), *Autonomy in the Law* (Springer, 2007) 141, 151–2.

159 Brölmann, 'Specialized Rules', 512. See generally eg T Sato, *Evolving Constitutions of International Organizations: A Critical Analysis of the Interpretive Frameworks of the Constituent Instruments of International Organizations* (Brill, 1996).

160 Klabbers, *An Introduction*, 269.

161 Elias, 'Who Can Make Treaties?', 90.

162 Arato, 'Treaty Interpretation', 353.

163 Ibid. cf AT Guzman, 'Against Consent' (2012) 52 VJIL 747, 753, warning against an 'excessive commitment' to the doctrine of consent.

164 Brölmann, 'Specialized Rules', 515; Villiger, *Customary International Law and Treaties* (1985), para 18.

165 Arato, 'Treaty Interpretation', 355.

of subsidiary organs,[166] including organs of limited membership such as the UN Security Council, has the same legal effect as the practice of the overarching organization, but may remove the States parties 'one step further from control of the IO "practice" '.[167] Organs of international organizations sometimes issue reports that explicitly exclude the responsibility of the larger organization and its individual member States.[168] Such documents clearly fail to qualify as subsequent practice, let alone practice capable of establishing an agreement between the members to the organization.

On the other hand, if an international organization takes a decision autonomously from its constituent States, the latter can object to the practice. *A contrario*, in the absence of such objection, the organizational practice could be said to represent collective State practice or constitute an approximation of State practice in the sense of Article 31(3)(b) VCLT. In the same vein, it is doubtful whether an instance of organizational practice unanimously supported by the organization's membership will still pose a problem of consent.[169] It can be argued that organizational practice can qualify as 'subsequent practice' within the meaning of Article 31(3)(b)[170] since the parties to the constitutive treaties are assumed to have agreed in becoming members to its decision-making mechanisms, even if they disagree with a particular decision:[171] 'States, on joining international organisations, impliedly accept the permissibility of constitutional development in this manner.'[172] Formal amendments of instruments such as the UN Charter are also passed by majority rather than by unanimity, but still become binding for all members of the organization.[173]

Thus, subsequent practice in relation to constitutive treaties can still be founded upon agreement or consent, even if the latter has to be implied.[174] This approach is also aligned with the principle of effectiveness in developing constitutional texts through practice,[175] given the growing importance of international organizations

[166] Draft Articles on the Responsibility of International Organizations, 52, Art 2(c), defines an 'organ' of an international organization as 'any person or entity which has that status in accordance with the rules of the international organization'.

[167] Brölmann, 'Specialized Rules', 515. See also *Certain Expenses Advisory Opinion*, Separate Opinion of Judge Spender, ICJ Reports 182, 189–90.

[168] See eg OECD, 'OECD Guidelines for Multinational Enterprises' (2008) <www.oecd.org/corporate/mne> accessed 24 June 2016: 'This work is published on the responsibility of the Secretary-General of the OECD. The opinions expressed and arguments employed herein do no necessarily reflect the official views of the Organisation or of the governments of its member countries.'

[169] Amerasinghe, *Principles*, 52, arguing that even when a large majority supports the practice, 'it is arguable that a small obstinate majority (...) cannot obstruct an interpretation given by the membership of the organ'. cf *Certain Expenses Advisory Opinion*, Separate Opinion of Judge Spender, 196.

[170] See eg Churchill, 'The Impact of State Practice', 92.

[171] Amerasinghe, *Principles*, 53. See also Lauterpacht, 'The Development of the Law of International Organization', 459 (suggesting that the practice of international organizations could still be established 'on the basis of majority voting and often against the dissenting views of a minority'); Greig, *Intertemporality*, 87. Acceptance may depend on the effect of the decisions (for instance, RFMOs have the possibility to opt out).

[172] Lauterpacht, 'The Development of the Law of International Organization', 460.

[173] See Arts 108 and 109 of the UN Charter. See further Section 3.3.4.

[174] Amerasinghe, *Principles*, 53.

[175] Ibid. 55; M Herdegen, 'Interpretation in International Law' in R Wolfrum (ed), *Max Planck Encyclopedia of Public International Law* (OUP, 2008). See further Section 2.5.1.

and of non-State actors in general. Article 31(3)(b) VCLT, after all, does not specify *whose* practice is to be taken into account when establishing an agreement between the parties.[176] In addition, the relevance of the practice will depend on the nature and relevance of the provision being interpreted, such as whether it is of an internal procedural nature, or whether it is of a general, substantive nature, in which case the practice of the international organization will have to be kept carefully in line with the will of the States parties to the treaty.

It is in any case clear that, since international organizations can conclude treaties on their own,[177] their practice in the application of those treaties to which they are *direct* parties should qualify as 'subsequent practice'. The European Union is a prime example: in the areas in which it has exclusive competences and acts in the place of its member States, its practice cannot be distinguished from theirs.[178] It is noteworthy in this respect that the formulation of Article 31(3)(b) of the 1969 Vienna Convention is identical to the corresponding article in the 1986 Vienna Convention.

A considerable number of scholars maintain that the practice of international organizations—which may include that of international dispute settlement institutions—can be captured as 'subsequent practice' in the sense of Article 31(3)(b) VCLT.[179] The ICJ seems to have at least implicitly endorsed this view in the case of *Legality of the Use by a State of Nuclear Weapons*,[180] triggering criticism from a number of commentators and judges.[181] The Court acknowledged the interpretative difficulties encountered in the context of international organizations:

[176] See also J Pauwelyn, RA Wessel, and J Wouters, 'Informal International Lawmaking: An Assessment and Template to Keep It Both Effective and Accountable' in J Pauwelyn, RA Wessel, and J Wouters (eds), *Informal International Lawmaking* (OUP, 2012) 500, 530.

[177] See eg Elias, 'Who Can Make Treaties?', 90–1; C Brölmann, *The Institutional Veil in Public International Law: International Organisations and the Law of Treaties* (Hart Publishing, 2007) 192–3.

[178] See eg F Hoffmeister, 'The Contribution of EU Practice to International Law' in M Cremona (ed), *Developments in EU External Relations Law* (OUP, 2008) 37; E Paasivirta and PJ Kuijper, 'Does One Size Fit All? The European Community and the Responsibility of International Organizations' (2005) 36 NYBIL 169.

[179] McGinley, 'Practice as a Guide to Treaty Interpretation', 212–13; Thirlway, 'Law and Procedure' (1991), 49; Amerasinghe, 'Interpretation of Texts in Open International Organizations', 198; Ress, 'The Interpretation of the Charter', 38–42; Churchill, 'The Impact of State Practice', 92; Linderfalk, *On the Interpretation of Treaties*, 166; Gardiner, *Treaty Interpretation*, 247–8; Sorel and Boré Eveno, 'Article 31', 826; Venzke, *How Interpretation Makes International Law*, 238, citing eg Karl, *Vertrag*, 114–17, 170–1; L Boisson de Chazournes, 'Subsequent Practice, Practices, and "Family-Resemblance": Towards Embedding Subsequent Practice in Its Operative Milieu' in G Nolte (ed), *Treaties and Subsequent Practice* (OUP, 2013) 53, 57. cf Villiger, *Customary International Law and Treaties* (1985), para 18; Brölmann, 'Specialized Rules', 515.

[180] *WHO Nuclear Weapons Advisory Opinion*, paras 19–27. See also P-M Dupuy, 'Le droit des Nations Unies et sa pratique dans la jurisprudence de la Cour internationale de Justice' in SFDI (ed), *La pratique et le droit international* (Pédone, 2004) 139, 144–5. See eg Sections 2.5.3(c) and 2.4.

[181] *Certain Expenses Advisory Opinion*, Separate Opinion of Judge Spender, 189–90; *Legal Consequences of the Continued Presence of South Legal Consequences for States of the Continued Presence of South Africa in Namibia (South West Africa) Notwithstanding Security Council Resolution 276 (1970)*, Advisory Opinion of 21 June 1971, Dissenting Opinion of Judge Fitzmaurice, ICJ Reports 220, 282; HG Schermers and NM Blokker, *International Institutional Law: Unity Within Diversity* (Martinus Nijhoff, 2003) 844.

[The constituent instruments of international organizations] can raise specific problems of interpretation owing, *inter alia*, to their character which is conventional and at the same time institutional; the very nature of the organization created, the objectives which have been assigned to it by its founders, the imperatives associated with the effective performance of its functions, *as well as its own practice*, are all elements which may deserve special attention when the time comes to interpret these constituent treaties.[182]

The Court proceeded to equate the practice of the organization in question—namely, the practice of the World Health Organization (WHO), consisting of 'reports and resolutions'—with subsequent practice in the sense of Article 31(3)(b) VCLT.[183] Its ultimate finding was that, under the circumstances, the practice did not relate sufficiently to the legality of the use of nuclear weapons to establish an agreement between the WHO members empowering the organization to address questions on such matters. However, an *a contrario* reading suggests that, under different circumstances, the organizational practice would have been capable of establishing the 'agreement of the parties' regarding the interpretation to include nuclear weapons issues under the organization's chapeau.

In a number of previous cases, in analysing the subsequent practice of an international organization, the Court did not refer explicitly to the State practice of the parties to the constitutive treaty and Article 31(3)(b) VCLT, thus equating the practice of the organization with relevant subsequent practice for purposes of interpretation. In *Competence of the General Assembly for the Admission of a State to the United Nations*, for instance, it stated that the organs entrusted with the 'judgment of the Organization in matters of admission have consistently interpreted the text in the sense that the General Assembly can decide to admit only on the basis of the recommendations of the Security Council'.[184] In *Constitution of the Maritime Safety Committee of the Inter-Governmental Maritime Consultative Organization*, the Court referred to the Organization's own practice in relation to the underlying treaty as a means of interpretation.[185] In its *Certain Expenses Advisory Opinion*, it relied on the 'consistent practice of the General Assembly' as a means of interpretation of the UN Charter.[186] And in its Advisory Opinion on the *Privileges and Immunities of the United Nations*, it conflated the practice of organs of the organization with that of the United Nations.[187]

Similarly, in the *Namibia Advisory Opinion*, the ICJ relied directly on the subsequent practice of the Security Council to arrive at an interpretation—bordering on, if not constituting, modification[188]—of Article 27(3) of the UN Charter that allowed for the adoption of resolutions even in the event of an abstention by a

[182] *WHO Nuclear Weapons Advisory Opinion*, para 19 (emphasis added).

[183] Ibid. para 27. See Gardiner, *Treaty Interpretation*, 247.

[184] *Competence of the General Assembly for the Admission of a State to the United Nations*, Advisory Opinion of 3 March 1950, ICJ Reports 4, 9.

[185] *Constitution of the Maritime Safety Committee of the Inter-Governmental Maritime Consultative Organization*, Advisory Opinion of 8 June 1960, ICJ Reports 150, 169.

[186] *Certain Expenses Advisory Opinion*, 160, 168.

[187] *Privileges and Immunities Advisory Opinion*, para 48.

[188] See Section 5.2.1.

permanent member.[189] However, in the latter case, the Court also referred to the fact that the Security Council's practice was 'generally accepted by Members of the United Nations and evidences a general practice of the Organization', thus combining the practice of the Security Council with State practice to support its conclusion.[190] Most recently, in the *Israeli Wall Advisory Opinion*, the Court recognized that UN political organs could shape the interpretation of underlying treaty provisions, in this case Article 12 of the UN Charter.[191] It should therefore be noted that the practice of (organs of) international organizations recognized by the ICJ as a form of 'subsequent practice' sometimes includes practice that may not establish the agreement of the parties to the treaty.[192] In the *Israeli Wall Advisory Opinion*, for instance, the Court refers to practice in the form of acts taken by an international organization despite the opposition of certain member States.[193] Such forms of subsequent practice could be categorized under Article 32 VCLT, as discussed further in this chapter.[194]

In sum, the Court has often relied on organizational practice, including the practice of organs such as the Security Council and non-representative bodies such as the office of the legal counsel, as a 'proxy' for State practice,[195] even if its *degree* of reliance on the organizational practice may vary. In doing so, the Court has 'developed a mechanism for affecting informal constitutional change (. . .) capable of skirting the stringent requirements of the formal amendment rule'.[196] This phenomenon is explored further in Chapter 3 of this book.[197]

Reverting back to the fact that Article 31(3)(b) VCLT does not specify *whose* practice must establish the agreement of the parties:

> A reasonable expectation is that relevant practice will usually be that of those on whom the obligation of performance falls, but obviously this depends on the nature of the obligation and treaty provision in issue. Hence where states by treaty entrust performance of activities to an organization, how those activities are conducted can constitute practice under the treaty; but whether such practice establishes agreement of the parties regarding the treaty's interpretation may require account to be taken of further factors. These may include assessment of the powers of the organ acting in the matter, the potential for any other body in the organization to control the organ, the manner in which states parties to the treaty participate in the activities of the organization, etc.[198]

[189] *Namibia Advisory Opinion*, 22. See also ibid. 36, discussing the practice of the General Assembly; Amerasinghe, *Principles*, 50. See further Sections 3.4.2 and 5.2.1.

[190] Nolte, Third Report on Subsequent Practice, para 52, citing *Namibia Advisory Opinion*, 22. For similar examples, see Nolte, Third Report on Subsequent Practice, paras 53–6, citing eg KG Bühler, *State Succession and Membership in International Organizations* (Kluwer Law International, 2001) 295, 298.

[191] *Israeli Wall Advisory Opinion*, paras 27–8. See further Gardiner, *Treaty Interpretation*, 248; Sorel and Boré Eveno, 'Article 31', 826.

[192] cf text to nn 179–80.

[193] *Israeli Wall Advisory Opinion*, para 27, referring to the adoption of UNGA Res 1600 (XV) of 15 April 1961, UN Doc A/RES/1600 (1961) and UNGA Res 1913 (XVIII) of 13 December 1963, UN Doc A/RES/1913 (1963). See Nolte, Third Report on Subsequent Practice, para 49.

[194] See also Section 2.3.5.

[195] Arato, 'Treaty Interpretation', 328. See further Sections 2.5.2, 5.2.1, and 5.2.5.

[196] Arato, 'Treaty Interpretation', 330.

[197] See also Sections 5.2.1 and 5.2.5.

[198] Gardiner, *Treaty Interpretation*, 246.

Therefore, whether decisions or activities of an organization will qualify as practice reflective of an agreement of the parties, will vary depending on the specific situation and a range of factors, including the degree of support for the practice. In the aforementioned *Namibia Advisory Opinion*, for instance, the practice seemed to have unanimous support.[199] States' reactions to the practice of the organization are in a sense assessed in light of their capacity as members of that organization, rather than as parties to the constitutive treaty.[200]

Even if its basis falls outside the scope of Article 31(3)(b) VCLT,[201] 'institutional' practice supplements 'classical' State practice.[202] Its relevance, and the reactions of member States to it, may have to be assessed on the basis of different standards than those applicable to other types of treaties.[203] This special character of institutional practice may carry implications for the relative weight it is accorded in the interpretative process, but cannot be excluded from consideration altogether due to a strict reading of Article 31(3)(b) VCLT.[204] This may simply mean that Article 31(3)(b) is not appropriate for all kinds of practice. In fact, it has been noted with regard to treaties constituting international organizations that it may be inferred that the 'wording of Article 31(3)(b) is not suitable for the interpretation of every treaty'.[205]

Institutional practice could instead be classified as relevant under Article 32 VCLT: '[t]he practice of organs in the application of a constituent instrument can thus, at a minimum, be conceived as being "other subsequent practice" under article 32.'[206] The practice of (organs of) international organizations could fall under Article 32 VCLT even if it does not evidence the agreement of the parties, for instance in the case of a dissenting minority: 'even if a majority vote cannot in the formal sense bind the minority, it can, if consistently exercised in a particular way, suffice to establish a settled practice which a tribunal can usefully and properly take account of'.[207] In the same vein, several ICJ judges in the *Whaling in the Antarctic* case were of the view that resolutions of the International Whaling Commission (IWC) adopted by a large majority of IWC members, as opposed to *all* the members, could still count as relevant, even if they fall outside the terms of Article 31(3)(b)

[199] Amerasinghe, *Principles*, 52.

[200] Boisson de Chazournes, 'Subsequent Practice', 58 (adding that this move would incidentally also allow 'the obstacles standing in the way of treaty modification through practice to be brushed away').

[201] Amerasinghe, *Principles*, 53. cf Venzke, *How Interpretation Makes International Law*, 238.

[202] See Boisson de Chazournes, 'Subsequent Practice', 58 (referring to subsequent practice and the practice of an organization as 'twins raised in two different contexts to one another'). See also eg C Peters, 'Subsequent Practice and Established Practice of International Organizations: Two Sides of the Same Coin?' (2011) 3 GoJIL 617. See further, by analogy, ILC, 'Fourth Report on Identification of Customary International Law, by Michael Wood, Special Rapporteur', UN Doc A/CN.4/695 (2016) [Wood, Fourth Report] para 20 (underlining that the practice of international organizations as such can contribute to the creation of customary international law); *Report of the International Law Commission on the work of its 68th session*, UN Doc A/71/10 (2016) Ch V [ILC Draft Conclusions on Customary International Law (2016)] ('Conclusion 4', para 2).

[203] Nolte, Annex A, para 18, citing Amerasinghe, *Principles*, 49, 290, 460.

[204] Crema, 'Subsequent Agreements and Subsequent Practice', 24–5.

[205] Ibid. 19.

[206] Nolte, Third Report on Subsequent Practice, para 49.

[207] *Certain Expenses Advisory Opinion*, Separate Opinion of Judge Fitzmaurice, 201–2. See also Greig, *Intertemporality*, 99. See further Section 2.4.

VCLT.[208] Thus, as long as it is analysed keeping the special character of constitutive treaties closely in mind, the practice of international organizations provides a useful source of examples for the 'repertoire' of practice in Chapter 5.[209]

Practice of other 'treaty bodies' and 'autonomous institutional arrangements'

Building upon the previous analysis of the relevance of the practice of (organs of) international organizations, a preliminary distinction must be made between different types of treaty bodies. First, there are treaty bodies[210] composed of *State representatives* constituting *organs of international organizations* (including institutionalized forms of Conferences of States Parties[211]), and, second, treaty bodies composed of *experts* constituting *organs of international organizations* (such as the Committee of Experts on the Application of Conventions and Recommendations of the International Labour Organization[212]). The practice of both these types of treaty bodies can, in principle, be attributed to the organization acting collectively, as well as to the individual member States, as discussed.[213] Third, there are treaty bodies composed of *State representatives* but *not* constituting organs of international organizations (such as those less institutionalized forms of Conferences of States Parties that are merely periodic review meetings by the States parties,[214] in particular those established under environmental treaties). Such treaty bodies therefore cannot be clustered with international organizations, and their practice amounts to State practice within that framework. A fourth category is that of treaty bodies consisting of *experts* serving in their personal capacity and *not* constituting organs of international organizations,[215] in particular bodies established under human rights treaties.[216] The previous section already dealt with the first two forms of practice of (treaty bodies constituting) organs of international organizations. The present section addresses the latter two forms of treaty bodies, which, by contrast, do not represent organs of international organizations.

208 See *Whaling in the Antarctic (Australia v Japan: New Zealand intervening)*, Judgment of 31 March 2014, General List No 148, Separate Opinion of Judge ad hoc Charlesworth, para 4; ibid. Separate Opinion of Judge Xue, para 12.

209 See eg Sections 5.2.1 and 5.3.1.

210 For an overview, see Nolte, Fourth Report on Subsequent Practice, paras 11–12.

211 See further Nolte, Second Report on Subsequent Practice, paras 77–8; Nolte, Fourth Report on Subsequent Practice, para 11.

212 See eg ILC, 'International Law Commission's study of the topic "Subsequent agreements and subsequent practice in relation to the interpretation of treaties"; selected examples provided by the International Labour Organization' (29 February 2016) <http://legal.un.org/ilc/sessions/68/pdfs/english/sasp_ilo.pdf> accessed 11 November 2016.

213 See text to n 155 on the difficulty of distinguishing State practice from organizational practice. See also Draft Articles on the Responsibility of International Organizations, Art 6(1).

214 cf n 211.

215 See Nolte, Fourth Report on Subsequent Practice, Annex, 47 ('Draft Conclusion 12'); ILC Draft Conclusions on Subsequent Agreements and Subsequent Practice (2016), 123 ('Conclusion 13', para 1). See also 'Statement of the Chairman of the Drafting Committee, Mr Pavel Šturma' (10 June 2016) <http://legal.un.org/docs/?path=../ilc/documentation/english/statements/2016_dc_chairman_statement_sasp.pdf> accessed 21 July 2016.

216 See eg N Rodley, 'The Role and Impact of Treaty Bodies' in D Shelton (ed), *The Oxford Handbook of International Human Rights Law* (OUP, 2013) 621, 622–3.

So-called 'autonomous institutional arrangements' (AIAs), such as conferences or meetings of the States parties,[217] particularly in the context of multilateral environmental agreements (MEAs), can generate subsequent practice.[218] Since they are often representative of the membership as a whole (though not organs of the organization), they can be regarded as a 'continuing common venue' for the exercise of the parties' collective will and a source of authoritative interpretations, as a mechanism for continuous treaty clarification, elaboration, and adaptation.[219]

Some commentators argue that AIAs effectively constitute international organizations.[220] Even if they do not, AIAs share certain key features with international organizations, such as autonomy from the States parties and the ability to create new obligations under the treaty by means of protocols and amendments, being 'both more informal and more flexible, and often innovative in relation to norm creation and compliance'.[221] Churchill and Ulfstein argue that there is no reason to believe that parties to MEAs meant to establish less effective bodies internally by not establishing formal international organizations.[222] The GATT may have presented a similar situation: though merely a treaty being applied provisionally, the GATT gradually became a *de facto* international organization, as the initial Agreement was developed over time by regular meetings of the Contracting Parties.[223] Likewise, the periodic meetings of the consultative parties to the Antarctic Treaty[224] have developed the original provisions through 'recommendations' and the elaboration of further treaties and protocols, effectively adapting the Antarctic regime.[225] It is still heavily debated whether the practice of such bodies is covered by international institutional law or compares to the practice of 'classical' international organizations.[226] In any case, it should be noted that there is no generally

[217] AIAs should be distinguished from plenary organs of international organizations, such as the UN General Assembly or the Ministerial Conference and General Council of the WTO, as well as from conferences of the parties of limited membership.

[218] RR Churchill and G Ulfstein, 'Autonomous Institutional Arrangements in Multilateral Environmental Agreements: A Little-Noticed Phenomenon in International Law' (2000) 94 AJIL 623; J Brunnée, 'COPing with Consent: Lawmaking under Multilateral Environmental Agreements' (2002) 15 LJIL 1; A Wiersma, 'The New International Law-Makers? Conference of the Parties to Multilateral Environmental Agreements' (2009) 31 MJIL 231; Bowman, '"Normalizing"', 293. See also Nolte, Second Report on Subsequent Practice, para 94; Nolte, Third Report on Treaties over Time, 378 ('When acting within the framework of a COP [conference of the parties], states parties can create subsequent agreements or subsequent practice in the sense of Art 31(3)(a) and (b) VCLT.').

[219] Nolte, Third Report on Treaties over Time, 365.

[220] See eg P Sands, *Principles of International Environmental Law: Framework, Standards and Implementation* (Manchester UP, 1995) 92.

[221] Churchill and Ulfstein, 'Autonomous Institutional Arrangements', 623. See also Bowman, '"Normalizing"', 332.

[222] Churchill and Ulfstein, 'Autonomous Institutional Arrangements', 633.

[223] See GATT Art XXV. See further Section 5.3.1(d).

[224] Art IX of the 1959 Antarctic Treaty System, 402 UNTS 71.

[225] Churchill and Ulftsein, 'Autonomous Institutional Arrangements', 656–8, citing RT Scully, 'Alternatives for Cooperation and Institutionalization in Antarctica: Outlook for the 1990s' in F Orrego Vicuña (ed), *Antarctic Resources Policy* (CUP, 1983) 281, 283.

[226] cf Bowman, '"Normalizing"', 331, citing F Morgenstern, *Legal Problems of International Organizations* (CUP, 1986) 22–3.

agreed definition of an international organization,[227] thus leaving these questions even more open for debate.

It has been argued, furthermore, that the practice of 'treaty bodies' composed of independent experts, in particular certain UN human rights treaty bodies such as the Human Rights Committee (HRC), the Committee on Economic, Social and Cultural Rights (CESCR), and the Committee against Torture (CAT), coupled with States' endorsements of their findings, should be regarded as constituting 'subsequent practice' in the sense of Article 31(3)(b) VCLT.[228] This argument is based on the unique role played by such committees as the main interpreters of the underlying human rights treaties—a role normally left to States in most other treaty regimes.[229] This is tied in with the special nature of human rights treaties, which, as is also the case for constitutive treaties, carries implications for the interpretative practices applicable, and for the role and nature of subsequent practice in that context.[230]

Such treaty bodies have been described as organs established by treaty—also treaties outside the human rights context—that do not represent international organizations, nor international dispute settlement bodies, but that nevertheless resemble international organizations in their functions and otherwise.[231] Little scholarly attention has been devoted to them, treaty law does not provide much guidance on their competences, and it is unclear to what extent international institutional law applies, if at all.[232] Nevertheless, these treaty bodies, such as the Commission on the Limits of the Continental Shelf under the LOSC,[233] certain 'compliance

[227] Churchill and Ulfstein, 'Autonomous Institutional Arrangements', 632. See also Bowman, '"Normalizing"', 331 (international organizations 'are of such variety that they virtually defy conjugation under any single, universally applicable definition').

[228] ILA, Committee on Human Rights Law and Practice, 'Final Report on the Impact of Findings of the United Nations Human Rights Treaty Bodies' (2004) 71 Intl L Assn Rep Conf 621, 628; M Craven, *The International Covenant on Economic, Social and Cultural Rights: A Perspective on Its Development* (Clarendon Press 1995) 91; M Scheinin, 'Human Rights Treaties and the Vienna Convention on the Law of Treaties – Conflicts or Harmony' in Vienna Commission (ed), *The Status of International Treaties on Human Rights* (Council of Europe Publishing, 2006) 43, 49; CK Hall, 'The Duty of States Parties to the Convention against Torture to Provide Procedures Permitting Victims to Recover Reparations for Torture Committed Abroad' (2007) 18 EJIL 921, 927; H Keller and L Grover, 'General Comments of the Human Rights Committee and Their Legitimacy' in H Keller and G Ulfstein (eds), *UN Human Rights Treaty Bodies: Law and Legitimacy* (CUP, 2012) 116, 130–2; MG Kohen, 'Keeping Subsequent Agreements and Practice in Their Right Limits' in G Nolte (ed), *Treaties and Subsequent Practice* (OUP, 2013) 34, 42. See also HRC, Draft General Comment No 33 (Second revised version as of 18 August 2008) UN Doc CCPR/C/GC//33/CRP.33 (2008) para 18 (the 'general body of jurisprudence generated by the Committee (...) or, alternatively, the acquiescence of States parties in those determinations' constitutes subsequent practice in the sense of Art 31(3)(b) VCLT). However, this statement was omitted from the ultimately adopted text of the general comment—HRC, General Comment No 33, UN Doc CCPR/C/GC//33 (2008). cf Nolte, Third Report on the Law of Treaties, 381.

[229] K Mechlem, 'Treaty Bodies and the Interpretation of Human Rights' (2009) 42 Vand J Transn'l L 905, 920–1.

[230] On the special nature of human rights treaties, see eg Section 3.5.1. See further eg M Fitzmaurice, 'Interpretation of Human Rights Treaties' in D Shelton (ed), *The Oxford Handbook of International Human Rights Law* (OUP, 2013) 739, 769–70.

[231] Ulfstein, 'Treaty Bodies' 428. See also Boisson de Chazournes, 'Subsequent Practice', 58–9.

[232] Ulfstein, 'Treaty Bodies', 429.

[233] See eg Section 5.3.2(a). A difference between UN human rights treaty bodies and the CLCS is that while the former provide 'views' regarding the interpretation of the treaty and are composed of

committees' under environmental treaties,[234] and the supervisory bodies of various human rights conventions,[235] may be a source of interpretative practice in relation to a treaty,[236] or may issue 'General Comments' with far-reaching interpretations for their constitutive treaties.[237]

These treaty bodies could be taken to represent a non-classical category of subsequent practice in the sense of Article 31(3)(b) VCLT,[238] perhaps especially if States do not challenge their practice over an extended period of time.[239] A more likely construction is that the practice of such treaty bodies triggers State practice establishing the parties' agreement in the sense of Article 31(3)(b) VCLT. In other words, it is the practice of States choosing to follow their practice, rather than the practice of the treaty bodies themselves, that effectively interprets or modifies the underlying treaties: 'their importance lies in the fact that they may either reflect or trigger subsequent agreements and practice of the parties'.[240] In this sense, the analysis reverts to 'classical' State practice. The practice of the treaty bodies can, however, be compared to that of international organizations in the sense that, while not amounting to practice of the States parties, its purpose is to contribute to the proper application of the treaty—and it can thus be qualified as 'other subsequent practice' under Article 32 VCLT.[241]

individuals of 'recognized competence in the field of human rights, consideration being given to the usefulness of the participation of some persons having legal experience' (Art 28(2) of the 1966 International Covenant on Civil and Political Rights, 999 UNTS 171), the Commission provides primarily 'scientific and technical advice' and is composed of 'experts in the fields of geology, geophysics or hydrography' (Art 2 of Annex II to the LOSC), although the advice of the Commission may very well relate to interpretation of the Convention—Nolte, Fourth Report on Subsequent Practice, paras 74–5.

234 See eg 1997 Kyoto Protocol to the United Nations Framework Convention on Climate Change, 2303 UNTS 162, Art 18, coupled with *Report of the Conference of the Parties on its seventh session* (2001) UN Doc FCCC/CP/2001/13/Add.3 (21 January 2002) vol III, Decision 24/CP.7, 64; 2000 Cartagena Protocol on Biosafety to the Convention on Biological Diversity, 2226 UNTS 208, Art 34.

235 See eg Keller and Grover, 'General Comments', 116.

236 Ulfstein, 'Treaty Bodies', 436.

237 Ibid. 437.

238 cf Nolte, Fourth Report on Subsequent Practice, paras 42–4.

239 D Shelton, 'The Legal Status of Normative Pronouncements of Human Rights Treaty Bodies' in H Hestermeyer and others (eds), *Coexistence, Cooperation and Solidarity: Liber Amicorum Rüdiger Wolfrum*, vol I (Martinus Nijhoff, 2012) 553, 563ff. cf Nolte, Third Report on Treaties over Time, 383; ILC Draft Conclusions on Subsequent Agreements and Subsequent Practice (2016), 123 ('Conclusion 13', para 3) ('Silence by a party shall not be presumed to constitute subsequent practice under article 31, paragraph 3(b), accepting an interpretation of a treaty as expressed in a pronouncement of an expert treaty body.').

240 Nolte, Third Report on the Law of Treaties, 381. See also ILC, 'Information provided by the Ministry for Foreign Affairs of Finland in response to Chapter III of the Report of the International Law Commission (A/69/10) detailing specific issues on which comments would be of particular interest to the Commission' (30 January 2015) <legal.un.org/ilc/sessions/67/pdfs/english/sasp_finland.pdf> accessed 11 November 2016 ('The interpretation of conventions can (...) be affected when organs supervising the implementation of human rights treaties give conclusions and recommendations concerning conventions and the governments in their turn engage in discussions with these organs.'); ILC Draft Conclusions on Subsequent Agreements and Subsequent Practice (2016), 123 ('Conclusion 13', para 3) (but see also ibid. para 4: '[t]his draft conclusion is without prejudice to the contribution that a pronouncement of an expert treaty body may otherwise make to the interpretation of a treaty.'). See further B Schlütter, 'Aspects of Human Rights Interpretation by the UN Treaty Bodies' in H Keller and G Ulfstein (eds), *UN Human Rights Treaty Bodies: Law and Legitimacy* (CUP, 2012) 261, 293, 318. cf Shelton, 'The Legal Status of Normative Pronouncements of Human Rights Treaty Bodies', 563.

241 Nolte, Fourth Report on Subsequent Practice, para 62.

Practice of other non-State actors and dispute settlement bodies

A final point is merited here with regard to the relevance of the practice of other non-State actors, a 'phenomenon *à la mode* in contemporary international law doctrine'.[242] There may be many other actors competent to assume obligations under formal international agreements, ranging from sub-federal states to private actors, including corporations, NGOs, and natural persons.[243] This goes to show that the notion of 'subsequent practice' is of 'variable geometry': State conduct amounting to subsequent practice depends on the conventional context and, more precisely, on the allocation of rights and obligations established under it.[244] This is of special significance in the context of human rights and investment treaties, the focus of which is to protect individuals or private entities. Private actors in the context of investment treaty arbitration even possess the ability to enter into arbitration agreements.[245]

One interesting example is the special role of the International Committee of the Red Cross (ICRC), legally a private association incorporated under Swiss law, akin to a non-governmental organization, and in certain ways resembling the workings of an international organization,[246] which has contributed to the development of international humanitarian law by providing interpretative guidance on the 1949 Geneva Conventions and their Additional Protocols, as well as through its actual work in the field.[247]

In 2009, for instance, the ICRC published a document on 'Interpretive Guidance on the Notion of Direct Participation in Hostilities under International Humanitarian Law', the product of a lengthy process of research and expert consultation. The document contains the ICRC's recommendations as to how international humanitarian law relating to the notion of the direct participation of civilians in

[242] Kohen, 'Keeping Subsequent Agreements and Practice in Their Right Limits', 41. See also Venzke, *How Interpretation Makes International Law*, 237.

[243] T Grant, 'Who Can Make Treaties? Other Subjects of International Law' in DB Hollis (ed), *The Oxford Guide to Treaties* (OUP, 2012) 125, 126; and see ibid. 144, arguing that although the VCLT does not directly cover their practice, its central propositions, including Art 31, may still apply to private actors by way of customary international law. See also C Tomuschat, 'Individuals' in J Crawford, A Pellet, and S Olleson (eds), *The Law of International Responsibility* (OUP, 2010) 985, 990.

[244] Boisson de Chazournes, 'Subsequent Practice', 56, citing A Roberts, 'Power and Persuasion in Investment Treaty Interpretation: The Dual Role of States' (2010) 104 AJIL 179, 207–15.

[245] Grant, 'Who Can Make Treaties?', 143–4. See eg *Republic of Ecuador v Occidental Petroleum & Production Co* [2005] EWHC Comm 774, para 61; *Republic of Ecuador v Occidental Petroleum & Production Co* [2006] EWHC Comm 345, para 8.

[246] R Giladi and S Ratner, 'The Role of the International Committee of the Red Cross' in A Clapham, P Gaeta, and M Sassòli, *The 1949 Geneva Conventions: A Commentary* (OUP, 2015) 525, 528. The international legal status of the ICRC is the subject of debate—see eg J-P Lavoyer, 'The International Committee of the Red Cross: Legal Status and Headquarters Agreements' in D Fleck (ed), *The Handbook of the Law of Visiting Forces* (OUP, 2001) 471; G Abraham, 'Yes, ... But Does It Have Personality? The International Committee of the Red Cross and Sovereign Immunity' (2007) 124 S Afr LJ 499; T Gazzini, 'A Unique Non-State Actor: The International Committee of the Red Cross' (2010) 4 HRILD 32.

[247] See eg H-P Gasser, 'International Committee of the Red Cross (ICRC)' in R Wolfrum (ed), *Max Planck Encyclopedia of Public International Law* (OUP, 2013); Nolte, Third Report on Treaties over Time, 321.

hostilities *should* be interpreted.[248] In theory, the Interpretive Guidance is not intended to change existing rules but to ensure that they are interpreted consistently, based on the hope that it will have a persuasive effect upon State practice.[249] The official mandate of the ICRC—'to work for the faithful application of international humanitarian law applicable in armed conflicts and (…) prepare any development thereof'[250]—backs up its authority in this regard. It remains to be seen what the impact of the ICRC's guidance—and the practice it elicits—will be on the development of international humanitarian law. The ICRC's proactive role as 'guardian' of international humanitarian law, which has surpassed its formally envisaged role,[251] is noted further in Chapters 3 and 5.[252]

As with treaty bodies, in general, and unless the treaty expressly provides otherwise, the role of non-State actors is only *indirectly* relevant to subsequent practice,[253] either by monitoring[254] and evidencing[255] subsequent practice—which does not exclude the possibility that, in doing so, such actors also (inadvertently or deliberately) contribute to shaping it[256]—or, indeed, by *influencing* the practice of the actual parties to the treaty.[257] In the case of treaties conferring directly enforceable rights (rather than merely benefits) upon non-State actors, such as human rights and investment treaties, subsequent practice could be assessed with an awareness

[248] ICRC, 'Interpretive Guidance on the Notion of Direct Participation in Hostilities under International Humanitarian Law' (ICRC 2009) <www.icrc.org/eng/assets/files/other/icrc-002-0990.pdf> accessed 28 June 2016.

[249] N Melzer, 'The ICRC's Clarification Process on the Notion of Direct Participation in Hostilities under International Humanitarian Law' (2008) <www.oas.org/dil/esp/XXXVI_curso_The_ICRC_Clarification_Process_Nils_Melzer.pdf> accessed 28 June 2016. See also R Giladi and S Ratner, 'The Role of the International Committee of the Red Cross' in A Clapham, P Gaeta, and M Sassòli, *The 1949 Geneva Conventions: A Commentary* (OUP, 2015) 525, 538.

[250] 1986 Statutes of the International Red Cross and Red Crescent Movement, as amended, <www.icrc.org/eng/assets/files/other/statutes-en-a5.pdf> accessed 28 June 2016, Art 5(2)(c) and (g).

[251] Giladi and Ratner, 'The Role of the International Committee of the Red Cross', 537ff.

[252] See Sections 3.3.2(b) and 5.3.2(d).

[253] *US and Iran*, Award No 108-A-16/582/591-FT (25 January 1984) 5 Iran-US CTR 57, cited in Nolte, Second Report on Treaties over Time, 229. cf Crema, 'Subsequent Agreements and Subsequent Practice', 26.

[254] An example is the work of the Landmine and Cluster Munition Monitor in identifying and collecting practice in relation to the 1997 Convention on the Prohibition of the Use, Stockpiling, Production and Transfer of Anti-Personnel Mines and on their Destruction, 2056 UNTS 211, and the 2008 Convention on Cluster Munitions, 2688 UNTS 39—Cluster Munition Coalition, *Cluster Munition Monitor 2015* (International Campaign to Ban Landmines 2015) <www.the-monitor.org/cmm/2011/pdf> accessed 28 June 2016. See also ILC, 'First Report on Subsequent Agreements and Subsequent Practice in Relation to Treaty Interpretation, by Georg Nolte, Special Rapporteur', UN Doc A/CN.4/660 (2013) [Nolte, First Report on Subsequent Practice] para 139.

[255] See eg UN High Commissioner for Refugees, *Handbook on Procedures and Criteria for Determining Refugee Status under the 1951 Convention and the 1967 Protocol relating to the Status of Refugees*, UN Doc HCR/IP/4/Eng/REV 1 (reedited, 1992), often taken as a reflection of State practice (see also Art 35(1) of the 1951 Geneva Convention relating to the Status of Refugees).

[256] See eg Nolte, First Report on Subsequent Practice, para 140 ('[NGOs] can try to shape subsequent practice by providing their reading of disputed provisions. (…) This does not exclude the fact that State practice gathered by non-governmental organizations is often a valuable source of evidence for the subsequent practice of all the parties.').

[257] Kohen, 'Keeping Subsequent Agreements and Practice in Their Right Limits', 41, citing ILC, 'Fourth Report on State Responsibility, by Mr Roberto Ago, Special Rapporteur' (1972) II YBILC 71, para 65. See also text to nn 248–52 on the influence of the ICRC.

of the inherent 'asymmetry of interests' between those holding the rights and those interpreting them.[258] In principle, however, what matters for determining relevant practice in the interpretation of a treaty is not the practice of private actors and investors as such, but rather what their effects are in terms of how the parties react in the application of the treaty as a result of that conduct.[259]

Similarly, it has been suggested that the totality of practice of courts and tribunals can be taken to amount to subsequent practice in the sense of Article 31(3)(b) VCLT.[260] This is difficult territory. Technically, judgments or awards are only final and binding for the parties to the specific dispute, but successive decisions between different parties could still contribute to a trend towards establishing the parties' agreement to a certain interpretation.[261] For instance, this can be noted in the WTO context, where the Member States, acting collectively as the Dispute Settlement Body (DSB), can, by consensus, reject panel and Appellate Body reports:

> WTO Members generally adjust their behaviour and interpretation of the WTO agreements to judicial interpretations in Appellate Body and panel reports because either they are disputants and bound by the decision at issue, or they accept and comply with the *jurisprudence constante* produced in those reports. The resulting practice in performing their treaty obligations can be defined as subsequent practice, if defined on the basis of the content of the practice. From a legal-technical point of view, the resulting practice develops from the subsequent agreement that is the DSB report adopting the panel or Appellate Body decision.[262]

Therefore, as with the activities of other non-State actors surveyed above, the value for present purposes of decisions of international courts and tribunals is indirect, and lies in their influence upon the subsequent practice of the parties to the treaty.[263] Moreover, a problem is that, for instance, the decision of a dispute settlement body operating within the framework of a larger international organization may be subject to the further decision-making power of a different organ of that organization.[264]

It is submitted that while the decisions of international courts and tribunals constitute an independent source of legal development, they are not capable of constituting an agreement between the treaty parties and thus subsequent practice. Further consideration of the question of the relevance of the practice of dispute

[258] Roberts, 'Power and Persuasion', 202.

[259] Kohen, 'Keeping Subsequent Agreements and Practice in Their Right Limits', 41–2. See also Crawford, 'A Consensualist Interpretation of Article 31(3)', 31.

[260] See eg Gardiner, *Treaty Interpretation*, 111; O Dörr, 'Article 31: General Rule of Interpretation' in O Dörr and K Schmalenbach (eds), *Vienna Convention on the Law of Treaties: A Commentary* (Springer, 2012) 521, 531 para 19. See further A Boyle and C Chinkin, *The Making of International Law* (OUP, 2007) 268; I Buga, 'Book Review of I Venzke, How Interpretation Makes International Law: On Semantic Change and Normative Twists' (2013) 83 BYBIL 190.

[261] Gardiner, *Treaty Interpretation*, 229–30.

[262] I Van Damme, *Treaty Interpretation by the WTO Appellate Body* (OUP, 2009) 341. Reference can be made to the practice of international criminal tribunals, namely, the ICTY, ICTR, and ICC, which have based certain assessments of subsequent practice not on State practice, but on the practice of international judicial bodies such as the ECtHR and IACtHR—Nolte, Second Report on Treaties over Time, 292–3. Such 'patterns' in the practice of judicial bodies that bring about change in treaty interpretation should be distinguished from interpretations the *substance* of which brings about change.

[263] cf Gardiner, *Treaty Interpretation*, 111; Dörr, 'Article 31', 531.

[264] Gardiner, *Treaty Interpretation*, 230.

settlement bodies for the definition in Article 31(3)(b) VCLT, coupled with the question of their interpretative authority and the value of precedent in international law,[265] goes beyond the scope of this book.

A broad notion of 'practice'

In light of these considerations, a broader concept of 'practice' is preferred, given the endless diversity of means by which consent to an international obligation can be expressed.[266] The practice of States, based strictly on consent, remains the main focal point, but flexibility should be maintained in applying the notion of practice—a concept that defies strict conceptual compartmentalization.[267]

The practice of domestic branches of State other than the executive, even sometimes that of actors that are not high-ranking officials, may count as subsequent practice.[268] Moreover, it is necessary at times to look beyond State practice to less 'traditional' categories of practice, such as that of international organizations and other institutional arrangements resembling international organizations, as the subjects sometimes most involved in the application of a treaty.[269] This gives fuller recognition to the interpretative importance of subsequent practice,[270] and to the fact that 'the body of practice under any given multilateral treaty may in fact have been created by a much more diverse set of hands than the original signatory states'.[271] The exclusion of such types of practice would fail to give a complete picture of the effects and nuances relating to the operation of subsequent practice in different contexts and regimes.

The notion of 'practice' will therefore be taken here to include all of the abovementioned forms of practice—whether they fall under the scope of Article 31(3)(b) or Article 32 VCLT—bearing in mind at all times their special characteristics and wider context. This is not to say, however, that subsequent practice is not subject to a number of important qualifications. These other 'constitutive elements' are covered in the ensuing sections.

2.3.2 The term 'subsequent'

The first issue that comes to mind in delineating the boundaries of the notion of 'subsequent' is how to pinpoint the beginning of the relevant period in which subsequent practice can influence a treaty. The term 'subsequent' refers to practice established after the point when the treaty was concluded,[272] rather than the point

[265] See eg Chua, 'Precedent and Principles', 171.

[266] See eg C Tomuschat, 'Obligations Arising for States Without or Against Their Will' (1993-IV) 241 RC 195, 277; L Boisson de Chazournes, 'Qu'est-ce que la pratique en droit international?' in SFDI, Colloque de Geneve, *La pratique et le droit international* (Pédone, 2004) 13, 14 ('la définition de la pratique est juridiquement très volatile').

[267] Boisson de Chazournes, 'Subsequent Practice', 68.

[268] See eg Venzke, *How Interpretation Makes International Law*, 238. See also nn 122–35.

[269] See eg Venzke, *How Interpretation Makes International Law*, 240.

[270] Crema, 'Subsequent Agreements and Subsequent Practice', 24.

[271] McLachlan, 'Evolution of Treaty Obligations', 73.

[272] See further Linderfalk, *On the Interpretation of Treaties*, 163.

when the treaty was ratified or entered into force,[273] unless something different must be gathered from the specific context.[274] Articles 18 and 25 VCLT suggest that a treaty can be regarded as 'concluded' when its text has been established as definite even before its entry into force.[275] In fact, subsequent practice in the period between the treaty's conclusion and its entry into force may be of great evidentiary value since at that stage the parties are not only still 'acutely aware' of their intentions under the treaty, but are also preparing its entry into force.[276]

On the other hand, this is also a period in which parties may attempt to make self-serving statements in order to influence the treaty's subsequent application, and a point when differences of opinion exist as to the 'correct' interpretation of the treaty.[277] Similar considerations may have prompted certain States to request clarification as to whether the provisional application of a treaty could result in its modification in the context of the current work of the ILC on the topic of 'Provisional Application of Treaties'[278]—a possibility envisaged by some commentators as an effect of provisional application.[279]

It can be difficult and perhaps unnecessary[280] to draw a strict distinction in a given case between what falls under 'context' in paragraph 2 of Article 31 VCLT, and what constitutes subsequent practice under paragraph 3 of the same article:

> The point in time from which a practice (or an agreement) is 'subsequent' in the sense of Article 31(3)(a) and (b) VCLT is not necessarily chronologically after the conclusion of the treaty. The respective practice (or agreement) may also be performed or agreed upon simultaneously with the conclusion of the treaty as long as it is formally subordinated to the treaty (...). In such cases subsequent practice (or agreements) can indistinguishably blend with the 'context' of the treaty in the sense of Article 31(2) VCLT.[281]

[273] See Art 24 VCLT.

[274] Koskenniemi, Fragmentation Report, para 232. See also JB Mus, 'Conflicts between Treaties in International Law' (1998) 45 NILR 208, 214–17; Aust, *Modern Treaty Law*, 183; SA Sadat-Akhavi, *Methods of Resolving Conflicts between Treaties* (Martinus Nijhoff, 2003) 75–82. cf M Sørensen, 'Le problème dit du droit intertemporel dans l'ordre international' (1973) 55 AFDI 1, 54.

[275] Nolte, Introductory Report on Treaties over Time, 189; S Rosenne, 'Treaties, Conclusion and Entry into Force' in R Bernhardt (ed), *Encyclopedia of Public International Law*, vol IV (North Holland, 2000) 933 ('Strictly speaking it is the negotiation that is concluded through a treaty.').

[276] Nolte, Introductory Report on Treaties over Time, 189.

[277] One may think of declarations in relation to the LOSC submitted before its entry into force.

[278] 'Statement by Mr. Luke Tang, Delegate to the 69th Session of the United Nations General Assembly on Agenda Item 78, Chapters X, XI, XII and XIII of the Report of the International Law Commission on the Work of its 66th Session, Sixth Committee', Permanent Mission of Singapore to the United Nations (3 November 2014) <https://papersmart.unmeetings.org/media2/4655007/singapore-rev.pdf> accessed 6 July 2016, para 9. See also ILC, 'First Report on the Provisional Application of Treaties, prepared by Mr Juan Manuel Gómez-Robledo, Special Rapporteur', UN Doc A/CN.4/664 (2013) para 30. cf ILC, *Report of the International Law Commission on the work of its 66th session*, UN Doc A/69/10 (2014) Ch XII, para 237; ILC, *Report of the International Law Commission on the work of its 67th session*, UN Doc A/70/10 (2015) Ch XI, para 277.

[279] See eg A Greslin, *La mise en application provisoire des traités* (Pédone, 2005) 32. See also ILC, 'Third Report on the Provisional Application of Treaties, by Juan Manuel Gómez-Robledo, Special Rapporteur', UN Doc A/CN.4/687 (2015) para 105. cf RE Dalton, 'Provisional Application of Treaties' in DB Hollis (ed), *The Oxford Guide to Treaties* (OUP, 2012) 221.

[280] See Gardiner, *Treaty Interpretation*, 204–5.

[281] Nolte, Second Report on Treaties over Time, 303; see ibid. 229. cf Crawford, 'A Consensualist Interpretation of Article 31(3)', 30.

For instance, in one case, the Iran-US Claims Tribunal qualified the Executive Order[282] issued by the President of the United States at the time of adherence by the United States to the Algiers Accords establishing the Tribunal's jurisdiction,[283] as constituting 'practice' in the sense of Article 31(3), despite the fact that the practice was simultaneous rather than strictly speaking 'subsequent' to the treaty.[284] Judges Holtzmann and Allison added in their Separate Opinion:

> That Executive Order is relevant to the interpretation of the General Declaration because the text was shown to Iran during the negotiations and thus is part of the 'context', as that term is used in Article 31, para. 2 of the Vienna Convention. Having been issued on the same day as the General Declaration as a step in implementing it, the Executive Order is also part of the 'practice' of a party in applying the General declaration (...).[285]

Another point here concerns the *end* of the relevant period in which subsequent practice can impact treaty obligations. State practice seems *prima facie* to lose its relevance in relation to the treaty once the latter has been terminated. Even the formulation of Article 31(3)(b) seems to rule this out by requiring practice 'in the application of the treaty', which assumes that the instrument is still in force. However, one can imagine situations in which the subsequent practice of the parties relates to a treaty that is no longer in force in the sense that it deals with consequences stemming from its previous operation that are still applicable following its termination.[286] The ICJ proceedings concerning the *Arbitral Award Made by the King of Spain* serve as an illustration.[287] The Court rejected Nicaragua's argument that, since the King of Spain's designation as arbitrator had taken effect ten days after the Treaty supposedly ceased to be in force, the arbitral proceedings and his resulting decision of 23 December 1906 had no effect.[288] It pointed out that no objection was made at the time on the ground that the Treaty had already expired, and concluded that the parties had intended the arbitral proceedings and resulting award to fall 'within the currency of the Treaty'.[289]

These rare situations where practice is subsequent to a treaty that has ceased to be in force, should be distinguished from those in which subsequent practice causes treaty provisions to fall into desuetude,[290] which still counts as practice 'in the application of the treaty': 'conduct which expresses the position of the parties that the treaty has

[282] Executive Order No 12281, 46 FR 7923 (1981).

[283] Declaration of the Government of the Democratic and Popular Republic of Algeria Concerning the Settlement of Claims by the Government of the United States of America and the Government of the Islamic Republic of Iran (1981) 20 ILM 223, 230 (Claims Settlement Declaration, Algiers Accords).

[284] *Islamic Republic of Iran and United States of America*, Partial Award No 529-A15-FT (6 May 1992) 28 Iran-US CTR 112, 129.

[285] *Islamic Republic of Iran and United States of America*, Partial Award No 529-A15-FT (6 May 1992) Separate Opinion of Howard M Holtzmann, George H Aldrich, and Richard C Allison, Dissenting in Part and Concurring in Part, 28 Iran-US CTR 142, 151 fn 7. cf Judge Aldrich's view that the Executive Order only forms part of the context of the Declarations, ibid. 144.

[286] Nolte, Introductory Report on Treaties over Time, 189–90.

[287] *Arbitral Award Made by the King of Spain*, 192.

[288] Ibid. 208.

[289] Ibid. 209.

[290] See eg Sections 3.3.1 and 3.3.2(b).

fallen into desuetude usually carries the same weight as (other) authentic subsequent conduct'.[291]

There are a number of additional scenarios in which subsequent practice can maintain its relevance after the termination of the original treaty. These relate mainly to treaty modification by subsequent practice, such as the (rare) circumstances in which tacit modifications of the original treaty may carry through to a second treaty with identical content, or apply to new States in the case of State succession. These possibilities are explored in Chapter 3 in the context of treaty modification by subsequent practice.[292]

2.3.3 'Subsequent practice' and 'subsequent agreements'

It has rightly been observed that the distinction between 'subsequent agreements' under Article 31(3)(a) VCLT and 'subsequent practice' under Article 31(3)(b) VCLT is a fluid one.[293] As a result, 'a lot of ink has been spilled on the difference between these two procedures'.[294] Both subsequent agreements and subsequent practice constitute forms of authentic interpretation, and extrinsic sources of objective evidence of the parties' common understanding of the treaty.[295] Authentic interpretations are a particularly reliable means of interpretation, endowed with binding force[296] and a potentially higher status in the interpretative process.[297] The parties, through authentic interpretation, are masters of their own treaty[298] and can even modify it by informal means.[299] In his notable work on authentic interpretation, Voicu explains:

> La raison fondamentale en est que les deux activités sont menées par les parties contractantes en vertu d'un même pouvoir de création, d'interprétation et de modification du droit (…). On pourrait même dire que rien n'empêche les parties contractantes de modifier par voie d'interprétation les instruments conventionnels qu'elles ont passés.[300]

The term 'agreement' in the concept of 'subsequent agreement' covers more than just treaties. It presumably also covers *non*-written agreements, as well as, for instance, decisions adopted by meetings of the States parties.[301] Nolte cites as an example

[291] Nolte, Introductory Report on Treaties over Time, 190, referring to France's position in *Nuclear Tests* (*New Zealand v France*), Provisional Measures, Order of 22 June 1973, ICJ Reports 135, para 16.

[292] See Sections 3.3.6(b)–(c).

[293] Nolte, Annex A, para 24.

[294] Hafner, 'Subsequent Agreements and Practice', 109.

[295] Villiger, *Commentary*, 429; A Orakhelashvili, *The Interpretation of Acts and Rules in Public International Law* (OUP, 2008) 105. See also ILC Draft Conclusions on Subsequent Agreements and Subsequent Practice (2016), 120 ('Conclusion 3').

[296] Villiger, 'The Rules on Interpretation', 111.

[297] Nolte, Introductory Report on Treaties over Time, 171-2.

[298] Villiger, *Commentary*, 429. See also McNair, *Law of Treaties*, 169; D Carreau, *Droit international* (9th edn, Pédone, 2007).

[299] See eg Tammelo, *Treaty Interpretation*, 6; Karl, *Vertrag*, 46. See further Section 3.3.2(a).

[300] I Voicu, *De l'interprétation authentique des traités internationaux* (Pédone, 1968) 87–8, citing eg Kelsen, *The Law of the United Nations*, 15 ('by authentic interpretation a legal norm may be replaced by another norm of totally different content').

[301] ILC, 'Summary record of the 769th meeting', *Summary records of the 16th session* (1964) I YBILC 308, paras 23 (Waldock) and 63 (Ago); *Methanex Corporation v United States of America*, UNCITRAL Arbitration under NAFTA Chapter Eleven, Final Award of the Tribunal on Jurisdiction and Merits of 3 August 2005 [*Methanex v US*] Part II(B), paras 19-21; MK Yasseen, 'L'interprétation des traités d'après

of the latter type of subsequent agreement, the case when the EU Member States changed the denomination of the ECU to the Euro.[302] Although it can take a range of different forms, the scope of the term 'subsequent agreement' is qualified by the fact that it presumably entails a higher degree of formality than subsequent practice, posing less of a challenge to legal certainty:

A formal written agreement between the parties agreeing to the meaning of an otherwise ambiguous term would likely fall within Article 31(3)(a). On the other hand, independent actions of both parties, temporally separated, that appear to demonstrate agreement between them on the meaning of the treaty is more likely to come within Article 31(3)(b).[303]

In the words of one tribunal, '[i]n sub-paragraph (a) the agreement is *ex hypothesi* conscious and express, in sub-paragraph (b) it arises by implication from the parties' actions.'[304] This entails that subsequent agreements and subsequent practice do not share the same evidentiary value in determining 'true' authentic interpretations: while subsequent agreements, as express and more formalized agreements, can *automatically* amount to authentic interpretation, subsequent practice only constitutes authentic interpretation if it evidences an implied agreement.[305] This could suggest that party agreement that falls under Article 31(3)(a) should be accorded more weight—or, at least, weight should more readily be accorded to it than to an apparent agreement in the sense of Article 31(3)(b)—in the interpretative process.[306]

One approach could therefore be to take 'subsequent agreements' to mean express agreements as to a treaty's interpretation,[307] and 'subsequent practice' as denoting the agreement of the parties in any other relevant shape or form.[308] As noted by one commentator, 'while substance is generally preferred over form in international law, the distinction between Articles 31(3)(a) and (b) concerns form rather than substance'.[309]

The case law suggests that the notion of subsequent practice is understood as the broader of the two, and is sometimes taken to *comprise* subsequent agreements.[310]

la Convention de Vienne sur le droit des traités' (1976-III) 151 RC 1, 37; Gardiner, *Treaty Interpretation*, 208; Villiger, *Commentary*, 430–1; Aust, *Modern Treaty Law*, 191. See also ILC, 'Permanent Mission of Austria to the United Nations, Statement by Gregor Schusterschitz—68th Session of the General Assembly Sixth Committee, Agenda Item 81' (28 October 2013) <http://legal.un.org/ilc/sessions/67/pdfs/english/sasp_austria.pdf> accessed 11 November 2016.

302 Nolte, Annex A, para 24, citing Aust, *Modern Treaty Law*, 192. See further Section 5.3.2(e).

303 R Moloo, 'When Actions Speak Louder Than Words: The Relevance of Subsequent Party Conduct to Treaty Interpretation' (2013) 31 Berkeley JIL 39, 50.

304 *HICEE BV v Slovak Republic*, UNCITRAL Arbitral Tribunal, PCA Case No 2009/11, Partial Award of 23 May 2011, para 134.

305 Nolte, Introductory Report on Treaties over Time, 173–4.

306 Moloo, 'When Actions Speak Louder Than Words', 50. See also Gardiner, *Treaty Interpretation*, 208–9.

307 Gardiner, *Treaty Interpretation*, 209; Sorel and Boré Eveno, 'Article 31', 1320 para 43.

308 Nolte, Introductory Report on Treaties over Time, 174.

309 Moloo, 'When Actions Speak Louder Than Words', 19 (footnotes omitted).

310 See eg *Maritime Delimitation in the Area between Greenland and Jan Mayen* (*Denmark v Norway*), Judgment of 14 June 1993, ICJ Reports 38 [*Greenland-Jan Mayen*] para 28; *Pulp Mills on the River Uruguay* (*Argentina v Uruguay*), Request for the Indication of Provisional Measures, Order of 13 July 2006, ICJ Reports 113, para 53. See further Nolte, Introductory Report on Treaties over Time,

The word 'agreement' in Article 31(3)(b) VCLT has also been used more liberally—in the sense of an 'understanding'[311] or 'concordance'[312]—than in the context of 'subsequent agreement' in Article 31(3)(a), which, though it contains no particular form requirement, is often presumed to entail a higher degree of formality.[313] Certain scholars argue that the reverse is true, namely, that subsequent practice falls under the 'generic expression' subsequent agreement.[314]

This may cause some confusion as to the precise relationship between subparagraphs (a) and (b) of Article 31(3) VCLT. The situation is not helped by the fact that international courts and tribunals have shown a reluctance to distinguish clearly between the two,[315] leading to the use of 'evasive terminology'.[316] The two terms were referred to collectively as 'subsequent conduct' by the ILC Study Group on 'Treaties over Time', which considered that 'it would not be fruitful, and even lead to confusion, if the term subsequent practice were used both in a narrower sense (in contradistinction to subsequent agreement) and in a broader sense (as encompassing subsequent agreement)'.[317]

It is submitted here that these two forms of authentic interpretation overlap substantially, given that subsequent practice can be taken to include subsequent agreements,[318] and that subsequent agreements may also take the form of non-written agreements.[319] Thus, subsequent practice and subsequent agreements fall along a spectrum[320] ranging from the implicit to the explicit, with passive conduct on one end and treaties on the other. Some forms of agreement are easy to classify: authoritative interpretations of NAFTA provisions issued by the Free Trade Commission qualify as subsequent agreements,[321] as do Implementation Agreements such as those adopted in relation to the Law of the Sea Convention.[322]

174; Nolte, Second Report on Treaties over Time, 216 and fn 22, citing eg *Mexico–Measures Affecting Telecommunications Services*, Report of the Panel (2 April 2004) WT/DS204/R [*Mexico–Telecoms*, Panel Report]; *United States–Measures Affecting the Cross-Border Supply of Gambling and Betting Services*, Report of the Appellate Body (7 April 2005) WT/DS285/AB/R [*US–Gambling*, AB Report]. cf H Fox, 'Article 31(3)(a) and (b) of the Vienna Convention and the *Kasikili/Sedudu Island* Case' in M Fitzmaurice, O Elias, and P Merkouris (eds), *Treaty Interpretation and the Vienna Convention on the Law of Treaties: 30 Years On* (Martinus Nijhoff, 2010) 59, 63–4.

311 See eg *Young Loan Arbitration* (*The Kingdom of Belgium, the French Republic, the Swiss Confederation, the United Kingdom and the United States of America v The Federal Republic of Germany*) (1980) 59 ILR 495, para 31.

312 Linderfalk, *On the Interpretation of Treaties*, 169.

313 cf Crawford, 'A Consensualist Interpretation of Article 31(3)', 30: 'There is no reason to think that the word "agreement" in para (b) has any different meaning as compared to the meaning it has in para (a). It is an agreement between the parties which establishes, as it may be, the interpretation of the treaty or the agreement of the parties regarding its interpretation.' See also *Kasikili/Sedudu Island* (*Botswana/Namibia*), Judgment of 13 December 1999, Dissenting Opinion of Vice-President Weeramantry, ICJ Reports 1153, para 23.

314 Crema, 'Subsequent Agreements and Subsequent Practice', 16 fn 12.

315 See eg *Libya/Chad*, paras 66ff; *Qatar v Bahrain*, Jurisdiction and Admissibility, para 28; *Gabčíkovo-Nagymaros Project*, para 138; *Indonesia/Malaysia*, para 61.

316 Nolte, Introductory Report on Treaties over Time, 173–4.

317 Ibid. 174.

318 See text to n 310.

319 See text to n 301.

320 See eg Moloo, 'When Actions Speak Louder Than Words', 50; R Crootof, 'Change Without Consent: How Customary International Law Modifies Treaties' (2016) 41 Yale JIL 237, 258.

321 See Section 5.2.3(c).

322 See Section 5.3.2(a).

The same can obviously be said of subsequent or successive treaties. When it comes to more informal types of practice, the classification largely depends on the specific circumstances of the case.

This book adopts a broad understanding of the term subsequent practice, in recognition of the inevitable overlap with subsequent agreements, to avoid terminological complications and fully take account of relevant practice going beyond the formal amendment procedures prescribed in the VCLT. To exclude those forms of practice clearly constituting informal subsequent agreements from the scope of this book would limit the exploration of the nuances and effects of practice too much, especially for the purposes of Chapter 3.

There are strong examples of subsequent agreements that go beyond prescribed formal amendment procedures and tacitly (or, perhaps more accurately, 'informally') modify treaty provisions; the only difference is that they show a higher degree of formality, and pose slightly less of a challenge to legal certainty and transparency, than modifications through (other forms of) subsequent practice. However, questions regarding, for example, successive treaties—subsequent agreements at the highest level of formality—are excluded from the scope of the present book. In any case, the examples explored in the analysis of examples in Chapter 5 usually fall closer to subsequent practice than to subsequent agreements on the spectrum of possible conduct. Where an instance of practice (also) qualifies as a subsequent agreement, this is specifically addressed.

2.3.4 Practice 'in the application of the treaty'

Article 31(3)(b) VCLT requires subsequent practice 'in the application of the treaty'. Article 31(3)(a) VCLT refers to subsequent agreements 'regarding the interpretation of the treaty or the application of its provisions'. It is not necessary for the purposes of the present analysis to delve into the (largely theoretical[323]) distinction between interpretation and application.[324] Suffice is to say that interpretation

[323] As stated by Judge Shahabuddeen in connection with a decision on the existence of a dispute as to the 'interpretation or application' of the Headquarters Agreement (1947 Agreement between the United Nations and the United States of America regarding the Headquarters of the United Nations, 11 UNTS 11), '[s]ince it is not possible to apply a treaty save with reference to some factual field (even if taken hypothetically) and since it is not possible to apply a treaty except on the basis of some interpretation of it, there is a detectable view that there is little practical, or even theoretical, distinction between the two elements of the formula.'—*Applicability of the Obligation to Arbitrate under Section 21 of the United Nations Headquarters Agreement of 26 June 1947*, Advisory Opinion of 26 April 1988, Separate Opinion of Judge Shahabuddeen, ICJ Reports 57, 59, citing LB Sohn, 'Settlement of Disputes relating to the Interpretation and Application of Treaties' (1976) 150 RC 195, 271. See also Section 1.1, n 10.

[324] This question arose in an Ecuador-US arbitration based on a BIT containing a compromissory clause referring to disputes regarding the 'interpretation or application of the treaty'. Ecuador argued there was jurisdiction since a dispute existed as to interpretation, though not as to application, but the Tribunal found it lacked jurisdiction 'due to the absence of the existence of a dispute falling within the ambit of Article VII of the Treaty'—see <www.state.gov/s/l/c53491.htm> accessed 10 July 2016 (arbitral award not public). *Arbitration under the Treaty between the United States of America and the Republic of Ecuador concerning the Encouragement and Reciprocal Protection of Investments and the UNCITRAL Arbitration Rules (1976) between the Republic of Ecuador and the United States of America*, PCA Case No 2012/5, Award of 29 September 2012.

could generally be described as the process of 'determining the meaning' of the text,[325] while application entails determining the consequences that follow from that meaning in a given case.[326] Thus, the act of application logically presupposes its interpretation.[327]

The requirement that relevant practice must occur 'in the application of the treaty' relates to the treaty as a whole, rather than only to the application of the provisions being interpreted.[328] It is unclear how closely or explicitly the practice must relate to the treaty concerned in order to count as practice in its application, such as in the case of practice that only vaguely relates to the interpretation of the treaty: 'the more specifically an agreement or a practice is related to a treaty the more probative or interpretative value it can acquire under articles 31(3)(a) and (b) and 32'.[329]

An example in which practice *appeared* not to relate directly to the interpretation of the treaty is the abundance of documents submitted by Georgia to the ICJ to prove the existence of a dispute in the *Georgia v Russia* case.[330] The Court dismissed the documented practice in its entirety as lacking 'legal significance' on account of the fact that, *inter alia*, the communications did not expressly mention the terms 'racial discrimination' or 'ethnic cleansing'.[331] Due to these terminological differences, the Court did not consider the practice to relate closely enough to the 1965 International Convention on the Elimination of All Forms of Racial Discrimination (CERD).[332] Without this practice, however, it could not be demonstrated that there

[325] See also the discussion in Section 2.5.

[326] Gardiner, *Treaty Interpretation*, 28. See also *Factory at Chorzów*, Jurisdiction, Judgment of 26 July 1927, Dissenting Opinion of M Ehrlich, PCIJ Series A, No 9, 35, 39. cf McNair, *The Law of Treaties*, 365 fn 1, arguing that when a treaty is clear, it is applied rather than interpreted. As rightly pointed out in Gardiner, *Treaty Interpretation*, 27–8, this seems to 'set on its head the natural sequence that is inherent in the process of reading a treaty: first ascribing meaning to its terms and then applying the outcome to a particular situation.' See also M Milanovic, 'The ICJ and Evolutionary Treaty Interpretation' (*EJIL: Talk!*, 14 July 2009) <www.ejiltalk.org/the-icj-and-evolutionary-treaty-interpretation> accessed 24 June 2016: '[Interpretation] is the activity of establishing the linguistic or semantic meaning of a text; [application] (…) the activity of translating that text into workable legal rules to be applied in a given case.'

[327] 1935 Harvard Draft Convention, 938; Yasseen, 'L'interprétation', 47; Distefano, 'La pratique subséquente', 41; U Linderfalk, 'Is the Hierarchical Structure of Articles 31 and 32 of the Vienna Convention Real or Not? Interpreting the Rules of Interpretation' (2007) 54 NILR 133, 141–4, 147; Gardiner, *Treaty Interpretation*, 27–9; P Sands and J Commission, 'Treaty, Custom and Time: Interpretation/Application?' in M Fitzmaurice, O Elias, and P Merkouris (eds), *Treaty Interpretation and the Vienna Convention on the Law of Treaties: 30 Years On* (Martinus Nijhoff, 2010) 39, 40. Either way, States parties assume a position regarding the interpretation of the treaty—Nolte, Second Report on Subsequent Practice, para 4; Gardiner, *Treaty Interpretation*, 235; Dörr, 'Article 31', 556 paras 80, 82.

[328] Gardiner, *Treaty Interpretation*, 232; Arato, 'Subsequent Practice and Evolutive Interpretation', 459.

[329] Nolte, Second Report on Subsequent Practice, para 10.

[330] *Application of the International Convention on the Elimination of All Forms of Racial Discrimination* (*Georgia v Russian Federation*), Preliminary Objections, Judgment of 1 April 2011, ICJ Reports 70. See B Simma, 'Miscellaneous Thoughts on Subsequent Agreements and Practice' in G Nolte (ed), *Treaties and Subsequent Practice* (OUP, 2013) 46, 47.

[331] *Georgia v Russia*, paras 53, 55–6, 59–60, 62, 65–8, 70, 75–6, 78, 80–2, 84–7, 89, 91–3, 108.

[332] 660 UNTS 195.

was a dispute regarding the interpretation or application of the Convention in order for the Court to be able to establish jurisdiction.[333]

By contrast, the ICJ seemed to adopt a very liberal approach to subsequent practice in the *Maritime Dispute* (*Peru v Chile*) case: it did not investigate the subsequent practice of the parties 'in the application of' the treaty, such as the 1952 Santiago Declaration,[334] but rather used it to establish the substance of a different tacit agreement of the parties.[335]

The condition that subsequent practice must relate directly to the treaty provision in question was applied in the *US–Zeroing* case, in which the WTO Panel took a relatively strict view:

> We note that the argument of the European Communities with respect to subsequent practice is based on the fact that the particular provisions in domestic laws and/or regulations that have been notified to the Committee on Anti-Dumping Practices that in the view of the European Communities correspond to Article 2.4.2 of the AD Agreement either do not include the phrase 'during the investigation phase' [the wording of the AD Agreement] or use the phrase 'during the investigation period'. In our view, this is simply not a sufficient basis to draw a conclusion as to whether or not the practice of a particular Member to apply Article 2.4.2 to the assessment of the amount of anti-dumping duties within the meaning of Article 9.3.[336]

The Panel also noted that many Members had signalled legislation predating the WTO Agreement,[337] which meant that the legislative practice could not be 'subsequent', nor could it be 'in the application of the treaty'. Moreover, subsequent practice that would take place *regardless* of the existence of the treaty obligation is probably not subsequent practice 'in the application of the treaty'.[338] Judge Fitzmaurice in his Separate Opinion in the *Certain Expenses Advisory Opinion*, for instance, pointed out that it is 'hardly possible to infer from the mere fact that Member States pay, that they necessarily admit in all cases a positive legal obligation to do so'.[339]

The criterion 'in the application of the treaty' can be better understood by contrasting it with types of practice that do not qualify as such. A distinction must be made between subsequent practice 'in the application of the treaty' pursuant to Article 31(3)(b) VCLT, and other subsequent developments which may have an influence on the treaty.[340] Subsequent rules or developments do not carry the same persuasive authority as subsequent practice relating directly to the treaty. In the

[333] See the criticism of this decision in *Application of the International Convention on the Elimination of All Forms of Racial Discrimination* (*Georgia v Russian Federation*), Preliminary Objections, Judgment of 1 April 2011, Separate Opinion of Judge Simma, ICJ Reports 188, paras 23–57.

[334] 1952 Santiago Declaration on the Maritime Zone, 1006 UNTS 325.

[335] See *Peru v Chile*, Judgment of 27 January 2014, General List No 137, Joint Dissenting Opinion of Judges Xue, Gaja, Bhandari, and Judge ad hoc Orrego Vicuña, paras 9–34.

[336] *United States–Measures Relating to Zeroing and Sunset Reviews*, Report of the Panel (20 September 2006) WT/DS322/R [*US–Zeroing*, Panel Report] para 7.217.

[337] Ibid. [338] See further Nolte, Second Report on Subsequent Practice, paras 7–10.

[339] *Certain Expenses Advisory Opinion*, Separate Opinion of Judge Sir Gerald Fitzmaurice, ICJ Reports 198, 201. See also *Certain Expenses Advisory Opinion*, Separate Opinion of Judge Spender, 189–95.

[340] Nolte, Introductory Report on Treaties over Time, 174–5, citing eg *Gabčíkovo-Nagymaros Project*, paras 133–4.

Gabčíkovo-Nagymaros Project case, however, the subsequent actions and omissions of the parties to the treaty in violation thereof, though not relevant as subsequent practice 'in the application of the treaty', did contribute to the creation of a certain factual situation that impacted the way in which the treaty was interpreted:

The Court (...) cannot disregard the fact that the Treaty has not been fully implemented by either party for years, and indeed that their acts of commission and omission have contributed to creating the factual situation that now exists. (...) What is essential, therefore, is that the factual situation as it has developed since 1989 shall be placed within the context of the preserved and developing treaty relationship, in order to achieve its object and purpose in so far as that is feasible. (...) What might have been a correct application of the law in 1989 or 1992, if the case had been before the Court then, could be a miscarriage of justice if prescribed in 1997.[341]

Another example is provided by the refusal of the Tribunal in the *Wintershall v Argentina* arbitration to take into account treaties between the Respondent and third States in interpreting the BIT in dispute.[342] Such treaties, *prima facie*, do not seem to qualify under Article 31(3)(a) or (b) VCLT, since they do not constitute practice 'in the application of the treaty'. However, they can still be relevant to interpretation if they evidence a consistent and common practice on the part of both parties.[343] A number of tribunals have followed this approach.[344] Such treaties are then likely to fall under Article 32 VCLT.[345]

Subsequent developments that do not occur strictly 'in the application of the treaty' may also fall under Article 31(3)(c) VCLT, which prescribes that the process of interpretation should take into account 'any [other] relevant rules of international law applicable in the relations between the parties'.[346] External rules relevant to the interpretation of a treaty may include other treaties applicable between the parties.[347] This shows that there is potential for overlap between Articles 31(3)(a) and 31(3)(b) VCLT on the one hand, and Article 31(3)(c) VCLT on the other: the interpretative value of other treaties applicable between the parties can fall under both Article 31(3)(c), as external rules relevant to the interpretation of the treaty, and Articles 31(3)(a) and 31(3)(b), as subsequent practice or agreements in relation to the treaty.[348]

'Other rules' within the meaning of Article 31(3)(c) VCLT also cover rules of customary international law.[349] This touches upon the distinction, to the extent that

341 *Gabčíkovo-Nagymaros Project*, paras 133–4.

342 *Wintershall v Argentina*, para 128.

343 Gazzini, 'Bilateral Investment Treaties', 123.

344 See eg *Emilio Agustín Maffezini v Kingdom of Spain*, ICSID Case No ARB/97/7, Decision of the Tribunal on Objections to Jurisdiction, 25 January 2000, particularly paras 57–61; *Aguas del Tunari SA v Bolivia*, paras 289–314.

345 See Section 2.4.

346 Article 31(3)(c) also covers rules between the parties that preceded the treaty and therefore do not qualify as 'subsequent'.

347 These differ from treaties between one of the parties and third States, which, as discussed, likely fall under Art 32.

348 Moloo, 'When Actions Speak Louder Than Words', 7–8, citing *Delimitation of the Abyei Area*, paras 651, 654–5.

349 ILC, 'Conclusions of the Work of the Study Group on the Fragmentation of International Law: Difficulties arising from the Diversification and Expansion of International Law', *Report of the*

it can be made, between subsequent customary law that has emerged *independently* of the treaty regime—as a subsequent development not specifically related to the treaty—and customary law stemming from the parties' *treaty-related* practice, based on subsequent practice within the meaning of Article 31(3)(b) VCLT capable of amounting to authentic interpretation. The nature and significance of this distinction is examined further in Chapter 4 of this book.[350]

An example of a tribunal taking into account subsequent developments is the approach of the ICTY Appeals Chamber in relation to the status of 'protected persons' under Article 4 of the 1949 Geneva Convention relative to the Protection of Civilian Persons in Time of War[351] in the *Tadić* case:

> [A]lready in 1949 the legal bond of nationality was not regarded as crucial and allowance was made for special cases. In the (...) case of refugees, the lack of both allegiance to a State and diplomatic protection of this State was regarded as more important than the formal link of nationality.[352]

Another example of a dispute settlement body relying on subsequent developments or customary law clearly extrinsic to the treaty can be found in the ICJ's *Namibia Advisory Opinion*:

> [T]he Court must take into consideration the changes which have occurred in the supervening half-century, and its interpretation cannot remain unaffected by the subsequent development of law, through the Charter of the United Nations and by way of customary law. (...) In the domain to which the present proceedings relate, the last fifty years (...) have brought important developments. These developments leave little doubt that the ultimate objective of the sacred trust was the self-determination and independence of the peoples concerned (...) and this the Court, if it is faithfully to discharge its functions, may not ignore.[353]

The relation between subsequent developments, Article 31(3)(c) VCLT, and subsequent practice is discussed further in this chapter with regard to the process of evolutionary interpretation.[354]

The scope of the criterion 'in the application of the treaty' is, in any case, broad, making it difficult to pinpoint the dividing line between subsequent practice in the sense of Article 31(3)(b), and subsequent developments that fall under Articles 31(3)(c) or 32 VCLT (as well as other types of developments[355]):

> [I]t cannot be disputed that there is no clear dividing line, but rather a continuum between subsequent conduct by the parties which specifically relates to a treaty and other practice which bears some meaningful but less immediate relationship with that treaty.[356]

International Law Commission on the work of its 58th session, UN Doc A/61/10 (2006) Ch XII, 407 ('Conclusion 18'); and see further 'Conclusion 21' on the interpretative value of other treaty rules.

350 See in particular Sections 4.5.1 and 4.6.

351 75 UNTS 287 (Fourth Geneva Convention).

352 *Prosecutor v Dusko Tadić*, Appeal Judgment, Case No IT-94-1-A (15 July 1999) para 165.

353 *Namibia Advisory Opinion*, para 53.

354 See Section 2.5.3.

355 For instance, the ECtHR often seems to link 'subsequent social developments' to a basis in State practice in the application of the treaty—Nolte, Second Report on Treaties over Time, 247–9. See eg *Christine Goodwin v United Kingdom* [GC] App no 28957/95 (ECtHR, 11 July 2002) [*Christine Goodwin v UK*] para 88.

356 Nolte, Introductory Report on Treaties over Time, 175.

Whether practice relates closely enough to the treaty or not is therefore a matter of degree—and interpretation.[357] This ambiguity once again highlights the importance of a case-by-case analysis of instances of practice in attempting to determine their interpretative weight.

2.3.5 The requirement of 'agreement'

The crucial condition for practice to constitute relevant subsequent practice is that it must establish the 'agreement of the parties'. The requirement of agreement is inherently linked to another qualification of the notion of subsequent practice in Article 31(3)(b) VCLT, namely, the question of how many parties are required to participate in the practice.[358] As discussed with regard to its drafting history,[359] Article 31(3)(b) requires agreement among *all* the parties, in order to ensure that the interpreter is attentive to the intention of the entire treaty membership. Thus, for instance, the ICJ in the *Whaling in the Antarctic* case took a highly restrictive view of certain resolutions of the IWC to which it refused to accord any interpretative weight on account of the fact that they had been adopted without the support of all the parties to the 1946 International Convention for the Regulation of Whaling (ICRW),[360] and consequently failed to establish the parties' agreement within the meaning of Article 31(3)(b) VCLT.[361] This is a rather extreme approach and one that seems unusual in light of the Court's previous jurisprudence.[362] As explored later in this chapter, practice that does not meet the strict conditions under Article 31(3)(b) VCLT can still be taken into account in the interpretative process pursuant to Article 32 VCLT.[363]

Particularly in the case of multilateral treaties, the requirement of 'all' the parties can still be attained even if, as usually happens, only some of the parties actively partake in the practice while the rest remain passive and may be taken to have accepted through acquiescence.[364] The number of parties that must actively engage in the practice varies from case to case.[365] This is logical given the size of the

357 cf Simma, 'Miscellaneous Thoughts on Subsequent Agreements and Practice', 47.

358 Greig, *Intertemporality*, 92 ('the weight and extent of the practice must be judged against the standard required to establish an agreement amongst the parties').

359 See Section 2.2. 360 161 UNTS 72.

361 See eg *Whaling in the Antarctic* (*Australia v Japan: New Zealand intervening*), Judgment of 31 March 2014, General List No 148, para 83; ibid. Separate Opinion of Judge Greenwood, para 6.

362 See eg J Arato, 'Subsequent Practice in the Whaling Case, and What the ICJ Implies about Treaty Interpretation in International Organizations' (*EJIL: Talk!*, 31 March 2014) <www.ejiltalk.org/subsequent-practice-in-the-whaling-case-and-what-the-icj-implies-about-treaty-interpretation-in-international-organizations> accessed 24 June 2016; L Crema, 'Is the Intention of the Parties at the Heart of Interpretation? Some News about Subsequent Practice from The Hague' (*SIDIBlog*, 9 May 2014) <www.sidiblog.org/wp-content/uploads/2016/04/Quaderni-Sidi-Blog_1_2014-1.pdf> accessed 24 June 2016.

363 See Section 2.4.

364 1966 Draft Articles on the Law of Treaties with Commentaries, 221–2. See further Section 2.3.5(b).

365 *European Communities–Customs Classification of Frozen Boneless Chicken Cuts*, Report of the Appellate Body (12 September 2005) WT/DS269/AB/R [*EC–Chicken Cuts*, AB Report] para 259. See also ILC Draft Conclusions on Subsequent Agreements and Subsequent Practice (2016), 122

membership of certain multilateral treaty regimes, as observed by the WTO Panel in *EC–Chicken Cuts*:

If (...) it were necessary to show the existence of practice common to all parties to a treaty (in this case, all 148 members of the WTO) in order to demonstrate the existence of 'subsequent practice' for the purpose of Article 31(3)(b) of the Vienna Convention, it is highly unlikely that subsequent practice could ever be proved in the WTO context with respect to schedules.[366]

Furthermore, it is not only the proportion of parties contributing to the practice that matters, but also the relevance of the participating parties and how their agreement is established.[367] But if the practice of some States is contradictory, to what extent does this cancel out the relevance of the subsequent practice of the other parties? This was already discussed with regard to the required degree of determinacy of practice.[368] According to the ILC, the effects of contradictory subsequent practice will vary according to the treaty regime concerned.[369] For example, the WTO Appellate Body usually discounts practice contradicted by the practice of any other party,[370] whereas the ECtHR only does so if the latter reflects the 'vast majority' of the parties to the European Convention on Human Rights.[371]

We have also seen that practice must be sufficiently concrete[372] and relate to the treaty provisions in question.[373] The latter criterion suggests that the practice should involve an element of intentionality or awareness in that it is connected to the relevant party's belief that its conduct expresses a position taken on the interpretation of the treaty,[374] and hence establishes the parties' common understanding in relation to a point of law.[375] This element overlaps with the *opinio juris* component required for the emergence of customary international law.[376]

('Conclusion 10', para 2): 'The number of parties that must actively engage in subsequent practice in order to establish an agreement under article 31, paragraph 3(b), may vary.'

366 *European Communities–Customs Classification of Frozen Boneless Chicken Cuts*, Report of the Panel (30 May 2005) WT/DS269/R [*EC–Chicken Cuts*, Panel Report] para 7.253. The Appellate Body later rejected the Panel's more liberal approach to subsequent practice, in *EC–Chicken Cuts*, AB Report, paras 251–76.

367 *North Sea Continental Shelf (Federal Republic of Germany/Denmark; Federal Republic of Germany/Netherlands)*, Judgment of 20 February 1969, ICJ Reports 3, para 74 ('states whose interests are specially affected'); AM Feldman, 'Evolving Treaty Obligations: A Proposal for Analyzing Subsequent Practice Derived from WTO Dispute Settlement' (2009) 41 NYU 655, 694.

368 See Section 2.3.1(b).

369 ILC Report on the Work of Its 64th Session, para 240.

370 See eg *European Communities–Customs Classification of Certain Computer Equipment*, Report of the Appellate Body (5 June 1998) WT/DS62/AB/R [*EC–Computer Equipment*, AB Report] paras 92–3.

371 See eg *Sigurdur A Sigurjónsson v Iceland* App no 16130/90 (ECtHR, 30 June 1993) para 35. See further Nolte, Second Report on Treaties over Time, 305 ('General Conclusion 16').

372 See Section 2.3.1(a). See also eg *United States–Subsidies on Upland Cotton*, Report of the Appellate Body (3 March 2005) WT/DS267/AB/R, para 625; Nolte, Introductory Report on Treaties over Time, 196–7; Nolte, Second Report on Treaties over Time, 221, 236.

373 See Section 2.3.4.

374 *Kasikili/Sedudu Island*, para 74; Crema, 'Subsequent Agreements and Subsequent Practice', 17. cf Arato, 'Treaty Interpretation', 304: 'constitutional transformation can occur through the less-than-intentional action of the constituted bodies. The issue is not the intentions of the actors but the *consequences* of their actions.' (Emphasis in the original.)

375 Nolte, Introductory Report on Treaties over Time, 190. See also *Certain Expenses Advisory Opinion*, Separate Opinion of Judge Fitzmaurice, 201.

376 See Sections 4.3.3 and 4.6.

A contrasting minority view is that practice should *not* be coupled with an intention to create law since that would make it the equivalent of customary law.[377] It is submitted here that this standpoint cannot be accepted: first, because we have seen that subsequent practice represents a source of authentic interpretation,[378] and, second, because there is indeed a strong analogy to be drawn between the process of subsequent practice and the process of customary international law, which is the subject of Chapter 4.[379]

In any case, the agreement established by the practice must be opposable to all the parties. Thus, Article 31(3)(b) VCLT appears to impose a high threshold for practice,[380] in line with a 'consensualist' notion of the law of treaties.[381] And yet it has been argued that the unanimity rule is 'honoured more in the breach than in the observance',[382] particularly with regard to the practice of international organizations, as opposed to that of its individual member States.[383] Moreover, subsequent practice in a given instance may constitute the parties' agreement to only *temporarily* not apply the treaty, or may create a practical arrangement that leaves the interpretation of the treaty open, and which may be subject to challenge by other States parties or before an international court or tribunal.[384]

A number of factors merit closer attention on the subject of establishing agreement through subsequent practice: (a) the role of silence, (b) the related notions of acquiescence and estoppel, and (c) the evidence required for agreement. These are each dealt with in turn.

2.3.5a The role of silence in establishing agreement

As mentioned, silence can under certain conditions contribute to relevant subsequent practice.[385] Passive conduct does not automatically imply acquiescence unless it can be shown, for instance, that the passive State was aware of the practice in

[377] Linderfalk, *On the Interpretation of Treaties*, 170–7. *Contra* eg R Bernhardt, 'Interpretation and Implied (Tacit) Modification of Treaties: Comments on Arts 27, 28, 29, and 38 of the ILC's 1966 Draft Articles on the Law of Treaties' (1967) 27 ZaöRV 491, 499; Yasseen, 'L'interprétation', 48, 52; I Sinclair, *The Vienna Convention on the Law of Treaties* (2nd edn, Manchester UP, 1984) 137; Nolte, Third Report on Treaties over Time, 341. This relates to the discussion in Section 2.3.1(b) regarding determinacy and context.

[378] See Section 2.3.3.

[379] See in particular Section 4.6.

[380] See also Section 3.3.4.

[381] Crawford, 'A Consensualist Interpretation of Article 31(3)', 30–1.

[382] E Schwelb, 'The Amending Procedure of Constitutions of International Organizations' 49 (1954) 31 BYBIL 49, citing PC Jessup, *A Modern Law of Nations: An Introduction* (Macmillan, 1948) 144.

[383] See Section 2.3.1(c). Note also that many treaties allow 'authoritative interpretations' of the treaty by only a majority of States parties (eg Art IX of the WTO Agreement). See eg J Pauwelyn, 'The Role of Public International Law in the WTO: How Far Can We Go?' (2001) 95 AJIL 535, 574. See also Section 5.2.3(c) (on the 2001 FTC Interpretation).

[384] Nolte, Third Report on Treaties over Time, 343–4; Nolte, Second Report on Subsequent Practice, para 71; ILC Draft Conclusions on Subsequent Agreements and Subsequent Practice (2016), 123 ('Conclusion 6', para 1).

[385] See eg *Prosecutor v Anto Furundžija* (TC) Judgment, Case No IT-17/1-T (10 December 1998) para 179; *EC–Chicken Cuts*, AB Report, para 272; *Rantsev v Cyprus and Russia* App no 25965/04 (ECtHR, 7 January 2010) para 285.

question:[386] *qui tacit consentire videtur si loqui debuisset ac potuisset* ('he who keeps silent is held to consent if he must and can speak').[387] In the words of the ICJ, 'silence may also speak, but only if the conduct of the other state calls for a response'.[388] Only such 'qualified' silence may constitute acquiescence upon which other States may come to rely.[389] This is tied closely to the notion of awareness or intentionality[390]—not only an awareness of the implications of the silence, but also an awareness of the practice that merits a reaction in the first place. For instance, the 'mere fact that a document is publicly accessible does not (...) mean that it can be assumed that another state has knowledge of it, or that another state has even adopted a position with respect to it'.[391]

Therefore, it is important to investigate the underlying reason for the lack of reaction on the part of non-participating States—an investigation also linked to the concept of good faith, central to Article 31 VCLT—to be able to infer whether their silence implies agreement:

> [W]e have misgivings about deducing, without further inquiry, agreement with a practice from a party's 'lack of reaction'. We do not exclude that, in specific situations, the 'lack of reaction' or silence by a particular treaty party may, in the light of attendant circumstances, be understood as acceptance of the practice of other treaty parties.[392]

Accordingly, though national legislation is in general capable of contributing to relevant subsequent practice,[393] a State cannot typically be expected to be aware of the internal conduct of another State, as reflected, for example, in the latter's parliamentary documents. The former State's silence cannot automatically be taken to imply a tacit acceptance of said practice.[394] For instance, in the *Sovereignty over Pulau Ligitan and Pulau Sipadan* case, the ICJ did not regard a map accompanying the draft legislation authorizing the ratification of the treaty in question as a subsequent agreement or practice under Article 31(3) VCLT.[395] It explained:

> The Court observes that the Explanatory Memorandum and map were never transmitted by the Dutch Government to the British Government, but were simply forwarded to the latter by its diplomatic agent in The Hague (...). This agent specified that the map had been published in the Official Journal of the Netherlands and formed part of a Report presented to the Second Chamber of the States-General. He added that 'the map seems to be the only interesting feature of a document which does not otherwise call for special comment'.

386 See Villiger, *Commentary*, 431–2 fn 69.

387 See further NS Marques Antunes, 'Acquiescence' in R Wolfrum (ed), *Max Planck Encyclopedia of Public International Law* (OUP, 2009) 1.

388 *Sovereignty over Pedra Branca/Pulau Batu Puteh, Middle Rocks and South Ledge* (*Malaysia v Singapore*), Judgment of 23 May 2008, ICJ Reports 12, para 121. See also ILC Draft Conclusions on Subsequent Agreements and Subsequent Practice (2016), 122 ('Conclusion 10', para 2): 'Silence (...) can constitute acceptance of the subsequent practice when the circumstances call for some reaction.'

389 Villiger, *Commentary*, 9. See also Wood, Third Report, paras 22ff; JP Müller and T Cottier, 'Acquiescence' in R Bernhardt (ed), *Encyclopedia of Public International Law*, vol VII (North Holland, 1984) 5.

390 See text to nn 374–5.

391 Nolte, Third Report on Treaties over Time, 318.

392 *EC–Chicken Cuts*, AB Reports, para 272.

393 See Section 2.3.1(a).

394 See eg *Greenland-Jan Mayen*, para 29; *Anglo-Iranian Oil*, 106–7.

395 *Indonesia/Malaysia*, paras 59–61.

However (…) [the agent] did not draw the attention of his authorities to the red line drawn on the map among other lines. (…) In these circumstances, such a lack of reaction [by the British government] to this line on the map appended to the Memorandum cannot be deemed to constitute acquiescence in this line.[396]

In the *Certain Expenses Advisory Opinion*, on the other hand, the ICJ took silence to imply acquiescence because the UN practice had been publicized to such an extent that States were presumed to know about it and had been given ample opportunity to object.[397] Likewise, in *Military and Paramilitary Activities in and against Nicaragua*, the Court ruled that Nicaragua had consented to its jurisdiction since the UN had 'regularly placed Nicaragua on the list of those States that have recognized the compulsory jurisdiction of the Court', a practice that had gone on for years and which had given Nicaragua and any other State 'every opportunity of accepting or rejecting' such claims.[398] This indicates that the more 'concordant, common and consistent' the silence is, the easier it can be taken to imply acquiescence.[399]

The *Temple of Préah Vihéar* case is particularly interesting in this respect.[400] It involved an instance of subsequent practice amounting to the tacit modification of a boundary: specifically, a map depicting the position of the Temple of Préah Vihéar on the Cambodian side of the boundary line, executed by French topographical officers at the request of Siamese authorities, duly communicated to the Siamese Government, and given 'wide publicity'.[401] The Court found that the specific circumstances of the case had warranted a reaction on the part of the Siamese authorities,[402] and that the extended absence of such a reaction was proof of Thailand's acquiescence to the practice reflected by the map:

It has been contended on behalf of Thailand that this communication of the maps by the French authorities was, so to speak, *ex parte*, and that no formal acknowledgment of it was either requested of, or given by, Thailand. In fact (…) an acknowledgment by conduct was undoubtedly made in a very definite way; but even if it were otherwise, it is clear that *the circumstances were such as called for some reaction*, within a reasonable period, on the part of the Siamese authorities, if they wished to disagree with the map or had any serious question to raise in regard to it. They did not do so, either then or for many years, and thereby must be held to have acquiesced. *Qui tacet consentire videtur si loqui debuisset ac potuisset.*[403]

The Court concluded that the Siamese authorities 'cannot therefore now plead any error vitiating the reality of their consent'.[404] The Court added that, even if it had indeed believed to have title over the Temple grounds at the time, due to the fact that it subsequently decided not to react, 'Thailand is now precluded by her conduct from asserting that she did not accept it (…) [since] France, and through her Cambodia, relied on Thailand's acceptance of the map.'[405] This, in other words, is a situation of estoppel, which entails that a State is precluded by its conduct from asserting that it

[396] Ibid. para 48. [397] *Certain Expenses Advisory Opinion*, 175.
[398] *Nicaragua v US*, Jurisdiction and Admissibility, para 36.
[399] Feldman, 'Evolving Treaty Obligations', 693. [400] See Section 5.2.1.
[401] *Temple of Préah Vihéar*, 20. [402] Ibid. 23–4. [403] Ibid. 23 (emphasis added).
[404] Ibid. 27. [405] Ibid. 32.

did not agree to or recognize a given situation.[406] The ICJ thus dismissed Thailand's argument that it had been in possession of the Temple at all material times and hence had felt no need to positively react to the practice.[407] This decision garnered a significant amount of criticism.[408] However, criticisms of the Court's judgment have not gained majority support.[409]

An objective[410] appraisal of the circumstances in which a reaction is required can be used to determine whether one can speak of qualified silence in the sense of the aforementioned maxim, *qui tacit consentire videtur si loqui debuisset ac potuisset*[411]—namely, whether the silent State had an obligation (*debuisset*) or the capacity (*potuisset*) to react to the practice in question.[412] Thus, the legal value of silence is 'disassociated (...) from the actual intention of the silent state',[413] although the presumption based on these objective circumstances could still be rebutted by proof of a contrary intention.

Conversely, in the *Cameroon v Nigeria* case, the ICJ considered that where a treaty establishes a determinate boundary, circumstances only exceptionally call for a reaction since preference must be given to the holder of the title, and concluded that Cameroon had not acquiesced in the abandonment of its title.[414] The presumption in this situation was that silence does not constitute agreement to the practice in question. The Tribunal in the *Delimitation of the Maritime Boundary between Guinea and Guinea-Bissau* arbitration, on the other hand, took full account of the difficulties faced by Guinea at the time, but found that these did not exempt it from the expectation to react to pertinent developments such as, in this case, a widely publicized boundary treaty.[415] Its silence could thus be taken as a sign of acquiescence to the practice in question. Most recently, in two cases between Nicaragua and Colombia, the ICJ found that no agreement in the sense of Article 31(3)(b) VCLT could be read into the absence of objection on the part of the States parties to the Pact of Bogotá[416] with regard to Colombia's notification of denunciation of

[406] See further *Dispute concerning Delimitation of the Maritime Boundary Between Bangladesh and Myanmar in the Bay of Bengal* (*Bangladesh/Myanmar*) Judgment of 14 March 2012, ITLOS Case No 16 [*Bay of Bengal*] para 124. See also Section 2.3.5(b).

[407] *Temple of Préah Vihéar*, 30.

[408] See eg PCW Chan, 'Acquiescence/Estoppel in International Boundaries: *Temple of Préah Vihéar* Revisited' (2004) 3 Chinese JIL 421, 439; A Buss, 'The Préah Vihéar Case and Regional Customary Law' (2010) 9 Chinese JIL 114.

[409] Nolte, Introductory Report on Treaties over Time, 194.

[410] See S Kopela, 'The Legal Value of Silence as State Conduct in the Jurisprudence of International Tribunals' (2010) 29 Aust YBIL 87, 133: 'International tribunals have stressed the importance of the conduct itself and the existence of objective criteria in order to establish whether the silence of a state may amount to acquiescence and produce legal effects in the relations among states [although they have not gone so far as to negate the existence or the importance of state intention].'

[411] See text to n 387.

[412] Kopela, 'The Legal Value of Silence', 87.

[413] Ibid. 112.

[414] *Cameroon v Nigeria*, Judgment, paras 64, 67–8, 70 (discussed further in Sections 3.5.1(a) and 5.2.1). The same reasoning had been applied in *Frontier Dispute* (*Burkina Faso/Republic of Mali*), Judgment of 22 December 1986, ICJ Reports 554, para 63. See also *Sovereignty over Pedra Branca*, paras 233–4, 239.

[415] *Case concerning the Delimitation of the Maritime Boundary between Guinea and Guinea-Bissau*, Award of 14 February 1985, 19 RIAA 149, para 65.

[416] 1948 American Treaty on Pacific Settlement (Pact of Bogotá), 30 UNTS 55.

the treaty.[417] As reinforced by the circumstances of the case—namely, the timing of Nicaragua's commencement of proceedings in both cases against Colombia before the Court—the Court concluded that Nicaragua's lack of reaction did not amount to acquiescence.[418]

Thus, the significance of silence when assessing subsequent practice evidencing the parties' agreement varies strongly with the general context and circumstances of the specific case. This was underscored in Judge Spender's Dissenting Opinion in the *Temple of Préah Vihéar* case:

> The circumstances in which the maps came into existence and were distributed is of importance as providing part of the background against which the conduct of France and Siam is to be evaluated. (...) In determining what inferences may or should be drawn from Thailand's silence and absence of protest regard must (...) be had to the period of time when the events we are concerned with took place, to the region of the world to which they related, to the general political conditions existing in Asia at this period, to political and other activities of Western countries in Asia at the time and to the fact that of the two States concerned one was Asian, the other European. It would not, I think, be just to apply to the conduct of Siam in this period objective standards comparable to those which reasonably might today be or might then have been applied to highly developed European States.[419]

A trickier issue is establishing relevant subsequent practice in the context of international organizations. This point relates closely to the previous discussion on the significance of the practice of international organizations vis-à-vis that of the States parties as such.[420] The constitutive instruments of international organizations raise specific problems due to their special institutional character.[421] For instance, they create higher expectations for States parties 'to accept that a lack of reaction to generally apparent developments would mean agreement'.[422] Therefore, dispute settlement bodies seem more willing to assume the consent of the parties to the organization based on the practice of the organization or its organs.[423]

The general conclusion that can be drawn from the foregoing considerations is that an analysis of the legal significance of silence in a given case will depend on the specific facts and relations between the States concerned.[424] Moreover, conclusions

[417] *Alleged Violations of Sovereign Rights and Maritime Spaces in the Caribbean Sea* (*Nicaragua v Colombia*), Preliminary Objections, Judgment of 17 March 2016, para 46; *Question of the Delimitation of the Continental Shelf between Nicaragua and Colombia beyond 200 Nautical Miles from the Nicaraguan Coast* (*Nicaragua v Colombia*), Preliminary Objections, Judgment of 17 March 2016, para 44.

[418] Ibid.

[419] *Temple of Préah Vihéar* (*Cambodia v Thailand*), Merits, Judgment of 15 June 1962, Dissenting Opinion of Sir Percy Spender, ICJ Reports 101, 128. See also eg M Kelly, 'The Temple Case in Historical Perspective' (1963) 39 BYBIL 471.

[420] See Section 2.3.1(c).

[421] Gardiner, *Treaty Interpretation*, 247.

[422] Nolte, Introductory Report on Treaties over Time, 195, citing *Nicaragua v US*, Jurisdiction and Admissibility, para 39.

[423] Arato, 'Subsequent Practice', 460, citing *Namibia Advisory Opinion*, paras 21–2. See also Gardiner, *Treaty Interpretation*, 247; Alvarez, *International Organizations*, 80. See further Sections 5.2.1 and 5.2.5.

[424] See further Marques Antunes, 'Acquiescence', 3.

from silence must be drawn with great caution to ensure that they are actually reflective of the parties' common understanding.[425]

2.3.5b The role of acquiescence and estoppel in establishing agreement

Acquiescence relates closely to what was previously discussed regarding the role of silence: it refers to a State's silence or failure to protest in a situation arising from other States' practice that may encroach upon its rights, and which calls for an active objection on the part of that State.[426] Hence, it gives rise to a rebuttable presumption of acceptance or recognition of a legal position claimed by another State:[427] 'acquiescence is equivalent to tacit recognition manifested by unilateral conduct which the other party may interpret as consent'.[428] Acquiescence can play a determinative role in a case by sealing the legality 'upon rules which were formerly in process of development and upon rights which were formerly in process of consolidation'.[429] Its effects are interrelated with those of subsequent practice and customary international law, in the sense that general tolerance by the international community of a certain norm may solidify the view that a new customary rule has emerged that modifies an earlier rule.[430] They 'share a common process of development which involves, on the one hand, the constant assertion of the right in question, and, on the other hand, consent in that assertion on the part of the affected States'.[431]

General acquiescence in a practice deviating from a treaty can modify or even terminate rights and duties, particularly if the practice is unopposed, as is explored in Chapter 3 of this book. For example, in the *Fisheries Jurisdiction* case, acquiescence led to the enlargement of maritime claims.[432] In the *Temple of Préah Vihéar* case, it led to a change in the land boundary, as discussed.[433] The far-reaching consequences of acquiescence—echoing the potential treaty modifying effects of subsequent practice—have been described as follows:

> [D]erogation of existing law would be entailed by general acquiescence in a practice initiated by a group of States in violation of established rules, provided that the practice affected the generality of States and met with no opposition. (…) [States must] maintain a scrupulous standard of vigilance in keeping with their rights and responsibilities, and, in their own interest, to exhibit a readiness to react unequivocally, by protest or similar measures, on the

[425] Nolte, Second Report on Subsequent Practice, para 66.

[426] The definition of 'acquiescence' adopted for present purposes excludes States' active conveyance of consent or approval.

[427] See IC MacGibbon, 'The Scope of Acquiescence in International Law' (1954) 31 BYBIL 143.

[428] *Delimitation of the Maritime Boundary in the Gulf of Maine Area* (*Canada/United States of America*), Judgment of 12 October 1984, ICJ Reports 246 [*Gulf of Maine*] para 130.

[429] Ibid. 145.

[430] Marques Antunes, 'Acquiescence', 2–3. See further IC MacGibbon, 'Customary International Law and Acquiescence' (1957) 33 BYBIL 115.

[431] MacGibbon, 'The Scope of Acquiescence', 150. See also M Sørensen, *Les sources du droit international: Étude sur la jurisprudence de la Cour Permanente de Justice Internationale* (Munksgaard 1946) 101.

[432] See Section 5.2.1.

[433] Ibid.

occasion of each and every encroachment on their rights (...) which they are concerned to defend.[434]

The fundamental problem with identifying acquiescence is determining when it actually reflects consent, as opposed to merely action or inaction by States based on various considerations, such as political expediency or simply a lack of occasion to react.[435] This relates to the earlier point concerning the preference for an objective assessment of the facts and circumstances of the case.[436] For instance, the inaction of a State in a situation regarded as provisional because negotiations are still ongoing should not be taken as acquiescence.[437]

The main conceptual difficulty, from which practical problems relating to the application of the concept stem, lies in the tension between two opposable maxims: *qui tacit consentire videtur* ('he who keeps silent is held to consent') and *qui tacit neque negat, neque utique fatetur* ('he who keeps silent is held neither to deny nor to accept'). The aforementioned 'qualified' notion of silence, namely, silence subject to the requirement of *si loqui debuisset ac potuisset* ('if one could have and should have spoken'), represents a compromise between the two maxims. The latter requirement is not always easy to apply. It may be discerned based on inferences that certain facts were, or should have been, known to the State in question ('notoriety'), are of direct interest to that State ('interest'), have existed for a significant period ('duration') without significant change ('consistency'), or are attributable to a representative of that State ('attribution').[438]

A highly debated issue is the difficult distinction between acquiescence and the related notion of estoppel,[439] as noted by the ICJ on multiple occasions.[440] The utility of distinguishing between the two notions is doubtful given that, as illustrated in the *Temple of Préah Vihéar* case, in most cases estoppel is deemed to *stem* from a State's acquiescing conduct:[441]

A claim of estoppel may—and indeed frequently does—relate to the existence, non-existence or deemed existence of a particular state of mind of the respondent State, and in particular its acceptance of, or consent to, a particular matter; but while a claim of acquiescence asserts that the State concerned *did* accept or agree on that point, a claim of estoppel accepts, by implication that the respondent State did *not* accept or agree, but contends that, having misled

[434] MacGibbon, 'The Scope of Acquiescence', 185–6.

[435] Ibid. 172; MG Kohen, 'Desuetude and Obsolescence of Treaties' in E Cannizzaro (ed), *The Law of Treaties Beyond the Vienna Convention* (OUP, 2011) 350.

[436] See text to nn 412–15.

[437] See eg *Rights of Nationals*, 200–1, where the ICJ considered that Morocco could not be taken to have acquiesced to the continued exercise of consular jurisdiction by the US as its legal right in light of the negotiations ongoing at the time between the US and France.

[438] Marques Antunes, 'Acquiescence', 4.

[439] See eg H Das, 'L'estoppel et l'acquiescement: assimilations pragmatiques et divergences conceptuelles' (1997) 30 RBDI 607, 608.

[440] See eg *Gulf of Maine*, para 130; *Temple of Préah Vihéar*, Dissenting Opinion of Judge Spender, 130–1. See further Marques Antunes, 'Acquiescence', 1, 4.

[441] See Marques Antunes, 'Acquiescence', 4; DW Bowett, 'Estoppel before International Tribunals and Its Relation to Acquiescence' (1957) 33 BYBIL 176; MacGibbon, 'The Scope of Acquiescence', 143; Chan, 'Acquiescence/Estoppel', 421.

the applicant State by behaving as though it did agree, it cannot be permitted to deny the conclusion which its conduct suggested.[442]

Estoppel, a general principle of international law,[443] is based on the notion that one should not benefit from one's own inconsistency, as reflected in the maxim *allegans contraria non audiendus est*.[444] It entails a detrimental reliance by one State on a certain factual situation, the appearance of which was created by the conduct of another State and the change of which could lead to undue prejudice.[445] As confirmed by ITLOS in its 2012 decision in the maritime delimitation case between Bangladesh and Myanmar,[446] and as already discussed with regard to the *Temple of Préah Vihéar* case,[447] the other State is consequently precluded by its own conduct from later asserting that it had not agreed to or recognized that situation.[448] Relevant conduct may consist of a positive act (such as a declaration), or an omission or silence. In the case of estoppel, silence operates 'as a condition of a rule which applies independently of the will of the parties'.[449] Thus, Nolte refers to estoppel as a 'non-consent based rule'.[450] This has led to a certain degree of confusion as to the meaning of estoppel, although the majority of scholars do not question its status as a general principle of international law.[451] In any case, the notable difference between acquiescence and the related notion of estoppel is that only the former requires the conveyance of consent.[452]

The case law demonstrates the close connection between estoppel and acquiescence,[453] as part of the process of subsequent practice more generally.[454] Thus, acquiescence and estoppel remain highly relevant to the reasoning of courts and tribunals, but caution must continue to be exercised in assessing their effects with regard to the value of silence or omissions in establishing an agreement through practice.[455]

442 HWA Thirlway, 'The Law and Procedure of the International Court of Justice: 1960–80, Part One' (1989) 60 BYBIL 1, 29–30. See also A Martin, *L'estoppel en droit international public* (Pédone, 1979) 259–60; I Sinclair, 'Estoppel and Acquiescence' in V Lowe and M Fitzmaurice (eds), *Fifty Years of the International Court of Justice: Essays in Honour of Sir Robert Jennings* (CUP, 1996) 120.

443 Brownlie, *Principles of Public International Law*, 616.

444 See eg McNair, *Law of Treaties*, 485. The literal translation of the Latin maxim would be 'one making contradictory statements is not to be heard'.

445 See eg *North Sea Continental Shelf*, para 30. This requirement is open to some debate—see eg M Koskenniemi, *From Apology to Utopia: The Structure of International Legal Argument* (CUP, 2005) 348, 356.

446 *Bay of Bengal*, paras 124–5, citing *North Sea Continental Shelf*, para 30; *Gulf of Maine*, para 145.

447 See text to nn 405–6.

448 The State invoking this argument may have to prove that the conduct 'caused it to change its position to its detriment or suffer some prejudice in reliance on such conduct'—*Bay of Bengal*, para 125.

449 Nolte, Introductory Report on Treaties over Time, 196.

450 Ibid. Bowett, 'Estoppel', 201.

451 See eg MacGibbon, 'The Scope of Acquiescence', 147–8; Brownlie, *Principles*, 616.

452 See eg *Temple of Préah Vihéar*, Dissenting Opinion of Judge Spender, 131; AD McNair, 'The Legality of the Occupation of Ruhr' (1924) 5 BYBIL 17, 34–5.

453 Sinclair, 'Estoppel and Acquiescence', 120.

454 Ibid. 104. See also Brownlie, *Principles*, 161.

455 Sinclair, 'Estoppel and Acquiescence', 120.

2.3.5c Evidence of 'agreement'

The ways in which agreement can be manifested are as diverse as the forms in which subsequent practice is manifested. No form requirements exist.[456] It is also clear that 'agreement' in the sense of Article 31(3)(b) VCLT can be established by the tacit acceptance of a practice involving only some of the parties to the treaty. This is reflected in the case law.[457] As explained in the *Beagle Channel Arbitration*:

> [T]he Court cannot accept the contention that no subsequent conduct (...) can have probative value as a subsidiary method of interpretation unless representing a formally stated or acknowledged 'agreement' between the Parties. The terms of the Vienna Convention do not specify the ways in which 'agreement' may be manifested. (...) Under these circumstances the silence of Argentina permits the inference that the acts [by Chile] tended to confirm an interpretation of the meaning of the Treaty (...).[458]

The WTO Appellate Body took a strict view in *Japan–Alcoholic Beverages*, according to which evidence of the parties' agreement requires practice to be 'concordant, common and consistent':[459]

> [T]he essence of subsequent practice in interpreting a treaty has been recognized as a 'concordant, common and consistent' sequence of acts or pronouncements which is sufficient to establish a discernable pattern implying the agreement of the parties regarding its interpretation.[460]

Generally, the higher the degree of concordance, commonness, and consistency, the higher the probative value of the practice, and the less corroborative evidence is needed to confirm that the subsequent practice in question reflects the agreement of the parties in relation to the interpretation of the treaty.[461] This also applies to the *silence* of non-participating parties.[462]

However, as pointed out by Nolte, the standard adopted by the Appellate Body is restrictive and has not, for instance, been applied by the ILC or the ICJ.[463] The Appellate Body's approach is tied to the particular character and context of the WTO Agreements and does not necessarily hold relevance for the application of the requirements in Article 31(3)(b) to most other treaties.[464] It is not the

[456] Yasseen, 'L'interprétation', 45; Distefano, 'La pratique subséquente', 47; A Aust, 'The Theory and Practice of Informal International Instruments' (1986) 35 ICLQ 787, 789; Gardiner, *Treaty Interpretation*, 208–9.

[457] See eg *Beagle Channel Arbitration*, paras 168(i), 169; *Heathrow Airport User Charges Arbitration*, para 6.8.

[458] *Beagle Channel Arbitration*, para 169(a).

[459] Yasseen, 'L'interprétation', 48; Sinclair, *Vienna Convention*, 137. See also *Japan–Alcoholic Beverages II*, AB Report, 13; *Chile–Price Band System and Safeguard Measures Relating to Certain Agricultural Products*, Report of the Appellate Body (23 September 2002) WT/DS207/AB/R [*Chile–Price Band System*, AB Report] para 214; *US–Gambling*, AB Report, paras 191–2; *EC–Chicken Cuts*, AB Report, paras 256–8. See further Section 3.3.3.

[460] *Japan–Alcoholic Beverages II*, AB Report, 13 (footnotes omitted). See also Canal-Forgues, 'Sur l'interprétation', 21. See further Section 2.3.1.

[461] See eg Feldman, 'Evolving Treaty Obligations', 697–9.

[462] See Section 2.3.1(a).

[463] Nolte, Second Report on Treaties over Time, 217. cf Nolte, Second Report on Subsequent Practice, paras 44–8.

[464] Nolte, Second Report on Subsequent Practice, para 48. See Section 2.5.2.

validity of the practice that depends on the criterion of 'concordance, commonness and consistency', but rather its evidentiary value.[465] In other words, this criterion does not represent a formal threshold for practice, but rather an indication of the circumstances in which subsequent practice could be relevant pursuant to Article 31(3)(b).[466]

The duration and frequency of practice are not independent conditions, but rather indicators of the existence of a consistent subsequent practice (and, potentially, customary international law).[467] The longer the duration, the more easily one can distinguish between consistent and inconsistent practice.[468] Moreover, the longer the period of time and the higher the frequency with which the practice occurs, the greater the opportunity for non-participating States to object to it, or for the participating States themselves to eventually alter it.[469] Sometimes, subsequent practice capable of establishing agreement can arise quickly, 'on account of the quickening pace of international relations, technological progress and social change',[470] if within that period, no matter how short, the practice was 'extensive and virtually uniform'.[471]

The notion of 'agreement' also raises the question of whether a one-time instance of practice can amount to relevant subsequent practice or whether additional treaty applications are required. Following the aforementioned passage regarding the 'concordant, common and consistent' requirement, the Appellate Body in *Japan–Alcoholic Beverages* considered that subsequent practice can only be established by a sequence of acts, rather than an isolated act.[472] Other commentators have expressed a different view:

> From a principle point of view, I find it difficult to see why *one* application cannot constitute a 'practice' but *two* can. (...) It seems to me to be the only reasonable interpretation that a 'practice' can consist of any number of applications, one or two or many—just as long as they 'establish the agreement of the parties regarding its interpretation'.[473]

[465] Nolte, Second Report on Subsequent Practice, para 47; *Islamic Republic of Iran and United States of America*, Interlocutory Award No ITL 83-B1-FT, para 114; Cot, 'La conduite subséquente des parties a un traité', 644–7 ('valeur probatoire'); Sinclair, *Vienna Convention*, 137.

[466] Nolte, Second Report on Subsequent Practice, para 47.

[467] M Sørensen, 'Principes de Droit International Public' (1960-III) 101 RC 1, 40; R Bernhardt, 'Ungeschriebenes Völkerrecht' (1976) 36 ZaöRV 50, 67; ME Villiger, *Customary International Law and Treaties: A Manual on the Theory and Practice of the Interrelation of Sources* (2nd rev edn, Kluwer International, 1997) para 61. cf *United States–Restrictions on Imports of Cotton and Man-Made Fibre Underwear*, Report of the Appellate Body (10 February 1997) WT/DS24/AB/R [*US–Restrictions on Imports of Cotton*, AB Report] 17.

[468] Villiger, *Customary International Law and Treaties* (1997), para 62.

[469] Ibid. See also R-J Dupuy, 'Coutume sage et coutume sauvage' in *Mélanges offerts à Charles Rousseau: La communauté internationale* (Pédone, 1974) 75, 84; MS McDougal, HHD Lasswell, and JC Miller, *The Interpretation of International Agreements and World Public Order: Principles of Content and Procedure* (Martinus Nijhoff, 1994) 271.

[470] Villiger, *Customary International Law and Treaties* (1997), para 61. See also Section 4.3.

[471] *North Sea Continental Shelf*, para 74.

[472] *Japan–Alcoholic Beverages II*, AB Report, 12–13. See also Canal-Forgues, 'Sur l'interprétation', 21.

[473] Linderfalk, *On the Interpretation of Treaties*, 166. See also JHH Weiler, 'Discussion' in A Cassese and JHH Weiler (eds), *Change and Stability in International Law-Making* (W de Gruyter, 1988) 8; J Pauwelyn, *Conflict of Norms in Public International Law: How WTO Law Relates to Other Rules of International Law* (CUP, 2003) 144.

The WTO Panel in *EC–Chicken Cuts* considered that the practice of a single party could be relevant for interpretation when it is the only State concerned in the matter.[474] Despite the fact that its decision was subsequently overruled by the Appellate Body,[475] the Panel 'merely reiterated a problem that has arisen in other contexts as well (...) [namely] that the practice of one individual State may have special cogency when it is related to the performance of an obligation incumbent on that State.'[476] This has also been recognized by the ICJ: '[i]nterpretations placed upon legal instruments by the parties to them, though not conclusive as to their meaning, have considerable probative value when they contain recognition by a party of its own obligations under an instrument.'[477]

One cannot view an instance of subsequent practice in isolation from its context: its relevance depends not only on the reaction of other parties, but also on the relevance of the obligation for the particular State carrying out the practice.[478] The higher the relevance of the participating States, the higher the probative value of the practice.[479] For instance, in *EC–Computer Equipment*,[480] the Appellate Body rejected the finding of the Panel that the classification practice of a number of main importers constituted subsequent practice, since certain other importers and the main exporter, as the relevant parties, did not follow the same practice.

However, it should be noted that it is often difficult to identify the relevant States whose practice is most important in order to establish agreement. For instance, in *US–Gambling*, the Appellate Body rejected the Panel's finding that certain Scheduling Guidelines could constitute subsequent practice, adding that it is generally 'unclear whose practice and whose agreement in which form would be sufficient to establish agreement [regarding WTO Schedules]', such as those States involved in the trade of the specific product, or those with a potential trading interest.[481] This also relates back to the discussion in Section 2.3.1(c) as to whose practice counts towards subsequent practice.

[474] *EC–Chicken Cuts*, Panel Report, para 7.255. See also Section 3.3.3(b).

[475] *EC–Chicken Cuts*, AB Report, para 259.

[476] Nolte, Annex A, para 29. See also Amerasinghe, *Principles*, 50; Tomuschat, 'Obligations', 290.

[477] *International Status of South West Africa*, Advisory Opinion of 11 July 1950, ICJ Reports 128, 135–6. See also McNair, *Law of Treaties*, 427.

[478] See also G Fitzmaurice, 'The General Principles of International Law Considered from the Standpoint of the Rule of Law' (1957-II) 92 RC 1, 114.

[479] *North Sea Continental Shelf*, para 74 ('states whose interests are specially affected'); Baxter, 'Treaties and Custom', 66 (referring to a State's size, volume of international relations, and general contribution to developing international law); AA D'Amato, *The Concept of Custom in International Law* (Cornell UP, 1971) 96 (referring to a State's 'degree of sophistication in international law'); E Jiménez de Aréchaga, 'Intervention' in A Cassese and JHH Weiler (eds), *Change and Stability in International Law-Making* (W de Gruyter, 1988) 48; Feldman, 'Evolving Treaty Obligations', 694, 697–9. But see Villiger, *Customary International Law and Treaties* (1997), para 41, citing Akehurst, 'Custom', 22: 'It is difficult to harmonize this view with the notion of the equality of States in international law, since the latter forestalls any *a priori* assumptions of "specially important" States in the law-making process. Moreover, the "sophistication" of one State's practice does not invariably result in general practice, because, as Akehurst has argued, small powers may equally well imitate other small nations.'

[480] *EC–Computer Equipment*, AB Report, para 92.

[481] *US–Gambling*, AB Report, para 193.

In addition, it can be argued that the practice should be sufficiently 'representative'[482] of the treaty parties—that is, reflective of the different socio-economic or political groupings of States.[483] The latter qualification may be of particular significance in the context of a treaty regime such as the WTO Agreement.[484] These regimes span an extremely wide membership with diverse and often conflicting interests across different categories of States, such as between developed and developing States. The same can be said of the Law of the Sea Convention, the quasi-universal membership of which often reflects opposing interests and views among the parties, categories of which include, *inter alia*, coastal versus landlocked States, maritime versus non-maritime powers, and developed versus developing States.

This also indicates that the type of treaty regime or provision can impact the scope and degree of practice necessary to evidence agreement.[485] An additional question in this respect is whether different rules should apply to subsequent practice in relation to treaties that create rights for (non-State) third party beneficiaries, such as human rights or investment treaties.[486] In the same vein, it is often assumed under contract law that contracting parties cannot act in a way that undermines third party rights once the 'beneficiary has accepted them or reasonably acted in reliance of them'.[487] The legitimate expectations of foreign investors built on the basis of the subsequent practice of the parties to the treaty should be protected.[488] The implications arising out of the special character of such treaties and the applicability of 'non-regression' are discussed further in Chapter 3.[489]

The foregoing analysis of the constitutive elements of subsequent practice is helpful in revealing the nuances and difficulties inherent in defining the parameters of subsequent practice. However, given the context-dependent nature of the process, those elements should not unduly narrow the perspective on the scope of practice relevant for treaty interpretation,[490] and, as discussed later

482 *North Sea Continental Shelf*, para 73.

483 Villiger, *Customary International Law and Treaties* (1997), para 35.

484 Marrakesh Agreement Establishing the World Trade Organization 1994, 1867 UNTS 3.

485 See also Section 3.5.1.

486 See eg *American Manufacturing and Trading, Inc v Republic of Zaire*, ICSID Case No ARB/93/1, Award of 21 February 1997, para 6.06.

487 International Institute for the Unification of Private Law, UNIDROIT Principles of International Commercial Contracts (2010), Art 5.2.5 <www.unidroit.org/english/principles/contracts/principles2010/integralversionprinciples2010-e.pdf> accessed 11 November 2016.

488 See Gazzini, 'Bilateral Investment Treaties', 116, citing eg *Técnicas Medioambientales Tecmed, SA v United Mexican States*, ICSID Case No ARB(AF)/00/2, Award of 29 May 2003 [*Tecmed v Mexico*] para 154; *Rumeli Telekom AS and Telsim Mobil Telekomunikasyon Hizmetleri AS v Republic of Kazakhstan*, ICSID Case No ARB/05/16, Award of 29 July 2008, para 609; E Snodgrass, 'Protecting Investors' Legitimate Expectations: Recognizing and Delimiting a General Principle' (2006) 21 ICSID Rev For Inv LJ 1; S Fietta, 'The "Legitimate Expectations" Principle under Article 1105 NAFTA: *International Thunderbird Gaming Corporation v The United American States*' (2006) 7 JWIT 423; I Tudor, *The Fair and Equitable Treatment Standard in International Foreign Investment Law* (OUP, 2008) 163–8. See also *Enron Corporation and Ponderosa Assets LP v Argentine Republic*, ICSID Case No ARB/01/3, Award of 22 May 2007 [*Enron Corporation and Ponderosa Assets*, Award] para 337; *Sempra Energy International v Argentine Republic*, ICSID Case No ARB/02/16 (Argentina-US BIT) Award of 28 September 2007, para 385; BM Clagett, 'Expropriation Issue before the Iran-United States Claims Tribunal: Is Just Compensation Required by International Law or Not' (1984) 16 L & Pol Intl Bus 813, 823.

489 See Section 3.5.

490 See also Nolte, Third Report on Treaties over Time, 311.

particularly in Chapter 3, treaty modification.[491] Subsequent practice in the sense of Article 31(3)(b) VCLT is thus generally taken to mean all applications of the treaty by the parties or other actors whose practice is attributable to the parties or can be considered as their collective practice (such as in the context of international organizations), subsequent to the conclusion of the treaty, and constituting the parties' agreement, be it tacit or explicit.

2.4 Subsequent Practice as a Supplementary Means under Article 32 VCLT

Article 32 VCLT deals with the supplementary means of interpretation, such as a treaty's drafting history and the circumstances of its conclusion. Supplementary means shed further light on the parties' intentions as to the meaning of the treaty.[492] Recourse is to be had to such means in order to confirm a meaning arrived at through the application of Article 31 VCLT, and to elucidate treaty terms when an interpretation according to Article 31 either leaves the meaning ambiguous or obscure (paragraph (a) of Article 32), or leads to a manifestly absurd or unreasonable result (paragraph (b) of Article 32). The drafting history suggests that the term 'supplementary' refers to the role of these interpretative means as 'complementary', rather than as 'subsidiary'.[493] It is therefore difficult to envisage situations in which Article 32 VCLT would not be applicable.[494] In fact, the ILC had envisaged automatic resort to the supplementary means in Article 32,[495] although States and dispute settlement bodies seem to have only limited recourse to it.[496]

The difference between subsequent practice in the narrow sense of Article 31(3)(b) VCLT and subsequent practice under Article 32 VCLT pertains to the interpretative weight accorded to practice in a given case.[497] A number of elements distinguish subsequent practice in the sense of Article 31(3)(b) from other types of practice falling under Article 32. As dealt with in Sections 2.3.1 to 2.3.3, the meaning of subsequent practice is extremely varied in terms of the type and form of practice, the actors of the practice, and the point at which the practice becomes relevant.

As seen in Section 2.3.4, a necessary criterion is that the practice must occur 'in the application of the treaty'. Moreover, as discussed at length in Section 2.3.5, the degree and type of practice—depending also on the extent to which it is 'concordant, common and consistent'—must be capable of establishing the agreement of all the parties as to the interpretation in question. Additionally, there must be an element of intentionality or awareness of the implications of the practice in order for it to qualify under Article 31(3)(b).[498]

491 See Section 3.3.3. 492 Waldock, Third Report on the Law of Treaties, 58 para 21.

493 ILC, 'Summary record of the 873rd meeting', *Summary records of the 18th session* (1966) I(2) YBILC 202, 206 para 41 (Waldock); Summary record of 884th meeting, 270 para 35 (Waldock).

494 Villiger, *Commentary*, 447. 495 Ibid. 448. 496 Ibid.

497 Nolte, Second Report on the Law of Treaties, 235. 498 See Section 2.3.5.

Practice that does not meet the above-mentioned requirements can still play a role under Article 32,[499] which goes to show the wider interpretative potential of subsequent practice.[500] The scope of Article 32 is wide.[501] It can include practice that does not strictly relate to the application of the treaty but still affects its interpretation.[502] And even when no agreement has been reached, recourse can still be had to subsequent practice in the interpretative process.[503] Moreover, the practice of international organizations, even if not deemed to constitute the States parties' agreement (for instance, if there is a dissenting minority[504]), can qualify as relevant practice under Article 32.[505] This goes to show that Article 31(3)(b) is not suited for the interpretation of any type of treaty,[506] perhaps especially not for treaties constituting international organizations.[507] In fact, a significant challenge lies in determining how to take into account new forms of practice that have come to characterize the evolution of present-day international law, 'much of which takes place outside the strict terms of art 31(3)(b)'.[508]

In the *Kasikili/Sedudu Island* case, for instance, the ICJ took into account the parties' subsequent practice relating to the boundary between them, though it was not shown that this established their agreement as to the interpretation of the treaty.[509] The Court relied on factual findings that were not disputed, and which confirmed the interpretation arrived at by the Court, but did not make explicit reference to Article 32 VCLT.[510] Panels and the Appellate Body have also taken a broader view of subsequent practice in certain cases, despite the Appellate Body's generally restrictive approach:[511]

> The fact that a certain practice does not fit the narrow *Japan–Alcoholic Beverages II* definition of 'subsequent practice' in the sense of Article 31(3)(b) VCLT and its relatively strict jurisprudential application does not mean that such practice is necessarily irrelevant as a means of interpretation.[512]

[499] See eg Torres Bernárdez, 'Interpretation of Treaties', 726; Villiger, *Commentary*, 446; Crema, 'Subsequent Agreements and Subsequent Practice', 17.

[500] Crema, 'Subsequent Agreements and Subsequent Practice', 26.

[501] Sorel and Boré Eveno, 'Article 31', 826. In *Greenland-Jan Mayen*, para 28, the practice taken into consideration included a press release by the Norwegian Ministry of Foreign Affairs and a subsequent treaty in the same field.

[502] See also Section 2.3.4.

[503] Moloo, 'When Actions Speak Louder Than Words', 39.

[504] *Certain Expenses Advisory Opinion*, Separate Opinion of Judge Fitzmaurice, 201–2: 'even if a majority vote cannot in the formal sense bind the minority, it can, if consistently exercised in a particular way, suffice to establish a settled practice which a tribunal can usefully and properly take account of'.

[505] See Section 2.3.1(c) (including the discussion on IWC resolutions in *Whaling in the Antarctic*). See also eg Greig, *Intertemporality*, 98.

[506] Crema, 'Subsequent Agreements and Subsequent Practice', 19.

[507] See eg *Certain Expenses Advisory Opinion*, 157. See also (text to) n 205.

[508] McLachlan, 'Evolution of Treaty Obligations', 81.

[509] *Kasikili/Sedudu Island*, paras 79–80. See also Fox, 'Article 31(3)(a) and (b)', 71.

[510] cf MN Shaw, 'Case concerning Kasikili/Sedudu Island (Botswana/Namibia)' (2000) 49 ICLQ 964, 975.

[511] See Section 2.3.5(c).

[512] *United States–Section 110(5) of US Copyright Act*, Report of the Panel (15 June 2000) WT/DS160/R, para 1.3.3.

In *US–Section 110(5) Copyright Act*, the WTO Panel referred to 'several examples from various countries of limitations in national [copyright] laws' to confirm its interpretation of the Berne Convention, despite the fact that there was no mention of an 'agreement of the parties' established by subsequent practice in the sense of Article 31(3)(b).[513] In fact, the Panel added that '[b]y enunciating these examples of state practice we do not wish to express a view on whether these are sufficient to constitute "subsequent practice" within the meaning of Article 31(3)(b) of the Vienna Convention.'[514] The Panel in *Mexico–Telecoms* considered that:

> In interpreting the scope of cross border supply in Article I:2(a) of the GATS, we need not decide whether the Explanatory Note provides 'context' (...) under paragraph 2 of Article 31 of the Vienna Convention, or whether it can be 'taken into account' (...) as a subsequent agreement or practice under paragraph 3 of the same provision. In any case, we consider that the source, content and use of the Explanatory Note make it part of the 'circumstances' of the conclusion of the GATS, within the meaning of Article 32 of the Vienna Convention.[515]

What the case law shows is that courts and tribunals oftentimes read Article 31(3)(b) VCLT liberally, without (explicitly) determining whether the conditions required according to a strict reading of the provision have been fulfilled.[516] Article 31(3)(b) comes to encapsulate a broader range of practice than appears at first sight. It has been argued that although this broad use of subsequent practice may go against the strict wording of Article 31(3)(b), it is more in line with the underlying principles of interpretation of the VCLT in placing greater emphasis on the principle of good faith: 'to base the rules of interpretation on the good faith principle, with a clear separation of textualism from originalism (the division between arts 31 and 32), while at the same time limiting the interpretive relevance of subsequent practice, is contradictory'.[517] Thus, the difference between the classification of practice as subsequent practice within the meaning of Article 31(3)(b), and as a supplementary means under Article 32, remains to some extent ambiguous.

2.5 Methods of Interpretation and the Role of Subsequent Practice

Interpretation must be capable of adapting the law to its constantly changing environment.[518] It plays a role in striking the balance between legal stability on the one hand, and the natural evolution of international law on the other[519]—a balance that falls differently per type of treaty and specific provision.[520] In the same vein,

513 Ibid. para 6.55. 514 Ibid. fn 68.

515 *Mexico–Telecoms*, Panel Report, paras 7.43–7.44. See also *EC–Computer Equipment*, AB Report, paras 89–90; Van Damme, *Treaty Interpretation*, 342.

516 See the ICJ's approach in eg *WHO Nuclear Weapons Advisory Opinion*, para 19; *Israeli Wall Advisory Opinion*, paras 25ff. See also *Peru v Chile*, paras 96–9, 103–11.

517 Crema, 'Subsequent Agreements and Subsequent Practice', 28.

518 C McLachlan, 'The Principle of Systemic Integration and Article 31(3)(c) of the Vienna Convention' (2005) 54 ICLQ 279, 282.

519 ES Yambrusic, *Treaty Interpretation: Theory and Reality* (UP of America, 1987) 239.

520 See eg Brunnée, 'Treaty Amendments', 351; Crema, 'Subsequent Agreements and Subsequent Practice', 19.

'one might well quip that interpretation is the continuation of treaty negotiations by other means'.[521] This reflects the political nature of treaty interpretation, inherent in the fact that a treaty's meaning continues to be the subject of change and debate even after the instrument's conclusion—the focus merely switches from the actual words to be employed in the treaty, to the meaning to be assigned to them.[522] The political aspect inherent in the process of according meaning to legal provisions under international law led one commentator to remark:

> One of the most fascinating strains in the theory of interpretation in international law is that of the 'freedom to interpret' vested in the State and in the other subjects of international law. (...) Pondering the subject, one once more gains the impression of a legal order in which conditions still prevail that, in national law, belong to an ancient past. And do even the best modern endeavours to regulate interpretation bring us any further than the stage of the medieval glossators and the freedom of interpretation they represented?[523]

Unsurprisingly, interpretation has been likened more to an art than an exact science[524]—'though it is part of the art that it should have the appearance of a science'.[525] Moreover, it has been argued that 'it is not entirely clear what interpretation is supposed to reveal': the true meaning of the text as intended by the drafters, or the scope of the rights and obligations of the parties, or both.[526] Thus, for the same reason that a treaty's meaning is not 'carved in stone' at the moment of the instrument's conclusion,[527] interpretation cannot be captured in 'strict, absolute rules':[528]

> The process of interpretation, rightly conceived, cannot be regarded as a mere mechanical one of drawing inevitable meanings from the words in a text, or of searching for and discovering some preexisting specific intention of the parties with respect to every situation arising under a treaty. It is precisely because the words used in an instrument rarely have exact and single meanings, and because all possible situations which may arise under it cannot be, or at least are not, foreseen and expressly provided for by the parties at the time of its drafting that the

[521] J Klabbers, 'On Rationalism in Politics: Interpretation of Treaties and the World Trade Organisation' (2005) 74 NJIL 405, 406, citing P Allot, 'The Concept of International Law' (1999) 10 EJIL 43.

[522] Klabbers, 'On Rationalism in Politics', 406.

[523] Bos, *A Methodology of International Law*, 127.

[524] Waldock, Third Report on the Law of Treaties, 54 para 6; 1966 Draft Articles on the Law of Treaties with Commentaries, 218 para 4; VD Degan, *L'Interprétation des accords en droit international*, vol II (Martinus Nijhoff, 1963) 163–4; C Rousseau, *Droit international public, Tome I: Introduction et sources* (Dalloz, 1970) 29; S Rosenne, 'On Multi-Lingual Interpretation' (1971) 6 Isr L Rev 360, 365; S Sur, *L'interprétation en droit international public* (LGDJ, 1974) 12; D Alland (ed), *Droit international public* (PUF, 2000) 237; P Merkouris, 'Introduction: Interpretation is a Science, is an Art, is a Science' in M Fitzmaurice, O Elias, and P Merkouris (eds), *Treaty Interpretation and the Vienna Convention on the Law of Treaties: 30 Years On* (Martinus Nijhoff, 2010) 1, 12–13. cf J Klabbers, 'Virtuous Interpretation' in M Fitzmaurice, O Elias, and P Merkouris (eds), *Treaty Interpretation and the Vienna Convention on the Law of Treaties: 30 Years On* (Martinus Nijhoff, 2010) 17, citing RY Jennings, 'General Course on Principles of International Law' (1967-II) 151 RC 323, 544.

[525] Jennings, 'General Course', 544. cf Klabbers, 'On Rationalism in Politics', 406: 'current tendencies suggest nonetheless that the scientific ambition has started to play first fiddle, and that deliberate attempts are being made to strip interpretation of its artsy connotations—and, more importantly perhaps, its political nature'.

[526] Klabbers, 'On Rationalism in Politics', 406 fn 4.

[527] Ibid. 406. See also Section 1.1.

[528] Klabbers, 'On Rationalism in Politics', 427.

necessity for interpretation occurs. In most instances therefore, interpretation involves *giving* a meaning to a text (...).[529]

The real question is what rules exist for practicing this 'art' of interpretation.[530] The answer requires an analysis of the main methods and policies of interpretation, and the different types of treaties and obligations (for instance, treaties constituting international organizations) that affect the role of subsequent practice in the interpretative process: 'Even if international law provides for a single set of rules of interpretation, the nature of the interpreted treaty may call for different approaches in its interpretation, and for different thresholds in the establishment of interpretive values of subsequent practice.'[531] This also establishes a starting point for the discussion on the factors that impact the process of modification by subsequent practice in Chapter 3.

A word on terminology is required. A distinction must be drawn between interpretative *means* (such as subsequent practice), *methods* (such as the 'textual' method, which downplays the role of subsequent practice in the interpretative process), and *policies* (such as a focus on identifying 'authentic interpretation').[532] The aim of Sections 2.5.1 and 2.5.2 is to clarify the implications of these notions for the operation of subsequent practice as a means of interpretation. Sections 2.5.3 and 2.5.4 then explore the special relation between subsequent practice on the one hand, and the respective doctrines of evolutionary interpretation and implied powers, on the other.

2.5.1 Overview of the main interpretative methods and the relevance of subsequent practice

Article 31 VCLT combines different means of interpretation, including subsequent practice, with different methods of employing them, each of which accord a different role to subsequent practice in the interpretative process. The article by no means sets out to provide an exhaustive statement of all possible interpretative methods.[533] It merely provides '*prima facie* guides' in the interpretative process,[534] avoiding the application of rigid interpretative rules—after all, interpretation is not a mechanical process,[535] nor is it a purely political one.[536] Article 31 represents a 'true example of a compromise'[537] between the different methods of interpretation. Its title—'General

[529] Waldock, Third Report on the Law of Treaties, 53 para 1, citing 1935 Harvard Draft Convention, 946 (emphasis in the original). See also eg M Bos, 'Theory and Practice of Treaty Interpretation' (1980) 27 NILR 3, 13–15.

[530] Gardiner, *Treaty Interpretation*, 5.

[531] Crema, 'Subsequent Agreements and Subsequent Practice', 19.

[532] See further Sorel and Boré Eveno, 'Article 31', 807.

[533] Koskenniemi, Fragmentation Report, para 427.

[534] McNair, *Law of Treaties*, 366.

[535] 1935 Harvard Draft Convention, 946; H Lauterpacht, 'Restrictive Interpretation and the Principle of Effectiveness in the Interpretation of Treaties' (1949) 26 BYBIL 48, 51.

[536] See Section 1.1. See also Koskenniemi, *From Apology to Utopia*, 333; Klabbers, 'On Rationalism in Politics', 405.

[537] Sorel and Boré Eveno, 'Article 31', 808.

rule', in the singular—may even 'stem from the difficulty of perceiving unity in "Rules" whereas the plural form hints at multiplicity and dispersion'.[538]

It is useful here to consider the main interpretative methods available. These can be loosely categorized into three basic types.[539] First, there is the *textual* or *objective* method, which emphasizes the literal meaning of the text, rooted in Article 31(1) VCLT, and is favoured by the ICJ.[540] It is associated with the plain meaning doctrine reflected in the famous 'Vattel principle', according to which: '*La première maxime générale sur l'interprétation est, qu'il n'est pas permis d'interpréter ce qui n'a pas besoin d'interprétation.*'[541] The textual interpretation has its disadvantages: the meaning inferred from the interpretation of the words of a treaty provision may vary with the context in which they are employed, the interpreter's frame of reference (a judge may give a different interpretation from a political State authority), and the nature of the treaty.[542] Subsequent practice has a varied impact upon the determination of the 'ordinary meaning' of the text of a treaty. Usually, it leads to the concretization or clarification of the range of possible meanings of the text,[543] particularly where the latter is obscure or formulated at a high level of generality.[544] But interpretation by subsequent practice can also expose the text to a broader interpretative range,[545] even in the case of seemingly clear terms.[546] Regardless of whether it results in a narrower or broader reading, the determination of the 'ordinary meaning' of the treaty arrived at through subsequent practice is taken as decisive in the case law.[547]

[538] Ibid. 814. See also Waldock, Sixth Report on the Law of Treaties, 95.

[539] This classification is endorsed by eg Jacobs, 'Varieties of Approach to Treaty Interpretation', 318; MN Shaw, *International Law* (6th edn, CUP, 2008) 932–3; M Fitzmaurice and P Merkouris, 'Canons of Treaty Interpretation: Selected Case Studies from the World Trade Organization and the North American Free Trade Agreement' in M Fitzmaurice, O Elias, and P Merkouris (eds), *Treaty Interpretation and the Vienna Convention on the Law of Treaties: 30 Years On* (Martinus Nijhoff, 2010) 153, 155. See the detailed classification of the different methods of interpretation in Bos, *A Methodology of International Law*, 139. See also Sørensen, *Les sources du droit international*, 210–36.

[540] See eg *Interpretation of Peace Treaties with Bulgaria, Hungary and Romania* (*Second Phase*), Advisory Opinion of 18 July 1950, ICJ Reports 221, 226–30; *Libya/Chad*, 22; *Qatar v Bahrain*, Jurisdiction and Admissibility, 21.

[541] 'The first general maxim of interpretation is, that it is not permissible to interpret what has no need of interpretation.'—E de Vattel, *Le droit des gens; ou Principes de la loi naturelle, appliqués à la conduite et aux affaires des nations et des souverains* (1758), vol II (trans CG Fenwick, Oceana Publications, 1964) Ch 17, para 263 (own translation). However, '[b]y recognising the need to interpret the clear text, [Article 31 of] the Vienna Convention distances itself from the Vattelian approach.'—Orakhelashvili, *Interpretation of Acts and Rules*, 318. See also the discussion at n 326.

[542] Yambrusic, *Treaty Interpretation*, 243.

[543] Nolte, Introductory Report on Treaties over Time, 181. See eg *Competence of the General Assembly*, 9; *WHO Nuclear Weapons Advisory Opinion*, para 55; *Land and Maritime Boundary between Cameroon and Nigeria* (*Cameroon v Nigeria: Equatorial Guinea intervening*), Preliminary Objections, Judgment of 11 June 1998, ICJ Reports 275 [*Cameroon v Nigeria*, Preliminary Objections] para 67.

[544] See eg *Arbitral Award Made by the King of Spain*, 208ff; *Certain Expenses Advisory Opinion*, Separate Opinion of Judge Spender, 189; *Costa Rica v Nicaragua*, Declaration of Judge ad hoc Guillaume, 290.

[545] Nolte, Introductory Report on Treaties over Time, 181. See eg *Rights of Nationals*, 211.

[546] Nolte, Introductory Report on Treaties over Time, 180, citing *Israeli Wall Advisory Opinion*, para 28.

[547] Nolte, Introductory Report on Treaties over Time, 179, citing *Certain Expenses Advisory Opinion*, 158ff (broad interpretation of 'expenses'), 164ff (narrow interpretation of 'action'). See also Nolte, Third Report on Treaties over Time, 334–5.

Second, the *subjective* method of interpretation seeks to determine the 'real' intention of the parties at the time of the treaty's conclusion, and, accordingly, encourages recourse to means such as the treaty's *travaux préparatoires* (Article 32 VCLT).[548] Subsequent practice can play a significant role here, both in its capacity as a primary means of interpretation under Article 31(3)(b) and as a supplementary means under Article 32.[549]

Third, the *teleological* or *purposive* method of interpretation, adopting a wider perspective, emphasizes the 'object and purpose' of the treaty (Article 31(1) VCLT) to discern the true meaning of its provisions. It entails that all the different interpretative means—including the preamble and the elements in Articles 31 and 32 VCLT—are combined to achieve a proper interpretation of the treaty.[550] Teleological interpretation is often used to interpret constitutive instruments of international organizations,[551] as well as other 'dynamic' types of treaties,[552] such as human rights and investment treaties.[553] This method is used increasingly by international courts and tribunals.[554] It was formulated as far back as 1935 in the Harvard Draft Convention on the Law of Treaties, Article 19 of which states:

> A treaty is to be interpreted *in the light of the general purpose which it is intended to serve*. The historical background of the treaty, *travaux préparatoires*, the circumstances of the parties at the time the treaty was entered into, the change in these circumstances sought to be effected, *the subsequent conduct of the parties in applying the provisions of the treaty*, and the conditions prevailing at the time interpretation is being made, are to be considered in connection with the general purpose which the treaty is intended to serve.[555]

The purposive method of interpretation is thus particularly interesting for present purposes, not only because it represents a form of 'dynamic' interpretation with implications resembling some of the more far-reaching effects of subsequent practice, but also because subsequent practice can, *inter alia*, be used to determine the 'object and purpose' of a treaty in the first place.[556] Fitzmaurice has termed the method of determining a treaty's object and purpose by means of subsequent practice 'emergent purpose', based on the idea that a treaty's object and purpose is bound to change or evolve 'as experience is gained in the operation and working of

[548] See eg G Fitzmaurice, 'Hersch Lauterpacht—The Scholar as Judge—Part III' (1963) 39 BYBIL 137.

[549] See Sections 2.3–2.4.

[550] Shaw, *International Law*, 932–3; Villiger, *Commentary*, 428.

[551] See eg E Suy, 'The Constitutional Character of Constituent Treaties of International Organizations and the Hierarchy of Norms' in R Bernhardt and others (eds), *Recht Zwischen Umbruch und Bewahrung: Festchrift für Rudolf Bernhardt* (Springer, 1995) 267. See also Section 2.5.4.

[552] See Section 2.5.3.

[553] See eg *Proposed Amendments to the Naturalization Provisions of the Constitution of Costa Rica*, Advisory Opinion OC-4/84, Inter-American Court of Human Rights Series A No 4 (19 January 1984) para 24; *WHO Nuclear Weapons Advisory Opinion*, para 18.

[554] See eg Section 2.5.2.

[555] 1935 Harvard Draft Convention, 937 (emphasis added).

[556] Nolte, Introductory Report on Treaties over Time, 181, citing *Namibia Advisory Opinion*, 179, *Oil Platforms*, Preliminary Objection, para 30, *Greenland-Jan Mayen*, para 27, *Cameroon v Nigeria*, Preliminary Objections, para 67, and *Israeli Wall Advisory Opinion*, para 109.

the convention'.[557] Fitzmaurice acknowledges that this notion of 'emergent purpose' can also come to modify a treaty's object and purpose[558]—a fundamental issue discussed in Section 3.3.5 of this book. This doctrine has mainly been used in the context of international organizations,[559] where it shares similarities with the doctrine of implied powers.[560]

The exercise of employing a treaty's object and purpose in interpreting its provisions finds its limits in the ordinary meaning(s) of the treaty terms. In this way, Article 31(1) VCLT ('a treaty shall be interpreted in good faith in accordance with the ordinary meaning to be given to the terms of the treaty in their context and in the light of its object and purpose') seems to stay clear of a far-reaching interpretation that could lead to gradual treaty modification. This is different for the means of 'authentic interpretation' in Article 31(2) and (3), including subsequent practice.[561]

Tied in with the teleological method, and coupled with the principle of good faith, is the principle of effectiveness,[562] as expressed in the maxim *ut res magis valeat quam pereat*.[563] This dynamic principle implies that a treaty should be construed so as to make sense of or give effect to its provisions. It was declared an important part of the law of treaties in the *Fisheries Jurisdiction* (*Spain v Canada*) case by the ICJ,[564] in arbitral awards such as the *Iron Rhine Railway Arbitration*,[565] and in the context of human rights treaties by the European Court of Human Rights.[566] The ICJ in the *South West Africa* case remarked:

> It may be urged that the Court is entitled to engage in a process of 'filling in the gaps', in the application of a teleological principle of interpretation, according to which instruments must be given their maximum effect in order to ensure the achievement of their underlying purposes.[567]

557 Fitzmaurice, 'The Law and Procedure of the International Court of Justice' (1957), 208. See also Bowman, '"Normalizing"', 240.

558 Ibid.

559 See eg *Namibia Advisory Opinion*, para 22, discussed further in Sections 3.4.2 and 5.2.1.

560 Nolte, Introductory Report on Treaties over Time, 182, citing S Rosenne, *Developments in the Law of Treaties 1945–1986* (CUP, 1989) 240. See further Section 2.5.4.

561 Villiger, *Commentary*, 428–9 (and see fn 54). See also eg Section 2.3.3.

562 See for early examples eg *Polish Postal Service in Danzig*, Advisory Opinion of 16 May 1925, PCIJ Series B, No 11, 39; *Cayuga Indians (Great Britain) v United States*, American and British Claims Arbitration Tribunal, Award of 22 January 1926 (1926) 20 AJIL 574, 587; *Interpretation of the Greco-Turkish Agreement of 1 December 1926 (Final Protocol, Article IV)*, Advisory Opinion of 28 August 1928, PCIJ Series B, No 16, 20; *Reparation for Injuries Suffered in the Service of the United Nations, Advisory Opinion, ICJ Reports 1949*, 174. See also S Rosenne, *The Law and Practice of the International Court, 1920–1996* (3rd edn, Martinus Nijhoff, 1997) 1148.

563 Fitzmaurice, 'The Law and Procedure of the International Court of Justice' (1957), 211–12. See also H Gutiérrez Posse, 'La maxime *ut res magis valeat quam pereat* (interpretation en fonction de "l'effet utile"); les interpretations "extensives" et "restrictives"' (1972) 23 ÖZöR 229.

564 *Fisheries Jurisdiction* (*Spain v Canada*), Jurisdiction, Judgment of 4 December 1998, ICJ Reports 432, 455.

565 See eg *Iron Rhine Railway Arbitration*, paras 49, 84.

566 See eg *Soering v United Kingdom* App no 14038/88 (ECtHR, 7 July 1989) [*Soering v UK*] 34.

567 *South West Africa* (*Ethiopia v South Africa; Liberia v South Africa*) (*Second Phase*), Judgment of 18 July 1966, ICJ Reports 6 [*South West Africa*] para 91.

The principle of effectiveness is not explicitly mentioned in the Vienna Convention's Articles 31 and 32 on interpretation, but the Commentary to the final ILC Draft Articles on the Law of Treaties deals with it in detail. The Commission explains that the principle was excluded from the text of the Convention not because it does not constitute a general rule of interpretation, but rather because, '[w]hen a treaty is open to two interpretations one of which does and the other does not enable the treaty to have appropriate effects, *good faith and the objects and purposes* of the treaty demand that the former interpretation should be adopted.'[568] Thus, the ILC found it unnecessary to codify the principle separately because it was considered already implied in Article 31 VCLT.[569] It added that '[p]roperly limited and applied, the maxim does not call for an "extensive" or "liberal" interpretation in the sense of an interpretation going beyond what is expressed or necessarily to be implied in the terms of the treaty.'[570]

The 'New Haven' or 'McDougal' School views treaty interpretation as a highly context-dependent, 'nontextual', and continuous process of authoritative decisions 'in which rules are continuously made and remade'.[571] It is based on the notion of identifying the shared expectations of the relevant political actors with regard to what is substantively and procedurally 'fitting' in a given situation subject to common societal values.[572]

This diverges sharply from the textual method described above, and to some extent combines the subjectivist focus on original intentions with the teleological notion that one should look to the purpose of the rules being interpreted:[573] 'if law as rules requires the application of outdated and inappropriate norms, then law as process encourages interpretation and choice that is more compatible with values we seek to promote and objectives we seek to achieve'.[574] This approach, which seems to favour more powerful States, has been criticized in light of the need to limit the influence of personal preferences on decision-making and ensure legal stability and consistency over time.[575]

The above makes clear that the range of views regarding the 'proper' method of interpretation is extremely wide:[576]

568 1966 Draft Articles on the Law of Treaties with Commentaries, 219 para 6 (emphasis added).

569 cf McDougal, Lasswell, and Miller, *Interpretation of International Agreements*, lxv.

570 1966 Draft Articles on the Law of Treaties with Commentaries, 219 para 6. See further D Rauschning, *The Vienna Convention on the Law of Treaties: Travaux Préparatoires* (Metzner, 1978) 251. See also the ICJ's statement at n 567.

571 MS McDougal, 'A Footnote' (1963) 57 AJIL 383. See also eg R Higgins, 'Policy Considerations and the International Judicial Process' (1968) 17 ICLQ 58, 59.

572 See McDougal, Lasswell, and Miller, *Interpretation of International Agreements*, 40–1. For a critical analysis of the New Haven School, see eg G Fitzmaurice, '*Vae Victis* or Woe to the Negotiator? Your Treaty or Our Interpretation of It' (review essay) (1971) 65 AJIL 358; SJ Toope, 'Confronting Indeterminacy: Challenges to International Legal Theory' (1990) 19 Can Council Intl L Proc 209.

573 McDougal, Lasswell, and Miller, *Interpretation of International Agreements*, 58–9.

574 R Higgins, 'International Law and the Avoidance, Containment and Resolution of Disputes' (1991-V) 230 RC 9, 34.

575 See D Kleimann, 'Positivism, the New Haven School, and the Use of Force in International Law' (2006) 3 BSIS J Intl Stud 3. See also n 572.

576 Sorel and Boré Eveno, 'Article 31', 836–7.

The highly divergent views (...) range from the Vattel principle of the 'clear sense' of words to the McDougal proposition that words as such are ambiguous. (...) The 'objectivists' use the text as the starting point of interpretation, seeking the 'apparent', 'objective' intention of the parties. The 'subjectivists', on the other hand, search for the 'actual' or 'subjective' intentions of the parties at the time of the treaty's conclusion, emphasizing the factual (extra-textual) context of the treaty. Neither approach, however, seems to have embraced the total context.[577]

No hierarchy exists among the different elements of interpretation, which are meant to be applied in a 'single combined operation'.[578] International law thus offers 'guidelines' for treaty interpretation, but does not prescribe any one of them in particular.[579] Accordingly, Articles 31 and 32 VCLT represent an 'attempt to assess the relative value and weight of the elements to be taken into account in the process of interpretation rather than to describe the process of interpretation itself'.[580] This non-obligatory character provides the interpreter with a significant amount of discretion and flexibility in the interpretative process.[581] One can speak of the tendency among dispute settlement bodies to place different emphasis on the various interpretative methods, depending, *inter alia*, on the context and treaty regime. For instance, the European Court of Justice (ECJ) seems disinclined to adopt the 'textual' method as a primary means of interpretation[582] in contrast to the WTO Appellate Body.[583] This does not, however, imply the existence of a hierarchy between the different approaches among courts.[584] These different interpretative approaches constitute the focus of the following section.

2.5.2 Interpretative 'policies' and the consequent role of subsequent practice in the interpretative process

Subsequent practice as an interpretative tool has been employed in the case law of the Permanent Court of International Justice,[585] which has had a tendency to use it to seek out the parties' original intention,[586] and in the decisions of the Iran-US Claims

[577] Yambrusic, *Treaty Interpretation*, 10–14. cf Orakhelashvili, *Interpretation of Acts and Rules*, 296.

[578] 1966 Draft Articles on the Law of Treaties with Commentaries, 219.

[579] As expounded eg in *Lake Lanoux* (*France v Spain*), Award of 16 November 1957, 12 RIAA 281, 285. See also Sorel and Boré Eveno, 'Article 31', 807–8.

[580] Sinclair, *Vienna Convention*, 117.

[581] Waldock, Third Report on the Law of Treaties, 54 para 6. See also Koskenniemi, *From Apology to Utopia*, 333–45.

[582] PJ Kuijper, 'The Court and the Tribunal of the EC and the Vienna Convention on the Law of Treaties 1969' (1998) 1 LIEI 2, 4.

[583] MM Slotboom, *Do Different Treaty Purposes Matter for Treaty Interpretation? A Comparison of WTO and EC Law*, Proefschrift (Cameron, 2005) 94.

[584] See also Sorel and Boré Eveno, 'Article 31', 835–7.

[585] *Competence of the ILO in regard to International Regulation of the Conditions of the Labour of Persons Employed in Agriculture*, Advisory Opinion of 12 August 1922, PCIJ Series B, No 2, 38–40; *Lausanne Advisory Opinion*, 24; *Jurisdiction of the European Commission of the Danube*, Advisory Opinion of 8 December 1927, PCIJ Series B, No 14, 27, 62–3; *Jurisdiction of the Courts of Danzig*, 18.

[586] See Nolte, Introductory Report on Treaties over Time, 175–7. See also Section 2.1.

Tribunal,[587] the International Tribunal for the Law of the Sea,[588] the European Court of Human Rights,[589] the International Criminal Tribunal for the former Yugoslavia,[590] WTO Panels and the Appellate Body,[591] and numerous other dispute settlement bodies.[592] National courts have also been known to refer to subsequent practice to determine the impact of treaties in the domestic legal order.[593] For instance, in *Medellín v Texas*, the US Supreme Court interpreted a treaty by relying on the parties' post-ratification 'understanding' of the Vienna Convention on Consular Relations.[594]

The present section places a certain emphasis on WTO case law on subsequent practice. The WTO context provides an excellent 'counter-weight' to the case law of dispute settlement bodies that adopt a more liberal and open approach to subsequent practice[595]—also, going further, in relation to subsequent practice as a means of treaty modification, as explored in Chapters 3 and 5.[596] This contrast facilitates a better understanding of the role subsequent practice can play in the interpretative process, depending on the specifics of the treaty regime and dispute settlement mechanism in question. Moreover, the WTO case law on subsequent practice is extensive and relatively consistent. This analysis sets the tone for that of the process of modification by subsequent practice in different treaty regimes, for which the WTO context also provides a valuable reference point.

The approach of different dispute settlement bodies varies depending on their specific 'environment' and, especially, their audience.[597] As a result of fragmentation

[587] *US and Iran*, Award No 108-A-16/582/591-FT, 71; *Houston Contracting Co and National Iranian Oil Co*, Award No 378-173-3 (22 July 1988) 20 Iran-US CTR 3, 56–7.

[588] *M/V 'Saiga' Case (No 2)* (*Saint Vincent and the Grenadines v Guinea*) Judgment of 2 July 1999, ITLOS Case No 2, paras 155–6.

[589] See eg *Loizidou v Turkey* App no 15318/89 (ECtHR, 18 December 1996), 2236; *Banković and others v Belgium and others* [GC] App no 52207/99 (ECtHR, 12 December 2001); *Öcalan v Turkey* [GC] App no 46221/99 (ECtHR, 12 May 2005) [*Öcalan v Turkey* (Grand Chamber Judgment)].

[590] See eg *Prosecutor v Dusko Tadić*, Appeal Judgment, para 165.

[591] See eg nn 82–4, 337, 336, 365–6, 459–60, 474–5, and 480–1.

[592] See eg *Affaire de l'indemnité russe* (*Russia v Turkey*), Award of 11 November 1912, 11 RIAA 431, 433; *Beagle Channel Arbitration*, 53; *Southern Bluefin Tuna* (*Australia and New Zealand v Japan*), Award on Jurisdiction and Admissibility of 4 August 2000, 22 RIAA 1, 45–6; *Tax Regime Governing Pensions to Retired UNESCO Officials*, para 70.

[593] See eg *Trans World Airlines, Inc v Franklin Mint Corp*, 466 US 243 (1984) Supreme Court; *R v Secretary of State for the Environment, Transport and the Regions, ex parte the Channel Tunnel Group and France Manche SA* [2001] EWCA Civ 1185; ILC, 'Comments of the Czech Republic on the specific issues raised in Chapter III of the Report of the International Law Commission on the work of its 67th session' (2015) <http://legal.un.org/ilc/sessions/68/pdfs/english/sasp_czech_republic.pdf> accessed 11 November 2016. See further Nolte Annex A, para 18, citing Amerasinghe, *Principles*, 372; JN Moore, 'Treaty Interpretation, the Constitution, and the Rule of Law' (2001) 42 VJIL 163. See also Nolte, Fourth Report on Subsequent Practice, paras 95ff.

[594] *Medellín v Texas*, 552 US 491, 511 (2008) Supreme Court. In the US, for instance, the issue is regarded as part of a broader question of the effects of the different sources of international law on domestic law and the consequent role of the Senate.

[595] Arato, 'Treaty Interpretation', 311–12 ('the interpretive practices of the WTO-AB provide a useful control to better gauge the breadth and effects of the more liberal approaches to subsequent practice of the ICJ and the ECtHR').

[596] See in particular Section 5.2.

[597] G Nolte, 'Subsequent Practice as a Means of Interpretation in the Jurisprudence of the Appellate Body' in E Cannizzaro (ed), *The Law of Treaties Beyond the Vienna Convention* (OUP, 2011) 138,

and the rise of new dispute settlement bodies in recent decades, the range of interpretative approaches has expanded, at the possible expense of consistency and coherence.[598] As a result, the role played by subsequent practice in the interpretative process will differ depending on the interpretative 'policy' employed.[599] One common thread, however, is that dispute settlement bodies rarely declare that subsequent practice has played a decisive role in the outcome of a decision, even when this is in fact the case.[600]

Three principal *policies*—which will, for present purposes, be roughly classified as 'conventional', 'textual', and 'purposive'—can be distinguished with regard to the way in which international courts and tribunals apply, and prioritize between, the different *methods* of interpretation. As a result, there is ongoing debate as to whether a narrow[601] or broad[602] role should be accorded to subsequent practice in the interpretative process.

First, a more or less 'conventional' policy can be detected in the case law of dispute settlement bodies such as the ICJ and the Iran-US Claims Tribunal. This approach amounts to a tendency to justify an interpretative approach 'in legalese',[603] by staying close to the terms of Article 31 VCLT, which imposes a high threshold for subsequent practice[604] and implies that the latter should be employed to the same extent as the other listed interpretative means.[605] The 'conventionality' of the approach adopted by the ICJ is observed only by contrast to the other two interpretative policies: namely, it appears rather conservative in comparison to the purposive approach adopted by dispute settlement bodies such as the ECtHR, but relatively liberal in comparison to the strict textual approach adopted in the WTO context, as we shall see.

The practice of dispute settlement bodies such as the ICJ and ITLOS is so diverse that it does not lend itself to the drawing of strict conclusions.[606] The fact that ITLOS, for instance, has referred to subsequent practice without commenting on the degree of practice necessary for it to qualify as relevant,[607] indicates that the

140, citing G Abi-Saab, 'The Appellate Body and Treaty Interpretation' in M Fitzmaurice, O Elias, and P Merkouris (eds), *Treaty Interpretation and the Vienna Convention on the Law of Treaties: 30 Years On* (Martinus Nijhoff, 2010) 99, 105. See also J Pauwelyn and M Elsig, 'The Politics of Treaty Interpretation: Variations and Explanations across International Tribunals' in JL Dunoff and MA Pollack (eds), *Interdisciplinary Perspectives on International Law and International Relations: The State of the Art* (CUP, 2012) 445.

[598] Sorel and Boré Eveno, 'Article 31', 807.

[599] Nolte, Statement 2011, 3–4. See also A Roberts, 'Subsequent Agreements and Practice: The Battle Over Interpretive Power' in G Nolte (ed), *Treaties and Subsequent Practice* (OUP, 2013) 95, 100.

[600] Nolte, Statement 2011, 6. But see eg *Namibia Advisory Opinion*, para 22.

[601] See eg Yasseen, 'L'interprétation', 48; Sinclair, *Vienna Convention*, 137.

[602] See eg Amerasinghe, 'Interpretation of Texts in Open International Organizations', 199, citing *Jurisdiction of the European Commission of the Danube*, 57–8, and *Inter-Governmental Maritime Consultative Organization Advisory Opinion*, 167–8. See also Lauterpacht, 'The Development of the Law of International Organization', 457.

[603] Arato, 'Treaty Interpretation', 306.

[604] See generally Section 2.3.

[605] See eg Torres Bernárdez, 'Interpretation of Treaties', 733.

[606] See eg Nolte, Second Report on Treaties over Time, 285.

[607] Ibid. See eg *'Tomimaru' Case (Japan v Russian Federation)* Prompt Release, Judgment of 6 August 2007, ITLOS Case No 15, para 72. cf *M/V 'Saiga' Case (No 2) (Saint Vincent and the Grenadines v*

Tribunal can be less conventional and strict in its approach,[608] yet it cannot be said to take the same interpretative liberties as, say, the ECtHR.

The ICJ often takes subsequent practice into account. However, its approach is varied, failing to demonstrate a consistent, common position on the role of subsequent practice.[609] This was also made apparent recently in the Court's very different decisions—one (overly) strict, the other liberal—in the *Whaling in the Antarctic* and *Maritime Dispute* (*Peru v Chile*) cases, respectively. Whilst in the *Whaling in the Antarctic* case, the Court refused to accord any weight to resolutions of the IWC because they did not demonstrate the agreement of *all* the parties pursuant to Article 31(3)(b),[610] in *Maritime Dispute* (*Peru v Chile*), it upheld a tacit agreement, based on rather thin evidence, that had not even been argued by the parties.[611] Indeed, in the past, the Court has sometimes preferred a highly textual reading of Article 31(3)(b) VCLT,[612] while in others it has opted for a broad approach to subsequent practice, without, for instance, specifying whether that practice establishes an agreement between the parties.[613] This is most notably the case with regard to treaties constituting international organizations,[614] and in particular with regard to the interpretation of the UN Charter, the Court's own constitutive instrument.[615] Thus, the interpretative policy of the ICJ is more 'conventional' than that of the ECtHR, but often still demonstrates liberality.[616]

A rather more conservative version of a 'conventional' policy[617] in respect of subsequent practice is encountered in the practice of the Iran-US Claims Tribunal, which largely follows the terms of Article 31 VCLT, remarking in one case that:

> [I]t is a recognized principle of treaty interpretation to take into account, together with the context, any subsequent practice in the application of an international treaty (...) which must, however, be a practice of the parties to the treaty and one that establishes the agreement of the parties regarding the interpretation of that treaty.[618]

Guinea) Judgment of 1 July 1999, ITLOS Case No 2, Separate Opinion of Judge Laing, paras 43–6 (offering an extensive analysis of subsequent practice).

608 Nolte Statement 2011, 5–6, citing *M/V 'Saiga' Case* (*No 1*) (*Saint Vincent and the Grenadines v Guinea*) Prompt Release, Judgment of 4 December 1997, ITLOS Case No 1, paras 57–9.

609 See eg AM Weisburd, 'The International Court of Justice and the Concept of State Practice' (2009) 31 U Penn J Intl L 295.

610 cf *Whaling in the Antarctic*, Separate Opinion of Judge ad hoc Charlesworth, para 4; ibid. Separate Opinion of Judge Xue, para 12.

611 cf *Peru v Chile*, Judgment of 27 January 2014, General List No 137, Declaration of President Tomka, paras 2, 25; ibid. Separate Opinion of Judge Owada, paras 5–6, 12.

612 See eg *Land, Island and Maritime Frontier Dispute* (*El Salvador/Honduras: Nicaragua intervening*) Judgment of 11 September 1992, ICJ Reports 350 [*El Salvador/Honduras*] para 380.

613 See *Kasikili/Sedudu Island*, paras 79–80; see also para 50 (referring to practice as an element of context). See further Nolte, 'Subsequent Practice', 141.

614 See eg *WHO Nuclear Weapons Advisory Opinion*, para 19; *Israeli Wall Advisory Opinion*, paras 25ff. See further Sections 2.3.1(c), 5.2.1, and 5.2.5.

615 See further Arato, 'Treaty Interpretation', 289.

616 Ibid. 294.

617 Yet it has recognized the modifying effect of subsequent practice, as discussed in Section 5.2.3(c).

618 *US and Iran*, Award No 108-A-16/582/591-FT, 71.

This policy limits the role of subsequent practice in the interpretative process.[619] The preference for this approach may be due to the fact that the Iran-US Claims Tribunal adjudicates in a bilateral setting that, at the same time, is 'rendered more open and indeterminate by the presence of para-statal actors and private persons whose property rights and interests are at issue'.[620] A similar trend can be observed in the context of the North American Free Trade Agreement (NAFTA).[621]

Second, certain adjudicatory bodies, most notably the WTO Appellate Body, prefer a 'textual' policy, placing the greatest emphasis on the words of the underlying treaty.[622] The Appellate Body's strict interpretative policy also directly reflects its view on the role to be accorded to subsequent practice in the interpretative process. As already mentioned, the Appellate Body has defined subsequent practice very narrowly,[623] as a ' "concordant, common and consistent" sequence of acts or pronouncements (. . .) sufficient to establish a discernable pattern implying the agreement of the parties'.[624] In *US–Gambling*,[625] the Appellate Body rejected the Panel's finding that certain Scheduling Guidelines could constitute subsequent practice, asserting that 'practice' had to be a common, consistent, discernable pattern of acts that imply the parties' agreement on the interpretation of the relevant provision.

In two other cases, the Appellate Body considered that the practice was not sufficiently uniform. In *EC–Computer Equipment*,[626] it rejected the finding of the Panel that the classification practice of a few main importers constituted relevant subsequent practice, since certain other importers and the main exporter did not follow the same practice.

In *Chile–Price Band System*, the question was whether Chile's price band system could be maintained given that it was 'required to be converted into ordinary customs duties' pursuant to Article 4.2 of the Agreement on Agriculture. Despite Chile's argument that no country with a price band system in place prior to the conclusion of the Uruguay Round had actually converted it into ordinary customs duties, the Appellate Body noted that neither the record of the Panel nor the parties' submissions pointed to a discernible pattern of practice implying an agreement among WTO Members to such an interpretation. It rejected the Panel's reasoning that a *lack of objection* by other States to Chile's form of determining customs duties was a sufficient indication of an agreement,[627] and concluded that the alleged practice did not amount to 'subsequent practice' within the meaning of Article 31(3)(b) VCLT.[628]

Similarly, the Appellate Body in the *EC–Chicken Cuts* case rejected the finding of the Panel that the (then) European Community's classification practice of certain

[619] J Wessel, 'Relational Contract Theory and Treaty Interpretation: End-Game Treaties v Dynamic Obligations' (2004) 60 NYU Ann Surv Am L 149, 181.

[620] Nolte, Second Report on Treaties over Time, 232. cf the discussion in Section 5.2.3(b).

[621] Ibid. 243–4. See Section 5.2.3(c).

[622] Abi-Saab, 'The Appellate Body and Treaty Interpretation', 106.

[623] See Section 2.3.5(c).

[624] *Japan–Alcoholic Beverages II*, AB Report, 12–13. See also Canal-Forgues, 'Sur l'interprétation', 21.

[625] *US–Gambling*, AB Report, para 193.

[626] *EC–Computer Equipment*, AB Report, para 92.

[627] *Chile–Price Band System*, AB Report, para 212.

[628] Ibid. paras 213–14.

chicken parts, which had remained unopposed for six years, could constitute subsequent practice.[629] The Appellate Body was of the view that, since the relevant headings of the Schedules represent the common agreement of all Members, it was necessary to consider how the agreement of the parties *not* actively engaged in the practice could be ascertained. By contrast to the Panel, it was of the opinion that such assent must be deduced from *affirmative* reactions to the practice, in the absence of which the EC's classification practice did not amount to subsequent practice.[630] Moreover, in the *US–Restrictions on Imports of Cotton* case, the Appellate Body did not take the practice of the parties into account because it regarded it as too recent.[631] Also, in *EC–Bananas III*, the Appellate Body rejected the respective Panel's finding that a waiver could constitute relevant subsequent practice.[632]

Thus, the textual policy of the Appellate Body is highly prudent when it comes to subsequent practice.[633] It demonstrates a tendency to 'limit or even largely exclude' subsequent practice as an interpretative tool, although a careful analysis of its reasoning reveals that subsequent practice remains relevant within the WTO system.[634] It is important to note that there have also been instances in which subsequent practice has been interpreted broadly in the WTO context.[635] In *US–Section 110(5) Copyright Act*, the WTO Panel referred to 'several examples from various countries of limitations in national [copyright] laws' to confirm its interpretation of the Berne Convention, without any mention of whether there was an agreement of the parties.[636] Similarly, in *Mexico–Telecoms*, the Panel took into account subsequent practice in a broader sense, falling under either Article 31(3)(b) or Article 32 VCLT.[637] The overall approach of the Appellate Body, however, is still 'probably more restrictive than what the ILC had contemplated when drafting the VCLT, and it is also more restrictive than the pertinent jurisprudence of the ICJ'.[638]

This prudent approach makes sense in light of the specific nature of the WTO legal regime: the particular need for legal certainty, the role that the Appellate Body plays in providing predictability and systemic coherence through its jurisprudence, the technical nature of certain provisions in the WTO agreements that perhaps lends itself more easily to textual methods, as well as the political and organizational framework surrounding them.[639] For instance, pursuant to Article IX:2 of the Marrakesh

[629] *EC–Chicken Cuts*, AB Report, para 272. [630] Ibid.

[631] *US–Restrictions on Imports of Cotton*, AB Report, 17.

[632] *European Communities–Regime for the Importation, Sale and Distribution of Bananas*, Second Recourse to Article 21.5 Appellate Body Report (26 November 2008) WT/DS27/AB/RW2/ECU and WT/DS27/AB/RW/USA [*EC–Bananas III* (Art 21.5 II), AB Report] para 389.

[633] Sorel and Boré Eveno, 'Article 31', 827.

[634] Nolte, 'Subsequent Practice', 139–40. See eg *EC–Chicken Cuts*, AB Report, para 251; *US–Section 110(5) Copyright Act*, Panel Report, para 6.55; *Brazil–Measures Affecting Desiccated Coconut*, Report of the Panel (17 October 1996) WT/DS22/R, para 255; *US–Zeroing*, Panel Report, para 7.218; Van Damme, *Treaty Interpretation by the WTO Appellate Body*, 338–50.

[635] See Section 2.4. See further Nolte, Second Report on Treaties over Time, 220.

[636] *US–Section 110(5) Copyright Act*, Panel Report, para 6.55.

[637] *Mexico–Telecoms*, Panel Report, paras 7.43–7.44. See also *EC–Computer Equipment*, AB Report, paras 89–90; Van Damme, *Treaty Interpretation by the WTO Appellate Body*, 342. See further Section 2.4.

[638] Nolte, Second Report on Treaties over Time, 224.

[639] See generally Nolte, 'Subsequent Practice', 142–4.

Agreement, the Ministerial Conference and General Council 'shall have the exclusive authority to adopt interpretations' regarding the WTO agreements. Moreover, with regard to certain WTO obligations such as the Schedules of commitments, 'it is generally unclear whose practice and whose agreement in which form would be sufficient to establish agreement'.[640]

In general, the reluctance to stray too much from the textual approach in favour of a more purposive interpretation 'may have to do with the attitude of a young institution which must establish its authority in a "member-driven organization"'.[641] Thus, the Appellate Body 'goes about its task of interpretation in an especially rigid way, generally eschewing dynamism in favor of strict deference to member state consent.'[642] It is submitted here, however, that, bearing the above-mentioned considerations in mind, the reluctance of the Appellate Body with regard to subsequent practice is harder to understand when it comes to interpretations carefully inferred from actual practice, reflective of the authority and stated intentions of the Members themselves.[643]

Finally, a third, 'purposive' policy is reflected in the practice of courts that focus on concepts such as 'object and purpose', '*effet utile*', and the nature of the treaty as a 'living instrument'. The prime example is the European Court of Human Rights.[644] The ECtHR has referred 'very widely'[645] to subsequent practice in its judgments.[646] As discussed in the next chapter, it has even acknowledged its treaty modifying potential.[647] As mentioned previously,[648] the ECtHR does not require that the practice be unanimous, as long as it is supported by a 'vast majority' of States.[649] This far-reaching approach contrasts with the requirement of the agreement of all the parties under Article 31(3)(b) VCLT.[650] Although it accords an important role to subsequent practice, the Court also often makes references to other types of subsequent developments,[651] such as the 'changing conditions in European societies'.[652]

640 *US–Gambling*, AB Report, para 193.

641 Nolte, 'Subsequent Practice', 123.

642 Arato, 'Treaty Interpretation', 312.

643 Nolte, Second Report on the Law of Treaties, 225.

644 Nolte, Statement 2011, 6–7; Sorel and Boré Eveno, 'Article 31', 827–8.

645 Sorel and Boré Eveno, 'Article 31', 827–8.

646 See eg *Engel and others v The Netherlands* App no 5100/71, 5101/71, 5102/71, 5354/72, 5370/72 (ECtHR, 8 June 1976) para 72; *Marckx v Belgium* App no 6833/74 (ECtHR, 13 June 1979) paras 41ff; *Rasmussen v Denmark* App no 8777/79 (ECtHR, 28 November 1984) paras 40–1; *Inze v Austria* App no 8695/79 (ECtHR, 28 October 1987) para 41; *Toth v Austria* App no 11894/85 (ECtHR, 25 November 1991) para 77. cf *James and others v United Kingdom* App no 8793/79 (ECtHR, 21 February 1986) para 65.

647 See Section 5.2.3(a).

648 See Section 2.3.5.

649 See eg *Sigurdur A Sigurjónsson v Iceland*, para 35; *Loizidou v Turkey*, paras 79–80; *Öcalan v Turkey* (Grand Chamber Judgment), para 163; *Al-Saadoon and Mufdhi v United Kingdom* App no 61498/08 (ECtHR, 2 March 2010) [*Al-Saadoon and Mufdhi v UK*] para 120. With regard to the contrary practice of the respondent State, see eg *Tyrer v United Kingdom* App no 5856/72 (ECtHR, 25 April 1978) [*Tyrer v UK*] para 31; *Demir and Baykara v Turkey* [GC] App no 34503/97 (ECtHR, 12 November 2008) paras 52, 85. See also Nolte Second Report on Treaties over Time, 305 ('General Conclusion 16').

650 Arato, 'Treaty Interpretation', 336–8.

651 On the distinction, see Section 2.3.4.

652 See Nolte, 'Subsequent Practice', 142; H Nottage and T Sebastian, 'Giving Legal Effect to the Results of WTO Trade Negotiations: An Analysis of the Methods of Changing WTO Law' (2006) 9 J Intl Econ L 989, 994ff.

This approach makes sense in light of the evolutionary nature of human rights treaties.[653]

International criminal courts also often adopt a broad notion of subsequent practice, and refer to subsequent developments, without explicitly relying on Articles 31 and 32 VCLT, sometimes even if the subsequent practice in question does not strictly relate to the application of the treaty or establish the agreement of all the parties.[654] References to subsequent developments in a broader sense are also frequently made by the Inter-American Court of Human Rights (IACtHR), while references to subsequent practice are minimal. The difference between the Inter-American Court and the European Court of Human Rights may pertain to the subject-matter usually dealt with by the former, with its focus on gross human rights violations that 'hardly lend themselves to considerations of subsequent state practice but rather to fact-finding and the evaluation of evidence',[655] as well as the fact that the subsequent practice of parties to the proceedings is often contradictory.[656]

A focus on 'object and purpose' is clear in the practice of international investment tribunals, which place particular emphasis on treaty titles and preambles.[657] This policy has mainly to do with the nature of investment treaties and their substantive provisions, such as fair and equitable treatment standards, as well as procedural provisions in dispute clauses providing access to arbitration exclusively to the investor. Their aim is to grant personal rights and protections to investors—the main beneficiaries of such treaties.[658] The 'asymmetrical' nature of investment treaties represents a 'deliberate choice' by the contracting States.[659] Therefore, tribunals have taken it as determinative of the object and purpose of investment treaties,[660] preferring interpretations favourable to investors.[661] Due to this focus on object and purpose, investment tribunals do not often rely on subsequent practice or agreements,[662] although it is noteworthy that the range of acts taken into account as relevant practice is remarkably broad.[663]

> Most investment treaty awards and commentaries hardly discuss appropriate interpretive approaches and, when they do (...) [the] interpretive relevance of subsequent agreements and practice is not commonly analyzed, with the notable exception of FTC's Notes of Interpretation.[664]

[653] See Sections 2.5.3 (evolutionary interpretation) and 3.5.1 (special nature of human rights treaties).

[654] See examples in Nolte, Second Report on Treaties over Time, 295.

[655] Ibid. 275.

[656] G Neuman, 'Import, Export, and Regional Consent in the Inter-American Court of Human Rights' (2008) 19 EJIL 101, 107. See further Nolte, Second Report on Treaties over Time, 275.

[657] Fauchald, 'The Legal Reasoning of ICSID Tribunals', 322; Roberts, 'Power and Persuasion', 179 fn 11; Schreuer, 'Diversity and Harmonization', 131.

[658] See eg Gazzini, 'Bilateral Investment Treaties', 107, citing *American Manufacturing*, para 6.06.

[659] Ibid.

[660] cf *Mondev v US*, para 43; *El Paso Energy International Company v Argentine Republic*, ICSID Case No ARB/03/15, Decision on Jurisdiction of 27 April 2006, para 70.

[661] See eg *Noble Ventures, Inc v Romania*, ICSID Case No ARB/01/11, Award of 12 October 2005, para 52.

[662] With certain notable exceptions, such as authoritative interpretation of the NAFTA FTC, discussed in Section 5.2.3(c). See eg Fauchald, 'The Legal Reasoning of ICSID Tribunals', 322–3, 348.

[663] Fauchald, 'The Legal Reasoning of ICSID Tribunals', 348–9.

[664] See eg Roberts, 'Power and Persuasion', 181 fn 11.

One explanation for this tendency may be that investment tribunals are cautious not to allow States to diminish the rights of private investors through their subsequent practice.[665] Nevertheless, we may see an increased reliance on subsequent practice in the investor treaty context in the future.[666]

The focus on the teleological method of interpretation is also central to the interpretative policy of the European Court of Justice, although, by contrast to most adjudicatory bodies, the ECJ has rarely made explicit reference to subsequent practice when interpreting and applying the EU founding treaties.[667] The Court's 'ends-focused interpretation' seeks to minimize the role of subsequent practice in favour of the underlying intentions of the EU treaties.[668] The ECJ therefore typically refers to subsequent practice only when dealing with treaties between the EU and third States.[669]

Thus, for a wide range of reasons, interpretative policies vary markedly across dispute settlement bodies—a situation that may also carry implications for the fragmentation of international law. These tendencies are revealing of the 'self-understanding' of different dispute settlement bodies.[670] This is especially true of the contrast observed between the dynamic, purposive styles of the ECtHR and ECJ, and the strict, textual approach of the Appellate Body. As a result, the diverse and often far-reaching effects of subsequent practice are manifested differently across different treaty regimes, depending on the considerations and structures at play in each case.

2.5.3 Subsequent practice and evolutionary interpretation

The 'evolutionary treaty' approach,[671] though still encountered quite rarely,[672] is of special relevance for the topic of subsequent practice and for the process

[665] Ibid. 210–18. See further Section 3.5 on the non-regression principle and treaties conferring rights upon third-party beneficiaries.

[666] Nolte, Second Report on Treaties over Time, 237.

[667] ILC, 'Contribution of the European Union on the topic of subsequent agreements and subsequent practice in relation to treaty interpretation' (2015) <http://legal.un.org/ilc/sessions/67/pdfs/english/sasp_eu.pdf> accessed 11 November 2016 [Comments by the EU to the ILC] 2–4, emphasizing, *inter alia*, that, since 'Union law represents an autonomous legal order and that the founding Treaties of the Union are not like ordinary international treaties', the ECJ 'refrains from taking into account of *Member States subsequent practice* when interpreting the founding Treaties' as well as the '*subsequent practice of institutions of the Union* (…) with regard to the proper interpretation and implementation of the relevant provisions of the founding Treaties' (emphasis added). See eg *International Fruit Company NV and others v Produktschap voor Groenten en Fruit* (Joined Cases C-21-24/72) [1972] ECR 1219. See further Nolte, 'Subsequent Practice', 142.

[668] Sorel and Boré Eveno, 'Article 31', 828. The ECJ has even dismissed subsequent practice where it conflicted with those underlying intentions—see *Commission of the European Communities v French Republic* (*Sheep Meat Case*) (Case C-232/78) [1979] ECR 2729. See also Section 3.5.1(a).

[669] Nolte, Statement 2011, 5, citing eg *Leonce Cayrol v Giovanni Rivoira & Figli* (Case C-52/77) [1977] ECR 2261, para 18, and *The Queen v Minister of Agriculture, Fisheries and Food, ex parte S P Anastasiou (Pissouri) Ltd and others* (Case C-432/92) [1994] ECR I-3087, paras 43, 50; Comments by the EU to the ILC, 5.

[670] Nolte, 'Subsequent Practice', 140.

[671] R Bernhardt, 'Evolutive Treaty Interpretation, Especially of the European Convention of Human Rights' (1999) 42 GYBIL 11.

[672] Nolte, 'Subsequent Practice', 143; SD Murphy, 'The Relevance of Subsequent Agreements and Subsequent Practice for the Interpretation of Treaties' in G Nolte (ed), *Treaties and Subsequent Practice* (OUP, 2013) 82, 87.

of treaty modification by subsequent practice in particular, as is made clear in Chapter 3.[673] Evolutionary interpretation is a form of dynamic treaty interpretation derived from the purposive method of interpretation discussed in Section 2.5.2. It is primarily rooted in Article 31(1) VCLT on 'object and purpose', and Article 31(3)(c) VCLT[674] on other 'relevant rules of international law'.[675] It may also be 'housed' in the 'ordinary meaning to be given to the terms of the treaty' under Article 31(1) VCLT.[676] It advocates that certain treaties must be interpreted according to the 'meaning attached to the expression by the law in force at any given time'.[677]

The Working Group on 'Treaties over Time' has noted that 'evolutionary interpretation is possible also for bilateral treaties whose main purpose is the delimitation of sovereign rights which, in principle, should be as clear and stable as possible'.[678] The process enables the interpreter to account for important legal developments—including subsequent practice and new customary law—without having recourse to treaty modification: 'an evolutive term is inherently dynamic, so giving it successive interpretations over time, even if these directly contradict one another, do not amount to modification but merely dynamism'.[679]

Evolutionary interpretation can serve the same purpose as the process of subsequent practice, allowing treaties to develop over time, ensuring the instrument's survival and adaptation to contemporary priorities.[680] However, the premises upon which the two mechanisms of subsequent practice and evolutionary interpretation operate can be very different. In principle, evolutionary interpretation looks to the parties' original intention to determine whether they meant to interpret and apply the treaty in a way that makes allowance for new developments,[681] including subsequent practice.[682]

The focus of evolutionary interpretation on the original intentions of the parties has been portrayed as a legal fiction,[683] since evolutionary 'changes are determined

[673] See eg Section 3.5.2.

[674] Most likely the primary purpose of Art 31(3)(c) was to use subsequent practice to shed light on the parties' original intentions, even where no question of evolutionary meaning(s) arose.

[675] Koskenniemi, Fragmentation Report, para 478(a).

[676] Simma, 'Miscellaneous Thoughts', 48.

[677] *Aegean Sea Continental Shelf* (*Greece v Turkey*), Jurisdiction of the Court, Judgment of 19 December 1978, ICJ Reports 3, 33.

[678] Nolte, Introductory Report on Treaties over Time, 207, citing *Dispute regarding Navigational and Related Rights* (*Costa Rica v Nicaragua*), Judgment of 13 July 2009, ICJ Reports 213 [*Costa Rica v Nicaragua*], discussed extensively in Section 2.5.3(c). But see *Dispute regarding Navigational and Related Rights* (*Costa Rica v Nicaragua*), Judgment of 13 July 2009, Separate Opinion of Judge Skotnikov, ICJ Reports 283, paras 5–6.

[679] Arato, 'Subsequent Practice', 453.

[680] P-M Dupuy, 'Evolutionary Interpretation of Treaties: Between Memory and Prophecy' in E Cannizzaro (ed), *The Law of Treaties Beyond the Vienna Convention* (OUP, 2011) 123, 125.

[681] Arato, 'Subsequent Practice', 445, 466.

[682] See eg *Aegean Sea Continental Shelf*, paras 74–5; Nolte, First Report on Subsequent Practice, para 38 ('Conclusion 3').

[683] See *Costa Rica v Nicaragua*, Declaration of Judge ad hoc Guillaume, para 16, and Separate Opinion of Judge Skotnikov, paras 9–10, discussed in Section 2.5.3(c). See also eg T Georgopoulos, 'Le

by developments independent of the intentions of the parties'.[684] One commentator has remarked:

> The necessary presumption that parties must have intended the meaning of a treaty to change as it did falls only slightly short of assuming that parties were clairvoyant at the moment of the treaty's conclusion. (...) What might certainly happen is that something deemed specific and precise at one time, later turns out to be 'generic' and therefore subject to evolution.[685]

Thus, it has been argued that the 'courts to which we owe the doctrine of evolutionary/dynamic interpretation [the ICJ and ECtHR], give a wrong explanation of what they are actually doing in this regard'.[686] What evolutionary interpretation really entails is 'to apply such meaning of a treaty provision to its environment, the changing and changed world around the treaty, within which it has to maintain its effect, and it is at that stage, the act of application, that the evolutionary/dynamic step is taken'.[687]

Most importantly, even if it significantly changes the contents of a provision, evolutionary interpretation, unlike subsequent practice, cannot amount to modification. Evolutionary interpretation remains bounded by the four corners of the text.[688] Subsequent practice, on the other hand, can elucidate *both* the original and the *contemporary* intentions of the parties,[689] and may thus also evidence the parties' agreement to *remove* a textual limit on the evolutionary potential of a treaty.[690]

Thus, while the primary focus of evolutionary interpretation is the parties' intention at the time of the conclusion of the treaty, 'arguments based on subsequent practice seek a more stable ground by looking at renewed manifestations of agreement'.[691] It is submitted that the process of evolutionary interpretation may therefore also involve a significant degree of 'guesswork' as to which treaty terms could have been intended as evolutionary.[692] These considerations are now dealt with in more detail.

2.5.3a Evidentiary standards for evolutionary interpretation

As in the case of subsequent practice, evolutionary (or 'evolutive') interpretation requires certain evidentiary standards to be met,[693] although these are still

droit intertemporel et les dispositions conventionnelles évolutives—Quelle thérapie contre la vieillesse des traités?' (2004) 108 RGDIP 123, 142.

684 Crema, 'Subsequent Agreements and Subsequent Practice', 22, citing G Distefano, 'L'interprétation évolutive de la norme internationale' (2011) 11 RGDIP 373.

685 Venzke, *How Interpretation Makes International Law*, 232–3 (references omitted).

686 Simma, 'Miscellaneous Thoughts', 49, citing Milanovic, 'The ICJ and Evolutionary Treaty Interpretation'.

687 Ibid. See generally E Bjorge, *The Evolutionary Interpretation of Treaties* (OUP, 2014).

688 See eg Orakhelashvili, *Interpretation of Acts and Rules*, 291.

689 See eg Section 2.1.

690 Arato, 'Subsequent Practice', 482. See also Section 5.2.3(a), (text to) n 279. See further Section 2.5.3(b).

691 Venzke, *How Interpretation Makes International Law*, 233.

692 See eg the discussion of the evolution of the term 'whaling' in Bowman, '"Normalizing"', 436. See also Section 2.5.3(c) on *Costa Rica v Nicaragua*; Milanovic, 'The ICJ and Evolutionary Interpretation'.

693 Arato, 'Subsequent Practice', 466.

developing.[694] According to the ILC, the interpreter is required to identify 'concrete evidence' of the parties' intentions. This may be found in the terms of the treaty, its object and purpose, context, *travaux*, and subsequent practice. These elements are merely indicators, not cumulative criteria.[695]

A first option is to deduce 'evolutionary intent' from the use of special terminology, for instance from generic terms such as 'commerce',[696] 'natural resources',[697] or 'dispute relating to territorial status'.[698] 'Generic' refers to terms that are inherently context-dependent. In the *Namibia Advisory Opinion*, for instance, the ICJ read the notions of 'strenuous conditions of the modern world', 'well-being and development of the peoples concerned', and 'sacred trust of civilization' in the context of the right of peoples to self-determination.[699] Such terms are deemed to be 'by definition, evolutionary'.[700] There are also other, more specific grounds for evolutionary interpretation.[701] In the *Iron Rhine Railway Arbitration*, a technical term was given an evolutionary meaning to allow for future technological advancements and render the agreement effective, in line with the principle of effectiveness.[702]

The language of a treaty may reflect its evolutionary character if obligations are couched in such general terms that they essentially operate 'a kind of *renvoi* to the state of the law at the time of its application'.[703] Such a general formulation can be found in Article XX of the GATT, which provides exceptions to WTO obligations for measures such as those 'necessary to protect human, animal or plant life or health' or 'relating to the conservation of exhaustible natural resources'.[704] Measures 'necessary' to protect life or health will evolve over time, as will natural resources considered 'exhaustible'.[705] Another indication of evolutionary tendencies is treaty language that conveys the fact that it was intended to be of 'continuing duration'.[706] The evidentiary standard for such deductions is significantly lower than that for the interpretation of generic terms discussed in the foregoing paragraph.[707]

694 M Fitzmaurice, 'Dynamic (Evolutive) Interpretation of Treaties' (2008) 2 Hague YB IL 101, 153.

695 See eg *Report of the International Law Commission on the work of its 57th session*, UN Doc A/60/10 (2005) Ch XI(C)(3), 219.

696 *Costa Rica v Nicaragua*, para 64.

697 *United States–Import Prohibition of Certain Shrimp and Shrimp Products*, Report of the Appellate Body (12 October 1998) WT/DS58/AB/R [*US–Shrimp/Turtle*, AB Report] para 130.

698 *Aegean Sea Continental Shelf*, para 77.

699 *Namibia Advisory Opinion*, paras 52–3.

700 Ibid. para 53. See also *US–Shrimp/Turtle*, AB Report, para 130.

701 Nolte, Introductory Report on Treaties over Time, 186.

702 *Iron Rhine Railway Arbitration*, para 80 ('in the present case it is not a conceptual or generic term that is in issue, but rather new technical developments relating to the operation and capacity of the railway'). See also eg the scientific terms discussed in *Gabčíkovo-Nagymaros Project*, para 112.

703 Koskenniemi, Fragmentation Report, para 478.

704 *US–Shrimp/Turtle*, AB Report, para 130.

705 See ibid. paras 127–33, where the Appellate Body rejected the Panel's interpretation of the term 'exhaustible natural resources'—which is both generally formulated and a generic term—as including only 'finite resources such as minerals', and adopted a more far-reaching interpretation that included both living and non-living resources (citing CITES Appendix I as evidence that sea turtles are exhaustible).

706 See eg *Costa Rica v Nicaragua*, para 66.

707 Arato, 'Subsequent Practice', 476.

Second, an interpreter can search the instrument's object and purpose for indications of whether the parties intended to '[commit] themselves to a programme of progressive development'.[708] Human rights treaties, for instance, have generally come to be considered evolutionary in nature, on account, *inter alia*, of their aim of protecting fundamental rights in the common interest of all mankind, the 'integral' nature of their obligations, and their 'quasi-constitutional' character.[709]

In the *Gabčíkovo-Nagymaros Project* case, the ICJ found that the parties had committed themselves to incorporating 'new environmental norms' into the treaty, and that, '[b]y inserting these evolving provisions in the Treaty, the parties recognized the potential necessity to adapt the Project. Consequently, the Treaty is not static, and is open to adapt to emerging norms of international law.'[710] We can also once again refer to the *Iron Rhine Railway Arbitration*: 'here, too, it seems that an evolutive interpretation, which would ensure an application of the treaty that would be effective in terms of its object and purpose [a stable border delimitation], will be preferred to a strict application of the intertemporal rule'.[711]

Another interesting example is the evolution of the 1884 Convention for the Protection of Submarine Telegraph Cables[712] so as to cover telephone cables, in accordance with a 'reasonable interpretation' of its object and purpose, given that the laying of telephone cables was not foreseeable at the time of the Convention's conclusion.[713]

The evolutionary standards and indicators are also dealt with in the Final Report of the ILC Study Group on the Fragmentation of International Law, which identifies three situations in which treaty language may require evolutionary interpretation: the use of concepts that imply taking into account subsequent technical, economic, or legal developments, concepts that set up an obligation for further progressive development of the law, or those of a very general nature or couched in such general terms that they can be taken to have been intended to account for changing circumstances.[714]

[708] Koskenniemi, Fragmentation Report, para 478(a), citing *Gabčíkovo-Nagymaros Project*, paras 132–47.

[709] See eg *Reservations to the Convention on the Prevention and Punishment of the Crime of Genocide*, Advisory Opinion of 28 May 1951, ICJ Reports 15, 23; Koskenniemi Fragmentation Report, para 387; Higgins, *Problems and Process*, 75; Arato, 'Subsequent Practice', 486; F Pocar, 'Some Remarks on the Continuity of Human Rights and International Humanitarian Law Treaties' in E Cannizzaro (ed), *The Law of Treaties Beyond the Vienna Convention* (OUP, 2011) 279, 282, 292. See also eg D Moeckli and others (eds), *International Human Rights Law* (2nd edn, OUP, 2014) 99–101.

[710] *Gabčíkovo-Nagymaros Project*, para 112.

[711] *Iron Rhine Railway Arbitration*, para 80.

[712] 14 March 1884, TS 380. Certain provisions of the Convention are considered of continuing relevance and reflective of customary law, and have been incorporated into Arts 113–15 LOSC. See further eg E Wagner, 'Submarine Cables and Protections Provided by the Law of the Sea' (1995) 19 Mar Policy 127, 134.

[713] District Court of Rotterdam, 17 January 1977, ECLI:NL:RBROT:1977:AJ1243 (finding that, based on a 'reasonable interpretation', the Convention covers not only telegraph but also telephone cables, the discovery of which was not foreseeable at the time of its conclusion), confirmed by The Hague Court of Appeal, 15 April 1983, ECLI:NL:GHSGR:1983:AJ4905, para 3.

[714] Koskenniemi, Fragmentation Report, para 478(a)–(b), citing the exceptions in GATT Art XX.

The significance of evolutionary interpretation may differ within and outside the context of international organizations. Dupuy contrasts evolutionary interpretation supported by 'memory', based on the original intent of the parties to allow the treaty to evolve, with evolutionary interpretation as 'prophecy'.[715] The latter refers to constitutive treaties establishing international organizations, which are 'designed to achieve a shared purpose', such that the interpreter should no longer be guided by the original will of the individual parties: the 'collective institution thus overrides individual consent'.[716]

This also provides a basis for the doctrine of implied powers (in turn closely linked to the principle of effectiveness) explored in Section 2.5.4.[717] The so-called *Mazilu* case has been cited as an example of evolutionary interpretation by subsequent conduct in the context of an international organization.[718] Namely, the ICJ found that, in practice, the UN entrusts missions to persons without official UN status, but who are nevertheless regarded as experts on mission in the sense of the provision being interpreted.[719]

In sum, if the requisite evidentiary standards are met, the parties' intention can be taken to allow for the interpretation of certain treaty provisions in accordance with relevant subsequent developments.[720] Although the meaning of a term may have changed significantly since the treaty's inception, such reinterpretations cannot be regarded as modifications because they adhere to the parties' *original* intention as embodied in the text.

2.5.3b Textual limits of evolutionary interpretation

While evolutionary interpretation relies on the parties' original intention of codifying treaty terms that are evolutionary in nature,[721] interpretation (or modification) by subsequent practice focuses on the intention of the parties at the time of application, in *addition* to their original intention.[722] Evolutionary interpretation cannot lead to modification of the treaty since it only allows reference to factors not excluded by the treaty itself.[723] For instance, a seven-judge dissenting opinion in the ECtHR's *Feldbrugge* case emphasized that the evolutionary approach 'does not allow entirely new concepts or spheres of application to be introduced into the Convention: that is a legislative function that belongs to the Member States of the Council of Europe'.[724] In the same vein, later that year in *Johnston v Ireland*, the

[715] Dupuy, 'Evolutionary Interpretation', 123. [716] Ibid. 131–2.

[717] See further Suy, 'Constituent Treaties', 267.

[718] Nolte, Introductory Report on Treaties over Time, 178.

[719] *Privileges and Immunities Advisory Opinion*, para 48.

[720] M Foster, *International Refugee Law and Socio-Economic Rights: Refugee from Deprivation* (CUP, 2007) 61.

[721] See eg *Case concerning the Delimitation of the Maritime Boundary between Guinea-Bissau and Senegal*, Award of 31 July 1989, 20 RIAA 119, para 85.

[722] See eg Section 2.1. [723] Orakhelashvili, *Interpretation of Acts and Rules*, 291.

[724] *Feldbrugge v The Netherlands* App no 8562/79 (ECtHR, 29 May 1986) (Joint Dissenting Opinion of Judges Ryssdal, Robert, Lagergren, Matscher, Evans, Bernhardt, and Gersing) [*Feldbrugge*, Joint Dissenting Opinion] paras 23–4.

Court rejected a request to interpret the 'right to marry' as covering the right to divorce and remarry on account of the fact that an evolutionary approach cannot go so far as to derive a right not originally included in the law.[725] In a sense, it could be said that the interpreter following the evolutionary approach must alter the meaning of treaty provisions without altering their nature.[726]

Since the ECtHR has made reference to evolutionary interpretation (a method still rarely employed in the case law) and subsequent practice (including modification by subsequent practice[727]) more frequently and more liberally than other dispute settlement bodies,[728] a number of its other cases may be noted here.

In *Tyrer v UK*[729] and *Loizidou v Turkey*,[730] respectively, the ECtHR distinguished between subsequent practice on the one hand, and evolutionary interpretation in light of 'modern-day conditions' on the other. It clearly asserted that the latter process could not lead to modification of the ECHR. As to the former process, in *Öcalan v Turkey*, the Grand Chamber stated that subsequent practice was capable of modifying, and in fact terminating, the ECHR provision regarding the death penalty,[731] thus *removing* a textual limit on the scope for evolutionary interpretation of the provision on the prohibition of torture and inhuman or degrading treatment or punishment.[732] In other words, had the provision permitting the death penalty been modified by subsequent practice, it would have meant that the provision prohibiting torture and inhuman or degrading treatment or punishment could also be interpreted as prohibiting the death penalty. Thus, the combination of subsequent practice and evolutionary interpretation is capable of leading to a harmonious result.[733]

The ECtHR also allowed certain derogations from the ECHR in *Ireland v United Kingdom*[734] based on the evolutionary approach in turn based on subsequent practice, acknowledging that some margin of discretion in progressive interpretation should be left to State practice.

Moreover, the Chamber of the ECtHR in *López-Ostra v Spain* read the right to freedom from environmental pollution as part of the right to a 'private and family life',[735] an interpretation also confirmed by the Grand Chamber in *Guerra and others v Italy*.[736] This was regarded as dynamic interpretation rather than modification, on account of the evolutive right to a private life. However, the ECtHR seems to have introduced a new concept here—contrary to what is allowed of evolutionary

[725] *Johnston and others v Ireland* App no 9697/82 (ECtHR, 18 December 1986) para 53.
[726] Dupuy, 'Evolutionary Interpretation', 125. [727] See Section 5.2.3(a).
[728] See Section 2.5.2. [729] *Tyrer v UK*, para 31.
[730] *Loizidou v Turkey* (Preliminary Objections) App no 15318/89 (ECtHR, 23 March 1995) para 71. See also *Feldbrugge*, Joint Dissenting Opinion, paras 23–4.
[731] See Section 5.2.3(a).
[732] *Öcalan v Turkey* (Grand Chamber Judgment), para 163. See Art 3 of the ECHR.
[733] Arato, 'Subsequent Practice', 456–7 fn 45.
[734] *Ireland v United Kingdom* App no 5310/71 (ECtHR, 18 January 1978) para 220.
[735] *López-Ostra v Spain* App no 16798/90 (ECtHR, 9 December 1994) paras 51, 58.
[736] *Guerra and others v Italy* [GC] Case no 116/1996/735/932 (ECtHR, 19 February 1998).

interpretation according to the *Feldbrugge* Joint Dissenting Opinion and the *Johnston v Ireland* decision—with significant practical consequences: 'from a quantitative perspective on the rights and obligations connoted by the treaty, the interpretation signals quite a large-scale reassessment of the obligations connoted by the right to a private life'.[737]

Overall, the case law suggests that the implications of expansive evolutionary interpretation can be similar to those resulting from (modification by) subsequent practice. This comparison is the subject of the ensuing section.

2.5.3c Costa Rica v Nicaragua: *The effects of evolutionary interpretation and subsequent practice compared*

The effects of evolutionary interpretation versus those of subsequent practice were highlighted in the 2009 *Dispute regarding Navigational and Related Rights* (*Costa Rica v Nicaragua*) before the International Court of Justice.[738] The dispute concerned Costa Rica's right of free navigation for commercial purposes on the San Juan River, over which Nicaragua has sovereignty pursuant to the bilateral 1858 Treaty of Limits delineating the boundary between the two States. One of the points in dispute involved interpreting the term 'commercial purposes' to determine the scope of Costa Rica's navigational rights on the river pursuant to the treaty. Nicaragua favoured a narrow definition, in line with the meaning of the term at the time of the treaty's conclusion in 1858, to limit its definition to trade in goods. Costa Rica argued for a broader interpretation, comprising 'any activity in pursuit of commercial purposes (…) [including] the transport of passengers, tourists among them, as well as goods'.[739]

The Court acknowledged both the process of modification by subsequent practice and the doctrine of evolutionary interpretation.[740] However, it based its reasoning solely on evolutionary interpretation[741] and did not address the question of modification by subsequent practice any further. It considered the term '*comercio*' to be inherently evolutionary, based on its high degree of generality and incorporation into a treaty 'entered into for a very long period' and 'of continuing duration'.[742] The term therefore had to be interpreted according to its broader contemporary meaning.[743] The Court arrived at the conclusion that Costa Rica's right to pursue navigation for commercial purposes on the river had evolved to include services such as the transport of tourists (though not the navigation of vessels for non-profit purposes).[744] Going further, it held that, in accordance with this right, Nicaragua

[737] Arato, 'Subsequent Practice', 456–7 fn 45.
[738] See also Section 5.2.1.
[739] *Costa Rica v Nicaragua*, para 59.
[740] Ibid. para 64 (emphasis added).
[741] Ibid. paras 66–7.
[742] Ibid. cf *Costa Rica v Nicaragua*, Separate Opinion of Judge Skotnikov, paras 5–6.
[743] Ibid. paras 67–70. cf *Costa Rica v Nicaragua*, Declaration of Judge ad hoc Guillaume, para 16 (arguing that the term had a broad meaning from the beginning).
[744] Ibid. para 71.

could not require visas for tourists aboard Costa Rican vessels, despite the former's consistent practice of requiring such visas over the years.[745]

Judge Skotnikov in his Separate Opinion in the case reaches a conclusion not far removed from that of the Court, but on the basis of subsequent practice rather than evolutionary interpretation. Judge Guillaume in his Declaration adopts a similar reasoning.[746] In contrast to the Court's judgment, Judge Skotnikov argues that the mere inclusion of a generic term in the treaty does not in itself demonstrate the parties' intention to give it an evolutionary character, adding, moreover, that limitations on a State's sovereignty (here, Nicaragua's) should not be presumed, especially in the case of a boundary treaty (by expanding an original right granted to Costa Rica back in 1858).[747]

Most importantly, Judge Skotnikov points out that Nicaragua's 'consistent practice' of allowing Costa Rica to use the river for tourist navigation would have sufficed to establish the parties' agreement to include services within the meaning of 'commercial purposes'[748]—which, it is submitted here, could be regarded as amounting to a treaty modification by subsequent practice. Moreover, following reasoning based on subsequent practice, Nicaragua would not have relinquished its right to require visas from tourists on Costa Rican vessels.[749]

Thus, the Court's conclusion on the basis of evolutionary interpretation led to a broader, more radical 'reinterpretation' of Costa Rica's navigational rights than that reached by Judge Skotnikov through subsequent practice.[750] The decision may also affect *future* interpretations of the treaty, 'since interpreting a treaty as "evolutive" entails a claim about the dynamic nature of the treaty itself'.[751] Moreover, the findings based on evolutionary interpretation—the effects of which, unlike subsequent practice, in principle carry relevance only for the specific treaty[752]—could influence the interpretation of similar terms in *other* treaties.[753] Therefore, reliance on subsequent practice would have been 'less speculative than conjecturing about what the parties had to foretell at the time of a treaty's conclusion',[754] minimizing recourse to presumptions,[755] and providing higher legitimacy.[756]

[745] Ibid. para 115. [746] Ibid. Declaration of Judge ad hoc Guillaume, para 16.

[747] Ibid. Separate Opinion of Judge Skotnikov, paras 4–6. See also *Costa Rica v Nicaragua*, para 48. cf Gardiner, *Treaty Interpretation*, 242–3.

[748] Ibid. Separate Opinion of Judge Skotnikov, paras 8–10; *Costa Rica v Nicaragua*, Declaration of Judge ad hoc Guillaume, para 16.

[749] Ibid. Separate Opinion of Judge Skotnikov, para 15.

[750] Arato, 'Subsequent Practice', 450. [751] Ibid.

[752] See Nolte, Third Report on Treaties over Time, 315 ('the effect which subsequent agreements or subsequent practice on a given treaty may have on a different treaty will be an element of the general effect of one treaty on another in the sense of Art 31(3)(c)').

[753] Arato, 'Subsequent Practice', fn 32 (arguing that the decision may set a *de facto* precedent: if in one case the Court determines 'commerce' to be inherently evolutive, it should do so again in interpreting other treaties, as should other judicial bodies in similar situations), 482 ('subsequent practice normally entails no vertical effects outside of the parties' control').

[754] Venzke, *How Interpretation Makes International Law*, 232–3.

[755] *Costa Rica v Nicaragua*, Declaration of Judge ad hoc Guillaume, para 15.

[756] Nolte, 'Subsequent Practice', 143.

2.5.3d Relation between evolutionary interpretation and subsequent practice

A first link between evolutionary interpretation and subsequent practice, as explained, is provided by the fact that the conclusion that a term or treaty was intended to be 'evolutionary' is often arrived at *by means of subsequent practice*.[757] In other words, subsequent practice can provide evidence to support an evolutionary interpretation. Judicial bodies such as the ICJ and the ECtHR have relied frequently on subsequent practice as a central tool in the process of evolutionary interpretation.[758]

In fact, subsequent practice plays a key role in some of the most important cases involving evolutionary interpretation.[759] In the *Aegean Sea Continental Shelf* case, for instance, the Court confirmed its reading of the generic term 'territorial dispute' by reference to UN and State practice.[760] Likewise, in the *Namibia Advisory Opinion*, the Court referred to the evolution of the right of peoples to self-determination as evidenced in State practice and the practice of certain UN bodies.[761] In his Declaration in *Costa Rica v Nicaragua*, Judge Guillaume looked to the historical practice of the parties to interpret the (evolutionary) intention of the drafters of the 1858 Treaty 'to cover the transport for profit of passengers as well as of goods when they referred to navigation for commercial purposes'.[762]

Second, and most importantly, evolutionary interpretation and subsequent practice have been applied *simultaneously* as interpretative tools in the case law, sometimes leading to differing results (*Costa Rica v Nicaragua*), other times pointing to the same conclusion (*Öcalan v Turkey*). The implications of the two approaches may differ depending on the text, object and purpose, context, and nature of the treaty, as well as the type of obligation, such as when a human rights treaty or constitutive instrument of an international organization is involved.[763] Further considerations, including the principles of good faith and stability of boundaries, may also be relevant.[764] These factors are considered further in Chapter 3 with regard to the operation of subsequent practice as a means of treaty modification.[765]

In any case, the conclusion that can be drawn from *Costa Rica v Nicaragua* is that an agreement by the parties through subsequent practice may provide more legitimacy than the evolutionary approach.[766] This is not only due to the fact that the

[757] See also ILC Draft Conclusions on Subsequent Agreements and Subsequent Practice (2016), 122 ('Conclusion 8').

[758] Nolte, Statement 2011, 7.

[759] Nolte, Introductory Report on Treaties over Time, 178, 207–8.

[760] *Aegean Sea Continental Shelf*, paras 74–5.

[761] *Namibia Advisory Opinion*, para 51.

[762] *Costa Rica v Nicaragua*, Declaration of Judge ad hoc Guillaume, para 16.

[763] Arato, 'Subsequent Practice', 478, 487 fn 122.

[764] See eg MG Kohen, 'The Decision on the Delimitation of the Eritrea/Ethiopia Boundary of 13 April 2002: A Singular Approach to International Law Applicable to Territorial Disputes' in MG Kohen (ed), *Promoting Justice, Human Rights and Conflict Resolution through International Law: Liber Amicorum Lucius Caflisch* (Brill, 2007) 767, 772–3. See also *Costa Rica v Nicaragua*, Separate Opinion of Judge Skotnikov, paras 5–6. On good faith and subsequent practice, see eg Crema, 'Subsequent Agreements and Subsequent Practice', 28.

[765] See further Section 3.5.

[766] Nolte, 'Subsequent Practice', 143. See also *Costa Rica v Nicaragua*, Declaration of Judge ad hoc Guillaume, paras 11–12, 15.

'vertical' effects (on future interpretations of the same treaty) and 'horizontal' effects (on future interpretations of similar treaties) of subsequent practice may be more limited than those of evolutionary interpretation, but also the fact that subsequent practice may provide a truer, more current reflection of the parties' intentions:

> The exclusive reference to a changed meaning, to the object and purpose of a treaty, and/or to changed legal framework and circumstances can result in the imposition of an external evaluation of this evolution upon the parties. To also take the subsequent practice of the parties into account in the assessment of this process allows for a consideration of *how* the parties themselves, that is, the subjects primarily involved in the application of the treaty, have faced and managed this change. It allows the intentions of the parties and a dynamic vision of international law to be taken together, avoiding the risk of arbitrary interpretations of the text, but also breaking up the common, static couplet of loyalty to the parties' intentions and strict textualism.[767]

Evolutionary interpretation not only overlaps with subsequent practice as an *interpretative* tool, but also with subsequent practice as a means of treaty *modification*, in seeking to find a balance between stability and flexibility of the law.[768] Evolutionary treaty provisions are less susceptible to modification by subsequent practice because they contain an inherent 'adaptation' mechanism from their inception—even seemingly divergent subsequent practice may be 'read into' the drafters' original intention to allow the treaty to evolve and may thus be regarded as an element in the interpretative process rather than as a reflection of a tacit modifying agreement:

> While evolutionary interpretation and the taking into account of subsequent conduct are, in principle, mutually complementary (...) it is noteworthy that subsequent conduct can play both a justificatory and a limiting role for evolutionary interpretation. The justificatory role consists in demonstrating that an evolved understanding of a treaty can—also—be based on subsequent conduct as an authentic means of interpretation. The limiting role of subsequent conduct emerges more clearly with the growing recognition of the possibility of an evolutive interpretation.[769]

It could be said that the more room there is for evolutionary interpretation, the less there may be for tacit modification by subsequent practice.[770] In any case, the higher the 'evolutionary' potential of a treaty or term, the more difficult it becomes to draw the line between interpretation and a tacit modification, to determine the point at which evolutionary interpretation has 'stretched' the meaning of the text beyond its boundaries and into the realm of modification.

Nevertheless, the fact that evolutionary interpretation remains based on concepts already contained in the treaty implies that its potential for extending the meaning of the text is inherently more limited than that of subsequent practice.[771] As already noted, the latter is capable of going further than, and even evidencing the

767 Crema, 'Subsequent Agreements and Practice', 23 (emphasis in the original).
768 Dupuy, 'Evolutionary Interpretation', 137.
769 Nolte, Introductory Report on Treaties over Time, 188.
770 Ibid. 207.
771 Gardiner, *Treaty Interpretation*, 243.

parties' agreement to remove a textual limit on, an evolutionary interpretation of the treaty.[772]

2.5.4 Subsequent practice and the doctrine of implied powers

It has already been explained that constitutive treaties of international organizations represent a special case for treaty interpretation in general, and for subsequent practice in particular.[773] The focus here, building upon the points made in relation to evolutionary interpretation, is on one specific aspect of the topic of international organizations: the doctrine of implied powers.[774]

Implied powers[775] are central[776] to any discussion on the powers of international organizations:[777]

> The constituent documents of organizations necessarily come with gaps, simply because the drafters cannot be expected to think of every possible contingency, and because it may be expected, perhaps even hoped, that internal dynamics will move the organization forward. In those circumstances, the organization should not be limited by those powers granted to it upon its creation; instead, the organization must be allowed some flexibility. It must be allowed certain powers which, while not expressly granted, are granted by implication.[778]

The notion of implied powers is strongly linked to the aforementioned principle of effectiveness.[779] Some commentators adopt the broad view that implied powers

[772] Arato, 'Subsequent Practice', 482. [773] See eg Sections 2.3.1(c) and 2.5.1.

[774] See eg B Rouyer-Hameray, *Les compétences implicites des organisations internationales* (LGDJ, 1962); R Khan, *Implied Powers of the United Nations* (Vikas 1970); J Makarczyk, 'The International Court of Justice on the Implied Powers of International Organizations' in J Makarczyk (ed), *Essays in International Law in Honour of Judge Manfred Lachs* (Martinus Nijhoff, 1984) 501; K Skubiszewski, 'Implied Powers of International Organizations' in Y Dinstein (ed), *International Law at a Time of Perplexity: Essays in Honour of Shabtai Rosenne* (Martinus Nijhoff, 1989) 855; C Denys, *Impliciete bevoegdheden in de Europese Economische Gemeenschap: een onderzoek naar de betekenis van de 'implied powers'* (Maklu, 1990); Schermers and Blokker, *International Institutional Law*, 158ff; Amerasinghe, *Principles*, 44–8; Klabbers, *An Introduction*, 67–81.

[775] The distinction between 'implied powers' and 'inherent powers' (powers not derived from any express provision or purpose laid down in the constitutive treaty, but rather intrinsic to organizations as such) is difficult. See eg F Seyersted, *Objective International Personality of Intergovernmental Organizations: Do Their Capacities Really Depend upon the Conventions Establishing Them?* (Krohns Bogtnykker, 1963); A Dashwood, 'Implied External Competence of the EC' in M Koskenniemi (ed), *International Law Aspects of the European Union* (Kluwer Law International, 1998) 113; Klabbers, *An Introduction*, 75–8.

[776] cf Klabbers, *An Introduction*, 79 ('at least in some of the more settled organizations, the doctrine has passed its heyday').

[777] This discussion could arguably be extended to 'autonomous institutional arrangements' (see Section 2.3.1(c)). AIAs may have implied powers in relation to their internal procedures, substantive obligations under their constitutive agreements, and external capacities such as treaty-making and international legal personality, and they have been known to take far-reaching, seemingly legally binding decisions without an express basis in the underlying agreement. However, such decisions, if unchallenged, could also be regarded 'as agreements in simplified form between parties to the MEA, rather than as decisions based on implied powers'—Churchill and Ulfstein, 'Autonomous Institutional Arrangements', 639–40, citing Sands, *Principles*, 380.

[778] Klabbers, *An Introduction*, 66. [779] See Section 2.5.1.

provide a means by which an organization can fulfil its function and purpose.[780] A more restrictive approach advocates that implied powers are limited to those powers strictly 'necessary' for the implementation of the powers expressly established by the treaty.[781] In the *Reparation for Injuries Advisory Opinion*, concerning the ability of the UN to bring external legal claims, the ICJ first acknowledged that powers can be conferred upon an organization 'by necessary implication as being essential to the performance of its duties',[782] concluding that:

> Upon examination of the character of the functions entrusted to the Organization and of the nature of the missions of its agents, it becomes clear that the capacity of the Organization to exercise a measure of functional protection of its agents arises *by necessary intendment* out of the Charter.[783]

The Court reaffirmed this broad interpretation in the *UN Administrative Tribunal Advisory Opinion*, in which it upheld the UN General Assembly's power to establish an administrative tribunal 'by necessary intendment' out of the Charter in order to ensure the efficient operation of the organization and its organs.[784] In the *Certain Expenses Advisory Opinion*, the ICJ emphasized the connection of implied powers to the fulfilment of the purposes of the organization, and thus the object of the underlying treaty.[785] Although it has been argued that recently the Court has begun to take a more restrictive approach to implied powers,[786] the ICJ once again acknowledged the implied powers doctrine in the *WHO Nuclear Weapons Advisory Opinion*:

> The powers conferred on international organizations are normally the subject of an express statement in their constituent instruments. Nevertheless, the necessities of international life may point to the need for organizations, in order to achieve their objectives, to possess subsidiary powers which are not expressly provided for in the basic instruments which govern their activities. It is generally accepted that international organizations can exercise such powers, known as 'implied powers'.[787]

The rationale used by the ICJ to assess the implied powers of international organizations can also be extended to international tribunals.[788] International

[780] See eg *Reparation for Injuries Suffered in the Service of the United Nations*, Advisory Opinion of 11 April 1949, ICJ Reports 174, 182: 'the Organisation must be deemed to have those powers which, though not expressly provided in the Charter, are conferred upon it by necessary implication as being essential to the performance of its duties'.

[781] *Reparation for Injuries Suffered in the Service of the United Nations*, Advisory Opinion of 11 April 1949, Dissenting Opinion of Judge Hackworth, ICJ Reports 196, 198.

[782] *Reparation for Injuries Advisory Opinion*, 182.

[783] Ibid. 184 (emphasis added).

[784] *Effects of Awards of Compensation Made by the United Nations Administrative Tribunal*, Advisory Opinion of 13 July 1954, ICJ Reports 47 [*UN Administrative Tribunal Advisory Opinion*] 57. See also *WHO Nuclear Weapons Advisory Opinion*, 79.

[785] *Certain Expenses Advisory Opinion*, 168.

[786] See eg *WHO Nuclear Weapons Advisory Opinion*, paras 20–1, where the Court found that the WHO's constitutive treaty did not allow it to tackle issues concerning the legality of nuclear weapons.

[787] Ibid. para 25.

[788] E Lauterpacht, '"Partial Judgments" and the Inherent Jurisdiction of the International Court of Justice' in AV Lowe and M Fitzmaurice (eds), *Fifty Years of the International Court of Justice* (CUP, 1996) 477; I Buga, 'Territorial Sovereignty Issues in Maritime Disputes: A Jurisdictional Dilemma for Law of the Sea Tribunals' (2012) 27 IJMCL 59, 77–8. See eg *UN Administrative Tribunal Advisory Opinion*, 56–7; *Certain Expenses Advisory Opinion*, 168. See also P Gaeta, 'Inherent Powers of International

tribunals may exercise competences not expressly conferred under their constitutive instrument, as long as they do not contradict the text or object of the treaty.[789] The ICJ has also at times adopted a teleological interpretation of its title of jurisdiction.[790] Once again, this approach is closely linked to the principle of effectiveness.[791]

Thus, when a treaty does not provide sufficient basis or guidance for an observed practice, 'it may be necessary to turn to principles of international institutional law'.[792] It is submitted that the law of treaties and institutional law principles such as the implied powers doctrine can be complementary, as illustrated by the fact that the basis for implied powers can be derived from the notion of 'object and purpose' in Article 31(1) VCLT.

This contrasts with the view that international institutional law principles could lead to modifications unforeseen or prohibited under the law of treaties—for example, the possibility of excluding a State from an international organization if that State is impeding its functioning, even in the absence of an express power to do so in the respective treaty or on the basis of a material breach in the sense of Article 60(2) VCLT.[793] The law of treaties is flexible enough to adapt to different contexts and regimes, as in the special case of international organizations.

Like the doctrine of evolutionary interpretation, the implied powers doctrine represents a form of dynamic, teleological interpretation. Implied powers apply when a term or competence is read into the instrument to give effect to what the parties had agreed to under the treaty, rather than to modify it.[794] Thus, implied powers, like evolutionary interpretation, provide an adaptation mechanism to ensure that a treaty remains effective without, in principle, modifying it. Moreover, both doctrines rely on powers or objectives established by the original drafters[795]

Courts and Tribunals' in LC Vohran and others (eds), *Man's Inhumanity to Man: Essays on International Law in Honour of Antonio Cassese* (Kluwer Law International, 2003) 353, 355; PC Rao, 'Delimitation Disputes under the United Nations Convention on the Law of the Sea: Settlement Procedures' in TM Ndiaye and R Wolfrum (eds), *Law of the Sea, Environmental Law and Settlement of Disputes* (Martinus Nijhoff, 2007) 896, 891.

789 Gaeta, 'Inherent Powers', 353; CF Amerasinghe, *Jurisdiction of International Tribunals* (Kluwer Law International, 2003) 394. See eg *LaGrand* (*Germany v USA*), 503.

790 *South West Africa*, 48 ('the Court is entitled to engage in a process of "filling in the gaps", in the application of a teleological principle of interpretation, according to which instruments must be given their maximum effect'). See also *Factory at Chorzów*, Jurisdiction, Judgment of 26 July 1927, PCIJ Series A, No 9, 21–2; *Corfu Channel*, 23–6; Higgins, 'International Law and Avoidance, Containment and Resolution of Disputes', 34.

791 *Polish Postal Service in Danzig*, 39; *Reparation for Injuries Advisory Opinion*, 174; *Fisheries Jurisdiction* (*Spain v Canada*), 455; *Iron Rhine Railway Arbitration*, paras 49, 84; Rosenne, *Law and Practice of the International Court*, 1148.

792 Ulfstein, 'Treaty Bodies', 433.

793 Schermers and Blokker, *International Institutional Law*, 104–5; Churchill and Ulfstein, 'Autonomous Institutional Arrangements', 634.

794 Skubiszewski, 'Implied Powers', 856–7.

795 Some scholars thus distinguish between 'implied powers', founded on powers attributed to the organization at its creation, and 'customary powers', attributed subsequently by the parties. See Schermers and Blokker, *International Institutional Law*, 181; ND White, *The Law of International Organisations* (2nd edn, Manchester UP, 2005) 71.

and find their limit in the text of the treaty.[796] In any case, they cannot add to or detract from the basic 'objectives' of the treaty (as distinct from 'powers').[797] Lastly, both evolutionary interpretation and implied powers can have far-reaching effects, pushing the boundary between interpretation and modification.[798]

Therefore, the implications of the implied powers doctrine are similar to those of evolutionary interpretation: the more room there is for an 'implicit' conferral of powers, and thus for adaptation of the constitutive treaty based on teleological interpretation, the less need there may be for tacit modification through subsequent practice. On the other hand, the significant attention paid to the practice of international organizations in the case law and doctrine suggests that these treaties may be adapted through means not envisaged by their founders.[799]

One popular example is the tacit modification of Article 27(3) of the UN Charter by the Security Council.[800] The crux lies in determining the scope and effects of implied powers in a given case. This requires differentiating between situations in which there is sufficient basis in the treaty to support an implied power, and interpretations that would extend the mandate or authority of the organization beyond that scope—thus becoming something more than mere interpretation.[801] This problem applies generally to distinguishing between interpretation and modification by subsequent practice. The issues involved in the process of modification by subsequent practice constitute the focus of the next chapter.

[796] *Certain Expenses Advisory Opinion*, Dissenting Opinion of Judge Moreno Quintana, ICJ Reports 239, 245. See also AIL Campbell, 'The Limits of the Powers of International Organizations' (2002) 32 ICLQ 523, 528. For a discussion of the further limitations of 'implied powers', see Schermers and Blokker, *International Institutional Law*, 181, 184–5 (implied powers must be 'essential' to the performance of the organization's functions, may be curtailed by explicit powers under the treaty, must not violate fundamental legal principles, and should not affect the distribution of functions within the organization). See also eg D Sarooshi, 'The Legal Framework Governing United Nations Subsidiary Organs' (1996) 76 BYBIL 428.

[797] Schermers and Blokker, *International Institutional Law*, 187.

[798] For instance, the Conference of the Parties of CITES has established subsidiary bodies despite the lack of any explicit power to do so. The COP is normally only entitled to 'make recommendations for improving the effectiveness' of the Convention. See 1973 Convention on International Trade in Endangered Species of Wild Fauna and Flora, 993 UNTS 243, Art XI(3)(e). See further Section 5.3.2(b).

[799] See eg Brölmann, 'Specialized Rules', 512. See also Amerasinghe, *Principles*, 48ff; Churchill and Ulfstein, 'Autonomous Institutional Arrangements', 632.

[800] See further Sections 3.4.2 and 5.2.1.

[801] See eg EP Hexner, 'Teleological Interpretation of Basic Instruments of International Organizations' in S Engel and RA Metall (eds), *Law, State and International Legal Order: Essays in Honor of Hans Kelsen* (University of Tennessee Press, 1964) 119, 123–4.

3

Subsequent Practice as a Means of Treaty Modification

3.1 Introduction

The preceding chapter addressed the role of subsequent practice in the process of treaty interpretation. The focus now turns to subsequent practice as a means of modifying treaty provisions.

The modification of treaties by subsequent practice is a reality in treaty relations, inherent in the role of States as 'masters' of their own treaty.[1] Despite its elusive nature, and the controversy at times associated with its recognition, the process has been acknowledged by a wide range of dispute settlement bodies and the majority of legal scholars. The International Court of Justice has effectively recognized the possibility of treaty modification by subsequent practice.[2] Other international judicial bodies such as the European Court of Human Rights[3] and the Iran-US Claims Tribunal[4] have explicitly acknowledged the process. Likewise, international arbitral tribunals have sustained the modifying effect of subsequent practice.[5] National courts have

[1] See eg I Sinclair, *The Vienna Convention on the Law of Treaties* (2nd edn, Manchester UP, 1984) 98, citing AD McNair, *The Law of Treaties* (Clarendon Press, 1961) 169; ME Villiger, *Commentary on the 1969 Vienna Convention on the Law of Treaties* (Martinus Nijhoff, 2009) 429.

[2] See eg *Costa Rica v Nicaragua*, para 64; *Cameroon v Nigeria*, Judgment, para 68; *El Salvador/Honduras*, para 80. See also, more implicitly, eg *Temple of Préah Vihéar*, 33–4; *Namibia Advisory Opinion*, para 22; *Israeli Wall Advisory Opinion*, paras 27–8. These cases are discussed in detail in Section 5.2.1 of this book. See also the PCIJ's statement in *The Payment of Various Serbian Loans Issued in France*, Judgment of 12 July 1929, PCIJ Series A, Nos 20/21 [*Serbian Loans*] 38. Individual ICJ judges have also recognized modification by subsequent practice. See eg *Certain Expenses Advisory Opinion*, Separate Opinion of Judge Spender, 191; *Certain Expenses Advisory Opinion*, Dissenting Opinion of Judge Winiarski, 230; *Namibia Advisory Opinion*, Dissenting Opinion of Judge Fitzmaurice, 282; *Kasikili/Sedudu Island* (*Botswana/Namibia*), Judgment of 13 December 1999, Dissenting Opinion of Judge Parra-Aranguren, ICJ Reports 1208, para 16. cf Nolte, Second Report on Subsequent Practice, paras 115, 124–9 (but see ibid. 138; ILC, 'Provisional summary record of the 3205th meeting', UN Doc A/CN.4/SR.3205 (2014) [Provisional summary record of 3205th meeting] 7 (Forteau)).

[3] *Soering v UK*, paras 103–4; *Öcalan v Turkey* App no 46221/88 (ECtHR, 12 March 2003) [*Öcalan v Turkey*] paras 196, 198; *Öcalan v Turkey* (Grand Chamber Judgment), para 163; *Al-Saadoon and Mufdhi v UK*, para 119; *Hassan v United Kingdom* [GC] App no 29750/09 (ECtHR, 16 September 2014) [*Hassan v UK*] para 101. See Section 5.2.3(a).

[4] *Iran and USA*, Interlocutory Award No ITL 83-B1-FT, para 132. See Section 5.2.3(b).

[5] See eg *Interpretation of the Air Transport Services Agreement between the United States of America and France* (*United States/France*), Award of 22 December 1963, 16 RIAA 5 [*Air Transport Services Arbitration* (*US/France*)] 63; *Interpretation of the Air Transport Services Agreement between the United*

also taken up the matter.[6] In addition, numerous international law scholars have recognized treaty modification by subsequent practice[7]—some of them have even

States of America and Italy (*United States/Italy*), Award of 17 July 1965, 16 RIAA 75 [*Air Transport Services Arbitration* (*US/Italy*)] 100; *Case concerning the Location of Boundary Markers in Taba between Egypt and Israel*, Award of 29 September 1988, 20 RIAA 1 [*Taba Arbitration*] paras 209–10, 235; *Decision regarding Delimitation of the Border between Eritrea and Ethiopia* [*Eritrea-Ethiopia Arbitration*] Award of 13 April 2002, 25 RIAA 110, paras 3.6, 3.8, 3.10. See Section 5.2.2.

[6] See eg *International Military Operations* (*German Participation*), Federal Constitutional Court, 90 BVerfGE 286 (Case Nos 2 BvE 3/92, 5/93, 7/93, and 8/93) Judgment of 12 July 1994, reproduced in English in (1997) 106 ILR 319, 338. See further Sections 5.2.4 and 5.3.1(b).

[7] See eg G Fitzmaurice, 'The Law and Procedure of the International Court of Justice 1951–4: Treaty Interpretation and Other Treaty Points' (1957) 33 BYBIL 203, 225; S Engel, '"Living" International Constitutions and the World Court (The Subsequent Practice of International Organs under their Constituent Instruments)' (1967) 16 ICLQ 865; FG Jacobs, 'Varieties of Approach to Treaty Interpretation: With Special Reference to the Draft Convention on the Law of Treaties Before the Vienna Diplomatic Conference' (1969) 18 ICLQ 318, 332; G Haraszti, *Some Fundamental Problems of the Law of Treaties* (Akadémiai Kiadó, 1973) 143–5; M Akehurst, 'The Hierarchy of the Sources of International Law' (1974–75) 47 BYBIL 273, 277; MK Yasseen, 'L'interprétation des traités d'après la Convention de Vienne sur le droit des traités' (1976-III) 151 RC 1, 51; W Karl, *Vertrag und spätere Praxis im Völkerrecht: Zum Einfluß der Praxis auf Inhalt und Bestand völkerrechtliche Verträge* (Springer, 1983) 292–3; Sinclair, *Vienna Convention*, 138; HWA Thirlway, 'The Law and Procedure of the International Court of Justice: 1960-1989, Part Three' (1991) 62 BYBIL 48, 52; DA Koplow, 'When Is an Amendment Not an Amendment? Modification of Arms Control Agreements Without the Senate' (1992) 59 U Chicago L Rev 981, 1023–4; G Distefano, 'La pratique subséquente des États parties à un traité' (1994) 40 AFDI 41, 54–67; P Reuter, *Introduction to the Law of Treaties* (2nd edn, Kegan Paul International, 1995) 137, para 211; Z Kivilcim-Forsman, 'Principe d'egalité entre le traité et la coutume en droit international public' (1996) 45 J Faculty of Law, Ankara Univ 211, 215; K Wolfke, 'Treaties and Custom: Aspects of Interrelation' in J Klabbers and R Lefeber (eds), *Essays on the Law of Treaties: A Collection of Essays in Honour of Bert Vierdag* (Martinus Nijhoff, 1998) 31, 34–5; M Byers, *Custom, Power and the Power of Rules: International Relations and Customary International Law* (CUP, 2001) 174–5; R Bernhardt, 'Völkerrechtliche und verfassungsrechtliche Aspekte konkludenter Vertrag-sänderungen' in H-W Arndt and others (eds), *Völkerrecht und Deutsches Recht: Festschrift für Walter Rudolf zum 70 Geburtstag* (Beck, 2001) 15, 16–17; I Brownlie, *Principles of Public International Law* (6th edn, OUP, 2003) 601; J Pauwelyn, *Conflict of Norms in Public International Law: How WTO Law Relates to other Rules of International Law* (CUP, 2003) 50; EJ Criddle, 'The Vienna Convention on the Law of Treaties in U.S. Treaty Interpretation' (2004) 44 VJIL 431, 439; DR Rothwell, 'The Impact of State Practice on the Jurisdictional Framework Contained in the LOS Convention: A Commentary' in AG Oude Elferink (ed), *Stability and Change in the Law of the Sea: The Role of the LOS Convention* (Martinus Nijhoff, 2005) 145, 148; A Laursen, *Changing International Law to Meet New Challenges: Interpretation, Modification and the Use of Force* (DJØF Publishing, 2006) 65, 67; U Linderfalk, *On the Interpretation of Treaties: The Modern International Law as Expressed in the 1969 Vienna Convention on the Law of Treaties* (Springer, 2007) 168; MN Shaw, *International Law* (6th edn, CUP, 2008) 931; MJ Bowman, '"Normalizing" the International Convention for the Regulation of Whaling' (2007–2008) 29 MJIL 293, 337; R Jennings and A Watts (eds), *Oppenheim's International Law: Peace* (9th edn, OUP, 2008) paras 624, 1254; A Bianchi, 'The International Regulation of the Use of Force: The Politics of Interpretive Method' (2009) 22 LJIL 651, 659; RK Gardiner, *Treaty Interpretation* (OUP, 2008) 243–5; Villiger, *Commentary*, 429; R Monaco and C Curti Gialdino, *Manuale di diritto internazionale pubblico* (3rd edn, UTET, 2009) 177; J Arato, 'Subsequent Practice and Evolutive Interpretation: Techniques of Treaty Interpretation over Time and Their Diverse Consequences' (2010) 9 LPICT 443, 464; T Gazzini, 'Interpretation of (Allegedly) Self-Judging Clauses in Bilateral Investment Treaties' in M Fitzmaurice, O Elias, and P Merkouris (eds), *Treaty Interpretation and the Vienna Convention on the Law of Treaties: 30 Years On* (Martinus Nijhoff, 2010) 239, 251; J Harrison, *Making the Law of the Sea: A Study in the Development of International Law* (CUP, 2011) 95; P Sands, 'Article 39—1969 Convention' in O Corten and P Klein (eds), *The Vienna Convention on the Law of Treaties: A Commentary*, vol I (OUP, 2011) 963, 972, 974; A Aust, *Modern Treaty Law and Practice* (3rd edn, CUP, 2013) 264; L Crema, 'Subsequent Agreements and Subsequent Practice Within and Outside the Vienna Convention' in G Nolte (ed), *Treaties and Subsequent Practice* (OUP, 2013) 13, 26; JY Qin, 'The Conundrum of WTO Accession Protocols: In Search of Legality and Legitimacy' (2015) 55 VJIL 369, 407; D Costelloe and M Fitzmaurice, 'Lawmaking by Treaty: Conclusion of Treaties and Evolution of Treaty Regimes in Practice' in C Brölmann and Y Radi (eds), *Research Handbook on the Theory and Practice of International Lawmaking* (Edward Elgar, 2016)

pointed to its customary law status.[8] What is more, it has been argued that the proliferation of cases and practice confirming the possibility of modification by subsequent practice has led to a reinterpretation through subsequent practice of the VCLT itself, 'to mean that under art. 31(3)(b) interpretation can shade into modification by subsequent practice'.[9]

As covered later in this chapter, the ILC acknowledged the modifying effect of subsequent practice in the context of its drafting of the Vienna Convention decades ago.[10] The process has also been taken note of more recently in the ongoing ILC discussions on subsequent practice. Specifically, the treaty modifying potential of subsequent practice has been examined in the context of a broader study by the ILC on 'Treaties over Time', established in 2008,[11] the working title and format of which was changed with effect from 2013 to 'Subsequent Agreements and Subsequent Practice in relation to the Interpretation of Treaties'.[12] Although the focus of the ILC topic is in principle limited to treaty interpretation, the issue of modification by subsequent practice has come up.[13] Following the proposal of the Special Rapporteur,[14] the ILC provisionally adopted a draft conclusion on 'possible effects of subsequent agreements and subsequent practice in interpretation',[15] paragraph 3 of which reads in relevant part as follows:

> It is presumed that the parties to a treaty, by an agreement subsequently arrived at or a practice in the application of the treaty, intend to interpret the treaty, not to amend or to modify it.

111, 130–1; R Kolb, *The Law of Treaties: An Introduction* (Edward Elgar, 2016) 193–4. *Contra* eg J Kammerhofer, *Uncertainty in International Law: A Kelsenian Perspective* (Routledge, 2011) 131–4; MG Kohen, 'Keeping Subsequent Agreements and Practice in Their Right Limits' in G Nolte (ed), *Treaties and Subsequent Practice* (OUP, 2013) 34.

[8] See eg Jacobs, 'Varieties of Approach to Treaty Interpretation', 332; Karl, *Vertrag*, 292–3; Pauwelyn, *Conflict of Norms*, 50; S Sur, *L'interprétation en droit international public* (LGDJ, 1974) 201; AM Feldman, 'Evolving Treaty Obligations: A Proposal for Analyzing Subsequent Practice Derived from WTO Dispute Settlement' (2009) 41 NYU J Intl L & Pol 655, 658, 705; Arato, 'Subsequent Practice', 464 and fn 73. See also *Summary records of the plenary meetings and of the meetings of the Committee of the Whole, Official Records of the United Nations Conference on the Law of Treaties—First Session (26 March–24 May 1968)* UN Doc A/CO NF.39/11, 38th Meeting of the Committee of the Whole (25 April 1968) 210 [38th Meeting of the Committee of the Whole], 214; Nolte, Second Report on Subsequent Practice, para 122. See further Section 3.3.7 and the sources cited in n 455.

[9] Arato, 'Subsequent Practice', fn 73.

[10] Section 3.2. See eg Waldock, Third Report on the Law of Treaties, 61–2; Waldock, Sixth Report on the Law of Treaties, 87–8; *Summary records of the plenary meetings and of the meetings of the Committee of the Whole, Official Records of the United Nations Conference on the Law of Treaties— First Session (26 March–24 May 1968)* UN Doc A/CO NF.39/11, 37th Meeting of the Committee of the Whole (24 April 1968) 203 [37th Meeting of the Committee of the Whole], paras 57, 59, 66; 38th Meeting of the Committee of the Whole, paras 28, 48, 55. See further ME Villiger, *Customary International Law and Treaties: A Study of Their Interactions and Interrelations, with Special Consideration of the 1969 Vienna Convention on the Law of Treaties* (Brill, 1985) paras 306–7, 310.

[11] See eg Nolte, Introductory Report on Treaties over Time, 200ff. The Study Group proceeded on the basis of an examination of three reports presented informally by the Chairperson (2010–12).

[12] ILC Report on the Work of Its 64th Session, paras 226–7. The Commission has thus far proceeded on the basis of four reports of the Special Rapporteur (2013–16).

[13] Nolte, Second Report on Subsequent Practice, paras 115–66. Many ILC members considered that the discussion of treaty modification may not be appropriate given that the topic under consideration related to treaty interpretation—see eg Provisional summary record of 3205th meeting, 7 (Forteau); ILC, 'Provisional summary record of the 3207th meeting', UN Doc A/CN.4/SR.3207 (2014) [Provisional summary record of 3207th meeting] 3 (Escobar Hernández), 5 (Tladi), 6 (Šturma); ILC, 'Provisional summary record of the 3208th meeting', UN Doc A/CN.4/SR.3208 (2014), 6 (Hmoud), 9 (Vásquez-Bermudez).

[14] Ibid. para 166 ('Draft conclusion 11').

[15] ILC, 'Provisional summary record of the 3215th meeting', UN Doc A/CN.4/SR.3215 (2015) 6.

The possibility of amending or modifying a treaty by subsequent practice of the parties has not been generally recognized. The present draft conclusion is without prejudice to the rules on the amendment or modification of treaties under the Vienna Convention on the Law of Treaties and under customary international law.[16]

The first sentence of the draft conclusion rightly provides that the modifying effect of subsequent practice (and subsequent agreements) should not be presumed.[17] Accordingly, 'States and courts should make every effort to conceive an agreed subsequent practice of the parties as an effort to interpret the treaty in a particular way.'[18] As we shall see in the present chapter, the strength of the presumption against modification will depend on many factors connected with the nature of the treaty regime and provision in question.[19] This presumption will be even stronger in exceptional cases where, for instance, a modification would affect the object and purpose of the treaty[20] or where formal amendment procedures have already been triggered.[21]

The second sentence of the ILC's draft conclusion states that the possibility of treaty modification by subsequent practice has not been generally recognized (although the Commentary acknowledges 'examples to the contrary in case law and diverging opinions in the literature'[22]). This raises some questions, as noted by certain ILC members[23] and delegations in their comments to the ILC[24]—not least given that the statement is difficult to square with the express acknowledgement

[16] ILC Draft Conclusions on Subsequent Agreements and Subsequent Practice (2016), 121–2 ('Conclusion 7', para 3).

[17] This links to the discussion on the definition of modification based on the notion of a 'genuine' conflict and the general presumption against conflicts under international law—see Sections 3.3.1 and 3.4.2. cf Provisional summary record of 3205th meeting, 7 (Forteau), arguing that 'it could not be presumed that subsequent agreements or subsequent practice had an interpretative rather than modifying effect: that depended on the circumstances'.

[18] Nolte, Second Report on Subsequent Practice, para 142. See also ILC, 'Permanent Mission of Austria to the United Nations, Statement by Ambassador Helmut Tichy—69th Session of the General Assembly Sixth Committee, Agenda Item 78' (29 October 2014) <http://legal.un.org/ilc/sessions/67/pdfs/english/sasp_austria.pdf> accessed 11 November 2016 [Comments by the Austrian Delegation to the ILC]; ILC Draft Conclusions on Subsequent Agreements and Subsequent Practice (2016), 174 para 24, 180 para 38.

[19] Section 3.5. See ILC Draft Conclusions on Subsequent Agreements and Subsequent Practice (2016), 179 para 35, citing I Buga, 'Subsequent Practice and Treaty Modification' in MJ Bowman and D Kritsiotis (eds), *Conceptual and Contextual Perspectives on the Modern Law of Treaties* (CUP, forthcoming): '[A] treaty may preclude the subsequent practice of the parties from having a modifying effect. (...) Conversely, (...) a treaty may permit the subsequent practice of the parties to have a modifying effect. Thus, ultimately, much depends on the treaty or on the treaty provisions concerned.'

[20] Section 3.3.5. [21] Section 3.3.4.

[22] ILC Draft Conclusions on Subsequent Agreements and Subsequent Practice (2016), 173 para 21.

[23] Provisional summary record of 3205th meeting, 7 (Forteau), finding the sentence unconvincing given the recognition in ICJ cases of the modifying effect of subsequent practice.

[24] See Comments by the Austrian Delegation to the ILC: 'The statement contained in the second sentence of draft conclusion 7 paragraph 3 (...) raises some questions. (...) In the view of the Austrian delegation, this effect [that subsequent practice may modify a treaty] may not be generally excluded. (...) [I]t seems clear that a "subsequent practice" establishing an *agreement* to modify a treaty should be regarded as a treaty modification and not merely an interpretation exercise.'

that the possibility of modification by subsequent practice cannot be precluded.[25] The sentence, it may be noted, also seems to indicate a certain change of course from the initial report on 'Treaties over Time'.[26] Furthermore, both the Special Rapporteur's work and the ILC's Commentary on the draft conclusions set out examples of a range of dispute settlement bodies acknowledging (albeit with varying degrees of explicitness), and in some cases also applying, modification by subsequent practice (and subsequent agreements)—despite the general reluctance of courts and tribunals to explicitly recognize modifying instances, discussed in detail in the ensuing sections,[27] and the significant differences in approach between dispute settlement bodies noted earlier.[28] It is also acknowledged that numerous legal scholars have recognized the process,[29] and that State practice outside of judicial proceedings reveals examples of modification by subsequent practice and subsequent agreements.[30] As explained at the outset of this book, the fact that potentially modifying instances of practice unrelated to judicial proceedings may be 'difficult to identify'[31] does not invalidate the process of modification by subsequent practice—in fact, it only further justifies the inquiry.

Furthermore, the possibility of modification by subsequent *agreements* is recognized in clear terms in the ILC's Commentary ('agreements subsequently arrived at may serve to amend or modify the treaty'[32]). In fact, as underscored by the Special Rapporteur, if sufficiently clear, a subsequent agreement 'may even contribute to modifying an essential element of a treaty'.[33] As explained in Section 2.3, however, no strict distinction is—or, it is submitted, *can*—be made between subsequent practice and subsequent agreements for present purposes; in both cases, the requirement of an agreement must be safeguarded.[34] Thus, if the possibility of modification by subsequent agreements is recognized—as the *a contrario*

[25] ILC Draft Conclusions on Subsequent Agreements and Subsequent Practice (2016), 179 paras 35–7. See also L Crema, 'Subsequent Practice in Hassan v United Kingdom: When Things Seem to Go Wrong in the Life of a Living Instrument' (*QIL*, 12 May 2015) <www.qil-qdi.org/subsequent-practice-in-hassan-v-united-kingdom-when-things-seem-to-go-wrong-in-the-life-of-a-living-instrument/> accessed 27 April 2017.

[26] See eg Nolte, Introductory Report on Treaties over Time, Section V.

[27] See in particular Section 5.2. See also Nolte Second Report on Subsequent Practice, paras 138, 142; ILC Draft Conclusions on Subsequent Agreements and Subsequent Practice (2016), eg 175 paras 24–6, 180 para 38.

[28] See Section 2.5. See also Nolte Second Report on Subsequent Practice, eg paras 138–9 ('the International Court of Justice seems to have recognized the possibility in general terms, without however clearly applying it in a specific case. (...) The WTO Appellate Body, on the other hand, has rejected the possibility of a modification of the WTO Covered Agreements by the subsequent practice of the parties, whereas the European Court of Human Rights has recognized and applied the possibility in at least one case.'). See, likewise, ILC Draft Conclusions on Subsequent Agreements and Subsequent Practice (2016), eg 179 para 35.

[29] Nolte, Second Report on Subsequent Practice, eg para 122; ILC Draft Conclusions on Subsequent Agreements and Subsequent Practice (2016), eg 175 para 26.

[30] Nolte, Second Report on Subsequent Practice, para 137.

[31] Ibid.

[32] ILC Draft Conclusions on Subsequent Agreements and Subsequent Practice (2016), 173 para 21 (and see ibid. 174 para 23). See likewise Nolte, Second Report on Subsequent Practice, para 144.

[33] Nolte, Second Report on Subsequent Practice, para 164. See further Section 3.3.5.

[34] This book employs a broad understanding of the term subsequent practice in recognition of the inevitable overlap with subsequent agreements. See Section 2.3.3.

reading of Conclusion 7 and the express statements in the Commentary thereto suggest—it is difficult to come to the opposite conclusion with regard to subsequent practice.

This point is further reinforced by the last sentence of the ILC's draft conclusion, which provides that its previous sentences are without prejudice to the rules on treaty amendment or modification under the VCLT and customary international law. First, as explored later in this chapter, the 'general rule regarding the amendment of treaties' in Article 39 VCLT, when read together with Article 31(3) VCLT, confirms that agreements reached subsequently by the parties, including those established by their practice in the application of the treaty, can legitimately modify treaties.[35] Second, as to the rules on treaty amendment or modification under customary international law, many writers have argued that the rule of treaty modification by subsequent practice has been relegated to the status of unwritten (customary) law. This is pointed out in the ILC's Commentary itself:

> Many writers came to the conclusion that the negotiating States simply did not wish to address this question in the 1969 Vienna Convention and that *treaties can, as a general rule under the customary law of treaties, indeed be modified by subsequent practice* that establishes the agreement of the parties to that effect.[36]

These discussions are still ongoing, as the topic and draft conclusions of the ILC are scheduled to be considered next at the Commission's 70th session in 2018, pending comments and observations from governments.[37]

Based on these considerations, it is submitted that the process of modification by subsequent practice is a reality, and oftentimes a practical necessity, in treaty relations. Its occurrence, however, must not be presumed, and its identification and application warrants a considerable degree of caution and sensitivity to the context and circumstances of the given case.

The analysis in this chapter begins with the drafting history of the original provision on modification by subsequent practice formulated by the ILC in its work leading up to the Vienna Convention on the Law of Treaties (Section 3.2). Section 3.3 deals with the validity, nature, and scope of the process, as well as the result of modification by subsequent practice. Section 3.4 then considers how to approach the distinction between interpretation and modification by subsequent practice. Lastly, Section 3.5 explores how crucial factors such as the type of treaty regime and specific provision can influence or limit the process, as well as how alternative treaty adaptation mechanisms can reduce the scope or need for recourse to modification by subsequent practice. Preliminary conclusions are set out in Section 3.6.

[35] See Section 3.3.4. See also Nolte, Second Report on Subsequent Practice, para 144; ILC Draft Conclusions on Subsequent Agreements and Subsequent Practice (2016), 174 para 23 (referring only to Art 31(3)(a) rather than Art 31(3) VCLT more generally); Kolb, *The Law of Treaties*, 194.

[36] ILC Draft Conclusions on Subsequent Agreements and Subsequent Practice (2016), 175 para 26 (emphasis added). See also ILC, 'Provisional summary record of the 3240th meeting', UN Doc A/CN.4/SR.3240 (2015) 5. See further Section 3.3.7 below.

[37] UNGA Res 71/140 of 19 December 2016, UN Doc A/RES/71/140 (2016) para 5.

3.2 The ILC Draft Provision on Treaty Modification by Subsequent Practice

In the course of its work on the law of treaties, the International Law Commission discussed in detail the extent to which the role of subsequent practice was to be codified in the envisioned convention. In the resulting Draft Articles on the Law of Treaties, the process of treaty modification by subsequent practice was recognized expressly in Article 68 of the ILC Draft of 1964 and Article 38 of the ILC Draft of 1966, respectively.[38] In its final version, the article read:

> A treaty may be modified by subsequent practice in the application of the treaty establishing the agreement of the parties to modify its provisions.

Together with what is now Article 31(3)(b) VCLT, this provision was meant to account for a fuller range of applications of subsequent practice in the law of treaties.[39] Its origin as a draft provision and evolution during the ILC discussions are considered in the ensuing sections, along with the reasons for its ultimate exclusion from the VCLT, which are illuminating for the discussion on the modifying effect of subsequent practice.

3.2.1 Genesis of the provision: Draft Article 56 on intertemporality

The origin of the provision on modification by subsequent practice stems from the first reading of the Draft Articles at the Commission's sixteenth session in 1964.[40] At its 728th[41] and 729th[42] meetings, the ILC produced a draft Article 56 on the 'intertemporal law'. This issue of intertemporality was first expressed by Judge Huber in the *Island of Palmas* arbitration,[43] regarding which it has been noted that '[f]ew arbitral *dicta* have been more widely cited, or have come to assume a more important place in international law.'[44] The *dictum* begins as follows:

> A juridical fact must be appreciated in the light of the law contemporary with it, and not of the law in force at the time when a dispute in regard to it arises or falls to be settled.[45]

38 1964 Draft Articles on the Law of Treaties, 198; 1966 Draft Articles on the Law of Treaties, 182.

39 See eg ILC, 'Summary record of the 876th meeting', *Summary records of the 18th session* (1966) I(2) YBILC 219 [Summary record of 876th meeting] paras 17–22.

40 ILC, *Summary records of the 16th session (11 May–24 July 1964)* (1964) I YBILC 1.

41 ILC, 'Summary record of the 728th meeting', *Summary records of the 16th session* (1964) I YBILC 33 [Summary record of 728th meeting].

42 ILC, 'Summary record of the 729th meeting', *Summary records of the 16th session* (1964) I YBILC 34 [Summary record of 729th meeting].

43 *Island of Palmas Case (Netherlands/USA)*, Award of 4 April 1928, 2 RIAA 829.

44 R Higgins, 'Time and the Law: International Perspectives on an Old Problem' (1997) 46 ICLQ 501, 515. See also P Merkouris, 'Introduction: Interpretation Is a Science, Is an Art, Is a Science' in M Fitzmaurice, O Elias, and P Merkouris (eds), *Treaty Interpretation and the Vienna Convention on the Law of Treaties: 30 Years On* (Martinus Nijhoff, 2010) 1, 4.

45 *Island of Palmas Case*, 845. This also reflects the general principle that laws should not be applied retroactively. There was some debate regarding the fact that a treaty is a juridical act, rather than a juridical fact, and that the question of intertemporality may thus not be relevant to treaty interpretation—see

Judge Huber then emphasizes the second aspect of the inter-temporal law:

> The same principle which subjects the act creative of a right to the law in force at the time the right arises, demands that the existence of the right, in other words its continued manifestation, shall follow the conditions required by the evolution of the law.[46]

In other words, a treaty must be viewed not only in light of the rules prevalent at the time of its conclusion, but also those in force at the time of application. This is, for example, why treaty provisions that come into conflict with a later *jus cogens* norm will become void.[47]

In line with Judge Huber's *dictum*, draft Article 56 was worded by ILC Special Rapporteur Sir Humphrey Waldock as follows:

Article 56—The Inter-Temporal Law

1. A treaty is to be interpreted in light of the law in force at the time when the treaty was drawn up.
2. Subject to paragraph 1, the application of a treaty shall be governed by the rules of international law in force at the time when the treaty is applied.[48]

The first paragraph of Article 56 represents the 'first leg' of the inter-temporal law, which deals with the *interpretation* of the treaty, by reference to the parties' original intention at the time of the treaty's conclusion. The second paragraph represents the 'second leg' of the inter-temporal law, which relates to the *application* of the treaty,[49] as governed by general rules of international law in force at the time of application.[50] The rationale behind each of the two branches of the inter-temporal law is difficult to contest, but pinpointing their exact relationship can be problematic.[51] This also

eg Summary record of 728th meeting, para 9 (Jiménez de Aréchaga). Other members disagreed, arguing that a treaty can be both a fact and a legal act and source of law—see eg Summary record of 729th meeting, paras 20–1 (Bartos).

46 *Island of Palmas Case*, 845.

47 See eg Art 64 VCLT.

48 Summary record of 728th meeting, 33; Summary record of 729th meeting, 34.

49 For the (largely theoretical) difference between interpretation and application, see Section 2.3.4, nn 325–7. See also Section 1.1, n 10.

50 This can be taken to include the possibility of modification by subsequent customary law. See Villiger, *Customary International Law and Treaties* (1985), para 293, citing Waldock, Third Report on the Law of Treaties, 9, para 4 (Commentary to Art 56). The inter-temporal rule should be differentiated from the question of conflicting norms stemming from different sources of international law. See Villiger, *Customary International Law and Treaties* (1985), para 293 fn 6.

51 Waldock, Third Report on the Law of Treaties, 9, para 4. See ibid. 9 para 2, citing *The North Atlantic Coast Fisheries Case* (*Great Britain/United States*), Award of 7 September 1910, 11 RIAA 167, 196, as an example of the application of the first inter-temporal rule. The Tribunal there applied an old 17th-century method of boundary delimitation to the exclusion of the so-called '10-mile rule' for bays, since the latter rule had only become established twenty-one years after the conclusion of the 1818 Treaty in question. The Treaty was intended to be a definitive settlement of the respective areas reserved to Canadian fisheries, dependent on the definition of 'bays'. Since no legal definition of 'bay' existed at the time of the treaty's conclusion, the Tribunal applied the geographical rather than legal concept, thus avoiding the question of which legal concept—temporal or contemporary—would have otherwise applied. Such problems seem especially relevant in fields such as the law of the sea, where there has been significant evolution in the law regarding coastal waters and the continental shelf.

relates to the question of the role of subsequent practice in elucidating the original and contemporary intentions of the parties:

> [W]hen States create a legal relationship, they undoubtedly do this bearing in mind the normative environment as it existed at the moment when the relationship was formed. Or in other words, deference to the law in force at the time when a treaty is concluded takes best account of the intent of the parties. Nevertheless, no legal relationship can remain unaffected by time. This is confirmed already by the need to take into account the subsequent practice of the parties.[52]

Numerous questions were raised regarding the two seemingly contradictory paragraphs of draft Article 56 during the ILC discussions. Several members insisted that the two paragraphs actually dealt with completely different problems, admitting that 'what caused a shock at first sight' was the fact that the two principles, though both correct, were placed alongside each other in the same article.[53] By contrast, another member pointed out that these two 'legs' of the inter-temporal law—one looking to the past, the other to the present—in fact operate for the same reason, namely, to determine the parties' actual intention:

> The intention of the parties should be controlling, and there seemed to be two possibilities so far as that intention was concerned: either they had meant to incorporate in the treaty some legal concept that would remain unchanged, or, if they had no such intention, the legal concepts might be subject to change and would then have to be interpreted not only in the context of the instrument, but also within the framework of the entire legal order to which they belong. *The free operation of the will of the parties should not be prevented by crystallizing every concept as it had been at the time when the treaty was drawn up.*[54]

Other ILC members insisted that it was not possible to draw a practical distinction between interpretation and application at all, as Waldock had attempted to do in the formulation of the draft article. What they considered relevant is whether international law had changed following the conclusion of the treaty, which relates not to application but rather to *modification* of treaties by subsequent law (*lex posterior derogat anteriori*).[55] This latter point must be qualified depending on the situation. For one thing, as already seen in Chapter 2, taking into account subsequent changes in the law or the meaning of certain terms in the process of treaty interpretation or application does not necessarily lead to treaty modification,[56] a topic also discussed at length in the present chapter.[57] Moreover, the fact that the law has changed does not necessarily mean the parties have to modify the treaty accordingly: for instance, the principle of *lex specialis derogat lege generali* dictates that even where a subsequent

[52] Koskenniemi, Fragmentation Report, para 476. The question of how the two branches of the inter-temporal law relate to the purpose of subsequent practice of shedding light on the original versus contemporaneous intention of the parties was discussed in eg Section 2.1.

[53] Summary record of 729th meeting, para 28 (De Luna). See also Summary record of 728th meeting, para 13 (Rosenne); Summary record of 729th meeting, paras 52 (Ago), 54 (Lachs).

[54] Summary record of 728th meeting, para 10 (Jiménez de Aréchaga) (emphasis added). See also Higgins, 'Time and the Law', 515–19.

[55] Summary record of 728th meeting, paras 6–7 (Verdross).

[56] See in particular Section 2.5.3. [57] See Section 3.4.

rule of customary law has emerged, unless it is one of *jus cogens*, the parties to a treaty can choose to ignore it in keeping with the treaty's provisions.[58] Nevertheless, the second branch of the inter-temporal law is undoubtedly relevant for the process of modification by subsequent practice, and indeed formed the basis for the draft provision on the topic, discussed below.

Certain members argued that tackling the substance of Article 56 might even require drafting a new text to address the relation between treaty and non-treaty rules. Article 56(2) posed the challenge of reconciling, as far as possible, 'the stability of conventional international law and the flexibility of customary international law'.[59] Most importantly, certain members of the Commission strongly in favour of recognizing the validity of tacit treaty modification underlined the frequency with which the process occurred in practice, underscoring that implicit in the scope of Article 56(2) was the 'problem of the possible transformation of the clauses of a treaty by custom and tacit agreement of the parties'.[60]

An interesting question was raised as to whether the principle in Article 56 applies in the same manner to 'law-making treaties', which tend to 'take on a life of [their] own, independent of the will of the parties at the time of conclusion'.[61] Another ILC member also noted that inter-temporality touched upon the general legal principle that new procedural rules automatically take precedence over previous ones as an application of the *lex posterior* maxim.[62] This posits a distinction between, on the one hand, substantive rules that create rights, and, on the other hand, procedural rules that enable them. In relation to the latter, the precedence between the first and second leg of the inter-temporal law is clear: had the parties, at the time of the conclusion of the treaty, been able to foresee changes that could have made it procedurally easier for them to carry out their obligations, they would have accepted them. Thus, modification by subsequent practice affecting procedural rather than substantive treaty provisions can be easier for States to recognize and accept. The extent to which different types of treaty regimes and treaty provisions vary the effects of subsequent practice are explored further below.[63]

A notable remnant of the inter-temporal rule, and specifically of its second leg, in the current Vienna Convention, can be found in the reference to 'any [other] relevant rules of international law applicable in the relations between the parties' contained in Article 31(3)(c) VCLT.[64] This provision, already touched upon in Chapter 2,[65] embodies the principle of 'systemic integration' and entails that rules

58 This was also pointed out by certain ILC members during the 1966 discussions. See further Ch 4.

59 Summary record of 729th meeting, paras 10 (Reuter), 24 (Tsuruoka).

60 Ibid. para 43 (Tunkin).

61 Summary record of 728th meeting, paras 6–7 (Verdross), referring to Art 27 of the UN Charter, discussed in Section 5.2.1 of this book, and Art 18 of the League of Nations Covenant, according to which treaties could not become binding without being registered with the Secretariat, both of which have been modified by practice.

62 Summary record of 728th meeting, paras 13–14 (Paredes).

63 See Section 3.5.

64 The temporal element was also considered to be 'implicitly covered by the concept of good faith'—ILC, 'Summary record of the 870th meeting', *Summary records of the 18th session* (1966) I(2) YBILC 185, para 72 (Jiménez de Aréchaga).

65 See eg Section 2.3.4.

that have developed subsequent to the conclusion of the treaty, such as subsequent customary law, are to be taken into account in the interpretation of the treaty. Its relevance for the present subject matter is discussed further in Chapter 4 with regard to the effects of subsequent customary law.[66]

Generally, these considerations reveal that the question of the inter-temporal law underscores the complexities involved in distinguishing between treaty interpretation, application, and modification by subsequent practice, as well as subsequent custom.

3.2.2 The 1964 Provision on Treaty Modification by Subsequent Agreement, Subsequent Practice, and Subsequent Customary Law: Draft Articles 73 and 69A

In his Third Report on the Law of Treaties, and following the discussions on draft Article 56, Special Rapporteur Waldock chose to deal with the two branches of the inter-temporal law in separate articles: one on treaty interpretation, the other based on the idea that 'the legal effects of a treaty, as of any other legal act, are influenced by the evolution of the law'.[67] With regard to the latter provision, Waldock stated that although sometimes an interpretation adopted by parties to a treaty can diverge from the 'natural and ordinary meaning of the terms', hence blurring the line between interpretation and modification, the two processes are nonetheless distinct.[68] Thus, he proposed Article 73 in place of what had been Article 56(2). The provision was discussed at the ILC's 765th,[69] 766th,[70] and 767th[71] meetings:

Article 73—Effect of a Later Customary Rule or of a Later Agreement on Interpretation of a Treaty

The interpretation at any time of the terms of a treaty (…) shall take account of:

(a) the emergence of any later rule of customary international law affecting the subject-matter of the treaty and binding upon all the parties;
(b) any later agreement between all the parties to the treaty and relating to its subject-matter;
(c) any subsequent practice in relation to the treaty evidencing the consent of all the parties to an extension or modification of the treaty.

Notably, the ILC members hardly questioned the substance of this provision on informal treaty modification. Rather, they focused mainly on the accuracy of its phrasing and on figuring out its proper location in the draft articles. The Special Rapporteur considered it 'prudent to state only the broad principle and not to attempt to define its results'.[72] He explained that Article 73 covered instances when

[66] See eg Section 4.4.2.
[67] Waldock, Third Report on the Law of Treaties, 61, para 31.
[68] Ibid. 60, para 25.
[69] ILC, 'Summary record of the 765th meeting', *Summary records of the 16th session* (1964) I YBILC 275.
[70] Summary record of 766th meeting, 282.
[71] ILC, 'Summary record of the 767th meeting', *Summary records of the 16th session* (1964) I YBILC 291 [Summary record of 767th meeting].
[72] Waldock, Third Report on the Law of Treaties, 61, para 32.

subsequent practice could not be reconciled with the ordinary meaning of a treaty, despite purporting to be an application of it.[73] In respect of sub-paragraph (c), he added that such modification by subsequent practice could eventually generate a norm of customary international law, in which case it would be more analogous to sub-paragraph (a) on modification by subsequent customary law. Despite the interconnectedness and overlap between subsequent practice and subsequent customary law,[74] he considered it 'more appropriate and more usual to classify it as a case of variation of the treaty by tacit agreement'.[75] This distinction is also mirrored in the approach of the present book: while the current chapter focuses on modification by subsequent practice, as reflected in draft Article 73(c), the issue of modification of treaties by subsequent customary law (draft Article 73(a))—and the corresponding analysis of the relevant ILC discussions—are dealt with separately in Chapter 4.

It was noted that the three elements contained in draft Article 73—namely, subsequent agreements, subsequent practice of the parties in the application of the treaty, and subsequent rules of customary law—related to treaty interpretation as well as treaty modification. As a result, the Special Rapporteur decided to codify the elements in draft Article 73(a) and (b) (subsequent agreements and subsequent practice) as means of treaty *interpretation* in what is now Article 31(3)(a) and (b) VCLT. All three elements in Article 73 were also included as means of treaty *modification* in a new draft Article 69A. This provision was introduced at the Commission's 769th[76] and 770th[77] meetings. It read:

Article 69A [subsequently Article 68[78]]—Modification of a Treaty by a Subsequent Treaty, by Subsequent Practice or by Customary Law

The operation of a treaty may also be modified:

(a) By a subsequent treaty between the parties relating to the same subject matter to the extent that their provisions are incompatible;
(b) By a subsequent practice of the parties in the application of the treaty establishing their tacit agreement to an alteration or extension of its provisions; or
(c) By the subsequent emergence of a new rule of customary law relating to matters dealt with in the treaty and binding upon all the parties.[79]

Waldock highlighted that the article dealt with the 'accidental' modification of the operation of a treaty by subsequent events, and that in two of the three cases covered by it—namely, sub-paragraph (a) on modification by a subsequent treaty, and sub-paragraph (c) on modification by subsequent customary law—there was no intention to amend the text of the treaty. Whereas sub-paragraph (b) concerned the subsequent practice of the parties in the application of the treaty, sub-paragraphs

[73] Summary record of 767th meeting, para 39. [74] See Ch 4, particularly Section 4.6.
[75] Waldock, Third Report on the Law of Treaties, 62, para 33.
[76] ILC, 'Summary record of the 769th meeting', *Summary records of the 16th session* (1964) I YBILC 308 [Summary record of 769th meeting].
[77] ILC, 'Summary record of the 770th meeting', *Summary records of the 18th session* (1966) I(2) YBILC 315 [Summary record of 770th meeting] 318.
[78] 1964 Draft Articles on the Law of Treaties, 198.
[79] Summary record of 769th meeting, 308; Summary record of 770th meeting, 318.

(a) and (c) concerned the 'impact on a treaty of acts done *outside* and *not in relation to it*'.[80] This brings us back to the question of whether an external rule, such as subsequently emerged customary law, can impact a treaty without the concurrent intention by the parties to that effect, an issue discussed further in Chapter 4.[81]

What is most significant is that the ILC thereby recognized the existence of the rules enshrined in the draft article, particularly sub-paragraph (b) regarding subsequent practice: 'The 1964 debate in the ILC never cast doubts on the concept of modification.'[82]

A proposal to delete the word 'tacit' in sub-paragraph (b) was adopted unanimously, although it is unclear whether the phrasing 'tacit agreement' was in itself problematic or—as seems more likely—simply posed an unnecessary limitation. Following this amendment, the article was adopted unanimously, and became Article 68 of the 1964 Draft Articles.[83]

3.2.3 The 1966 Provision on Treaty Modification by Subsequent Agreement, Subsequent Practice, and Subsequent Customary Law: Draft Article 68

In 1966, discussions on the provision on treaty modification resumed during the second reading of the Draft Articles on the Law of Treaties at the ILC's eighteenth session.[84] Waldock's Sixth Report on the Law of Treaties contains comments by various governments,[85] as well as the Special Rapporteur's own observations and proposals regarding draft Article 68 (formerly Article 69A). These deliberations are noteworthy. As the Special Rapporteur was keen to point out, no government had questioned the content of the provision.[86] The United States, for instance, expressly acknowledged that paragraph (b) of Article 68 reflected 'long-standing and widely accepted practice'.[87] However, some governments argued that sub-paragraph (b) on modification by subsequent practice was redundant since it was indistinguishable in its practical effects from draft Article 69(3)(b), now Article 31(3)(b) VCLT, on interpretation by subsequent practice.[88]

80 Waldock, Sixth Report on the Law of Treaties, 97, para 14 (emphasis added).

81 See in particular Section 4.5.1.

82 Villiger, *Customary International Law and Treaties* (1985), para 294.

83 Summary record of 770th meeting, paras 45, 49.

84 ILC, *Summary records of the 18th session (4 May–19 July 1966)* (1966) I(2) YBILC 1.

85 'Comments by Governments on parts I, II and III of the draft articles on the law of treaties drawn up by the Commission at its fourteenth, fifteenth and sixteenth sessions' (1966) II YBILC 279 [Comments by Governments on the 1966 Draft Articles] eg 300 (Israel), 323 (Pakistan), 335 (Portugal), 342 (Turkey), 345 (UK), 358 (US).

86 Waldock, Sixth Report on the Law of Treaties, 89, para 7.

87 Ibid. *Contra* M Sorel and V Boré Eveno, 'Article 31 (1969)' in O Corten and P Klein (eds), *The Vienna Conventions on the Law of Treaties: A Commentary*, vol I (OUP, 2011) 805, 828, citing *Gabčíkovo-Nagymaros Project*, paras 100, 114 (but acknowledging that the *Namibia Advisory Opinion* contradicts this conclusion).

88 Waldock, Sixth Report on the Law of Treaties, 89 para 7 (on the views of the Government of Israel). See further Bowman, '"Normalizing"', 337, citing TO Elias, *The International Court of Justice and Some Contemporary Problems: Essays on International Law* (Martinus Nijhoff, 1983) 98–100.

Waldock's observation highlights one of the most important points to be drawn from the discussions in the ILC, namely, that objections to the provision on modification by subsequent practice related more to concerns regarding its overlap with other rules in the Draft Articles, than to the belief that its inclusion would constitute an incorrect reflection of international law.[89] This may also reflect a misunderstanding on the part of certain governments as to the scope of the respective provisions on interpretation and modification by subsequent practice.

Like governments, most ILC members considered that subsequent practice is undoubtedly capable of modifying treaties.[90] They underscored, however, that it could only do so under certain conditions.[91] Namely, the practice must provide evidence of agreement to modify the treaty provisions, and such agreement should comprise (nearly) all the parties to the treaty.[92] Other important considerations in this respect included the distinction between modification among all the parties and modification *inter se*,[93] and whether a distinction regarding the possibility of modification by subsequent practice should be made between essential and secondary or minor treaty provisions[94]—to the extent that one can determine which provisions are to be qualified as 'essential'.[95] While expressing his appreciation for these 'judicious' remarks, Waldock emphasized that they raised extremely delicate, and perhaps unnecessary, issues with regard to draft Article 68:

> While appreciating the reasons that lay behind those comments, as a draughtsman he would shrink from the task of having to cover the points in the text of sub-paragraph (b). Nor was it even certain that the attempt would be justified.[96]

In his own comments, Waldock noted that the substance of Article 68 and its relation to other draft articles—notably, Article 63 on the application of treaties having incompatible provisions, Articles 65 to 67 on formal treaty amendment and agreements to modify between certain of the parties only, and Article 69 containing the general rule of interpretation—would require close and careful examination by the Commission.[97]

There was significant debate as to the overlap between Article 68(b) and Article 65 containing the general rule on formal treaty amendment.[98] The latter draft article provided that 'a treaty may be amended by agreement between the parties', unless the treaty stipulates otherwise. A number of ILC members suggested that the two provisions be combined by moving Article 68 back to the 'more essential'

[89] J Wessel, 'Relational Contract Theory and Treaty Interpretation: End-Game Treaties v Dynamic Obligations' (2004) 60 NYU Ann Surv Am L 149, 165.

[90] ILC, 'Summary record of the 866th meeting', *Summary records of the 18th session* (1966) I(2) YBILC 163 [Summary record of 866th meeting] para 17 (Tunkin).

[91] Ibid. paras 17–19 (Tunkin), 45 (El-Erian).

[92] Ibid. para 17 (Tunkin).

[93] Ibid. paras 18–19 (Tunkin).

[94] Ibid. para 18 (Tunkin).

[95] An indication could be if derogation from a specific provision requires derogation from the object and purpose of the treaty as a whole—ibid.

[96] Ibid. para 64 (Waldock).

[97] Waldock, Sixth Report on the Law of Treaties, 88–91.

[98] The overlap between Arts 65 and 68 was also a prominent subject of debate during the discussions on Art 68 at the ILC's 866th Meeting—see eg Summary record of 866th meeting, paras 37 (Yasseen), 55 (Tunkin), 29–34, 61 (Tsuruoka). Most members agreed that Art 68 was partly covered by Art 65.

Article 65.[99] However, other members of the Commission, including the Special Rapporteur,[100] were keen to point out that the ideas in the two articles were very different, underlining, for instance, that while Article 65 dealt with treaty amendment, Article 68 dealt with questions relating to treaty operation. Following the ILC's 866th meeting, the Drafting Committee decided not to combine the two articles so as to emphasize the distinction between informal treaty modification by subsequent practice and formal treaty amendments.[101]

The other principal overlap was considered to be between Article 68(b) and Article 69(3)(b) on interpretation by subsequent practice.[102] It had already been pointed out in the ILC discussions in 1964 in relation to the draft article on interpretation that subsequent practice is capable of transforming a treaty 'so profoundly that it was made to serve a purpose diametrically opposed to the one for which it had been concluded',[103] especially in the context of international organizations.[104] This also provides one answer to the question of whether subsequent practice can affect the object and purpose of a treaty.[105] One ILC member expressed the opinion that the distinction between the two provisions was merely one of degree, given that in both cases the change is achieved by stretching the meaning of treaty terms.[106] Many ILC members refuted this remark, stressing the fundamental and necessary, albeit difficult, distinction between interpretation and modification.[107] In the comments by governments, the Israeli representative had also expressed the opinion that the contents of Article 68(b) were already covered by the provision on interpretation by subsequent practice. In response, Waldock emphasized that the Commission had already made clear that, though the line may sometimes be blurred, the two processes are legally distinct and must be codified separately. Case law was cited in support of this view,[108] such as the *Temple of Préah Vihéar* case and the 1963 *Air Transport Services Arbitration* (*US/France*), both of which are discussed in Chapter 5.[109]

In this connection, it was suggested that in the case of bilateral treaties, the distinction between subsequent practice evidencing an agreement to *modify* the treaty and subsequent practice evidencing an agreement as to an *authentic interpretation* of the treaty may not be relevant for practical purposes.[110] Thus, in the *Temple of*

[99] ILC, 'Summary record of the 859th meeting', *Summary records of the 18th session* (1966) I(2) YBILC 112, paras 9 (Verdross), 12 (Rosenne), 16 (De Luna).

[100] Ibid. paras 18 (Jiménez de Aréchaga), 29 (Briggs), 33 (Amado), 34–5 (Waldock).

[101] Summary record of 876th meeting, 220ff.

[102] Summary record of 866th meeting, paras 22 (De Luna), 26–7 (Briggs).

[103] Summary record of 766th meeting, paras 45–6 (Lachs). See ibid. paras 38–9 (De Luna).

[104] See ibid. para 39 (De Luna): 'The subsequent practice of the parties [to international organizations] had in many cases led to interpretations which in effect amended the instruments concerned. Nothing said in the draft articles on interpretation should be capable in any way of preventing that progressive development within international organizations.'

[105] See in particular Section 3.3.5.

[106] Summary record of 866th meeting, para 26 (Briggs).

[107] See eg ibid. para 56 (Tunkin) (radically opposing the view that Art 68 was in any way merely a matter of interpretation, since it related to practice deviating from the letter of the treaty and could not be examined through the prism of the treaty's own provisions).

[108] Waldock, Sixth Report on the Law of Treaties, 89–90, para 8.

[109] See Sections 5.2.1–5.2.2.

[110] Waldock, Sixth Report on the Law of Treaties, 89, para 8.

Préah Vihéar case,[111] despite the parties' manifest divergence from one of the points of the boundary delimited by the bilateral treaty, the ICJ held that their practice represented an authentic interpretation that prevailed over the relevant treaty provision, without calling it an outright modification.[112] But it is not the case that all instances of subsequent practice, however much at variance with the treaty text, can be classified as authentic interpretation.[113] In the *Air Transport Services Arbitration* (*US/France*),[114] the tribunal expressly held that the bilateral treaty in question had been modified by subsequent practice. Thus, for bilateral treaties, the distinction between interpretation and modification is less relevant and less controversial. Subsequent practice in relation to multilateral treaties often warrants closer scrutiny.

Moreover, Waldock pointed out that the requirement of the practice of *all* the parties in Article 69(3)(b) on interpretation by subsequent practice did not apply to Article 68(b) on modification by subsequent practice:

> Many multilateral treaties operate in practice bilaterally in the relations between each party and each other party; and it may happen that different parties apply the treaty in somewhat different ways; or that some parties apply the treaty in a way which the others do not accept as a correct interpretation of it. Clearly, on the plane of interpretation, the treaty has only one correct interpretation. But in practice it may have applications between particular parties which diverge from the interpretation and application of it by the general body of the parties. It hardly seems possible to classify such cases under the head of 'interpretation by subsequent practice' without seeming to throw overboard the essential concept of the integrity of the text of a multilateral treaty. (…) Accordingly, it is thought that the Commission was right in 1964 to distinguish between the 'interpretation' and the 'modification' of a treaty by subsequent practice.[115]

Waldock had also remarked earlier, in relation to the draft article on the effect of an amending or revising instrument on the rights and obligations of the parties, in his Third Report on the Law of Treaties to the ILC, that:

> History furnishes many instances of treaty regimes amended or revised by a new treaty concluded between some only of the parties to the earlier treaty. (…) The rule requiring the unanimous consent of all the original parties for revision (…) has in the past been honoured more in the breach than in the observance.[116]

[111] See Section 5.2.1.

[112] See Waldock, Sixth Report on the Law of Treaties, 89, para 8: 'If this reasoning may seem somewhat artificial (…) the case does perhaps show that for practical purposes it may not be of much moment whether in bilateral treaties subsequent practice is regarded as having its effect in the context of an interpretation or a modification of the treaty.' Of course, what courts and tribunals say in practice does not always fully reflect the effects of subsequent practice in a given case. However, this book is also not the place to speculate as to underlying reasons for specific decisions. See Sections 5.1–5.2, in particular the interim conclusions in Section 5.2.5.

[113] Waldock, Sixth Report on the Law of Treaties, 89, para 8.

[114] See Section 5.2.2.

[115] Waldock, Sixth Report on the Law of Treaties, 90, para 9.

[116] Waldock, Third Report on the Law of Treaties, 49, para 7. See also 1966 Draft Articles on the Law of Treaties, 235 para 1 (Commentary to Art 37): 'History furnishes a number of instances of *inter se* agreements which substantially changed the regime of the treaty and which overrode the objections of interested States.'

Thus, Waldock underlined an important aspect of the discussion on the potential effects of subsequent practice: the distinction between a treaty modification among all the parties and a modification *inter se*.[117] The latter is typically used to adapt the treaty to new needs or establish different, usually higher, standards among certain parties.[118] This depends on the nature of the respective treaty. For a treaty such as the Vienna Convention on Diplomatic Relations, for instance, an application that differentiates between one party and another may *ipso facto* amount to a breach of the treaty.[119] This would presumably be the same with, say, concessions under the WTO Agreements subject to the 'most favoured nation' principle.[120]

Some members argued that Article 68 could not allow for the possibility of *inter se* modification in light of Article 65 on amendment of treaties, which required the approval of the majority or all of the parties. Moreover, the concern was expressed that the provision on *inter se* modification would go too far given that not all the procedural safeguards set out in Article 67 on 'agreements to modify multilateral treaties between certain of the parties only',[121] that is, formal *inter se* modifications, could be extended to Article 68 on informal modification. Specifically, the concern was that *inter se* modification by subsequent practice could circumvent the requirement to notify the other parties, potentially leaving some parties unaware of the change that has taken place between the modifying parties. The Special Rapporteur agreed that the relation between Article 68 and formal amendment procedures required further clarification.

3.2.4 The 1966 Provision on Treaty Modification by Subsequent Practice: Draft Article 38

The comments by governments on the text of Article 68 and the Special Rapporteur's own reflections prompted significant changes to the provision. First, sub-paragraph (a) on modification by a subsequent treaty was dropped due to the fact that it coincided with the more comprehensive Article 63 ('application of treaties having incompatible provisions'), a change supported by virtually all members of the

117 See eg 1964 Draft Articles on the Law of Treaties with Commentaries, 197; 1966 Draft Articles on the Law of Treaties with Commentaries, 235ff.

118 Villiger, *Commentary*, 531. For instance, Art 19(1) of the 1928 Havana Convention on Treaties adopted by the Sixth International Conference of American States (1928) 29 AJIL Supp 138, cited in 1935 Harvard Draft Convention, 1203, stated that 'two or more States may agree that their relations are to be governed by rules other than those established in general conventions celebrated by them with other States'.

119 Waldock, Sixth Report on the Law of Treaties, 90, para 9.

120 See further eg Section 3.5.1(a).

121 Art 67 stated: '1. Two or more of the parties to a multilateral treaty may conclude an agreement to modify the treaty as between themselves alone if: (a) the possibility of such a modification is provided for by the treaty; or (b) the modification in question: (i) does not affect the enjoyment by the other parties of their rights under the treaty or the performance of their obligations; (ii) does not relate to a provision derogation from which is incompatible with the effective execution of the objects and purposes of the treaty as a whole; and (iii) is not prohibited by the treaty. 2. Unless in a case falling under paragraph 1(a), *the parties in question shall notify the other parties of their intention to conclude the agreement and of the modifications to the treaty for which it provides*.' (Emphasis added.)

Commission.[122] Sub-paragraph (c) was also dropped for the aforementioned reason that it overlapped with the provision on interpretation by subsequent practice.[123] Thus, as approved by the Drafting Committee following the discussions at the ILC's 866th meeting, Article 68 was confined to modification by subsequent practice alone.

The Special Rapporteur had proposed a new title and text for Article 68 based on sub-paragraph (b) alone, including a new sentence addressing the possibility of *inter se* modification:

Article 68—Modification of a Treaty by Subsequent Practice

The operation of a treaty may be modified by subsequent practice of the parties in the application of the treaty establishing their agreement to an alteration or extension of its provisions. In the case of a multilateral treaty, the rules set out in article 67, paragraph 1, apply to an alteration or extension of its provisions as between certain of the parties alone.[124]

However, following the disagreements regarding *inter se* modifications discussed earlier,[125] the second sentence on *inter se* modification was deleted, and the reference to an 'alteration or extension' of the provisions of the treaty was replaced by 'modification'. With regard to the latter, it was noted that the word 'modification' was employed to differentiate it as a *process* from formal amendments of treaty terms.[126] Thus, at the second reading of the draft articles at the ILC's 876th meeting, Briggs, Chairman of the Drafting Committee, proposed the following new title and text for Article 68:

Article 68—Modification of Treaties by Subsequent Practice

A treaty may be modified by subsequent practice of the parties in the application of the treaty establishing their agreement to modify its provisions.[127]

The main question raised was whether 'all' the parties would need to overtly contribute to the subsequent practice. Most members considered that treaty modification by subsequent practice represented what Tunkin termed the 'customary way of modifying treaties': it is not necessary that all the parties follow the practice, but it must at least be tolerated, if not accepted, by all of them.[128] The Special Rapporteur, along with most other ILC members, argued that to require the consent of all the parties, rather than tacit acceptance or tolerance, would go beyond existing practices in relation to multilateral treaties by conferring upon Article 68 a 'rigidity that was quite uncharacteristic of contemporary international law in the matter'.[129] The reference to the practice of the parties was sufficiently clear, and adding the word 'all' would introduce an unreasonable rule into the draft.[130] Overall, the majority of ILC members agreed that Article 68 did not require *all* the parties to actively participate

[122] See text to n 72. [123] See further Section 4.2.
[124] Waldock, Sixth Report on the Law of Treaties, 91, para 15. [125] Section 3.2.3.
[126] Summary record of 883rd meeting, para 74 (Waldock). See also ibid. para 77 (Jiménez de Aréchaga).
[127] Summary record of 876th meeting, para 11.
[128] Ibid. eg paras 24 (Tunkin), 36 (Briggs), 40 (Reuter), 42 (De Luna), 43, 55 (Waldock), 56 (Briggs).
[129] Ibid. para 55 (Waldock). See also Feldman, 'Evolving Treaty Obligations', 669.
[130] Summary record of 883rd meeting, para 81 (Ago).

in the practice; it is sufficient that the practice establish the *agreement* of all the parties.[131]

It was further suggested that the requirements for establishing modifications by subsequent practice had to be equally stringent to those for establishing formal amendments.[132] This would also imply that the conditions for formal *inter se* modification under Article 41 VCLT would apply to tacit *inter se* modification by subsequent practice.[133] If so, tacit *inter se* modifications would have to meet two conditions: first, such a modification must not affect the rights or add to the burdens of the other parties (Article 41(1)(b)(i) VCLT);[134] second, it must 'not relate to a provision, derogation from which would be incompatible with the effective execution of the object and purpose of the treaty as a whole' (Article 41(1)(b)(ii)).[135] The question of the relation between modification by subsequent practice and formal amendments was not addressed further by the Commission.

At the Commission's 883rd meeting, Article 68, in its revised form,[136] was adopted by 11 votes to none, with 4 abstentions. The final text of the article, renumbered, was then adopted without comments at the 893rd meeting.[137] It read:

Article 38: Modification of Treaties by Subsequent Practice

A treaty may be modified by subsequent practice in the application of the treaty establishing the agreement of the parties to modify its provisions.[138]

The Commentary to Article 38 reiterates that even if not every party actively participates in the practice, the practice must be such as to establish the agreement of the parties as a whole to the modification in question.[139] The Commentary also makes clear that subsequent practice modifying a treaty must be consistent and must establish the common consent of the parties to the application of the treaty in a manner different from what is laid down in its provisions—a process distinct from treaty interpretation.[140] This is one important difference with Article 68: in the latter case, the Commission had emphasized that modification takes place when the subsequent practice of the parties diverges from treaty interpretation to such an extent that the application of the treaty becomes incompatible with its express provisions. This definition of modification was attenuated in the Commentary to Article 38 in 1966, which mentioned only that the provision concerns the application of the treaty in a way not envisioned in its provisions.[141] This definition could

131 Ibid. para 85 (Waldock).

132 Summary record of 876th meeting, paras 25 (Tunkin), 59 (Reuter).

133 Shaw, *International Law*, 931. See also the previous discussion in Section 3.2.3.

134 See I Voicu, *De l'interprétation authentique des traités internationaux* (Pédone, 1968) 93–4.

135 Aust, *Modern Treaty Law*, 222. See also Shaw, *International Law*, 931. See eg Art 311(3) LOSC, which allows States to conclude agreements modifying the operation of the Convention, as long as there is no incompatibility with the object and purpose of the Convention or the rights and obligations of other parties. cf Koskenniemi, Fragmentation Report, para 279, on the 'rather loosely' formulated reference to compatibility in Art 311 LOSC.

136 ILC, 'Revised Draft Articles' (1966) II YBILC 112, 119.

137 Summary record of 893rd meeting, 330. See also Summary record of 894th meeting, 336.

138 1966 Draft Articles on the Law of Treaties, 236.

139 Summary record of 894th meeting, paras 1–2.

140 1966 Draft Articles on the Law of Treaties, 236 para 1 (Commentary to Art 38).

141 Ibid.

be regarded as providing an even broader scope for modification by subsequent practice.

3.2.5 The 1968–1969 Vienna Conference on the Law of Treaties: Deletion of Article 38

At the end of its 18th session in 1966, the International Law Commission completed the second and final reading of the draft articles on the law of treaties. It submitted its final report to the General Assembly, with the recommendation that the latter convene an international conference to discuss the articles and conclude a convention on the law of treaties. By means of General Assembly resolution 2287 (XXII) of 6 December 1967,[142] the first session of the United Nations Conference on the Law of Treaties was convened in Vienna in March 1968, attended by representatives of over 100 States.

Draft Article 38 was discussed at the 37th and 38th meetings of the 1968 session of the Conference.[143] A majority of State representatives expressed opposition to the article, rehashing many of the arguments discussed in the ILC in 1964 and 1966. A number of States submitted amendments for its deletion, and one amendment, by France, proposed the insertion of certain qualifications to the article.[144] A few delegates went so far as to argue that Article 38 did not reflect an existing rule of international law.[145] However, many more States disagreed with this statement and argued that modification by subsequent practice was based on an existing principle of international law and a 'legal fact'.[146]

Some State representatives also considered that the case law confirming such modification was not yet soundly established: 'an arbitral award, however well-founded, was not sufficient to make the solution applicable to a specific case into a general norm of international law'.[147] Since the case law confirming informal modification was still recent at the time, the rule may have been difficult to regard as already having 'ripened' into customary international law.[148] As Tunkin points out, 'it may well be that the Commission went too far and frightened the Conference by such a sweeping proposal'.[149]

[142] UNGA Res 2287 (XXII) of 6 December 1967, UN Doc A/RES/2287(XXII).

[143] 37th Meeting of the Committee of the Whole, 207ff; 38th Meeting of the Committee of the Whole, 210ff.

[144] See text to n 159. The following amendments were submitted: UN Doc A/CONF.39/*C*.1/L.143 (Finland); UN Doc A/CONF.39/*C*.1/L.200 (Japan); UN Doc A/CONF.39/*C*.1/L.206 (Venezuela); UN Doc A/CONF.39/*C*.1/L.220 (Vietnam); UN Doc A/CONF.39/*C*.1/L.241 (France).

[145] 37th Meeting of the Committee of the Whole, para 208 (Japan); 38th Meeting of the Committee of the Whole, paras 27 (Turkey), 36 (Uruguay), 47 (The Netherlands).

[146] See eg 38th Meeting of the Committee of the Whole, paras 8 (Iraq), 22 (Italy), 33 (Austria), 48 (Israel), 49 (Cambodia), 50 (Switzerland), 51 (Argentina).

[147] Ibid. para 36 (Uruguay). cf ibid. para 51 (Argentina).

[148] This situation may since have changed. See eg Feldman, 'Evolving Treaty Obligations', 705, noting 'the growing acceptance of informal modification (…) under customary law since the adoption of the VCLT.'

[149] G Tunkin, 'Is General International Law Customary Law Only?' (1993) 4 EJIL 534, 540 (adding that, although instances of modification by subsequent practice 'are not rare and nobody considers them unlawful', it may not be advisable to codify such an 'unlimited rule'). See also Section 3.3.7.

A number of delegates argued that Article 38 could 'open the door to all kinds of interpretations, in the course of which the treaty might lose its substance', which could lead to uncertainty or instability in treaty relations in various respects.[150] These representatives emphasized the importance of the element of certainty inherent in formal amendment procedures, outside of which any modification would lack a legal basis.[151] This latter argument seems to reflect the fact that, at the time, many delegates did not fully appreciate the necessity of such modification in certain circumstances for the purpose of overcoming the obstacles to formal amendments, and thus may not have perceived the full significance of the process codified in Article 38.[152]

Some representatives also considered that the process of modification by subsequent practice could threaten the principle of *pacta sunt servanda*[153] and 'nullify written law'.[154] This point met with opposition from many other State representatives. One of them highlighted that international law is 'not a slave to formalism and by reason of its nature must adapt itself to practical realities'.[155] Generally, the concern regarding *pacta sunt servanda* is misguided in light of the fact that any modification by subsequent practice is based on the agreement of the parties—and on the principle of good faith.[156] As Sir Humphrey Waldock, as an Expert Consultant at the Conference, pointed out, many of the criticisms advanced by certain delegations show that they were not taking into account the final words 'establishing the agreement of the parties to modify its provisions' in Article 38.[157] The article was compatible with general principles of international law, fundamental rules of treaty law, and, especially, with the *pacta sunt servanda* principle.[158]

Another question arose as to whether the unqualified recognition of modification by subsequent practice in Article 38 would make redundant the specific provisions on amendment procedures contained in many international agreements. This prompted the aforementioned proposal by France to insert in Article 38 the qualification that the principle codified therein would not apply when a treaty itself specifies the manner in which it is to be revised, nor when the form and conditions of its conclusion bar its modification under different conditions.[159] This proposal is

150 37th Meeting of the Committee as a Whole, paras 62 (Vietnam), 74 (Spain); 38th Meeting of the Committee of the Whole, paras 31 (Guinea), 40 (Cuba), 42 (Portugal).

151 37th Meeting of the Committee of the Whole, paras 60 (Venezuela), 62 (Vietnam).

152 38th Meeting of the Committee of the Whole, para 53 (Czechoslovakia) ('it might be asked why, if the parties agreed to modify a treaty on the basis of their practice, and if in most cases they had to resort to a formal agreement to do so, they should not simply revise the treaty').

153 37th Meeting of the Committee of the Whole, para 75 (Chile); 38th Meeting of the Committee of the Whole, paras 30–2 (Guinea), 35 (Uruguay), 40 (Cuba), 42 (Portugal).

154 38th Meeting of the Committee of the Whole, para 40 (Cuba).

155 Ibid. para 22 (Italy). See also 37th Meeting of the Committee of the Whole, para 10 (Iraq); 38th Meeting of the Committee of the Whole, paras 49 (Cambodia), 51 (Argentina), 55 (Waldock).

156 Ibid. para 56 (Waldock).

157 Ibid. para 55 (Waldock).

158 Ibid. para 10 (Iraq); see also ibid. para 51 (Argentina).

159 37th Meeting of the Committee of the Whole, para 64 (France). A number of delegates expressed support for the proposed amendment, or in any case their lack of opposition to it—see 38th Meeting of the Committee of the Whole, eg paras 25 (Italy), 33 (Austria), 49 (Cambodia), 51 (Argentina), 75 (Chile), 76 (Canada). One delegate noted the difficulty in practice of determining, according to the

one worth considering and is examined, along with other factors that may limit or exclude recourse to modification by subsequent practice, further below.[160]

Moreover, a large number of States expressed the fear that the process of modification by subsequent practice would violate their national constitutional law by circumventing national procedures for the approval of treaties and subsequent amendments thereto.[161] This was a point that had not been brought up during the ILC discussions, although it was linked to the concern that Article 38 would allow State officials—even relatively low-ranking ones—to modify treaty obligations without their respective States being aware of it,[162] an issue that *had* been discussed in the ILC.[163] As to the point regarding low-ranking officials, the presumption against change in legal rules implies that a significant amount of practice is required to modify a treaty provision, consistent with the requirement of 'agreement' in Article 38, allowing higher State authorities to react to the practice, and thus providing an effective safeguard.[164]

Waldock, in his capacity as Expert Consultant at the Conference, did not regard the domestic constitutional law objection to the draft article as a valid problem. He noted that modifications by subsequent practice 'had never raised any constitutional problem', nor did they usually affect the main basis of the treaty or give rise to any objections from parliaments.[165] Another potential consideration, to supplement Waldock's practical observation, is that modification by subsequent practice is not very different in this sense from the operation of customary international law.[166] Customary international law often becomes binding upon States without the active involvement of most States' legislative or executive organs, even when its content diverges from that of existing treaty provisions.[167] While the constitutional argument raised during the Conference is certainly a practical or political concern, it is not a valid reason for the deletion of Article 38.[168]

Most States hardly objected to the substance of the provision, but rather pointed out the problem of the lack of specificity and methodology for analysing subsequent practice in the draft provision. Various definitional and functional issues arose

proposed amendment, 'whether the provisions of a treaty or the conditions of its conclusion were such as to constitute a bar to its modification by subsequent practice.'—ibid. para 16 (Poland).

160 See Section 3.5.

161 37th Meeting of the Committee of the Whole, paras 58 (Japan), 63 (France), 68 (Spain); 38th Meeting of the Committee of the Whole, paras 1 (Soviet Union), 17 (Poland), 21 (Colombia), 36 (Uruguay), 41 (Cuba), 43 (Philippines).

162 37th Meeting of the Committee of the Whole, para 68 (Spain); 38th Meeting of the Committee of the Whole, para 6 (United States). cf 38th Meeting of the Committee of the Whole, para 9 (Iraq): '[Article 38] provided that agreement to modify a treaty was established by practice, that was to say by a series of acts: not just any practice, but one which could be attributed to States. That excluded an act by a consul or other official who exceeded his powers.'

163 See further Section 3.3.3(a).

164 Akehurst, 'Hierarchy of the Sources', 277; Villiger, *Customary International Law and Treaties* (1985), para 19.

165 38th Meeting of the Committee of the Whole, para 57 (Waldock).

166 See also the comment discussed in Section 3.2.4 that modification by subsequent practice could be termed the 'customary way of modifying treaties'—Summary record of 876th meeting, eg para 24 (Tunkin).

167 See generally Ch 4, in particular Section 4.3.

168 See further Section 3.3.2(a).

regarding the use of specific terms in Article 38, including the concept of 'practice', the meaning of 'parties', the notion of 'consistency' of practice, and the length of time necessary to establish it.[169] Another problem was the unclear relation between the formation of customary law and the implied agreement contemplated in the draft article.[170] The question from previous ILC discussions of whether modification by subsequent practice should be restricted to 'secondary' treaty provisions, as opposed to 'essential' provisions, was also raised.[171] Moreover, many State representatives pointed out that Article 38 overlapped with too many other proposed articles. A recurrent argument, mirroring the preceding ILC discussions, was that it was an unnecessary duplication of Article 31(3)(b) VCLT (then draft Article 27(3)(b)), and that, moreover, the processes of interpretation and modification covered by the respective articles were indistinguishable in their practical effects.[172] However, as Waldock pointed out at the Conference, the ILC had repeatedly emphasized that, although the line between modification and interpretation may sometimes be blurred, the two processes are legally distinct and must be codified separately.[173]

For the abovementioned reasons, many of the State representatives pointed to the difficulty of trying to codify the process of modification by subsequent practice, which some considered 'far too complicated to be solved satisfactorily in a single article which simply stated that a treaty might be modified by subsequent practice'.[174] One representative argued that, though it was true that subsequent practice could modify treaties, the process of modification by subsequent practice fell outside the scope of the envisioned convention, which would be limited to treaties concluded between States in written form.[175] This statement touches upon the question of the nature of the result of a treaty modification by subsequent practice and its relation to the underlying treaty.[176] In any case, the qualifications found to be lacking in Article 38 posited Waldock to comment that if the Commission had been able to devote more time to the law of treaties, 'it might have examined the problem again and drafted a more elaborate text'.[177] These statements speak to the underlying validity of the provision, and the mainly practical rather than substantive reasons for which it was considered problematic.

Contrary to what certain comments by State representatives at the Conference appear to indicate, Article 38 contained sufficient qualifications to at least ensure the consensual nature of the process of modification by subsequent practice—safeguards that State representatives at the Conference seem to have failed to fully

[169] 37th Meeting of the Committee of the Whole, paras 71–3 (Spain); 38th Meeting of the Committee of the Whole, para 35 (Uruguay).

[170] 37th Meeting of the Committee of the Whole, paras 72 (Spain), 57 (Finland).

[171] Ibid. para 69 (Spain), citing Summary record of 866th meeting, para 18 (Tunkin). See also Section 3.2.3.

[172] 37th Meeting of the Committee of the Whole, paras 57 (Finland), 59 (Venezuela), 66 (Spain); 38th Meeting of the Committee of the Whole, paras 28 (Turkey), 48 (Israel).

[173] 38th Meeting of the Committee of the Whole, para 55 (Waldock).

[174] Ibid. para 15 (Poland).

[175] Ibid. para 14 (Poland).

[176] See further Section 3.3.6(a).

[177] 38th Meeting of the Committee of the Whole, para 55 (Waldock).

appreciate.[178] As one ILC member had pointed out during the drafting of the article prior to the Conference, modifications envisaged by Article 38, though not formal amendments, were still to some extent 'formalized' by the requirement that subsequent practice establish the agreement of the parties to modify treaty provisions.[179] Generally, the ILC members involved in the drafting process prior to the UN Conference had taken a rather more open approach to the issue of modification by subsequent practice than State representatives in 1968, focused more on the technicalities of its codification than on the implications of codifying it as such.

Amendments to delete Article 38 were ultimately adopted by 53 votes to 15, with 26 abstentions.[180] Conclusions must be drawn not from the number of States that rejected the codification of modification by subsequent practice,[181] nor from the mere fact of the draft article's deletion,[182] but rather from their reasons for doing so.[183] As discussed below, these indicate that most participants did not reject the underlying process itself.[184]

3.2.6 Conclusions based on the 1964–1968 discussions

Two main lines of reasoning led to the deletion of Article 38 from the final provisions on the law of treaties at the Vienna Conference—these reasons are, in fact, similar to those pointed out in relation to the draft conclusion[185] regarding modification by subsequent practice currently under discussion in the ILC.[186] First, the 1964 and

[178] Feldman, 'Evolving Treaty Obligations', 671–2. See also 38th Meeting of the Committee of the Whole, para 55 (Waldock): 'Several of the criticisms made seemed (...) to show that certain delegations were not taking account of the final words "establishing the agreement of the parties to modify its provisions".' See further ibid. para 49 (Cambodia): 'initially, his [Mr. Chea Den's] delegation had had some doubts about the value of article 38, for at first glance it was difficult to accept that subsequent practice could modify treaty provisions. (...) However (...) his delegation had come around to the view (...) in favour of retaining the article. For in fact, the modification contemplated (...) the unanimous agreement of the parties.'.

[179] Summary record of 876th Meeting, para 31 (Briggs).

[180] 38th Meeting of the Committee of the Whole, para 60.

[181] cf Kohen, 'Keeping Subsequent Agreements and Practice in Their Right Limits', 36–7; G Hafner, 'Subsequent Agreements and Practice: Between Interpretation, Informal Modification, and Formal Amendment' in G Nolte (ed), *Treaties and Subsequent Practice* (OUP, 2013) 105, 116.

[182] See eg A Bianchi, 'Law, Time, and Change: The Self-Regulatory Function of Subsequent Practice' in G Nolte (ed), *Treaties and Subsequent Practice* (OUP, 2013) 133, 136: 'I surmise that even if art 38 had been adopted and included in the VCLT, we would still be struggling with its underlying interpretive "riddles". (...) Subsequent practice, by definition, hardly lends itself to be formalized. When one tries to constrain its operation, it may cease to perform its function of regulatory device and collective "meaning-fixer" '.

[183] See Section 3.2.6.

[184] See eg Villiger, *Customary International Law and Treaties* (1985), paras 294, 302; DW Greig, *Intertemporality and the Law of Treaties* (British Institute of International and Comparative Law, 2003) 90, 118; Gazzini, 'Interpretation', 251; J Arato, 'Treaty Interpretation and Constitutional Transformation' (2013) 38 Yale JIL 311.

[185] See Section 3.1.

[186] See eg 'Provisional summary record of 3205th meeting, 9 (Murase, noting the difficulty of codification while striking the balance between flexibility and clarity); Provisional summary record of 3207th meeting', 3 (Escobar Hernandez, pointing out that the draft conclusion 'duplicated provisions found in other draft conclusions'). See also Section 6.2.1 of this book.

1966 preliminary versions of the article, as well as the final version, were found to overlap with or touch upon issues already covered, explicitly or implicitly, in other draft provisions. Second, the provisions on modification by subsequent practice and subsequent customary law triggered questions that were considered either too difficult or too risky to tackle at the time. The States at the UN Conference preferred not to take a concrete stance on this 'problematic' topic.[187] In any case, the Conference 'hardly disagreed on principle' with regard to the possibility of modification by subsequent practice.[188] This could also be inferred from the fact that draft Article 38 is 'merely a corollary' to current VCLT Article 31(3)(b), which was adopted as part of the Convention by a unanimous vote.[189]

The same conclusion that the provision was excluded from the VCLT for reasons of practicality more than substance was reached by Professor Nolte in the context of the ILC's work on the topic:

> [P]aragraphs 3(a) and (b) of Article 31 (...) were the remnants of a more ambitious plan by the Commission to deal also with the inter-temporal law and the modification of treaties. This more ambitious plan could not be realized (...) in particular [due to] the difficulties of formulating in an appropriate way a general rule on the inter-temporal law and the resistance by States during the Vienna Conference to accept an explicit rule on the informal modification of treaties by way of subsequent practice. It does not seem, however, that clear differences in substance led to the abandoning of the initial, more ambitious plan.[190]

Most writers agree with this view:

> After the Vienna Conference, writers discussed the question whether the rejection of draft article 38 at the Vienna Conference means that the possibility of a modification of a treaty by subsequent practice of the parties was thereby excluded. They mostly came to the conclusion that the negotiating States simply did not wish to address this question in the Convention and that treaties can, as a general rule under the customary law of treaties, indeed be modified by subsequent practice which establishes the agreement of the parties to that effect.[191]

The article's exclusion from the final Convention has not detracted from the importance of the process of modification by subsequent practice.[192] Despite its 'tacit' nature, it represents a source of dynamic development in international law. It could

[187] DJ Bederman, *The Spirit of International Law* (University of Georgia Press, 2002) 44. See also Voicu, *De l'interprétation authentique*, 94.

[188] Villiger, *Customary International Law and Treaties* (1985), para 302. See also eg Greig, *Intertemporality*, 90 ('The Commission certainly regarded the draft provision as representing the then current legal position, and it is difficult to accept that its rejection by the Conference had the legislative effect of abolishing the principle.'), 118 ('The objections mainly concentrated on more formal aspects of the problems it would cause (...) [and that] Article 38 was either duplicated, or that its role could be performed, by what became Article 31(3)(b) of the Convention.'); Gazzini, 'Interpretation', 251. See also n 184.

[189] Villiger, *Customary International Law and Treaties* (1985), para 302.

[190] ILC, *Report of the International Law Commission on the work of its 62nd session*, UN Doc A/65/10 (2010) Ch X ('Treaties over Time') para 352.

[191] Nolte, Second Report on Subsequent Practice, para 122.

[192] In fact, the article's inclusion in the VCLT could possibly have led to 'less, rather than greater, flexibility in the attitude of States towards a treaty'—Greig, *Intertemporality*, 119, citing 37th Meeting of the Whole, paras 61 (Vietnam), 63 (France).

be said that, since the article's deletion in Vienna in 1968, the process of modification by subsequent practice has been relegated to the realm of custom, lying just beyond the sphere of what is now the Vienna Convention on the Law of Treaties.[193]

These nuanced discussions reveal not only the inherent political difficulties involved in codifying the process of treaty modification by subsequent practice, but also the abstract legal notions underlying its practical effects and the challenge of identifying them. Nevertheless, the discussions do not cast doubt on the possibility of modification by subsequent practice.[194] Instead, they serve as an important starting point for an investigation into the process. A number of crucial distinctions came to light during the ILC discussions, such as whether subsequent practice affects procedural or substantive provisions, rules of secondary importance or 'essential' ones, and whether its effects are limited by amendment provisions or even non-amendable provisions in the treaty itself. Another factor is the degree of clarity of the treaty provisions in question—the less ambiguous a treaty's provisions are, the easier it is to spot diverging subsequent practice. Other distinctions relate to the nature of the treaty, for instance as to whether it is bilateral or multilateral, or of a technical or more general character (such as law-making or 'standard-setting' treaties, like those on human rights). Furthermore, it matters if the nature of the treaty is such that any *inter se* divergence from its provisions would inherently affect the non-participating parties' rights and obligations under the treaty. The ILC drafting history thus gives an overview of the diverse, complex, and interrelated questions that arise with regard to the process of treaty modification by subsequent practice. These considerations form the foundation for the ensuing discussion.

3.3 Treaty Modification by Subsequent Practice: General Framework

Having taken a detailed look at the historical discussions in the ILC context, points of reference must be identified to further guide the inquiry into the process of modification by subsequent practice—a framework to be applied directly in the analysis of the compilation of examples of modification by subsequent practice in Chapter 5. The following sections deal with the definition of 'modification' by subsequent practice (Section 3.3.1), the validity of the process of treaty modification and termination by subsequent practice (Section 3.3.2), its constitutive elements and evidentiary standards, including the crucial requirement of agreement, building upon the groundwork laid in Chapter 2 (Section 3.3.3), as well as its relation to formal amendment procedures (Section 3.3.4) and a treaty's object and purpose (Section 3.3.5). Moreover, the result of modification by subsequent practice is examined in relation to the original treaty, subsequent treaties, and subsequent parties to the

[193] See eg Qin, 'The Conundrum of WTO Accession Protocols', 407 ('Short of codification in the VCLT, the issues concerning modifications of a treaty by subsequent practice are left to customary international law.'); G Distefano, 'L'accord tacite ou l'univers parallèle du droit des traités' (2015) 18 QIL 17, 30 and fn 77. See further Section 3.3.7.

[194] Villiger, *Customary International Law and Treaties* (1985), paras 294, 302.

treaty (Section 3.3.6), before, lastly, turning to an inquiry into the potential status of the underlying rule on modification by subsequent practice (Section 3.3.7).

3.3.1 Defining 'modification'

It is important to make clear what is meant by 'modification' in the present book.[195] The term 'modification' is taken here to mean *altering* treaty provisions, as well as *supplementing* them with an important 'novel' element or direction (as opposed to a mere clarification).[196] Moreover, 'modification' includes the effect of tacitly *terminating* treaty provisions (desuetude). In addition, the term comprises later modifications to *previously* established modifications by subsequent practice (which could, imaginably, even change the respective rule back to its original meaning).[197]

First, 'modification' includes the *alteration* of the original treaty provision(s) by subsequent practice. Treaty alteration implies the existence of a true conflict[198]—conflicts, after all, serve as 'conduits for legal change'[199]—between the contents of the original treaty provision on the one hand, and the substance of the modification by subsequent practice on the other. This entails that the two cannot be reconciled through 'harmonious interpretation'.[200] Reference can be made in this respect to the principle of 'systemic integration' reflected in Article 31(3)(c) VCLT.[201] This

[195] See also Section 1.3.

[196] I Venzke, *How Interpretation Makes International Law: On Semantic Change and Normative Twists* (OUP, 2012) 236.

[197] See further Section 3.3.3(b).

[198] Conflicts of norms are inherent in international law, given its horizontal, decentralized structure, coupled with its high pace of development. This applies to normative clashes of all kinds, also between treaty rules and rules of customary law. See Villiger, *Customary International Law and Treaties* (1985), para 311, referring to F Capotorti, 'L'extinction et la suspension des traités' (1971-III) 134 RC 417, 517. There are three general categories: conflicts between successive norms (eg *lex posterior*), conflicts between general and special law (*lex specialis*), and conflicts with higher norms (*lex superior*). Numerous provisions deal with resolution or consequences of conflict (notably, Art 103 of the UN Charter, Arts 30 and 59 VCLT, and countless conflict clauses in individual treaties), but there is no official *definition* of 'conflict' under international law. Likewise, the case law is not explicit as to criteria for defining and ascertaining the existence of a conflict, with the major exception of WTO case law—see eg *European Communities–Regime for Importation, Sale and Distribution of Bananas*, Report of the Panel (9 September 1997) DS27/R/USA, 338, fn 401; *Indonesia–Certain Measures Affecting the Automobile Industry*, Report of the Panel (2 July 1998) WT/DS64/R, 334, 347; *Guatemala–Anti-Dumping Investigation regarding Portland Cement from Mexico*, Report of the Appellate Body (2 November 1998) WT/DS60/AB/R, para 65; *Turkey–Restriction on Imports of Textile and Clothing Products*, Report of the Panel (31 May 1999) WT/DS34/R, 124–5; *United States–Tax Treatment for Foreign Sales Corporations*, Report of the Appellate Body (24 February 2000) WT/DS108/AB/R, para 159.

[199] S Ranganathan, 'Between Philosophy and Anxiety? The Early International Law Commission, Treaty Conflict and the Project of International Law' (2013) 83 BYBIL 82, 91. See also ibid. 86, 114, on the reasoning behind Art 30 VCLT on conflicting treaties, namely, that a flexibly formulated rule would promote legal discourse as a means of settling conflicting claims.

[200] See eg JB Mus, 'Conflicts between Treaties in International Law' (1998) 45 NILR 208, 211; J Klabbers, 'Beyond the Vienna Convention: Conflicting Treaty Provisions' in E Cannizzaro (ed), *The Law of Treaties Beyond the Vienna Convention* (OUP, 2011) 192, 193 (referring to conflict as between provisions that 'cannot be resolved through such mechanisms as "reconciling interpretation" or even "balancing" or "proportionality" ').

[201] Koskenniemi, Fragmentation Report, para 413; C McLachlan, 'The Principle of Systemic Integration and Article 31(3)(c) of the Vienna Convention' (2005) 54 ICLQ 279.

provision requires the interpreter to take into account 'any other rules of international law' applicable between the parties, also when there is 'an inconsistency, a conflict, an overlap between two or more norms, and no other interpretative means provides a resolution'.[202] But 'harmonious' or 'reconciling' interpretation can only resolve *apparent* conflicts, not genuine conflicts.[203] One can only speak of a 'genuine' conflict when the rules in question cannot sensibly be read together and thus cannot be complied with simultaneously without in effect breaching one of them.[204] This includes situations in which the result of a modification by subsequent practice conflicts with the treaty's (original) object and purpose.[205] Moreover, the existence of a conflict (and, hence, scope for modification by subsequent practice[206]), even taken in its widest sense,[207] must not be presumed: '[t]he wide definition of conflict (...) must be tempered by the generally accepted presumption against conflict.'[208] Accordingly, conflicts, and therefore alterations to treaty provisions through modification by subsequent practice, should be construed narrowly. But, to be clear, the presumption is 'against the *existence* of conflict, not a presumption in favour of the

[202] Koskenniemi, Fragmentation Report, para 420.

[203] CJ Borgen, 'Resolving Treaty Conflicts' (2005) 37 GWILR 573, 640. See also *Application of the Interim Accord of 13 September 1995 (the former Yugoslav Republic of Macedonia v Greece)*, Judgment of 5 December 2011, ICJ Reports 644, 678–9; CW Jenks, 'The Conflict of Law-Making Treaties' (1953) 29 BYBIL 425, 427.

[204] See eg Art 59(1)(b) VCLT. See also eg Villiger, *Customary International Law and Treaties* (1985), para 311; SA Sadat-Akhavi, *Methods of Resolving Conflicts between Treaties* (Martinus Nijhoff, 2003) 241. The definition of a 'genuine' conflict as the impossibility of joint compliance applies regardless of whether the conflict is only between mutually exclusive *obligations* (strict view) or between mutually exclusive *norms*, ie rights and obligations (broader view). For the 'strict' view, see eg Jenks, 'The Conflict of Law-Making Treaties', 425 (but see ibid. 428); W Karl, 'Conflicts between Treaties' in R Bernhardt (ed), *Encyclopedia of Public International Law*, vol 7 (North-Holland, 1984) 468; Mus, 'Conflicts between Treaties', 211; G Marceau, 'WTO Dispute Settlement and Human Rights' (2002) 13 EJIL 753, 791–4. For the broader view, see eg Art 30 VCLT (referring to 'rights and obligations'); W Czaplinski and G Danilenko, 'Conflicts of Norms in International Law' (1990) 21 NYBIL 3, 13; Pauwelyn, *Conflict of Norms*, 175; E Vranes, 'The Definition of "Norm Conflict" in International Law and Legal Theory' (2006) 17 EJIL 395, 402; Villiger, *Commentary*, 402, 674, 727. According to a still broader view, conflict occurs when one treaty frustrates the goals of another, entailing 'functional interference' (rather than mutual exclusiveness) between (sets of) norms with clashing policy objectives. See Koskenniemi, Fragmentation Report, paras 24–5; M Prost, *The Concept of Unity in Public International Law* (Bloomsbury, 2012) 66. cf R Michaels and J Pauwelyn, 'Conflict of Norms or Conflict of Laws? Different Techniques in the Fragmentation of Public International Law' in T Broude and Y Shany (eds), *Multi-Sourced Equivalent Norms in International Law* (Hart Publishing, 2011) 19, 21; S Linton and FK Tiba, 'The International Judge in an Age of Multiple International Courts and Tribunals' (2009) 9 Chi J Intl L 407, 441. See further eg NT Tulcer, 'The Definition of Norm Conflict in Public International Law: The Case of World Trade Organization Law' (2012) 9 Ankara L Rev 27.

[205] Koskenniemi, Fragmentation Report, para 24; Pauwelyn, *Conflict of Norms*, 50.

[206] Since the alteration of treaty provisions as a form of modification by subsequent practice is distinguished from interpretation by assessing the extent to which there is a *conflict* between the original treaty provisions and the substance of the modification, a presumption against conflict entails a presumption against modification by subsequent practice. See also Section 3.1.

[207] See nn 204–5.

[208] Pauwelyn, *Conflict of Norms*, 240. See also Koskenniemi, Fragmentation Report, para 37, citing eg C Rousseau, 'De la compatibilité des normes juridiques contradictoires dans l'ordre international' (1932) 39 RGDIP 133, 153. As a result of this presumption, it is for the party relying on the conflict (or modification by subsequent practice) to prove its existence, rather than for the other party to prove the continuing existence of the old law. See Pauwelyn, *Conflict of Norms*, 244.

earlier rule in the event there is a real conflict'.[209] Of course, determining the existence of a conflict is precisely the root of the problem, as such determination is itself a matter of interpretation: '[r]ules appear to be compatible or in conflict *as a result of interpretation*.'[210] This discussion also lies at the heart of the distinction between interpretation and modification explored in Section 3.4 below.

Second, during the drafting of the Vienna Convention, the ILC considered not only alterations, but also *extensions* of treaty provisions, as a form of modification by subsequent practice.[211] As noted by one ILC member:

> [A] modification was not always necessarily the reversal of a rule in the amended instrument (amendment *contra legem*); the effect of the modification might be to add something that was consistent with that instrument (amendment *secundum legem*) (...) [or] to remove doubts which had arisen (amendment *praeter legem*).[212]

The elaboration or supplementation of a rule by subsequent practice constitutes modification if it adds a new 'dimension' to the rule or to the treaty's object and purpose(s) rather than merely a concretization or clarification of the text. When the effects of an extension of the treaty by subsequent practice are far-reaching, the situation can be more easily qualified as modification. For instance, as an example of subsequent practice taken in its broadest sense to include successive treaties, or otherwise by analogy, Article 3 of the 2001 UNESCO Convention on the Protection of the Underwater Cultural Heritage[213] states that its provisions shall not prejudice the Law of the Sea Convention, yet concerns have been expressed that the rights it confers go beyond coastal States' rights and jurisdiction under the LOSC.[214]

On the other hand, where an issue is not covered by the terms of the treaty and subsequent practice is used to fill in the gap, it more likely represents an interpretation than a modification.[215] One can take the following theoretical example: if the text of a constituent treaty provides that two different organs cannot deal with the same issue in parallel, and yet a practice is established whereby the two organs do so anyway, this can be seen as an alteration of the treaty text amounting to modification through the practice of the organization.[216] If the treaty were silent on the issue, however, would the practice of the two organs working in parallel constitute modification of the treaty by adding a new rule or procedure? Or would it merely supplement the treaty without modifying it, since it does not go against the letter

[209] Ibid. 242 (emphasis in the original), explaining that 'this presumption should not form an excuse to *define* conflict narrowly' (emphasis in the original) or interpret the 'new' norm restrictively.

[210] Koskenniemi, Fragmentation Report, para 412.

[211] 1964 Draft Articles on the Law of Treaties with Commentaries, 198, Art 68(b) (referring to 'alteration or extension').

[212] ILC, 'Summary record of the 764th meeting', *Summary record of the 16th session* (1964) I YBILC 267, para 104 (De Luna).

[213] (2002) 41 ILM 40.

[214] See eg T Scovazzi, 'The Protection of Underwater Cultural Heritage: Article 303 and the UNESCO Convention' in D Freestone, R Barnes, and DM Ong (eds), *The Law of the Sea: Progress and Prospects* (OUP, 2006) 120, 134.

[215] Greig, *Intertemporality*, 91–2.

[216] See Section 5.2.1 on the *Israeli Wall Advisory Opinion*.

or spirit of its text? The distinction between supplementing and extending or modifying the text or scope of the treaty is difficult to establish.

A concrete example relates to Article 18(2) of the Charter of the Arab League, which provides for the expulsion of members following a unanimous decision of all the other parties, but says nothing about the possibility of suspension of membership.[217] In practice, the League has suspended members using a lower majority requirement than that prescribed for expulsion,[218] without any specific basis under the treaty.[219] It is debatable whether this should be regarded as a modification or an extension of the Charter. At least in theory, the granting of new powers to an international organization by means of subsequent practice would constitute more than a mere addition to the text, amounting to a clear modification of the instrument, to the extent that it surpasses what can already be read into the treaty through interpretation based on implied powers.[220] Once again, this is a complex matter of interpretation that relates to the distinction between interpretation and modification by subsequent practice discussed further below.[221]

The distinction between an 'alteration' and an 'extension' of treaty provisions may carry implications for the threshold needed to establish a modification by subsequent practice.[222] Where subsequent practice supplements the treaty text, it may require a lower evidentiary threshold to establish the agreement of the parties than in cases where subsequent practice establishes a modification derogating from *existing* text. In the former case, no pre-existing rule is actually being modified. Similarly, it has been argued, in the context of national constitutional law, that the threshold for unwritten law to *derogate* from written law or rules that have external working should be quantitatively higher than in the case of unwritten rules that merely *supplement* without a *contra legem* character or only have internal (procedural) working.[223]

Third, subsequent practice can lead to the termination of treaty provisions, denoted here as 'desuetude'.[224] Desuetude thus refers to a special form of modification by subsequent practice, whereby the treaty-related conduct of the parties

[217] Pact of the League of Arab States 1945, 70 UNTS 237.

[218] The suspension of Egypt's membership took place in 1979 (readmitted in 1989), Libya's on 22 February 2011 (readmitted later that same year), and Syria's on 12 November 2011 (interestingly, the seat has, since 2013, been offered to the opposition Syrian National Coalition—see eg H Droubi and R Gladstone, 'Syrian Opposition Joins Meeting of Arab League' (*New York Times*, 26 March 2013) <www.nytimes.com/2013/03/27/world/middleeast/syrian-opposition-group-takes-seat-at-arab-league.html> accessed 29 March 2017). See eg D Batty and J Shenker, 'Syria suspended from Arab League' (*The Guardian*, 12 November 2011) <www.theguardian.com/world/2011/nov/12/syria-suspended-arab-league> accessed 29 March 2017.

[219] Moreover, these decisions appear to contrast with Art 7 of the Arab Charter, which prescribes that 'decisions of the Council taken by a unanimous vote shall be binding on all the member States of the League; those that are reached by a majority vote shall bind only those that accept them.'

[220] See Sections 2.5.4 and 3.5.2. [221] See Section 3.4.

[222] See further Section 3.3.3(b).

[223] DJ Elzinga, 'Grondwet en ongeschreven staatsrecht' in CJ Bax and MC de Voogd (eds), *Van constitutionalisme en anarchisme: Opstellen aangeboden aan Th Holterman en GFM van der Tang* (Kluwer, 2003) 5; DJ Elzinga, R de Lange, and HG Hoogers (eds), *Van der Pot, Handboek van het Nederlandse Staatsrecht* (16th edn, Kluwer, 2013) 190.

[224] The term applies equally to customary international law.

implies their consent to render the treaty—or a provision thereof—obsolete.[225] Kontou points out that treaty modification by subsequent practice leads both to the extinction of the prior rule and its replacement by a new one, such that 'authors sometimes use the term desuetude broadly to describe both situations'.[226] Similarly, Villiger distinguishes between the scenario whereby 'modification includes, and implies, desuetude of the conventional rule' (desuetude as a stage in the process of modification), and 'desuetude of a conventional rule alone, without substitution' (desuetude as the end result of the modification).[227]

In his 1957 Second Report on the Law of Treaties, Special Rapporteur Fitzmaurice described the process of desuetude as follows:

> [T]he parties themselves, without denouncing or purporting actually to terminate the treaty, have, over a long period, conducted themselves in relation to it more or less as though it did not exist, by failing to apply or invoke it [which constitutes a special case of renunciation of rights] (. . .) [so that] there exists what amounts to a tacit agreement of the parties, by conduct, to disregard the treaty and to consider it as being at an end.[228]

Later, the ILC defined desuetude as 'the consent of the parties to abandon the treaty, which is to be implied from their conduct in relation to the treaty'.[229] By contrast, Kohen, based on a historical elucidation of the term, defines it not as termination by tacit agreement, but as termination purely by way of the passing of a significant amount of time during which the treaty is not applied, and claims that it has no place in treaty law.[230] It is the former understanding of desuetude—as a consensually implied agreement—that is employed presently.[231]

In sum, the notion of 'modification'[232] here is taken to encompass alterations or extensions of treaty provisions between (all or a subset of) the treaty parties, as well as desuetude, referring generally to a situation in which the operation of a treaty or individual provisions is tacitly varied by means of subsequent practice (or, as we shall see in Chapter 4, by subsequent customary law[233]).

[225] See generally A Vamvoukos, *Termination of Treaties in International Law: The Doctrine of* Rebus Sic Stantibus *and Desuetude* (Clarendon Press, 1985) 325; R Kolb, 'La désuétude en droit international public' (2007) 111 RGDIP 577. cf Capotorti, 'L'extinction', 417.

[226] N Kontou, *The Termination and Revision of Treaties in the Light of New Customary International Law* (Clarendon Press, 1994) 28.

[227] Villiger, *Customary International Law and Treaties* (1985), paras 313–14 (emphasis omitted).

[228] ILC, 'Second Report on the Law of Treaties, by Mr GG Fitzmaurice, Special Rapporteur' (1957) II YBILC 16 [Fitzmaurice, Second Report on the Law of Treaties] 48, para 86. This view influenced the work of the ILC—see 1966 Draft Articles on the Law of Treaties with Commentaries, 237, para 5.

[229] 1966 Draft Articles on the Law of Treaties with Commentaries, 237, para 5. See also Kivilcim-Forsman, 'Principe d'egalité', 217.

[230] MG Kohen, 'Desuetude and Obsolescence of Treaties' in E Cannizzaro (ed), *The Law of Treaties Beyond the Vienna Convention* (OUP, 2011) 350, 351–2. See also JAC Thomas, 'Desuetudo' (1965) 12 RIDA 469.

[231] See Section 2.3.5(a).

[232] See Section 1.3 on terminology.

[233] As explained in Ch 4, treaty 'modification' by subsequent customary law differs from treaty modification by subsequent practice, *inter alia*, in that the former displaces or substitutes the treaty provision without becoming 'part and parcel' of the treaty, whereas the latter actually modifies the treaty's substance. Yet the process of customary law is intricately linked to that of subsequent practice, and this overlap adds an extra dimension to the discussion on subsequent practice. For convenience, the outcome of both processes is denoted here as 'modification'.

3.3.2 Validity of the process

It is already well established that subsequent practice can shed light on the meaning of treaty provisions and in that way play a clarifying and 'gap-filling' role.[234] But as the international case law and doctrine show,[235] subsequent practice in the application of a treaty is also well capable of modifying (and terminating) treaty provisions: 'la pratique crée, la pratique modifie, la pratique interprète, la pratique prouve, la pratique éteint la règle de droit'.[236] Moreover, subject to the same requirements as those applicable to the modification of treaty provisions, subsequent practice can also modify *previous* modifications by subsequent practice.[237] The following section discusses the validity of the process of treaty modification (Section 3.3.2(a)), and of treaty modification specifically through termination (Section 3.3.2(b)), by subsequent practice.

3.3.2a The process of treaty modification by subsequent practice

It should be noted here, as a preliminary observation, that the reference to modification by subsequent practice *ipso facto* implies that the respective practice is established and lawful. The extent to which initial (unauthorized) deviations can eventually crystallize into relevant subsequent practice constituting a modification of the treaty is discussed in other sections of this book.[238] The central question, therefore, is not *whether* the process of tacit treaty modification by subsequent practice exists or is legitimate; rather, the focus is on an attempt to sketch how this phenomenon operates, and determine its main boundaries.

There are various reasons for the existence of modification by subsequent practice, and the prevalence in certain situations of legitimate expectations resulting from subsequent conduct.[239] As emphasized by Judge Alvarez, '[w]e have to choose between the maintenance of texts as immutable, even if they lead to unreasonable consequences, and the modification of these texts, if that becomes necessary. There cannot be any doubt as to the choice.'[240] The practical impossibility of formal amendment in certain cases, the premise of *pacta sunt servanda*, the fluid interchange between interpretation and modification, and the need to respect the contemporaneous intentions of the parties, all lead to this conclusion, as explained in turn below.

First, in many cases, it is unfeasible to negotiate adjustments to treaty terms by means of formal amendment processes, and States cannot be expected to foresee all potential modifications in advance of a treaty's conclusion. Even treaty regimes

[234] See Ch 2, in particular Section 2.5. [235] See Section 3.1.

[236] MG Kohen, 'La pratique et la théorie des sources du droit international' in MG Kohen, L Boisson de Chazournes, and G Buzzini (eds), *La Pratique et le Droit International, Société Française pour le Droit International, Colloque de Genève* (Pédone, 2004) 81, 110.

[237] See Section 3.3.3(b). [238] Ibid. See also Section 2.3.5 and text to nn 259–61.

[239] See eg Brownlie, *Principles*, 601.

[240] *Competence of the General Assembly for the Admission of a State to the United Nations*, Advisory Opinion of 3 March 1950, Dissenting Opinion of Judge Alvarez, ICJ Reports 12, 18.

with only a small number of parties, such as NAFTA with its three States parties,[241] may prove difficult if not impossible to amend by means of formal processes.[242] And yet no legal relationship can remain unchanged over time. States find alternative ways to accommodate treaty change, which explains the need to take into account subsequent practice.[243] These changes respond to a 'blind spot in the construction of sources doctrine and (...) [offer] a complementary account on where international law comes from'.[244] In other words, the process of modification by subsequent practice can be seen as a development that helps legitimize the practice of those international actors (States, international organizations, etc) engaging in treaty interpretation or application that stretches the limits of the text to the point where it can be said to constitute tacit modification.[245]

The issue of formal amendments also relates to the concern that, by circumventing national procedures for the approval of treaty amendments, modification by subsequent practice can lead to domestic constitutional problems.[246] Though seemingly counter-intuitive, subsequent *agreements*, with regard to which the role of the executive branch is likely to be more pronounced, may raise more constitutional concerns than less formalized types of subsequent practice.[247] However, as already discussed in Section 3.2.5 above,[248] the domestic constitutional law objection was not regarded by Sir Humphrey Waldock, Expert Consultant at the 1968 Vienna Conference, as a valid problem.[249] The same has been pointed out in the doctrine.[250] For one thing, '[s]maller modifications usually do not require ratification and larger ones would attract the attention of states, who will then have the opportunity to object or to proceed with ratifications.'[251] The operation of modification by subsequent practice is

[241] Feldman, 'Evolving Treaty Obligations', 657 fn 3.

[242] Ibid. 656. See Section 5.2.3(c) on NAFTA FTC 'interpretations'.

[243] Koskenniemi, Fragmentation Report, para 476.

[244] Venzke, *How Interpretation Makes International Law*, 196. See further AV Lowe, 'The Politics of Law-Making: Are the Method and Character of Norm Creation Changing?' in M Byers (ed), *The Role of Law in International Politics* (OUP, 2000) 207.

[245] See Venzke, *How Interpretation Makes International Law*, 225.

[246] See eg Section 3.2.5.

[247] See eg I Wuerth, 'Treaty Interpretation, Subsequent Agreements and Practice, and Domestic Constitutions' in G Nolte (ed), *Treaties and Subsequent Practice* (OUP, 2013) 154, 158.

[248] See 37th Meeting of the Committee of the Whole, paras 58 (Japan), 63 (France), 68 (Spain); 38th Meeting of the Committee of the Whole, paras 1 (Soviet Union), 17 (Poland), 21 (Colombia), 36 (Uruguay), 41 (Cuba), 43 (Philippines). See also eg S Kadelbach, 'Domestic Constitutional Concerns with Respect to the Use of Subsequent Agreements and Practice at the International Level' in G Nolte (ed), *Treaties and Subsequent Practice* (OUP, 2013) 145, 145–8; Wuerth, 'Treaty Interpretation', 154–9; H Ruiz Fabri, 'Subsequent Practice, Domestic Separation of Powers, and Concerns of Legitimacy' in G Nolte (ed), *Treaties and Subsequent Practice* (OUP, 2013) 160, 165–6.

[249] 38th Meeting of the Committee of the Whole, para 57 (Waldock).

[250] See eg Wuerth, 'Treaty Interpretation', 158 ('generally the record would seem to suggest that constitutional problems are the rare exception, not an ongoing problem'); Kadelbach, 'Domestic Constitutional Concerns', 147; OA Hathaway and others, 'Tacit Amendment' (2011) *White Paper for Yale Law School Center for Global Legal Studies* 1, 24 <https://law.yale.edu/system/files/documents/pdf/cglc/TacitAmendments.pdf> accessed 30 March 2017 ('the Senate has generally recognized that unratified amendment processes, including those providing for tacit amendments, provide a necessary and flexible tool to develop robust treaty regimes').

[251] J Liang, 'Modifying the UN Charter through Subsequent Practice: Prospects for the Charter's Revitalisation' (2012) 81 NJIL 1, 17.

not different in this sense from that of customary international law, which becomes binding upon States often without formal procedures at the national level, even if it contravenes existing treaty provisions.[252] Once again, it must be emphasized that modification by subsequent practice becomes established on the basis of the parties' agreement, which in turn is evidenced by their practice at the national level—in other words, the legislative, executive, or judicial branches of State act in a sufficiently consistent manner, whether expressly through special domestic procedures or not, such that their overall combined practice transpires at the international level as an intention to modify the treaty. Therefore, while the constitutional argument is a (political) concern, it is not a valid reason to reject the possibility of modification by subsequent practice.

Second, the principle of *pacta sunt servanda* 'cannot rule out change'.[253] That treaties must be fulfilled in good faith is a natural law principle that exists independently of State parties' consent, let alone their subsequent practice.[254] It 'says nothing about *what* qualifies as a treaty in the first place, *who* can make one, or *how* a treaty should be applied, interpreted, avoided, or ended'.[255] The very premise is that agreements should be respected, but this does not mean that the content of those agreements cannot change over time, by both formal and tacit means.[256] Modification by subsequent practice is rooted precisely in the agreement of the parties, and, moreover, in the principle of good faith.[257] The view that subsequent practice cannot modify a treaty even if it establishes the parties' agreement to do so, is untenable:

> The meaning and application of a treaty are as much subject to the common will of the parties as was its initial formation. As international law does not place any restriction upon how obligations are assumed whether by agreement or otherwise, nor are any imposed on the making of treaties or their modification by the Vienna Convention, changes to a treaty may be achieved by the tacit consent of the parties.[258]

[252] See generally Ch 4.

[253] Villiger, *Customary International Law and Treaties* (1985), para 322. cf DP O'Connell, 'Reflections on the State Succession Convention' (1979) 39 ZaöRV 725, 739. See also eg *Award in the Matter of an Arbitration between Kuwait and the American Independent Oil Company (Aminoil)*, Award of 24 March 1982 (1982) 21 ILM 976 [*Aminoil Arbitration*] para 97.

[254] G Fitzmaurice, 'Some Problems Regarding the Formal Sources of International Law' in FM van Asbeck and others (eds), *Symbolae Verzijl: Présentées au Professeur JHW Verzijl à l'occasion de son LXX-ième anniversaire* (Martinus Nijhoff, 1958) 153, 164 ('the rule *pacta sunt servanda* (…) is not dependent on consent, for it would exist without it').

[255] DB Hollis, 'Introduction' in DB Hollis (ed), *The Oxford Guide to Treaties* (OUP, 2012) 1, 2 (emphasis in the original).

[256] This was also made clear during the ILC discussions—see Section 3.2.5.

[257] 38th Meeting of the Committee of the Whole, para 56 (Waldock). See further Section 3.2.5.

[258] Greig, *Intertemporality*, 90, citing *Legal Status of Eastern Greenland (Denmark v Norway)*, Judgment of 5 April 1933, PCIJ Series A/B, No 53, 70–1; *Temple of Préah Vihéar*, 31–2; *Nuclear Tests (Australia v France)*, Judgment of 20 December 1974, ICJ Reports 253, 267–8; *Aegean Sea Continental Shelf*, 39; *Burkina Faso/Republic of Mali*, 573–4; *Maritime Delimitation and Territorial Questions between Qatar and Bahrain (Qatar v Bahrain)*, Jurisdiction and Admissibility, Judgment of 1 July 1994, ICJ Reports 112, paras 23ff.

Moreover, just as divergent interpretations might initially occur in relation to treaty provisions that are ambiguous and eventually crystallize into accepted dynamic treaty interpretations,[259] the *pacta sunt servanda* principle is only violated in the initial few instances of modification, as more States acquiesce or actively contribute to the practice, until *consuetudo est servanda*.[260] The same idea applies to the modification of *previous* treaty modifications by subsequent practice.[261]

With each potential modification by subsequent practice, legitimate expectations are created as States come to rely on the new meaning of the modified provision. In accordance with good faith, enunciated in Article 31(1) VCLT, legitimate expectations raised in other parties shall be honoured (*Vertrauensschutz*).[262] The fundamental principle of *pacta sunt servanda* is part of this broader principle of legitimate expectations,[263] which also encapsulates the notion of consent and effects such as estoppel.[264]

Third, the subsequent practice of parties to a treaty often reflects a fluid interchange between interpretation and modification,[265] as pointed out by Voicu in his notable work on authentic interpretation.[266] Determining the point in time when this switch from interpretation to modification occurs is inherently an act of interpretation in itself.[267] As already explained, subsequent practice establishing the parties' agreement is capable of constituting an authentic interpretation of the treaty.[268] Authentic interpretations can have binding effect in the same way as formal amendments and in a sense remove the gap between interpretation and modification:[269] 'authentic interpretations come from the law-makers themselves [and thus] (...) are not interpretations but rather new legal enactments'.[270]

Voicu also argues that the 'danger' of this tacit process lies in the fact that there is often a marked inequality between contracting parties, so a modification is more likely to disadvantage less powerful States.[271] This could make it more difficult to

[259] Voicu, *De l'interprétation authentique*, 96.

[260] ME Villiger, *Customary International Law and Treaties: A Manual on the Theory and Practice of the Interrelation of Sources* (2nd rev edn, Kluwer International, 1997) para 333. See also B Simma and CJ Tams, 'Reacting against Treaty Breaches' in DB Hollis (ed), *The Oxford Guide to Treaties* (OUP, 2012) 576 ('almost all nations, almost all the time, consider their rights under a given treaty to be violated'). cf Fitzmaurice, 'The Law and Procedure of the International Court of Justice' (1957), 113. See also the previous discussion in Section 2.3.5 on the frequency of applications before conduct amounts to 'subsequent practice'.

[261] See further Section 3.3.3.

[262] Villiger, *Commentary*, 426, citing JP Müller, *Vertrauensschutz im Völkerrecht* (Heymann, 1971) 128.

[263] Byers, *Custom*, 176–7.

[264] Ibid.

[265] See eg B Kunoy, 'The 10 Year Time Frame to Disputed Areas' (2009) 40 ODIL 131, 138. See further Section 3.4.

[266] Voicu, *De l'interprétation authentique*, 100.

[267] See Ch 1.

[268] See Section 2.3.3.

[269] See eg Karl, *Vertrag*, 46. See also Voicu, *De l'interprétation authentique*, 87–8.

[270] I Tammelo, *Treaty Interpretation and Practical Reason: Towards a General Theory of Legal Interpretation* (Law Book Co, 1967) 6. This corresponds with the view in R Higgins, *Problems and Process: International Law and How We Use It* (Clarendon Press, 1994) of international law as a continuous, dynamic process of authoritative decisions.

[271] Voicu, *De l'interprétation authentique*, 90.

set limits for legitimacy, particularly since the interchange between interpretation and modification can be said to be effectuated more under a political umbrella than a legal one.[272] Voicu warns that the subtlety of the process of authentic interpretation could enable States to achieve by this 'back-door' what they could not achieve during the original negotiation of the treaty.[273] However, and once again, it should not be forgotten that the modifying potential of subsequent practice is kept in check by the requirement of the agreement of the parties, the result of which can only be to bypass the original negotiations if the parties subsequently decide that this is desirable.

Fourth, denying that changes can be brought about tacitly through subsequent practice would in some cases mean prioritizing the original intention of the treaty parties over their later intention (and that of later parties to the treaty). For instance, as early as 1964, many of the provisions of the UN Charter, at that point almost two decades old, were being construed very differently from what had been envisaged at their inception.[274] As pointed out during the 1964 ILC discussions on the law of treaties:

> [T]he original parties to the Charter were now outnumbered by the States that had acceded to the Charter since 1945; it would be going too far to claim that the original signatories had a greater say in the interpretation of the Charter than the majority. The burden of the operation of a treaty, in the light of the realities of international relations, fell upon all its signatories; there was therefore no reason for giving a higher standing to the intentions of the original parties in the matter of interpretation.[275]

It is, moreover, not only a change in circumstances, but also simply the lack of foreseeability or information regarding the implications of certain treaty terms, that provides cause for treaty adjustment through subsequent practice. Treaty interpretation and application is a 'learning process', particularly in fields where the visibility and understanding of the implications of treaty practice is reduced by the structures and processes in place in that specific context.[276]

The basis of the process of modification by subsequent practice is rooted in the 'dynamism of international life'.[277] If kept in check by the requirement of the

[272] Ibid. See also Ch 1, n 17; McNair, *Law of Treaties*, 534 ('treaty revision is a matter for politics and diplomacy'); Brownlie, *Principles*, 625 ('the issue is primarily one of politics').

[273] Voicu, *De l'interprétation authentique*, 89.

[274] See Section 5.3.1(a).

[275] Summary record of 766th meeting, para 46 (Lachs). See also *Competence of the General Assembly*, Dissenting Opinion of Judge Alvarez, 18; *Certain Expenses Advisory Opinion*, Separate Opinion of Judge Spender, 186.

[276] See eg K Gordon and J Pohl, 'Investment Treaties over Time—Treaty Practice and Interpretation in a Changing World' (2015) 2 OECD Working Papers on International Investment 1, 10 (referring to the investment law context, where 'countries that, at one time and for various reasons, had not given in-depth consideration to investment treaties' language prior to adoption (...) may now feel a need to adjust treaty practice'). The more informed States become of treaty practice, the more they tend to reassess their own practice. Note that in this sense, dispute settlement may be not an alternative adaptation mechanism (Section 3.5.2), but a *complementary* one, contributing to informing practice about itself and thus triggering new directions in subsequent practice.

[277] *Competence of the General Assembly*, Dissenting Opinion of Judge Alvarez, 18.

agreement of the parties, it is aligned with fundamental principles such as *pacta sunt servanda*, and, in fact, a natural consequence thereof.[278]

3.3.2b The process of treaty modification through termination by subsequent practice

If subsequent practice can modify treaties by means of tacit agreement, it can also be capable of terminating them.[279] Modification 'merges into termination at one extreme and into interpretation at the other extreme.'[280] As defined in Section 3.3.1, this form of modification by subsequent practice is referred to here as 'desuetude'.

The only provisions dealing with treaty termination in the VCLT are to be found in its Part V, most notably in Articles 42(2), 54(b), and 59. During the 1966 ILC discussions on modification by subsequent practice, 'all members seemed to admit that in one way or another obsolescence and desuetude could be used as a means of bringing a treaty to an end, and *a fortiori* as a means of modifying it'.[281] But the Commission did not consider it necessary to expressly include a provision on tacit termination in the Convention.[282] Its Commentary to what is now Article 42 VCLT on 'validity and continuance in force of treaties' states that desuetude is already covered by Article 54(b) VCLT, according to which termination can take place 'at any time by consent of all the parties after consultation with the other contracting States'.[283] The article does not require such consent to be established expressly: the parties are 'free to choose the form of their agreement to terminate the treaty' and may choose to do so implicitly.[284] In fact, the Commission substituted the term 'agreement' with 'consent' in Article 54(b) precisely to allow for the possibility of tacit termination.[285] As for the consultation requirement, this merely entails that, in line with the principle of good faith, 'the contracting States must be informed in

[278] See eg 38th Meeting of the Committee of the Whole, paras 10 (Iraq), 51 (Argentina), 55–6 (Waldock), discussed in Section 3.2.5.

[279] J Leca, *Les techniques de révision des conventions internationales* (LGDJ 1961) 10; Villiger, *Customary International Law and Treaties* (1985), para 304; M Akehurst, *A Modern Introduction to International Law* (6th edn, Harper Collins Academic, 1987) 204–5.

[280] Akehurst, 'Hierarchy of the Sources', 277. See also Villiger, *Customary International Law and Treaties* (1985), para 313 ('As a result, *modification includes, and implies, desuetude* of the conventional rule'; emphasis in the original), citing eg Capotorti, 'L'extinction', 516; P de Visscher, 'Cours général de droit international public' (1972-II) 136 RC 1, 79; Karl, *Vertrag*, 257.

[281] Summary record of 866th meeting, paras 12–14 (Rosenne).

[282] See further eg Villiger, *Commentary*, 541–9; MG Kohen and S Heathcote, 'Article 42—1969 Convention' in O Corten and P Klein (eds), *Vienna Conventions on the Law of Treaties: A Commentary* (OUP, 2010) 1015.

[283] 1966 Draft Articles on the Law of Treaties with Commentaries, 236–7. See also Villiger, *Customary International Law and Treaties* (1985), para 303.

[284] T Giegerich, 'Article 54' in O Dörr and K Schmalenbach (eds), *Vienna Convention on the Law of Treaties: A Commentary* (Springer, 2012) 945, para 40. See also *Nuclear Tests (New Zealand v France)*, Judgment of 20 December 1974, Joint Dissenting Opinion of Judges Onyeama, Dillard, Jiménez de Aréchaga and Sir Humphrey Waldock, ICJ Reports 494, paras 53–4 (addressing the claim by France that the General Act of 1928 had fallen into desuetude with the demise of the League of Nations); Sinclair, *Vienna Convention*, 164 para 23; V Chapaux, 'Article 54 (1969)' in O Corten and P Klein (eds), *Vienna Conventions on the Law of Treaties: A Commentary* (OUP, 2010) 1236, 1244.

[285] Summary record of 876th meeting, para 94.

good time of the intention to terminate the treaty or withdraw from it'.[286] It does make clear that *all* the parties must be in agreement. Desuetude, in the sense of termination by tacit consent, is therefore implicitly covered by Article 54(b) VCLT. Moreover, Article 59 VCLT, which provides for the (implied or express) termination of a treaty by the conclusion of a later treaty, can also constitute a form of tacit termination.[287]

In his report, Fitzmaurice emphasized that the attitude and conduct of the parties must establish 'beyond doubt' that the condition of 'long continued disregard' is present.[288] Though relevant in assessing the parties' intention, age and desuetude as such do not constitute the basis for termination. This is based instead on the underlying tacit agreement of the parties. The same applies when a treaty falls into desuetude as a result of new customary law; it is not the customary law as such that terminates the treaty provisions, but rather the underlying consent of the parties.[289] Likewise, Kohen underscores that silence or lack of invocation of the treaty must be *qualified*,[290] meaning that it must be supported by clear evidence of the parties' will to terminate the treaty.[291] Termination should not be inferred simply from prolonged non-application.[292] Compelling evidence is if the parties were faced with situations where they could have applied the treaty, but instead chose various other solutions.[293] There may be other explanations for the observed (lack of) practice in relation to the treaty, such as special political considerations or 'inertia' in reacting to a breach,[294] or simply the lack of occasion to apply it.[295]

A good example is the matter of 'protecting powers'[296] under the 1949 Geneva Conventions[297] and Additional Protocol I.[298] A 'protecting power' is a State not

[286] Giegerich, 'Article 54', para 44.

[287] cf Section 2.3.3 on the notion of 'subsequent agreement'.

[288] 1966 Draft Articles on the Law of Treaties with Commentaries, 237 para 87. Even the reciprocal non-compliance of parties to a bilateral treaty may not suffice for its termination—Giegerich, 'Article 54', para 40, citing *Gabčíkovo-Nagymaros Project*, para 114.

[289] Kontou, *Termination and Revision of Treaties*, 28. See also R Plender, 'The Role of Consent in the Termination of Treaties' (1986) 57 BYBIL 133, 142; Chapaux, 'Article 54', 1244 para 24. See further Ch 4, in particular Section 4.5.1.

[290] See Section 2.3.5(a) on the role of silence in establishing agreement through subsequent practice.

[291] Kohen, 'Desuetude', 350. cf Villiger, *Customary International Law and Treaties* (1985), para 315; MJ Glennon, 'How International Rules Die' (2005) 93 Geo LJ 939.

[292] Kohen, 'Desuetude', 355.

[293] Villiger, *Customary International Law and Treaties* (1985), para 315.

[294] *Yuille Shortridge and Co (Great Britain/Portugal)*, Award of 21 October 1861, in A de Lapradelle and N Politis, *Recueil des arbitrages internationaux*, vol II (Pédone, 1923) 78, 105, underscoring, in sum, that if no significant consequences flow from a State's breach of the treaty for another State, lack of reaction on the latter's part would be a matter of courtesy, not an act of renunciation of the treaty.

[295] Kohen, 'Desuetude', 356–7.

[296] See H-J Heintze, 'Protecting Power' (2009) MPEPIL <http://mpepil.com>.

[297] Geneva Convention for the Amelioration of the Condition of the Wounded and Sick in Armed Forces in the Field 1949, 75 UNTS 31 (First Geneva Convention); Geneva Convention for the Amelioration of the Condition of the Wounded, Sick and Shipwrecked Members of the Armed Forces at Sea 1949, 75 UNTS 85 (Second Geneva Convention); Geneva Convention relative to the Treatment of Prisoners of War 1949, 75 UNTS 135 (Third Geneva Convention); Geneva Convention relative to the Protection of Civilian Persons in Time of War 1949, 75 UNTS 287 (Fourth Geneva Convention).

[298] Protocol Additional to the Geneva Conventions of 12 August 1949, and relating to the Protection of Victims of International Armed Conflicts 1977, 1125 UNTS 3 (Additional Protocol I).

party to an armed conflict but designated by a party thereto and accepted by the adverse party to fulfil certain tasks set out under the Convention,[299] a role that can also be fulfilled by the International Committee of the Red Cross.[300] Despite the fact that the language of the Geneva Conventions suggests that there is an *obligation* to appoint protecting powers,[301] such powers have rarely been appointed.[302] Nevertheless, the obligation was reaffirmed in Additional Protocol I.[303] Since then, the appointment of protecting powers has continued to remain scarce.[304] The fact that the obligation was reaffirmed indicates that its lack of implementation is not tantamount to desuetude. Other factors confirm this as well. For instance, the 'pragmatic approach' adopted by the ICRC has led it to fulfil many of the tasks assigned to protecting powers.[305] This shows that desuetude should not be easily inferred from a lack of implementation, especially where 'subsequent practice demonstrates that the purpose of the obligation is being fulfilled in similar ways, thereby indicating a continuing sense of obligation'.[306]

Certainly, the age of a treaty as such is 'no bar to its continuing legal force'.[307] It can even be argued that in certain cases the lack of new practice in relation to a treaty confirms its continued relevance: '[t]he non-invocation of a treaty may in fact be due to its efficiency in obviating disputes between the parties—and thereby constitute the best evidence of its continuance in force.'[308]

The character of a treaty is important in interpreting relevant State practice (or a lack thereof). It provides indication of whether the treaty is one that the parties would be likely to regard as outdated or as having fallen into desuetude.[309] Certain types of treaties constitute special cases. For instance, tacit termination of a human rights treaty to the detriment of the rights-holders would go against the alleged non-regression principle.[310] Something similar could be said of boundary treaties.[311] The implications of the nature of different types of treaties and treaty obligations are discussed further in Section 3.5. In any case, subsequent practice resulting in desuetude must be determined with great caution, taking into account the context and aims of the specific treaty.

[299] See eg Arts 102 and 126 of the Third Geneva Convention.

[300] Common Arts 10/10/10/11(3) of the 1949 Geneva Conventions.

[301] See Common Arts 8/8/8/9 of the 1949 Geneva Conventions: 'The present Convention shall be applied with the cooperation and under the scrutiny of the Protecting Powers (...).' See further Heintze, 'Protecting Power', para 17.

[302] F Bugnion, *Le comité international de la Croix-Rouge et la protection des victims de la guerre* (CICR 2000) 1008–11.

[303] Art 5 of Additional Protocol I.

[304] In fact, since 1977, protecting powers have been appointed only once, in the UK-Argentina Falkland/Malvinas conflict in 1982.

[305] Nolte, Third Report on Treaties over Time, 357. See eg Art 126 of the Third Geneva Convention and Art 143 of the Fourth Geneva Convention. See also H-P Gasser, 'Respect des garanties judiciaires fondamentales en temps de conflit armé: Le rôle du délégué du CICR' (1992) 74 RICR 129.

[306] Nolte, Third Report on Treaties over Time, 358. See also Section 5.3.2(d).

[307] Kohen, 'Desuetude', 355 (referring to treaties still in force since as far back as the 1600s).

[308] *Nuclear Tests (Australia v France)*, Judgment of 20 December 1974, Dissenting Opinion of Judge De Castro, ICJ Reports 372, 381 fn 1.

[309] 1966 Draft Articles on the Law of Treaties with Commentaries, 237, para 88.

[310] See Section 3.5.1(a).

[311] See eg *Libya/Chad*, paras 72ff.

3.3.3 Constitutive elements and evidentiary standards

The constitutive elements of subsequent practice were discussed at length in Chapter 2.[312] Most of them apply equally to subsequent practice as a means of treaty interpretation and subsequent practice resulting in treaty modification. A certain degree of repetition is warranted here. The different elements are dealt with briefly, only to the extent that there is more to be said about them in the specific context of modification by subsequent practice.

3.3.3a Type of practice, determinacy, and relevant actors

As already discussed in Chapter 2, the notion of 'practice' is extremely wide: '[a]nything can count as practice unless the treaty's constituent instrument says it cannot or the practice was conducted with the understanding it would not change legal rights or relations.'[313] The relevance of a certain practice depends on whether its nature makes it capable of establishing the parties' tacit agreement to informally modify a treaty. For instance, some statements and practice may be purely for publicity or political purposes, such as a claim based on practice in relation to an expressly non-binding UN General Assembly resolution.[314] This issue has already been discussed in Section 2.3.1(b) with regard to subsequent practice in Article 31(3)(b) VCLT, in terms of the types and degree of determinacy of relevant practice. The ambivalence of certain types of practice—namely, the difficulty of determining a State's underlying intention based on practice, especially in cases where the practice appears contradictory or insufficiently concrete—prompted a Singaporean representative in the General Assembly's Sixth Committee, during recent discussions on subsequent practice, to comment as follows:

> Practice may of course be reflective of a shared binding understanding on the part of the parties of how their obligations have been varied subsequent to the conclusion of the Treaty. But this is not always the only conclusion one can reach from the conduct of the parties. First, they may be motivated by reasons of pure political expediency, and as such, may simply not reflect the intent of the parties. Second, what seems to be a departure affecting the interpretation of a Treaty may be temporary, and after some time, revert to a state of conformity with the provisions of the Treaty. Third, practice, and the motivations thereof, are usually not properly recorded, and while it can sometimes be inferred from particular acts, there are many instances where the exact contours cannot be clearly ascertained. (...) Practice should therefore only amend (...) in exceptional circumstances.[315]

[312] Sections 2.3.1–2.3.5 and 2.4.

[313] Feldman, 'Evolving Treaty Obligations', 696. See Section 2.3.1(a).

[314] See Section 2.3.1(b) on the value of political statements and General Assembly resolutions. See also Feldman, 'Evolving Treaty Obligations', 695, arguing that soft law cannot directly constitute subsequent practice since often the reason for consensus on non-binding agreements is owed to their non-binding nature.

[315] Statement by Mr Lionel Yee, Director-General, International Affairs Division, Attorney-General's Chambers of Singapore, on Chapters X, XI, and XII of the Report of the ILC on the Work of its 62nd Session, Sixth Committee, Permanent Mission of the Republic of Singapore (1 November 2010) <www.mfa.gov.sg/content/mfa/overseasmission/newyork/nyemb_statements/sixth_committee/2010/201011/press_201011.html> accessed 30 March 2017. See also eg Comments by the EU to the ILC, 3,

Another essential consideration is *whose* practice can validly contribute to subsequent practice capable of modifying a treaty[316]—a question of attribution.[317] Although this was already discussed in the context of subsequent practice as a means of treaty interpretation in Section 2.3.1(c), it is useful to consider here some additional aspects in the context of modification by subsequent practice. As previously noted, some writers have argued that subsequent practice, whether its effect is to interpret or modify, should be carried out by the 'properly authorized organs' of the State in question.[318] Haraszti, for instance, mentions the Security Council's practice of modifying Article 27(3) of the UN Charter[319] as an exceptional case in which subsequent practice led to treaty modification. What makes this situation exceptional in Haraszti's view is that clear conclusions could be drawn from the Security Council's subsequent practice regarding the common intention of the 'properly authorized organs of the parties' to modify the Charter provision.[320] He also considers that the Tribunal in the *Air Transport Services Arbitration* (*US/France*)[321] was correct in asserting that subsequent practice can serve as a means of treaty modification, but went too far in taking into account the practice of certain administrative bodies, consisting of relatively low-ranking officials, as a deciding factor.[322]

By contrast, in the arbitration on the *Tax Regime Governing Pensions Paid to Retired UNESCO Officials Residing in France* (*France v UNESCO*), the Tribunal was indisposed to regard the conduct of low-ranking State organs as subsequent practice that had led to a modification of the treaty.[323] At issue in the case was the question of whether Article 22(b) of the Headquarters Agreement[324] had been modified by subsequent practice. According to that article, officials governed by the provisions of the UNESCO Staff Regulations were 'exempt from all direct taxation on salaries and emoluments paid to them by the Organization'. The French tax administration had for decades also applied this exemption to retired UNESCO officials, thus allegedly modifying the provision through practice. France argued, and the Tribunal agreed, that only the practice of the State organs vested with 'treaty making power' and involved in concluding the Agreement was relevant, not that of subsidiary State organs like the French tax authorities. It was considered that, since the tax-free

that 'according to consistent case-law, the fact that the European Commission, in her general task of guardian of the Treaties, has not reacted against an infringement of European law on the part of a Member State does not imply [approval] on her side (…).'

316 See in this respect Kohen, 'La pratique', 88ff.

317 *Topical summary of the discussion held in the Sixth Committee of the General Assembly during its 65th session*, UN Doc A/CN.4/638 (19 January 2011) Ch II(G), para 109. See the earlier discussion in Section 2.3.1(c).

318 Haraszti, *Some Fundamental Problems of the Law of Treaties*, 145.

319 See Sections 3.4.2 and 5.2.1.

320 Haraszti, *Some Fundamental Problems of the Law of Treaties*, 145.

321 See Section 5.2.2.

322 Haraszti, *Some Fundamental Problems of the Law of Treaties*, 145.

323 *Tax Regime Governing Pensions to Retired UNESCO Officials*, paras 67–77. See also R Kolb, 'La modification d'un traité par la pratique subséquente des parties' (2004) 14 *Schweizerische Zeitschrift für Internationales und Europäisches Recht* 9.

324 1954 Agreement Regarding the Headquarters of UNESCO and the Privileges and Immunities of the Organization on French Territory, 357 UNTS 5103.

residence in France of retired officials had been granted temporarily and had not been 'officially' accepted, no modification of Article 22(b) had occurred.[325]

As noted in Section 3.2 above, the issue of low-ranking officials was also raised in the 1966 ILC discussions. One concern was that a very wide admission of the possibility of modification by subsequent practice might allow even minor State officials to alter formally agreed treaty obligations.[326] Apprehension was also expressed by the US delegation during the discussions on modification by subsequent practice at the first session of the UN Conference on the Law of Treaties in 1968.[327] The US voiced the concern that the proposed article on modification by subsequent practice might allow 'relatively low-ranking officials such as vice-consuls and third secretaries [to] interpret a treaty erroneously and follow a course of conduct that, unknown to governments, could lead to the modification of a treaty'.[328] The Chairman, Mr. Yasseen, was correct in responding that the article was sufficiently clear in requiring that agreement to modify be established by 'not just any practice, but one which could be attributed to States'. This excludes the acts of (lower-ranking) officials exceeding their powers,[329] but includes, depending on the circumstances, the acts of lower-ranking officials charged with applying the treaty, and hence conducted with the (tacit) consent of higher authorities.[330]

3.3.3b The requirement of agreement

The fundamental requirement for subsequent practice to be able to result in treaty modification is that it must establish the agreement of (all[331]) the parties. Different factors influence the 'threshold' required for practice to constitute agreement in a given case, depending, *inter alia*, on the type[332] and scope[333] of modification envisioned and the nature of the treaty provisions in question.[334]

325 This relates to issues of determinacy and intentionality, given also that France argued this policy was based on politeness, not intended as a legal act. See *Tax Regime Governing Pensions to Retired UNESCO Officials*, para 74.

326 Summary record of 866th meeting, paras 6–10 (Jiménez de Aréchaga).

327 38th Meeting of the Committee of the Whole, para 6. See Section 3.2.6. Note also the proposal by Special Rapporteur Fitzmaurice in 1956 to introduce a draft Art 9, the third paragraph of which read: 'No State is obliged, or, strictly speaking, entitled, to accept as internationally authentic the acts of another State in relation to a treaty, *unless they are the acts of the executive authority*.'—ILC, 'Report on the Law of Treaties by Mr GG Fitzmaurice, Special Rapporteur' (1956) II YBILC 104, 108–9. This provision sparked debate and was eventually deleted—ILC, 'Summary record of the 369th meeting', *Summary records of the 8th session* (1956) I YBILC 219, paras 4 (Krylov), 59 (Zourek); ILC, 'Summary record of the 482nd meeting', *Summary records of the 11th session* (1959) I YBILC 12, paras 40 (Tunkin), 47–8 (Fitzmaurice).

328 38th Meeting of the Committee of the Whole, para 6. 329 Ibid. para 9.

330 See Section 2.3.1(c). See also eg J-P Cot, 'La conduite subséquente des parties à un traité' (1966) 70 RGDIP 632, 665; Gardiner, *Treaty Interpretation*, 228 ('[a]ny body charged with the authority of the state may carry out relevant acts if these demonstrate a position in relation to the state's treaty commitments or entitlements.'). Moreover, as suggested during the ILC discussions as early back as 1959, 'surely, every State had the undisputed right to determine for itself what authority was empowered to represent it in such matters [in relation to a treaty]'—Summary record of 482nd meeting, para 40.

331 See further the discussion in Section 3.3.4 as to whether different thresholds for modification could apply depending on the voting majority imposed by formal amendment procedures.

332 See eg text to n 196. 333 See eg Sections 3.3.4–3.3.5. 334 See Section 3.5.

For present purposes a higher 'threshold' refers not only to the quantity and quality of the practice (a substantive threshold), but also to the burden on the interpreter, usually a dispute settlement body, of clarifying and justifying why a modification has occurred in that case (a procedural threshold). It should be noted in this respect that the modification of a treaty provision that reflects customary law does not as such entail a higher threshold. Rather, modification of the declaratory treaty provision and the pre-existing customary rule requires two separate modifying instances, since the norms stem from independent sources of law.[335] For certain types of provisions, however, such as the (declaratory) Law of the Sea Convention provisions establishing the outer limits of the various maritime zones, treaty modification would naturally entail a corresponding modification of the underlying customary rules. These provisions provide an example of where modification of the treaty and customary international law coincide, on account of the large number of parties to the LOSC, coupled with the fact that the articles set up an objective regime, which can only function based on generally respected rules. The threshold for modification of such provisions is only higher in the sense that the modification of the customary rule also requires the practice of States *not* parties to the treaty. In other words, modifying the underlying customary norm poses an additional requirement concerning the practice of third States, *not* a higher threshold for the treaty modification itself.

There are two basic elements applicable to the analysis of subsequent practice in the process of treaty modification, reflected in the notion of a 'concordant, common and consistent' practice.[336] As explained previously, this notion does not constitute a formal threshold for practice but rather an indication of its evidentiary value as subsequent practice reflective of the parties' agreement to modify the treaty.[337] The first element is that it must be common or discernable in the general practice of the contracting parties, that is, common and concordant, so as to be capable of establishing their agreement.[338] As set out earlier, this does not, therefore, require the active practice of all the parties, but rather that of some of the parties combined with acceptance on the part of the rest.[339] It could even be argued that a small number of objecting States, akin to 'persistent objectors',[340] would not rule out the

[335] See Section 4.4.1.

[336] See Section 2.3.5(c). See further *Japan–Alcoholic Beverages II*, AB Report, 13; *Chile–Price Band System*, AB Report, para 214; *US–Gambling*, AB Report, paras 191–2; *EC–Chicken Cuts*, AB Report, paras 256–8; Sinclair, *Vienna Convention*, 137, citing Yasseen, 'L'interprétation', 48. cf Nolte, Second Report on Treaties over Time, 217, arguing that this criterion is restrictive and has not been confirmed by the ICJ or ILC.

[337] See Section 2.3.5(c).

[338] See in particular *Air Transport Services Arbitration* (*US/France*), 248–55. cf Sinclair, *Vienna Convention*, 79–80, citing eg H Blix, 'The Rule of Unanimity in the Revision of Treaties' (1956) 5 ICLQ 447.

[339] See Section 2.3.5.

[340] See Section 4.3.2. The effect of a State's timely objection to the formation of new customary law is that it will not become bound by that rule itself, *not* that it would prevent the rule from crystallizing, although in the case of very influential States, this distinction may be less clear—see P Dumberry 'Incoherent and Ineffective: The Concept of Persistent Objector Revisited' (2010) 59 ICLQ 779, 781, citing P Weil, 'Le droit international en quête de son identité: cours général de droit international public' (1992) 237 RC 129, 196–7.

possibility of a modification (also interesting is that 'persistent objectors' eventually phase out over time[341]). A second basic criterion is that there be a sequence of acts or pronouncements constituting the practice, i.e. a certain consistency, also linked to the factor of *time*: the longer the duration, the more time there is for a consistent sequence of acts to develop indicating that a treaty provision has been modified. As previously discussed, notions such as estoppel and acquiescence can play a significant role in solidifying claims of tacit agreements through subsequent practice,[342] although they should be applied carefully.[343]

As discussed in Section 2.3.5(c), the notion of 'agreement' also raises the question of whether a one-time application of a treaty can be regarded as sufficient to amount to relevant practice, or whether additional applications are required. There is no immediate reason why the former possibility should be ruled out as long as the practice is sufficient to establish the agreement of the parties,[344] especially if it is the practice of the only States to which the matter in question is relevant.[345]

A first, isolated instance of practice deviating from the text—depending also on the form of that practice[346] and on whether the transition from interpretation in the direction of modification is gradual or abrupt[347]—may initially be regarded as a violation under the law of treaties,[348] and could trigger consequences under the law of State responsibility.[349] However, once the practice becomes established as

[341] See eg JI Charney, 'The Persistent Objector Rule and the Development of Customary International Law' (1985) 56 BYBIL 1, 11–15, 22 ('no case is cited for a circumstance in which the objector effectively maintained its status after the rule became well accepted in international law'); P Cahier, 'Changement et continuité du droit international: cours général de droit international public' (1985) 195 RC 9, 236; TL Stein, 'The Approach of the Different Drummer: The Principle of the Persistent Objector in International Law' (1985) 26 Harv ILJ 457, 468; P-M Dupuy, 'A propos de l'opposabilité de la coutume générale: enquête brève sur l'objecteur persistant' in *Mélanges Michel Viraly* (Pédone, 1991) 257, 264; Weil, 'Le droit international', 191, 197. cf K Wolfke, *Custom in Present International Law* (Martinus Nijhoff, 1993) 66–7 (arguing that this 'does not undermine the principle of the persistent objector').

[342] See by analogy Section 2.3.5. See also Nolte, Annex A, para 25; I Sinclair, 'Estoppel and Acquiescence' in V Lowe and M Fitzmaurice (eds), *Fifty Years of the International Court of Justice: Essays in Honour of Sir Robert Jennings* (CUP, 1996) 104, 108–12; Feldman, 'Evolving Treaty Obligations', 664 fn 36.

[343] See eg E Gordon, 'Article 2(4) in Historical Context' (1985) 10 Yale JIL 271.

[344] Linderfalk, *On the Interpretation of Treaties*, 166. See also Pauwelyn, *Conflict of Norms*, 144; Weiler, 'Discussion', 8.

[345] *EC–Chicken Cuts*, AB Report, para 7.255. See also Section 2.3.5(c) of this book.

[346] See eg Villiger, *Customary International Law and Treaties* (1985), para 321, pointing out that statements in the UN context contradicting treaty rules *in abstracto* do not automatically constitute violations.

[347] Ibid. See also para 331. Villiger refers to gradual modification through interpretation ('modificatory practice via adaptation'), which starts off as compatible with the treaty rule, and modifying practice whereby 'the initial derogation is *a priori* incompatible with the written rule' and eventually crystallizes into a modification. It is not immediately clear why 'modification by derogation' would be a separate category from 'modification by interpretation', since both will at some point or another entail divergence from, and potential breach of, the treaty.

[348] See eg ibid. para 318; BI Bonafé and P Palchetti, 'Relying on General Principles in International Law' in C Brölmann and Y Radi (eds), *Research Handbook on the Theory and Practice of International Lawmaking* (Edward Elgar, 2016) 160, 175 ('at the formative stage the dividing line between changing the law and breaching it becomes extremely thin').

[349] The relation between the law of State responsibility and the law of treaties may be one of the most difficult in international law. See *Gabčíkovo-Nagymaros Project*, paras 47, 101, on the distinction and complementarity between the two. See also *Case concerning the Difference between New Zealand and*

part of a sequence of acts, it can contribute towards a (lawful) tacit modification,[350] establishing the parties' agreement to that end,[351] and hence raise questions of legitimacy but not legality:[352]

> [T]he line which divides conduct which international law permits from that which it prohibits is in many cases not susceptible of precise delimitation. A course of action which in one period may have been expressly prohibited may, by dint of its continued repetition coupled with the consent of other States, be acceptable under the rules obtaining in a later period.[353]

The same applies to an established modification by subsequent practice that eventually subsequently *reverts* to the meaning of the original provision. The cut-off date is presumably the moment at which the practice has established a change. After this point, disagreement with an established modification would no longer be relevant or would even violate the terms of the modification; but it could also provide the starting point for a *new* change, including a reversal of the modification.

The issue of when a modification can be said to have crystallized arose recently with respect to the question of the potential modification of Article 2(4) of the UN Charter[354] on the prohibition on the use of force with regard to the issue of military intervention in Syria, *inter alia* on grounds of humanitarian intervention in response to its use of chemical weapons:

> There is no doubt that in the present situation, military strikes against Syria would be in violation of international law as it has been understood since 1945. (...) [An] option is to present the strikes as part of a process of reconstruction of the law on the use of force, and more in particular as a revival of the right to humanitarian intervention. (...) Present international law may prohibit it, but international law is not static and can change by being breached. *The unlawful act may contain the seeds of a new rule allowing for humanitarian intervention.*[355]

France concerning the Interpretation or Application of Two Agreements, Concluded on 9 July 1986 between the Two States and which Related to the Problems Arising from the Rainbow Warrior Affair, Award of 30 April 1990, 20 RIAA 215, para 75. See further eg J Crawford and S Olleson, 'The Exception of Non-Performance: Links between the Law of Treaties and the Law of State Responsibility' (2000) 21 Aust YBIL 55; M Fitzmaurice, 'Exceptional Circumstances and Treaty Commitments' in DB Hollis (ed), *The Oxford Guide to Treaties* (OUP, 2012) 605, 606.

[350] See eg Section 3.3.2(a).

[351] This situation should of course be differentiated from situations where the parties' intention was merely to deviate from the treaty temporarily. See Section 2.3.5. See also Nolte, Third Report on Treaties over Time, 343–4; Nolte, Second Report on Subsequent Practice, para 71.

[352] See Section 3.3.1(a) explaining that 'modification' *ipso facto* implies that the effect of the practice is established and lawful. See also eg JE Alvarez, 'Limits of Change by Way of Subsequent Agreements and Practice' in G Nolte (ed), *Treaties and Subsequent Practice* (OUP, 2013) 123, 130.

[353] IC MacGibbon, 'The Scope of Acquiescence in International Law' (1954) 31 BYBIL 143.

[354] See Section 5.3.1(a).

[355] A Nollkaemper, 'Intervention in Syria and International Law: Inside or Out?' (*Opinio Juris*, 1 September 2013) <http://opiniojuris.org/2013/09/01/syria-insta-symposium-andre-nollkaemper-intervention-syria-international-law-inside/> accessed 5 April 2017 (emphasis added). See also E Heffes and BE Frenkel, 'The Decision-Making Process of the R2P Doctrine: Towards New (Old) Paths in the Use of Force in International Law' (*Opinio Juris*, 2 September 2013) <http://opiniojuris.org/2013/09/02/syria-insta-symposium-ezequiel-heffes-brian-e-frenkel-decision-making-process-r2p-doctrine-towards-new-old-paths-use-force-international-law/> accessed 5 April 2017.

The discussions at the national and international level in general triggered by the situation in Syria—as recently as 2017—may indicate dissatisfaction with the current state of the law. On the other hand, past violations of Article 2(4) have not changed the fact that it is still being taken as a 'first baseline for justifying or critiquing action or inaction'.[356] Modification of the article by subsequent practice—and the concomitant modification of the underlying peremptory[357] (or, in any case, customary[358]) norm[359]—has not (yet) occurred and would, in light of the nature and importance of the provision, in practice entail an extremely high threshold.[360]

Another pertinent reflection can be found in the *North Sea Continental Shelf* cases, where the Court dealt with the question of whether the subsequent practice of parties to the Geneva Convention on the Continental Shelf of 1958 had given rise to a customary rule—a consideration that applies by analogy to the process of modification by subsequent practice. The Court answered in the negative. It declared that time is not in itself a decisive factor: only three years had elapsed since the proceedings had been initiated.[361] The duration of the practice is a relative requirement. This makes sense in light of the quickening pace of international relations, technological progress, and communication in the current era, which can considerably speed up the process of establishing agreement through practice. What matters most is not duration as such, but that it be sufficient to distinguish between consistent and inconsistent practice, allow the content of the new rule or modification to crystallize, and enable other States to become aware and react to it, or provide 'a certain stability of practice upon which States may come to rely'.[362] As explained previously, the longer the period of time and frequency with which the practice occurs, the higher the opportunity and reason for non-participating States to express disagreement or for the participating States themselves to eventually alter the practice.[363] If the practice remains consistent over a lengthy period of time, it can more easily and accurately be taken to reflect the intention and tacit agreement of the parties to informally modify the treaty.

The Court in the *North Sea Continental Shelf* cases highlights another factor that indicates whether practice is capable of establishing agreement,[364] namely, the issue

[356] Nollkaemper, 'Intervention in Syria'. See also Section 5.3.1(a) on UN Charter Art 2(4).

[357] B Simma, 'NATO, the UN and the Use of Force: Legal Aspects' (1999) 10 EJIL 1, 3; ID Seiderman, *Hierarchy in International Law: The Human Rights Dimension* (Intersentia, 2001) 62; M Bossuyt and J Wouters, *Grondlijnen van Internationaal Recht* (Intersentia, 2005) 92; A Cassese, *International Law* (2nd edn, OUP, 2005) 202; T Ruys, *'Armed Attack' and Article 51 of the UN Charter: Evolutions in Customary Law and Practice* (CUP, 2011) 267; A Orakhelashvili, *Peremptory Norms in International Law* (OUP, 2006) 51. Others are of the view that peremptory status only applies to the prohibition of 'aggression'—see Ruys, *'Armed Attack'*, 26, 380, citing L Hannikainen, *Peremptory Norms (Jus Cogens) in International Law: Historical Development, Criteria, Present Status* (Finnish Lawyers' Publishing Company, 1988) 356; PH Kooijmans, *Internationaal Publiekrecht in Vogelvlucht* (Wolters-Noordhoff, 1996) 29.

[358] *Nicaragua v US*, Merits, para 202.

[359] See text to n 335.

[360] Simma, 'NATO', 3; Ruys, *'Armed Attack'*, 267; D Akande, 'The Legality of Military Action in Syria: Humanitarian Intervention and the Responsibility to Protect' (*OXPOL*, 29 August 2013) <http://blog.politics.ox.ac.uk/legality-military-action-syria-humanitarian-intervention-responsibility-protect/> accessed 22 April 2017.

[361] *North Sea Continental Shelf*, para 74.

[362] Villiger, *Commentary*, 9.

[363] See Section 2.3.5(c).

[364] Ibid.

of the practice of States 'whose interests are specially affected'.[365] One must look at the main actors subject to the treaty obligations in question to see whether they are participating in the practice: 'it is not the number of parties that is essential, but the relevance of the parties and how agreement is established.'[366]

A potential indication of an intention to modify the treaty is the observance of a widespread practice among *third* States that coincides with the divergent practice of the treaty parties in relation to the original provision.[367] This applies to some extent by analogy to modification by subsequent customary law, the focus of Chapter 4: when trying to identify customary law that has emerged as a result of treaty-related practice, one could also seek evidence *outside* of the practice of the treaty parties alone.[368] The question of the relevance of the practice of third States in determining whether a modification has taken place was considered during the 1964 ILC discussions by Special Rapporteur Sir Humphrey Waldock.[369] His answer, in the affirmative, was that the growing interdependence of States 'makes it desirable that at any rate those States which are substantially interested in the functioning of the [treaty-based] regime' should be allowed a voice in its revision, amendment, or desuetude.[370] He added that this only applied in respect of those provisions of the treaty affecting the actual functioning of the regime. Let us imagine that an influential State, such as the United States,[371] follows the (divergent) practice of parties to a treaty, such as the LOSC, in relation to a provision not capable of, or not yet, generating customary law,[372] and which is not of a strictly internal or procedural nature (in which case it would not be of relevance to third States). The practice of the United States, as the relevant third State in this scenario, could provide an indication that a potentially modifying practice has become the standard among the parties to the treaty. Evidently, it is still the practice of the treaty parties that determines whether a modification actually occurs.

The considerations above form the basis for Feldman's suggested 'three-step approach' that attempts to find a uniform way of analysing subsequent practice.[373] Drawing from relevant WTO jurisprudence—which takes a very strict approach to subsequent practice[374]—he first presents a two-step analysis, the 'double-consent

[365] *North Sea Continental Shelf*, para 74. See further Section 2.2.5(c).

[366] Feldman, 'Evolving Treaty Obligations', 694.

[367] cf Resolution on 'Problems Arising from a Succession of Codification Conventions on a Particular Subject' (1995) 66 AIDI 435, 443 ('Conclusion 13'), cited by Y Dinstein, 'The Interaction between Customary International Law and Treaties' (2006) 322 RC 243, para 217.

[368] Villiger, *Customary International Law and Treaties* (1985), 183–4; RR Churchill, 'The Impact of State Practice on the Jurisdictional Framework Contained in the LOS Convention' in AG Oude Elferink (ed), *Stability and Change in the Law of the Sea: The Role of the LOS Convention* (Martinus Nijhoff, 2005) 91, 98; Rothwell, 'The Impact of State Practice', 147. Granted, this could pose difficulties in the rare cases of treaties that have achieved near-universality—see *North Sea Continental Shelf*, 3ff.

[369] Waldock, Third Report on the Law of Treaties, 34, para 24. [370] Ibid.

[371] See Rothwell, 'The Impact of State Practice', 147: 'Some [States] still remain outside of the Convention, and here inevitably the State practice of the United States falls under the spotlight. Whilst the US still formally remains outside of the Convention, it is clear that it has in many areas warmly embraced its provisions if not *de jure* then certainly *de facto*.'

[372] A provision could, by its very nature, be non-generalizable. See further Sections 4.3 and 4.4.1.

[373] Feldman, 'Evolving Treaty Obligations', 655.

[374] See in particular Sections 2.3.5(c) and 2.5.2.

model', the initial step of which is to check if the practice is 'concordant, common and consistent', and the second, to look for overt evidence that it constitutes agreement based on the nature of the practice. Due to the rigidity of this two-step analysis,[375] Feldman proposes a 'three-step approach'. The three steps involve looking at the character of the practice, then at the degree of its concordance, commonness, and consistency (depending also on the relevance of the participating parties), and, lastly, at the extent to which the practice implies agreement. As pointed out in the preceding chapter, the last two steps are inter-related: the higher the degree of concordance, commonness, and consistency, the higher the evidentiary value of the practice in establishing agreement between the parties.[376] Accordingly, and by contrast to the WTO Appellate Body's definition of subsequent practice, the 'concordant, common and consistent' criterion is not a formal threshold for practice, but rather an indication of the circumstances in which subsequent practice could constitute agreement.[377]

The three-step approach makes consent the focal point of the analysis.[378] It thus stays true to the wishes expressed by States in the ILC discussions on the draft article on modification by subsequent practice and to Sir Humphrey Waldock's argument that concordant, common, and consistent practice, coupled with evidence of an implied agreement, can lead to modification that accords with party consent.[379] Since the great advantage of subsequent practice—its flexibility—also creates the danger of a 'reinterpretation' of the treaty beyond the actual consent of the parties, the aforementioned 'three-step' analysis based on the conservative approach adopted by the Appellate Body establishes a safe balance between stability and change in treaty relations. However, this approach does not distinguish between the various effects of subsequent practice, such as when it can be said to have surpassed the scope of interpretation, nor does it determine some of its limitations. These issues are considered in Sections 3.4 and 3.5, respectively.

3.3.4 Relation to formal amendment procedures

It is difficult to see why a treaty would have to be amended exclusively by means of an instrument of equivalent form or level of formality.[380] In fact, often, the more sophisticated the treaty, the broader the range of adaptation mechanisms employed.[381] Reference can be made to the open formulation of the general rule

[375] Feldman, 'Evolving Treaty Obligations', 700. [376] See Section 2.3.5(c).

[377] Ibid. See also eg Nolte, Second Report on Subsequent Practice, para 47.

[378] Feldman, 'Evolving Treaty Obligations', 700.

[379] Ibid. 699, citing Waldock, Third Report on the Law of Treaties, 59–60.

[380] 1966 Draft Articles on the Law of Treaties with Commentaries, 249; Bowman, '"Normalizing"', 337. See also Nolte, Second Report on Subsequent Practice, para 144. cf Kammerhofer, *Uncertainty in International Law*, 134; Hafner, 'Subsequent Agreements and Practice', 115. cf also *Whaling in the Antarctic*, Separate Opinion of Judge Greenwood, para 7, stating that the nature of the ICRW as a 'living instrument' does not permit undercutting its rules on formal amendment and evolution. This stance contrasts with the ECtHR's view as expressed in its case law, according to which the nature of the ECHR as a 'living instrument' renders it more open to change by informal means—see Section 5.2.3(a).

[381] See eg MJ Bowman, 'The Multilateral Treaty Amendment Process—A Case Study' (1995) 44 ICLQ 540, 542; J Brunnée, 'Treaty Amendments' in DB Hollis (ed), *The Oxford Guide to Treaties* (OUP, 2012) 347, 351. Some treaties do not provide for their own amendment at all. One example is the 1971 Ramsar Convention, to which an amendment procedure was added by means of the 1982 Protocol of Amendment. See Ch 1, n 26 and Section 3.5 on alternative adaptation mechanisms.

regarding treaty amendment in Article 39 VCLT. The article provides merely that '[a] treaty may be amended by agreement between the parties', without requiring any particular form of adaptation.[382] It does not specify that the amendment must take place by means of an equal act or by the same authority: '[t]he term agreement serves as a common denominator of all forms of amending a treaty.'[383]

The existence of formal amendment procedures prescribed by the treaty does not exclude the possibility of modification by subsequent practice,[384] in the same way that express interpretation clauses in a treaty do not exclude recourse to interpretation based on subsequent practice pursuant to Article 31(3)(b) VCLT.[385] Domestic constitutional concerns in this respect have already been addressed in the preceding sections.[386] Indeed, when taken together with Article 31(3)(a) and (b) VCLT, Article 39 VCLT confirms that agreements reached subsequently by the parties, also through their practice, can legitimately modify treaties[387]—especially since there is no reason why the meaning of 'agreement' in Article 31(3)(a) and (b)[388] should be regarded as different from that in Article 39 VCLT.[389]

Recourse to subsequent practice despite the existence of formal amendment provisions may be prompted by the rigidity or unfeasibility of those very procedures.[390] Difficulties with formal amendments can be observed in a wide range of contexts, from the rigid formal amendment procedures prescribed by the Law of the Sea Convention, leading States to resort to other mechanisms to bring

[382] See eg *Methanex v US*, Part IV(C), para 21.

[383] Villiger, *Commentary*, 513, citing ILC, 'Summary record of the 752nd meeting', *Summary records of the 16th session* (1964) I YBILC 184, para 69 (Ago), and 'Summary record of the 753rd meeting', *Summary records of the 16th session* (1964) I YBILC 191, para 23 (Yasseen).

[384] See eg Engel, '"Living" International Constitutions', 909; Karl, *Vertrag*, 344–5; Churchill, 'The Impact of State Practice', 97; H Fox, 'Article 31(3)(a) and (b) of the Vienna Convention and the *Kasikili/Sedudu Island* Case' in M Fitzmaurice, O Elias, and P Merkouris (eds), *Treaty Interpretation and the Vienna Convention on the Law of Treaties: 30 Years On* (Martinus Nijhoff, 2010) 59, 61.

[385] See Nolte, Second Report on Subsequent Practice, para 114; ILC, 'Statement by Professor August Reinisch, Delegation of Austria—67th Session of the General Assembly Sixth Committee, Agenda Item 79' (2 November 2012) <http://legal.un.org/ilc/sessions/67/pdfs/english/sasp_austria.pdf> accessed 11 November 2016, 6; *Beagle Channel Arbitration*, paras 169, 173; *EC–Chicken Cuts*, AB Report, para 273; E Pan, 'Authoritative Interpretation of Agreements: Developing More Responsive International Administrative Regimes' (1997) 38 Harv ILJ 519; Hafner, 'Subsequent Agreements and Practice', 120.

[386] See in particular Section 3.3.2(a).

[387] Nolte, Second Report on Subsequent Practice, para 144 (referring only to Art 31(3)(a)), citing SD Murphy, 'The Relevance of Subsequent Agreements and Subsequent Practice for the Interpretation of Treaties' in G Nolte (ed), *Treaties and Subsequent Practice* (OUP, 2013) 82, 88.

[388] As explained in Section 2.3.3, subsequent practice can be taken to comprise subsequent agreements. See also eg J Crawford, 'A Consensualist Interpretation of Article 31(3) of the Vienna Convention on the Law of Treaties' in G Nolte (ed), *Treaties and Subsequent Practice* (OUP, 2013) 29, 30.

[389] Nolte, Second Report on Subsequent Practice, paras 144–5. See also eg Aust, *Modern Treaty Law*, 233; Kolb, *The Law of Treaties*, 194.

[390] Bowman, 'The Multilateral Treaty Amendment Process', 540; C McLachlan, 'The Evolution of Treaty Obligations in International Law' in G Nolte (ed), *Treaties and Subsequent Practice* (OUP, 2013) 69, 71; Liang, 'Modifying the UN Charter', 1; Arato, 'Treaty Interpretation', 355. cf *Namibia Advisory Opinion*, Dissenting Opinion of Judge Fitzmaurice, 191.

about treaty change,[391] to the stalemates in trade negotiations encountered at the Doha Round, impeding further amendments to WTO obligations.[392] The same fundamental problem applies to the UN Charter, Articles 108 and 109 of which provide extremely rigid amendment procedures.[393] From a practical standpoint, certain formal amendments are not worth the procedural hassle of notification, negotiation, and implementation, as set out for instance in Article 40 VCLT.[394] After all, the argument that informal modification might be used to circumvent formal amendment procedures must be posited against the fact that international law is no slave to formalism—it adapts by formal and informal means, as long as those means remain rooted in the agreement of the parties.[395]

Thus, for instance, the States parties to certain treaty-based international telecommunications satellite organizations, such as INMARSAT[396] and INTELSAT,[397] managed to privatize them in ways that clearly diverged from the amendment and termination provisions in the constitutive treaties.[398] Similarly, the ECtHR in the *Al-Saadoon* case expressly recognized that subsequent practice could in certain circumstances take precedence over formal amendment procedures under the ECHR.[399] There have even been instances where the treaty's formal amendment procedures themselves seem to have been modified by subsequent practice.[400]

The ICJ's *Pulp Mills* case raises the question of whether the existence of formal amendment procedures requires modifying subsequent practice to reflect the specific intention of the parties to bypass the formal procedures. The parties in *Pulp Mills* had, subsequent to the relevant treaty, established a High-Level Technical Group, possibly in order to circumvent the duties of information and notification required by the Administrative Commission of the River Uruguay (CARU). Argentina argued that the Group process was not meant to substitute, but rather

[391] See Buga, 'Between Stability and Change in the Law of the Sea Convention', 46ff. See also OR Young, 'Commentary on Shirley V Scott "The LOSV Convention as a Constitutional Regime for the Oceans"' in AG Oude Elferink (ed), *Stability and Change in the Law of the Sea: The Role of the LOS Convention* (Martinus Nijhoff, 2005) 39, 44; Rothwell, 'The Impact of State Practice' 149; Y Tanaka, *The International Law of the Sea* (CUP, 2012) 33.

[392] See Ch 1, n 18. See also eg H Nottage and T Sebastian, 'Giving Legal Effect to the Results of WTO Trade Negotiations: An Analysis of the Methods of Changing WTO Law' (2006) 9 J Intl Econ L 989.

[393] Articles 108 and 109 require a two-thirds majority vote, ratification by two-thirds of members, as well as the affirmative vote of all five permanent members of the Security Council. See eg H Kelsen, *The Law of the United Nations: A Critical Analysis of its Fundamental Problems* (Steven & Sons, 1951) 818–19; Laursen, *Changing International Law*, 65–6; Liang, 'Modifying the UN Charter', 2; Arato, 'Treaty Interpretation', 317. See further Section 5.3.1(a).

[394] See eg Koskenniemi, Fragmentation Report, para 49.

[395] See n 155. See further Section 3.3.2(a).

[396] 1976 Convention and Operating Agreement on the International Maritime Satellite Organization (INMARSAT), 1143 UNTS 105. See further D Sagar, 'Provisional Application in an International Organization' (1999) 27(2) J Space L 99.

[397] 1971 Operating Agreement relating to the International Telecommunications Satellite Organization (INTELSAT), 1220 UNTS 149. See further F Lyall, 'On the Privatization of INTELSAT' (2001) 5 Sing JICL 111.

[398] Crawford, 'A Consensualist Interpretation of Article 31(3)', 31.

[399] *Al-Saadoon and Mufdhi v UK*, para 126. See further Section 5.2.3(a).

[400] See Section 5.3.2(b) regarding the 1987 Montreal Protocol.

to complement, existing CARU procedures.[401] The Court refused to displace the CARU procedures prescribed by the treaty in favour of the informal arrangement set up in the form of the High-Level Technical Group.[402] There are, however, examples where an explicit choice is made for subsequent practice as an alternative to formal amendment, manifesting the parties' clear intention to opt for one over the other.[403] Such a choice is implied in cases where a proposal for formal amendment is rejected, but the proposed change is subsequently brought about by means of modification by subsequent practice.[404]

It is submitted here that it is not necessary for practice in a given case to demonstrate the parties' intention to modify the treaty, *as well as* their concurrent rejection of the formal amendment procedures prescribed by it.[405] However, where formal amendment procedures have already been triggered, a different evidentiary threshold applies. Namely, once formal amendment procedures are initiated, any parallel modification by subsequent practice can only occur if the parties' intention to opt for it over formal amendment is manifest. This may apply particularly with regard to certain types of treaties concerning, for instance, boundary delimitations and shared watercourses, as in the *Pulp Mills* case.[406] In the aforementioned *Al-Saadoon* case, the ECtHR considered the parties' practice, establishing their agreement to modify the Convention, sufficiently manifest to also take precedence over the ongoing, parallel formal amendment procedure.[407]

There is often a difference between the threshold needed for formal amendments, usually requiring a certain *majority*, and the threshold required for modifications by subsequent practice, entailing the agreement of *all* the parties.[408] Akehurst argues that where a treaty prescribes a certain majority for the adoption of formal amendments, this should be applied 'by analogy' to modifications of that treaty by subsequent practice.[409] This would entail a lower threshold for modification than in cases where the treaty is silent as to its own amendment, given that, by default, subsequent practice must establish the agreement of *all* the parties. Akehurst's reasoning therefore suggests that the exact threshold required for modification by subsequent practice will vary from treaty to treaty, but should be at least as high as that applicable to formal amendments. A problem with this approach is that assessing whether a specific threshold has been attained (for instance, a two-thirds majority) would often be impracticable given the tacit nature of modifications by subsequent practice. Apart from this practical consideration, the requirement of agreement of all the parties is meant to ensure that modification by subsequent practice reflects

[401] *Pulp Mills*, paras 132–5. [402] Ibid. paras 138–50.

[403] See Section 5.3.2(a) regarding the 2001 SPLOS decision.

[404] See eg Section 5.3.2(d) regarding Art 118 of the Third Geneva Convention.

[405] This is not to say, however, that a different threshold may not apply to establishing the parties' agreement where subsequent practice modifies, rather than merely supplementing, existing text—as in cases where it overrides formal amendment procedures. See in particular text to nn 222–3.

[406] Crawford, 'A Consensualist Interpretation of Article 31(3)', 32. See also B Simma, 'Miscellaneous Thoughts on Subsequent Agreements and Practice' in G Nolte (ed), *Treaties and Subsequent Practice* (OUP, 2013) 46, 47.

[407] See Section 5.2.3(a). [408] See Section 2.3.5.

[409] Akehurst, 'Hierarchy of the Sources', 277–8.

the parties' actual intention, precisely in light of the elusive nature of the process. Moreover, subsequent practice establishing the agreement of 'all' the parties does not necessarily require 'unanimity of opinion' in the way that active voting does, but rather consensus[410] by means of the active practice of certain parties combined with acceptance on the part of the rest.[411] It could even be argued that a small number of objecting States would not rule out the possibility of a modification.[412] Furthermore, the general premise for treaty change is that all parties are entitled to participate in the (informal) modification or (formal) amendment. The fact that formal amendment procedures often only require a (qualified) majority—or even weighted voting, where the parties are unequal from the outset—creates a special situation that differs from the default premise of inclusiveness of all the parties, and which cannot be applied, *mutatis mutandis*, to the tacit process of modification by subsequent practice.

Certain extensive treaty changes may still require implementation by means of formal amendment where modification by subsequent practice is either not possible (see especially the limitations discussed in Section 3.5 below) or the parties feel the need to specify the modification in clear and detailed terms.[413] For instance, formal amendment procedures were initiated to implement the specifics of a decision taken by the COP to the Basel Convention on the Control of Transboundary Movements of Hazardous Wastes and Their Disposals,[414] constituting a subsequent agreement that affected a key provision of the Convention[415]—an example that is analysed in detail in Chapter 5.[416] It suggests that States may be inclined to opt for formal amendment procedures when an important substantive provision is at issue and the modification in question carries significant economic and political consequences that must be set out with a great degree of clarity.

3.3.5 Relation to the object and purpose of the treaty

There is considerable debate as to how far modifications by subsequent practice can reach—could they go so far as to affect a treaty's object and purpose? The answer appears to be affirmative.[417] As pointed out in the ILC discussions, 'occasionally,

[410] See eg Section 5.3.2(b) regarding Art 4 of the Basel Convention.

[411] See Section 2.3.5. cf R Wolfrum and N Matz, *Conflicts in International Environmental Law* (Springer, 2010) 141.

[412] See Section 3.3.3(b), in particular (text to) nn 340–1.

[413] See further eg A Chanaki, *L'adaptation des traités dans le temps* (Bruylant, 2013).

[414] 1989 Basel Convention on the Control of Transboundary Movements of Hazardous Wastes and Their Disposals, 1673 UNTS 125.

[415] This amendment has still not entered into force.

[416] See Section 5.3.2(b).

[417] G Fitzmaurice, 'The Law and Procedure of the International Court of Justice' (1951) 28 BYBIL 8, fn 2 ('emergent purpose'); S Rosenne, *Developments in the Law of Treaties 1945–1986* (CUP, 1989) 240; T Sato, *Evolving Constitutions of International Organizations: A Critical Analysis of the Interpretive Frameworks of the Constituent Instruments of International Organizations* (Brill, 1996) 33; Bowman, '"Normalizing"', 340–2 (citing the examples of the Ramsar Convention and the mandate of the World Organization for Animal Health); Nolte, Introductory Report on Treaties over Time, 182; Nolte, Second Report on Subsequent Practice, para 164 (noting that if a subsequent agreement is clear, it 'may even contribute to modifying an essential element of a treaty').

the subsequent practice of the parties transformed a treaty so profoundly that it was made to serve a purpose diametrically opposed to the one for which it had been concluded'.[418] Even so, such practice is subject to certain crucial limitations.[419] Moreover, as previously noted, a modification *inter se* cannot affect the object and purpose of the treaty.[420]

For one thing, it is entirely conceivable that States may prefer to retain an existing treaty framework and its accompanying infrastructure in order to pursue new objectives. This is especially true for treaties constituting international organizations, where change brought about through subsequent practice often confers upon provisions of the constitutive treaty a meaning far removed from that originally intended.[421] For instance, NATO's 'new strategic concept' appears to go beyond the original purpose of the 1949 North Atlantic Treaty of collective defence and deterrence oriented towards the Soviet Union.[422] NATO's adaptation to a broad range of global issues and security tasks in recent years indicates a marked modification by subsequent practice of its original mandate,[423] a point that has also surfaced in national proceedings.[424] Similarly, the original purpose of the International Whaling Convention may have changed over time from a focus on the sustainable management of resources to conservation.[425] Lastly, the classic example of the development of the GATT into a *de facto* international organization through the practice of the parties over time furnishes another instance of modification of the object and purpose of a constituent treaty producing a result diametrically opposed to that originally intended by the drafters.[426]

Examples outside the context of international organizations can also be identified. For instance, during the ILC discussions on the law of treaties, one member gave the example of the 1948 Treaty between Belgium, France, Luxembourg, the Netherlands, and the United Kingdom of Great Britain and Northern Ireland for Collaboration in Economic, Social and Cultural Matters and for Collective Self-Defence.[427] Although the Treaty had originally been intended as a protection *against* Germany, the Federal Republic of Germany subsequently became a party. The Treaty

[418] Summary record of 766th meeting, para 45 (Lachs).

[419] For instance with regard to the balance established under the treaty between the rights and obligations of the States parties—Sadat-Akhavi, *Methods of Resolving Conflicts*, 131, cited in Koskenniemi, Fragmentation Report, para 109.

[420] Art 41 VCLT is clear on this. See Section 3.2.4. See also Koskenniemi, Fragmentation Report, 250.

[421] Summary record of 766th meeting, para 46 (Lachs); see also ibid. paras 38–9 (De Luna).

[422] North Atlantic Treaty (Washington Treaty) 1949, 34 UNTS 243. See Section 5.3.1(b).

[423] See eg L Condorelli, 'Conclusions Générales' in SFDI (ed), Colloque de Genève, *La pratique et le droit international* (Pédone, 2004) 304; RD Asmus and RC Holbrooke, 'Re-reinventing NATO', *Riga Papers* (2006) 1 <http://trends.gmfus.org/doc/A4_Holbrooke_c.pdf> accessed 10 April 2016; SC Hofmann, 'Debating Strategy in NATO: Obstacles to Defining a Meaningful New Strategic Concept' (IFRI, 2008) 1–4, 11. cf C Brölmann, 'Specialized Rules of Treaty Interpretation: International Organizations' in DB Hollis (ed), *The Oxford Guide to Treaties* (OUP, 2012) 507, 523.

[424] *PDS v Federal Government*, German Federal Constitutional Court (Case No 2 BvE 6/99) Judgment of 22 November 2001, 104, 151.

[425] See eg Bowman, '"Normalizing"', 293.

[426] See Section 5.3.1(d).

[427] 19 UNTS 51.

was hence transformed into a treaty of *alliance* with Germany as a direct result of the parties' changed intention as expressed in their subsequent practice.[428] Another interesting example, applicable only by analogy because it concerned a contract granting oil concessions, is the *Aminoil Arbitration*.[429] Here, the Tribunal found that the parties, through their practice in accordance with external developments, had modified the very nature of the contract, and 'brought about a metamorphosis in the whole character of the Concession'.[430]

Another consideration regarding the modification of a treaty's object and purpose by subsequent practice is that the very notion of 'object and purpose' is elusive and context dependent.[431] Complex multilateral treaties, such as the LOSC or the UN Charter,[432] often have several objects and purposes (which can each be formulated in specific as well as more general terms), many of which are not easily discernable, and, in any case, can hardly be determined exhaustively.[433] Moreover, the notion of 'object and purpose' is linked to the concept of 'essential' provisions, a relation underlined in Article 60(3)(b) VCLT on material breach, which refers to a 'violation of a provision essential to the accomplishment of the object or purpose of the treaty'.[434] The problem is that determining which provisions can be considered 'essential' is just as elusive. Neither the VCLT nor the ILC Commentary deals with this issue. It is also, by its very nature, subjective: provisions considered by a party as essential to the effective execution of the treaty and which may have induced it to become a party in the first place, may be of a merely ancillary character.[435] The implications of 'essential provisions' are discussed further in Section 3.5.2 below. In sum, determining what constitutes 'object and purpose' is inherently a matter of interpretation. It seems unnecessary to attempt to draw a strict distinction between modifications that affect a treaty's object and purpose, and those that affect other, less important provisions.

This may of course be different in cases where the treaty itself specifies that a provision or principle embodied in the treaty cannot be derogated from—for instance, Article 311(6) LOSC expressly prohibits derogation from the cornerstone principle of the 'common heritage of mankind', laid down in Article 136 of the Convention. It is sufficient here to note that certain fundamental provisions reflective of the treaty's object and purpose cannot be modified by subsequent practice in certain cases, either because this is expressly stated in the instrument, or as a consequence

[428] Summary record of 766th meeting, para 45 (Lachs). See further Section 5.3.2(e).

[429] See Section 5.2.2.

[430] *Aminoil Arbitration*, para 97; and see paras 98–9.

[431] See eg I Buffard and K Zemanek, 'The "Object and Purpose" of a Treaty: An Enigma?' (1998) 3 ARIEL 311.

[432] See eg *Certain Expenses Advisory Opinion*, para 168, referring to the 'other purposes' of the Charter as dependent on the primary place ascribed to international peace and security.

[433] Take eg the Bonn Convention example in Section 5.3.2(b): is the reading of 'species' as including non-migrant species something that impacts upon the treaty's 'object and purpose' or only upon an important substantive provision?

[434] See eg *Nicaragua v US*, Merits, para 273; B Simma and CJ Tams, 'Article 60 (1969)' in O Corten and P Klein (eds), *The Vienna Convention on the Law of Treaties* (OUP, 2011) 1350, 1358–9.

[435] 1966 Draft Articles on the Law of Treaties with Commentaries, 255 para 9, pointing out that the ILC preferred the term 'material' to 'fundamental' to avoid limiting the article only to breach of a provision touching upon the central purposes of the treaty.

of other mechanisms preventing derogation, such as the non-regression principle. These and other limitations are discussed at length in Section 3.5 below.

Based on these considerations, and subject to key limitations, subsequent practice can, in exceptional circumstances, modify the object and purpose(s) of a treaty. However, a higher threshold may be required for practice to establish the agreement of the parties in such cases.[436] This entails that the interpreter must identify the constitutive elements of subsequent practice with precision and justify that a modification has occurred more carefully—in this sense, the higher threshold represents a procedural rather than substantive hurdle.[437] It should be noted, however, that courts and tribunals rarely acknowledge modifications by subsequent practice of a treaty's object and purpose in so many words, given, *inter alia*, the often far-reaching implications of such modifications.

3.3.6 The result of modification

3.3.6a Relation to the original treaty

Another essential question pertains to the nature of the result of a modification by subsequent practice—and how it relates to the original treaty.[438] Do treaty modifications by subsequent practice constitute a new basis of obligation, or should they be conceived as having preserved the same—albeit transformed—basis in the original treaty?[439] This is, for instance, of direct relevance to the jurisdictional issue mentioned in the introduction to this book.[440] Namely, a dispute settlement body may have trouble asserting jurisdiction in a case submitted based on a referral clause relating to disputes regarding the 'interpretation and application of the treaty', but which actually concerns a modification thereof. If the modification by subsequent practice were to be regarded as an independent source of legal obligation, the treaty would no longer constitute the basis of the dispute invoked pursuant to its compromissory clause.[441] Of course, parties could always agree in advance that the compromissory clause will cover disputes relating to the interpretation or application of the treaty, including agreements to modify the treaty's provisions by subsequent practice.[442] But where parties have not done so, if the result of their subsequent practice constitutes a basis of obligation in its own right, the court will not have jurisdiction under the original treaty.

[436] Parallel formal amendment procedures may set this threshold even higher, as discussed in Section 3.3.4. The threshold may also be higher due to other factors—see Section 3.5.

[437] See Section 3.3.3(b).

[438] Subsequent practice may also modify a previous modification by subsequent practice.

[439] See Nolte, Introductory Report on Treaties over Time, 209. Note also the reference to '*supersession* of treaties by subsequent practice' in Crawford, 'A Consensualist Interpretation of Article 31(3)', 29 (emphasis added).

[440] Section 1.2.

[441] *Heathrow Airport User Charges Arbitration*, para 6.8; Nolte, Introductory Report on Treaties over Time, 207–8; Crawford, 'A Consensualist Interpretation of Article 31(3)', 33.

[442] Crawford, 'A Consensualist Interpretation of Article 31(3)', 33.

The same applies to the competence of certain treaty supervisory mechanisms and complaint commissions, such as the Inter-American Commission under the 1978 American Convention on Human Rights (ACHR).[443] Article 44 of the ACHR grants persons and nongovernmental entities the right to lodge petitions with the Commission containing denunciations or complaints of violation of the *Convention* by one of the States parties. If a modification by subsequent practice of the allegedly violated provision of the Convention were to be regarded as an independent source of legal obligation, the treaty would no longer constitute the basis of the complaint procedure initiated under Article 44.

Thus, two different views on the nature of the result of modification by subsequent practice exist. According to the first view, the modified original agreement remains the basis of obligation. Pursuant to the second view, subsequent practice creates an independent source of obligation rendering ineffective the provisions of the original agreement concerned. The result has to be determined on a case-by-case basis:

> The correct interpretation seems to be that both approaches are possible and that the answer depends on the understanding of the parties and on the context of each case whether the subsequent conduct was 'intended to establish a source of title independent of the terms of the treaty'. Such would be the case, for example, if the modification gave the treaty a new element or a new direction which affected its original program, or its object and purpose. On the other hand, if a modification by subsequent conduct is limited to spelling out further, or adapting, the original program of a treaty, the presumption would be that this does not change the character of the obligation deriving from the original treaty.[444]

In this view, the question of whether the original treaty remains the basis of obligation or whether the modification applies independently also relates to the explanations in Section 3.3.1 above regarding modifications in the form of 'alterations' or 'extensions' of treaty provisions by subsequent practice. Modification by subsequent practice may have been intended to establish an independent source of title if it gives the treaty a new 'direction' that perhaps even affects its object and purpose, rather than merely elaborating upon it. On the other hand, it is not clear why the result of a modification by subsequent practice that takes place in the context of implementation of the treaty would produce something 'outside' of the treaty; modification changes the content of a provision without changing its text, but still arguably falls within the total package of the treaty.

The result of a modification may also depend on the nature of the subsequent practice in question. Presumably, if it resembles a subsequent agreement in form and scope, it is more likely to be found to constitute a separate basis of obligation than if it resembles a 'tacit amendment', in which case it is more likely to be viewed as an integral part of the existing treaty framework.[445] In the *Heathrow Airport User*

[443] 1144 UNTS 123.

[444] Nolte, Introductory Report on Treaties over Time, 207–8, citing *Beagle Channel Arbitration*, para 169.

[445] There is, for example, an interesting discussion with regard to the basis for the powers of 'autonomous institutional arrangements', discussed in Section 2.3.1(c), to develop their underlying treaties through practice. It has been argued that, while sometimes their decisions can be regarded as interpretations, where their practice creates new obligations, 'the more persuasive explanation would treat the

Charges Arbitration, the Tribunal held that it could not have decided the case had the original agreement been modified by the parties' subsequent MoU, since the treaty's jurisdictional provision referred only to disputes 'arising under the Treaty'.[446] In other words, depending on the nature of the understanding in question, an MoU could be classified as a subsequent agreement that displaces the original treaty as the relevant basis of obligation.[447] Conversely, this could suggest that modifications in the form of more 'classical' types of subsequent practice tend to remain within the boundaries of the treaty regime, and do not constitute an independent source of international law. In this sense, subsequent practice represents a procedure in *relation* to a source.[448] The discussion as to whether modification results in a separate basis of obligation also relates to the distinction between modification by subsequent practice and modification by subsequent customary law, the latter of which always represents an independent basis of obligation—an issue discussed in detail in Chapter 4.[449]

3.3.6b 'Transferability' to subsequent treaties

The result of modification by subsequent practice also raises questions concerning the 'transferability' of such a modification from one treaty to another. One can imagine a scenario in which the original treaty becomes tacitly modified, following which a second treaty with identical content is concluded by the same States. An example could be the transition from the PCIJ Statute[450] to the ICJ Statute,[451] or GATT practice to WTO practice, or the transition between certain civil liability treaties. Does the tacit modification applicable to the first treaty carry through to the second treaty? This would not regularly be the case when the (same) parties to a treaty conclude another treaty, for, presumably, if they had wanted the modification to the original treaty to take effect, they would have explicitly included it in the subsequent instrument.[452] However, this may be different in certain circumstances.

powers of a COP or MOP as a type of a secondary legislation adopted under a primary treaty, or perhaps even constituting a new treaty, depending on the decision at hand.'—D Costelloe and M Fitzmaurice, 'Lawmaking by Treaty: Conclusion of Treaties and Evolution of Treaty Regimes in Practice' in C Brölmann and Y Radi (eds), *Research Handbook on the Theory and Practice of International Lawmaking* (Edward Elgar, 2016) 111, 119. See further the examples in Section 5.3.2(b).

[446] *Heathrow Airport User Charges Arbitration*, para 6.8 (referring to Art 17 of the Treaty).

[447] See also Section 2.3.1(a).

[448] See eg *Land and Maritime Boundary between Cameroon and Nigeria (Cameroon v Nigeria: Equatorial Guinea intervening)*, Judgment of 10 October 2002, Dissenting Opinion of Judge Ajibola, ICJ Reports 538 [*Cameroon v Nigeria*, Dissenting Opinion of Judge Ajibola] para 59 ('it must be clear that the *effectivités* of Nigeria in the Lake Chad basin is not meant to displace the conventional title (…) [but] will only vary or adjust the conventional title boundary'), suggesting that the modification resulting from the boundary practice becomes part and parcel of the treaty rather than displacing the treaty provision.

[449] See in particular Section 4.6. It has also been suggested that subsequent practice could be said to constitute 'special' customary law.

[450] Statute of the Permanent Court of International Justice 1920, 6 LNTS 379, 390.

[451] Statute of the International Court of Justice 1945 (1945) 39 AJIL Supp 215.

[452] This also relates to the point in Section 3.3.3(b) that a modification may subsequently revert to the original provision.

For instance, when it comes to transitions between treaties with the same wording, such as the PCIJ and ICJ Statutes, operating in an organizational context, the parties may not have wanted to modify the wording of the subsequent treaty based on other considerations (expediency, symbolic value, etc).[453] The corresponding modifications can thus still carry through to the later instrument.

3.3.6c Applicability to subsequent parties

Another question concerns the effect of a tacit treaty modification for a third State that becomes party to the treaty after the modification has taken place. Could the new State party subsequently deny the applicability of the modification to the extent that the State could not (reasonably be expected to) have known about it? According to principles of due diligence and good faith, new parties must look into the kind of treaty regime they sign up to. It will be difficult to invoke the excuse that they could not reasonably have been expected to know about a modification established by the other parties' practice. Moreover, Article 40(5) VCLT could be applied here by analogy: 'Any state which becomes a party to the treaty after the entry into force of the amending agreement shall, failing an expression of a different intention by that state: (a) be considered as a party to the treaty as amended'. In any case, this puts the onus on the acceding State.

A similar question relates to the issue of succession. Is the new State bound by the same (tacitly modified) treaty obligations as its predecessor State? This issue is not explored further in this book, but it is useful to note that, in any case, human rights treaties have come to be regarded as automatically applicable to new States in the case of succession, presumably along with any accompanying modifications.[454]

3.3.7 A customary rule on treaty modification by subsequent practice?

It has been speculated whether there is a rule of customary international law—or perhaps a general principle of international law—on treaty modification by subsequent practice. Numerous legal scholars have referred to a (customary or pre-existing) rule or principle of international law recognizing treaty modification by subsequent practice evidenced in the case law and practice.[455] Several ILC members also seemed

[453] See also the discussion in Section 5.3.1(d) on the WTO practice of accession protocols, presumably a remnant of the GATT, but which, given the differences in structure between the WTO and its predecessor, may not work in the same way in the WTO context. See Qin, 'The Conundrum of WTO Accession Protocols', 373.

[454] F Pocar, 'Some Remarks on the Continuity of Human Rights and International Humanitarian Law Treaties' in E Cannizzaro (ed), *The Law of Treaties Beyond the Vienna Convention* (OUP, 2011) 279.

[455] See eg Jacobs, 'Varieties of Approach to Treaty Interpretation', 332; Karl, *Vertrag*, 292–3; Pauwelyn, *Conflict of Norms*, 50; T Ruys, *The Intangible 'Armed Attack': Evolutions in Customary Practice Pertaining to the Right of States to Self-Defense and the Quest for a Definition of 'Armed Attack' under Article 51 UN Charter* (PhD, Catholic University of Leuven, 2009) 100 ('It is generally accepted that treaty modification by subsequent practice of the parties constitutes a rule of customary law.'); Arato, 'Subsequent Practice', 464 and fn 73. See also eg Fitzmaurice, 'The Law and Procedure of the International Court of Justice' (1957), 225; Capotorti, 'L'extinction', 519; Sur, *L'interprétation*, 201; Villiger, *Customary International Law and Treaties* (1985), para 302 and fn 58; Feldman, 'Evolving Treaty

to have supported this notion during the drafting of the law of treaties, prompted by Special Rapporteur Sir Humphrey Waldock,[456] as did a number of delegations at the ensuing Vienna Conference in 1968.[457] Pauwelyn therefore argues that despite the absence of a codifying provision in the Vienna Convention, the possibility of modifying treaties through subsequent practice by means of implicit agreement is generally understood to be a rule of customary international law.[458] Kohen, by contrast, argues that the rejection of the draft article on modification by subsequent practice by so many different States at the Vienna Conference in 1968 proves that it cannot be part of customary law.[459] Yet this argument cannot stand given the actual reasons for the article's rejection and the overall support for the substance of the article despite that decision.[460] During the drafting of the VCLT, there was insufficient time and political will to deal with the rules on subsequent practice in more detail. States expressed the fear that retaining the provision would require pinpointing the nature and operation of the process with a degree of specificity and accuracy too difficult to codify, as compared to the convenience of leaving the matter to the realm of customary law.[461]

It is true that there were only limited references to case law and State practice in support of the view that modification by subsequent practice represents a customary rule, and none of the judgments referred to explicitly recognize its customary status.[462] However, the relevant practice, case law, and doctrine were less extensive when the Vienna Convention was being drafted than they are today, as well as perhaps too recent at the time to be regarded as reflective of customary international law.[463] They may since have become established.[464] If the process of treaty modification by subsequent practice can be said to have developed into a customary rule, it could be read into the Vienna Convention via its Preamble, which provides that 'the rules of customary international law will continue to govern questions not regulated by the provisions of the present Convention'.[465] The process of modification by

Obligation', 658, 705. See moreover Nolte, Second Report on Subsequent Practice, para 122: 'After the Vienna Conference, writers (...) mostly came to the conclusion that (...) treaties can, as a general rule under the customary law of treaties, indeed be modified by subsequent practice (...).'

[456] Summary record of 866th meeting, paras 8 (Jiménez de Aréchaga), 17 (Tunkin), 36 (Yasseen).

[457] 38th Meeting of the Committee of the Whole, paras 8 (Iraq), 22 (Italy) (referring to 'a legal fact which had always existed'), 33 (Austria), 48 (Israel), 50 (Switzerland), 51 (Argentina).

[458] Pauwelyn, *Conflict of Norms*, 50.

[459] Kohen, 'Keeping Subsequent Agreements and Practice in Their Right Limits', 37.

[460] See Section 3.2.

[461] See in particular Section 3.2.6.

[462] *Namibia Advisory Opinion, Temple of Préah Vihéar*, and *Air Transport Services Arbitration* (*US/France*), discussed extensively in Section 5.2.

[463] It could also be argued that the fact that one of the ILC's main tasks is to codify existing customary international law in addition to 'progressive development', coupled with the fact that a rule of modification was included in the Draft Articles on the Law of Treaties, which was, moreover, recognized by the majority of members as a rule of international law, implies the existence of a customary rule of modification by subsequent practice. See also Statute of the International Law Commission, UNGA Res 174 (II) of 21 November 1947, UN Doc A/RES/174(II), Art 15.

[464] Feldman, 'Evolving Treaty Obligations', 705.

[465] This does not pertain to the question of legality of modification by subsequent practice, for even if it is not a customary rule, it is not prohibited by the VCLT. See eg Distefano, 'L'accord tacite', 30 and fn 77.

subsequent practice could also be seen as the effect of the application of general principles of law. Overall, it remains unclear whether this process can be said to have crystallized into customary international law, or whether it is even capable of constituting such a norm in the first place. Nevertheless, the politically and legally sensitive nature of the issue makes unwritten (customary) law a more adequate medium for such a process than conventional law.

3.4 Identifying Modification by Subsequent Practice: Distinguishing between Interpretation and Modification

The distinction between treaty interpretation and modification lies at the heart of the present endeavour—as we have seen, the very definition of modification is set out relative to interpretation.[466] Despite the concomitant difficulties, making the distinction is necessary, for the legal effects of interpretation and modification are distinct. The ensuing section looks at the relevance and process of doing so—a stepping-stone for further analysis of the nature and scope of modifications by subsequent practice.

3.4.1 Relevance of distinguishing between interpretation and modification

It has been pointed out that, '[w]hile interpretation uncovers what is out there, modification places something new into the world.'[467] Interpretation and modification may sometimes appear indistinguishable in practice—although, as we shall see, there are cases in which the distinction can easily be made. But the two can have very different legal (and practical) effects.[468]

It has been argued, for one thing, that modifications constitute an integral part of the treaty, with automatic effect in all situations in which the treaty is applied, whereas the parties' agreement to a given interpretation '*may* have a legal effect (...) limited to the particular case at hand'.[469] Under certain circumstances, modification could conceivably even create a basis of obligation outside of the underlying

[466] See Section 3.3.1 on the requirement for modification through alteration of a 'genuine' conflict that cannot be reconciled through interpretation.

[467] Venzke, *How Interpretation Makes International Law*, 236, citing GE do Nascimento e Silva, 'Le Facteur Temps et les Traités' (1977) 154 RC 215, 269.

[468] See eg Section 1.2. See also *Kasikili/Sedudu Island*, Dissenting Opinion of Judge Parra-Aranguren, para 16; G Scelle, *Theorie juridique de la revision des traités* (Librairie du Recueil Sirey, 1936) 11; Yasseen, 'L'interprétation', 45; Linderfalk, *On the Interpretation of Treaties*, 168. cf Engel, '"Living" International Constitutions', 909.

[469] Linderfalk, *On the Interpretation of Treaties*, 168. This implies that interpretations, as opposed to modifications, do not become part and parcel of the treaty. See by analogy the argument in Nottage and Sebastian, 'WTO Trade Negotiations', 17, that decisions of the Ministerial Council, constituting subsequent agreements, can be relevant as interpretations, but may not be invocable as the basis of a legal claim or defence in WTO dispute settlement proceedings.

treaty.[470] It was already explained in Section 3.3.6(a) that this can impact the work of international courts and tribunals in their ability to assert jurisdiction in a given case, as well as that of other actors such as treaty supervisory mechanisms: the dispute settlement body in question will have to assess whether the case concerns a modification as an independent source of legal obligation falling outside the scope of the treaty's compromissory clause on disputes relating to its 'application and interpretation', in which case it lacks jurisdiction.[471]

Moreover, crucially, a 'true' *interpretation* explains what a treaty (provision) has always been, whereas modification brings about a *change* in the meaning it held before.[472] Thus, 'modification normally only generates consequences for the future'.[473] Pursuant to the principle of non-retroactivity, a modification may not apply in legal proceedings in which the provision at issue was modified *subsequent* to the initiation of the proceedings.[474] In other words, if the result of the subsequent practice is regarded as an interpretation, it may be relevant to the proceedings, whereas the application of a modification may be limited temporally due to the fact that it reflects a concrete change in the previous meaning of the affected provisions, and thus, unlike interpretation, will not be applicable retroactively.[475]

Another consideration, as discussed in Section 2.5.3(c) above, is that, while the interpretation of one treaty could be expected to influence the interpretation of similar terms in other treaties, modification by subsequent practice does not, in principle, have 'horizontal' effects, since it carries relevance only for the specific treaty. However, circumstances could be imagined in which treaties are interrelated or overlapping in terms of substance and composition of States parties, such that subsequent practice in relation to one treaty influences that of the other. Moreover, the assertion that modifications pertain in principle only to the specific treaty does not hold in those cases where the subsequent practice of the treaty parties generates customary international law.

470 See the discussion in Section 3.3.6(a). See eg *Heathrow Airport User Charges Arbitration*, para 6.8; Nolte, Introductory Report on Treaties over Time, 207–8; Crawford, 'A Consensualist Interpretation of Article 31(3)', 33.

471 See further Sections 1.2 and 3.3.6(a).

472 G Kaufmann-Kohler, 'Interpretive Powers of the NAFTA Free Trade Commission—Necessary Safety Valve or Infringement of the Rule of Law?' in F Bachand (ed), *Fifteen Years of NAFTA Chapter 11 Arbitration, IAI Conference Proceedings* (JurisNet, 2011) 175, 192. See also Ruys, '*Armed Attack*', 22. This applies even in the case of evolutionary interpretation, which is still based on the original intention of the parties—see Section 2.5.3.

473 Ruys, '*Armed Attack*', 22, citing Sur, *L'interprétation*, 202; Yasseen, 'L'interprétation', 47, 52.

474 This scenario may be especially relevant in cases where a modification crystallizes in a relatively short period of time.

475 In special cases of treaties such as BITs creating rights for investors as third-party beneficiaries, it is especially important to take into account whether a treaty modification by subsequent practice accords temporally with the timing of the acts in dispute. See T Gazzini, 'Bilateral Investment Treaties' in T Gazzini and E De Brabandere (eds), *International Investment Law: The Sources of Rights and Obligations* (Martinus Nijhoff, 2012) 99, 117, citing eg *Enron Corporation and Ponderosa Assets*, Award, para 337: 'Even if the interpretation [of Article IX of the BIT in question] were shared today by both parties to the Treaty, it would still not result in a change of its terms. States are of course free to amend the Treaty by consenting to another text, but this would not affect rights acquired under the Treaty by investors or other beneficiaries.'

The utility of distinguishing between interpretation and modification also lies in the ability to establish when a certain body entitled to interpret or apply a treaty has gone beyond its competence and veered into the realm of actual treaty change.[476] In other words, functionally, knowledge of a modification can be used for contestation. Moreover, the knowledge that a modification has occurred can prompt additional confirmation of the modification by means of formal treaty amendment.[477]

Perhaps most importantly, as mentioned in the introduction to this work,[478] the effects of modification often reach further than interpretation[479] (interpretation, in principle, does not alter the rights and obligations enshrined under the treaty[480]), although this is not always so—see for instance the discussion on the ICJ's judgment in the *Costa Rica v Nicaragua* case.[481] In principle, modifications are not bound by the 'four corners' of the text, and can therefore significantly change key treaty provisions, give rise to entirely new obligations, or even create new institutions and international organizations, as in the case of the GATT.[482] These effects, and the functionality of distinguishing them from interpretation, are observed further in the collection of examples of practice in Chapter 5.

3.4.2 Distinguishing between interpretation and modification in practice

The constitutive elements and evidentiary standards outlined in Sections 2.3 and 3.3.3 of this book provide a solid basis for identifying—and filtering—relevant subsequent practice. But they do not provide a full basis for identifying subsequent practice in the process of *modifying* as distinguished from *interpreting* treaties[483]—in other words, for pinpointing where determining the meaning of a provision ends and change begins.[484]

The term 'modification' was previously defined in Section 3.3.1 for present purposes as an alteration, extension, or termination of treaty provisions by subsequent practice. As explained, an 'alteration' entails determining the existence of a 'true' conflict between the contents of the treaty provision affected and the substance of the agreement established by subsequent practice. A 'true' conflict exists when the norms in question cannot sensibly be read together and complied with simultaneously; this is itself a matter of interpretation. The existence of such conflict, and hence the occurrence of modification by subsequent practice, must not be presumed.[485] An 'extension' of treaty provisions by subsequent practice, meanwhile, constitutes modification where it supplements the treaty with a novel element or

[476] See eg Section 5.3.2(b) on examples in the context of MEAs.

[477] Ibid. See also Section 3.3.4. See further R Crootof, 'Change Without Consent: How Customary International Law Modifies Treaties' (2016) 41 Yale JIL 237, 276 (making the same point with regard to treaty modification by subsequent customary law, which 'may also prompt states to engage in more traditional means of treaty modification').

[478] See Section 1.2.

[479] See eg C Djeffal, *Static and Evolutive Treaty Interpretation: A Functional Reconstruction* (CUP, 2015) 42.

[480] Ruys, '*Armed Attack*', 22.

[481] See Sections 2.5.3(c) and 5.2.1.

[482] See Section 5.3.1(d).

[483] Feldman, 'Evolving Treaty Obligations', 655.

[484] Kammerhofer, *Uncertainty in International Law*, 125.

[485] See Section 3.3.1.

direction, be it a procedure, obligation, or right—especially where its effects are far-reaching, such as where it creates a new institution.[486] By contrast, where subsequent practice merely amounts to a clarification or concretization of treaty terms, it is to be characterized as an interpretation.[487]

Of course, there are instances where practice has clearly or even explicitly led to modification, but such instances are relatively rare.[488] Given the breadth and flexibility of the interpretative means available, in most cases there is sufficient room to construe the result of subsequent practice as a form of 'dynamic' interpretation, no matter how far-fetched the result.[489] Thus, distinguishing between these two outcomes of subsequent practice is a complex, open-ended task, ultimately bypassed by the ILC in its 1966 Draft Articles on the Law of Treaties, as discussed.[490]

The distinction is complicated further by the fact that States typically prefer that their practice be regarded as an interpretation of the treaty,[491] especially where an organization such as the UN or WTO is involved.[492] Thus, tacit modification is likely to occur under the guise of interpretative practice[493]—a good example would be the controversial interpretation of Article 1105 of NAFTA by the Federal Trade Commission in 2001.[494] The same applies in certain cases of actual treaty *breaches*, which States might prefer to treat as interpretative disagreements.[495] Determining

[486] See the discussion in Section 5.3.1(d) concerning the GATT. [487] See Section 3.3.1.

[488] See eg Sections 5.2.1 (*Israeli Wall Advisory Opinion*), 5.3.1(d) (GATT), and 5.3.2(a) (1958 Geneva Conventions on the Law of the Sea).

[489] See Nolte, Second Report on Subsequent Practice, para 142.

[490] Section 3.2. See eg R Bernhardt, 'Interpretation and Implied (Tacit) Modification of Treaties: Comments on Arts. 27, 28, 29 and 38 of the ILC's 1966 Draft Articles on the Law of Treaties' (1967) 27 ZaöRV 491, 499.

[491] For one thing, it has been argued that more justification goes into acting upon an alleged treaty modification than a treaty interpretation. See eg Crootof, 'Change Without Consent', 293, arguing that, as opposed to modifications, 'states are free to propose interpretations and act on them', without awaiting international approval of that interpretation. Although 'the action may later be determined to be unlawful (...) the state that acted on an unapproved interpretation is unlikely to be punished'. By contrast, a State justifying action on the basis of an alleged modification must to a greater extent 'respect the international community's consensus' (ibid. 297), such that, 'somewhat counterintuitively, arguments based on modification by subsequently developed customary international law may be less destabilizing and spur states to show greater respect for the consensus of the international community' (ibid. 299).

[492] Akehurst, *Modern Introduction*, 204. See also eg YZ Blum, *Eroding the United Nations Charter* (Martinus Nijhoff, 1993) 243–4 (referring, in the context of the UN Charter, to the 'widespread tendency to present even the most far-reaching departure from the plain meaning of the provisions' as interpretation, despite the fact that modifications of the Charter by subsequent practice are an 'undeniable fact'); Shaw, *International Law*, 88. This point also relates to the discussion in Ch 2 that one must look at the motivations underlying the respective practice, as touched but not elaborated upon in the 1966 ILC discussions.

[493] See eg Voicu, *De l'interprétation authentique*, 89; Akehurst, *Modern Introduction*, 204, 268; A Orakhelashvili, *The Interpretation of Acts and Rules in Public International Law* (OUP, 2008) 105.

[494] Notes of Interpretation of Certain Chapter Eleven Provisions (Free Trade Commission, 31 July 2001) <www.sice.oas.org/tpd/nafta/Commission/CH11understanding_e.asp> accessed 19 April 2017. See eg CH Brower, 'Why the FTC Notes of Interpretation Constitute a Partial Amendment of NAFTA Article 1105' (2006) 46 VJIL 347, 349–50. See further the extensive discussion in Section 5.2.3(c).

[495] Rosenne, *Breach of Treaty*, 119–20. For instance, a State might prefer not to react to another State's breach to avoid terminating the treaty or leading to a deterioration of relations between the parties.

whether an act of treaty application has strayed so far from the treaty's terms that it amounts to a *violation* may, in substance, involve essentially the same exercise as identifying whether subsequent practice has led to a *modification* of the treaty—in both cases, one looks for a 'genuine' conflict[496] between the practice observed and the terms of the treaty (the crucial difference being the requirement of a general practice evidencing the parties' agreement in the case of a modification). Indeed, as previously discussed, initial instances of practice deviating from the treaty may at first be regarded as violations thereof, up until the point when the practice of the treaty parties crystallizes into a modification.[497] Another analogy can be drawn here to the challenge of determining whether an interpretative declaration, purporting mainly to 'specify and clarify',[498] is actually a treaty reservation in disguise, with the effect to 'exclude or modify'.[499] Both distinctions—namely, between an interpretative declaration and a reservation in disguise, and between an interpretation by subsequent practice and a modification in disguise—require essentially the same exercise of carefully examining the substance and context of the statement or practice.

Moreover, courts and tribunals seem disinclined to acknowledge tacit modification by subsequent practice where it has occurred,[500] most likely due to the perception that States are wary of the possibility of judicial bodies using tacit modification as a way of changing the law.[501] Instead, courts and tribunals often prefer recourse to alternative adaptation mechanisms, such as evolutionary interpretation,[502] and favour explicit treaty rules over the more contentious process of identifying implied agreements by subsequent practice or new customary law.[503] Even when courts explicitly recognize a tacit modification, they fail to provide generalizable criteria for identifying it.[504]

In sum, tribunals are reluctant, and States are wary, of admitting that modification has occurred: 'states and tribunals may be inclined to shoe-horn a situation of "modification" into one of "interpretation" instead, making it difficult to identify precedents in this area'.[505]

These underlying considerations aside, many scholars have pointed out the inherent difficulty of fixing the dividing line between 'interpretation properly so called and modification effected under the pretext of interpretation'.[506] But the fact that

496 See Section 3.3.1. 497 See text to nn 348–50.

498 ILC, *Report of the International Law Commission on the work of its 59th session*, UN Doc A/62/10 (2007) Ch IV(C), 48 ('Definition 1.2').

499 Article 2(1)(d) VCLT. See eg LDM Nelson, 'Declarations, Statements and "Disguised Reservations" with Respect to the Convention on the Law of the Sea' (2001) 50 ICLQ 767.

500 With notable exceptions—see eg Section 3.1.

501 Murphy, 'Subsequent Agreement and Subsequent Practice', 83, 87. See also Nolte, Second Report on Subsequent Practice, para 137.

502 See eg *Costa Rica v Nicaragua*, discussed in Sections 2.5.3(c) and 5.2.1.

503 Pauwelyn, *Conflict of Norms*, 141.

504 See the cases cited at nn 2–5. See also eg Nolte, Second Report on Subsequent Practice, para 165; Kadelbach, 'Domestic Constitutional Concerns', 148.

505 Murphy, 'Subsequent Agreement and Subsequent Practice', 90. But see Fitzmaurice, 'The Law and Procedure of the International Court of Justice' (1957), 225.

506 Sinclair, *Vienna Convention*, 138. See also eg Voicu, *De l'interprétation authentique*, 100; Brownlie, *Principles*, 601. cf Karl, *Vertrag*, 3.

the boundary between interpretative and modifying practice is often blurred does not mean that it cannot be established:

The fact that subsequent agreements and practice lie somewhere between interpretation, informal modification, and formal amendment is a truism that makes almost any international lawyer content and relieved not to have to dig any further into the question. All the more so if the same attitude is taken up by international courts and decision-makers alike.[507]

Numerous authors[508] reject this resignation to the impossibility of distinguishing treaty modification from treaty interpretation: 'one can only show that we experience difficulty in ascertaining the borderline, not that it does not exist'.[509] There has to be a way of identifying the moment where subsequent practice in the application of a treaty results in its modification, even if only by means of reference points applicable on a case-by-case basis. Identifying such indicators is the focal point of the ensuing sections and of the compilation of examples analysed in Chapter 5.

A convenient point of departure to distinguish between interpretation and modification is determining whether practice diverges significantly from (a plausible interpretation of) the 'natural and ordinary meaning' of the treaty terms.[510] This entails adopting a 'textual' interpretation as a starting point for the distinction, also in order to arrive at the parties' intention, to the extent that it can be said to have been expressed in words.[511] Accordingly, a manifest divergence from the ordinary meaning of a provision will indicate a treaty modification by subsequent practice. One example is the 'accepted practice' at issue in the *Israeli Wall Advisory Opinion*, which was contrary to the express and straightforward terms of Article 12(1) of the UN Charter.[512] However, the line between interpretation and modification can be blurred even when dealing with seemingly clear terms or situations.[513] Determining when terms can be considered 'clear' is a matter of interpretation in

[507] Bianchi, 'Law, Time, and Change', 131.

[508] See eg Bernhardt, 'Interpretation', 499, 501; Wolfke, 'Treaties and Custom', 34; Linderfalk, *On the Interpretation of Treaties*, 168–9; Akehurst, *Modern Introduction*, 204.

[509] Kammerhofer, *Uncertainty in International Law*, 243–4. cf Karl, *Vertrag*, 9–10.

[510] Waldock, Third Report on the Law of Treaties, 61 para 25; Nolte, Introductory Report on Treaties over Time, 181; Linderfalk, *On the Interpretation of Treaties*, 169. See also ILC, *Topical summary of the discussion held in the Sixth Committee of the General Assembly during its 66th session*, UN Doc A/CN.4/650 (20 January 2012) para 54 (on the need to clarify the extent to which subsequent practice can depart from the literal meaning of the treaty without amending or violating the treaty); Wolfke, 'Treaties and Custom', 34 ('by accepting this simple criterion the number of true interpretations [ie modifications] by means of practice will be rather rare').

[511] See eg *Namibia Advisory Opinion*, 31, emphasizing the parties' intentions. See also A Barak, *Purposive Interpretation in Law* (Princeton UP, 2005) 18, 65, citing, *inter alia*, LH Tribe, *American Constitutional Law* (3rd edn, Foundation Press, 2000) 92 ('[M]y position is that the limits of the text set the limits of interpretation in law (...). An activity is interpretive if it confers meaning on a text that is consistent with one of its (explicit or implicit) meanings, in the (public or private) language of the text. (...) [W]e must insist that interpretation confer upon the text a meaning that it is capable of bearing in the language in which it is expressed.'); R Goode, H Kronke, and E McKendrick (eds), *Transnational Commercial Law: Text, Cases, and Materials* (OUP, 2007) 121.

[512] See Section 5.2.1.

[513] Nolte, Introductory Report on Treaties over Time, 202. See the cases discussed in Sections 3.5.1(a), 5.2.1, and 5.2.2 of this book.

itself,[514] just as rules appear to be compatible with each other or in conflict '*as a result of interpretation*'.[515]

In the aforementioned example of the *Israeli Wall Advisory Opinion*, the ICJ considered the 'increasing tendency' of the General Assembly and Security Council to 'deal in parallel with the same matter concerning the maintenance of international peace and security',[516] in particular with regard to recommendations,[517] to be consistent with Article 12(1) of the UN Charter—despite the fact that the practice contradicts the clear wording of the article, which specifically precludes the General Assembly from making recommendations with regard to disputes or situations in respect of which the Security Council is exercising its functions. This indicates a tacit modification.[518] The Court nonetheless avoided construing it as more than 'accepted practice' amounting to an interpretative exercise.[519] Likewise, in the *Temple of Préah Vihéar* case, the ICJ held that the boundary line accepted by the parties through their subsequent practice, though clearly at variance with the ordinary meaning of the text of the boundary treaty, constituted an authentic interpretation that prevailed over the relevant treaty provision.[520] It did not, however, refer to an outright modification (though authentic interpretations constitute new legal enactments rather than mere interpretations).[521]

As an example unrelated to judicial proceedings, subsequent practice seems to have expanded the definition of 'migratory species' in Article I(1)(a) of the Convention on Migratory Species (CMS)[522] to include species that become *non*-migratory due to climate change, as well as classical *sedentary* species subject to 'transboundary, climate-induced range shifts', which are not, *stricto sensu*, covered by the provisions of the Convention.[523] This seems to have led to a broadening of the scope of the CMS regime to such an extent that it could arguably even affect the treaty's object and purpose.[524] This strongly suggests modification over interpretation.[525]

514 See eg Greig, *Intertemporality*, 93–4, citing *Namibia Advisory Opinion*. cf Bianchi, 'Law, Time, and Change', 137, arguing that 'a text is clear not so much because its meaning is uncontroversial', but 'because the text is uncontested'.

515 Koskenniemi, Fragmentation Report, para 412 (emphasis in the original). See Section 3.3.1 on the definition of a 'true' conflict.

516 *Israeli Wall Advisory Opinion*, para 27.

517 Ibid. paras 25–33.

518 See eg Liang, 'Modifying the UN Charter', 10; Nolte, Introductory Report on Treaties over Time, 180, 201–2; Arato, 'Treaty Interpretation', 326–7; Qin, 'The Conundrum of WTO Accession Protocols', 409.

519 *Israeli Wall Advisory Opinion,* para 28.

520 *Temple of Préah Vihéar*, 33.

521 Tammelo, *Treaty Interpretation*, 6. See also eg Waldock, Sixth Report on the Law of Treaties, 89, para 8; Orakhelashvili, *Interpretation of Acts and Rules*, 515; Karl, *Vertrag*, 46. *Temple of Préah Vihéar* was also cited by the ILC in support of treaty modification by subsequent practice—Waldock, Sixth Report on the Law of Treaties, 90, para 8. See also *Cameroon v Nigeria*, Dissenting Opinion of Judge Ajibola, paras 52–4.

522 Bonn Convention on the Conservation of Migratory Species of Wild Animals 1979 (1980) 19 ILM 15 (CMS).

523 M Bowman, P Davies, and C Redgwell, *Lyster's International Wildlife Law* (2nd edn, CUP, 2011) 540–1; A Trouwborst, 'Transboundary Wildlife Conservation in a Changing Climate: The Adaptation of the Bonn Convention on Migratory Species and its Daughter Instruments to Climate Change' (2012) 4 Diversity 258, 287–8.

524 See eg Preamble and Art 2 of the CMS.

525 See further Section 5.3.2(b).

The approach of taking the text of the treaty as the main point of departure fails to account for the issue of ambiguous provisions, complicated further by the diversity of authentic texts and languages in modern treaty practice. The wider the range of interpretations available due to the ambiguity of certain provisions,[526] the more difficult it will be to tell when a modification has occurred.[527] The same can be said of terms that are inherently 'evolutionary' or which can be expanded by means of the doctrine of implied powers.[528] And yet, as already discussed, dynamic interpretation has its limits:

[W]ords are not infinitely elastic. As new norms become widely accepted, certain inflexible treaty obligations will appear progressively more absurd or impractical, and proposed [dynamic] interpretations attempting to resolve discrepancies between treaty law and state action will appear less plausible and convincing.[529]

In other words:

[O]ne must take account of the aforementioned possibility of dynamic treaty interpretation and of the fact that a treaty term may possess many "ordinary meanings". Modification can arguably be defined as a the situation where the new rule cannot be fit into *any* of the plausible meanings that could be given to the treaty text, nor into the special meaning which the parties intended to give to the text at the time of its adoption.[530]

Moreover, as explained in Section 3.3.1 above, modification is not only a process of altering existing provisions; it can also supplement them with a novel element or direction. Thus, subsequent practice creating new obligations, or even new institutions,[531] cannot be understood by reference to the treaty text alone; rather, such new developments must be seen in the context of the treaty regime and its underlying purposes—hence the relation to the issue of implied powers.

One could take the example of the voting practice of the Security Council in relation to UN Charter Article 27(3).[532] Article 27(3) requires the 'concurring votes'

[526] See *Legal Consequences of the Continued Presence of South Africa in Namibia (South West Africa) Notwithstanding Security Council Resolution 276 (1970)*, Advisory Opinion of 21 June 1971, Separate Opinion Judge Dillard, ICJ Reports 150, 154 fn 1: 'It has been observed that the word "ambiguous" is in itself not free from ambiguity. Much depends on the nature of the subject-matter to be interpreted (...). Much depends also on the character of the applicable norms (...), and much depends on the expectations aroused in light of the entire text and the social interests involved.'

[527] See Ford, 'Legal Processes of Change', 104, citing E Zoller, 'The "Corporate Will" of the United Nations and the Rights of the Minority' (1987) 81 AJIL 610, 616; F Salerno, 'Treaties Establishing Objective Regimes' in E Cannizzaro (ed), *The Law of Treaties Beyond the Vienna Convention* (OUP, 2011) 225. See also, by analogy, Rosenne, *Breach of Treaty*, 121, discussing how political compromise leads to ambiguity, making it harder to distinguish treaty breaches from interpretation.

[528] See Sections 2.5.3–2.5.4 on the relation between subsequent practice and, respectively, evolutionary interpretation and implied powers. See further Section 3.5.2 on evolutionary interpretation and implied powers as alternative adaptation mechanisms.

[529] Crootof, 'Change Without Consent', 247–8.

[530] Ruys, '*Armed Attack*', 23. cf Waldock, Sixth Report on the Law of Treaties, 90, para 9 ('Clearly, on the plane of interpretation, the treaty has only one correct interpretation.').

[531] See Sections 1.2 and 5.3.1(d). See also eg *Effect of Awards of Compensation Made by the UN Administrative Tribunal*, 47, 56–8.

[532] See Section 5.2.1.

of the permanent members of the Security Council for certain decisions. The word 'concurrence' does not, at first sight, leave much room for ambiguity.[533] In practice, however, the Council has taken 'concurring' to mean 'non-objection', contrary to what was originally intended by the drafters.[534] This enabled it, for instance, to recommend intervention in the 1950 Korean War in the absence of the Soviet Union.[535] The practice could be said to conform to the principle of effectiveness.[536] According to this principle, paying insufficient regard to—or, conversely, placing undue emphasis on—the text, the parties' (believed) intentions, or the treaty's object and purpose,[537] is unlikely to lead to a result that reflects the 'real area of treaty operation'.[538] In the case of UN Charter Article 27(3), the 'reinterpreted' voting procedure allows the Council to adopt decisions faster, while preserving the permanent members' veto power, and perhaps also granting permanent members the discretion to support a politically sensitive decision without expressly endorsing it. From this vantage point, the Council's practice may be seen as a 'dynamic' interpretation.[539] Indeed, in the *Namibia Advisory Opinion*, the ICJ implied that this voting practice falls within the interpretative bounds of the Charter,[540] despite the fact that the *travaux préparatoires* indicate otherwise.[541] This allowed the Court to avoid any 'slippery slopes of reasoning' or claims of treaty breach.[542] A majority of writers, however, believe that Article 27(3) has been effectively modified.[543]

Once more, the discussion regarding Charter Article 27(3) demonstrates that determining whether a tacit agreement by subsequent practice merely interprets a treaty or actually modifies it can be a difficult question of interpretation even when the circumstances appear straightforward at first sight. An analysis of the practice in

[533] Ford, 'Legal Processes of Change', 105. cf Greig, *Intertemporality*, 94–5, referring to *Namibia Advisory Opinion*, Separate Opinion of Judge Dillard, 153–4.

[534] See Section 1.2. [535] See Section 5.2.1. [536] See Section 2.5.1.

[537] Aust, *Modern Treaty Law*, 185.

[538] DP O'Connell, *International Law*, vol I (2nd edn, Stevens and Sons, 1970) 253.

[539] See eg B Simma, S Brunner, and H-P Kaul, 'Article 27' in B Simma (ed), *The Charter of the United Nations: A Commentary* (2nd edn, OUP, 2002) 476; CF Amerasinghe, *Principles of the Institutional Law of International Organizations* (2nd edn, CUP, 2005) 55.

[540] *Namibia Advisory Opinion*, para 22.

[541] See eg LM Goodrich, E Hambro, and AP Simons (eds), *Charter of the United Nations: Commentary and Documents* (3rd edn, Columbia UP, 1969) 229; Gardiner, *Treaty Interpretation*, 245; Aust, *Modern Treaty Law*, 216.

[542] Venzke, *How Interpretation Makes International Law*, 73.

[543] See eg *Legal Consequences of the Continued Presence of South Legal Consequences for States of the Continued Presence of South Africa in Namibia (South West Africa) Notwithstanding Security Council Resolution 276 (1970)*, Advisory Opinion of 21 June 1971, Separate Opinion of Judge De Castro, ICJ Reports 170 [*Namibia Advisory Opinion*, Separate Opinion of Judge De Castro] 186; *Cameroon v Nigeria*, Dissenting Opinion of Judge Ajibola, paras 52–3; G Fitzmaurice, 'The Law and Procedure of the International Court of Justice, 1951-54: General Principles and Sources of Law' (1953) 30 BYBIL 1, 50; L Gross, 'Voting in the Security Council: Abstention in the Post-1965 Amendment Phase and its Impact on Article 25 of the Charter' (1968) 62 AJIL 315, 328; Goodrich, Hambro, and Simons, *Charter of the United Nations*, 229; DW Greig, *International Law* (Butterworths, 1970) 382–3; E Lauterpacht, 'The Waning of the Requirement of Consent' (1991) 85 ASIL Proc 38, 39–41; J Klabbers, *The Concept of Treaty in International Law* (Kluwer, 1996) 91; Byers, *Custom,* 173; Wolfke, 'Treaties and Custom', 34; Tunkin, *Theory of International Law*, 339–40; Gardiner, *Treaty Interpretation*, 245; Aust, *Modern Treaty Law*, 216; Alvarez, 'Limits of Change', 127; Arato, 'Treaty Interpretation', 323; Distefano, 'L'accord tacite', 31. See further Section 5.2.1.

question must take into account the extent to which the practice diverges from the textual meaning of the provision (according to the basic, 'textual' method of interpretation), the intentions of the parties as reflected in that provision (the 'subjective' method), and the provision as interpreted in light of the object and purpose of the treaty (the 'purposive' method).[544]

Simply put, the more that subsequent practice, analysed according to the 'three-step approach' discussed in Section 3.3.3(b), diverges from the letter and/or object of the treaty, the more likely it is that a tacit modification has occurred.[545]

In the 'grey areas' between authentic interpretation and modification,[546] where the degree of divergence from the 'letter and object' of the treaty is difficult to determine, it becomes necessary to look for other distinctions and indicators of the effects of subsequent practice:

> The most reasonable approach seems to be that the line between interpretation and modification cannot be determined by abstract criteria but must rather be derived, in the first place, from the treaty itself, the character of the specific treaty provision at hand, and the legal context within which the treaty operates, and the specific circumstances of the case.[547]

These factors and distinctions constitute the central focus of the next section.

3.5 Analysing Modification by Subsequent Practice: Essential Distinctions, Non-Derogability, and Alternative Adaptation Mechanisms

As explained, in most cases treaty modification by subsequent practice can be identified not by means of abstract criteria, but on a case-by-case basis, by reference to a large array of factors and limitations. The following has been noted with regard to the limitations of the process of modification by subsequent practice:

> Some believe that there is effectively no limit on the effects of subsequent practice. For some, if that practice is compelling, clear, and consistent, intended to affect the interpretation of a treaty, and accurately reflects the views or at least the acquiescence of all the parties and not just a few of them, such practice can modify the text of the treaty. On this view, the state parties always remain the legislators of a treaty and continue to be fully in control of its meaning over time, irrespective of what the original text of their agreement or the negotiating history states.[548]

As explained in Chapter 1, there are, theoretically, no limits to the effects of subsequent practice, which is rooted in the agreement of the parties, who are masters of their own treaty. In reality, however, the process of modification of treaties by

544 See Section 2.5 on the different interpretative methods.
545 See eg *Interpretation of Peace Treaties Advisory Opinion*, 229.
546 See eg the debate regarding the aforementioned 2001 NAFTA FTC Interpretation—see (text to) n 494 and Section 5.2.3(c).
547 Nolte, Second Report on Subsequent Practice, para 165.
548 Alvarez, 'Limits of Change', 130.

subsequent practice faces important limitations. In the same way that it is unlikely that in practice a current *jus cogens* norm will cease to exist or revert back to a weaker peremptory norm as a result of the agreement of the international community, so it is unlikely that certain fundamental principles and rules enshrined, for instance, in human rights treaties, would be undermined through tacit modification by subsequent practice. Subsequent practice could, on the other hand, supplement such norms rather than override them, modifying them to the benefit of the rights-holders or the international community in general. With these considerations in mind, this section sets out to determine the degree to which a treaty is amenable to modification by subsequent practice. It does so by investigating the limits of modification in light of the character of the treaty, its subject matter, the type of (multilateral) treaty provision affected, and 'in-built' adaptation mechanisms contained in various treaties. These considerations will help to develop the analysis of the examples of potential modifications by subsequent practice in Chapter 5.

3.5.1 Implications of different types of treaties and treaty provisions

Subsequent practice is a complex, 'cross-cutting' issue[549] because it covers so many areas and underlying principles of law. A proper analysis of analogous cases of subsequent practice requires drawing distinctions between certain types of treaties and treaty provisions[550]—distinctions important for the compilation of examples analysed in Chapter 5.

3.5.1a Type of treaty regime

It has been remarked that modification by subsequent practice has for the most part been recognized in relation to certain categories of treaty, namely, boundary treaties and treaties constituting international organizations.[551] Yet it is clear that the examples encountered are sufficiently diverse to conclude that they are based on the same process.[552] Indeed, modifications by subsequent practice have been recognized in relation to many other types of treaties.[553] For instance, a significant number of examples below relate to the Law of the Sea Convention, a large, complex multilateral treaty regime that exhibits many special characteristics affecting the operation of the process of modification by subsequent practice.

It must be noted from the outset that the Vienna Convention on the Law of Treaties does not offer much guidance on differentiating between different types

[549] Nolte, Annex A, para 45.

[550] See eg J Leca, *Les techniques de révision des conventions internationales* (LGDG, 1961). See also ILC, 'Information submitted by the Netherlands on "Subsequent agreements and subsequent practice in relation to the interpretation of treaties"' (2015) <http://legal.un.org/ilc/sessions/67/pdfs/english/sasp_netherlands.pdf> accessed 11 November 2016, para 6, pointing out that whether modification of a treaty by subsequent agreements or practice is possible 'will depend to a large extent on the provisions of the treaty concerned'.

[551] Nolte, Introductory Report on Treaties over Time, 202.

[552] Ibid. 206.

[553] See the extensive examples in Ch 5.

of treaties or treaty obligations,[554] but 'conceive[s] of the treaty as a single, uniform concept'.[555] Nevertheless, countless treaty differentiations have been suggested, such as bilateral versus multilateral, 'law-making' versus technical, special categories such as treaties constituting international organizations, and divisions in terms of subject matter.[556] There is a difference, for instance, between the effects of subsequent practice in relation to technical treaties, in which case the process of modification by practice may be easier to survey,[557] and more general treaties, such as those concerned with ensuring international peace and security or human rights.[558] This also relates to the difference between more 'contractual' treaties and 'standard-setting' or 'law-making' ones—multilateral treaties that purport to codify and concurrently develop general substantive rules and seek to attract as many parties as possible.[559] A classic example is the LOSC, which both codifies the international law of the sea and develops it. Law-making treaties often tend to be intrinsically evolutionary in nature (like treaties constituting international organizations or human rights treaties[560]). It is debatable in how far the dichotomy between law-making and contractual treaties, though a frequently used analytical tool,[561] can be useful,[562] particularly with regard to analysing subsequent practice.[563] It will nevertheless be kept in mind throughout this section.

One fundamental consideration is whether a treaty is bilateral or multilateral. Modification by subsequent practice is easier to determine and less contentious in the former case.[564] In this sense, the distinction between interpretation and modification by subsequent practice is also less relevant for bilateral treaties.[565] Many of the treaties that provide key illustrations of modification by subsequent practice are

[554] See I Buga, 'A Critical Look at the Law of Treaties: Giving Recognition to Informal Means of Treaty Adaptation' in E Molenaar and others (eds), *What's Wrong with International Law? Liber Amicorum Prof AHA Soons* (Martinus Nijhoff, 2015) 231. The VCLT does contain a number of rules pertaining to special types of treaties, but these are limited—see eg Arts 40, 41, 58, and 60 on bilateral versus multilateral treaties, Arts 5 and 20(3) on constitutive treaties, Art 60(5) referring to humanitarian treaties, Art 62(2)(a) on boundary treaties, and Art 64 preventing derogation from *jus cogens* norms. See also Koskeniemmi, Fragmentation Report, 251.

[555] DB Hollis, 'Defining Treaties' in DB Hollis, *The Oxford Guide to Treaties* (OUP, 2012) 11, 36. See also C Brölmann, 'Law-Making Treaties' (2005) 74 NJIL 383, 390, pointing out that this may have been due to the focus during the VCLT's drafting on 'form' over 'function'.

[556] See eg AD McNair, 'The Functions and Differing Legal Character of Treaties' (1930) 11 BYBIL 100, 101–18; Hollis, 'Defining Treaties', 36.

[557] See eg 37th Meeting of the Committee of the Whole, para 64 (France).

[558] See the discussion in Section 3.4.2 on clear versus ambiguous terms.

[559] cf Brölmann, 'Law-Making Treaties', 383.

[560] See eg Pocar, 'Some Remarks', 279. See also Section 2.5.3(a).

[561] See eg McNair, 'Functions and Differing Legal Character of Treaties', 103–4; L Sohn, 'The Many Faces of International Law' (1963) 57 AJIL 868.

[562] Nolte, Introductory Report on Treaties over Time, 183.

[563] Jenks, 'The Conflict of Law-Making Treaties', 401; Brölmann, 'Law-Making Treaties', 383; Villiger, *Commentary*, 427 para 11. cf J Pauwelyn, 'How to Win a WTO Dispute Based on Non-WTO Law' (2003) 37 JWT 997.

[564] See eg Gazzini, 'Bilateral Investment Treaties', 106; Murphy, 'Subsequent Agreement and Subsequent Practice', 92.

[565] See Section 3.2.3.

bilateral in nature.[566] But there is nevertheless no shortage of instances where *multilateral* treaties have been modified by subsequent practice,[567] as becomes apparent in Chapter 5.[568] The operation of subsequent practice in multilateral treaty regimes merits closer attention due to the fact that the more States parties there are, the higher the threshold is for establishing agreement to a tacit modification.

Moreover, older treaty regimes are more susceptible to tacit modification.[569] This can arise with greater frequency once multilateral treaties reach a certain age, as the context evolves and the risk increases of 'losing their foundation in the agreement of the parties'.[570] The older the treaty, the higher the chance it will eventually need to be adapted to modern developments and the changing intentions of the parties—intentions that are mirrored in their subsequent practice. Generally, adjustments by means of tacit modification are likely to be more prevalent in 'rigid' treaty regimes in which formal procedures and the injection of new issues is more problematic, than for example in a context such as the WTO, where States are constantly negotiating new areas of international trade.[571] It should also be noted that formal amendment procedures with regard to *some* WTO provisions are considerably more flexible—though not for the core substantive provisions of the GATT,[572] GATS,[573] or TRIPS Agreement,[574] and Articles IX and X of the WTO Agreement, the modification of which still requires unanimity—than those in other large multilateral treaties, such as the UN Charter.[575]

Another distinction can be made between treaties that do and do not provide their own dispute settlement mechanism.[576] Where the former is the case, there is an accompanying tendency to develop specialized rules of interpretation (and of, or against, modification) that cannot be applied outside the context of the specific treaty regime. For instance, Panel and Appellate Body reports concerning subsequent practice must be understood in the specific context of the WTO framework, which, as discussed in Chapter 2, contains its own rules and systemic limitations.[577] The policy of the European Court of Justice with regard to the EU founding treaties, also discussed in Chapter 2, likewise serves as an example.[578] As highlighted by

[566] See eg *Temple of Préah Vihéar*, *Air Transport Services Arbitration* (*US/France*), and *Taba Arbitration*, discussed in Section 5.2.

[567] See eg *Israeli Wall Advisory Opinion* and *Namibia Advisory Opinion*, discussed in Section 5.2.1. See also Nolte Introductory Report on Treaties over Time, 206.

[568] See eg Sections 5.3.1(a) and 5.3.2(a).

[569] Nolte, Annex A, para 31; Murphy 'Subsequent Agreement and Subsequent Practice', 94.

[570] Nolte, Annex A, para 6.

[571] Feldman, 'Evolving Treaty Obligations', 702. See also Section 3.5.2 on 'in-built' adaptation mechanisms in the WTO context. But see n 392 on the stalemates in negotiations encountered in the WTO context.

[572] General Agreement on Tariffs and Trade 1994, WTO Agreement, Annex 1A, 1867 UNTS 190.

[573] General Agreement on Trade in Services 1994, WTO Agreement, Annex 1B, 1869 UNTS 183.

[574] Agreement on Trade-Related Aspects of Intellectual Property Rights 1994, 1869 UNTS 299.

[575] Arato, 'Treaty Interpretation', 317 fn 122. See Art X of the WTO Agreement.

[576] See Section 3.5.2 on dispute settlement as an 'in-built' adaptation mechanism and alternative to subsequent practice.

[577] See Section 2.5.2.

[578] Ibid. See also Nolte, Third Report on Subsequent Practice, para 28. This pertains to the significance of the nature of a treaty in determining the role of subsequent practice, as discussed below.

the EU's recent comments to the ILC, the ECJ minimizes the role of subsequent practice in the interpretation and modification of the founding treaties due to the nature of EU law as an 'autonomous legal order' and the resulting structure of the Union.[579] Thus, it rejected, for instance, a subsequent agreement by all Member States containing a timetable for fulfilling the obligation to equalize the pay of men and women by 31 December 1964 and amounting to a modification of the 31 December 1961 deadline envisaged in the founding treaty.[580] Likewise, the practice of the EU institutions, not just of the Member States, 'cannot derogate from the rules laid down in the Treaty'.[581] These considerations are important as a note of caution when attempting to generalize observations from such self-contained regimes.[582]

The nature of a treaty regime can pose further limitations on the modifying potential of subsequent practice.[583] 'Non-reciprocal' treaties, for instance, are treaties every breach of which undermines the position of all the other parties.[584] Whether a treaty is 'non-reciprocal' in nature can be inferred from the treaty's object and purpose(s).[585] This is the case under the WTO tariff schedules due to the 'most favoured nation' principle, a bedrock principle of the organization.[586] The same applies with regard to the 1963 Vienna Convention on Consular Relations, or to disarmament (arms control) treaties, where performance by one party is a prerequisite for performance by all the other parties, and, conversely, a breach by one party is a breach vis-à-vis all the others.[587] Human rights treaties contain 'integral' or 'absolute' obligations, a subset of obligations *erga omnes partes*,[588] which are 'independent of any expectation of reciprocity' from the other States parties.[589] The same applies to obligations *erga omnes* generally. *Inter se* modifications are therefore usually

[579] Comments by the EU to the ILC, 2–4. However, the role accorded to subsequent practice is different where the ECJ deals with treaties between the EU and *third* States—see Section 2.5.2, (text to) n 669.

[580] *Gabrielle Defrenne v Société anonyme belge de navigation aérienne Sabena* (Case 43/75) [1976] ECR 455, para 57 ('the Resolution of [the Conference of] the Member States of 30 December 1961 was ineffective to make any valid modification of the time-limit fixed by the Treaty').

[581] *United Kingdom of Great Britain and Northern Ireland v Council of the European Communities* (Case C-68/86) [1988] ECR 855, para 24 (citing further case law). See also *French Republic v Commission of the European Communities* (Case C-327/91) [1994] ECR I-3641, paras 31, 36; *French Republic v Commission of the European Communities* (Case T-240/04) [2007] ECR II-4035, paras 22, 45; Nolte, Annex A, para 34.

[582] Nolte, Annex A, para 33; Arato, 'Treaty Interpretation', 289.

[583] See eg Fitzmaurice, Second Report on the Law of Treaties, 40 para 76; ILC, 'Third Report on State Responsibility, by Mr James Crawford, Special Rapporteur' (2000) II(1) YBILC 3 [Crawford, Third Report on State Responsibility] paras 99–108; Nolte, First Report on Subsequent Practice, para 16.

[584] Koskenniemi, Fragmentation Report, para 312.

[585] See eg Art 60(2)(c) VCLT, allowing the invocation of a breach 'if the treaty is of such a character that a material breach of its provisions by one party radically changes the position of every party with respect to the further performance of its obligations under the treaty'. See also Art 42(b)(ii) of the ILC Articles on State Responsibility and Commentary.

[586] See eg GATT Arts I:1 and XIII. cf Section 5.3.1(d) on the discussion of modification through WTO accession protocols.

[587] Koskenniemi, Fragmentation Report, para 312.

[588] Crawford, Third Report on State Responsibility, 47.

[589] Koskenniemi, Fragmentation Report, paras 312–13.

not permitted in respect of treaties containing non-reciprocal obligations—see also Article 41(1)(b)(ii) VCLT—as these 'might more easily be understood to be contrary to the object and purpose of the treaty'.[590] Generally, modification by subsequent practice is much more difficult in relation to 'non-reciprocal' obligations.[591] This issue is discussed further in relation to special types of treaty obligations in Section 3.5.1(b) below.

Moreover, a treaty like the Law of the Sea Convention may create 'an expectation of non-derogation'.[592] This can be deduced from its nature as a 'package deal' and the character of certain of its core obligations. A higher degree of practice may be required for tacit modification to occur in such cases, in order to safeguard the integrity of the treaty.[593] Of course, in a case such as that of the LOSC, total consistency of practice is next to impossible to achieve, 'given the breadth, extent, and goals of the Convention and the vastly different expectations the Convention holds for many different States which have become parties'.[594] A contributing factor may be whether the practice is spread out across the different geopolitical groupings of States parties, which relates to the discussion in Section 2.3.5 above on the degree of representativeness of the practice and relevance of the contributing parties.[595]

As explained in Chapter 2, subsequent practice plays a special role in the context of international organizations.[596] Although modification by subsequent practice (also referred to as 'transformation'[597]) occurs often in relation to constitutive treaties,[598] it has been remarked, especially with regard to international organizations, that modification should not 'disrupt the balance established under the general treaty between the rights and obligations of States parties thereto'.[599] On the other hand, implied powers often allow constitutive treaties to be adapted to a great extent without

[590] Ibid. para 311. [591] Ibid. para 385. [592] Ibid. para 109.

[593] Churchill, 'The Impact of State Practice', 104.

[594] Rothwell, 'The Impact of State Practice', 147.

[595] Churchill, 'The Impact of State Practice', para 105.

[596] See eg Art 2(1)(j) VCLTIO, referring to 'established practice' as a means of determining how rules of the organization emerge. See also Jennings and Watts, *Oppenheim's International Law*, 1268. See in particular Sections 2.3.1(c) and 2.5.4 of this book. As discussed, it is necessary to bear in mind the distinction between the practice of the organization itself and that of individual States.

[597] See eg Arato, 'Treaty Interpretation', 289.

[598] See eg Sections 5.2.1 and 5.3.1. States' views in the Sixth Committee were varied as to modification of constitutive treaties by subsequent practice in reaction to Nolte, Third Report on Subsequent Practice—see eg 'Summary record of the 21st meeting', UN GAOR, 17th Session, UN Doc A/C.6/70/SR.21 (2015) paras 44–5 (The Netherlands, recognizing that 'the conduct of an organ of an international organization could influence that organization's practice (…) [which] could result in an implicit modification of the constituent instrument', but that 'it was often difficult to determine whether (…) [it] had been taken by an organ of the organization or by the Member States'), 60 (Singapore, stating that 'it was advisable to avoid circumventing the amendment mechanisms' in constitutive treaties); 'Summary record of the 22nd meeting', UN GAOR, 17th Session, UN Doc A/C.6/70/SR.22 (2015) paras 27 (Jamaica), 33 (New Zealand), 88 (Chile) (arguing in favour of formal amendment); 'Summary record of the 23rd meeting', UN GAOR, 17th Session, UN Doc A/C.6/70/SR.23 (2015) paras 49 (Malaysia, expressing its concern regarding the modifying effect of subsequent practice outside the scope of Arts 39 and 41 VCLT), 68 (Iran, underscoring the importance of assessing the member States' intention to 'modify the instrument's original mandate').

[599] Sadat-Akhavi, *Methods of Resolving Conflicts*, 131, cited in Koskenniemi, Fragmentation Report, para 109.

the need for modification by subsequent practice.[600] These complex aspects of the operation of subsequent practice in relation to treaties establishing international organizations are explored in detail in Chapter 5.

It has also been argued that the role of subsequent practice is different in the case of boundary treaties, where a presumption of non-derogability applies in light of the principle of stability of boundaries.[601] Yet this principle has not impeded arbitral tribunals from upholding boundary modifications by subsequent practice. In fact, the Tribunal in the *Taba Arbitration* relied on the stability of boundaries to *sustain* a modification of the boundary pillar, contrary to the clear wording of the '1906 Agreement', on the basis of 'long accepted' practice on which the parties had come to rely.[602] Similarly, the Boundary Commission tasked with settling the dispute in the *Eritrea-Ethiopia Arbitration* found that subsequent practice served to mark a modification of the treaty between the parties.[603] The tacit modification of a boundary treaty was likewise central to the ICJ's judgment in the *Temple of Préah Vihéar* case.[604]

In the *Cameroon v Nigeria* judgment, the ICJ also confirmed that the possibility of a State acquiescing 'in the establishment of a change in treaty title (…) cannot be wholly precluded as a possibility in law'.[605] However, it added that, where a boundary has previously been delimited, preference must be given to the holder of the title in assessing whether practice amounts to conduct acquiescing in a change thereof.[606] This entails a presumption against modification in favour of the title-holder under the treaty. In this sense, the Court may distinguish 'between boundary treaties which are not yet delimited or demarcated (and are, therefore, more open to interpretation and modification by way of subsequent conduct) and those boundary treaties where the boundary has already been demarcated'.[607] In sum, if there is no legal title to modify to begin with, subsequent (boundary) practice can be more easily determinative, whereas if there is a legal title, a presumption applies in favour of the holder of the legal title. Ultimately, the Court found that Cameroon's (lack of) practice did not amount to acquiescence in the abandonment of its title in the areas

600 See further Section 2.5.4.

601 *Libya/Chad*, para 72; MG Kohen, 'The Decision on the Delimitation of the Eritrea/Ethiopia Boundary of 13 April 2002: A Singular Approach to International Law Applicable to Territorial Disputes' in MG Kohen (ed), *Promoting Justice, Human Rights and Conflict Resolution through International Law: Liber Amicorum Lucius Caflisch* (Martinus Nijhoff, 2007) 767, 772–3. cf MN Shaw, 'Title, Control, and Closure? The Experience of the Eritrea-Ethiopia Boundary Commission' (2007) 56 ICLQ 755, 777.

602 *Taba Arbitration*, paras 210, 235 (citing *Temple of Préah Vihéar*).

603 *Eritrea-Ethiopia Arbitration*, paras 3.8, 3.10, 4.60. cf Kohen, 'Decision on the Limitation of the Eritrea/Ethiopia Boundary', 772–3.

604 See Section 5.2.1. See also Nolte, Introductory Report on Treaties over Time, 204–6.

605 *Cameroon v Nigeria*, Judgment, para 68, citing *El Salvador/Honduras*, 408–9.

606 *Cameroon v Nigeria*, Judgment, para 68, citing *Burkina Faso/Republic of Mali*, para 63. See ibid. para 223. cf *Cameroon v Nigeria*, Dissenting Opinion of Judge Ajibola, para 52.

607 Nolte, Introductory Report on Treaties over Time, 205, citing *Cameroon v Nigeria*, Judgment, para 64 ('now that it [the Court] has made its findings that the frontier in Lake Chad was delimited (…) it follows that any Nigerian *effectivités* are indeed to be evaluated for their legal consequences as acts *contra legem*'). This also relates to the point in Section 3.5.2 that the provision for delimitation by a boundary commission can constitute an alternative mechanism that leaves less room for modification of the boundary treaty by subsequent practice.

in question.[608] In relation to a different area of the boundary, however, the Court found, in effect, that the parties had (tacitly) accepted that the area be delimited differently from the text of the relevant agreement.[609] The *Cameroon v Nigeria* judgment also 'confirmed and clarified'[610] the view expressed by the Chamber in the *Land, Island and Maritime Frontier Dispute* that States could subsequently vary treaty-delimited boundaries between them by agreement.[611] These cases confirm that the subsequent practice of boundary States demonstrating their agreement as to the course of a boundary inconsistent with the treaty 'may be recognized as an authoritative alteration of the boundary'.[612]

It is therefore submitted that the principle of stability of boundaries can, depending on the circumstances, be used to sustain a subsequent modification of the boundary agreed by the parties derogating from the original treaty text, and that boundary treaties can be more susceptible to modification by subsequent practice precisely due to the need for stability and clarity:

> [T]he reason (...) for the modificatory effect of subsequent conduct even with respect to boundary treaties does not seem to lie in their inherently more dynamic nature but rather in a consideration why boundary treaties are designed to be particularly clear and stable in the first place. (...) Thus, as far as boundary treaties are concerned the issue underlying the question of how, whether and how far the text of a treaty may be modified by subsequent conduct is mainly a matter of balancing one type of means for ensuring stability (text) against another type of means for ensuring stability (subsequent conduct).[613]

However, the modification of a boundary treaty requires a clear and compelling assertion of subsequent practice evidencing the parties' intention to deviate from the treaty, given the presumption against modification, particularly in such cases—the establishment of a permanent boundary constitutes 'a matter of grave importance and agreement is not easily to be presumed'.[614] It may also be noted that the examples above are based on bilateral treaties, in relation to which, as explained, modification by subsequent practice is less contentious. On the other hand, boundary treaties can also be categorized as treaties establishing 'objective regimes',[615] setting up 'objective

[608] *Cameroon v Nigeria*, Judgment, paras 70 and 224, respectively. See Section 5.2.1.

[609] Ibid. paras 144–6. The Court concluded that the relevant agreement had to be 'interpreted' accordingly and thus did not explicitly distinguish between interpretation and modification. See also MN Shaw, 'Self-Determination, Human Rights, and the Attribution of Territory' in U Fastenrath and others (eds), *From Bilateralism to Community Interest: Essays in Honour of Judge Bruno Simma* (OUP, 2011) 590, 606. See further Section 5.2.1 of this book.

[610] Shaw, 'Self-Determination', 606.

[611] *El Salvador/Honduras*, para 80.

[612] Shaw, 'Self-Determination', 606. See also *Cameroon v Nigeria*, Dissenting Opinion of Judge Ajibola, paras 52–3, 59, 61.

[613] Nolte, Introductory Report on Treaties over Time, 205.

[614] *Nicaragua v Honduras*, para 253. See also JG Merrills, 'Land and Maritime Boundary between Cameroon and Nigeria (Cameroon v Nigeria, Equatorial Guinea Intervening), Merits, Judgment of October 10, 2002' (2003) 52 ICLQ 788, 796 ('once a treaty boundary is in place, a heavy burden lies on the party seeking to argue for its displacement').

[615] Waldock, Third Report on the Law of Treaties, 26–34. Likewise, treaties on freedom of navigation in international rivers or waterways constitute examples of objective regimes. See further eg F Salerno, 'Treaties Establishing Objective Regimes' in E Cannizzaro (ed), *The Law of Treaties Beyond the Vienna Convention* (OUP, 2011) 225; G Gaja, 'Article 38 (1969)' in O Corten and P Klein (eds), *The Vienna Convention on the Law of Treaties* (OUP, 2011) 949, 957.

rules' with *erga omnes* effects.[616] Other examples of such treaties include the 1959 Antarctic Treaty System (ATS)[617] and the LOSC provisions establishing the outer limits of the various maritime zones.[618]

The stability of boundaries is one example of a principle that can, depending on the nature of the practice, make certain types of treaties less amenable to modification by subsequent practice. Reference could also perhaps be made to the concept of non-regression, which may apply to human rights law,[619] and, even more contentiously, to environmental law.[620] According to the idea of non-regression, beneficiaries upon whom certain rights or protected interests have been bestowed can no longer be deprived of them, even in cases of State succession.[621] This also applies if subsequent practice supports or reverts back to an interpretation intended at the time when the treaty was concluded.[622] In sum, non-regression would create a presumption against modification to the detriment of the rights-holders.[623] More generally, there is a prohibition on derogation from treaties benefiting third parties,

[616] 1966 Draft Articles on the Law of Treaties with Commentaries, 231 para 4. See also H Mosler, 'The International Society as a Legal Community' (1974) 140 RC 234; P Cahier, 'Le problème des effets des traités à l'égard des Etats tiers' (1974) 143 RC 660; P Subedi, 'The Doctrine of Objective Regimes in International Law and the Competence of the United Nations to Impose Territorial or Peace Settlements on States' (1994) 37 GYIL 174; Salerno, 'Treaties Establishing Objective Regimes', 225, citing McNair, *Law of Treaties*, 259. cf Waldock, Third Report on the Law of Treaties, 25: 'A treaty establishes an objective regime when it appears from its terms and from the circumstances of its conclusion that the intention of the parties is to create in the general interest general obligations and rights relating to a particular region, State, territory, locality, river, waterway, or to a particular area of sea, sea-bed, or air-space (. . .).' Ultimately, the ILC decided to leave this question aside, as 'to lay down a rule recognizing the possibility of the creation of objective regimes directly by treaty might be unlikely to meet with general acceptance', and, moreover, the possibility was considered already covered, *inter alia*, by the provision on 'treaties intended to create rights in favour of States generally'—1966 Draft Articles on the Law of Treaties with Commentaries, 231 para 4. See likewise 1964 Draft Articles on the Law of Treaties with Commentaries, 184–5 para 3.

[617] 402 UNTS 71.

[618] See eg LOSC Arts 4, 33, 57, and 76.

[619] See Art 30 of the 1948 Universal Declaration of Human Rights, UNGA Res 217A (III), UN Doc A/810, 71 (1948) (UDHR); Arts 17 and 53 of the Convention for the Protection of Human Rights and Fundamental Freedoms (European Convention on Human Rights, as amended) 1950, 213 UNTS 221 (ECHR); Art 5 of the 1966 International Covenant on Civil and Political Rights, 999 UNTS 171 (ICCPR) and of the 1966 International Covenant on Economic, Social and Cultural Rights 1966, 993 UNTS 3 (ICESCR).

[620] M Prieur and G Sozzo, *La non régression en droit de l'environnement* (Bruylant, 2012). See also *Gabčíkovo-Nagymaros Project* (*Hungary/Slovakia*), Judgment of 25 September 1997, Separate Opinion of Vice-President Weeramantry, ICJ Reports 88, 114 ('environmental rights are human rights').

[621] Pocar, 'Some Remarks', 279. See also eg HRC, General Comment No 26 ('Continuity of Obligations') UN Doc CCPR/C/21/Rev.1/Add.8/Rev.1 (1977) [HRC General Comment No 26] para 4; Koskenniemi, Fragmentation Report, para 108.

[622] See eg *Gabčíkovo-Nagymaros Project*, Separate Opinion of Vice-President Weeramantry, 114: 'A Court cannot endorse actions which are a violation of human rights by the standards of their time merely because they are taken under a treaty which dates back to a period when such action was not a violation of human rights.' See further R Higgins, 'Some Observations on the Inter-Temporal Rule in International Law' in J Makarczyk (ed), *Theory of International Law at the Threshold of the 21st Century* (Kluwer Law International, 1996) 173.

[623] HRC General Comment No 26, para 108; Karl, 'Treaties, Conflicts between', 939; Sadat-Akhavi, *Methods of Resolving Conflicts*, 213; I Hachez, *Le principe de standstill dans le droit des droits fondamentaux: une irréversibilité relative* (Bruylant, 2008).

such as investor protection under bilateral investment treaties.[624] The same applies based on the principle that the legitimate expectations of such actors as to the non-derogation from certain provisions must be respected.[625] Thus, 'treaty parties may still be masters of the treaty, but one cannot assume no harm, no foul in accepting their interpretations of nonstate actors' rights'.[626] This also relates to what was stated earlier regarding the fact that while, theoretically, there are no 'inherent' limits to the effects of subsequent practice, in practice, there are significant limitations.[627]

3.5.1b Type of treaty provision

Certain types of treaty provisions[628] either (implicitly or explicitly) set a very high bar for, or altogether prohibit, derogation, including modification by subsequent practice.

A primary example is that of provisions reflective of *jus cogens* norms. As already discussed with regard to the special nature of certain types of treaties, the impact of modification by subsequent practice is restricted, though not completely, in respect of obligations *erga omnes* (towards the international community as a whole[629]) or *erga omnes partes* (aimed at protecting the collective interests of all the treaty parties[630]), including 'integral' obligations ('according to which any breach undermines the position of all the other parties, to an extent that justifies treating each State party as individually injured'[631]).[632] The same applies to obligations that are 'non-reciprocal' ('independent of any expectation of reciprocity or performance on the part of other parties'[633]). The Law of the Sea Convention furnishes a number of interesting examples, such as the 'peaceful purposes' requirement and the invalidity

[624] See eg Art 37 VCLT; Gazzini, 'Bilateral Investment Treaties', 107, citing *American Manufacturing*, para 6.06. See further Higgins, *Problems and Process*, 54; E De Brabandere, 'Non-State Actors in International Dispute Settlement: Pragmatism in International Law' in J d'Aspremont (ed), *Participants in the International Legal System: Multiple Perspectives on Non-State Actors in International Law* (Routledge, 2011) 342.

[625] Gazzini, 'Bilateral Investment Treaties', 116, citing eg *Tecmed v Mexico*, para 154; *Rumeli Telekom*, para 609; E Snodgrass, 'Protecting Investors' Legitimate Expectations: Recognizing and Delimiting a General Principle' (2006) 21 ICSID Rev 1; S Fietta, 'The "Legitimate Expectations" Principle under Article 1105 NAFTA: *International Thunderbird Gaming Corporation v The United American States*' (2006) 7 JWIT 423; I Tudor, *The Fair and Equitable Treatment Standard in International Foreign Investment Law* (OUP, 2008), in particular 163–8.

[626] AE Roberts, 'Power and Persuasion in Investment Treaty Interpretation: The Dual Role of States' (2010) 104 AJIL 179, 202.

[627] See Section 1.4.

[628] This section is developed from Buga, 'Between Stability and Change', 46ff.

[629] *Barcelona Traction, Light and Power Company, Limited (Belgium v Spain) (New Application: 1962)*, Judgment (Second Phase) of 5 February 1970, ICJ Reports 3, para 33; Crawford, Third Report on State Responsibility, 46. See further Koskenniemi, Fragmentation Report, para 387 (highlighting that *erga omnes* norms are 'not necessarily distinguished by the importance of their substance' but rather by their 'procedural thrust', a certain 'generality of standing'; citing eg *Prosecutor v Anto Furundžija*, para 153); J Frowein, 'Obligations *Erga Omnes*' in R Bernhardt (ed), *Encyclopaedia of International Law*, vol III (Elsevier, 1997) 757; M Byers, 'Conceptualising the Relationship between *Jus Cogens* and *Erga Omnes* Rules' (1997) 66 NJIL 211, 230.

[630] Crawford, Third Report on State Responsibility, 47.

[631] Ibid. 47 fn 195.

[632] See Koskenniemi, Fragmentation Report, para 390, and further eg para 154.

[633] Ibid. paras 311–12, and further eg paras 154, 385.

of sovereignty claims over the high seas, respectively enshrined in Articles 88 and 89 LOSC. Likewise, the general obligation in Article 192 LOSC to 'protect and preserve the marine environment', albeit vague, can be characterized as an integral obligation. As a core environmental provision, it may also be subject to an additional presumption against modification based on the alleged principle of non-regression.[634]

Sometimes treaty provisions explicitly rule out the possibility of modification by subsequent practice (or any form of modification for that matter). For instance, in the LOSC context, Article 311(6) LOSC expressly prohibits derogation from the cornerstone principle of the 'common heritage of mankind' laid down in Article 136 LOSC. Article 311(3) LOSC highlights that the modifying potential of subsequent practice is also very limited with regard to other 'core' LOSC principles.[635]

Importantly, modification by subsequent practice seems to be more easily accepted with regard to procedural rather than substantive provisions—to the extent that this distinction is workable.[636] This issue was discussed during the drafting of the Vienna Convention in the ILC.[637] Generally, 'provisions that are central to the integrity of a treaty, such as its main substantive provisions and procedural infrastructure, will be less amenable to change than technical or administrative standards'.[638] This applies also to 'essential' provisions,[639] which lie at the 'heart' of the treaty.[640] A higher threshold would therefore be required for practice to modify essential provisions of the LOSC, such as those on the various maritime zones.[641] These provisions balance diverse State interests and sovereignty over resources on the one hand, with the goal of multilateralism under the LOSC on the other[642]—a balance reflective of the aims of the Convention as a 'package deal'. Moreover, as already discussed, the LOSC provisions on the outer limits of the maritime zones reflect customary international law. Given the number of States parties to the LOSC, and the fact that these provisions set up objective regimes, their modification would require the concurrent modification of the underlying customary norms,[643] which entails also taking into account the practice of third States.[644]

The notion of 'essential' provisions, as highlighted in Section 3.3.5 above, is linked to that of 'object and purpose', another enigmatic term.[645] However, essential provisions do not have to regulate a central purpose of the treaty. They can also be

[634] See generally Prieur and Sozzo, *La non régression en droit de l'environnement*, and Section 3.5.1(a).

[635] See also n 135.

[636] cf Koplow, 'When is an Amendment Not an Amendment?', 1044 ('the crucial distinction between "big" and "small" changes in a treaty regime, while superficially plausible, is ephemeral in practice').

[637] Summary record of 866th meeting, paras 18, 64; 37th Meeting of the Committee of the Whole, para 69.

[638] Brunnée, 'Treaty Amendments', 351.

[639] Ibid. See also Bowman, '"Normalizing"', 333.

[640] Simma and Tams, 'Article 60 (1969)', 1360.

[641] Rothwell, 'The Impact of State Practice', 149; Buga, 'Between Stability and Change', 51.

[642] See further eg Y Tanaka, *A Dual Approach to Ocean Governance: The Cases of Zonal and Integrated Management in International Law of the Sea* (Ashgate Surrey, 2008).

[643] See Section 3.3.3(b).

[644] See Section 3.3.1.

[645] Buffard and Zemanek, 'The "Object and Purpose" of a Treaty', 311. See further D Kritsiotis, 'The Concept of a Treaty's Object and Purpose' in MJ Bowman and D Kritsiotis (eds), *Conceptual and Contextual Perspectives on the Modern Law of Treaties* (CUP, forthcoming).

of an ancillary nature, yet still considered 'essential to the effective execution of the treaty', and thus an important reason for a party to have joined the treaty in the first place.[646] Dispute settlement provisions constitute an example of essential provisions with an *ancillary* character, the violation of which could constitute grounds for a material breach in the sense of Article 60 VCLT.[647] One major problem is that, in the case of complex multilateral treaties, essential provisions are often difficult to identify:

> In cases of treaties dealing with a limited subject matter, this test [of identifying essential provisions] will usually lead to clear results. Hence, the duty to extradite would be essential to the accomplishment of an extradition treaty, as would the obligation to carry out works to a joint construction project. Outside these clear-cut cases, the meaning of the term is difficult to ascertain.[648]

Examples of modifications by subsequent practice affecting procedural, substantive, and 'essential' provisions, to the extent that such distinctions are tenable, are explored in Chapter 5.

As already mentioned with regard to the relevance of the nature of certain types of treaties, a general prohibition exists on derogation from obligations benefiting third parties.[649] One potential example—to supplement those given earlier contained in human rights, environmental, and investment treaties—is the right of innocent passage established by the LOSC for 'ships of all States' or 'foreign ships'. This restricts the sovereignty of coastal States in favour of rights for (private) vessels, even presumably those of non-parties.[650] There are other similarly generic terms in the Convention.[651]

Interestingly, a careful study of the Law of the Sea Convention reveals that certain types of provisions are more amenable to modification by subsequent practice on account of various other reasons. Parts of the LOSC that are more susceptible to change by subsequent practice include some of the more 'novel' issues codified in the Convention, such as the straight baselines system.[652] These had not been fully established by practice prior to the Third United Nations Conference on the Law of the Sea (UNCLOS III), by contrast to certain other provisions in Part II LOSC that codify issues established well before UNCLOS III.[653] Moreover, provisions on subjects such as 'conservation' require frequent adaptation to maintain their

[646] 1966 Draft Articles on the Law of Treaties with Commentaries, 255 para 9. See also ILC, 'Second Report on the Law of Treaties, by Sir Humphrey Waldock, Special Rapporteur' (1963) II YBILC 36 [Waldock, Second Report on the Law of Treaties] 75 para 11; Rosenne, *Breach of Treaty*, 21. See eg Arts 41(1)(b)(ii), 44(3)(b), 60(3)(b), and 62(1)(a) VCLT.

[647] Waldock, Second Report on the Law of Treaties, 75, para 11.

[648] Simma and Tams, 'Article 60 (1969)', 1360.

[649] Koskenniemi, Fragmentation Report, para 154.

[650] See eg Art 17 LOSC.

[651] See further N St Skourtos, 'Legal Effects for Parties and Nonparties: The Impact of the Law of the Sea Convention' in MH Nordquist and JN Moore (eds), *Entry into Force of the Law of the Sea Convention* (Kluwer, 1995) 187, 195ff.

[652] JRV Prescott, 'Straight and Archipelagic Baselines' in G Blake (ed), *Maritime Boundaries and Ocean Resources* (Croom Helm, 1987) 38, 49 (referring to Art 7 LOSC as 'effectively a dead letter'); Churchill, 'The Impact of State Practice', 108.

[653] Rothwell, 'The Impact of State Practice', 145.

relevance, and also appear more amenable to tacit modification (as well as dynamic interpretation).[654] With regard to those provisions for which the threshold required for modification by subsequent practice is extremely high or effectively unattainable, States would have to resort to formal amendment procedures,[655] or at least to more 'formalized' types of practice.[656]

3.5.2 Availability and implications of alternative treaty adaptation mechanisms

A treaty's formal amendment procedures represent the most obvious type of in-built adaptation mechanism.[657] Examples include Articles 312 and 313 LOSC, Article X of the WTO Agreement, or Articles 108 and 109 of the UN Charter. A default for such rules is provided in Article 40 VCLT. The thresholds set for amendment vary per treaty.[658] The relation between subsequent practice and formal amendment procedures was already explored in Section 3.3.4 above and does not require further elaboration in the present section. Rather, the emphasis here is on the numerous informal means of treaty adaptation available to States, in addition to the mechanisms of modification by subsequent practice and formal amendment.

Indeed, treaties often contain 'in-built' mechanisms that can facilitate adaptation, removing some of the 'appeal' of subsequent practice:

> It is possible that certain kinds of treaties do not lend themselves for the possibility of their modification by way of subsequent conduct, either because of their character or because of their having been provided with special mechanisms for their modification which exclude informal modification by subsequent conduct.[659]

Such alternative adaptation mechanisms include special institutions and processes, dispute settlement, evolutionary interpretation or implied powers, and incorporation by reference to external standards. Even ambiguous provisions can be characterized as an 'in-built' mechanism, granting States 'leeway' in interpreting and implementing the treaty and thus reducing the need to achieve flexibility through modification by subsequent practice.[660] These are illustrated here by reference to treaties such as the LOSC, the complexity and breadth of which provides fruitful examples of how such mechanisms operate in relation to subsequent practice.

An obvious example of an adaptive mechanism is dispute settlement (note that the relevance of treaties with a specialized judicial system has already been discussed[661]).

[654] Buga, 'Between Stability and Change', 67.

[655] See Section 3.3.4.

[656] In the context of the LOSC, this includes eg implementation agreements. See Section 2.3.3. See further Section 5.3.2(a).

[657] This section is developed from Buga, 'Between Stability and Change', 65–6.

[658] Some treaty regimes even have a 'tacit acceptance' system by means of which amendments are automatically approved unless States 'opt out' within a certain period of time, as 'a more efficient alternative to traditional amendment procedures.'—Costelloe and Fitzmaurice, 'Lawmaking by Treaty', 118.

[659] Nolte, Introductory Report on Treaties over Time, 206. See also Venzke, *How Interpretation Makes International Law*, 236.

[660] What diplomats may refer to as 'constructive ambiguity' gives parties more freedom to interpret provisions in a way that suits their interests. See text to and nn 526–7.

[661] Section 3.5.1(a).

Once again, reference can be made to the law of the sea context. For instance, the 'equidistance/relevant circumstances' method of maritime boundary delimitation was developed in the case law in order to further specify or supplement Articles 74(1) and 83(1) LOSC, which merely refer to achieving an 'equitable solution'.[662] Another interesting development is that ITLOS, by means of Article 138 of its Rules of procedure,[663] introduced the possibility for an authorized 'body' to request an advisory opinion on a legal question based on an agreement related to the purposes of the Convention[664]—a major innovation, with a basis in Article 21 of the ITLOS Statute,[665] and a broad mandate, as compared, for instance, to the advisory procedure of the ICJ. Leaving aside the question of whether the Tribunal exceeded its powers under the Convention in construing Article 138 in this way, the new competence offers an additional means of facilitating regime interaction and adaptation without having to rely on modification by subsequent practice. The decision of the European Court of Human Rights in *Mamatkulov and Askarov v Turkey* also springs to mind. The Court relied on the practice of other courts to confirm its competence to order binding interim measures, a decision criticized by a number of judges as an impermissible exercise of a legislative function.[666]

Treaties—particularly multilateral environmental agreements—are also informally adapted through the practice of so-called 'autonomous institutional arrangements', such as certain conferences or meetings of the State parties, discussed in Chapter 2.[667] Since they are open to all the parties, such conferences provide a continuing expression of the parties' collective will and thus serve as vehicles for treaty adaptation.[668] Such quasi-autonomous arrangements can modify treaty obligations, *inter alia* by means of protocols and amendments.[669] The review mechanism that has evolved over time on the basis of Article XII of the 1972 Biological Weapons Convention (BWC),[670] in contrast with the treaty's formal amendment procedure prescribed in Article XI, is another interesting example of a framework for developing and adapting the treaty more informally. Similarly, various 'treaty bodies', especially

[662] See eg *Bay of Bengal*, paras 229–33, 238.

[663] ITLOS, Rules of the Tribunal, Doc ITLOS/8 (as amended on 17 March 2009).

[664] See eg the recent Request for an Advisory Opinion by the Sub-Regional Fisheries Commission (SRFC), 27 March 2013, ITLOS Case No 21, based on the 2012 Convention on the Determination of the Minimal Conditions for Access and Exploitation of Marine Resources within the Maritime Areas under Jurisdiction of the Member States of the Sub-Regional Fisheries Commission (CMAC). See for a recent discussion M Lando, 'The Advisory Jurisdiction of the International Tribunal for the Law of the Sea: Comments on the Request for an Advisory Opinion Submitted by the Sub-Regional Fisheries Commission' (2016) 29 LJIL 441.

[665] United Nations Law of the Sea Convention, Annex VI, 1833 UNTS 3.

[666] *Mamatkulov and Askarov v Turkey* [GC] App nos 46827/99 and 46951/99 (ECtHR, 4 February 2005) (Dissenting Opinion of Judges Caflish, Türmen, and Kovler) para 12.

[667] See Section 2.3.1(c). See also eg Hathaway and others, 'Tacit Amendment', 9–10.

[668] Nolte, Third Report on Treaties over Time, 365.

[669] Bowman, 'The Multilateral Treaty Amendment Process', 544; RR Churchill and G Ulfstein, 'Autonomous Institutional Arrangements in Multilateral Environmental Agreements: A Little-Noticed Phenomenon in International Law' (2000) 94 AJIL 623; A Wiersema, 'The New International Law-Makers? Conference of the Parties to Multilateral Environmental Agreements' (2009) 31 MJIL 231.

[670] Convention on the Prohibition of the Development, Production and Stockpiling of Bacteriological and Toxin Weapons and on their Destruction, 1015 UNTS 1963.

in the field of human rights, arguably engage in lawmaking through interpretative recommendations and resolutions.[671] Leaving aside the question of whether the activities of such bodies can constitute 'subsequent practice' within the meaning of Article 31(3)(b) VCLT,[672] their impact on the evolution of treaties reduces—but does not necessarily exclude—the need for modification by (other types of) subsequent practice. A number of examples of modification by means of special institutional arrangements in the context of MEAs are considered in Chapter 5.[673]

On a more general level, a treaty like the LOSC is developed through the activities of States parties and bodies or institutions such as the Meeting of States Parties, Commission on the Limits of the Continental Shelf, International Seabed Authority, and the UN Informal Consultative Process on Oceans and the Law of the Sea—even if mostly in ways not exceeding the realm of interpretation. For instance, a 2011 Advisory Opinion of the ITLOS Seabed Disputes Chamber demonstrates how certain parts of the LOSC, in that case those relating to the Area, are susceptible to development by subsequent practice through the International Seabed Authority, most notably through the promulgation of the 'Mining Code'.[674] Similarly, the practice of the Commission on the Limits of the Continental Shelf in relation to its Rules of Procedure[675] and coastal States' submissions may have led to the tacit modification of certain parts of Article 76 LOSC.[676] Even *de facto* amendments by the Meeting of States Parties to the LOSC, if regarded as rooted in implied powers rather than as modifications by subsequent practice, could constitute a special adaptation mechanism. These examples are discussed further in Chapter 5. The point here is to show how different processes can develop a treaty by means of—or, rather, instead of—subsequent practice.

In the context of the WTO, a number of alternative mechanisms were explicitly provided or subsequently devised to facilitate the adaptation of WTO law, given the rigidity of its formal amendment procedures.[677] One possibility is the modification of schedules annexed to GATT 1994 and the GATS by means of protocols (in addition to modifications pursuant to Article XXVIII of the GATT and Article XXI of the GATS, and various certification procedures).[678] Moreover, decisions of the Ministerial Conference have been a source of adaptation in the WTO context.

[671] K Mechlem, 'Treaty Bodies and the Interpretation of Human Rights' (2009) 42 Vand JIL 905, 920–1; G Ulfstein, 'Treaty Bodies and Regimes' in DB Hollis (ed), *The Oxford Guide to Treaties* (OUP, 2012) 436–7.

[672] See Section 2.3.1(c).

[673] Section 5.3.2.

[674] Regulations on Prospecting and Exploration for Polymetallic Nodules in the Area, ISBA/6/A/18 (4 October 2000) Art 31(2); Regulations on Prospecting and Exploration for Polymetallic Sulphides in the Area, ISBA/16/A/12/Rev1 (7 May 2010) Art 33(2). See also *Responsibilities and Obligations of States Sponsoring Persons and Entities with respect to Activities in the Area (Request for Advisory Opinion submitted to the Seabed Disputes Chamber)*, Advisory Opinion of 1 February 2011, ITLOS Case No 17, paras 122, 125–35.

[675] Rules of Procedure of the Commission on the Limits of the Continental Shelf, Doc CLCS/40/Rev.1 (17 April 2008).

[676] See eg A Serdy, 'The Commission on the Limits of the Continental Shelf and its Disturbing Propensity to Legislate' (2011) 26 IJMCL 367.

[677] See Art X of the WTO Agreement. cf text to n 575.

[678] See further Nottage and Sebastian, 'WTO Trade Negotiations', 989.

Such decisions have supplemented or modified the WTO agreements, for instance by means of authoritative interpretations and waivers (Articles IX:2 and IX:3 of the WTO Agreement, respectively), but also through other decisions under Article IV:1 of the WTO Agreement.[679] The latter decisions could also be qualified as subsequent practice (or, more specifically, subsequent agreements), and are discussed briefly in Chapter 5.[680] Due to the existence of these quasi-formal adaptation mechanisms in the WTO context, there is less need for other, more 'classical' forms of subsequent practice in order to modify WTO agreements, or, on the other side of the spectrum, for recourse to formal amendment.[681]

A key mechanism for adaptation and regime interaction, encountered frequently in the LOSC, is a system of 'rules of reference'.[682] For instance, many provisions in Part XII LOSC direct States to give effect to 'generally accepted international rules and standards' or look to 'competent international organizations' from other regimes. The International Convention for the Prevention of Pollution from Ships (MARPOL 73/78),[683] as amended by the 1978 MARPOL Protocol,[684] are the principal sources of 'rules and standards' on pollution from vessels referred to in Articles 194, 211, 218, and 220 LOSC. Likewise, Article 237 LOSC works as an umbrella provision for the protection of the marine environment, enhancing the function of the LOSC as a framework convention. This openness to external norms through 'rules of reference' is an adaptation mechanism that reduces the need for modification by subsequent practice.

Generally, as discussed, 'evolutionary interpretation' provides an effective treaty adaptation device that sometimes rivals the process of subsequent practice.[685] Like subsequent practice, it can significantly alter the meaning of a provision.[686] However, evolutionary interpretation cannot amount to modification; it relies on the parties' original intention to render the treaty evolutionary[687] and never leaves the confines of the text.[688] This also applies to the principle of 'systemic integration' rooted in Article 31(3)(c) VCLT, which, in turn, (partly) provides the roots for 'evolutionary interpretation', and allows for external norms to be read into the treaty without modifying it.[689] The doctrine of implied powers, another form of 'dynamic'

[679] Ibid. 1004–9. See also ME Footer, 'The Making of International Trade Law' in C Brölmann and Y Radi (eds), *Research Handbook on the Theory and Practice of International Lawmaking* (Edward Elgar, 2016) 395, 403ff.

[680] See Section 5.3.1(d).

[681] See Section 3.5.1(a), in particular text to n 571.

[682] See further BH Oxman, 'Tools for Change: The Amendment Procedure' in *Proceedings of the Twentieth Anniversary Commemoration of the Opening for Signature of the UNCLOS* (UN 2003) 195.

[683] 1973 International Convention for the Prevention of Pollution from Ships, 1340 UNTS 184.

[684] Protocol of 1978 Relating to the International Convention for the Prevention of Pollution from Ships, 1340 UNTS 61 (1978 MARPOL Protocol).

[685] See in particular Section 2.5.3.

[686] The result of evolutionary interpretation can sometimes even be more drastic than that of subsequent practice—see *Costa Rica v Nicaragua*, 213, and Separate Opinion of Judge Skotnikov, paras 8–10; Arato, 'Subsequent Practice', 450.

[687] Arato, 'Subsequent Practice', 453.

[688] See eg Gardiner, *Treaty Interpretation*, 243; Orakhelashvili, *Interpretation of Acts and Rules*, 291.

[689] See Section 4.4.2. See also Section 2.3.4.

interpretation, has a similar effect with regard to treaties establishing international organizations: it permits terms to be 'read into' the text in order to give effect to what was agreed under the treaty, without technically modifying it.[690] Thus, the more room there is for evolutionary interpretation or implied powers under the treaty, the less room or need there may be for modification by subsequent practice.[691] In the LOSC regime, which often interacts with other regimes in fields such as environmental law and human rights,[692] 'evolutionary' terms contained in the treaty also operate as implicit rules of reference, with the effect of importing general international law into the Convention without the need for recourse to modification by subsequent practice. Terms that could be deemed evolutionary include 'pollution' and 'protection of the marine environment', 'conservation of living resources', 'natural resources', and 'generally accepted rules and standards' (also an express rule of reference). The more flexibility that can be achieved through evolutionary interpretation and Article 31(3)(c) VCLT as gateways to regime interaction, the less of a need there is for either formally or tacitly modifying the Convention.[693]

Special adaptation mechanisms could even arise in the case of treaties describing a boundary in 'abstract' terms, without establishing an actual line, and leaving the delimitation to a boundary commission.[694] This could result in excluding, or creating a presumption against, other forms of specifying the boundary, including modification by subsequent practice[695]—a presumption disregarded, however, in the *Temple of Préah Vihéar* case,[696] and refuted in the *Beagle Channel Arbitration*.[697]

Perhaps a final note is warranted here with regard to the doctrine of 'approximate application', first expounded by Lauterpacht,[698] which serves mostly as an alternative to *formal* treaty amendment. The doctrine applies in situations similar to that in *Gabčíkovo-Nagymaros Project*.[699] When parties to a treaty are faced with a clear situation of breach, they are obliged to redraft or reformulate the treaty, whether on

[690] K Skubiszewski, 'Implied Powers of International Organizations' in Y Dinstein (ed), *International Law at a Time of Perplexity: Essays in Honour of Shabtai Rosenne* (Martinus Nijhoff, 1989) 855, 856–7.

[691] Nolte, Introductory Report on Treaties over Time, 207.

[692] Just the issue of sustainable fishing alone, for instance, involves the law of the sea, the related FAO regime that manages data on fishing and promotes sustainable practices, the CITES species protection regime and sanctions, the WTO trade regime that impacts trade in fish, and many others. See eg MA Young, 'Regime Interaction in Creating, Implementing and Enforcing International Law' in MA Young (ed), *Regime Interaction in International Law: Facing Fragmentation* (CUP, 2012) 85, 87.

[693] See eg Section 2.5.3.

[694] Nolte, Introductory Report on Treaties over Time, 208. It is relevant to note the distinction between 'delimitation' (the definition of the boundary in a treaty or judgment) and 'demarcation' (the physical marking of the boundary on the ground). See eg D Rushworth, 'Mapping in Support of Frontier Arbitration: Delimitation and Demarcation' (1997) 5 IBRU Boundary and Security Bulletin 61.

[695] Nolte, Introductory Report on Treaties over Time, 208.

[696] The Court held that the use of a certain map coupled with acquiescence had determined the course of the boundary, although the envisioned boundary commission had not delimited it. See Section 5.2.1.

[697] *Beagle Channel Arbitration*, para 169.

[698] *Admissibility of Hearings of Petitioners by the Committee on South West Africa*, Advisory Opinion of 1 June 1956, Separate Opinion of Sir Hersch Lauterpacht, ICJ Reports 35, 46.

[699] *Gabčíkovo-Nagymaros Project*, para 114. See further Section 5.2.1.

their own or by means of a competent organ, 'so as to ensure its continued effective application':[700]

> The doctrine of approximate application (...) if skilfully used may serve as a prod to the re-negotiation, reinterpretation or readaptation of a treaty which in its general lines remains desirable to all parties but which in its details cannot stand up to the wear and tear of daily life.[701]

This method is in keeping with the spirit of Article 60 VCLT, namely, with the idea that a treaty's existence does not automatically end in the case of a breach, in order to safeguard stability in treaty relations.[702]

Overall, where the aforementioned 'in-built' treaty mechanisms—most of which remain bounded by the four corners of the text—fail to go far enough in facilitating adaptation or are unavailable, modification by subsequent practice remains a possibility, and, moreover, a strategic tool for adaptation at the parties' disposal.

3.6 Interim Conclusions

In spite of the difficulties associated with its identification, the process of modification by subsequent practice—in the sense of an alteration, extension, or termination of treaty provisions or previous modifications—has been acknowledged by a wide range of courts and tribunals, a majority of legal scholars, and ILC members on various occasions. The practical difficulty (even impossibility) often encountered with formal amendment, the premise of *pacta sunt servanda*, the fluid interchange between interpretation and modification, and the significance of the contemporaneous intention of the parties (as well as of later treaty parties), all reinforce the validity of and need for the process of treaty modification by subsequent practice.[703] Moreover, the drafting history of the initial ILC article on modification by subsequent practice underscores the validity of the process. However, that history also reveals its complex, elusive nature. It is precisely that nature that made the process resistant to codification in the eyes of many ILC members and States in the first place, and constituted the main reason for its exclusion from the VCLT.[704]

While the process remains a reality in treaty relations, and a necessity in treaty evolution, it must be kept firmly in line with the parties' intention, in accordance with the constitutive elements and evidentiary standards discussed.[705] The modifying effect of subsequent practice is not to be presumed and can be taken to have occurred in exceptional circumstances where these requirements are met.[706] The

700 Rosenne, *Breach of Treaty*, 100. 701 Ibid. 702 Ibid.
703 See Section 3.3.3.
704 See Sections 3.2.6 and 3.3.7. See also Section 6.2.1 on the feasibility of codifying the process of modification by subsequent practice.
705 The constitutive elements were discussed in Section 3.3.3, building upon their more extensive treatment in Section 2.3.
706 See Section 3.1.

strength of the presumption against modification will, as stated, vary per treaty regime and provision; modification may even be prohibited altogether.[707] In any case, the presumption against modification will be particularly strong—though, as we have seen, not insurmountable—where a potential modification would affect the treaty's object and purpose[708] or formal amendment procedures have already been triggered.[709] In sum, it should not be assumed lightly that subsequent practice has led to a modification of the treaty—but such effect can by no means be wholly precluded. The 'threshold' required for practice to constitute agreement to a modification will depend on the type[710] and scope[711] of the envisioned modification, and the nature of the treaty and provisions in question.[712] This threshold refers not only to the quantity and quality of the practice (a substantive threshold), but also to the onus on the interpreter, often a dispute settlement body, to identify and apply the constitutive elements necessary for modifying practice, and substantiate clearly whether a modification has occurred (a procedural threshold).[713] It must be noted, however, that the modification by subsequent practice of a declaratory treaty provision does not require a higher threshold in order to modify the corresponding customary norm; rather, it poses an additional requirement (for a separate modifying act) with regard to the concurring practice of third States.[714]

The greatest conceptual difficulty lies in distinguishing between the two functions of subsequent practice discussed extensively in this book: treaty interpretation and treaty modification, the different effects of which may carry significant practical implications.[715] This distinction is to be approached on a case-by-case basis by reference to a range of factors and considerations that serve as reference points in analysing the examples in Chapter 5. Namely, one must look not only at the extent to which practice in a given case diverges from the text of the treaty and its object and purpose, but also—crucially—at key factors such as the nature and subject matter of the treaty, as well as the nature and substance of its provisions.[716] An example is the 'non-reciprocal' nature of certain treaties, or the 'integral' or 'interdependent' nature of certain multilateral obligations. Moreover, one must take into account the extent to which a treaty contains 'in-built' adaptation mechanisms that provide potential alternatives to modification by subsequent practice. Such mechanisms can include dispute settlement or forms of 'dynamic' interpretation such as evolutionary interpretation and implied powers.[717]

While it may be difficult to specify a list of concrete criteria to pinpoint modifications by subsequent practice—particularly in light of the ever-increasing

[707] See Section 3.5.
[708] See Section 3.3.5.
[709] See Sections 3.1 and 3.3.4.
[710] See Section 3.3.1.
[711] See eg Sections 3.3.4–3.3.5.
[712] See Section 3.5.
[713] See Section 3.3.3(b).
[714] See Section 3.3.1. See further Ch 4.
[715] See Section 3.4.1.
[716] See Section 3.5.1.
[717] See Section 3.5.2.

array of legal fields, topics, and types of instruments in international law—the aforementioned factors, applied systematically, can contribute to a more consistent approach to determining the effects of subsequent practice. Dispute settlement bodies could (and should) achieve a better understanding of how subsequent practice operates and impacts conventional law. Even more importantly, States themselves could (and should) achieve a better understanding of the impact of (their own) subsequent practice, as they shape and re-shape their treaty-related expectations[718]—hence also the aim of 'informing practice about itself'[719] intended from the outset of this book.[720]

718 Feldman, 'Evolving Treaty Obligations', 659 ('consent to obligations under treaty law will be better protected when states have greater awareness of how subsequent practice may change their treaty obligations').

719 Venzke, *How Interpretation Makes International Law*, 265.

720 See eg Section 1.4.

4

Subsequent Customary Law as a Means of Treaty Modification

4.1 Introduction

Subsequent customary international law can, under certain circumstances, lead to treaty modification[1]—a process that, despite drawing increasing attention, remains underexplored. Although this process is distinct from that of modification by

[1] See eg *Fisheries Jurisdiction* (*United Kingdom of Great Britain and Northern Ireland v Iceland*), Merits, Judgment of 25 July 1974 [*Fisheries Jurisdiction* (*UK v Iceland*), Merits] paras 50–3; *Delimitation of the Continental Shelf between the United Kingdom of Great Britain and Northern Ireland and the French Republic* (*UK/France*), Decisions of 30 June 1977 and 14 March 1978, 18 RIAA 3 [*Anglo-French Continental Shelf Arbitration*] para 47. The process has also been recognized by national courts. See eg Cour d'appel de Rennes [Rennes Regional Court of Appeal], 26 March 1979, *Rego Sanles Andres c/ Ministère public* (1980) AFDI 809, 823. See also Waldock, Sixth Report on the Law of Treaties, 88–91; Koskenniemi, Fragmentation Report, para 224 and fn 288; Comments by the Austrian Delegation to the ILC (referring to a 'generally accepted phenomenon'); G Fitzmaurice, 'The Law and Procedure of the International Court of Justice 1951–4' (1957) 33 BYBIL 203, 225; F Capotorti, 'L'extinction et la suspension des traités' (1971-III) 134 RC 417, 516ff; C Rousseau, *Droit international public, Tome I: Introduction et sources* (Dalloz, 1970) 283; HWA Thirlway, *International Customary Law and Codification: An Examination of the Continuing Role of Custom in the Present Period of Codification of International Law* (AW Sijthoff International Publishing, 1972) 125; M Akehurst, 'The Hierarchy of the Sources of International Law' (1974–75) 47 BYBIL 273, 274–8; DW Bowett, 'Reservations to Non-Restricted Multilateral Treaties' (1976) 48 BYBIL 67, 84; W Karl, *Vertrag und spätere Praxis im Völkerrecht: Zum Einfluß der Praxis auf Inhalt und Bestand völkerrechtliche Verträge* (Springer, 1983) 86; I Sinclair, *The Vienna Convention on the Law of Treaties* (2nd edn, Manchester UP, 1984) 163ff; RR Churchill and NG Foster, 'European Community Law and Prior Treaty Obligations of Member States: The Spanish Fishermen's Cases' (1987) 36 ICLQ 504, 516; GM Danilenko, *Law-Making in the International Community* (Martinus Nijhoff, 1993) 139–40; K Wolfke, 'Treaties and Custom: Aspects of Interrelation' in J Klabbers and R Lefeber (eds), *Essays on the Law of Treaties: A Collection of Essays in Honour of Bert Vierdag* (Martinus Nijhoff, 1998) 31; N Kontou, *The Termination and Revision of Treaties in the Light of New Customary International Law* (Clarendon Press, 1994) 145ff; P Daillier and A Pellet (eds), *Droit international public* (*NQ Dinh*) (6th rev edn, LGDJ, 1999) 266; M Byers, *Custom, Power and the Power of Rules: International Relations and Customary International Law* (CUP, 2001) 174–5; Y Dinstein, 'The Interaction between Customary International Law and Treaties' (2006) 322 RC 243, 383–416; MJ Bowman, '"Normalizing" the International Convention for the Regulation of Whaling' (2007–2008) 29 MJIL 293, 305; ME Villiger, *Commentary on the 1969 Vienna Convention on the Law of Treaties* (Martinus Nijhoff, 2009) 433; T Ruys, *'Armed Attack' and Article 51 of the UN Charter: Evolutions in Customary Law and Practice* (CUP, 2011) 19, 24. cf P Sands, 'Article 39 (1969)' in O Corten and P Klein (eds), *The Vienna Conventions on the Law of Treaties: A Commentary*, vol I (OUP, 2011) 963, 973–4; J Kammerhofer, *Uncertainty in International Law: A Kelsenian Perspective* (Routledge, 2011) 135–6; K Odendahl, 'Article 39' in O Dörr and K Schmalenbach (eds), *Vienna Convention on the Law of Treaties: A Commentary* (Springer, 2012) 699, 704.

subsequent practice, the significant conceptual and practical overlap and interrelation between the two—which has even posited certain commentators to refer to modification by subsequent practice as a 'customary' process[2]—adds an additional dimension to the discussion on subsequent practice.

Treaty modification by subsequent customary law occurs when a non-identical, conflicting norm of customary international law emerges in respect of the subject matter covered by a pre-existing treaty—whether as a result of the treaty-related practice of the parties, or practice related to an external norm[3]—and the parties intend for it to be overriding.[4] One classic example is the acceptance as law of the 200-mile exclusive economic zone in deviation from the 1958 Geneva Convention on the High Seas.[5] The result here is mainly one of disapplication rather than validity: the treaty rule is set aside to the extent it conflicts[6] with the customary norm (whereas conflict with a *jus cogens* norm would render the treaty rule invalid[7]). But the supervening customary norm does not become an integral part of the treaty;[8] it maintains a separate existence.[9] The term 'modification'[10] by subsequent customary law therefore differs from treaty modification by subsequent practice, in that the former 'displaces' or 'substitutes' the treaty provision in question without becoming part and parcel of the treaty, whereas the latter actually modifies its contents.[11]

The present chapter begins by reviewing the background of the deleted ILC provision on modification by subsequent customary law (Section 4.2).[12] Next, Section 4.3 gives an overview of the general process of formation and identification of customary international law. Section 4.4 considers the complex interaction between treaties and customary international law (4.4.1), and the identification (4.4.2) and basis (4.4.3) of the process of treaty modification by customary law by reference to that interplay. Section 4.5 discusses certain crucial requirements and distinctions in relation to modification by subsequent customary law—most notably, 'external' versus 'treaty-related' customary law and the intention of the parties (4.5.1), the

[2] See eg Summary record of 876th meeting, para 24. See also R Kolb, *Interprétation et création du droit international* (Bruylant, 2006) 507.

[3] Villiger, *Commentary*, 433. See further Section 4.5.1.

[4] *Jus cogens* norms are an exception—see Section 4.3.4.

[5] See Section 5.3.2(a).

[6] The concept of a 'genuine' conflict was discussed in Section 3.3.1.

[7] Article 64 VCLT.

[8] This is different in the case of modifications by subsequent practice, the result of which in most instances will not be regarded as an independent source of obligation. See Section 3.3.6(a).

[9] Pauwelyn argues that this separate existence may explain why a modifying later customary rule may not be able to form the basis for a claim of breach before a WTO panel with substantive jurisdiction covering only claims strictly regarding the WTO agreements—J Pauwelyn, *Conflict of Norms in Public International Law: How WTO Law Relates to Other Rules of International Law* (CUP, 2003) 142 (and see also, by analogy, Nottage and Sebastian, 'Giving Legal Effect to the Results of WTO Trade Negotiations', 17, discussed in Section 3.4.1, n 469). This conclusion seems to neglect to take into account the relevance of customary international law in the WTO context. See eg *US–Gasoline*, AB Report, 16 (stating that the WTO agreements cannot be read 'in clinical isolation from public international law'); *Korea–Measures Affecting Government Procurement*, Report of the Panel (19 January 2000) WT/DS163/R, para 7.96. cf JP Trachtman, 'The Domain of WTO Dispute Resolution' (1999) 40 Harv ILJ 333, 342; L Bartels, 'Applicable Law in WTO Dispute Settlement Proceedings' (2001) 35(3) JWT 499.

[10] See the definition of 'modification' set out in Section 1.3.

[11] This would presumably be coupled with the parallel modification or desuetude of the provision.

[12] See also Section 3.2.2.

issue of 'special' customary law (4.5.2), and the necessary evidentiary threshold for modification (4.5.3). Finally, Section 4.6 examines the extent to which a distinction can be made between treaty modification by subsequent customary law and treaty modification by subsequent practice, especially since the latter may itself lead to the emergence of a rule of customary international law. The findings are summarized in Section 4.7.

4.2 The ILC Draft Provision on Treaty Modification by Subsequent Customary Law

At the ILC's sixteenth session in 1964, Special Rapporteur Sir Humphrey Waldock proposed draft Article 73. In addition to the provision on modification by subsequent practice,[13] it contained a provision on modification by a subsequent rule of customary law.[14] The relevant text read:

Article 73: Effect of a Later Customary Rule or of a Later Agreement on Interpretation of a Treaty

The interpretation at any time of the terms of a treaty (...) shall take account of:

(a) the emergence of any later rule of customary international law affecting the subject-matter of the treaty and binding upon all the parties (...).

The draft provision was adopted unanimously at the 1964 ILC session, which is partly why its subsequent deletion by the ILC came as somewhat of a surprise.[15]

In preparation for the Commission's eighteenth session in 1966, the article was redrafted and included as part of Article 68:

Article 68: Modification of a Treaty by a Subsequent Treaty, by Subsequent Practice or by Customary Law

The operation of a treaty may be modified:

(...)

(c) By the subsequent emergence of a new rule of customary law relating to matters dealt with in the treaty and binding upon all the parties.

The article does not specify how exactly a treaty rule would come to be affected by such a modification.[16] During the discussions, Waldock drew the distinction between modification by subsequent practice and modification by subsequent customary law by arguing that, unlike in the case of modification by subsequent practice, sub-paragraph (c) of Article 68 dealt with the 'accidental modification of the

[13] See Section 3.2. [14] Summary record of 765th, 766th, and 767th meetings, 275ff.

[15] ME Villiger, *Customary International Law and Treaties: A Study of Their Interactions and Interrelations, with Special Consideration of the 1969 Vienna Convention on the Law of Treaties* (Brill, 1985) para 297.

[16] 1964 Draft Articles on the Law of Treaties with Commentaries, 198 para 3; Summary record of 866th meeting, para 41 (Yasseen).

operation of the treaty by subsequent events'.[17] His reasoning was that modification by subsequent customary law did not involve an intention to change the text of the treaty, but rather concerned the 'impact on a treaty done outside and in relation to it'.[18] However, drawing a distinction between subsequent practice and subsequent customary law based on the presence or absence of an intention to modify the treaty is controversial. While the *emergence* of customary law requires a general practice that does not have to be of all the parties, treaty *modification* by customary law requires the intention of all of them. The 'accidental' modification of a treaty through subsequent customary law could only occur in the case of a subsequently emerged peremptory norm of general international law (*jus cogens*). This matter is discussed in the next section.[19]

In the comments by governments on the Draft Articles, the main objections to the inclusion of sub-paragraph (c) of Article 68 were advanced by Pakistan (without stated reasons), the United Kingdom, and the United States.[20] Of these, only the United Kingdom questioned the principle of modification itself.[21] The aforementioned characterization by the Special Rapporteur of subsequent customary law as an extrinsic means of modifying treaties prompted the United Kingdom to comment that treaties should not be modified without the parties' consent.[22] As we shall see, and as already noted, this is indeed correct—and a point with which the process of modification by subsequent customary law is actually fully in conformity. The United Kingdom also stressed the difficulty of determining the exact point in time when a new rule of customary law could be said to have emerged.[23] Of course, albeit a problematic aspect of customary law generally, this point in no way constitutes a valid reason to deny the effects of subsequent customary law.[24]

The United States argued that, though 'literally accurate' and 'in keeping with the long-recognized principle that treaties are to be applied in the context of international law and in accordance with its evolution', the provision could be problematic due to the existence of too broad a range of views as to what constitutes customary law.[25] It thus proposed to delete sub-paragraph (c), 'leaving the principle to be applied "under the norms of international law in general" rather than as a specific provision in a convention on treaty law'.[26] The United States therefore did not contest the substance of the provision, but advised not to codify it.

The Special Rapporteur did not regard the uncertainty as to the rules of customary law as constituting a 'cogent objection'.[27] He insisted that, regardless of any uncertainties regarding its operation, customary law 'looms large' in international law and its constant and undeniable impact on the operation of treaties 'unquestionably exists'.[28]

[17] Summary record of 859th meeting, para 35 (Waldock). See also Summary record of 866th Meeting, para 24 (De Luna).

[18] Waldock, Sixth Report on the Law of Treaties, 97, para 14.

[19] See Section 4.3.4.

[20] Waldock, Sixth Report on the Law of Treaties, 87–8.

[21] Villiger, *Customary International Law and Treaties* (1985), 210.

[22] Waldock, Sixth Report on the Law of Treaties, 88.

[23] Ibid.

[24] See also text to nn 27–8.

[25] Waldock, Sixth Report on the Law of Treaties, 88.

[26] Ibid.

[27] Ibid. 90, para 11.

[28] Ibid.

At the Commission's 865th and 866th meetings in 1966, a number of members endorsed the view that any attempt at an adequate formulation of the rule of modification by subsequent customary law would require dealing with 'controversial' and 'extremely difficult problems'[29]—a clear parallel to the ILC discussions on the provision on modification by subsequent *practice*.

One member expressed concern at the prospect of including any article relating to the controversial relationship between customary and treaty law that would go beyond what was already included in relation to *jus cogens* norms.[30] He also underscored the diplomatic nature of the conference.[31] Some ILC members pointed out that *not* acknowledging the possibility of treaty modification by subsequent customary law would endorse a formal hierarchy between treaties and customary international law—thus, 'sub-paragraph (c) touched on a problem of capital importance, the competition between sources of international law'.[32] Others emphasized that it is not the source as such that determines the hierarchy between a customary and a treaty norm, but rather the substance of the rules in each specific case that decides which will take priority in a given case. Sub-paragraph (c) did not sufficiently clarify the conditions under which customary law can take precedence over conventional law.[33]

Still on this issue, a member argued that sub-paragraph (c) was unnecessary, since a treaty could only be modified by subsequent customary law if the latter represents a *jus cogens* norm—an issue already covered by then draft Article 53(bis), now Article 64 VCLT—and that, for the rest, derogations from customary law are allowed, so that a pre-existing treaty containing conflicting provisions could still stand.[34] Once again, various members highlighted the point that it is not the emergence of the subsequent customary rule as such, but rather the tacit *will of the parties*, which is capable of terminating or modifying:

> [Except for when a new rule of *jus cogens* has emerged,] if the parties agreed to modify the treaty so as to bring its provisions into conformity with the new rule of customary law, they were at liberty to do so; otherwise, the emergence of a new customary rule of general international law would have no effect on the existence of the treaty.[35]

Another member argued that in some cases, parties to a treaty may contribute to the formation of a new rule of customary law without intending to derogate from the treaty provisions as *lex specialis*, bearing in mind that *lex specialis derogat legi generali*.[36] It is difficult—though not impossible—to imagine situations in which parties continue fulfilling their obligations under a treaty while simultaneously contributing to the formation of a customary rule conflicting with the contents of those very provisions.[37]

29 Summary record of 866th meeting, para 24 (De Luna).
30 Ibid. para 58 (Rosenne).
31 Ibid. para 59 (Rosenne).
32 Ibid. para 40 (Yasseen).
33 Ibid. paras 40–1 (Yasseen), pointing to the question of intentionality or consent.
34 Ibid. para 32 (Tsuruoka).
35 Ibid. para 50 (Ago); see also para 51 (Amado).
36 Ibid. para 24 (De Luna).
37 See Section 4.5.3 referring to situations in which, for instance, the parties apply the treaty rule *inter se* and contribute to the formation of a rule of customary law in relation to non-parties.

In any case, there was widespread agreement as to the intentionality- or consent-based argument that a treaty can be modified as a result of the emergence of a new customary norm if there is evidence of the intention of the parties to that effect—otherwise, the treaty is presumed to remain unaffected, as *lex specialis*.

It was also argued that sub-paragraph (c) should be dropped because it could already be read into sub-paragraph (b) on modification by subsequent practice, wherein 'the idea of a customary norm was already present'.[38] The idea that the process of modification by subsequent practice overlaps with, or contains crucial elements of, the process of modification by customary law is explored in the ensuing sections. This also raises the distinction between customary law originally developed through treaty-oriented subsequent practice, and custom *contra legem*, developed outside the treaty regime, but which comes to impact upon its application.[39]

In addition, in its comments on the 1964 text of Article 68,[40] Israel had pointed to the connection between sub-paragraph (c) of Article 68, as an expression of the 'second leg' of the inter-temporal law, and Article 69 on interpretation by subsequent practice, as the 'first leg'.[41] It was in favour of bringing the provision in sub-paragraph (c) closer to and following Article 69, rather than retaining it in Article 68 on treaty modification.[42] A number of ILC members also proposed that sub-paragraph (c) be discussed under Article 69.[43]

Waldock agreed, in as far as the provision regarding subsequent customary law did not relate to modification in the same way that the provision on subsequent practice did, and consequently did not belong in Article 68 on modification.[44] He acknowledged that the emergence of a new rule of customary law also represents a source of treaty interpretation, and that, further, it raises the problematic question of relative priority between conventional and customary law, as discussed.[45] These considerations prompted the Rapporteur to delete sub-paragraph (c), bestowing upon it the same fate as that of the provision on modification by subsequent practice.[46]

Overall, the drafting history of the Vienna Convention reveals that the ILC excluded the provision dealing with modification by customary law from the Draft Articles for two reasons. First, the article was excluded due to the difficulty associated with attempts at codifying the interplay between treaty and customary law, an issue dealt with in a 'perfunctory' manner in the provision without any indication of scope or conditions, and which the Commission had long agreed to try and avoid.[47]

[38] Summary record of 866th meeting, para 20 (Tunkin). [39] See Section 4.5.1.

[40] Waldock, Sixth Report on the Law of Treaties, 97. [41] See also Section 3.2.1.

[42] Waldock, Sixth Report on the Law of Treaties, 97, paras 11–12.

[43] Summary record of 866th meeting, eg paras 10 (Jiménez de Aréchaga), 20 (Tunkin), and 25 (Briggs). cf ibid. para 24 (De Luna).

[44] Waldock, Sixth Report on the Law of Treaties, 91, para 14. [45] Ibid. 91, para 15.

[46] See Section 3.2.

[47] Summary record of 866th meeting, paras 25 (Briggs), 40–2 (Yasseen), 48 (Ago), 58–9 (Rosenne), and 67 (Waldock); *Report of the International Law Commission on the work of its 18th session* (1966) II YBILC 172, Ch II, 177, para 34; 1966 Draft Articles on the Law of Treaties with Commentaries, 236, para 3.

In fact, difficulties associated with the notion were still perceived to exist as recently as 1998, when the topic was listed in an unofficial ILC survey on 'items that should not be inscribed on the ILC's agenda', stating that '[i]t is counterproductive, and may be impossible, to codify the relatively flexible processes by which rules of customary international law are formed.'[48] These past difficulties prompted the Commission to take up the topic again in 2012, when it placed the 'Formation and Evidence of Customary International Law' on its current programme of work.[49]

Second, the draft article was excluded due to the fact that many members preferred to leave the provision aside on the understanding that the issue would instead be discussed in relation to the article on interpretation:[50]

> The 1966 ILC Commentary twice justified this deletion by noting the complexity of the relationship of customary law and treaties, a subject beyond the scope of a convention on the law of treaties (...) [referring also] to the special circumstances of each case. An additional factor in favour of deletion was the confusion in the ILC as to the intertemporal implications, and the distinction between the application and interpretation of treaties.[51]

Nevertheless, the deliberations in the ILC did not call into question the principle of modification:

> The text [of Article 68(c)] may not shed light on the phenomenon of modification, but, in view of its legislative history, discloses *general recognition* both by the ILC and the State community of the process of modification. In hindsight, omission of the provision may well have been the most expedient course of action.[52]

At least Article 64 VCLT still remains, denoting one potential form of customary rules—newly emerged rules of *jus cogens*—with automatic effect on pre-existing treaty provisions.[53] As for the effects of subsequent customary international law more generally, the ILC drafting history serves as a reminder that the process exists, and will persist, even if it never made it into the Vienna Convention.[54]

[48] *Report of the Study Group on the Future Work of the International Law Commission* (unofficial survey), para 104, in MR Anderson and others (eds), *The International Law Commission and the Future of International Law* (British Institute of International and Comparative Law, 1998) 1, 42, as cited in ILC, 'First Report on Formation and Evidence of Customary International Law, by Michael Wood, Special Rapporteur', UN Doc A/CN.4/663 (2013) [Wood First Report] para 10.

[49] UNGA Res 66/98 of 9 December 2011, UN Doc A/RES/66/98 (2012); ILC, 'Provisional summary record of the 3132nd meeting', UN Doc A/CN.4/SR.3132 (2012), 16; ILC, 'Formation and evidence of customary international law—Note by Michael Wood, Special Rapporteur', UN Doc A/CN.4/653 (2012), paras 1–7; Wood First Report, para 10.

[50] See eg Summary record of 866th meeting, paras 10 (Jiménez de Aréchaga), 20 (Tunkin), 25 (Briggs), 42 (Yasseen), and 68 (Waldock).

[51] Villiger, *Customary International Law and Treaties* (1985), para 298, citing, *inter alia*, Capotorti, 'L'extinction', 519.

[52] Villiger, *Customary International Law and Treaties* (1985), para 298 (emphasis in the original).

[53] Byers, *Custom*, 174.

[54] Villiger, *Commentary* 15; J Crawford, 'A Consensualist Interpretation of Article 31(3) of the Vienna Convention on the Law of Treaties' in G Nolte (ed), *Treaties and Subsequent Practice* (OUP, 2013) 29.

4.3 Formation and Identification of Customary Law and the Role of Practice

The formation and identification of customary international law is a highly dynamic process.[55] As with subsequent practice, the lack of precision inherent in the emergence and identification of customary international law brings with it the advantage of flexibility,[56] but also legal uncertainty—hence the reference to 'coutume sauvage'.[57] The tedious process of identification involves a number of elements that must be properly applied to be able to understand the treaty modifying effect of customary international law in the ensuing sections.

4.3.1 The two-element approach

Customary international law is defined in Article 38 of the Statute of the International Court of Justice as 'evidence of a general practice accepted as law'.[58] This definition contains an objective element, *usus* ('a general practice'), and a subjective element, *opinio juris* ('accepted as law'), which are discussed in turn. The two elements taken together represent 'the conjunction of behavioral regularities and convergent expectations'[59]—also a fitting description for subsequent practice capable of treaty modification.[60] According to the ILC, whose own work provides evidence of customary international law,[61] sources of evidence of (the two elements of) customary international law may include 'treaties, decisions of national and international courts, national legislation, diplomatic correspondence, opinions of national legal advisers, practice of international organizations'.[62] Their relevance must be assessed carefully in light of the circumstances of the given case.[63]

The 'two-element' approach to customary international law remains dominant, as exemplified in the case law, literature, and practice,[64] and reaffirmed recently by the ILC.[65] However, the interplay between the two elements—which are admittedly

[55] See eg *North Sea Continental Shelf* (*Federal Republic of Germany/Denmark; Federal Republic of Germany/Netherlands*), Judgment of 20 February 1969, Dissenting Opinion of Judge Sørensen, ICJ Reports 241, 243; AA D'Amato, *The Concept of Custom in International Law* (Cornell UP, 1971) 12.

[56] See eg J Pearce, 'Customary International Law: Not Merely Fiction or Myth' (2003) Aust ILJ 125.

[57] R-J Dupuy, 'Coutume sage et coutume sauvage' in *Mélanges offerts à Charles Rousseau: La communauté internationale* (Pédone, 1974) 75. See also Z Kivilcim-Forsman, 'Principe d'egalité entre le traité et la coutume en droit international public' (1996) 45 J Faculty of Law, Ankara Univ 211, 218.

[58] See further A Pellet, 'Article 38' in A Zimmermann, C Tomuschat, and K Oellers-Frahm (eds), *The Statute of the International Court of Justice: A Commentary* (2nd edn, OUP, 2012) 812–32.

[59] Byers, *Custom*, 150, citing OR Young, *International Cooperation: Building Regimes for Natural Resources and the Environment* (Cornell UP, 1989) 81.

[60] As explored in Section 4.6, the notion of *opinio juris* resembles the element of intentionality in the 'agreement' requirement for subsequent practice discussed in Sections 2.3.5 and 3.3.3(b).

[61] Villiger, *Customary International Law and Treaties* (1985), para 19. See also eg Wood, Fourth Report, para 26.

[62] *Report of the International Law Commission covering its 2nd session* (1950) II YBILC 364, 368ff.

[63] Wood, Second Report, paras 29–31. See also eg ILC Draft Conclusions on Customary International Law (2016) ('Conclusion 3', para 1).

[64] Ibid. eg paras 3, 21–31. See, likewise, Wood, Third Report, para 17.

[65] ILC Draft Conclusions on Customary International Law (2016) ('Conclusion 2').

closely, if not often impossibly, entangled[66]—is still the subject of significant debate.[67] In order to explain the (chronological) separation between practice and *opinio juris*, attempts have been made to describe the process of formation of customary international law in terms of phases.[68] According to this theory, at the initial stage, practice determines the content of the emerging rule (formative stage). In the second stage, States become conscious of the fact that they are contributing to the creation of a legal norm (stage of intent to be bound). Finally, in the third stage, the content becomes a legal norm—that is, the rule becomes cognizable as customary law (law-creating stage).[69]

Certain scholars have proposed alternative, 'deductive'[70] approaches to the 'traditional' or 'inductive'[71] two-element approach to customary international law. These various 'modern' approaches to customary law favour one constitutive element over the other, or exclude one of the two altogether.[72] For instance, some scholars focus only on the notion of *opinio juris*,[73] particularly in fields such as human rights,[74] humanitarian law,[75] and international criminal law,[76] while others are of the opinion that *opinio juris* is hardly provable in practice and thus bears little relevance for the actual identification of customary international law.[77] Another suggestion is the 'sliding scale' approach, according to which the stronger the evidence

[66] ILA, Committee on Formation of Customary (General) International Law, 'Final Report of the Committee: Statement of Principles Applicable to the Formation of General Customary International Law' (2000) 69 Intl L Assn Rep Conf 714 [ILA London Statement of Principles on Customary International Law] para 10(c); Wood, Second Report, para 3; HWA Thirlway, *The Sources of International Law* (OUP, 2014) 62.

[67] Wood, Second Report, para 3. Nevertheless, 'each of the two constituent elements must be separately ascertained'—ILC Draft Conclusions on Customary International Law (2016) ('Conclusion 3', para 2).

[68] H Meijers, 'How Is International Law Made? The Stages of Growth of International Law and the Use of its Customary Rules' (1978) 9 NYBIL 3.

[69] See further GJH van Hoof, *Rethinking the Sources of International Law* (Kluwer, 1983).

[70] Wood, Second Report, para 98. [71] Ibid. para 96.

[72] Ibid. para 27. For an overview, see Wood, First Report, paras 97–101.

[73] See eg B Cheng, 'Epilogue' in B Cheng (ed), *International Law: Teaching and Practice* (Stevens & Sons, 1982) 223; AT Guzman, 'Saving Customary International Law' (2005) 27 MJIL 115, 153.

[74] See eg RB Lillich, 'The Growing Importance of Customary International Human Rights Law' (1995–96) 25 Ga J Intl & Comp L 1.

[75] See eg T Meron, *The Making of International Criminal Justice: A View from the Bench: Selected Speeches* (OUP, 2011) 32; J d'Aspremont, 'An Autonomous Regime of Identification of Customary International Humanitarian Law: Do Not Say What You Do or Do Not Do What You Say?' in R van Steenbergh (ed), *Droit international humanitaire: un regime special de droit international?* (Bruylant, 2013) 67.

[76] See eg W Schabas, 'Customary Law or "Judge-Made" Law: Judicial Creativity at the UN Criminal Tribunals' in J Doria and others (eds), *The Legal Regime of the International Criminal Court: Essays in Honour of Professor Igor Blishchenko* (Martinus Nijhoff, 2009) 77. cf G Boas, *Public International Law: Contemporary Principles and Perspectives* (Edward Elgar, 2012) 90. See further Wood, First Report, para 68.

[77] See eg P Guggenheim, 'Les deux éléments de la coutume en droit international' in C Rousseau (ed), *La technique et les principes du droit public: etudes en l'honneur de Georges Scelle* (LGDJ, 1950) 272, 280; R Müllerson, 'The Interplay of Objective and Subjective Elements in Customary Law' in K Wellens (ed), *International Law: Theory and Practice. Essays in Honour of Eric Suy* (Martinus Nijhoff, 1998) 161; AA D'Amato, 'Customary International Law: A Reformulation' (1998) 4 ILT 1; MN Shaw, *International Law* (6th edn, CUP, 2008) 75.

of one of the two elements, the less evidence is required for the other to prove the existence of a customary rule.[78]

In connection with this issue, there has been debate regarding the notion of so-called 'instant custom', premised on the idea that customary rules may develop so rapidly—subject to the specific context and reception by the international community—that they may be regarded as 'instant', such that only the element of *opinio juris* is required.[79] The classic example is the formation of customary international law through *opinio juris* on the basis of UN General Assembly resolutions.[80] Confusion stems from the fact that in many cases *usus* and *opinio juris* seem indistinguishable, making the discussion overly abstract. Nevertheless, the two represent separate requirements and the element of State practice should not be neglected. A customary norm cannot be proclaimed to be in force without being respected in actual practice. Accordingly, statements and views expressed in General Assembly resolutions do not carry decisive value in and of themselves if they are not also supported by practice.[81] Otherwise, General Assembly resolutions would in effect automatically constitute hard law.[82] This does not mean that General Assembly resolutions and other such verbal statements cannot constitute relevant practice; rather, it means that their evidentiary value relates to the degree of determinacy of the practice, as discussed at length in Chapter 2[83] and further in Section 4.3.2.

'Modern' approaches to customary international law have received a significant amount of criticism, as they neglect to properly take into account the essential roles played by both practice and *opinio juris*.[84] Indeed, it is submitted here that despite the fact that in reality more emphasis is placed on the practice element,[85] both constitutive elements are indispensable to the process of customary law formation.

[78] See eg FL Kirgis, Jr, 'Custom on a Sliding Scale' (1987) 81 AJIL 146, 146–51. cf AE Roberts, 'Traditional and Modern Approaches to Customary International Law: A Reconciliation' (2001) 95 AJIL 757, 774.

[79] See especially B Cheng, 'United Nations Resolutions on Outer Space: "Instant" International Customary Law?' (1965) 5 IJIL 23, 36. See also eg B Langille, 'It's "Instant Custom": How the Bush Doctrine Became Law After the Terrorist Attacks of September 11, 2001' (2003) 26 BC Intl & Comp L Rev 151, 151–6. cf *North Sea Continental Shelf (Federal Republic of Germany/Denmark; Federal Republic of Germany/Netherlands)*, Judgment of 20 February 1969, Dissenting Opinion of Judge Lachs, ICJ Reports 218, 230; *North Sea Continental Shelf*, Dissenting Opinion of Judge Sørensen, 240; M Scharf, 'Seizing the Grotian Moment: Accelerated Formation of Customary International Law in Times of Fundamental Change' (2010) 43 Cornell ILJ 446, 446–8.

[80] See eg *Nicaragua v US*, Merits, para 188 (relying as evidence of *opinio juris* principally on the 'Declaration on Principles of International Law concerning Friendly Relations and Co-operation among States in Accordance with the Charter of the United Nations', UNGA Res 2625 (XXV) of 24 October 1970, UN Doc A/RES/25/2625 (1970)).

[81] See Sections 2.3.1(b) and 3.3.3(a). See also Wood, Third Report, paras 47ff. cf M Bos, *A Methodology of International Law* (North-Holland, 1984) 86.

[82] See eg D'Amato, *The Concept of Custom*, 118.

[83] See Sections 2.3.1(a)–(b) and 2.3.5.

[84] See eg RY Jennings, 'The Identification of International Law' in B Cheng (ed), *International Law: Teaching and Practice* (Stevens, 1982) 3, 5; B Simma and P Alston, 'The Sources of Human Rights Law: Custom, *Jus Cogens*, and General Principles' (1988–89) 12 Aust YBIL 83, 107.

[85] Wood, First Report, para 96. See also G Fitzmaurice, 'The Law and Procedure of the International Court of Justice, 1951–54: General Principles and Sources of Law' (1953) 30 BYBIL 1, 68; Simma and Alston, 'The Sources of Human Rights Law', 88; ME Villiger, *Customary International Law and Treaties: A Manual on the Theory and Practice of the Interrelation of Sources* (2nd rev edn, Kluwer International, 1997) 16; RY Jennings and A Watts (eds), *Oppenheim's International Law: Peace*, vol I (9th edn, OUP, 2008) 25; Roberts, 'Traditional and Modern Approaches', 758.

Without *opinio juris*, practice would not amount to a *rule* of international law, and without practice, a rule would not be one of *customary* law:[86]

Without practice (*consuetudo*), customary international law would obviously be a misnomer, since practice constitutes precisely the main *differentia specifica* of that kind of international law. On the other hand, without the subjective element (...) the difference between international custom and simple regularity of conduct (*usus*) or other non-legal rules of conduct would disappear.[87]

Thus, the two-element approach adopted in this book remains, as Wood has put it, 'loyal to a classical understanding of customary law formation as an empirical, decentralized, and bottom-up process.'[88]

4.3.2 The element of practice

Practice, the objective element, constitutes the 'raw material'[89] of customary international law—it both constitutes and limits it.[90] The definition of 'practice' coincides with what was already extensively discussed in relation to subsequent practice in Chapters 2 and 3,[91] and therefore does not require detailed treatment in the present section. As we have seen, the meaning of 'practice' is extremely broad, and can be taken to include practice on the international plane as well as relevant domestic practice.[92] It covers action, both physical and verbal, and inaction, as long as it 'discloses the State's conscious attitude with respect to—its recognition of—a customary rule'.[93]

As discussed, the weight to be accorded to different types of practice will depend on the circumstances of each case,[94] including the extent to which the practice is sufficiently determinate.[95] This may also depend on the legal field in question. For instance, the ICTY Appeals Chamber in the *Tadić* case explained the following in relation to the law of armed conflict:

Before pointing to some principles and rules of customary law that have emerged in the international community for the purpose of regulating civil strife, a word of caution on the law-making process in the law of armed conflict is necessary. When attempting to ascertain State practice with a view to establishing the existence of a customary rule or a general principle, it is difficult, if not impossible, to pinpoint the actual behaviour of the troops in the

86 Van Hoof, *Rethinking the Sources*, 93, citing Meijers, 'How Is International Law Made?', 13.
87 K Wolfke, *Custom in Present International Law* (Martinus Nijhoff, 1993) 40–1.
88 Wood, First Report, para 96, citing eg L Henkin, *How Nations Behave: Law and Foreign Policy* (2nd edn, Columbia UP, 1979) 34.
89 Villiger, *Customary International Law and Treaties* (1985), para 18.
90 *Right of Passage over Indian Territory* (*Portugal v India*), Merits, Judgment of 12 April 1960, Dissenting Opinion of Judge Sir Percy Spender, ICJ Reports 97, 99.
91 See in particular Sections 2.3.1(a) and 3.3.3(a). See further Wood, Second Report, para 48 ('Draft conclusion 7').
92 See Section 2.3.1(c).
93 Villiger, *Customary International Law and Treaties* (1985), para 18.
94 Wood, First Report, para 19; Wood, Second Report, para 49.
95 See Section 2.3.1(b).

field for the purpose of establishing whether they in fact comply with, or disregard, certain standards of behaviour.[96]

As mentioned in Section 4.3.1, in certain fields such as human rights[97] or armed conflict,[98] the centrality of practice and the two-element approach do not fully account for why customary rules seem to require a lower degree of supporting practice to emerge and adapt.[99] Koskenniemi argues that the normal rules for customary international law formation are not applicable when it comes to certain fundamental norms:

> [I]t is really our certainty that genocide or torture is illegal that allows us to understand state behaviour and to accept or reject its legal message, not state behaviour itself that allows us to understand that these practices are prohibited by law. It seems to me that if we are uncertain of the latter *fact*, then there is really little in this world we can feel confident about.[100]

Different 'modern' approaches have been advanced to account for this issue regarding customary law formation, but these are not explored further in the present chapter.[101] Suffice it to mention that in such fields, the threshold for practice may be lower, if not merely a formality,[102] and the requirement of agreement among members of the international community is more easily assumed.

As to the question of *whose* practice can contribute to the formation of customary international law,[103] the term can be taken to refer primarily to the practice of States.[104] The practice of international organizations can be taken into account as well—in any case to the extent to which the practice of international organizations as such can be distinguished from the individual practice of States within the organization,[105] but not only.[106] Caution is required when determining the *weight* to be accorded to the practice of international organizations in identifying customary law.[107] For instance, distinctions in terms of evidentiary weight can be made

[96] *Prosecutor v Dusko Tadić*, Appeal on Jurisdiction, para 99.

[97] See eg IT Winkler, *Human Right to Water: Significance, Legal Status, and Implications for Water Allocation* (Hart, 2014) 67.

[98] O Schachter, 'New Custom: Power, *Opinio Juris* and Contrary Practice' in J Makarczyk (ed), *Theory of International Law at the Threshold of the 21st Century: Essays in Honour of Krzysztof Skubiszewski* (Kluwer, 1996) 531, 539; Meron, *The Making of International Criminal Justice*, 32.

[99] Byers, *Custom*, 163.

[100] M Koskenniemi, 'The Pull of the Mainstream' (1990) 88 Mich L Rev 1946, 1952 (emphasis in the original). See also eg J Klabbers, 'The Curious Condition of Custom' (2002) 8 ILT 29, 34; J Wouters and C Ryngaert, 'Impact on the Process of Formation of Customary International Law' in MT Kamminga and M Scheinin (eds), *The Impact of Human Rights Law on General International Law* (OUP, 2009) 111, 129–30.

[101] See eg Simma and Alston, 'The Sources of Human Rights Law', 82; N Petersen, 'Customary Law Without Custom? Rules, Principles, and the Role of State Practice in International Norm Creation' (2008) 23 Am U Intl Rev 275.

[102] Petersen, 'Customary Law', 279.

[103] See Sections 2.3.1(c) and 3.3.3(a).

[104] See eg Wood, Second Report, paras 33, 36; Dinstein, 'The Interaction between Customary Law and Treaties', 242, 266; Villiger, *Customary International Law and Treaties* (1985), para 18.

[105] Villiger, *Customary International Law and Treaties* (1985), para 19.

[106] Wood, Second Report, para 48 ('Draft conclusion 7', para 4).

[107] Ibid. para 43, referring to J Wouters and P De Man, 'International Organizations as Law-Makers' in J Klabbers and A Wallendahl (eds), *Research Handbook on the Law of International Organizations* (Edward Elgar, 2011) 190, 208.

between practice relating to internal matters of the organization itself, and its external, 'operational' activities;[108] between the practice of organs composed of State representatives and those composed of individuals serving in their personal capacity (for instance, the ILC, though an authoritative source of knowledge of the law, does not theoretically contribute to the formation of customary law);[109] and between the practice of the secretariat of an international organization versus that of its intergovernmental organs.[110] The significance of the practice of international organizations has already been discussed *in extenso* with regard to subsequent practice in Chapter 2.[111] Moreover, as discussed in that chapter, non-State actors such as individuals and NGOs can incentivize States to follow a certain course of action, but do not, in principle, directly contribute to the formation of customary international law.[112]

Practice capable of giving rise to a customary norm must be 'general',[113] as well as consistent,[114] and include the practice of 'specially affected States'.[115] Potentially significant but by no means singly decisive factors are the frequency and duration of the practice, and the absence of protest by interested States.[116] These considerations, which also apply to the identification of relevant subsequent practice as seen in Chapters 2 and 3,[117] are discussed in turn.

Regarding the required duration of the practice, while in many national legal systems timescales are laid down as to the required duration for a certain usage to become a customary rule, no such provision exists in international law. As highlighted in the *North Sea Continental Shelf* cases, the duration must be sufficient to allow States to become aware and react to the practice, which can occur over a very short time span:[118]

> [A]n indispensable requirement would be that within the period in question, short though it might be, State practice, including that of States whose interests are specially affected, should

[108] Wood, Second Report, para 43; I Johnstone, 'Law-Making through the Operational Activities of International Organizations' (2008) 40 Geo Wash L Rev 87, 94.

[109] Wood, Second Report, para 43. [110] Ibid. [111] See Section 2.3.1(c).

[112] Ibid. See also Wood, Second Report, para 45; AC Arend, *Legal Rules and International Society* (OUP, 1999) 176; T Buergenthal and SD Murphy, *Public International Law in a Nutshell* (5th edn, West, 2013) 75.

[113] Article 38 of the ICJ Statute. See also ILC Draft Conclusions on Customary International Law (2016) ('Conclusion 8').

[114] See eg American Law Institute, *Restatement of the Law (Third), The Foreign Relations Law of the United States* (American Law Institute Publishers, 1987) [Restatement (Third) of US Foreign Relations Law] Section 102.2; Wood, Second Report, para 59 ('Draft conclusion 9').

[115] *North Sea Continental Shelf*, para 73. See also WT Worster, 'The Transformation of Quantity into Quality: Critical Mass in the Formation of Customary International Law' (2013) 31 BU Intl LJ 1, 63. On the definition of 'specially affected', see Meijers, 'How Is International Law Made?', 7; Danilenko, *Law-Making*, 95.

[116] See also Section 2.3.5(c). [117] See in particular Sections 2.3 and 3.3.3.

[118] *North Sea Continental Shelf*, para 74. See also D'Amato, *The Concept of Custom*, 59. cf BD Lepard, 'Customary International Law as a Dynamic Process' in CA Bradley (ed), *Custom's Future: International Law in a Changing World* (CUP, 2016) 62, arguing that customary law requires State practice that is 'longstanding' and *opinio juris* that is 'well grounded and consistent through time', which 'gives customary norms permanence and rootedness' and makes them more resilient to change.

have been both extensive and virtually uniform (...) and should moreover have occurred in such a way as to show a general recognition that a rule of law or legal obligation is involved.[119]

Thus, duration is usually not a crucial element,[120] but it contributes to the 'persuasiveness' of the change; in other words, it carries evidentiary value.[121] This also relates to the issue of so-called 'instant custom' discussed in Section 4.3.1.

As mentioned, another element of uncertain significance is the frequency of the practice.[122] While, like duration, it lends greater evidentiary weight to the practice in question,[123] 'the degree of frequency has to be weighted against the frequency with which the circumstances arise in which the action constituting practice has to be taken, or is appropriate'.[124] It is even conceivable that a single act can suffice to give rise to new customary law.[125] This is similar to the discussion on modification by subsequent practice.[126] Much more important is the level of *generality* of the practice: 'the practice from which it is possible to deduce custom is that of the generality of States and not of all of them'.[127] Thus, as explained in relation to subsequent practice in Chapter 2,[128] the practice must be sufficiently widespread[129] and representative.[130] To the extent that this requirement is different from that of generality,[131] the practice must also be *uniform and consistent*,[132] which does not

[119] *North Sea Continental Shelf*, para 74.

[120] ILA London Statement of Principles on Customary International Law, Commentary to Principle 12, para (b); D'Amato, *The Concept of Custom*, 56–8; M Akehurst, 'Custom as a Source of International Law' (1974–75) 47 BYBIL 1, 15–16; Shaw, *International Law*, 76–8; O Corten, *Méthodologie du droit international public* (Editions de l'Université de Bruxelles, 2009) 150–1. cf *Dispute regarding Navigational and Related Rights* (*Costa Rica v Nicaragua*), Judgment of 13 July 2009, Separate Opinion of Judge Sepúlveda-Amor, ICJ Reports 273, 279; Jennings, 'The Identification of International Law', 5; S Rosenne, *Practice and Methods of International Law* (Oceana Publications, 1984) 55; LB Sohn, 'Unratified Treaties as a Source of Customary International Law' in A Bos and H Siblesz (eds), *Realism in Law-Making: Essays in International Law in Honour of Willem Riphagen* (Martinus Nijhoff, 1986) 231, 234.

[121] D'Amato, *The Concept of Custom*, 25.

[122] Wood, Second Report, para 55. cf Meijers, 'How Is International Law Made?', 13.

[123] Wood, Second Report, para 56.

[124] Thirlway, *The Sources of International Law*, 65.

[125] Cheng, 'United Nations Resolutions', 23; G Abi-Saab, 'La coutume dans tous ses états ou le dilemme du développement du droit international général dans un monde éclaté' in *Le droit international à l'heure de sa codification: Etudes en l'honneur de Robert Ago*, vol I (Dott A Giuffrè, 1987) 53, 60; Shaw, *International Law*, 78. See *contra* eg NQ Dinh, P Daillier, and A Pellet, *Droit international public* (7th edn, LGDJ, 2002) 325–6.

[126] See eg Section 3.3.3(b).

[127] *Barcelona Traction, Light and Power Company, Limited* (*Belgium v Spain*) (*New Application: 1962*), Judgment (Second Phase) of 5 February 1970, Separate Opinion of Judge Ammoun, ICJ Reports 286, 330.

[128] See eg Section 2.3.5.

[129] See eg *Gulf of Maine*, para 111; *Maritime Delimitation and Territorial Questions between Qatar and Bahrain* (*Qatar v Bahrain*), Merits, Judgment of 16 March 2001, ICJ Reports 40 [*Qatar v Bahrain*, Merits] para 205.

[130] *North Sea Continental Shelf*, para 73; Wood, Second Report, para 52.

[131] See DP Fidler, 'Challenging the Classical Concept of Custom: Perspectives on the Future of Customary International Law' (1996) 39 GYBIL 198, 202 (arguing that uniformity and generality 'meld together in a unitary analytical process').

[132] See eg *Asylum Case* (*Colombia/Peru*), Judgment of 20 November 1950, ICJ Reports 266, 276–7; *Fisheries Case* (*United Kingdom v Norway*), Judgment of 18 December 1951, ICJ Reports 116 [*Anglo-Norwegian Fisheries*] 131, 138; *Right of Passage over Indian Territory* (*Portugal v India*), Merits, Judgment of 12 April 1960, ICJ Reports 6, 40; *North Sea Continental Shelf*, para 74.

mean that full universality or absolute consistency has to be achieved.[133] In fact, particularly if there is little opposition, 'it very well may be that only a relatively small number of States engage in a practice, and the inaction of others suffices to create a rule of customary international law'.[134]

It is not necessary to prove that a State has actively participated or even deliberately acquiesced in the practice in order for it to become binding upon it as customary international law.[135] In principle, new States, and States that remain silent during its formation, are bound by pre-existing customary law even if they did not have the opportunity to, or did not explicitly, consent to it at the time of its inception. However, a State that openly and repeatedly opposes being bound by a customary rule at the time of its formation[136] may attain the status of 'persistent objector'.[137] Some commentators see this notion as a practical solution:

> As a matter of policy, the persistent objector rule could be regarded as a useful compromise. It respects States' sovereignty and protects them from having new law imposed on them against their will by a majority; but at the same time, if the support for the new rule is sufficiently widespread, the convoy of the law's progressive development can move forward without having to wait for the slowest vessel.[138]

Thus, as also discussed in Chapter 3, a small number of objecting States, in this context termed 'persistent objectors', would not rule out the emergence of a rule of customary international law.[139] Moreover, once a customary norm has formed, 'subsequent objectors' are not allowed;[140] States will by then have come to rely on the subsequently objecting States conforming to the customary rule, in line with the principle of legitimate expectations. Although a few subsequent objectors could not call the customary rule into question, they could potentially indicate the gradual emergence of a *new* customary rule modifying or terminating the previous one.[141]

[133] Wood, Second Report, para 57, citing eg Fitzmaurice, 'The Law and Procedure of the International Court of Justice' (1953), 45; Villiger, *Customary International Law and Treaties* (1997), 44; J Crawford, *Brownlie's Principles of Public International Law* (8th edn, OUP, 2012) 24. See also *Nicaragua v US*, Merits, para 186 ('The Court does not consider that, for a rule to be established as customary, the corresponding practice must be in absolutely rigorous conformity with the rule.').

[134] Wood, Second Report, para 53. See also Akehurst, 'Custom', 18.

[135] See eg ILA London Statement of Principles on Customary International Law, Principle 14(ii).

[136] ILA London Statement of Principles on Customary International Law, Principle 15; Charney, 'The Persistent Objector Rule', 1. See also JB McClane, 'How Late in the Emergence of a Norm of Customary International Law May a Persistent Objector Object?' (1989) 13 ILSA JIL 1, 7.

[137] See eg *Asylum Case*, 277–8; *Anglo-Norwegian Fisheries*, 131. See also eg Wood, Third Report, paras 85–95; Rousseau, *Droit international public*, 326; Danilenko, *Law-Making*, 109–13; Villiger, *Customary International Law and Treaties* (1997), 33–7; Wolfke, 'Treaties and Custom', 66–7; GI Tunkin, *Theory of International Law* (2nd rev edn, Wildy, Simmonds, and Hill, 2003) 130; Jennings and Watts, *Oppenheim's International Law*, 29. cf D'Amato, *The Concept of Custom*, 233–63; Charney, 'The Persistent Objector Rule', 1.

[138] ILA London Statement of Principles on Customary International Law, Principle 15 para (c).

[139] See Section 3.3.3(b).

[140] Wood, Third Report, para 93, pointing out that a 'State should object to a developing rule as early as possible.' See also eg A Kaczorowska, *Public International Law* (4th edn, Routledge, 2010) 41. cf CA Bradley and M Gulati, 'Withdrawing from International Custom' (2010) 120 Yale LJ 202.

[141] Villiger, *Customary International Law and Treaties* (1985), para 52, citing Fitzmaurice, 'The Law and Procedure of the International Court of Justice' (1953), 99. See also Section 3.3.3(b), text to nn 350ff.

The ICJ in the *Nicaragua* case noted that, 'to deduce the existence of customary rules (...) instances of State conduct inconsistent with a given rule should generally have been treated as breaches of that rule, not as indications of the recognition of a new rule'.[142] Therefore, the *violation* of a customary rule could indicate the beginning of a new rule—once again, a parallel with the discussion on (modification by) subsequent practice in the previous chapter.[143]

What may be of further influence in the formation of customary international law is the relative power of the States contributing to the practice,[144] which likewise applies to modification by subsequent practice.[145] Byers argues that States' 'differing abilities to engage in State practice' favours more powerful States in the process of customary law formation[146]—a similar argument to that postulated by Voicu.[147] Koskenniemi is of the view that customary international law thus acts as a 'smoke-screen' masking subjective political preferences.[148] Due to the sheer size of the international community, 'a survey of customary international law is often highly selective and takes into account only major powers and the most affected states.'[149] Thus, any analysis of practice contributing to the formation of customary international law may inevitably suffer from a certain degree of bias or subjectivity. On the other hand, the requirements of generality, consistency, representativeness, and determinacy, should ensure that the practice in question is sufficiently established to provide a trustworthy indication of emerging customary rules.

Generally, the required threshold for the emergence of customary law will vary according to the nature of the respective usage. The threshold for practice may be higher depending on the 'strength of the prior rule which is purportedly over-thrown,'[150] if indeed such a contrary prior rule exists and must be surmounted.[151] As explained in Chapter 3, this applies generally whenever a change entails an alteration of existing rules rather than an extension thereof.[152] This point also relates to the threshold required for treaty modification by subsequent customary law in cases where customary law comes to displace existing treaty rules.[153]

4.3.3 The element of *opinio juris*

The concept of *opinio juris sive necessitatis*,[154] the subjective or psychological element of customary law, requires that the practice observed be 'accepted as law', in the sense that it be coupled with a sense of legal obligation.[155] *Opinio juris* can

[142] *Nicaragua v US*, Merits, para 186. [143] See eg Section 3.3.3(b).

[144] C de Visscher, *Theory and Reality in Public International Law* (Princeton UP, 1957) 149; Wolfke, *Custom*, 81; Byers, *Custom*, 46–9; Shaw, *International Law*, 79–80.

[145] See Section 3.3.3(b). See also Section 2.3.5, text to n 367. [146] Byers, *Custom*, 205.

[147] See Section 3.3.2(a). [148] Koskenniemi, 'The Pull of the Mainstream', 1946.

[149] Petersen, 'Customary Law', 277.

[150] Shaw, *International Law*, 78. See also Akehurst, 'Custom', 19; D'Amato, *The Concept of Custom*, 60–1. cf Section 4.5.3.

[151] Shaw, *International Law*, 56. [152] See Section 3.3.1. [153] See Section 4.5.3.

[154] First formulated in F Gény, *Méthode d'interprétation et sources en droit privé positif: essai critique* (1st edn, LGDJ, 1899) para 110. See also eg Continental Shelf (Libyan Arab Jamahiriya/Malta), Judgment of 3 June 1985, ICJ Reports 13 [*Libya/Malta*], 13, 29.

[155] See eg *North Sea Continental Shelf*, paras 76, 78.

be thought of as 'those shared understandings which enable States to distinguish between legally relevant and legally irrelevant State practice'.[156] In other words, practice must reflect an awareness of, or be motivated by, the existence or creation of a legal rule, rather than purely by extralegal (political, ideological, or practical) considerations.[157] The same was explained in relation to subsequent practice in the previous chapters.[158]

Moreover, the practice must be motivated by the formation of a *customary* rule, rather than, for example, solely by the need of the treaty parties to comply with the treaty's rules.[159] Thus, in a sense, 'it can be more difficult to appraise practice in relation to a norm that has a pre-existing treaty basis, as the practice of parties to the treaties *inter se* can be attributed to the existence of the treaty'.[160] Conversely, the practice of non-parties in accordance with rules contained in a treaty can indicate the parallel emergence of a customary rule with the same content.[161]

The concept of *opinio juris* is certainly not free from ambiguity,[162] and grasping its meaning and function as the '"extra ingredient" necessary to transform a repetitive practice into a binding norm' has been labelled the 'central problem' with customary law.[163] It is debated, for instance, whether *opinio juris* stands for States' belief (or opinion) or consent (or will),[164] the latter of which brings the notion closer to the 'agreement' required for subsequent practice.[165] Moreover, a common criticism of *opinio juris* is that it is difficult to prove.[166] However, this is not always so, particularly in the case of express statements, but also with regard to other types of practice, including treaties.[167] Its determination 'may depend upon the nature of the rule and the circumstances in which the rule falls to be applied'.[168] The ICJ has maintained a

[156] Byers, *Custom*, 166.

[157] See eg *Asylum Case*, 285–6; *North Sea Continental Shelf*, para 77; *Fisheries Jurisdiction* (*United Kingdom of Great Britain and Northern Ireland v Iceland*), Merits, Judgment of 25 July 1974, Separate Opinion of Judge Dillard, ICJ Reports 53, 58; *Nicaragua v US*, Merits, para 207. See further Wood, Second Report, paras 61–2; GI Tunkin, 'Remarks on the Juridical Nature of Customary Norms of International Law' (1961) 49 CLR 419, 422; Crawford, *Brownlie's Principles*, 23–4.

[158] See Sections 2.3.5 and 3.3.3(b).

[159] *Rights of Nationals*, 199–200; *North Sea Continental Shelf*, para 76; Wood, Second Report, para 62. See also eg O Schachter, 'Entangled Treaty and Custom' in Y Dinstein and M Tabory (eds), *International Law at a Time of Perplexity: Essays in Honour of Shabtai Rosenne* (Martinus Nijhoff, 1989) 717, 729; A Orakhelashvili, *The Interpretation of Acts and Rules in Public International Law* (OUP, 2008) 81.

[160] R Cryer, 'Of Custom, Treaties, Scholars and the Gavel: The Influence of the International Criminal Tribunals on the ICRC Customary Law Study' (2006) 11 JCSL 239, 244.

[161] Wood, Second Report, para 62.

[162] See eg M Mendelson, 'The Subjective Element in Customary International Law' (1995) 66 BYBIL 177, 194, 207.

[163] E Kadens and EA Young, 'How Customary Is Customary International Law?' (2013) 54 Wm & Mary L Rev 885, 907.

[164] Wood, Second Report, para 66, noting that PCIJ and ICJ cases refer to both will and belief, and citing eg O Elias, 'The Nature of the Subjective Element in Customary International Law' (1995) 44 ICLQ 501.

[165] See Section 2.3.5.

[166] Wood, Second Report, para 66, citing Akehurst, 'Custom', 36, and H Taki, '*Opinio Juris* and the Formation of Customary International Law: A Theoretical Analysis' (2010) 51 GYBIL 447.

[167] Wood, Second Report, paras 75–6.

[168] Ibid. para 71.

high threshold for establishing *opinio juris*, often looking at whether the legality of the practice is supported by treaties, UN resolutions, or ILC reports.[169]

It has been argued that the process of judging the existence of a customary rule and interpreting its content, ie extracting the rights and obligations applicable in the given case,[170] particularly when evaluating the element of *opinio juris*, grants the judge a significant degree of latitude.[171] One scholar has remarked that the validity of a newly identified customary norm 'lies less in the conviction of the States than in that of the judges'.[172] Moreover, 'both treaty and judicial practice have repeatedly neglected to distinguish between the conditions which must be fulfilled, on the one hand for the creation of international customary law, and on the other, for its existence'.[173] It is clear that the process of identifying and interpreting customary law entails a difficult balancing act of objective and subjective elements, and a certain dose of (judicial) discretion. This seems to provide yet another conceptual link between the process of formation and identification of new customary law and that of subsequent practice as discussed in earlier chapters.

4.3.4 A note on *jus cogens*

The formation and identification of customary international law, as well as its interaction with treaty law, also relates to the topic of peremptory norms of general international law (*jus cogens*). This concept is defined in Article 53 VCLT as 'a norm accepted and recognized by the international community of States as a whole as a norm from which no derogation is permitted and which can be modified only by a subsequent norm of general international law having the same character'.[174]

The existence of *jus cogens*, a form of *lex superior*, is now well-established,[175] but much debate still exists as to the content of such norms and the evidentiary challenges involved in identifying them.[176] Many commentators consider them a sub-category

[169] See eg *Nicaragua v US*, Merits, paras 187ff.

[170] CF de Casadevante Romani, *Sovereignty and Interpretation of International Norms* (Springer, 2007) 88.

[171] Ibid. 90. See also eg R Haggenmacher, 'La doctrine du droit coutumier dans la pratique de la Cour internationale' (1986) 1 RGDIP 117.

[172] De Casadevante Romani, *Sovereignty and Interpretation*, 89. See also Shaw, *International Law*, 76.

[173] Meijers, 'How Is International Law Made?', 11.

[174] The VCLT definition is of general application. See Wood, First Report, para 24 fn 43.

[175] See eg Koskenniemi, Fragmentation Report, paras 346ff; Wood, First Report, para 25; J Frowein, 'Jus Cogens' in R Bernhardt (ed), *Encyclopaedia of International Law*, vol III (Elsevier, 1997) 65. See also eg *Armed Activities on the Territory of the Congo*, 52; *Questions relating to the Obligation to Prosecute or Extradite* (*Belgium v Senegal*), Judgment of 20 July 2012, ICJ Reports 422, para 99.

[176] See eg AA D'Amato, 'It's a Bird, It's a Plane, It's Jus Cogens' (1990) 6 Conn JIL 1; Villiger, *Customary International Law and Treaties* (1997), 491, 493; S Kadelbach, '*Jus Cogens*, Obligations *Erga Omnes* and Other Rules—The Identification of Fundamental Norms' in C Tomuschat and JM Thouvenin (eds), *The Fundamental Rules of the International Legal Order:* Jus Cogens *and Obligations* Erga Omnes (Martinus Nijhoff, 2006) 21; H Charlesworth, 'Law-Making and Sources' in J Crawford and M Koskenniemi (eds), *The Cambridge Companion to International Law* (CUP, 2012) 187, 191.

of customary international law,[177] or regard customary law as one possible source of *jus cogens*,[178] depending also on one's view of customary international law.[179]

For present purposes, the most important aspect of the operation of peremptory norms is laid down in Article 64 VCLT, namely, that any existing treaty in conflict with a newly emerged *jus cogens* norm becomes void and terminates. This contrasts with the effects of (other types of) customary international law, which are not automatic and only serve to *displace* conflicting treaty provisions, as already explained.[180] In view of the scope of the present topic, the linkages between customary law and *jus cogens*, and the general process of emergence of the latter, do not require further elaboration. Reference will only be made to them in specific cases when relevant.

4.4 Treaty Modification by Subsequent Customary Law: The Interplay between Treaties and Customary International Law

4.4.1 Treaties and customary international law: No formal hierarchy

Article 38 of the ICJ Statute confirms that there is no hierarchy between the primary sources of international law, particularly between treaty and customary international law.[181] The various items in Article 38 are listed in order of logical progression, reflecting the degree of certainty with which their existence can be discerned. The equality between treaty and customary international law is manifested in different ways in practice: if a customary norm and a treaty norm conflict, the norm that will prevail in a given case will depend on their normative content, context, and the parties bound by them.[182]

[177] See eg AD McNair, *The Law of Treaties* (Clarendon Press, 1961) 213–15; D'Amato, *The Concept of Custom*, 132; J Paust, 'The Reality of *Jus Cogens*' (1991) 7 Conn JIL 81, 82; MH Mendelson, 'The Formation of Customary International Law' (1998) 272 RC 155, 181; Jennings and Watts, *Oppenheim's International Law*, 7–8; RB Baker, 'Customary International Law in the 21st Century: Old Challenges and New Debates' (2010) 21 EJIL 173, 177; Crawford, *Brownlie's Principles*, 594. *Contra* eg Van Hoof, *Rethinking the Sources*, 164; U Linderfalk, 'The Creation of *Jus Cogens*: Making Sense of Article 53 of the Vienna Convention' (2011) 71 ZaöRV 359; ME O'Connell, '*Jus Cogens*: International Law's Higher Ethical Norms' in DE Childress III (ed), *The Role of Ethics in International Law* (CUP, 2012) 13, 26.

[178] See eg Akehurst, 'Hierarchy of the Sources', 282–4; A Orakhelashvili, *Peremptory Norms in International Law* (OUP, 2006) 126; Shaw, *International Law*, 127.

[179] Wood First Report, para 25, citing Van Hoof, *Rethinking the Sources*, 163–4.

[180] See Section 4.1.

[181] The role of general principles as a primary source carries less practical importance than treaties and customary law. General principles are usually applied in the absence of (specific) rules of treaty or customary law, or to interpret the latter. On the other hand, general principles may sometimes be more specific than broad principles in treaties or customary law, in which case the *lex specialis* maxim can lead to the application of general principles instead. See eg *Russian Claim for Interest on Indemnities* (*Russia v Turkey*), Award of 11 November 1912, 11 RIAA 433, where it was held that a State must pay moratory interest on its debts based on a general principle, despite the customary presumption in favour of liberty of State action.

[182] Kivilcim-Forsman, 'Principe d'égalité', 212. See also G Fitzmaurice, 'Some Problems Regarding the Formal Sources of International Law' in FM van Asbeck and others (eds), *Symbolae Ve rzijl: Présentées au Professeur JHW Verzijl à l'occasion de son LXX-ième anniversaire* (Martinus Nijhoff, 1958) 153, 154.

The two sources share a complex and dynamic relationship. As to the impact of treaties upon customary law, the former have been characterized as 'records' of State practice that continually impact upon the contents of the latter.[183] Treaties may evidence or codify existing customary law,[184] crystallize emerging customary law,[185] and lead to the creation of new customary law.[186] In this sense, treaties do not 'harden' into customary law, but rather 'generate' it—a theoretical distinction.[187] Once this occurs, the customary norm takes on a life of its own, independent of the original treaty provision.[188] Thus, even if a State opts out of the treaty, it remains bound by the given rule under customary law. Conversely, customary norms can lead to an expansive interpretation, modification, or even desuetude of treaty provisions.[189] Moreover, treaty and customary law can derogate from each other as *lex specialis*.[190]

D'Amato argues that a majority of customary rules have their roots in treaty provisions.[191] Even bilateral treaties could theoretically generate customary rules.[192] Only certain types of provisions, however, are capable of generating customary law,

[183] D'Amato, *The Concept of Custom*, 105, 115, citing *Lauritzen et al v Government of Chile*, Supreme Court of Chile, 19 December 1955 (1956) 23 ILR 708, 729. See generally Wood, Third Report, para 35, stating that treaties may (come to) reflect a customary rule in at least three ways: by codifying an existing rule, crystallizing an emerging rule, or generating a new rule; ILC Draft Conclusions on Customary International Law (2016) ('Conclusion 11', para 1).

[184] See eg *Fisheries Jurisdiction* (*UK v Iceland*), Merits, para 58; *Nicaragua v US*, Merits, paras 187ff.

[185] See Wood, Third Report, para 38, citing eg *North Sea Continental Shelf*, Dissenting Opinion of Judge Sørensen, 243 ('a treaty purporting to create new law may be based on a certain amount of State practice and doctrinal opinion which has not yet crystallized into customary law (…) a customary rule in *statu nascendi*'), and the example of the development of the concept of the exclusive economic zone at UNCLOS III and its acceptance as customary international law by States even before the adoption of the LOSC (see further Section 5.3.2(a)).

[186] Koskenniemi, Fragmentation Report, para 224, citing *North Sea Continental Shelf*, para 71; *Continental Shelf* (*Libyan Arab Jamahiriya/Malta*), Judgment of 3 June 1985, ICJ Reports 13, para 27; RR Baxter, 'Treaties and Custom' (1970-I) 129 RC 25. See also Wood, Third Report, paras 39–43 (cautioning that this requires a careful examination of the circumstances).

[187] D'Amato, *The Concept of Custom*, 120.

[188] *Nicaragua v US*, Merits, paras 177–8. See also *North Sea Continental Shelf*, paras 63, 68–73.

[189] Koskenniemi, Fragmentation Report, para 224; Bowman, '"Normalizing"', 305; Byers, *Custom*, 172–80. Note that the termination of *customary international law* by *treaty* seems unlikely, since the former is generally binding upon all States, while a treaty binds only the specific parties (this may be different for near-universal treaties). If the entire legal community would want a customary rule displaced, modification through the emergence of new customary law would be more likely. Other features of customary law also make such an effect unlikely, such as the difficulty of determining the precise moment of formation of customary law and the fact that its content may be vague compared to treaties. See Wolfke, 'Treaties and Custom', 31.

[190] The most basic case is the adoption of a treaty in an area previously covered by customary law, which prevails over the customary rule between the treaty parties as *lex specialis*. This does not automatically imply the extinction of the prior customary law, which remains valid for States not parties to the (codifying) treaty, and may occasionally apply between treaty partners if, for instance, the treaty covers the subject matter only partially. Conversely, it is conceivable that a customary rule may be more specific than a treaty rule, or that a 'special' customary rule binding a small number of States may conflict with a multilateral treaty with many States parties. In such cases, the customary rule will prevail over the treaty according to the *lex specialis* maxim. See also Section 4.4.2.

[191] AA D'Amato, *International Law: Prospect and Progress* (Transnational, 1987) 125.

[192] *Nottebohm* (*Liechtenstein v Guatemala*) (*Second Phase*), Judgment of 6 April 1955, ICJ Reports 4, 21–3. cf C de Visscher, 'Coutume et traité en droit international public' (1955) 59 RGDIP 353.

namely, those containing 'generalizable' rules.[193] Examples of non-generalizable provisions are procedural clauses specific to a treaty (such as entry into force requirements), provisions regarding the competences and internal procedures of international organizations (such as UN Charter articles regulating the various functions of the Security Council), and technical obligations such as trade schedules under the GATT. Other provisions may give rise only to 'special', 'regional', or 'local' customary law, further discussed[194]—one example would be 'objective regimes' established by treaties regulating navigational rights on a river or specifying inter-State boundaries.[195] Some scholars have suggested that a treaty cannot generate customary law 'unless (...) [it] regulates some aspect of behavior the international community (or its most important members) has an interest in enforcing'.[196] The ICJ in the *North Sea Continental Shelf* cases, in dealing with the question of whether the equidistance principle in Article 6 of the 1958 Geneva Convention on the Continental Shelf could apply to a non-ratifying party (Germany), applied what has been termed the 'manifest intent' test:[197] if it appears from the wording or structure of the treaty that a provision is secondary or subsidiary in nature, contains ambiguities (in this case, the concept of 'special circumstances'), and, moreover, if the treaty parties have the option to unilaterally withdraw from it, then the norm-generating potential of the provision is significantly weakened.[198]

Thus, on the one hand, treaties may be part of the process of creation of customary law. On the other hand, customary behaviour influences the interpretation and application of treaties, and can even come to modify them. The latter interaction is most important for present purposes. Since no general hierarchy exists between treaty and customary law, the result of this interaction will always remain to be decided on a case-by-case basis.

4.4.2 Identifying modifications by subsequent customary law: Conflicts between treaties and subsequent customary norms

The process of identifying (emerging) customary international law was discussed in Section 4.3. The present section takes the analysis a step further, dealing with the issue of identifying *modifying* subsequent customary law. In particular, it looks at situations in which subsequent customary law displaces existing treaty provisions.[199] It is only after the existence and substance of a customary norm have

[193] D'Amato, *The Concept of Custom*, 105. cf Villiger, *Customary International Law and Treaties* (1985), para 286. This point says something about the difference between subsequent practice and subsequent customary law—see further Section 4.6.

[194] See Section 4.5.2. [195] See Section 3.5.1(a).

[196] MA Kaplan and N Katzenbach, *The Political Foundations of International Law* (John Wiley & Sons, 1961) 241.

[197] D'Amato, *The Concept of Custom*, 108. [198] *North Sea Continental Shelf*, paras 63ff.

[199] Customary international law may also come to supplement the content of the treaty with a novel element or direction. The required threshold is higher for a customary rule to *displace*, rather than to significantly supplement or *extend*, an existing treaty rule (see Section 4.5.3). This is in line with the definition of modification in Section 3.3.1 as an alteration, extension, or termination of treaty provisions by subsequent practice or subsequent customary law.

been ascertained that its relation to a pre-existing treaty—and the extent to which there is 'genuine' conflict (that is, a true incompatibility) between the customary and treaty rules in question—can be assessed. If such a conflict is present, there is potential for modification by subsequent customary law, subject to the requirements discussed in Section 4.5.

The Vienna Convention does not provide much guidance on conflicts between treaty and customary law, which are endemic to international law,[200] with *jus cogens* norms as a notable exception.[201] As determined in the previous section,[202] 'hierarchies must only be established ad hoc and with a view to resolving particular problems as they arise'.[203] Wherever possible, one should first attempt to reconcile a treaty rule with a seemingly conflicting subsequent customary norm through harmonious interpretation, and in line with the principle of effectiveness,[204] in a way that causes 'minimal disturbance' to the functioning of the international legal system.[205] Moreover, one must seek to allow the norm that is set aside to remain 'in the background', continuing to influence the interpretation of the norm to which priority is accorded.[206] This could be done by reference to 'collision rules' or 'conflict-resolution' techniques such as *lex specialis derogat lege generali* and *lex posterior derogat priori*, or, notably, by means of the principle of 'systemic integration' in Article 31(3)(c).[207] When the incompatibility cannot be resolved by means of interpretation, one can speak of a 'genuine' conflict, a notion already explored in the previous chapter.[208]

The aforementioned 'collision rules' offer a tool to help understand normative conflict,[209] although they arguably constitute policy arguments rather than organizing principles.[210] Pursuant to the *lex specialis* maxim, treaties may remain unaffected by a later, conflicting customary rule (just as, conceivably, customary law could constitute *lex specialis* vis-à-vis treaty rules[211]).[212] However, the principle does not apply automatically.[213] For instance, it may not necessarily hold

[200] Koskenniemi, Fragmentation Report, para 486.
[201] Article 64 VCLT.
[202] See Section 4.4.1.
[203] Koskenniemi, Fragmentation Report, para 485.
[204] See Section 2.5.1.
[205] Koskenniemi, Fragmentation Report, para 410.
[206] Ibid. para 411.
[207] See eg C McLachlan, 'The Principle of Systemic Integration and Article 31(3)(c) of the Vienna Convention' (2005) 54 ICLQ 279.
[208] See Section 3.3.1.
[209] See eg Q Wright, 'Conflict between International Law and Treaties' (1917) 11 AJIL 579; C Rousseau, 'De la compatibilité des normes juridiques contradictoires dans l'ordre international' (1932) 39 RGDIP 133, 150; Akehurst, 'Hierarchy of the Sources', 273; Sinclair, *Vienna Convention*, 98; Pauwelyn, *Conflict of Norms*, 335ff.
[210] See eg S Ranganathan, 'Between Philosophy and Anxiety? The Early International Law Commission, Treaty Conflict and the Project of International Law' (2013) 83 BYBIL 82, 94.
[211] See (text to) n 190.
[212] See eg *INA Corporation v Government of the Islamic Republic of Iran*, Award No 184-161-1 (13 August 1985) 8 Iran-US CTR 373, 378. See also ILC, 'Conclusions of the work of the Study Group on the Fragmentation of International Law: Difficulties arising from the Diversification and Expansion of International Law', *Report of the International Law Commission on the work of its 58th session*, UN Doc A/61/10 (2006) Ch XII [Conclusions of the Study Group on Fragmentation] 408; DP O'Connell, *The International Law of the Sea*, vol I (Clarendon Press, 1982) 46–7.
[213] Koskenniemi, Fragmentation Report, paras 22–6.

true that special law (in our case, treaty provisions vis-à-vis customary law), being more concrete, takes better account of the particular context in which it is to be applied.[214] Moreover, according to the principle of *lex posterior derogat priori*, a new customary rule could, under the right circumstances, replace a treaty provision.[215] Yet this maxim, too, 'fails to render itself applicable in any mechanical way'.[216] As mentioned earlier, subsequent customary law must satisfy certain conditions to override a prior treaty rule.[217] In each case, a balancing act is necessary between these various considerations. The question may boil down to an 'assessment of which aspect "speciality" or "temporality"—seems more important in this connection'.[218] Of course, ultimately, the issue is to be resolved by interpreting the will of the parties.[219] Conversely, a pre-existing treaty could take priority over (that is, remain unaffected by) subsequent customary law as *lex prior*.[220] Once again, there is no automaticity here: the result will be subject to the intention of the parties and the subject matter in question. It will depend, *inter alia*, on the status and degree of generality of the treaty (multilateral treaties such as the UN Charter, with the character of a legislative enactment relevant to the entire international community, are more difficult to override),[221] as well as the nature of individual provisions and, evidently, their normative status (such as *jus cogens* norms).[222] For instance, in the case of a conflict between human rights norms, 'the one that is more favourable to the protected interest is usually held overriding'.[223] Finally, this brings us to the more straightforward issue of *lex superior*. A customary norm that represents *jus cogens* will automatically invalidate any contrary pre-existing treaty provision. The same is true of Article 103 of the UN Charter and most likely also of *erga omnes* obligations.[224]

It suffices here to conclude that there is 'nothing automatic or mechanical' about the process of resolving normative conflicts between treaties and subsequent customary law.[225] Any analysis must take into account the nature of the treaty, its subject matter and constituency, and, especially, the will of the parties, with a view to establishing its level of specificity (*lex specialis*), temporality (*lex posterior* or *lex prior*), and status (*lex superior*) through interpretation.[226]

This is where the role of Article 31(3)(c) VCLT becomes relevant to the interaction between (pre-existing) treaties and (subsequent) customary norms, though it

214 Conclusions of the Study Group on Fragmentation, 408–9; Koskenniemi, Fragmentation Report, para 224 fn 289; Akehurst, 'Hierarchy of the Sources', 275.

215 See eg Thirlway, *International Customary Law*, 131.

216 Koskenniemi, Fragmentation Report, para 250.

217 See Section 4.5.

218 Koskenniemi, Fragmentation Report, para 233.

219 Ibid. para 243. See further Section 4.5.1.

220 Ibid. para 227; see further para 241.

221 Ibid. para 259.

222 See eg Section 3.5 on the nature of different types of treaty regimes and obligations. See further Koskenniemi, Fragmentation Report, para 108; Crawford, Third Report on State Responsibility, paras 99–108; SA Sadat-Akhavi, *Methods of Resolving Conflicts between Treaties* (Martinus Nijhoff, 2003) 213–31.

223 Koskenniemi, Fragmentation Report, para 108. See also Karl, 'Treaties, Conflicts between', 939.

224 See ibid. para 241.

225 Ibid. para 410. See also Kivilcim-Forsman, 'Principe d'égalité', 218.

226 Koskenniemi, Fragmentation Report, para 412; see also para 410. cf J Klabbers, *Treaty Conflict and the European Union* (CUP, 2009) 90.

has been argued that it 'scarcely covers this aspect with the degree of clarity requisite to so important a matter'.[227] Article 31(3)(c), still only seldom referred to in judicial practice, requires the interpreter to take into account 'any relevant rules of international law applicable in the relations between the parties', a formulation broad enough to include customary norms.[228] The article reflects the principle of 'systemic integration'.[229] The underlying notion is that rules cannot be understood in isolation from the larger body of norms of general international law.[230] This provides a way of reading new norms, even those from different legal fields, into the treaty without having to modify it—a 'cross-fertilization' of international law.[231] Thus, the overall process of Article 31(3)(c) arguably already includes techniques such as *lex specialis* and *lex posterior*.[232] In addition, it should be noted that external norms could also be interpreted into the terms of the treaty by reference to their 'ordinary meaning' (Article 31(1) VCLT) or 'special meaning' (Article 31(4) VCLT).[233]

In this sense, Article 31(3)(c) provides an alternative mechanism for treaty adaptation, as discussed in the previous chapter[234]—especially in relation to evolutionary interpretation, which is (partly) rooted in Article 31(3)(c).[235] Indeed, by means of the evolutionary approach, treaty provisions can undergo change in line with subsequent customary law without the need for actual modification:

> The existence and the interpretation of a treaty obligation by which the parties have attempted to codify a rule of customary international law may be influenced by the continuing formation of the respective parallel rule of customary international law.[236]

For instance, investment tribunals have considered that the meaning of certain declaratory provisions in investment treaties, such as the 'fair and equitable treatment' standard, is constantly evolving in accordance with changing customary international law.[237]

[227] *Gabčíkovo-Nagymaros Project*, Separate Opinion of Vice-President Weeramantry, 114.

[228] Sands, 'Treaty, Custom and the Cross-Fertilization of International Law', 95. The provision is primarily meant to address *treaty* interpretation, but can also apply to the interpretation of customary rules since Art 31(3)(c) itself reflects customary international law. See eg *Certain Questions of Mutual Assistance in Criminal Matters (Djibouti v France)*, Judgment of 4 June 2008, ICJ Reports 177, para 112; P Merkouris, 'Article 31(3)(c) of the VCLT and the Principle of Systemic Integration' (PhD, Queen Mary University of London, 2010). Any references to Art 31(3)(c) here can therefore be taken to refer to its customary counterpart.

[229] See eg Merkouris, 'Article 31(3)(c)', 1; McLachlan, 'Principle of Systemic Integration', 279.

[230] Sands, 'Treaty, Custom', 95.

[231] See generally ibid. 85ff.

[232] Merkouris, 'Article 31(3)(c)', 186; CJ Borgen, 'Treaty Conflicts and Normative Fragmentation' in DB Hollis (ed), *The Oxford Guide to Treaties* (OUP, 2012) 448, 454.

[233] M Paparinskis, 'Sources of Law and Arbitral Interpretations of *Pari Materia* Investment Protection Rules' in OK Fauchald and A Nollkaemper (eds), *The Practice of International and Nationals Courts and the (De-)Fragmentation of International Law* (Hart, 2012) 87, 112.

[234] See Section 3.5.2.

[235] See Section 2.5.3.

[236] Nolte, Third Report on Treaties over Time, 353 ('Conclusion 12').

[237] *Pope & Talbot Inc v Canada*, UNCITRAL Arbitration under Chapter Eleven of NAFTA, Award on Damages, 31 May 2002 [*Pope & Talbot*] paras 46, 54–62; *ADF Group Inc v United States of America*, ICSID Case No ARB(AF)/00/1, Award of 9 January 2003 [*ADF v US*] para 184; *International Thunderbird Gaming Corporation v The United Mexican States*, UNCITRAL Arbitration under NAFTA Chapter Eleven, Award of 26 January 2006 [*International Thunderbird Gaming*] para 194. See further Section 2.5.3 on evolutionary interpretation.

Customary law can be accounted for under Article 31(3)(c) VCLT as long as it is relevant to the subject matter of the treaty and applicable between the parties in question.[238] This can be interpreted broadly and at a high level of abstraction to include customary norms that pertain to related rather than identical matters, thus providing even more opportunity for the incorporation of external rules.[239] On the other hand, it could be argued that where a customary rule and a treaty rule clearly differ in that the latter is much more stringent than the former, the customary norm, as *lex generalis*, should not be read into treaty provisions intended precisely to provide a different standard as *lex specialis*.[240]

Article 31(3)(c) VCLT bears another important caveat: it entails that the customary norm is read into the treaty provision, not applied instead of it ('take into account'). Thus, the customary norm plays only a secondary role to the treaty.[241] Its scope does not extend to modification by subsequent customary law. Accordingly, treaty modification by customary law can be said to have occurred when a non-identical customary rule emerges in respect of the same subject matter covered by the treaty, and interpretation pursuant to Article 31(3)(c) is no longer sufficient to account for the observed practice.[242] In other words, the demarcation between dynamic or evolutionary interpretation, and modification by customary law, occurs beyond the realm of Article 31(3)(c), once the respective customary norm can no longer be reconciled through interpretation as 'secondary' to the treaty provision in question. If a genuine incompatibility between the treaty provision and the subsequent customary norm, irreconcilable through interpretation, is proven to exist, and the will of the parties so dictates, the customary norm can come to displace the conventional norm.

4.4.3 Validity of the process of treaty modification by subsequent customary law

Just as treaties do not usually make explicit any departures from existing customary law,[243] so too are States reluctant to admit, for a multitude of reasons, that their practice represents a departure from the provisions of a treaty in favour of a new, divergent customary norm—as we have seen, the same can be said of States' general attitude towards modifications by subsequent practice.[244] This reluctance stems at least partly from the fact that 'customary modification', like modification by

[238] See n 228. This point also relates to the identification of customary law—see Section 4.3.

[239] M Paparinskis, 'Investment Treaty Arbitration and the (New) Law of State Responsibility' (2013) 24 EJIL 617, 642. See also *Oil Platforms (Islamic Republic of Iran v United States of America)*, Merits, Judgment of 6 November 2003, Separate Opinion of Judge Simma, ICJ Reports 324, para 9 ('provisions of any treaty have to be interpreted and applied in the light of the treaty law applicable between the parties as well as of the rules of general international law "surrounding" the treaty').

[240] Paparinskis, 'Sources of Law', 23.

[241] Sands, 'Treaty, Custom', 102–3.

[242] Ibid. 86.

[243] RR Baxter, 'Multilateral Treaties as Evidence of Customary International Law' (1965–66) 41 BYBIL 291; D'Amato, *The Concept of Custom*, 127.

[244] See eg Section 3.4.

subsequent practice, implies deviation from the treaty and, at least initially, a potential violation of the principle of *pacta sunt servanda*:[245]

> It is submitted that *pacta sunt servanda* is breached only in the initial few instances of modification (...). The violative nature of the initial instances of modificatory development is neutralized, as additional States acquiesce or participate in the practice (...). Eventually, the conventional rule will have passed out of use (...). Of course, if this development does not occur, the breaches continue to violate *pacta sunt servanda*. Hence, whether a derogation constitutes a breach of obligation depends, *inter alia*, on the reactions of other parties.[246]

Other issues with treaty modification by subsequent customary law have been invoked, such as the internal constitutional problem addressed in the context of the discussion on modification by subsequent practice,[247] namely, that treaties should be modified by the same State organ responsible for their ratification.[248]

The principle of *pacta sunt servanda* may give rise to a presumption against treaty modification by subsequent customary law[249]—a presumption applicable both ways, that is, also against the (albeit unlikely[250]) replacement of *customary* law by *treaty* law.[251] This may have been Oppenheim's meaning in recognizing that the codification of international law through treaties 'interferes with the so-called organic growth of the law through usage into custom'.[252] The presumption could be understood in the sense that one must first strive to reconcile the conflicting norms through interpretation.[253] In any case, as discussed in the previous chapter,[254] the principle of *pacta sunt servanda* must be viewed in the context of the overarching principle of legitimate expectations, which lies 'at the heart of all customary and treaty rules'.[255] After all, customary international law, like the duty to perform obligations as agreed, is rooted in the consent of the parties:

245 As explained in relation to modification by subsequent practice, whether an initial derogation constitutes a breach may depend on the nature of the acts involved and the abruptness of the change. In any case, continual breaches of a treaty by its parties may indicate newly emerging customary law, which can come to modify or even terminate the instrument—Dinstein, 'The Interaction between Customary International Law and Treaties', para 216. See also eg E Giraud, 'Exposé préliminaire: Modification et terminaison des traités collectifs' (1961-I) 49 AIDI 5. See further Section 3.3.3(b).

246 Villiger, *Customary International Law and Treaties* (1997), para 333.

247 See Section 3.3.2(a).

248 Kivilcim-Forsman, 'Principe d'égalité', 215.

249 Villiger, *Customary International Law and Treaties* (1985), paras 343–6; Byers, *Custom*, 176. See Section 3.1 on the general presumption against modification, entailing, *inter alia*, that perceived modifications are, as far as reasonably possible, to be conceived as interpretations. See also Section 4.5.3 on the threshold(s) required for modification by subsequent customary law.

250 See n 189.

251 RMM Wallace and O Martin-Ortega, *International Law* (6th edn, Sweet & Maxwell, 2009) 22.

252 L Oppenheim, *International Law: A Treatise*, E Lauterpacht (ed), vol I (Peace) (8th edn, Longmans, Green & Co, 1955) 58–9. In the same vein, according to Thirlway, *International Customary Law*, 143, 'codification may sometimes prove to have been the purchase of immediate consistency and order at the price of later difficulty and divergence'.

253 See nn 204–8 and Section 3.3.1 on 'genuine' normative conflicts. See also Koskenniemi, Fragmentation Report, para 412; Wallace and Martin-Ortega, *International Law*, 22.

254 See Section 3.3.2(a).

255 Byers, *Custom*, 109.

Given the necessity of combining legal stability with innovation while avoiding abrupt change, modification represents a *desirable* process for the international legal order, *a fortiori* since customary law corresponds by definition with the interests of States.[256]

Thus, '[t]here is no reason to feel any unease about custom trumping a treaty (with the tacit consent of the Contracting Parties).'[257] The possibility must exist, and legitimate expectations stemming from subsequent customary law should under certain circumstances be capable of rebutting the presumption against change.[258]

A short excursion is warranted here to note the debate in the *Institut de Droit International* in 1994[259] during the process of drafting the 1 September 1995 Resolution on 'Problems Arising from a Succession of Codification Conventions on a Particular Subject.'[260] The final version of 'Conclusion 11' of the 1995 Resolution, which deals with the hierarchy of sources, states from the outset that 'there is no *a priori* hierarchy between treaty and custom as sources of international law'.[261] The Resolution itself does not expressly address the potential treaty modifying effect of subsequent customary law. However, in the Institute's prior set of draft conclusions in 1994, the corresponding Conclusion read:

Relevant norms deriving from a treaty binding upon the parties to the dispute will prevail over norms deriving from customary law, save where the norm deriving from a treaty contravenes a rule of *jus cogens*, or has been subsequently modified by a later norm of customary law.[262]

The Conclusion thus confirmed treaty modification by later customary law.[263] Many members of the Institute initially rejected the proposal by Rosalyn Higgins to remove this latter part of the phrase.[264] Some participants argued that sustaining the proposal would endorse a hierarchy between treaty law and customary law.[265] Notably, Higgins had based the proposition to delete the reference to modification by later customary law on the grounds that such a complex and important issue is 'inappropriate for the Institute to deal with (...) as an ancillary point at the end of a Conclusion'.[266]

[256] Villiger, *Customary International Law and Treaties* (1985), para 333 (emphasis in the original), citing K Venkata Raman, 'Toward a General Theory of International Customary Law' in WM Reisman and BH Weston (eds), *Toward World Order and Human Dignity: Essays in Honor of MS McDougal* (Free Press, 1976) 365, 366 ('Custom (...) is of indispensable value for accomplishing changes informally.').

[257] Dinstein, 'The Interaction between Customary International Law and Treaties', para 277. Note the argument in Crootof, 'Change Without Consent', 283, that Art 62 VCLT (fundamental change in circumstances) could provide a legal basis for treaty termination by subsequent customary law (citing Kontou, *Termination and Revision of Treaties*, 32–3); however, this seems doubtful given the qualifiers in Art 62.

[258] Villiger, *Customary International Law and Treaties* (1985), para 345; Byers, *Custom*, 109, 176. See also Sections 3.1 and 3.3.1 of this book on the general presumption against modification or conflict.

[259] Institut de Droit International (1995) 66(I) AIDI 208.

[260] Institut de Droit International, Resolution of 1 September 1995 on 'Problems Arising from a Succession of Codification Conventions on a Particular Subject' (1995) 66(I) AIDI 245 [1995 IDI Resolution]. See further R Higgins, 'Report on the Legal Consequences for Member States of the Non-fulfilment by International Organizations of their Obligations toward Third Parties' (1995) 66(I) AIDI 251, 254; Pauwelyn, *Conflict of Norms*, 133.

[261] 1995 IDI Resolution, 248.

[262] Ibid.

[263] See also Pauwelyn, *Conflict of Norms*, 138–9.

[264] Institut de Droit International (1995) 66(II) AIDI 210.

[265] Ibid. 208.

[266] Ibid. 207.

From a practical and political standpoint, customary modification is necessary in view of the fact that treaties may be nearly impossible to formally amend, '[giving] over the development of international law almost entirely into the hands of custom, operating upon and beyond the codifying treaties'.[267] Moreover, customary rules may become so well established that States do not consider it necessary to codify them or amend conflicting older treaties anymore. What is more, denying the possibility of treaty modification through customary law ignores the very purpose of the numerous (declarative) treaties codifying customary law:

> If codification treaties are part of a larger endeavour to promote co-operation and the peaceful resolution of disputes, they should not bind States to outmoded statements of customary international law in areas where the interests of most States, as manifested through their practice, have clearly and significantly changed.[268]

It should also be mentioned that the possibility of modification by subsequent customary law does not affect the option of recourse to formal amendment processes.[269] The two can be regarded as complementary or alternative adaptation mechanisms.[270] For one thing, modification by customary law, like modification by subsequent practice, may be better suited for the gradual or fractional change of treaty provisions, due to its flexible, informal nature.[271]

Based on these considerations, subsequent customary law can constitute a tacit but legitimate source of lawmaking. As St Thomas Aquinas noted, an accumulation of acts constituting custom *contra legem* (contrary to existing law) can amount to custom *praeter legem* (alongside the law) where, in light of social development, 'the law is found wanting, and yet so to act will not be wrongful'.[272] Nevertheless, the modifying effect of newly emerged customary law must be qualified by certain important considerations. These are dealt with in the ensuing section.

4.5 Treaty Modification by Subsequent Customary Law: Requirements and Distinctions

A number of distinctions and reference points can be used to determine when new customary norms may come to modify incompatible pre-existing treaty provisions. These build upon the foregoing analysis of the elements of customary law, most notably the constitutive element of practice—the driving force behind both customary law formation and 'customary' modification.[273]

Once again, as highlighted in the ILC,[274] subsequent customary law cannot modify treaties automatically, but rather only subject to the will of the parties (the only exception being that of *jus cogens* norms, which automatically render conflicting

[267] Thirlway, *International Customary Law*, 146. [268] Byers, *Custom*, 177.
[269] The same applies to modification by subsequent practice. See Section 3.3.4.
[270] cf Villiger, *Customary International Law and Treaties* (1985), para 313.
[271] Ibid. 226. [272] As cited in Thirlway, *International Customary Law*, 130–1.
[273] See eg C Parry, 'The Practice of States' (1958) 44 TGS 145, 165.
[274] See Section 4.2.

treaty provisions invalid[275]). Indeed, as suggested in the case law, it is insufficient for the parties to show that the new customary rule has emerged and is binding upon them.[276] They must provide additional evidence of their intention to modify or terminate provisions of the treaty[277]—a higher standard of proof.[278] Such intention must be 'clearly manifested'[279] in their statements or 'abundant and consistent practice'.[280] This mirrors the discussion on treaty modification by subsequent practice: the practice must be concordant, common, and consistent, and establish an intention to modify the treaty—an implied agreement.[281] Once again, it is the tacit consent of the parties, not the customary rule per se, which is capable of modifying the treaty. Otherwise, the treaty provisions in question prevail *qua lex specialis*.[282]

4.5.1 'External' versus 'treaty-related' customary law

The present section aims to highlight the relevance of a basic distinction, also underscored in the ILC during the drafting of the VCLT,[283] between the two ways in which subsequent customary law can come to impact a treaty: through treaty-related subsequent practice or through subsequent practice in relation to an external customary norm. This relates to the origin and scope of subsequent customary law, as well as its parallels to the process of modification by subsequent practice, as explored in Section 4.6.

First, modification by 'treaty-related' customary law derives from the subsequent practice of the parties in the application of a treaty.[284] To that extent, it fully overlaps with modification by subsequent practice.[285] Indeed, as long as the nature of the provision so allows,[286] there is no reason why a further result of modification by subsequent practice cannot be to produce a parallel, identical norm of customary law; a general customary norm when in conjunction with the practice of third States, and otherwise a special or regional customary norm. An example is the modification of many substantive provisions of the 1958 Geneva Conventions on the Law of the Sea by the subsequent practice of the treaty parties, which, coupled with that

[275] Again, this would endorse a hierarchy between customary and treaty law.

[276] Kontou, *Termination and Revision of Treaties*, 132ff, citing eg *Fisheries Jurisdiction* (*UK v Iceland*), Merits, 3; *Anglo-French Continental Shelf Arbitration*, 3; *Filleting within the Gulf of St Lawrence between Canada and France* ('*La Bretagne*'), Award of 17 July 1986, 19 RIAA 225.

[277] See eg Orakhelashvili, *Interpretation of Acts and Rules*, 129. See also Section 4.5.3 on the 'double consent' requirement.

[278] Akehurst, 'Hierarchy of the Sources', 275–6; Kontou, *Termination and Revision of Treaties*, 132–3, 145–6. See *contra* Pauwelyn, *Conflict of Norms*, 140.

[279] Restatement (Third) of US Foreign Relations Law, Section 102, comment (j).

[280] Akehurst, 'Hierarchy of the Sources', 275–6.

[281] See eg Sections 2.3.5 and 3.3.3(b).

[282] See also eg MG Kohen, 'Desuetude and Obsolescence of Treaties' in E Cannizzaro (ed), *The Law of Treaties Beyond the Vienna Convention* (OUP, 2011) 350, 353.

[283] Summary record of 866th meeting, eg para 41 (Yasseen). See Section 4.2.

[284] See eg Bos, *A Methodology of International Law*, 67. See also Art 38 VCLT, which prescribes that 'nothing in articles 34 to 37 precludes a rule set forth in a treaty from becoming binding upon a third State as a customary rule of international law, recognized as such'.

[285] See also Nolte, Third Report on Treaties over Time, 350–1. See further Section 4.6.

[286] See eg Section 4.4.1 on 'generalizable' treaty provisions.

of third States, led to the emergence of customary international law in the wake of UNCLOS III.[287] In such cases, treaty-related subsequent practice capable of modification cannot be distinguished from practice as a constitutive element of a new customary rule. This also facilitates the harmonious development of substantive treaty law (as modified by subsequent practice) together with customary law (as shaped by the same modifying subsequent practice).[288]

The second possibility, 'external' customary law, is a customary norm that comes into existence through the practice of States *outside* of the treaty regime, the content of which conflicts with the rules codified therein, and which is eventually taken up by the treaty parties as well.[289] This latter category does not fully overlap with treaty-related subsequent practice, since the 'external' customary norm is originally derived from the (non-treaty-related) practice of (in principle[290]) non-parties. However, it shares various conceptual similarities with it, in the sense that modification of the treaty can only occur if eventually the practice of the treaty parties becomes aligned with the external customary rule. The subsequent practice that drives the modification is different from subsequent practice that contributes to 'treaty-related' customary law, as just discussed: it cannot be said to constitute subsequent practice in relation to the treaty. Rather, it constitutes the treaty parties' practice *in relation to the external customary norm*. For instance, it has been pointed out that the practice of the United States on targeting military objects cannot be regarded as practice in relation to the Hague Convention of 1907,[291] to which it is a party, but rather in relation to the *customary norm* corresponding to Article 57 of Additional Protocol I to the Third Geneva Convention, to which it is not a party, which impacts upon the contents of the 1907 Hague Convention as a result.[292]

The process of modification by 'external' customary law may be more controversial than that of 'treaty-related' customary law.[293] 'External' customary law is akin to subsequent practice (or external developments) not in relation to the treaty,

[287] See Section 5.3.2(a). See also the example concerning the 'Minorities Treaties' in Section 5.3.2(c).

[288] Nolte, Third Report on Treaties over Time, 350.

[289] Thus, one could seek evidence of a general practice supporting the customary rule outside the practice of the treaty parties. See Waldock, Third Report on the Law of Treaties, 34 para 24; Villiger, *Customary International Law and Treaties* (1985), para 284; Dinstein, 'The Interaction between Customary International Law and Treaties', para 217.

[290] As previously explained, it is difficult to imagine parties to a treaty contributing to the formation of a conflicting customary rule of general application while simultaneously applying their obligations under that treaty—but see further Section 4.5.3.

[291] 1907 Hague Convention (IX) concerning Bombardment by Naval Forces in Time of War, 205 CTS 345.

[292] Nolte, Third Report on Treaties over Time, 351, discussing US practice in this respect: '[i]t is difficult to consider this statement [from the 2007 US Naval Handbook] as subsequent practice to the Hague Convention of 1907. Instead, it is clearly based on the assumption of customary status of Art. 57 Additional Protocol I.'

[293] See eg Karl, *Vertrag*, 106–10; Thirlway, *International Customary Law*, 132, 139; Byers, *Custom*, 242. See also Kammerhofer, *Uncertainty in International Law*, 136, on the preference to 'accord the privilege of modificability only to "treaty-specific" (*inter se*) customary law, ie particular customary law created by (all) the parties to a given treaty'. This approach is premised upon a misunderstanding of extrinsic customary law: if the latter initially develops independently of the treaty, but is eventually taken up by the treaty parties, there is no reason why it may not also come to impact upon the treaty in accordance with the parties' will.

rather than subsequent practice 'in the application of the treaty', as described in Chapter 2[294]—in other words, practice in the sense of Article 32 VCLT rather than Article 31(3) VCLT.[295] This implies that its *evidentiary weight* is lower than practice in relation to modification by treaty-related customary law, since, in the latter case, the customary law stems in the first instance from the practice of the treaty parties themselves 'in the application of the treaty'. By contrast, in the case of 'external' customary law, the subsequent practice relates to an *already* emerged customary rule, which only later comes to affect the treaty. Therefore, the significance of the connection to what was discussed in Chapter 2 with regard to practice 'in the application of the treaty' is that 'external' customary law may require a higher threshold for modification than 'treaty-related' customary law.[296]

This distinction between 'external' and 'treaty-related' customary law may pose difficulties in the case of treaties of near-universality in relation to which a new rule of customary international law can rarely be conceived as 'external': *ipso facto*, a significant number of the parties to such a global treaty must have participated in its creation.[297] Nevertheless, the relevance of the distinction lies in the difference in evidentiary threshold: with 'treaty-related' customary law, the intent of the parties (whose practice contributes to its emergence in the first place) to modify the treaty is already assumed, whereas customary law that has emerged independently of the treaty can only impact upon the treaty if there is clear evidence that the parties subsequently so intended. Otherwise, the treaty will continue to operate alongside the customary rule as *lex specialis*,[298] a situation that in practice is relatively easy to establish.[299]

4.5.2 Special customary law

The term 'special' or 'particular' customary law—recognized by the ICJ, the ILC, and in the scholarship[300]—refers to a customary rule that does not, by its nature, apply universally to all States, but concerns only a smaller set of States: '*special* customary international law deals with non-generalizable topics such as title to or rights in specific portions of world real estate [such as boundary delimitations] (. . .) or with rules expressly limited to countries of a certain region (such as the law of asylum

294 See Section 2.3.4. 295 See generally Sections 2.3–2.4.

296 See Section 3.3.3(b) for the definition of 'threshold'.

297 See Villiger, *Customary International Law and Treaties* (1985), para 324.

298 Kontou, *Termination and Revision of Treaties*, 147. See also eg Waldock, Sixth Report on the Law of Treaties, 91 para 13; Villiger, *Customary International Law and Treaties* (1985), para 328.

299 Pauwelyn, *Conflict of Norms*, 141.

300 See eg Wood, Third Report, para 80 (noting that 'particular' customary law 'has been recognized by the International Court of Justice and by individual judges of the Court, as well as national courts, Governments and writers' (references omitted)); ILC Draft Conclusions on Customary International Law (2016) ('Conclusion 16'); *Asylum Case*, 266; *Right of Passage*, 39. See likewise the Restatement (Third) of US Foreign Relations Law, Section 102, comment (b): 'Failure of a significant number of important states to adopt a practice can prevent a principle from becoming general customary law though it might become "particular customary law" for the participating states.'

in Latin America)'.[301] More specifically, 'regional' customary law applies between States of a particular geographical region and 'local' customary law applies bilaterally,[302] while non-regional special customary law applies between States sharing other interests, such as socio-economic ones.[303]

A treaty can come to be modified in accordance with an 'external' (general or special) customary norm between certain of the parties only—*inter se* modification in line with subsequent customary law. Moreover, subsequent practice diverging from a treaty could *generate* (hence 'treaty-related') 'special' or 'particular' customary law. The *Spanish Fishermen's Cases* brought before the ECJ are an example. Here, the Court found that the evolution of international law regarding fishing in the high seas had brought about a revision of the fisheries regime governing the relations between Spain and the then European Community (EC).[304] The judgment shows that multilateral treaty provisions may be revised between some of the parties only (*inter se*) by supervening customary norms applicable between them, in this case with regard to Spain's fishing rights in EC waters.

The ICJ's reasoning in the *Asylum Case*[305] indicates that special customary law requires a high threshold of proof: the State relying on it must provide not only evidence of its existence, but also some degree of proof of 'opposability' to the State against which it is invoked.[306] It only becomes binding on those States who have (tacitly) agreed to it through their subsequent practice in deviation from the treaty, and who are regarded as members of the same 'community' in which the special customary rule has been established, as long as they have not consistently protested against it.[307] Presumably, the conditions set out in Article 41 VCLT on agreements to modify multilateral treaties between certain of the parties apply by analogy to such situations. Accordingly, an *inter se* modification must not affect the other parties' enjoyment of their rights or performance of their obligations under the treaty, nor relate to provisions derogation from which would be incompatible with the execution of the object and purpose of the treaty (Article 41(1)(a) and (b) VCLT).

It may be difficult in some cases to clearly distinguish between a widespread but still 'regional' customary rule modifying a treaty regime, and a new rule of supervening customary law of general application. This also raises a problem with regard to the position of new States, in terms of whether they are considered automatically bound by 'local' customary rules, or whether they must first express their position to that effect. Such issues inevitably involve a certain degree of uncertainty.[308]

301 AA D'Amato, 'The Concept of Special Custom in International Law' (1969) 63 AJIL 211 (emphasis in the original).

302 See eg *Right of Passage*, 39.

303 See eg Villiger, *Customary International Law and Treaties* (1997), para 81.

304 See further Section 5.2.3(d).

305 *Asylum Case*, 266.

306 Thirlway, *International Customary Law*, 139.

307 Ibid.

308 See eg I Voicu, *De l'interprétation authentique des traités internationaux* (Pédone, 1968) 97; Thirlway, *International Customary Law*, 143.

4.5.3 Evidentiary threshold for modification

The threshold for establishing an agreed treaty interpretation is lower than that required for establishing a treaty modification by subsequent customary law:[309] 'the guiding principle must be that the more we move up the interpretive continuum towards overt modification, the higher the evidentiary standard that must be reached in terms of State practice and *opinio juris*'.[310] Moreover, the threshold required for a modification by subsequent customary law that entails the displacement of existing treaty provisions is presumably higher than the threshold for customary modification that expands or supplements (the scope of) the treaty.[311] The threshold for modification by subsequent customary law may also be higher than that for modification by subsequent practice: one must establish not only (the parties' agreement concerning the substance of) the new customary rule, but also their intention to modify the treaty accordingly—a 'double consent' requirement.[312]

Detecting 'double consent' may be tricky, since presumably parties demonstrate their intent to override or modify the treaty precisely by adhering to the new customary rule, a process that can also occur very gradually.[313] Therefore, 'it may be difficult to assess whether a certain practice by a state [party] (...) constitutes subsequent practice to the respective treaty or adds to a development of customary law, or both'.[314] The 'double consent' requirement may nevertheless be useful given that, as pointed out during the ILC discussions, parties to a treaty may conceivably contribute to the formation of a new customary rule without intending to derogate from the treaty provisions as *lex specialis*.[315] On the other hand, it is difficult to imagine situations in which parties continue fulfilling their obligations under the treaty while simultaneously contributing to the formation of a customary rule of general application conflicting with the substance of those same obligations. Such a situation could be envisaged if the scope of the treaty would be limited to a specific aspect of the general customary rule or to a particular geographical region—in which case the treaty and the customary norm would not actually conflict—or if the parties apply the treaty rule *inter se* while contributing to the formation of a rule of customary law in relation to non-parties to the treaty. Akehurst cautions:

In all cases, what counts is the practice followed *inter se* by the parties to the treaty; the practice which they follow in their dealings with States which are not parties to the treaty, and

309 Nolte, Third Report on Treaties over Time, 352.

310 Ruys, *'Armed Attack'*, 29. The same applies by analogy to modification versus interpretation by subsequent practice—see Section 3.3.1.

311 See Section 3.3.1 on the definition of 'modification' as altering, extending, or terminating treaty provisions.

312 See eg Kontou, *Termination and Revision of Treaties*, 132ff (and the case law cited therein); Orakhelashvili, *Interpretation of Acts and Rules*, 129. cf Villiger, *Customary International Law and Treaties* (1985), 345, 449–52, arguing that such a requirement seems inconsistent with the lack of hierarchy between treaty and customary law. In any case, such a presumption would be irrelevant to non-parties to the treaty.

313 Villiger, *Customary International Law and Treaties* (1985), para 313, citing eg Capotorti, 'L'extinction', 516; Akehurst, 'Hierarchy of the Sources', 275; Karl, *Vertrag*, 257; Thirlway, *International Customary Law*, 132 fn 24.

314 Nolte, Third Report on Treaties over Time, 352. See also Wood, Third Report, para 41.

315 Summary record of 866th meeting, para 24 (De Luna). See text to nn 36–7.

the practice of the latter States, may give rise to a rule of customary law, but such a rule has no effect on the treaty unless it is followed by the parties to the treaty in their relations with one another.[316]

Therefore, the 'double consent' requirement may require a higher quality and quantity of practice for modification by subsequent customary law than for the initial emergence of the customary norm.[317] This higher threshold may be impractical in cases of only partial change of a treaty rule by means of customary law.[318] Indeed, the condition should not be applied so prohibitively that it impedes legal development, not to mention the possibility of modification by subsequent customary law altogether.[319]

If subsequent customary law comes to modify a *declaratory* treaty provision, the modification may entail changing not only the contradictory treaty rule, but also the underlying conflicting customary rule.[320] The modification of two parallel rules may take longer and require a higher degree of practice than other treaty modifications.[321] This is because they require the creation of a 'completely new body of State practice', coupled with *opinio juris*, in favour of the new customary rule.[322]

Furthermore, it has already been stated that the threshold for modification may be higher depending on the nature of the treaty and provision concerned, including its object and purpose, States parties, any special provisions on non-derogability, and other considerations such as third-party rights created by the treaty.[323]

This higher threshold requirement is often not applied in practice. For instance, the ILC considers the 'non-responsibility' rule in Article 4 of the 1930 Hague Convention on Certain Questions relating to the Conflict of Nationality Laws,[324] which reflected customary international law at the time of its codification,[325] modified by 'the present customary rule' on 'effective nationality' reflected in Article 7 of the 2006 Draft Articles on Diplomatic Protection.[326] Aside from references to case

[316] Akehurst, 'Hierarchy of the Sources', 276.

[317] Ibid. 275; Villiger, *Customary International Law and Treaties* (1985), para 328.

[318] Villiger, *Customary International Law and Treaties* (1985), para 328. Examples include the (arguably only partial) modification of the 1930 Hague Convention by the rule reflected in Art 7 of the ILC Draft Articles on Diplomatic Protection, discussed further and in Section 5.3.2(e), and the modification of Art 85 of the Third Geneva Convention by the addition of an exception, reflected in Art 44(2)–(4) of Additional Protocol I, discussed further and in Section 5.3.2(d).

[319] Villiger, *Customary International Law and Treaties* (1985), para 329.

[320] See also Section 3.3.3(b).

[321] Villiger, *Customary International Law and Treaties* (1985), 117. See also Byers, *Custom*, 126.

[322] Ibid. para 331.

[323] See Section 4.4.2. These factors have already been discussed with regard to modification by subsequent practice in Section 3.5 and do not require separate treatment here.

[324] 179 LNTS 89. According to Art 4 of the Convention, 'a State may not afford diplomatic protection to one of its nationals against a State whose nationality such person also possesses'.

[325] Nolte, Third Report on Treaties over Time, 350. See also Harvard Research in International Law, 'Draft Convention on the Law of Responsibility of States for Damage done in their Territory to the Person or Property of Foreigners' (1929) 23 AJIL Special Supp 133, Art 16(a). See further *Reparation for Injuries Advisory Opinion*, 186.

[326] ILC, 'Draft Articles on Diplomatic Protection with commentaries', UN Doc A/61/10 (2006) [Draft Articles on Diplomatic Protection] Art 7, Comment 4. According to Art 7, '[a] State of nationality

law, it is not clearly substantiated in terms of degree of practice how this change came about (admittedly, the Commission discusses the matter not in terms of modification of one rule by another, but in terms of the parallel development of two separate rules). According to Nolte, what is significant in any case is that parties to the original Hague Convention contributed to the trend towards the 'effective nationality' rule.[327] This evidences how 'practice which contributes to the development of customary international law can, under certain circumstances, also be interpreted as simultaneously constituting subsequent treaty practice'.[328] The overlap between subsequent practice and subsequent customary law (through subsequent practice) as two separate processes is discussed in detail in Section 4.6 below.

4.6 The Processes of Modification by Subsequent Practice and Subsequent Customary Law Compared

Parallels between the two modification processes—subsequent practice as an independent process and subsequent customary law—have already been drawn throughout this chapter. The present section summarizes some of the primary observations.

The conceptual relation between customary international law and subsequent practice is evident.[329] The two processes share similarities from their inception, leading some commentators to characterize subsequent practice as a sub-category of customary law.[330] It has been explained that 'practice' as a constitutive element of customary international law is just as broad as, and in fact coincides with, practice capable of constituting relevant subsequent practice with the potential for treaty modification.[331] From an evidentiary standpoint, the requirement in the former case that practice in principle be general and consistent, mirrors the standard in the latter case that the evidentiary value of the practice increases with the extent to which it is concordant, common, and consistent.[332] In both cases, the practice must be determinate and sufficiently visible or accessible to other States.[333] The time or duration element is equally non-determinative for subsequent practice and subsequent customary law.[334]

may not exercise diplomatic protection in respect of a person against a State of which that person is also a national unless the nationality of the former State is predominant, both at the date of injury and at the date of the official presentation of the claim.'

[327] Nolte, Third Report on Treaties over Time, 350 and fn 276. [328] Ibid.

[329] cf Wood, First Report, para 17, stating that, despite their linkages, the dividing line between the ILC topics 'Formation and identification of customary international law' and 'Subsequent agreements and subsequent practice' is reasonably clear.

[330] See eg Kolb, *Interprétation*, 507.

[331] See Sections 2.3.1(a) and 4.3.2. See also Section 3.3.3(a).

[332] See eg M Paparinskis, *The International Minimum Standard and Fair and Equitable Treatment* (OUP, 2013) 144–5 (pointing out that treaty modification can take place either by 'widespread and consistent practice supporting a new rule of customary law or concordant, common, and consistent subsequent practice supporting a new content of treaty law').

[333] See Sections 2.3.1(b) and 4.3.2. See also Section 3.3.3(a).

[334] See Sections 2.3.5(c) and 4.3. See also Section 3.3.3(b).

Moreover, both processes involve the element of awareness or intentionality to contribute to the creation of a legal norm or consequence.[335] Accordingly, the notion of *opinio juris*, which, as noted earlier, has been taken to refer to both the belief and the *will* of States,[336] bears a strong conceptual parallel to the requirement of an agreement pursuant to Article 31(3)(b) VCLT in relation to subsequent practice.[337]

> Both the circumstances relevant to practice formation and the prerequisites for the former to count as practice are determined on the basis of the paradigm of customary rules formation. (…) In requiring the repetition of a certain conduct, coupled with some form of recognition by the parties, art 31(3)(b) repeats the normative criteria regarding the development of customary rules.[338]

Above all, both modification by subsequent practice and modification by subsequent customary law are premised upon the parties' intention to *modify* the treaty. During the ILC discussions on the drafting of the VCLT, Special Rapporteur Waldock argued that while modification by subsequent practice operates based on the parties' implied consent, modification by subsequent customary law is 'accidental' in that it relates to acts done outside and not in relation to the treaty.[339] However, as discussed extensively, subsequent rules of customary international law, with the major exception of *jus cogens* norms, do not automatically displace conflicting treaty provisions.[340] The process of modification by subsequent customary law is not accidental. On the contrary, it is strictly subject to the treaty parties' will. Where their consent is absent, the treaty will remain standing *qua lex specialis*. Thus, the distinction between the two processes drawn by Waldock cannot be sustained.

The process of modification by subsequent customary law therefore mirrors the discussion on modification by subsequent practice in that practice must be sufficient to establish the parties' agreement to modify the treaty—a similarity also noted in the ILC.[341] Moreover, it is difficult to imagine having a uniform, constant practice without the presence of *opinio juris*, which would, consequently, reflect a tacit agreement between the parties that 'might equally be included within the term "agreement" in Article 39 [VCLT]'.[342] On the other hand, while cases of general and consistent practice 'may indeed *give rise to* the acceptance of the practice as law, they do not embody such acceptance in and of themselves'.[343]

[335] See Sections 2.3.5 and 4.3. See also Section 3.3.3(b). See further eg Arato, 'Treaty Interpretation and Constitutional Transformation', 315. In this sense, modification by subsequent practice could be compared to the process of modification by special customary law. See Karl, *Vertrag*, 109.

[336] See eg Wood, Second Report, para 66 (and the case law and literature cited therein).

[337] See Section 4.3.3.

[338] L Boisson de Chazournes, 'Subsequent Practice, Practices, and "Family-Resemblance": Towards Embedding Subsequent Practice in its Operative Milieu' in G Nolte (ed), *Treaties and Subsequent Practice* (OUP, 2013) 53. See also eg Kolb, *Interprétation*, 507.

[339] Waldock Sixth, Report on the Law of Treaties, 97, para 14.

[340] See eg Section 4.5.1.

[341] Summary record of 876th meeting, para 44 (Waldock). See also eg Kolb, *Interprétation*, 507; Sands, 'Article 39', 973 para 38; Boisson de Chazournes, 'Subsequent Practice', 53–4, 58.

[342] Sands, 'Article 39', 973.

[343] Wood, Second Report, para 73 (emphasis in the original). See also eg *North Sea Continental Shelf*, para 77.

Certain scholars have argued that while a tacit agreement established by subsequent practice takes effect instantaneously, modification by customary law requires time.[344] It is respectfully submitted here that, contrary to this statement, we have already seen how both processes can occur seemingly 'instantaneously', with the time factor providing merely an indication, rather than a prerequisite, for modification.[345]

The threshold for treaty modification by subsequent customary law and subsequent practice can also be compared. The general presumption against modification applies to both processes. Likewise, the threshold for both is higher where the modification alters (or, more accurately in the case of subsequent customary law, displaces) existing treaty provisions, than where it expands or supplements them.[346] On the other hand, the threshold for modification by subsequent customary law is arguably higher than that for modification by subsequent practice in the sense that practice must establish not only the parties' agreement concerning the substance of the new customary rule, but also their intention to modify the treaty ('double consent').[347] In addition, just as with modification by subsequent practice,[348] the threshold for modification by subsequent customary law may be higher depending on the nature of the treaty and provision in question, including its object and purpose, States parties, any special provisions on non-derogability, as well as other considerations such as third-party rights created by the treaty.[349]

The processes of modification by subsequent customary law and modification by subsequent practice thus overlap on a conceptual and practical level—hence the reference to modification by subsequent practice as the 'customary way of modifying treaties'[350] (and to subsequent practice as a 'sub-category' of customary law[351]).

But the two processes must also be carefully distinguished. We have already seen that subsequent practice has the independent ability—also *outside* of the process of customary law—to hold legal relevance and modify treaty provisions:

> It is commonplace to discuss the criteria of practice's normativity in connection with the theory of custom development. In particular, the genesis of 'practice' is often conflated into the process of rule production through practice. (...) Other than according to custom logic [i.e. the paradigm of customary rules formation], little or no room, therefore, remains for a legally relevant practice to arise. However, one may doubt whether this assumption accurately reflects the international legal order we live in today.[352]

[344] Dinh, Dailler, and Pellet, *Droit international public*, 296–7.

[345] See eg Sections 2.3.5(c), 3.3.3(b), and 4.3, particularly the discussion on 'instant' custom in Section 4.3.1.

[346] See text to nn 150–3 and n 199. See further Section 3.3.1.

[347] See Section 4.5.3.

[348] See eg Section 3.5.1.

[349] See eg Sections 4.4.2 and 4.5.3.

[350] Summary record of 876th meeting, eg para 24. See also eg the characterization of the modification by subsequent practice of Article 27(3) of the UN Charter as modification by customary law, discussed in Section 5.2.1, text to nn 48–9. See further Section 3.2.4.

[351] Kolb, *Interprétation*, 507.

[352] Boisson de Chazournes, 'Subsequent Practice', 53. See also eg RR Churchill, 'The Impact of State Practice on the Jurisdictional Framework contained in the LOS Convention' in AG Oude Elferink (ed), *Stability and Change in the Law of the Sea: The Role of the LOS Convention* (Martinus Nijhoff, 2005) 91, 92.

The two processes, modification by subsequent practice and modification by subsequent customary law, differ in terms of their scope of operation in various ways. In terms of constituency, of course, a general customary norm extends to the entire international community (unless it is a special or regional customary rule), whereas modification by subsequent practice applies only to the parties to the treaty. Granted, in the case of a treaty of near-universality or legislative nature, such as the UN Charter or the LOSC, the two processes may converge.[353]

Moreover, some confusion stems from the implications of how a conflicting customary rule has emerged vis-à-vis the subsequent practice of the parties to the treaty, as discussed.[354] 'Treaty-related' subsequent practice can lead to the modification of the treaty, as well as to the emergence of a corresponding treaty-derived customary norm (a general norm if non-parties contribute to its emergence, and a special or regional one if it applies to the treaty parties only). In such cases, practice that constitutes treaty-related subsequent practice capable of modification cannot be distinguished from practice as a constitutive element of the new customary rule. The situation is different where a customary norm is formed through the (non-treaty-related) practice of non-parties to a treaty ('external' customary law). Even if the treaty parties eventually decide to modify the operation of the treaty in line with the 'external' customary rule, their practice would not constitute subsequent practice *in relation to the treaty*, but rather in relation to the *external customary norm*.[355] It may, accordingly, be difficult to discern whether it is their intention to contribute only to the development of the external customary norm, or also to subsequent practice in relation to the treaty.[356]

Another key difference pertains to the legal effect of subsequent treaty practice and subsequent customary law. While modification by subsequent customary law displaces treaty provisions, modification by subsequent practice modifies their content.[357] Even if a later customary norm 'modifies' an earlier treaty and becomes the applicable law on the issue, it does not become 'part and parcel of the treaty',[358] maintaining a separate existence. Thus, by contrast to modification by subsequent practice, treaty modification by customary law *always* constitutes a different basis of obligation than the original treaty.[359] Therefore, in cases where practice constitutes subsequent practice capable of treaty modification and simultaneously contributes to the development of customary international law, it leads to the 'harmonious parallel development, as far as possible, of customary international law and treaty law'.[360]

Moreover, the type of provision the two processes can modify may differ. Treaty-oriented subsequent customary law, for instance, relates to provisions with content capable of generating customary law, whether general or special/regional.[361]

353 Villiger, *Customary International Law and Treaties* (1985), para 337. See also Wood, Third Report, para 41.

354 See Section 4.5.1.

355 Ibid.

356 Nolte, Third Report on Treaties over Time, 352. See also Section 4.5.3.

357 See eg Paparinskis, *The International Minimum Standard*, 144–5.

358 Pauwelyn, *Conflict of Norms*, 142.

359 cf Section 3.3.6(a).

360 Nolte, Report on Treaties over Time, 350.

361 See the discussion on 'generalizable' provisions in Section 4.4.1.

Treaty-specific, strictly procedural provisions are unlikely to be modified by subsequent customary law. By contrast, subsequent practice can impact all types of provisions (subject to the limitations discussed regarding the nature of the treaty and type of provision, etc), though often its effects remain limited to procedural, non-essential ones.

Some commentators allege that, while the process of modification by subsequent practice, though not free of difficulties, is 'largely recognized and accepted by States and in the practice of international law',[362] modification by subsequently emerged rules of customary law is more controversial.[363] The present author respectfully disagrees with the latter stance. The mainly practical reasons for the deletion of the ILC draft provisions dealing with the two processes have previously been discussed.[364] As long as the intention of the parties is kept carefully within view, both processes, though not identical, converge significantly. They constitute logical, valid, and recognized mechanisms for treaty adaptation and the evolution of international law more generally. In fact, subsequent customary law can often be viewed as one of multiple possible outcomes[365] of subsequent practice in the application of a treaty, rather than a phenomenon operating exclusively outside of it.[366]

4.7 Interim Conclusions

The foregoing analysis of the modifying effect of subsequent customary law endeavoured to demonstrate the conditions in which an emerging customary rule could come to modify a prior treaty rule. First, the chapter set out to show, based on, *inter alia*, the drafting history of the ultimately deleted ILC article on modification by customary international law, that modification by customary law is a well-recognized process. It was deliberately not codified in the Vienna Convention for practical and political reasons.[367]

Second, we have seen that the formation and identification of customary international law, based on the elements of practice and *opinio juris*, is a highly complex process in itself, yet a necessary step towards understanding its modifying potential.[368] The constitutive element of practice is the driving force behind not only the formation of customary law, but also modification by customary law.[369] Moreover, the process of formation of customary law bears significant conceptual parallels to that of subsequent practice.

362 See Section 3.1.

363 Sands, 'Article 39', 973, citing Waldock, Sixth Report on the Law of Treaties, 88–91. cf Crootof, 'Change Without Consent', 264.

364 See Sections 3.2 and 4.2, respectively.

365 On the various effects of subsequent practice, including those explored in Chs 2 and 3 of this book, see generally Kohen, 'La pratique et la théorie des sources du droit international', 81; Boisson de Chazournes, 'Subsequent Practice', 53.

366 See eg Nolte, Annex A, para 4; Nolte, Third Report on Treaties over Time, 350–1.

367 See Section 4.2. 368 See Section 4.3.

369 See eg Parry, 'The Practice of States', 165.

Third, the modifying potential of customary law was examined by reference to its non-hierarchical relation to treaty law. International obligations are becoming more extensive, intricate, and intertwined.[370] At the same time, it is often difficult if not impossible to formally amend treaties.[371] This increases the likelihood of conflicts between treaties and customary norms, and with it, the need for harmonization through interpretation and, increasingly, informal modification, such as tacit modification through subsequent customary law. Accordingly, customary modification can only be said to occur in a situation of genuine incompatibility between customary and treaty norms. Determining when 'customary modification' could be said to have occurred can be difficult. Normative conflicts such as those between subsequent customary law and pre-existing treaties are highly sensitive to context and require a balanced, holistic analysis of the norms involved. They should be resolved on a case-by-case basis with regard to the quality and quantity of practice, the nature of the treaty and provisions affected, and that which poses 'minimal disturbance to the operation of the legal system'.[372] The 'genuine' conflict requirement constitutes a preliminary step in identifying instances of modification by subsequent customary law and distinguishing them from mere interpretations (for instance via Article 31(3)(c) VCLT).

Fourth, as demonstrated, the requirements for treaty modification by subsequent customary law are strict, also in light of the general presumption against change. This places a higher evidentiary burden on the interpreter in situations where a customary modification is said to have occurred than in those where customary law is merely found to have emerged. The requirements are more stringent still in order for customary law to come to displace, rather than supplement, treaty provisions. The crucial condition is that the parties' practice must demonstrate their *intention* to displace the treaty provision in favour of the subsequent customary rule, and attain the necessary evidentiary threshold. This threshold is understood to contain a 'double consent' requirement: the practice must establish not only the content of the customary norm, but also its intended treaty modifying effect. It was also explained that such modification might occur through either 'treaty-related' or 'external' customary law.[373] There is an obvious overlap between the two, especially in the case of treaty regimes with a large number of States parties, in relation to which a newly emerged customary rule could hardly be conceived as 'extrinsic'. Subsequent practice in divergence of a treaty could potentially even constitute an instance of 'special' customary law.[374] No matter how the customary rule initially emerged, however, the determining factor is the intention of the parties to displace the treaty provisions in line with the customary norm.

Thus, several basic scenarios can be envisioned with regard to the interaction between treaties and customary law, and the processes of modification by subsequent

[370] See also M Footer, 'Treaty Interrelationships' in MJ Bowman and D Kritsiotis (eds), *Conceptual and Contextual Perspectives on the Modern Law of Treaties* (CUP, forthcoming).

[371] See eg Ch 1 and Section 3.3.4.

[372] Koskenniemi, Fragmentation Report, para 410.

[373] Villiger, *Commentary*, 433.

[374] See also Conclusions of the Study Group on Fragmentation, 411.

practice and modification by subsequent customary law. A conflicting customary rule may emerge independently of a treaty regime through the practice of non-parties, leaving the treaty unaffected, as *lex specialis*. The external customary norm may come to modify the treaty if the subsequent practice of the parties so determines (modification by 'external' custom, be it general or special). Moreover, modifying subsequent customary law may emerge as a direct result of the 'treaty-related' practice of the parties, potentially also coupled with the practice of third States (modification by 'treaty-related' customary law, be it general or special). Furthermore, treaty provisions may come to be displaced by a supervening customary norm among certain of the parties only (*inter se* modification by subsequent customary law).

Lastly, the convergence between the processes of modification by subsequent practice and modification by subsequent customary law was highlighted in detail. While significant differences between these two distinct processes must be acknowledged, subsequent practice is the 'raw material' that fuels both, coupled with the crucial requirement of the parties' intention. From this perspective, subsequent customary law could be regarded as one of the multiple potential outcomes of subsequent practice in relation to a treaty.

5

A Systematic Analysis of Examples of Modification by Subsequent Practice

5.1 Introduction: General Approach

The present chapter is intended to further illustrate the treaty modifying potential of subsequent practice by applying the considerations identified in previous chapters to the analysis of a non-exhaustive collection of examples—a 'repertoire' of practice.[1] It aims, first, to explore the modifying potential of subsequent practice systematically in different contexts, facilitating identification and analysis of analogous cases.[2] The wealth of pertinent material can be more easily analysed in this way. Second, this chapter serves more than an illustrative purpose: it aims to both combine and build upon the analysis in the preceding chapters in order to derive—with the focus on international practice as such—guidelines that provide future reference points to better understand the modifying potential of subsequent practice.[3] A third objective is to examine the way in which modifications have been dealt with by dispute settlement bodies in particular, but also States and other international actors.[4]

To facilitate a systematic analysis, the examples are firstly categorized according to whether they relate to practice assessed *within* or *outside* of judicial or quasi-judicial proceedings. Although one would expect subsequent practice outside of the judicial context to be the theoretical point of departure,[5] for practical purposes, subsequent practice as assessed in the case law is considered first. This order was chosen so as to investigate whether the reasoning of various dispute settlement bodies provides indications of methodology or reference points to assess modifications by subsequent practice. Even a case in which a dispute settlement body denies a certain interpretation by a State arguing that something falls within the scope of the treaty in question, could provide indication of what can constitute interpretation versus modification. The decisions of courts and tribunals provide a source of examples of potential modifications by subsequent practice, not a source of subsequent practice in themselves.

[1] The term 'repertory' was employed in the context of the work of the ILC Study Group on 'Treaties over Time'. See Nolte, Annex A, paras 20–2, 37–8.
[2] Nolte, Annex A, para 20. [3] Ibid. para 22.
[4] For different interpretative policies with regard to subsequent practice, see Section 2.5 of this book.
[5] Nolte, Annex A, para 40.

Although judicial discourse provides an essential starting point for the analysis, some of the most interesting instances of modification by subsequent practice are often to be found outside of the dispute settlement context. The likelihood of identifying instances of modification is also higher outside of this context: first, for the simple reason that States have limited recourse to third party dispute settlement in such situations; and second, because dispute settlement bodies are for various reasons reluctant to acknowledge such instances as modifications even when they do surface in legal proceedings[6]—with notable exceptions.[7] This is most likely due to the perception that States are wary of dispute settlement bodies using tacit modification as a tool to 'evolve the law'.[8] As a result, both States and dispute settlement bodies tend to characterize situations tantamount to modification as interpretation, which often makes it more complicated to discern what is actually going on in practice.[9]

Thus, the first part of the chapter, Section 5.2, deals with examples assessed in the case law. First, it reviews the ICJ case law relating to modification by subsequent practice (Section 5.2.1) and that of various ad hoc arbitral tribunals (Section 5.2.2). These examples are supplemented by pronouncements of dispute settlement bodies in the context of special treaty regimes (Section 5.2.3) and a number of national court decisions regarding modification by subsequent practice (Section 5.2.4). The main observations based on examples taken from the case law are summarized in Section 5.2.5. The second part of the 'repertoire' of practice, Section 5.3, consists of examples of subsequent practice outside of judicial or quasi-judicial proceedings. These instances are divided into two categories, based on whether they can be placed within (Section 5.3.1) or outside (Section 5.3.2) the context of international organizations. The latter category is further subdivided into sections on the law of the sea, environmental law, human rights, and humanitarian law—key sources of examples of modification by subsequent practice—as well as other fields. Preliminary conclusions are presented in Section 5.3.3.

Of course, a certain degree of overlap between these different categories and sections is inevitable. For instance, examples from the UN context are explored both in the ICJ case law (Section 5.2.1) and outside the judicial arena in the general context of international organizations (Section 5.3.1). Likewise, law of the sea examples are explored within the dispute settlement context in Section 5.2, as well as in Section 5.3.2(a), which focuses specifically on instances of modification in that field. Such links are made explicit where necessary and overlaps are explored further in the conclusions.

The analysis of the collected examples is based on the conclusions drawn from the previous chapters, where applicable. First, the nature and form of practice in question must be identified, including its form of manifestation (positive act or

[6] See Section 3.4.2. [7] See Section 5.2 generally. See also Section 3.1.

[8] SD Murphy, 'The Relevance of Subsequent Agreements and Subsequent Practice for the Interpretation of Treaties' in G Nolte (ed), *Treaties and Subsequent Practice* (OUP, 2013) 82, 83, 87. See also Nolte, Second Report on Subsequent Practice, para 137.

[9] Ibid. 90.

omission), the relevant State organs or international actors involved, the extent to which it can be classified as subsequent practice or also, more specifically, as a subsequent agreement, the extent to which it is common, concordant, and consistent, and the extent to which it specifically relates to the treaty.[10] A second set of distinctions concerns the nature, age, and field of the treaty regime, including whether it is bilateral, multilateral, or regional, technical or 'law-making', reciprocal or non-reciprocal, and whether it contains special adaptation mechanisms or in-built obstacles to modification by subsequent practice.[11] A third set of distinctions pertains to the nature of the specific provisions affected, based, for example, on whether they are procedural or substantive, essential or non-essential, or integral or interdependent in nature—to the extent that these distinctions are generally feasible in the first place—as well as their degree of ambiguity, the presence of generic terms, and any other special factors that can affect the process of tacit modification by subsequent practice.[12] Fourth, as already mentioned, the cases taken from within the judicial context serve a dual purpose: as examples of potential modifications as such, as well as illustrations of how they are dealt with by dispute settlement bodies. Thus, where applicable, it is relevant to identify the judicial approach or mechanism used, for instance by distinguishing explicit references to modification by subsequent practice from indirect recognition or references to interpretation, and determining whether the dispute settlement body accepted or rejected a certain interpretation or argumentation, or whether any specific reasoning or set of criteria was applied. Fifth, and most importantly, the scope of the effects of the practice must be carefully assessed with a view to distinguishing between (dynamic) interpretation, modification by subsequent practice (including desuetude), modification by subsequent customary law, and establishing how the change relates to the object and purpose of the treaty and the underlying instrument as a whole.

5.2 Treaty Modification by Subsequent Practice as Assessed in the Case Law

It is useful to examine certain key cases in which dispute settlement bodies dealt with potential treaty modifications by subsequent practice. Case law of dispute settlement bodies adopting a restrictive stance towards modification by subsequent practice—an immediate example is the WTO Appellate Body—has been included as an occasional reference point.[13] The intention is not to speculate with regard to individual cases as to whether the 'real' reasons underlying a decision differ from those stated in the judgment, but to draw conclusions from trends observed in the case law in general. The focus remains on describing how the process of modification

[10] See the various elements of subsequent practice discussed in Section 2.3.

[11] See Sections 3.5.1–3.5.2.

[12] See Section 3.5.

[13] Certain cases touching upon this issue have been included as counterfactual examples—see eg Section 5.2.1 on *Gabčíkovo-Nagymaros Project*.

by subsequent practice has been recognized and justified. In that sense, the approach is purely descriptive.

The first set of cases is taken from the ICJ case law (Section 5.2.1).[14] The next section is a compilation of decisions of various ad hoc arbitral tribunals dealing with tacit modification, mainly with regard to bilateral treaties (Section 5.2.2). These are supplemented by examples of pronouncements of judicial bodies operating in the context of 'special regimes', such as the European Court of Human Rights (Section 5.2.3). As previously explained,[15] subsequent practice is approached differently by different dispute settlement bodies, particularly within treaty regimes that provide their own standing dispute settlement mechanism, such as the ECJ, ECtHR, or the WTO Appellate Body. In such areas an accompanying tendency exists to develop specialized rules for treaty adaptation.[16] For instance, we have seen in earlier chapters that the WTO Appellate Body has firmly rejected the possibility of modification by subsequent practice in relation to the covered agreements. Its approach is a product of the specific circumstances prevalent in the WTO context—hence the word of caution on treaty regimes that operate in their own specific context and develop specialized rules. Lastly, there is a brief section on examples from the case law of various national courts (Section 5.2.4). Taken together, these cases represent a crucial first part of the analysis on treaty modification by subsequent practice.

5.2.1 International Court of Justice

The *Namibia Advisory Opinion* and Article 27(3) of the UN Charter

The UN Charter has given rise to numerous instances of modification by subsequent practice,[17] as shown further in Section 5.3.1. The classic example is the voting practice of the Security Council in relation to Article 27(3) of the UN Charter.[18] The provision states:

[14] Although ICJ interpretations of the UN Charter could also be characterized as a dispute settlement mechanism under a special regime (Section 5.2.3 below), due to the Court's broad jurisdiction these cases are dealt with separately (Section 5.2.1).

[15] See eg Sections 2.5.2 and 3.5.2.

[16] See eg S Engel, '"Living" International Constitutions and the World Court (The Subsequent Practice of International Organs under their Constituent Instruments)' (1967) 16 ICLQ 865; T Sato, *Evolving Constitutions of International Organizations: A Critical Analysis of the Interpretive Frameworks of the Constituent Instruments of International Organizations* (Brill, 1996) xiii; CF Amerasinghe, *Principles of the Institutional Law of International Organizations* (2nd edn, CUP, 2005) 24; RK Gardiner, *Treaty Interpretation* (OUP, 2008) 247.

[17] See eg S Engel, 'Procedures for *De Facto* Revision of the Charter' (1965) 59 ASIL Proc 108; ME Villiger, *Customary International Law and Treaties: A Study of Their Interactions and Interrelations, with Special Consideration of the 1969 Vienna Convention on the Law of Treaties* (Brill, 1985) para 305. See further M Akehurst, *A Modern Introduction to International Law* (6th edn, Harper Collins, Academic 1987) 202.

[18] See generally C Stavropoulos, 'The Practice of Voluntary Abstentions by Permanent Members of the Security Council under Article 27, Paragraph 3, of the Charter of the United Nations' (1967) 61 AJIL 737, citing, *inter alia*, H Kelsen, 'Organization and Procedure of the Security Council' (1946) 59 Harv L Rev 1087, 1098; YL Liang, 'Abstention and Absence of a Permanent Member in Relation to the Voting Procedure in the Security Council' (1950) 44 AJIL 694; L Gross, 'Voting in the Security Council: Abstention from Voting and Absence from Meetings' (1951) 60 Yale LJ 209; MS McDougal

Decisions of the Security Council on all other [non-procedural] matters shall be made by an affirmative vote of seven members [now nine members] including the concurring votes of the permanent members; provided that, in decisions under Chapter VI, and under paragraph 3 of Article 52, a party to a dispute shall abstain from voting.

Article 27(3) is formulated in 'active' language[19] that clearly requires the 'concurring votes' of the permanent members of the Security Council for certain decisions. The word 'concurrence' does not, at first sight, leave much room for ambiguity.[20] Despite the fact that different words are employed in the provision, namely, 'affirmative' and then 'concurring', the drafting history confirms that the two were intended as synonyms to mean 'affirmative'.[21] However, the Council has in practice taken 'concurring' to mean 'non-objection' rather than 'affirmative vote',[22] contrary to its literal meaning[23] and the drafters' original intention.[24] This may even have been contrary to the intention of some of the States contributing to the development of the practice. For instance, in one case of voluntary abstention, the Soviet representative stated that:

[B]earing in mind (...) that my voting against the Australian draft resolution would make its adoption impossible, I shall abstain from voting. I consider it necessary to draw attention of the Security Council to the fact that my abstention (...) may in no way be regarded as a precedent capable of influencing in any way the question of the abstention of permanent members of the Security Council.[25]

and RN Gardner, 'The Veto and the Charter: An Interpretation for Survival' Meetings' (1951) 60 Yale LJ 258, 278ff. See also the previous discussion on UN Charter Art 27(3) in Section 3.4.2.

[19] J Arato, 'Treaty Interpretation and Constitutional Transformation: Informal Change in International Organizations' (2013) 38 Yale JIL 289, 323.

[20] L Gross, 'Voting in the Security Council: Abstention from Voting and Absence from Meetings' (1951) 60 Yale LJ 209, 210, 224, 247, 249; S Ford, 'Legal Processes of Change: Article 2(4) and the Vienna Convention on the Law of Treaties' (1999) 4 JCSL 75, 105. cf McDougal and Gardner, 'The Veto and the Charter', 262; DW Greig, *Intertemporality and the Law of Treaties* (British Institute of International and Comparative Law, 2003) 94–5.

[21] See LM Goodrich, E Hambro, and AP Simons, *Charter of the United Nations: Commentary and Documents* (3rd edn, Columbia UP, 1969) 229; Gardiner, *Treaty Interpretation*, 245; A Aust, *Modern Treaty Law and Practice* (3rd edn, CUP, 2013) 216.

[22] See eg UN, *Repertory of Practice of United Nations Organs* (1945–54) vol 2, paras 46–52; Supp no 1 (1954–55) vol 1, para 11; Supp no 2 (1955–59) vol 2, para 11; Supp no 3 (1959–66) vol 2, para 19; Supp no 4 (1966–69) vol 1, para 10; Supp no 5 (1970–78) vol 2, para 10; Supp no 6 (1979–84) vol 3, para 10; Supp nos 7–9 (1985–99) vol 3, para 3; Supp no 10 (2000–09) vol 3, para 5.

[23] See (text to) nn 19–20. See also A Laursen, *Changing International Law to Meet New Challenges: Interpretation, Modification and the Use of Force* (DJØF, 2006) 77 ('It is hard to accept that the word 'concurring' can be interpreted to include abstentions.'). cf Amerasinghe, *Principles*, 55 ('The practice in fact adopted resulted in giving the meaning "not negative" to the term "affirmative" which is less removed and may be construed as development rather than amendment.').

[24] See n 21. See also *Namibia Advisory Opinion*, Separate Opinion of Judge de Castro, 186; G Fitzmaurice, 'The Law and Procedure of the International Court of Justice, 1951–54: General Principles and Sources of Law' (1953) 30 BYBIL 1, 50; Stavropoulos, 'The Practice of Voluntary Abstentions', 739–40; K Wolfke, 'Treaties and Custom: Aspects of Interrelation' in J Klabbers and R Lefeber (eds), *Essays on the Law of Treaties: A Collection of Essays in Honour of Bert Vierdag* (Martinus Nijhoff, 1998) 31, 34; J Klabbers, *The Concept of Treaty in International Law* (Kluwer, 1996) 16; JE Alvarez, 'Limits of Change by Way of Subsequent Agreements and Practice' in G Nolte (ed), *Treaties and Subsequent Practice* (OUP, 2013) 123, 127.

[25] *Repertoire of the Practice of the Security Council* (1946–51) Ch IV, Part III, 173, Case 180.

However, most States contributing to the practice made clear that they were acting with awareness and intentionality in perpetuating the practice of voluntary abstentions.[26] Although in its early stages some questions had been raised, 'no objections to it were ever sustained, and it appears to have been supported automatically, without any question, since the end of 1949'.[27] One commentator found that abstentions by permanent members of the Security Council were not considered a negative vote on 319 occasions by 2001.[28] Thus, the practice concerning voluntary abstentions under Article 27(3) of the UN Charter emerged as 'one of the most clearly established practices in the Security Council'.[29]

This practice enabled the Council, for instance, to adopt a decision recommending intervention in the 1950 Korean War despite the absence of the Soviet Union.[30] In fact, as pointed out by Stavropoulos, without this accepted practice, numerous States would not have become UN members or parties to the ICJ Statute, UN forces in various countries would have lacked legal foundation, and countless other examples relating to virtually all non-procedural issues dealt with by the Security Council would have been affected.[31] Thus, we can see the far-reaching implications of the practice on voluntary abstentions developed in the Security Council over time.

The question of voluntary abstentions under Article 27(3) was raised in the ICJ *Namibia Advisory Opinion*.[32] The Court confirmed that this reading of the article had become established practice, referring to the continuity, consistency, and uniformity of the practice as evidence that it represents practice generally accepted by all members of the organization,[33] not just by those of the Security Council:

> [T]he proceedings of the Security Council extending over a long period supply abundant evidence that presidential rulings and the positions taken by members of the Council, in particular its permanent members, have consistently and uniformly interpreted the practice of voluntary abstention by a permanent member as not constituting a bar to the adoption of resolutions. (…) This procedure followed by the Security Council, which has continued unchanged after the amendment in 1965 of Article 27 of the Charter, has been generally accepted by Members of the United Nations and evidences a general practice of that Organization.[34]

Regrettably, the ICJ did not elaborate on the legal effect of the Security Council practice in relation to Article 27(3), ie whether it constituted modification or

[26] Ibid. 173–5, Cases 182 (United States), 183 (Syria), 185 (France), and 186 (United Kingdom).

[27] Stavropoulos, 'The Practice of Voluntary Abstentions', 746.

[28] TM Franck, *Recourse to Force: State Action Against Threats and Armed Attacks* (CUP, 2002) 8.

[29] Ibid.

[30] See eg UNSC Res 82 (1950) of 25 June 1950, UN Doc S/1501 (1950); UNSC Res 83 (1950) of 27 June 1950, UN Doc S/1511 (1950); UNSC Res 84 (1950) of 7 July 1950, UN Doc S/1588 (1950). See also SD Bailey and S Daws, *The Procedure of the United Nations Security Council* (3rd edn, Clarendon Press, 1998) 257.

[31] Stavropoulos, 'The Practice of Voluntary Abstentions', 745.

[32] *Namibia Advisory Opinion*, para 22.

[33] However, a number of States did raise objections to this voting practice with regard to the adoption of *specific* resolutions—ibid. paras 20–1.

[34] Ibid. para 22.

interpretation. It implied in its Advisory Opinion that the observed practice falls within the interpretative bounds of the Charter provision,[35] despite the fact that the text and *travaux* indicate otherwise.[36] This approach, as noted by one commentator, may have allowed it to avoid any 'slippery slopes of reasoning' or claims of treaty breach.[37] The case illustrates the reluctance of judicial and quasi-judicial bodies to deal with the distinction between interpretation and modification by subsequent practice and acknowledge the latter.

Some scholars support the view that the Security Council's practice in relation to Article 27(3) is merely a 'dynamic' interpretation of the provision.[38] This could be said to conform to the principle of effectiveness.[39] As stated previously, according to this principle, paying insufficient regard to—or, conversely, placing undue emphasis on—the text, the parties' (believed) intentions, or the treaty's object and purpose,[40] is unlikely to lead to a result that reflects the 'real area of treaty operation'.[41] In this case, the 'reinterpreted' voting procedure allows the Council to adopt decisions more effectively while preserving the permanent members' veto power, and perhaps also granting permanent members the discretion to support a politically sensitive decision without expressly endorsing it by abstaining. Conversely, the effect of the voting practice may simply go to show that the modification of Article 27(3) is in line with the Charter's object and purpose(s), and only affects the content of the one provision.

It has also been argued that the practice relating to Article 27(3) amounts to interpretation rather than modification in light of the fact that the last sentence of the provision, concerning obligatory abstentions, obliges any Security Council member involved in a dispute to abstain from voting in certain circumstances, in which case the 'concurring votes of the permanent members' will be counted without that State. It is contended that for this reason, the first sentence of Article 27(3) cannot be taken to always require 'all' the concurring votes of the permanent members, and may suggest that members have the discretion to voluntarily abstain in other circumstances as well.[42] In other words, the possibility of *obligatory* abstentions in the second sentence of Article 27(3) would impact its first sentence, which appears to rule out *voluntary* abstentions, creating a certain degree of ambiguity in the text that can be resolved by recourse to subsequent practice, leaving more room for interpretation.[43] As discussed earlier, ambiguity can thus constitute a mechanism that narrows the scope or need for modification by subsequent practice.[44]

[35] Ibid. [36] See (text to) nn 23–4.

[37] I Venzke, *How Interpretation Makes International Law: On Semantic Change and Normative Twists* (OUP, 2012) 73.

[38] See eg B Simma, S Brunner, and H-P Kaul, 'Article 27' in B Simma (ed), *The Charter of the United Nations: A Commentary* (2nd edn, OUP, 2002) 476. cf Laursen, *Changing International Law*, 77; Venzke, *How Interpretation Makes International Law*, 73.

[39] See Section 2.5.1. [40] Aust, *Modern Treaty Law*, 185.

[41] ME O'Connell, *The International Law of the Sea*, vol I (Clarendon Press, 1982) 253.

[42] Greig, *Intertemporality*, 94–5.

[43] Ibid. 95, referring to *Namibia Advisory Opinion*, Separate Opinion of Judge Dillard, 153–4.

[44] See Section 3.5.

A majority of commentators, however, believe that Article 27(3) has been effectively modified.[45] Indeed, it is submitted here that, since the practice in question is difficult to square with the plain, active language employed in the text of the provision and contradicts its *travaux*, it constitutes an instance of modification of a provision of a constitutive treaty by the member States. This is underscored further by the significant implications of the change in question: 'the practice of the Council has transformed abstentions into an affirmative vote—with dramatic consequences for the effectiveness of the Council and the UN as a whole'.[46] Moreover, the argument that, in light of the provision's second sentence on obligatory abstentions, Article 27(3) cannot be taken to require the concurring votes of 'all' permanent members in all circumstances, does not sufficiently explain why the article has been taken to mean that it does not require the concurring votes of all permanent members in *any* circumstances if they choose to abstain, ie also when the second sentence does not apply. The two sentences of Article 27(3) deal with separate scenarios: the first requires unanimity in all cases not covered by the second sentence, although practice now allows for voluntary abstentions, while the second requires obligatory abstentions in certain cases.

Furthermore, the process that has taken place in relation to Article 27(3) has also been characterized as (modification by) subsequent (treaty-related[47]) customary law, once again demonstrating the potential overlap, conceptually and practically, between the processes of subsequent practice and subsequent customary law:[48]

> The constant practice of the Security Council of not treating the voluntary abstention of a permanent member of the Security Council as a vote against a substantive draft resolution before the Council is, it is submitted, customary law, and was the valid customary law of the United Nations long before the Security Council resolutions of 1968, 1969 and 1970 on the subject of Namibia were adopted.[49]

[45] See eg *Namibia Advisory Opinion*, Separate Opinion of Judge De Castro, 186; *Cameroon v Nigeria*, Dissenting Opinion of Judge Ajibola, paras 52–3; Fitzmaurice, 'The Law and Procedure of the International Court of Justice' (1953), 50; Gross, 'Voting in the Security Council', 328; Goodrich, Hambro, and Simons, *Charter of the United Nations*, 229; DW Greig, *International Law* (Butterworths, 1970) 382–3; E Lauterpacht, 'The Waning of the Requirement of Consent' (1991) 85 ASIL Proc 38, 39–41; Klabbers, *The Concept of Treaty*, 91; M Byers, *Custom, Power and the Power of Rules: International Relations and Customary International Law* (CUP, 2001) 173; Wolfke, 'Treaties and Custom', 34; GI Tunkin, *Theory of International Law* (2nd rev edn, Wildy, Simmonds and Hill, 2003) 339–40; Gardiner, *Treaty Interpretation*, 245; Alvarez, 'Limits of Change', 127; Aust, *Modern Treaty Law*, 216; Arato, 'Treaty Interpretation', 323; G Distefano, 'L'accord tacite ou l'univers parallèle du droit des traités' (2015) 18 QIL 17, 31.

[46] Alvarez, 'Limits of Change', 127. cf Summary record of 766th meeting, paras 46 (Lachs) and 38–9 (De Luna); *Competence of the General Assembly*, Dissenting Opinion of Judge Alvarez, 18.

[47] As discussed at length in Ch 4, this term refers to the situation in which the (modifying) practice of the parties to the treaty *in relation to the treaty*, in conjunction with the practice of non-parties, leads to the emergence of new customary law. See in particular Section 4.5.1. In this case, the subsequent practice could be said to have resulted in both a modification of the treaty and the emergence of the subsequent customary rule.

[48] See Section 4.6.

[49] *Legal Consequences for States of the Continued Presence of South Africa in Namibia (South West Africa) Notwithstanding Security Council Resolution 276 (1970)*, Oral Statement by Mr Stavropoulos, ICJ Pleadings (vol II) 30, 39. See also eg K Wolfke, 'Some Reflections on Kinds of Rules and International Law-Making by Practice' in J Makarczyk (ed), *Theory of International Law at the Threshold of the 21st Century: Essays in Honour of Krzysztof Skubiszewski* (Kluwer Law International, 1996) 588, 590; ME

As to the type of treaty, provision, and practice involved, it is worth noting that this example concerns an instance of tacit modification of an expansive multilateral treaty regime, as opposed to cases involving bilateral treaties for which evidence of an implied agreement is much easier to establish. The provision in question is also of an internal procedural nature, the modification of which, as discussed, is likewise less contentious. Moreover, the example concerns practice within an international organization, and, what is more, of an organ of limited membership within that organization.[50] As discussed in Chapter 2, the practice of the Security Council is in principle capable of constituting relevant practice establishing the agreement of the parties to a modification of the UN Charter in respect of its own voting procedures.[51] In this case, moreover, the ICJ highlighted that the practice was also 'generally accepted by Members of the United Nations' and qualified as a 'general practice' of the organization as a whole[52]—hence combining the Security Council's practice with the practice of the States parties to the constitutive treaty ('classical' State practice[53]) to confirm the agreement of all the parties to the Charter on the changed reading of Article 27(3). The effect of the modification could be regarded both as altering the contents of the first sentence of Article 27(3) and as supplementing them with the qualification of voluntary abstentions.[54] In any case, the example of Article 27(3) of the Charter demonstrates the amount of discussion that even a reasonably clear-cut distinction between an act of modification and interpretation can generate.

Israeli Wall Advisory Opinion

The ICJ's *Israeli Wall Advisory Opinion* also involved the interpretation of a UN Charter provision, this time Article 12(1). The meaning of the Article has been impacted by the subsequent practice of the Security Council and General Assembly—a practice acquiesced in by the general membership of the organization and capable of establishing the agreement of all the parties.

Pursuant to Article 12(1) of the UN Charter, 'while the Security Council is exercising in respect of any dispute or situation the functions assigned to it in the present Charter, the General Assembly shall not make any recommendation with regard to that dispute or situation'—a seemingly non-ambiguous treaty provision.[55]

Villiger, *Customary International Law and Treaties: A Manual on the Theory and Practice of the Interrelation of Sources* (2nd rev edn, Kluwer International, 1997) para 314. See also HWA Thirlway, 'The Law and Procedure of the International Court of Justice: 1960–1989, Part Three' (1991) 62 BYBIL 1, 48–9, referring to both the process of modification by subsequent practice and that of new customary law.

[50] This relates to the discussion on the nature of organizational practice relative to the notion of 'subsequent practice' in the sense of Art 31(3)(b) VCLT—see Section 2.3.1(c).

[51] Ibid.

[52] *Namibia Advisory Opinion*, para 22. See also Nolte, Third Report on Subsequent Practice, para 52; Greig, *Intertemporality*, 94.

[53] See Section 2.3.1(c) on the distinction between the practice of States parties within an international organization and the practice of the organization 'itself'—a distinction that the ICJ has yet to (explicitly) make.

[54] See Section 3.3.1 on the meaning of 'modification'.

[55] Nolte, Introductory Report on Treaties over Time, 180. See also Arato, 'Treaty Interpretation', 326.

Initially, practice confirmed this seemingly clear wording.[56] Only later did the practice change to allow the General Assembly and Security Council to proceed in parallel on the same issues, in particular with regard to 'recommendations'.[57] In the *Israeli Wall Advisory Opinion*, the ICJ considered that this 'increasing tendency'[58] was consistent with Article 12(1)[59]—despite the fact that the practice contradicts its clear wording. The Court reasoned as follows:

> As regards the practice of the United Nations, both the General Assembly and the Security Council initially interpreted and applied Article 12 to the effect that the Assembly could not make a recommendation on a question concerning the maintenance of international peace and security while the matter remained on the Council's agenda. (...)
>
> However, this interpretation of Article 12 has evolved subsequently. Thus the General Assembly deemed itself entitled in 1961 [and 1963] to adopt recommendations (...) while those cases still appeared on the Council's agenda, without the Council having adopted any recent resolution concerning them. (...) [T]he Legal Counsel of the United Nations confirmed that the Assembly interpreted the words 'is exercising the functions' in Article 12 of the Charter as meaning 'is exercising the functions at this moment' (...). Indeed, the Court notes that there has been an increasing tendency over time for the General Assembly and the Security Council to deal in parallel with the same matter concerning the maintenance of international peace and security [citing several examples]. (...) It is often the case that, while the Security Council has tended to focus on the aspects of such matters related to international peace and security, the General Assembly has taken a broader view, considering also their humanitarian, social and economic aspects.[60]

Thus, the ICJ concluded that 'the accepted practice of the GA, as it has evolved, is consistent with Article 12, paragraph 1, of the Charter.'[61] As appears from the passage above, the Court relied not only on the practice of the Security Council and General Assembly, but also on that of the Legal Counsel of the United Nations, a body not representative of the organization's membership. In this sense, the Court went a step further with regard to assigning value to institutional practice than in its previous decisions.[62]

Once again, the Court did not elaborate upon the legal effect of the practice or whether it constituted interpretation or modification. It avoided construing it as anything more than 'accepted practice' impliedly amounting to an exercise of interpretation. Nevertheless, it is difficult to deny, based on the wording and background of the provision, that the subsequent practice in question represents a modification, in the sense of a tacit alteration or termination, of the Charter provision: 'Article 12 of the UN Charter is a provision whose text does not indicate what the subsequent practice of the General Assembly is suggesting.'[63] Indeed, subsequent practice in relation to Article 12(1) is frequently cited as an example of modification or desuetude

[56] *Israeli Wall Advisory Opinion*, para 27. [57] Ibid. paras 25–33. [58] Ibid. para 27.
[59] Ibid. para 28. [60] Ibid. para 27. [61] Ibid. para 28.
[62] See also the case law discussed in Section 2.3.1(c).
[63] Nolte, Introductory Report on Treaties over Time, 180.

in the doctrine,[64] and as a provision that, as a result of practice, has effectively been turned into a dead letter.[65] As to the implications of the modification, though the change cannot be said to have affected the object and purpose(s) of the UN Charter, it certainly appears to have led to a reordering of the relations and competences between the General Assembly and Security Council.[66] Thus, the practice can be said to have led to a substantive, far-reaching modification to the text of Article 12(1) of the Charter.

WHO Nuclear Weapons Advisory Opinion

The *WHO Nuclear Weapons Advisory Opinion* involved a request for an advisory opinion by the World Health Organization[67] set forth in Resolution WHA46.40[68] as to whether, in light of health and environmental effects, the use of nuclear weapons by a State in armed conflict is a breach of its obligations under international law and the WHO Constitution.[69] The ICJ rejected the request on account of the fact that the question did not fall within the scope of the WHO's activities pursuant to Article 96(2) of the UN Charter.[70] It did not find any implication in the text or object and purpose of the constitutive instrument of the Organization, or in the overall system of the UN Charter,[71] of its competence to address the legality of the use of nuclear weapons, even under the doctrine of implied powers.[72]

Most interesting for present purposes is the Court's assessment of WHO practice confirming this conclusion. The Court pointed out that the reports and resolutions referred to in Resolution WHA46.40 were not in the nature of a WHO practice regarding the legality—as opposed to the effects—of the threat or use of nuclear weapons, nor could it find such practice elsewhere.[73] The Court added:

> Resolution WHA46.40 itself, adopted, not without opposition, (...) could not be taken to express or to amount on its own to a practice establishing an agreement between the members of the Organisation to interpret its Constitution as empowering it to address the question of the legality of the use of nuclear weapons.[74]

Although the case does not as such involve an instance of modification by subsequent practice, it has been argued that 'the general tenor of the Court's approach (...) endorsed the possibility of the tacit modification of an international constitution

[64] See eg J Liang, 'Modifying the UN Charter through Subsequent Practice: Prospects for the Charter's Revitalisation' (2012) 81 NJIL 1, 10; Alvarez, 'Limits of Change', 127; Arato, 'Treaty Interpretation', 326–7; Nolte, Introductory Report on Treaties over Time, 180, 201–2; Distefano, 'L'accord tacite', 31; JY Qin, 'The Conundrum of WTO Accession Protocols: In Search of Legality and Legitimacy' (2015) 55 VJIL 369, 409.

[65] Alvarez, 'Limits of Change', 127.

[66] Arato, 'Treaty Interpretation', 330.

[67] *Legality of the Use by a State of Nuclear Weapons in Armed Conflict*, Request for Advisory Opinion of 3 September 1993, ICJ Pleadings 2.

[68] World Health Assembly, Res WHA46.40 of 14 May 1993, 'Health and Environmental Effects of Nuclear Weapons', *13th Plenary Meeting of the Forty-Sixth World Health Assembly* (1993).

[69] Constitution of the World Health Organization 1946, 14 UNTS 185 (WHO Constitution).

[70] *WHO Nuclear Weapons Advisory Opinion*, paras 21–6.

[71] Ibid. para 26.

[72] Ibid. para 25.

[73] Ibid. para 27.

[74] Ibid.

through the practice of its members'.[75] An *a contrario* reading may suggest that, had Resolution WHA46.40 been supported by sufficient practice, it could have granted the WHO the power to address the question of legality of the use of nuclear weapons—hence modifying the Organization's constitutive instrument. This may be regarded as an example of indirect recognition of the possibility of treaty modification by subsequent practice, and, specifically, in relation to a special category of treaty—the constitutive instrument of an international organization.

South West Africa Voting Procedure Advisory Opinion

The 1955 *South West Africa Voting Procedure Advisory Opinion* is also worthy of note.[76] It concerned a request by the General Assembly for a clarification of the ICJ's previous 1950 Advisory Opinion on the legal status of South West Africa.[77] Following the 1950 Advisory Opinion, the General Assembly had adopted 'Rule F' on the voting procedure for decisions regarding reports and petitions concerning the territory of South West Africa. According to this Rule, such decisions were to be taken pursuant to the two-thirds majority voting rule in Article 18(2) of the UN Charter. The ICJ found Rule F to be a correct interpretation of the statement in its 1950 Advisory Opinion that '[t]he degree of supervision to be exercised by the General Assembly (…) should conform as far as possible to the procedure followed in this respect by the Council of the League [of Nations].'[78] The Court stated that this was not intended to transplant the Council's unanimity rule upon the General Assembly, which would have posed 'insurmountable' problems of a juridical nature given the differences between the two organs:[79]

> Taking decisions by a two-thirds majority vote or by a simple majority is one of the distinguishing features of the General Assembly, while the unanimity rule was one of the distinguishing features of the Council of the League of Nations. These two systems are characteristic of different organs, and one system cannot be substituted for the other without constitutional amendment.[80]

The Court also pointed out that it was 'legally impossible' for the General Assembly to derive its competence to exercise its supervisory authority from the Charter, while reaching decisions relating to that exercise 'in accordance with a voting system entirely alien to that prescribed by the Charter'.[81] As for the words 'as far as possible' in its 1950 Opinion, the Court explained that these had been intended 'to allow for adjustments or modifications' made necessary by the fact that the General Assembly

[75] Greig, *Intertemporality*, 90.

[76] *Voting Procedure on Questions relating to Reports and Petitions concerning the Territory of South West Africa*, Advisory Opinion of 7 June 1955, ICJ Reports 67 [*South West Africa Voting Procedure Advisory Opinion*].

[77] *Voting Procedure on Questions relating to Reports and Petitions concerning the Territory of South West Africa*, Request for Advisory Opinion of 6 December 1954, ICJ Pleadings 8.

[78] *South West Africa Voting Procedure Advisory Opinion*, 72, 75, 77, citing *International Status of South West Africa Advisory Opinion*, 128.

[79] *South West Africa Voting Procedure Advisory Opinion*, 75. [80] Ibid. [81] Ibid. 76.

and the Council were governed by different instruments.[82] The 1950 Opinion therefore 'left the General Assembly with Article 18 of the Charter as the sole legal basis for the voting system applicable to decisions in connection with its supervisory functions'.[83] The adoption of 'Rule F' hence fell within the 'bounds of legal possibility' of the Court's 1950 Opinion.[84]

Judge Klaestad in his Separate Opinion considered that the unanimity rule in Article 5 of the League's Covenant applied instead of the proposed two-thirds majority prescribed in Article 18(2) of the Charter, 'as the practice of the Council does not disclose any such exception'.[85] This implies that, *a contrario*, the Council's practice could have modified the unanimity rule. Moreover, he added that '[i]t is not for the Court to consider whether the Council would have been justified in modifying the rule of absolute unanimity.'[86] Meanwhile, Judge Lauterpacht in his Separate Opinion arrived at the same conclusion as the Court regarding compatibility between 'Rule F' and the 1950 Opinion, only by a different route. By contrast to Judge Klaestad, he implied that the unanimity rule in Article 5 of the Covenant had been modified (though the word employed was 'interpretation') by the League's subsequent practice:

> There is no doubt that, in the course of time and without any formal amendment, the rule of absolute unanimity ceased to be a factor to which there was invariably attached decisive importance. (...) A proper interpretation of a constitutional instrument must take into account not only the formal letter of the original instrument, but also its operation in actual practice and in the light of the revealed tendencies in the life of the Organization.[87]

Judge Lauterpacht also added that there is room for modification of the General Assembly's voting procedure to achieve a result 'half-way between qualified unanimity and a two-thirds majority'[88] (unanimity as such would have been wholly inconsistent with the Charter[89]):

> [I]t cannot be said (...) that in no circumstances may the General Assembly act by a system of voting other than that laid down in the Charter. There is no room for any emphasis of language suggesting that any such modification of the voting procedure is a juridical impossibility. Frequent practice of the League of Nations accomplished that juridical impossibility (...). [90]

Both potential instances of modification under discussion concerned voting practices in relation to large multilateral treaty regimes constituting international organizations.[91] First, the Covenant of the League, according to Judge Lauterpacht,

[82] Ibid. 77. [83] Ibid. [84] Ibid.

[85] *Voting Procedure on Questions relating to Reports and Petitions concerning the Territory of South West Africa*, Advisory Opinion of 7 June 1955, Separate Opinion of Judge Klaestad, ICJ Reports 84, 86.

[86] Ibid.

[87] *Voting Procedure on Questions relating to Reports and Petitions concerning the Territory of South West Africa*, Advisory Opinion of 7 June 1955, Separate Opinion of Judge Lauterpacht, ICJ Reports 90, 105–6.

[88] Ibid. 113. [89] Ibid. 114. [90] Ibid. 111.

[91] See also eg L Kopelmanas, 'Custom as a Means of Creation of International Law' (1937) 18 BYBIL 127, 139–40, discussing examples relating to the practice of the Council of the League of Nations, as well as an old example relating to the practice of the Congress of the Universal Postal Union, the main

had been modified with regard to the unanimity rule, and, as seemingly implied by Judge Klaestad, *could* have been modified by subsequent practice. Second, the UN Charter, according to Lauterpacht, could have been modified to allow for a different voting procedure not wholly inconsistent with the Charter from both a legal and practical standpoint, given that 'the number of States required for unanimity in the General Assembly is about four times as large as in the Council of the League'.[92]

One year later, the General Assembly submitted another request for the interpretation of the 1950 Advisory Opinion in the case of *Admissibility of Hearings of Petitioners by the Committee on South West Africa*.[93] The Court here recognized the competence of the Council of the League to introduce, 'had it seen fit to do so', a right of petition into the Mandates System—'an innovation designed to render the supervisory function of the Council more effective'.[94] With regard to the General Assembly's Committee on South West Africa, it noted:

[U]nder the compulsion of practical considerations arising out of the lack of co-operation by the Mandatory, the Committee on South West Africa provided by Rule XXVI of its Rules of Procedure an alternative procedure for the receipt and treatment of petitions. (...) This Rule enabled the Committee on South West Africa to receive and deal with petitions notwithstanding that they had not been transmitted by the Mandatory and involved a departure in this respect from the procedure prescribed by the Council of the League.[95]

The Court thus concluded that there was no incompatibility between the decision to authorize a procedure for granting hearings to petitioners by the Committee on South West Africa and its 1950 Advisory Opinion.[96] Its decision could be taken as implicitly accepting the possibility of significant modifications to the relevant text by the practice of the Council and the General Assembly.[97] However, Judge Lauterpacht pointed out that the departure from the original legal procedure 'is less drastic when viewed in the light of the cessation of that system as the result of the attitude of non co-operation (*sic*) as adopted by South Africa [the Mandatory]'.[98] He referred to the principle of approximate application:[99]

It is a sound principle of law that whenever a legal instrument of continuing validity cannot be applied literally owing to the conduct of one of the parties, it must (...) be applied in a way approximating most closely to its primary object. To do that is to interpret and to give effect to the instrument—not to change it.[100]

meeting of parties to the Union, which replaced the unanimity rule with majority voting. As a result, States opposed to a decision had no choice but to accept it or leave the Union.

[92] *South West Africa Voting Procedure Advisory Opinion*, Separate Opinion of Judge Lauterpacht, 113.

[93] *Admissibility of Hearings of Petitioners by the Committee on South West Africa*, Request for Advisory Opinion of 19 December 1955, ICJ Pleadings 8.

[94] *Admissibility of Hearings of Petitioners by the Committee on South West Africa*, Advisory Opinion of 1 June 1956, ICJ Reports 23, 29.

[95] Ibid. 31. [96] Ibid. 32. [97] Engel, '"Living" International Constitutions', 906.

[98] *Admissibility of Hearings of Petitioners by the Committee on South West Africa*, Separate Opinion of Sir Hersch Lauterpacht, 43.

[99] See Section 3.5.2.

[100] *Admissibility of Hearings of Petitioners*, Separate Opinion of Judge Lauterpacht, 46.

Judge Lauterpacht also discussed the special nature of multilateral instruments of a law-making character or creating an international regime, in relation to which 'the principle of separability of their provisions with a view to ensuring the continuous operation of the treaty as a whole has been increasingly recognized by international practice'.[101] Such treaties may be more adaptable to changing circumstances, such as non-cooperation of one of the parties, than ordinary treaties. This reasoning suggests that changes of the kind at issue here are less likely to be regarded as outright modifications by subsequent practice, and certainly not modifications that affect the treaty's object and purpose.

Costa Rica v Nicaragua

The *Costa Rica v Nicaragua* case, as discussed in Chapter 2,[102] concerned an old bilateral boundary treaty—the 1858 Treaty of Limits[103]—between Costa Rica and Nicaragua. In question pursuant to that treaty was the extent of Costa Rica's navigational rights for commercial purposes on the San Juan River. Nicaragua argued in favour of the original definition of the term 'commercial purposes' as comprising only trade in goods, while Costa Rica militated in favour of a broader interpretation comprising 'any activity in pursuit of commercial purposes', including the transport of tourists.[104]

In its analysis, the ICJ effectively recognized the process of treaty modification by subsequent practice, which it contrasted with evolutionary interpretation:[105]

> On the one hand, the subsequent practice of the parties, within the meaning of Article 31(3)(b) of the Vienna Convention, can result in a departure from the original intent on the basis of a tacit agreement between the parties. On the other hand, there are situations in which the parties' intent upon conclusion of the treaty was, or may be presumed to have been, to give the terms used—or some of them—a meaning or content capable of evolving (...). In such instances it is indeed in order to respect the parties' common intention at the time the treaty was concluded, not to depart from it, that account should be taken of the meaning acquired by the terms in question upon each occasion on which the treaty is to be applied.[106]

The relation between the processes of treaty modification by subsequent practice and evolutionary interpretation has already been discussed.[107] As explained, the Court in *Costa Rica v Nicaragua* chose to rely solely on evolutionary interpretation,[108] without further addressing the question of modification by subsequent practice. Thus, its statement above remains an *obiter dictum*.

By means of the evolutionary technique, the Court held that the term '*comercio*' had evolved to include services such as tourism.[109] It further held that Nicaragua

[101] Ibid. 49. [102] See Section 2.5.3(c).

[103] 1858 Treaty of Territorial Limits between Costa Rica and Nicaragua, 118 CTS 439.

[104] *Costa Rica v Nicaragua*, para 59.

[105] As explained in Section 2.5.3, subsequent practice can also be a means to arrive at evolutionary interpretation.

[106] *Costa Rica v Nicaragua*, para 64.

[107] See Section 2.5.3.

[108] *Costa Rica v Nicaragua*, paras 66–7.

[109] Ibid. paras 66–71. cf *Costa Rica v Nicaragua*, Separate Opinion of Judge Skotnikov, paras 5–6, and Declaration of Judge ad hoc Guillaume, para 16.

could not require visas for such tourists—despite Nicaragua's consistent practice of doing so.[110] Had the Court instead relied on modification by subsequent practice, it would likewise have upheld Costa Rica's right to use the river for tourism but would not have prohibited Nicaragua from requiring tourist visas.[111] As Judge Skotnikov pointed out, Nicaragua's 'consistent practice' of allowing Costa Rica to use the river for tourist navigation would have sufficed to establish the parties' agreement to include services within the meaning of 'commercial purposes'.[112] Judge Guillaume in his Declaration adopted a similar reasoning.[113] Thus, the result of modification by subsequent practice would have been less drastic and more in tune with the parties' intention,[114] in this way providing higher legitimacy.[115] The case highlights both the mutually reinforcing relationship between the two processes, in that subsequent practice can evidence evolutionary interpretation, and their sometimes mutually exclusive nature, as separate processes that can lead to different results. Although once again the case seems to illustrate a reluctance to acknowledge modification by subsequent practice head on, most notable is that the Court expressly recognized the potential for subsequent practice to diverge from the original treaty text and intention of the parties.

Worthy of note is also Judge Skotnikov's argument that limitations on a State's (Nicaragua's) sovereignty should not be presumed by expanding the original right granted to Costa Rica in 1858, especially in the case of a boundary treaty.[116] It is submitted here that, while such a treaty may be less susceptible to change over time, the effects of subsequent practice are more likely and easier to deduce in relation to a bilateral treaty, especially with regard to an old regime the provisions of which no longer adequately cater to the parties' needs and interests.[117] It is not surprising, therefore, that the 1858 Treaty of Limits was prone to informal change over time, *inter alia* in light of the new economic activities undertaken by the parties.

Temple of Préah Vihéar

The *Temple of Préah Vihéar* case between Cambodia and Thailand, discussed extensively in Chapter 2,[118] concerned a bilateral boundary treaty, the Treaty of 13 February 1904, which established the general character of the frontier between the two States (along the watershed line), the corresponding boundary of which was to be delimited by a Franco-Siamese Mixed Commission.[119] The ICJ here found

[110] Ibid. para 115. See also J Arato, 'Subsequent Practice and Evolutive Interpretation: Techniques of Treaty Interpretation over Time and Their Diverse Consequences' (2010) 9 LPICT 443, 450.

[111] Ibid. Separate Opinion of Judge Skotinkov, para 15.

[112] Ibid. paras 8–10; *Costa Rica v Nicaragua*, Declaration of Judge ad hoc Guillaume, para 16.

[113] Ibid. Declaration of Judge ad hoc Guillaume, para 16.

[114] Ibid. para 15; Venzke, *How Interpretation Makes International Law*, 232–3.

[115] Nolte, 'Subsequent Practice as a Means of Interpretation in the Jurisprudence of the WTO Appellate Body', 143.

[116] *Costa Rica v Nicaragua*, Separate Opinion of Judge Skotnikov, paras 4–6. See also *Costa Rica v Nicaragua*, para 48. cf Gardiner, *Treaty Interpretation*, 242–3.

[117] See Section 3.5.1(a).

[118] See Section 2.3.5(b).

[119] 1904 Convention between France and Siam Modifying the Stipulations of the Treaty of 3 October 1893 Concerning the Territories and the Other Agreements, 195 CTS 47.

a manifest divergence between the boundary line accepted by the parties through their subsequent practice[120] (specifically, a map depicting the position of the Temple on the Cambodian side of the boundary) and that laid down in the bilateral treaty: '[b]oth parties, by their conduct, recognized the [former] line and thereby in effect agreed to regard it as being the frontier line.'[121] It held as follows:

> The Court considers that the acceptance of the Annex I map by the Parties caused the map to enter the treaty settlement and to become an integral part of it. It cannot be said that this process involved a departure from, and even a violation of, the terms of the Treaty of 1904, wherever the map line diverged from the line of the watershed, for, as the Court sees the matter, the map (...) was accepted by the Parties (...) as constituting the result of the interpretation given by the two Governments to the delimitation which the Treaty itself required. In other words, the Parties at that time adopted an interpretation of the treaty settlement which caused the map line, in so far as it may have departed from the line of the watershed, to prevail over the relevant clause of the treaty.[122]

Thus, first of all, the Court regarded the result of the subsequent practice as having become an integral part of the treaty (rather than an independent basis of obligation), a consideration also potentially relevant to the discussion on the result of a modification by subsequent practice in relation to the original treaty.[123] It has, however, been argued that, since the treaty only prescribed the 'general character of the frontier', which was to follow the watershed line (Article 1 of the 1904 Treaty), while the 'exact course of that frontier' was to be delimited by a Mixed Commission (Article 3 of the 1904 Treaty),[124] the Court implicitly characterized the relationship between Articles 1 and 3 as one of *lex generalis* and *lex specialis*, such that the latter (taken to refer generally to the actual delimitation of the boundary) ultimately prevails as a matter of interpretation.[125] In this sense, the ambiguity of the former, which can constitute an in-built treaty adaptation mechanism,[126] left more room for interpretation and less for alteration by subsequent practice. However, it is submitted that the treaty-prescribed watershed criterion provided for a 'non-demarcated, but objectively determinable boundary',[127] and was thus relatively unambiguous.

The Court further considered that the parties' subsequent practice—which was clearly at variance with the ordinary meaning of the text—established an authentic interpretation of the treaty that prevailed over the original provision.[128] Although the statement that the result of the practice 'prevail(s) over the relevant clause of the treaty' already alludes to a modification by alteration of the treaty provision, the Court did not refer to a modification outright. But authentic interpretations constitute new legal enactments rather than mere interpretations.[129] Following this

[120] In Thailand's case, through acquiescence or estoppel. See *Temple of Préah Vihéar*, 23, 30–2. See further Section 2.3.5(b).

[121] *Temple of Préah Vihéar*, 33.

[122] Ibid. 33–4.

[123] See Section 3.3.6(a) on modification in relation to the underlying treaty.

[124] *Temple of Préah Vihéar*, 17.

[125] Laursen, *Changing International Law*, 74.

[126] See Section 3.5.2.

[127] Nolte, Introductory Report on Treaties over Time, 205.

[128] Laursen, *Changing International Law*, 74.

[129] I Tammelo, *Treaty Interpretation and Practical Reason: Towards a General Theory of Legal Interpretation* (Law Book Co, 1967) 6. See also eg Waldock, Sixth Report on the Law of Treaties, 89 para 8; A Orakhelashvili, *The Interpretation of Acts and Rules in Public International Law* (OUP, 2008)

line of reasoning, authentic interpretations close the gap between interpretation and modification of treaties.[130] Thus, the case shows that, at least with regard to bilateral treaties, the effect of subsequent practice evidencing the parties' subsequent agreement to modify a treaty can be indistinguishable from subsequent practice evidencing their agreement to an authentic interpretation of it:

If this reasoning [of the Court] may seem somewhat artificial (...) the case does perhaps show that for practical purposes it may not be of much moment whether in bilateral treaties subsequent practice is regarded as having its effect in the context of an interpretation or a modification of the treaty.[131]

Regarding the nature and form of practice concerned, it may be noted that the Court's emphasis on subsequent practice did not relate directly to the interpretation of the 1904 Treaty, but was raised as evidence of the agreement of the parties to a certain map line as constituting the correct boundary in the disputed area. In this sense, the subsequent practice was not, strictly speaking, 'in the application of the treaty', a constitutive element of subsequent practice pursuant to Article 31(3)(b) VCLT.[132] Another aspect, as discussed, is that, in assessing relevant practice, the Court took into account the acts of lower ranking officials, though it also deemed higher officials to have been aware of those acts at the time.[133] As to the form of practice in question, the case partly concerned Thailand's lack of reaction and the related notions of acquiescence and estoppel. The Court found that the specific circumstances had warranted a reaction on the part of the Siamese authorities, and that the extended absence of such reaction was proof of Thailand's acquiescence to the practice.[134] It also found that, in any case and in accordance with the notion of estoppel, Thailand was precluded by its subsequent practice from asserting otherwise, as the other party had come to rely on its acceptance of the respective map.[135]

Interestingly, the Court relied on subsequent practice to determine the course of the boundary despite the fact that a boundary commission was prescribed by the treaty to delimit it—which, as discussed, could constitute a special adaptation mechanism with the potential effect of excluding other forms of specifying the boundary and giving rise to a (further) presumption against modification by subsequent practice.[136]

Also noteworthy is that the principle of stability of boundaries did not impede the Court from upholding changes to the treaty boundary on the basis of subsequent practice, a point discussed in Chapter 3.[137] On the contrary, the Court used

515; W Karl, *Vertrag und spätere Praxis im Völkerrecht: Zum Einfluß der Praxis auf Inhalt und Bestand völkerrechtliche Verträge* (Springer, 1983) 46.

[130] Karl, *Vertrag*, 46; Orakhelashvili, *Interpretation of Acts and Rules*, 515. See further Sections 3.2.3 and 3.3.2(a).

[131] Waldock, Sixth Report on the Law of Treaties, 89 para 8.

[132] See Section 2.3.4 of this book.

[133] *Temple of Préah Vihéar*, 25. cf ibid. 30 (finding the practice of local authorities insufficient to establish that Thailand had been in possession of the Temple at all material times). See Section 2.3.1(c).

[134] Ibid. 23–4. [135] Ibid. 32. See Section 2.3.5(a). See also Section 2.3.5(b).

[136] See Section 3.5.2. [137] See Section 3.5.1(a).

precisely the stability argument to justify the prevalence of the line established by practice over that set out in the treaty: '[i]t is precisely to achieve this [stability and finality] that delimitations and map lines are resorted to.'[138] This serves to confirm, as stated earlier, that the principle of stability of boundaries can, depending on the circumstances, be used to sustain a subsequent modification of the boundary originally laid down in the treaty.[139] While this generally requires a clear and compelling practice evidencing the parties' intention to deviate from the treaty,[140] in the case of bilateral treaties such modifications are less contentious.[141] Thus, the Court held:

> There is (...) no reason to think that the Parties attached any special importance to the line of the watershed as such, as compared with the overriding importance, in the interests of finality, of adhering to the map line as eventually delimited and as accepted by them. The Court, therefore, feels bound, as a matter of treaty interpretation, to pronounce in favour of the line as mapped in the disputed area.[142]

In sum, the parties' subsequent practice amounted to a clear modification of a technical provision in the boundary treaty, despite the Court's characterization of the situation as a matter of 'ordinary treaty interpretation'.[143] Indeed, the *Temple of Préah Vihéar* judgment has been invoked frequently in the case law as an example of modification by subsequent practice,[144] as well as by the ILC in support of the draft article on treaty modification by subsequent practice discussed in Chapter 3.[145]

Cameroon v Nigeria and *El Salvador/Honduras*

The *Cameroon v Nigeria* case concerned a number of issues pertaining to the land and maritime boundary between the two States. Although the Court found that certain contested areas were already delimited in favour of Cameroon, Nigeria nevertheless claimed sovereignty based, *inter alia*, on 'effective administration [or peaceful possession] by Nigeria, acting as sovereign, and an absence of protest [by Cameroon]', coupled with 'manifestations of sovereignty by Nigeria together with the acquiescence by Cameroon in Nigerian sovereignty' over the areas in question.[146] The ICJ confirmed that it 'cannot be wholly precluded' that a State may acquiesce 'in the establishment of a change in treaty title'.[147] It thus acknowledged the possibility of modification by subsequent practice, in this case, again, in relation to a treaty

138 *Temple of Préah Vihéar*, 34.

139 See Section 3.5.1(a).

140 See eg *Nicaragua v Honduras*, para 253; JG Merrills, 'Land and Maritime Boundary between Cameroon and Nigeria (Cameroon v Nigeria, Equtorial Guinea Intervening), Merits, Judgment of October 10, 2002' (2003) 52 ICLQ 788, 796.

141 See Section 3.5.1(a).

142 *Temple of Préah Vihéar*, 35.

143 Ibid. 34.

144 See eg *Air Transport Services Agreement* (*US/France*), 63 fn 1; *Eritrea-Ethiopia Arbitration*, para 3.9. See also *Cameroon v Nigeria*, Dissenting Opinion of Judge Ajibola, paras 52–4. See further Section 5.2.2.

145 Waldock, Sixth Report on the Law of Treaties, 90 para 8. See also eg Nolte, Introductory Report on Treaties over Time, 205 ('the ICJ [in the *Temple* case] left considerable room for the parties to modify the treaty by way of subsequent conduct tacitly accepted or acquiesced to'). See further Section 3.2.

146 *Cameroon v Nigeria*, Judgment, paras 62 and 218, relating, respectively to the Chad and Bakassi areas (quoting Nigeria's submissions).

147 Ibid. para 68, citing *El Salvador/Honduras*, 408–9.

boundary. However, the Court added that, where a boundary has previously been delimited, preference must be given to the holder of the title in assessing whether practice amounts to conduct acquiescing in a change thereof.[148] This entails that, if there is no legal title to modify to begin with, subsequent (boundary) practice can more easily be determinative, whereas if there is a legal title, a presumption applies in favour of the title-holder. The Court ultimately found that Cameroon had not acquiesced in the abandonment of its title in relation to the areas of Lake Chad[149] and the Bakassi Peninsula.[150]

In relation to another area of the boundary, however, the Court, in effect, found that the parties had (tacitly) accepted that the area be delimited differently from the text of the relevant agreement.[151] As in previous cases, it concluded that the relevant agreement was to be 'interpreted' accordingly and did not refer to modification.[152] Not unlike the discussion in relation to *Temple of Préah Vihéar* above,[153] it could be argued here that the underlying agreements were incomplete, such that the resulting delimitation could not be properly effectuated without resorting to the parties' practice. This would mean that their subsequent practice, to the extent there was no treaty provision to modify in the first place, played a gap-filling rather than altering (that is, modifying) role, and that, even where it did modify, the modification was corrective of an inaccuracy in the underlying agreements, which would presumably lower the threshold for modification to occur. The case therefore constitutes an example of effective recognition of the possibility of treaty modification by subsequent practice, and, potentially, of an actual modification.

The *Cameroon v Nigeria* judgment also 'confirmed and clarified'[154] the view expressed by the Chamber in *El Salvador/Honduras* that States could, evidently, vary treaty-delimited boundaries between them by agreement through subsequent practice, and that such modification was sustained in light of the circumstances of the case:

> It was obviously open to those States to vary the boundaries between them by agreement; and some forms of activity, or inactivity, might amount to acquiescence in a boundary other than that of 1821. (...) The situation was susceptible of modification by acquiescence in the lengthy intervening period; and the Chamber finds that the conduct of Honduras from 1881 until 1972 may be regarded as amounting to such acquiescence in a boundary corresponding to the boundary between the Tepanguisir lands granted to Citala and those of Ocotepeque.[155]

These cases confirm—as a follow-up to the *Temple of Préah Vihéar* case above—that the subsequent practice of boundary States demonstrating their agreement on the course of a boundary inconsistent with the treaty 'may be recognized as an

[148] *Cameroon v Nigeria*, Judgment, para 68, citing *Burkina Faso/Republic of Mali*, para 63. See ibid. para 223. cf *Cameroon v Nigeria*, Dissenting Opinion of Judge Ajibola, para 52.

[149] Ibid. para 70.

[150] Ibid. paras 221–4.

[151] Ibid. paras 144–6.

[152] Ibid. para 146.

[153] See text to nn 124–5.

[154] MN Shaw, 'Self-Determination, Human Rights, and the Attribution of Territory' in U Fastenrath and others (eds), *From Bilateralism to Community Interest: Essays in Honour of Judge Bruno Simma* (OUP, 2011) 590, 606.

[155] *El Salvador/Honduras*, para 80.

authoritative alteration of the boundary',[156] and that the principle of stability of boundaries does not impede subsequent modification of a boundary agreed by the parties in derogation from the original treaty text.[157]

Sovereignty over Certain Frontier Land

The *Sovereignty over Certain Frontier Land*[158] case between Belgium and the Netherlands has also been cited as accepting modification by subsequent practice.[159] The case concerned sovereignty over two disputed plots of land. The Netherlands argued that even if sovereignty over the plots belonged to Belgium pursuant to the 1843 Boundary Convention, 'acts of sovereignty exercised by the Netherlands since 1843 have established sovereignty in the Netherlands.'[160] In response, the Court noted:

> This is a claim to sovereignty in derogation of title established by treaty. Under the Boundary Convention, sovereignty resided in Belgium. The question for the Court is whether Belgium has lost its sovereignty, by non-assertion of its rights and by acquiescence in acts of sovereignty alleged to have been exercised by the Netherlands at different times since 1843.[161]

The instances of subsequent practice invoked included maps, national survey documents and registers, taxation practices, legal proceedings, the application of domestic laws to houses on the plots, and the granting of a railway concession.[162] In assessing the weight of said instances, the Court noted the manifest 'difficulties confronting Belgium in detecting encroachments upon, and in exercising, its sovereignty over these two plots, surrounded as they were by Netherlands territory.'[163] Thus, it assessed whether Belgium's silence (lack of reaction) could be taken to constitute relevant practice evidencing its acquiescence in relinquishing its sovereignty. It also conversely took note of assertions of sovereignty by Belgium of which the Netherlands had been aware but which it did not repudiate—a lack of reaction that the Court assessed as relevant.[164] On this basis, it concluded that Belgium's sovereignty had not been extinguished.[165] Nevertheless, as in the *Cameroon v Nigeria* case and others, the Court recognized the possibility of a State acquiescing in a change in treaty title. In other words, although it did not sustain a modification by subsequent practice in the case, the Court once again effectively recognized the possibility that subsequent practice could, depending on the circumstances, modify the underlying bilateral boundary treaty.

[156] Shaw, 'Self-Determination', 606. See also *Cameroon v Nigeria*, Dissenting Opinion of Judge Ajibola, paras 52–3, 59, 61 ('this *effectivité* will serve a corrective or amending role in this case by modification, adjustment and variation as the case may be in all the relevant places').

[157] *Cameroon v Nigeria*, Dissenting Opinion of Judge Ajibola, para 62. See further Section 3.5.1(a) of this book.

[158] *Case concerning Sovereignty over Certain Frontier Land (Belgium/Netherlands)*, Judgment of 20 June 1959, ICJ Reports 209 [*Sovereignty over Certain Frontier Land*].

[159] Laursen, *Changing International Law*, 72.

[160] *Sovereignty over Certain Frontier Land*, 227. [161] Ibid. [162] Ibid. 227–9.

[163] Ibid. 229. [164] Ibid. 229–30. [165] Ibid. 227–30.

Gabčíkovo-Nagymaros Project

The case concerning the *Gabčíkovo-Nagymaros Project* may be an interesting counterfactual example. Hungary and Slovakia (Czechoslovakia at the time the treaty was signed[166]) had agreed, under a bilateral treaty dated 16 September 1977,[167] on the construction of a system of locks on the Danube, which constituted a significant part of the boundary between the two States. The main purpose of the project was to establish the joint operation of two hydroelectric power plants. In May 1989, for what it regarded as pertinent ecological and political reasons, the Hungarian government decided to suspend work on the project. After Hungary's material breach of the 1977 Treaty in refusing to continue the construction of the system of locks, and following a series of fruitless talks between the two governments, Czechoslovakia decided to take unilateral action by carrying out the operation of the so-called 'Gabčíkovo' system, which it referred to as the 'provisional solution' or 'Variant C'.[168] It did so despite the fact that the 'joint regime' represented a basic element under the terms of the treaty.[169]

The ICJ pointed out that Czechoslovakia's actions, '[i]n spite of having a certain external physical similarity with the original Project (...) thus differed sharply from it in its legal characteristics.'[170] Czechoslovakia was not interpreting and applying the treaty, but deviating from it, which amounted to a violation of its treaty obligations:

> The basic characteristic of the 1977 treaty is (...) to provide for the construction of the Gabčíkovo-Nagymaros System of Locks as a joint investment constituting a single and indivisible operational system of works. (...) By definition all this could not be carried out by unilateral action.
>
> (...) Czechoslovakia submitted that Variant C was essentially no more than what Hungary had already agreed to and that the only modifications made were those which had become necessary by virtue of Hungary's decision not to implement its treaty obligations. (...) The suspension and withdrawal of that [Hungary's] consent constituted a violation of Hungary's legal obligations, demonstrating, as it did, the refusal by Hungary of joint operation; but that cannot mean that Hungary forfeited its basic right to an equitable and reasonable sharing of the resources of an international watercourse.
>
> The Court accordingly concludes that Czechoslovakia, in putting Variant C into operation, was not applying the 1977 Treaty but, on the contrary, violated certain of its express provisions, and, in so doing, committed an internationally wrongful act.[171]

Thus, through their subsequent practice in the form of positive acts as well as omissions, both parties had undertaken steps diverging from the treaty, which, moreover, set up an objective regime with implications for third States.[172] The ICJ

[166] The succession of the Slovak Republic from the former Czechoslovakia took place in January 1993.
[167] 1977 Treaty on the Construction and Joint Operation of the Gabčíkovo-Nagymaros System of Locks on the Danube between Hungary and Czechoslovakia, 1109 UNTS 236.
[168] *Gabčíkovo-Nagymaros Project*, eg paras 72–4. [169] Ibid. paras 144–5.
[170] Ibid. para 77. [171] Ibid. paras 77–8.
[172] Ibid. para 123 ('The Treaty also established the navigational regime for an important sector of an international waterway (...). In so doing, it inescapably created a situation in which the interests of other users of the Danube were affected.').

had to address the question of whether and how this combined non-compliance had affected the legal regime. The continuous diverging practice of the parties could arguably have led to the desuetude of the 1977 Treaty. Indeed, Hungary maintained that the parties had, through their subsequent practice, agreed to terminate the treaty, and that 'a bilateral treaty repudiated by both parties cannot survive.'[173] This view seems extreme, however, since the parties disagreed as to their obligations under the treaty. Accordingly, the Court found that the treaty could not be terminated 'on grounds of reciprocal non-compliance'; this would have been otherwise had the parties' practice reflected their 'mutual consent' to terminate the treaty.[174] Thus, the treaty was still in force and continued to govern the parties' relations.[175] In other words, the subsequent practice did not amount to the parties' agreement to alter or terminate the treaty, but merely demonstrated their 'reciprocal wrongful conduct'.[176]

According to the Court, the subsequent practice and subsequent developments in question could not impact upon the operation and contents of the 1977 Treaty, which continued to govern the parties' rights and obligations, due to the fact that the very nature of the treaty prohibited unilateral action. This implied, in effect, that the subsequent factual conduct of the parties, in particular Czechoslovakia's 'provisional solution' could not be considered 'in the application of the treaty' (as a requirement for relevant subsequent practice) and thus did not affect the treaty regime.[177] Nolte supports this approach of treating 'subsequent mutual treaty violations'—which seem feasible only in the case of a bilateral treaty—as a modification of the 'factual situation' surrounding the treaty as opposed to an authentic interpretation or modification of the treaty by subsequent practice, arguing that a distinction must be made between subsequent practice in the sense of Article 31(3)(a) and (b), and 'other subsequent developments'.[178] The Court explained further:

The Court (...) cannot disregard the fact that the Treaty has not been fully implemented by either party for years, and indeed that their acts of commission and omission have contributed to creating the factual situation that now exists. Nor can it overlook that factual situation—or the practical possibilities and impossibilities to which it gives rise—when deciding on the legal requirements for the future conduct of the Parties.

This does not mean that facts—in this case facts which flow from wrongful conduct—determine the law. The principle *ex injuria jus non oritur* is sustained by the Court's finding that the legal relationship created by the 1977 Treaty is preserved and cannot in this case be treated as voided by unlawful conduct.

What is essential, therefore, is that the factual situation as it has developed since 1989 shall be placed within the context of the preserved and developing treaty relationship, in order to achieve its object and purpose in so far as that is feasible.[179]

[173] Ibid. para 114. [174] Ibid. [175] Ibid. para 132. [176] Ibid. para 114.

[177] See Nolte, Annex A, para 5 ('the conditions under which subsequent acts or developments can affect the existence or content of a treaty should be well defined.').

[178] Nolte, Introductory Report on Treaties over Time, 174–5. See further Section 2.3.4.

[179] Nolte, Introductory Report on Treaties over Time, para 133.

Thus, the Court incorporated the subsequent practice of the parties as 'factual context' into the legal framework of the 1977 Treaty, giving the practice relevance only to the extent that it accorded with the treaty regime. The Court based its reasoning on the 'flexibility of the treaty regime, as opposed to the general principle that allows adapting law to subsequent facts'.[180] This amounted to a 'judicial adjustment' of the 1977 Treaty as originally intended, which had become unsustainable in light of Czechoslovakia's unilateral implementation of 'Variant C', as well as new scientific developments and changes in environmental law.[181] By means of this 'integration' of the parties' subsequent practice into the existing treaty regime, the Court seems to have circumvented the issue of the possibility of modification. In fact, pursuant to the doctrine of 'approximate application'—which requires parties to redraft or reformulate the treaty when faced with a clear situation of breach 'to ensure its continued effective application'[182]—this approach could constitute an alternative treaty adaptation mechanism that rules out modification by subsequent practice.[183]

Fisheries Jurisdiction Cases

The 1974 *Fisheries Jurisdiction Cases*[184] provide further insight into how dispute settlement bodies deal with the issue of modification by subsequent customary law. Their relevance becomes clearer after examining the background of the dispute. Following the Second UN Conference on the Law of the Sea in 1960 (UNCLOS II), Iceland announced its intention to reserve the right of fishing within an area of 12 miles from its baselines exclusively for Icelandic fishermen, and to thereafter further extend this zone. It had already issued a Regulation to this effect on 30 June 1958.[185] The UK would not accept this measure and continued to allow its fishing vessels to enter the 12-mile zone, which sparked a series of incidents. After numerous negotiations between Iceland and the UK, a settlement was reached in 1961 in the form of an Exchange of Notes. It entailed that the UK would no longer object to the 12-mile fishery zone and in return would be granted fishing rights within that zone, subject to certain restrictions. In this Exchange of Notes, the UK recognized the 'exceptional dependence of the Icelandic nation upon coastal fisheries for their livelihood and economic development'.[186]

However, in 1971, Iceland declared that its agreements on fisheries jurisdiction with the UK, as well as with Germany, would be terminated. It went on to claim an extension of its fishery limits to 50 nautical miles. It did so despite the UK's objection that the Exchange of Notes was not open to unilateral termination and that Iceland's subsequent extension lacked any foundation in international law.[187]

[180] Orakhelashvili, *Interpretation of Acts and Rules*, 132.

[181] D Reichert-Facilides, 'Down the Danube: The Vienna Convention on the Law of Treaties and the *Case Concerning the Gabcïkov-Nagymaros Project*' (1998) 47 ICLQ 837.

[182] S Rosenne, *Breach of Treaty* (Grotius Publications, 1985) 100.

[183] See Section 3.5.2.

[184] *Fisheries Jurisdiction* (*UK v Iceland*), Merits, 3, and *Fisheries Jurisdiction* (*Federal Republic of Germany v Iceland*), Merits, Judgment of 25 July 1974, ICJ Reports 175.

[185] *Fisheries Jurisdiction* (*UK v Iceland*), Merits, para 23.

[186] Ibid. para 26.

[187] Ibid. paras 27–8.

Further negotiations with the Icelandic government proved fruitless. The UK was willing to accept preferential rights for Iceland due to its economic dependency on fishing, but could not agree on the extent and scope of these rights and the methods for their enforcement.[188] In accordance with the compromissory clause in the 1961 Exchange of Notes, the UK submitted the dispute to the ICJ in April 1972. The Court upheld jurisdiction in its Judgment of 2 February 1973, at which point it, too, emphasized 'the exceptional dependence of Iceland on its fisheries and the principle of conservation of fish stocks'.[189]

Due to increasingly frequent incidents between British and Icelandic vessels on the fishing grounds concerned, the two countries concluded an 'Interim Agreement' relating to fisheries in the disputed area in November 1973. This was adopted without prejudice to either of the parties' rights. The Court took these provisional measures into account in its Order of 12 July 1973.[190]

In its Judgment on the Merits of 25 July 1974, the ICJ began by examining the provisions of the 1958 Geneva Convention on the High Seas.[191] Article 2 provides that all nations have equal access to the high seas and that the freedom of the high seas applies likewise to coastal and non-coastal States, qualified only by 'reasonable regard' for the interests of other States.[192] Thus, there was no specific international law obligation in force at the time addressing the conservation of fish stocks on the high seas. Nor did the 1958 Territorial Sea Convention define the breadth of the territorial sea, leaving this point (and the related question regarding the fisheries jurisdiction of coastal States) unsettled at both the First UN Conference on the Law of the Sea in 1958 (UNCLOS I) and in 1960 at UNCLOS II. Interestingly, the ICJ pointed out that, since UNCLOS II, the law had evolved on the basis of near-agreements reached at the Conference:

> Two concepts have crystallized as customary law in recent years arising out of the general consensus revealed at that Conference. The first is the concept of the fishery zone, the area in which a State may claim exclusive fishery jurisdiction independently of its territorial sea; the extension of that fishery zone up to a 12-mile limit from the baselines appears now to be generally accepted. The second is the concept of preferential rights of fishing in adjacent waters in favour of the coastal State in a situation of special dependence on its coastal fisheries, this preference operating in regard to other States concerned in the exploitation of the same fisheries (...).[193]

The Court went on to explain the meaning and scope of 'preferential rights', as evidenced abundantly by State practice. It concluded that the Icelandic regulations, which aimed at setting up an exclusive fishery zone rather than merely claiming

[188] Ibid. para 32.

[189] *Fisheries Jurisdiction* (*UK v Iceland*), Jurisdiction, para 42. The Court had also implied this earlier in its Order indicating interim measures of protection—*Fisheries Jurisdiction* (*United Kingdom v Iceland*), Provisional Measures, Order of 17 August 1972, ICJ Reports 12.

[190] *Fisheries Jurisdiction* (*United Kingdom v Iceland*), Continuance of Interim Measures of Protection, Order of 12 July 1973, ICJ Reports 302, para 7.

[191] 1958 Convention on the High Seas (Geneva High Seas Convention), 450 UNTS 11. The Law of the Sea Convention had not been concluded at the time.

[192] *Fisheries Jurisdiction* (*UK v Iceland*), Merits, para 50.

[193] Ibid. para 52.

priority with regard to Iceland's fishing rights, exceeded the accepted limits of this concept.[194] This was found particularly true given the importance of fishing for the UK's economy, and in light of the lack of alternative fishing opportunities for the UK.[195] Iceland's unilateral claim was not justified, particularly since Iceland itself had acknowledged the UK's historic and special interests in the waters adjacent to its 12-mile zone.[196] The Court found that the UK was not under obligation to accept Iceland's claim to an exclusive fisheries zone extending 50 miles from the baselines, though Iceland did have preferential rights in the waters adjacent to the 12-mile limit.[197] Nor was the UK obliged to accept Iceland's unilateral termination of the 1961 Exchange of Notes agreement.[198] An equitable balance had to be struck between two co-existing sets of rights, neither of which were absolute: first, the preferential rights of coastal States, assessed with regard to their economic development and degree of dependency on fishing, and, second, the established rights of other fishing States, qualified by the coastal State's special dependence and the 'due regard' principle.[199]

This illustrates that new customary rules can emerge following economic changes or dissatisfaction with a treaty provision, resulting in a modification of the operation of a treaty rule. Specifically, the ICJ decided that, since the adoption of the High Seas Convention in 1958, the right of States to establish 12-mile fishing zones had crystallized into customary law. Moreover, it concluded that the 'preferential rights' principle had emerged through subsequent practice as a new customary rule deviating from Article 2(2) of the 1958 Convention, which does not specify any other restriction on the freedom of the high seas aside from the 'due regard' principle. These findings provide a clear case of supervening subsequent customary law significantly altering or supplementing a treaty provision, despite the fact that the ICJ seems to have only implicitly acknowledged the concept here.[200]

5.2.2 Ad hoc arbitral tribunals

Air Transport Services Arbitration (US/France)

A frequently cited instance of treaty modification by subsequent practice occurred in relation to the 1963 Award on the *Air Transport Services Arbitration (US/France)*.[201] The dispute before the Tribunal concerned the interpretation of the special unilateral procedure provided for in Section VII of the Annex to the 1946 'Air Services Agreement', a bilateral treaty between France and the United States regulating civil air flights between the two States.[202] In its decision, the Tribunal stated that the

194 Ibid. paras 61–2. 195 Ibid. para 64. 196 Ibid. para 65.

197 Ibid. The case must also be viewed in the (political) context of the negotiations ongoing at the time at UNCLOS III in relation to the emergence of the 200-mile zone.

198 Ibid. paras 67–8. 199 Ibid. para 71.

200 Villiger, *Customary International Law and Treaties* (1985), para 308. See also RR Churchill, 'The Fisheries Jurisdiction Cases: The Contribution of the International Court of Justice to the Debates on Coastal States' Fisheries Rights' (1975) 24 ICLQ 86.

201 *Air Transport Services Arbitration* (*US/France*), 5ff.

202 1946 Agreement with France on Air Transport Services, 61 Stat 3445.

special unilateral procedure 'cannot be used to add to a route points of call which, like those called into question in the present arbitration, do not come within the limits of the general path of the route'.[203] Otherwise, this would amount, both in terms of the literal meaning and the essential purpose of the provision, to a modification of the Annex and, accordingly, of the Agreement itself.[204] Thus, such a measure of adding 'points of call' could only be done on a consensual basis between the parties. The Tribunal found further confirmation of this interpretation of the Annex in the parties' subsequent practice.[205]

More importantly, however, with regard to the concession from 1955 onwards of the right to serve Tehran, the Tribunal noted that careful consideration must be given to the subsequent conduct of the parties in the application of the Agreement:

> This course of conduct may, in fact, be taken into account not merely as a means useful for interpreting the Agreement, but also as something more: that is, as a *possible source of a subsequent modification*, arising out of certain actions or certain attitudes, having a bearing on the juridical situation of the parties and on the rights that each of them could properly claim.[206]

In terms of the form of subsequent practice, the Tribunal specified that it was not solely referring to subsequent agreements (thus implicitly characterizing subsequent agreements as part of the broader concept of subsequent practice), such as Exchanges of Notes modifying the 1946 Agreement and the wording of Schedules of Routes, or Minutes of the negotiations:

> What the Tribunal particularly has in mind are cases where express or implied consent has been given to a certain claim or the exercise of a certain activity, or cases where an attitude (...) certainly has the same effects on the resulting juridical situation between the Parties as consent properly speaking would have.[207]

Following a detailed analysis of the parties' practice and the conferral of their implied consent, the Tribunal concluded as follows:

> Thus an analysis of the conduct of the Parties leads the Tribunal to conclude that, as a result of the attitude adopted by the French authorities from and after May 14, 1955, the right to serve Tehran via Paris, Rome, Beirut and Damascus had been established and could no longer be contested save in exceptional circumstances. But the Tribunal also believes that it should once again state that, in its opinion, *it was not by virtue of the Agreement of 27 March, 1946, but rather by virtue of an agreement that implicitly came into force at a later date*, that the right in question was in fact accorded; and precisely by the effect of the consent given by the French authorities from and after May 14, 1955 to the timetables (...) which made provision for the Tehran service, consent which was constantly confirmed by the attitude of these authorities in the course of the years that followed.[208]

[203] *Air Transport Services Arbitration* (*US/France*), 60. [204] Ibid.

[205] As was done prior to the VCLT, the Tribunal treated 'subsequent practice' only as a *supplementary* rather than primary means of interpretation. It was thus not deemed necessary to consider the practice of other States in applying analogous provisions contained in aviation agreements.

[206] *Air Transport Services Arbitration* (*US/France*), 62–3 (emphasis added). [207] Ibid. 63.

[208] Ibid. 66–7 (emphasis added).

The Tribunal therefore expressly recognized that the subsequent practice of the parties had altered the substance of the treaty. As in many of the aforementioned cases, the treaty in question constituted a bilateral, technical treaty, in relation to which tacit modification is both easier to identify and less controversial.[209]

Air Transport Services Arbitration (US/Italy)

The Award in the arbitration concerning the *Air Transport Services Arbitration (US/Italy)* involved somewhat similar issues to those in the *Air Transport Services Arbitration (US/France)*.[210] The main issue was whether the 1948 Agreement between the United States and Italy[211]—again, a bilateral, technical treaty—allowed for the operation of flights carrying cargo only ('all-cargo' flights). Italy argued that the phrase 'passengers, cargo *and* mail' in Section III of the Annex to the Agreement should be taken to refer to 'mixed' flights only, to the exclusion of all-cargo flights.

In analysing the parties' practice, the Tribunal noted that treaty interpretation by subsequent practice requires less time to become authoritative than a modification leading to the emergence of a bilateral customary rule, which requires constant practice sustained over a lengthier period:

> It is correct that only a constant practice, observed in fact and without change can constitute a rule of customary international law. (…) However, in the case in point the matter at issue is not to deduce a legal standard from the practice followed but merely to reveal the interpretation the parties gave to the provisions in dispute, which can serve as additional evidence in ascertaining the intentions of the parties and illustrate their intent as of the time the Agreement was concluded. For this purpose a shorter period of continuity is sufficient.[212]

However, the Tribunal seemed to imply that it was not the time element as such, but the degree of continuity of the practice over the period concerned, that mattered most in assessing the value of the practice: '[w]hat counts is that throughout the periods (…) the said practice was followed without exception. For this reason, continuity in practice cannot be denied.'[213] In this case, the parties in their practice had from the beginning treated all-cargo flights as being covered by the Agreement alongside 'mixed' flights also carrying passengers and mail.

The Tribunal indicated that these requirements apply more stringently for modification by subsequent practice than for interpretation. It referred specifically to the *Air Transport Services Arbitration (US/France)* in support of the possibility of a 'subsequent amendment' of the 1948 Agreement. However, it found that 'in the case before us neither the Tribunal nor the parties would wish to draw such a conclusion from the conduct of the parties.'[214] Based on a careful analysis of the text, context, practice of the parties, and other factors, which all pointed to the same conclusion,

[209] See eg Section 3.5.1.

[210] *Air Transport Services Arbitration (US/Italy)*, 75. See generally eg PB Larsen, 'The United States-Italy Air Transport Arbitration: Problems of Treaty Interpretation and Enforcement' (1967) 61 AJIL 496.

[211] Air Transport Agreement with Italy of 1948, 62 Stat 3729.

[212] Ibid. 100.

[213] Ibid.

[214] Ibid.

the Tribunal held that the 1948 Agreement permitted all-cargo services. The parties' practice was therefore shown to be in the interpretation of the treaty rather than going beyond it.

At times, the Tribunal seemed restrained with regard to the prospect of treaty change:

> It is not for the Tribunal to pronounce on the question of whether the disputed Agreement (...) still constitute[s] an appropriate, fair and equitable solution, in view of the development of civil aviation and the growing importance of all-cargo services. This question has not been submitted to the Tribunal; it is a question for Governments. If any amendment appears appropriate it can only be effected following negotiations between the two Governments and the conclusion of a new Agreement.[215]

Nevertheless, and although a modification was not sustained in this case, the Tribunal confirmed the holding in the *Air Transport Services Arbitration (US/France)* and the possibility of modification by subsequent practice more generally.

Taba Arbitration

The *Taba Arbitration* between Egypt and Israel concerned a bilateral boundary treaty, the 1906 Agreement.[216] It provided that the disputed demarcation pillars along the shared border of Egypt and Israel on the Sinai Peninsula should be erected at 'intervisible' points. The main point of contention between the parties concerned the 'Taba pillar', referred to as the 'final boundary pillar' under the Arbitration Agreement. The Tribunal ultimately interpreted the 'final pillar' to be located at a point termed the 'Parker pillar', which, contrary to the clear text, was *not* intervisible with the preceding pillar to its north.

The Tribunal acknowledged that the 1906 Agreement did not provide any exception to the rule of 'intervisibility' between the pillars. Nevertheless, it found that the location of the pillar had come to be recognized and accepted by the parties during the critical period,[217] as demonstrated by their subsequent practice in the application of the Agreement.[218] With regard to the subsequent practice in question, the Tribunal stated:

> [W]here the States concerned have, *over a period of more than fifty years*, identified a marker as a boundary pillar and acted upon that basis, it is no longer open to one of the Parties or to third States to challenge that long held assumption on the basis of an alleged error. The *principle of the stability of boundaries,* confirmed by the International Court of Justice [in the

[215] Ibid. 101.

[216] Agreement of Rafeh of 1 October 1906 between the Turkish Sultanate and the Egyptian Khediviate, concerning the Fixing of a Separating Administrative Line between the Vilayet of Hejaz and Governorate of Jerusalem and the Sinai Peninsula, 99 BFSP 482.

[217] The 'critical period' refers to the period in which the Mandate for Palestine was applicable, as approved by the Council of the League of Nations in July 1922, entering into force in September 1923, and lasting until May 1948, when the State of Israel came into existence.

[218] *Taba Arbitration*, para 237. The Tribunal provided evidence in support of the possibility that the two parties to the Agreement had themselves ignored the intervisibility requirement when construing the pillars—ibid. paras 236–7.

Temple of Préah Vihéar case] (...) requires that boundary markers, long accepted as such by the States concerned, should be respected and not open to challenge indefinitely on the basis of error.[219]

The respective boundary marker had been enforced over an extended period of time in a certain way, such that the original error could no longer be challenged, and could be taken to have been tacitly accepted or acquiesced in by the parties.[220] Although the Tribunal did not explicitly state that treaty provisions could, as a matter of *principle*, be altered by diverging subsequent practice, the sustained practice of the parties clearly seems to have modified the instrument, given the degree of clarity and precision, as well as the technical nature, of the provisions concerned.

Once again, the principle of stability of boundaries was used to argue that a boundary evidenced by subsequent practice prevailed over that indicated under the treaty.[221] The Tribunal argued that it would be going against this principle by altering the tacit agreement of the parties as to the location of the final pillar.[222] The significance of the sanctity of borders, especially in a case involving a territorial boundary, was reflected in the weight attached to the respective practice, in this case in relation to the erroneously labelled location of the disputed pillar. Thus, the Tribunal did not explicitly make reference to modification by subsequent practice, but rather upheld the modification by reason of the underlying existence of the stability of boundaries principle. The *Taba Arbitration* nevertheless provides another often-cited example of treaty modification by subsequent practice.

Eritrea-Ethiopia Arbitration

Subsequent practice also modified the treaty relations between the parties in the 2002 *Eritrea-Ethiopia Arbitration*.[223] At issue was the precise location of extensive parts of the shared boundary between the two States. Eritrea and Ethiopia concluded an Agreement on 12 December 2000 (the 'December Agreement')[224] establishing an Eritrea-Ethiopia Boundary Commission to settle the dispute. According to the Agreement, the Commission was to base its decision on the three relevant treaties of 1900,[225] 1902,[226] and 1908,[227] which together covered the entire boundary (the central, western, and eastern sectors, respectively), and on 'applicable international law'. The Commission interpreted the latter term broadly to take subsequent practice into account, not only as a means of treaty interpretation, but also as a potential

[219] Ibid. para 235 (emphasis added).

[220] See Section 2.3.5(b) on the notions of acquiescence and estoppel.

[221] See eg the analysis of the *Temple of Préah Vihéar* case in Section 5.2.1.

[222] *Taba Arbitration*, paras 210, 235.

[223] *Eritrea-Ethiopia Arbitration*, 110ff.

[224] Agreement between the Government of the Federal Democratic Republic of Ethiopia and the Government of the State of Eritrea 2000, 2138 UNTS 94.

[225] Frontier Delimitation Agreement of 10 July 1900, Ethiopia-Italy, 189 CTS 6.

[226] Treaty for the Delimitation of the Frontiers between Ethiopia and Eritrea and the Sudan of 15 May 1902, Ethiopia–Great Britain–Italy, 191 CTS 180.

[227] Convention between Ethiopia and Italy for the Settlement of the Frontier between the Italian Colony of Eritrea and Ethiopia of 16 May 1908, 207 CTS 28.

source of treaty modification. Its reference to subsequent practice went beyond the parameters set out in Article 31(3)(b) VCLT:[228]

> The function of such [subsequent] practice is not, it must be emphasised, relevant exclusively to the interpretation of the [1900, 1902, and 1908] Treaties. It is quite possible that practice or conduct may affect the legal relations of the Parties even though it cannot be said to be practice in the application of the Treaty or to constitute an agreement between them. As the Permanent Court of International Justice said in relation to loan agreements which, for present purposes, are analogous to treaties: 'If the subsequent conduct of the Parties is to be considered, it must be not to ascertain the terms of the loans, but whether the Parties by their conduct have altered or impaired their rights.'[229]

Citing the aforementioned *Namibia Advisory Opinion*, the Commission declared as a general principle that:

> [T]he effect of subsequent conduct may be so clear in relation to matters that appear to be the subject of a given treaty that the application of an otherwise pertinent treaty provision may be varied, or may even cease to control the situation, regardless of its original meaning.[230]

The Commission seemed to imply that treaty modification by subsequent practice can only be identified based on the specific context rather than based on objective or generalizable criteria, which gives dispute settlement bodies a considerable degree of discretion: '[t]he nature and extent of the conduct effective to produce a variation of the treaty is, of course, a matter of appreciation by the tribunal in each case.'[231] The Commission also referred to *Temple of Préah Vihéar* and the *Taba Arbitration* in support of the view that the parties' tacit agreement could modify even clear treaty provisions.[232] It explained that even the unilateral practice of a party to a bilateral treaty could come to modify it when certain elements are present, namely:

> [A]n act, course of conduct or omission by or under the authority of one party indicative of its view of the content of the applicable legal rule—*whether of treaty or customary origin*; the knowledge, actual or reasonably to be inferred, of the other party, of such conduct or omission; and a failure by the latter party within a reasonable time to reject, or dissociate itself from, the position taken by the first.[233]

The Commission thus also acknowledged the potential treaty modifying effect of new customary law. It reinforced this finding by reference to the *Kasikili/Sedudu Island* case,[234] which it interpreted in a rather striking way: it took it to mean that, within the scope of the applicable law clause in the parties' Compromis, it was

228 Specifically with regard to the Commission's statement that modifying practice 'cannot be said to be in the application of the Treaty or to constitute an agreement [between the parties]', it is submitted, as explained extensively in the preceding chapters, that such practice can still be in the application of the treaty and indeed *must* constitute the parties' agreement in order to have a modifying effect.

229 *Eritrea-Ethiopia Arbitration*, para 3.6, citing *Serbian Loans*, 38, where the PCIJ considered whether subsequent practice had led to the termination of a treaty obligation by way of estoppel, effectively recognizing the possibility of modification by subsequent practice (though not sustaining it in the case).

230 *Eritrea-Ethiopia Arbitration*, para 3.8.

231 Ibid. para 3.9.

232 Ibid. paras 3.9–3.10.

233 Ibid. para 3.9 (emphasis added).

234 Ibid. para 3.14, citing *Kasikili/Sedudu Island*, paras 91–3.

required to decide the case not only based on the rules of treaty interpretation, but also any customary norms with a bearing on the case, 'even if such rules might involve a departure from the position prescribed by the relevant treaty provisions'.[235] Although the Court in *Kasikili/Sedudu Island* did not find sufficient evidence to support such divergence, the Commission considered it significant that it had read the applicable law provision in a way that could allow for the variation of the treaty on the basis of customary rules on prescription.[236]

The Commission adopted a similarly wide interpretation of the scope of the 'applicable international law' clause in the Arbitration Agreement. It denied Ethiopia's claim that the boundary should be determined exclusively on the basis of the three treaties in question, as 'it is required also to apply those rules of international law applicable generally to the determination of disputed borders including, in particular, the rules relating to the effect of conduct of the parties'.[237] The Commission identified three broad categories of subsequent practice:[238] first, maps relating to the disputed area, second, diplomatic exchanges and records between the parties, and, third, any activities by a State—*effectivités*—comprising 'legislative, administrative or judicial assertions of authority over the disputed area (...) [for which] there is no set standard of duration and intensity'.[239] With regard to *effectivités*, it noted that:

> It is also important to bear in mind that conduct does not by itself produce an absolute and indefeasible title, but only a title relative to that of the competing State. The conduct of one Party must be measured against that of the other. Eventually, but not necessarily so, the legal result may be to vary a boundary established by a treaty.[240]

In light of these three types of subsequent practice, the Commission verified whether a departure from the boundary established by each of the three treaties was warranted. Most notable are its findings with regard to the 1900 Treaty, in relation to which the Commission upheld tacit modifications to the boundary in two regions of the covered sector.[241] With regard to the 1902 Treaty, it found that Italy's subsequent unilateral action, replacing one boundary point (the Sittona boundary) with another (the Mai Tomsa), had become binding upon Ethiopia by 1935. The Commission stated that this 1935 agreed boundary had not been altered since.[242] Lastly, in respect of the 1908 Treaty, the Commission found only a minor adjustment to the treaty boundary to be necessary.[243]

[235] Ibid.

[236] Ibid. cf MG Kohen, 'The Decision on the Delimitation of the Eritrea/Ethiopia Boundary of 13 April 2002: A Singular Approach to International Law Applicable to Territorial Disputes' in MG Kohen (ed), *Promoting Justice, Human Rights and Conflict Resolution through International Law: Liber Amicorum Lucius Caflisch* (Martinus Nijhoff, 2007) 767, 772.

[237] *Eritrea-Ethiopia Arbitration*, para 3.15.

[238] Ibid. paras 3.16–3.30.

[239] Ibid. para 3.29.

[240] Ibid.

[241] Ibid. paras 4.78, 4.85. First, the Commission made two alterations to the boundary on the western part of the 'Belesa' projection: the northern (Tserona) and southern (Acran region and Fort Cadorna) sections were placed in Eritrean territory. Second, regarding the 'Endeli' part of the boundary projection, the Commission upheld two further adjustments: one in respect of the town of Zalambessa, and the other in respect of the 'more southerly and easterly parts' of the projection, both of which were attributed to Ethiopia.

[242] Ibid. para 5.91.

[243] Ibid. para 6.32.

The Commission's approach has garnered criticism from some commentators, who argue that modification by subsequent practice is inappropriate in the context of boundary treaties, as it undermines presumptions in favour of, *inter alia*, the finality of boundaries.[244] Kohen considers the Commission's approach tantamount to saying that conventional boundaries must be confirmed through subsequent practice.[245] Admittedly, the Commission had liberal recourse to subsequent practice (including its reference to practice not necessarily 'in the application of the treaty' or constituting the parties' agreement[246]), as evidenced by its statement that it would examine the parties' subsequent practice to determine whether any variations or adjustments of the treaty boundaries were required.[247] Nevertheless, as discussed extensively in Chapter 3[248] and in relation to cases such as *Temple of Préah Vihéar, Cameroon v Nigeria*, and the *Taba Arbitration* above, the same principles of stability and finality can in fact be used, depending on the circumstances, precisely in order to uphold modifications of treaty boundaries by subsequent practice. There is thus no immediate reason why parties cannot subsequently rely on a different boundary in their mutual practice from which legitimate expectations may flow. The stringent requirements imposed upon such tacit agreements by subsequent practice ensure that the resulting boundary reflects the principles of stability and finality.

It should be noted that, rather than expressly acknowledging the treaty modification by subsequent practice, the Commission seems to have based the modification of the treaty provisions establishing the disputed boundary on 'underlying' customary norms, such as the principle of sovereignty over territory.[249] In this sense, the case also relates to the discussion in Chapter 4 regarding the overlap between subsequent practice and 'treaty-related' customary law.[250]

Anglo-French Continental Shelf Arbitration

In the 1977 *Arbitration on the Delimitation of the Continental Shelf* between the UK and France, the Court of Arbitration found that the 1958 Geneva Convention on the Continental Shelf was in force between the parties to the dispute.[251] This was contrary to France's argument that the treaty had been rendered obsolete by recent developments in customary international law, accelerated by UNCLOS III. However, the Court did concede the relevance of those customary developments:

> [T]he Court recognises both the importance of the evolution of the law of the sea which is now in progress and the possibility that a development in customary law may, under certain

[244] Kohen, 'Decision on the Delimitation of the Eritrea/Ethiopia Boundary', 772–3.

[245] Ibid. 772, citing P Weckel, 'Chronique de jurisprudence internationale, Cour permanente d'arbitrage, Commission du tracé de la frontière Erythrée-Ethiopie' (2002) 106 RGDIP 696.

[246] *Eritrea-Ethiopia Arbitration*, para 3.6, discussed at n 229. [247] Ibid. para 4.60.

[248] See Section 3.5.1(a).

[249] This is analogous to the principle of stability of boundaries referred to in the *Taba Arbitration*.

[250] See in particular Section 4.6. See also Section 4.5.1 on the notion of 'treaty-related' customary law.

[251] 1958 Convention on the Continental Shelf (Geneva Continental Shelf Convention), 499 UNTS 311.

conditions, evidence the assent of the States concerned to the modification, or even termination, of previously existing treaty rights and obligations.[252]

The Court further noted that, given how recently the 1958 Convention had entered into force at the time and indications that the parties also regarded it as an existing treaty in force, 'only the most conclusive indications of the intention of the parties to the 1958 Convention to regard it as terminated could warrant this Court in treating it as obsolete and inapplicable [between the parties]'.[253] The Court concluded that the subsequent practice in question and the developments at UNCLOS III did not evidence such agreement to the termination of the 1958 Convention.[254] As emphasized during the ILC discussions on the law of treaties, a new rule of customary law, with the exception of *jus cogens*, cannot supersede a pre-existing treaty provision without evidence of the intention to this effect of the parties to the treaty.[255] Most importantly, the Court here recognized the possibility of treaty modification and termination by subsequent practice, and, specifically, by subsequent customary law.[256]

Aminoil Arbitration

Another noteworthy case—applicable only by analogy to the present study because it concerned a contract granting oil concessions rather than a treaty—is the 1982 *Aminoil Arbitration*. Here, the Tribunal found that the parties, through their practice, had modified the very nature of the contract:

> While attributing its full value to the fundamental principle of *pacta sunt servanda*, the Tribunal has felt obliged to recognize that the contract of Concession has undergone great changes since 1948 (...). They were introduced into the contractual relations between the Government and Aminoil through the play of Article 9, or else as the result of at least tacit acceptances by the Company, which entered neither objections nor reservations in respect of them. These changes must not simply be viewed piece-meal, but on the basis of their total effect, and they brought about a metamorphosis in the whole character of the Concession.[257]

[252] *Anglo-French Continental Shelf Arbitration*, para 47.

[253] Ibid.

[254] Ibid.

[255] See Section 4.2.

[256] The Court then set out to consider the effect of France's reservations to Art 6 of the Continental Shelf Convention, dealing with delimitation between opposite and adjacent States. France claimed that the reservations were meant to ensure recourse to the customary law principles set out in *North Sea Continental Shelf*, but the UK objected, claiming instead that the legal principles contained in Art 6 were fully relevant to the boundary delimitation (*Anglo-French Continental Shelf Arbitration*, paras 49ff). The Court upheld the admissibility of the reservations, stating that they modified the legal effect of Art 6, rendering it inapplicable as between the two States to the extent of the reservations, as long as the result still rested upon an 'equitable' foundation (ibid. paras 55, 59–61). cf DW Bowett, 'Reservations to Non-restricted Multilateral Treaties' (1976) 48 BYBIL 67, 78. The Court found that with regard to other points Art 6 still applied to the delimitation, complemented by the customary law principles discussed in *North Sea Continental Shelf* (ibid. para 75). The Court thus based its conclusion on a 'merger' between the relevant rules of customary international law, the meaning of Art 6 of the Convention, and subsequent practice. See DA Colson, 'The United Kingdom-France Continental Shelf Arbitration' (1978) 72 AJIL 95, 111. See also AE Boyle, 'The Law of Treaties and the Anglo-French Continental Shelf Arbitration' (1980) 29 ICLQ 498.

[257] *Aminoil Arbitration*, para 97.

The 'total effect' of the changes had been to transform the very character and purpose of the agreement into an instrument essential to the country's economic and social process of development,[258] a fact that carried direct consequences for Aminoil's undertaking and the allocation of the parties' rights and interests.[259] The Tribunal considered that the parties were acting in accordance with the agreement as it stood at the time of application, and hence '[i]t is not a case of change involving a departure from a contract, but of a change in the nature of the contract itself, brought about by time, and the acquiescence or conduct of the Parties.'[260] Thus, the Tribunal concluded that at the time of the decision in 1977, the nationalization of Aminoil's enterprise could not be regarded as inconsistent with the contract as it stood at the time of application, on account of the latter's changed character.[261] The case indicates that external developments or third-party practice can play an important role in the interpretation and modification of an agreement, subject to the parties' consent thereto.[262]

Japanese House Tax Arbitration

The *Japanese House Tax Arbitration* concerned three bilateral treaties between Japan on the one side, and Germany (of 1896),[263] France (of 1896),[264] and Great Britain (of 1894)[265] on the other.[266] Based on those treaties, Japan had agreed to designate certain pieces of land for perpetual lease to foreign nationals and exempt the lands from further conditions such as taxes and charges not specified in the leases. The question was, as contended by Germany, France, and Great Britain, whether the *buildings* constructed on such land enjoyed the same exemptions as the land itself.[267]

The Tribunal treated the three treaties as basically the same instrument, without according significance to the differences in the text of the earlier treaty between Japan and Great Britain, as compared, in particular, to the later treaty between Japan and Germany. Namely, certain protective clauses contained in the 1894 Treaty with Great Britain were lacking in the 1896 Treaty with Germany. The Tribunal considered that 'the British Delegate, in presenting a draft drawn up on the basis of the said proposal, intended that a reservation should be made with regard to buildings',[268] and that 'it

[258] Ibid. para 98. [259] Ibid. para 99. [260] Ibid. para 101.

[261] Ibid. para 102.

[262] See eg Section 3.3.3(b) and generally Ch 4 on the impact of 'external customary law' on treaty provisions.

[263] Treaty of Commerce and Navigation between Japan and Germany of 4 April 1896 in *Treaties and Conventions between the Empire of Japan and Other Powers. Compiled by the Foreign Office* (ZP Maruya & Co, Ltd, 1899) 131.

[264] Treaty of Commerce and Navigation between Japan and France of 4 August 1896 in *Treaties and Conventions between the Empire of Japan and Other Powers. Compiled by the Foreign Office* (ZP Maruya & Co, Ltd, 1899) 267.

[265] Treaty of Commerce and Navigation between Japan and Great Britain of 16 July 1894 in *Treaties and Conventions between the Empire of Japan and Other Powers. Compiled by the Foreign Office* (ZP Maruya & Co Ltd, 1899) 37.

[266] *Japanese House Tax* (*France, Germany and Great Britain v Japan*), Award of 22 May 1905, 11 RIAA 51, available in English at <https://pca-cpa.org/en/cases/69/> accessed 25 May 2017.

[267] Ibid. 3. [268] Ibid. 4.

cannot be supposed that the German Government intended to renounce privileges conceded to Great Britain by the new Treaty, which would besides be incompatible with the clause securing most-favoured-nation treatment to Germany'.[269] The Tribunal based this on the parties' presumed intention and on the overall text of the treaty in its broader context, including the MFN clause.

In light of these considerations, Japan's practice, coupled with the earlier treaty between Japan and Great Britain containing the protective clauses in question, was found to have overridden the provisions in Japan's later treaties with Germany and France that limited the exemption from taxes to the leased land only. The Tribunal considered that 'the will of the parties consequently formed the law in the matter and, in order to ascertain how the instruments have really been interpreted, it is necessary to refer to the treatment to which the holders of the land have in fact been subjected'.[270] It concluded:

> [I]t is unquestionable that, in accordance with a practice which has not varied and which has existed for a long series of years, not only the land in question, but also the buildings erected on the land, have been exempt from all imposts, taxes, charges, contributions, or conditions whatsoever, other than those expressly stipulated in the leases in perpetuity.[271]

It should be noted that, although the Tribunal referred to the consistency and longevity of the practice, it did not account for the fact that the practice was not strictly 'in the application' of the respective treaties. However, since it seemed to treat the three treaties as the same instrument, practice in the application of one treaty was counted as relevant in interpreting the others. Thus, subsequent practice was taken to have overridden or otherwise extended the text of the later treaties concluded by Japan with Germany and France. The Tribunal referred to the prior 1894 Treaty between Japan and Great Britain—in an application of the *lex priori* principle—as a basis for the prevailing reading of the subsequent two treaties. In this sense, the case is not only a potential example of modification (in the form of an alteration *or* extension) by subsequent practice of the treaties with Germany and France, but also an example of the use of subsequent practice to confirm and shed light on the original intention of the parties to the prior treaty between Japan and Great Britain. Moreover, the subsequent practice had the effect of *supplementing* the 1894 Treaty between Japan and Great Britain, by leading to the conclusion that:

> The provisions of the Treaties (...) exempt not only the land held in virtue of the leases in perpetuity granted by or on behalf of the Government of Japan, but they exempt the land and buildings of every description constructed or which may hereafter be constructed on such land, from all imposts, taxes, charges, contributions, or conditions whatsoever, other than those expressly stipulated in the leases in question.[272]

The Tribunal also stated that if the parties had wanted to override this conclusion arrived at on the basis of established practice (and of the inference of what the parties to the later two treaties could have intended), they would have had to explicitly stipulate that the scope of the exemption from taxes and charges would be limited

[269] Ibid. 5. [270] Ibid. 4. [271] Ibid. [272] Ibid. 5.

only to the land itself: 'in the clauses in question, the Powers have not spoken of land, as they must necessarily have done if the immunity, *contrary to the practice obtaining up to then,* was to be restricted to the land'.[273]

In sum, it appears not only that the later treaties were modified, but that the earlier treaty with Great Britain was supplemented—or at least, according to another reading, clarified or interpreted—by subsequent practice. However, the Tribunal did not make any explicit reference to the process of modification by subsequent practice. Rather, it equated the three different treaties with Japan as 'one' treaty, and proceeded to analyse their meaning according to the intention of the parties, stating, *inter alia*, that the parties 'used expressions wide enough to include the whole situation created by the leases for the lessees'[274] (a feature that can constitute an in-built treaty adaptation mechanism[275]). In other words, although this may be a situation where subsequent practice modified the respective treaty provisions, the Tribunal implicitly characterized it as an interpretation thereof.

5.2.3 Courts and tribunals under special regimes

5.2.3a European Court of Human Rights

Capital punishment cases

The landmark judgment of the European Court of Human Rights in *Soering v UK* is an important example of a pronouncement in relation to subsequent practice of a dispute settlement body operating within a special treaty regime—in this case, a major human rights regime. The Court was faced here with the question of whether the extradition of a German citizen, Jan Soering, by the United Kingdom to the United States to face capital murder charges—which the Court referred to as the 'death row phenomenon'[276]—amounted to a breach of Article 3 of the ECHR on the prohibition of torture and inhuman and degrading treatment.[277] Since the Convention had to be read as a whole, Article 3 had to be interpreted in harmony with Article 2(1) ECHR on the 'right to life (...), save in the execution of a sentence of a court following his conviction of a crime for which this penalty is provided by law'.[278] This meant that Article 3 could not be interpreted as generally prohibiting the death penalty.

Most significant in the present context is the Court's *obiter dictum* expressly accepting that an established practice among the parties to the ECHR could give rise to an amendment of the Convention; that is, a modification by subsequent practice. Specifically, it held that a general abolition of capital punishment reflected in

[273] Ibid. (emphasis added). [274] Ibid. [275] See Section 3.5.2.

[276] *Soering v UK*, para 105.

[277] The ECHR does not have an express provision on non-refoulement, but the Court considers it 'inherent' in Art 3, as reaffirmed in cases concerning not only extradition but also immigration (see eg *Cruz Varas and others v Sweden* App no 15576/89 (ECtHR, 20 March 1991) paras 69–70; *Vilvarajah and others v United Kingdom* App nos 13163/87, 13164/87, 13165/87, 13447/87, 13448/87 (ECtHR, 30 October 1991) [*Vilvarajah and others v UK*] para 103). This could potentially also constitute an example of informal supplementation or alteration of the Convention.

[278] *Soering v UK*, para 103.

the parties' national penal policies could constitute subsequent practice establishing their agreement to abrogate the exception in Article 2(1) ECHR, 'and hence to remove a textual limit on the scope for evolutive interpretation of Article 3'.[279] This touches upon the relationship discussed between evolutionary interpretation and modification by subsequent practice, highlighting the latter's capacity to go beyond even the most dynamic forms of interpretation.[280]

However, since the Parties to the ECHR had chosen to follow the formal procedure for amending the text of the Convention by means of an optional instrument, 'Protocol No. 6',[281] regarding the abolishment of the death penalty in peacetime, the Court ultimately saw no need to pronounce a final ruling on whether the practice of the parties had tacitly led to a change in the respective provisions:

> Protocol No. 6, as a subsequent written agreement, shows that the intention of the Contracting Parties (…) was to adopt the normal method of amendment of the text in order to introduce a new obligation to abolish capital punishment in time of peace and, what is more, to do so by an optional instrument allowing each State to choose the moment when to undertake such an engagement. In these conditions, notwithstanding the special character of the Convention (…) Article 3 cannot be interpreted as generally prohibiting the death penalty.[282]

The potential for treaty modification by subsequent practice, again with regard to the death penalty, was reaffirmed by both the Chamber[283] and Grand Chamber[284] in *Öcalan v Turkey*. While in *Soering v UK* the Court had recognized the *possibility* of modification by subsequent practice, here it recognized that a modification had occurred. The parties' subsequent practice was now even more pronounced than at the time of the *Soering v UK* judgment, and a considerable amount of time had passed, which set the scene for *Öcalan v Turkey*:

> [T]he concepts of inhuman and degrading treatment and punishment have evolved considerably since the Convention came into force in 1950 and indeed since the Court's *Soering v the United Kingdom* judgment in 1989. (…) Equally the Court observes that the legal position as regards the death penalty has undergone a considerable evolution since the *Soering* case was decided.[285]

The ECtHR looked at the national practice of the parties as well as that of the Council of Europe. Although the *ratification* of Protocol No. 6 was not completely unanimous, its unanimous *signature*, coupled with the *de jure* (in 43 States) and *de facto* (Russia's moratorium) abolition of the death penalty in all the parties' territories, was sufficient to constitute subsequent practice capable of modifying the Convention.[286] This carried implications for Article 2(1) ECHR:

[279] Ibid. See also Section 2.5.3, text to n 690.

[280] See Section 2.5.3. See also eg *Johnston and others v Ireland*, para 53.

[281] Protocol No 6 to the Convention for the Protection of Human Rights and Fundamental Freedoms concerning the Abolition of the Death Penalty (28 April 1983) CETS No 114.

[282] *Soering v UK*, para 103.

[283] *Öcalan v Turkey*, paras 192–8.

[284] *Öcalan v Turkey* (Grand Chamber Judgment), para 163.

[285] Ibid. citing *Öcalan v Turkey*, paras 194–5.

[286] Ibid. para 195.

Such a marked development could now be taken as signaling the *agreement of the Contracting States to abrogate, or at the very least to modify*, the second sentence of Article 2 § 1 (...). It may be questioned whether it is necessary to await ratification of Protocol No. 6 by the three remaining States before concluding that the death penalty exception in Article 2 has been significantly modified. Against such a consistent background, it can be said that capital punishment in peacetime has come to be regarded as an unacceptable (...) form of punishment that is no longer permissible under Article 2.[287]

This reasoning is particularly noteworthy in light of the fact that, as discussed, already triggered formal amendment procedures give rise to a strong presumption against a parallel modification by subsequent practice.[288] The decision reveals the Court's liberal approach towards subsequent practice—one that may at times potentially stray from the strict requirements for modification by subsequent practice. The ECtHR's willingness to presume the existence of agreement among all the parties to abolish capital punishment, despite the fact that three States had not ratified the Protocol (Turkey, Armenia, and Russia) and one party had not officially abolished the death penalty (Russia), may be seen as far-reaching. The judgment also illustrates how subsequent practice and evolutionary interpretation—in this case, with regard to the notions in Article 3 ECHR—can be mutually reinforcing.

Even here, the Court did not actually sustain the modification by subsequent practice identified, due to the fact that the use of the death penalty in times of war had not yet been ruled out by practice. This was reflected in the fact that, at the time of the judgment, 'Protocol No. 13'[289] on the abolishment of the death penalty in all circumstances (including in times of war) was not yet unanimously supported by the parties. However, the Court predicted a trend in the direction of an actual modification of the Convention:

The Court notes that by opening for signature Protocol No. 13 concerning the abolition of the death penalty in all circumstances the Contracting States have chosen the traditional method of amendment of the text of the Convention in pursuit of their policy of abolition. At the date of this judgment, three member States have not signed this Protocol and sixteen have yet to ratify it. However, this final step towards complete abolition of the death penalty—that is to say both in times of peace and in times of war—can be seen as confirmation of the abolitionist trend in the practice of the Contracting States. It does not necessarily run counter to the view that Article 2 has been amended in so far as it permits the death penalty in times of peace. (...) For the time being, the fact that there is still a large number of States who have yet to sign or ratify Protocol No. 13 may prevent the Court from finding that it is the established practice of the Contracting States to regard the implementation of the death penalty as inhuman and degrading treatment contrary to Article 3 of the Convention, since no derogation may be made from that provision, even in times of war.[290]

[287] Ibid. para 196 (emphasis added). [288] See Section 3.3.4.

[289] Protocol No 13 to the Convention for the Protection of Human Rights and Fundamental Freedoms, concerning the Abolition of the Death Penalty in all Circumstances (3 May 2002) CETS No 187.

[290] *Öcalan v Turkey* (Grand Chamber Judgment), paras 164–5.

In turn, this judgment set the scene for the Court's subsequent ruling in *Al-Saadoon and Mufdhi v UK*, just as *Soering v UK* had done for *Öcalan v Turkey*. At issue once again was whether the transfer of a person, an Iraqi citizen, by a State party to the Convention (the UK) to a non-party (Iraq), where he would face the risk of the death penalty, was permissible under Article 3 ECHR, read in light of Article 2 ECHR. Recalling its 1989 judgment in *Soering v UK*, the Court reiterated that 'an established practice within the member States could give rise to an amendment of the Convention'.[291] However, based on the fact that the parties' subsequent practice had evolved even further, the Court now reached a different conclusion:

> [T]he Grand Chamber in *Öcalan* did not exclude that Article 2 had already been amended so as to remove the exception permitting the death penalty. Moreover, as noted above, the position has evolved since then. All but two of the Member States have now signed Protocol No. 13 and all but three of the States which have signed have ratified it. These figures, together with consistent State practice in observing the moratorium on capital punishment, are strongly indicative that Article 2 has been amended so as to prohibit the death penalty in all circumstances. Against this background, the Court does not consider that the wording of the second sentence of Article 2 § 1 continues to act as a bar to its interpreting the words 'inhuman or degrading treatment or punishment' in Article 3 as including the death penalty (...).[292]

The Court therefore relied on the fact that *most* parties had signed *and* ratified the Protocol—observing simply that 'Azerbaijan and Russia are alone in not having signed the Protocol'[293]—coupled with the fact that they *all* observed the 'moratorium' on capital punishment. Once again, the Court's approach was liberal to consider the parties' practice unanimous in establishing their agreement to modify Article 2 ECHR—*despite* the fact that two States had not signed, and three had not ratified, the respective Protocol, as well as the strong presumption against modification in situations in which formal amendment procedures have been initiated. As a consequence, the transfer of a person by a party to the ECHR, even in time of war, to a country where they would face a real risk of the death penalty, amounted to a violation of Article 3 ECHR. This provision could potentially lead, or may already have led, to the creation of a special or regional customary norm on the subject.[294]

The Court's approach may still leave open the question of whether the practice occurred in relation to the treaty and in fulfilment of a legal obligation (for instance, with regard to the moratorium), which the Court seemed to presume, or whether it was motivated by other considerations or beliefs.[295] However, the fact that the practice occurred so explicitly makes the parties' stance with regard to capital punishment sufficiently manifest and overcomes the fact that formal amendment procedures were already triggered. This illustrates how subsequent practice can displace formal amendment procedures,[296] although, as the procedures were not yet

[291] *Al-Saadoon and Mufdhi v UK*, para 119.

[292] Ibid. para 120.

[293] Ibid. para 117.

[294] See eg AC Emilianides, 'Can the European Convention on Human Rights be Modified by Subsequent Customary Law?' (2006) CYBIR 83, 93.

[295] Nolte, Second Report on Treaties over Time, 265–6.

[296] Ibid. 268. cf ibid. 265.

complete at the time of the modification, it could also be taken to demonstrate that the two means of treaty adaptation should not be regarded as mutually exclusive.

The extent to which the Court's reasoning is generalizable to other treaties, given the special nature of the ECHR, depends on the weight accorded to the nature of the treaty regime and constituency in question. The ECHR is a human rights treaty, a type of treaty that is inherently dynamic[297] (hence the reference to a 'living instrument'[298]), with a relatively homogeneous set of parties among which agreement by subsequent practice is easier to achieve.[299] The capital punishment cases do show the Court's awareness of the elements required for subsequent practice,[300] especially when it comes to its modifying effect[301]—namely, determinacy, the degree to which the practice is common and consistent (which is, in itself, a requirement stricter than necessary[302]), and its ability to establish agreement of all the parties, though perhaps less with regard to making explicit whether the practice is 'in the application of the treaty'.[303] From this perspective, the Court's approach to subsequent practice is applicable also outside of the ECHR regime.

Hassan v UK

A recent ECtHR case to expressly confirm modification by subsequent practice is *Hassan v UK*, where the Court was faced with a request by the UK to disapply or interpret Article 5 ECHR (right to liberty and security) in light of powers of detention under international humanitarian law.[304] In the absence of derogation based on Article 15 ECHR, the UK argued that Article 5 had been modified to allow for the capture and detention of actual or suspected combatants in accordance with the Third and Fourth Geneva Conventions. The Court, among other things, considered that the absence of derogation from Article 5 ECHR in States' practice when detaining in the context of international armed conflicts (viewed also in light of Article 31(3)(c) VCLT on other relevant rules) indicates that the provision is not deemed to exclude detentions pursuant to international humanitarian law:

> [T]he Court has previously stated that a consistent practice on the part of the High Contracting Parties, subsequent to their ratification of the Convention, could be taken as establishing their agreement not only as regards interpretation but even to modify the text of the Convention. (...) The practice of the High Contracting Parties is not to derogate from their obligations under Article 5 in order to detain persons on the basis of the Third and Fourth Geneva Conventions during international armed conflicts. (...) [And] although there have been a number of military missions involving Contracting States acting extraterritorially since their ratification of the Convention, no State has ever made a derogation

[297] See eg Sections 2.5.3 and 3.5.1. [298] See Section 5.2.5.

[299] See R Bernhardt, 'The Convention and Domestic Law' in R Macdonald and F Matscher (eds), *The European System for the Protection of Human Rights* (Martinus Nijhoff, 1993) 35.

[300] See generally Section 2.3.

[301] For an analysis of the Court's 'softened requirement of a common agreement' and 'of a sufficiently determinate position', see Nolte, Second Report on Treaties over Time, 266–8. See also eg L Helfer, 'Consensus, Coherence and the European Convention on Human Rights' (1993) 26 Cornell ILJ 140; P Carozza, 'Uses and Misuses of Comparative Law in International Human Rights: Some Reflections on the Jurisprudence of the European Court of Human Rights' (1998) 73 Notre Dame L Rev 1217, 1224ff.

[302] See Section 2.3.5(c), text to nn 463–6.

[303] Nolte, Second Report on Treaties over Time, 266. [304] *Hassan v UK*, para 99.

pursuant to Article 15 of the Convention in respect of these activities (...) Moreover, it would appear that the practice of not lodging derogations under Article 15 of the Convention in respect of detention under the Third and Fourth Geneva Conventions during international armed conflicts is mirrored by State practice in relation to the International Covenant for the Protection of Civil and Political Rights. (...) [N]o State has explicitly derogated under Article 4 of the Covenant in respect of such detention (...).[305]

Thus, according to the Court, Article 5 ECHR was modified to allow for detentions in conformity with the Third and Fourth Geneva Conventions. That this result falls within the realm of modification rather than interpretation is clear based on the text of Article 5 itself, which provides in no uncertain terms that '[n]o one shall be deprived of his liberty save in the following cases', and proceeds to list six specific grounds for detention. In light of this express and seemingly exhaustive list, the (tacit) addition, by subsequent practice, of detention pursuant to international humanitarian law to the list of grounds of permitted deprivation of liberty, constitutes a modification (in the form of an alteration or, more likely, an extension[306]) of Article 5 ECHR.[307] This is further confirmed by the critical remarks of the four dissenting judges on the case that the powers under the Third and Fourth Geneva Conventions 'are in direct conflict' with[308] and 'flatly' contradict the nature of[309] Article 5(1) of the Convention:

[O]n the facts of this case, the powers of internment under the Third and Fourth Geneva Conventions (...) are in direct conflict with Article 5 § 1 of the Convention. (...) By attempting to *reconcile the irreconcilable*, the majority's finding today does not, with respect, reflect an accurate understanding of the scope and substance of the fundamental right to liberty under the Convention (...).[310]

In line with this Dissenting Opinion, certain commentators have questioned whether the Court's approach was not too far-reaching:

[T]he Court's reinterpretation of Article 5 is tantamount to its amendment, and puts some states that have started to criticize the Court for an extravagant approach to interpretation (e.g. the UK) in a somewhat curious position—approval for the result in *Hassan* (which the UK did win, even if not in the way it wanted to win) may also be seen as approval for the Court's own interpretative self-empowerment.[311]

An issue with the Court's analysis of subsequent practice is its deduction of the modifying intent *inter alia* from the absence of derogations under Article 5 ECHR—the

[305] Ibid. para 101. [306] See text to ns 323–5 on non-regression.

[307] See *Hassan v United Kingdom* [GC] App no 29750/09 (ECtHR, 16 September 2014) (Partly Dissenting Opinion of Judge Spano Joined by Judges Nicolaou, Bianku and Kalaydjieva) [*Hassan v UK*, Dissenting Opinion] 66 ('It effectively disapplies or displaces the fundamental safeguards underlying the exhaustive and narrowly interpreted grounds for permissible detention under the Convention by judicially creating a new, unwritten ground for a deprivation of liberty (...) in direct conflict with the Convention provision.').

[308] Ibid. [309] Ibid. 65. [310] Ibid. 66 (emphasis in the original).

[311] M Milanovic, 'A Few Thoughts on Hassan v. United Kingdom' (*EJIL: Talk!*, 22 October 2014) <www.ejiltalk.org/a-few-thoughts-on-hassan-v-united-kingdom/> accessed 26 May 2017.

practice in question constituted solely 'negative' conduct.[312] This ties in with the difficulty of determining whether practice in cases of silence is *in the application of the treaty* and evidences the *parties' intention to modify it*, and the resulting need to exercise caution when drawing inferences from acts of omission.[313] Thus, it is difficult to say whether, for one thing, States' lack of notifications under Article 15 ECHR in relation to Article 5 detentions constitutes practice in relation to the Convention evidencing their agreement to modify the provision: 'in the present case it is hard to see how a practice of not performing a formal requirement can be linked to the application of the ECHR'.[314] The absence of derogations may be explained by other reasons,[315] such as not wanting to concede extraterritoriality of the Convention.[316]

Moreover, the Court referred to the practice of States parties to the ICCPR to compare State conduct in similar situations in relation to other agreements.[317] Such practice is in principle not directly relevant to the analysis of potentially modifying subsequent practice in relation to the ECHR, especially since it includes the practice of third States, and, moreover, relates to a provision that differs in wording and scope from the Convention.[318] It could, however, be argued that, to the extent that the ECHR parties are concerned, their practice under one instrument could indicate their intention in relation to the other, and that, in any case, the practice of third States can also provide an indication of emerging modifications, particularly in cases involving fundamental provisions.[319] However, the Court did not specify whose State practice it was referring to or how this point fits in with the requisite elements for subsequent practice under the VCLT.[320]

The Court's highly liberal approach is, again, especially notable in light of the nature of the ECHR as a human rights treaty with third-party beneficiaries, which entails a higher threshold for modification and signals that any potential modifications, particularly those to the detriment of the rights-holders, must be assessed very carefully.[321] Such 'non-regression' considerations were also implicit in the Dissenting Opinion:

> Furthermore, and most importantly in my view, in assessing whether a State practice fulfils the criteria flowing from Article 31 § 3 (b), and thus plausibly modifies the text of the Convention (...), there is, on the one hand, a fundamental difference between a State

[312] L Crema, 'Subsequent Practice in Hassan v United Kingdom: When Things Seem to Go Wrong in the Life of a Living Instrument' (2015) 15 QIL 3, 9.

[313] See eg Sections 2.3.5(a) and 3.3.3(b).

[314] Crema, 'Hassan v United Kingdom', 10.

[315] See eg L Hill-Cawthorne, 'The Grand Chamber Judgment in Hassan v UK' (*EJIL: Talk!*, 16 September 2014) <www.ejiltalk.org/the-grand-chamber-judgment-in-hassan-v-uk/> accessed 26 May 2017; C De Koker, '*Hassan v United Kingdom*: The Interaction of Human Rights Law and International Humanitarian Law with regard to the Deprivation of Liberty in Armed Conflicts' (2015) 31 Utrecht J Intl & Eur L 90, 94.

[316] Hill-Cawthorne, 'Hassan v UK', citing *Hassan v UK*, Dissenting Opinion, paras 61–2.

[317] *Hassan v UK*, para 101.

[318] *Hassan v UK*, Dissenting Opinion, 63.

[319] See eg Section 3.3.3(b).

[320] See E Bjorge, 'What is Living and What is Dead in the European Convention on Human Rights? A Comment on *Hassan v United Kingdom*' (2015) 15 QIL 23, 35–6 ('Whilst (...) subsequent practice could legitimately lead to the kind of extreme interpretative results which were the outcome in *Hassan* (...) it is far from clear that the requisite practice was actually obtained in *Hassan*.').

[321] See eg Section 3.5.1(a).

practice clearly manifesting a concordant, common and consistent will of the Member States to collectively modify the fundamental rights enshrined in the Convention, towards a more *expansive or generous understanding of their scope than originally envisaged*, and, on the other, a State practice that *limits or restricts those rights*, as in the present case, in direct contravention of an exhaustive and narrowly tailed limitation clause of the Convention protecting a fundamental right.[322]

It is debatable whether the modification in question amounts to a case of regression:

[T]he *Hassan* decision does not seem to fit the description of a regressive interpretation of the Convention. The Court decided to fix one of the issues arising from the application of the Convention in conflicts abroad, a situation not foreseen when the Convention was adopted, and to which Article 15 was not written to apply. (…) By saying that the concept of lawful in Article 5(1) also covers a IHL during conflicts abroad, the Court did not lower the protection of the individual, but adjusted the applicability of the Convention to a new situation not envisaged by its drafters.[323]

If it is accepted that the modification relates to an unforeseen situation in the ECHR, it likely constitutes an *extension* rather than an alteration of the treaty.[324]

Once again, the Court did not analyse these various aspects in detail, but rather referred to the practice in generic terms.[325] The four dissenting judges on the case, who, by contrast, took a restrictive view towards subsequent practice, considered the Court's approach in the previous capital punishment cases to be more cautious than in *Hassan v UK*, which supposedly strayed further from the criteria in Article 31(3)(b) VCLT.[326] Other commentators, present author included, consider the decision overall consistent with the Court's—albeit highly liberal—approach towards subsequent practice in its previous decisions, although it may not be an approach commonly found in the decisions of other dispute settlement bodies.[327]

5.2.3b Iran-US Claims Tribunal

The Iran-US Claims Tribunal functions in a bilateral setting that can be classified as an international economic regime. Given the sheer volume of its caseload (thousands of cases), its longevity (since 1981), and its established case law, the Tribunal cannot be qualified as 'ad hoc' in the sense of the examples explored in Section 5.2.2 above.[328] Established as part of the resolution of the Iran hostage crisis, with its jurisdictional basis founded upon the Claims Settlement Declaration (CSD) under the Algiers Accords,[329] the Tribunal deals with inter-State cases as well as those involving

322 *Hassan v UK*, Dissenting Opinion, 63 (emphasis in the original).
323 Crema, 'Hassan v United Kingdom', 21–2 (footnotes omitted).
324 See further Section 3.3.1.
325 Crema, 'Hassan v United Kingdom', 9.
326 *Hassan v UK*, Dissenting Opinion, 63.
327 Crema, 'Hassan v United Kingdom', 10. See also eg A Mowbray, 'The Creativity of the European Court of Human Rights' (2005) 5 HR L Rev 57.
328 Nolte, Second Report on Treaties over Time, 226.
329 Declaration of the Government of the Democratic and Popular Republic of Algeria Concerning the Settlement of Claims by the Government of the United States of America and the Government of the Islamic Republic of Iran 1981 (1981) 20 ILM 223, 230 (Claims Settlement Declaration, Algiers Accords).

non-State actors regarding large financial claims between, on the one hand, the United States and its nationals, and, on the other, Iran and its nationals.[330]

In a 2004 case dealing with an inter-State claim between Iran and the US, Iran's first preliminary objection was that the Iran-US Tribunal did not have jurisdiction to hear 'official counterclaims' under the CSD.[331] In an *obiter dictum*, the Tribunal first recognized the treaty modifying potential of subsequent practice and agreements:

> [I]f the two Parties that created the Tribunal, i.e., Iran and the United States, were to agree to submit a case to the Tribunal, then this would arguably be sufficient to grant the Tribunal jurisdiction over such case [concerning matters not conferred on it by the Algiers Declarations], as it would constitute an international agreement modifying the Algiers Declarations with respect to the particular case. But this is not the issue here.[332]

In casu, the Tribunal found that the parties' subsequent practice had led only to an *interpretation* of Article II(2) of the CSD, providing the Tribunal with jurisdiction to hear official counterclaims. Article II(2) grants the Tribunal jurisdiction over 'official claims of the United States and Iran against each other arising out of contractual arrangements between them for the purchase and sale of goods and services'. The provision makes no mention of the ability to bring counterclaims, nor can this possibility be derived from the context or object and purpose of the provision.[333] However, the Tribunal found decisive support for such an ability in the parties' subsequent practice,[334] which demonstrated 'their common understanding that such counterclaims were allowed'.[335] The Tribunal thus also rejected Iran's argument regarding the principle of restrictive interpretation of provisions conferring jurisdiction.[336] Iran's argument nevertheless remains a valid question as to whether the threshold for subsequent practice is higher in relation to jurisdictional provisions as a special type of treaty provision. Moreover, the question remains whether the Tribunal's expansive interpretation of Article II(2), the content of which it supplemented by means of the parties' subsequent practice, does not border on modification in the form of a significant extension.[337]

Iran also raised the question of the significance of practice not intended by the acting State as legally relevant. Namely, it argued that the submission of official counterclaims by the parties did not constitute relevant subsequent practice in the sense of Article 31(3)(b) VCLT since these were purely part of a 'defence strategy'.[338] This also relates to the issue of determinacy of practice discussed in Chapter 2, especially with regard to positions taken in the context of legal proceedings.[339] The Tribunal rejected Iran's argument, *inter alia* on the grounds that the subjective intention of the parties is not pertinent to the process of identifying relevant subsequent practice.[340] Although the Tribunal's assertion regarding the irrelevance of the

[330] See further eg G Aldrich, *The Jurisprudence of the Iran-United States Claims Tribunal* (Clarendon Press, 1996).
[331] *Iran and USA*, Interlocutory Award No ITL 83-B1-FT, para 15.
[332] Ibid. para 132; see also para 113. [333] Ibid. para 134. [334] Ibid.
[335] Ibid. para 117. [336] Ibid. para 135. [337] See Section 3.3.1.
[338] *Iran and USA*, Interlocutory Award No ITL 83-B1-FT, para 129.
[339] See Section 2.3.1(b).
[340] *Iran and USA*, Interlocutory Award No ITL 83-B1-FT, para 130.

parties' subjective intention may be debatable,[341] it indicates the Tribunal's openness to assessing subsequent practice, particularly given the complex setting within which it operates, which appears primarily bilateral but involves a wide range of private actors and State entities in the proceedings.[342]

Overall, given its conservative policy of staying close to the terms of Article 31 VCLT,[343] particularly in comparison to other dispute settlement bodies, the Tribunal's approach of according subsequent practice a decisive role in the case and, moreover, of acknowledging the *possibility* of treaty modification by subsequent practice, makes the example noteworthy.

5.2.3c North American Free Trade Agreement

The North American Free Trade Agreement is a regional, trilateral treaty establishing a trade bloc between the United States, Canada, and Mexico, qualified as an international economic regime.[344] NAFTA's inter-governmental Free Trade Commission (FTC), established by Article 2001 of the Agreement, is tasked with supervising the implementation of the Agreement and resolving disputes regarding its interpretation or application. Pursuant to Article 1131(2) of the NAFTA, the FTC can issue interpretations that are binding upon arbitral tribunals set up in accordance with NAFTA Chapter 11. Its practice constitutes 'relevant' subsequent practice[345] reflective of the collective will of all the parties: 'the FTC is an emanation of the States parties to the NAFTA'.[346]

The interpretative powers of the FTC are similar to constitutive treaties setting up non-judicial bodies tasked with issuing binding interpretations thereof, such as the Ministerial Conference and General Council in the context of the WTO.[347] As discussed in Section 2.5.2 above with regard to the WTO, such interpretations are not to be used in a manner that undermines formal amendment procedures,[348] or adds to or diminishes the rights and obligations of the organization's members.[349]

[341] See eg Sections 2.3.1(b) and 3.3.3(a) on the relevance of the parties' intention in assessing the weight to be accorded to practice.

[342] See eg *Iran and USA*, Interlocutory Award No ITL 83-B1-FT, para 128, where the Tribunal had to deal with the attribution of the practice of Iranian respondents in filing official counterclaims to Iran in light of Art VII(3) of the CSD.

[343] See Section 2.5.2.

[344] North American Free Trade Agreement 1992 (1993) 32 ILM 289, 605.

[345] See Sections 2.3.1(c) and 2.3.5.

[346] G Kaufmann-Kohler, 'Interpretive Powers of the NAFTA Free Trade Commission—Necessary Safety Valve or Infringement of the Rule of Law?' in F Bachand (ed), *Fifteen Years of NAFTA Chapter 11 Arbitration, IAI Conference Proceedings* (JurisNet, 2011) 175, 191. See also AE Roberts, 'Power and Persuasion in Investment Treaty Interpretation: The Dual Role of States' (2010) 104 AJIL 179, 194. cf S Matiation, 'Arbitration with Two Twists: Loewen v United States and Free Trade Commission Intervention in NAFTA Chapter 11 Disputes' (2003) 24 U Pa J Intl Econ L 451, 477.

[347] Art IX(2) of the WTO Agreement. See further Sections 2.5.2 and 3.5.2.

[348] Art IX(2) of the WTO Agreement.

[349] Van Damme, *Treaty Interpretation by the WTO Appellate Body*, 28, citing *EC–Bananas III* (Art 21.5 II), AB Report, para 383. See also eg T Gazzini, 'Can Authoritative Interpretation Under Article IX:2 of the Agreement Establishing the WTO Modify the Rights and Obligations of Members?' (2008) 57 ICLQ 169, 175, 179. cf G Sacerdoti, 'The Dispute Settlement System of the WTO: Structure and

On 31 July 2001, the FTC issued an 'Interpretation' regarding, *inter alia*, the 'minimum standard of treatment' in Article 1105 of the NAFTA.[350] The first paragraph of the Article obliges the parties to accord investors 'treatment in accordance with international law, including fair and equitable treatment and full protection and security.' The FTC's Interpretation states that 'fair and equitable treatment' and 'full protection and security' 'do not require treatment in addition to or beyond that which is required by the customary international law minimum standard of treatment of aliens.' It also states, among other things, that the 'breach of another provision of the NAFTA, or of a separate international agreement, does not establish that there has been a breach of Article 1105(1).'

The FTC Interpretation triggered debate as to whether it falls within the scope of Article 1131(2) NAFTA or, rather, constitutes an informal modification of Article 1105.[351] A number of arbitral tribunals have addressed this reading of Article 1105 in their awards, referring to the Interpretation as everything ranging from a subsequent agreement in the sense of Article 31(3)(a) and an authentic interpretation, to a (legitimate) informal modification of the Agreement, to an impermissible amendment of the NAFTA.[352] The Tribunal in *Pope & Talbot*, for instance, held that the Interpretation represents an amendment in disguise, based on a reading of the NAFTA text and its *travaux*. It did not, however, address the issue further, since its conclusion in the award could stand regardless of this characterization:

> [W]ere the Tribunal required to make a determination whether the Commission's action is an interpretation or an amendment, it would choose the latter. However, (...) this determination is not required. Accordingly, the Tribunal has proceeded on the basis that the Commission's action was an 'interpretation'.[353]

The Tribunal in *Merrill & Ring Forestry v Canada* also considered the Interpretation to be 'closer to an amendment of the treaty, than a strict interpretation,'[354] but did not elaborate or attach any consequences to the observation.

By contrast, the Tribunal in *Mondev v US* had no difficulty accepting the FTC's Interpretation as an interpretation, without further explanation.[355] In *ADF v US*, the Tribunal (expressly) preferred not to engage in distinguishing between 'interpretation' and 'amendment'.[356] It referred to the FTC's Interpretation as a subsequent agreement constituting the most 'authentic and authoritative source' of the

Function in the Perspective of the First 10 Years' (2006) 5 LPICT 49; J Pauwelyn, *Conflict of Norms in Public International Law: How WTO Law Relates to other Rules of International Law* (CUP, 2003) 112.

[350] Notes of Interpretation of Certain Chapter Eleven Provisions (FTC, 31 July 2001) <www.sice.oas.org/tpd/nafta/Commission/CH11understanding_e.asp> accessed 19 April 2017.

[351] For a sharp critique, see *Methanex Corporation v United States of America*, UNCITRAL Arbitration under NAFTA Chapter Eleven, Second Opinion of Professor Sir Robert Jennings, QC, 6 September 2001.

[352] See further eg Brower, 'Why the FTC Notes of Interpretation Constitute a Partial Amendment of NAFTA Article 1105', 347ff.

[353] *Pope & Talbot*, para 47.

[354] *Merrill & Ring Forestry LP v Government of Canada*, UNCITRAL Arbitration under NAFTA Chapter Eleven, Award of 31 March 2010, para 192.

[355] *Mondev v US*, para 121.

[356] *ADF v US*, para 177.

parties' intention in relation to the NAFTA provisions,[357] and deferred to the fact that the FTC's Note *claimed* to be an interpretation:

> [T]he FTC Interpretation of 31 July 2001 expressly purports to be an interpretation of several NAFTA provisions, including Article 1105(1), and not an 'amendment,' or anything else. (...) There is, therefore, no need to embark upon an inquiry into the distinction between an 'interpretation' and an 'amendment' of Article 1105(1). But whether a document submitted to a Chapter 11 tribunal purports to be an amendatory agreement (...) or an interpretation (...), we have the parties themselves—all the Parties—speaking to the Tribunal. No more authentic and authoritative source of instruction on what the Parties intended to convey in a particular provision of NAFTA, is possible.[358]

In fact, the Tribunal took a restrictive view of its very competence to determine whether an FTC Interpretation is actually an interpretation or a modification:

> Nothing in NAFTA suggests that a Chapter 11 tribunal may determine for itself whether a document submitted to it as an interpretation by the Parties acting through the FTC is in fact an 'amendment' (...). We do not find persuasive the Investor's submission that a tribunal is impliedly authorized to do that as part of its duty to determine the governing law of a dispute.[359]

The Tribunal in *Methanex v US* also characterized the FTC Interpretation as a subsequent agreement between the NAFTA parties in the sense of Article 31(3)(a) VCLT, though it expressly objected to attaching any requirement of formality to it or differentiating it from the notion of 'agreement' as a constitutive element of subsequent practice.[360] It referred to the Interpretation as authentic interpretation that 'overrides the ordinary principles of interpretation',[361] hence also highlighting that such authentic interpretations are possible even without a basis in NAFTA Article 1131(2). However, the Tribunal emphasized that this characterization of the FTC Interpretation was put forward 'without here deciding Methanex's claim that the interpretation of 31st July 2001 is in truth an amendment, not an interpretation'.[362] It did, however, note the lack of authority cited for the argument that 'far-reaching changes in a treaty must be accomplished only by formal amendment rather than by some form of agreement between all of the parties',[363] and the fact that Article 39 VCLT does not require any particular form for treaty amendment by agreement.[364] The Tribunal may have implicitly recognized the possibility of modification by subsequent agreement or practice, but it did not sustain it in the specific case. These considerations are in line with the previous discussion regarding the relation between modification by subsequent practice and formal amendment procedures.[365]

Other tribunals dealt with the substance of the Interpretation without questioning its nature.[366] Many of them considered that the 'minimum standard of

[357] Ibid. [358] Ibid.

[359] Ibid. cf G Fitzmaurice, 'The Law and Procedure of the International Court of Justice 1951–4: Treaty Interpretation and Other Treaty Points' (1957) 33 BYBIL 203, 225.

[360] *Methanex v US*, Part IV(C), para 20. [361] Ibid. para 23. [362] Ibid.

[363] Ibid. para 20. [364] Ibid. para 21. [365] See Section 3.3.4.

[366] See eg *Mondev v US*, para 100; *United Parcel Service of America Inc v Government of Canada*, UNCITRAL Arbitration under NAFTA Chapter Eleven, Award on Jurisdiction of 22 November 2002, paras 175–92; *Loewen Group, Inc and Raymond L Loewen v United States of America*, ICSID Case

treatment' in Article 1105 is evolutionary in character.[367] The Tribunal in *ADF v US*, for instance, noted:

In considering the meaning and implications of the 31 July 2001 FTC Interpretation, it is important to bear in mind that the Respondent United States accepts that the customary international law referred to in Article 1105(1) is not 'frozen in time' and that the minimum standard of treatment does evolve. The FTC Interpretation of 31 July 2001, in the view of the United States, refers to customary international law 'as it exists today'. It is equally important to note that Canada and Mexico accept the view of the United States on this point (...). Put in slightly different terms, what customary international law projects is not a static photograph of the minimum standard of treatment of aliens as it stood in 1927 when the Award in the *Neer* case was rendered. For both customary international law and the minimum standard of treatment of aliens it incorporates, are constantly in a process of development.[368]

As discussed in Chapters 2 and 3 of this book, evolutionary interpretation entails that even far-reaching changes may be qualified as interpretation rather than modification.[369] Indeed, the 'minimum treatment standard' seems to have changed significantly since the 1926 *Neer Arbitration*,[370] according to which, to constitute a violation, the treatment must 'amount to an outrage, to bad faith, to wilful neglect of duty, or to an insufficiency of governmental action so far short of international standards that every reasonable and impartial man would readily recognise its insufficiency'.[371] Following this reasoning, the 2001 FTC Interpretation could be qualified as an evolutionary interpretation of the 'minimum treatment standard'. This again demonstrates the grey areas between the latter process and modification by subsequent practice. The arbitral awards discussing the issue also reveal the reluctance or failure to adequately deal with instances of modification by subsequent practice.

Overall, the FTC Interpretation can be deemed tantamount to a modification of the NAFTA by subsequent practice (more specifically, by subsequent agreement).[372] This seems to be the case, despite the fact that the threshold for modification by subsequent practice may be higher with regard to treaties that create third-party beneficiaries and a dispute settlement mechanism, as discussed in Chapter 3.[373] Several commentators have argued that the Interpretation represents an *ultra vires*

No ARB(AF)/98/3 (NAFTA), Award of 26 June 2003, paras 124–8; *Waste Management, Inc v United Mexican States* ('Number 2'), ICSID Case No ARB(AF)/00/3 (NAFTA), Award of 30 April 2004, paras 90–9.

[367] See eg *Mondev v US*, para 125; *ADF v US*, para 179; *Waste Management v Mexico*, paras 91–3, 98; *International Thunderbird Gaming*, para 194.

[368] *ADF v US*, para 179 (footnotes omitted).

[369] See in particular Sections 2.5.3 and 3.5.1.

[370] See eg *Merrill & Ring Forestry v Canada*, paras 210, 213. cf *Glamis Gold, Ltd v United States of America*, UNCITRAL Arbitration under NAFTA, Award of 8 June 2009, para 616. See further eg DA Gantz, 'The Evolution of FTA Investment Provisions: From NAFTA to the United States-Chile Free Trade Agreement' (2004) 19 Am U Intl L Rev 679.

[371] *USA (LF Neer) v United Mexican States*, 15 October 1926, 4 RIAA 60, para 4.

[372] See eg *Methanex v US*, Second Opinion of Professor Sir Robert Jennings, 8; *Pope & Talbot*, para 47; CH Brower, 'Fair and Equitable Treatment Under NAFTA's Investment Chapter' (2002) ASIL Proc 9, 10–11.

[373] See Section 3.5.

act by the FTC because it supplements the provision in Article 1105 in a way that goes beyond the text and its drafting history.[374] It is submitted that while the FTC Interpretation may be tantamount to a modification by subsequent practice, it is not *ultra vires*. As explained, FTC practice coincides with the relevant subsequent practice of the parties to the NAFTA, such that 'an amendment by way of an FTC interpretation amounts to an amendment by the contracting States themselves'.[375] Such modifications are binding upon arbitral tribunals established under Chapter 11 of the NAFTA—although the modifications will not have retroactive effect if the FTC 'interpretation' is issued after the conduct in dispute in a specific arbitration has already occurred.[376] This should assuage the concern that such FTC interpretations could enable the NAFTA parties to change their positions after an investor has brought a claim, 'and has therefore relied, to his detriment, on the original rights accorded directly to investors under that treaty.'[377]

5.2.3d European Court of Justice

The *Spanish Fishermen's Cases* constitute a potential example of treaty modification by subsequent practice and subsequent customary law in the context of the (then) European Community.[378] In these cases, the European Court of Justice had to decide the compatibility of certain Community regulations governing fishing by Spanish vessels in Community waters (put into force while the EEC-Spain Fisheries Agreement was still being negotiated) with three prior fisheries treaties to which the individual member States were parties—namely, the 1958 Convention on Fishing and Conservation of the Living Resources of the High Seas,[379] the 1964 Fisheries Convention,[380] and the 1967 Franco-Spanish General Fisheries Agreement.[381]

In the *Burgoa* case, the Court held that:

> [T]he interim régime which the Community set up under its own rules falls within the framework of the relations established between the Community and Spain in order to resolve the problems inherent in conservation measures and the extension of exclusive fishery limits and in order to ensure reciprocal access by fishermen to the waters subject to such measures. *Those relations were superimposed on the régime which previously applied in those zones in order*

[374] See eg T Weiler, 'NAFTA Investment Arbitration and the Growth of International Economic Law' (2002) 36 CBLJ 405, 428; Brower, 'FTC Notes of Interpretation', 348.

[375] Kaufmann-Kohler, 'Interpretive Powers', 191.

[376] Ibid. 192, 194. See also Section 3.4.1.

[377] Alvarez, 'Limits of Change', 131, citing CH Brower, 'Investor-State Disputes under NAFTA: The Empire Strikes Back' (2001) 40 Colum J Transnat'l L 43.

[378] See eg *Attorney General v Juan C Burgoa* (Case C-812/79) [1980] ECR 2787; *Tome v Procureur de la République, Procureur de la République v Yurrita* (Joined Cases 180 and 266/80) [1981] ECR 2997 [*Tome and Yurrita*]; *Procureur général près la Cour d'Appel de Pau and others v José Arbelaiz-Emazabel* (Case C-181/80) [1981] ECR 2961 [*Procureur général v Arbelaiz-Emazabel*].

[379] 1958 Convention on Fishing and Conservation of Living Resources of the High Seas (Geneva Convention on Fishing and Conservation of Living Resources), 559 UNTS 285.

[380] 1964 Fisheries Convention, 581 UNTS 57.

[381] Exchange of Notes Constituting a General Fisheries Agreement between France and Spain 1967, 712 UNTS 365.

to take account of the general development of international law in the field of fishing on the high seas.[382]

Moreover, in the *Arbelaiz-Emazabel* case, the Court stated:

Those relations, which were confirmed by the Agreement on Fisheries concluded between the Community and Spain and were progressively developed with the concurrence of the Spanish authorities following the decisions (...) [adopted] to deal with the increasingly urgent need to conserve the living resources of the sea and to take into account the general evolution of international law in the field of sea fishing, *replaced the prior international obligations existing between certain Member States, such as France, and Spain.*[383]

Likewise, in *Tome and Yurrita*, the Court found that those relations between Spain and the Community had been 'substituted for the regime which previously applied in those zones in order to take account of the general development of international law in relation to fishing on the high seas'.[384]

Thus, the Court in the abovementioned cases found that the evolution of international law on fishing on the high seas had altered the regime governing the relations between Spain and the European Community. It therefore concluded that the Spanish fishermen were no longer able to rely on the prior international agreements between France and Spain to prevent the application of the Community's 'interim regulations' in the case of conflict between the two 'categories of provisions'.[385] This was reaffirmed in subsequent cases.[386] These cases suggest that subsequent practice in the form of the Community regulations constituting the 'interim regime' governing fisheries on the high seas had modified—more specifically, *altered* or even *terminated* ('superimposed', 'substituted', 'replaced')—the prior treaties of 1958, 1964, and 1967, to which the Community was not even itself a party.[387]

Equally interesting is that Advocate General Capotorti in his opinions in the *Burgoa* and *Arbelaiz-Emazabel* cases implied that the relevant provisions of the prior treaties on fishing on the high seas had been terminated by the emergence of the subsequent customary rule on the 200-mile economic or fishing zone:

I reiterate the conviction, already expressed in the opinion of the *Burgoa* case, that recent developments in general international maritime law have caused the earlier incompatible provisions, both general and particular, to be abrogated; and it seems to me that provisions such as Article 7 of the Geneva Convention, which deal with the question of conservation of biological resources on the basis of the traditional division between territorial waters and the

382 *Attorney General v Juan C Burgoa*, para 24 (emphasis added).

383 *Procureur général v Arbelaiz-Emazabel*, para 30 (emphasis added).

384 *Tome and Yurrita*, para 18.

385 *Procureur général v Arbelaiz-Emazabel*, para 31; *Tome and Yurrita*, para 20.

386 See eg *Directeur des affaires maritimes du littoral du Sud-Ouest and Procureur de la République v Javier Marticorena-Ortazo and Manuel Prego Parada* (Joined Cases 138 and 139/81) [1982] ECR 3819; *Administrateur des affaires maritimes v Dorca Marina and others* (Joined Cases 50-58/82) [1982] ECR 3949.

387 See eg RCA White, 'Fishing Rights of Non-Member States in Community Waters' (1981) 6 ELR 398, 401–02. cf P Daillier, 'La CEE et le respect des droits acquis' (1979) 4 Ann Droit Mar Aér 211, 216–17; RR Churchill and NG Foster, 'European Community Law and Prior Treaty Obligations of Member States: The Spanish Fishermen's Cases' (1987) 36 ICLQ 504, 517–18.

high seas, can no longer be regarded as being in force now that that division has been rendered extremely uncertain by recognition of the 'exclusive economic zone'.[388]

The Court did not elaborate further on the relationship between the subsequent practice and the prior treaties concluded by individual member States. It also did not refer explicitly to the process of treaty modification by subsequent practice or customary law. Generally, as discussed in previous chapters,[389] the ECJ takes a highly conservative approach to subsequent practice, on account of the special character of EU law and the conception that primary EU law should govern the practice of the member States rather than the other way around.[390] Again, such considerations are important as a note of caution when attempting to generalize observations from such self-contained regimes.[391]

5.2.4 National courts

Various national courts have recognized modification by subsequent practice.[392] It is sufficient to explore a few examples here, also given the difficulties associated with the identification of and access to domestic cases.

US courts on Article 17 of the Warsaw Convention

It has been pointed out that US courts have come to regard the liability coverage under the 1929 Convention for the Unification of Certain Rules Relating to International Carriage by Air (Warsaw Convention)[393] as modified by subsequent practice.[394] Article 17 of the Convention provides:

The carrier is liable for damage sustained in the event of the death or wounding of a passenger or any other bodily injury (...) if the accident which caused the damage so sustained took place on board the aircraft or in the course of any of the operations of embarking or disembarking.

Based on subsequent practice, one US court, in *Husserl v Swiss Air Transport,* held that, '[a]lthough hijacking was probably not within the specific contemplation of

[388] *Procureur général près la Cour d'Appel de Pau and others v José Arbelaiz-Emazabel* (Case C-181/80) [1981] ECR 2988 (Opinion of Mr Advocate General Capotorti of 15 September 1981). cf Churchill and Foster, 'European Community Law', 516–17.

[389] See Sections 2.5.2 and 3.5.1(a).

[390] Nolte, Second Report on Treaties over Time, 301. See also Comments by the EU to the ILC regarding subsequent agreements and subsequent practice (2015), 2–4. See further eg N Fennelly, 'Legal Interpretation at the European Court of Justice' (1997) 20 Fordham ILJ 656, 672.

[391] Nolte, Annex A, para 33; Arato, 'Treaty Interpretation', 289.

[392] The decisions of national courts are used here as a means of identifying recognized examples of modification by subsequent practice, rather than as a form of practice in themselves.

[393] 137 LNTS 11.

[394] See eg Murphy, 'Subsequent Agreements and Subsequent Practice', 89 and fn 39, citing *Husserl v Swiss Air Transport*, 702, and *Day v Trans World Airlines*, 528 F.2d 31 (1975) Court of Appeals, Second Circuit. See further eg M Frankowska, 'The Vienna Convention on the Law of Treaties Before United States Courts' (1988) 28 VJIL 281, 341–52; Laursen, *Changing International Law*, 83.

the parties at the time the Warsaw Convention was promulgated, the Montreal Agreement seems to resolve whatever doubt might have existed over the construction of the word "accident".'[395] Thus, the 'practice' in question related to the 'Montreal Agreement'.[396] This Agreement is neither a treaty nor a protocol; it is not signed by States, but was developed by them under the auspices of the International Air Transport Association (IATA) as an agreement between the American Civil Aeronautics Board (CAB) and airline industry carriers. In *Husserl v Swiss Air Transport*, the Court admitted that the Agreement was not binding with the 'effect of a treaty', but that 'it is difficult to question the modification effectuated by the Montreal Agreement of the contractual relationship between the parties within the Warsaw Convention system of liability'.[397] The United States Court of Appeals for the Second Circuit, in *Day v Trans World Airlines*, explained that, '[a]lthough it was the foreign airlines, and not their respective governments, who signed the agreement implementing these modifications, the governments whose carriers were to participate in the plan formally assured the United States (...) that they would permit the new plan to go into effect.'[398] However, neither court addressed the fact that only some parties to the Warsaw Convention had adhered to the Agreement, which would, *stricto sensu*, imply that any modification by subsequent practice would apply only to them.[399]

The Court in *Husserl v Swiss Air Transport* thus concluded that as a result of the practice surrounding the Montreal Agreement, hijacking is now 'within the ambit of the term "accident", and sufficient to raise the presumption of liability under the Warsaw Convention as modified'.[400] In *Day v Trans World Airlines*, the Court likewise concluded on a result of subsequent practice that diverged from the parties' original intention.[401]

One commentator has suggested that the decision's referral to Article 31(3)(b) VCLT demonstrates that the issue was one of interpretation.[402] However, as discussed, the elements of Article 31(3)(b) VCLT are relevant for discussions on modification by subsequent practice. It is also noteworthy that US courts deciding on the issue of the Warsaw Convention have invoked the following extract:

> A court might even feel obliged to sustain (the parties' later) construction of a treaty differing widely from that which it was in fact possible to prove to have been the design of the parties at the time when the agreement was concluded.[403]

This quote was followed up by the mention that, in doing so, 'the court does not, of course, impose its own values upon the parties (...) [but] does no more than respect

[395] *Husserl v Swiss Air Transport*, 706.

[396] Agreement between the carrier and the United States Civil Aeronautics Board, CAB Agreement No 18990 (Montreal Agreement). See eg AF Lowenfeld and AI Mendelsohn, 'The United States and the Warsaw Convention' (1967) 80 Harv L Rev 497.

[397] *Husserl v Swiss Air Transport*, 707.

[398] *Day v Trans World Airlines*, para 28 fn 15.

[399] Frankowska, 'The Vienna Convention on the Law of Treaties Before United States Courts', 350.

[400] *Husserl v Swiss Air Transport*, 707.

[401] *Day v Trans World Airlines*, 35–6.

[402] Murphy, 'Subsequent Agreements and Subsequent Practice', 89 fn 39.

[403] C Hyde, *International Law Chiefly as Interpreted and Applied by the United States* (Little, Brown, 1922) 72, as cited in *Day v Trans World Airlines*, para 21 fn 13.

and implement the goals and intentions of the parties'[404]—an acknowledgment that subsequent practice can provide an accurate and authoritative reflection of the contemporaneous will of the parties.

It is not fully clear from the aforementioned considerations whether the reading of Article 17 of the Warsaw Convention by US courts indicates an interpretation or modification. The Court in *Husserl v Swiss Air Transport* also pointed out, for instance, that the 'policy underpinnings' of the Convention led to the same conclusion that hijacking fell within its scope.[405] While this could suggest that a purposive interpretation of the Convention would lead to the same result, it may also indicate simply that the modification in question does not affect the object and purpose of the Convention. Moreover, the same Court chose not to attach significance to the argument that the 1971 Guatemala City Protocol, which never came into force,[406] had substituted the word 'event' for 'accident' in Article 17, suggesting that the intention was to exclude precisely such incidents of sabotage or hijacking.[407] These factors point to a subsequent modification of the intended meaning of Article 17 of the Convention. This view also finds support in the doctrine.[408]

Swiss Federal Supreme Court on Article 9 VCDR

The decision of the Swiss Federal Supreme Court regarding Article 9 of the Vienna Convention on Diplomatic Relations (VCDR) is also interesting for present purposes.[409] Article 9(1) of the Convention provides as follows:

> The receiving State may at any time (...) notify the sending State that the head of the mission or any member of the diplomatic staff of the mission is persona non grata or that any other member of the staff of the mission is not acceptable. In any such case, the sending State shall, as appropriate, either recall the person concerned or terminate his functions with the mission. (...)

The Court found that States had, through their practice, and as masters of their own treaty, acted 'contrary to the wording of Article 9 VCDR by ordering expulsion without previously demanding recall by the sending State'.[410] One commentator has argued that the Court's explicit referral to Article 31(3)(b) VCLT in its judgment means that 'it understood this particular conduct as a case of interpretation and not as a modification of the treaty'.[411] Once again, it is respectfully submitted

[404] *Day v Trans World Airlines*, para 21 fn 13. [405] 351 F.Supp 707.

[406] Protocol to Amend the Convention for the Unification of Certain Rules Relating to International Carriage by Air 1971 (1971) 10 ILM 613 (Guatemala City Protocol).

[407] *Husserl v Swiss Air Transport*, 707 fn 5.

[408] See eg Frankowska, 'The Vienna Convention', 341, 346 ('Neither the *Husserl* nor the *Day* court had difficulty accepting the subsequent practice evidenced by the Montreal Agreement as a *de facto* modification of the Warsaw Convention.'). See also the sources in n 394.

[409] 1961 Vienna Convention on Diplomatic Relations, 500 UNTS 95.

[410] *A v B*, Appeal judgment, Case No 4C.140/2003, BGE 130 III 430, ILDC 343 (CH 2004), 8 April 2004, Swiss Federal Supreme Court, para 3.5, cited by G Hafner, 'Subsequent Agreements and Practice: Between Interpretation, Informal Modification, and Formal Amendment' in G Nolte (ed), *Treaties and Subsequent Practice* (OUP, 2013) 105, 112 (unofficial translation by OUP).

[411] Hafner, 'Subsequent Agreements and Practice', 112.

that references to Article 31(3)(b) VCLT do not necessarily indicate an interpretation, especially here, given the Court's reference to the role of the parties as masters of their own agreements, and its express admission that the practice observed was 'contrary' to Article 9 VCDR. Under these circumstances, the practice observed is likely to have modified the strict wording of the provision.

German Constitutional Court on the NATO Treaty

The issue of modification by subsequent practice has repeatedly come up in proceedings before the Federal Constitutional Court of Germany, as also discussed in Section 5.3.1(b) on the NATO regime below. An important ruling by the Court in 1994 concerned the legality of the deployment of German armed forces outside of German territory and the NATO area. In turn, this involved the question of whether the joint practice of the NATO parties, as reflected in the 1991 Strategic Concept,[412] had tacitly extended the scope of the North Atlantic Treaty to such an extent that it amounted to a treaty amendment requiring (renewed) parliamentary approval in accordance with Germany's constitutional procedure—in other words, whether the changed practice in relation to the NATO Treaty required a new treaty.

The Court held that the fact that the parties had extended the scope of the NATO Treaty while declaring that they were acting within its scope, did not amount to a treaty amendment of the kind requiring parliamentary approval.[413] In doing so, it recognized the possibility of changing the NATO Treaty through subsequent practice, without recourse to formal amendment:

> In practice, international law is characterized by a fluid transition from treaty interpretation to treaty amendment (...). Within this borderline area, a change in the contents of an international treaty is occasionally brought about by interpretation of an existing international treaty [i.e. modification] rather than by an amendment of the treaty. (...) [I]n certain instances this practice can have the same effect on a treaty as a proper amendment. In these circumstances, there are insufficient indications (...) to conclude that by their specific actions or statements the Parties intended to enter into *new* treaty obligations.[414]

This suggests that, even where practice has 'the same effect on a treaty as a proper amendment', the result of a treaty modification by subsequent practice remains part of the treaty rather than creating an independent treaty obligation outside of it: '[t]hus it cannot be ruled out that the Government [in concert with the governments of other Contracting Parties], by legally pertinent actions *"within the framework of" existing treaties*, creates for the Federal Republic of Germany new international rights and duties.'[415] The Court then proceeded to explain that such a process does not undermine parliamentary authority.[416]

[412] 'The Alliance's New Strategic Concept' (8 November 1991) <www.nato.int/cps/en/natohq/official_texts_23847.htm> accessed 4 June 2017 [1991 Strategic Concept].

[413] *International Military Operations*, 338–9.

[414] Ibid. (emphasis in the original).

[415] Ibid. 339 (emphasis added). See the discussion in Section 3.3.6(a).

[416] Ibid. 340.

These finds were reaffirmed in subsequent decisions in 2001 and 2007,[417] this time in relation to the 1999 Strategic Concept.[418] Once again, the Court recognized the possibility of modification by subsequent practice as 'legally relevant action' falling 'below the level of a formal amendment' that 'brings about a gradual change of the content of the Treaty', and which in this case resulted in 'far-reaching consequences for the command and structure of the armed forces of the partners in the Alliance'.[419] Again, it found insufficient evidence of the parties' intention to *formally* amend the NATO Treaty by means of the new Strategic Concept:

> If commitments that are made in the 1999 Strategic Concept are, in an insurmountable and clearly discernible manner, inconsistent with the area of operation that is defined in the Treaty, or if they contain an expansion of the Treaty beyond the scope that has been binding to this point, this indicates the parties' consent to amend the Treaty. (…) This is not the case here. In particular, the issue that is at the centre of the *Organstreit* proceedings, i.e., the expansion of the Alliance's security policy approach to crisis response operations, constitutes only a further development of the NATO Treaty, which cannot be interpreted, at any rate with the degree of certainty required for assuming the existence of a consent to amend the Treaty that can be inferred from acts of the parties, as an inconsistency with, or as an expansion of, the content of the existing Treaty.[420]

Thus, the changes brought about by the 1999 Strategic Concept did not amount to a modification of the kind requiring parliamentary approval, also in light of the fact that the North Atlantic Council had explicitly declared in the 'Washington Declaration' that the purpose and nature of the Alliance would remain unchanged. Of course, we have seen that sometimes what States declare to be an interpretation may be a modification in disguise.[421] Moreover, it is unclear whether the Court's reasoning still applies following the 2010 Strategic Concept,[422] which fundamentally shifted the emphasis from collective defence to other essential concerns of NATO members.[423]

Furthermore, in a 2015 decision, the Federal Constitutional Court reaffirmed, based on a combined reading of Articles 31(3)(b) and 39 VCLT,[424] the 'possibility under international law to (implicitly) modify the content or at least the

[417] *PDS v Federal Government*, Federal Constitutional Court, 104 BVerfGE 151 (Case No 2 BvE 6/99) Judgment of 22 November 2001 (English excerpts at <www.bundesverfassungsgericht.de/entscheidungen/es20011122_2bve000699en.html> accessed 4 June 2017); *PDS/Die Linke v Federal Government*, Federal Constitutional Court, 118 BVerfGE 244 (Case No 2 BvE 2/07) Judgment of 3 July 2007, ILDC 819 (DE 2007) (with English translation). See further S Kadelbach, 'Die parlamentarische Kontrolle des Regierungshandelns bei der Beschlussfassung internationaler Organisationen' in R Geiger (ed), *Neuere Probleme der parlamentarischen Legitimation im Bereich der auswärtigen Gewalt* (Nomos, 2003) 41.

[418] 'The Washington Declaration', *NATO Press Release* NAC-S(99)63 (23 April 1999) <www.nato.int/docu/pr/1999/p99-063e.htm> accessed 4 June 2017.

[419] *PDS v Federal Government* (English excerpts), para 21.

[420] Ibid. para 10.

[421] See eg Section 3.4.2.

[422] 'Active Engagement, Modern Defence—Strategic Concept for the Defence and Security of the Members of the North Atlantic Treaty Organization' (19 November 2010) <www.nato.int/cps/nl/natohq/topics_82705.htm> accessed 4 June 2017.

[423] See Section 5.3.1(b).

[424] See Section 3.3.4.

interpretation of a treaty with respect to certain specific points by the practice of its application with the agreement of the other parties'.[425]

Although these cases before the German Federal Constitutional Court confirm the possibility of modification by subsequent practice, they also illustrate the general concern of States that their national treaty approval procedures could be bypassed by tacit modifications through subsequent practice,[426] the implications of which have not yet been comprehensively and systematically analysed.[427] As explained in Chapter 3, subsequent practice in the form of subsequent agreements—in this case, the Strategic Concepts—can trigger greater legitimacy concerns than other forms of subsequent practice due to the prominent role played by the executive branch.[428] As noted earlier, the German Constitutional Court here considered that parliament retained sufficient control over the operation and development of the Alliance to invalidate constitutional concerns. Overall, this series of judgments by the German Federal Constitutional Court demonstrates that—like international judicial bodies—national courts often take a pragmatic view, if any, towards modification by subsequent practice.[429]

5.2.5 Interim conclusions

The cases analysed above serve a dual purpose. First, they represent an important source of examples of modifications by subsequent practice. Second, they reveal how such modifications have been dealt with in the case law of different dispute settlement bodies. The case law shows that courts and tribunals accord varying degrees of importance not only to subsequent practice in the interpretative process,[430] but also to subsequent practice and subsequent customary law as a means of treaty modification.

Many cases in which a modification by subsequent practice was explicitly recognized involved bilateral treaties of a rather technical nature in relation to which modification is more easily identifiable and accepted.[431] On the other hand, these cases primarily involved boundary treaties, which represent a special category of treaty that, depending on the circumstances, may entail a stronger presumption against modification by subsequent practice.[432] Other cases, such as the *Namibia Advisory Opinion* and the *Israeli Wall Advisory Opinion*, concerned practice within an international organization in relation to a constitutive treaty—the UN Charter. As discussed in Chapter 2, subsequent practice can play a special role in

[425] German Federal Constitutional Court (Case No 2 BvL 1/12) Judgment of 15 December 2015 (unpublished), available at <www.bverfg.de/e/ls20151215_2bvl000112.html> accessed 2 July 2016, para 90, as translated in Nolte, Fourth Report on Subsequent Practice, para 98.

[426] Nolte, Annex A, para 17.

[427] See eg the discussion in Sections 3.2.5 and 3.3.2(a).

[428] See eg Section 3.3.2(a).

[429] S Kadelbach, 'Domestic Constitutional Concerns with Respect to the Use of Subsequent Agreements and Practice at the International Level' in G Nolte (ed), *Treaties and Subsequent Practice* (OUP, 2013) 145, 148.

[430] See Section 2.5.2.

[431] See Section 3.5.1.

[432] Ibid.

the international institutional context.[433] In cases concerning the practice of UN organs, notably the Security Council and General Assembly, significant emphasis is placed on the acceptance of the practice by the member States rather than just the practice of the organ(s) concerned.

Overall, the case law reveals an acceptance of the possibility of modification by subsequent practice and demonstrates the frequency with which this process impacts treaties,[434] in relation to both clear and concrete provisions[435] and more ambiguous ones.[436] Cases such as the *Air Transport Services Arbitration (US/France)*, the ECtHR's capital punishment and *Hassan v UK* cases, and judgments such as those of the Iran-US Claims Tribunal, demonstrate that the relevance of subsequent practice has been recognized in very different contexts and in relation to a diverse range of treaties. Thus, the foregoing examples taken from the case law are already sufficiently different 'to permit the conclusion that they are based on a general rule'.[437]

It also becomes evident from the case law of standing dispute settlement bodies operating under special regimes and interpreting their own constitutive treaties, such as the ICJ, ECJ, and ECtHR, that by recognizing changes that have taken place through subsequent practice, they can give effect to changes ranging from 'minor readjustments to sweeping systemic reorganization'.[438] That these judicial bodies have developed their own, specific approaches to modification by subsequent practice in relation to their constituent instruments is reflected, for instance, in the fact that the ICJ's approach to subsequent practice appears to be more liberal in cases involving the UN Charter than in those that do not.

The ICJ effectively recognized the possibility of modification by subsequent practice in *Costa Rica v Nicaragua*, as well as in *Cameroon v Nigeria* and *El Salvador/ Honduras*, and, implicitly, by acknowledging its effects, in cases such as the *Namibia Advisory Opinion* and *Temple of Préah Vihéar*. In respect of the UN Charter in the *Namibia Advisory Opinion* and, especially, in the *Israeli Wall Advisory Opinion*, the Court seems to have taken a dynamic, transformative approach to the Charter.[439] Through such judgments, it sends an important signal to other principal organs of the organization that their consistent practice can constitute a source of authoritative interpretation and, accordingly, change.[440] It also seems to have relied on a

[433] See Section 2.3.1(c). See also eg Art 2(1)(j) VCLTIO (referring to 'established practice' as a means of determining how rules of an organization may emerge); RY Jennings and A Watts (eds), *Oppenheim's International Law: Peace*, vol I (9th edn, OUP, 2008) 1268.

[434] Nolte, Introductory Report on Treaties over Time, 202.

[435] See Section 5.2 on the *Namibia Advisory Opinion, Israeli Wall Advisory Opinion, Eritrea-Ethiopia Arbitration*, and *Taba Arbitration.*

[436] See *Certain Expenses Advisory Opinion*, Separate Opinion of Judge Spender, 189.

[437] Nolte, Introductory Report on Treaties over Time, 206. See also Distefano, 'L'accord tacite', 30 ('d'une jurisprudence malgré tout relativement constante et uniforme').

[438] Arato, 'Treaty Interpretation', 304. See eg Section 5.2.1 on the *Israeli Wall Advisory Opinion*, which entailed a reordering of the relation and competences of the General Assembly and Security Council.

[439] See also eg *Certain Expenses Advisory Opinion*, 157. See further Arato, 'Treaty Interpretation', 294–5.

[440] See eg Arato, 'Treaty Interpretation', 295, 331–2, arguing that the Court has thus sanctioned a 'second track of constitutional change, outside of the formal amendment rule (...) [which is] available to the other organs than to the Court itself'.

broad definition of subsequent practice, taking into account not only the practice of UN organs, but also that of certain non-representative UN bodies.[441] In fact, it has been argued that the Court is increasingly reliant on forms of practice that shift the focus away from direct reference to State practice.[442] By implicitly recognizing the modifying potential of the established practice of UN organs like the Security Council, it may place greater weight on their practice than on that of (other) States, even if the rest of the membership can be said to have acquiesced in that practice. As discussed, however, in most cases the Court portrays instances likely to constitute modifications as interpretations—despite the seemingly clear wording of the provisions affected, which makes the shift from interpretation to modification more obvious.[443] Even in *Costa Rica v Nicaragua*, the Court opted for the evolutionary approach over subsequent practice, despite the fact that the former option led to more far-reaching results than the latter[444]—a decision that triggered criticism from a number of judges.[445]

The European Court of Human Rights, by contrast, has not only acknowledged the existence of the process of modification by subsequent practice; it has also sustained it in the *Al-Saadoon and Mufdhi v UK* and *Hassan v UK* cases. What is more, in the former case, it did so even in light of a parallel, ongoing formal amendment procedure, and in the latter case, despite, *inter alia*, potential non-regression considerations given the nature of the ECHR as a human rights treaty with third-party beneficiaries. Although the ECtHR usually relies on (direct) State practice rather than that of organs of international organizations as a 'proxy' like in the ICJ case law, its overall approach to subsequent practice, as discussed extensively in Chapter 2 and the present chapter,[446] is significantly more liberal than that of the ICJ. Thus, it has in the past relied on the practice of *most* rather than *all* States to establish a common standard or 'emerging consensus' among the parties,[447] despite the presence of contradictory practice,[448] as evidenced also by its willingness in the capital punishment cases to assume unanimous acceptance of the practice despite discrepancies in the ratification of the protocol concerned.[449] This approach starkly contrasts, for instance, with that of the WTO Appellate Body.[450] It implicitly grants the Court itself more power and discretion to determine when subsequent practice

441 See *Israeli Wall Advisory Opinion*, discussed in Section 5.2.1. See by contrast the ICJ's approach in the *Whaling in the Antarctic* case, discussed in Section 2.3.5.

442 AM Weisburd, 'The International Court of Justice and the Concept of State Practice' (2009) 31 U Penn J Intl L 295, 352, 360.

443 See eg *Israeli Wall Advisory Opinion*, discussed in Section 5.2.1.

444 See Sections 2.5.3(c) and 5.2.1.

445 See *Costa Rica v Nicaragua*, Separate Opinion of Judge Skotnikov and Declaration of Judge ad hoc Guillaume, discussed in Section 2.5.3(c).

446 See Sections 2.5.2 and 5.2.3(a).

447 See eg *Demir and Baykara v Turkey*, para 85; *Christine Goodwin v UK*, paras 84–5; *Sigurdur A Sigurjónsson v Iceland*, para 35; Nolte, Second Report on Treaties over Time, 305, 'General Conclusion 16'. See also Section 2.3.5 of this book.

448 See eg *Loizidou v Turkey* (Preliminary Objections), paras 79–80, 89; *Öcalan v Turkey* (Grand Chamber Judgment), para 163; *Al-Saadoon and Mufdhi v UK*, para 120. See also eg Mowbray, 'The Creativity of the European Court of Human Rights', 61.

449 See Section 5.2.3(a).

450 See eg *EC–Computer Equipment*, AB Report, paras 92–3.

is sufficient to modify the ECHR, thus in a sense, if not aligned with the general requirements for (modification by) subsequent practice, 'diluting the parties' mastery over the treaty'.[451] The Court's approach is influenced by the nature of the treaty as a human rights regime,[452] its character as a 'living instrument'[453] and a 'constitutional instrument of European public order',[454] and the relatively homogeneous nature of its States parties.

The case law also shows that international economic regimes, such as that established by the Algiers Accords within which the Iran-US Claims Tribunal operates, as well as NAFTA, can be prone to modifications by subsequent practice. The NAFTA example also illustrates how an authoritative intergovernmental body like the FTC can issue far-reaching interpretations bordering on—and in the present author's opinion, constituting—modification. However, arbitral decisions concerning the 2001 FTC Interpretation reveal a lack of consistency in dealing with potential modifications—and even regarding the extent to which tribunals consider the issue *can* be dealt with in the first place.[455] Even dispute settlement bodies operating in special economic regimes, such as in the context of the WTO and the EU, which have traditionally adopted a conservative stance with regard to subsequent practice, seem to have implicitly upheld modifications in the past. The ECJ's *Spanish Fishermen* string of cases is one indication: although these cases were not portrayed as concerning modification, the Court did not provide any other justification for the 'substitution' of prior treaties for Community regulations.[456]

For various reasons already discussed,[457] dispute settlement bodies are overall reluctant to acknowledge modifications by subsequent practice—with notable exceptions, as seen above. One reason is likely due to the perception that States are wary of dispute settlement bodies using tacit modification as a tool to 'evolve the law'.[458] Indeed, it is 'entirely reasonable to postulate, for example, that States are very reluctant to permit dispute settlers to use subsequent conduct to modify a treaty relationship, but that States are quite happy amongst just themselves to view a treaty as modified based on mutual understandings'.[459] Not surprisingly,

[451] Arato, 'Treaty Interpretation', 350.

[452] See eg IE Koch and J Vedsted-Hansen, 'International Human Rights and National Legislatures—Conflict or Balance?' (2006) 75 NJIL 3, 11–12; G Letsas, *A Theory of Interpretation of the European Convention on Human Rights* (2nd edn, OUP, 2009) 79.

[453] See eg *Tyrer v UK*, para 183.

[454] *Loizidou v Turkey* (Preliminary Objections), para 75. See also generally *South West Africa Voting Procedure Advisory Opinion*, Separate Opinion of Judge Lauterpacht, 105–6: 'A proper interpretation of a constitutional instrument must take into account not only the formal letter of the original instrument, but also its operation in actual practice and in the light of the revealed tendencies in the life of the Organization.'

[455] See *ADF v US*, para 177, discussed in Section 5.2.3(c), where the Tribunal considered that it did not have the competence to decide whether the FTC Interpretation constituted an interpretation or modification.

[456] See Section 5.2.3(d).

[457] See Sections 3.4.2 and 5.1. This also applies with regard to evolutionary interpretation—see eg Section 2.5.3, n 686, and Section 5.2.1, nn 114–15.

[458] Murphy, 'Subsequent Agreement and Subsequent Practice', 83, 87. See also Nolte, Second Report on Subsequent Practice, para 137.

[459] Murphy, 'Subsequent Agreement and Subsequent Practice', 83.

dispute settlement bodies seem to favour the more explicit treaty rule over the more contentious process of identifying treaty modifying implied agreements by subsequent practice[460]—perhaps especially when dealing with a potential alteration of a treaty by customary law. The reluctance in the latter scenario may also stem from the fact that it may require two findings: first, that a customary norm has emerged, and, second, that there is evidence of the parties' intention to modify the treaty accordingly.[461]

Instead, dispute settlement bodies often prefer recourse to alternative adaptation mechanisms,[462] such as evolutionary interpretation,[463] 'approximate application',[464] or ambiguous provisions.[465] Such 'mechanisms' also allow courts and tribunals to avoid issues of subsequent practice extending beyond the terms of a treaty, and to state merely that such instances fall within the treaty's interpretative scope.[466] Some dispute settlement bodies have, as pointed out earlier, even explicitly stated that they lack the competence to ascertain whether a given practice constitutes interpretation or modification in the first place.[467] Others have emphasized that their duty is to interpret rather than revise treaties[468] (with the possible exception of cases in which there are ambiguities or gaps in the treaty text[469]). In particular this latter consideration does not, and should not, prohibit dispute settlement bodies from recognizing modification by subsequent practice where it has occurred—that is, from observing that a modification has taken place based on the will of the parties as evidenced by their practice, not by the decision of the court or tribunal itself.

Furthermore, despite their potential reluctance to deal with and recognize modifications by subsequent practice for practical and 'political' reasons, dispute settlement bodies must nevertheless do so from a judicial and legal perspective:

> [Just as] it is the duty of a tribunal 'to interpret treaties, not to revise them', it is equally the duty of a tribunal to interpret them *as* revised, and to give effect to any revision arrived at by the parties (...) [as] there is little doubt that agreement can result from conduct.[470]

The importance of recognizing modifications where they have occurred goes hand in hand with the 'higher threshold' requirement discussed in Chapter 3, which is especially applicable to certain types of modifications, such as those affecting a treaty's

[460] Pauwelyn, *Conflict of Norms*, 141. [461] See Section 4.5.3.
[462] See generally Section 3.5.2.
[463] See eg *Costa Rica v Nicaragua*, discussed in Section 5.2.1.
[464] See *Gabčíkovo-Nagymaros Project*, discussed in Section 5.2.1.
[465] See eg *Japanese House Tax Arbitration*, discussed in Section 5.2.2.
[466] See eg Venzke, *How Interpretation Makes International Law*, 73 (arguing that such reasoning enabled the ICJ in the *Namibia Advisory Opinion* to avoid any 'slippery slopes of reasoning' or claims of treaty breach).
[467] See eg *Air Transport Services Arbitration (US/Italy)*, paras 100–1, discussed in Section 5.2.2, or *ADF v US*, para 177, discussed in Section 5.2.3(c).
[468] See eg *Interpretation of Peace Treaties Advisory Opinion*, 229; *Rights of Nationals*, 196; *South West Africa (Second Phase)*, 49; *Delimitation of the Maritime Boundary between Guinea-Bissau and Senegal*, para 85.
[469] *Delimitation of the Maritime Boundary between Guinea-Bissau and Senegal*, para 85.
[470] Fitzmaurice, 'The Law and Procedure of the International Court of Justice' (1957), 225. See also Gardiner, *Treaty Interpretation*, 225–49; Arato, 'Treaty Interpretation', 309.

object and purpose.[471] In those cases, the judge or interpreter must meet a higher (evidentiary) standard in the identification of the requirements necessary for modification to occur and in the justification based on the constitutive elements of subsequent practice of the conclusion reached.[472]

All in all, the examples in the foregoing sections show that numerous dispute settlement bodies have indeed explicitly (or effectively) recognized the possibility of treaty modification by subsequent practice (or by subsequent customary law), even if sometimes they did not sustain a modification in the specific case.[473] However, even where dispute settlement bodies do actually recognize that a modification by subsequent practice has occurred, they are not consistent in referring to or applying the constitutive elements of subsequent practice discussed in Chapter 2.[474] Moreover, the relevant passages are usually too brief to draw generalizable conclusions and only indicate how the change affects the content of the treaty, without specifying any criteria or circumstances used to determine that a treaty modification has occurred.[475] This has prompted one scholar to remark: 'international courts and tribunals (...) very rarely deal with the matter and, if so, take a favourable view of subsequent practice, tending not to even question modification by practice.'[476] Thus, it is difficult to develop from such an array of cases a consistent approach as to how to identify modification by subsequent practice or subsequent customary law.

5.3 Treaty Modification by Subsequent Practice Outside of Judicial and Quasi-Judicial Proceedings

The second part of this chapter is concerned with examples of potential modifications by subsequent practice outside of the case law, spanning a wide range of fields of international law. In relatively recent discussions on the topic in the UN General Assembly's Sixth Committee, many delegations highlighted the importance of considering practice that has not been assessed in judicial or arbitral proceedings.[477] While a major focus in the first part of the chapter was on describing how courts and tribunals have dealt with the issue of modification by subsequent practice, the focus in the present part is on conducting an independent analysis of practice. As discussed in Chapter 3,[478] States typically portray their practice as an interpretation of the treaty even where it leads to modification,[479] perhaps especially in the context

471 See Section 3.3.5. 472 See Section 3.3.3(b).

473 See eg the examples in Sections 2.5.1, 5.2.2, and 5.2.3(a).

474 See generally Section 2.3.

475 See eg Nolte, Second Report on Subsequent Practice, para 165.

476 Kadelbach, 'Domestic Constitutional Concerns', 148.

477 *Topical summary of the discussion held in the Sixth Committee of the General Assembly during its 65th session*, UN Doc A/CN.4/638 (19 January 2011) Ch II(G), para 107.

478 See Section 3.4.2.

479 See eg Voicu, *De l'interprétation authentique des traités internationaux*, 89; Akehurst, *Modern Introduction*, 204, 268; Orakhelashvili, *Interpretation of Acts and Rules*, 105.

of international organizations.[480] Therefore, an investigation into subsequent practice must be conducted carefully, keeping closely in mind its constitutive elements to ensure in as far as possible that the result stays true to the parties' actual intentions.

The first part of this section explores further the role of subsequent practice in the international institutional context. Examples are taken from the context of the UN, NATO, the International Labour Organization (ILO), the (former) GATT, the WTO, and certain international financial institutions (Section 5.3.1). The conclusions also refer back to the examples involving international organizations already explored in Section 5.2 above. The second part of this section looks for trends outside the context of international organizations, in particular at examples in the fields of the law of the sea, human rights, and environmental law (Section 5.3.2). Once again, the overlap with the case law examples explored in Section 5.2 is taken into account. Interim conclusions are discussed in Section 5.3.3.

5.3.1 Examples within the context of international organizations

5.3.1a UN Charter

The UN Charter, drafted in 1945, is a 'law-making' treaty of near-universality, as well as a constitutive treaty, containing countless ambiguous provisions and political compromises. Like the ECHR, the Charter has been characterized as a 'living' instrument,[481] requiring continual evolution:

> Flexibility is the life blood that sustains and perpetuates constitutions. Concepts as to the nature of the foundations of peace and freedom change. This underlies the advisability of letting the United Nations Charter evolve, little by little, case by case.[482]

Indeed, as discussed in Chapter 3, 'the flexibility with respect to the use of subsequent practice in the course of interpreting the Charter has much to do with the nature of the UN itself'.[483] For one thing, the Charter's procedures for formal amendment are regarded as notoriously ineffective.[484] Pursuant to Article 108 of the Charter, formal amendments must be adopted and ratified by two-thirds of the

480 Akehurst, *Modern Introduction*, 204; YZ Blum, *Eroding the United Nations Charter* (Martinus Nijhoff, 1993) 243–4; MN Shaw, *International Law* (6th edn, CUP, 2008) 88.

481 UN Secretary-General Kofi Annan, Speech delivered at his Annual Report to the opening meeting of the General Assembly (20 September 1999) <www.un.org/press/en/1999/19990920.sgsm7136.html> accessed 28 April 2017. See also S Chesterman, TM Franck, and DM Malone, *Law and Practice of the United Nations: Documents and Commentary* (OUP, 2008) 11.

482 EA Gross, 'Revising the Charter: Is It Possible? Is It Wise?' (1954) 32 Foreign Affairs 203, 216.

483 Alvarez, 'Limits of Change', 128.

484 See eg Kelsen, *The Law of the United Nations*, 818–19; R Zacklin, *The Amendment of the Constitutive Instruments of the United Nations and Specialized Agencies* (Sijthoff, 1968) 171; Laursen, *Changing International Law*, 65–6; Liang, 'Modifying the UN Charter', 2. However, there have been a number of successful Art 108 amendments. See E Schwelb, 'Amendments to Articles 23, 27 and 61 of the Charter of the United Nations' (1965) 59 AJIL 834; W Karl, B Mützelburg, and G Witschel, 'Article 108' in B Simma and others (eds), *The Charter of the United Nations: A Commentary*, vol II (2nd edn, OUP, 2002) 1341. See also G Schwarzenberger, *The Dynamics of International Law* (Professional Books, 1976), 10 (referring to the amendment process as 'a complicated and protracted affair (...) yet, whenever the necessary consensus exists, the feat can, and has been, accomplished').

General Assembly, including all the permanent members of the Security Council, which have veto power. For more substantial amendments, Article 109 provides the possibility of a General Conference of all the member States, subject to the same requirements as in Article 108.[485] As a result of these cumbersome requirements, and despite the enormous changes that international society has undergone since the UN's inception—positing one commentator to remark that the Charter 'bears little more resemblance to the modern world than does a Magellan map'[486]—the Charter has not been formally amended since 1971.[487]

Its characteristics, including its age, nature, and rigid amendment provisions, have rendered the UN Charter more susceptible to modification by subsequent practice;[488] 'a *runway* from which change takes off'.[489] In fact, few treaties have been as susceptible to informal change as the UN Charter: 'the UN Charter has, in roughly a half century, seen more changes than the US Constitution has experienced in over 200 years'.[490] As Judge Spender commented back in 1962, '[t]he wisest of them could never have anticipated the tremendous changes which politically, militarily, and otherwise have occurred in the comparatively few years that have elapsed since 1945.'[491] Prominent UN Charter modifications by subsequent practice have already been discussed in Section 5.2.1 above in the context of the ICJ's *Namibia Advisory Opinion* in relation to Article 27(3) of the UN Charter, and the *Israeli Wall Advisory Opinion* in relation to Article 12(1). Thus, 'it is established that the Charter may not only be subject to formal amendments under Arts 108 or 109, but may also be changed by informal or *de facto* modifications'.[492] These modifications are constantly portrayed as mere interpretations of the Charter.[493]

At the same time, the abovementioned characteristics of the Charter further blur the line between modification and dynamic interpretation, sometimes making it difficult to settle on the precise effects of subsequent practice.

As discussed extensively in previous chapters,[494] and in relation to the *Namibia Advisory Opinion* in the present chapter,[495] the practice of organs of international organizations, as distinguished from that of the individual member States, can provide a valuable source of interpretation and modification by subsequent practice. A broader concept of subsequent practice, taken to include the practice of UN organs such as the Security Council and the General Assembly, accords with the principle of effectiveness and the related doctrine of implied powers.[496] In the case

[485] See eg R Kolb, *An Introduction to the Law of the United Nations* (Hart, 2010) 170.

[486] See TM Franck, 'Who Killed Article 2(4)' (1970) 64 AJIL 809, 811.

[487] See 'Introductory Note' <https://integrity.unodc.org/pdf/iaol/charter_un.pdf> accessed 2 June 2017. See further J Müller (ed), *Reforming the United Nations: The Struggle for Legitimacy and Effectiveness* (Martinus Nijhoff, 2006).

[488] Nolte, Annex A, para 31. See also Laursen, *Changing International Law*, 65. See further Section 3.5.1.

[489] IL Claude, *The Changing United Nations* (Random House, 1967) xvi.

[490] Ibid. 127.

[491] *Certain Expenses Advisory Opinion*, Separate Opinion of Judge Spender, 186. cf MJ Glennon, *Limits of Law, Prerogatives of Power: Interventionism After Kosovo* (Palgrave, 2001) 138.

[492] Karl, Mützelburg, and Witschel, 'Article 108', para 10.

[493] Blum, *Eroding the United Nations Charter*, 243–4, 250; Liang, 'Modifying the UN Charter', 6.

[494] See Section 2.3.1(c).

[495] See Section 5.2.1.

[496] Alvarez, 'Limits of Change', 128.

of the UN, the practice of its organs has led to radical changes to the substance of the Charter's provisions, though (arguably) not to its principal purposes and objectives.

Article 2(4) of the UN Charter

An interesting case is that of Article 2(4) of the UN Charter,[497] which is of customary,[498] and arguably also peremptory,[499] status and embodies the fundamental prohibition on the use of force:

> All Members shall refrain in their international relations from the threat or use of force against the territorial integrity or political independence of any state, or in any other manner inconsistent with the Purposes of the United Nations.

Instances of subsequent practice in violation of Article 2(4) have occurred frequently since its inception, starting with the UK's derogation at issue in the 1946 *Corfu Channel* case. Other examples in the decades that followed include the North Korean invasion of South Korea, Indonesia's invasion of East Timor, as well as invasions by the Soviet Union in Hungary, Czechoslovakia, and Afghanistan, and the invasions by the US of the Dominican Republic, Grenada, and Panama.[500] A recent example is the issue of military intervention in Syria in response to its use of chemical weapons, as discussed in Chapter 3.[501]

These frequent violations led one scholar to argue that State practice after 1945 had 'so severely shattered' the meaning of Article 2(4) that 'only the words remain'.[502] Likewise, another commentator concluded that Article 2(4) had by the 1990s been effectively nullified.[503] A less extreme position regarding the status of Article 2(4) is taken by commentators arguing that Article 2(4) has been altered (rather than terminated) by subsequent practice to legally allow for threats of force[504] or even armed attacks in certain situations.[505] A further nuance is introduced by commentators suggesting that Article 2(4) may still be in the *process* of being modified by subsequent practice,[506] as 'unlawful act[s] may contain the seeds of a new rule allowing for humanitarian intervention'.[507]

[497] See generally eg A Bianchi, 'The International Regulation of the Use of Force: The Politics of Interpretive Method' (2009) 22 LJIL 651. See also Section 3.3.3(b).

[498] *Nicaragua v US*, Merits, para 202 ('though examples of trespass against this principle are not infrequent, the Court considers that it is part and parcel of customary international law').

[499] See sources cited in Section 3.3.3(b), n 357.

[500] Ford, 'Legal Processes of Change', 82.

[501] See Section 3.3.3(b).

[502] Franck, 'Who Killed Article 2(4)', 809.

[503] AC Arend, 'International Law and the Recourse to Force: A Shift in Paradigms' (1990) 27 Stan J Intl L 1, 25–8. See also AA D'Amato, 'Trashing Customary Law' (1987) 81 AJIL 101, 104–5.

[504] O Schachter, 'The Right of States to Use Armed Force' (1984) 82 Mich L Rev 1620, 1625; R Sadurska, 'Threats of Force' (1988) 82 AJIL 239.

[505] Ford, 'Legal Processes of Change', 114–15, arguing that 'a majority of writers accept that Article 2(4) has been changed by State practice', citing Arend, 'International Law', 25–7.

[506] E Heffes and BE Frenkel, 'The Decision-Making Process of the R2P Doctrine: Towards New (Old) Paths in the Use of Force in International Law' (*Opinio Juris*, 2 September 2013) <http://opiniojuris.org/2013/09/02/syria-insta-symposium-ezequiel-heffes-brian-e-frenkel-decision-making-process-r2p-doctrine-towards-new-old-paths-use-force-international-law/> accessed 5 April 2017.

[507] A Nollkaemper, 'Intervention in Syria and International Law: Inside or Out?' (*Opinio Juris*, 1 September 2013) <http://opiniojuris.org/2013/09/01/syria-insta-symposium-andre-nollkaemper-intervention-syria-international-law-inside/> accessed 5 April 2017.

It is submitted that, although violations of Article 2(4) have been widespread, the 'careful statements of intent' accompanying most such violations indicate that alteration—let alone termination—of the provision was not the intention behind the divergent subsequent practice.[508] As discussed with regard to the concept of desuetude,[509] 'to reject the legal norm because of a lack of enforcement is not only contrary to the expressed intent of the states of the world, but akin to throwing out the baby with the bath water'.[510] In fact, as remarked by the ICJ, the substance of the provision may only be further solidified if such practice is invoked as an exception *reinforcing* that rule:

If a State acts in a way prima facie incompatible with a recognized rule, but defends its conduct by appealing to exceptions or justifications contained within the rule itself, then whether or not the State's conduct is in fact justifiable on that basis, the significance of that attitude is to confirm rather than to weaken the rule.[511]

Therefore, past violations of Article 2(4) have not changed the fact that it is still being taken as a 'first baseline for justifying or critiquing action or inaction',[512] and that Article 2(4) remains legally pertinent: 'while violations have been widespread and enforcement sporadic, most states have rejected the attempts of others to change the prohibition on the use of force'.[513] This is reinforced by the fact that a modification of Article 2(4) by subsequent practice, and the concomitant modification of the underlying peremptory (or, in any event, customary) norm, would, given the nature and significance of the provision, require an extremely high threshold.[514]

Article 2(7) of the UN Charter

A similar issue can be said to exist with regard to Article 2(7) of the UN Charter, which states:

Nothing contained in the present Charter shall authorize the United Nations to intervene in matters which are essentially within the domestic jurisdiction of any state or shall require the Members to submit such matters to settlement under the present Charter; but this principle shall not prejudice the application of enforcement measures under Chapter VII.

One commentator has argued that this article has given rise to more controversy than any other provision in the UN Charter.[515] In practice, a number of different tests are applied to determine what falls within the scope of the non-intervention principle: a matter is unlikely to be regarded as within a State's domestic jurisdiction

[508] Ford, 'Legal Processes of Change', 115. [509] See Sections 2.3.5(a) and 3.3.2(b).
[510] Ford, 'Legal Processes of Change', 116.
[511] *Nicaragua v US*, Merits, para 186. See also ibid. para 202. cf C Gray, *International Law and the Use of Force* (3rd edn, OUP, 2008) 25.
[512] Nollkaemper, 'Intervention in Syria'. [513] Ford, 'Legal Processes of Change', 115.
[514] Simma, 'NATO', 3; T Ruys, *'Armed Attack' and Article 51 of the UN Charter: Evolutions in Customary Law and Practice* (CUP, 2011) 267; D Akande, 'The Legality of Military Action in Syria: Humanitarian Intervention and the Responsibility to Protect' (*OXPOL*, 29 August 2013) <http://blog.politics.ox.ac.uk/legality-military-action-syria-humanitarian-intervention-responsibility-protect/> accessed 22 April 2017. See Section 3.3.3(b) for a discussion of the threshold required in such situations, and Section 3.5 on the implications of the nature and type of treaty provision.
[515] Akehurst, *Modern Introduction*, 207–8.

if it constitutes a breach of international law, an infringement of the interests of other States, a threat to international peace, a gross violation of human rights, or an interference with progress towards self-determination in a colony. However, the general practice has been to interpret the concept of 'domestic jurisdiction' narrowly—the opposite of the drafter's intention.[516] Given the essential nature of the principle enshrined in Article 2(7), such a substantive change to its original scope of operation arguably amounts to a modification by subsequent practice.

It may also be noted that Article 2(7) states that the principle of non-intervention in matters of domestic jurisdiction 'shall not prejudice the application of enforcement measures under Charter VII', in relation to action with respect to threats to or breaches of the peace and acts of aggression. Pursuant to UN practice, this proviso at the end of Article 2(7) is unnecessary, since a threat to the peace, breach of the peace, or act of aggression is automatically treated as not constituting a matter of domestic jurisdiction.[517] This development with regard to the last sentence of Article 2(7) does not appear to go beyond the bounds of the treaty text and amounts merely to clarification through interpretative practice.

Peacekeeping operations

Peacekeeping operations have no express basis in the UN Charter, but have nevertheless become established practice.[518] They are often said to fall under so-called 'Charter VI ½',[519] a term famously coined by former Secretary-General Dag Hammarskjöld during the 1960 Congo Crisis. The label stems from the fact that peacekeeping operations have been authorized under Chapter VI of the Charter on the 'pacific settlement of disputes' (traditional peacekeeping operations), as well as under Chapter VII on 'action with respect to threats to the peace, breaches of the peace, and acts of aggression' (peacekeeping with a broader mandate, to secure delivery of humanitarian assistance, disarm militias, etc).[520]

The competence to authorize peacekeeping operations has been interpreted as flowing from the implied powers of the Security Council and General Assembly.[521] However, some commentators have regarded them as a 'practical experiment invented out of necessity'.[522] This brings us back to the discussions in Chapter 2

[516] Ibid. [517] Ibid.

[518] M Bothe, 'Peace-keeping' in B Simma (ed), *The Charter of the United Nations: A Commentary* (2nd edn, OUP, 2002) 648; H Nasu, *International Law on Peacekeeping: A Study of Article 40 of the UN Charter* (Martinus Nijhoff, 2009) 28; Venzke, *How Interpretation Makes International* Law, 72; C Brölmann, 'Specialized Rules of Treaty Interpretation: International Organizations' in DB Hollis (ed), *The Oxford Guide to Treaties* (OUP, 2012) 507, 521.

[519] UN, *The Blue Helmets: A Review of United Nations Peacekeeping* (UN Department of Public Information 1985) 5; Kolb, *An Introduction*, 171.

[520] See further on the evolution of the practice of peacekeeping operations eg M Katayanagi, *Human Rights Functions of United Nations Peacekeeping Operations* (Martinus Nijhoff, 2002) 37–66; O Engdahl, *Protection of Personnel in Peace Operations: The Role of the 'Safety Convention' Against the Background of General International Law* (Martinus Nijhoff, 2006) 15–17.

[521] *Certain Expenses Advisory Opinion*, 164; ND White, 'The UN Charter and Peacekeeping Forces: Constitutional Issues' (1996) 3 International Peacekeeping 43, 46–9.

[522] Nasu, *International Law on Peacekeeping*, 28, citing eg EC Luck, *UN Security Council: Practice and Promise* (Routledge, 2006) 36–7.

on implied powers and Chapter 3 on distinguishing between interpretation and modification. The crux lies in determining when the effects of subsequent practice can be said to go beyond a reasonable interpretation on the basis of implied powers and amount to modification.[523] The practice of peacekeeping operations has supplemented the UN Charter in a way that constitutes a significant change to its substantive provisions, though not to the Charter's object and purpose(s). The lack of a concrete textual basis, coupled with the gradual evolution of peacekeeping operations towards a more expansive mandate—and even the institutionalization of the notion in the form of the intergovernmental Peacebuilding Commission established in 2005 by General Assembly and Security Council resolutions[524]—could be regarded as a modification in the form of a significant extension[525] of the Charter by means of subsequent practice.

Threats to 'international peace and security' under Chapter VII of the Charter

According to Article 39 of Chapter VII of the UN Charter, the Security Council may only take non-military measures under Article 41 or military measures under Article 42 once it has determined the existence of a threat to the peace, breach of the peace, or act of aggression, 'in order to maintain or restore international peace and security'. Chapter VII appears to limit such action to threats to *international* peace and security, defined by the 2004 High Level Panel on Threats, Challenges and Change as 'any event or process that leads to large-scale death or lessening of life chances and undermines States as the basic unit of the international system'.[526] The notion of threats to international peace and security presumably rules out intervention in a State's internal affairs, even when it comes to protecting defenceless civilians (a State cannot be an aggressor on its own territory). What is more, the intention of the drafters, as reflected in the original purpose of the Security Council, was to take action against States engaging in aggressive acts against other States,[527] and maintain the 'negative peace'; that is, maintenance of the *status quo* and prevention of the use of force.[528]

Since the Cold War, however, the view has taken hold 'that the "negative peace" cannot be maintained in the light of continued flagrant and mass violations of human rights'.[529] It has therefore been argued that the original, narrowly conceived notion of 'peace and security' enshrined as the essential object and purpose of the Charter has been transformed over time into a more positive, active concept with a 'preventive dimension',[530] to reflect a new conception of collective

[523] See in particular Section 2.5.4.

[524] UNGA Res 60/180 of 20 December 2005, UN Doc A/RES/60/180 (2005); UNSC Res 1645 (2005) of 20 December 2005, UN Doc S/RES/1645 (2005).

[525] See Section 3.3.1.

[526] UNGA, 'A More Secure World: Our Shared Responsibility', *Report of the High-level Panel on Threats, Challenges and Change*, UN GAOR, 59th session, UN Doc A/59/565 (2004) 12.

[527] M Payandeh, 'The United Nations, Military Intervention, and Regime Change in Libya' (2012) 52 VJIL 355, 364, citing J Frowein and N Krisch, 'Article 39' in B Simma (ed), *The Charter of the United Nations: A Commentary*, vol I (2nd edn, OUP, 2002) 717.

[528] N Schrijver, 'The Future of the Charter of the United Nations' (2006) 10 Max Planck UNYB 1, 16.

[529] Ibid 17.

[530] Liang, 'Modifying the UN Charter', 12, citing Schrijver, 'The Future of the Charter', 9–10.

security.[531] Moreover, it has become 'routine' Security Council practice—tacitly accepted by the UN membership[532]—to treat not only inter-State conflicts, but also *intra*-State conflicts, such as human rights violations and civil wars, as potential threats to 'international peace and security' under Article 39.[533]

The Security Council has sometimes justified measures taken under Chapter VII by reference to their destabilizing effects on the region. As early as 1960, the Security Council declared that South Africa's apartheid regime and large-scale racially motivated killings could endanger international peace and security[534]—although South Africa's policy led to military conflicts with other States, which constitutes an international element. In 1965, it labelled the situation resulting from the unilateral declaration of independence by the authorities in Southern Rhodesia as a threat to international peace and security.[535] The bulk of the practice, however, emerged in the 1990s. In 1991, for instance, the Security Council qualified the human rights violations committed by Iraq against the Iraqi civilian population as a threat to international peace and security.[536] The same occurred in relation to the civil war in Yugoslavia in the early 1990s.[537] The Security Council also seems to have regarded the magnitude of the human tragedy and suffering in Somalia and Rwanda as such threats.[538] The same applied to the humanitarian situation in Haiti.[539] More recently, the humanitarian crisis and human rights violations in Darfur were regarded as threats to international peace and security.[540] In the majority of such cases, the Security Council authorized 'all necessary measures', a phrase that includes military action.[541] Another recent example is the 2011 Security Council resolution authorizing military action in Libya, allowing the use of 'all necessary measures' to protect the civilian population.[542] The situation did not constitute a threat to 'international peace and security' in the sense envisioned by the founders of the Charter, but corresponded with the settled practice of the Security Council to include seemingly 'internal' human rights violations within its definition.[543]

[531] UNGA, 'A More Secure World', paras 7, 44–58; UNGA, 'In Larger Freedom: Towards Development, Security and Human Rights for All', *Report of the Secretary-General*, 21 March 2005, UN Doc A/59/2005, para 78.

[532] Payandeh, 'The United Nations', 366, citing Frowein and Krisch, 'Article 39', 724.

[533] Payandeh, 'The United Nations', 364–6, citing PH Kooijmans, 'The Enlargement of the Concept "Threat to the Peace"' in RJ Dupuy (ed), *The Development of the Role of the Security Council* (Kluwer, 1993) 111; Frowein and Krisch, 'Article 39', 723–6; C Gray, 'The Use of Force and the International Legal Order' in MD Evans (ed), *International Law* (3rd edn, OUP, 2010) 615, 623.

[534] UNSC Res 134 (1960) of 1 April 1960, UN Doc S/RES/134 (1960) paras 1, 4.

[535] UNSC Res 217 (1965) of 20 November 1965, UN Doc S/RES/217 (1965) para 1.

[536] UNSC Res 688 (1991) of 5 April 1991, UN Doc S/RES/688 (1991) paras 3, 9–14.

[537] See eg UNSC Res 713 (1991) of 25 September 1991, UN Doc S/RES/713 (1991) paras 3–4.

[538] See eg UNSC Res 794 (1992) of 3 December 1992, UN Doc S/RES/794 (1992); UNSC Res 918 (1994) of 17 May 1994, UN Doc S/RES/918 (1994).

[539] UNSC Res 940 (1994) of 31 July 1994, UN Doc S/RES/940 (1994).

[540] UNSC Res 1556 (2004) of 30 July 2004, UN Doc S/RES/1556 (2004).

[541] A Cassese and JHH Weiler (eds), *International Law* (2nd edn, OUP, 2005) 350; Payandeh, 'The United Nations', 368.

[542] UNSC Res 1973 (2011) of 17 March 2011, UN Doc S/RES/1973 (2011).

[543] Payandeh, 'The United Nations', 393.

When the ICTY dealt with the preliminary question of whether the Security Council had the power to establish the ICTY pursuant to Article 41 of Chapter VII of the UN Charter in the *Tadić* case, it held:

> [E]ven if it [the armed conflict in the Former Yugoslavia] were considered merely as an 'internal armed conflict', it would still constitute a 'threat to the peace' according to the settled practice of the Security Council and the common understanding of the United Nations membership in general. Indeed, the practice of the Security Council is rich with cases of civil war or internal strife which it classified as 'threat to the peace' and dealt with under Chapter VII, with the encouragement or even at the behest of the General Assembly (...). It can thus be said that there is a common understanding, manifested by the 'subsequent practice' of the membership of the United Nations at large, that the 'threat to the peace' of Article 39 may include, as one of its species, internal armed conflicts.[544]

Thus, this Security Council practice, generally accepted by the UN Member States, has 'departed significantly from the system of collective security envisioned by the founders of the Charter (...) [through] an expansive reading of Article 39' to include *internal* disturbances such as humanitarian crises.[545] The implications of this changed concept of threat to the peace are far-reaching:

> The fact that the political organs of the United Nations thus assumed the power to determine that serious violations of human rights constitute a threat to peace can be viewed as one of the most fundamental policy changes within the United Nations system, if not in international relations as a whole.[546]

There is debate as to whether this practice constitutes a dynamic interpretation or tacit modification of Article 39 of the UN Charter. Arguments in favour of interpretation include the fact that the wording of the provision is open-ended,[547] that the Charter (and the competences of the Security Council[548]) should be interpreted in a purposive or evolutionary manner in light of the end goal of maintaining international peace and security,[549] that human rights violations have now become a matter of international concern,[550] that the Security Council has considerable discretion to characterize a situation as a 'threat to peace and

[544] *Prosecutor v Dusko Tadić*, Appeal on Jurisdiction, para 30. See further JE Alvarez, 'Nuremberg Revisited: The Tadić Case' (1996) 7 EJIL 245.

[545] Payandeh, 'The United Nations', 364.

[546] Schrijver, 'The Future of the Charter', 17.

[547] WM Reisman, 'Report, Tenth Commission: Present Problems of the Use of Armed Force in International Law, Sub-group on Humanitarian Intervention' (2007) 72 AIDI 237, 243.

[548] See eg the formulation of Art 42 of the UN Charter: 'it may take action (...) as may be necessary to maintain or restore international peace and security'.

[549] See eg *Namibia Advisory Opinion*, para 31; G Ress, 'The Interpretation of the Charter' in B Simma (ed), *The Charter of the United Nations: A Commentary*, vol I (2nd edn, OUP, 2012) 13, 23–5; M Payandeh, 'With Great Power Comes Great Responsibility? The Concept of Responsibility to Protect Within the Process of International Lawmaking' (2010) 35 Yale JIL 469, 496, 506–8.

[550] Frowein and Krisch, 'Article 39', 720–1.

security',[551] and references to the controversial notion of 'responsibility to protect'.[552]

On the other hand, the word 'international' seems to require some kind of justification of the trans-boundary effects of the crisis or situation in question. What complicates matters further is that the Security Council has avoided characterizing internal conflicts as the basis for measures in response to 'international' threats.[553] It has at times justified measures taken on account of massive human rights violations, humanitarian crises, and civil wars by referring to their destabilizing effects on the region, taking into account consequences such as outflows of refugees.[554] Thus, it has relied on negative effects stemming from 'internal' threats to validate measures to prevent 'international' ones.[555] In some cases, however, the Council's practice has gone even further, determining that the sheer scale of human tragedy is sufficient to amount to a threat to international peace and security, such as in the case of Somalia, without referring to any trans-boundary or destabilizing effects on the region.[556] It also declined to provide such justification in the case of Libya.[557] In this sense, the subsequent practice of the Security Council seems to diverge from the ordinary meaning of the text of Article 39 by failing to base action taken under Chapter VII in terms of what would (at least traditionally) be regarded as 'international' elements of such conflicts.[558] This practice has led to the 'continuous enlargement of the concept of threats to the peace, particularly in terms of allowing for various forms of humanitarian intervention in domestic situations, to the point of its becoming a new feature of the action of the United Nations'.[559]

Chapter VII provisions could even be interpreted to include climate change. The argument is based on the fact that to 'determine the existence of any threat to the peace, breach of the peace, or act of aggression' pursuant to Article 39, the Council looks to the 'root causes of conflict',[560] which can include 'non-military sources of instability in the economic, social, humanitarian and ecological fields'.[561] In 2005, then Secretary-General Kofi Annan also referred to climate change as a viable threat,[562] and in 2007, the concern was expressed that '[a]n unstable climate

551 See eg United Nations Conference on International Organization (25 April–26 June 1945) *Report of the Rapporteur of Committee 3 to Commission III*, UNCIO Doc 881, III/3/46 of 10 June 1945; E De Wet, *The Chapter VII Powers of the United Nations Security Council* (Hart, 2004) 133ff; M Wood, 'United Nations, Security Council' in R Wolfrum (ed), *Max Planck Encyclopedia of Public International Law* (OUP, 2007) paras 18, 25–30.

552 Payandeh, 'With Great Power Comes Great Responsibility?', 495–6.

553 See eg KM Manusama, *The United Nations Security Council in the Post-Cold War Era: Applying the Principle of Legality* (*Legal Aspects of International Organization*) (Martinus Nijhoff, 2006) 47; Payandeh, 'The United Nations', 355, 371.

554 See eg S Chesterman, '"Leading from Behind": The Responsibility to Protect, the Obama Doctrine, and Humanitarian Intervention after Libya' (2011) 25 Ethics & Intl Aff 279.

555 See eg Frowein and Krisch, 'Article 39', 725; Payandeh, 'The United Nations', 370.

556 See eg Payandeh, 'The United Nations', 371.

557 Ibid. 393.

558 Frowein and Krisch, 'Article 39', 717.

559 F Orrego Vicuña, *International Dispute Settlement in an Evolving Global Society: Constitutionalization, Accessibility, Privatization* (CUP, 2004) 23.

560 Statement by the President of the Security Council, 12 July 2005, UN Doc S/PRST/2005/30.

561 Note by the President of the Security Council, 31 January 1992, UN Doc S/23500. See also eg Venzke, *How Interpretation Makes International Law*, 72.

562 UNGA, 'In Larger Freedom: Towards Development, Security and Human Rights for All', *Report of the Secretary-General*, 21 March 2005, UN Doc A/59/2005, para 78.

will exacerbate some of the core drivers of conflict, such as migratory pressures and competition for resources.'[563] Additionally, in 2009, the General Assembly unanimously passed a resolution confirming the possible security implications of climate change,[564] followed by a Report of the Secretary-General.[565] The HIV/AIDS epidemic has also been declared a threat to international peace and security in the sense of Chapter VII.[566]

In any event, the practice of the Security Council has strayed considerably from the original focus of Article 39 on inter-State conflicts[567] and the maintenance of the 'negative' peace,[568] with far-reaching implications.[569] This change points to a gradual, tacit modification by subsequent practice (arguably in the form of an extension, rather than an alteration, of the treaty text[570])—even if the development is fully legitimate on account of the fact that these 'threats' were not foreseeable at the time of its inception.

The enforcement mechanism under Chapter VII of the Charter

The peace enforcement mechanism originally envisioned under Chapter VII—once a threat to peace and security has been determined—also raises further issues of modification by subsequent practice. For instance, the drafters envisioned a military enforcement mechanism under Article 43 of the UN Charter pursuant to which UN members must provide the Security Council with armed forces to be placed under the latter's command, which has, however, never been used.[571] Instead, the Security Council has, *inter alia*, established a practice of providing broad authorization—'all necessary measures'—for the use of force intended to prevent or contain humanitarian catastrophes, at least since the intervention in Iraq in the 1990s,[572] and as in the more recent case of Libya.[573] This practice of the Security Council strays significantly from the original enforcement mechanism envisioned by the drafters, which placed restrictive exceptions on the prohibition on the use of force (this links to the previous discussion regarding the question of the potential gradual erosion of Article 2(4) of the Charter).[574] The effects of this practice, though perhaps, strictly speaking, not completely at odds with the text of the respective provisions, may carry

563 UNSC, Letter dated 5 April 2007 from the Permanent Representative of the United Kingdom of Great Britain and Northern Ireland to the United Nations addressed to the President of the Security Council (S/2007/186), UN SCOR, 62nd sess, 5663rd meeting, 17 April 2007, UN Doc S/PV.5663.

564 UNGA Res 63/281 of 3 June 2009, 'Climate Change and Its Possible Security Implications', UN Doc A/RES/63/281 (2009).

565 UNGA, 'Climate Change and Its Possible Security Implications', *Report of the Secretary-General*, 11 September 2009, UN Doc A/64/350. See also Statement by the President of the Security Council, 20 July 2011, UN Doc S/PRST/2011/15.

566 UNSC Res 1308 (2000) of 17 July 2000, UN Doc S/RES/1308 (2000).

567 Payandeh, 'The United Nations', 392.

568 Schrijver, 'The Future of the Charter', 16.

569 See text to n 559 above.

570 See Section 3.3.1.

571 A similar remark can be made with regard to the Military Staff Committee provided for in Article 47 of the UN Charter, which has been effectively inactive since 1947. For the time being, these provisions are regarded as dormant rather than as having fallen into desuetude. See generally the repertoire of the practice of the Security Council with regard to the provisions of Chapter VII of the UN Charter, available at <www.un.org/en/sc/repertoire/actions.shtml> accessed 4 June 2017.

572 See UNSC Res 678 (1990) of 29 November 1990, UN Doc S/RES/678 (1990).

573 Payandeh, 'The United Nations', 398–400, 403.

574 Ibid. 403.

significant implications and raise 'questions that touch upon the very foundations of the international order'.[575]

[T]here are now, within the UN's terms, several precedents for recommendatory military action, and it is arguable that the Security Council has by its practice established a power to authorize states to take 'necessary measures' with regard to a particular conflict or situation. On the other hand, it is arguably legally unacceptable to imply a power which goes against the express provisions of the Charter which clearly envisage collective security in the form of the centralisation of armed force.[576]

Moreover, pursuant to Article 24(1), the UN Charter bestows the primary responsibility for the maintenance of peace and security on the Security Council, in accordance with the powers granted, *inter alia*, under Chapter VII. However, the Security Council has not retained a significant degree of authority or control over the various interventions, but seems instead to have transferred it to the intervening States. This practice prompted a Member State to argue that '[t]he Security Council has no right to deprive itself of its own authority, or to delegate that authority to a number of states, unless the Charter is properly amended.'[577] The Security Council practice further enlarges the scope of its authorization to use force,[578] despite the narrowly intended scope of Article 2(4), and appears to contravene the provision in Article 24(1) of the Charter. Moreover, on account of its new 'normative reality', the sentence in Article 42 of the UN Charter providing, *inter alia*, that the Security Council 'may take such action by air, sea, or land forces as may be necessary to maintain or restore international peace and security', may effectively be replaced by the phrase 'may authorize all Member States to take all measures necessary (...)'.[579] Thus, the Security Council's practice of not actively controlling or delegating in such situations, accompanied by the overall acceptance of the Member States, may constitute a modification (most likely in the form of an alteration[580]) of, *inter alia*, Article 42 of the Charter.[581]

In any event, it is no longer possible to deny that the meaning of threats to 'international peace and security' under Article 39 of the Charter and the application of the peace enforcement mechanism provisions in Chapter VII have changed significantly over time.[582] The fact that provisions in Chapter VII are open-textured allows

[575] Ibid. 402.

[576] ND White, *Keeping the Peace: The United Nations and the Maintenance of International Peace and Security* (2nd edn, Manchester UP, 1997) 128.

[577] Iraq's statement in UNSC, *Provisional Verbatim Record of the 2938th Meeting*, 25 August 1990, UN Doc S/PV.2938, 71 (in relation to the adoption of UNSC Res 665 (1990) of 25 August 1990, UN Doc S/RES/665 (1990)). See also eg ibid. 12-13/15 (Cuba), 22–5 (Colombia), and, to a lesser degree, 37 (Malaysia). See further NM Blokker, 'Is the Authorization Authorized? Powers and Practice of the UN Security Council to Authorize the Use of Force by "Coalitions of the Able and Willing"' (2000) 11 EJIL 541, 555–60.

[578] Distefano, 'L'accord tacite', 32.

[579] Ibid. (Own translation.)

[580] See Section 3.3.1.

[581] See Distefano, 'L'accord tacite', 32, referring to Art 42 of the Charter as a primary example of modification by (unopposed) subsequent practice.

[582] See eg Kooijmans, '"Threat to the Peace"', 111; Frowein and Krisch, 'Article 39', 723–6; Gray, 'The Use of Force', 615, 623; Brölmann, 'Specialized Rules of Treaty Interpretation', 521; Payandeh, 'The United Nations', 364–6; Venzke, *How Interpretation Makes International* Law, 72.

for more liberal interpretations, which in turn makes it more difficult to discern whether subsequent practice has gone beyond its interpretative range and crossed into the realm of modification. As explained in Section 3.5 of this book, both the ambiguity and evolutionary potential of certain treaty provisions provide adaptation mechanisms that serve as alternatives to treaty modification by subsequent practice. Moreover, any discussion of the competences of the Security Council will include the doctrine of implied powers, which again enlarges the scope of possible interpretations under Chapter VII. Nevertheless, some of the central terms of Chapter VII of the UN Charter have changed so significantly that they can reasonably be said to go beyond dynamic interpretations, into the realm of modification by subsequent practice—a 'normative transformation' of the UN Charter over time.[583]

Other examples relating to the UN Charter

Other examples of potential modifications by subsequent practice of the UN Charter may be mentioned here briefly. For instance, Article 19 of the Charter on the suspension of voting rights when a member falls behind on its payment of certain financial contributions to the organization, such as with regard to peacekeeping operations, is no longer applied, and may represent an example of modification, in the form of termination, by 'negative' subsequent practice.[584] Similarly, treaty modification by subsequent practice arguably took place in the aftermath of the ICJ's *Certain Expenses Advisory Opinion*.[585] The ICJ had upheld the textual interpretation of Article 17(2) of the Charter, according to which '[t]he expenses of the Organization shall be borne by the Members as apportioned by the General Assembly.' By contrast to the ICJ's view, the compromise that was later reached through States' subsequent conduct may have effectively altered the application of Article 17(2) to such an extent that the obligation has since fallen into desuetude.[586]

In discussions in the UN Sixth Committee on 'treaties over time', it was also pointed out that Articles 53, 77, and 107 of the UN Charter—'former enemies clauses'—are now considered to have fallen into desuetude.[587] Moreover, the decision to seat Russia in the place of the Soviet Union as a permanent member of the Security Council can be seen as a modification of the express wording of Article 23 of the UN Charter, which provides that the 'Republic of China, France, the Union of Soviet Socialist Republics, the United Kingdom of Great Britain and Northern Ireland, and the United States of America shall be permanent members

583 Liang, 'Modifying the UN Charter', 12.

584 See A Verdross and B Simma, *Universelles Völkerrecht: Theorie und Praxis* (3rd edn, Duncker & Humblot, 1984) 162; Villiger, *Customary International Law and Treaties* (1985), para 305.

585 See *Certain Expenses Advisory Opinion*, 179–80.

586 TM Franck, *Nation Against Nation: What Happened to the UN Dream and What the US Can Do About It* (OUP, 1985) 259. See also PJ Kuijper, 'Law of GATT as a Special Field of International Law, Ignorance, Further Refinement or Self-Contained System of International Law?' (1994) 25 NYBIL 227, 231 (questioning eg if GATT Art V on freedom of road transit has not fallen into desuetude between the EU Member States—ie *inter se* modification).

587 *Topical summary of the discussion held in the Sixth Committee of the General Assembly during its 64th session*, UN Doc A/CN.4/620 (26 January 2010) Ch II(I), para 87.

of the Security Council'.[588] On the other hand, the Russian Federation is seen as a continuation of the Soviet Union.[589] The same issue exists in relation to the tacit replacement in Article 23(1) of the Republic of China (now Taiwan) with the People's Republic of China.[590]

As these examples show, the diversity of tacit modifications of the UN Charter—relating to substantive and procedural provisions, ranging from less consequential to far-reaching changes, and constituting modification in the form of alterations, extensions, and terminations by subsequent practice—illustrates how the characteristics of the Charter make it highly prone to informal change, and a prime subject for observing the impact of subsequent practice.

5.3.1b NATO

There is fervent debate as to whether the scope of action of the North Atlantic Treaty Organization is expanding beyond its mandate—an issue already touched upon in Section 5.2.4 above. The crux lies in the fact that during the Cold War, NATO mainly focused on collective defence and deterrence oriented towards the Soviet Union. At the same time, it carried out certain narrowly defined 'political' functions, including the democratization of its member States, and managed peaceful relations among NATO allies.[591] At its inception, Article 5 of the North Atlantic Treaty, its collective defence provision, was the Alliance's central tenet. The Article provides:

> The Parties agree that an armed attack against one or more of them in Europe or North America shall be considered an attack against them all and consequently they agree that, if such an armed attack occurs, each of them, in exercise of the right of individual or collective self-defence recognised by Article 51 of the Charter of the United Nations, will assist the Party or Parties so attacked by taking forthwith, individually and in concert with the other Parties, such action as it deems necessary, including the use of armed force, to restore and maintain the security of the North Atlantic area. (...)

With the end of the Cold War, however, the primary purpose of the Alliance disappeared. Consequently, in recent years, NATO has adapted to a new range of global issues, especially in the aftermath of 11 September 2001. By means of subsequent practice, NATO has significantly changed its purpose from collective defence to a much broader set of security-related tasks.[592] The aforementioned 1991, 1999, and 2010 'Strategic Concepts'—amounting to subsequent agreements—mark this gradual shift from a collective defence system to a cooperative defence system, re-interpreting the 1949 North Atlantic Treaty to adapt it to the current

[588] Alvarez, 'Limits of Change', 127.

[589] See eg M Koskenniemi and M Lehto, 'La succession d'états dans l'ex-URSS, en ce qui concerne particulièrement les relations avec la Finlande' (1992) 38 AFDI 179, 186–9; AG Oude Elferink, *The Law of Maritime Boundary Delimitation: A Case Study of the Russian Federation* (Martinus Nijhoff, 1994) 7; BA Boczek, *International Law: A Dictionary* (Scarecrow Press, 2005) 131.

[590] Karl, Mützelburg, and Witschel, 'Article 108', para 10.

[591] SC Hofmann, 'Debating Strategy in NATO: Obstacles to Defining a Meaningful New Strategic Concept' (IFRI, 2008) 3.

[592] Ibid. 1.

geopolitical and strategic context.[593] For instance, the 1991 New Strategic Concept recognized that, '[i]n contrast with the predominant threat of the past, the risks to Allied security that remain are multi-faceted in nature and multi-directional, which makes them hard to predict and assess.'[594] Moreover, the updated and revised 2010 Strategic Concept, entitled 'Active Engagement, Modern Defence', can be further distinguished from its 1991 and 1999 precursors by the fact that it lists collective defence as only one of NATO's three 'essential core tasks', the other two being 'crisis management' and 'cooperative security'.

Thus, the present-day focus of NATO is no longer merely on collective defence under Article 5, but on a much broader range of global problems, such as combating terrorism, non-proliferation of weapons of mass destruction, and organized crime—a new functional scope. NATO's *geographical* scope of action has also changed from a focus on the relevant territories of the member States to the international plane to reflect its new focus on issues of global purport,[595] and generally as a result of changing power distributions in the international system,[596] including the emergence of the EU.[597] These developments concerning the organization's structure and scope indicate a marked modification by subsequent practice—in the form of both an alteration and a significant extension—of the Alliance's original mandate.[598] In fact, when compared to NATO's purposes and objectives during the Cold War period, subsequent practice seems to have both altered and supplemented the Treaty's original object and purpose, transforming the organization into one tailored to the needs of modern international society.[599]

As discussed,[600] the question of whether subsequent practice has led to a modification of the North Atlantic Treaty has also come up in national proceedings before the German Federal Constitutional Court. The Court focused on whether there was sufficient evidence of the parties' intention to *formally amend* the Treaty. In its 1994 judgment, it found that, although the 1991 Strategic Concept may have had

[593] See further eg G Nolte, 'The "New Tasks" of NATO and WEU: International Law and German Constitutional Law Aspects' (1994) 54 ZaöRV 122; J Ringsmose and S Rynning (eds), *NATO's New Strategic Concept: A Comprehensive Assessment* (DIIS, 2011).

[594] 1991 Strategic Concept, Part II, para 20.

[595] Hofmann, 'Debating Strategy in NATO', 4.

[596] DS Yost, *NATO Transformed: The Alliance's New Roles in International Security* (United States Institute for Peace Press, 1998).

[597] Hofmann, 'Debating Strategy in NATO', 2. The institutional overlap between NATO's current mandate and the EU's Common Security and Defence Policy has triggered debates in light of talks of further expansion pushed by the US, who argues in favour of NATO becoming a global security institution, while most European States oppose this view, insisting that NATO should be confined to the Euro-Atlantic area. See RD Asmus and RC Holbrooke, 'Re-reinventing NATO', *Riga Papers* (2006) 1 <www.gmfus.org/doc/A4_Holbrooke_c.pdf> accessed 10 April 2016.

[598] Hofmann, 'Debating Strategy in NATO', 4. cf Nolte, 'The "New Tasks" of NATO and WEU', 122.

[599] See eg L Condorelli, 'Conclusions générales' in SFDI (ed), Colloque de Genève, *La pratique et le droit international* (Pédone, 2004) 304 ('En effet, le traité O.T.A.N. d'aujourd'hui, tel que métamorphosé par la pratique, n'est plus le même accord international par rapport auquel les Etats membres avaient exprimé leur consentement à être liés conformément aux dispositions constitutionnelles internes pertinentes.').

[600] See Section 5.2.4.

the same effect as a formal amendment, it did not constitute a modification of the kind that would require renewed parliamentary approval under German law.[601] In its 2001 decision, the Court dealt with similar questions, this time with regard to the 1999 Strategic Concept. In line with its prior judgment, the Court considered that the developments in subsequent practice had not gone beyond the scope of a legitimate reinterpretation of the treaty to the point where a *formal* amendment was required—even though crisis response operations, not premised upon an attack on the territory of a NATO party, clearly did not fall within the scope of the Treaty's essential collective defence provision. It is unclear whether this reasoning would still apply in relation to the 2010 Strategic Concept (not examined by the Court), which, as mentioned, fundamentally shifts the emphasis from collective defence to other essential concerns of NATO members. On the one hand, the Court referred to the open-textured nature of the NATO Treaty,[602] a feature that makes it more difficult to identify modification by subsequent practice by expanding the interpretative range of the treaty provisions in question. On the other hand, it recognized that the 1999 Strategic Concept drastically expanded upon the meaning and scope of the original provisions. In the words of the Court, '[t]he possibility of so-called crisis response operations (…) constitutes an important expansion of NATO's tasks, *which has not been implied in the Treaty*'.[603] Again, this suggests that the Strategic Concept modified—by significantly supplementing—the underlying treaty of the Alliance (but fell short of a formal amendment).

Thus, in light of the fundamental changes that have taken place by means of subsequent practice and agreements to the organization's structure and functional and geographical scope—and, accordingly, to the object and purpose of its founding Treaty—the example of NATO points in the direction of a modification.[604]

5.3.1c ILO Constitution

Another example of modification by subsequent practice within an international organization is the voting procedure followed in the International Labour Organization (ILO) for the election of the Governing Body of the International Labour Office (the organization's executive body), pursuant to Article 7(7) of the ILO Constitution, and of the President of the International Labour Conference, pursuant to Article 17(1) of the same instrument.[605] These procedures are elaborated in the rules of the Organization by means of Standing Orders. These dictate that, under Article 7[606] and Article 17,[607] voting must be carried out by means of a secret ballot. However, the

601 *International Military Operations*, 339.

602 *PDS v Federal Government* (English excerpts), para 12.

603 Ibid. (Emphasis added.)

604 cf Brölmann, 'Specialized Rules of Treaty Interpretation', 523.

605 International Labour Organization Constitution 1919, 15 UNTS 40.

606 ILO, *Compendium of Rules Applicable to the Governing Body of the International Labour Office* (2016) <http://www.ilo.org/wcmsp5/groups/public/---dgreports/---jur/documents/genericdocument/wcms_429623.pdf> accessed 4 June 2017, 15–16, Art 1.4.

607 ILO, *Standing Orders of the International Labour Conference* (2002) <www.ilo.org/public/english/standards/relm/ilc/ilc-so.htm> accessed 4 June 2017, Art 19(10), stating clearly that '[a]ny vote on the election of the President shall be by secret ballot.'

established practice of ILO members diverges from this rule.[608] The Chairperson of the Governing Body and the President of the Conference have for many years been elected by the Governing Body and the Conference, respectively, *without* following a voting procedure. Instead, the regional groups of the 'Government group' conduct in-depth consultations in order to appoint a Chairperson by consensus, without holding a ballot vote as stipulated in the Organization's texts.[609] This practice is carried out in accordance with the unwritten rule of fair geographical rotation, which allows each of the regions—the Americas, Africa, Asia, and Europe—to accede to the Office of Chairperson of the Governing Body based on a four-year cycle.[610]

As confirmed in the Standing Orders of the ILO itself, this practice pursuant to the principle of geographical rotation has, through regular use and over an extended period of time, become an established—albeit unwritten—procedural 'rule'.[611] Therefore, the subsequent practice of the ILO members can be said to have effectively modified the aforementioned voting provisions of the Organization's constitutive treaty—provisions of a procedural rather than a substantive nature. It would be going too far to argue that these provisions have fallen into desuetude, since the codified voting procedures can still be reverted to should the need arise. They remain in operation as a default option if, for instance, a regional group is unable to reach a decision on the appointment of a candidate as Chairperson of the Governing Body.[612]

A much older example of modification by subsequent practice in the ILO context is the practice that emerged with regard to requesting the opinion of the International Labour Office on matters concerning the interpretation of the ILO Constitution.[613] Article 37(1) of the ILO Constitution assigned this task to the PCIJ (it has now been modified to refer to the ICJ):

> Any question or dispute relating to the interpretation of this Constitution or of any subsequent Convention concluded by the Members in pursuance of the provisions of this Constitution shall be referred for decision to the Permanent Court of International Justice.[614]

This option was rarely used and was seen as a last resort.[615] Yet it cannot be said to have fallen into desuetude since the same rule exists and is regarded as valid today. Rather, the practice triggered the emergence of the *parallel* procedure of requesting opinions from the International Labour Office, even on topics of importance, despite the lack of a concrete basis in the organization's constitutive text (unless it is taken

[608] L Picard, 'La pratique comme fondement de l'action du Bureau International du Travail' in SFDI (ed), Colloque de Genève, *La pratique et le droit international* (Pédone, 2004) 209, 217.

[609] *Compendium of Rules Applicable to the Governing Body of the International Labour Office*, para 16.

[610] Ibid. para 15.

[611] Ibid. para 3 ('The consolidation of the rules (...) contains not only texts, but also practical solutions that (...) through repetition, have become precedents that the Governing Body follows, as in the case of the "rule" of geographical rotation of the office of Chairperson of the Governing Body.').

[612] Ibid. para 17.

[613] CW Jenks, 'The Interpretation of International Labour Conventions by the International Labour Office' (1939) 20 BYBIL 132, 133.

[614] Pursuant to Art 37(2) ILO Constitution, a tribunal can also be established to determine such questions or disputes.

[615] Jenks, 'Interpretation of International Labour Conventions', 133.

to fall under implied powers, which in this case seems doubtful given the Office's clear lack of interpretative authority under the ILO Constitution).[616] This practice led to a substantial 'jurisprudence' of opinions of the International Labour Office, which remained unchallenged by the member States.[617] Hence, it amounted to subsequent practice establishing the agreement of the member States to the respective procedure.[618] The practice thus modified Article 37(1) of the ILO Constitution by *supplementing* it with a new procedure (the procedure established is in principle parallel to the Article 37 procedure, so it does not as such alter it).[619]

Both practices mentioned with regard to the ILO represent procedural modifications—primarily in the form of extensions rather than alterations—of provisions of the constitutive text that clarify and facilitate the decision-making process and general operation of the organization, but do not affect its object and purpose. The threshold for such modifications is therefore significantly lower than in the case of other modifications of constitutive treaties explored above.

5.3.1d GATT/WTO Context

Given the rigidity of WTO amendment procedures,[620] States have turned to various alternative mechanisms for adaptation of the WTO regime,[621] including treaty modification by subsequent practice—despite the Appellate Body's reluctance to recognize the possibility in dispute settlement proceedings.[622] First, a brief reference can be made to the practice of consensus decisions that replaced majority voting in the organization, a procedural modification similar to that identified in the context of the ILO.[623] Second, as we have seen in Chapter 2, it is possible for treaties to collectively amount to relevant subsequent practice, though this notion remains open to discussion.[624] Accordingly, the conclusion of an extensive amount of BITs with largely similar if not identical substantive provisions, coupled with the acquiescence of non-participating States, may have led collectively to subsequent practice—'a discernable pattern implying the agreement of the parties'[625]—potentially

[616] Although the power to interpret the ILO Constitution in principle lies with the Court (or a tribunal established pursuant to Art 37(2)), requests to the Office often arguably merely relate to obtaining information or clarification. Thus, 'it would seem that the interpretation of [the] Convention by the Office does not constitute a derogation from their [the Court or tribunal's] powers'—E Osieke, *Constitutional Law and Practice in the International Labour Organisation* (Martinus Nijhoff, 1985) 208–9.

[617] Jenks, 'Interpretation of International Labour Conventions', 133.

[618] See eg ILO, *Minutes of the 9th Session of the Governing Body of the International Labour Office* (Geneva, October 1921) 365–6; ILO, *Official Bulletin*, Vol 23 (1938) No 1 <www.ilo.org/public/libdoc/ilo/P/09604/09604(1938-23).pdf> accessed 4 June 2017, 32.

[619] See n 616.

[620] See Art X of the WTO Agreement.

[621] H Nottage and T Sebastian, 'Giving Legal Effect to the Results of WTO Trade Negotiations: An Analysis of the Methods of Changing WTO Law' (2006) 9 J Intl Econ L 989.

[622] See eg Section 2.5.2.

[623] Pauwelyn, *Conflict of Norms*, 49.

[624] See eg Section 2.3.1(a).

[625] T Gazzini, 'Bilateral Investment Treaties' in T Gazzini and E De Brabandere (eds), *International Investment Law: The Sources of Rights and Obligations* (Martinus Nijhoff, 2012) 99, fn 9, citing eg *Japan–Taxes on Alcoholic Beverages II*, 13.

modifying the MFN clause in Article II:1 of the GATS,[626] and even impacting customary international law.[627]

A third, somewhat related, example pertains to the curious status of WTO accession protocols.[628] An accession protocol is a bilateral agreement between the WTO and an acceding State (and thus, on its own, does not fall within the definition of subsequent practice adopted for the purposes of this book[629]). Such protocols impose on acceded members country-specific rules that are different and more stringent than those applicable to the organization's original members. Given the non-reciprocal nature of the underlying agreements,[630] by varying the rules under the WTO agreements per acceded member, the accession protocols 'alter the rights and obligations of *all* members under the WTO agreements', even if the extent differs per protocol.[631] Moreover, because these rules are often more stringent than those applicable to the organization's original members, the accession protocols lead to less favourable treatment for acceded members 'in derogation of the WTO principle of nondiscrimination'.[632] All country-specific rules altering the rights or obligations under the WTO agreements derogate from the general MFN principle.[633]

Yet it is unclear what the basis is for the accession protocols.[634] The constitutive treaty provides only that accession is based on 'terms to be agreed' between the acceding State and the WTO,[635] and the actual accession instruments declare themselves an 'integral part' of the WTO Agreement.[636] However, the implications of purported 'integration' between a bilateral treaty between a State and an international organization and an inter-State multilateral treaty 'has proven highly controversial'.[637] This lack of clarity 'creates uncertainties over the rights and obligations of acceded members vis-à-vis those of other members'.[638]

Based on the above, the accession protocols can be said to modify the WTO agreements.[639] Collectively, this practice could potentially be qualified as treaty-related subsequent practice of the organization—as 'a continued and unchanged

[626] Gazzini, 'Bilateral Investment Treaties', 101.

[627] Ibid. 6, citing *Mondev v US*, para 43. See further SM Schwebel, 'The Influence of Bilateral Investment Treaties on Customary International Law' (2004) 98 ASIL Proc 27; JE Alvarez, 'A BIT on Custom' (2009) 42 NYU J Intl L & Pol 17.

[628] See generally Qin, 'WTO Accession Protocols', 369ff.

[629] See Section 2.3.3.

[630] See Section 3.5.1(a) on the nature of non-reciprocal treaties.

[631] Qin, 'WTO Accession Protocols', 400 (emphasis added).

[632] Ibid. 374.

[633] Ibid. 401.

[634] Note that, as a matter of WTO institutional law, the Ministerial Council may have acted *ultra vires* in light of Art IX:2 of the WTO Agreement, and implicitly undermined formal amendment provisions, by approving accession terms that effectively modify the WTO agreements. See ibid. 412, citing S Charnovitz, 'Mapping the Law of WTO Accession' in ME Janow, V Donaldson, and A Yanovich (eds), *The WTO: Governance, Dispute Settlement, and Developing Countries* (Juris Publishing, 2008) 855, 900–1, and M Tyagi, 'Flesh on a Legal Fiction: Early Practice in the WTO on Accession Protocols' (2012) 15 J Intl Econ L 391, 412–14.

[635] Art XII:1 of the WTO Agreement.

[636] See WTO, *Technical Note on the Accession Process—Note by the Secretariat, Addendum*, Doc WT/ACC/10/Rev.4/Add.1 (25 May 2010). See also Qin, 'WTO Accession Protocols', 414, arguing that, '[i]n essence, the integration clause is another example of subsequent practice of the WTO that effectively amends the WTO Agreement.'

[637] Qin, 'WTO Accession Protocols', 373.

[638] Ibid.

[639] Ibid. 372, 401–4.

practice' since China's 2001 accession that is 'generally accepted by the members of the WTO'[640]—modifying, in the sense of *altering*, the WTO agreements.[641] This result goes against the original intention of the parties to the WTO Agreement.[642] Moreover, the practice not only alters a large number of provisions affecting the substantive rights and obligations of WTO members, but it constitutes a major departure from a fundamental principle of the organization—the MFN provisions under the WTO agreements.[643] This also affects the constitutive treaty's object and purpose. In sum, the collective practice of accession protocols may constitute a modification, in the form of an alteration, of key substantive provisions and the object and purpose(s) of a large constitutive treaty that is non-reciprocal in nature. This entails a very high threshold for modification. As such, it represents a 'significant development in contemporary treaty practice'.[644]

Fourth, other alternative mechanisms for adaptation of the WTO agreements, namely, modifications of the Schedules and certain decisions of the Ministerial Council, may qualify as subsequent practice (more specifically, subsequent agreements).[645] The use of protocols to supplement and modify existing concessions under the Schedules, an integral part of the GATT,[646] represents a long-standing practice in the organization.[647] It may be compared to the subsequent implementation agreements concluded in relation to the Law of the Sea Convention,[648] as subsequent agreements bypassing overly rigid formal amendment procedures. There is no specific basis for such practice of modification through protocols under the WTO Agreement: 'these Protocols are subsequent or supplemental agreements, which have their basis in the residual rules on amendments in [general] treaty law and practice'.[649]

As mentioned, the Ministerial Council is a source of treaty adaptation in the WTO regime. It can, for instance, issue authoritative interpretations, waivers, as well as other types of decisions specifically provided for in the WTO Agreement.[650] Most interesting for present purposes is its general decision-making competence under Article IV:1 of the WTO Agreement:

> The Ministerial Conference shall carry out the functions of the WTO and take actions necessary to this effect. The Ministerial Conference shall have the authority to take decisions on all matters under any of the Multilateral Trade Agreements, if so requested by a Member (…).

Unlike other provisions setting out specific decision-making powers of the Ministerial Council, Article IV:1 does not specify in how far such decisions can

[640] Ibid. 410.

[641] See ibid. 407–11 (and 404–7, as to whether the accession protocols could also be characterized as a subsequent agreement).

[642] Ibid. 446. [643] Ibid. 410. [644] Ibid. 411. [645] See Section 3.5.

[646] *EC–Chicken Cuts*, AB Report, para 145 (referring to Article II:7 GATT 1994). See likewise Art XX:3 of the GATS.

[647] Nottage and Sebastian, 'Giving Legal Effect to the Results of WTO Trade Negotiations', 998.

[648] See Section 5.3.2(a).

[649] M Footer, *An Institutional and Normative Analysis of the World Trade Organization* (Martinus Nijhoff, 2006) 221–30.

[650] See Section 3.5.2.

modify the rights and obligations of the member States. Read in conjunction with Article IX:1 of the WTO Agreement, such decisions only require a simple majority, a much lower requirement than that needed for formal amendment.[651] They presumably only qualify as relevant subsequent agreements or practice[652] capable of treaty modification if they are taken by consensus (which also relates to the argument that, unless they are based on consensus, Article IX:1 decisions are unlikely to be recognized as a basis for a legal claim in WTO dispute settlement proceedings[653]). Moreover, they have often been adopted without reference to a specific legal basis.[654] Nevertheless, a number of these decisions have effectively modified WTO obligations, either by adding new obligations or by adding exceptions to existing obligations to the covered agreements.[655] It seems reasonable to conclude that this process is specific to the WTO context, since it does not satisfy the general requirements for modification by subsequent practice or agreements. The (former) GATT Contracting Parties also used to adopt such decisions to modify rights and obligations and avoid formal amendment.[656] The most prominent example is the decision on the 'Enabling Clause', which permitted an important exception to Article I of the GATT on MFN treatment, allowing certain types of preferential treatment to developing countries.[657]

Finally, and perhaps most interestingly, the GATT itself constitutes an example of the treaty modifying effects of subsequent practice. GATT 1947 was never meant to be an international organization; it was intended only as a tariff deal, or rather as a multilateral treaty setting up, and subordinate to, the International Trade Organization.[658] But the ITO Charter was never ratified, largely due to the fact that the United States government, its main initiator, could not persuade Congress to approve it.[659] Instead, the GATT, which has never actually come into force, was applied on a provisional basis by means of a separate Protocol of Provisional Application.[660] This alone indicates that it was never intended as an organization. In fact, its provisions were redrafted early on to 'eliminate the suggestion of an

651 Article IX:1 of the WTO Agreement.

652 Nottage and Sebastian, 'Giving Legal Effect to the Results of WTO Trade Negotiations', fn 68.

653 Ibid. 106–10.

654 Ibid. 105. See also PJ Kuijper, 'Some Institutional Issues Presently Before the WTO' in D Kennedy and J Southwick (eds), *The Political Economy of International Trade Law: Essays in Honor of Robert E Hudec* (CUP, 2002) 82, 106–7, pointing out that the 'WTO presently abounds in "decisions" which have no legal basis whatsoever'.

655 See eg WTO, Doha Work Programme: Ministerial Declaration, 18 December 2005, Doc WT/MIN(05)/DEC (22 December 2005) paras 36, 47, and Annex F, Proposals 36 and 84, cited in Nottage and Sebastian, 'Giving Legal Effect to the Results of WTO Trade Negotiations', 106.

656 See eg O Long, *Law and Its Limitations in the GATT Multilateral Trade System* (Martinus Nijhoff, 1985) 107.

657 See Nottage and Sebastian, 'Giving Legal Effect to the Results of WTO Trade Negotiations', 107.

658 JJ Jackson, *The World Trading System: Law and Policy of International Economic Relations* (2nd edn, MIT Press, 1997) 38.

659 Ibid. See further SA Aaronson, *Trade and the American Dream: A Social History of Postwar Trade Policy* (UP of Kentucky, 1996).

660 It may also be noted that the PPA contained two clauses that altered the impact of the GATT itself. First, it required only sixty days' notice for withdrawal; second, it stated that Part II of the GATT, containing important substantive obligations, was subject to the 'existing legislation' exception in Article 1(b) of the PPA, which granted 'grandfather rights' for any national legislative provision in

organization'[661]—hence the reference to the 'contracting parties acting jointly', rather than an organizational body, in Article XXV of GATT 1947, and generally to 'contracting parties' rather than 'members'.

Nevertheless, the GATT evolved to fill the gap of the absent ITO, as more nations joined and increasingly turned to it as a forum for resolving trade problems.[662] Through the practice of the parties, a *de facto* Secretariat emerged, formed by an appointed Director-General, supported by employed staff, and funded by the parties' contributions.[663] A complex network of subsidiary bodies developed, including committees, working parties, and panels.[664] Moreover, the PPA States decided on the basis of GATT Article XXII:2—according to which the 'Contracting Parties may (...) consult with any contracting party or parties in respect of any matter for which it has not been possible to find a satisfactory solution'—to establish periodic meetings and create a decision-making process. This eventually evolved into the GATT dispute settlement system.[665] The development first began with disputes being submitted to the plenary semi-annual meeting of the Contracting Parties, then to their 'intercessional committee', and later to a designated working party. Then disputes began to be referred to panels composed of independent representatives that would act in their own capacity, indicating a shift towards more 'judicial' dispute settlement.[666] Panels were established on the basis of unanimity, with consensus required both for the formation of the panel and the adoption of final reports, which were largely respected in practice.[667] Since the parties still could not agree to make the GATT legally binding, they used negotiating rounds to further reduce tariff barriers, and adopted standalone agreements ('side codes') on non-tariff barriers.[668]

Thus, the GATT gradually developed through subsequent practice into the *de facto* central organization for international trade[669]—despite its 'flawed' treaty basis, and despite the founders' clear intention to the contrary:

> [T]he GATT has limped along for nearly fifty years with almost no basic constitution designed to regulate its organizational activities and procedures. Even so, the GATT by any

existence at the time a State became a party that was inconsistent with GATT Part II obligations. These clauses persisted for a long time and caused difficulties, but eventually became extinct.

661 Jackson, *The World Trading System*, 37.

662 Ibid. 41; M Matsushita, TJ Schoenbaum, and P Mavroidis, *The World Trade Organization: Law, Practice, and Policy* (2nd edn, OUP, 2006) 2.

663 Jackson, *The World Trading System*, 42; Matsushita, Schoenbaum, and Mavroidis, *The World Trade Organization*, 2.

664 Jackson, *The World Trading System*, 63.

665 On the development of the GATT dispute settlement system, see further RE Hudec, *Enforcing International Trade Law: The Evolution of the Modern GATT Legal System* (Butterworth Legal, 1993); E-U Petersmann, 'The Dispute Settlement System of the World Trade Organization and the Evolution of the GATT Dispute Settlement System since 1948' (1994) 31 CMLR 1157.

666 Matsushita, Schoenbaum, and Mavroidis, *The World Trade Organization*, 106.

667 Ibid.

668 This led to increased complexity and fragmentation in the GATT system due to the optional nature of individual agreements ('GATT à la carte'), ultimately resolved with the 'single-package' approach of the WTO agreements. See also Jackson, *The World Trading System*, 121, regarding certain subsequent formal agreements, such as the Tokyo Round subsidies code and antidumping codes, which purported to interpret the GATT but in fact effectively modified it.

669 D Carreau, P Juillard, and T Flory, *Droit international economique* (2nd edn, LGDJ, R Pichon et R Durand-Auzias, 1980) 258; Long, *Law and Its Limitations*, 45; F Roessler, 'The Competence of

fair definition must be deemed to have been a de facto international organization. Through trial and error it has evolved some fairly elaborate procedures for conducting its business. That it could be so, despite the flawed basic documents on which it had to build, is a tribute to the pragmatism and ingenuity of many of its leaders over the years.[670]

Until the entry into force of the WTO Agreement in 1995, the GATT continued to operate on this basis. Due to its provisional nature and the consequent uncertainty regarding its precise status and authority, it suffered from a number of inherent weaknesses that were largely resolved with the WTO Agreement. These difficulties illustrate the downside of (fundamental) treaty changes through subsequent practice, namely, the indeterminacy it may produce on account of its tacit operation.

The GATT provides an example of a treaty implemented very differently from its original text and intended purpose. As a result, an international organization arose from a provisionally applied treaty. Even the complex dispute settlement system that emerged was the result of State practice. This practice was not necessarily *contrary* to, but certainly not originally part of, the GATT's initial object and purpose of supporting the ITO. Although implementation through the PPA served the GATT's basic purposes, it evolved into something far beyond that originally envisioned. The object and purpose of the GATT was therefore supplemented and altered by subsequent practice in accordance with its evolved structure and function. This illustrates the far-reaching effects of informal change through subsequent practice, and its ability to create vital international institutions.

5.3.1e International financial institutions

The 'unparalleled'[671] expansion of the original scope of operation of the World Bank in the post-1945 era could be compared to the 'normative transformation'[672] of the UN Charter.[673] The World Bank seems to have expanded its functions beyond the text of its constitutive Articles of Agreement[674] to tackle modern social and governance issues not originally within its range[675]—although these changes do not go beyond the organization's broadly framed underlying purposes.[676] There is increasing pressure to extend this mandate even further,[677] for instance by considering

GATT' (1987) 21 JWTL 73; GM Berrisch, 'The Establishment of New Law through Subsequent Practice in GATT' (1991) 16 NC J Intl L & Comm Reg 497, 522; Jackson, *The World Trading System*, 31, 59; Matsushita, Schoenbaum, and Mavroidis, *The World Trade Organization*, 2ff; AH Qureshi and AR Ziegler, *International Economic Law* (2nd edn, Sweet & Maxwell, 2007) 275.

670 Jackson, *The World Trading System*, 42.

671 I Shihata, 'The Dynamic Evolution of International Organizations: The Case of the World Bank' (2000) 2 J Hist Intl L 217, 247.

672 Liang, 'Modifying the UN Charter', 12.

673 See Section 5.3.1(a).

674 Articles of Agreement of the International Bank for Reconstruction and Development 1945, 2 UNTS 134 (IBRD Articles of Agreement).

675 See eg Shihata, 'The Dynamic Evolution of International Organizations', 241.

676 See eg I Shihata (ed), *The World Bank in a Changing World. Volume I* (Martinus Nijhoff, 1991) viii; G Handl, 'The Legal Mandate of Multilateral Development Banks as Agents for Change Toward Sustainable Development' (1998) 92 AJIL 642.

677 Shihata, 'The Dynamic Evolution of International Organizations', 242.

a country's human rights record in loan agreements, which could be justified on the basis that human rights law is intended to prevail as 'external customary law' over the prohibition in the Bank's Articles of taking political considerations into account,[678] or even as other applicable rules in the sense of Article 31(3)(c) VCLT.[679] The latter idea illustrates the potential overlap between subsequent practice and subsequent developments.[680] Other examples of modification (through alteration and termination) by subsequent practice have been identified in relation to the World Bank's Articles of Agreement, but are not elaborated upon further in this book.[681]

Another example in the context of international financial institutions concerns the International Monetary Fund. When, in 1971, exchange rates between the major world currencies became floating, which was clearly inconsistent with the fixed exchange rate system in force under the IMF Statute at the time,[682] there was all-round support for the practice among the participating States and from the side of the IMF Executive Directors.[683] However, the practice was only formally incorporated into the IMF Statute years later.

Once again, this shows that international organizations—such as the UN, NATO, and various international financial institutions—have in the past been required to make (sometimes sudden) adjustments to the provisions and purposes of their constitutive instruments in order to adapt to their changing international environment. More generally, this illustrates how subsequent practice can modify and terminate rights and obligations to adapt to major changes in the global community.[684]

5.3.2 Examples outside the context of international organizations

5.3.2a Law of the sea

The law of the sea[685] provides an abundance of examples of modification by subsequent practice, specifically under the regime of the Law of the Sea Convention, as well

678 See further eg Section 4.5.1.

679 Shihata, 'The Dynamic Evolution of International Organizations', 246 and fn 76.

680 See Section 2.3.4.

681 See Shihata, 'The Dynamic Evolution of International Organizations', 220–1, discussing examples where subsequent practice has resulted in 'informal modification' or termination of provisions of the IBRD Articles of Agreement. See eg Art IV, Section 4(a), regarding commissions for the Special Reserve under Art IV, Section 6, which have been effectively reduced to zero; Art V, Section 6, on the Advisory Council consisting of experts advising the Bank on general policy issues, which has not been reconstituted for decades; and Art IV, Section 3, on the financing of the local cost of projects, which has been modified by subsequent practice. See further I Shihata (ed), *The World Bank in a Changing World. Volume III* (Martinus Nijhoff, 1999).

682 Articles of Agreement of the International Monetary Fund (Bretton Woods Agreement) 1945, 2 UNTS 39.

683 Executive Board Decision, 'Central Rates and Wider Margins: A Temporary Regime', Decision No 3463-(71/126) of 18 December 1971, *IMF Annual Report 1972*, 85.

684 J Gold, 'The "Dispensing" and "Suspending" Powers of International Organizations' (1972) 19 NTIR 181, 182–4; Karl, *Vertrag*, 232. cf Berrisch, 'The Establishment of New Law', 509 (referring to this development as internal customary international law).

685 This section is developed from I Buga, 'Between Stability and Change in the Law of the Sea Convention: Subsequent Practice, Treaty Modification and Regime Interaction' in DR Rothwell and others (eds), *The Oxford Handbook on the Law of the Sea* (OUP, 2015) 46ff.

as in relation to the 1958 Geneva Conventions on the Law of the Sea. The examples reflect varying degrees of formality, ranging from informal instances of subsequent practice to more 'formalized' ones constituting subsequent agreements, such as implementation agreements. As previously explained,[686] the LOSC in particular contains numerous explicit and implicit mechanisms to deal with change, from the formal amendment procedures in Articles 312 and 313 LOSC, to its dispute settlement system, and the activities of bodies such as, *inter alia*, the Meeting of States Parties (SPLOS), the Commission on the Limits of the Continental Shelf (CLCS), and the International Seabed Authority (ISA). There are important limits on the extent to which these rules and institutions can ensure the responsiveness of the Convention to the changing needs of the international community. For instance, formal amendments can be cumbersome, if not altogether unworkable in practice,[687] and the procedures in Articles 312 and 313 LOSC have yet to be utilized.[688] Thus, complex, dynamic treaty regimes like the LOSC tend to be amenable to subsequent change through a range of mechanisms beyond formal amendment—most notably, subsequent practice.

1958 Geneva Conventions on the Law of the Sea

UNCLOS III provided a catalyst for the emergence of new modifying practice and subsequent customary law, to the extent that the provisions of the LOSC had already become declaratory before the Convention had even entered into force. These new norms came to modify numerous provisions of the 1958 Geneva Conventions on the Law of the Sea: the Convention on the Territorial Sea and the Contiguous Zone, the Convention on the High Seas, the Convention on Fishing and Conservation of the Living Resources of the High Seas, and the Convention on the Continental Shelf, the product of the first United Nations Conference on the Law of the Sea (UNCLOS I). Some examples are briefly considered below.

The emergence of the concept of the exclusive economic zone as customary international law was first confirmed by the ICJ in 1982[689] and 1985.[690] It provides coastal States with the exclusive right to regulate fishing up to 200 nautical miles from their baselines. This constituted an important modification of the 1958 High Seas Convention, in particular Article 1, which defines the high seas as 'all parts of the sea that are not included in the territorial sea or in the internal waters of a State', and Article 2(2) on freedom of fishing on the high seas.[691] The emergence of the

[686] See Section 3.5.2.

[687] See eg MJ Bowman, 'The Multilateral Treaty Amendment Process—A Case Study' (1995) 44 ICLQ 540; C McLachlan, 'The Evolution of Treaty Obligations in International Law' in G Nolte (ed), *Treaties and Subsequent Practice* (OUP, 2013) 69, 71.

[688] OR Young, 'Commentary on Shirley V Scott "The LOSV Convention as a Constitutional Regime for the Oceans"' in AG Oude Elferink (ed), *Stability and Change in the Law of the Sea: The Role of the LOS Convention* (Martinus Nijhoff, 2005) 39, 44; DR Rothwell, 'The Impact of State Practice on the Jurisdictional Framework Contained in the LOS Convention: A Commentary' in AG Oude Elferink (ed), *Stability and Change in the Law of the Sea: The Role of the LOS Convention* (Martinus Nijhoff, 2005) 145, 149; Y Tanaka, *The International Law of the Sea* (CUP, 2012) 33.

[689] *Tunisia/Libya*, para 100. [690] *Libya/Malta*, para 34.

[691] Villiger, *Customary International Law and Treaties* (1985), para 306, citing eg E Jiménez de Aréchaga, 'International Law in the Past Third of a Century' (1978-I) 159 RC 1, 21; C Hudson, 'Fishery

customary rule on the 12-mile breadth of the territorial sea could likewise be said to have modified the operation of the 1958 High Seas Convention.[692] The customary status of a 12-mile fishery zone was also recognized in the aforementioned ICJ *Fisheries Jurisdiction* case.[693] Similarly, the principle of the common heritage of mankind, now enshrined in Article 136 LOSC, modified the freedom of the high seas in the sense of Article 1 of the Convention on the High Seas, which previously entailed free access to non-living resources on the seabed of the high seas.[694] Moreover, the rule now contained in Article 33(2) LOSC on the contiguous zone extending up to 24 nautical miles from the baselines from which the breadth of the territorial sea is measured, modified Article 24(2) of the 1958 Territorial Sea Convention,[695] which only allowed for a contiguous zone of 12 nautical miles from the baseline.[696]

Another example is the relation between Article 1 of the 1958 Continental Shelf Convention and the subsequent rule enshrined in Article 76(1) LOSC. Article 76(1) LOSC prescribes that the outer limit of the continental shelf extends to 200 nautical miles from the baselines from which the breadth of the territorial sea is measured in cases where the outer edge of the continental margin does not extend that far. Article 1 of the 1958 Continental Shelf Convention, by contrast, provides a different definition of the outer limit, referring to the 200-metre isobath in addition to the so-called 'exploitability' criterion.[697] It in principle applies to non-LOSC parties like the United States vis-à-vis LOSC parties. However, the United States applies Article 76 LOSC on account of the fact that it represents customary international law.[698] This practice indicates that the (potential) customary norm underlying the

and Economic Zones as Customary International Law' (1980) 17 San Diego L Rev 661; GM Danilenko, *Law-Making in the International Community* (Martinus Nijhoff, 1993) 168–9; RR Churchill, 'The Impact of State Practice on the Jurisdictional Framework Contained in the LOS Convention' in AG Oude Elferink (ed), *Stability and Change in the Law of the Sea: The Role of the LOS Convention* (Martinus Nijhoff, 2005) 91, 96.

692 Byers, *Custom*, 174; Churchill, 'The Impact of State Practice', 96.

693 *Fisheries Jurisdiction* (*UK v Iceland*), Merits, paras 52, 54, discussed in Section 5.2.1.

694 ILC, *Report of the International Law Commission covering the work of its 8th session* (1956) II YBILC 253, Ch II (III) [Articles concerning the Law of the Sea with Commentaries (1956)] 278 (Commentary to Art 27); DW Arrow, 'The Customary Norm Process and the Deep Seabed, Ocean Development and International Law' (1981) 9 ODILA 1, 21, 38; J van Dyke and C Yuen, ' "Common Heritage" v "Freedom of the High Seas": Which Governs the Seabed?' (1982) 19 San Diego L Rev 493; A Verdross and B Simma, *Universelles Völkerrecht: Theorie und Praxis* (3rd edn, Duncker & Humblot, 1984) 550; Villiger, *Customary International Law and Treaties* (1985), para 306.

695 J Laylin, 'Emerging Customary Law of the Sea' (1976) 10 TIL 610, 672; L Caflisch, 'Les zones maritimes sous jurisdiction nationale, leurs limites et leurs délimitations' (1980) 84 RGDIP 68; Villiger, *Customary International Law and Treaties* (1985), para 306; Byers, *Custom*, 174; Danilenko, *Law-Making*, 168–9.

696 See also I Brownlie, *Principles of Public International Law* (6th edn, OUP, 2003) 601, referring to the modification by practice of the 1958 Territorial Sea Convention to include 'fishing zones' as part of the contiguous zone. See likewise Amerasinghe, *Principles*, 462. The present author submits that the connection between the two concepts seems unclear. Rather, the establishment of fishing zones can be viewed as a modification of the Convention on the High Seas as it applies to areas previously part of the high seas that are not claimable by any State.

697 Villiger, *Customary International Law and Treaties* (1985), para 306.

698 See eg 'United States Policy Governing the Continental Shelf of the United States of America' (17 November 1987), reprinted in JA Roach and RW Smith, *US Responses to Excessive Maritime Claims* (2nd edn, Martinus Nijhoff, 1996) 201–2.

subsequent rule reflected in Article 76(1) LOSC may have modified Article 1 of the 1958 Convention.

The obligation to remove abandoned oil platforms in Article 5(5) of the 1958 Geneva Convention on the Continental Shelf has arguably been modified by subsequent practice—an important issue given the growing number of oil installations in recent decades, and the consequent increase of abandoned platforms at sea.[699] The formulation of the last sentence of Article 5(5) is clear and categorical: '[a]ny installations which are abandoned or disused must be entirely removed.' However, the subsequent practice of the parties seems to have led to a different rule, namely, that abandoned oil platforms may be left in place as long as appropriate safety measures are taken. This is to some extent covered by Article 60(3) LOSC, which prescribes:

> Any installations or structures which are abandoned or disused shall be removed to ensure safety of navigation, taking into account any generally accepted international standards established in this regard by the competent international organization. (...) Appropriate publicity shall be given to the depth, position and dimensions of any installations or structures not entirely removed.[700]

Therefore, Article 60(3) seems to impose a *partial* removal obligation in cases where the safety of navigation could be affected.[701] Alternatively, it has been argued that the provision only allows for non-removal as an exception,[702] but this latter interpretation does not accord with State practice, which seems to point to a partial removal obligation.[703] Such practice accords with the flexible, case-by case approach[704] adopted in the IMO-issued 1989 Guidelines and Standards for the Removal of Offshore Installations and Structures on the Continental Shelf and in the Exclusive Economic Zone,[705] incorporated into the LOSC by the rule of reference in Article 60(3) LOSC on 'generally accepted international standards'.[706] The IMO Guidelines require the removal of abandoned offshore installations under

[699] S Trevisanut, 'L'Enlèvement et la gestion des plates-formes et installations offshore abandonnées ou désaffectées' in G Andreone, A Caligiuri, and G Cataldi (eds), *Law of the Sea and Environmental Emergencies* (Editoriale Scientifica, 2012) 193, 193–4.

[700] RR Churchill and AV Lowe, *The Law of the Sea* (2nd rev edn, Manchester UP, 1988) 129; R Higgins, *Problems and Process: International Law and How We Use It* (Clarendon Press, 1994) 31–2; Byers, *Custom*, 173–4.

[701] See eg P McDade, 'The Removal of Offshore Installations and Conflicting Treaty Obligations as a Result of the Emergence of the New Law of the Sea: A Case Study' (1987) 24 San Diego L Rev 645; GC Kasoulides, 'Removal of Offshore Platforms and the Development of International Standards' (1989) 13 Mar Policy 249 (criticizing Art 60(3) LOSC for this reason).

[702] R Wolfrum and N Matz, *Conflicts in International Environmental Law* (Springer, 2010) 110–11.

[703] Trevisanut, 'Plates-formes et installations offshore abandonnées ou désaffectées', 201.

[704] T Treves, 'Codification du droit international et pratique des états dans le droit de la mer' (1990-IV) 223 RC 9, 205.

[705] IMO Assembly Res A.672(16) of 16 October 1989. See further S Rosenne, 'The International Maritime Organization Interface with the Law of the Sea Convention' in MH Nordquist and JN Moore (eds), *Current Maritime Issues and the International Maritime Organization* (Martinus Nijhoff, 1999) 260.

[706] As discussed in Section 3.5.2, the system of 'rules of reference' in the LOSC provides an alternative mechanism to subsequent practice. In this sense, State practice in relation to the IMO Guidelines falls within the realm of interpretation of the LOSC and its incorporated external standards.

certain circumstances, but also allow for partial or non-removal depending on the technical, financial, or environmental considerations involved. Another possibility is the conversion of decommissioned offshore installations into artificial reefs for environmental purposes.

Overall, practice with regard to the legal regime governing the removal of offshore installations is not uniform, either in relation to global instruments, such as the LOSC and the 1972 Convention on the Prevention of Marine Pollution by Dumping of Wastes and Other Matter[707] and its 1996 Protocol,[708] or between global and regional conventions; for instance, the OSPAR Convention[709] and the Helsinki Convention[710] have enacted more stringent rules in their respective areas. Nevertheless, it is clear that in any case subsequent practice does not support an *absolute* obligation to remove abandoned offshore installations as originally prescribed in Article 5(5) of the 1958 Continental Shelf Convention.[711] It can be concluded that, although practice is not yet sufficiently uniform and determinate for its contents to have fully crystallized, the general trend points to a modification of the strict rule in Article 5(5) by subsequent practice, if not by means of 'treaty-related' customary law.[712]

The aforementioned examples constitute modifications by subsequent practice and subsequent customary law of various substantive and, notably, *essential* provisions of the 1958 Geneva Conventions.[713] In such cases, involving, for instance, the creation of new maritime zones or expansion of existing maritime zones, divergence from the original treaty text is so clear that there can be little doubt that subsequent practice or subsequent customary law has led to modification.

The SPLOS

An important source of modification of the LOSC by subsequent practice is the Meeting of States Parties. As discussed in Chapter 2, such meetings can qualify as relevant subsequent practice capable of interpretation and modification.[714] Decisions of the SPLOS have effectively altered the Convention in several ways, despite the fact that the LOSC appears to grant the SPLOS merely an informational and administrative role.[715] In light of the formal functions of the SPLOS, it is unlikely that these decisions can be regarded as falling within the scope of

[707] 1046 UNTS 120 (London Convention).

[708] Protocol to the Convention on the Prevention of Marine Pollution by Dumping of Wastes and Other Matter 1996 (1997) 36 ILM 1 (London Protocol).

[709] Convention for the Protection of the Marine Environment of the North-East Atlantic 1992, 2354 UNTS 67.

[710] Convention on the Protection of the Marine Environment of the Baltic Sea Area 1992, 1507 UNTS 167.

[711] Trevisanut, 'Plates-formes et installations offshore abandonnées', 216.

[712] Byers, *Custom*, 174. See generally Section 4.5.1 of this book.

[713] See, by contrast, text to nn 839–40 on the maritime zone provisions in the LOSC.

[714] See Section 2.3.1(c).

[715] See eg LOSC Annex II, Art 2, and Annex VI, Arts 4, 6, 18, 19. Article 319(2)(e) LOSC is admittedly vague.

implied powers and, hence, interpretation of the Convention.[716] Since they were adopted by consensus, the decisions could be said to satisfy the requirement that subsequent practice must evidence the agreement of all the parties to modify the LOSC.[717]

In 1994, the SPLOS decided, for policy reasons,[718] on a 'one-time deferment' of the first election of the International Tribunal for the Law of the Sea beyond the date imposed by Article 4(3) of Annex VI LOSC.[719] It also provisionally varied Article 4(2) of Annex VI LOSC to allow States still in the process of *becoming* parties to the LOSC to nominate candidates for the Tribunal.[720] Similarly, in 1996, the SPLOS postponed the first election of the members of the CLCS, thus deviating from Annex II, Article 2(2) LOSC.[721] What is more, at the first elections of the CLCS in 1997, the SPLOS agreed on a composition of the Commission that departed from the geographical distribution requirement contained in Annex II, Article 2(3) LOSC.[722] Once again, it was emphasized that this was a one-off measure that should not be interpreted as, nor constitute a precedent for, derogation from the LOSC.[723] Nevertheless, the decision clearly (though temporarily) derogated from the Convention.[724] These four SPLOS decisions constitute modifications—in the form of alterations—by subsequent practice, even if only with regard to relatively minor procedural provisions.[725]

More importantly, in 2001, the SPLOS extended the time limit prescribed by the Convention for coastal States' submissions on the outer limits of their continental shelf to the CLCS.[726] Article 76 LOSC requires coastal States whose continental margin extends beyond 200 nautical miles to submit information on those outer limits to the CLCS, which then issues a recommendation on the matter. Article 4 of Annex II LOSC requires submission 'as soon as possible but in any case within ten years of the entry into force of this Convention for that State'. Accordingly, for certain States, the specified ten-year period would have expired in 2004, as calculated from the point of the Convention's entry into force in 1994. However,

[716] cf J Harrison, *Making the Law of the Sea: A Study in the Development of International Law* (CUP, 2011) 84.

[717] Theoretically, Rule 52 of the Rules of Procedure for Meetings of States Parties, Doc SPLOS/2/Rev.4 (24 January 2005), provides for voting if 'all efforts to achieving general agreement have been exhausted'. However, this 'would have the effect of altering the established treaty rights of those [dissenting] states against their will'—Harrison, *Making the Law of the Sea*, 82.

[718] See eg Treves, 'The General Assembly and the Meeting of States Parties in the Implementation of the LOS Convention', 69–70.

[719] *Report of the First Meeting of States Parties*, Doc SPLOS/3 (28 February 1995) para 16(a).

[720] Ibid. para 16(b).

[721] *Report of the Third Meeting of States Parties*, Doc SPLOS/5 (22 February 1996) para 20.

[722] *Report of the Sixth Meeting of States Parties*, Doc SPLOS/20 (29 March 1997) paras 12–13.

[723] Ibid. para 13.

[724] Harrison, *Making the Law of the Sea*, 79; Tanaka, *The International Law of the Sea*, 34.

[725] Harrison, *Making the Law of the Sea*, 80.

[726] *Decision regarding the Date of Commencement of the Ten-Year Period for Making Submissions to the Commission on the Limits of the Continental Shelf Set Out in Article 4 of Annex II to the United Nations Convention on the Law of the Sea*, Doc SPLOS/72 (29 May 2001) [*Decision regarding the Date of Commencement of the Ten-Year Period* (2001)].

many developing coastal States were finding it difficult to meet this deadline.[727] A formal amendment was not an option for legal and political reasons.[728] In view of these difficulties, the SPLOS decided that the ten-year submission period should be calculated from the date of adoption by the Commission of its Scientific and Technical Guidelines,[729] granting disadvantaged States significantly more time (until 2009).[730]

The decision was formulated as an interpretation, but its terms undeniably diverge from Article 4, which unambiguously states that the ten-year period shall commence from the date of entry into force of the Convention. This 'could raise questions concerning the competence of the Meeting to take such an action and might set an unwelcome precedent'.[731] This is likely why calls for a second extension of the time limit have been denied,[732] as this would have been even more difficult to pass off as a mere interpretation: '[a] further decision of the Meeting to extend the time limit almost certainly would have been considered to be an amendment. That view seems also to be implied in the opinions expressed at the 11th Meeting of States Parties which adopted the 2001 decision.'[733] States want to avoid the impression that the LOSC can be modified by an SPLOS decision rather than by formal amendment as envisaged in the Convention.[734]

In fact, the SPLOS had previously considered four procedures for adopting the initial decision, in descending order of formality: the formal amendment procedures in Articles 312 and 313 LOSC, an implementation agreement, and, finally, an SPLOS decision.[735] In opting for the latter solution, it relied on the precedents set by the aforementioned decisions deferring the first elections of the CLCS and ITLOS[736]—despite the fact that these were allegedly not intended to function as precedents.[737] In light of the fact that formal amendment procedures were expressly considered, it is difficult to deny that the SPLOS

[727] *Issues with respect to Article 4 of Annex II to the United Nations Convention on the Law of the Sea; Background paper prepared by the Secretariat*, Doc SPLOS/64 (1 May 2001) para 7.

[728] AG Oude Elferink, '"Openness" and Article 76 of the Law of the Sea Convention: The Process Does Not Need to Be Adjusted' (2009) 40 ODIL 36, 45.

[729] *Decision regarding the Date of Commencement of the Ten-Year Period* (2001). This applies to States for which the Convention entered into force prior to May 1999.

[730] *Report of the Eleventh Meeting of States Parties*, Doc SPLOS/73 (14 June 2001) para 70.

[731] AG Oude Elferink, 'Current Legal Developments: Meeting of States Parties to the UN Law of the Sea Convention' (2008) 23 IJMCL 769, 770. See also eg D Freestone and AG Oude Elferink, 'Flexibility and Innovation in the Law of the Sea—Will the LOS Convention Amendment Procedures Ever Be Used?' in AG Oude Elferink (ed), *Stability and Change in the Law of the Sea: The Role of the LOS Convention* (Martinus Nijhoff, 2005) 169, 208–9.

[732] See eg *Decision regarding the Workload of the Commission on the Limits of the Continental Shelf and the Ability of States, Particularly Developing States, to Fulfill the Requirements of Article 4 of Annex II to the United Nations Convention on the Law of the Sea, as well as the Decision Contained in SPLOS/72, Paragraph (a)*, Doc SPLOS/183 (20 June 2008) [*Decision regarding the Workload of the CLCS* (2008)] Preamble, para 8.

[733] Oude Elferink, 'Current Legal Developments', 777.

[734] Oude Elferink, '"Openness"', 45 and fn 68. See also *Report of the Eleventh Meeting of States Parties*, para 70.

[735] *Report of the Eleventh Meeting of States Parties*, para 78.

[736] Ibid.

[737] See *Report of the Sixth Meeting of States Parties*, para 13.

decision is effectively a modification.[738] Also difficult to deny, as mentioned, is that it diverges from the wording of the procedural requirement in Article 4. The 2001 SPLOS decision appears to modify a procedural rather than a substantive provision, which is relevant because modifications in relation to procedural provisions are more easily accepted.[739] However, some participants considered the decision to be more than procedural, pointing out that it carried direct relevance for States' rights and obligations under the Convention.[740]

Furthermore, in 2008, the SPLOS decided to grant States experiencing 'financial and technical difficulties' the option of submitting only 'preliminary information' in fulfilment of the CLCS submission deadline[741]—a possibility clearly not contained in the Convention. The CLCS has the obligation under the Convention to consider the information submitted by coastal States under Article 4, Annex II, and then issue recommendations on the basis of those submissions. Contrary to this obligation, the 2008 SPLOS decision requires the Commission to *refrain* from making a decision on the basis of the preliminary information submitted to it under the newly envisaged procedure, pending the final submissions of the coastal States concerned.

Thus, both the 2001 and the 2008 decisions of the Meeting of States Parties represent modifications advanced under the guise of interpretations. Their effects could be regarded as procedural in nature,[742] in the sense that they facilitate the substantive objectives of the treaty, potentially improving the Commission's effectiveness and the quality of States' submissions to it.[743] Either way, they institute more extensive changes than the prior SPLOS decisions with regard to the CLCS and ITLOS. Moreover, the more recent decisions had 'neither the same urgency nor the *de minimis* character as the previous instances'.[744] It is thus difficult to see them as anything less than modifications of the LOSC.

1994 Implementation Agreement and 1995 Fish Stocks Agreement

The 1994 Agreement relating to the Implementation of Part XI of the United Nations Convention on the Law of the Sea of 10 December 1982 (1994 Implementation

[738] See eg Churchill, 'The Impact of State Practice', 97; Oude Elferink, '"Openness"', 132; B Kunoy, 'The 10 Year Time Frame to Disputed Areas' (2009) 40 ODIL 131, 132; Harrison, *Making the Law of the Sea*, 80–1; Tanaka, *The International Law of the Sea*, 34–5. Kunoy also deals with the question of whether certain provisions of the Rules of Procedure of the Commission on the Limits of the Continental Shelf, Doc CLCS/40/Rev.1 (17 April 2008), established based on the CLCS's implicit powers, constitute subsequent practice not only *interpreting* the Convention, but also *overriding* certain of its provisions. Specifically, he considers whether, on the basis of the Convention and the Rules of Procedure of the Commission, States may be exempted from the explicit treaty obligation to submit all data to the Commission within the ten-year time frame where an area is disputed, concluding that no such modification has yet occurred.

[739] See eg Section 3.5.1.

[740] *Report of the Eleventh Meeting of States Parties*, para 79. cf Oude Elferink, '"Openness"', 45.

[741] *Decision regarding the Workload of the CLCS* (2008), para 1(a). See further *Report of the Eighteenth Meeting of States Parties*, Doc SPLOS/184 (21 July 2008) paras 85–99.

[742] Oude Elferink, '"Openness"', 45.

[743] Oude Elferink, 'Current Legal Developments', 774.

[744] Harrison, *Making the Law of the Sea*, 82.

Agreement)[745] was adopted as a result of the refusal by many States, including the United States, to become parties to the LOSC until changes were made to the deep seabed mining regime under Part XI of the Convention. The 1994 Implementation Agreement is to be interpreted and applied together with the LOSC 'as a single instrument'.[746] In conjunction with the subsequent practice of States that are parties to the LOSC but not also to the 1994 Implementation Agreement,[747] the latter represents a subsequent agreement.[748]

According to Article 2(1) of the 1994 Implementation Agreement, coupled with its Annex, certain LOSC provisions are to be disapplied[749] or replaced,[750] and a number of structural and institutional changes are to be implemented.[751] For instance, Section 2, paragraph 3, of the Agreement, declares the LOSC obligation to fund one mine site of the Enterprise inapplicable, providing expressly that the parties shall be under no such obligation. Likewise, the LOSC provisions on the transfer of technology are declared inapplicable (Section 5, paragraph 2) and replaced with new principles (Section 5, paragraph 1). These examples constitute clear changes to the substantive obligations created under the (original) LOSC regime.[752] The 1994 Implementation Agreement also extensively changes, for instance, the regime and division of tasks originally envisioned by the LOSC in relation to the three principal organs of the ISA, namely, the Assembly, Council, and Secretariat.[753] In addition, it establishes new organs, such as the Finance Committee pursuant to Section 9, paragraph 1, of the Annex to the Agreement. It therefore alters the roles of existing institutions established by the LOSC and supplements them by establishing new organs. The 1994 Implementation Agreement can therefore be said to alter, extend, as well as terminate various procedural and substantive provisions of the LOSC, in line with the definition of modification in Chapter 3.[754] However, it does not as such modify the essential underlying purposes of the LOSC, including the principle of the common heritage of mankind, the purpose to benefit mankind as a whole, the prohibition on claiming sovereignty or sovereign rights in the Area, or the peaceful purposes requirement.[755]

Confusion may stem from the fact that the 1994 Implementation Agreement was 'carefully drafted to avoid any clear indication that what states were doing was amending Part XI of the Convention'.[756] For instance, the reference in Section 2, paragraph 6, of the Agreement to the 'interpretation' of LOSC provisions relating to the Enterprise in accordance with that section, does not detract from the fact that the implications are so extensive compared to the original text and aims of the LOSC

[745] 1836 UNTS 3. [746] Art 2 of the 1994 Implementation Agreement.

[747] See text to nn 759–61. [748] See Section 2.3.3.

[749] See eg 1994 Implementation Agreement, Annex Section 2, para 3; Section 3, para 8 and para 16; Section 4; Section 5, para 2; Section 6, para 7; Section 8, para 2.

[750] See eg 1994 Implementation Agreement, Annex Section 5, para 2; Section 6, para 1(a).

[751] See eg 1994 Implementation Agreement, Annex Section 1, paras 2, 4; Section 2; Section 3, paras 1, 2, 5; Section 4, para 1.

[752] Freestone and Oude Elferink, 'Flexibility and Innovation', 187.

[753] Article 158 of the LOSC. [754] See Section 3.3.1.

[755] LDM Nelson, 'The New Deep Sea-Bed Mining Regime' (1995) 10 IJMCL 189, 203; Harrison, *Making the Law of the Sea*, 93; Tanaka, *The International Law of the Sea*, 182–4.

[756] Harrison, *Making the Law of the Sea*, 92.

provisions concerned, that it is difficult to square them with a mere interpretation. Thus, 'the politically prudent label of an "implementing agreement" is a euphemism for the word "amendment" which would have been more correct from the legal point of view'.[757] Overall, there can be no doubt that the 1994 Implementation Agreement represents a modification of the LOSC by subsequent agreement.[758]

The operation of the 1994 Implementation Agreement further illustrates the effects of modification by subsequent practice in a different way. According to Article 4(1) of the Agreement, States that ratify the LOSC *subsequent* to the adoption of the 1994 Implementation Agreement automatically also become parties to the latter. This leaves unclear whether the Agreement also binds States that became parties to the LOSC *prior* to the Agreement, since many of them have not formally consented to such effect.[759] Nevertheless, 'members of the [International Seabed] Authority [pursuant to the LOSC] which are not parties to the 1994 Agreement necessarily participate in the work of the Authority under arrangements based on the Agreement'.[760] In other words, by participating in ISA activities in this way, ie in relation to the new activities rather than their original LOSC obligations, non-parties to the Agreement can be deemed to have consented to the Agreement as a result of their subsequent practice.[761]

The 1995 Agreement for the Implementation of the Provisions of the United Nations Convention on the Law of the Sea of 10 December 1982 relating to the Conservation and Management of Straddling Fish Stocks and Highly Migratory Fish Stocks (1995 Fish Stocks Agreement or FSA)[762] may provide another example of treaty adaptation by means of subsequent agreement going beyond the formal amendment procedures in the LOSC. It introduces significant changes to the Convention,[763] although it seems to remain faithful, and mainly only supplement, the basic provisions, illustrating the difficulty of pinpointing the 'switch' from interpretation to tacit modification.

Article 2 of the FSA declares its objective to be to 'ensure the long-term conservation and sustainable use of straddling fish stocks and highly migratory fish stocks'. It

[757] Nelson, 'The New Deep Sea-Bed Mining Regime', 192–3; T Scovazzi, 'The Evolution of International Law of the Sea: New Issues, New Challenges' (2000) 286 RC 39, 125; Freestone and Oude Elferink, 'Flexibility and Innovation', 184; AE Boyle, 'Further Development of the 1982 Law of the Sea Convention' in D Freestone, R Barnes, and D Ong (eds), *The Law of the Sea: Progress and Prospects* (OUP, 2006) 40, fn 14.

[758] See eg DH Anderson, 'Further Efforts to Ensure Universal Participation in the United Nations Convention on the Law of the Sea' (1994) 43 ICLQ 886, 889; Nelson, 'The New Deep Sea-Bed Mining Regime', 192–3, 203; Scovazzi, 'The Evolution of International Law of the Sea', 125; Treves, 'The General Assembly', fn 4; Churchill, 'The Impact of State Practice', 97; Freestone and Oude Elferink, 'Flexibility and Innovation', 184, 187; Boyle, 'Further Development', 41, 49; Harrison, *Making the Law of the Sea*, 92; Tanaka, *The International Law of the Sea*, 33, 178–84. See also Nolte, Third Report on Treaties over Time, 323.

[759] See eg *Report of the Secretary-General of the International Seabed Authority*, Doc ISBA/6/A/9 (6 June 2000) para 4. See also Harrison, *Making the Law of the Sea*, 93–4.

[760] *Report of the Secretary-General of the International Seabed Authority*, Doc ISBA/15/A/2 (23 March 2009) para 5.

[761] Harrison, *Making the Law of the Sea*, 95–6. This argument stands separate from the question of whether the LOSC Part XI regime has created an 'objective regime' applicable to all States.

[762] 2167 UNTS 3.

[763] Anderson, 'Further Efforts', 886; Nelson, 'The New Deep Sea-Bed Mining Regime', 767; Scovazzi, 'The Evolution of International Law of the Sea', 39; Freestone and Oude Elferink, 'Flexibility

has been argued that the contemporary meaning of 'sustainable use' may amount to a modification of the term 'maximum sustainable yield' contained in Articles 61(3) and 119(1)(a) of the LOSC.[764] Moreover, the FSA, which admittedly only applies to certain species or stocks, adopts an 'ecosystem' approach (see Article 5(d)-(f)) that goes beyond the provisions of Part VII LOSC.[765] It also introduces the precautionary principle, discussed further in the next section.[766]

This does not necessarily lead to incompatibility between the FSA and the LOSC. Wolfrum and Matz argue that the LOSC—as a framework convention—is sufficiently flexible to incorporate these approaches, as it lays down only minimum standards (see Articles 192 or 194(5) LOSC).[767] Moreover, Article 237 LOSC provides that Part XII is without prejudice to the specific obligations assumed by States under special conventions and agreements concerning the protection of the marine environment. As always, the question of whether these examples constitute modification or 'dynamic' interpretation, is itself a matter of interpretation.

But the FSA also contains provisions such as Article 21, allowing members of regional management organizations to board and inspect vessels suspected of engaging in unauthorized fishing on the high seas—deemed a 'landmark' in fisheries management enforcement.[768] It is difficult to say whether this provision alters or supplements the LOSC; in either case, it establishes concrete rights that the LOSC does not itself provide. Thus, in accordance with the definition of the notion of modification in Chapter 3 as including alteration, extension, and termination, it appears to qualify as treaty modification by subsequent practice.

Moreover, pursuant to Article 8(4) FSA, only States members of a regional fisheries management organization (RFMO) or which have agreed to the conservation measures established by an RFMO, 'shall have access to the fishery resources to which those measures apply'. Some commentators have questioned whether the practice of restricting access to fisheries is compatible with Article 116 LOSC (granting every State the right to fish on the high seas) and Article 119(3) LOSC ('conservation measures and their implementation (...) [should] not discriminate against the fishermen of any State').[769] These provisions may once again point more in the direction of a tacit modification.

Overall, there does not seem to be a strict incompatibility between the text of the LOSC and that of the FSA. Thus, the latter blurs the line between modification and interpretation more than the 1994 Implementation Agreement. But it still introduces

and Innovation', 184–5; Boyle, 'Further Development', fn 14; Harrison, *Making the Law of the Sea*, 86–92.

764 Freestone and Oude Elferink, 'Flexibility and Innovation', 193.

765 Y Takei, *Filling Regulatory Gaps in High Seas Fisheries: Discrete High Seas Fish Stocks, Deep-sea Fisheries and Vulnerable Marine Ecosystems* (Brill, 2013) 88–9.

766 The FSA thus also has to be viewed in the broader context of the development of the relevant law after the adoption of the LOSC.

767 Wolfrum and Matz, *Conflicts*, 30.

768 Freestone and Oude Elferink, 'Flexibility and Innovation', 201.

769 See eg PGG Davies and C Redgwell, 'The International Legal Regulation of Straddling Fish Stocks' (1996) 67 BYBIL 199, 265; Takei, *Filling Regulatory Gaps*, 67.

'novel' elements and objectives that can be said to constitute modifications of the LOSC by subsequent agreement,[770] as per the definition of modification discussed.[771] According to some commentators, the FSA may even come to undermine certain basic principles of the LOSC, like the freedom of fishing on the high seas.[772] As a form of subsequent practice, the Implementation Agreement represents an effective way of implementing changes to the operation of the treaty regime without resorting to formal amendment procedures.[773] On the other hand, the differing membership of the FSA as compared to the LOSC may to some extent limit its effect upon the latter.[774] It may be interesting to note that this limitation would also apply to formal amendments, which do not bind States parties that have not accepted them.[775] Although this may be seen to create a risk of fragmentation within the law of the sea, the FSA is placed in the context of the broader development of international law, and thus rather seems to result in a greater degree of coherence.[776]

Article 105 LOSC

The current practice in relation to Article 105 LOSC on piracy, granting universal jurisdiction to any State to 'seize a pirate ship or aircraft', constitutes another potential instance of tacit modification. The article specifies that prosecution may be carried out by 'the courts of the State which carried out the seizure'. It is unclear from the text—in particular, due to the use of the word 'may'—whether it is only the courts of the arresting State that have such jurisdiction. However, the *travaux préparatoires* strongly indicate that this is the case.[777]

In practice, there have been numerous instances of pirates arrested by one State and prosecuted by another. Memoranda of understanding were concluded by the United States,[778] the United Kingdom,[779] and the European Union[780]

[770] See eg Young, 'Commentary', 44; Treves, 'The General Assembly', fn 4; Freestone and Oude Elferink, 'Flexibility and Innovation', 203, 209, 219.

[771] See Section 3.3.1.

[772] See further Freestone and Oude Elferink, 'Flexibility and Innovation', 203.

[773] If the provisions of the FSA had been adopted by formal amendment under the LOSC, a much higher number of accessions would have been required than there are currently parties to the Agreement. See ibid. 219.

[774] The FSA has had a significant impact upon the constitutive instruments of RFMOs, also where the members are not parties to the FSA.

[775] Art 316 LOSC. See also Art 40(4) VCLT.

[776] See eg n 766.

[777] Articles concerning the Law of the Sea with Commentaries (1956): 'This article gives any State the right to seize pirate ships (...) and to have them adjudicated upon by its courts. This right cannot be exercised at a place under the jurisdiction of another State.' cf JA Roach, 'Countering Piracy off Somalia: International Law and International Institutions' (2010) 104 AJIL 397, 404–5.

[778] Memorandum of Understanding between the United States of America and the Republic of Kenya concerning the conditions of transfer of suspected pirates and armed robbers and seized property in the western Indian Ocean, the Gulf of Aden, and the Red Sea (16 January 2009), Termination notice 30 March 2010. See also D Morgan, 'U.S. Delivers Seven Somali Pirate Suspects to Kenya' (*Reuters*, 5 March 2009) <www.reuters.com/article/worldNews/idUSTRE52480N20090305> accessed 9 June 2017.

[779] See further eg E Kontorovich, 'International Legal Responses to Piracy off the Coast of Somalia' (2009) 13 ASIL Insights 1.

[780] See also Exchange of Letters between the European Union and the Government of Kenya on the Conditions and Modalities for the Transfer of Persons Suspected of Having Committed Acts of Piracy

with Kenya in 2008 and 2009, as well as agreements with other States in the region, such as the Seychelles[781] and Mauritius,[782] to arrange such transfers of captured pirates for trial.[783] In fact, Kenya has taken custody of hundreds of pirates captured by other countries in recent years.[784] It should be noted that Kenya is a party to the LOSC, while the United States is a (very influential) non-party.[785] Both Kenya and the United States are parties to the 1958 Geneva Convention on the High Seas,[786] which contains near-identical piracy provisions that apply between them.[787] Moreover, as discussed, there is no reason in principle to ignore the practice of non-parties, even if it is not equal in (evidentiary) value to the practice of the parties.[788]

Likewise, pirates captured by Denmark and Russia have been handed over to Yemen,[789] France has transferred pirates for trial to Somalia,[790] a Dutch court in Rotterdam asserted jurisdiction over pirates arrested by a Danish frigate,[791] and in 2012, ten Somali pirates arrested by a Dutch frigate were handed over to Germany and prosecuted.[792] Some States 'catch and release' suspected pirates.[793] Other

and Detained by the European Union-led Naval Force (EUNAVFOR), and seized property in the possession of EUNAVFOR, from EUNAVFOR to Kenya and for their treatment after such transfer (6 March 2009) OJ (L 79) 49, approved by Council Decision 2009/293/CFSP (2009) OJ (L 79) 47. See further E Kontorovich, 'Introductory Note to Exchange of Letters between the European Union and the Government of Kenya' (2009) 48 ILM 747.

[781] See eg Memorandum of Understanding between the United States of America and the Republic of the Seychelles concerning the conditions of transfer of suspected pirates and armed robbers and seized property in the western Indian Ocean, the Gulf of Aden, and the Red Sea (14 July 2010); Exchange of Letters between the European Union and the Republic of Seychelles on the Conditions and Modalities for the Transfer of Suspected Pirates and Armed Robbers from EUNAVFOR to the Republic of Seychelles and for their Treatment after such Transfer (2 December 2009) OJ (L 315) 37, approved by Council Decision 2009/877/CFSP (2009) OJ (L 315) 35. See also eg E Pineau, 'France Asks Seychelles to Help with Pirate Trials' (*Reuters,* 18 October 2009) <www.reuters.com/article/2009/10/18/idUSLI622681> accessed 9 June 2017.

[782] See eg 'Signing of Piracy Agreement with Mauritius' (*Gov.uk*, 8 June 2012) <www.gov.uk/government/news/signing-of-piracy-agreement-with-mauritius> accessed 9 June 2017; Exchange of letters between the European Union and the Republic of Mauritius on the Conditions and Modalities for the Transfer of Suspected Pirates and Associate Seized Property from the European-led Naval Force to the Republic of Mauritius and on the Conditions of Suspected Pirates after Transfer (14 July 2011).

[783] Kenya has since withdrawn from some of these agreements, but continues to accept pirates for prosecution on a case-by-case basis. See *Report of the Secretary-General on specialized anti-piracy courts in Somalia and other States in the Region*, UN Doc S/2012/50 (20 January 2012) para 78.

[784] E Kontorovich, '"A Guantanamo on the Sea": The Difficulties of Prosecuting Pirates and Terrorists' (2010) 98 CLR 243, 263, citing C Philp, 'Captured Somali Pirates Are Being Dumped in Kenya, Officials Say' (*The Times* (*London*), 12 June 2009) 41; S McGregor, 'Somali Pirates' Kenya Trial Postponed Until October (Update 1)' (*Bloomberg*, 7 August 2009).

[785] See Rothwell, 'The Impact of State Practice', 147.

[786] 450 UNTS 11.

[787] Article 30(4)(b) VCLT.

[788] See eg Section 3.3.3(b).

[789] Kontorovich, 'A Guantanamo on the Sea', 255, 268.

[790] D Guilfoyle, 'Piracy Off Somalia: A Sketch of the Legal Framework' (*EJIL: Talk!*, 20 April 2009) <www.ejiltalk.org/piracy-off-somalia-a-sketch-of-the-legal-framework/> accessed 9 June 2017.

[791] *Somali Pirates Case*, District Court of Rotterdam, 17 June 2010, Judgment No 10/600012-09, LJN: BM8116.

[792] C Ahlborn, 'Adjudicating Somali Piracy Cases—German Courts in a Double Bind' (*CJICL Blog*, 3 January 2013) <www.sharesproject.nl/adjudicating-somali-piracy-cases-german-courts-in-a-double-bind/> accessed 9 June 2017.

[793] Roach, 'Countering Piracy off Somalia', 403 and fn 35.

solutions, including the establishment of specialized anti-piracy courts in Somalia and the region, have also been considered.[794]

Overall, it seems to be the preferred practice of States involved in combating piracy to hand over arrested pirates to other States for prosecution.[795] These trends are based on practical considerations: 'Concerns include logistical difficulties, the possibility that pirates could request asylum from the prosecuting state, the possibility that they would invoke the Geneva Conventions, the difficulties of proving a criminal case when the arrest was made by military personnel [and more].'[796]

Some writers argue that this practice conflicts with Article 105 of the LOSC,[797] while others point out that the provision does not prohibit such transfers.[798] It has been argued that the stance that non-capturing States lack jurisdiction to prosecute pirates, though feasible, is not convincing, given the customary norm regarding universal jurisdiction.[799] A strict interpretation of Article 105 may also not give full effect to the duty to cooperate in Article 100 LOSC, nor to calls by the Security Council for such cooperation to combat piracy.[800] The LOSC drafters may have considered 'large-scale high seas piracy a thing of the past'.[801] If Article 105 is indeed undergoing a gradual modification by subsequent practice—as the contrast between current practice and the article's text and *travaux* suggests[802]—this change is more than merely procedural, given that Article 105 derogates from flag State jurisdiction. Nevertheless, its effect is to enhance the performance of LOSC obligations

[794] See UNSC Res 1976 (2011) of 11 April 2011, UN Doc S/RES/1976 (2011) para 26; *Report of the Secretary-General on the modalities for the establishment of specialised Somali anti-piracy courts*, UN Doc S/2011/360 (15 June 2011); C Massarella, 'UN Security Council Resolution 1976 (2011) and Efforts to Support Piracy Prosecutions' (2011) 26 IJMCL 679.

[795] See eg *Report of the Secretary-General on specialized anti-piracy courts in Somalia and other States in the Region*, paras 78, 124; Roach, 'Countering Piracy', 404; A Middelburg, *Piracy in a Legal Context: Prosecution of Pirates Operating off the Somali Coast* (Wolf Legal, 2011) 55; R Geiss and A Petrig, *Piracy and Armed Robbery at Sea* (OUP, 2011) 21, 30–3, 168; E Papastavridis, *The Interception of Vessels on the High Seas: Contemporary Challenges to the Legal Order of the Oceans* (Hart, 2013) 169, 171.

[796] Kontorovich, 'Introductory Note', 747.

[797] E Kontorovich, 'Case Report: *United States v Shi*' (2009) 103 AJIL 734, 739; E Papastavridis, 'Piracy Off Somalia: The "Emperors and the Thieves of the Oceans" in the 21st Century' in A Abass (ed), *Protecting Human Security in Africa* (OUP, 2010) 122, 142.

[798] Roach, 'Countering Piracy', 403; Y Dinstein, 'Piracy *Jure Gentium*' in H Hestermeyer and others (eds), *Coexistence, Cooperation and Solidarity: Liber Amicorum Rüdiger Wolfrum* (Martinus Nijhoff, 2012) 1125, 1141; T Treves, 'Piracy and the International Law of the Sea' in D Guilfoyle (ed), *Modern Piracy: Legal Challenges and Responses* (Edward Elgar, 2013) 117, 122. See also D Guilfoyle, 'Combating Piracy: Executive Measures on the High Seas' (2011) 53 JYBIL 149, 164 ('the limited reference in UNCLOS Article 105 to the seizing State's adjudication/curial jurisdiction does not preclude the existence of other valid jurisdictions nor prevent transfers between them. Nothing, for example, precludes a "receiving" State exercising its own jurisdiction which has an independent basis in customary international law once a suspect is within its territory.').

[799] L Azubuike, 'International Law Regime Against Piracy' (2009) 15 Ann Surv Intl & Comp L 43, 54–5.

[800] See eg UNSC Res 1897 (2009) of 30 November 2009, UN Doc S/RES/1897 (2009) paras 12–14.

[801] Kontorovich, 'A Guantanamo on the Sea', 270.

[802] Note that the contrast between current practice and the *travaux* is precisely the basis upon which the ICJ's *Namibia Advisory Opinion* is characterized as an example of modification by subsequent practice rather than interpretation—see eg Aust, *Modern Treaty Law*, 243. See further Sections 3.4.2 and 5.2.1.

in the light of present-day concerns, leaving the essential aims and purposes of the Convention intact.

Other LOSC provisions impacted by subsequent practice

Article 7 of the LOSC allows for the use of a system of straight baselines along deeply indented coastlines or where there is a fringe of islands in the immediate vicinity of the coast, setting out several conditions for this purpose. The system of straight baselines in Article 7 has attracted an extensive amount of State practice, although its effects may still be ambiguous. The ICJ has emphasized that straight baselines should only be used in cases involving exceptional geographical circumstances.[803] Nevertheless, a large proportion of States have used straight baselines contrary to the requirements in Article 7.[804] Moreover, straight baselines are applied differently by different States. This practice has triggered objections from non-participating States. Thus, the practice in relation to Article 7 fails to qualify as 'concordant, common and consistent' amounting to an agreement of the parties,[805] and cannot be said to have modified the LOSC. It also cannot result in an *inter se* modification between the States that have taken a broad view of Article 7, since, aside from the inconsistency of their practice, this would affect other States' rights and obligations under the LOSC. The practice has nonetheless had a certain impact, in the sense that it has significantly 'weakened the authority' of Article 7.[806]

Numerous other aspects of the LOSC raise similar questions. For instance, a divisive issue is the question of whether warships passing through a coastal State's territorial sea require prior authorization (or notification). It is unclear from the *travaux* or the text of the LOSC whether such a right of passage exists, although it may be implied by certain provisions.[807] A significant number of States currently require prior authorization, which would seem to contradict the Convention. However, as discussed in Chapter 2, subsequent practice must be sufficiently determinate and consistent to be capable of treaty interpretation and modification.[808] The current practice is not yet sufficiently widespread or consistent (especially in light of persistent objections from certain States) to draw any firm conclusions.[809]

Principles of ocean governance and environmental law: the dynamic character of the LOSC as a framework Convention

As mentioned, fields such as the law of the sea, and 'framework' or 'law-making' instruments such as the LOSC,[810] are more dynamic and require a greater degree of

[803] See eg *Qatar v Bahrain*, Merits, paras 212–15.

[804] Churchill, 'The Impact of State Practice', 107.

[805] See eg Section 2.3.5.

[806] Churchill, 'The Impact of State Practice', 108. See also JRV Prescott, 'Straight and Archipelagic Baselines' in G Blake (ed), *Maritime Boundaries and Ocean Resources* (Croom Helm, 1987) 38, 49 (referring to LOSC Art 7 as 'effectively a dead letter').

[807] Churchill, 'The Impact of State Practice', 111–13, citing eg LOSC Arts 17, 19(2), and 20.

[808] See eg Sections 2.3.1(b) and 2.3.5.

[809] See Churchill, 'The Impact of State Practice', 91ff for further examples. See also Rothwell, 'The Impact of State Practice', 145.

[810] See the discussion on 'law-making' treaties in Section 3.5.1. See also eg Brölmann, 'Law-Making Treaties', 383.

responsiveness than other fields or treaties.[811] One reason is because the law of the sea interacts with numerous other regimes, including international environmental law,[812] human rights,[813] trade law,[814] and security law.[815] Subsequent practice can serve as a vehicle for interaction between these different regimes, adapting the LOSC in line with external developments.[816] It can also help reconcile norms *within* the law of the sea.[817] As discussed, it seems to have led to the (tacit) adherence by all LOSC parties to the 1994 Implementation Agreement, promoting consistency between the two instruments.[818]

Taken in its broadest sense to include subsequent agreements in the form of successive treaties, subsequent practice can impact LOSC provisions by means of other treaties.[819] For instance, Article 3 of the 2001 UNESCO Convention on the Protection of the Underwater Cultural Heritage[820] states that its provisions shall not prejudice the LOSC, yet concerns have been expressed that the rights it confers go beyond coastal States' rights and jurisdiction under the LOSC.[821] Similarly, Article 22(1) of the 1992 Convention on Biological Diversity (CBD)[822] declares that the LOSC shall prevail, *unless* it poses a serious threat or damage to biodiversity. It takes a protective, 'ecosystem' approach that goes beyond the LOSC's more management-oriented one.[823] To this extent, the CBD could modify the operation of LOSC Parts V and VII, while remaining compatible with the LOSC's object and purpose.[824]

The impact of the precautionary principle on the LOSC may be a good example of regime interaction through modification by subsequent practice in the environmental law context. The principle was endorsed in Principle 15 of the 1992 Rio Declaration on Environment and Development.[825] In its 2011 Advisory Opinion

811 See Buga, 'Between Stability and Change', 46ff.

812 See eg T Stephens, *International Courts and Environmental Protection* (CUP, 2009) Ch 9; Wolfrum and Matz, *Conflicts*, 13–61.

813 See eg BH Oxman, 'Human Rights and the United Nations Convention on the Law of the Sea' (1998) 36 Colum J Transnat'l L 399; T Treves, 'Human Rights and the Law of the Sea' (2010) 28 Berkeley JIL 1.

814 See eg the *Swordfish Cases* brought before the WTO and ITLOS: *Chile–Measures Affecting the Transit and Importing of Swordfish*, Request for the Establishment of a Panel by the European Communities (7 November 2000) WT/DS193/2, and *Conservation and Sustainable Exploitation of Swordfish Stocks in the South-Eastern Pacific Ocean* (*Chile/European Community*) Order 2000/3 of 20 December 2000, ITLOS Case No 7, 148. See generally MA Young, *Trading Fish, Saving Fish: The Interaction between Regimes in International Law* (CUP, 2011).

815 See eg Convention for the Suppression of Unlawful Acts against the Safety of Maritime Navigation (SUA Convention) 1988, 1678 UNTS 221.

816 Wolfrum and Matz, *Conflicts*, 140; Buga, 'Between Stability and Change', 60–3.

817 Koskenniemi, Fragmentation Report, para 278 ('accommodation is easiest between two instruments within a regime').

818 See text to nn 760–1. See also Section 3.1.

819 Buga, 'Between Stability and Change', 62.

820 (2002) 41 ILM 40.

821 See eg T Scovazzi, 'The Protection of Underwater Cultural Heritage: Article 303 and the UNESCO Convention' in D Freestone, R Barnes, and DM Ong (eds), *The Law of the Sea: Progress and Prospects* (OUP, 2006) 120, 134.

822 1760 UNTS 79.

823 See eg Wolfrum and Matz, *Conflicts*, 15–30.

824 Boyle, 'Further Development', 40.

825 (1992) 31 ILM 874.

on *Responsibilities and Obligations of States with Respect to Activities in the Area*, the ITLOS Seabed Disputes Chamber declared that the Nodules and Sulphides Regulations[826] have turned the 'precautionary approach'[827] in Rio Principle 15 into a binding obligation in relation to activities in the Area.[828] As mentioned earlier, the precautionary approach was also introduced in the context of fisheries law by means of the 1995 FSA (admittedly, within the narrow scope of fish stocks covered by the Agreement), and other international fisheries instruments followed suit.[829] Indeed, in the *Southern Bluefin Tuna* case, ITLOS seemed to suggest that the precautionary approach might have modified the LOSC's fisheries provisions.[830] The precautionary approach is also linked to the aforementioned ecosystem approach.[831]

It could be argued that these trends indicate that conservation measures are 'being gradually taken for the purposes of conservation as such, rather than conservation with a view to utilization'.[832] Following this reasoning, the concept of 'conservation of living resources' under the LOSC may be undergoing modification by subsequent practice, mirroring developments in environmental law on the precautionary and ecosystem approaches, sustainable use, and biodiversity.[833]

Concluding remarks on the LOSC regime

The LOSC establishes an intricate treaty regime, covering a wide range of substantive issues and objectives, setting up new institutional arrangements, and spanning an extensive membership with diverse interests. The Convention already contains numerous 'in-built' adaptation mechanisms that provide (partial) alternatives to subsequent practice.[834] It includes provisions prohibiting or limiting the possibility of modification by subsequent practice—its very nature as a 'package deal' is an example—and provisions that are 'evolutionary' in nature, importing general

[826] Regulations on Prospecting and Exploration for Polymetallic Nodules in the Area, Doc ISBA/6/A/18 (4 October 2000) Art 31(2); Regulations on Prospecting and Exploration for Polymetallic Sulphides in the Area, Doc ISBA/16/A/12/Rev1 (7 May 2010) Art 33(2).

[827] It is unclear whether the content of the 'precautionary approach' differs from that of the 'precautionary principle'.

[828] *Responsibilities and Obligations of States Sponsoring Persons and Entities with Respect to Activities in the Area (Request for Advisory Opinion Submitted to the Seabed Disputes Chamber)* Advisory Opinion of 1 February 2011, ITLOS Case No 17, paras 122, 125–35.

[829] See eg FAO Code of Conduct for Responsible Fisheries 1995, FAO Doc 95/20/Rev/1, Arts 6.5, 7.5; 2001 Reykjavik Declaration on Responsible Fisheries in the Marine Ecosystem, para 5; UNGA Res 67/79 of 11 December 2012, UN Doc A/RES/67/79 (2013).

[830] *Southern Bluefin Tuna (Australia v Japan; New Zealand v Japan)* Provisional Measures, Order of 27 August 1999, ITLOS Case Nos 3 and 4, paras 77–80; ibid. Separate Opinion of Judge Laing, paras 16–19; ibid. Separate Opinion of Judge Treves, para 9. See *Responsibilities and Obligations of States with Respect to Activities in the Area*, para 132; MH Nordquist (ed), *United Nations Convention on the Law of the Sea 1982: A Commentary*, vol III (Martinus Nijhoff, 2005) 2888; Boyle, 'Further Development', 51.

[831] See eg Art 5(d)–(f) FSA; FAO Code of Conduct for Responsible Fisheries, Art 6.2.

[832] Takei, *Filling Regulatory Gaps*, 103.

[833] Ibid. 79–80, 103.

[834] See Section 3.5.2.

international law into the LOSC, and curtailing the need for recourse to subsequent practice. Nevertheless, the LOSC is highly impacted by subsequent practice with regard to both individual provisions and the regime as a whole.[835] This is because other informal adaptation mechanisms and formal amendment procedures often fail to go far enough in facilitating adaptation.

The parts of the LOSC more susceptible to modification include some of the more 'novel' issues codified in the Convention, such as the straight baselines system discussed above. These were not supported by longstanding practice prior to UNCLOS III, unlike provisions such as those in Part II LOSC, which codify issues established well before UNCLOS III.[836] Moreover, provisions on subjects such as 'conservation' require frequent adaptation to maintain their relevance and accordingly seem more amenable to tacit modification.[837] In addition, procedural provisions—to the extent the distinction between procedural and substantive provisions is practicable—are much more prone to modification by subsequent practice.[838]

By contrast, it would be more difficult for subsequent practice to modify 'essential'[839] provisions such as the outer limits of the various maritime zones.[840] These provisions balance diverse State interests and sovereignty over resources on the one hand, with the goal of multilateralism under the LOSC on the other—a balance reflective of the aims of the Convention as a 'package deal'.[841] Likewise, as discussed, the modifying potential of subsequent practice is highly limited in relation to 'core' LOSC principles, such as the common heritage of mankind or the peaceful purposes requirement. Many of these provisions also reflect customary international law, entailing—given the expansive range of States parties to the LOSC—that subsequent practice would have to modify both the treaty and the corresponding customary norm.[842] With regard to provisions for which the required modification threshold is unattainable, States would have to resort to formal amendment under the LOSC, or at least to more 'formalized' types of practice such as implementation agreements.[843]

Based on the examples above, it is submitted that the process of modification by subsequent practice has had a significant impact on the development of the LOSC framework, and will continue to do so in the future. If approached with due caution, it can contribute to developing the Convention in accordance with the evolving needs of the international community, enabling the instrument to fulfil its purpose as a 'Constitution for the Oceans'.[844]

835 As explained, the general environmental approach of the LOSC is gradually changing through regime interaction fuelled by subsequent practice.

836 Rothwell, 'The Impact of State Practice', 145.

837 Buga, 'Between Stability and Change', 67.

838 See Section 3.5.1(b).

839 Ibid.

840 Rothwell, 'The Impact of State Practice', 149.

841 See Section 3.5.1(b).

842 See Section 3.3.3(b).

843 Treves, 'The General Assembly', 73.

844 DOALOS, 'A Constitution for the Oceans—Remarks by T Koh' <www.un.org/depts/los/convention_agreements/convention_overview_convention.htm> accessed 9 June 2017.

5.3.2b Environmental law: MEAs

International environmental law is a dynamic, rapidly evolving field: 'given that the international community's understanding of environmental problems is continually evolving, and that the very nature and extent of those problems are themselves in a state of flux, there is an enhanced requirement for speedy and effective mechanisms for the adaptation of treaty provisions to developing needs'.[845] Many developments are driven by the practice of meetings and conferences of the parties to multilateral environmental agreements (MEAs). As discussed extensively,[846] such conferences of the parties (COPs) have a somewhat 'hybrid' status as institutions: they bear more of a resemblance to international organizations if regarded as 'autonomous institutional arrangements'[847] than mere 'diplomatic conferences'.[848] In this sense, the present section could have been placed in the preceding section on international organizations. However, many of the examples relating to decisions by COPs can be compared to the effects of the SPLOS decisions discussed in the LOSC context.[849] Many qualify as '*ad hoc* conferences' rather than 'treaty-management organizations', since they do not have a separate secretariat or broad powers, express or implied, under the constitutive treaty, nor the power to supervise its implementation.[850] They have therefore been placed outside the context of 'classic' international organizations.

Most important for present purposes is that COPs are open to all the treaty parties, making them a 'vehicle for the continuing and evolving expression of the will of the parties, and allowing for the concretization and adaptation of treaty provisions over time'.[851] Their practice, as explained in Chapter 2, can thus constitute relevant subsequent practice in relation to the underlying treaty.[852] Although they do not expressly have the power to change substantive obligations in their constitutive instruments, they have done so extensively in practice.[853] A factor in these cases is whether their decisions qualify as tacit modifications by subsequent practice or fall instead under the doctrine of implied powers.[854]

[845] Bowman, 'The Multilateral Treaty Amendment Process', 542. Of course, this argument can be applied by analogy to other fields such as the law of the sea.

[846] See Sections 2.3.1(c) and 3.5.2.

[847] See RR Churchill and G Ulfstein, 'Autonomous Institutional Arrangements in Multilateral Environmental Agreements: A Little-Noticed Phenomenon in International Law' (2000) 94 AJIL 623.

[848] See eg AE Boyle, 'Saving the World? Implementation and Enforcement of International Environmental Law through International Institutions' (1991) 3 J Envtl L 229, 233. See further Section 2.3.1(c).

[849] See Section 5.3.2(a).

[850] See the typology in J Sommer, 'Environmental Law-Making by International Organizations' (1996) 56 ZaöRV 628, 629–33.

[851] Nolte, Third Report on Treaties over Time, 365.

[852] See Section 2.3.1(c).

[853] See Sections 2.5.4 and 3.5.2. See also eg Churchill and Ulfstein, 'Autonomous Institutional Arrangements', 641, arguing that many such decisions approach the status of 'legislation'.

[854] See also Section 2.5.4.

Article 4 of the Basel Convention

The 1989 Basel Convention on the Control of Transboundary Movements of Hazardous Wastes and Their Disposal[855] provides a good example of a multilateral treaty impacted by subsequent practice (more specifically, subsequent agreement) through the decisions of its COP. In 1994, the COP adopted Decision II/12 by consensus.[856] The decision entailed a modification of the contents of Article 4 ('General obligations') of the Basel Convention, a key substantive provision, by banning the transboundary movement of hazardous waste from OECD to non-OECD States. The decision did not affect the object and purpose of the Convention, which aims to reduce the movement of hazardous waste, especially from developed to less developed countries.

The fact that the COP decision bypassed the formal amendment procedures prescribed in Article 17 of the Convention triggered criticism from a number of States.[857] By contrast, certain commentators argued that the decision was merely an interpretation of Article 4 and thus did not require formal amendment.[858] The fact that the decision constituted more than just interpretation soon became evident, however, when, following the criticism regarding the appropriateness of the form of the decision, at its next meeting in 1995 the COP triggered the formal amendment procedure under the Convention in order to implement the aims of Decision II/12.[859] This entailed the insertion of a new paragraph 7bis in the Preamble and a new Article 4A in the Convention. However, the formal amendment has still not entered into force.

The fact that Decision II/12 was adopted by consensus indicates that it was capable of establishing the general agreement of the parties, though it does not necessarily reflect 'unanimity of opinion' on the substantive issue in question.[860] Certain States objected to the form in which the decision was taken mainly based on practical and political concerns,[861] given that Article 4 represents a central substantive provision of

[855] 1673 UNTS 126.

[856] UNEP, *Report of the Second Meeting of the Conference of the Parties to the Basel Convention on the Control of Transboundary Movements of Hazardous Wastes and Their Disposal*, UN Doc UNEP/CHW.2/30 (25 March 1994) Decision II/12, 20.

[857] UNEP, *Decisions adopted by the Third Meeting of the Conference of the Parties to the Basel Convention on the Control of Transboundary Movements of Hazardous Wastes and Their Disposal*, UN Doc UNEP/CHW.3/35 (28 November 1995) Decision III/1 (Amendment to the Basel Convention), 1–2. See further G Handl, 'International "Lawmaking" by Conferences of the Parties and Other Politically Mandated Bodies' in R Wolfrum and V Röben (eds), *Developments of International Law in Treaty Making* (Springer, 2005) 127, 132.

[858] K Arts and J Gupta, 'Climate Change and Hazardous Waste Law: Developing International Law of Sustainable Development' in NJ Schrijver and F Weiss (eds), *International Law and Sustainable Development: Principles and Practice* (Martinus Nijhoff, 2004) 519, 538, pointing to Decision II/12, Preamble, para 2, which states that 'transboundary movements of hazardous wastes from OECD to non-OECD States have a high risk of not constituting an environmentally sound management of hazardous wastes as required by the Basel Convention.' See also the Greenpeace claim discussed in Wolfrum and Matz, *Conflicts*, 141.

[859] Decision III/1 (Amendment to the Basel Convention).

[860] UN Secretariat, Office of Legal Affairs, *Comments on Some Procedural Questions* <http://legal.un.org/ola/media/GA_RoP/GA_RoP_EN.pdf> accessed 10 June 2017, para 8 (rather, '[consensus] is used to describe the practice under which every effort is made to achieve general agreement').

[861] See Handl, 'International "Lawmaking" ', 132.

the Convention, the modification of which carries considerable politico-economic implications. Subsequent discussions revealed that many definitional questions remained regarding the implications of Decision II/12.[862] For these reasons, some States preferred a higher degree of formality and precision in undertaking the modification, and turned to the procedures prescribed by the treaty:

> The case of the Basel Convention must not necessarily be interpreted as an *ex post* recognition by the parties that the decision by the COP required a formal amendment, but can also be seen as an effort to avoid disagreement and to use a 'safe' way of proceeding even if it is not strictly necessary.[863]

The relation between modification by subsequent practice and formal amendment procedures was discussed in Chapter 3. As explained, the mere existence of formal amendment procedures under a treaty does not exclude the possibility of (informal) modification by subsequent practice. However, once formal amendment procedures have been *initiated*, any parallel modification by subsequent practice can only occur if the parties' intention to apply it over formal amendment is manifest.[864] At the third COP meeting in 1995, many delegates argued that Decision II/12 was legally binding pending formal amendment,[865] while others disagreed.[866] Given the parallel formal amendment initiated by the COP, Decision II/12, as a subsequent agreement in relation to the treaty, does not seem to fulfil the requirement of demonstrating the parties' clear intention to bypass formal amendment for the modification to take effect.

It has been argued that the recourse to formal amendment here underscored the limits of informal adaptation mechanisms, in this case the prior COP decision.[867] However, the fact that a number of States objected to the form of the decision should not immediately be taken to mean that the latter did not amount to relevant subsequent practice capable of treaty modification, particularly since it constituted the agreement of (all) the parties. Rather, the recourse to formal amendment further solidified what had already been established by subsequent practice. According to a similar view, 'decision II/12 stands on its own and is written in the strongest legal terms short of an amendment. (…) [A]mendment will not replace Decision II/12, but will enshrine it within the formal Convention itself, strengthen it and protect it against future attempts at sabotage'.[868] The initiation of the formal amendment

[862] UNEP, *Report of the Third Meeting of the Conference of the Parties to the Basel Convention Convention on the Control of Transboundary Movements of Hazardous Wastes and Their Disposal*, UN Doc UNEP/ CHW.3/34 (17 October 1995) paras 3, 51. For instance, while acknowledging the binding nature of COP decisions, the Brazilian delegate argued that 'to transform decision II/12 into a disposition of the Basel Convention through an amendment would be desirable only if that decision was perfect and not as it stands nowadays.'—ibid. para 51(i).

[863] Nolte, Third Report on Treaties over Time, 356.

[864] See Section 3.3.4. See also Section 5.2.3(a) discussing *Al-Saadoon and Mufdhi v UK*.

[865] See eg *Report of the Third Meeting of the Conference of the Parties to the Basel Convention*, para 51(i)–(ii) (Malaysia, Brazil).

[866] Ibid. para 51.

[867] Wolfrum and Matz, *Conflicts*, 141.

[868] Greenpeace, 'The Basel Ban—The Pride of the Basel Convention: An Update on Implementation and Amendment—September 1995', as cited in Arts and Gupta, 'Climate Change', 538–9. See also J Puckett, 'The Basel Ban: A Triumph over Business-as-Usual' (Basel Action Network, 1997) <http://wiki.ban.org/The_Basel_Ban:_A_Triumph_Over_Business-As-Usual> accessed 3 September 2014.

procedure also confirmed that the decision concerned a modification rather than a mere interpretation of Article 4 of the Basel Convention. Nevertheless, the case highlights the need to proceed with caution when assessing the means by which treaty adaptation unfolds.[869]

Amendments to the Montreal Protocol

Another example concerns the 1990 amendments to the 1987 Montreal Protocol on Substances that Deplete the Ozone Layer,[870] adopted by means of Decision II/2 of the Meeting of the Parties (MOP)[871]—a subsequent agreement. These amendments and the accompanying procedure for their entry into force are specified in Annex II to the MOP decision,[872] Article 2 of which states:

> This Amendment shall enter into force on 1 January 1992, provided that at least twenty instruments of ratification, acceptance or approval of the Amendment have been deposited by States or regional economic integration organizations that are Parties to the Montreal Protocol on Substances that Deplete the Ozone Layer. In the event that this condition has not been fulfilled by that date, the Amendment shall enter into force on the ninetieth day following the date on which it has been fulfilled.

This contrasts with the procedure set out in Article 9(5) of the 1985 Vienna Convention for the Protection of the Ozone Layer,[873] which provides that:

> [Amendments to the Montreal Protocol] shall enter into force between parties having accepted them on the ninetieth day after the receipt by the Depository of notification of their ratification, approval or acceptance (...) by at least two-thirds of the parties to the protocol concerned, except as may otherwise be provided in such protocol.

Since its 1990 decision, the MOP has employed the same entry into force procedure to adopt successive amendments to the Protocol.[874] These decisions, taken together, may constitute a modification by subsequent practice of the procedural provisions on amendment of the Montreal Protocol in the 1985 Vienna Convention.[875] Alternatively, they could be said to have given rise to a supplementary new

[869] Wolfrum and Matz, *Conflicts*, 141.

[870] 1522 UNTS 3 (Montreal Protocol). See further eg Churchill and Ulfstein, 'Autonomous Institutional Arrangements', 641; J Brunnée, 'COPing with Consent: Lawmaking under Multilateral Environmental Agreements' (2002) 15 LJIL 1, 31.

[871] UNEP, *Report of the Second Meeting of the Parties to the Montreal Protocol on Substances that Deplete the Ozone Layer*, UN Doc UNEP/OzL.Pro.2/3 (7 June 1990) Decision II/2, 32. See Art 11 of the Montreal Protocol.

[872] Amendment to the Montreal Protocol on Substances that Deplete the Ozone Layer 1990, 1598 UNTS 469 (London Amendment to the Montreal Protocol).

[873] The MOP can in certain cases also have recourse to a separate 'adjustment' procedure set out in Art 11(4)(b) of the Montreal Protocol.

[874] See Amendment to the Montreal Protocol on Substances that Deplete the Ozone Layer 1992, 1785 UNTS 517 (Copenhagen Amendment to the Montreal Protocol); Amendment to the Montreal Protocol on Substances that Deplete the Ozone Layer 1997, UN Doc UNEP/OzL.Pro.9/12 (Montreal Amendment to the Montreal Protocol); Amendment to the Montreal Protocol on Substances that Deplete the Ozone Layer 1999, 2173 UNTS 183 (Beijing Amendment to the Montreal Protocol).

[875] Nolte, Third Report on Treaties over Time, 355.

amendment procedure. In any event, they amount to a procedural modification of the Convention.

The UNFCCC 'financial mechanism'

Article 11 of the 1992 United Nations Framework Convention on Climate Change (UNFCCC)[876] provides as follows:

> A mechanism for the provision of financial resources on a grant or concessional basis (…) is hereby defined. It shall function under the guidance of and be accountable to the Conference of the Parties, which shall decide on its policies, programme priorities and eligibility criteria related to this Convention.

The COP considered that additional institutional arrangements had to be established in order to govern financial activities under the regime of the Convention. In 2001, the parties, operating by means of the COP, created structures such as the Special Climate Change Fund and the Least Developed Countries Fund,[877] as well as the Green Climate Fund[878] in 2010, which was intended to become 'the main global fund for climate change finance'.[879] Thus, the financial mechanism originally foreseen in Article 11 of the UNFCCC has now become a 'totality of legal, institutional and procedural arrangements'[880] through decisions of the COP.

These decisions go further than merely fulfilling the tasks of the COP as provided under Article 11. They build new structures that facilitate the implementation of important substantive obligations under the Convention. On the other hand, these changes brought about by the COP create mainly internal mechanisms that, from a procedural standpoint, increase efficiency and facilitate the financial architecture of the Convention, and could arguably be interpreted as falling within the scope of the COP's implied powers.[881] By streamlining the regulation of financial activities, and providing settings in which to give effect to certain substantive obligations,[882] the COP decisions facilitate the aims of the UNFCCC. They also establish mechanisms for providing financial support to developing States, in accordance with the principle of 'common but differentiated responsibilities and capabilities' enshrined in the UNFCCC.[883] In any case, these institutional arrangements do not affect the object and purpose of the UNFCCC, but rather facilitate it. Overall, the COP decisions relating to the implementation of Article 11 are likely to be regarded as far-reaching procedural modifications to the structures and processes of the UNFCCC framework.

[876] 1771 UNTS 107.

[877] UNFCCC, *Report of the Conference of the Parties on its seventh session* (2001) UN Doc FCCC/CP/2001/13/Add.1 (21 January 2002) Section II, Decision 7/CP.7 op 1.

[878] UNFCCC, *Report of the Conference of the Parties on its sixteenth session* (2010) UN Doc FCCC/CP/2010/7/Add.1 (15 March 2011) Decision 1/CP.16 op 102.

[879] UNFCCC, *Report of the Conference of the Parties on its seventeenth session* (2011) UN Doc FCCC/CP/2011/9/Add.1 (15 March 2012) Decision 3/CP.17, Annex para 32.

[880] F Yamin and J Depledge, *The International Climate Change Regime: A Guide to Rules, Institutions and Procedures* (CUP, 2004) 283.

[881] See Sections 2.5.4 and 3.5.2.

[882] Nolte, Third Report on Treaties over Time, 367.

[883] Ibid.

'Migratory species' under the Bonn Convention and the issue of climate change

Climate change concerns have given rise to the question of whether the 1979 Convention on the Conservation of Migratory Species of Wild Animals (CMS or Bonn Convention)[884] should be adapted to play a role with regard to the conservation of the process of migration, as separate from the conservation of migratory *species*.[885] This would entail expanding the treaty's focus on preventing the loss of migratory species to that of migratory *behaviour* in general, an issue recently acknowledged by the CMS Conference of the Parties.[886] Such an expansion of the Convention's scope of operation may stretch the bounds of the CMS beyond its reasonable interpretative range and into the realm of modification. This issue is somewhat comparable to that encountered in the context of the discussion on the 'normative transformations' undergone by the UN Charter, the NATO Treaty, and the World Bank's Articles of Agreement in light of major societal changes over the past decades.[887]

Article I(1)(a) of the CMS defines 'migratory species' as follows:

> '[M]igratory species' means the entire population or any geographically separate part of the population of any species or lower taxon of wild animals a significant proportion of whose members cyclically and predictably cross one or more national jurisdictional boundaries.

The rather open-ended notions of 'cyclically and predictably' allow for significant flexibility.[888] The terms 'cyclically and predictably' were further specified in a subsequent interpretation issued by the Convention's COP, which was sufficiently broad to enable the coverage of more species than would have been the case subject to a strict reading of the provision.[889] It should be noted, however, that during the drafting of Article I CMS, the term initially employed had been 'periodically', but was replaced with 'cyclically and predictably' precisely to avoid a reading of the article that would allow for coverage of relatively sedentary species.[890]

More remarkable is the subsequent practice surrounding the definition of migratory species reflected in the fact that certain species have been included within the scope of the CMS despite doubts as to whether their movements across national boundaries are sufficiently 'cyclical and predictable'. The CMS may be a particularly interesting case study because the State that did much to dictate the terms of

[884] (1980) 19 ILM 15.

[885] A Trouwborst, 'Transboundary Wildlife Conservation in a Changing Climate: The Adaptation of the Bonn Convention on Migratory Species and its Daughter Instruments to Climate Change' (2012) 4 *Diversity* 258, 286.

[886] CMS COP Resolution 10.19 on Migratory Species Conservation in the Light of Climate Change (25 November 2011) Doc UNEP/CMS/Res.10.19, Preamble, noting the concern that 'climate change is already having an adverse impact on migratory species and the phenomenon of animal migration'.

[887] See Section 5.3.1.

[888] MJ Bowman, P Davies, and C Redgwell, *Lyster's International Wildlife Law* (2nd edn, CUP, 2010) 539.

[889] CMS COP Resolution 2.2 on Guidelines for the Application of Certain Terms of the Convention (13 October 1988) Doc UNEP/CMS/ScCAP/Inf.2, Res.2.2, para 1(a).

[890] Bowman, Davies, and Redgwell, *Lyster's International Wildlife Law*, 540, citing *Report of the US Delegation to the Conference to Conclude a Convention on the Conservation of Migratory Species of Wild Animals* (US Department of State, 17 October 1979) 2–4. cf Art IV(4) CMS.

the negotiations, the United States, ultimately declined to participate.[891] It would therefore be less of a surprise if the parties felt a 'freer hand' to drift away from the text through subsequent practice, as seems indeed to have occurred in relation to the definition of migratory species.[892] For instance, practice has led to the inclusion of species like the mountain gorilla and the South Andean huemul, the latter being considered migratory merely because the habitat of certain populations is located on the border area between Argentina and Chile:[893]

> Animals like these, which do not portray anything resembling regular migrations in the classical sense, but periodically cross national boundaries for the simple reason that their range overlaps more than one country, are sometimes referred to as 'technical migrants'.[894]

The inclusion of species that merely cross boundaries under the scope of the CMS seems to indicate a change of focus to the conservation of transboundary rather than migratory species to the point where '"Convention on Transboundary Wildlife Conservation" might indeed have been a more accurate title for the Bonn Convention'.[895] Thus, due to climate change concerns, the CMS is likely to play a role in the future not only in respect of the conservation of species that *become* non-migratory, and hence, *stricto sensu*, no longer qualify as 'migratory',[896] but also classical *sedentary* species that shift across national boundaries as a result of climate change.[897] This would seem to go against not only the wording of Article I, but also its *travaux*, as indicated by the replacement of the more open-ended term 'periodically' with 'cyclically and predictably'.[898]

On the other hand, it should be noted that practice has not been completely consistent in this respect.[899] For instance, a proposal to include the Asian elephant under the scope of protection of the CMS was rejected by the COP because it was not considered to be a truly migratory species, given its mere 'oscillation' across national borders.[900] As discussed, the degree of determinacy of a practice influences its evidentiary weight in the process of establishing whether an interpretation or modification by subsequent practice has occurred.[901] These inconsistencies in practice relating to the expansive definition of migratory species under the CMS regime may indicate that the concept, while currently *undergoing* change, has not yet fully crystallized in its modified form.

The new definition of 'migratory species'—a technical, substantive, albeit rather open-textured, provision in a multilateral treaty—seems to imply a broadening of

[891] Bowman, Davies, and Redgwell, *Lyster's International Wildlife Law*, 547.

[892] Ibid. 538–41.

[893] See Preamble to the Memorandum of Understanding between the Argentine Republic and the Republic of Chile on the Conservation of the South Andean Huemul (4 December 2010) <www.cms.int/huemul/en/node/4140> accessed 11 June 2017, used to justify the inclusion of the species under the umbrella of the CMS Appendices.

[894] Trouwborst, 'Transboundary Wildlife Conservation', 288. [895] Ibid.

[896] Ibid. 286. [897] Ibid. 287–8. [898] See n 890.

[899] See Bowman, Davies, and Redgwell, *Lyster's International Wildlife Law*, 538–9.

[900] Secretariat of the Convention on Migratory Species, *Proceedings of the Fourth Meeting of the Conference of the Parties* (Nairobi, Kenya, 7–11 June 1994) para 105.

[901] See Sections 2.3.1(b) and Section 2.3.5.

the scope of the CMS regime to such an extent that it could arguably even modify its object and purpose, though by supplementing (rather than altering) it. In any case, it provides a strong indication that a modification of Article I(1)(a) of the CMS by subsequent practice is underway to include even sedentary species within the Convention's scope, contrasting with the text and drafting history of the provision.

The general discussion on the CMS regime in light of climate change also applies to the 1979 Convention on the Conservation of European Wildlife and Natural Habitats (Bern Convention),[902] a large multilateral treaty regime that aims to 'conserve wild flora and fauna and their natural habitats' (Article 1(1)). Like the CMS, the Bern Convention does not contain express provisions regarding adaptation to climate change, which makes sense given the age of the treaty.[903] Instead, the parties to the Bern Convention addressed the issue of climate change in a series of non-binding decisions taken by the treaty's representative body, the Standing Committee.[904]

The contents of the Bern Convention could either be updated by means of the instrument's onerous formal amendment procedures[905] or by subsequent practice, such as decisions of the relevant treaty bodies.[906] Trouwborst illustrates the influence of COP decisions by means of a Dutch case involving the interpretation of Article 3 of the Ramsar Convention.[907] In that case, an infringement of the Convention was identified based on the failure to conduct an environmental impact assessment, despite the fact that Article 3 did not appear to require one. The Court reasoned that Article 3 had to be carried out in light of the Convention's aims and the 'resolutions, recommendations and guidelines' subsequently adopted at conferences of the parties.[908] The Court's approach, based on the practice of the COP, is generous, since

[902] 1284 UNTS 209.

[903] A Trouwborst, 'Conserving European Biodiversity in a Changing Climate: The Bern Convention, the EU Birds and Habitats Directives and the Adaptation of Nature to Climate Change' (2011) 20 RECIEL 62, 68.

[904] See eg Recommendation No 122 (2006) of the Standing Committee on the Conservation of Biological Diversity in the Context of Climate Change (30 November 2006); Recommendation No 135 (2008) of the Standing Committee on Addressing the Impacts of Climate Change on Biodiversity (27 November 2008); Recommendation No 142 (2009) of the Standing Committee Interpreting the CBD Definition of Invasive Alien Species to Take into Account Climate Change (26 November 2009); Recommendation No 143 (2009) of the Standing Committee on Further Guidance for Parties on Biodiversity and Climate Change (26 November 2009); Recommendation No 145 (2010) of the Standing Committee on Guidance for Parties on Biodiversity and Climate Change in Mountain Regions (9 December 2010); Recommendation No 146 (2010) of the Standing Committee on Guidance for Parties on Biodiversity and Climate Change in European Islands (9 December 2010); Recommendation No 147 (2010) of the Standing Committee on Guidance for Parties on Wildland Fires, Biodiversity and Climate Change (9 December 2010).

[905] Trouwborst, 'Conserving European Biodiversity', 7.

[906] Ibid. fn 37, citing Churchill and Ulfstein, 'Autonomous Institutional Arrangements', 641; A Wiersema, 'The New International Law-Makers? Conference of the Parties to Multilateral Environmental Agreements' (2009) 31 MJIL 231.

[907] Trouwborst, 'Conserving European Biodiversity', 7–8.

[908] Netherlands Crown Decision in the case lodged by the Competent Authority for the Island of Bonaire on the annulment of two of its decisions on the Lac wetland by the Governor of the Netherlands Antilles, KB 11 September 2011, *Staatsblad* 2007, no 347 (*Lac/Sorobon*). See further JM Verschuuren, 'Ramsar Soft Law Is Not Soft at All: Discussion of the 2007 Decision by the Netherlands Crown on the Lac Ramsar Site on the Island of Bonaire' (2008) 35 *Milieu en Recht* 28.

its interpretation of Article 3 results in an 'actual contradiction of the language employed in the treaty'.[909] It demonstrates how, by analogy, provisions in the Bern Convention could be interpreted in light of COP practice to impose new measures necessary for climate change adaptation. A similar argument has been made with regard to the expansive interpretation of the EU Birds and Habitats Directives.[910]

It is not completely clear whether such adjustments to regimes like the Bern Convention require modification by subsequent practice or merely dynamic interpretation in line with their object and purpose.[911] Again, this discussion relates back to the 'normative transformation' discussion relating to the constitutive instruments of international organizations such as the UN, NATO, and the World Bank, as well as the CMS.[912]

Other examples in relation to MEAs

Numerous other examples of potentially modifying practice by COPs or MOPs can be identified in relation to MEAs. For instance, the Consultative Meeting of the Parties to the London Convention on the Prevention of Marine Pollution by Dumping of Wastes and Other Matter has effectively expanded the definition of 'dumping' so as to include the disposal of waste into the seabed from the sea.[913] The COP of CITES[914] has also been a source of decisions constituting subsequent practice bordering on modification. The Conference, which can only make recommendations for improving the Convention's effectiveness,[915] has for instance established subsidiary bodies without any express power to do so.[916] It is unlikely that this could be accounted for on the basis of the doctrine of implied powers alone, given the extensive powers exercised by the COP in practice as compared to those formally conferred upon it.[917] Similarly, it has adopted a quota system for trade in various animal products, including ivory, which also falls somewhere between interpretation based on implied powers and modification.[918] Likewise, 'clarifications' provided by the CITES COP in relation to primary treaty obligations, such as the issue of species that can be regarded as captive stock, 'go far beyond the mere interpretation of key terms (as one might find in the definition of the section of a treaty) to establish a form of regulatory regime for "captive bred" or "artificially propagated" species'.[919]

It may still be debatable whether some of the individual decisions mentioned above amount to modification. However, the sheer amount of examples in relation

[909] Trouwborst, 'Conserving European Biodiversity', 8. [910] Ibid. 13, 16.

[911] Ibid. 21. [912] See eg Section 5.3.1(a)–(b) and (e).

[913] Churchill and Ulfstein, 'Autonomous Institutional Arrangements', 641, citing London Consultative Meeting of the Parties (1990) Res LDC.41(13), reprinted in (1990) 6 *International Organizations and the Law of the Sea: Documentary Yearbook* 332. The definition does not include the disposal of waste from land through tunnelling.

[914] See Section 2.5.4, n 798. [915] Art XI(3)(e) CITES.

[916] cf Churchill and Ulfstein, 'Autonomous Institutional Arrangements', fn 69, citing eg HG Schermers and NM Blokker, *International Institutional Law: Unity Within Diversity* (Martinus Nijhoff, 2003) 743.

[917] See text to n 915.

[918] P Sands, *Principles of International Environmental Law: Framework, Standards and Implementation* (Manchester UP, 1995) 380; Churchill and Ulfstein, 'Autonomous Institutional Arrangements', 639.

[919] P Davies, 'Non-Compliance—a Pivotal or Secondary Function of COP Governance?' (2013) 15 ICL Rev 77, 81–2, cited in D Costelloe and M Fitzmaurice, 'Lawmaking by Treaty: Conclusion

to substantive provisions in MEAs clearly indicates that subsequent practice, as reflected in the decisions of representative bodies such as COPs, is changing the normative scope and content of these treaties in line with the needs of international society.

5.3.2c Human rights

A number of examples of modification by subsequent practice in the context of human rights treaties have already been explored above. Although such instances have indeed occurred in the special context of the ECHR,[920] it was explained in Chapter 3 that the special nature of human rights treaties could generally have a limiting effect on the operation of the process of modification by subsequent practice. For one thing, human rights treaties can be regarded as inherently evolutionary.[921] This makes their adaptation easier without the need for actual modification. They often contain 'integral' or 'absolute' obligations that are non-reciprocal in nature.[922] Such provisions are more difficult to modify by subsequent practice[923] and do not permit *inter se* modifications.[924] Another reason for the more limited impact of modification by subsequent practice in this context may be found in the concept of non-regression, which prohibits changes to the detriment of the rights-holders.[925] Of course, this (disputed) concept still permits subsequent practice to supplement human rights norms rather than override them, and thus modify them to the benefit of the rights-holders or States. A number of additional examples of potential modifications of human rights treaties may be mentioned. The above considerations will be taken into account in assessing them.

The principle of *non-refoulement*

The principle of *non-refoulement* dictates that persons may not be transferred from one State to another if they face a risk of torture or persecution. It is codified in various human rights and refugee law instruments. In refugee law, one important source is Article 33 of the 1951 Geneva Convention relating to the Status of Refugees,[926] as amended by the 1967 Protocol relating to the Status of Refugees:[927]

1. No Contracting State shall expel or return ('refouler') a refugee in any manner whatsoever to the frontiers of territories where his life or freedom would be

of Treaties and Evolution of Treaty Regimes in Practice' in C Brölmann and Y Radi (eds), *Research Handbook on the Theory and Practice of International Lawmaking* (Edward Elgar, 2016) 111, 124.

920 See Section 5.2.3(a).

921 See eg *Gabčíkovo-Nagymaros Project*, Separate Opinion of Vice-President Weeramantry, 114–15; Pocar, 'Some Remarks on the Continuity of Human Rights and International Humanitarian Law Treaties', 279. See also Section 5.2.1(c) on the ECtHR and the nature of the ECHR as a 'living instrument'.

922 See Section 3.5.1. See also eg Koskenniemi, Fragmentation Report, paras 312–13.

923 Koskenniemi, Fragmentation Report, para 385.

924 Ibid. para 311. See further Section 3.5.1.

925 See Section 3.5.1 for an analysis of the alleged non-regression principle.

926 189 UNTS 137.

927 606 UNTS 267.

threatened on account of his race, religion, nationality, membership of a particular social group or political opinion.

2. The benefit of the present provision may not, however, be claimed by a refugee whom there are reasonable grounds for regarding as a danger to the security of the country in which he is, or who, having been convicted by a final judgment of a particularly serious crime, constitutes a danger to the community of that country.

Paragraph 2 of the Article thus allows for exceptions to the principle of *non-refoulement*. By contrast, under human rights law, the principle is derived from an *absolute* prohibition on torture and other inhuman treatment, and is not subject to any exceptions. This is implicitly as well as explicitly recognized in, among other human rights instruments, Article 3 of the 1984 Convention against Torture and Other Cruel, Inhuman or Degrading Treatment or Punishment,[928] Article 22(8) of the ACHR, Article 7 of the ICCPR, and Article 3 of the ECHR (as touched upon in Section 5.2.1 above in relation to the ECtHR string of cases on capital punishment[929]). The relation between the human rights and refugee law concepts of *non-refoulement* has been characterized as 'complementary protection',[930] suggesting that the two obligations operate in parallel.[931] It has even been argued that there has been an emergence of a customary principle of *non-refoulement* with differing content in the refugee and human rights law context.[932]

It has also been suggested that subsequent practice, or even 'treaty-related' customary law,[933] is in the process of impacting the meaning and scope of Article 33 of the 1951 Refugee Convention,[934] and potentially 'superseding the wishes expressed by states in Article 33(2)'.[935] Through a process of gradual alteration and extension, modifying subsequent practice or 'customary international law regarding *non-refoulement* might require states to protect individuals who would not qualify as refugees under relevant treaties, extending state obligations beyond treaties' explicit

[928] 1465 UNTS 85.

[929] See eg *Soering v UK*, para 91; *Cruz Varas and others v Sweden*, paras 69–70; *Vilvarajah and others v UK*, paras 102–10; *Chahal v United Kingdom* [GC] App no 22414/93 (ECtHR, 15 November 1996) para 74. The ECtHR also dealt with this issue in relation to migrants and refugee law—see eg *Hirsi Jamaa and others v Italy* [GC] App no 27765/09 (ECtHR, 23 February 2012).

[930] See GS Goodwin-Gill and J McAdam, *The Refugee in International Law* (3rd edn, OUP, 2007) 285.

[931] See eg C Droege, 'Transfers of Detainees: Legal Framework, *Non-Refoulement* and Contemporary Challenges' (2008) 90 IRRC 669, 676.

[932] E Lauterpacht and D Bethlehem, 'The Scope and Content of the Principle of Non-Refoulement: Opinion' in E Feller, V Türk, and F Nicholson (eds), *Refugee Protection in International Law: UNHCR's Global Consultations on International Protection* (CUP, 2003) 87, paras 217–53.

[933] See Section 4.5.1.

[934] See eg UN High Commissioner for Refugees, *Advisory Opinion on the Extraterritorial Application of* Non-Refoulement *Obligations under the 1951 Convention relating to the Status of Refugees and its 1967 Protocol* (26 January 2007) para 12, citing eg UNGA Res 51/75 of 12 February 1997, UN Doc A/RES/51/75 (1997) para 3, and UNGA Res 52/132 of 12 December 1997, UN Doc A/RES/52/132 (1997) Preamble, para 12; J Hathaway, *The Law of Refugee Status* (Butterworths, 1991) 24–7.

[935] A Farmer, 'Non-Refoulement and *Jus Cogens*: Limiting Anti-Terror Measures that Threaten Refugee Protection' (2009) 23 Geo Immigr LJ 1, 29 (arguing that *non-refoulement* has acquired the status of a *jus cogens* norm).

definitions'.[936] Such modification by subsequent customary law would require evidence of the parties' intention to modify the treaty rather than have it operate as *lex specialis*.[937] In any case, there may be an emerging trend against exceptions to the principle of *non-refoulement*,[938] in line with the principle of non-regression.[939]

For now, as subsequent practice is not sufficiently determinate, this entails mainly that exceptions under Article 33(2) of the 1951 Refugee Convention must be read very narrowly.[940] Thus, the effects of subsequent practice here do not yet seem to have gone beyond interpretation. This example also links back to the issue of fragmentation, demonstrating how different regimes—in this case, human rights and refugee law—can interact by way of subsequent practice.[941]

Minorities Treaties under the League of Nations

Another example is the impact of human rights concepts on the so-called Treaties on the Protection of National Minorities or 'Minorities Treaties' concluded after World War I under the chapeau of the League of Nations.[942] These treaties imposed obligations regarding the protection of members of minorities in their territory mainly as individuals[943] (although they also included rights such as freedom of religion and language). However, over time, the States parties 'succeeded in evading, eroding or eventually nullifying most of their obligations [under the Minorities Treaties].'[944] Eventually, new 'treaty-related' customary law emerged by tacit agreement through their subsequent practice, reflecting the development of new human rights concepts focusing on the 'idea of protecting and promoting individual (rather than group) human rights'.[945] According to a 1950 study by the UN Secretary-General:

> [T]his whole system [of minorities protection during the League of Nations] was overthrown by the Second World War. All the international decisions reached since 1944 have been

[936] R Crootof, 'Change Without Consent: How Customary International Law Modifies Treaties' (2016) 41 Yale JIL 237, fn 217, citing D Perluss and JF Hartman, *Temporary Refuge: Emergence of a Customary Norm* (1986) 26 VJIL 551.

[937] See eg Sections 4.4.2 and 4.5.1.

[938] Lauterpacht and Bethlehem, 'The Principle of *Non-Refoulement*', paras 151, 157.

[939] See Section 3.5.1(a).

[940] Lauterpacht and Bethlehem, 'The Principle of *Non-Refoulement*', paras 158–9.

[941] See eg Section 3.1.

[942] This label refers to the treaties, League of Nations mandates (regarded as treaties), and unilateral declarations (equated to treaties in that context) by States applying for membership to the League of Nations and the UN, concerning the protection of minority rights. See eg H Rosting, 'Protection of Minorities by the League of Nations' (1923) 17 AJIL 641. For a compilation of these treaties, see League of Nations, *Protection of Linguistic, Racial and Religious Minorities by the League of Nations* (League of Nations Publications, IB Minorities 1927) I.B.2.

[943] F Capotorti, 'Study of the Rights of Persons Belonging to Ethnic, Religious and Linguistic Minorities, Sub-Commission on Prevention of Discrimination and Protection of Minorities', UN ESCOR, 30th session, UN Doc E/CN.4/Sub.2/384/REV.1 (1979) para 101.

[944] RB Bilder, 'Can Minorities Treaties Work?' in Y Dinstein and M Tabory (eds), *The Protection of Minorities and Human Rights* (Martinus Nijhoff, 1992) 59, 66.

[945] Ibid. 67. See also Villiger, *Customary International Law and Treaties* (1985), para 309. cf IL Claude, *National Minorities: An International Problem* (Harvard UP, 1955) 29–33; A Spiliopoulou Akermark, *Justifications of Minority Protection in International Law* (Martinus Nijhoff, 1997) 119–23.

inspired by a different philosophy. The idea of a general and universal protection of human rights and fundamental freedoms is emerging. It is therefore no longer only the minorities in certain countries which receive protection (...). Reviewing the situation as a whole, therefore, one is led to conclude that between 1939 and 1947 circumstances as a whole changed to such an extent that generally speaking the system should be considered as having ceased to exist.[946]

These subsequent changes in customary international law, which conformed to the (alleged) principle of non-regression,[947] provided grounds for modification, also in the form of termination, of the original substantive obligations under the 'Minorities Treaties'.

5.3.2d Humanitarian law

Similar considerations as discussed in relation to human rights treaties above also apply to the process of modification by subsequent practice in the context of humanitarian law[948]—specifically, in relation to the 1949 Geneva Conventions.

For instance, Article 85 of the Third Geneva Convention provides that '[p]risoners of war prosecuted under the laws of the Detaining Power for acts committed prior to capture shall retain, even if convicted, the benefits of the present Convention.' However, subsequent practice has created an exception to this rule, which can either be seen as an alteration of or a supplement to the existing provision: where combatants fail to distinguish themselves from civilians, in breach of international humanitarian law, they no longer have the right to prisoner-of-war status. According to Rule 106 of the ICRC study on customary international humanitarian law, this practice now constitutes customary international law.[949] The practice was subsequently codified in Article 44(2)–(4) of Additional Protocol I of 1977, and also explicitly recognized by States not parties to the Protocol.[950] Thus, the exception to Article 85 of the Third Geneva Convention can be said to constitute an instance of (partial) modification of a substantive treaty provision by subsequent practice, which has apparently also given rise to ('treaty-related') subsequent customary law.[951]

[946] UN Commission on Human Rights, 'Study of the Legal Validity of the Undertakings Concerning Minorities', Memorandum by the Secretary-General, UN Doc E/CN.4/367 (7 April 1950) 70–1. See also T Modeen, *The International Protection of Minorities in Europe* (Åbo Akademi, 1969) 72–3; P Thornberry, *International Law and the Rights of Minorities* (Clarendon Press, 1991) 53–4. cf *Report of the Working Group on Minorities on its First Session*, UN Doc E/CN.4/Sub.2/1996/2 (30 November 1995) para 46.

[947] See eg Section 3.5.1(a).

[948] A discussion of the nature of the relation and interplay between human rights and humanitarian law goes beyond the scope of this book.

[949] JM Henckaerts and L Doswald-Beck (eds), *Customary International Humanitarian Law, Volume 1: Rules* (ICRC and CUP, 2005) 384.

[950] See eg Israel, *Public Committee against Torture in Israel v Government of Israel*, High Court of Justice, HCJ 769/02, Judgment of 14 December 2006 ('*Targeted Killings* case'), cited in ICRC, *Customary IHL Database* <www.icrc.org/customary-ihl/eng/docs/v2_rul_rule106_sectiona> accessed 12 June 2017 ('Practice Relating to Rule 106. Conditions for Prisoner-of-War Status').

[951] See Section 4.5.1.

A similar process has occurred in relation to Article 118 of the same Geneva Convention. It provides that '[p]risoners of war shall be released and repatriated without delay after the cessation of active hostilities.' At the time of drafting of the Convention, a proposed amendment to give prisoners a choice of whether or not to return to their home country was rejected by a large majority.[952] It is clear that at the time the Convention was not intended to provide for that right. However, through subsequent practice, in the form of a special agreement in 1953 established between the parties to the conflict in the Korean War, reflected in a 1952 General Assembly resolution,[953] and evidenced by State practice during the Gulf War in 1991,[954] Article 118 was radically reinterpreted to such an extent that the practice of granting prisoners of war the choice of whether to be repatriated has now become a basic 'point of departure'.[955] It is even considered to be customary international law.[956]

This result goes against both the text and the *travaux* of the provision, particularly in light of its express rejection by the drafters. It can be qualified as modification by subsequent practice—and 'treaty-related' customary law—of a substantive provision, and, moreover, one that according to the ICRC Commentary on the 1949 Geneva Conventions represents 'one of the most important Articles in the Convention'.[957] The modification does not affect the Convention's object and purpose. In fact, the practice is in line with the spirit of the modified provision, namely, of preventing unreasonable prolonged detention of prisoners in captivity with a view to their interests[958] and the Convention as a whole.[959]

Furthermore, Article 23 of the Fourth Geneva Convention, concerning the passage of consignments of medical supplies, food, and clothing, has arguably been modified by customary international law as reflected in Article 70 of Additional Protocol I (to which not all parties to the Convention are party).[960] Article 70 expands the obligations related to relief operations in non-occupation situations beyond what was originally envisaged in Article 23 of the Convention by prescribing a broader category of relief supplies[961]—a 'broadening [that] is generally accepted,

[952] See JS Pictet (ed), *Geneva Convention relative to the Treatment of Prisoners of War: Commentary* (ICRC, 1960) 542–4 (Art 118, Commentary of 1960).

[953] UNGA Res 610 (VII) of 3 December 1952, UN Doc A/RES/610 (1952).

[954] See eg P Rowe (ed), *The Gulf War in International and English Law* (Sweet and Maxwell, 1993) 203.

[955] Y Dinstein, 'Refugees and the Law of Armed Conflict' (1982) 12 IsrYbHR 94, 102. See also Pictet, *Geneva Convention*, 546–7.

[956] Y Dinstein, 'The Interaction between Customary International Law and Treaties' (2006) 322 RC 243, para 271.

[957] Pictet, *Geneva Convention*, 540–1. [958] Ibid. 541.

[959] See eg S Jaquemet, 'The Cross-Fertilization of International Humanitarian Law and International Refugee Law' (2001) 83 IRRC 651, 662.

[960] Crootof, 'Change Without Consent', 272.

[961] See eg Israel, *Physicians for Human Rights and Others v Prime Minister of Israel and Others*, High Court of Justice, HCJ 201/09 and 248/09, Judgment of 19 January 2009, para 21 ('Article 70 of the First Protocol provides a more general and broader duty [than Article 23 of the Convention], whereby parties to a conflict are obliged to allow the passage of articles that are essential for the civilian population, at the earliest opportunity and without delay.').

including by States not (...) party to Additional Protocol I'.[962] Moreover, Article 70 limits the exceptions under Article 23 (namely, if 'consignments may be diverted from their destination', 'control may not be effective', or 'a definite advantage may accrue to the military efforts or economy of the enemy through the substitution of the (...) consignments for goods') by prescribing that a State 'shall, in no way whatsoever, divert relief consignments from the purpose for which they are intended nor delay their forwarding, except in cases of urgent necessity in the interest of the civilian population concerned'. The ICRC has recognized the rule in Article 70 as customary international law,[963] as has, *inter alia*, Israel's High Court of Justice in a case concerning the government's decision to limit the supply of fuel and electricity to the Gaza Strip.[964] Thus, an 'external' customary norm appears to have emerged that has come to modify—by altering and significantly expanding—substantive obligations under the Convention.[965]

A more minor example relates to Article 38 of the First Geneva Convention. The Article provides that the 'heraldic emblem of the red cross on a white ground (...) is retained as the emblem and distinctive sign of the Medical Service of armed forces', but allows States already using the emblem of the red crescent or red lion and sun to continue doing so. However, certain States that did *not* already do so, eventually came to adopt the crescent, a practice uncontested by other States: '[i]t must therefore be admitted that well before the adoption of [Additional Protocol III[966]] (...) the content of Art 38 had been modified by state practice.'[967] The 2016 ICRC Commentary confirms that the current application of Article 38 'may be considered a rule that has been modified by a subsequent rule of customary international law, as well as by the tacit agreement of the High Contracting Parties'. Generally, however, as also cautioned with respect to the issue of 'protecting powers' under the Geneva Conventions in Chapter 3,[968] such conclusions should not be inferred lightly from a lack of implementation:

> Certain provisions of the [First Geneva] Convention do not seem to have been applied extensively in the past six decades. However, the absence of practice in the application of a provision does not, in and of itself, lead to the falling into desuetude of such a provision. Desuetude means that a treaty rule is no longer applicable or has been modified, a conclusion that should not be reached lightly. It is subject to stringent conditions and requires the

[962] ICRC, *Customary IHL Database* <https://ihl-databases.icrc.org/customary-ihl/eng/docs/v1_rul> accessed 4 June 2017, Rules 55 and 56.

[963] Ibid.

[964] Israel, *Gaber Albasyouni Ahmad and Others v Prime Minister and Others*, High Court of Justice, HCJ 9132/07, Judgment of 30 January 2008, para 13.

[965] See Section 4.5.1 on the notion of (modification by) 'external' customary law.

[966] Protocol Additional to the Geneva Conventions of 12 August 1949, and relating to the Adoption of an Additional Distinctive Emblem (Protocol III) 2005, 2404 UNTS 261. Protocol III, relating to the adoption of an additional emblem, puts the various emblems on the same level.

[967] A Clapham, P Gaeta, and M Sassòli, *The 1949 Geneva Conventions: A Commentary* (OUP, 2015) 859 fn 18.

[968] See Section 3.3.2(b).

agreement, at least tacit, of the Parties or the emergence of an inconsistent rule of customary international law.[969]

In the case of Article 38, an inconsistent, 'treaty-related' customary norm appears to have emerged and modified the Convention provision.[970]

On the topic of distinctive emblems, a further example illustrating how subsequent practice can lead to the *partial* modification of a treaty provision—namely, by creating an exception to an otherwise respected rule—relates to Article 12 of Additional Protocol II to the 1949 Geneva Conventions.[971] It provides that the distinctive emblem of the red cross, crescent, or lion and sun 'shall be displayed by medical and religious personnel and medical units, and on medical transports.' The language of the provision is clear and categorical as to the fact that the emblem must always be displayed: '[i]t shall be respected in all circumstances.' However, in practice, an exception to this rule has emerged, allowing States not to mark such convoys with the distinctive emblem where there is a risk of targeting of such medical transports by armed groups.[972] This is a minor modification of the rule in Article 12 of Protocol II.[973]

Finally, and more generally, it is necessary in this context to acknowledge the special role and status of the ICRC, already explored in Chapter 2.[974] As discussed there, the Committee's practice does not in itself constitute subsequent practice—but it may (inadvertently or deliberately) contribute to shaping it,[975] and, indeed, can be taken to reflect, or at least influence, State practice.[976] It is clear that the ICRC's proactive role as 'guardian' of international humanitarian law has surpassed its formally envisaged role,[977] such that 'a wide gap separates the meagre language of the [Geneva] Conventions' provisions mandating ICRC operations from the broad perception and exercise in practice of that mandate by the ICRC'.[978] One straightforward example is Article 123 of the Third Geneva Convention on the creation of a Central Prisoners of War Information Agency. The article authorizes the ICRC merely to 'propose (...) the organization of such an Agency'—and then only 'if it deems [it] necessary'. However, '[i]n practice, the ICRC operates the Central

969 ICRC, *Commentary on the First Geneva Convention* (ICRC, 2nd edn, 2016) <https://ihl-databases.icrc.org/ihl/full/GCi-commentary> accessed 12 June 2017, Introduction, para 51.

970 See further Section 4.5.1.

971 Protocol Additional to the Geneva Conventions of 12 August 1949, and relating to the Protection of Victims of Non-International Armed Conflicts (Protocol II) 1977, 1125 UNTS 609.

972 Nolte, Second Report on Subsequent Practice, para 36.

973 cf ibid. para 37, characterizing this example as a situation where subsequent practice confirmed an *interpretation* 'according to which article 12 does not contain an obligation to use the protective emblem in all circumstances, and thereby indicates a margin of discretion for the parties'. (Footnotes omitted.) It is respectfully submitted that such a reading of the provision does not seem to fall within its interpretative range given the clear and categorical wording of Art 12, and amounts to modification.

974 See Section 2.3.1(a), text to nn 246–52.

975 See eg Nolte, First Report on Subsequent Practice, para 140.

976 Kohen, 'Keeping Subsequent Agreements and Practice in Their Right Limits', 41. See Section 2.3.1(a).

977 See eg R Giladi and S Ratner, 'The Role of the International Committee of the Red Cross' in A Clapham, P Gaeta, and M Sassòli, *The 1949 Geneva Conventions: A Commentary* (OUP, 2015) 525, 537ff.

978 Clapham, Gaeta, and Sassòli, *The 1949 Geneva Conventions*, 531.

Tracing Agency itself.'[979] Similarly, the ICRC's offers of good offices may go beyond the interpretative realm of Article 23 of the First Geneva Convention and Article 14 of the Third Geneva Convention.[980] Generally, the ICRC's interpretative guidance and work in the field of humanitarian law has thus had a far-reaching impact upon the Geneva Conventions, in some instances even venturing into the realm of treaty modification.

5.3.2e Other fields

Various other examples of potential modifications by subsequent practice can be mentioned here briefly. One interesting case is the practice surrounding Article 5 of the 1944 Chicago Convention on International Civil Aviation,[981] a large multilateral treaty regime.[982] The article does not require charter airlines to seek permission to land in cases where they are not carrying passengers or cargo, stating, *inter alia*, that:

> Each contracting State agrees that all aircraft of the other contracting States, being aircraft not engaged in scheduled international air services, shall have the right (…) to make flights into or in transit non-stop across its territory and to make stops for non-traffic purposes without the necessity of obtaining prior permission, and subject to the right of the State flown over to require landing.

However, based on the practice of the parties to the Convention, the provision is taken to require that airlines request permission in all cases.[983] Such practice appears unopposed and has even been explicitly recognized in several bilateral Air Service Agreements.[984] It can thus be said to be common and consistent among the treaty parties.

The practice could be regarded as constituting merely an interpretation of Article 5 of the Convention by way of a mere procedural elaboration, given the qualification in the provision to the 'right of the State flown over to require landing'. However, it is more plausible, given the nature and scope of the practice, that subsequent practice has deviated from the treaty provision, establishing an implicit agreement between the parties to modify the law as codified in the Chicago Convention. In light of the extensive number of States parties to the treaty, the practice would even be capable of generating a norm of customary international law.[985] Moreover, the application of Article 5 of the Convention has been regarded as 'a virtually dead provision in

[979] Ibid. 532.

[980] Ibid. citing eg T Fischer, 'The ICRC and the 1962 Cuban Missile Crisis' (2001) 83 IRRC 842.

[981] 15 UNTS 295.

[982] The Convention currently has 190 Contracting States. See <www.icao.int/publications/pages/doc7300.aspx> accessed 4 June 2017.

[983] Feldman, 'Evolving Treaty Obligations', 664; Aust, *Modern Treaty Law*, 194, 242. See further B Cheng and R Austin, 'Air Law' in M Bos (ed), *The Present State of International Law and Other Essays* (Kluwer, 1989) 183.

[984] PPC Haanappel, *The Law and Policy of Air Space and Outer Space: A Comparative Approach* (Kluwer Law International, 2003) 110–11.

[985] Pauwelyn, *Conflict of Norms*, 50.

international air law',[986] and could be qualified as an instance of modification in the form of desuetude.[987] In any case, the example concerns a procedural change in the Convention, concerning a provision that is not 'essential' in the sense discussed in Chapter 3, nor likely to affect the instrument's object and purpose.

Another example of modification relates to Article 4 of the 1930 Hague Convention on Certain Questions relating to the Conflict of Nationality Laws,[988] a relatively old multilateral treaty regime. According to the article, 'a State may not afford diplomatic protection to one of its nationals against a State whose nationality such person also possesses'. It reflects the customary norm that existed at the time of its codification.[989] According to the ILC, through subsequent practice, this 'non-responsibility' rule in Article 4 came to be modified and replaced with the 'effective nationality' rule, which represents the current customary norm.[990] The latter is reflected in Article 7 of the Draft Articles on Diplomatic Protection, which provides:

> A State of nationality may not exercise diplomatic protection in respect of a person against a State of which that person is also a national unless the nationality of the former State is predominant, both at the date of injury and at the date of the official presentation of the claim.[991]

This represents an instance of treaty modification by subsequent practice of a *declaratory* treaty provision, which, as explained in earlier chapters, requires two separate modifying instances, namely, of the treaty provision and of the pre-existing customary rule.[992] Indeed, practice here eventually led to the emergence of a new (treaty-related[993]) customary norm that replaced the previous one.[994] References to case law aside, the ILC did not clearly substantiate in terms of degree of practice how this change had come about. Admittedly, the Commission discussed the matter not in terms of modification of one rule by another, but in terms of the parallel development of two separate rules. However, given the fact that the parties to the original Convention contributed to the practice that led to the 'effective nationality' rule, it is difficult to see the situation as anything but modification of the original rule by their subsequent practice.[995]

A much older illustration of the modifying effect of subsequent practice is noted by Kontou,[996] who cites the example of the extradition regime set up in the East Indies between France and Great Britain in the Convention of 7 March 1815,[997] followed by a new general extradition regime established by the Convention of 14

[986] Haanappel, *Law and Policy of Air Space*, 110–11. [987] See Section 3.3.1.
[988] 179 LNTS 89.
[989] Nolte, Third Report on Treaties over Time, 350. See likewise 1929 Harvard Draft Convention, Art 16(a).
[990] Draft Articles on Diplomatic Protection, Art 7, Comment 4. [991] Ibid.
[992] See Sections 3.3.3(b) and 4.4.1. [993] See Section 4.5.1.
[994] See further Section 4.6 on the overlap between subsequent practice and customary law.
[995] See eg Council of Europe, *Explanatory Report of the European Convention on Nationality*, ETS No 166, para 102, cited in Nolte, Third Report on Treaties over Time, 350.
[996] N Kontou, *The Termination and Revision of Treaties in the Light of New Customary International Law* (Clarendon Press, 1994) 72–4.
[997] J De Clercq, *Recueil des traités de la France*, vols 2 and 11 (A Durand et Pedone-Lauriel, 1880) 452.

August 1876.[998] Although initially the 1815 Convention was to continue to apply in the East Indies *qua lex specialis*, in derogation of the 1876 Convention, it was, in due course, altered and eventually tacitly terminated through the subsequent general practice of the parties.[999] Thus, the modification took place by desuetude, reflecting developments over time in the general law on extradition.[1000]

As a relatively minor example of modification by subsequent practice in the field of diplomatic law, Article 22(3) of the Vienna Convention on Diplomatic Relations provides in clear terms that the 'means of transport of the mission shall be immune from search, requisition, attachment or execution'. However, it appears to have become accepted practice to tow diplomatic cars for obstructing traffic or endangering public safety.[1001] This may have created an exception to the rule in Article 22(3).[1002]

Subsequent practice led to a much more far-reaching change in the general regime as well as the object and purpose of a 1948 Treaty between Belgium, France, Luxembourg, the Netherlands, and the United Kingdom of Great Britain and Northern Ireland for Collaboration in Economic, Social and Cultural Matters and for Collective Self-Defence.[1003] Although the treaty was originally intended as protection against Germany, the Federal Republic of Germany subsequently became a party. Thus, the treaty was transformed into a treaty of alliance with Germany, as a direct result of the parties' changed intentions expressed in their subsequent practice.[1004]

A less significant change took place in the case of the 1957 Treaty of Rome establishing the European Economic Community (subsequently the Treaty establishing the European Community),[1005] which referred to the 'European Currency Unit' (ECU). To avoid the lengthy ratification and parliamentary procedures involved in amending the Treaty, the Member States decided in 1995 to change the name of the currency from 'ECU' to 'euro' by more informal means, namely, by a decision in a European Council meeting. The resulting Conclusions of the Presidency, constituting a subsequent agreement, stated:

> The European Council therefore decides that (...) the name given to the European currency shall be Euro. (...) The specific name Euro will be used instead of the generic term 'ECU' used by the Treaty to refer to the European currency unit. The Governments of the fifteen Member States have achieved the common agreement that this decision is the agreed and definitive interpretation of the relevant Treaty provisions.[1006]

[998] Ibid. vol 11, 454.

[999] L Holz, 'L'Extradition entre l'Inde française et l'Empire anglo-indien' (1910) 17 RGDIP 449.

[1000] Kontou, *Termination and Revision of Treaties*, 72–3.

[1001] See E Denza, *Diplomatic Law: Commentary on the Vienna Convention on Diplomatic Relations. Oxford Commentaries on International Law* (3rd edn, OUP, 2008) 160. See also Nolte, Second Report on Subsequent Practice, para 33.

[1002] cf Nolte, Second Report on Subsequent Practice, para 33 (referring to this practice as an instance where subsequent practice *clarified* the meaning of the term 'execution' in Art 22(3)).

[1003] 19 UNTS 51.

[1004] Summary record of 766th meeting, para 45 (Lachs).

[1005] EC Treaty (Treaty of Rome, as amended).

[1006] Madrid European Council, 'Presidency Conclusions' (15 and 16 December 1995) <www.europarl.europa.eu/summits/mad1_en.htm> accessed 10 June 2017.

Despite the reference to the decision as an 'interpretation' of the Treaty, it clearly constitutes a modification, even if it concerns only a change of title.[1007]

5.3.3 Interim conclusions

Examples considered in the second part of this chapter, namely, those outside the judicial or quasi-judicial context, illustrate the extent to which subsequent practice can blur the line between interpretation and modification. For instance, sometimes practice diverges from the text and *travaux* of the provision in question, but could arguably still be regarded as dynamic interpretation in light of the treaty's evolutionary nature or broadly-framed object and purpose. A notable example is the expanding definition of threats to international peace and security under Chapter VII of the UN Charter.[1008] Often, such cases are complicated by the fact that States attempt to label their actions as interpretations. These characterizations are not determinative of the actual legal effect of their practice.

The 'blurring' of the distinction between interpretation and modification occurs especially where fundamental societal changes take place that were unforeseen at the time of a treaty's drafting. By contrast, in cases where the drafters deliberately excluded certain (foreseeable) issues from a treaty's scope, as in the example of Article 118 of the Third Geneva Convention,[1009] their later incorporation in the treaty through subsequent practice will more readily point towards a modification.

Modifications are easier to identify in relation to clear or technical provisions, such as the procedural provisions of the LOSC modified by the SPLOS and many of the changes to the 1958 Geneva Conventions on the Law of the Sea in the wake of UNCLOS III.[1010] But modifications can also be identified in relation to more open-textured provisions; the definition of 'migratory species' under the CMS provides a good example.[1011] Modification of more ambiguous provisions tends to occur gradually, rather than as an abrupt divergence from the original text. This also applies where dynamic interpretation on the basis of an evolutionary approach or implied powers has already significantly stretched the meaning of the text.

The examples reveal the complex relationship between modification by subsequent practice and formal amendment procedures.[1012] In the case of the 2001 SPLOS decision, recourse to formal amendment procedures was expressly rejected in favour of modification by subsequent practice.[1013] In *Al-Saadoon and Mufdhi v UK*, the ECtHR considered that modification by subsequent practice had already achieved the result envisioned by the already triggered formal amendment procedures.[1014] By contrast, with regard to the changes envisaged to Article 4 of the Basel Convention, States opted for formal amendment following the modifying subsequent agreement in question in order to provide greater clarity and certainty.[1015] As the example of

1007 Hafner, 'Subsequent Agreements and Practice', 109–10, 117. See also Aust, *Modern Treaty Law*, 239.

1008 See Section 5.3.1(a).

1009 See Section 5.3.2(d).

1010 See Section 5.3.2(a).

1011 See Section 5.3.2(b).

1012 See further Section 3.3.4.

1013 See Section 5.3.2(a).

1014 See Section 5.2.3(a).

1015 See Section 5.3.2(b).

the 1987 Montreal Protocol demonstrates, subsequent practice can even come to modify a treaty's formal amendment procedures themselves.[1016]

Subsequent practice or customary law rarely revises entire treaty regimes or multiple treaty provisions simultaneously. It often affects procedural rather than substantive provisions, regarding, for instance, voting practices, notification requirements, or time limits—provisions not strictly speaking 'essential' to the objectives of the treaty. Granted, practice has also shown that the latter characterization is difficult to determine given the far-reaching, substantive consequences of 'mere' procedural changes, as seen, for instance, in relation to Article 27(3) of the UN Charter.[1017] Through such 'procedural' modifications, subsequent practice develops the law and ensures its effectiveness by facilitating changes that further the broader aims of the treaty in question, as we have seen with many of the examples relating to the LOSC.

But there are also numerous cases in which practice impacts substantive provisions—and even the framework of the entire treaty. Such pragmatic and creative solutions are especially noticeable in the context of international organizations, where existing structures are retained but adapted to serve modern objectives, as in the case of NATO.[1018]

Numerous illustrations of the modifying effect of subsequent practice were identified in the context of international organizations, including the UN, NATO, the ILO, the WTO, the World Bank, and the IMF. Cornerstone instruments of international law—in particular, the UN Charter—have been significantly impacted by subsequent practice. This is demonstrated by the (far-reaching) procedural and substantive changes in relation, for instance, to Articles 12(1) and 27(3) of the Charter,[1019] or to Chapters 'VI½' and VII of the Charter.[1020] Here, once more, we see how subsequent practice can alter, terminate, and supplement treaties with a novel element or direction.[1021] Subsequent practice can serve as a tool for the revitalization of constitutive treaties of international organizations. One may think in particular of the 'normative transformations' that have affected the constitutive instruments of post-1945 institutions. Through subsequent practice, international organizations such as the UN (the expansive meaning of 'threats to international peace and security' and the application of the enforcement mechanism under Chapter VII[1022]), NATO (the increasing mandate reflected in the new strategic concept[1023]), and the World Bank (the broadened scope to tackle new socio-economic and socio-political issues[1024]) have considerably expanded their scope of operation. The case of NATO is especially illustrative of how subsequent practice can alter and supplement the functional and structural reach of international institutions. Perhaps most dramatically, in the case of the GATT, subsequent practice led to a result beyond anything imagined at the time of inception of the 1947 Agreement: the creation of a *de facto* international organization that became the key institution for international trade at the time.[1025]

[1016] Ibid. [1017] See Section 5.2.1. [1018] See Section 5.3.1(b).
[1019] See Section 5.2.1. [1020] See Section 5.3.1(a). [1021] See Section 3.3.1.
[1022] Section 5.3.1(a). [1023] Section 5.3.1(b). [1024] Section 5.3.1(e).
[1025] See Section 5.3.1(d).

Meanwhile, examples *outside* of the institutional context indicate that treaty modification by subsequent practice or subsequent customary law is most likely to arise in rapidly developing fields like the law of the sea and environmental law. Initial codifications of norms in such fields serve as catalysts for the evolution of new concepts with the potential to diverge from the original provisions. Sometimes this evolution occurs by means of more institutionalized or formalized types of subsequent practice, such as decisions of conferences of the States parties or subsequent implementation agreements, meant to bypass formal amendment procedures.

The examples confirm that provisions in 'law-making' treaties (as with treaties constituting international organizations and law of the sea and human rights treaties generally) often tend to be evolutionary in nature. This seems particularly true in the human rights context, where it appears more difficult to identify examples of modification by subsequent practice. Nevertheless, as seen in the context of the ECHR and other examples,[1026] as well as in the field of humanitarian law,[1027] modifications of such treaties do occur, particularly when the modifications benefit the treaty's rights-holders, and then often by means of subsequent customary international law.

Even outside the context of classical international organizations, one can still encounter instances where subsequent practice has led to what could be considered 'normative transformations'—examples include the adaptation of MEAs in light of climate change[1028] and the injection of a new environmental approach into the LOSC.[1029] Subsequent practice has also led to the creation of new institutions and processes, as in the case of the UNFCCC 'financial mechanism'.[1030] There are even examples where subsequent practice has led to an 'overhaul' of the original treaty, as with the 1948 Treaty for collective self-defence initially intended as protection against Germany, but which Germany subsequently joined.[1031]

In most cases, it is clear that modification by subsequent practice does not go so far as to undermine or detract from a treaty's object and purpose(s) or from the effects of fundamental provisions. Rather, subsequent practice helps strike a balance between the core concepts of treaties as complex as the LOSC, and contemporary norms that have subsequently emerged in other treaty regimes and the realm of customary law. Thus, through its various legal effects, subsequent practice serves as a vehicle for regime interaction, as seen in the context of the law of the sea[1032] and in relation to *non-refoulement* in human rights and refugee law.[1033] Crosscutting issues requiring a large degree of coordination between regimes can be more effectively dealt with in this way. This helps mitigate issues such as fragmentation and treaty congestion in international law.

The many examples in this chapter demonstrate, above all, that regardless of the legal field or context, there is a diversity of circumstances in which subsequent

[1026] See Sections 5.2.3(a) and 5.3.2(c). [1027] See Section 5.3.2(d).
[1028] See Section 5.3.2(b). [1029] See Section 5.3.2(a). [1030] See Section 5.3.2(b).
[1031] See Section 5.3.2(e). [1032] See Section 5.3.2(a). [1033] See Section 5.3.2(c).

practice and subsequent customary law are capable of bringing about variations (or even termination) in bilateral and multilateral, reciprocal and non-reciprocal, treaties—resulting in partial or total modifications, procedural or substantive changes, coordination between different fields, the creation of new institutions and processes, and, occasionally, modification of the scope of operation of the treaty regime as a whole.

6

Conclusion

6.1 Overview

6.1.1 The concept of subsequent practice and treaty interpretation

The process of modification by subsequent practice forms part of the greater process of treaty evolution over time, and thus, more generally, the evolution of international law. This book set out to achieve a better understanding of subsequent practice and its treaty modifying potential. The starting point for the analysis was the notion of subsequent practice itself, as well as its interpretative role pursuant to Articles 31(3)(b) and 32 VCLT. Consideration of the constitutive elements of subsequent practice included the scope of the terms 'practice' and 'subsequent', the relation between 'subsequent practice' and 'subsequent agreement', and the two basic qualifications of practice 'in the application of the treaty' and establishing the 'agreement of the parties'—parameters that are likewise instrumental for understanding the process of *modification* by subsequent practice.

For one thing, the notion of 'practice' cannot be exhaustively defined: the means by which States can manifest their understanding of treaty rights and obligations are too diverse.[1] Thus, the relevance of practice is determined by the qualifications attached to it.[2] For instance, the degree of determinacy and consistency of practice is crucial for assessing its evidentiary weight.[3] As for *whose* practice counts—a question inherently linked to the previous two points—one may look not only at 'classical' State practice, but, depending on the circumstances, also at certain forms of 'institutional' practice.[4] The latter notion may include the practice of (organs of) international organizations and that of certain treaty bodies and institutional arrangements, such as conferences of the parties, particularly where supported by member States' practice—although these may be subject to somewhat different standards. This wider notion of practice gives recognition to the interpretative potential of subsequent practice and the actions that actually contribute to its development—in other words, a recognition of political realities and the need to ensure effectiveness in the international legal system.

[1] See Section 2.3.1(a). [2] See Sections 2.3.1–2.3.5. [3] See Section 2.3.1(b).
[4] See Section 2.3.1(c).

We have also seen that the concepts of subsequent practice and subsequent agreement are not distinct notions as much as they are indications of the formality of the practice, on a spectrum ranging from the implicit to the explicit.[5] Both can generate authentic interpretations expressing States' understanding of the treaty, even if their evidentiary weight differs according to the clarity of that expression of consent. In this sense, subsequent practice may be taken to comprise subsequent agreements. Thus, informal subsequent agreements—short of subsequent agreements constituting successive treaties—were taken to fall within the scope of this book, and indeed provided an important source of cases and insight for the 'repertoire' in Chapter 5.[6]

The requirement of 'subsequent' practice places certain temporal restrictions upon what may count as relevant interpretative practice.[7] The requirement that practice be 'in the application' of the treaty posits a differentiation between subsequent practice and subsequent developments.[8] Moreover, relevant practice must demonstrate a certain intentionality or awareness on the part of the acting States that their conduct expresses a position taken with regard to a point of law, an element conceptually analogous to *opinio juris*.[9] Finally, and vitally, subsequent practice must establish the agreement of the parties. This requires caution as to what may be inferred from silence and based on notions such as acquiescence and estoppel.[10] The higher the degree of concordance, commonness, and consistency of the practice, the higher its probative value in establishing the parties' agreement in relation to the treaty.[11] Thus, subsequent practice is an open-textured and internally diverse notion, requiring careful analysis in accordance with strict requirements.

International case law confirms the usefulness of subsequent practice as an interpretative means. However, in the absence of an agreement on a single, 'proper' method of treaty interpretation, striking differences can be observed in the approach taken to subsequent practice across international dispute settlement bodies, particularly those operating in the context of special regimes, such as the WTO Appellate Body and the ECtHR.[12] These differences are even more acute when it comes to subsequent practice as a means of treaty modification.[13]

Lastly, the relation between subsequent practice on the one hand, and evolutionary interpretation and implied powers on the other hand, is double-sided. These latter techniques—themselves sometimes developed through subsequent practice—may serve to expand a treaty's interpretative range, thus reducing the need or room for separate recourse to interpretation or modification by subsequent practice.[14] As seen in Chapter 5, they often play a role in relation to important multilateral conventions on the law of the sea, environmental law, and human rights, as well

[5] See Section 2.3.3.
[6] See eg the examples in Sections 5.2.3(c), 5.3.1(b) and (d), and 5.3.2(a)–(b).
[7] See Section 2.3.2. [8] See Section 2.3.4. [9] See Sections 2.3.5 and 4.6.
[10] See Section 2.3.5(a) and (b). [11] See Section 2.3.5(c).
[12] See Sections 2.5.1–2.5.2.
[13] See Section 5.2, particularly the interim conclusions in Section 5.2.5.
[14] See Sections 2.5.3–2.5.4.

as in relation to constitutive treaties, which are shaped and adapted by decisions of organs that sometimes push the boundaries of interpretation.

6.1.2 Subsequent practice and treaty modification

The silence of the Vienna Convention on the Law of Treaties as to the process of treaty modification by subsequent practice has triggered a longstanding debate. The discussions in the ILC during the VCLT's drafting reveal not only political difficulties inherent in delineating the effects of subsequent practice, but also the abstract legal notions underlying it. Debates ran high as to whether to codify the principle of treaty modification by subsequent practice (and subsequent customary law). The result was draft Article 38 on treaty modification by subsequent practice.[15] At the ensuing UN Conference, where the fate of the provision was decided, the draft article was ultimately deleted for mainly two reasons, neither of which implied that it did not adequately reflect the current state of international law. First, the article was thought to overlap with too many other VCLT provisions. Second, it triggered questions considered too difficult to tackle at the time, particularly given the time constraints. The article's exclusion from the final Convention thus does not detract from the importance of the process it attempted to codify, but suggests that customary international law or general principles may be a more adequate medium to account for its operation.[16] In fact, as was shown, this drafting history demonstrates the validity of modification by subsequent practice, as well as its complex, elusive nature—a nature that does not lend itself easily to codification.[17]

The process of modification by subsequent practice is a reality, and at times a practical necessity, in treaty relations. It is acknowledged by a wide range of dispute settlement bodies and the majority of legal scholars.[18] The practical difficulty (even impossibility) often encountered with regard to formal amendment, the premise of *pacta sunt servanda*, the fluid interchange between interpretation and modification, and the need to respect the parties' contemporaneous intention reinforce its validity.[19] The modifying effect of subsequent practice in a given case, however, is not to be presumed. The strength of this presumption against modification will vary depending on the treaty regime or provision. The presumption will be stronger in exceptional cases where a modification may affect the object and purpose of the treaty[20] or where formal amendment procedures have already been triggered.[21] Thus, the threshold required for practice to constitute agreement to a modification will depend on the type and scope of the envisioned modification, and the nature of the respective treaty and provision. This threshold refers not only to the quantity and quality of the practice (a substantive threshold), but also to the onus on the interpreter, often a dispute settlement body, to identify and apply the constitutive elements necessary for modifying practice, and clearly substantiate whether a

[15] See Sections 3.2.1–3.2.4. [16] See Sections 3.2.6 and 3.3.7.
[17] See Sections 3.2.5–3.2.6. See further Section 6.2.1. [18] See Section 3.1.
[19] See Section 3.3.2. [20] See Section 3.3.5. [21] See Section 3.3.4.

modification has occurred (a procedural threshold).[22] The identification of modification by subsequent practice therefore warrants a considerable degree of caution and sensitivity to the context and circumstances of the given case, in accordance with the constitutive elements and evidentiary standards discussed.[23]

The greatest conceptual difficulty lies in distinguishing between the two functions of subsequent practice discussed extensively in this book: treaty interpretation and treaty modification. The effects of this distinction may carry significant implications.[24] While some scholars argue that interpretation and modification are indistinguishable in practice, others have volunteered criteria for making the distinction. Though not conclusive, these suggested approaches provide a provisional framework for future research.[25]

Differentiating between these two outcomes is, in any case, a complex, open-ended task, to be approached on a case-by-case basis by reference to a wide range of factors and considerations. Often, this task is complicated further by the fact that States typically prefer that their modifying practice be labelled as interpretation.[26] This difficulty can be compared to that of distinguishing between treaty *reservations* and interpretative statements, or, in a sense, even between treaty *violations* and mere interpretations: determining whether an act of treaty application has strayed so far from the treaty's terms that it amounts to a *violation* may, in substance, involve essentially the same exercise as identifying whether subsequent practice has led to a *modification*—in both cases, one looks for a genuine conflict between the practice observed and the terms of the treaty (the crucial difference, evidently, being the requirement of a general practice evidencing the parties' agreement in the case of modification).

Of course, there are instances where practice has clearly or even explicitly led to modification.[27] Modifications are easier to identify in relation to clear or technical provisions, such as procedural provisions on voting practices or time limits;[28] but they are also sometimes obvious in relation to more open-textured provisions,[29] including those susceptible to change on the basis of evolutionary interpretation or implied powers. However, given the breadth and flexibility of the interpretative means available, in most cases there is sufficient room to construe the result of subsequent practice as a form of 'dynamic' interpretation. The blurring of the distinction between interpretation and modification takes place particularly where fundamental societal changes occur that were unforeseen at the time of a treaty's drafting. This can be contrasted with cases where (foreseeable) issues deliberately excluded by the drafters are later tacitly incorporated into the treaty by subsequent practice; here the tendency towards modification is clearer.[30]

[22] See Section 3.3.3(b). [23] See Sections 2.3 and 3.3.3. [24] See Section 3.4.1.
[25] See Section 3.4. [26] See eg Sections 3.4 and 5.3.
[27] See eg Sections 5.3.1(d) (GATT) and 5.3.2(a) (1958 Geneva Conventions on the Law of the Sea).
[28] See eg Section 5.3.2(a) (SPLOS decisions; 1958 Geneva Conventions on the Law of the Sea).
[29] See eg Section 5.3.2(b) (definition of 'migratory species' under the CMS).
[30] See eg Sections 5.2.1 (Art 27(3) of the UN Charter), 5.3.1(d) (WTO accession protocols), and 5.3.2(d) (Art 118 of the Third Geneva Convention).

The 'repertoire' in Chapter 5 shows that, in identifying modification by subsequent practice, one must look not only at the extent to which practice diverges from the text, *travaux*, and object and purpose of the treaty, but also—crucially—at other aspects concerning the nature and subject matter of the treaty and its provisions. Factors such as the age, field, and type of treaty (including whether it is technical or general, bilateral or multilateral, 'reciprocal' or 'non-reciprocal'), as well as the applicability of special principles (including the stability of boundaries and non-regression), can affect the modifying potential of subsequent practice and determine the degree of controversy involved in its identification.[31] The same applies with regard to the nature of specific treaty provisions and whether they are procedural or substantive, essential or non-essential, and integral or interdependent in nature.[32] Moreover, the presence of 'in-built' adaptation mechanisms may detract from the potential for modification by subsequent practice, providing alternative outlets for treaty change.[33] These range from dispute settlement, evolutionary interpretation, implied powers, and ambiguous provisions, to other treaty-specific mechanisms encountered, for instance, in the context of the LOSC, WTO, and various MEAs.

The relationship between modification by subsequent practice and formal amendment procedures is complex.[34] The two can play complementary roles, serve as alternatives, or even directly impact each other,[35] as when formal amendment procedures themselves come to be modified by subsequent practice.[36] While the mere *existence* of formal amendment procedures under the treaty does not exclude the possibility of modification by subsequent practice,[37] once they have been triggered, the parties' intention to have recourse to modification by subsequent practice for the same change must be manifest.[38] For instance, in the case of the 2001 SPLOS decision, recourse to formal amendment procedures was expressly rejected in favour of modification by subsequent practice.[39] And in *Al-Saadoon and Mufdhi v UK*, the ECtHR considered that modification by subsequent practice had already achieved the result pursued by means of the previously triggered formal amendment procedure.[40] By contrast, States parties to the Basel Convention expressed a preference for formal amendment with regard to the changes envisaged to Article 4.[41]

As explained in Chapter 3 and confirmed by examples in Chapter 5, subsequent practice can alter, supplement, and terminate treaty provisions or even entire treaty frameworks, as well as previously established modifications by subsequent practice.[42] It can also generate customary law and fuel regime interaction. Depending on the treaty and modification in question, subsequent practice may arguably even create a new basis of obligation outside of the treaty, although in most cases it is conceived as an integral part of the underlying instrument.[43]

[31] See eg Section 3.5.1(a). [32] See eg Section 3.5.1(b). [33] See eg Section 3.5.2.
[34] See Section 3.3.4. [35] See Sections 5.2.3(a) and (c), 5.3.2(a)–(b), and 5.3.3.
[36] See Section 5.3.2(b) (1987 Montreal Protocol). [37] See Section 3.3.4.
[38] See eg Sections 3.3.4 and 5.3.1(c). [39] See Section 5.3.2(a).
[40] See Section 5.2.3(a). [41] See Section 5.3.2(b). [42] See eg Section 3.3.1.
[43] See Section 3.3.6(a). See also eg Sections 5.2.1 (*Temple of Préah Vihéar*) and 5.2.4 (German Constitutional Court on NATO).

Subsequent practice rarely revises multiple treaty provisions simultaneously or impacts the object and purpose or fundamental provisions of a treaty. It also often affects procedural rather than substantive provisions.[44] Nevertheless, in some cases, its impact can be profound. Examples include the adaptation of MEAs in light of climate change[45] or the injection of a new environmental approach into the LOSC.[46] Subsequent practice also led to an overhaul of a 1948 treaty for collective self-defence initially intended as protection against Germany, but which Germany subsequently joined.[47] Even cornerstone instruments of international law have undergone far-reaching changes, as seen with Articles 12(1) and 27(3),[48] or Chapters 'VI½' and VII,[49] of the UN Charter. Likewise, modifications of a treaty's object and purpose are not unheard of. Particularly where international organizations are concerned, subsequent practice has led to 'normative transformations', retaining existing structures but adapting them to serve new objectives or significantly broader mandates, as with NATO or the World Bank.[50] Perhaps most radically, subsequent practice has led to the inception of altogether new institutions. In the case of the GATT, the result went beyond anything intended or envisioned at the time of the instrument's conclusion: the creation of a *de facto* international organization that became the key institution for international trade at that time.[51]

Once more, it should not be lightly assumed that subsequent practice has led to the modification of a treaty—but such effect can by no means be wholly precluded. And while it may be difficult to specify a list of exact criteria for analysing modifications by subsequent practice—particularly in light of an ever-increasing array of fields and types of instruments in international law—the aforementioned considerations, taken systematically, can contribute to a more consistent approach to determining the effects of subsequent practice.

6.1.3 Subsequent customary law and treaty modification

The process of customary law is intricately linked to that of subsequent practice, and both processes can lead to treaty modification. The significant overlap between the two adds an additional dimension to the discussion on subsequent practice. Modification by subsequent customary law occurs when a non-identical customary norm emerges in respect of the subject matter covered by a pre-existing treaty, and the parties intend for it to be overriding. The modification of the 1958 Geneva Conventions on the Law of the Sea in the wake of UNCLOS III is one example.[52] Where 'customary modification' occurs, its effect is to displace the contents of the treaty rule, without becoming 'part and parcel' of the treaty itself.[53] This is different

[44] See the various examples in Sections 5.2.1(a), 5.3.1(c)–(d), 5.3.2(a)–(b) and (e).
[45] See Section 5.3.2(b).
[46] See Section 5.3.2(a). See also eg Section 5.3.2(b) (UNFCCC 'financial mechanism').
[47] See Section 5.3.2(e). [48] See Section 5.2.1. [49] See Section 5.3.1(a).
[50] See Sections 5.3.1(a) (UN Charter), (b) (NATO), and (e) (World Bank).
[51] See Section 5.3.1(d). [52] See Section 5.3.2(a). [53] See Sections 4.1 and 4.4.3.

in the case of modification by subsequent practice, the result of which can rarely be seen as creating a basis of obligation independent of the underlying treaty.[54]

As with modification by subsequent practice, the drafting history of the initial ILC article on modification by customary international law confirms the validity of the process, which is rooted, *inter alia*, in the lack of hierarchy between treaties and customary law. The ultimate exclusion of the draft article from the Vienna Convention, for practical and political reasons, in no way detracts from this conclusion.[55]

The formation and identification of customary international law, premised upon the 'two-element approach', not only highlights the complexity of the process, and provides a first step towards understanding the treaty modifying potential of customary international law, but also underscores its innate similarities and overlap with the process of subsequent practice.[56] Its relation to *jus cogens* is a further point of consideration.[57] Once the pitfalls involved in identifying customary law are understood, the analysis can turn to identifying its treaty modifying potential, by reference to its non-hierarchical, dynamic relation to treaty law.[58] Treaty modification by customary law could be said to have occurred, for instance, when a non-identical customary rule emerges in respect of the subject matter covered by a treaty and interpretation pursuant to Article 31(3)(c) VCLT can no longer account for such developments—the customary rule can no longer be regarded as secondary to the treaty provision.[59] The increasing likelihood of normative conflict between treaties and customary international law—as international obligations become more intricate and intertwined, while formal amendment remains difficult if not impossible—has heightened the need for harmonization through interpretation and, increasingly, informal modification. Determining where 'customary modification' has occurred requires a holistic assessment, on a case-by-case basis, of the nature and content of the norms involved, the quality and quantity of the practice, and the implications of any eventual modification for the operation of the legal system.

The conditions for modification by subsequent customary law, like those for modification by subsequent practice, are strict, also in light of the general presumption against change.[60] The parties' intention to displace the treaty provision in favour of the subsequent customary rule is paramount. The latter must attain the necessary evidentiary threshold, which is understood to contain a 'double consent' requirement: the practice must establish not only the content of the customary norm, but also its modification of the treaty rule.[61] The evidentiary burden to sustain a modification by customary law is thus higher than to prove only that a customary rule has emerged. It may be even higher in the case of non-reciprocal obligations and other special treaty rules.

Treaty modification by (general or special) customary international law can occur by means of either 'treaty-related' or 'external' customary law, although the two are practically indistinguishable with regard to treaty regimes of near-universal membership.[62] 'Treaty-related' customary law is derived directly from the treaty-related

[54] See Section 3.3.6(a). [55] See Section 4.2. [56] See Sections 4.3.1–4.3.3.
[57] See Section 4.3.4. [58] See Section 4.4. [59] See Section 4.4.3.
[60] See Section 4.5. [61] See Section 4.5.3. [62] See Section 4.5.1.

subsequent practice of the parties (and may be supplemented by the practice of third States to generate a customary norm of general application). In such cases, subsequent practice capable of modification is indistinguishable from practice as a constitutive element of the new customary rule. By contrast, 'external' modifying customary law is derived from the subsequent practice of the parties *in relation to that customary norm* rather than to the treaty. Therefore, evidence of external customary law requires more careful analysis to determine whether modification has occurred. Regardless of the origin or nature of the modifying customary norm, the determining factor is always the intention of the parties. If their intention to modify is unclear, the treaty will be presumed to remain unaffected as *lex specialis*.

The conceptual relationship between customary international law and subsequent practice is evident. Likewise, the processes of *modification* by subsequent customary law and by subsequent practice overlap on a conceptual and practical level.[63] Both constitute valid, recognized mechanisms for treaty adaptation. But the two processes must also be carefully distinguished in terms of their scope of operation.[64] Subsequent practice is nevertheless the 'raw material' that fuels both processes, subject always to the crucial requirement of the will of the parties. From this perspective, subsequent customary law can be regarded as one of the multiple potential outcomes of subsequent practice in relation to a treaty.

6.1.4 The need for recognition by dispute settlement bodies of modifications by subsequent practice and subsequent customary law

The case law demonstrates recognition of the possibility of modification by subsequent practice in different contexts and in relation to a diverse range of treaties.[65] It also shows that dispute settlement bodies take different approaches to modification by subsequent practice and subsequent customary law, particularly within treaty regimes with a standing dispute settlement mechanism. For instance, while the ECtHR has adopted a liberal approach, the WTO Appellate Body has consistently rejected alleged modifications by subsequent practice. That judicial bodies tend to develop their own approach to modification by subsequent practice regarding their constitutive treaty is also reflected in the ICJ's more open approach towards subsequent practice in cases involving the UN Charter than those that do not.

Recognition by dispute settlement bodies of the process of modification by subsequent practice is oftentimes limited to an *obiter dictum*. Even when they actually sustain a modification by subsequent practice in the given case, dispute settlement bodies are not consistent in referring to the constitutive elements of subsequent practice.[66] Moreover, the relevant passages are usually too brief to draw generalizable conclusions and only indicate how the change affects the content of the treaty, without specifying criteria or circumstances used to determine that a treaty

[63] See Section 4.6. [64] Ibid. [65] See generally Section 5.2.
[66] See Section 2.3.

modification has occurred.[67] This makes it difficult to develop a consistent approach to identifying modification by subsequent practice or subsequent customary law.

With notable exceptions,[68] it is clear from the case law that dispute settlement bodies are overall circumspect with regard to the possibility of treaty modification by subsequent practice and subsequent customary law, for reasons already discussed.[69] Not surprisingly, they seem to favour the more explicit treaty rule over the more contentious process of identifying treaty modifying implied agreements by subsequent practice.[70] They are particularly reticent with regard to modification by subsequent customary law. This may be on account of the fact that the latter requires two different findings: first, as to (the content of) the new customary legal norm, and second, as to the parties' intention to modify the treaty accordingly.[71]

Instead, dispute settlement bodies often leave the issue unaddressed[72] or have recourse to alternative adaptation mechanisms,[73] such as evolutionary interpretation,[74] 'approximate application',[75] or ambiguous provisions.[76] Such techniques allow them to avoid issues of modification by subsequent practice and classify the relevant instances as interpretation.[77] Some dispute settlement bodies have even explicitly stated that they lack the competence to ascertain whether a given practice constitutes interpretation or modification.[78] Others have emphasized that their duty is to interpret rather than to revise.[79]

This latter consideration, in particular, is not at issue in recognizing treaty modifications by subsequent practice where they have occurred. The modification is not effected by the dispute settlement body itself; its role in such cases is merely to take note that a modification has taken place by the parties' agreement as evidenced in their practice and apply the treaty *as modified*, leaving the revision of the treaty to the parties. In fact, to properly discharge their judicial function, dispute settlement bodies must interpret and give effect to treaty provisions as modified if they are to give effect to the parties' will.[80] This also sends a signal to States, as well as organs of international organizations, that their practice can constitute a source of authoritative interpretation and, accordingly, legal change.[81] The importance of recognizing

[67] See Section 5.2.5. [68] See Section 5.2.

[69] See Sections 2.5.5, 3.4.2, 5.1, and 5.2.5.

[70] J Pauwelyn, *Conflict of Norms in Public International Law: How WTO Law Relates to Other Rules of International Law* (CUP, 2003) 141.

[71] See Section 4.5.3.

[72] See eg Section 5.2.3 (ECJ's approach in*Spanish Fishermen's Cases*).

[73] See generally Section 3.5.2. [74] See Section 5.2.1 (*Costa Rica v Nicaragua*).

[75] Ibid. (*Gabčíkovo-Nagymaros Project*).

[76] See eg Section 5.2.2 (*Japanese House Tax Arbitration*).

[77] See eg I Venzke, *How Interpretation Makes International Law: On Semantic Change and Normative Twists* (OUP, 2012) 73 (arguing that this enabled the ICJ in the *Namibia Advisory Opinion* to avoid 'slippery slopes of reasoning' or claims of treaty breach).

[78] See eg Sections 5.2.2 (*Air Transport Services Arbitration (US/Italy)*) and 5.2.3(c) (*ADF v US*).

[79] See eg *Interpretation of Peace Treaties Advisory Opinion*, 229; *Rights of Nationals*, 196; *South West Africa*, 49; *Delimitation of the Maritime Boundary between Guinea-Bissau and Senegal*, para 85.

[80] G Fitzmaurice, 'The Law and Procedure of the International Court of Justice 1951–4: Treaty Interpretation and Other Treaty Points' (1957) 33 BYBIL 203, 225; J Arato, 'Treaty Interpretation and Constitutional Transformation: Informal Change in International Organizations' (2013) 38 Yale JIL 289, 309.

[81] See Section 5.2.5.

modifications where they have occurred is even more acute in cases where a higher evidentiary threshold for modification applies, such as when subsequent practice affects a treaty's object and purpose[82] or appears to bypass already triggered formal amendment procedures.[83] In those cases, the interpreter must meet a higher (evidentiary) standard in the identification of the requirements necessary for modification and justification based on the constitutive elements of subsequent practice.[84]

The attempt here is to inject a bit of certainty into the identification of a process that requires certain safeguards, not to advocate formalism—for the process of treaty modification by subsequent practice by its very nature goes against formalism. A more systematic approach to the recognition of modification by subsequent practice by dispute settlement bodies would be a welcome development in light of the inconsistencies encountered in the case law. The answer is thus not to avoid, but to deal with the possibility of modification by subsequent practice more consistently, with a greater sensitivity to context and circumstance.

6.2 Concluding Remarks

6.2.1 The process of treaty modification by subsequent practice: Assessing the feasibility of codification

The foregoing considerations, coupled with the conclusions drawn from the examples in Chapter 5, paint a larger picture of the workings of the process of subsequent practice, its dynamism, and its variables. One could attempt to present these findings by way of a provision on treaty modification by subsequent practice and subsequent customary law, building upon, and further specifying, the terms of the original provisions proposed by the ILC during the drafting of the VCLT. The relevant ILC draft articles provided, respectively, that a treaty 'may be modified by subsequent practice of the parties in the application of the treaty establishing their agreement to modify its provisions',[85] and that the 'operation of a treaty may be modified (…) by the subsequent emergence of a new rule of customary law relating to matters dealt with in the treaty and binding upon all the parties'.[86] These provisions, though broadly formulated, already contained certain essential safeguards and qualifications,[87] including, crucially, the requirement of the agreement of (all) the parties.[88]

In light of the requirements, factors, and limitations revealed in this book with regard to subsequent practice, it is submitted that it would be exceedingly difficult—perhaps even undesirable—to attempt to codify the process of treaty modification by subsequent practice and subsequent customary law. Many of the considerations and distinctions that have come to light in the previous chapters cannot be fully

[82] See Section 3.3.5. [83] See Sections 3.3.4 and 5.3.1(c).
[84] See Section 3.3.3(b). [85] See Section 3.2.4. [86] See Section 4.2.
[87] See eg Section 3.2.5. See the constitutive elements discussed in Section 2.3.
[88] See Section 2.3.5.

accounted for in codified form. They provide reference points to be weighed against each other, not fixed rules to achieve a clear-cut determination in every case. Only some of the findings reached seem to readily lend themselves to codification and express clarification. Based on those findings, a possible formulation of a provision on treaty modification by subsequent practice and subsequent customary law could read as follows:

Modification of Treaties by Subsequent Practice or Subsequent Customary Law

(a) A treaty may be modified by clear and determinate subsequent practice in relation to the application of the treaty establishing the agreement of the parties to the alteration, extension, or termination of certain or all of its provisions. In determining the existence of such agreement, regard must be had to the nature of the treaty and its provisions, and in particular to their object and purpose, any parallel formal amendment procedures initiated with regard to the same subject matter, and implicit or explicit prohibitions contained in the treaty regarding provisions or principles from which derogation is not permitted.

(b) The content of a treaty may be modified by subsequent customary law if the agreement of the parties to such effect is manifestly clear.

This draft article, though perhaps helpful as an introduction to the topic, remains incomplete. It does not adequately account for the numerous considerations that may influence, limit, or provide alternatives to the modifying effect of subsequent practice.[89] Indeed, such factors cannot be listed exhaustively. They can only be denoted by means of flexible reference points and examples, as done in the preceding chapters. Nor is it feasible to elaborate upon the evidentiary thresholds required for modification in the context of such a provision. Moreover, it would be difficult to account for the theoretical and practical differences between modification by subsequent practice and 'modification' by subsequent customary law,[90] or the distinction between 'treaty-related' and 'external' customary law.[91] Finally, the draft article does not allow for a comprehensive overview of the full range of effects of modifications by subsequent practice, including the creation of new institutions, normative transformations of the original treaty, and regime interaction.

It is reasonable to conclude that the nuances and variables involved in dealing with this complex process cannot adequately be presented in codified form. In fact, these difficulties are still being encountered in relation to the draft conclusion regarding modification by subsequent practice currently under discussion in the ILC.[92] This puts into perspective the challenges faced by the ILC at the time of drafting of the Vienna Convention, and the complexity of the present topic.

[89] See eg Section 3.5.

[90] As explained, the result of 'modification' by subsequent customary law differs from modification by subsequent practice in that the former leads to the 'displacement' or 'disapplication' of the treaty rule, whereas the latter modifies its content.

[91] See Section 4.5.1.

[92] See eg Provisional summary record of 3205th meeting, 9 (Murase, noting the difficulty of striking the balance between flexibility and clarity in formulating the draft conclusion, and positing more generally 'whether it might not be better to adopt draft guidelines rather than draft conclusions'). See further Section 3.1.

6.2.2 Striking the balance between the stability of treaties and the organic evolution of international law

Though subsequent practice, in both its interpretative and modifying capacities, can at times be a source of uncertainty, it is much more importantly a tool for facilitating greater coherence.[93] It plays a role in striking the delicate balance between legal stability and the need to allow for the natural evolution of the law—a balance that falls differently per treaty regime. The array of interests and developments in the international arena, and the plethora of instruments and rules created as a result, pose a challenge for the law, both customary and conventional, to evolve accordingly, concordantly, and at a fast enough pace. This innate lack of homogeneity and hierarchy has its advantages: it allows for flexibility and 'contextual sensitivity', facilitating progressive development. The growing interdependence of the international community means that acts of States and non-State actors can influence others and gradually gather sufficient momentum to steer the development of international norms. Such changes through practice often occur gradually, giving States the opportunity to take note and react.[94] However, the workings of such processes are complex and often tacit, making subsequent practice politically sensitive. Although it was not the aim of this book to consider the political implications of, or the underlying reasons for, the process of informal change by subsequent practice, these considerations informed some of the trends observed in how States and dispute settlement bodies have chosen to deal with its effects.[95]

Our understanding of subsequent practice remains limited, and opinions on the topic diverge significantly. While some scholars consider it a logical and vital process, others reject the possibility of modification by subsequent practice altogether. Moreover, while some commentators insist on distinguishing between treaty interpretation and modification, others have resigned themselves to the impossibility of doing so, or have denied the utility and relevance of such a distinction. These contrasts demonstrate the necessity of the present study—hopefully one of many to follow, not least in the light of the ILC's ongoing work on subsequent practice. This book has also attempted to highlight its relation to, *inter alia*, the tenets of treaty law, issues of interpretation including the evolutionary approach, the sources of international law and the complicated relationship between treaties and customary law, the question of fragmentation of international law, and the role of non-State actors and institutions in bringing about legal change—issues which themselves remain the subject of continuous study and doctrinal debate.

The book endeavours to provide flexible criteria and reference points to determine the value of subsequent practice, its interpretative and modifying effects, and its limitations and alternatives. It may be concluded that no categorical line can

[93] This section is developed from I Buga, 'Subsequent Practice and Treaty Modification' in MJ Bowman and D Kritsiotis (eds), *Conceptual and Contextual Perspectives on the Modern Law of Treaties* (CUP, forthcoming) Section 5.

[94] Where modification is relatively abrupt, it is usually effectuated by means of a clear decision, such as a subsequent agreement—see eg the SPLOS decisions discussed in Section 5.3.2(a).

[95] See eg Sections 2.3.1(b), 3.3.2(b), and 3.3.3(a).

generally be drawn between interpretation and modification by subsequent practice. The effects of subsequent practice cannot be established *in abstracto*, but by reference to the circumstances of the given case: the line between interpretative practice and modifying practice is thin and inherently context-dependent. The same could be said of the distinction between modification by subsequent practice and subsequent customary law. A deeper awareness of the nuances involved would enhance stability and clarity in the application of treaty obligations, and make international actors increasingly mindful of the consequences of their actions or reactions to an emerging practice.

The creation, continuation, and renewal of obligations in international law is a complex, fluid process, due to the lack of fixed legislative procedures and the horizontal structure of the international legal system. Treaties are snapshots of international law at a given point in time. They must be able to undergo transformation and modernization even if recourse to formal amendment procedures is unavailable or unworkable in practice. To say otherwise would mean underestimating the dynamism of international relations, and the organic development of international law through normative collisions. Subsequent practice can only be understood by means of a systematic exploration of its nature, repercussions, and legal underpinnings in relation to treaty law; this should remain the subject of further research. This book aims to contribute towards a better understanding of the variables involved, and confirms that—no matter how difficult to grasp in absolute terms—the dynamic process of modification by subsequent practice is valid, vital, and very much alive.

Bibliography

Abi-Saab G, 'La coutume dans tous ses états ou le dilemme du développement du droit international général dans un monde éclaté' in *Le droit international à l'heure de sa codification: Etudes en l'honneur de Robert Ago*, vol I (Dott A Giuffrè, 1987) 53.

——— 'The Appellate Body and Treaty Interpretation' in M Fitzmaurice, O Elias, and P Merkouris (eds), *Treaty Interpretation and the Vienna Convention on the Law of Treaties: 30 Years On* (Martinus Nijhoff, 2010) 99.

Abraham G, 'Yes, ... But Does It Have Personality? The International Committee of the Red Cross and Sovereign Immunity' (2007) 124 S Afr LJ 499.

Ahlborn C, 'Adjudicating Somali Piracy Cases—German Courts in a Double Bind' (*CJICL Blog*, 3 January 2013) <http://cjicl.org.uk> accessed 9 June 2017.

Akande D, 'The Legality of Military Action in Syria: Humanitarian Intervention and the Responsibility to Protect' (*OXPOL*, 29 August 2013) <http://blog.politics.ox.ac.uk/legality-military-action-syria-humanitarian-intervention-responsibility-protect/> accessed 22 April 2017.

Akehurst M, 'Custom as a Source of International Law' (1974–75) 47 BYBIL 1.

——— 'The Hierarchy of the Sources of International Law' (1974–75) 47 BYBIL 273.

——— *A Modern Introduction to International Law* (6th edn, Harper Collins Academic, 1987).

Aldrich GH, *The Jurisprudence of the Iran-United States Claims Tribunal* (Clarendon Press, 1996).

Alland D (ed), *Droit international public* (Presses Universitaires de France, 2000).

Allot P, 'The Concept of International Law' (1999) 10 EJIL 31.

Alvarez JE, 'Nuremberg Revisited: The *Tadic* Case' (1996) 7 EJIL 245.

——— *International Organizations as Law-Makers* (OUP, 2005).

——— 'A BIT on Custom' (2009) 42 NYU J Intl L & Pol 17.

——— 'Limits of Change by Way of Subsequent Agreements and Practice' in G Nolte (ed), *Treaties and Subsequent Practice* (OUP, 2013) 123.

Amerasinghe CF, 'Interpretation of Texts in Open International Organizations' (1994) 65 BYBIL 175.

——— *Jurisdiction of International Tribunals* (Kluwer Law International, 2003).

——— *Principles of the Institutional Law of International Organizations* (2nd edn, CUP, 2005).

American Law Institute, *Restatement of the Law (Third), The Foreign Relations Law of the United States* (American Law Institute Publishers, 1987).

Anderson DH, 'Further Efforts to Ensure Universal Participation in the United Nations Convention on the Law of the Sea' (1994) 43 ICLQ 886.

Anderson MR and others (eds), *The International Law Commission and the Future of International Law* (British Institute of International and Comparative Law, 1998).

Antippas S, 'A Background Report on Codification of the Law of Treaties at the Vienna Conference' (1969) 43 Tul L Rev 798.

Arato J, 'Subsequent Practice and Evolutive Interpretation: Techniques of Treaty Interpretation over Time and Their Diverse Consequences' (2010) 9 LPICT 443.

——— 'Treaty Interpretation and Constitutional Transformation' (2013) 38 Yale JIL 289.

——— 'Subsequent Practice in the Whaling Case, and What the ICJ Implies about Treaty Interpretation in International Organizations' (*EJIL: Talk!*, 31 March 2014) <www.ejiltalk.org/subsequent-practice-in-the-whaling-case-and-what-the-icj-implies-about-treaty-interpretation-in-international-organizations> accessed 4 September 2014.

Arend AC, 'International Law and the Recourse to Force: A Shift in Paradigms' (1990) 27 Stan J Intl L 1.

——— *Legal Rules and International Society* (OUP, 1999).

Arrow DW, 'The Customary Norm Process and the Deep Seabed, Ocean Development and International Law' (1981) 9 ODILA 1.

Arts K and J Gupta, 'Climate Change and Hazardous Waste Law: Developing International Law of Sustainable Development' in NJ Schrijver and F Weiss (eds), *International Law and Sustainable Development: Principles and Practice* (Martinus Nijhoff, 2004) 519.

Asmus RD and RC Holbrooke, 'Re-reinventing NATO', *Riga Papers* (2006) 1 <www.gmfus.org/doc/A4_Holbrooke_c.pdf> accessed 10 April 2016.

Aust A, 'The Theory and Practice of Informal International Instruments' (1986) 35 ICLQ 787.

——— 'Domestic Consequences of Non-Treaty (Non-Conventional) Law-Making' in R Wolfrum and V Röben (eds), *Developments of International Law in Treaty Making* (Springer, 2005) 487.

——— 'Amendment of Treaties' in A Orakhelashvili and S Williams (eds), *40 Years of the Vienna Convention on the Law of Treaties* (British Institute of International and Comparative Law, 2010) 41.

——— 'Alternatives to Treaty-Making: MOUs as Political Commitments' in DB Hollis (ed), *The Oxford Guide to Treaties* (OUP, 2012) 46.

——— *Modern Treaty Law and Practice* (3rd edn, CUP, 2013).

Aust HP and G Nolte (eds), *The Interpretation of International Law by Domestic Courts: Uniformity, Diversity, Convergence* (OUP, 2016).

Azubuike L, 'International Law Regime Against Piracy' (2009) 15 Ann Surv Intl & Comp L 43.

Bahar M, 'Attaining Optimal Deterrence at Sea: A Legal and Strategic Theory for Naval Anti-Piracy Operations' (2007) 40 VJTL 36.

Bailey SD and S Daws, *The Procedure of the United Nations Security Council* (3rd edn, Clarendon Press, 1998).

Baker RB, 'Customary International Law in the 21st Century: Old Challenges and New Debates' (2010) 21 EJIL 173.

Barak A, *Purposive Interpretation in Law* (Princeton UP, 2005).

Bartels L, 'Applicable Law in WTO Dispute Settlement Proceedings' (2001) 35(3) JWT 499.

Bastid S, *Les traités dans la vie internationale: conclusion et effets* (Économica, 1985).

Batty D and J Shenker, 'Syria suspended from Arab League' (*The Guardian*, 12 November 2011) <https://www.theguardian.com/world/2011/nov/12/syria-suspended-arab-league> accessed 29 March 2017.

Baxter RR, 'Multilateral Treaties as Evidence of Customary International Law' (1965–66) 41 BYBIL 275.

——— 'Treaties and Custom' (1970-I) 129 RC 25.

Bederman DJ, 'Revivalist Canons and Treaty Interpretation' (1994) 41 UCLA L Rev 953.

——— *The Spirit of International Law* (University of Georgia Press, 2002).

——— 'Third Party Rights and Obligations in Treaties' in DB Hollis (ed), *The Oxford Guide to Treaties* (OUP, 2012) 328.

Bernhardt R, 'Interpretation and Implied (Tacit) Modification of Treaties: Comments on Arts. 27, 28, 29 and 38 of the ILC's 1966 Draft Articles on the Law of Treaties' (1967) 27 ZaöRV 491.
——— 'Ungeschriebenes Völkerrecht' (1976) 36 ZaöRV 50.
——— 'The Convention and Domestic Law' in R Macdonald and F Matscher (eds), *The European System for the Protection of Human Rights* (Martinus Nijhoff, 1993) 35.
——— 'Evolutive Treaty Interpretation, Especially of the European Convention of Human Rights' (1999) 42 GYBIL 11.
——— 'Völkerrechtliche und verfassungsrechtliche Aspekte konkludenter Vertragsänderungen' in H-W Arndt and others (eds), *Völkerrecht und Deutsches Recht: Festschrift für Walter Rudolf zum 70 Geburtstag* (Beck, 2001) 15.
Berrisch GM, 'The Establishment of New Law through Subsequent Practice in GATT' (1991) 16 NC J Intl L & Comm Reg 497.
Bethlehem D, 'The Secret Life of International Law' (2012) 1 CJICL 23.
——— 'Interpretation and Implied (Tacit) Modification of Treaties; Comments on Arts. 27, 28, 29 and 38 of the ILC's 1966 Draft Articles on the Law of Treaties' (1967) 27 ZaöRV 491.
Bianchi A, 'The International Regulation of the Use of Force: The Politics of Interpretive Method' (2009) 22 LJIL 651.
——— 'Law, Time, and Change: The Self-Regulatory Function of Subsequent Practice' in G Nolte (ed), *Treaties and Subsequent Practice* (OUP, 2013) 133.
Bilder RB, 'Can Minorities Treaties Work?' in Y Dinstein and M Tabory (eds), *The Protection of Minorities and Human Rights* (Martinus Nijhoff, 1992) 59.
Bjorge E, *The Evolutionary Interpretation of Treaties* (OUP, 2014).
——— 'What Is Living and What Is Dead in the European Convention on Human Rights? A Comment on *Hassan v United Kingdom*' (2015) 15 QIL 23.
Bleckmann A, 'Zur Feststellung und Auslegung von Völkergewohnheitsrecht' (1977) 37 ZaöRV 504.
Blix H, 'The Rule of Unanimity in the Revision of Treaties' (1956) 5 ICLQ 447.
Blokker NM, 'Is the Authorization Authorized? Powers and Practice of the UN Security Council to Authorize the Use of Force by "Coalitions of the Able and Willing"' (2000) 11 EJIL 541.
Blum YZ, *Eroding the United Nations Charter* (Martinus Nijhoff, 1993).
Boas G, *Public International Law: Contemporary Principles and Perspectives* (Edward Elgar, 2012).
Boczek BA, *International Law: A Dictionary* (Scarecrow Press, 2005).
Boisson de Chazournes L, 'Qu'est-ce que la pratique en droit international?' in Société francaise pour le droit international, Colloque de Geneve, *La pratique et le droit international* (Pédone, 2004) 13.
——— 'Subsequent Practice, Practices, and "Family-Resemblance": Towards Embedding Subsequent Practice in its Operative Milieu' in G Nolte (ed), *Treaties and Subsequent Practice* (OUP, 2013) 53.
Bonafé BI and P Palchetti, 'Relying on General Principles in International Law' in C Brölmann and Y Radi (eds), *Research Handbook on the Theory and Practice of International Lawmaking* (Edward Elgar, 2016) 160.
Borgen CJ, 'Resolving Treaty Conflicts' (2005) 37 GWILR 573.
——— 'Treaty Conflicts and Normative Fragmentation' in DB Hollis (ed), *The Oxford Guide to Treaties* (OUP, 2012) 448.

Bos M, 'The Hierarchy among the Recognized Manifestations ("Sources") of International Law' in *Estudios de Derecho Internacional: Homenaje al Profesor Miaja de la Muela* (Editorial Tecnos, 1979) 363.
——— 'Theory and Practice of Treaty Interpretation' (1980) 27 NILR 3.
——— *A Methodology of International Law* (North-Holland, 1984).
Bossuyt M and J Wouters, *Grondlijnen van Internationaal Recht* (Intersentia, 2005).
Bothe M, 'Peacekeeping' in B Simma (ed), *The Charter of the United Nations: A Commentary* (2nd edn, OUP, 2002) 648.
Bouwens WHACM, MS Houwerzijl, and WL Roozendaal, *HL Bakels, Schets van het Nederlandse Arbeidsrecht* (21st edn, Kluwer, 2011).
Bowett DW, 'Estoppel before International Tribunals and Its Relation to Acquiescence' (1957) 33 BYBIL 176.
——— 'Reservations to Non-Restricted Multilateral Treaties' (1976) 48 BYBIL 67.
Bowman MJ, 'The Multilateral Treaty Amendment Process—A Case Study' (1995) 44 ICLQ 540.
——— '"Normalizing" the International Convention for the Regulation of Whaling' (2007–2008) 29 MJIL 293.
———, P Davies, and C Redgwell, *Lyster's International Wildlife Law* (2nd edn, CUP, 2010).
Boyle AE, 'The Law of Treaties and the Anglo-French Continental Shelf Arbitration' (1980) 29 ICLQ 498.
——— 'Saving the World? Implementation and Enforcement of International Environmental Law through International Institutions' (1991) 3 J Envtl L 229.
——— 'Further Development of the 1982 Law of the Sea Convention' in D Freestone, R Barnes, and DM Ong (eds), *The Law of the Sea: Progress and Prospects* (OUP, 2006) 40.
——— and C Chinkin, *The Making of International Law* (OUP, 2007) 246.
Bradley CA and M Gulati, 'Withdrawing from International Custom' (2010) 120 Yale LJ 202.
Brierly JL, 'Some Considerations on the Obsolescence of Treaties' (1926) 11 TGS 4.
——— *The Law of Nations* (6th edn, H Waldock, ed, OUP, 1963).
Briggs HW, 'Procedures for Establishing the Invalidity or Termination of Treaties under the International Law Commission's ILC Draft Articles on the Law of Treaties' (1967) 61 AJIL 976.
——— 'Reflections on the Codification of International Law by the International Law Commission and Other Agencies' (1969-I) 126 RC 233.
Brölmann C, 'Law-Making Treaties: Form and Function in International Law' (2005) 74 NJIL 383.
——— *The Institutional Veil in Public International Law: International Organisations and the Law of Treaties* (Hart Publishing, 2007).
——— 'Specialized Rules of Treaty Interpretation: International Organizations' in DB Hollis (ed), *The Oxford Guide to Treaties* (OUP, 2012) 507.
——— and Y Radi (eds), *Research Handbook on the Theory and Practice of International Lawmaking* (Edward Elgar, 2016).
Brower CH, 'Investor-State Disputes under NAFTA: The Empire Strikes Back' (2001) 40 Colum J Transnat'l L 43.
——— 'Fair and Equitable Treatment Under NAFTA's Investment Chapter' (2002) 96 ASIL Proc 9.
——— 'Why the FTC Notes of Interpretation Constitute a Partial Amendment of NAFTA Article 1105' (2006) 46 VJIL 347.
Brown PM, 'The Codification of International Law' (1935) 29 AJIL 25.
Brownlie I, *Principles of Public International Law* (6th edn, OUP, 2003).

Brunnée J, 'COPing with Consent: Lawmaking under Multilateral Environmental Agreements' (2002) 15 LJIL 1.

——— 'Treaty Amendments' in DB Hollis (ed), *The Oxford Guide to Treaties* (OUP, 2012) 347.

Buergenthal T and SD Murphy, *Public International Law in a Nutshell* (5th edn, West, 2013).

Buffard I and K Zemanek, 'The "Object and Purpose" of a Treaty: An Enigma?' (1998) 3 ARIEL 311.

Buga I, 'Territorial Sovereignty Issues in Maritime Disputes: A Jurisdictional Dilemma for Law of the Sea Tribunals' (2012) 27 IJMCL 59.

——— 'Book Review of I Venzke, How Interpretation Makes International Law: On Semantic Change and Normative Twists' (2013) 83 BYBIL 190.

——— 'Subsequent Practice and Treaty Modification' in MJ Bowman and D Kritsiotis (eds), *Conceptual and Contextual Perspectives on the Modern Law of Treaties* (CUP, forthcoming).

——— 'Between Stability and Change in the Law of the Sea Convention: Subsequent Practice, Treaty Modification and Regime Interaction' in DR Rothwell and others (eds), *The Oxford Handbook on the Law of the Sea* (OUP, 2015) 46.

——— 'A Critical Look at the Law of Treaties: Giving Recognition to Informal Means of Treaty Adaptation' in E Molenaar and others (eds), *What's Wrong with International Law? Liber Amicorum Prof AHA Soons* (Martinus Nijhoff, 2015) 231.

Bugnion F, *Le comité international de la Croix-Rouge et la protection des victimes de la guerre* (CICR, 2000).

Bühler KG, *State Succession and Membership in International Organizations* (Kluwer Law International, 2001).

Burdeau G, 'Vers l'épilogue de l'affaire de Taba: la sentence arbitrale du 29 septembre 1988 entre Israël et l'Egypte' (1988) 34 AFDI 195.

Buss M, 'The Préah Vihéar Case and Regional Customary Law' (2010) 9 Chinese JIL 114.

Byers M, 'Conceptualising the Relationship between *Jus Cogens* and *Erga Omnes* Rules' (1997) 66 NJIL 211.

——— *Custom, Power and the Power of Rules: International Relations and Customary International Law* (CUP, 2001).

——— 'Policing the High Seas: The Proliferation Security Initiative' (2004) 98 AJIL 526.

Caflisch L, 'Les zones maritimes sous jurisdiction nationale, leurs limites et leurs délimitations' (1980) 84 RGDIP 68.

Cahier P, 'Le problème des effets des traités à l'égard des Etats tiers' (1974) 143 RC 660.

——— 'Changement et continuité du droit international: cours général de droit international public' (1985) 195 RC 9.

Çali B, 'Specialized Rules of Treaty Interpretation: Human Rights' in DB Hollis (ed), *The Oxford Guide to Treaties* (OUP, 2012) 525.

Caminos C and MR Molitor, 'Progressive Development of International Law and the Package Deal' (1985) 79 AJIL 871.

Campbell AIL, 'The Limits of the Powers of International Organizations' (2002) 32 ICLQ 523.

Canal-Forgues E, 'Sur l'interprétation dans le droit de l'OMC' (2001) 1 RGDIP 21.

Capotorti F, 'L'extinction et la suspension des traités' (1971-III) 134 RC 417.

Carozza P, 'Uses and Misuses of Comparative Law in International Human Rights: Some Reflections on the Jurisprudence of the European Court of Human Rights' (1998) 73 Notre Dame L Rev 1217.

Carreau D, P Juillard, and T Flory, *Droit international économique* (2nd edn, Librairie générale de droit et de jurisprudence, R Pichon et R Durand-Auzias, 1980).

——— *Droit international* (9th edn, Pédone, 2007).

Casanovas La Rosa O, 'La modificación de los acuerdos internacionales por la práctica posterior' (1968) 21 *Revista española de derecho internacional* 328.

Cassese A and JHH Weiler (eds), *Change and Stability in International Law-Making* (W de Gruyter, 1988).

——— *International Law* (2nd edn, OUP, 2005).

Chan PCW, 'Acquiescence/Estoppel in International Boundaries: *Temple of Preah Vihear* Revisited' (2004) 3 Chinese JIL 421.

Chanaki A, *L'adaptation des traités dans le temps* (Bruylant, 2013).

Chapaux V, 'Article 54 (1969)' in O Corten and P Klein (eds), *Vienna Conventions on the Law of Treaties: A Commentary* (OUP, 2010) 1236.

Charlesworth H, 'Law-Making and Sources' in J Crawford and M Koskenniemi (eds), *The Cambridge Companion to International Law* (CUP, 2012) 187.

Charney JI, 'The Persistent Objector Rule and the Development of Customary International Law' (1985) 56 BYBIL 1.

——— 'The Impact on the International Legal System of the Growth of International Courts and Tribunals' (1999) 31 NYU J Intl L & Pol 697.

Charnovitz S, 'Mapping the Law of WTO Accession' in ME Janow, V Donaldson, and A Yanovich (eds), *The WTO: Governance, Dispute Settlement, and Developing Countries* (Juris Publishing, 2008) 855.

Cheng B, 'United Nations Resolutions on Outer Space: "Instant" International Customary Law?' (1965) 5 IJIL 23.

——— 'Epilogue' in B Cheng (ed), *International Law: Teaching and Practice* (Stevens & Sons, 1982) 223.

——— 'Custom: The Future of General State Practice in a Divided World' in RSJ MacDonald and DM Johnston (eds), *The Structure and Process of International Law: Essays in Legal Philosophy, Doctrine and Theory* (Martinus Nijhoff, 1983) 513.

——— and R Austin, 'Air Law' in M Bos (ed), *The Present State of International Law and Other Essays* (Kluwer, 1989) 183.

Chesterman S, TM Franck, and DM Malone, *Law and Practice of the United Nations: Documents and Commentary* (OUP, 2008).

——— '"Leading from Behind": The Responsibility to Protect, the Obama Doctrine, and Humanitarian Intervention after Libya' (2011) 25 Ethics & Intl Aff 279.

Chua ATL, 'Precedent and Principles of WTO Panel Jurisprudence' (1998) 16 Berkeley JIL 171.

Churchill RR, 'The Fisheries Jurisdiction Cases: The Contribution of the International Court of Justice to the Debates on Coastal States' Fisheries Rights' (1975) 24 ICLQ 86.

——— and NG Foster, 'European Community Law and Prior Treaty Obligations of Member States: The Spanish Fishermen's Cases' (1987) 36 ICLQ 504.

——— and AV Lowe, *The Law of the Sea* (2nd rev edn, Manchester UP, 1988).

——— and G Ulfstein, 'Autonomous Institutional Arrangements in Multilateral Environmental Agreements: A Little-Noticed Phenomenon in International Law' (2000) 94 AJIL 623.

——— 'The Impact of State Practice on the Jurisdictional Framework Contained in the LOS Convention' in AG Oude Elferink (ed), *Stability and Change in the Law of the Sea: The Role of the LOS Convention* (Martinus Nijhoff, 2005) 91.

Clagett BM, 'The Expropriation Issue Before the Iran-United States Claims Tribunal: Is "Just Compensation" Required by International Law or Not?' (1984) 16 L & Pol Intl Bus 813.

Clapham A, P Gaeta, and M Sassòli, *The 1949 Geneva Conventions: A Commentary* (OUP, 2015).

Claude IL, *National Minorities: An International Problem* (Harvard UP, 1955).

——— *The Changing United Nations* (Random House, 1967).

Cluster Munition Coalition, *Cluster Munition Monitor 2015* (International Campaign to Ban Landmines 2015) <www.the-monitor.org/cmm/2011/pdf> accessed 28 June 2016.

Colson DA, 'The United Kingdom-France Continental Shelf Arbitration' (1978) 72 AJIL 95.

Condorelli L, 'Conclusions Générales' in Société française pour le droit international (ed), Colloque de Genève, *La pratique et le droit international* (Pédone, 2004).

Corten O, 'Quels droits et quels devoirs pour les Etats tiers? Les effets juridiques d'une assistance à une acte d'agression' in K Bannelier and others (eds), *L'intervention en Irak et le droit international* (Pédone, 2004) 104.

——— *Méthodologie du droit international public* (Editions de l'Université de Bruxelles, 2009).

Costelloe D and M Fitzmaurice, 'Lawmaking by Treaty: Conclusion of Treaties and Evolution of Treaty Regimes in Practice' in C Brölmann and Y Radi (eds), *Research Handbook on the Theory and Practice of International Lawmaking* (Edward Elgar, 2016) 111.

Cot J-P, 'La conduite subséquente des parties à un traité' (1966) 70 RGDIP 632.

Craven M, *The International Covenant on Economic, Social and Cultural Rights: A Perspective on Its Development* (Clarendon Press, 1995).

Crawford J, 'Book Review of *L'Estoppel en droit international public. Précédé d'un apercu de la theorie de l'estoppel en droit anglais*, by Antoine Martin' (1980) 51 BYBIL 290.

——— and S Olleson, 'The Exception of Non-Performance: Links between the Law of Treaties and the Law of State Responsibility' (2000) 21 Aust YBIL 55.

——— *Brownlie's Principles of Public International Law* (8th edn, OUP, 2012).

——— 'A Consensualist Interpretation of Article 31(3) of the Vienna Convention on the Law of Treaties' in G Nolte (ed), *Treaties and Subsequent Practice* (OUP, 2013) 29.

Crema L, 'Subsequent Agreements and Subsequent Practice Within and Outside the Vienna Convention' in G Nolte (ed), *Treaties and Subsequent Practice* (OUP, 2013) 13.

——— 'Is the Intention of the Parties at the Heart of Interpretation? Some News about Subsequent Practice from the Hague' (9 May 2004) <www.sidi-isil.org/sidiblog/?p=897#more-897> accessed 4 September 2014.

——— 'Subsequent Practice in Hassan v United Kingdom: When Things Seem to Go Wrong in the Life of a Living Instrument' (2015) 15 QIL 3.

Criddle EJ, 'The Vienna Convention on the Law of Treaties in U.S. Treaty Interpretation' (2004) 44 VJIL 431.

Crootof R, 'Change Without Consent: How Customary International Law Modifies Treaties' (2016) 41 Yale JIL 237.

Cryer R, 'Of Custom, Treaties, Scholars and the Gavel: The Influence of the International Criminal Tribunals on the ICRC Customary Law Study' (2006) 11 JCSL 239.

Czaplinski W and G Danilenko, 'Conflicts of Norms in International Law' (1990) 21 NYBIL 3.

D'Amato AA, 'The Concept of Special Custom in International Law' (1969) 63 AJIL 211.

——— *The Concept of Custom in International Law* (Cornell UP, 1971).

——— *International Law: Prospect and Progress* (Transnational, 1987).

——— 'Trashing Customary Law' (1987) 81 AJIL 101.

——— 'It's a Bird, It's a Plane, It's Jus Cogens' (1990) 6 Conn JIL 1.

——— 'The Invasion of Panama Was a Lawful Response to Tyranny' (1990) 84 AJIL 516.

——— 'Customary International Law: A Reformulation' (1998) 4 ILT 1.

D'Aspremont J, 'An Autonomous Regime of Identification of Customary International Humanitarian Law: Do Not Say What You Do or Do Not Do What You Say?' in R van Steenbergh (ed), *Droit international humanitaire: un regime special de droit international?* (Bruylant, 2013) 67.

——— *Formalism and the Sources of International Law: A Theory of the Ascertainment of Legal Rules* (OUP, 2011).

Daillier P, 'La CEE et le respect des droits acquis' (1979) 4 Ann Droit Mar Aér 211.

——— and A Pellet (eds), *Droit international public* (*NQ Dinh*) (6th rev edn, LGDJ, 1999).

Dalton RE, 'Provisional Application of Treaties' in DB Hollis (ed), *The Oxford Guide to Treaties* (OUP, 2012).

Danilenko GM, *Law-Making in the International Community* (Martinus Nijhoff, 1993).

Das H, 'L'*estoppel* et l'acquiescement: assimilations pragmatiques et divergences conceptuelles' (1997) 30 RBDI 607.

Dashwood A, 'Implied External Competence of the EC' in M Koskenniemi (ed), *International Law Aspects of the European Union* (Kluwer Law International, 1998) 113.

Davies PGG and C Redgwell, 'The International Legal Regulation of Straddling Fish Stocks' (1996) 67 BYBIL 199.

——— 'Non-Compliance—A Pivotal or Secondary Function of COP Governance?' (2013) 15 ICL Rev 77.

De Brabandere E, 'Non-State Actors in International Dispute Settlement: Pragmatism in International Law' in J d'Aspremont (ed), *Participants in the International Legal System: Multiple Perspectives on Non-State Actors in International Law* (Routledge, 2011) 342.

De Casadevante Romani CF, *Sovereignty and Interpretation of International Norms* (Springer, 2007).

De Clercq J, *Recueil des traités de la France*, vols 2 and 11 (A Durand & Pedone-Lauriel, 1880).

De Koker C, '*Hassan v United Kingdom*: The Interaction of Human Rights Law and International Humanitarian Law with regard to the Deprivation of Liberty in Armed Conflicts' (2015) 31 Utrecht J Intl & Eur L 90.

De Vattel E, *Le droit des gens; ou Principes de la loi naturelle, appliqués à la conduite et aux affaires des nations et des souverains* (1758), vol II (trans CG Fenwick, Oceana Publications, 1964).

De Visscher C, 'Coutume et traité en droit international public' (1955) 59 RGDIP 353.

——— *Theory and Reality in Public International Law* (Princeton UP, 1957).

De Visscher P, 'Cours général de droit international public' (1972-II) 136 RC 1.

De Wet E, *The Chapter VII Powers of the United Nations Security Council* (Hart, 2004).

De Witte B, 'Rules of Change in International Law: How Special Is the European Community?' (1994) 25 NYBIL 299.

——— 'Treaty Revision in the European Union: Constitutional Change through International Law' (2004) 35 NYBIL 51.

Degan VD, *L'Interprétation des accords en droit international*, vol II (Martinus Nijhoff, 1963).

Denys C, *Impliciete bevoegdheden in de Europese Economische Gemeenschap. Een onderzoek naar de betekenis van 'implied powers'* (Maklu, 1990).

Denza E, *Diplomatic Law: Commentary on the Vienna Convention on Diplomatic Relations. Oxford Commentaries on International Law* (3rd edn, OUP, 2008).

Dicey AV, *Introduction to the Study of the Law of the Constitution* (8th edn, Macmillan, 1915).

Dinh NQ, P Daillier, and A Pellet, *Droit international public* (7th edn, LGDJ, 2002).

Dinstein Y, 'Refugees and the Law of Armed Conflict' (1982) 12 Isr Yb HR 94.

——— 'The Interaction between Customary International Law and Treaties' (2006) 322 RC 243.

——— 'Piracy *Jure Gentium*' in H Hestermeyer and others (eds), *Coexistence, Cooperation and Solidarity: Liber Amicorum Rüdiger Wolfrum* (Martinus Nijhoff, 2012) 1125.

Distefano G, 'La pratique subséquente des États parties à un traité' (1994) 40 AFDI 41.

——— 'L'interprétation évolutive de la norme internationale' (2011) 11 RGDIP 373.

——— 'L'accord tacite ou l'univers parallèle du droit des traités' (2015) 18 QIL 17.

Dixon R, 'Partial Constitutional Amendments' (2011) 13 U Pa J Const L 643.

——— 'Updating Constitutional Rules' (2011) 1 Sup Ct Rev 319.

Djeffal C, *Static and Evolutive Treaty Interpretation: A Functional Reconstruction* (CUP, 2015).

Do Nascimento e Silva GE, 'Le facteur de temps et les traités' (1977) 154 RC 217.

Donnan S, 'World Trade Organisation Moves on from Stalled Doha Round' *Financial Times* (19 December 2015) <www.ft.com/cms/s/0/4ccf5356-9eaa-11e5-8ce1-f6219b685d74.html> accessed 22 June 2016.

Dörr O, 'Article 31: General Rule of Interpretation' in O Dörr and K Schmalenbach (eds), *Vienna Convention the Law of Treaties: A Commentary* (Springer, 2012) 521.

Droege C, 'Transfers of Detainees: Legal Framework, *Non-Refoulement* and Contemporary Challenges' (2008) 90 IRRC 669.

Droubi H and R Gladstone, 'Syrian Opposition Joins Meeting of Arab League' (*New York Times*, 26 March 2013) <www.nytimes.com/2013/03/27/world/middleeast/syrian-opposition-group-takes-seat-at-arab-league.html> accessed 29 March 2017.

Dumberry P, 'Incoherent and Ineffective: The Concept of Persistent Objector Revisited' (2010) 59 ICLQ 779.

Dupuy P-M, 'A propos de l'opposabilité de la coutume générale: enquête brève sur l'objecteur persistant' in *Mélanges Michel Viraly* (Pédone, 1991) 257.

——— 'Le droit des Nations Unies et sa pratique dans la jurisprudence de la Cour internationale de Justice' in Société française pour le droit international (ed), *La pratique et le droit international* (Pédone, 2004) 139.

——— 'Evolutionary Interpretation of Treaties: Between Memory and Prophecy' in E Cannizzaro (ed), *The Law of Treaties Beyond the Vienna Convention* (OUP, 2011) 123.

Dupuy R-J, 'Coutume sage et coutume sauvage' in *Mélanges offerts à Charles Rousseau: La communauté internationale* (Pédone, 1974) 75.

Elias O, 'The Nature of the Subjective Element in Customary International Law' (1995) 44 ICLQ 501.

Elias TO, 'The Doctrine of Intertemporal Law' (1980) 74 AJIL 285.

——— *The International Court of Justice and Some Contemporary Problems: Essays on International Law* (Martinus Nijhoff, 1983).

——— 'Who Can Make Treaties? International Organizations' in DB Hollis (ed), *The Oxford Guide to Treaties* (OUP, 2012) 73.

Elkins Z, T Ginsburg, and J Melton, *The Endurance of National Constitutions* (CUP, 2009).

Elzinga DJ, 'Grondwet en ongeschreven staatsrecht' in CJ Bax and MC de Voogd (eds), *Van constitutionalisme en anarchisme: Opstellen aangeboden aan Th Holterman en GFM van der Tang* (Kluwer, 2003) 5.

———, R de Lange, and HG Hoogers (eds), *Van der Pot, Handboek van het Nederlandse Staatsrecht* (16th edn, Kluwer, 2013).

Emilianides AC, 'Can the European Convention on Human Rights Be Modified by Subsequent Customary Law?' (2006) CYBIR 83.

Engdahl O, *Protection of Personnel in Peace Operations: The Role of the 'Safety Convention' Against the Background of General International Law* (Martinus Nijhoff, 2006).

Engel S, 'Procedures for *De Facto* Revision of the Charter' (1965) 59 ASIL Proc 108.

——— '"Living" International Constitutions and the World Court (The Subsequent Practice of International Organs under their Constituent Instruments)' (1967) 16 ICLQ 865.

Farmer A, 'Non-Refoulement and *Jus Cogens*: Limiting Anti-Terror Measures that Threaten Refugee Protection' (2009) 23 Geo Immigr LJ 1.

Fauchald OK, 'The Legal Reasoning of ICSID Tribunals—An Empirical Analysis' (2008) 19 EJIL 301.

Feldman AM, 'Evolving Treaty Obligations: A Proposal for Analyzing Subsequent Practice Derived from WTO Dispute Settlement' (2009) 41 NYU J Intl L & Pol 655.

Fennelly N, 'Legal Interpretation at the European Court of Justice' (1997) 20 Fordham ILJ 656.

Fidler DP, 'Challenging the Classical Concept of Custom: Perspectives on the Future of Customary International Law' (1996) 39 GYBIL 198.

Fietta S, 'The "Legitimate Expectations" Principle under Article 1105 NAFTA: *International Thunderbird Gaming Corporation v The United American States*' (2006) 7 JWIT 423.

Fitzmaurice G, 'The Law and Procedure of the International Court of Justice: Treaty Interpretation and Certain Other Treaty Points' (1951) 28 BYBIL 8.

——— 'The Law and Procedure of the International Court of Justice, 1951–54: General Principles and Sources of Law' (1953) 30 BYBIL 1.

——— 'The Law and Procedure of the International Court of Justice 1951–4: Treaty Interpretation and Other Treaty Points' (1957) 33 BYBIL 203.

——— 'The General Principles of International Law Considered from the Standpoint of the Rule of Law' (1957-II) 92 RC 1.

——— 'Some Problems Regarding the Formal Sources of International Law' in FM van Asbeck and others (eds), *Symbolae Verzijl: Présentées au Professeur JHW Verzijl à l'occasion de son LXX-ième anniversaire* (Martinus Nijhoff, 1958) 153.

——— 'Hersch Lauterpacht—The Scholar as Judge—Part III' (1963) 39 BYBIL 133.

——— '*Vae Victis* or Woe to the Negotiator? Your Treaty or Our Interpretation of It' (review essay) (1971) 65 AJIL 358.

Fitzmaurice M, 'Actors and Factors in the Evolution of Treaty Norms (An Empirical Study)' (1999) 4 ARIEL 1.

——— 'Dynamic (Evolutive) Interpretation of Treaties' (2008) 2 Hague Yb IL 101.

——— and O Elias, *Contemporary Issues in the Law of Treaties* (Eleven International, 2005).

——— and P Merkouris, 'Canons of Treaty Interpretation: Selected Case Studies from the World Trade Organization and the North American Free Trade Agreement' in M Fitzmaurice, O Elias, and P Merkouris (eds), *Treaty Interpretation and the Vienna Convention on the Law of Treaties: 30 Years On* (Martinus Nijhoff, 2010) 153.

——— 'Exceptional Circumstances and Treaty Commitments' in DB Hollis (ed), *The Oxford Guide to Treaties* (OUP, 2012) 605.

——— 'Interpretation of Human Rights Treaties' in D Shelton (ed), *The Oxford Handbook of International Human Rights Law* (OUP, 2013) 739.

Footer M, *An Institutional and Normative Analysis of the World Trade Organization* (Martinus Nijhoff, 2006).

——— 'The Making of International Trade Law' in C Brölmann and Y Radi (eds), *Research Handbook on the Theory and Practice of International Lawmaking* (Edward Elgar, 2016) 395.

——— 'Treaty Interrelationships' in MJ Bowman and D Kritsiotis (eds), *Conceptual and Contextual Perspectives on the Modern Law of Treaties* (CUP, forthcoming).

Ford S, 'Legal Processes of Change: Article 2(4) and the Vienna Convention on the Law of Treaties' (1999) 4 JCSL 75.

Foster M, *International Refugee Law and Socio-Economic Rights: Refugee from Deprivation* (CUP, 2007).

Fox H, 'Article 31(3)(a) and (b) of the Vienna Convention and the *Kasikili/Sedudu Island* Case' in M Fitzmaurice, O Elias, and P Merkouris (eds), *Treaty Interpretation and the Vienna Convention on the Law of Treaties: 30 Years On* (Martinus Nijhoff, 2010) 59.

Franck TM, 'Who Killed Article 2(4)' (1970) 64 AJIL 809.

——— *Nation Against Nation: What Happened to the UN Dream and What the US Can Do About It* (OUP, 1985).

——— *Recourse to Force: State Action Against Threats and Armed Attacks* (CUP, 2002).

Frankowska M, 'The Vienna Convention on the Law of Treaties Before United States Courts' (1988) 28 VJIL 281.

Freestone D and AG Oude Elferink, 'Flexibility and Innovation in the Law of the Sea – Will the LOS Convention Amendment Procedures Ever Be Used?' in AG Oude Elferink (ed), *Stability and Change in the Law of the Sea: The Role of the LOS Convention* (Martinus Nijhoff, 2005) 169.

French, D, 'Treaty Interpretation and the Incorporation of Extraneous Legal Rules' (2006) 55 *ICLQ* 281.

Frowein J, 'Jus Cogens' in R Bernhardt (ed), *Encyclopaedia of International Law*, vol III (Elsevier, 1997) 65.

——— 'Obligations *Erga Omnes*' in R Bernhardt (ed), *Encyclopaedia of International Law*, vol III (Elsevier, 1997) 757.

——— 'Are There Limits to the Amendment Procedures in Treaties Constituting International Organisations?' in G Hafner and others (eds), *Liber Amicorum Professor Seidl-Hohenveldern in Honour of his 80th Birthday* (Kluwer Law International, 1998) 201.

——— and N Krisch, 'Article 39' in B Simma (ed), *The Charter of the United Nations: A Commentary*, vol I (2nd edn, OUP, 2002) 717.

Gaeta P, 'Inherent Powers of International Courts and Tribunals' in LC Vohran and others (eds), *Man's Inhumanity to Man: Essays on International Law in Honour of Antonio Cassese* (Kluwer Law International, 2003) 353.

Gaja G, 'Article 38 (1969)' in O Corten and P Klein (eds), *The Vienna Conventions on the Law of Treaties: A Commentary* (OUP, 2011) 949.

Gantz DA, 'The Evolution of FTA Investment Provisions: From NAFTA to the United States-Chile Free Trade Agreement' (2004) 19 Am U Intl L Rev 679.

Gardiner RK, *Treaty Interpretation* (OUP, 2008).

——— 'The Vienna Convention Rules on Treaty Interpretation' in DB Hollis (ed), *The Oxford Guide to Treaties* (OUP, 2012) 475.

Gasser H-P, 'International Committee of the Red Cross (ICRC)' in R Wolfrum, *Max Planck Encyclopedia of Public International Law* (OUP, 2013).

——— 'Respect des garanties judiciaires fondamentales en temps de conflit armé: Le rôle du délégué du CICR' (1992) 74 RICR 129.

Gazzini T, 'A Unique Non-State Actor: The International Committee of the Red Cross' (2010) 4 HRILD 32.

——— 'Can Authoritative Interpretation Under Article IX:2 of the Agreement Establishing the WTO Modify the Rights and Obligations of Members?' (2008) 57 ICLQ 169.

——— 'Interpretation of (Allegedly) Self-judging Clauses in Bilateral Investment Treaties' in M Fitzmaurice, O Elias, and P Merkouris (eds), *Treaty Interpretation and the Vienna Convention on the Law of Treaties: 30 Years On* (Martinus Nijhoff, 2010) 239.

——— 'Bilateral Investment Treaties' in T Gazzini and E De Brabandere (eds), *International Investment Law: The Sources of Rights and Obligations* (Martinus Nijhoff, 2012) 99.

Geiss R and A Petrig, *Piracy and Armed Robbery at Sea* (OUP, 2011).
Gény F, *Méthode d'interprétation et sources en droit privé positif: essai critique* (1st edn, Librairie générale de droit et de jurisprudence, 1899).
Georgiev GS, 'The Award in *Saluka Investments v. Czech Republic*' in GA Alvarez and WM Reisman (eds), *The Reasons Requirement in International Investment Arbitration: Critical Case Studies* (Martinus Nijhoff, 2008) 149.
Georgopoulos T, 'Le droit intertemporel et les dispositions conventionnelles évolutives—Quelle thérapie contre la vieillesse des traités?' (2004) 108 RGDIP 123.
Giegerich T, 'Article 54' in O Dörr and K Schmalenbach (eds), *Vienna Convention on the Law of Treaties: A Commentary* (Springer, 2012) 945.
Giladi R and S Ratner, 'The Role of the International Committee of the Red Cross' in A Clapham, P Gaeta, and M Sassòli, *The 1949 Geneva Conventions: A Commentary* (OUP, 2015) 525.
Giraud E, 'Exposé préliminaire: Modification et terminaison des traités collectifs' (1961-I) 49 AIDI 5.
Glennon MJ, *Limits of Law, Prerogatives of Power: Interventionism After Kosovo* (Palgrave, 2001).
——— 'How International Rules Die' (2005) 93 Geo LJ 939.
Gold J, 'The "Dispensing" and "Suspending" Powers of International Organizations' (1972) 19 NTIR 181.
Golsong H, 'Interpreting the European Convention on Human Rights Beyond the Confines of the Vienna Convention on the Law of Treaties?' in RStJ Macdonald, F Matscher, and H Petzold (eds), *The European System for the Protection of Human Rights* (Martinus Nijhoff, 1993) 147.
Goode R, 'Usage and Its Reception in Transnational Commercial Law' (1997) 46 ICLQ 1.
———, H Kronke, and E McKendrick (eds), *Transnational Commercial Law: Text, Cases, and Materials* (OUP, 2007).
Goodrich LM, E Hambro, and AP Simons, *Charter of the United Nations: Commentary and Documents* (3rd edn, Columbia UP, 1969).
Goodwin-Gill GS, *The Refugee in International Law* (OUP, 1996).
——— and J McAdam, *The Refugee in International Law* (3rd edn, OUP, 2007).
Gordon E, 'Article 2(4) in Historical Context' (1985) 10 Yale JIL 271.
Gormley WP, 'The Modification of Multilateral Conventions by Means of "Negotiated Reservations" and Other "Alternatives": A Comparative Study of the ILO and Council of Europe' (1970) 39 Fordham L Rev 59.
Gottlieb G, 'The Interpretation of Treaties by Tribunals' (1969) 63 ASIL Proc 122.
Gottlieb S, 'The Dutch Want Pirates in Court' (*Radio Netherlands Worldwide*, 16 January 2009) <www.rnw.nl/international-justice/article/dutch-want-pirates-court> accessed 2 December 2014.
Grant T, 'Who Can Make Treaties? Other Subjects of International Law' in DB Hollis (ed), *The Oxford Guide to Treaties* (OUP, 2012) 125.
Gray C, *International Law and the Use of Force* (3rd edn, OUP, 2008).
——— 'The Use of Force and the International Legal Order' in MD Evans (ed), *International Law* (3rd edn, OUP, 2010) 615.
Greig DW, *International Law* (Butterworths, 1970).
——— *Intertemporality and the Law of Treaties* (British Institute of International and Comparative Law, 2003).
Greslin A, *La mise en application provisoire des traités* (Pédone, 2005).
Gross EA, 'Revising the Charter: Is It Possible? Is It Wise?' (1954) 32 Foreign Affairs 203.
Gross L, 'Voting in the Security Council: Abstention from Voting and Absence from Meetings' (1951) 60 Yale LJ 209.

——— 'Voting in the Security Council: Abstention in the Post-1965 Amendment Phase and its Impact on Article 25 of the Charter' (1968) 62 AJIL 315.

Guggenheim P, 'Les deux éléments de la coutume en droit international' in C Rousseau (ed), *La technique et les principes du droit public: études en l'honneur de Georges Scelle* (LGDJ, 1950) 272.

Guilfoyle D, 'Piracy Off Somalia: A Sketch of the Legal Framework' (*EJIL:Talk!*, 20 April 2009) <www.ejiltalk.org> accessed 9 June 2017.

——— 'Combating Piracy: Executive Measures on the High Seas' (2011) 53 JYBIL 149.

Gutiérrez Posse H, 'La maxime *ut res magis valeat quam pereat* (interpretation en fonction de "l'effet utile"); les interpretations "extensives" et "restrictives"' (1972) 23 ÖzöR 229.

Guzman AT, 'Saving Customary International Law' (2005) 27 MJIL 115.

——— 'Against Consent' (2012) 52 VJIL 747.

Haanappel PPC, *The Law and Policy of Air Space and Outer Space: A Comparative Approach* (Kluwer Law International, 2003).

Hachez I, *Le principe de standstill dans le droit des droits fondamentaux: une irréversibilité relative* (Bruylant, 2008).

Hafner G, 'Subsequent Agreements and Practice: Between Interpretation, Informal Modification, and Formal Amendment' in G Nolte (ed), *Treaties and Subsequent Practice* (OUP, 2013) 105.

Haggenmacher R, 'La doctrine du droit coutumier dans la pratique de la Cour internationale' (1986) 1 RGDIP 117.

Hall CK, 'The Duty of States Parties to the Convention against Torture to Provide Procedures Permitting Victims to Recover Reparations for Torture Committed Abroad' (2007) 18 EJIL 921.

Handl G, 'The Legal Mandate of Multilateral Development Banks as Agents for Change Toward Sustainable Development' (1998) 92 AJIL 642.

——— 'International "Lawmaking" by Conferences of the Parties and Other Politically Mandated Bodies' in R Wolfrum and V Röben (eds), *Developments of International Law in Treaty Making* (Springer, 2005) 127.

Hannikainen L, *Peremptory Norms (Jus Cogens) in International Law: Historical Development, Criteria, Present Status* (Finnish Lawyers' Publishing Company, 1988).

Haraszti G, *Some Fundamental Problems of the Law of Treaties* (Akadémiai Kiadó, 1973).

Hardy MJL, *Modern Diplomatic Law* (Manchester UP, 1968).

Harrison J, *Making the Law of the Sea: A Study in the Development of International Law* (CUP, 2011).

Harvard Research in International Law, 'Draft Convention on the Law of Responsibility of States for Damage done in their Territory to the Person or Property of Foreigners' (1929) 23 AJIL Special Supp 133.

Harvard Research in International Law, 'Draft Convention on the Law of Treaties' (1935) 29 AJIL Special Supp 653.

Hathaway J, *The Law of Refugee Status* (Butterworths, 1991).

Hathaway OA and others, 'Tacit Amendment' (2011) *White Paper for Yale Law School Center for Global Legal Studies* 1 <www.law.yale.edu/documents/pdf/cglc/TacitAmendments.pdf> accessed 18 September 2014.

Heffes E and BE Frenkel, 'The Decision-Making Process of the R2P Doctrine: Towards New (Old) Paths in the Use of Force in International Law' (*Opinio Juris*, 2 September 2013) <http://opiniojuris.org/2013/09/02/syria-insta-symposium-ezequiel-heffes-brian-e-frenkel-decision-making-process-r2p-doctrine-towards-new-old-paths-use-force-international-law/> accessed 5 April 2017.

Heintze H-J, 'Protecting Power' in R Wolfrum (ed), *Max Planck Encyclopedia of Public International Law* (OUP, 2009).

Helfer LR, 'Consensus, Coherence and the European Convention on Human Rights' (1993) 26 Cornell ILJ 140.

——— 'Terminating Treaties' in DB Hollis (ed), *The Oxford Guide to Treaties* (OUP, 2012) 634.

Helmersen ST, 'Evolutive Treaty Interpretation: Legality, Semantics and Distinctions' (2013) 6 EJLS 127.

Henckaerts JM and L Doswald-Beck (eds), *Customary International Humanitarian Law, Volume 1: Rules* (ICRC and CUP, 2005).

Henkin L, *How Nations Behave: Law and Foreign Policy* (2nd edn, Columbia UP, 1979).

Herdegen M, 'Interpretation in International Law' in R Wolfrum (ed), *Max Planck Encyclopedia of Public International Law* (OUP, 2008).

Hexner EP, 'Teleological Interpretation of Basic Instruments of International Organizations' in S Engel and RA Metall (eds), *Law, State and International Legal Order: Essays in Honor of Hans Kelsen* (University of Tennessee Press, 1964) 119.

Higgins R, 'The Development of International Law by the Political Organs of the United Nations' (1965) 59 ASIL Proc 116.

——— 'Policy Considerations and the International Judicial Process' (1968) 17 ICLQ 58.

——— 'International Law and the Avoidance, Containment and Resolution of Disputes' (1991-V) 230 RC 9.

——— *Problems and Process: International Law and How We Use It* (Clarendon Press, 1994).

——— 'Report on the Legal Consequences for Member States of the Non-fulfilment by International Organizations of their Obligations toward Third Parties' (1995) 66(I) AIDI 251.

——— 'Some Observations on the Inter-Temporal Rule in International Law' in J Makarczyk (ed), *Theory of International Law at the Threshold of the 21st Century* (Kluwer Law International, 1996) 173.

——— 'Time and the Law: International Perspectives on an Old Problem' (1997) 46 ICLQ 501.

——— *Themes and Theories: Selected Essays, Speeches and Writings in International Law* (OUP, 2009).

Hijma J and others, *Rechtshandeling en Overeenkomst* (7th edn, Kluwer, 2013).

Hill-Cawthorne L, 'The Grand Chamber Judgment in Hassan v UK' (*EJIL: Talk!*, 16 September 2014) <www.ejiltalk.org/the-grand-chamber-judgment-in-hassan-v-uk/> accessed 26 May 2017.

Hoffmeister F, 'The Contribution of EU Practice to International Law' in M Cremona (ed), *Developments in EU External Relations Law* (OUP, 2008) 37.

Hofmann SC, 'Debating Strategy in NATO: Obstacles to Defining a Meaningful New Strategic Concept' (Institut Français des Relations Internationales, 2008).

Hollis DB, 'Introduction' in DB Hollis (ed), *The Oxford Guide to Treaties* (OUP, 2012) 1.

——— 'Defining Treaties' in DB Hollis (ed), *The Oxford Guide to Treaties* (OUP, 2012) 11.

Holz L, 'L'Extradition entre l'Inde francaise et l'Empire anglo-indien' (1910) 17 RGDIP 449.

Houlard M, *La nature juridique des traités internationaux et son application aux théories de la nullité, de la caducité et de la révision des traités* (Bordeaux, 1936).

Hoyt EC, *The Unanimity Rule in the Revision of Treaties: A Re-examination* (Martinus Nijhoff, 1959).

Hudec RE, *The GATT Legal System and World Trade Diplomacy* (Praeger, 1975).

——— *Enforcing International Trade Law: The Evolution of the Modern GATT Legal System* (Butterworth Legal, 1993).

Hudson C, 'Fishery and Economic Zones as Customary International Law' (1980) 17 San Diego L Rev 661.
Hyde C, *International Law Chiefly as Interpreted and Applied by the United States* (Little, Brown, 1922).
Jackson JJ, *The World Trading System: Law and Policy of International Economic Relations* (2nd edn, MIT Press, 1997).
Jacobs FG, 'Varieties of Approach to Treaty Interpretation: With Special Reference to the Draft Convention on the Law of Treaties Before the Vienna Diplomatic Conference' (1969) 18 ICLQ 318.
Jaquemet S, 'The Cross-Fertilization of International Humanitarian Law and International Refugee Law' (2001) 83 IRRC 651.
Jenks CW, 'The Interpretation of International Labour Conventions by the International Labour Office' (1939) 20 BYBIL 132.
——— 'The Conflict of Law-Making Treaties' (1953) 29 BYBIL 425.
Jennings RY, 'General Course on Principles of International Law' (1967-II) 151 RC 323.
——— 'The Identification of International Law' in B Cheng (ed), *International Law: Teaching and Practice* (Stevens, 1982) 3.
——— and A Watts (eds), *Oppenheim's International Law: Peace*, vol I (9th edn, OUP, 2008).
Jessup PC, *A Modern Law of Nations: An Introduction* (Macmillan, 1984).
Jiménez de Aréchaga E, 'International Law in the Past Third of a Century' (1978-I) 159 RC 1.
——— 'Customary International Law and the Conference on the Law of the Sea' in J Makarczyk (ed), *Essays in International Law in Honour of Judge Manfred Lachs* (Martinus Nijhoff, 1984) 575.
——— 'Intervention' in A Cassese and JHH Weiler (eds), *Change and Stability in International Law-Making* (W de Gruyter, 1988) 48.
Johnstone I, 'Law-Making through the Operational Activities of International Organizations' (2008) 40 Geo Wash L Rev 87.
Kaczorowska A, *Public International Law* (4th edn, Routledge, 2010).
——— 'Die parlamentarische Kontrolle des Regierungshandelns bei der Beschlussfassung internationaler Organisationen' in R Geiger (ed), *Neuere Probleme der parlamentarischen Legitimation im Bereich der auswärtigen Gewalt* (Nomos, 2003) 41.
Kadelbach S, '*Jus Cogens*, Obligations *Erga Omnes* and Other Rules—The Identification of Fundamental Norms' in C Tomuschat and JM Thouvenin (eds), *The Fundamental Rules of the International Legal Order:* Jus Cogens *and Obligations* Erga Omnes (Martinus Nijhoff, 2006) 21.
——— 'The Interpretation of the Charter' in B Simma and others (eds), *The Charter of the United Nations: A Commentary* (3rd edn, OUP, 2012) 71.
——— 'Domestic Constitutional Concerns with Respect to the Use of Subsequent Agreements and Practice at the International Level' in G Nolte (ed), *Treaties and Subsequent Practice* (OUP, 2013) 145.
Kadens E and EA Young, 'How Customary Is Customary International Law?' (2013) 54 Wm & Mary L Rev 885.
Kammerhofer J, 'Book Review on A Orakhelashvili, The Interpretation of Acts and Rules in Public International Law' (2009) 20 EJIL 1282.
——— *Uncertainty in International Law: A Kelsenian Perspective* (Routledge, 2011).
Kamto M, 'La volonté de l'Etat en droit international' (2004) 310 RC 133.
Kaplan MA and N Katzenbach, *The Political Foundations of International Law* (John Wiley & Sons, 1961).

Karagiannis S, 'À propos de la révision du Traité sur l'Union européenne effectuée de manière non conforme à la procédure de révision' (2008) 61 RHDI 239.

Karl W, *Vertrag und spätere Praxis im Völkerrecht: Zum Einfluß der Praxis auf Inhalt und Bestand völkerrechtliche Verträge* (Springer, 1983).

——— 'Conflicts between Treaties' in R Bernhardt (ed), *Encyclopedia of Public International Law*, vol 7 (North-Holland, 1984) 468.

———, B Mützelburg, and G Witschel, 'Article 108' in B Simma and others (eds), *The Charter of the United Nations: A Commentary*, vol II (2nd edn, OUP, 2002) 1341.

Kasoulides GC, 'Removal of Offshore Platforms and the Development of International Standards' (1989) 13 Mar Policy 249.

Katayanagi M, *Human Rights Functions of United Nations Peacekeeping Operations* (Martinus Nijhoff, 2002).

Kaufmann-Kohler G, 'Interpretive Powers of the NAFTA Free Trade Commission—Necessary Safety Valve or Infringement of the Rule of Law?' in F Bachand (ed), *Fifteen Years of NAFTA Chapter 11 Arbitration, IAI Conference Proceedings* (JurisNet, 2011) 175.

Kearney RD and RE Dalton, 'The Treaty on Treaties' (1970) 64 AJIL 495.

Keller H and L Grover, 'General Comments of the Human Rights Committee and Their Legitimacy' in H Keller and G Ulfstein (eds), *UN Human Rights Treaty Bodies: Law and Legitimacy* (CUP, 2012) 116.

Kelly M, 'The Temple Case in Historical Perspective' (1963) 39 BYBIL 471.

Kelsen H, 'Theorie du droit international coutumier' (1939) 1 Rev Intl Théorie Droit 253.

——— 'Organization and Procedure of the Security Council' (1946) 59 Harv L Rev 1087.

——— *The Law of the United Nations: A Critical Analysis of its Fundamental Problems* (Steven & Sons, 1951).

Khan R, *Implied Powers of the United Nations* (Vikas Publications, 1970).

Kirgis FL, Jr, 'Custom on a Sliding Scale' (1987) 81 AJIL 146.

Kivilcim-Forsman Z, 'Principe d'egalité entre le traité et la coutume en droit international public' (1996) 45 J Faculty of Law, Ankara Univ 211.

Klabbers J, *The Concept of Treaty in International Law* (Kluwer, 1996).

——— 'The Curious Condition of Custom' (2002) 8 ILT 29.

——— 'On Rationalism in Politics: Interpretation of Treaties and the World Trade Organization' (2005) 74 NJIL 405.

——— *Treaty Conflict and the European Union* (CUP, 2009).

——— 'Checks and Balances in the Law of International Organizations' in M Sellers (ed), *Autonomy in the Law* (Springer, 2007) 141.

——— *An Introduction to International Institutional Law* (2nd edn, CUP, 2009).

——— 'Law-Making and Constitutionalism' in J Klabbers, A Peters, and G Ulfstein (eds), *The Constitutionalization of International Law* (OUP, 2009) 81.

——— 'Virtuous Interpretation' in M Fitzmaurice, O Elias, and P Merkouris (eds), *Treaty Interpretation and the Vienna Convention on the Law of Treaties: 30 Years On* (Martinus Nijhoff, 2010) 17.

——— 'Beyond the Vienna Convention: Conflicting Treaty Provisions' in E Cannizzaro (ed), *The Law of Treaties Beyond the Vienna Convention* (OUP, 2011) 192.

Kleimann D, 'Positivism, the New Haven School, and the Use of Force in International Law' (2006) 3 BSIS J Intl Stud 3.

Koch IE and J Vedsted-Hansen, 'International Human Rights and National Legislatures—Conflict or Balance?' (2006) 75 NJIL 3.

Kohen MG, 'La codification du droit des traités: quelques elements pour un bilan global' (2000) 3 RGDIP 589.

——— 'Uti possidetis, prescription et pratique subséquente à un traité dans l'affaire de l'Ile de Kasikili/Sedudu devant la Cour internationale de Justice' (2000) 43 GYBIL 253.

——— 'La pratique et la théorie des sources du droit international' in MG Kohen, L Boisson de Chazournes, and G Buzzini (eds), *La pratique et le droit international, Société française pour le droit international, Colloque de Genève* (Pédone, 2004) 81.

——— 'The Decision on the Delimitation of the Eritrea/Ethiopia Boundary of 13 April 2002: A Singular Approach to International Law Applicable to Territorial Disputes' in MG Kohen (ed), *Promoting Justice, Human Rights and Conflict Resolution through International Law: Liber Amicorum Lucius Caflisch* (Martinus Nijhoff, 2007) 767.

——— and S Heathcote, 'Article 42 (1969)' in O Corten and P Klein (eds), *Vienna Conventions on the Law of Treaties: A Commentary* (OUP, 2010) 1015.

——— 'Desuetude and Obsolescence of Treaties' in E Cannizzaro (ed), *The Law of Treaties Beyond the Vienna Convention* (OUP, 2011) 350.

——— 'Keeping Subsequent Agreements and Practice in Their Right Limits' in G Nolte (ed), *Treaties and Subsequent Practice* (OUP, 2013) 34.

Kolb R, *La bonne foi en droit international public: Contribution à l'étude des principes généraux de droit* (Graduate Institute Publications, 2000).

——— 'La modification d'un traité par la pratique subséquente des parties' (2004) 14 *Schweizerische Zeitschrift für Internationales und Europäisches Recht* 9.

——— *Interprétation et création du droit international* (Bruylant, 2006).

——— 'La désuétude en droit international public' (2007) 111 RGDIP 577.

——— *An Introduction to the Law of the United Nations* (Hart, 2010).

——— *The Law of Treaties: An Introduction* (Edward Elgar, 2016).

Kontorovich E, 'International Legal Responses to Piracy off the Coast of Somalia' (2009) 13 ASIL Insights 1.

——— 'Case Report: *United States v Shi*' (2009) 103 AJIL 734.

——— 'Introductory Note to Exchange of Letters Between European Union and Kenya to Prosecute Pirates' (2009) 48 ILM 747.

——— ' "A Guantanamo on the Sea": The Difficulties of Prosecuting Pirates and Terrorists' (2010) 98 CLR 243.

Kontou N, *The Termination and Revision of Treaties in the Light of New Customary International Law* (Clarendon Press, 1994).

Kooijmans PH, 'The Enlargement of the Concept "Threat to the Peace" ' in R-J Dupuy (ed), *The Development of the Role of the Security Council* (Kluwer, 1993) 111.

——— *Internationaal Publiekrecht in Vogelvlucht* (Wolters-Noordhoff, 1996).

Kopela S, 'The Legal Value of Silence as State Conduct in the Jurisprudence of International Tribunals' (2010) 29 Aust YBIL 87.

Kopelmanas L, 'Custom as a Means of Creation of International Law' (1937) 18 BYBIL 127.

Koplow DA, 'When Is an Amendment Not an Amendment? Modification of Arms Control Agreements Without the Senate' (1992) 59 U Chi L Rev 981.

Koskenniemi M, 'The Pull of the Mainstream' (1990) 88 Mich L Rev 1946.

——— and M Lehto, 'La succession d'états dans l'ex-URSS, en ce qui concerne particulièrement les relations avec la Finlande' (1992) 38 AFDI 179.

——— and P Leino, 'Fragmentation of International Law? Postmodern Anxieties' (2002) 15 LJIL 553.

——— *From Apology to Utopia: The Structure of International Legal Argument* (CUP, 2005).

——— 'Hegemonic Regimes' in MA Young (ed), *Regime Interaction in International Law: Facing Fragmentation* (CUP, 2012) 305.

Kotzur M, 'Intertemporal Law' in R Wolfrum (ed), *Max Planck Encyclopaedia of Public International Law* (OUP, 2008).

Krishan D, 'A Notion of ICSID Investment' in TJ Grierson Weiler (ed), *Investment Treaty Arbitration and International Law* (Juris Publishing, 2008) 61.

Kritsiotis D, 'The Concept of a Treaty's Object and Purpose' in MJ Bowman and D Kritsiotis (eds), *Conceptual and Contextual Perspectives on the Modern Law of Treaties* (CUP, forthcoming).

Kuijper PJ, 'Law of GATT as a Special Field of International Law, Ignorance, Further Refinement or Self-Contained System of International Law?' (1994) 25 NYBIL 227.

——— 'The Court and the Tribunal of the EC and the Vienna Convention on the Law of Treaties 1969' (1998) 1 LIEI 2.

——— 'Some Institutional Issues Presently Before the WTO' in D Kennedy and J Southwick (eds), *The Political Economy of International Trade Law: Essays in Honor of Robert E Hudec* (CUP, 2002) 82.

Kunoy B, 'The 10 Year Time Frame to Disputed Areas' (2009) 40 ODIL 131.

Lachs M, 'Le problème de la révision de la Charte des Nations Unies' (1956-II) 90 RC 307.

Lando M, 'The Advisory Jurisdiction of the International Tribunal for the Law of the Sea: Comments on the Request for an Advisory Opinion Submitted by the Sub-Regional Fisheries Commission' (2016) 29 LJIL 441.

Lang J, '*Le plateau continental de la mer du Nord: Arrêt de la Cour internationale de Justice* (Librairie générale de droit et de jurisprudence, 1970).

Langille B, 'It's "Instant Custom": How the Bush Doctrine Became Law After the Terrorist Attacks of September 11, 2001' (2003) 26 BC Intl & Comp L Rev 151.

Larsen PB, 'Arbitration of the United States-France Air Traffic Rights Dispute' (1964) 30 J Air L & Comm 231.

——— 'The United States-Italy Air Transport Arbitration: Problems of Treaty Interpretation and Enforcement' (1967) 61 AJIL 496.

Laursen A, *Changing International Law to Meet New Challenges: Interpretation, Modification and the Use of Force* (DJØF, 2006).

Lauterpacht E, 'The Development of the Law of International Organization by the Decisions of International Tribunals' (1976-IV) 152 RC 377.

——— 'The Waning of the Requirement of Consent' (1991) 85 ASIL Proc 38.

——— '"Partial Judgments" and the Inherent Jurisdiction of the International Court of Justice' in AV Lowe and M Fitzmaurice (eds), *Fifty Years of the International Court of Justice* (CUP, 1996) 477.

——— and D Bethlehem, 'The Scope and Content of the Principle of Non-Refoulement: Opinion' in E Feller, V Türk, and F Nicholson (eds), *Refugee Protection in International Law: UNHCR's Global Consultations on International Protection* (CUP, 2003) 87.

Lauterpacht H, 'Restrictive Interpretation and the Principle of Effectiveness in the Interpretation of Treaties' (1949) 26 BYBIL 48.

——— 'De l'interprétation des traités: Rapport' (1950-II) 43 AIDI 366.

Lavoyer J-P, 'The International Committee of the Red Cross: Legal Status and Headquarters Agreements' in D Fleck (ed), *The Handbook of the Law of Visiting Forces* (OUP, 2001) 471.

Laylin J, 'Emerging Customary Law of the Sea' (1976) 10 TIL 610.

League of Nations, *Protection of Linguistic, Racial and Religious Minorities by the League of Nations* (League of Nations Publications, IB Minorities, 1927).

Leca J, *Les techniques de révision des conventions internationales* (LGDJ, 1961).

Lepard BD, *Customary International Law: A New Theory with Practical Application* (CUP, 2010).

——— 'Customary International Law as a Dynamic Process' in CA Bradley (ed), *Custom's Future: International Law in a Changing World* (CUP, 2016) 62.

Letsas G, *A Theory of Interpretation of the European Convention on Human Rights* (2nd edn, OUP, 2009).
Levinson S, 'How Many Times Has the United States Constitution Been Amended? (A) <26; (B) 26; (C) 27; (D) >27: Accounting for Constitutional Change' in S Levinson (ed), *Responding to Imperfection: The Theory and Practice of Constitutional Amendment* (Princeton UP, 1995) 13.
Liang J, 'Modifying the UN Charter through Subsequent Practice: Prospects for the Charter's Revitalisation' (2012) 81 NJIL 1.
Liang YL, 'Abstention and Absence of a Permanent Member in Relation to the Voting Procedure in the Security Council' (1950) 44 AJIL 694.
Lillich RB, 'The Growing Importance of Customary International Human Rights Law' (1995–96) 25 Ga J Intl & Comp L 1.
Linderfalk U, 'Is the Hierarchical Structure of Articles 31 and 32 of the Vienna Convention Real or Not? Interpreting the Rules of Interpretation' (2007) 54 NILR 133.
——— *On the Interpretation of Treaties: The Modern International Law as Expressed in the 1969 Vienna Convention on the Law of Treaties* (Springer, 2007).
——— 'Doing the Right Thing for the Right Reason—Why Dynamic or Static Approaches Should be Taken in the Interpretation of Treaties' (2008) 10 ICL Rev 109.
——— 'The Application of International Legal Norms Over Time: The Second Branch of Intertemporal Law' (2011) 58 NILR 147.
——— 'The Creation of *Jus Cogens*: Making Sense of Article 53 of the Vienna Convention' (2011) 71 ZaöRV 359.
Linton S and FK Tiba, 'The International Judge in an Age of Multiple International Courts and Tribunals' (2009) 9 Chi J Intl L 407.
Long O, *Law and Its Limitations in the GATT Multilateral Trade System* (Martinus Nijhoff, 1985).
Lowe AV, 'The Politics of Law-Making: Are the Method and Character of Norm Creation Changing?' in M Byers (ed), *The Role of Law in International Politics* (OUP, 2000) 207.
——— *International Law* (OUP, 2007).
Lowenfeld AF and AI Mendelsohn, 'The United States and the Warsaw Convention' (1967) 80 Harv L Rev 497.
Luck EC, *UN Security Council: Practice and Promise* (Routledge, 2006).
Lutz DS, *Toward a Theory of Constitutional Amendment* (1994) 88 Am Pol Sci Rev 355.
Lyall F, 'On the Privatization of INTELSAT' (2001) 5 Sing JICL 111.
MacGibbon IC, 'The Scope of Acquiescence in International Law' (1954) 31 BYBIL 143.
——— 'Customary International Law and Acquiescence' (1957) 33 BYBIL 115.
Makarczyk J, 'The International Court of Justice on the Implied Powers of International Organizations' in J Makarczyk (ed), *Essays in International Law in Honour of Judge Manfred Lachs* (Martinus Nijhoff, 1984) 501.
Manusama KM, *The United Nations Security Council in the Post-Cold War Era: Applying the Principle of Legality* (*Legal Aspects of International Organization*) (Martinus Nijhoff, 2006).
Marceau G, 'WTO Dispute Settlement and Human Rights' (2002) 13 EJIL 753.
Marques Antunes NS, 'Acquiescence' in R Wolfrum (ed), *Max Planck Encyclopedia of Public International Law* (OUP, 2009) 1.
Martin A, *L'estoppel en droit international public* (Pédone, 1979).
Massarella C, 'UN Security Council Resolution 1976 (2011) and Efforts to Support Piracy Prosecutions' (2011) 26 IJMCL 679.
Matiation S, 'Arbitration with Two Twists: Loewen v United States and Free Trade Commission Intervention in NAFTA Chapter 11 Disputes' (2003) 24 U Pa J Intl Econ L 451.

Matsushita M, TJ Schoenbaum, and P Mavroidis, *The World Trade Organization: Law, Practice, and Policy* (2nd edn, OUP, 2006).

Matz-Lück N, 'Norm Interpretation across International Regimes: Competences and Legitimacy' in MA Young (ed), *Regime Interaction in International Law: Facing Fragmentation* (CUP, 2012) 201.

McClane JB, 'How Late in the Emergence of a Norm of Customary International Law May a Persistent Objector Object?' (1989) 13 ILSA JIL 1.

McDade P, 'The Removal of Offshore Installations and Conflicting Treaty Obligations as a Result of the Emergence of the New Law of the Sea: A Case Study' (1987) 24 San Diego L Rev 645.

McDougal MS and RN Gardner, 'The Veto and the Charter: An Interpretation for Survival' (1951) 60 Yale LJ 258.

——— 'The Hydrogen Bomb Tests and the International Law of the Sea' (1955) 49 AJIL 356.

——— 'A Footnote' (1963) 57 AJIL 383.

——— 'The International Law Commission's Draft Articles upon Interpretation: Textuality Redivivus' (1967) 61 AJIL 992.

——— and others, *The Interpretation of Agreements and World Public Order* (Yale UP, 1980).

——— and M Reisman, 'The Prescribing Function in World Constitutive Process: How International Law is Made' (1980) 6 Yale Stud W Pub Ord 249.

———, HHD Lasswell, and JC Miller, *The Interpretation of International Agreements and World Public Order: Principles of Content and Procedure* (Martinus Nijhoff, 1994).

McGinley G, 'Practice as a Guide to Treaty Interpretation' (1985) 9 *The Fletcher Forum of World Affairs* 211.

McGregor S, 'Somali Pirates' Kenya Trial Postponed Until October (Update 1)' (*Bloomberg*, 7 August 2009).

McLachlan C, 'The Principle of Systemic Integration and Article 31(3)(c) of the Vienna Convention' (2005) 54 ICLQ 279.

——— 'The Evolution of Treaty Obligations in International Law' in G Nolte (ed), *Treaties and Subsequent Practice* (OUP, 2013) 69.

McNair AD, 'The Functions and Differing Legal Character of Treaties' (1930) 11 BYBIL 100.

——— 'The Legality of the Occupation of Ruhr' (1924) 5 BYBIL 17.

——— *The Law of Treaties* (Clarendon Press, 1961).

McRae D, 'Treaty Interpretation by the WTO Appellate Body: The Conundrum of Article 17(6) of the WTO Antidumping Agreement' in E Cannizzaro (ed), *The Law of Treaties Beyond the Vienna Convention* (OUP, 2011) 164.

Mechlem K, 'Treaty Bodies and the Interpretation of Human Rights' (2009) 42 Vand JIL 905.

Meijers H, 'How Is International Law Made? The Stages of Growth of International Law and the Use of its Customary Rules' (1978) 9 NYBIL 3.

——— 'On International Customary Law in the Netherlands' in IF Dekker and HHG Post (eds), *On the Foundations and Sources of International Law* (Asser Press, 2003) 77.

Melzer N, 'The ICRC's Clarification Process on the Notion of Direct Participation in Hostilities under International Humanitarian Law' (2008) <www.oas.org/dil/esp/XXXVI_curso_The_ICRC_Clarification_Process_Nils_Melzer.pdf> accessed 28 June 2016.

Mendelson MH, 'State Acts and Omissions as Explicit or Implicit Claims' in *Le droit international au service de la paix, de la justice et du développement: Mélanges Michel Virally* (Pédone, 1991) 373.

——— 'The Subjective Element in Customary International Law' (1995) 66 BYBIL 177.

——— 'The Formation of Customary International Law' (1998) 272 RC 155.

Merkouris P, 'Article 31(3)(c) of the VCLT and the Principle of Systemic Integration' (PhD, Queen Mary University of London, 2010).

——— 'Introduction: Interpretation is a Science, is an Art, is a Science' in M Fitzmaurice, O Elias, and P Merkouris (eds), *Treaty Interpretation and the Vienna Convention on the Law of Treaties: 30 Years On* (Martinus Nijhoff, 2010) 1.

Meron T, *The Making of International Criminal Justice: A View from the Bench: Selected Speeches* (OUP, 2011).

Merrills JG, 'Land and Maritime Boundary between Cameroon and Nigeria (Cameroon v Nigeria, Equtorial Guinea Intervening), Merits, Judgment of October 10, 2002' (2003) 52 ICLQ 788.

Michaels R and J Pauwelyn, 'Conflict of Norms or Conflict of Laws? Different Techniques in the Fragmentation of Public International Law' in T Broude and Y Shany (eds), *Multi-Sourced Equivalent Norms in International Law* (Hart, 2011) 19.

Middelburg A, *Piracy in a Legal Context: Prosecution of Pirates Operating off the Somali Coast* (Wolf Legal Nijmegen, 2011) 55.

Milanovic M, 'The ICJ and Evolutionary Treaty Interpretation' (*EJIL: Talk!*, 14 July 2009) <www.ejiltalk.org/the-icj-and-evolutionary-treaty-interpretation> accessed 24 June 2016.

——— 'A Few Thougts on Hassan v. United Kingdom' (*EJIL: Talk!*, 22 October 2014) <www.ejiltalk.org/a-few-thoughts-on-hassan-v-united-kingdom/> accessed 26 May 2017.

Modeen T, *The International Protection of Minorities in Europe* (Åbo Akademi, 1969).

Moeckli D and others (eds), *International Human Rights Law* (2nd edn, OUP, 2014).

Moloo R, 'When Actions Speak Louder Than Words: The Relevance of Subsequent Party Conduct to Treaty Interpretation' (2013) 31 Berkeley JIL 39.

Monaco R and C Curti Gialdino, *Manuale di diritto internazionale pubblico* (3rd edn, UTET, 2009).

Moore JN, 'Treaty Interpretation, the Constitution, and the Rule of Law' (2001) 42 VJIL 163.

Morgan D, 'U.S. Delivers Seven Somali Pirate Suspects to Kenya' (*Reuters*, 5 March 2009) <www.reuters.com/article/worldNews/idUSTRE52480N20090305> accessed 9 June 2017.

Morgenstern F, *Legal Problems of International Organizations* (CUP, 1986).

Mortenson JD, 'The Meaning of "Investment": ICSID's *Travaux* and the Domain of International Investment Law' (2001) 51 Harv ILJ 257.

Mosler H, 'The International Society as a Legal Community' (1974) 140 RC 234.

Moussalli M, 'The Evolving Functions of the Office of the High Commissioner for Refugees' in V Gowlland and K Samson (eds), *Problems and Prospects of Refugee Law* (The Graduate Institute of International Studies, 1992) 81.

Mowbray A, 'The Creativity of the European Court of Human Rights' (2005) 5 HRL Rev 57.

Müller J (ed), *Reforming the United Nations: The Struggle for Legitimacy and Effectiveness* (Martinus Nijhoff, 2006).

Müller JP, *Vertrauensschutz im Völkerrecht* (Heymann, 1971).

Müller JP and T Cottier, 'Acquiescence' in R Bernhardt (ed), *Encyclopedia of Public International Law*, vol VII (North Holland, 1984).

Müllerson R, 'The Interplay of Objective and Subjective Elements in Customary Law' in K Wellens (ed), *International Law: Theory and Practice. Essays in Honour of Eric Suy* (Martinus Nijhoff, 1998) 161.

Murphy SD, 'The Relevance of Subsequent Agreements and Subsequent Practice for the Interpretation of Treaties' in G Nolte (ed), *Treaties and Subsequent Practice* (OUP, 2013) 82.

Mus JB, 'Conflicts between Treaties in International Law' (1998) 45 NILR 208.

Nastase A, 'The Role of Interpretation in the Application of Treaties' (1989) 33 *Revue Roumaine* 49.

Nasu H, *International Law on Peacekeeping: A Study of Article 40 of the UN Charter* (Martinus Nijhoff, 2009).

Nelson LDM, 'The New Deep Sea-Bed Mining Regime' (1995) 10 IJMCL 189.

——— 'Declarations, Statements and "Disguised Reservations" with Respect to the Convention on the Law of the Sea' (2001) 50 ICLQ 767.

Neuman G, 'Import, Export, and Regional Consent in the Inter-American Court of Human Rights' (2008) 19 EJIL 101.

Newcombe A and L Paradell, *Law and Practice of Investment Treaties: Standards of Treatment* (Kluwer Law International, 2009).

Nollkaemper A, 'Inside or Out: Two Types of International Legal Pluralism' in J Klabbers and T Piiparinen (eds), *Normative Pluralism and International Law: Exploring Global Governance* (CUP, 2013) 94.

——— 'Intervention in Syria and International Law: Inside or Out?' (*Opinio Juris*, 1 September 2013) <http://opiniojuris.org/2013/09/01/syria-insta-symposium-andre-nollkaemper-intervention-syria-international-law-inside/> accessed 5 April 2017.

Nolte G, 'The "New Tasks" of NATO and WEU: International Law and German Constitutional Law Aspects' (1994) 54 ZaöRV 122.

——— and HP Aust, 'Equivocal Helpers—Complicit States, Mixed Messages and International Law' (2009) 58 ICLQ 1.

——— 'Between Contemporaneous and Evolutive Interpretation: The Use of "Subsequent Practice" in the Judgment of the International Court of Justice Concerning the Case of Costa Rica v. Nicaragua (2009)' in HP Hestermeyer and others (eds), *Coexistence, Cooperation and Solidarity*, vol II (Martinus Nijhoff, 2011) 1675.

——— 'Subsequent Practice as a Means of Interpretation in the Jurisprudence of the WTO Appellate Body' in E Cannizzaro (ed), *The Law of Treaties Beyond the Vienna Convention* (OUP, 2011) 138.

——— 'Introductory Report for the ILC Study Group on Treaties over Time: Jurisprudence of the International Court of Justice and Arbitral Tribunals of Ad Hoc Jurisdiction Relating to Subsequent Agreements and Subsequent Practice' in G Nolte (ed), *Treaties and Subsequent Practice* (OUP, 2013) 169.

——— 'Second Report for the ILC Study Group on Treaties over Time: Jurisprudence Under Special Regimes Relating to Subsequent Agreements and Subsequent Practice' in G Nolte (ed), *Treaties and Subsequent Practice* (OUP, 2013) 210.

——— 'Third Report for the ILC Study Group on Treaties over Time: Subsequent Agreements and Subsequent Practice of States Outside of Judicial or Quasi-Judicial Proceedings' in G Nolte (ed), *Treaties and Subsequent Practice* (OUP, 2013) 307.

Nordquist MH (ed), *United Nations Convention on the Law of the Sea 1982: A Commentary*, vol III (Martinus Nijhoff, 2005).

Nottage H and T Sebastian, 'Giving Legal Effect to the Results of WTO Trade Negotiations: An Analysis of the Methods of Changing WTO Law' (2006) 9 J Intl Econ L 989.

O'Connell DP, *International Law*, vol I (2nd edn, Stevens and Sons, 1970).

——— 'Reflections on the State Succession Convention' (1979) 39 ZaöRV 725.

——— *The International Law of the Sea*, vol I (Clarendon Press, 1982).

O'Connell ME, '*Jus Cogens*: International Law's Higher Ethical Norms' in DE Childress III (ed), *The Role of Ethics in International Law* (CUP, 2012) 13.

Odendahl K, 'Article 39' in O Dörr and K Schmalenbach (eds), *Vienna Convention on the Law of Treaties: A Commentary* (Springer, 2012) 699.

Oellers-Frahm K, 'The Evolving Role of Treaties in International Law' in R Miller and R Bratspies (eds), *Progress in International Law* (Martinus Nijhoff, 2008) 173.
Oppenheim L, *International Law: A Treatise*, E Lauterpacht (ed), vol I (Peace) (8th edn, Longmans, Green & Co, 1955).
Orakhelashvili A, *Peremptory Norms in International Law* (OUP, 2006).
——— *The Interpretation of Acts and Rules in Public International Law* (OUP, 2008).
Orrego Vicuña F, *International Dispute Settlement in an Evolving Global Society: Constitutionalization, Accessibility, Privatization* (CUP, 2004).
——— 'In Memory of Triepel and Anzilotti: The Use and Abuse of Non-Conventional Lawmaking' in R Wolfrum and V Röben (eds), *Developments of International Law in Treaty Making* (Springer, 2005) 497.
Osieke E, *Constitutional Law and Practice in the International Labour Organisation* (Martinus Nijhoff, 1985).
Oude Elferink AG, 'Current Legal Developments: Meeting of States Parties to the UN Law of the Sea Convention' (2008) 23 IJMCL 769.
——— ' "Openness" and Article 76 of the Law of the Sea Convention: The Process Does Not Need to Be Adjusted' (2009) 40 ODIL 36.
——— *The Law of Maritime Boundary Delimitation: A Case Study of the Russian Federation* (Martinus Nijhoff, 1994).
Oxman BH, 'Human Rights and the United Nations Convention on the Law of the Sea' (1998) 36 Colum J Transnat'l L 399.
——— 'Tools for Change: The Amendment Procedure' in *Proceedings of the Twentieth Anniversary Commemoration of the Opening for Signature of the UNCLOS* (United Nations, 2003) 195.
Paasivirta E and PJ Kuijper, 'Does One Size Fit All? The European Community and the Responsibility of International Organizations' (2005) 36 NYBIL 169.
Pan E, 'Authoritative Interpretation of Agreements: Developing More Responsive International Administrative Regimes' (1997) 38 Harv ILJ 519.
Paparinskis M, 'Investment Treaty Interpretation and Customary Law: Preliminary Remarks' in C Brown and K Miles (eds), *Evolution in International Investment Treaty Law and Arbitration* (CUP, 2011) 65.
——— 'Sources of Law and Arbitral Interpretations of *Pari Materia* Investment Protection Rules' in OK Fauchald and A Nollkaemper (eds), *The Practice of International and Nationals Courts and the (De-)Fragmentation of International Law* (Hart, 2012) 87.
——— 'Investment Treaty Arbitration and the (New) Law of State Responsibility' (2013) 24 EJIL 617.
——— *The International Minimum Standard and Fair and Equitable Treatment* (OUP, 2013).
Papastavridis E, 'Piracy Off Somalia: The "Emperors and the Thieves of the Oceans" in the 21st Century' in A Abass (ed), *Protecting Human Security in Africa* (OUP, 2010) 122.
——— *The Interception of Vessels on the High Seas: Contemporary Challenges to the Legal Order of the Oceans* (Hart, 2013).
Parry C, 'The Practice of States' (1958) 44 TGS 145.
Paust J, 'The Reality of *Jus Cogens*' (1991) 7 Conn JIL 81.
Pauwelyn J, 'The Role of Public International Law in the WTO: How Far Can We Go?' (2001) 95 AJIL 535.
——— *Conflict of Norms in Public International Law: How WTO Law Relates to Other Rules of International Law* (CUP, 2003).
——— 'How to Win a WTO Dispute Based on Non-WTO Law' (2003) 37 JWT 997.
——— and M Elsig, 'The Politics of Treaty Interpretation: Variations and Explanations across International Tribunals' in JL Dunoff and MA Pollack (eds), *Interdisciplinary*

Perspectives on International Law and International Relations: The State of the Art (CUP, 2012) 445.
———, RA Wessel, and J Wouters, 'Informal International Lawmaking: An Assessment and Template to Keep It Both Effective and Accountable' in J Pauwelyn, RA Wessel, and J Wouters (eds), *Informal International Lawmaking* (OUP, 2012) 500.
Payandeh M, 'With Great Power Comes Great Responsibility? The Concept of Responsibility to Protect Within the Process of International Lawmaking' (2010) 35 Yale JIL 469.
——— 'The United Nations, Military Intervention, and Regime Change in Libya' (2012) 52 VJIL 355.
Pearce J, 'Customary International Law: Not Merely Fiction or Myth' (2003) Aust ILJ 125.
Pellet A, 'Article 38' in A Zimmermann, C Tomuschat, and K Oellers-Frahm (eds), *Statute of the International Court of Justice: A Commentary* (2nd edn, OUP, 2012) 812.
Perluss D and JF Hartman, *Temporary Refuge: Emergence of a Customary Norm* (1986) 26 VJIL 551.
Peters C, 'Subsequent Practice and Established Practice of International Organizations: Two Sides of the Same Coin?' (2011) 3 GoJIL 617.
Petersen N, 'Customary Law Without Custom? Rules, Principles, and the Role of State Practice in International Norm Creation' (2008) 23 Am U Intl L Rev 275.
Petersmann E-U, 'The Dispute Settlement System of the World Trade Organization and the Evolution of the GATT Dispute Settlement System since 1948' (1994) 31 CMLR 1157.
Philp C, 'Captured Somali Pirates Are Being Dumped in Kenya, Officials Say' (*The Times (London)*, 12 June 2009) 41.
Picard L, 'La pratique comme fondement de l'action du Bureau International du Travail' in Société française pour le droit international, Colloque de Genève, *La pratique et le droit international* (Pédone, 2004) 209.
Pictet JS (ed), *Geneva Convention relative to the Treatment of Prisoners of War: Commentary* (ICRC, 1960).
Pineau E, 'France Asks Seychelles to Help with Pirate Trials' (*Reuters*, 18 October 2009) <www.reuters.com/article/2009/10/18/idUSLI622681> accessed 9 June 2017.
Plender R, 'The Role of Consent in the Termination of Treaties' (1986) 57 BYBIL 133.
Pocar F, 'Some Remarks on the Continuity of Human Rights and International Humanitarian Law Treaties' in E Cannizzaro (ed), *The Law of Treaties Beyond the Vienna Convention* (OUP, 2011) 279.
Prescott JRV, 'Straight and Archipelagic Baselines' in G Blake (ed), *Maritime Boundaries and Ocean Resources* (Croom Helm, 1987) 38.
Prieur M and G Sozzo, *La non régression en droit de l'environnement* (Bruylant, 2012).
Prost M, *The Concept of Unity in Public International Law* (Bloomsbury, 2012).
Puckett J, 'The Basel Ban: A Triumph over Business-as-Usual' (Basel Action Network, 1997) <http://wiki.ban.org/The_Basel_Ban:_A_Triumph_Over_Business-As-Usual> accessed 3 September 2014.
Qin JY, 'The Conundrum of WTO Accession Protocols: In Search of Legality and Legitimacy' (2015) 55 VJIL 369.
Qureshi AH and Ziegler AR, *International Economic Law* (2nd edn, Sweet & Maxwell, 2007).
Ranganathan S, 'Between Philosophy and Anxiety? The Early International Law Commission, Treaty Conflict and the Project of International Law' (2013) 83 BYBIL 82.
Rao PC, 'Delimitation Disputes under the United Nations Convention on the Law of the Sea: Settlement Procedures' in TM Ndiaye and R Wolfrum (eds), *Law of the Sea, Environmental Law and Settlement of Disputes* (Martinus Nijhoff, 2007) 896.

Rauschning D, *The Vienna Convention on the Law of Treaties—Travaux Préparatoires* (Metzner, 1978).
Reichert-Facilides D, 'Down the Danube: The Vienna Convention on the Law of Treaties and the *Case Concerning the Gabčikov-Nagymaros Project*' (1998) 47 ICLQ 837.
Reisman WM, 'The Constitutional Crisis in the United Nations' (1993) 87 AJIL 83.
——— 'Report, Tenth Commission: Present Problems of the Use of Armed Force in International Law, Sub-group on Humanitarian Intervention' (2007) 72 AIDI 237.
Ress G, 'The Interpretation of the Charter' in B Simma (ed), *The Charter of the United Nations: A Commentary*, vol I (2nd edn, OUP, 2002) 13.
Reuter P, *Introduction au droit des traités* (Armand Colin, 1972).
——— *Introduction to the Law of Treaties* (2nd edn, Kegan Paul International, 1995).
Riedel E, 'Standards and Sources: Farewell to the Exclusivity of the Sources Triad in International Law?' (1991) 2 EJIL 58.
Rigaux A and D Simon, 'Article 41 (1969)' in O Corten and P Klein (eds), *The Vienna Conventions on the Law of Treaties: A Commentary* (OUP, 2011) 986.
Ringsmose J and S Rynning (eds), *NATO's New Strategic Concept: A Comprehensive Assessment* (Danish Institute for International Studies, 2011).
Roach JA and RW Smith, *US Responses to Excessive Maritime Claims* (2nd edn, Martinus Nijhoff, 1996).
——— 'Countering Piracy off Somalia: International Law and International Institutions' (2010) 104 AJIL 397.
Roberts AE, 'Traditional and Modern Approaches to Customary International Law: A Reconciliation' (2001) 95 AJIL 757.
——— 'Power and Persuasion in Investment Treaty Interpretation: The Dual Role of States' (2010) 104 AJIL 179.
——— 'Subsequent Agreements and Practice: The Battle over Interpretive Power' in G Nolte (ed), *Treaties and Subsequent Practice* (OUP, 2013) 95.
Robinson J, 'Metamorphosis of the United Nations' (1958-II) 94 RC 493.
Rodley N, 'The Role and Impact of Treaty Bodies' in D Shelton (ed), *The Oxford Handbook of International Human Rights Law* (OUP, 2013) 621.
Roessler F, 'The Competence of GATT' (1987) 21 JWTL 73.
Rosand E, 'The Security Council as "Global Legislator": Ultra Vires or Ultra Innovative?' (2005) 28 Fordham ILJ 542.
Rosenne S, 'On Multi-Lingual Interpretation' (1971) 6 Isr L Rev 360.
——— *Practice and Methods of International Law* (Oceana Publications, 1984).
——— *Breach of Treaty* (Grotius Publications, 1985).
——— *Developments in the Law of Treaties 1945–1986* (CUP, 1989).
——— *The Law and Practice of the International Court, 1920–1996* (3rd edn, Martinus Nijhoff, 1997).
——— 'The International Maritime Organization Interface with the Law of the Sea Convention' in MH Nordquist and JN Moore (eds), *Current Maritime Issues and the International Maritime Organization* (Martinus Nijhoff, 1999) 260.
——— 'Treaties, Conclusion and Entry into Force' in R Bernhardt (ed), *Encyclopaedia of Public International Law*, vol IV (North Holland, 2000) 933.
Rosting H, 'Protection of Minorities by the League of Nations' (1923) 17 AJIL 641.
Rothwell DR, 'The Impact of State Practice on the Jurisdictional Framework Contained in the LOS Convention: A Commentary' in AG Oude Elferink (ed), *Stability and Change in the Law of the Sea: The Role of the LOS Convention* (Martinus Nijhoff, 2005) 145.

Rousseau C, 'De la compatibilité des normes juridiques contradictoires dans l'ordre international' (1932) 39 RGDIP 133.

——— *Droit international public, Tome I: Introduction et sources* (Dalloz, 1970).

Rouyer-Hameray B, *Les compétences implicites des organisations internationales* (LGDJ, 1962).

Rowe P (ed), *The Gulf War in International and English Law* (Sweet and Maxwell, 1993).

Ruiz Fabri H, 'Subsequent Practice, Domestic Separation of Powers, and Concerns of Legitimacy' in G Nolte (ed), *Treaties and Subsequent Practice* (OUP, 2013) 160.

Rushworth D, 'Mapping in Support of Frontier Arbitration: Delimitation and Demarcation' (1997) 5 IBRU Boundary and Security Bulletin 61.

Ruys, T, *The Intangible 'Armed Attack': Evolutions in Customary Practice Pertaining to the Right of States to Self-Defense and the Quest for a Definition of 'Armed Attack' under Article 51 UN Charter* (PhD, Catholic University of Leuven 2009).

——— *'Armed Attack' and Article 51 of the UN Charter: Evolutions in Customary Law and Practice* (CUP, 2011).

Sacerdoti G, 'The Dispute Settlement System of the WTO: Structure and Function in the Perspective of the First 10 Years' (2006) 5 LPICT 49.

Sadat-Akhavi SA, *Methods of Resolving Conflicts between Treaties* (Martinus Nijhoff, 2003).

Sagar D, 'Provisional Application in an International Organization' (1999) 27 J Space L 99.

Salerno F, 'Treaties Establishing Objective Regimes' in E Cannizzaro (ed), *The Law of Treaties Beyond the Vienna Convention* (OUP, 2011) 225.

Sandholtz W, *Prohibiting Plunder: How Norms Change* (OUP, 2007).

Sands P, *Principles of International Environmental Law: Framework, Standards and Implementation* (Manchester UP, 1995).

——— 'Treaty, Custom and the Cross-Fertilization of International Law' (1998) 1 Yale HR & Dev LJ 85.

——— and J Commission, 'Treaty, Custom and Time: Interpretation/Application?' in M Fitzmaurice, O Elias, and P Merkouris (eds), *Treaty Interpretation and the Vienna Convention on the Law of Treaties: 30 Years On* (Martinus Nijhoff, 2010) 39.

——— 'Article 39 (1969)' in O Corten and P Klein (eds), *The Vienna Conventions on the Law of Treaties: A Commentary*, vol I (OUP, 2011) 963.

Sarooshi D, 'The Legal Framework Governing United Nations Subsidiary Organs' (1996) 76 BYBIL 428.

Sato T, *Evolving Constitutions of International Organizations: A Critical Analysis of the Interpretive Frameworks of the Constituent Instruments of International Organizations* (Brill, 1996).

Scelle G, *Theorie juridique de la revision des traités* (Librairie du Recueil Sirey, 1936).

Schabas W, 'Customary Law or "Judge-Made" Law: Judicial Creativity at the UN Criminal Tribunals' in J Doria and others (eds), *The Legal Regime of the International Criminal Court: Essays in Honour of Professor Igor Blishchenko* (Martinus Nijhoff, 2009) 77.

Schachter O, 'The Twilight Existence of Nonbinding International Agreements' (1977) 71 AJIL 296.

——— 'The Right of States to Use Armed Force' (1984) 82 Mich L Rev 1620.

——— 'Entangled Treaty and Custom' in Y Dinstein and M Tabory (eds), *International Law at a Time of Perplexity: Essays in Honour of Shabtai Rosenne* (Martinus Nijhoff, 1989) 717.

——— 'New Custom: Power, *Opinio Juris* and Contrary Practice' in J Makarczyk (ed), *Theory of International Law at the Threshold of the 21st Century: Essays in Honour of Krzysztof Skubiszewski* (Kluwer Law International, 1996) 531.

Scharf M, 'Seizing the Grotian Moment: Accelerated Formation of Customary International Law in Times of Fundamental Change (2010) 43 Cornell ILJ 446.

Scheinin M, 'Human Rights Treaties and the Vienna Convention on the Law of Treaties-Conflicts or Harmony' in Vienna Commission (ed), *The Status of International Treaties on Human Rights* (Council of Europe Publishing, 2006) 43.
Schermers HG and NM Blokker, *International Institutional Law: Unity within Diversity* (Martinus Nijhoff, 2003).
Schlütter B, 'Aspects of Human Rights Interpretation by the UN Treaty Bodies' in H Keller and G Ulfstein (eds), *UN Human Rights Treaty Bodies: Law and Legitimacy* (CUP, 2012) 261.
Schmalenbach K, 'Art. 5 Treaties Constituting International Organizations and Treaties Adopted within an International Organization' in O Dörr and K Schmalenbach (eds), *Vienna Convention on the Law of Treaties: A Commentary* (Springer, 2012) 89.
Schreuer C, 'Diversity and Harmonization of Treaty Interpretation in Investment Arbitration' in Treaty, Custom and Time: Interpretation/Application?' in M Fitzmaurice, O Elias, and P Merkouris (eds), *Treaty Interpretation and the Vienna Convention on the Law of Treaties: 30 Years On* (Martinus Nijhoff, 2010) 129.
Schrijver N, 'The Future of the Charter of the United Nations' (2006) 10 Max Planck UNYB 1.
Schwarzenberger G, 'Myths and Realities of Treaty Interpretation: Articles 27–29 of the Vienna Draft Convention on the Law of Treaties' (1968) 9 VJIL 1.
——— *The Dynamics of International Law* (Professional Books, 1976).
Schwebel SM, 'The Influence of Bilateral Investment Treaties on Customary International Law' (2004) 98 ASIL Proc 27.
Schwelb E, 'The Amending Procedure of Constitutions of International Organizations' 49 (1954) 31 BYBIL 49.
——— 'Charter Review and Charter Revision—Recent Developments' (1958) 8 ICLQ 303.
——— 'Amendments to Articles 23, 27 and 61 of the Charter of the United Nations' (1965) 59 AJIL 834.
Scott GL and CL Carr, 'Multilateral Treaties and the Formation of Customary International Law' (1996) 25 Denver JIL & Policy 71.
Scovazzi T, 'The Evolution of International Law of the Sea: New Issues, New Challenges' (2000) 286 RC 39.
——— 'The Protection of Underwater Cultural Heritage: Article 303 and the UNESCO Convention' in D Freestone, R Barnes, and DM Ong (eds), *The Law of the Sea: Progress and Prospects* (OUP, 2006) 120.
Scully RT, 'Alternatives for Cooperation and Institutionalization in Antarctica: Outlook for the 1990s' in F Orrego Vicuña (ed), *Antarctic Resources Policy* (CUP, 1983) 281.
Sadurska R, 'Threats of Force' (1988) 82 AJIL 239.
Seiderman ID, *Hierarchy in International Law: The Human Rights Dimension* (Intersentia, 2001).
Serdy A, 'The Commission on the Limits of the Continental Shelf and its Disturbing Propensity to Legislate' (2011) 26 IJMCL 367.
Seyersted F, *Objective International Personality of Intergovernmental Organizations: Do Their Capacities Really Depend upon the Conventions Establishing Them?* (Krohns Bogtnykker, 1963).
Sharma SP, 'Treaties as a Source of International Law' (1979) 19 IJIL 500.
Shaw MN, 'Case concerning Kasikili/Sedudu Island (Botswana/Namibia)' (2000) 49 ICLQ 964.
——— 'Title, Control, and Closure? The Experience of the Eritrea-Ethiopia Boundary Commission' (2007) 56 ICLQ 755.
——— *International Law* (6th edn, CUP, 2008).

——— 'Self-Determination, Human Rights, and the Attribution of Territory' in U Fastenrath and others (eds), *From Bilateralism to Community Interest: Essays in Honour of Judge Bruno Simma* (OUP, 2011) 590.

Shelton D, 'The Legal Status of Normative Pronouncements of Human Rights Treaty Bodies' in H Hestermeyer and others (eds), *Coexistence, Cooperation and Solidarity: Liber Amicorum Rüdiger Wolfrum*, vol I (Martinus Nijhoff, 2012) 553.

Shihata I (ed), *The World Bank in a Changing World. Volume I* (Martinus Nijhoff, 1991).

——— *The World Bank in a Changing World. Volume III* (Martinus Nijhoff, 1999).

——— 'The Dynamic Evolution of International Organizations: The Case of the World Bank' (2000) 2 J Hist Intl L 217.

Simma B, 'Consent: Strains in the Treaty System' in RSJ MacDonald and DM Johnston (eds), *The Structure and Process of International Law: Essays in Legal Philosophy, Doctrine and Theory* (2nd edn, Martinus Nijhoff, 1986) 484.

——— and P Alston, 'The Sources of Human Rights Law: Custom, *Jus Cogens*, and General Principles' (1988–89) 12 Aust YBIL 83.

——— 'NATO, the UN and the Use of Force: Legal Aspects' (1999) 10 EJIL 1.

———, S Brunner, and H-P Kaul, 'Article 27' in B Simma (ed), *The Charter of the United Nations: A Commentary* (OUP, 2002) 476.

——— and CJ Tams, 'Article 60 (1969)' in O Corten and P Klein (eds), *The Vienna Conventions on the Law of Treaties: A Commentary* (OUP, 2011) 1350.

——— and CJ Tams, 'Reacting against Treaty Breaches' in DB Hollis (ed), *The Oxford Guide to Treaties* (OUP, 2012) 576.

——— 'Miscellaneous Thoughts on Subsequent Agreements and Practice' in G Nolte (ed), *Treaties and Subsequent Practice* (OUP, 2013) 46.

Simon D, *L'interpretation judiciaire des traités d'organisations internationals* (Pédone, 1981).

Sinclair I, *The Vienna Convention on the Law of Treaties* (2nd edn, Manchester UP, 1984).

——— 'Estoppel and Acquiescence' in V Lowe and M Fitzmaurice (eds), *Fifty Years of the International Court of Justice: Essays in Honour of Sir Robert Jennings* (CUP, 1996) 104.

Skourtos N St, 'Legal Effects for Parties and Nonparties: The Impact of the Law of the Sea Convention' in MH Nordquist and JN Moore (eds), *Entry into Force of the Law of the Sea Convention* (Kluwer, 1995) 187.

Skouteris T, 'The Force of a Doctrine: Art. 38 of the PCIJ Statute and the Sources of International Law' in F Johns, R Joyce, and S Pahuja (eds), *Events: The Force of International Law* (Routledge, 2011) 69.

Skubiszewski K, 'Implied Powers of International Organizations' in Y Dinstein (ed), *International Law at a Time of Perplexity: Essays in Honour of Shabtai Rosenne* (Martinus Nijhoff, 1989) 855.

Slaughter A-M, *A New World Order* (Princeton UP, 2004).

Slotboom MM, *Do Different Treaty Purposes Matter for Treaty Interpretation? A Comparison of WTO and EC Law*, Proefschrift (Cameron, 2005).

Snodgrass E, 'Protecting Investors' Legitimate Expectations: Recognizing and Delimiting a General Principle' (2006) 21 ICSID Rev 1.

Sohn LB, 'The Many Faces of International Law' (1963) 57 AJIL 868.

——— 'Settlement of Disputes relating to the Interpretation and Application of Treaties' (1976) 150 RC 195.

——— 'Unratified Treaties as a Source of Customary International Law' in A Bos and H Siblesz (eds), *Realism in Law-Making: Essays in International Law in Honour of Willem Riphagen* (Martinus Nijhoff, 1986) 231.

Sommer J, 'Environmental Law-Making by International Organizations' (1996) 56 ZaöRV 628.

Sorel M and V Boré Eveno, 'Article 31 (1969)' in O Corten and P Klein (eds), *The Vienna Conventions on the Law of Treaties: A Commentary*, vol I (OUP, 2011) 805.

Sørensen M, *Les sources du droit international: Étude sur la jurisprudence de la Cour Permanente de Justice Internationale* (Munksgaard, 1946).

——— 'Principes de Droit International Public' (1960-III) 101 RC 1.

——— 'Le problème dit du droit intertemporel dans l'ordre international' (1973) 55 AFDI 1.

Spiliopoulou Akermark A, *Justifications of Minority Protection in International Law* (Martinus Nijhoff, 1997).

Stavropoulos C, 'The Practice of Voluntary Abstentions by Permanent Members of the Security Council under Art. 27, paragraph 3 of the Charter of the United Nations' (1967) 61 AJIL 737.

Stein TL, 'The Approach of the Different Drummer: The Principle of the Persistent Objector in International Law' (1985) 26 Harv ILJ 467.

Stephens T, *International Courts and Environmental Protection* (CUP, 2009).

Stern B, 'Interpretation in International Trade Law' in Treaty, Custom and Time: Interpretation/Application?' in M Fitzmaurice, O Elias, and P Merkouris (eds), *Treaty Interpretation and the Vienna Convention on the Law of Treaties: 30 Years On* (Martinus Nijhoff, 2010) 111.

Stone J, 'Fictional Elements in Treaty Interpretation' (1955) 1 Syd L Rev 344.

Strauss DA, 'The Irrelevance of Constitutional Amendments' (2001) 114 Harv L Rev 1457.

Subedi P, 'The Doctrine of Objective Regimes in International Law and the Competence of the United Nations to Impose Territorial or Peace Settlements on States' (1994) 37 GYBIL 174.

Sur S, *L'interprétation en droit international public* (LGDJ, 1974).

Suy E, 'The Constitutional Character of Constituent Treaties of International Organizations and the Hierarchy of Norms' in R Bernhardt and others (eds), *Recht Zwischen Umbruch und Bewahrung: Festchrift für Rudolf Bernhardt* (Springer, 1995) 267.

Swart M, 'Judicial Lawmaking at the Ad Hoc Tribunals: The Creative Use of the Sources of International Law and "Adventurous Interpretation"' (2010) 70 ZaöRV 459.

Takei Y, *Filling Regulatory Gaps in High Seas Fisheries: Discrete High Seas Fish Stocks, Deep-sea Fisheries and Vulnerable Marine Ecosystems* (Brill, 2013).

Taki H, '*Opinio Juris* and the Formation of Customary International Law: A Theoretical Analysis' (2010) 51 GYBIL 447.

Tammelo I, *Treaty Interpretation and Practical Reason: Towards a General Theory of Legal Interpretation* (Law Book Co, 1967).

Tanaka Y, *A Dual Approach to Ocean Governance: The Cases of Zonal and Integrated Managent in International Law of the Sea* (Ashgate Surrey, 2008).

——— *The International Law of the Sea* (CUP, 2012).

Thirlway HWA, *International Customary Law and Codification: An Examination of the Continuing Role of Custom in the Present Period of Codification of International Law* (AW Sijthoff International Publishing, 1972).

——— 'The Law and Procedure of the International Court of Justice: 1960–80, Part One' (1989) 60 BYBIL 1.

——— 'The Law and Procedure of the International Court of Justice: 1960–1989, Part Three' (1991) 62 BYBIL 1.

——— *The Sources of International Law* (OUP, 2014).

Thomas JAC, 'Desuetudo' (1965) 12 RIDA 469.
Thornberry P, *International Law and the Rights of Minorities* (Clarendon Press, 1991).
Tobin HJ, 'The Role of the Great Powers in Treaty Revisions' (1934) 28 AJIL 487.
Tomka P, 'Custom and the International Court of Justice' (2013) 12 LPICT 195.
Tomuschat C, 'Obligations Arising for States Without or Against Their Will' (1993-IV) 241 RC 195.
——— 'Individuals' in J Crawford, A Pellet, and S Olleson (eds), *The Law of International Responsibility* (OUP, 2010) 985.
Toope S, 'Confronting Indeterminacy: Challenges to International Legal Theory' (1990) 19 Can Council Intl L Proc 209.
——— 'Formality and Informality' in D Bodansky, J Brunnée, and E Hey (eds), *The Oxford Handbook of International Environmental Law* (OUP, 2007) 107.
Torres Bernárdez S, 'Interpretation of Treaties by the International Court of Justice following the Adoption of the 1969 Vienna Convention on the Law of Treaties' in G Hafner and others (eds), *Liber Amicorum Professor Seidl-Hohenveldern in Honour of his 80th Birthday* (Kluwer Law International, 1998) 721.
Trachtman JP, 'The Domain of WTO Dispute Resolution' (1999) 40 Harv ILJ 333.
Treves T, 'Codification du droit international et pratique des États dans le droit de la mer' (1990-IV) 223 RC 9.
——— 'The General Assembly and the Meeting of States Parties in the Implementation of the LOS Convention' in AG Oude Elferink (ed), *Stability and Change in the Law of the Sea: The Role of the LOS Convention* (Martinus Nijhoff, 2005) 55.
——— 'Piracy, Law of the Sea, and Use of Force: Developments off the Coast of Somalia' (2009) 30 EJIL 399.
——— 'Human Rights and the Law of the Sea' (2010) 28 Berkeley JIL 1.
——— 'Customary International Law' in R Wolfrum (ed), *Max Planck Encyclopedia of Public International Law* (OUP, 2012).
——— 'Piracy and the International Law of the Sea' in D Guilfoyle (ed), *Modern Piracy: Legal Challenges and Responses* (Edward Elgar, 2013) 117.
Trevisanut S, 'L'Enlèvement et la gestion des plates-formes et installations offshore abandonnées ou désaffectées' in G Andreone, A Caligiuri, and G Cataldi (eds), *Law of the Sea and Environmental Emergencies* (Editoriale Scientifica, 2012) 193.
Tribe LH, 'Taking Text and Structure Seriously: Reflections on Free-Form Method in Constitutional Interpretation' (1995) 108 Harv L Rev 1221.
——— *American Constitutional Law* (3rd edn, Foundation Press, 2000).
Trouwborst A, 'Conserving European Biodiversity in a Changing Climate: The Bern Convention, the EU Birds and Habitats Directives and the Adaptation of Nature to Climate Change' (2011) 20 RECIEL 62.
——— 'Transboundary Wildlife Conservation in a Changing Climate: The Adaptation of the Bonn Convention on Migratory Species and its Daughter Instruments to Climate Change' (2012) 4 *Diversity* 258.
Tudor I, *The Fair and Equitable Treatment Standard in International Foreign Investment Law* (OUP, 2008).
Tulcer NT, 'The Definition of Norm Conflict in Public International Law: The Case of World Trade Organization Law' (2012) 9 Ankara L Rev 27.
Tunkin GI, 'Remarks on the Juridical Nature of Customary Norms of International Law' (1961) 49 CLR 419.
——— 'Is General International Law Customary Law Only?' (1993) 4 EJIL 534.
——— *Theory of International Law* (2nd rev edn, Wildy, Simmonds and Hill, 2003).

Tyagi M, 'Flesh on a Legal Fiction: Early Practice in the WTO on Accession Protocols' (2012) 15 J Intl Econ L 391.

Tzanakopulos A, 'Judicial Dialogue as a Means of Interpretation' in HP Aust and G Nolte (eds), *The Interpretation of International Law by Domestic Courts: Uniformity, Diversity, Convergence* (OUP, 2016) 72.

Ulfstein G, 'Treaty Bodies and Regimes' in DB Hollis (ed), *The Oxford Guide to Treaties* (OUP, 2012) 428.

United Nations, *The Blue Helmets: A Review of United Nations Peacekeeping* (United Nations Department of Public Information, 1985).

United States Embassy to Kenya, Press Release, Capture of Suspected Somali Pirates, 2 February 2006 <http://nairobi.usembassy.gov/pr_20060202.html>.

Vamvoukos A, *Termination of Treaties in International Law: The Doctrine of* Rebus Sic Stantibus *and Desuetude* (Clarendon Press, 1985) 325.

Van Damme I, *Treaty Interpretation by the WTO Appellate Body* (OUP, 2009).

Van Dyke J and C Yuen, '"Common Heritage" v "Freedom of the High Seas": Which Governs the Seabed?' (1982) 19 San Diego L Rev 493.

Van Hoof GJH, *Rethinking the Sources of International Law* (Kluwer, 1983).

Vandevelde KJ, 'Treaty Interpretation from a Negotiator's Perspective' (1988) 21 Vand JIL 281.

Venkata Raman K, 'Toward a General Theory of International Customary Law' in WM Reisman and BH Weston (eds), *Toward World Order and Human Dignity: Essays in Honor of MS McDougal* (Free Press, 1976) 365.

Venzke I, *How Interpretation Makes International Law: On Semantic Change and Normative Twists* (OUP, 2012).

Verdross A and B Simma, *Universelles Völkerrecht: Theorie und Praxis* (3rd edn, Duncker & Humblot, 1984).

Vermeer-Künzli A, 'The Merits of Reasonable Flexibility: The Contribution of the Law of Treaties to Peace' in G Nolte (ed), *Peace through International Law: The Role of the International Law Commission. A Colloquium at the Occasion of its Sixtieth Anniversary* (Springer, 2009) 67.

Verschuuren JM, 'Ramsar Soft Law is Not Soft at All: Discussion of the 2007 Decision by the Netherlands Crown on the Lac Ramsar Site on the Island of Bonaire' (2008) 35 *Milieu en Recht* 28.

Villiger ME, *Customary International Law and Treaties: A Study of Their Interactions and Interrelations, with Special Consideration of the 1969 Vienna Convention on the Law of Treaties* (Brill, 1985).

——— *Customary International Law and Treaties: A Manual on the Theory and Practice of the Interrelation of Sources* (2nd rev edn, Kluwer Law International, 1997).

——— *Commentary on the 1969 Vienna Convention on the Law of Treaties* (Martinus Nijhoff, 2009).

——— 'The Rules on Interpretation: Misgivings, Misunderstandings, Miscarriage? The "Crucible" Intended by the International Law Commission' in E Cannizzaro (ed), *The Law of Treaties Beyond the Vienna Convention* (OUP, 2011) 105.

Voicu I, *De l'interprétation authentique des traités internationaux* (Pédone, 1968).

Vranes E, 'The Definition of "Norm Conflict" in International Law and Legal Theory' (2006) 17 EJIL 395.

Vranken J, 'Exciting Times for Legal Scholarship' (2012) 2 *Recht en Methode in Onderzoek en Onderwijs* 42.

Vukas B, 'Generally Accepted International Rules and Standards' in AHA Soons (ed), *Implementation of the Law of the Sea Convention through International Institutions* (The Law of the Sea Institute, 1990) 405.

Wagner E, 'Submarine Cables and Protections Provided by the Law of the Sea' (1995) 19 *Marine Policy* 127.

Waibel M, 'International Investment Law and Treaty Interpretation' in R Hofmann and CJ Tams (eds), *International Investment Law and General International Law: From Clinical Isolation to Systemic Integration?* (Nomos, 2011) 29.

Wallace RMM and O Martin-Ortega, *International Law* (6th edn, Sweet & Maxwell, 2009).

Watson A, *The Evolution of Law* (Blackwell, 1985).

Weckel P, 'Chronique de jurisprudence internationale, Cour permanente d'arbitrage, Commission du tracé de la frontière Erythrée-Ethiopie' (2002) 106 RGDIP 696.

Weeramantry RJ, *Treaty Interpretation in Investment Arbitration* (OUP, 2012).

Weil P, 'Le droit international en quête de son identité: cours général de droit international public' (1992) 237 RC 129.

Weiler JHH, 'Discussion' in A Cassese and JHH Weiler (eds), *Change and Stability in International Law-Making* (W de Gruyter, 1988) 8.

——— 'The Interpretation of Treaties—A Re-examination' (2010) 21 EJIL 507.

Weiler T, 'NAFTA Investment Arbitration and the Growth of International Economic Law' (2002) 36 CBLJ 405.

Weisburd AM, 'Customary International Law: The Problem of Treaties' (1988) 21 Vand J Transn'l L 1.

——— 'The International Court of Justice and the Concept of State Practice' (2009) 31 U Penn J Intl L 295.

Wessel J, 'Relational Contract Theory and Treaty Interpretation: End-Game Treaties v Dynamic Obligations' (2004) 60 NYU Ann Surv Am L 149.

White ND, 'The UN Charter and Peacekeeping Forces: Constitutional Issues' (1996) 3 *International Peacekeeping* 43.

——— *Keeping the Peace: The United Nations and the Maintenance of International Peace and Security* (2nd edn, Manchester UP, 1997).

——— *The Law of International Organisations* (2nd edn, Manchester UP, 2005).

White RCA, 'Fishing Rights of Non-Member States in Community Waters' (1981) 6 ELR 398.

Wiersma A, 'The New International Law-Makers? Conference of the Parties to Multilateral Environmental Agreements' (2009) 31 MJIL 231.

Winkler IT, *Human Right to Water: Significance, Legal Status, and Implications for Water Allocation* (Hart, 2014).

Wolfke K, *Custom in Present International Law* (Martinus Nijhoff, 1993).

——— 'Some Persistent Controversies regarding Customary International Law' (1993) 24 NYBIL 1.

——— 'Some Reflections on Kinds of Rules and International Law-Making by Practice' in J Makarczyk (ed), *Theory of International Law at the Threshold of the 21st Century: Essays in Honour of Krzysztof Skubiszewski* (Kluwer Law International, 1996) 588.

——— 'Treaties and Custom: Aspects of Interrelation' in J Klabbers and R Lefeber (eds), *Essays on the Law of Treaties: A Collection of Essays in Honour of Bert Vierdag* (Martinus Nijhoff, 1998) 31.

Wolfrum R and V Röben (eds), *The Development of International Law in Treaty Making* (Springer, 2005).

——— and N Matz, *Conflicts in International Environmental Law* (Springer, 2010).

Wood M, 'United Nations, Security Council' in R Wolfrum (ed), *Max Planck Encyclopedia of Public International Law* (OUP, 2007).

——— 'The Law of Treaties and the UN Security Council: Some Reflections' in E Cannizzaro (ed), *The Law of Treaties Beyond the Vienna Convention* (OUP, 2011) 244.

Worster WT, 'The Transformation of Quantity into Quality: Critical Mass in the Formation of Customary International Law' (2013) 31 BU Intl LJ 1.

Wouters J and C Ryngaert, 'Impact on the Process of Formation of Customary International Law' in MT Kamminga and M Scheinin (eds), *The Impact of Human Rights Law on General International Law* (OUP, 2009) 111.

——— and P De Man, 'International Organizations as Law-Makers' in J Klabbers and A Wallendahl (eds), *Research Handbook on the Law of International Organizations* (Edward Elgar, 2011) 190.

Wright Q, 'Conflict between International Law and Treaties' (1917) 11 AJIL 566.

Wuerth I, 'Treaty Interpretation, Subsequent Agreements and Practice, and Domestic Constitutions' in G Nolte (ed), *Treaties and Subsequent Practice* (OUP, 2013) 154.

Yambrusic ES, *Treaty Interpretation: Theory and Reality* (UP of America, 1987).

Yamin F and J Depledge, *The International Climate Change Regime: A Guide to Rules, Institutions and Procedures* (CUP, 2004).

Yasseen MK, 'L'interprétation des traités d'après la Convention de Vienne sur le droit des traités' (1976-III) 151 RC 1.

Yost DS, *NATO Transformed: The Alliance's New Roles in International Security* (United States Institute for Peace Press, 1998).

Young MA, *Trading Fish, Saving Fish: The Interaction between Regimes in International Law* (CUP, 2011).

——— 'Regime Interaction in Creating, Implementing and Enforcing International Law' in MA Young (ed), *Regime Interaction in International Law: Facing Fragmentation* (CUP, 2012) 85.

Young OR, *International Cooperation: Building Regimes for Natural Resources and the Environment* (Cornell UP, 1989).

——— 'Commentary on Shirley V Scott "The LOSV Convention as a Constitutional Regime for the Oceans"' in AG Oude Elferink (ed), *Stability and Change in the Law of the Sea: The Role of the LOS Convention* (Martinus Nijhoff, 2005) 39.

Zacklin R, *The Amendment of the Constitutive Instruments of the United Nations and Specialized Agencies* (Sijthoff, 1968).

Zemanek K, 'What Is "State Practice" and Who Makes It?' in U Beyerlin and others (eds), *Recht zwischen Umbruch und Bewahrung: Völkerrecht, Europarecht, Staatsrecht—Festschrift für Rudolf Bernhardt* (Springer, 1995) 289.

——— 'The Metamorphosis of *Jus Cogens*: From an Institution of Treaty Law to the Bedrock of the International Legal Order' in E Cannizzaro (ed), *The Law of Treaties Beyond the Vienna Convention* (OUP, 2011) 381.

Ziegler AR, *International Economic Law* (2nd edn, Sweet & Maxwell, 2007).

Zoller E, 'The "Corporate Will" of the United Nations and the Rights of the Minority' (1987) 81 AJIL 610.

Index

Blast Cleaning Technology

A. Momber

Blast Cleaning Technology

With 385 Figures and 169 Tables

Springer

Andreas Momber
Privatdozent Dr.-Ing. habil.
Hamburg
Germany

ISBN: 978-3-642-09280-0 e-ISBN: 978-3-540-73645-5

Cover design: eStudio Calamar, Girona, Spain

Printed on acid-free paper

9 8 7 6 5 4 3 2 1

springer.com

Contents

Chapter 1
Introduction

1.1 Motivation

Reams (1939), in his book *Modern Blast Cleaning and Ventilation*, and Rosenberger (1939), in his book *Impact Cleaning*, probably delivered the first serious state-of-the-art reviews about the industrial fundamentals of blast cleaning. They were followed by Plaster (1972) with his two-volume compendium on '*Blast Cleaning and Allied Processes*'. In Germany, Horowitz' (1982) book about *Oberflächenbehandlung mittles Strahlmitteln* (*Surface Treatment with Blasting Media*) became very popular and is still a widely used reference. Since then, 25 years of intense progress in both industrial applications and scientific research have passed. The aim of this book is to provide an extensive up-to-date engineering-based review about the fundamental principles of blast cleaning.

This book is concerned with the blast cleaning of metallic substrates prior to the application of protective coatings or adhesives.

1.2 Introductory Remarks

From the point of view of the material removal mechanism, blast cleaning can be considered to be an erosion process. "Erosion", as a tribological term, is the removal of materials due to the action of impinging solid particles. Erosion is a natural phenomenon [the correct designation in terms of geology is *corrasion* (Bates and Jackson, 1980)] and there exist a number of impressive examples about the material removal capability of natural erosion. One example, the erosion of rock columns, is illustrated in Fig. 1.1.

Blast cleaning is one of the most frequently utilised treatment methods in modern industry. The starting point of the utilisation of blast cleaning for industrial purposes was Tilghman's patent on "*Improvement in cutting and engraving stone, metal, glass, etc.*" (Tilghman, 1870). Benjamin Chew Tilghman (1821–1901), an American scientist, invented the "*cutting, boring, grinding, dressing pulverizing, and engraving stone, metal, glass, wood, and other hard or solid substances, by means of a stream of sand or grains of quartz, or of other suitable materials, artificially driven*

Fig. 1.1 The natural erosion (corrasion) of rock columns in Palmyra (Photograph: University of Tokyo)

Fig. 1.2 Benjamin C. Tilghman (Copyright: ATT-Net)

as projectiles rapidly against them by any suitable method of propulsion" (Patent No. 108,408, October 18, 1870). It is not only the general idea of what we today call blast cleaning, or grit blasting, covered by this invention, Tilghman also mentioned a number of methods how to propel the solid particles against the material surface. He wrote: "*The means of propelling the sand . . . is by a rapid jet or current of steam, air, water, or other suitable gaseous or liquid medium; but any direct propelling force may be used, as, for example, the blows of the blades of a rapidly-revolving fan, or the centrifugal force of a revolving drum or tube, or any other suitable machine*" (Patent No. 108, 408, October 18, 1870). Benjamin Tilghman is portrayed in Fig. 1.2.

The industrial applications mentioned by Tilghman included the following: "*Articles of cast or wrought metal may have their surfaces smoothed and cleaned from slag, scale, or other incrustions.*" Reviews about the early developments in industrial blast cleaning were provided by Plaster (1972, 1993). Early applications included applications in the foundry industry, steel industry and corrosion protection industry. Today's applications include the use for micro-machining, polishing, maintenance and surface preparation for coating applications. A recent advanced application in the machining industry is grit blast assisted laser milling (Li et al., 2005).

1.3 Blast Cleaning Methods and Applications

Blast cleaning methods, according to corrosion protection applications, can be subdivided as listed in Table 1.1. Blast cleaning is by definition a method "*where blasting media (as tools) are accelerated in blasting devices of different blasting systems, and where they are forced to impinge the surface of a target (substrate) to be treated*" (ISO 12944-4, 1998). To define a blast cleaning method completely, the following information is required:

Table 1.1 Blast cleaning methods according to ISO 12944-4 (1998)

Blast cleaning methods	Dry abrasive blast cleaning	– Centrifugal abrasive blast cleaning – Compressed-air abrasive blast cleaning – Vacuum or suction-head abrasive blast cleaning
	Moisture-injection abrasive blast cleaning	(No further subdivision)
	Wet abrasive blast cleaning	– Compressed-air wet abrasive blast cleaning – Slurry blast cleaning – Pressurised-liquid blast cleaning
	Particular applications of blast cleaning	– Sweep blast cleaning – Spot blast cleaning

- purpose of blasting;
- blasting system;
- blasting medium type.

A blast cleaning system is designated according to the method, and respectively the medium, that accelerates the abrasive particles up to the required velocity. From that point of view, blast cleaning systems can be subdivided into compressed-air blast cleaning, centrifugal blast cleaning and vacuum or suction-head blast cleaning.

The book deals with the application of compressed-air blast cleaning for the treatment of metallic substrates. This includes the two following applications:

- removal of mill scales, slags and coatings;
- substrate preparation for the subsequent application of coating systems or adhesive systems.

An application example is shown in Fig. 1.3. Coating systems to be applied to blast cleaned substrates include basically corrosion protective coatings and wear resistant coatings. The examples provided in Table 1.2 and in Figs. 1.4 and 1.5 very well illustrate the effects of surface preparation methods on the performance of coating systems.

Figure 1.4 shows the effects of different surface preparation methods on the degree of rusting for a variety of coating materials. It can clearly be seen that blast cleaning to a high surface preparation standard (Sa $2^1/_2$) could notably improve

Fig. 1.3 Application of blast cleaning for the surface preparation of steel (Photograph: Muehlhan AG, Hamburg)

Table 1.2 Effect of pipe surface cleanliness on cathodic disbonding; conditions: 30 days/38°C (Neal, 1999)

Coating	Cathodic disbonding in mm		
	Surface cleanliness		
	Blast cleaning (white metal)[a]	Blast cleaning (near-white blast)[a]	Power wire brush
Epoxy polymer concrete	–	5.0	17.1
Fusion bonded epoxy (FBE)	6.1	8.9	>40
Heat shrink sleeve	12.7	18.0	27.3
Tape	14.9	31.8	28.5
Coal tar urethane	13.6	16.5	26.9

[a]See Sect. 8.2.3 for surface preparation grades

the resistance of the coatings against rusting compared to the coatings applied over untreated substrate (mill scale) and over power tool cleaned (St 2 and St 3) substrates. The situation in Fig. 1.5 is more complex. It can be seen that a light blast cleaning (sweep blasting) did not succeed for all coating materials. If a PVC-based coating system was applied to the substrate, washing was more effective than blast cleaning. For the alky-based coatings, however, a preparation performed by blast cleaning substantially improved the resistance of the coating material against flaking.

Results of cathodic disbonding tests on coating materials for pipelines are listed in Table 1.2. It can be recognised that a thorough blast cleaning could notably reduce the delamination widths for all applied coating systems.

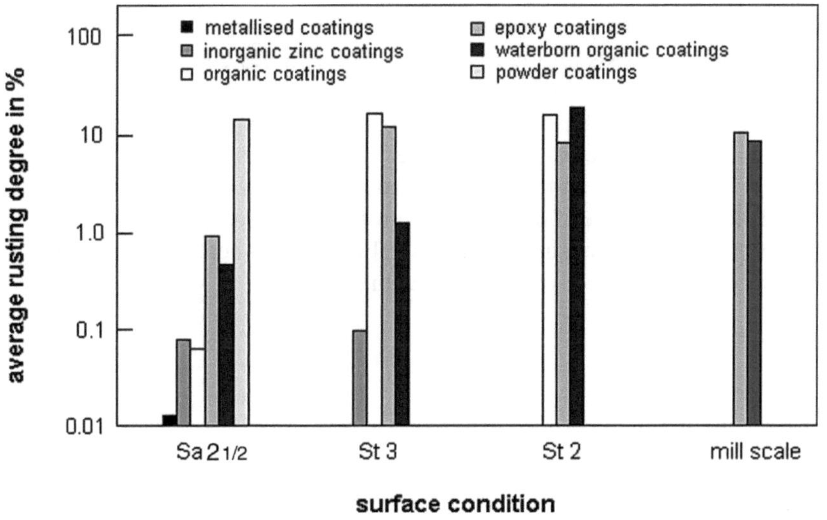

Fig. 1.4 Effects of steel substrate quality on the performance of corrosion protective coatings (Kogler et al., 1995)

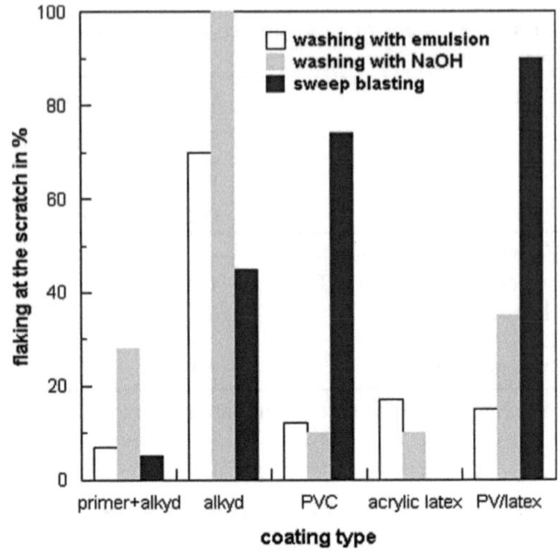

Fig. 1.5 Effects of surface preparation methods on the performance of a duplex coating system (Foghelin, 1990)

Table 1.3 Effects of surface preparation methods on the performance of a zinc-dust-based protective coating system (Brauns et al., 1964)

Surface preparation	Time to complete rusting in months		
	Splash zone	Transition zone	Underwater zone
Mill scale	5	16	10
Acid pickling	8	8	>24
Flame cleaning	8	8	>24
Blast cleaning[a]	24	>24	>24

[a] Abrasive: steel cut wire

Experimental results plotted in Table 1.3 illustrate the effects of different surface preparation methods on the rusting of steel samples coated with a zinc-dust-containing paint. The time of rusting was estimated in three corrosive maritime zones, which are typical for the corrosive loading of offshore constructions. These zones included, in particular, splash zone, water exchange zone and permanent underwater exposure. It can be seen that blast cleaning with steel cut wire notably improved the performance of the corrosion protection system. The time till complete rusting of the paint film occurred could notably be extended if the substrates have been blast cleaned irrespectively of the loading zone.

Chapter 2
Abrasive Materials

2.1 Classification and Properties of Abrasive Materials

A large number of different types of abrasive materials is available for blast cleaning applications. Most frequently applied abrasive materials are listed in Table 2.1. Table 2.2 lists numerous physical, chemical and technical properties of commercial abrasive materials. Basically, there can be distinguished between *metallic* abrasive materials and *non-metallic* abrasive materials.

The evaluation of an abrasive material for blast cleaning applications includes the following important parameters:

- material structure;
- material hardness;
- material density;
- mechanical behaviour;
- particle shape;
- particle size distribution;
- average grain size.

2.2 Abrasive Material Structure and Hardness

2.2.1 Structural Aspects of Abrasive Materials

Structural aspects of abrasive materials include the following features:

- lattice parameters;
- crystallographical group and symmetry;
- chemical composition;
- crystallochemical formula;
- cleavage;
- inclusions (water–gas inclusion and mineral inclusion).

Table 2.1 Annual abrasive consumption in the USA for blast cleaning processes (Hansink, 2000)

Abrasive type	Consumption in Mio. of tonnes
Coal boiler slag	0.65
Copper slag	0.1–0.12
Garnet	0.06
Hematite	0.03
Iron slag	0.005
Nickel slag	0.05
Olivine	0.03
Silica sand	1.6
Staurolite/zirconium	0.08–0.09
Steel grit and steel shot	0.35

Table 2.3 lists typical values for some abrasive materials. Table 2.4 displays a commercial technical data and physical characteristics sheet for a typical blast cleaning abrasive material.

Abrasive particles contain structural defects, such as microcracks, interfaces, inclusions or voids. Very often, these defects are the result of the manufacturing process. Strength and fracture parameters of materials can be characterised through certain distribution types. A widely applied distribution is the Weibull distribution, and it was shown by Huang et al. (1995) that this distribution type can be applied to abrasive materials. The authors derived the following relationship between fracture probability, particle strength and particle volume:

$$F(\sigma_F) = 1 - \exp\left[-V_P \cdot \left(\frac{\sigma_F}{\sigma^*}\right)^{m_W}\right] \quad (2.1)$$

The strength parameter σ^* is a constant, which is related to the defects distribution. The power exponent m_W is the so-called Weibull modulus; it can be read from a graphical representation of (2.1). Low values for m indicate a large intrinsic variability in particle strength. A Weibull plot for aluminium oxide abrasive particles, based on the results of compressive crushing tests, is displayed in Fig. 2.1. Values for the Weibull modulus estimated for different abrasive materials are listed in Table 2.5. There is a notable trend in the values that both fracture strength and Weibull modulus drop with increasing particle size. Therefore, scatter in strength of abrasive particles can be assumed to be wider for larger particles. The relationship between abrasive particle size and fracture strength of the particles is shown in Fig. 2.2. This phenomenon can be explained through the higher absolute number of defects in larger particles. The probability that a defect with a critical dimension (for example, a critical crack length in a fracture mechanics approach) exists increases with an increasing number of defects.

This effect was also observed by Larssen-Basse (1993). This author found also that the Weibull modulus of abrasive particles depended on the atmospheric humidity. Larssen-Basse (1993) performed crushing tests with SiC-particles, and he found that, if humidity increased, the Weibull modulus and the number of fragments both

Table 2.2 Selected abrasive properties (References: manufacturer data)

Brand name	Bulk density[a] in t/m^3	Apparent density in t/m^3	Hardness[b–e]	Melting point in °C	Grain size min–max in mm	Major composite in %	Technical name
Abrablast	–	4.3	9[b]	1,900	–	Al_2O_3 (71.9)	Zirconium corundum
Abramax	1.0–2.0	3.95	2,200[c]	2,000	–	Al_2O_3(99.6)	Corundum
Abrasit	1.1–2.3	3.96	2,100[c]	2,000	–	Al_2O_3 (96.4)	Corundum
Afesikos	1.4	2.6	8[b]	–	0.04–1.4	SiO_2 (53)	Aluminium silica
Afesikos HS	2.83	4.1	8[b]	–	0.04–1.4	SiO_2 (36)	Garnet
Afesikos SK	1.8	3.96	9[b]	–	0.06–2.8	Al_2O_3 (99.3)	Corundum
Asilikos	1.3	2.5–2.6	7–8[b]	–	0.06–2.8	SiO_2 (51)	Aluminium silica
Cast steel	–	–	60[d]	–	0.12–3.36	–	–
Garnet	–	3.9–4.1	8–9[b]	1,315	–	SiO_2 (41.3)	Garnet
Glass beads	1.5	2.45	6[b]	–	0.07–0.4	SiO_2 (73)	–
GSR	3.7–4.3	7.4	44–58[d]	–	0.1–2.24	–	Cast steel
Cast iron	2.7–4.3	7.4	56–64[d]	–	up to 3.15	–	–
Ceramic spheres	2.3	3.8	60–65[d]	–	0.07–0.25	ZrO_2 (67)	Ceramics
MKE	1.75	3.92	1,800–2,200[e]	–	0.001–2.8	Al_2O_3 (99.6)	Corundum
Olivine	1.7–1.9	5.3	6.5–7[b]	1,760	0.09–1.0	MgO (50)	–
Scorex	1.35	–	–	–	0.5–2.8	SiO_2 (40)	Refinery slag
Steel grit	–	7.5	48–66[d]	–	0.2–1.7	–	–
Steel shot	–	7.3	46–51[d]	–	0.2–2.0	–	–
Testra	1.2–1.4	2.5–2.7	7[b]	–	0.09–2.0	SiO_2 (54)	Melting chamber slag

[a]Depends on grain size
Hardness parameter: [b]Mohs; [c]Vickers; [d]Rockwell; [e]Knoop

Table 2.3 Structural properties of abrasive materials (Vasek et al., 1993)

Material	Damaged grains (%)	Lattice constant (Å)	Cell volume (Å^3)
Almandine	5–60	11.522 (0.006)	1,529.62
Spessartine	–	11.613 (0.005)	1,566.15
Pyrope	–	11.457 (0.005)	1,503.88
Grossular	30	11.867 (0.005)	1,671.18
Andradite	80–90	12.091 (0.009)	1,767.61

increased. This feature can be attributed to moisture-assisted sharpening of the tips of surface defects present in the particles.

The presence of defects, such as cracks and voids, affects the cleaning and degradation performance of abrasive materials. Number and size of defects are,

Table 2.4 Data sheet for a garnet blast cleaning abrasive material (Reference: GMA Garnet)

Parameter	Value
Average chemical composition	
SiO_2^a	36%
Al_2O_3	20%
FeO	30%
Fe_2O_3	2%
TiO_2	1%
MnO	1%
CaO	2%
MgO	6%
Physical characteristics	
Bulk density	2,300 kg/m^3
Specific gravity	4.1
Hardness (Mohs)	7.5–8
Melting point	1,250°C
Grain shape	Sub-angular
Other characteristics	
Conductivity	10–15 mS/m
Moisture absorption	Non-hydroscopic
Total chlorides	10–15 ppm
Ferrite (free iron)	<0.01%
Lead	<0.002%
Copper	<0.005%
Other heavy metals	<0.01%
Sulphur	<0.01%
Mineral composition	
Garnet (Almandine)	97–98%
Ilmenite	1–2%
Zircon	0.2%
Quartz (free silica)	<0.5%
Others	0.25%

[a]Refers to SiO_2 bound within the lattice of the homogeneous garnet crystal (no free silica)

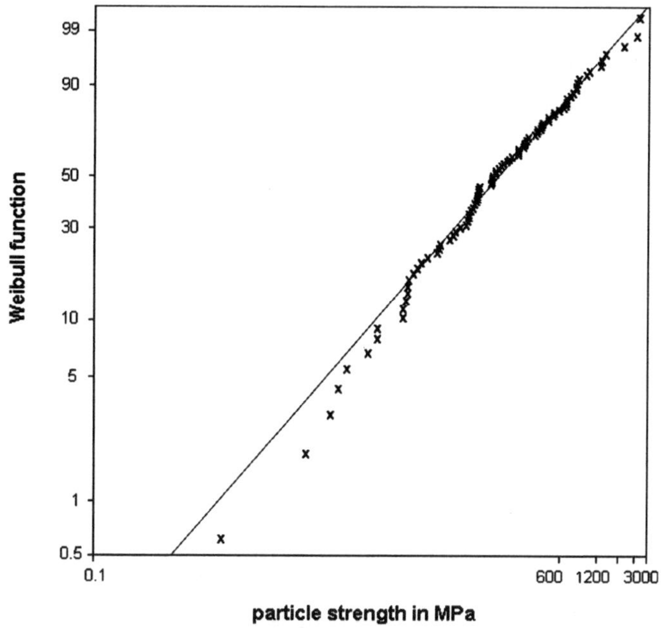

Fig. 2.1 Weibull plot for the strength of aluminium oxide particles (Verspui et al., 1997). Abrasive particle size: 10–500 μm

therefore, important assessment criteria. Cast steel shot, for example, should not contain cracked particles, as illustrated in Fig. 2.3, in excess of 15%. Cast steel grit should not contain cracked particles, as shown in Fig. 2.4, in excess of 40% (SFSA, 1980). Requirements for the defects of particles of metallic abrasive materials are listed in Table 2.6.

Table 2.5 Strength parameters for abrasive materials (Yashima et al., 1987; Huang et al., 1995)

Abrasive material	Grain size in mm	Fracture strength in MPa	Weibull modulus	*[a] in MPa/mm³
Brown corundum	2.58	67.5	1.98	228.8
	1.85	78.6	2.47	142.8
	1.29	115.4	2.88	135.1
	0.78	200.5	3.47	149.0
Rounded corundum	1.85	96.1	3.41	160.8
White corundum	1.29	79.5	2.57	127.3
Sintered corundum	1.85	110.8	3.85	174.9
Green silicon carbide	1.85	62.2	1.92	155.5
Quartz	0.1–2.0	–	21.0	–
Glass beads	–	–	5.90	–

[a]Defect distribution parameter

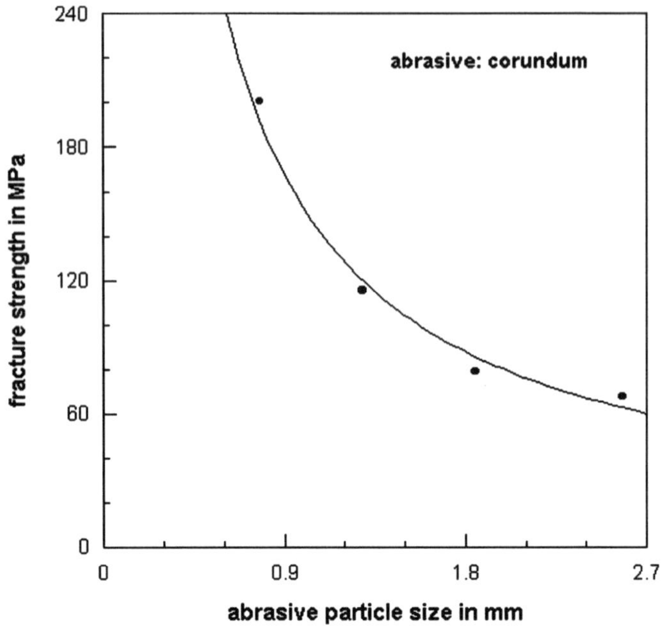

Fig. 2.2 Relationship between abrasive particle size and particle fracture strength (values from Huang et al., 1995)

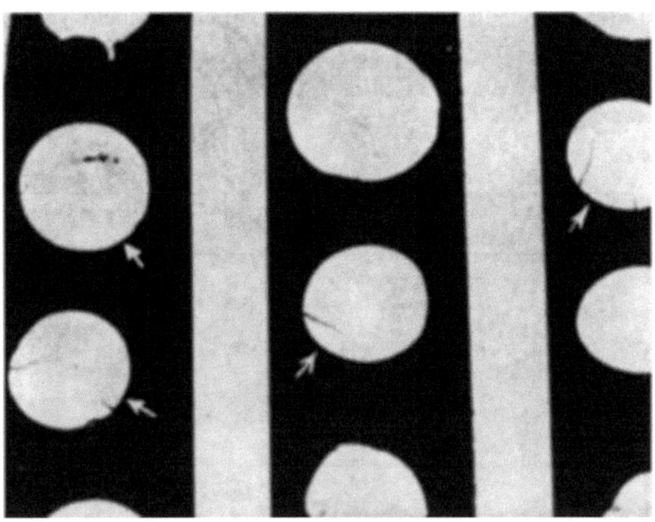

Fig. 2.3 Cracks in cast steel shot particles; magnification: 10× (SFSA, 1980)

Fig. 2.4 Cracks in cast steel grit particles; magnification: 10× (SFSA, 1980)

2.2.2 Hardness of Abrasive Materials

The hardness of abrasive materials is usually estimated by two types of tests: a scratching test for non-metallic abrasive materials, which delivers the *Mohs hardness*, and indentation tests for metallic materials, which deliver either the *Knoop hardness* or the *Vickers hardness*. Respective values for commercial abrasive materials are listed in Table 2.2.

Mohs hardness is based on a scale of ten minerals, which is provided in Table 2.7. The hardness of a material is measured against the scale by finding the hardest

Table 2.6 Particle defect requirements for metallic abrasive materials (ISO 11124/2-4)

Property	Chilled iron grit	High-carbon cast steel shot	High-carbon cast steel grit	Low-carbon cast steel shot
Particle shape	Max. 10% shot or more than half-round	Max. 5% non-round	Max. 10% shot or more than half-round for grit up to 700 HV; max. 5% for grit above 700 HV	Max. 5% non-round
Voids	Max. 10%	Max. 10%	Max. 10%	Max. 15%
Shrinkage defects	Max. 10%	Max. 10%	Max. 10%	Max. 5%
Cracks	Max. 40%	Max. 15%	Max. 40%	None
Total defects	Max. 40%	Max. 20%	Max. 40%	Max. 20%

Table 2.7 Mohs scale (Tabor, 1951)

Material	Mohs hardness
Talc	1
Gypsum	2
Calcite	3
Fluorite	4
Apatite	5
Orthoclase (Feldspar)	6
Quartz	7
Topaz	8
Corundum	9
Diamond	10

material that the given material can scratch, and/or the softest material that can scratch the given material. For example, if some material is scratched by quartz but not by feldspar, its hardness on Mohs scale is 6.5. In abrasive standardisation, abrasive particles are being rubbed against a glass plate having a Mohs hardness corresponding to 7. If the particles can scratch the plate, their hardness is >Mohs 7. If they do not scratch the plate, their hardness is <Mohs 7. It is because of this procedure that data sheets for mineral abrasive materials often list the Mohs hardness as >7 only.

The principles of two frequently applied indentation hardness tests are illustrated in Table 2.8. In laboratory practice, an abrasive particle is embedded in a special resin matrix, and it is then being polished in order to obtain an even

Table 2.8 Indentation hardness measurement methods (Images: TWI, Cambridge, UK)

Method	Brinell	Vickers
Principle	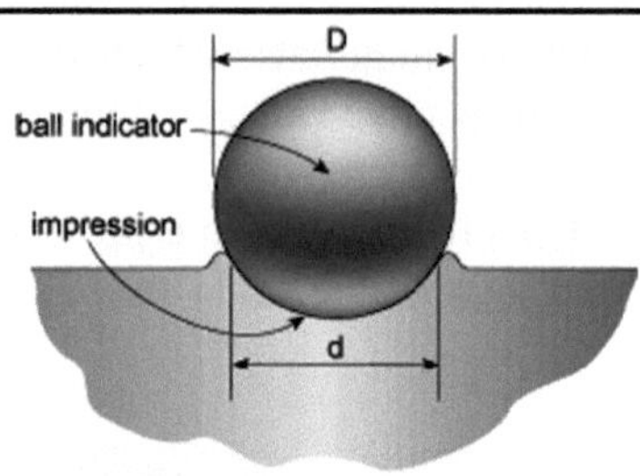	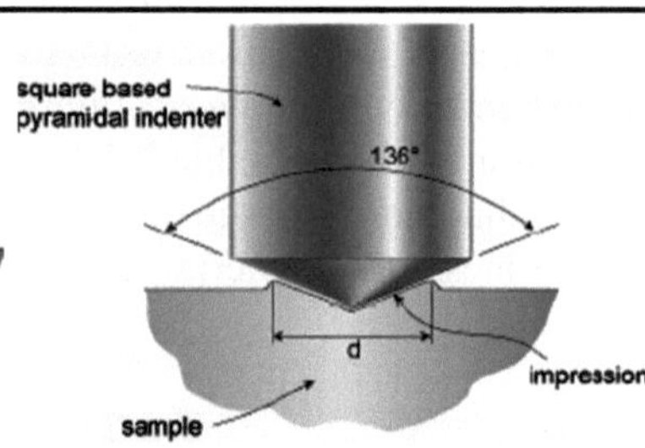
Measurement	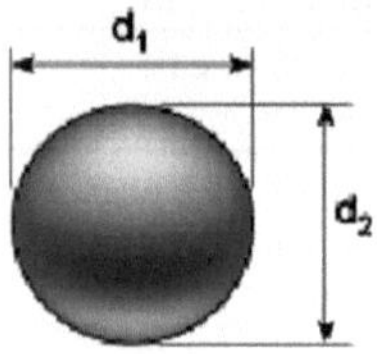	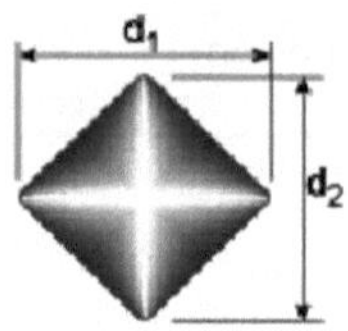
Calculation[a]	$H_B = \dfrac{F}{\frac{\pi}{2} \cdot D \cdot \left[D - (D^2 - d^2)^{1/2}\right]}$	$H_V = \dfrac{2 \cdot F \cdot \sin(136°/2)}{d^2}$

[a]F= indentation load

$d = \text{indentation size} = \dfrac{d_1 + d_2}{2}$

D = indenter size

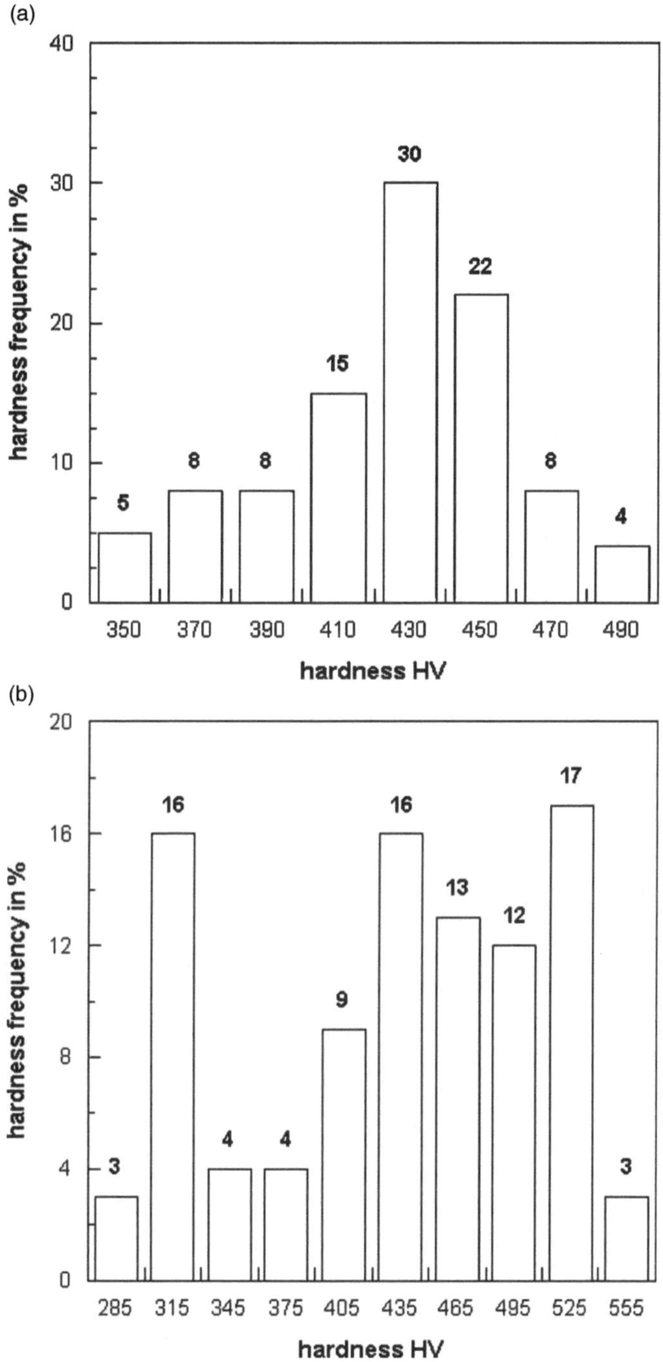

Fig. 2.5 Vickers hardness distributions of two cut wire samples (Gesell, 1979). (**a**) Laboratory sample; (**b**) Work sample

smooth cross-section where the actual indentation test is being performed. Indentation hardness values are always dependent on indentation load, and care should be taken to provide the certain applied indentation load in data sheets. Values from indentation hardness tests and from Mohs hardness tests can be related to each other; exceptions are diamond and corundum (Bowden and Tabor, 1964).

The hardness of metallic abrasive particles is a probabilistic parameter, and the hardness values mentioned in data sheets are mainly mean values only. Two typical abrasive hardness distribution diagrams of cut wire samples are provided in Fig. 2.5. Figure 2.5a shows the distribution of a laboratory sample, whereas Fig. 2.5b illustrates the distribution of a working sample. Although both materials had equal hardness designations of 420 HV, the distributions differed widely. The laboratory sample had a unimodal distribution with a maximum at a Vickers hardness of about 430 HV, whereas the working sample featured a multimodal distribution. The hardness distribution of the laboratory sample can be expressed through a Normal distribution – this is shown in Fig. 2.6. This result points to a rather homogeneous response of the wire material to the indentation with the Vickers pyramid, which is not always the case (Lange and Schimmöller, 1967). Such a distribution was also reported by Flavenot and Lu (1990) for steel wire shot.

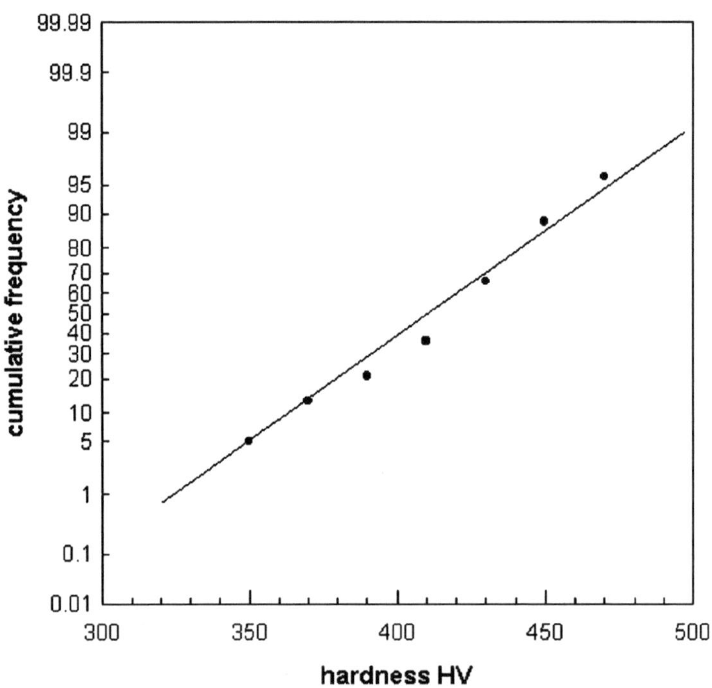

Fig. 2.6 Normal distribution function for the laboratory cut wire sample plotted in Fig. 2.5a

2.3 Abrasive Particle Shape Parameters

2.3.1 Basic Shape Definitions

The following three basic shape definitions are provided for abrasive particles used for blast cleaning applications:

- shot;
- grit;
- cylindrical.

The corresponding designations are listed in Table 2.9. Examples for two shape definition are displayed in Fig. 2.7. The term *shot* characterises grains with a predominantly spherical shape. Their length-to-diameter ratio is <2, and they do not exhibit sharp edges or broken sections. The term *grit* characterises grains with a predominantly angular shape. These grains exhibit sharp edges and broken sections. The term *cylindrical* denotes grains that are manufactured by a cutting process. Their length-to-diameter ratio is ∼1. This shape can only be found with cut steel wire pellets.

2.3.2 Relative Proportions of Particles

Shape parameters characterise the shape of individual particles. Wadell (1933) and Heywood (1933) were probably the first who gave rigorous analyses of shape parameters. Heywood (1933) considered the shape of a particle to have the following two distinct characteristics:

- the relative proportions of length, breadth and thickness;
- the geometrical form.

The relative proportion includes two parameters: (1) the *elongation ratio* (r_E) and (2) the *flatness ratio* (r_F). Both parameters are defined and illustrated in Table 2.10. Bahadur and Badruddin (1990) applied the elongation ratio to investigate the influence of the abrasive particle shape on particle impact erosion processes. They found notable relationships between abrasive type, abrasive particle diameter and abrasive particle shape. Some results of their study are provided in Fig. 2.8. Silica carbide particles became more elongated and less circular with an increase in the particle size, while the opposite was the case with aluminium oxide particles. The general variation of silica oxide was similar to that of silica carbide particles, though not as systematic. The elongation ratios for the silica carbide particles and for the

Table 2.9 Grain shape designations

Designation	Grain shape	Symbol
Shot	Spherical, round	S
Grit	Angular, irregular	G
Cylindrical	Sharp-edged	C

(a)  (b)

Fig. 2.7 Basic shape designations for abrasive particles (Photographs: Kuhmichel GmbH). (**a**) Grit; (**b**) Shot

aluminium oxide were very sensitive to the particle size in the range of small particles. For equal grain sizes, silica oxide particles featured much higher elongation ratios than silica carbide particles. For a particle diameter of $d_P = 300\,\mu m$, as an example, the elongation ratio was $r_E = 0.53$ for silica carbide, and $r_E = 0.7$ for silica oxide. A relationship between particle abrasive size and shape was also noted by Djurovic et al. (1999). For starch media, these authors found that smaller particles were less elongated than larger particles. These results clearly show that particle shape may be considered an abrasive material characteristic.

2.3.3 Geometrical Forms of Particles

The geometrical form is a volumetric shape factor, representing the degree to which a particle approximates an ideal geometric form (cube, sphere or tetrahedron). The following two parameters can describe the geometrical form of particles: (1) the *sphericity* (S_P) and (2) the *roundness* (S_R).

Table 2.10 Shape parameters for abrasive particles

Parameter and definition	Graphical expression
Shape factor $F_{\text{shape}} = \frac{d_{\min}}{d_{\max}}$	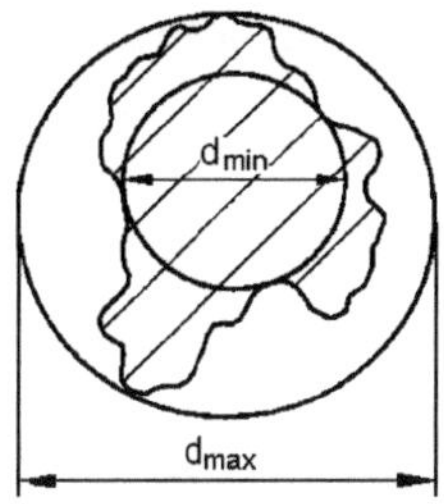
Circularity factor $F_0 = \frac{4 \cdot \pi \cdot A_P}{\text{Perimeter}^2}$	
Roundness $S_R = \frac{\sum\left(\frac{2 \cdot r_{\text{corner}}}{d_P}\right)}{N_{\text{corner}}}$	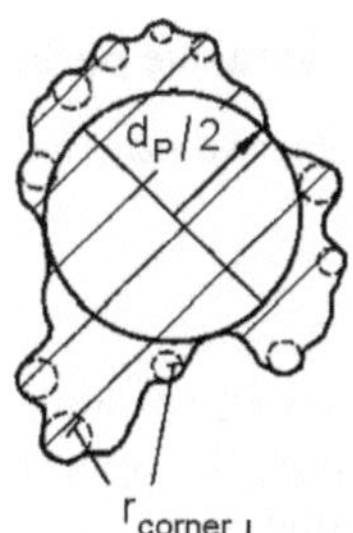
Sphericity $S_P = \frac{\sqrt{\frac{4}{\pi} \cdot b_P \cdot l_P}}{d_{\text{circle}}}$	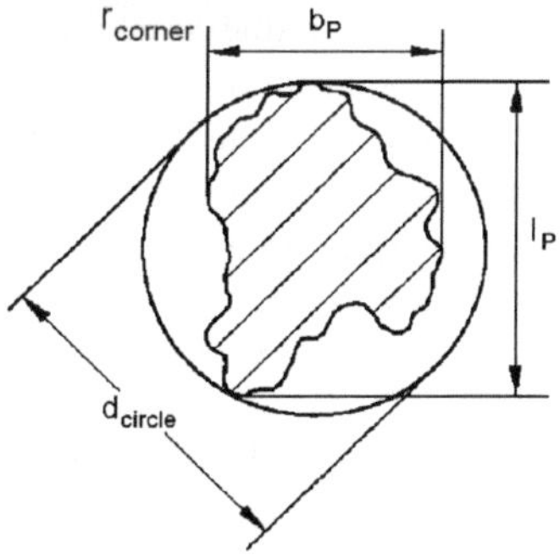
Elongation ratio $r_E = \frac{l_P}{b_P}$ Flatness ratio $r_F = \frac{l_P}{t_P}$	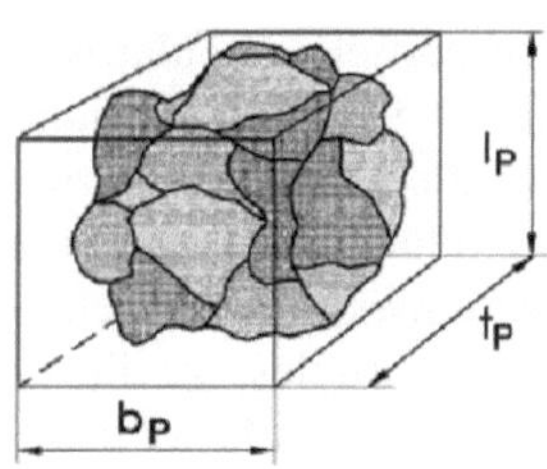

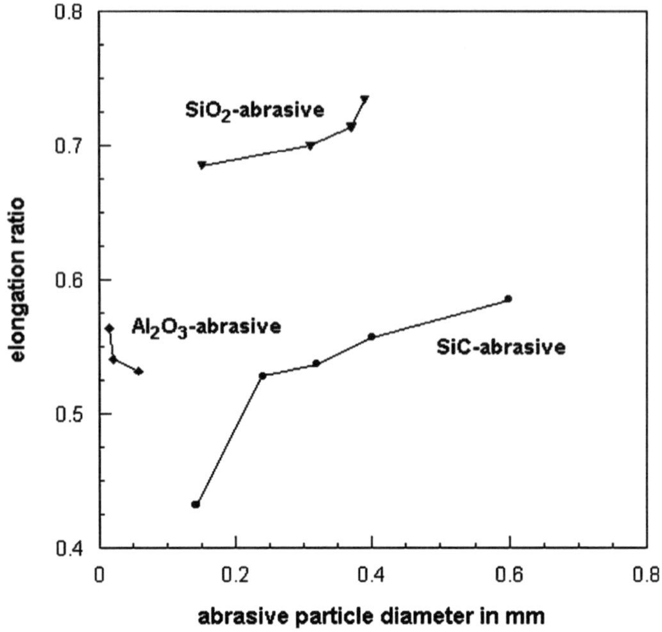

Fig. 2.8 Relationships between abrasive material, particle size and particle shape (Bahadur and Badruddin, 1990)

The sphericity, introduced by Wadell (1933), is defined and illustrated in Table 2.10. In two dimensions, the sphericity is related to the projection area of the sphere yielding the roundness, which is defined and illustrated in Table 2.10 as well. Both sphericity and roundness range from "0" for very angular particles to "1" for ideally round particles. Hansink (1998) defined an alternative roundness scale, which is illustrated in Fig. 2.9, for the assessment of the shapes of abrasive particles. This scale defines and quantifies the often used qualitative terms *angular* or *rounded*. Several references used roundness–sphericity diagrams in order to characterise the shape of abrasive particles. Such a roundness–sphericity diagram is illustrated in Fig. 2.10.

Vasek et al. (1993) and Martinec (1994) suggested a circularity factor, which was originally developed by Cox (1927), and a shape factor in order to characterise abrasive particles. The *circularity factor* (F_0) is defined and illustrated in Table 2.10. For a perfectly round particle, circularity factor will be unity. Gillespie (1996) and Gillespie and Fowler (1991) applied image analysis in order to estimate circularity factors (which they called "shape factors" in their papers) for shot peening media, and they defined any value for the circularity parameter $F_0 > 0.83$ as acceptable for shot peening applications. Some of their results, featuring circularity factors for a number of real abrasive particles, are illustrated in Fig. 2.11, and it can be seen that a notable number of particles would not meet the critical circularity factor. Figure 2.12 shows a histogram of circularity factors based on an automatic image analysing

Designation	Very angular	Angular	Sub-angular
Definition	0.5	1.5	2.5
Shape image	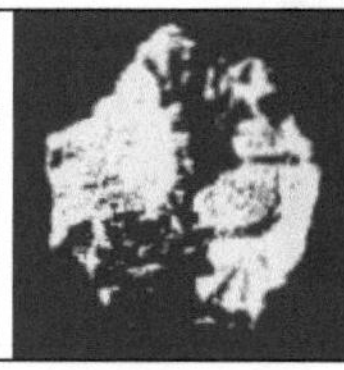	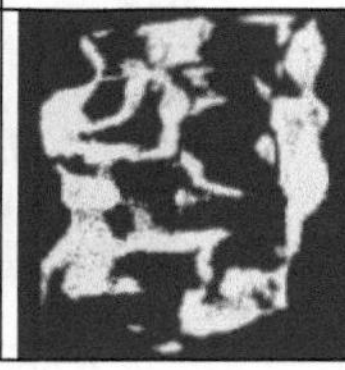	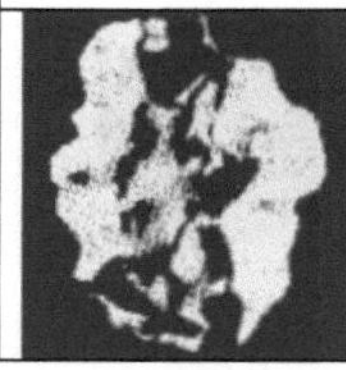

Designation	Sub-rounded	Rounded	Well rounded
Definition	3.5	4.5	5.5
Shape image	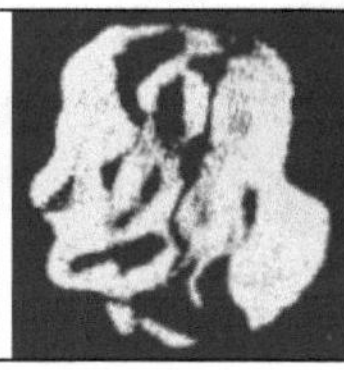	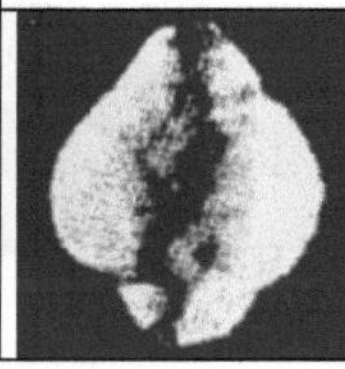	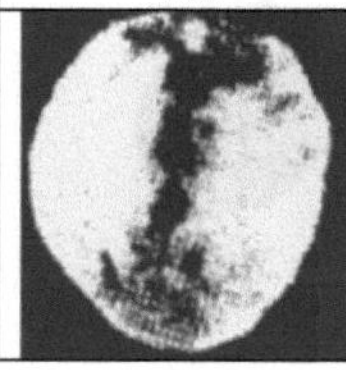

Fig. 2.9 Designations for angular and rounded particle shapes (Hansink, 1998)

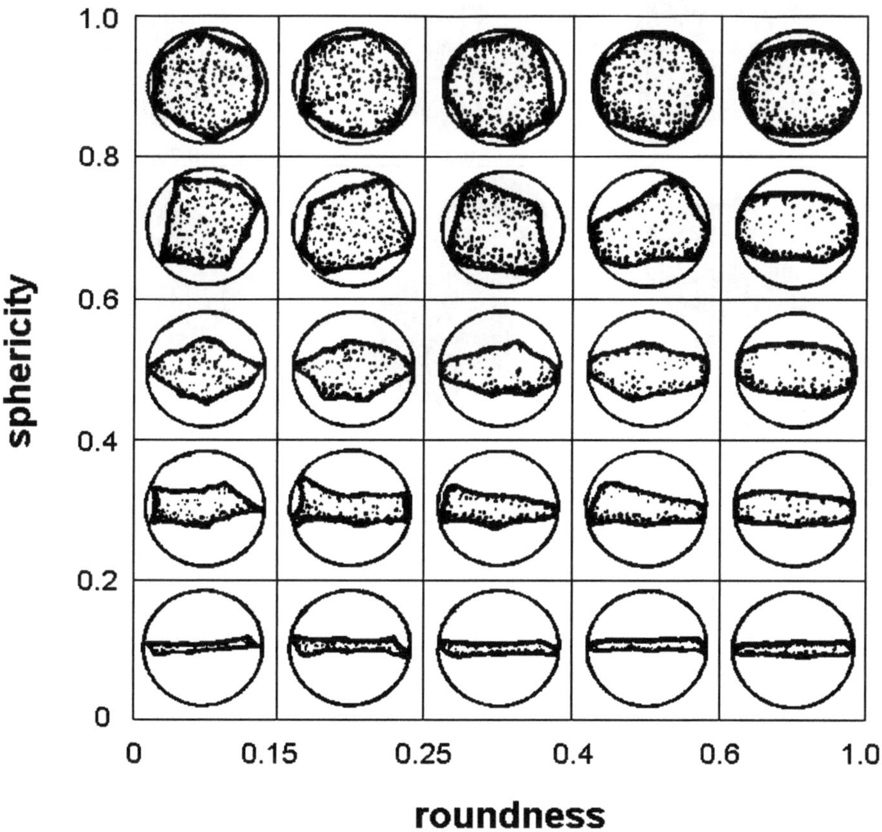

Fig. 2.10 Roundness-sphericity diagram for a garnet abrasive material (Reference: Bohemia Garnet)

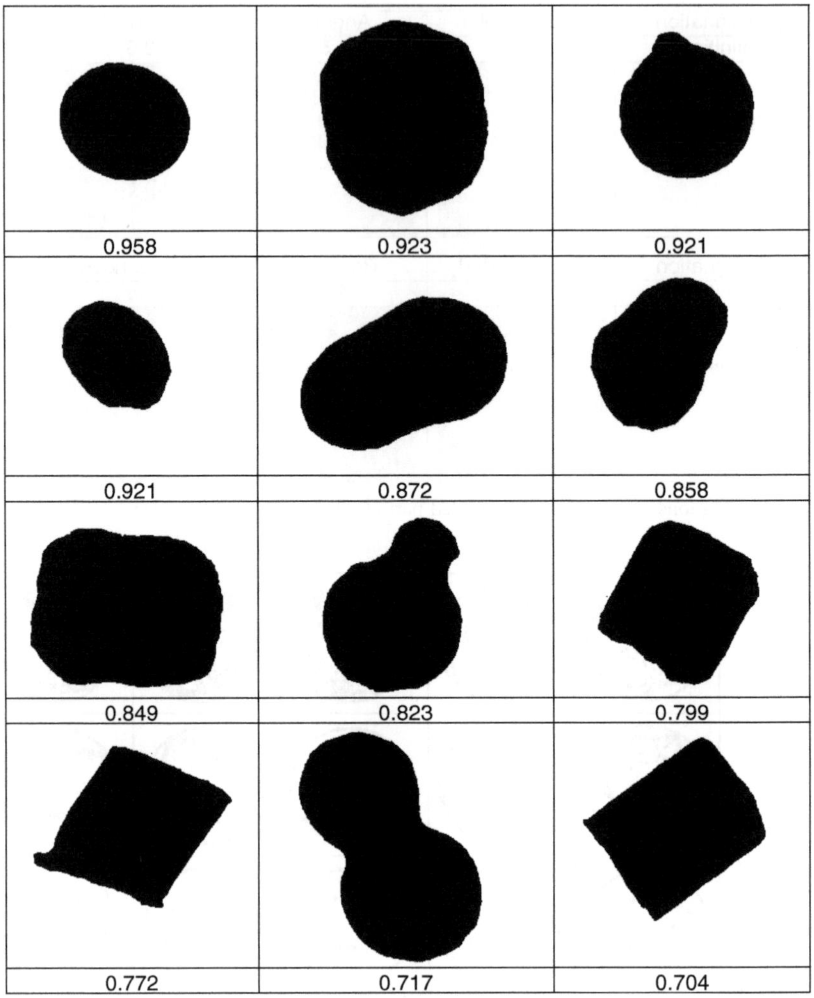

Fig. 2.11 Circularity factors of steel shot particles, assessed with image processing technique (Gillespie, 1996)

procedure. It can clearly be seen that "shape" is not a well-defined standard property for a given abrasive material. Shape parameters in general are rather characterised by distributions with certain statistical parameters. Typical statistical parameters for an assessment procedure are listed in Table 2.11; the listing very well illustrates the high number of assessment parameters delivered by an automatic image analysis procedure.

The *shape factor* (F_{shape}) is also defined and illustrated in Table 2.10. For circles, the shape factor is unity. Table 2.12 lists some typical values for circularity and shape factors for a number of different abrasive materials.

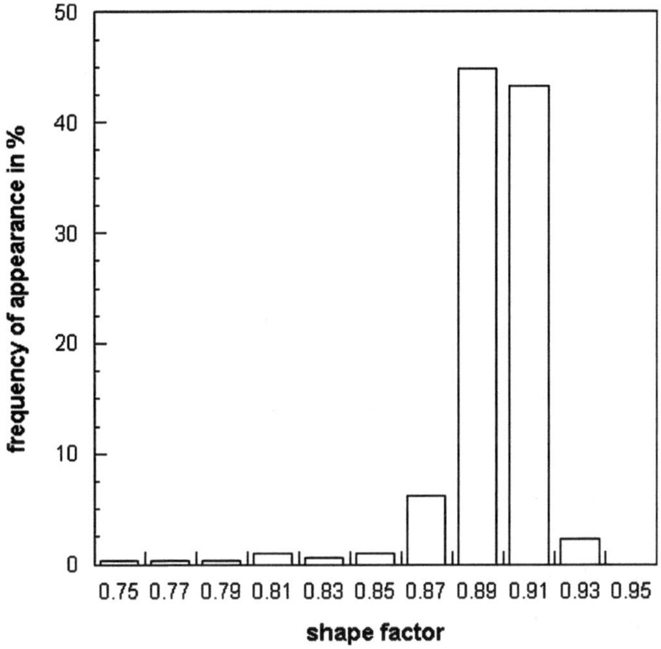

Fig. 2.12 Frequency distribution functions of shape factors (Gillespie and Fowler, 1991)

Table 2.11 Statistics of circularity factors of cast steel shot S-280, based on automatic image analysis (Gillespie and Fowler, 1991)

Parameter	Value
Minimum	0.487
Maximum	0.926
Median	0.898
25% quartile	0.890
75% quartile	0.906
Total value	577
Mean	0.894
Geometric mean	0.893
Harmonic mean	0.893
Sample variance	0.00083
Sample standard variation	0.029
Population variance	0.00083
Population standard variation	0.02
Standard deviation of the mean	0.0011
Relative standard error	0.0013
Skew	$-17,402$
Kurtosis	0.000057

Table 2.12 Shape factors and shape characteristics of garnet abrasive materials (Vasek et al., 1993)

Mineral	Subtype	Shape parameter	
		F_0	F_{shape}
Almandine	B	0.66	0.65
	M	0.69	0.67
	K	0.68	0.66
	G	0.66	0.64
Grossular	–	0.71	0.70
Andradite	V–A	0.67	0.65
	V–B	0.68	0.68
	V–C	0.65	0.68

2.4 Abrasive Particle Size Distribution and Abrasive Particle Diameter

2.4.1 Particle Size Distribution

2.4.1.1 General Definitions

In general, the term "diameter" is specified for any equidimensional particle. By conversion, particle sizes are expressed in different units depending on the size ranges involved. Coarse grains are measured in inches or millimetres, fine particles in terms of screen size, very fine particles are measured in micrometer or manometer. A number of "diameter" definitions are known. The diameter is defined either in terms of some real property of the particle, such as its volume or surface area, or in terms of behaviour of the particle in some specific circumstances, such as settling in water under defined conditions (Kelly and Spottiswood, 1982). In the area of blast cleaning, the particle size is usually given in mesh designation (according to the Tyler-Standard-Screen sieve series), which barely mentions the related particle size distributions or the shape of the particles. A regression study made to link the Tyler sieve series to the corresponding average particle diameter delivers the following relationship:

$$\mathrm{d_P} = 17{,}479 \cdot \mathrm{mesh}^{-1.0315} \tag{2.2}$$

with a regression coefficient of 0.998. The particle diameter is in μm in this equation. A mesh number 180 would correspond to an average particle diameter of $d_\mathrm{p} = 82\,\mu\mathrm{m}$.

2.4.1.2 Sieve Analysis

Because it is impracticable to individually estimate each particle, size analysis is carried out by dividing the particles into a number of suitably narrow size ranges. Table 2.13 presents results of sieve analyses for abrasive particle samples used in

Table 2.13 Sieve analyses results for two abrasive mixtures (Metabrasive Ltd.)

Sieve size in μm	Weight in %	
	Alumina 700	Metagrit 65
125	–	2
150	–	5
212	–	20
300	4	28
425	26	35
600	45	10
850	22.5	–
1,180	2.5	–
Total	100	100

blast cleaning. Graphically, data are conventionally presented by plotting the particle size horizontally and the measured quantity of property vertically. Two approaches are used to present the quantity: (1) plotting the absolute amount in each size fraction (Fig. 2.13a) and (2) plotting the cumulative amount above or below a certain size (Fig. 2.13b).

2.4.1.3 Particle Size Distribution Models

A number of models were developed to mathematically describe the size distributions of fine-grained comminution products, which include abrasive particles. These models have empirical relationships, which to a greater or lesser extent were found capable of describing comminution products size distributions. Table 2.14 lists the most frequently used models. These equations are all of the general type:

$$M_0(d_P) = f\left(\frac{d_P}{d^*}\right)^{n_M} \tag{2.3}$$

The size modulus, d^*, is an indication of an average particle diameter. When the equation has an upper size limit, d^* is in fact the maximum particle size in the distribution. Equation (2.3) also includes a second parameter, n_M, that is frequently called the distribution modulus, since it is a measure of the spread of particle sizes. The higher the value for n_M, the more homogeneous is the grain size structure of the sample. For $n_M \rightarrow \infty$, the sample consists of grains with equal diameters. Figure 2.14a, b shows fits for the sieve analysis from Table 2.13 by two common particle-size distribution functions. The Rosin–Rammler–Sperling–Bennett (RRSB) distribution is of particular interest because its distribution parameters are utilised by some authors as a measure of the ageing and reusability of metallic abrasive particles (Wellinger et al., 1962).

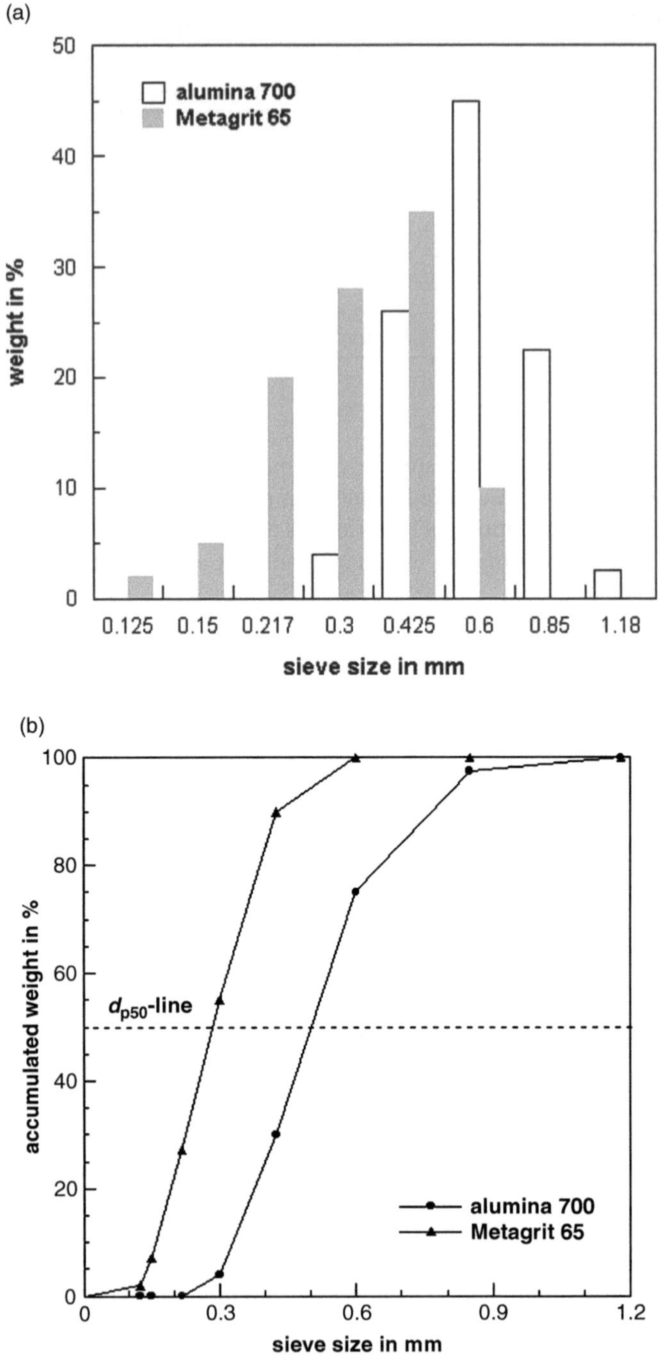

Fig. 2.13 Graphical representations of sieve analysis results (see Table 2.13). (**a**) Absolute distribution; (**b**) Cumulative distribution

Table 2.14 Particle-size distribution functions (Kelly and Spottiswood, 1982; Schubert, 1988)

Function	Formula $M_0(d_P)$	Significance of $d*$	Equation
Logarithmic probability	$\mathrm{erf}\left[\frac{\ln \frac{d_P}{d^*}}{\sigma}\right]$	Medium particle diameter	2.3a
Rosin–Rammler–Sperling–Bennett (RRSB)	$1-\exp\left[\left(\frac{d_P}{d^*}\right)^{n_M}\right]$	Particle diameter at $M_0 = 63.2\%$	2.3b
Gates–Gaudin–Schumann (GGS)	$\left(\frac{d_P}{d^*}\right)^{n_M}$		2.3c
Gaudin–Meloy	$1-\left[1-\frac{d_P}{d^*}\right]^2$	Maximum particle diameter	2.3d
Broadbent–Callcott	$\frac{1-\exp\left[-\frac{d_P}{d^*}\right]}{1-\exp(-1)}$	–	2.3e

2.4.2 Particle Diameter

According to regulations in ISO 1117, the particle diameter is defined according to a particle "size class". A size class of "140", for example, means a particle diameter of 1.4 mm.

If the particle size distribution is known from the sieve analysis, several "average" diameter values of the particle sample can be estimated. The *median diameter*, d_{50}, is the 50% point on any cumulative distribution curve (Fig. 2.13b). For the examples presented in Table 2.13 and Fig. 2.13, this diameter is $d_{P50} = 510\ \mu m$ (Alumina 700) and $d_{P50} = 280\ \mu m$ (MG 65), respectively. The *geometric mean diameter*, d_{PG}, is based on the assumption of an even graduation in size from maximum to minimum, and it assumes an equal number of particles in each size average:

$$d_{PG} = \frac{d_{P\,max} + d_{P\,min}}{2} \tag{2.4}$$

In the examples given in Table 2.13 and Fig. 2.13, this diameter is $d_{PG} = 740\ \mu m$ (Alumina 700) and $d_{PG} = 362\ \mu m$ (MG 65), respectively. A third approach is the definition of a *statistical diameter*, d_{PSt}, which follows the equation:

$$d_{PSt} = \frac{\sum_{i=1}^{n} (m_i \cdot d_{Pi})}{100} \tag{2.5}$$

For the examples in Table 2.13 and Fig. 2.13, the statistical diameter is $d_{PSt} = 613\ \mu m$ (Alumina 700) and $d_{PSt} = 345\ \mu m$ (MG 65), respectively.

2.4.3 Alternative Abrasive Particle Size Assessment Methods

Particle sizes, but also particle size distributions, can be assessed also by applying image analysis methods. This alternative approach is not a standard in

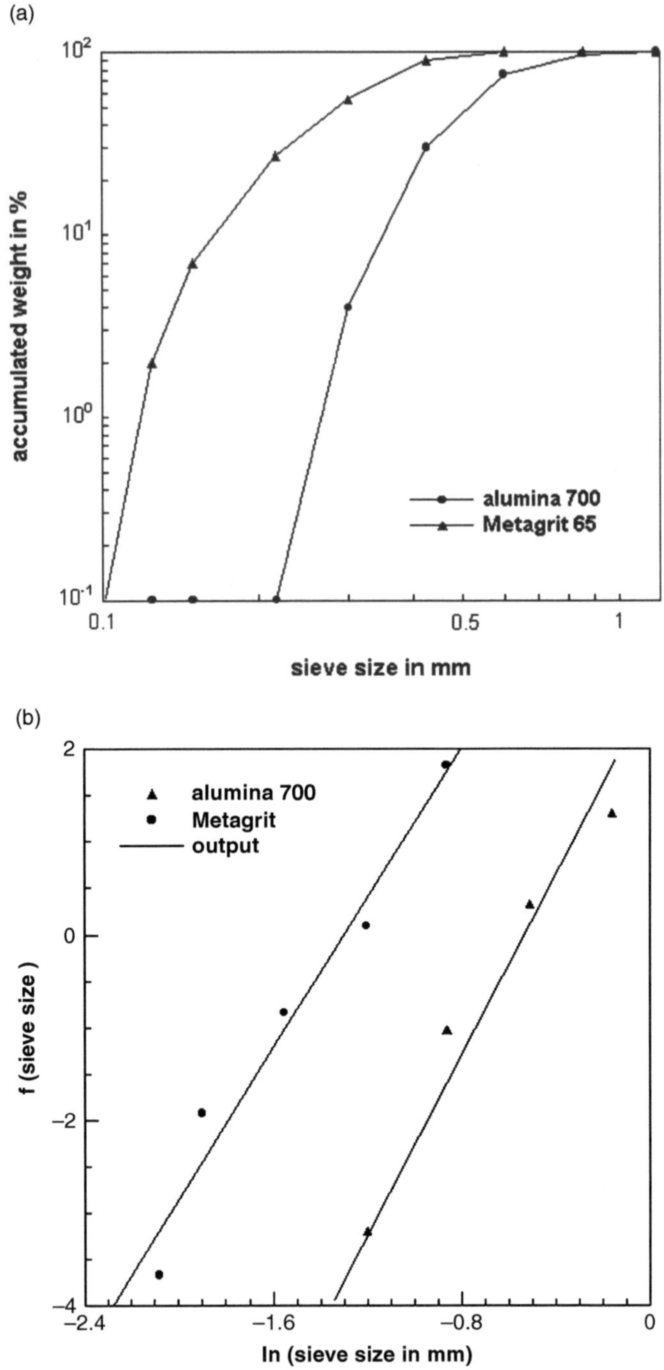

Fig. 2.14 Distribution functions for sieve analysis results (see Table 2.12). (**a**) Gates–Gaudin–Schumann (GGS) distribution; (**b**) Rosin–Rammler–Sperling–Bennett (RRSB) distribution

the blast cleaning industry, although promising results have been reported for the image analysis of shot peening media. Gillespie (1996) and Gillespie and Fowler (1991) performed comparative size measurements by using conventional sieve analysis, a digital micrometer and image analysis. Some results are displayed in Fig. 2.15. The agreement between the three methods depended on the sieve size; it was very good (less than 2 wt.%) for the smaller sieve sizes. The average difference between sieve analysis and image analysis was 2.71 wt.%. Image analysis is of definite interest because this method can deliver information on particle size as well as on particle shape. Promising experience is available on the shape assessment of particles, either of shot peening media (Gillespie and Fowler, 1991; Gillespie, 1996) or of erosion debris (Momber and Wong, 2005b), with image analysis methods. Further details on this application are provided in Sect. 2.3.

Optical methods for the assessment of particle sizes are very familiar in particle technology. Sparks and Hutchings (1993) have, however, shown that these methods must be applied with caution to broken abrasive particles. Especially glass particles show different optical properties whether they are round (e.g. glass beads) or broken (e.g. glass grit). Broken glass particles would, in a correct orientation with respect to a laser beam, diffract light in such a way so as to suggest that they were of larger diameter.

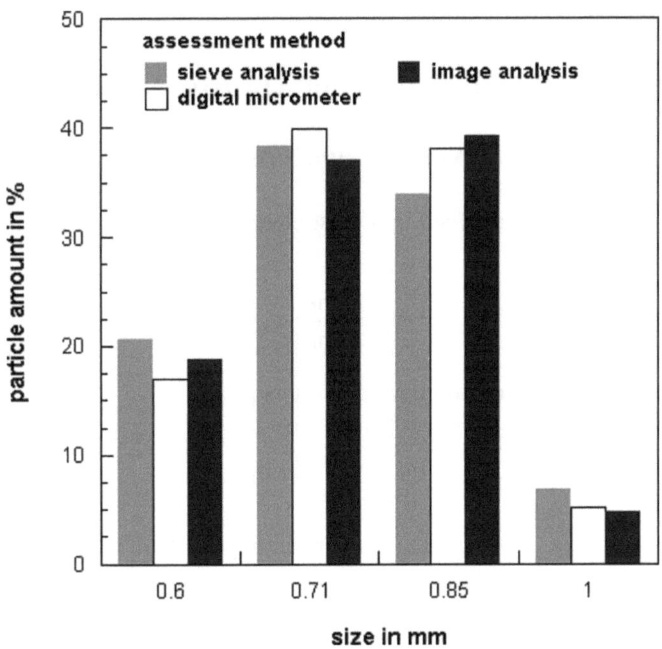

Fig. 2.15 Comparison between abrasive size assessment methods (Gillespie, 1996)

2.5 Density of Abrasive Materials

The following two density parameters are defined for abrasives:

- apparent density;
- bulk density.

The apparent density is the ratio between mass and volume of a single abrasive grain:

$$\rho_P = \frac{m_P}{V_P} = \frac{6 \cdot m_P}{\pi \cdot d_P^3} \tag{2.6}$$

It can be estimated with well-defined methods. This density parameter includes flaws, pores and cracks. Therefore, it is a physical constant of the material. The apparent density must, for example, be used if kinetic energy of an impinging grain is calculated.

The bulk density is the mass of a volume of a group of individual grains. Bulk density depends on packing density of the grain sample. It is affected, for example, by grain size and grain shape. Exactly seen, it is not a material property. However, some values for typical blasting media are listed in Table 2.2, based on standard grain samples. A typical ratio between apparent density and bulk density is ~2 for many abrasive materials.

2.6 Number and Kinetic Energy of Abrasive Particles

2.6.1 Abrasive Particle Number and Frequency

The number of particles involved in a blast cleaning process can be approximated as follows:

$$N_P = \frac{\dot{m}_P}{m_P} \cdot t_E \tag{2.7}$$

The mass of an individual abrasive particle is:

$$m_P = \frac{\pi}{6} \cdot d_P^3 \cdot \rho_P \tag{2.8}$$

for spherical particles. If, for example, the median particle diameter d_{P50} is utilised, the number of particles in a transversal (y-direction) moving blast cleaning jet is:

$$N_P = \frac{6 \cdot \dot{m}_P \cdot y}{\pi \cdot \rho_P \cdot d_{P50}^3 \cdot v_T} \tag{2.9}$$

For a given traverse distance, the higher the abrasive mass flow rate, the higher the number of abrasive particles. The higher the abrasive material density and average abrasive particle diameter, the lower the number of abrasive particles. The abrasive particle impact frequency is simply:

$$\dot{N}_P = \frac{N_P}{t_E} = \frac{\dot{m}_P}{m_P} \tag{2.10}$$

For a given exposure time, the impact frequency increases with an increase in abrasive mass flow rate and with a decrease in average particle diameter. If abrasive material density increases, the impact frequency decreases. Henning and Brauer (1986) introduced a particle frequency number:

$$\dot{n}_P = \frac{\dot{N}_P}{A_C} \tag{2.11}$$

which considers geometrical effects. The unit of this parameter is $1/(s \cdot m^2)$. Glatzel and Brauer (1978) defined a dimensionless collision number, which characterised the collision between reflected and incident abrasive particles:

$$c_K = \frac{c_R \cdot d_N}{d_P \cdot \cos\varphi} \tag{2.12}$$

The variable c_R is the particle concentration in the impinging stream. This variable can be calculated as follows:

$$c_R = \frac{4}{\pi} \cdot \frac{\dot{m}_P}{v_P \cdot \rho_P \cdot d_N^2} \tag{2.13}$$

The collision number is high for a high particle concentration, for a small nozzle diameter, for small abrasive particles, and for high angles of impingement.

2.6.2 Kinetic Energy of Abrasive Particles

The kinetic energy of a spherical abrasive particle is simply:

$$E_P = \frac{\pi}{12} \cdot d_P^3 \cdot \rho_P \cdot v_P^2 \tag{2.14}$$

Data plotted in Fig. 2.16 illustrate typical values for kinetic energies. The kinetic energy of a glass bead with a density $\rho_P = 2{,}450\,\mathrm{kg/m^3}$, a diameter $d_P = 1.5\,\mathrm{mm}$ and an impingement velocity $v_P = 100\,\mathrm{m/s}$ reads $E_P = 0.022\,\mathrm{J}$ as marked in the graph. It may, however, be noted that abrasive particle size and abrasive particle velocity cannot be varied independently on each other in most blast cleaning devices. This special topic is discussed in Sect. 3.6.3. The power delivered to the cleaning site by

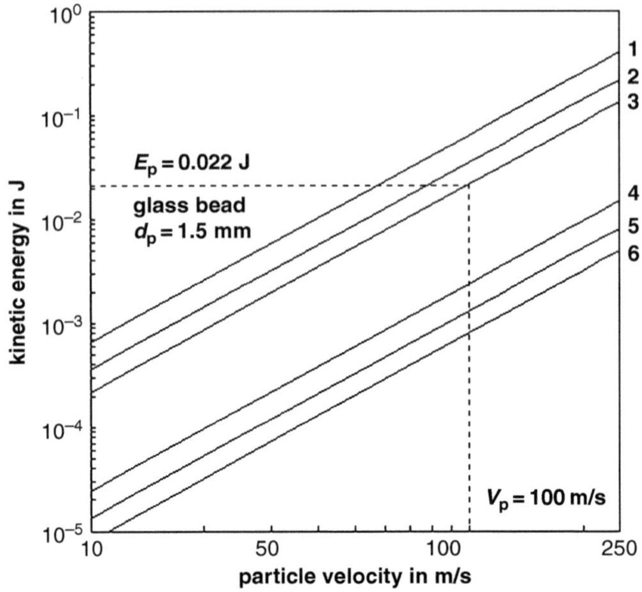

Fig. 2.16 Kinetic energies of abrasive particles; calculated with (2.14). 1 to 3: particle diameter $d_P = 1.5\,mm$; 4 to 6: particle diameter $d_P = 0.5\,mm$; 1+4: steel ball ($\rho_P = 7{,}300\,kg/m^3$); 3 + 6: glass bead ($\rho_P = 2{,}450\,kg/m^3$); 2 + 5: garnet ($\rho_P = 4{,}000\,kg/m^3$)

an abrasive particle stream is given through the following relationship:

$$P_P = \frac{\dot{m}_P}{2} \cdot v_P^2 = E_P \cdot \dot{N}_P \tag{2.15}$$

This is a simplified relationship, which assumes abrasive particles of equal sizes. The situation for such a case is illustrated in Fig. 2.17. If a certain power is available, it can be divided between individual abrasive particle energy and abrasive particle number (frequency). If a power of $P_P = 1.25\,kW$ is available, it can be seen from Fig. 2.17 that this power can either be spread over 765,000 particles per second, each with a kinetic energy of $E_P = 0.002\,J$; or it can be spread over 19,400 particles per second, each with a kinetic energy of $E_P = 0.06\,J$. Therefore, *loading intensity* (kinetic energy) and *loading frequency* (particle number) can be controlled. This control is mainly due to variations in abrasive particle size and abrasive particle material density.

2.6.3 Power Availability

Equation (2.15) characterises the power available at the nozzle exit. This amount of power is not available at the impact site. In order to consider this difference, Ciampini et al. (2003b) introduced the *power availability* for a target impinged by a

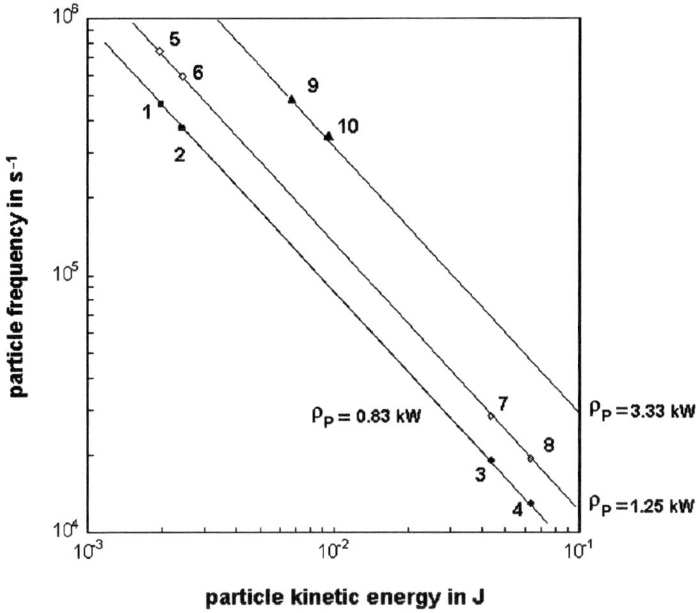

Fig. 2.17 Relationship between loading intensity (particle kinetic energy) and loading frequency (particle frequency) for three power values 1: $\dot{m}_P = 10\,\text{kg/min}$, $v_P = 100\,\text{m/s}$; 2: $\dot{m}_P = 10\,\text{kg/min}$, $v_P = 100\,\text{m/s}$; 3: $\dot{m}_P = 10\,\text{kg/min}$, $v_P = 100\,\text{m/s}$; 4: $\dot{m}_P = 10\,\text{kg/min}$, $v_P = 100\,\text{m/s}$; 5: $\dot{m}_P = 15\,\text{kg/min}$, $v_P = 100\,\text{m/s}$; 6: $\dot{m}_P = 15\,\text{kg/min}$, $v_P = 100\,\text{m/s}$; 7: $\dot{m}_P = 15\,\text{kg/min}$, $v_P = 100\,\text{m/s}$; 8: $\dot{m}_P = 15\,\text{kg/min}$, $v_P = 100\,\text{m/s}$; 9: $\dot{m}_P = 10\,\text{kg/min}$, $v_P = 200\,\text{m/s}$; 10: $\dot{m}_P = 10\,\text{kg/min}$, $v_P = 200\,\text{m/s}$

stream of abrasive particles. This parameter can be calculated as follows:

$$P^* = \frac{2 \cdot P_T}{m_P \cdot v_P^2 \cdot \dot{N}_P} \tag{2.16}$$

The numerator is equal to (2.15). The denominator is the power of the abrasive particle stream available at the impinged surface, including the effect of interference between incident and rebound streams:

$$P_T = f(\dot{N}_P; d_N; d_P; m_P; v_P; x; e_R; f_C) \tag{2.17}$$

The variables listed in the brackets can be replaced by dimensionless values as shown in Sect. 3.5.5. The value for P^* is a measure of the degree to which incident particles are scattered by rebounding ones. A high value of P^* is a necessary (but not sufficient) condition for an effective blast cleaning process. Figure 2.18 shows the dependence of the dimensionless power availability on the ratio between nozzle radius and abrasive particle radius for a range of stream densities (see Sect. 3.5.5) and impact angles. At low stream densities, the dependence on r_N/r_P is rather weak; but at higher stream densities, the dependence becomes weak only when $r_N/r_P > 15$,

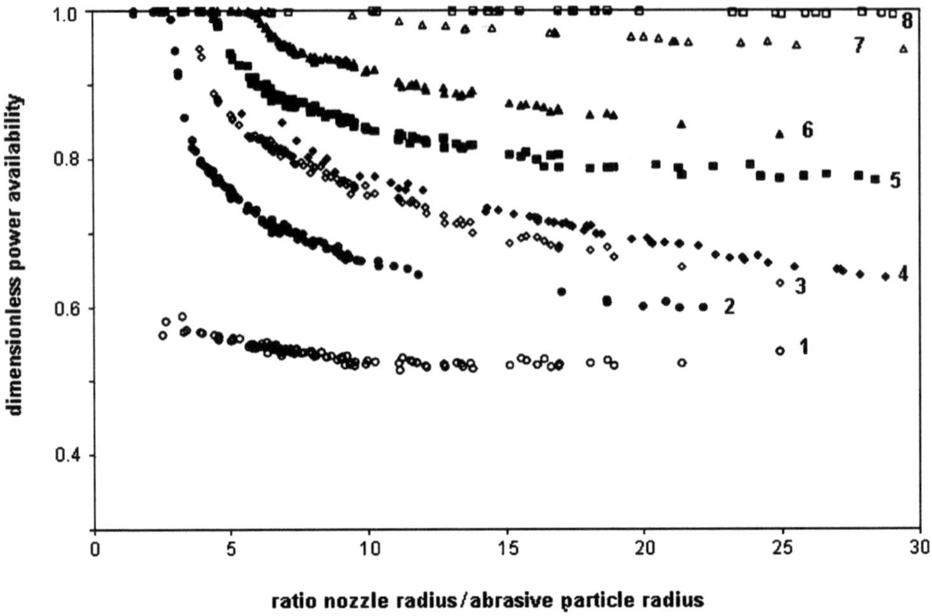

Fig. 2.18 Effects of nozzle diameter, particle diameter and particle stream density on power availability (Ciampini et al., 2003b). Ratio ρ_S/φ: 1 – 0.01/90°; 2 – 0.03/45°; 3 – 0.01/60°; 4 – 0.001/90°; 5 – 0.01/45°; 6 – 0.001/15°; 7 – 0.001/45°; 8 – 0.0001/45°

regardless of the impact angle. A more detailed discussion of these effects is provided by Ciampini et al. (2003b). The authors found, among others, that power availability decreased at higher impact angles and with larger relative distances between individual abrasive particles. There was, however, a certain value for the relative distance between individual particles at about $L^* = 20$, where the power availability reached unity.

2.7 Impurities

Impurities can deteriorate quality and efficiency of blast cleaning particles; they are in particular of importance if recycled abrasive material is being used. Impurities to be considered include non-abrasive residue, lead, water soluble contaminants and

Table 2.15 Requirements for recycled abrasives (SSPC-AB 2, 2004)

Matter	Limitation
Non-abrasive residue	1% by weight
Lead content	0.1% by weight
Water soluble contaminants	1,000 $\mu\Omega$/cm (electric conductivity)
Oil content	No presence, either on the surface of the water or as an emulsion in the water after 10 min

Table 2.16 Maximum permissible content of hazardous substrates (BGV D26)

Substrate	Permissible content (wt.%)
Total content	
Antimon, arsen, beryllium, lead, cadmium, chromate, cobalt, nickel, tin	2%
Arsen, beryllium, chromate, cobalt, nickel	0.2%
Individual contents	
Beryllium	0.1%
Cadmium	0.1%
Chromate	0.1%
Cobalt	0.1%
Free crystalline silica	
Cristobalit	2%
Quartz	2%
Tridymit	2%

oil. Some limits are listed in Table 2.15. Data sheets very often present impurities in mass percentage. Foreign solid matter can easily be estimated for metallic particles by use of magnets. Soluble foreign matter, however, such as salts, are more difficult to estimate. Basically, conductivity measurements or chemical analyses are required to quantify these parameters.

Table 2.16 lists critical amounts of hazardous substances that should not be exceeded. The limits being listed must be undershoot as far as possible. Blast cleaning abrasives must not contain more than 2 wt.% of free crystalline silica. Free silica includes the modifications listed in Table 2.16.

Contamination of abrasive particles is a critical issue if the abrasive material is being recycled. Table 2.17 gives results of measurements performed on six different recycled abrasive materials. It can be seen that the values for lead content and the values for electric conductivity exceeded critical regulatory limits. Further results are published by Johnson (1990).

Jopp (1995) measured the pH-values of numerous abrasive materials. He mixed 100 g abrasive material into 100 ml demineralised water and stored the suspension for 4 weeks at room temperature. Results of these measurements are provided in Fig. 2.19. Glass beads and glass powder caused a high alkalinity which may increase the probability of corrosion of the blast cleaned steel substrate at elevated

Table 2.17 Contamination of recycled abrasive field work mixes (Boocock, 1994)

Sample No.	Lead in ppm[a]	Electric conductivity in μS/cm[b]
1	8,200	480
2	220	480
3	8,400	540
4	<50	120
5	1,100	400
6	2,600	700

[a]Limit: 200 ppm
[b]Limit: 1,000 μS/cm

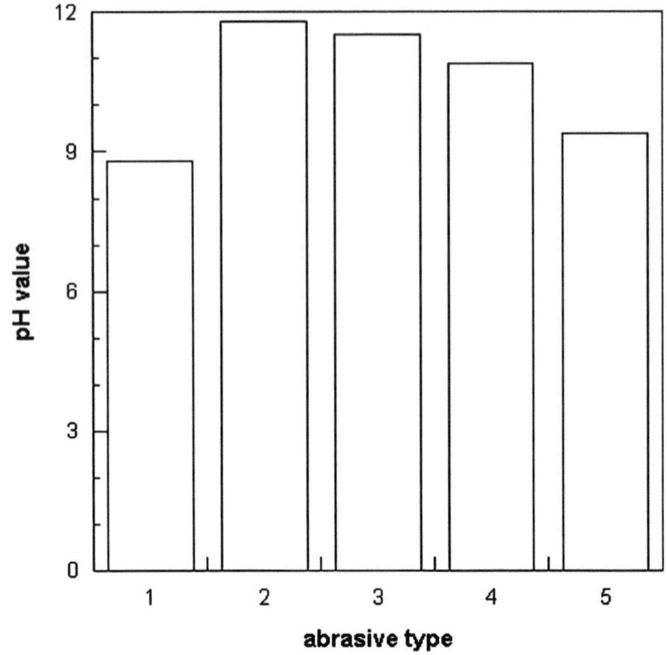

Fig. 2.19 pH-values for different abrasive materials (Jopp, 1995). Abrasive material: 1 – corundum; 2 – glass beads; 3 – glass powder; 4 – steel shot; 5 – steel grit

temperatures. It was shown that the pH-values of abrasive materials had a direct relationship to the durability of epoxy-based adhesive joints. Joints prepared with an abrasive material having a high pH-value exhibited the lowest durability values, and vice versa (Jopp, 1995).

2.8 Global Abrasive Evaluation Parameter

A global abrasive assessment parameter does not exist for blast cleaning processes. For a similar machining process – hydro-abrasive machining – Agus et al. (1995) introduced the following global assessment parameter to evaluate abrasive materials:

$$\chi_P = H_P^{a_1} \cdot S_P^{a_2} \cdot \rho_P^{a_3} \cdot d_P^{a_4} \cdot \dot{m}_P^{a_5} \qquad (2.18)$$

This equation includes the following variables:

- abrasive material hardness;
- abrasive particle shape;
- abrasive material density;
- abrasive particle diameter;
- abrasive mass flow rate.

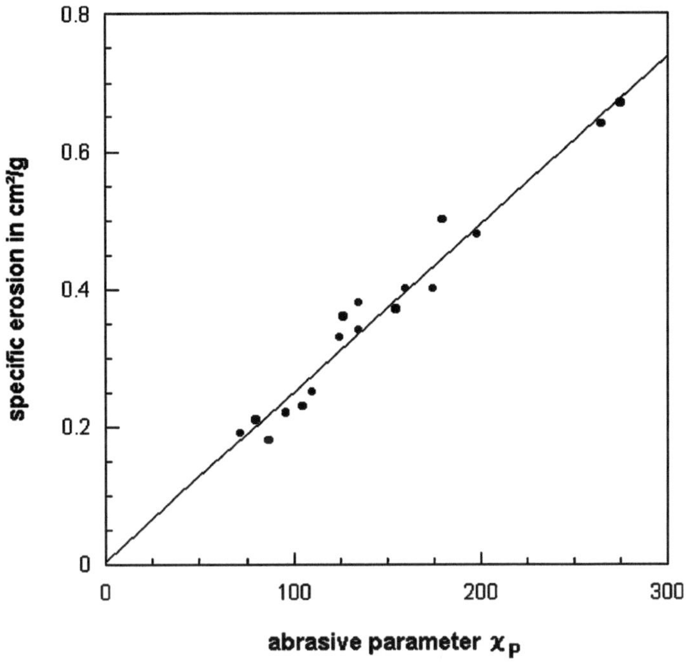

Fig. 2.20 Relationship between erosion rate and global abrasive assessment parameter for hydro-abrasive machining (Agus et al., 1995)

In (2.18), H_P is the Knoop hardness, and S_P is a particle shape factor. The evaluation parameter χ_P can be directly related to the specific erosion capability of hydro-abrasive jets (Agus et al., 1995). Some results are displayed in Fig. 2.20. For this special erosion case, abrasive material hardness and abrasive particle shape showed the most remarkable effects on the erosion process. For harder substrate materials, abrasive material hardness was predominant; whereas particle shape was most important for softer materials. Although corresponding relationships are not known for blast cleaning processes, the approach may form some basics for further research.

2.9 Process Behaviour of Abrasive Particles

2.9.1 Fracture Zones

Abrasive particles fracture during the blast cleaning process. This fracture process modifies certain properties of the particles, namely size and shape. These changes affect the reusability of the materials.

Figure 2.21 shows a simplification of the fracture structure in a non-regular particle subjected to impact. In the figure, two fracture zones can be distinguished. The *primary zone* is a result of high-velocity stress waves generated during the

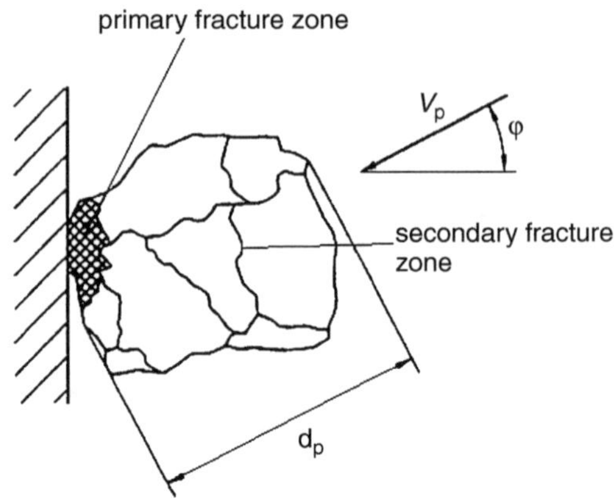

Fig. 2.21 Geometric situation and fracture structure of a particle subjected to impact (adapted from Buhlmann, 1970)

impact. On their way through the particle, the waves decelerated and reflected on the rear side of the particle. The reflected waves hit the fracture front. When the reflected waves partially stopped the fracture front, coarser fragments formed on the rear side of the particles which is defined as the *secondary zone*. Among others, Reiners (1960) documented these processes by using a high-speed photography technique. Salman and Gorham (2000) rationalised the appearance of damage and fracture features for impinging glass beads. The authors found that fracture appearance depended on impact velocity. For lower impact velocities ($v_P = 25$ m/s), only crack figures (Hertzian crack systems) could be observed; whereas fragment formation and powder formation took part at higher velocities ($v_P = 50$ m/s). Sparks and Hutchings (1993) reported that the initial fracture of impinging glass spheres ($v_P = 98$ m/s) occurred in two ways: by the detachment of a small cap, and by splitting across the whole sphere, forming almost hemispherical fragments. Many smaller fragments, with flat faces and sharp angular corners, were also observed.

Calboreanu (1991) found notable differences in the behaviour of steel shot whether it was impinged against a hard target surface (65 HRC) or against a soft target surface (22 HRC). In case of the hard target surface, he observed well-developed deformation bands on the shot particles, and the main breakdown mechanism was accomplished by internal crack extension. Shot impacted against the soft target surface presented small peripheral radial cracks (50–100 μm in length). The author also found that steel shot impacted against a softer surface had a higher amount of facets and a longer average size of the facets than the shot propelled against a harder surface. Results of these investigations are shown in Fig. 2.22.

Figure 2.23 illustrates the change in hardness of cut steel shot after a number of impact cycles. A significant increase in hardness can be seen for the first cycles, which probably corresponded to work hardening of the metal during the initial plastic deformation cycles. The hardness then stabilised, but finally started to drop at about 1,000 cycles, probably because the metal was softened after a high number of deformation cycles.

Wellinger and Gommel (1967) also performed deformation studies on cut steel wire abrasives. They measured the changes in hardness in the rim region as well

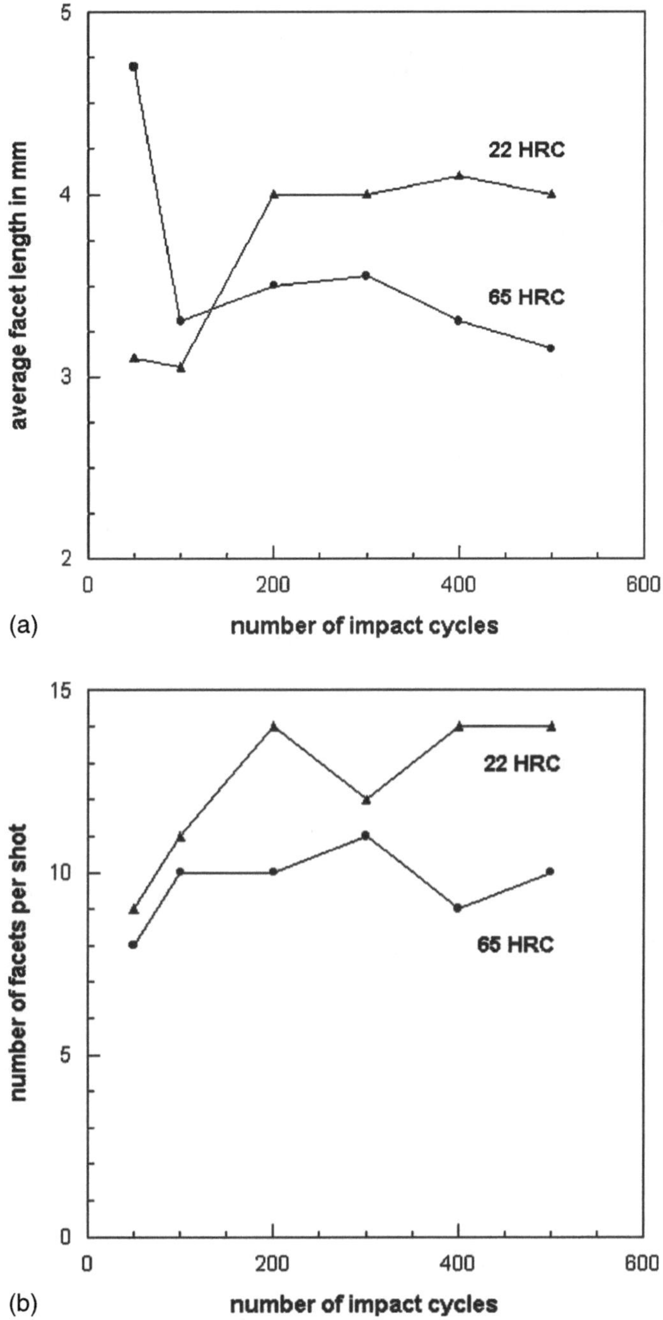

Fig. 2.22 Effects of target plate hardness and number of cycles on facet parameters for steel shot (Calboreanu, 1991); impact velocity: 61 m/s; shot designation: S 460. (**a**) Average facet length; (**b**) Average number of facets

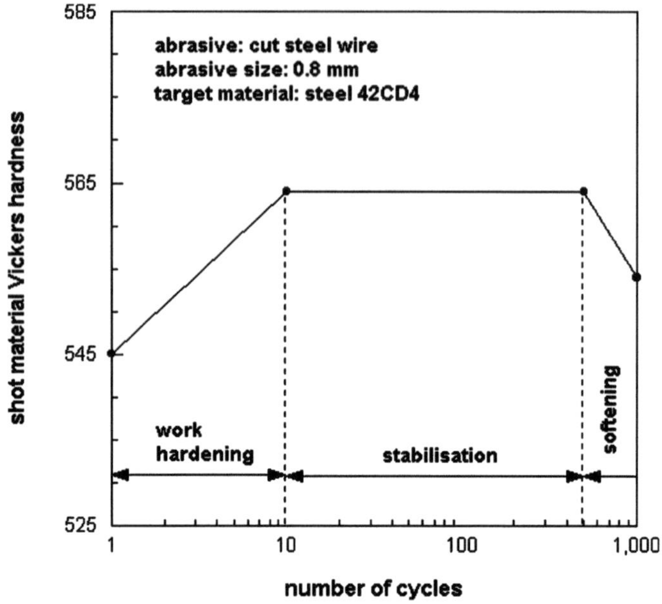

Fig. 2.23 Hardness modification of cut steel wire during shot peening (Flavenot and Lu, 1990)

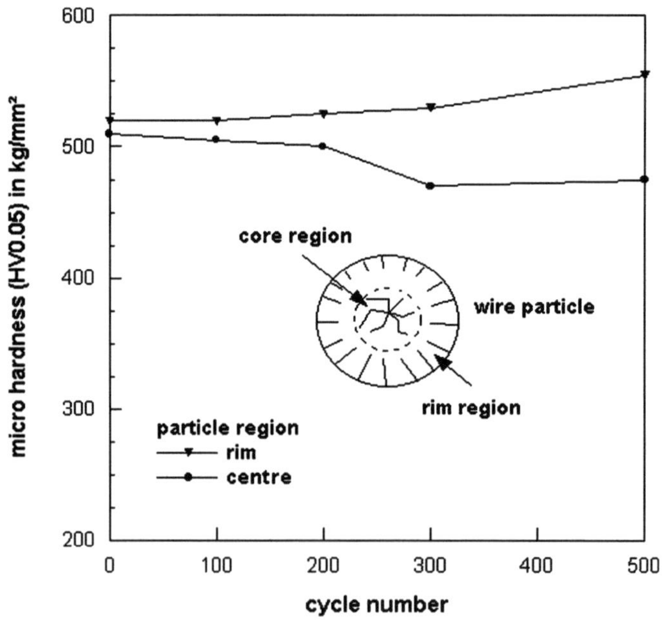

Fig. 2.24 Hardness modification of cut steel wire during the impingement on a steel plate (Wellinger and Gommel, 1967); abrasive size: 900 μm; impact speed: 70 m/s; wire strength: 170 kg/mm^2; substrate hardness: 750 kg/mm^2 (VH10)

as in the core region of the particles as a function of the number of impact cycles. Results of this study are displayed in Fig. 2.24. It can be seen that the hardness increased in the rim region with an increasing number of impact cycles, whereas the hardness in the core region decreased. The hardness decrease in the core region is assumed to be a measure of material fatigue. The difference in the hardness values between rim and core first increased with an increase in the number of cycles, but it reached a saturation level at about 500 cycles. At this cycle number, the authors observed the first fragmentation of abrasive particles. Obviously, the deformation capability of the material was exhausted at this cycle level.

2.9.2 Fracture Probability of Abrasive Particles

The major kinematic parameter in impact comminution is the impact velocity which is equal to the velocity of the impinging abrasive particle. The particle hits the solid surface whereby stresses are generated not only on the target surface, but also in the particle. Figure 2.21 illustrates the geometrical situation. A certain probability exists that an impinging grain fractures during the impact. This fracture probability strongly depends on impact velocity, impact angle and particle diameter. Experimental results are reported by Rumpf (1965) and Ruppel and Brauer (1990). Figure 2.25 shows the effects of impact velocity and impact angle on the fracture probability of non-regular quartz particles. The fracture probability increased with an increase in the impact velocity and an increase in the impact angle. Two critical velocity values can be distinguished in this graph.

The first value is a *threshold velocity*. In the graph, it is about $v_P = 40\,\text{m/s}$ for the glass sphere impinging the target at an angle of $\varphi = 89°$. This velocity must be exceeded in order to introduce fracture of individual particles. The threshold velocity is rather constant for most artificial abrasive materials, say glass beads; but it shows some scatter for natural abrasive materials, say quartz. The reason is the irregular uncontrolled distribution of flaws in the natural materials. Yashima et al. (1987) have shown that the threshold velocity depended on the particle size, and they derived the following relationship:

$$\frac{m_P}{2} \cdot v_P^2 \propto d_P^{\frac{3 \cdot m_F - 5}{m_F}} \tag{2.19}$$

This relationship delivers:

$$v_{Pt} \propto d_P^{\frac{1}{2} \cdot \left(\frac{3 \cdot m_F - 5}{m_F} - 3\right)} \tag{2.20}$$

Here, m_F is a flaw size distribution parameter of the abrasive material. Typical values are $m_F = 5.9$ for glass beads and $m_F = 21$ for quartz particles (with particle sizes between $d_P = 100$ and $2{,}000\,\mu\text{m}$). With these m_F-values, (2.20) delivers $v_{Pt} \propto d_P^{-0.42}$ for glass beads and $v_{Pt} \propto d_P^{-0.12}$ for quartz.

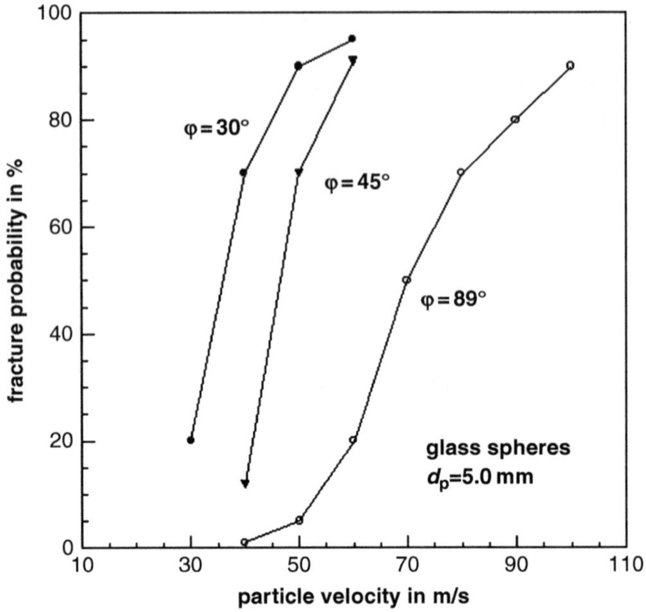

Fig. 2.25 Relationships between fracture probability, impact velocity and impact angle (Ruppel and Brauer, 1990)

The threshold velocity also depends on a large amount of the target material properties. Shipway and Hutchings (1993b) investigated the effects of substrate hardness and found a notable influence of the hardness on the threshold velocities for glass beads. Results of their study are summarised in Table 2.18. It can be seen that the threshold velocity was rather low for target materials featuring a high hardness.

The second critical value, which is illustrated in Fig. 2.25, is a *saturation velocity*. If this velocity is being exceeded, any impinging abrasive particle will be fractured; the fracture probability is unity. This saturation velocity is not being reached in any of the conditions considered in Fig. 2.25.

Relationships between impact velocity, particle size and fragmentation behaviour of impinging particles were in detail investigated by Andrews and Kim (1998, 1999)

Table 2.18 Effect of target material hardness on threshold velocity of 700-μm glass beads (Shipway and Hutchings, 1993b)

Target material	Vickers hardness in GPa	Threshold velocity in m/s
Aluminium alloy	1.75	216–240
Brass	1.22	216–289
Copper	0.89	250–288
Glass	6.14	175–200
Mild steel	1.98	201–218
Zirconia	14.0	41–48
Silicone carbide	30.5	47–82
Titanium alloy	3.25	174–203

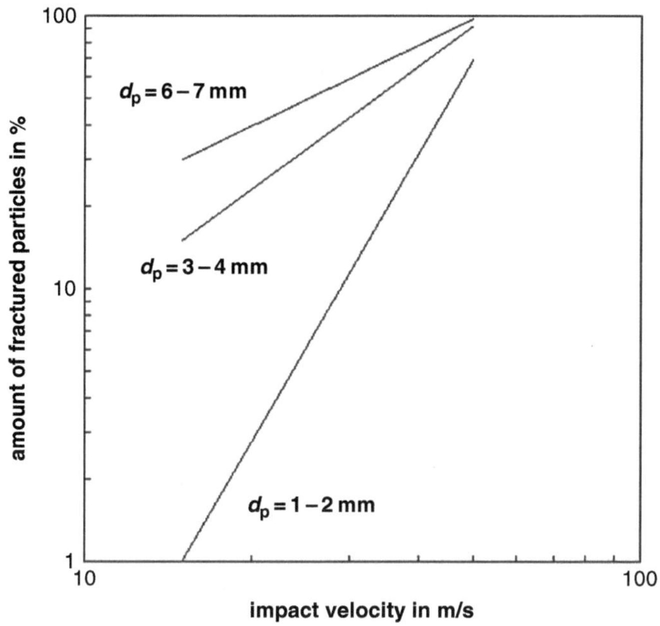

Fig. 2.26 Effects of impact velocity and particle diameter on the fracture probability of quartz particles (Rumpf, 1965)

and Rumpf (1965). Figure 2.26 illustrates relationships between fracture probability, particle velocity and particle diameter. As the figure shows, fracture probability is very sensitive to particle size. Because the curves are plotted in a bi-logarithmic mode in Fig. 2.26, straight lines can be drawn through the experimental points. It is evident that the ascent of these lines decreased with an increase in particle size. The ascent of the lines may be considered to describe the homogeneity of grain fragmentation. Whenever the particles contain a rather high number of cracks with different length, or of other flaws, the probability function will exhibit a low progress in a log-log-net.

Hutchings (1992) suggested that beyond a critical particle size and a critical particle velocity, the fragmentation of the particle is introduced. Particles smaller than a threshold size cannot be fractured, but will deform plastically; this threshold diameter is:

$$\mathrm{d_{Ppl}} = 30 \cdot \left(\frac{\mathrm{K_{Ic/P}}}{\mathrm{H_P}}\right)^2 \tag{2.21}$$

The following expressions for the critical particle size above which fracture will occur on impact at a given velocity can be derived for three cases (Hutchings, 1992):

(1) For $H_P > H_M$ and for an angular particle:

$$d_{Pf} \propto \left(\frac{K_{Ic/P}}{H_P}\right)^2 \cdot \frac{H_P^{1/2}}{H_M^{1/6}} \cdot \rho_P^{-1/3} \cdot v_P^{-2/3} \tag{2.22}$$

(2) For $H_P > H_M$ and for a rounded particle:

$$d_{Pf} \propto \left(\frac{K_{Ic/P}}{H_P}\right)^2 \cdot \frac{H_P^{1/2}}{H_M^{1/4}} \cdot \rho_P^{-1/4} \cdot v_P^{-1/2} \tag{2.23}$$

This relationship corresponds well with (2.20) for $m_F = 5.9$ for glass beads.

(3) For $H_P < H_M$ and for any geometry of the particle:

$$d_{Pf} \propto \left(\frac{K_{Ic/P}}{H_P}\right)^2 \cdot H_P^{1/4} \cdot \rho_P^{-1/4} \cdot v_P^{-1/2} \tag{2.24}$$

These conditions for abrasive particle fracture can be represented graphically. The case (1) for hard angular particles, shown in Fig. 2.27, illustrates three regimes of behaviour. The sloping line between the regimes III and II represents the condition for particle fracture given by (2.23). Within regime III, particle fracture will occur. Slikkerveer (1999) investigated the fragmentation behaviour of fused alumina powder ($d_P = 29$–44 μm), and he found a rather high threshold velocity for powder particle fragmentation of about $v_P = 125$ m/s.

Bandaru (2004) considered the volume loss of abrasive particles as a fragmentation criterion, and he investigated the effects of numerous process parameters on the

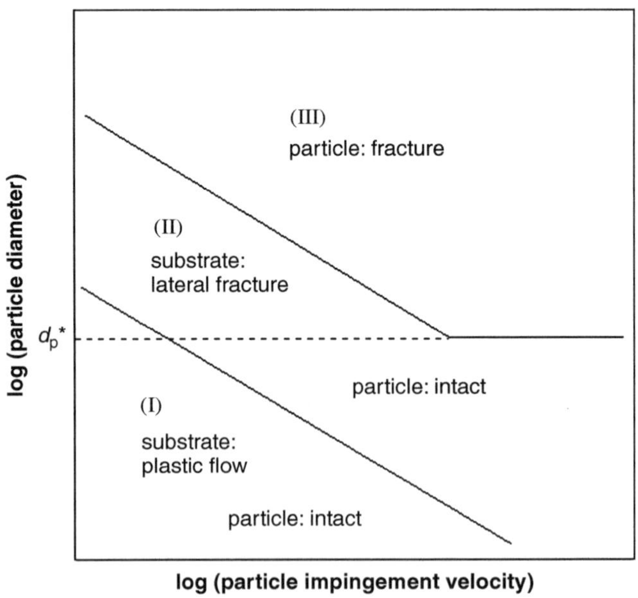

Fig. 2.27 Graphical representation of (2.24) for hard angular abrasive particles

volume loss. He found that volume loss increased linearly with increases in impact velocity, impact angle and abrasive particle size.

2.9.3 Effects of Abrasive Material Structure

The fracture probability of abrasive particles also strongly depends on their structure, in particular on the number and distribution of non-regularities, such as micro-cracks, grain boundaries and dislocations. Figure 2.28 illustrates how particle threshold velocity depends on the particle size and on abrasive material. A quartz particle with a diameter of $d_P = 500\ \mu m$ requires a critical velocity of $v_P = 25$ m/s, whereas a quartz glass particle of equal size requires a critical velocity of $v_P = 50$ m/s. It is known that the number of flaws in an abrasive grain depends on the volume of the abrasive particle (Huang et al., 1995). Equation (2.1) is an expression to this relationship. Experimental results by Martinec (1994) showed the validity of this concept for the fragmentation of abrasive particles. The author found that garnet particles with very small diameters were extremely homogeneous, and thus they showed good stability in size and shape during the acceleration process in mixing nozzles.

Cleaver and Ghadiri (1993) suggested a reduced impact fragmentation for particles with lower hardness, lower density, larger fracture toughness and lower

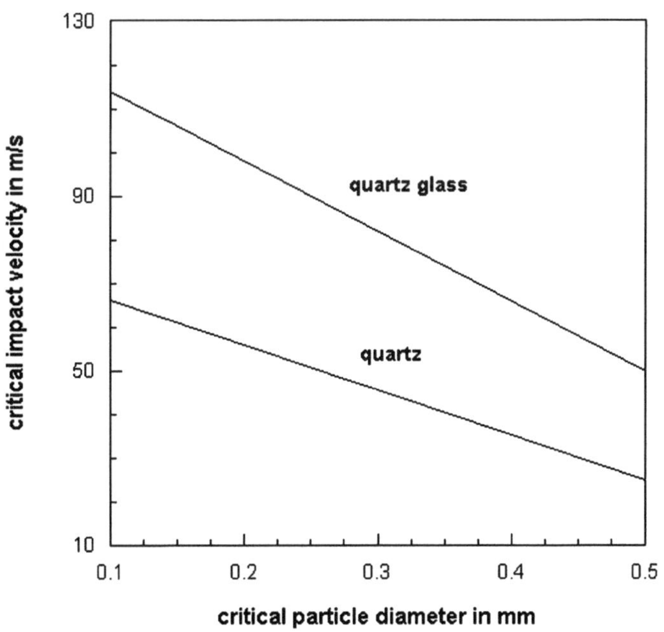

Fig. 2.28 Effects of abrasive material on threshold conditions for impact fragmentation (Yashima et al., 1987)

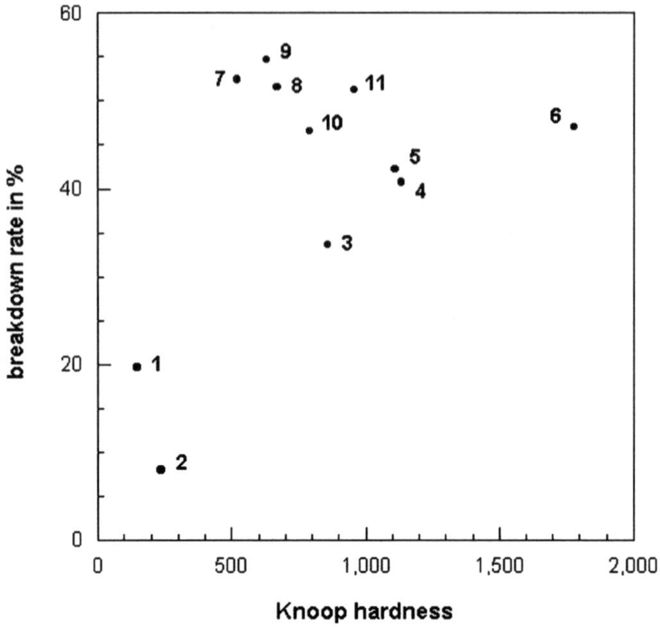

Fig. 2.29 Relationship between breakage ratio and abrasive material hardness (Fairfull and Weldon, 2001). Abrasive type; 1 – staurolite; 2 – steel grit; 3 – olivine; 4 – iron oxide; 5 – garnet. (A); 6 – garnet (B); 7 – copper slag; 8 – coal slag (A); 9 – coal slag (B); 10 – silica sand; 11 – nickel slag

particle diameter. Murugesh et al. (1991) reported similar relationships. Kiesskalt and Dahlhoff (1965) and Dahlhoff (1967) found significant relationships between the wave velocity in minerals and their resistance against impact comminution. The higher the wave velocity, the higher was the resistance against fragmentation. Figure 2.29 shows results for breakdown experiments performed by Fairfull and Weldon (2001) on a number of abrasive materials. It can be seen that the breakdown rate was low for abrasives having a low Knoop hardness. No trend could be recognised in the area of moderate and high hardness values. In that range, the effects of structural properties probably covered those of the hardness.

2.9.4 Debris Size

Reiners (1960) analysed debris generated during the impact of glass spheres. For not very high impact velocities ($v_P = 100\,\text{m/s}$), this author found large portions of sharp-shaped particles in all grain-size classes. At higher impact velocities ($v_P = 650\,\text{m/s}$), the debris consisted mainly of cubic and rectangular grains. Debris size decreased according to a power function if impact velocity increased. Reiners (1960) also found that the target material and geometry affected the average debris size. Debris size was largest for a copper substrate compared with a steel substrate.

2.9.5 Disintegration Numbers

Gommel (1967a) introduced a so-called *shatterability*, a parameter which quantifies the particle fragmentation during the impingement on a substrate. It was shown that shatterability depended on substrate hardness and impact velocity. If substrate hardness and impact velocity increased, shatterability increased. However, particle fragmentation was independent of impact velocity if the substrate hardness approached the hardness of the abrasive particle material (Gommel, 1967a).

Ohlsen (1997) introduced a *disintegration number* as follows:

$$\phi_D = 1 = \frac{\bar{d}_{Pout}}{\bar{d}_{Pin}} \qquad (2.25)$$

$$0 < \phi_D < 1$$

If $\phi_D = 0$, no disintegration of the particles occurs. The particle size parameter can be substituted by the particle parameters discussed in Sect. 2.4, for example, by d_{P50}. Results, based on steel shot tests, are displayed in Fig. 2.30. The disintegration numbers are rather low, pointing to a high size stability of the particles. It can also be noted that the disintegration number depended on the number of impact cycles, but also on the hardness of the target material. For the soft target material, the disintegration number was almost one order of magnitude larger than for the

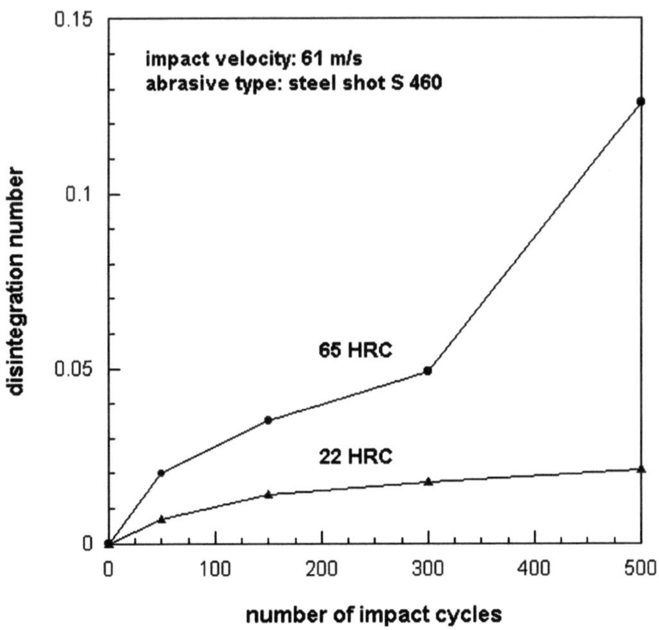

Fig. 2.30 Effects of number of impacts and target material hardness on the disintegration number (based o the sieve curves displayed in Fig. 2.33)

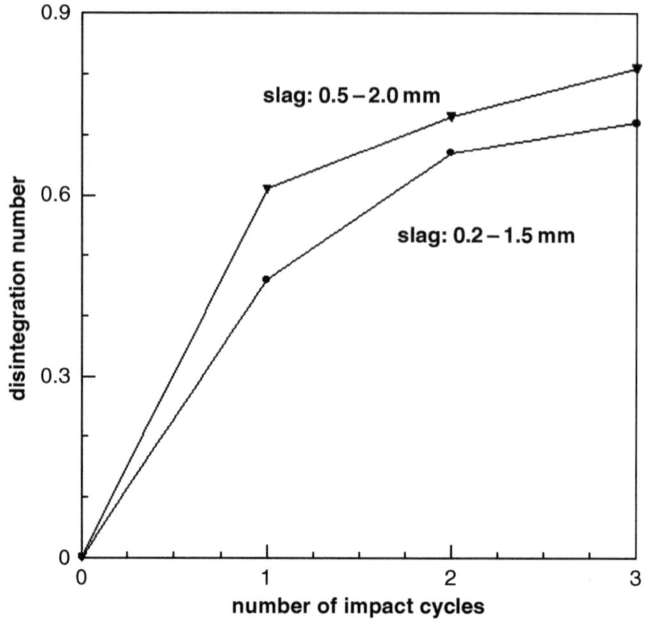

Fig. 2.31 Effects of number of impacts and abrasive particle size on the disintegration number (calculation is based on results reported by Hareux and Riac, 1986)

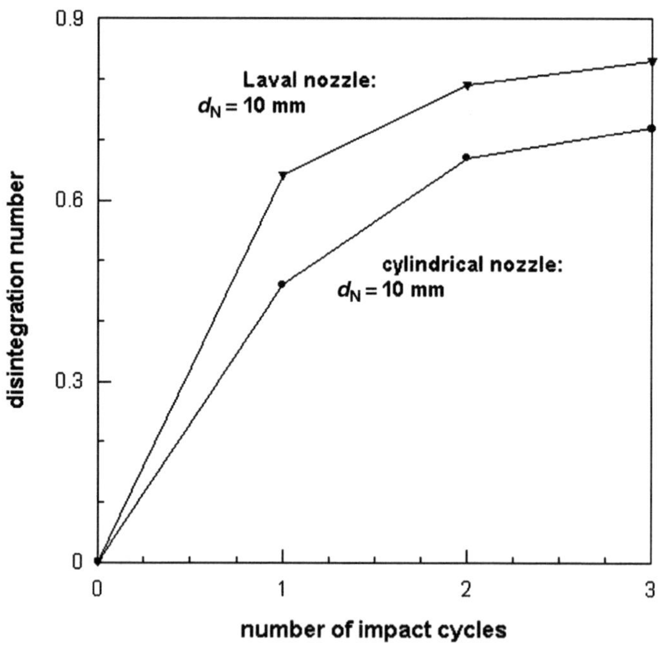

Fig. 2.32 Effects of number of impacts and nozzle type on the disintegration number (calculation is based on results reported by Hareux and Riac, 1986)

hard target material. Figure 2.31 illustrates the effect of the particle size of a slag material on its disintegration number. As could be expected from the results of the previous sections, disintegration number increased with an increase in the particle size. Another aspect is illustrated in Fig. 2.32 which shows the effect of nozzle type on the disintegration number. The disintegration of the abrasive material was more severe if the acceleration took part in a Laval nozzle. Laval-type nozzles can accelerate abrasive particles to higher speeds compared with cylindrical nozzles (see Sect. 3.3), and this results in a higher impingement speed and in a more severe fragmentation of the particles.

Repeated impingement of abrasive particles also affects the entire size distribution function of abrasive samples. An example is shown in Fig. 2.33. The amount of fine particles (left part of the graph) notably increased with an increase in number of impingement cycles. In recycling units, these rather fine particles are being removed from the sample if a certain amount is exceeded.

2.9.6 Particle Shape Modification During Abrasive Fragmentation

Another important aspect of the abrasive fragmentation is the *change in the shape* of the individual grains that may significantly influence the mechanism for material removal.

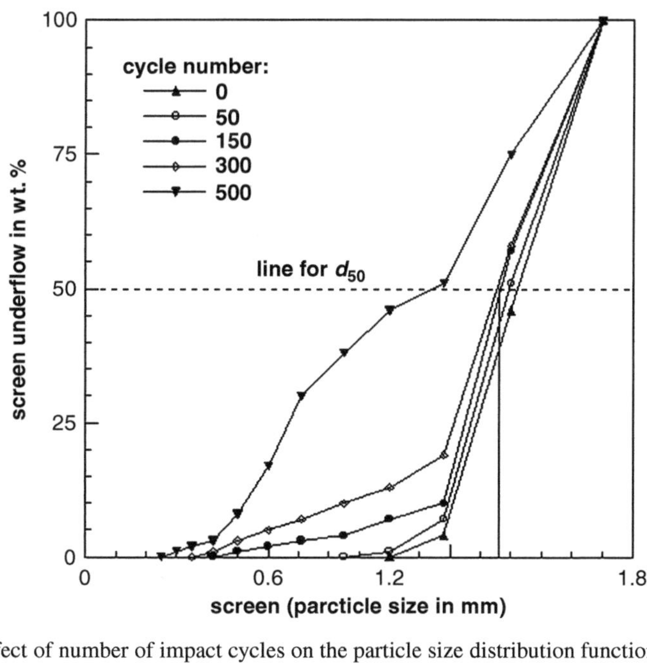

Fig. 2.33 Effect of number of impact cycles on the particle size distribution functions

Calboreanu (1991) who utilised round steel shot (S 460) for the impingement on cast iron samples noted a change of the shot contour from round to polygonal after 50 impact cycles (v_P = 61 m/s). A representative SEM-image of a polygonal shot contour is provided in Fig. 2.34.

Beitelman (2003) propelled very angular crushed steel grit (G 50) particles against carbon steel plates. He observed the following limiting cycle numbers: initial (zero cycles): very angular; after six cycles: angular; after 11 cycles: sub-angular; after 30 cycles: sub-rounded; after 200 cycles: rounded (see Fig. 2.9 for the particle shape designations). The author also investigated the effects of shape modifications on substrate profile and on the adhesion of coating systems; see Sects. 8.6.4 and 9.2.3 for the results. Wellinger and Gommel (1967) investigated the fragmentation behaviour of cut steel wires with a size of d_P = 900 µm at a moderate impact speed

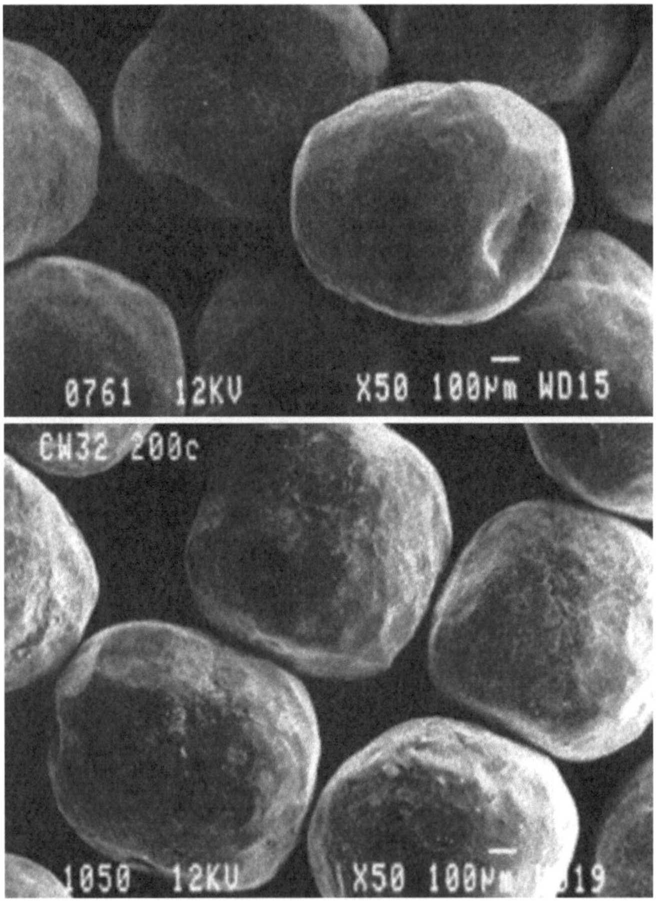

(a)

(b)

Fig. 2.34 SEM-images of shot particles (Flavenot and Lu, 1990); shot designation: S 460. (**a**) New, conditioned shot; (**b**) After 50 impact cycles (impact velocity: v_P = 61 m/s) on a cast iron target

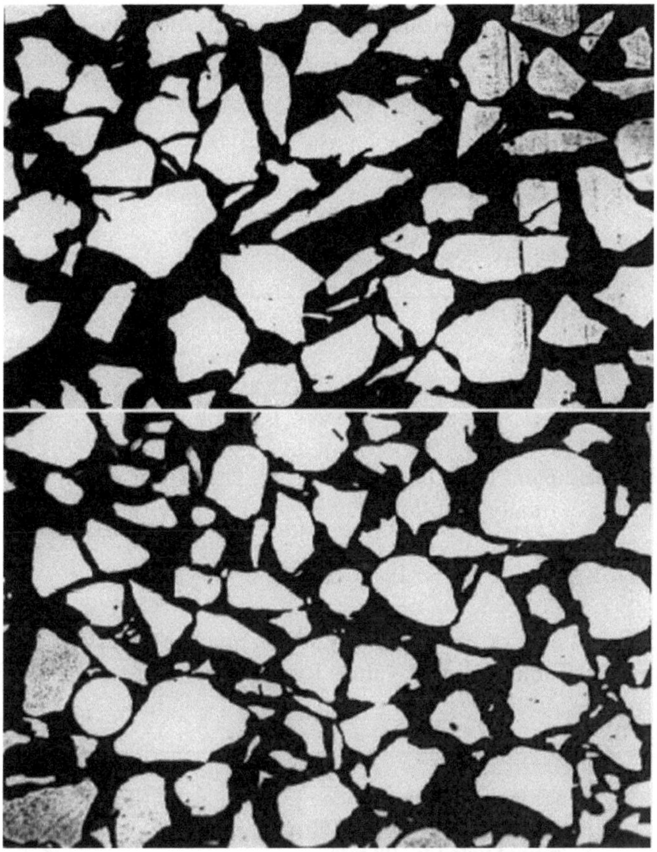

Fig. 2.35 SEM-images of stainless steel grit particles (Reference: Vulkan Inox GmbH, Hattingen); upper image: new particles; lower image: particles after one year of operation

of $v_P = 70\,\mathrm{m/s}$, and they found that the original wire shape changed into an almost spherical shape after about 150 impact cycles. Figure 2.35 illustrates the change in grain shape of stainless steel particles after one year in operation. A rounding of the originally irregular particles can be recognised in the lower image.

2.9.7 Energy Absorption During Abrasive Fragmentation

The process of abrasive fragmentation absorbs a certain amount of the kinetic energy of the particles. If the original grain-size distribution of the particle mixture and that of the mixture after the blast cleaning process are known, Bond's (1953, 1961) comminution formula can be applied to approximate the energy involved in this fragmentation process. The specific absorbed energy is then given by:

Table 2.19 Workability indices of minerals (Bond, 1953)

Material	Workability index in kWh/t
Ferrochromite	7.64
Ferromagnesite	8.30
Glass	12.31
Gravel	16.06
Quartzite	13.57
Slag	9.39
Silica carbide	25.87
Silica sand	14.10

$$E_F = w_i \cdot \frac{\sqrt{d_{P80in}} - \sqrt{d_{P80out}}}{\sqrt{d_{P80in}}} \cdot \sqrt{\frac{100}{d_{P80out}}} \qquad (2.26)$$

The particle diameters must be given in μm. The power absorbed by the fragmentation process is finally as follows:

$$P_F = E_F \cdot \dot{m}_P \qquad (2.27)$$

In (2.26), w_i is the index of workability which must be estimated with a standard comminution tests. Table 2.19 lists values for some materials. Figure 2.36 displays

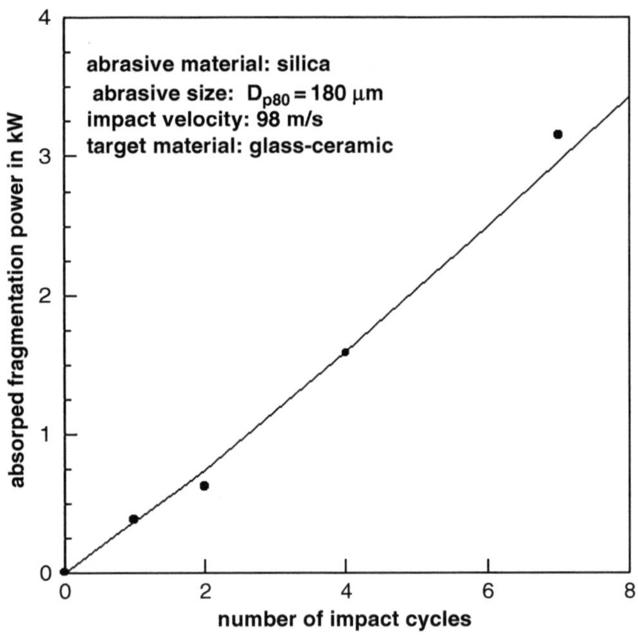

Fig. 2.36 Absorbed abrasive particle fragmentation power (calculation based on results reported by Sparks and Hutchings, 1993)

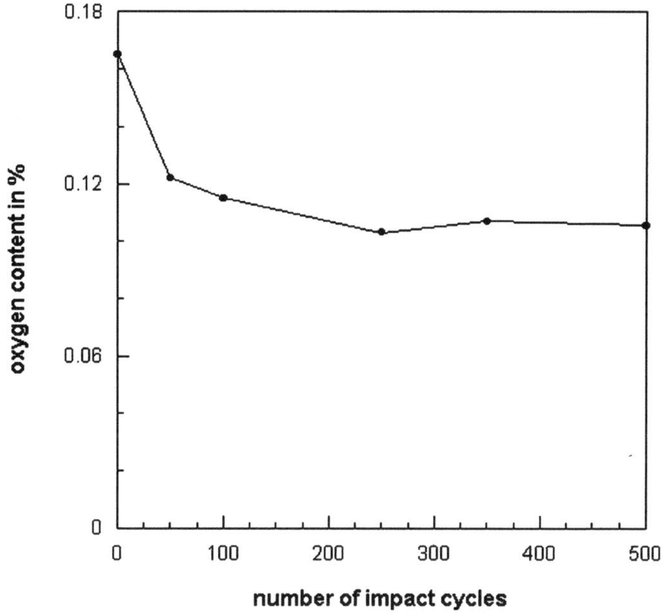

Fig. 2.37 Variation of oxygen content in steel shot after the impingement on cast iron (Calboreanu, 1991). Impact velocity: 61 m/s; shot designation: S 460

results of calculations performed with (2.27). The particle size parameters d_{P80in} and d_{P80out} for silica particles were taken from a detailed repeated impact study performed by Sparks and Hutchings (1993). The impact speed of the particles was $v_P = 98$ m/s, and the abrasive mass flow rate was assumed to be 10 kg/min. A Bond index of $w_i = 14.1$ kWh/t for silica sand was applied (see Table 2.19). For one impact cycle, the calculation delivers $P_F = 0.38$ kW. The power of the impinging abrasive particles can be calculated with (2.15), which delivers $P_P = 0.8$ kW. Therefore, almost 50% of the power delivered to the erosion site is dissipated into particle fragmentation. This rather high value is, however, caused by the high hardness of the target material, and it cannot be applied to other applications.

2.9.8 Chemical Degradation

Calboreanu (1991) investigated the behaviour of steel shot, impacted against cast iron, and found that the shot did not show chemical degradation after 500 cycles, except for a diminishment of the oxygen content due to the removal of the surface oxide layer. Results of this study are displayed in Fig. 2.37.

Chapter 3
Air and Abrasive Acceleration

3.1 Properties of Compressed Air

Air is a colourless, odourless and tasteless gas mixture. It consists of many gases, but primarily of oxygen (21%) and nitrogen (78%). Air is always more or less contaminated with solid particles, for example, dust, sand, soot and salt crystals. Typical properties of air are listed in Table 3.1. If air is considered to be an ideal gas, its behaviour can be described based on the general law of state:

$$\mathrm{p} \cdot \upsilon_{\mathrm{S}} = \mathrm{R_i} \cdot \mathrm{T} \tag{3.1}$$

where p is the static air pressure, υ_S is the specific volume of the gas, R_i is the individual gas constant and T is the absolute temperature. It can be distinguished between three pressure levels, which are illustrated in Fig. 3.1. The relationships between these pressure levels are as follows:

$$\mathrm{p} = \mathrm{p_0} + \mathrm{p_G} \tag{3.2}$$

The parameter p is the absolute pressure, the parameter p_G is the gauge pressure usually read by the pressure gages in the blast cleaning pressure systems, and the parameter p_0 is the atmospheric pressure. The atmospheric pressure is a function of altitude. It is important not to confuse the absolute pressure and the gauge pressure. For theoretical calculations, the absolute pressure must be used.

The parameter R_i in (3.1) is the individual gas constant, which is the energy delivered by a mass of 1 kg of air if its temperature is increased by +1°C (K) at constant pressure. Its value for air is provided in Table 3.1. The individual gas constant is the difference between isobaric heat capacity and isochoric heat capacity of the gas:

$$\mathrm{R_i} = \mathrm{c_P} - \mathrm{c_V} \tag{3.3}$$

The ratio between isobaric heat capacity and isochoric heat capacity is the isentropic exponent of the gas:

$$\kappa = \frac{\mathrm{c_P}}{\mathrm{c_V}} \tag{3.4}$$

Table 3.1 Properties of air

Parameter	Symbol	Unit	Value
Density[a]	ρ_A	kg/m^3	1.225
Dynamic viscosity[a]	η_0	Ns/m^2	1.72×10^{-5}
Isobaric specific heat capacity[b]	c_P	Nm/(kg K)	1,004
Isochoric specific heat capacity[b]	c_V	Nm/(kg K)	717
Gas constant	R_i	Nm/(kg K)	287
Adiabatic exponent	κ	–	1.4
Critical pressure ratio	β	–	0.528
Kinematic viscosity	ν_A	m^2/s	1.82×10^{-5}
Specific evaporation heat	q_V	Nm/kg	1.97×10^{-5}
Speed of sound[a]	c	m/s	331
Sutherland parameter	C_S	K	113

[a]Thermodynamic standard (Table 3.2: $\vartheta = 0°\text{C}$, $p = 0.101325$ MPa)
[b]For $T = 273$ K

Values for the heat capacities and for the isentropic exponent of air can be found in Table 3.1. The absolute temperature is given as follows:

$$T = \vartheta + 273.2 \tag{3.5}$$

Its physical unit is K. The parameter ϑ is the temperature at the Celsius scale (°C). With $\upsilon_S = 1/\rho_A$, (3.1) reads as follows:

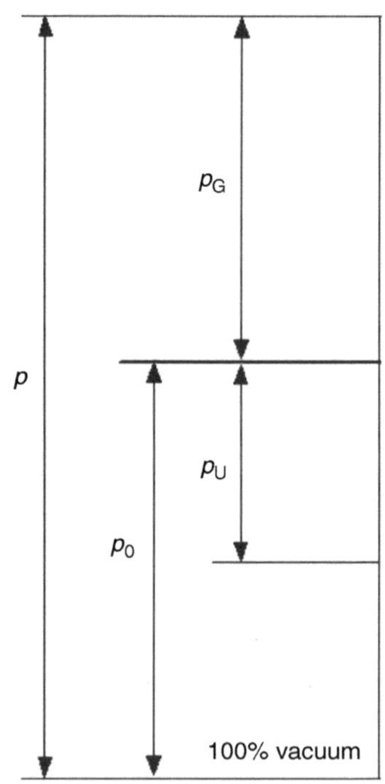

Fig. 3.1 Pressure levels

$$\frac{p}{\rho_A} = R_i \cdot T \tag{3.6}$$

This equation suggests that air density depends on pressure and temperature. These relationships are displayed in Fig. 3.2. For $T = 288.2\,\text{K}$ ($\vartheta = 15°\text{C}$) and $p = p_0 = 0.101325\,\text{MPa}$, the density of air is $\rho_A = 1.225\,\text{kg/m}^3$ according to (3.6).

The volume of air depends on its state. The following four standards can be distinguished for the state of air:

- physical normal condition (DIN 1343, 1990);
- industry standard condition (ISO 1217, 1996);
- environmental condition;
- operating condition.

These standards are defined in Table 3.2. It can be seen that the physical normal condition and the industry standard condition both apply to dry air only with a relative humidity of 0%. For wet air, corrective factors must be considered (see DIN 1945-1).

The dynamic viscosity of air is independent of pressure for most technical applications, but it depends on temperature according to the following relationship (Albring, 1970):

$$\eta_A = \eta_0 \cdot \left(\frac{T}{T_0}\right)^{1/2} \cdot \frac{1 + (C_S/T_0)}{1 + (C_S/T)} \tag{3.7}$$

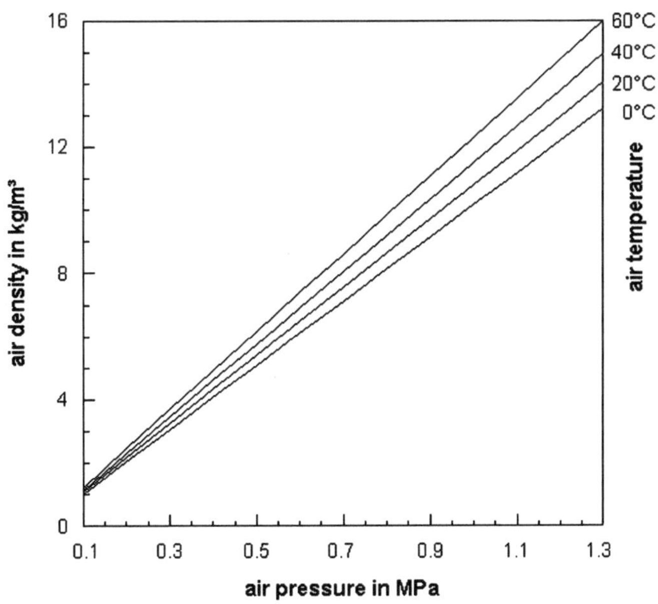

Fig. 3.2 Relationship between air pressure, air temperature and air density

Table 3.2 Conditions of state for air (DIN 1343, ISO 1217)

State	Temperature	Air pressure	Relative humidity	Air density
Physical standard (Normative standard)	0°C = 273.15 K	1.01325 bar = 0.101325 MPa	0%	1.294 kg/m³
Industry standard	20°C = 293.15 K	1.0 bar = 0.1 MPa	0%	–
Environmental condition	Environmental temperature	Environmental pressure	Environmental humidity	Variable
Operating condition	Operating temperature	Operating pressure	Variable	Variable

The Sutherland parameter C_S for air is listed in Table 3.1. Results of (3.7) are plotted in Fig. 3.3, and it can be seen that dynamic viscosity rises almost linearly with an increase in temperature (in contrast to water, where dynamic viscosity decreases with an increase in temperature). The kinematic viscosity of air depends on pressure, and the relationship is as follows:

$$\nu_A = \frac{\eta_A}{\rho_A} \tag{3.8}$$

with $\rho_A = f(p, T)$.

The speed of sound in air is a function of the gas properties and absolute temperature:

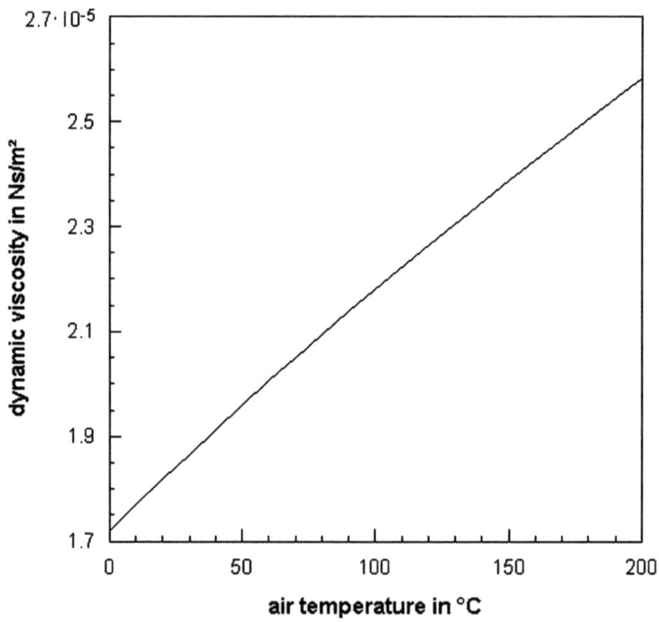

Fig. 3.3 Relationship between air temperature and dynamic viscosity of air

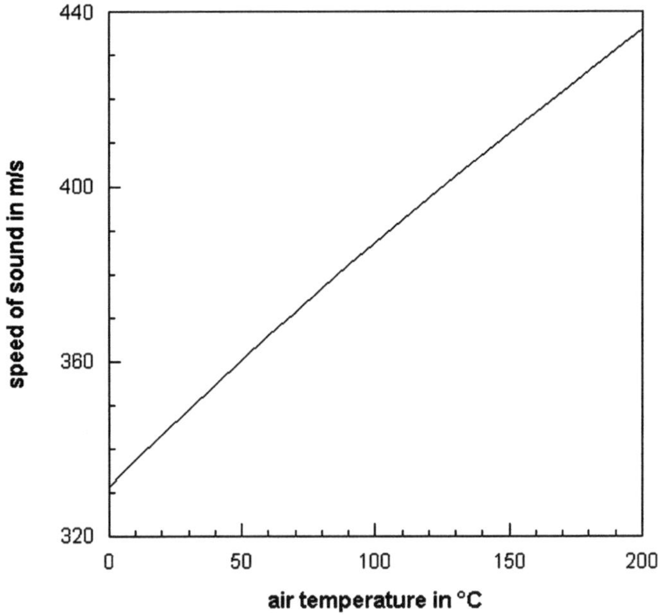

Fig. 3.4 Relationship between air temperature and speed of sound in air

$$c = (\kappa \cdot R_i \cdot T)^{1/2} \tag{3.9}$$

Results of (3.9) for different air temperatures are plotted in Fig. 3.4. The ratio between the actual local flow velocity and the speed of sound is the Mach number, which is defined as follows:

$$Ma = \frac{v_F}{c} \tag{3.10}$$

For $Ma < 1$, the flow is subsonic, and for $Ma > 1$, the flow is supersonic. For $Ma = 1$, the flow is sonic.

3.2 Air Flow in Nozzles

3.2.1 Air Mass Flow Rate Through Nozzles

Because air is a compressible medium, volumetric flow rate is not a constant value, and mass flow rate conversion counts for any calculation. The theoretical mass flow rate of air through a nozzle is given by the following equation (Bohl, 1989):

$$\dot{m}_{Ath} = \frac{\pi}{4} \cdot d_N^2 \cdot \left(2 \cdot \rho_A \cdot p\right)^{1/2} \cdot \underbrace{\left\{\frac{\kappa}{\kappa - 1} \cdot \left[\left(\frac{p_0}{p}\right)^{\frac{2}{\kappa}} - \left(\frac{p_0}{p}\right)^{\frac{\kappa+1}{\kappa}}\right]\right\}^{1/2}}_{\text{outflow function } \Psi} \tag{3.11}$$

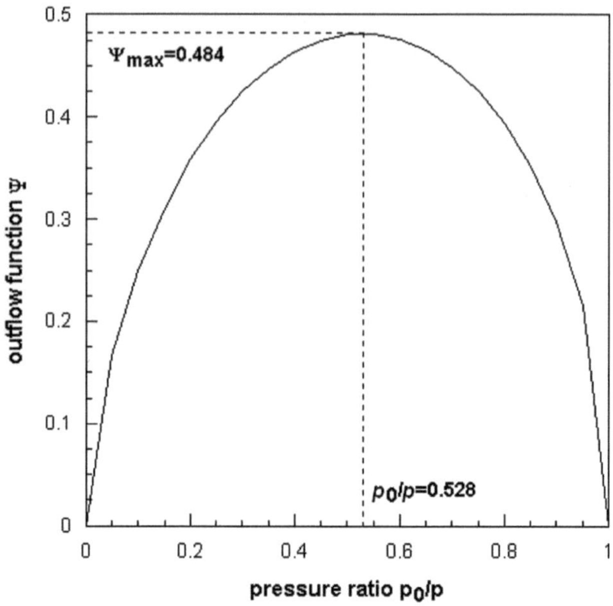

Fig. 3.5 Outflow function $\Psi = \mathrm{f}(p_0/p)$ for air

The outflow function $\Psi = \mathrm{f}(p_0/p)$ is plotted in Fig. 3.5. It is a parabolic function with a typical maximum value at a critical pressure ratio p_0/p. This critical pressure ratio is often referred to as *Laval pressure ratio*. It can be estimated as follows:

$$\left(\frac{\mathrm{p_0}}{\mathrm{p}}\right)_{\mathrm{crit}} = \left(\frac{2}{\kappa + 1}\right)^{\frac{\kappa}{\kappa - 1}} \tag{3.12a}$$

With $\kappa = 1.4$ for air, (3.12a) delivers the following value for the Laval pressure ratio:

$$\left(\frac{\mathrm{p_0}}{\mathrm{p}}\right)_{\mathrm{crit}} = 0.528 \tag{3.12b}$$

The corresponding value for the outflow function is $\psi_{\max}(0.528) = 0.484$. The graph plotted in Fig. 3.5 does not describe reality. In reality, air mass flow rate does not drop for pressure ratios < 0.528. The air mass flow rate rather follows the horizontal dotted line for $\psi_{\max} = 0.484$. Equation (3.11) can, therefore, be simplified for the condition $p_0/p < 0.528$ (respectively $p > 0.19\,\mathrm{MPa}$ for $p_0 = 0.1\,\mathrm{MPa}$):

$$\dot{\mathrm{m}}_{\mathrm{Ath}} = \frac{\pi}{4} \cdot \mathrm{d_N^2} \cdot (2 \cdot \rho_{\mathrm{A}} \cdot \mathrm{p})^{1/2} \cdot 0.484 \tag{3.13}$$

Equation (3.13) delivers the theoretical mass flow rate. The real mass flow rate includes a nozzle exit parameter:

Table 3.3 Nozzle exit coefficient α_N (Schwate, 1986)

Nozzle geometry	α_N-value
Sharp-edged opening	0.6
Opening with $l_N = 1.5 \cdot d_N$	0.8
Conical entry opening with rounded edges	0.9
Very smooth surface; rounded edges with radius = $0.5 \cdot d_N$	0.95

$$\dot{m}_A = \alpha_N \cdot \frac{\pi \cdot 0.484}{4} \cdot d_N^2 \cdot \left(2 \cdot \rho_A \cdot p\right)^{1/2} \tag{3.14}$$

The values for the nozzle exit coefficient α_N depend on nozzle geometry. Some values are listed in Table 3.3. Calculated theoretical air mass flow rates are plotted in Fig. 3.6. It can be seen that the mass flow rate linearly increases with an increase in nozzle pressure.

3.2.2 Volumetric Air Flow Rate

The volumetric air flow rate can be calculated as follows:

$$\dot{Q}_A = \frac{\dot{m}_A}{\rho_A} \tag{3.15}$$

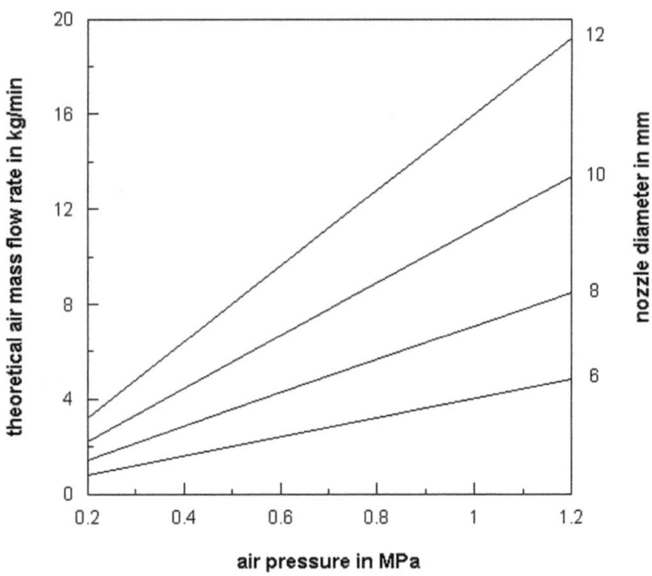

Fig. 3.6 Theoretical mass flow rates for a blast cleaning nozzle as functions of pressure and nozzle diameter (air temperature: 20 °C)

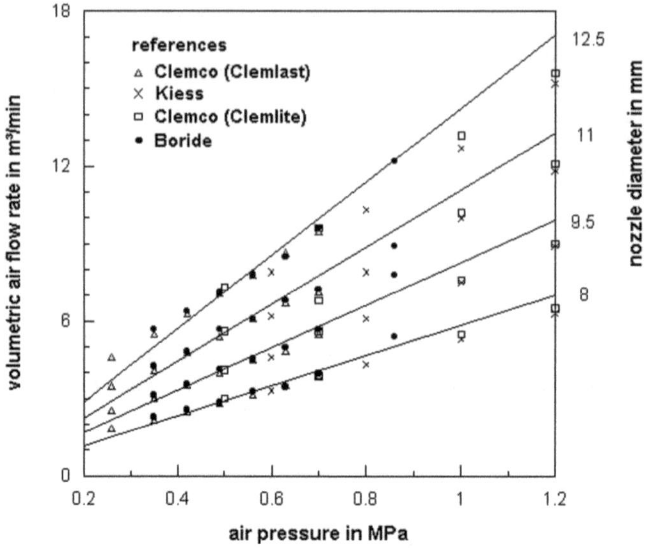

Fig. 3.7 Theoretical volumetric flow rates for a compressor (for an ambient air temperature of $\vartheta = 20°C$) and recommended values from equipment manufacturers

The density is given through (3.6). If the volumetric flow rate, which must be delivered by a compressor, is requested, the density ρ_A for the environmental conditions (see Table 3.2) must be inserted in (3.15). Because air density depends on temperature, the ambient air temperature in the vicinity of a compressor may affect the volumetric air rate. A change in ambient air temperature of $\Delta T = 10\,K$ ($\Delta\vartheta = 10\,°C$), however, leads to a 3%-change in the volumetric air flow rate.

Results of (3.14) and (3.15) for typical parameter configurations are plotted in Fig. 3.7 together with recommendations issued by equipment manufacturers. The deviations between calculation and recommendation cannot be neglected for nozzle pressures higher than $p = 0.9\,\text{MPa}$. Results obtained with (3.14) and (3.15) correspond very well with results of measurements reported by Nettmann (1936). For $p = 0.5\,\text{MPa}$ (gauge pressure) and $d_N = 10\,\text{mm}$, this author reported a value of $\dot{Q}_A = 5.65\,\text{m}^3/\text{min}$. The calculation (based on industry standard, $\vartheta = 20\,°C$) delivers $\dot{Q}_A = 5.63\,\text{m}^3/\text{min}$. Nettmann (1936) was probably the first who published engineering nomograms for the assessment of compressor volumetric air flow rate and of compressor power rating for varying gauge pressures and nozzle diameters. Equations (3.14) and (3.15) can be utilised to calculate nozzle working lines. Working lines for three different nozzles are plotted in Fig. 4.3.

If abrasive material is added to the air flow, it occupies part of the nozzle volume and displaces part of the air. This issue was in detail investigated experimentally by Adlassing (1960), Bae et al. (2007), Lukschandel (1973), Uferer (1992) and Plaster (1973); and theoretically by Fokke (1999). Fokke (1999) found that the abrasive particle volume fraction in the nozzle flow depended on abrasive mass flow rate, and it had values between $F_P = 0.01$ (1 vol.%) and 0.04 (4 vol.%).

Uferer (1992) derived a critical abrasive volume fraction for blast cleaning processes, and he suggested that the value of $F_P = 0.12$ (12 vol.%) should not be exceeded in order to guarantee a stable blast cleaning process.

Due to the dislocation effect, the air flow rate through a nozzle reduces if abrasive material is added to the flow, and a modified relationship reads as follows:

$$\dot{Q}_{A(P)} = \Phi_P \cdot \dot{Q}_A \tag{3.16}$$

The reduction parameter has typical values between $\Phi_P = 0.7$ and 0.9; it depends mainly on abrasive mass flow rate (Adlassing, 1960; Lukschandel, 1973; Plaster, 1973; Uferer, 1992; Bae et al., 2007). Fokke (1999) found that particle size had a very small influence on the air mass flow rate if rather high air pressures were applied.

Uferer (1992) recommended the following relationship for the estimation of the reduction parameter:

$$\Phi_P = \frac{1}{\left(1 + \frac{V_P}{V_A} \cdot \frac{\dot{m}_P}{\dot{m}_A}\right)^{1/2}} \tag{3.17}$$

For typical blast cleaning parameters ($\dot{m}_P/\dot{m}_A = 2,\ \nu_P/\nu_A = 0.3$), this equation delivers $\Phi_P = 0.79$, which is in agreement with the reported experimental results. Values estimated by Uferer (1992) are listed in Table 3.4. It can be seen that the value of the reduction parameter depended on abrasive type, nozzle geometry and mass flow ratio abrasive/air. For the range $R_m = 1.5$ to 3, which is recommended for blast cleaning processes, the values for the reduction parameter were between $\Phi_P = 0.75$ and 0.85.

Bae et al. (2007) and Remmelts (1968) performed measurements of volumetric air flow rates as a function of abrasive mass flow rate. Their results, partly plotted in Fig. 3.11, can be fitted with the following exponential regression:

$$\Phi_{P(Laval)} = \frac{\dot{Q}_{A(P)}}{\dot{Q}_A} = 0.98^{\dot{m}_P} \tag{3.18a}$$

Table 3.4 Reduction parameter values for different blast cleaning conditions (Uferer, 1992)

Abrasive type	Nozzle geometry	Mass flow ratio abrasive/air	Φ_P
Slag and quartz sand	Cylindrical	< 1.5	0.8
		1.5–3	0.75
	Convergent-divergent (Laval)	< 1.5	0.9
		1.5–3	0.85
Cut steel wire	Cylindrical	< 1.5	0.8
		1.5–3.5	0.75
		3.5–5.5	0.7
		> 5.5	0.6

The abrasive mass flow rate must be inserted in kg/min. The coefficient of regression is as high as 0.95 for all fits. It can be seen that $\Phi_P = 1$ for $\dot{m}_P = 0$. For a typical abrasive mass flow rate of $\dot{m}_P = 10\,\text{kg/min}$, the equation delivers $\Phi_P = 0.82$, which corresponds well with the values cited earlier. The regression is valid for Laval nozzles fed with steel grit. The basic number 0.98 in (3.18a) is independent of the dimensions of the nozzles (d_N, l_N), and it can be assumed to be typical for Laval nozzles. However, the basic number may change if other abrasive materials than steel grit are utilised.

Results of measurements of volumetric flow rates performed by some authors are presented in Figs. 3.8 and Fig. 3.9. The results provided in Fig. 3.8 demonstrate the effects of different abrasive types on the volumetric air flow rate. The addition of chilled iron was more critical to the volumetric air flow rate compared with the addition of the non-ferrous abrasive material. The results plotted in Fig. 3.9 showed that air volumetric flow rate depended on abrasive type, nozzle type and air pressure, if abrasive material was added. Interestingly, the effect of the abrasive material type was only marginal for small nozzle diameters. This effect was also reported by Adlassing (1960). The reduction in air flow rate was more severe if a Laval nozzle was utilised instead of a standard nozzle. Laval nozzles consumed approximately 10% more air volume than conventional cylindrical nozzles, if abrasives (quartz, SiC, corundum and steel grit) were added (Lukschandel, 1973). This result agrees with measurements provided in Table 3.4. Based on these results, the following very preliminary approach can be made:

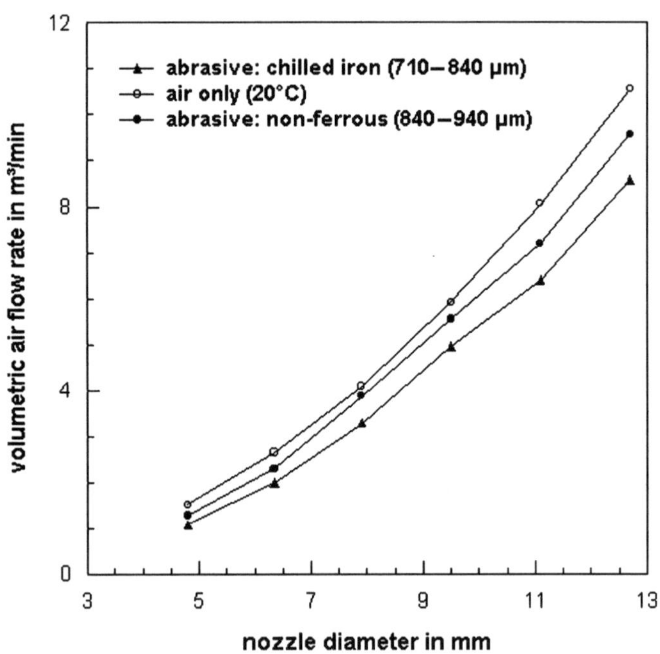

Fig. 3.8 Effect of abrasive type on volumetric air flow rate (Plaster, 1973)

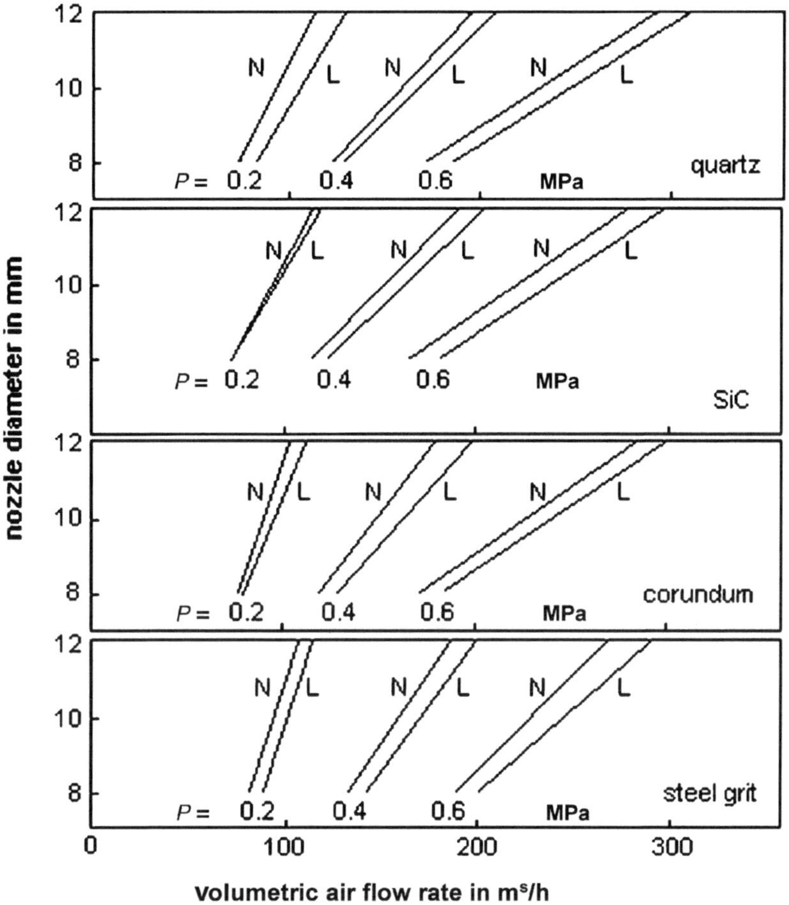

Fig. 3.9 Effects of air pressure, nozzle diameter, nozzle geometry and abrasive type on volumetric air flow rate (Lukschandel, 1973). "N" – cylindrical nozzle; "L" – convergent–divergent (Laval) nozzle

$$\Phi_{\mathrm{P(cylinder)}} = 0.9 \cdot \Phi_{\mathrm{P(Laval)}} \tag{3.18b}$$

More experimental evidence is provided in Figs. 3.10 and 3.11. Figure 3.10 illustrates the effect of nozzle layout on the air volume flow, if abrasive material (crushed cast iron) was added. The deviation in air volume flow rate was about 10%. The effects of varying nozzle geometries on the volumetric air flow rates were further investigated by Bae et al. (2007). Some of their results are displayed in Fig. 3.11. The effect of nozzle geometry parameters is much more pronounced compared with the results plotted in Fig. 3.10. The graphs also illustrate the effects of abrasive mass flow rate on the volumetric air flow rate. The more the abrasive material added, the lesser the air volume flow through the nozzle. The curves ran parallel to each

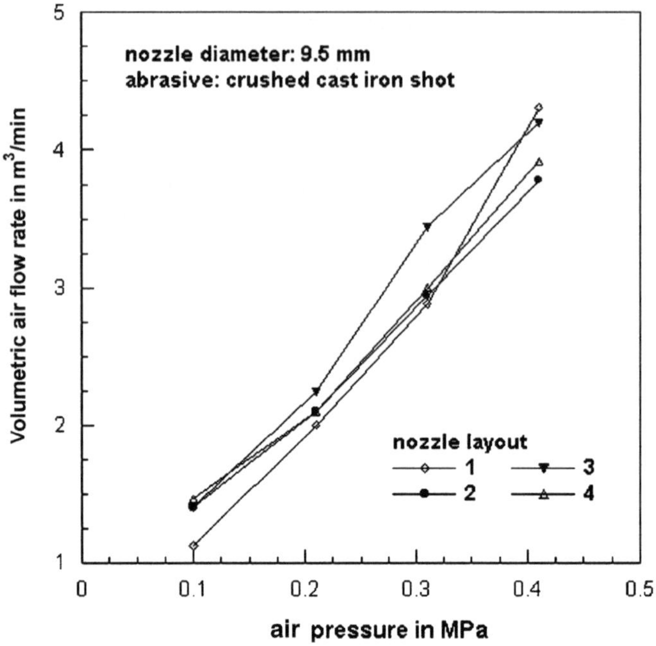

Fig. 3.10 Effects of nozzle geometry on volumetric air flow rate (Plaster, 1973); abrasive type: crushed chilled cast iron shot; $d_N = 9.5$ mm. Nozzle layout: "1" – convergent–divergent; "2" – bell-mouthed + convergent; "3" – bell-mouthed + divergent; "4": bell-mouthed + convergent–divergent

other; thus, the general trend was almost independent of the nozzle geometry. These relationships are expressed through (3.18a).

3.2.3 *Air Exit Flow Velocity in Nozzles*

For an isotropic flow (no heat is added or taken and no friction), the velocity of an air jet exiting a pressurised air reservoir through a small opening can be expressed as the enthalpy difference between vessel and environment as follows:

$$v_A = (2 \cdot \Delta h_A)^{1/2} \tag{3.19}$$

After some treatment, the velocity of air flow at the exit of a nozzle can be calculated with the following relationship (Kalide, 1990):

$$v_A = \left(2 \cdot \frac{\kappa}{\kappa - 1} \cdot \frac{p}{\rho_A} \cdot \left[1 - \left(\frac{p_0}{p}\right)^{\frac{\kappa-1}{\kappa}}\right]\right)^{1/2} \tag{3.20}$$

As an example, if compressed air at a temperature of $\vartheta = 27°C$ ($T = 300$ K) and at a pressure of $p = 0.6$ MPa flows through a nozzle, its theoretical exit velocity is about $v_A = 491$ m/s.

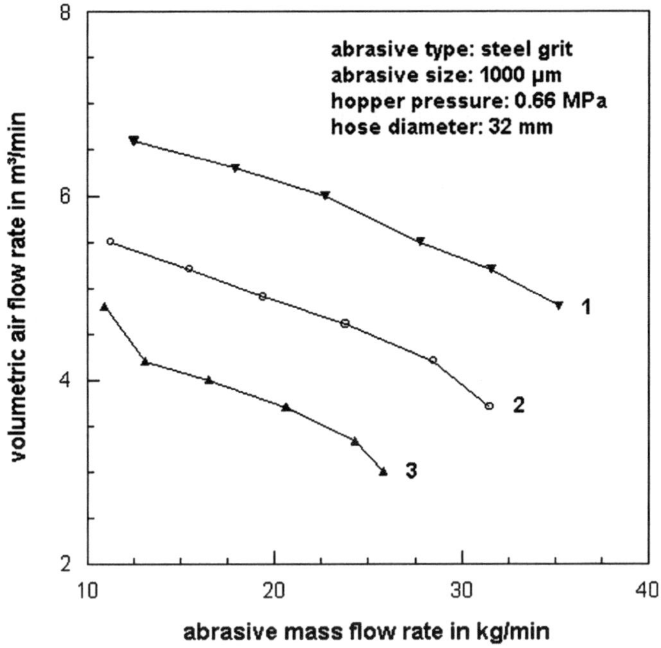

Fig. 3.11 Effects of abrasive mass flow rate and nozzle geometry on the air volume flow rate in convergent–divergent nozzles (Bae et al., 2007). Nozzle "1" – nozzle length: 150 mm, throat (nozzle) diameter: 11.5 mm, divergent angle: 2.1°, convergent angle: 9.3°; Nozzle "2" – nozzle length: 216 mm, throat (nozzle) diameter: 11.0 mm, divergent angle: 1.3°, convergent angle: 7.9°; Nozzle "3" – nozzle length: 125 mm, throat (nozzle) diameter: 12.5 mm, divergent angle: 7.6°, convergent angle: 3.9°

The maximum exit velocity, however, occurs at the point of maximum mass flow rate, which happens under the following conditions: Ψ_{max} and $(p_0/p)_{crit}$ (see Fig. 3.5). If the Laval pressure ratio $(p_0/p)_{crit}$ is introduced into (3.20), the following maximum limit for the air velocity in parallel cylindrical nozzles results:

$$v_{A\,max} = \left(2 \cdot \frac{\kappa}{\kappa+1} \cdot \frac{p}{\rho_A}\right)^{1/2} \tag{3.21}$$

After further treatment, the final equation reads as follows:

$$v_{A\,max} = v_L = (\kappa \cdot R_i \cdot T)^{1/2} \tag{3.22}$$

The equation is equal to (3.9). This critical air velocity is frequently referred to as *Laval velocity* (v_L). It cannot be exceeded in a cylindrical nozzle. It depends not on pressure, but on gas parameters and gas temperature. Figure 3.4 presents results for calculated Laval velocities. For the example mentioned in relationship with (3.20), the critical air flow velocity is $v_L = 347$ m/s, which is much lower than the velocity of $v_A = 491$ m/s calculated with (3.20).

If the exit air velocity needs to be increased further in order to exceed the Laval velocity given by (3.22), the nozzle exit region must be designed in a divergent shape. Nozzles which operate according to this design were independently developed by the German engineer Ernst Körting (1842–1921) and the Swedish engineer Gustav de Laval (1845–1913). In honour of the latter inventor, they are called Laval nozzles.

3.2.4 Air Flow in Laval Nozzles

If air velocities higher than the Laval velocity ($v_A > v_L$) are to be achieved, the cross-section of the nozzle must be extended in a way that smooth adiabatic expansion of the air is possible. Such a nozzle geometry is called convergent–divergent (Laval) nozzle. An example is shown in Fig. 3.12. The figure shows an image that was taken with X-ray photography. The flow direction is from right to left. The nozzle consists of a convergent section (right), a throat (centre) and a divergent section (left). The diameter of the throat, which has the smallest cross-section in the system, is considered the nozzle diameter (d_N). For this type of nozzle, (3.20) can be applied without a restriction. For practical cases, a nozzle coefficient φ_L should be added, which delivers the following equation for the calculation of the exit velocity of the air flow:

$$v_A = \varphi_L \cdot \left(2 \cdot \frac{\kappa}{\kappa - 1} \cdot \frac{p}{\rho_A} \cdot \left[1 - \left(\frac{p_0}{p}\right)^{\frac{\kappa-1}{\kappa}}\right]\right)^{1/2} \tag{3.23}$$

The Laval nozzle coefficient φ_L is a function of a dimensionless parameter ω. Relationships for two nozzle qualities are exhibited in Fig. 3.13. The parameter ω depends on the pressure ratio p_0/p (Kalide, 1990). Examples for certain pressure levels are plotted in Fig. 3.14. It can be seen that the dimensionless parameter takes values between $\omega = 0.5$ and 1.0 for typical blast cleaning applications. The parameter ω decreases if air pressure increases. A general trend is that nozzle efficiency decreases for higher air pressures. Results of (3.23) are displayed in the left graph in Fig. 3.15. The right graph displays results of (3.22). One result is that air flowing through a cylindrical nozzle at a high temperature of $\vartheta = 200°C$ and at a rather low pressure of $p = 0.2$ MPa obtains an exit velocity which is equal to that of air which

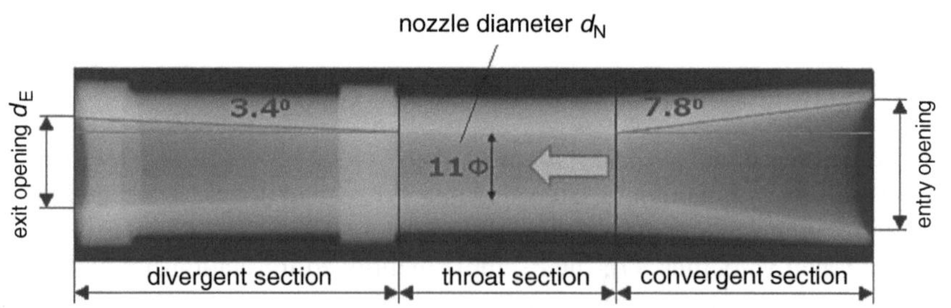

Fig. 3.12 X-ray image of a convergent–divergent (Laval) nozzle design (Bae et al., 2007)

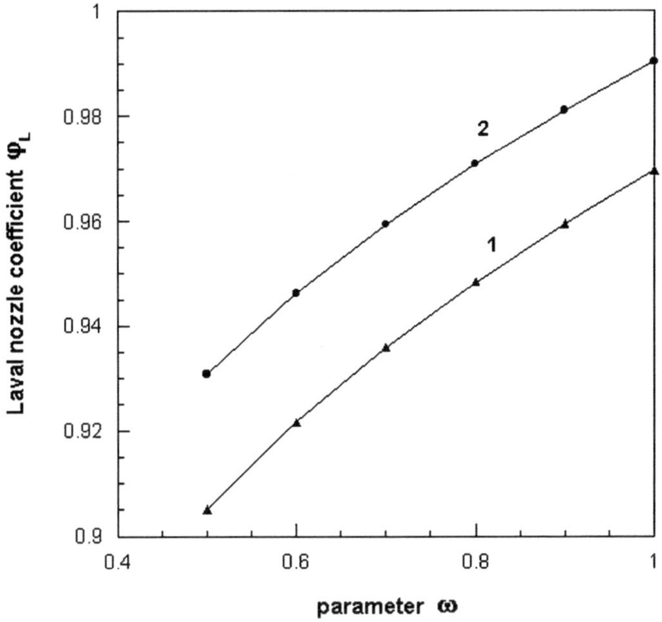

Fig. 3.13 Relationship between φ_L and ω (Kalide, 1990). "1" – Straight nozzle with smooth wall; "2" – curved nozzle with rough wall

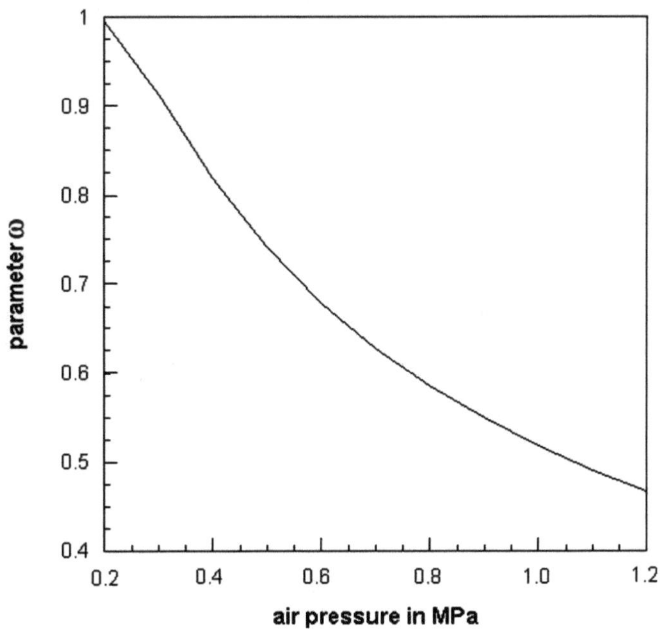

Fig. 3.14 Function ω =f(p) for p_0 = 0.1 MPa; according to a relationship provided by Kalide (1990)

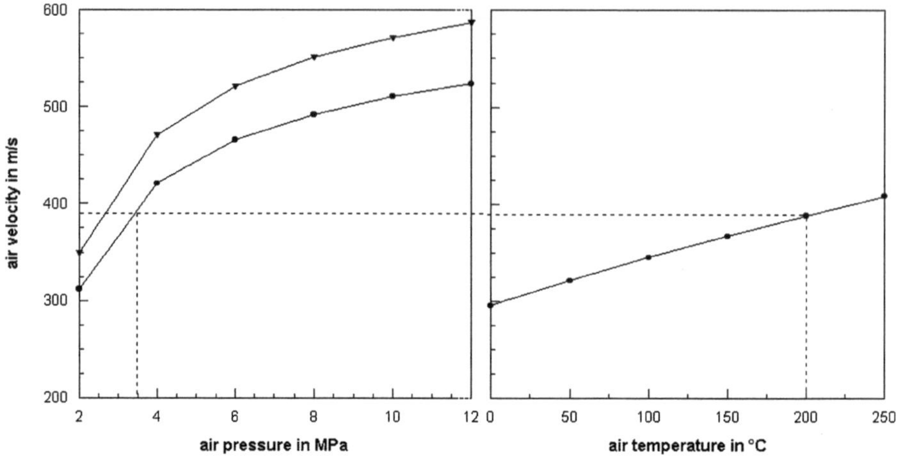

Fig. 3.15 Theoretical air exit velocities in Laval nozzles. Left: air temperature effect; upper curve: ϑ =100°C; lower curve: $\vartheta = 20°C$; Right: air pressure effect; $p = 0.2$ MPa

is flowing through a Laval nozzle at a temperature of $\vartheta = 20°C$ and at a much higher pressure of $p = 0.35$ MPa.

The air mass flow rate through a Laval nozzle can be calculated with (3.14), whereby d_N is the diameter of the narrowest cross-section (throat) in the nozzle. For air at a pressure of $p = 0.6$ MPa and a temperature of $\vartheta = 27°C$ ($T = 300$ K) flowing through a Laval nozzle with $d_N = 11$ mm and $\alpha_N = 0.95$, (3.14) delivers a mass flow rate of about $\dot{m}_A = 0.133$ kg/s.

The flow and thermodynamics either in cylindrical nozzles or in Laval nozzles can be completely described with commercially available numerical simulation programs, which an example of is presented in Fig. 3.16a. In that example, the progresses of Mach number, air density, air pressure and air temperature along the nozzle length are completely documented. It can be seen that pressure, density and temperature of the air are all reduced during the flow of the air through the nozzle.

The flow regimes that are set up in a convergent–divergent nozzle are best illustrated by considering the pressure decay in a given nozzle as the ambient (back) pressure is reduced from rather high to very low values. All the operating modes from wholly subsonic to underexpanded supersonic are shown in sequences "1" to "5" in Fig. 3.26, which will be discussed later in Sect. 3.4.3.

3.2.5 Power, Impulse Flow and Temperature

The power of the air stream exiting a nozzle is simply given as follows:

$$P_A = \frac{\dot{m}_A}{2} \cdot v_A^2 \tag{3.24}$$

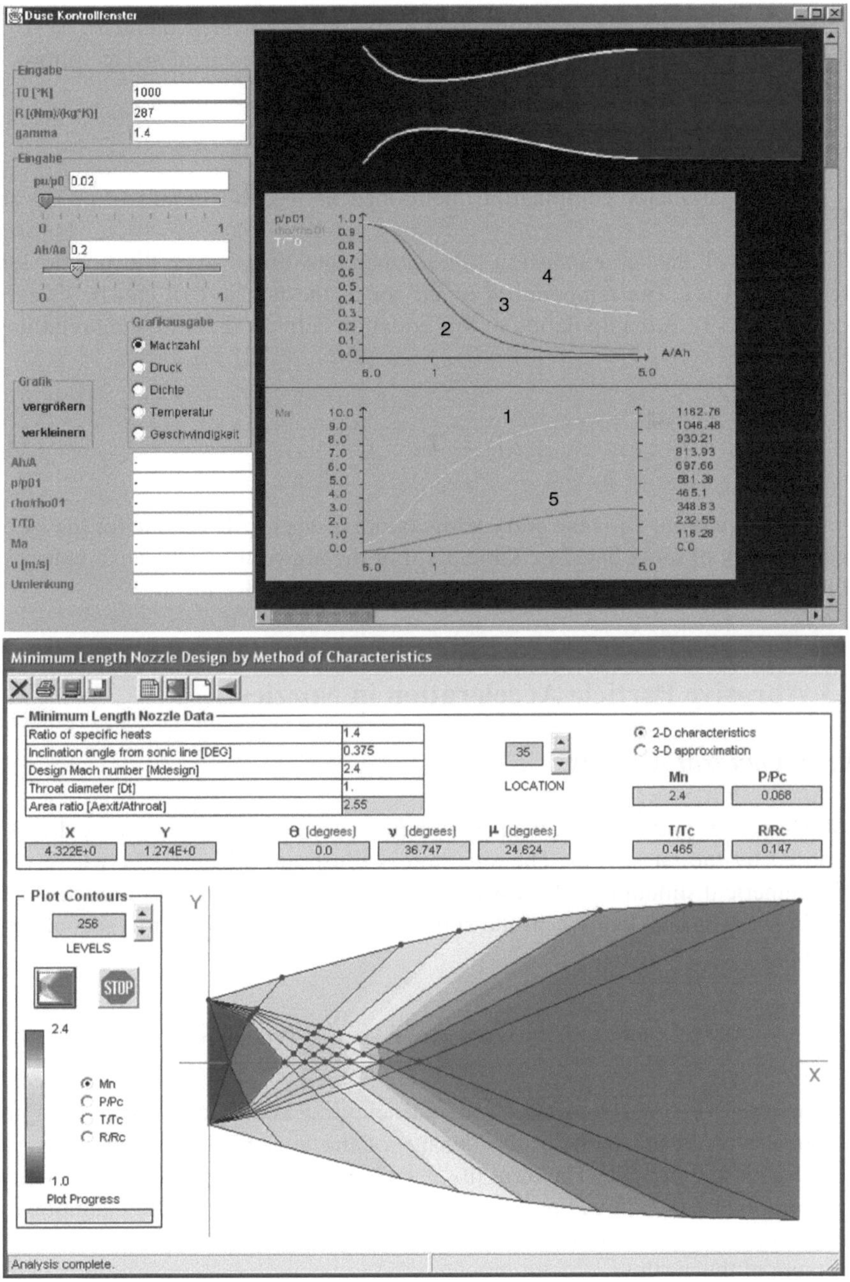

(a) (b)

Fig. 3.16 Results of numerical simulations of the air flow in convergent–divergent nozzles (Laval nozzles). (**a**) Gradients for Mach number (1), pressure (2), density (3), temperature (4) and air velocity (5): image: RWTH Aachen, Aachen, (Germany); (**b**) Complete numerical nozzle design including shock front computation (Aerorocket Inc., Citrus Springs, USA)

For the above-mentioned example, the air stream power is about $P_A = 16\,\text{kW}$. The impulse flow of an air stream exiting a nozzle can be calculated as follows:

$$\dot{I}_A = \dot{m}_A \cdot v_A \tag{3.25}$$

For the parameter combination mentioned above, the impulse flow is about $\dot{I}_A = 65\,\text{N}$.

Because of the air expansion, air temperature drops over the nozzle length (see Fig. 3.16a). The temperature of the air at the nozzle exit can be calculated based on (3.19). A manipulation of this equation delivers the following relationship (Bohl, 1989):

$$T_E = T_N - \frac{v_A^2}{2 \cdot c_P} \tag{3.26}$$

In that equation, T_N is the entry temperature of the air. The value for the isobaric heat capacity of air is listed in Table 3.1. For the above-mentioned example, (3.26) delivers an air exit temperature of $T_E = 180\,\text{K}$ ($\theta_E = -93°\text{C}$).

3.3 Abrasive Particle Acceleration in Nozzles

3.3.1 General Aspects

Solid abrasives particles hit by an air stream do accelerate because of the drag force imposed by the air stream. The situation is illustrated in Fig. 3.17 where results of a numerical simulation of pressure contours and air streamlines around a sphere are shown. The acceleration of the sphere is governed by Newton's second law of motion:

$$m_P \cdot \frac{dv_P}{dt} = F_D = c_D \cdot A_P \cdot \frac{\rho_A}{2} \cdot |v_A - v_{P0}|^2 \tag{3.27}$$

The drag force F_D depends on the particle drag coefficient, the average cross-sectional area of the particle, the density of the air and on the relative velocity between air and particle. The term $|v_A - v_{P0}| = v_{rel}$ is the relative velocity between gas flow and particle flow. For very low particles flow velocities, for example, in the entry section of a nozzle, $v_{rel} = v_A$. The term $1/2 \cdot \rho_A \cdot v_{rel}^2$ is equal to the dynamic pressure of the air flow.

The drag coefficient is usually unknown and should be measured. It depends on Reynolds number and Mach number of the flow: $c_D = f(Re, Ma)$, whereby the Mach number is important if the air flow is compressible. Settles and Geppert (1997) provided some results of measurements performed on particles at supersonic speeds.

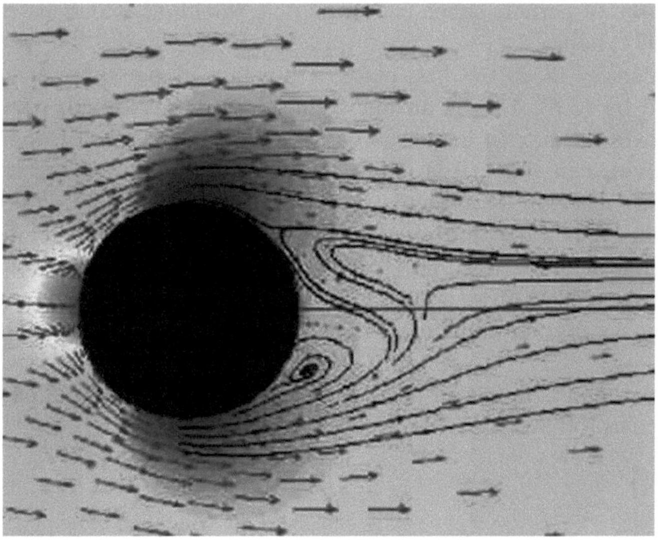

Fig. 3.17 Numerically simulated pressure contours and flow streamlines on a solid particle in a high-speed air flow (image: H.A. Dwyer, University of California, Davis)

Their results, plotted in Fig. 3.18, suggest that the drag coefficient only weakly depends on Reynolds number, but is very sensitive to changes in the Mach number. The c_D-value is rather low at low Mach number values, but it dramatically increases after a value of $Ma = 1$. It finally levels off around a value of unity for Mach numbers greater than $Ma = 1.4$. More information on this issue is delivered by Bailey and Hiatt (1972), who published c_D–Ma–Re data for different nozzle geometries, and by Fokke (1999). Other notable effects on the drag coefficient are basically those

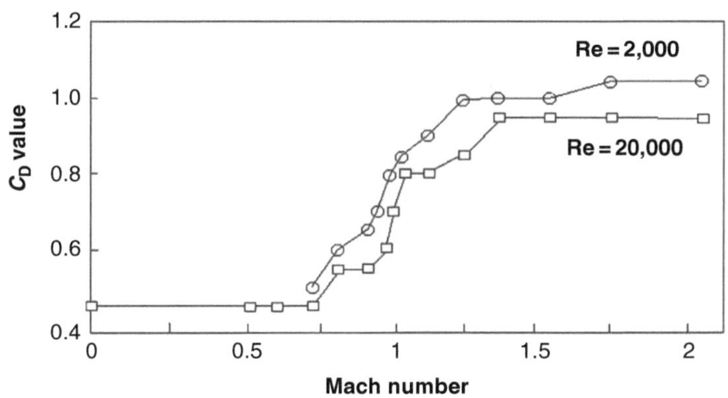

Fig. 3.18 Effects of Mach number and Reynolds number on friction parameter (Settles and Geppert, 1997)

of acceleration, of particle shape and of particle shielding, which are discussed in Brauer's (1971) book.

The air density is, in the first place, a function of pressure and temperature as expressed by (3.6). This is an interesting point because both parameters notably vary over the nozzle length as witnessed by the results of numerical simulations provided in Fig. 3.16a. Both air pressure and air temperature drop if they approach the exit. The relative velocity can, for practical purposes, be replaced by the velocity of the air flow ($v_A \gg v_{P0}$), if the acceleration process starts. In cylindrical nozzles, this velocity cannot exceed the speed of sound (see Sect. 3.2). However, because speed of sound depends on gas temperature (3.9), a theoretical possibility for an increase in drag force due to gas temperature increase exists.

The acceleration acting on a particle during the particle–air interaction can be approximated as follows:

$$a_P = \dot{v}_P = \frac{F_D}{m_P} \tag{3.28}$$

This condition delivers the following relationship:

$$\dot{v}_P \propto \frac{c_D \cdot \rho_A \cdot v_A^2}{d_P \cdot \rho_P} \tag{3.29}$$

Acceleration values for convergent–divergent nozzles were calculated by Achtsnick (2005), who estimated values as high as $a_P = 10^7$ m/s^2. This author could also verify the trend expressed in (3.29) for the particle diameter. The particle acceleration increased extraordinarily when the abrasive particle diameter was reduced below $d_P = 10$ µm. If particles get smaller, they start to follow the trajectories of air flow they are suspended, and the slip between particles and air flow reduces. The acceleration period required to realise a given final particle speed can be approximated as follows:

$$t_a \propto \frac{v_P \cdot d_P \cdot \rho_P}{c_D \cdot \rho_A \cdot v_A^2} \tag{3.30}$$

Acceleration is, of course, not a constant value over the nozzle length, but (3.29) depicts that acceleration effects are, in general, less severe if particles with larger diameter and larger density are entrained into the air flow. For a desired particle speed, acceleration period (nozzle length) must be increased if heavy (ρ_P), respectively large (d_P), abrasive particles are injected. Acceleration period (nozzle length) can be reduced if air flow density (ρ_A), air flow velocity (v_A) and drag coefficient (c_D) feature high values.

Equation (3.27) must be solved by numerical methods, and numerous authors (Kamzolov et al., 1971; Ninham and Hutchings, 1983; Settles and Garg, 1995; Settles and Geppert, 1997; Johnston, 1998; Fokke, 1999; Achtsnick et al., 2005) utilised such methods and delivered appropriate solutions. Results of such calculation procedures are provided in the following sections.

3.3.2 Simplified Solution

Iida (1996) and Kirk (2007) provided an approximation for the velocity of particles accelerated in a cylindrical blast cleaning nozzle. The solution of Iida (1996) neglects effects of friction parameter and air density. Kirk's (2007) approximation reads as follows:

$$\left(\frac{v_P}{v_A - v_P}\right)^2 = \frac{c_D \cdot L_N}{d_P} \cdot \frac{\rho_A}{\rho_P} \tag{3.31}$$

Due to certain simplifications, this equation can only serve for the assessment of trends, but cannot deliver suitable quantitative results. A solution to (3.31) delivers the following trends:

$$v_P \propto p^{0.68} \tag{3.32a}$$

$$v_P \propto d_P^{-0.36} \tag{3.32b}$$

$$v_P \propto \rho_P^{-0.38} \tag{3.32c}$$

Uferer (1992) applied a simplified numerical procedure for the calculation of abrasive particles accelerated in blast cleaning nozzles. Some results of these calculations for two nozzle layouts are provided in Fig. 3.19. The graphs demonstrate that the utilisation of a Laval nozzle increases the velocities of air and abrasive particles, but the gain is much higher for the air acceleration. The reason is the drop in air density in the divergent section of the Laval nozzle (see Fig. 3.16a). According to (3.27), this causes a reduction in the drag force acting at the particles to be accelerated. Thus, although Laval nozzles are very efficient in air acceleration, they do not increase the abrasive exit speed at an equally high ratio.

3.3.3 Abrasive Flux Rate

The abrasive flux rate through a nozzle (in kg/s per unit nozzle area passing through the nozzle) can be approximated as follows (Ciampini et al., 2003b):

$$\dot{m}_N = \rho_P \cdot v_P \cdot \rho_S^* \tag{3.33}$$

Thus, for a given abrasive material and incident abrasive velocity, interference effects resulting from changes in flux are described by the dimensionless stream density (see Sect. 3.5.5).

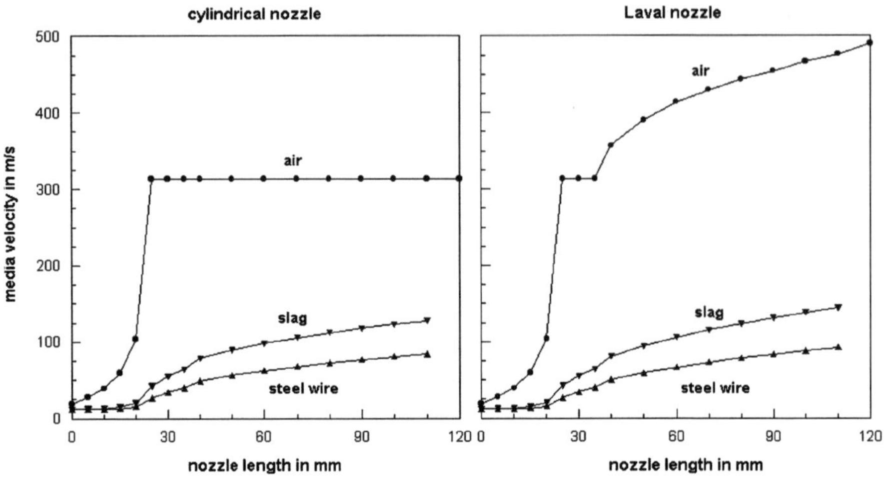

Fig. 3.19 Effects of nozzle layout on calculated air and abrasive velocities (Uferer, 1993)

3.3.4 Abrasive Particle Spacing

The average distance between individual abrasive particles in a blast cleaning nozzle can be approximated as follows (Shipway and Hutchings, 1994):

$$L_P = \left(\frac{m_P \cdot v_P \cdot \pi \cdot r_N^2}{\dot{m}_P} \right)^{1/3} \tag{3.34}$$

Results obtained by Shipway and Hutchings (1994) are listed in Table 3.5. The ratio between spacing distance and abrasive particle diameter had a typical value of about $L_P/d_P = 15$. For a low abrasive mass flow rate, this value increased up to $L_P/d_P = 23$.

Table 3.5 Average distances between abrasive particles in a blast cleaning nozzle (Shipway and Hutchings, 1994)

Particle diameter in μm	Particle velocity in m/s	Abrasive mass flow rate in g/min	Average distance in μm	L_P/d_P
63–75	70	50	900	~ 13
125–150	52	6	3,200	~ 23
212–250	45	31	4,000	~ 17
650–750	29	37	7,900	~ 13

3.4 Jet Structure

3.4.1 Structure of High-speed Air Jets

A schematic sketch of a free air jet is shown in Fig. 3.20. The term "free jet" designates systems where a fluid issues from a nozzle into a stagnant medium, which consists of the same medium as the jet. Two main regions can be distinguished in the jet: an initial region and a main region. The *initial region* is characterised by a potential core, which has an almost uniform mean velocity equal to the exit velocity. The velocity profile is smooth in that region. Due to the velocity difference between the jet and the ambient air, a thin shear layer forms. This layer is unstable and is subjected to flow instabilities that eventually lead to the formation of vertical structures. Because of the spreading of the shear layer, the potential core disappears at a certain stand-off distance. Ambient air entrains the jet, and entrainment and mixing processes continue beyond the end of the potential core. In the *main region*, the radial velocity distribution in the jet finally changes to a pronounced bell-shaped velocity profile as illustrated in Fig. 3.20. The angle θ_J is the expansion angle of the jet. In order to calculate this angle, the border between air jet and surrounding air flow must be defined. One definition is the half-width of the jet defined as the distance between the jet axis and the location where the local velocity $[v_J(x,r)]$ is equal to the half of the local maximum velocity situated on the centreline $[v_J(x, r = 0)]$. Achtsnick (2005) who applied this definition estimated typical expansion angles between $\theta_J = 12.5°$ and $15°$.

Shipway and Hutchings (1993a) took schlieren images from acetone-air plumes exiting cylindrical steel nozzles at rather low air pressures up to $p = 0.09$ MPa, and they could prove that the plume shape differed just insignificantly if the gas exited either from a nozzle with a low internal roughness ($R_a = 0.25$ μm) or from a nozzle with a rough wall structure ($R_a = 0.94$ μm). This situation changed if abrasive particles were added to the air flow.

The structure of an abrasive jet is disturbed due to rebounding abrasive particles if the nozzle is being brought very close to the specimen surface. This was

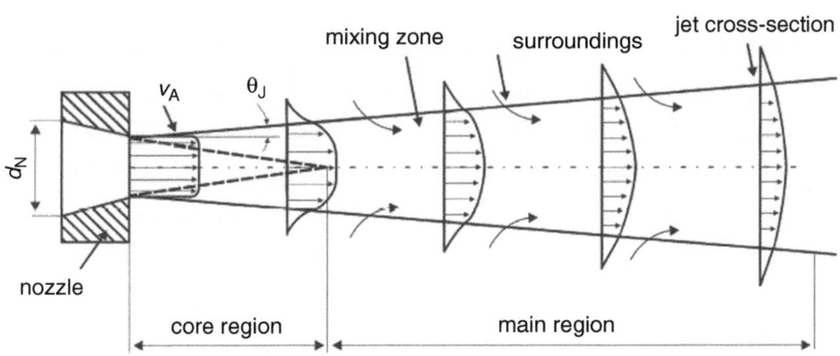

Fig. 3.20 Structure of an air jet issued from a nozzle into stagnant air (adapted from Achtsnick, 2005)

verified by Shipway and Hutchings (1994) who took long-exposure photographs of the trajectories of glass spheres in an air jet and observed many particle trajectories, which deviated strongly from the nozzle axis. It was supposed that these are particles rebounding from the target.

3.4.2 Structure of Air-particle Jets

Plaster (1972) was probably the first who advised the blast cleaning industry into the effect of nozzle configuration on the structure of air-particle jets. The images shown in Fig. 3.21 clearly illustrate the influence of nozzle design on jet stability. Figure 3.21a shows a jet exiting from a badly designed nozzle, which results in a shock wave at the tip (central image) and in an erratic projection of abrasives (right image). A correctly designed nozzle is shown in Fig. 3.21b. This nozzle produces a smooth flow as can be seen by the configuration of the air stream (central image) and by the even projection of the abrasives (right image).

The width (radius) of high-speed air-particle jets at different jet lengths was measured by Fokke (1999) and Slikkerveer (1999). Kirk and Abyaneh (1994) and Slikkerveer (1999) provided an empirical relationship as follows:

(a)

(b)

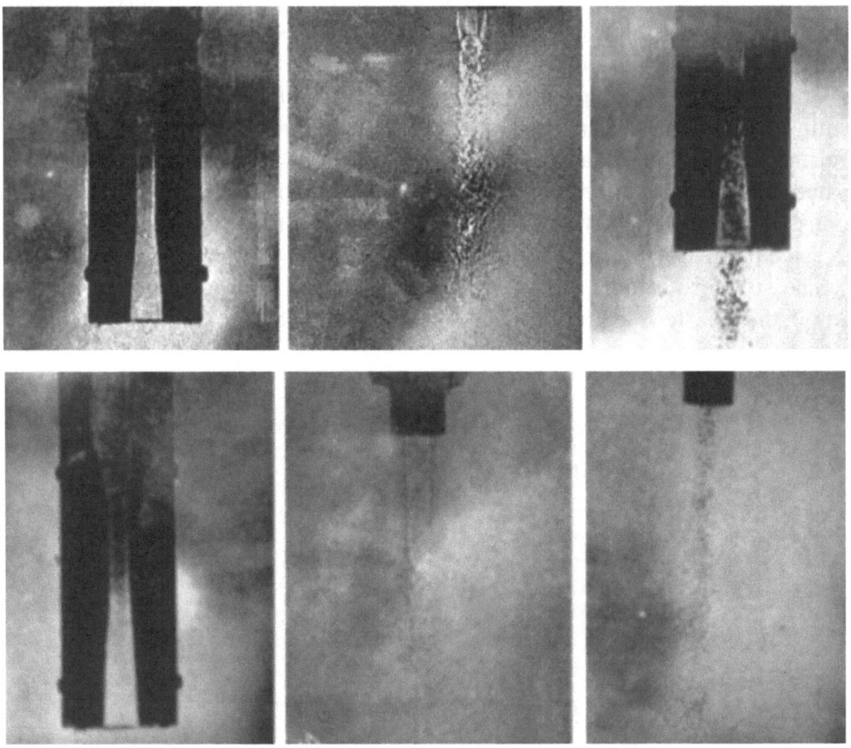

Fig. 3.21 Effect of nozzle design on jet structure and abrasive acceleration (Plaster, 1972). (**a**) Badly designed nozzle; (**b**) Correctly designed nozzle

$$d_J = d_N + 2 \cdot x \cdot \tan\theta_J \tag{3.35}$$

The expansion angle can be considered to be between $\theta_J = 3°$ and $7°$ (Slikkerveer, 1999; Achtsnick et al., 2005). Therefore, it is smaller than for a plain air jet. Results of calculations based on (3.35) for $\theta_J = 5°$ are displayed in Fig. 3.22.

Fokke (1999) found an almost linear relationship between jet half width and jet length. The air mass flow rate showed marginal effects on the half width at longer jet lengths: with an increase in air mass flow rate, half width slightly decreased. Some relationships are illustrated in Fig. 3.23. These results corresponded to that of Mellali et al. (1994) who found a linear relationship between stand-off distance and the area of the cross-section hit by a blast cleaning jet.

Shipway and Hutchings (1993a) took schlieren images from glass bead plumes exiting cylindrical steel nozzles at air pressures up to $p = 0.09$ MPa. They noted a distinct effect of the nozzle wall roughness on the plume shape as a result of the differences in the interaction of the particles with the nozzle wall. Variations in the rebound behaviour of the glass beads on impact with the nozzle wall caused the particles to leave the nozzle exit with different angular distributions. These authors also defined a "plume spread parameter", respectively a "focus coefficient":

$$\beta_P = \alpha_P \cdot x \tag{3.36}$$

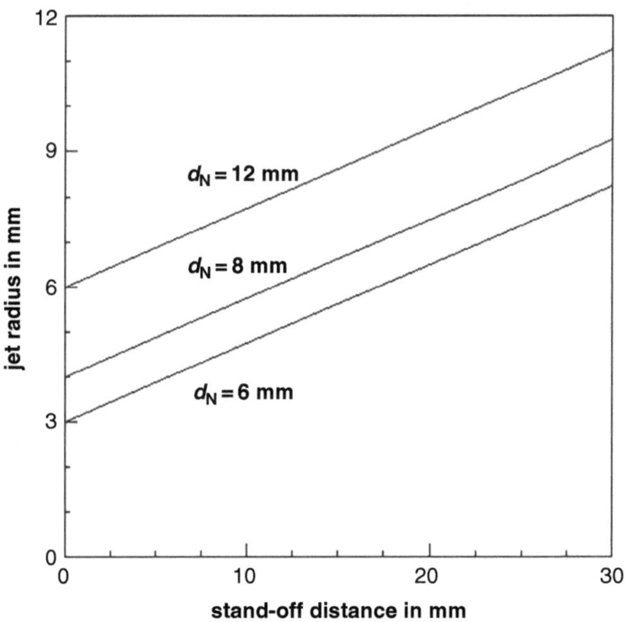

Fig. 3.22 Radius of a particle-air jet according to (3.35)

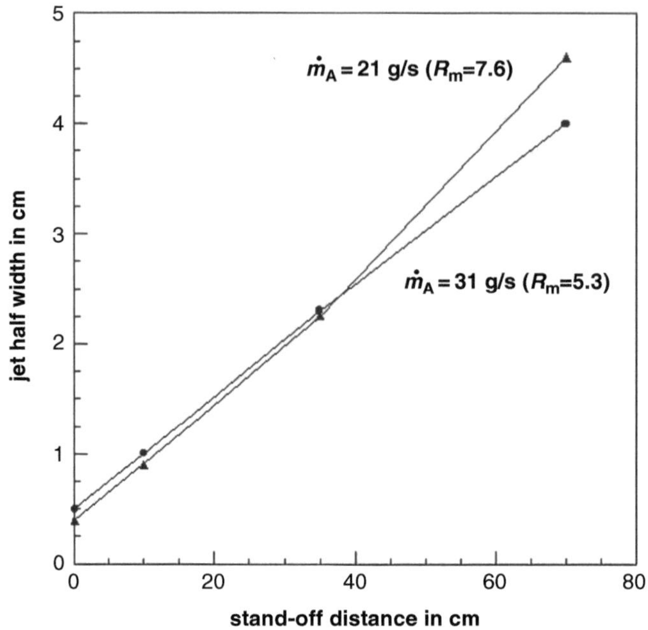

Fig. 3.23 Effects of stand-off distance and air mass flow rate (respectively mass flow ratio abrasive/air) on jet radius (Fokke, 1999)

Here, α_P is a constant that depends on the nozzle configuration. Lower values for α_P mean less spread and vice versa. Shipway and Hutchings (1993a) provided a method for the estimation of the dimensionless *focus coefficient*. It could be shown experimentally that the focus coefficient depended on the roughness of the nozzle wall surface. Results of this investigation are listed in Table 3.6. It was also shown by Stevenson and Hutchings (1995b) that the focus coefficient depended on nozzle length and abrasive particle velocity. It exhibited maximum values at moderate nozzle lengths. If abrasive particle velocity increased, the focus coefficient decreased notably.

3.4.3 Design Nozzle Pressure

Each Laval nozzle (convergent–divergent nozzle) has a so-called *design nozzle pressure* that enables it to produce a supersonic jet of air into the atmosphere with

Table 3.6 Relationships between nozzle wall roughness, abrasive particle type and *focus coefficient* (Shipway and Hutchings, 1993a)

Wall roughness in μm	Focus coefficient	
	Silica	Glass beads
0.94	14	8.7
0.25	22.3	15.2

minimum disturbance. The design criterion is the air pressure at the nozzle exit (P_E). The value for this pressure should be equal to the pressure of the surrounding air (called *back pressure* in the flow dynamics literature). The situation is characterised by the curve "1" in Fig. 3.26. For blast cleaning applications, the back pressure is usually the atmospheric pressure. The design criterion can be written as follows [modified from Bohl's (1989) book]:

$$\left(\frac{d_E}{d_N}\right)^2 = \left(\frac{\kappa+1}{2}\right)^{\frac{1}{\kappa-1}} \cdot \left(\frac{p_E}{p}\right)^{\frac{1}{\kappa}} \cdot \left\{\frac{\kappa+1}{\kappa-1} \cdot \left[1 - \left(\frac{p_E}{p}\right)^{\frac{\kappa-1}{\kappa}}\right]\right\}^{1/2} \quad (3.37)$$

For $p_E = p_0$, this equation delivers a ratio between exit diameter and nozzle (throat) diameter, which must be maintained in order to allow an undisturbed air flow at the given nozzle inlet pressure. A graphical solution to (3.37) is provided in Fig. 3.24. If the nozzle dimensions (d_N, d_E) are known, the corresponding *design pressure* can be read from this graph. Only data points located at the solid line correspond to the expansion condition characterised by Fig. 3.25d and by line "1" in Fig. 3.26.

It must be noted, however, that these relationships apply to the flow of plain air only. If solid particles are added, the effects of the particle flow must be considered. Fokke (1999) performed numerical simulations of the nozzle flow, and he could show that the addition of abrasive particles (steel balls, $d_P = 50$–1,000 µm;

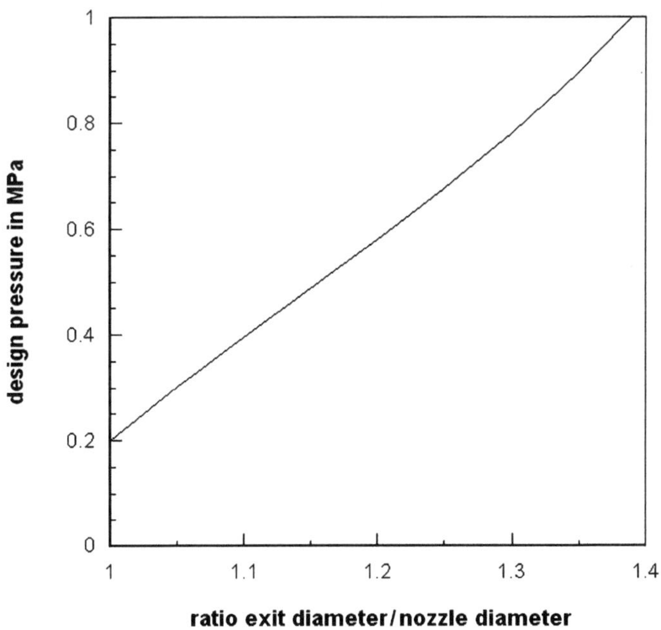

Fig. 3.24 Relationship between nozzle geometry and design pressure for convergent–divergent nozzles. Based on (3.37)

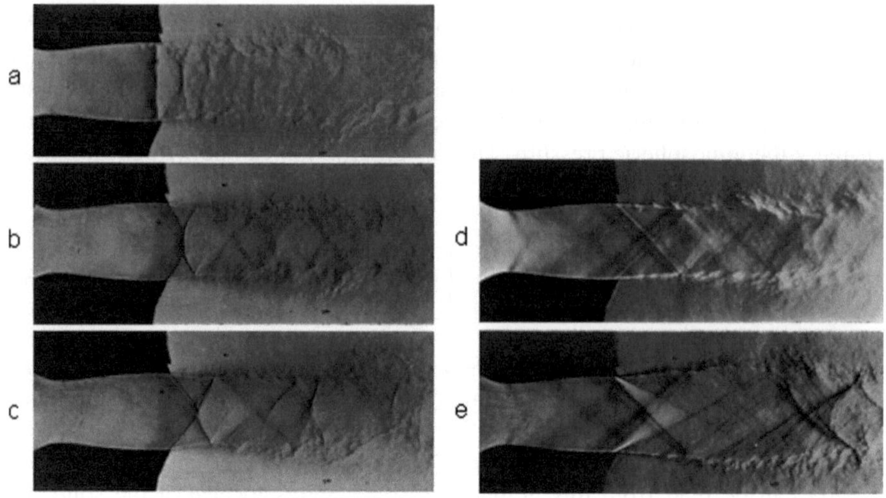

Fig. 3.25 Flow situation near the exit of a convergent–divergent nozzle (Oosthuizen and Carscallen, 1997) (**a**) Overexpanded flow with shock front leaving the nozzle exit; (**b**) Overexpanded flow with disappearing normal central shock front outside the nozzle; (**c**) Overexpanded with oblique shocks outside the nozzle; (**d**) Almost isentropic nozzle flow; (**e**) Underexpanded flow with severe expansion waves outside the nozzle

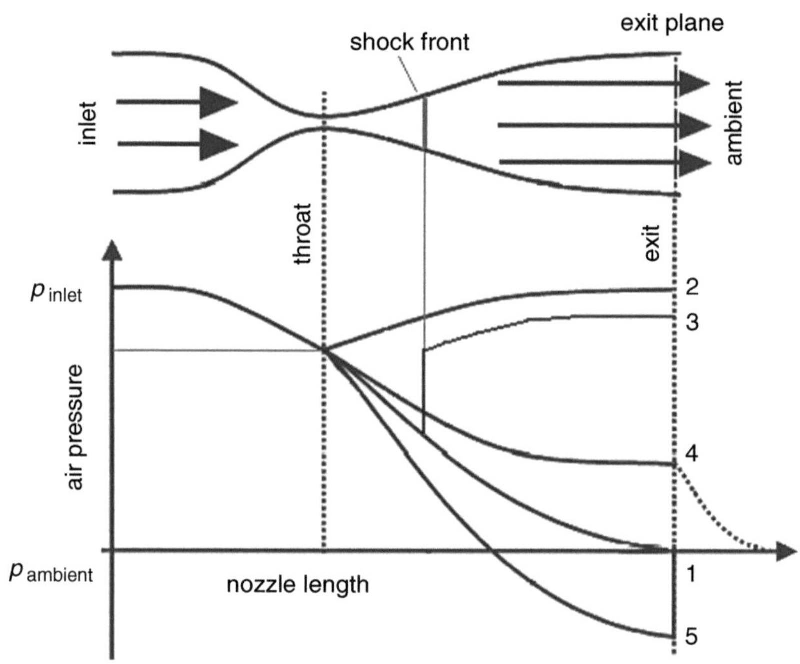

Fig. 3.26 Operating conditions of a convergent–divergent nozzle; see text for "1" to "5" (adapted from Oertel, 2001)

R_m = 0.1–6) was sensitive to the nozzle exit pressure. For all loading ratios, exit pressure increased with decreasing particle size. Exit pressure also increased with an increase in the mass flow ratio abrasive/air. Although the nozzle in Fokke's (1999) work was designed in a way that the air exit pressure would meet the atmospheric pressure, the exit pressures were all well below the atmospheric pressure as the abrasive particles were added. Effects of abrasive particle on the gas flow properties in the nozzle vanished for small mass flow rates abrasive/air ($R_m \ll 1$).

It is recommended to run a Laval nozzle at least at the design pressure for the nozzle being used, and at higher pressure if possible. When the nozzle is operated below the design pressure, the flow forms shock waves that slow down air flow as well as abrasive particles. Schlieren optics has been utilised by several authors to reveal such shock wave structures (Settles and Garg, 1995; Mohamed et al., 2003; Kendall et al., 2004). Some images are provided in Figs. 3.25 and 3.27.

Figure 3.26 summarises possible pressure decay modes along a convergent–divergent nozzle operating between nozzle inlet pressure and ambient pressure. Up to the throat, in the divergent section, the nozzle pressure decreases for all flow conditions. If the nozzle is being designed in a way that the nozzle exit pressure meets the atmospheric (back) pressure, the gas exits the nozzle as an undisturbed flow with parallel flow patterns. The flow is isentropic and shock-free. This situation is illustrated through the curve "1" in Fig. 3.26 and the image in Fig. 3.25d. In the situation characterised by the line "2" in Fig. 3.26, the back pressure is higher than the nozzle exit pressure (and also higher than the Laval pressure), but is reduced sufficiently to make the flow reach sonic conditions at the throat (Ma = 1). The flow in the divergent section is still subsonic because the back pressure is still high. Under ideal flow conditions (no friction), the exit nozzle pressure is equal to the

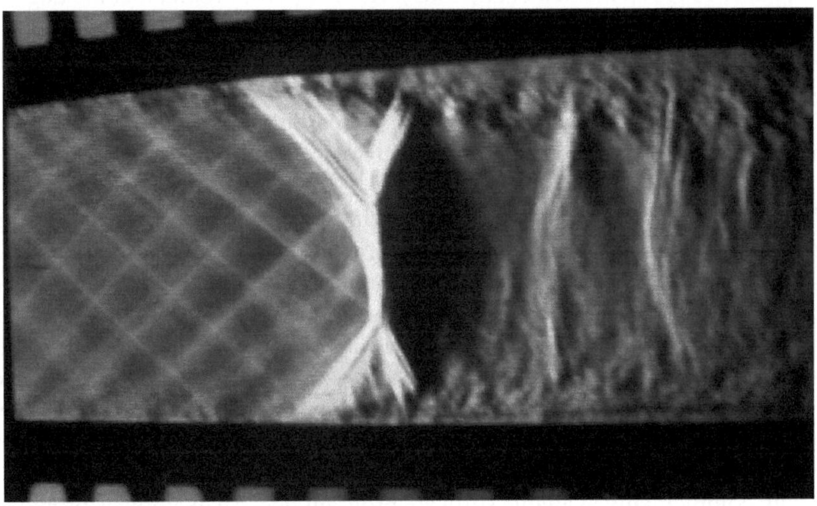

Fig. 3.27 Shock wave in the divergent section of a nozzle, followed by flow separation (image: Mechanical and Aerospace Engineering, University of California, Irvine)

nozzle entry pressure. The line "3" illustrates the situation if the back pressure is further reduced. In that case, a compression shock occurs in the flow in the divergent section of the nozzle. An example for such a shock front is provided in Fig. 3.27. This compression shock front in the divergent part of the nozzle develops normal to the flow, and it generates a "pressure jump", which is illustrated by the vertical line between line "1" and line "3" in Fig. 3.26. In front of this shock front, the flow is supersonic, whereas the flow behind the shock front moves at subsonic speed. Precise location and strength of the shock front depend on the back pressure. Decreasing the back pressure moves the shock wave downstream, and it finally reaches the nozzle exit plane (see image in Fig. 3.25a). If the back pressure is further reduced, the shock wave moves outside the nozzle, and the "pressure jump" takes places through a series of oblique shock waves. This type of nozzle flow is termed *over-expanded.* Line "4" in Fig. 3.26 and the images in Fig. 3.25b and c illustrate this case. The central shock wave head is at an almost normal position as shown in Fig. 3.25b, but the shock trajectories start to incline as in Fig. 3.25c for the lower back pressure. If the back pressure is further reduced and becomes less than the nozzle exit pressure, the flow expands, and the expansion takes place through a series of expansion waves outside the nozzle. This case is expressed through the line "5" in Fig. 3.26. Such a nozzle flow is termed *under-expanded.* Figure 3.25e provides an example. The system of expansion waves can clearly be distinguished in front of the nozzle exit. More illustrative photographs for the different types of pressure distribution can be found in Oertel (2001), where some very early schlieren images, taken by Ludwig Prandtl in 1907, are presented.

It was found, however, by some investigators that air expansion regime and shock location depended on abrasive parameters as well, namely on abrasive mass flow rate and abrasive particle size and density (Komov 1966; Myshanov and Shirokov, 1981; Fokke, 1999; Achtsnick et al., 2005). Komov (1966) found that the degree of air expansion was less for a particle-laden flow compared with the plain gas flow. This difference increased as the mass flow ratio abrasive/air increased. The authors also took images from shock fronts in a flow of air as well as in a particle-laden air flow, and they found that the shock front in the particle-laden air flow was located further upstream. They noted that this effect was most pronounced for high mass flow rates abrasive/air and smaller particles.

The operating characteristics of convergent nozzles and convergent–divergent nozzles are in detail described and discussed by Oosthuizen and Carscallen (1997). Schlieren images of shock waves formed in nozzles and in the exiting air jets under certain operating conditions can be found in Oertel's (2001) book. Examples of air jets formed under different operating conditions are shown in Fig. 3.25. Sakamura et al. (2005) have shown that pressure-sensitive paint technique can very well capture pressure maps for the two-dimensional flow in a convergent–divergent nozzle, and these results offer the opportunity for adding more knowledge to this issue. The shock characteristics in blast cleaning nozzles can be modelled with commercially available software programmes. An example is provided in Fig. 3.16b.

3.5 Composition of Particle Jets

3.5.1 Radial Abrasive Particle Distribution

Adlassing (1960) designed a special device for the assessment of the radial distribution of abrasive particles in an air jet exiting from blast cleaning nozzles. Interestingly, no distinguished effects of nozzle geometry (e.g. nozzle length) could be noted. General results were as follows: the inner core (24 cm^2 cross-section) consumed between 20 and 25 wt.% of all particles; the medium section (76 cm^2 cross-section) consumed between 45 and 45 wt.% of all abrasives; the external section (2,150 cm^2 cross-section) consumed between 25 and 30 wt.% of all abrasives. A curvature of the entry section of the nozzle did not change the distribution. The width of the particle-occupied section of a jet decreased if air pressure rose.

Particle density distribution over the nozzle exit cross-section is difficult to measure directly, and no systematic experimental study is known dealing with this issue. Achtsnick (2005) has subjected a polished glass plate to an abrasive particle flow formed in a blast cleaning nozzle. The visible impacts were microscopically detected and counted regardless their sizes. The results are presented in Fig. 3.28, and they demonstrated that the particles were essentially centred near the nozzle axis. Outside the centre, the number of impacts decreased sensitively towards the borders of the flow. The resulting particle concentration inside a cylindrical nozzle exit was of a bell-shape type. Outside the circle, drawn in Fig. 3.28, particle impacts occurred only incidentally. The same test was repeated for the perpendicular scanning direction and delivered equal results.

In order to get further information on the particle distribution, numerical simulations have been performed for different nozzle configurations by Achtsnick et al. (2005) and McPhee (2001). Results of these simulations are provided in Figs. 3.29 and 3.30. It can be seen that abrasive particle density distribution notably depended on nozzle layout and abrasive particle size. Effects of nozzle layout are illustrated in Fig. 3.29. According to these images, a Laval nozzle with a modified abrasive entry channel and a rectangular nozzle exit cross-section provided a more even distribution of the particles over the cross-section, whereas the conventional cylindrical nozzle design resulted in a concentration of abrasive particles in the central area of the nozzle cross-section. Some comparative measurements verified these trends (Achtsnick et al., 2005). The images in Fig. 3.30 characterise the effects of abrasive diameter on the particle density distribution in conventional round nozzles. In both cases, particles were concentrated in the centre of the nozzle cross-section, but the particle distribution was more favourable for the smaller abrasives.

3.5.2 Particle Velocity Distribution Function

Achtsnick (2005), Hamed and Mohamed (2001), Linnemann (1997), Linnemann et al. (1996), Slikkerveer (1999), Stevenson and Hutchings (1995) and Zinn et al.

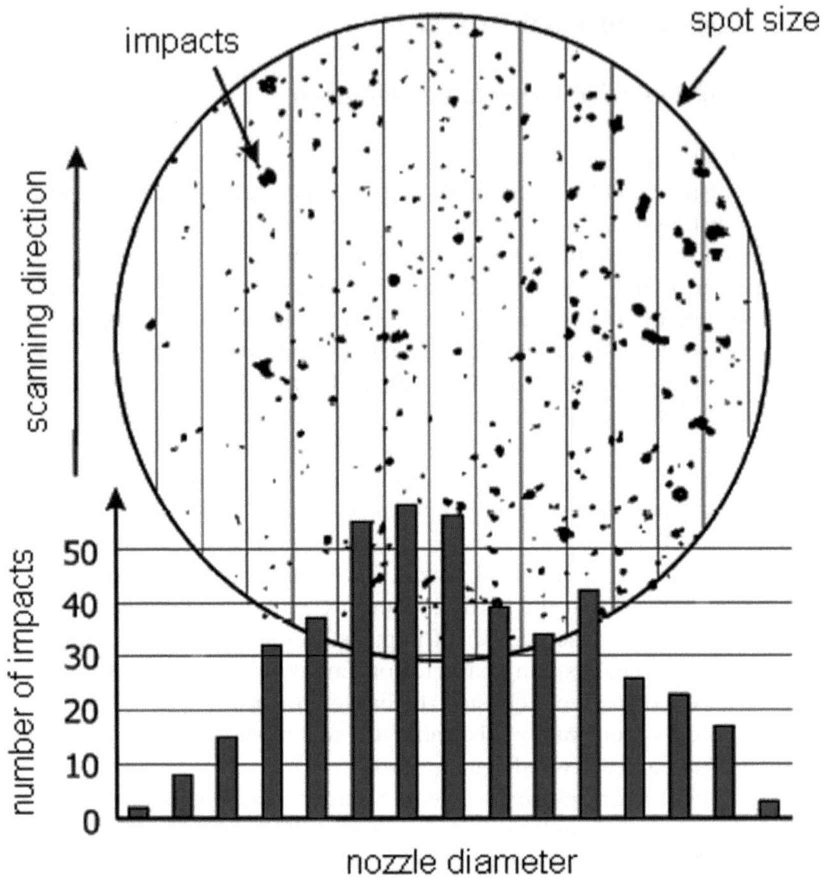

Fig. 3.28 Suggested abrasive particle distribution in the exit plane of a blast cleaning nozzle, based on impact spot inspections (Achtsnick, 2005)

(2002) experimentally investigated the statistical distribution of abrasive particle velocities in air-abrasive jets. The authors found velocity distributions as shown in Figs. 3.31 and 3.32. Figure 3.31 displays results of measurements of the velocities of aluminium oxide powder particles (mesh 360) accelerated in a convergent–divergent nozzle at two different air pressures. As expected, the average particle velocity increased with an increase in air pressure. Similar is the situation for the two graphs plotted in Fig. 3.32. In that case, silica sand particles were accelerated in a convergent-parallel nozzle. A Gaussian normal distribution could be applied to mathematically characterise the distribution of the axial particle velocity:

$$f(v_P) = \frac{1}{\sqrt{2 \cdot \pi} \cdot \sigma_{V_P}} \cdot \exp\left[\frac{-(v_P - \bar{v}_P)^2}{2 \cdot \sigma_{V_P}^2}\right] \tag{3.38}$$

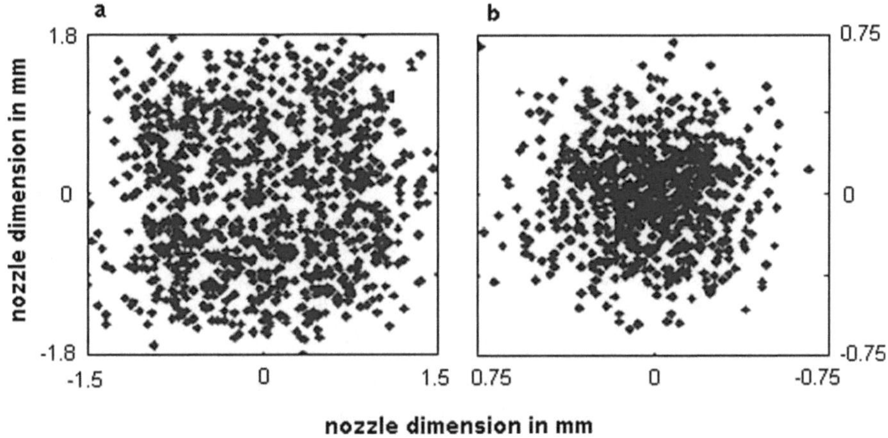

Fig. 3.29 Abrasive particle distributions in the exit planes of blast cleaning nozzles (Achtsnick et al., 2005). (**a**) Square convergent–divergent nozzle; (**b**) Conventional cylindrical nozzle

Typical values were $\bar{v}_P = 75\,\text{m/s}$ for the average axial particle velocity and $\sigma_{VP} = \pm 10\,\text{m/s}$ for the standard deviation of the axial abrasive particle velocity (Stevenson and Hutchings, 1995); and $\bar{v}_P = 15\,\text{m/s}$ for the average axial particle velocity and $\sigma_{VP} = \pm 5\,\text{m/s}$ for the standard deviation of the axial abrasive particle velocity (Linnemann, 1997). Lecoffre et al. (1993) found that the spreading of axial velocity distribution decreased as the nozzle diameter increased. Fokke (1999) has shown that particle velocity standard deviation slightly increased if air pressure rose, and he also found that the standard deviation did not change notably when the mass flow ratio abrasive/air ($R_m = 1.0$–4.5) or the stand-off distance (up to $x = 80\,\text{mm}$) was varied.

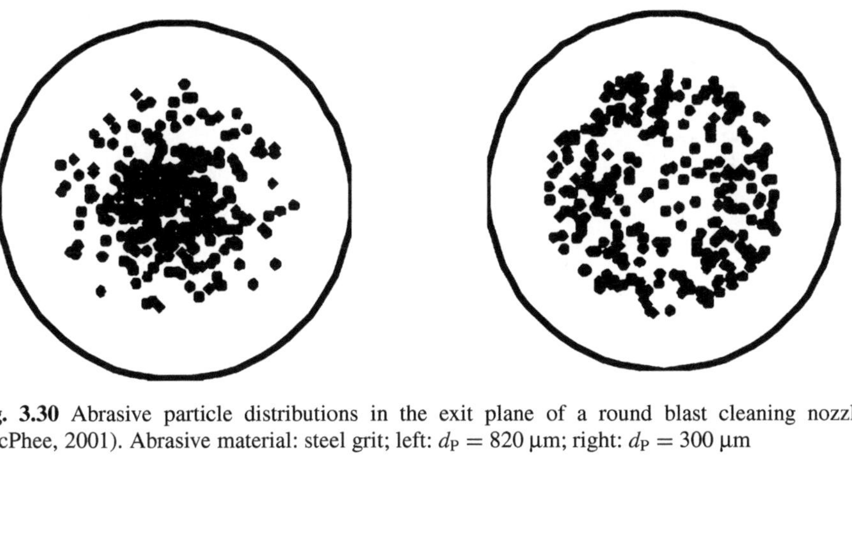

Fig. 3.30 Abrasive particle distributions in the exit plane of a round blast cleaning nozzle (McPhee, 2001). Abrasive material: steel grit; left: $d_P = 820\,\mu\text{m}$; right: $d_P = 300\,\mu\text{m}$

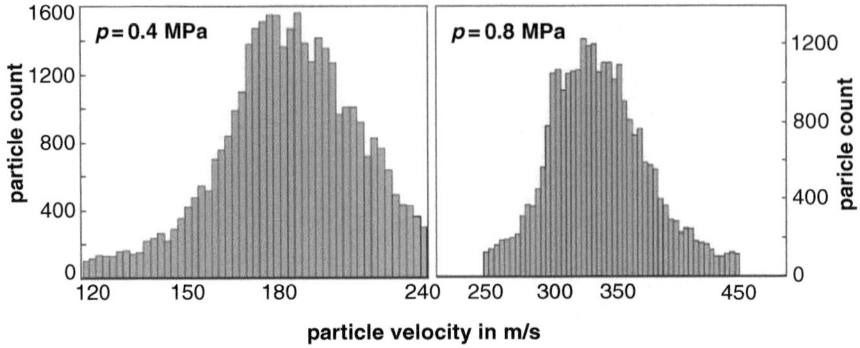

Fig. 3.31 Abrasive particle distributions in abrasive air jets; measurements with aluminium oxide powder (mesh 360) for two pressure levels in a convergent–divergent nozzle (Achtsnick, 2005)

Average particle velocity and abrasive particle velocity standard deviation are not independent on each other; this was shown by Zinn et al. (2002) based on experimental results with rounded-off wire shot. Typical values for the standard deviation were between $\sigma_{VP} = 1.2$ and 2.7 m/s for average abrasive velocities between $\bar{v}_P = 20$ and 47 m/s. The relationships were complex, and parameters which affected these relationships included nozzle type, abrasive particle size and abrasive mass flow rate.

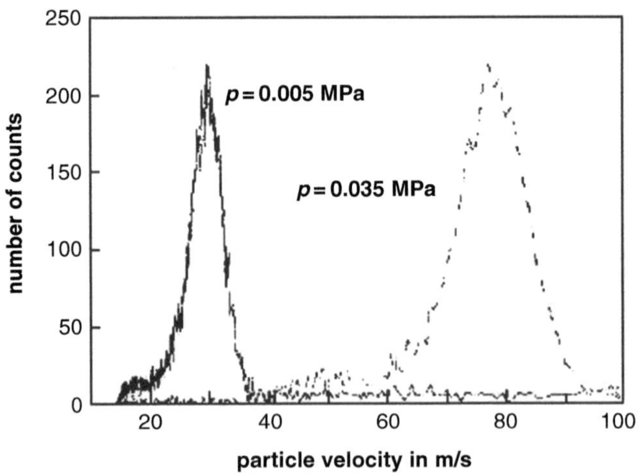

Fig. 3.32 Abrasive particle distributions in abrasive air jets; measurements with silica particles ($d_P = 125$–150 μm) for two low pressure levels in a cylindrical nozzle (Stevenson and Hutchings, 1995). Pressure is gauge pressure

3.5.3 Radial Abrasive Particle Velocity Distribution

Results of measurements of abrasive particle velocities over the cross-sections of two nozzles are plotted in Fig. 3.33. Radial abrasive velocity depended notably on nozzle design and air pressure. It can be seen that the cylindrical nozzle (left graph) featured a typical bell-shaped velocity profile. Such profiles are typical for standard Laval nozzles as well (Johnston, 1998). The modified Laval nozzle with a rectangular cross-section (right graph), however, approached a more favourable rectangular velocity distribution. It can also be seen that high air pressure deteriorated the particle velocity profile. The bell-shape was most pronounced for the highest air pressure.

Figure 3.34 shows results of erosion spot topography measurements performed by Johnston (1998). The term "erosion potential" is equal to the local material

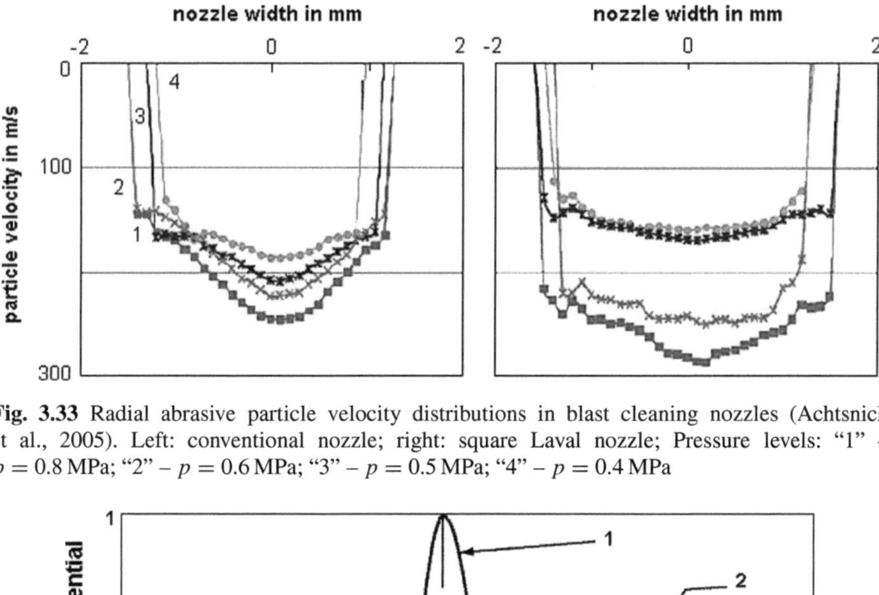

Fig. 3.33 Radial abrasive particle velocity distributions in blast cleaning nozzles (Achtsnick et al., 2005). Left: conventional nozzle; right: square Laval nozzle; Pressure levels: "1" – $p = 0.8\,\text{MPa}$; "2" – $p = 0.6\,\text{MPa}$; "3" – $p = 0.5\,\text{MPa}$; "4" – $p = 0.4\,\text{MPa}$

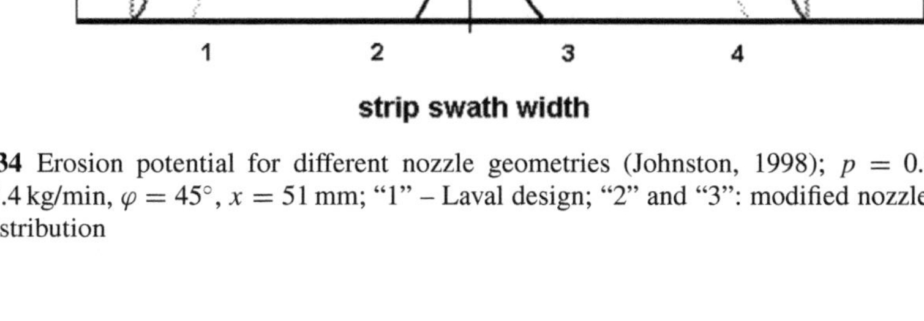

Fig. 3.34 Erosion potential for different nozzle geometries (Johnston, 1998); $p = 0.28\,\text{MPa}$, $\dot{m}_P = 5.4\,\text{kg/min}$, $\varphi = 45°$, $x = 51\,\text{mm}$; "1" – Laval design; "2" and "3": modified nozzles; "4" – ideal distribution

removal depth in a special model material. The standard Laval nozzle (designated "1") generated a small but deep spot formed due to a highly uneven localised erosion potential. The erosion potential was very high at the centre, but was restricted to this central range only. The two "modified" nozzles generated a much more even distribution. The erosion potential was equally distributed over almost the entire width. Only at the rim, there was an increase in the erosion potential. The curve "4" illustrates the erosion potential of an "ideal" blast cleaning nozzle. Here, the erosion potential was equally distributed over the entire strip swath width.

3.5.4 Area Coverage

Aspects of area coverage are illustrated in Figs. 3.35 and 3.36. Figure 3.35 shows images of two dent distributions, whereby the dents are the impressions formed on the target surface due to abrasive particle impingement. Measurements performed by Tosha and Iida (2001) have shown that dent distribution density [dent number/(s · m^2)] decreased if abrasive particle diameter increased. Figure 3.36 is a typical area coverage graph, where the area coverage is plotted against the exposure time. The area coverage can be calculated as follows (Kirk and Abyaneh, 1994; Karuppanam et al., 2002):

$$C_A(t_E) = 100 \cdot \left[1 - \exp\left(-\frac{3 \cdot r_I^2 \cdot \dot{m}_P \cdot t_E}{4 \cdot A_G \cdot r_P^3 \cdot \rho_P}\right)\right] \tag{3.39}$$

The trend between area coverage and abrasive mass flow rate was experimentally verified by Hornauer (1982). The author also found that values for the area coverage decreased if the traverse rate of the blast cleaning nozzle increased. Because of $t_E \propto v_T^{-1}$, this result also supports the validity of (3.39).

A typical area coverage function can be subdivided into two sections: (1) initial area coverage and (2) full area coverage. This is illustrated in Fig. 3.36. It was experimentally verified (Tosha and Iida, 2001) that the initial area coverage depended, among others, on abrasive particle diameter (initial area coverage dropped if abrasive diameter increased) and abrasive particle velocity (initial area coverage increased if abrasive particle velocity increased). The critical exposure time, where full area coverage started, depended on process parameters as follows (Tosha and Iida, 2001):

$$t_F \propto \frac{d_P^{1/2} \cdot H_M^{1/2}}{v_P} \tag{3.40}$$

3.5.5 Stream Density

Ciampini et al. (2003a) introduced a dimensionless stream density, the geometric basis of which is illustrated in Fig. 3.37a, and derived the following expression:

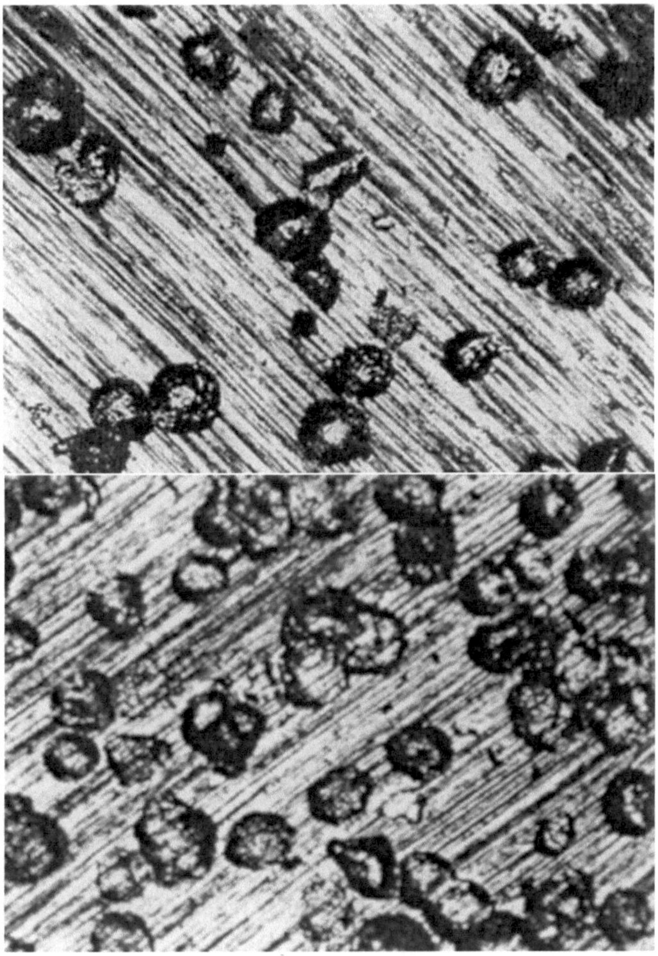

(a)

(b)

Fig. 3.35 Aspects of area coverage (Meguid and Rabie, 1986). (**a**) Coverage: 16%; (**b**) Coverage: 52%

$$\rho_S^* = \frac{4 \cdot r_P^{*3}}{3 \cdot r_N^{*2} + 3 \cdot r_N^* \cdot x^* \cdot \tan\,\theta_J + x^{*2} \cdot \tan^2\theta_J} \tag{3.41}$$

The dimensionless numbers in (3.41) read as follows. The dimensionless nozzle radius is defined as follows:

$$r_N^* = \frac{\dot{N}_P \cdot r_N}{v_P} \tag{3.42}$$

It is the number of particles launched in the time taken for a particle of average velocity to travel a distance equal to the nozzle radius. The dimensionless particle radius is defined as follows:

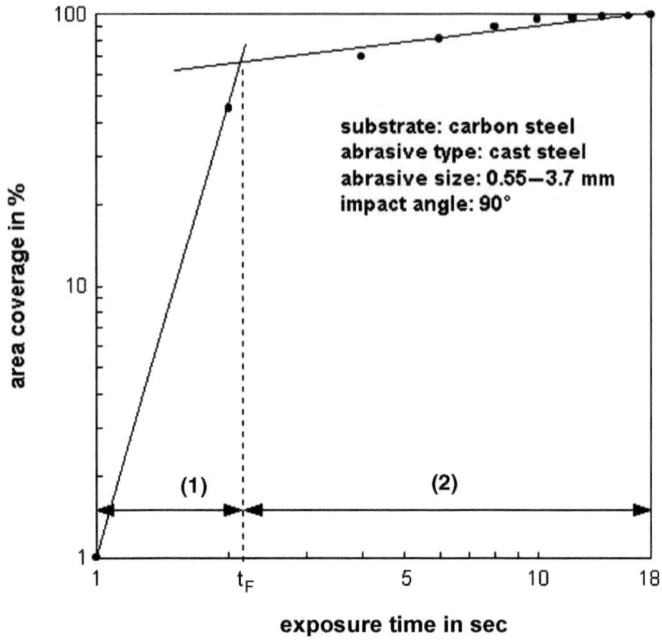

Fig. 3.36 Relationship between exposure time and area coverage (Tosha and Iida, 2001)

$$r_P^* = \frac{\dot{N}_P \cdot r_P}{v_P} \tag{3.43}$$

It is the number of particles launched in the time taken for a particle of average velocity to travel a distance equal to the particle radius. The dimensionless stand-off distance is defined as follows:

$$x^* = \frac{\dot{N}_P \cdot x}{v_P} \tag{3.44}$$

It is the number of particles launched in the time taken for a particle of average velocity to travel a distance equal to the stand-off distance between nozzle exit and target surface. The stream density can be applied to the calculation of a relative distance between abrasive particles as follows:

$$L_P^* = \frac{L_P}{d_P} = \left(\frac{\pi}{6 \cdot \rho_S^*}\right)^{1/3} \tag{3.45}$$

This parameter characterises the ratio between the average distance of two incident particles and the particle diameters.

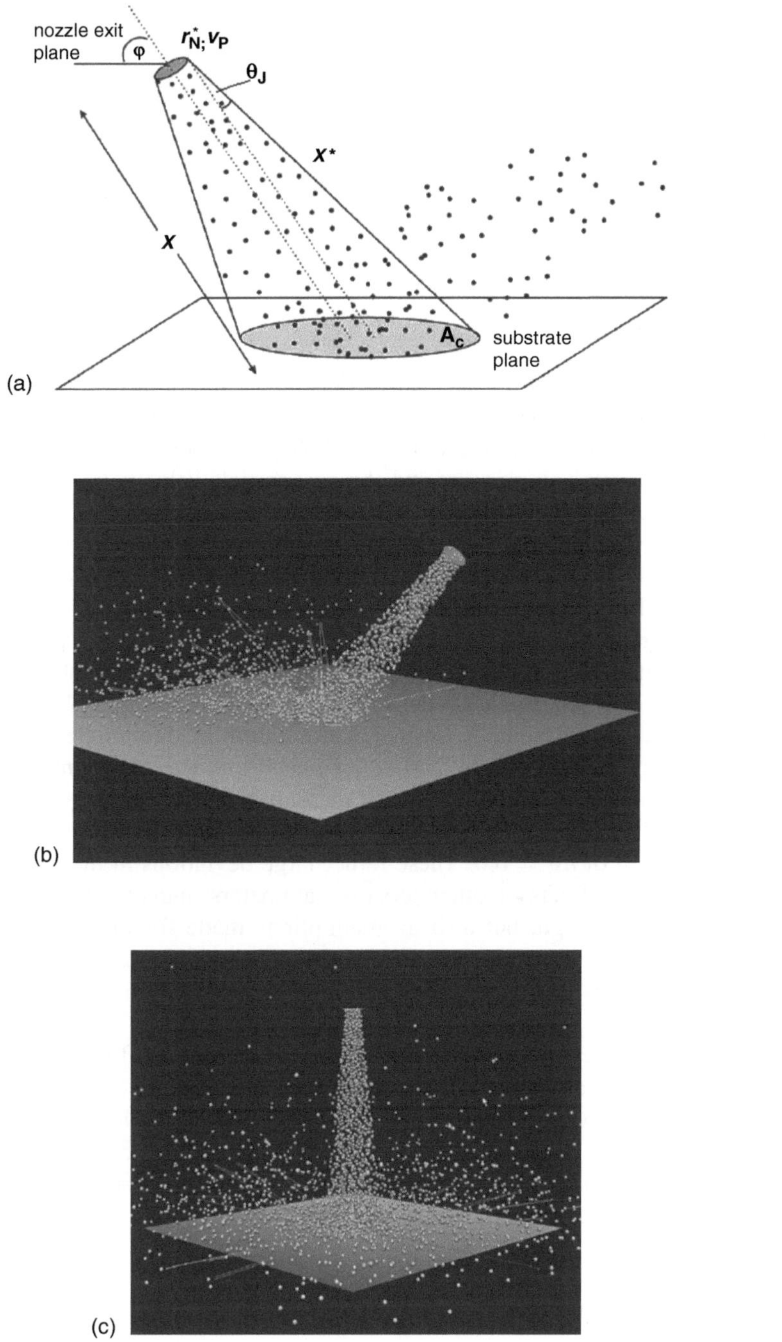

Fig. 3.37 Stream density (Ciampini et al., 2003a). (**a**) Geometric condition; (**b**) Simulation for oblique impact; (**c**) Simulation for normal impact

3.6 Parameter Effects on Abrasive Particle Velocity

3.6.1 Effects of Air Pressure on Particle Velocity

Tilghman (1870), in his original patent, wrote: "*The greater the pressure of the jet the bigger will be the velocity imparted to the grains of sand.*" Generally, the relationship between air pressure and particle velocity can be described as follows:

$$v_P \propto p^{n_V} \tag{3.46}$$

The power exponent n_V seemed to depend on numerous process parameters, among them the abrasive mass flow rate. Some authors (Green et al., 1981; Lecoffre et al., 1993; Linnemann, 1997; Remmelts, 1969; Ruff and Ives, 1975) found a linear relationship between air pressure and abrasive particle velocity ($n_V = 1$). Remmelts (1969) reported that the coefficient of proportionality depended on abrasive type. It was high for slag material (low material density) and low for cut steel wire (high material density). Results delivered by Belloy et al. (2000), Clausen and Stangenberg (2002), Linnemann et al. (1996), Ninham and Hutchings (1983), Stevenson and Hutchings (1995) and Zinn et al. (2002), however, suggest a power exponent $n_V < 1$ for numerous abrasive materials (e.g. glass beads, steel shot and ceramic abrasives). A solution to (3.31) delivers $n_V = 0.68$. Achtsnick (2005) performed a regression of experimentally estimated aluminium oxide particle (mesh 360) velocities in a cylindrical nozzle, and he estimated a power exponent of $n_V = 0.52$. Results of numerical simulations and of measurements performed by Fokke (1999) are displayed in Figs. 3.38 and 3.39. The results plotted in Fig. 3.39 suggest a power exponent of $n_V = 0.6$. These rather large deviations in the values could be attributed to the effects of other process parameters, namely abrasive mass flow rate and nozzle design, but also to assumptions made for the calculation procedures. Figure 3.39 illustrates the effect of the abrasive particle size on the power exponent. There is only a marginal effect of the particle diameter on the power exponent.

A rise in air pressure increases air density as well as air flow velocity; both effects contribute to an increase in the drag force according to (3.27). Measurements performed by Bothen (2000) have shown the following (particle diameter between $d_P = 23$ and 53 µm): abrasive particle velocity increased by +35% if the air pressure rose from $p = 0.2$ to 0.4 MPa; if air pressure rose from $p = 0.4$ to 0.6 MPa, abrasive particle velocity increased by +25%.

3.6.2 Effects of Abrasive Mass Flow Rate on Particle Velocity

Experimental results have shown that abrasive particle velocity dropped with an increase in the abrasive mass flow rate (Pashatskii et al., 1970; Green et al., 1981;

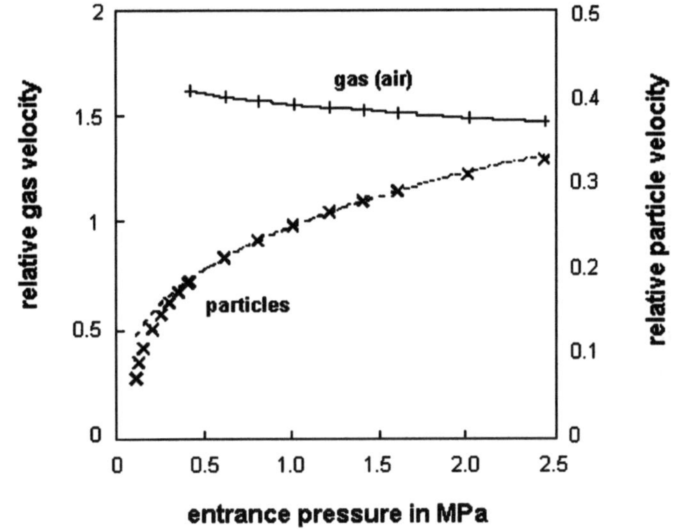

Fig. 3.38 Effect of air pressure on relative air velocity and relative particle velocity (Fokke, 1999). (Relative velocity is the ratio between actual velocity and velocity of sound.)

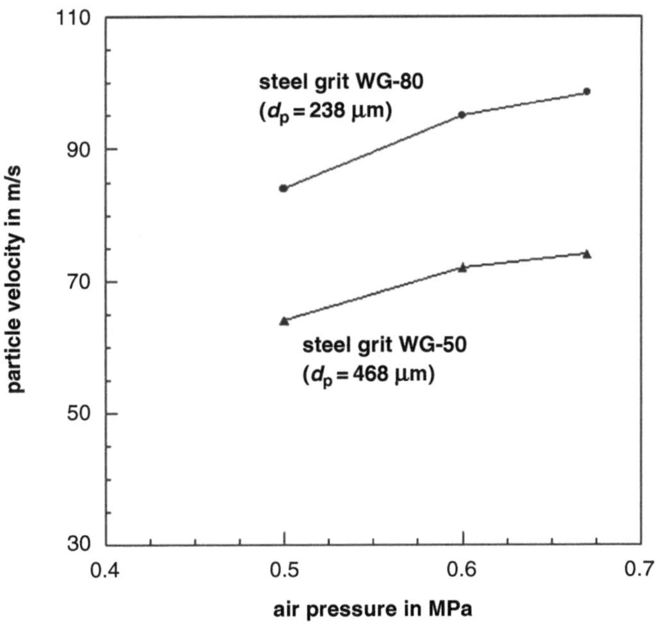

Fig. 3.39 Effects of air pressure and abrasive particle size on particle velocity (Fokke, 1999)

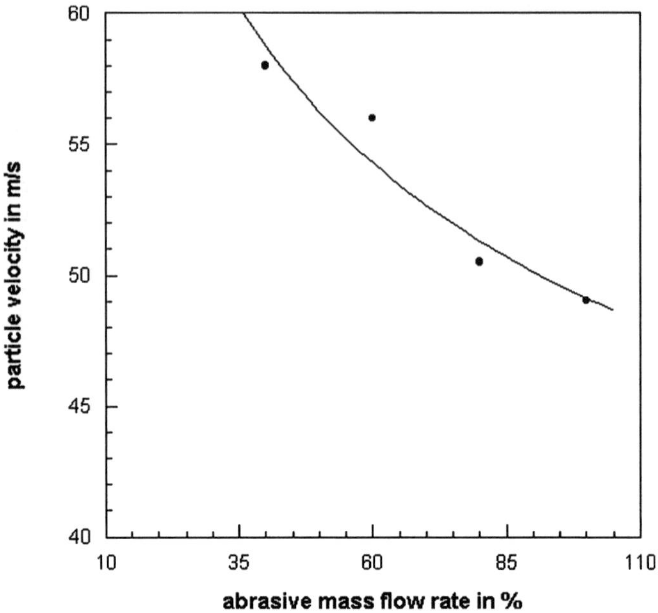

Fig. 3.40 Effect of relative abrasive mass flow rate on particle velocity (Lecoffre et al., 1993)

Lecoffre et al., 1993; Linnemann et al., 1996; Zinn et al., 2002). An example is shown in Fig. 3.40. The general trend is as follows:

$$v_P \propto \dot{m}_P^{-n_m} \tag{3.47}$$

The power exponent has values of $0 < n_m \leq 1$. If the impulse flow (respectively force) of the air flow according to (3.25) is considered, a value for the power exponent of $n_m = 1$ could be derived as a preliminary number.

Figure 3.41 shows the effects of changes in the mass flow ratio abrasive/air on the particle velocity. It can be seen that the particle velocity dropped if the mass flow ratio abrasive/air increased. This trend was observed by Hauke (1982), Pashatskii et al. (1970) and Wolak et al. (1977). The trend seemed to depend on the nozzle diameter for rather small R_m-values, and the influence of the nozzle diameter seemed to vanish for high values of R_m. Wolak et al. (1977) derived the following empirical relationship:

$$v_P \propto \exp(-k_R \cdot R_m) \tag{3.48}$$

Numerical simulations performed by Fokke (1999) for mass flow ratios up to $R_m = 6$ verified this trend: particle velocity dropped if mass flow ratio was increased. The author could also show that the effect of the mass flow ratio abrasive/air on particle velocity was largest for ratios between $R_m = 0.1$ and 3.0.

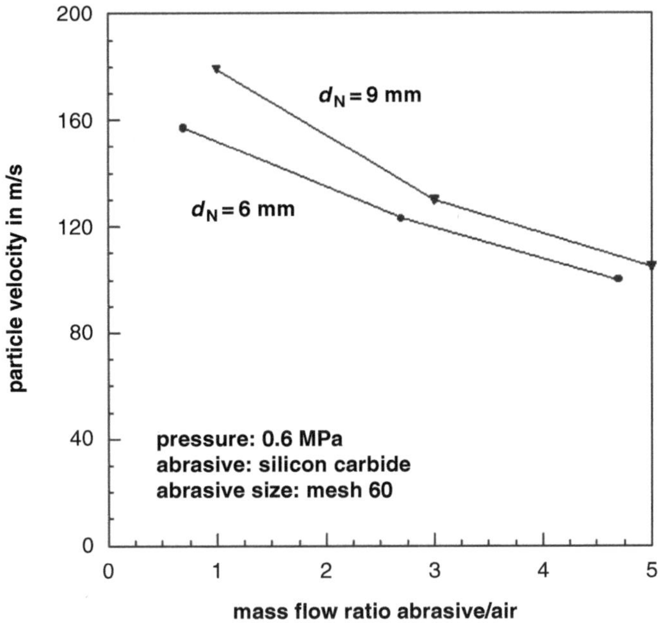

Fig. 3.41 Effects of mass flow ratio abrasive/air and nozzle diameter on particle velocity (Wolak et al., 1977)

3.6.3 Effects of Abrasive Particle Size on Particle Velocity

Measurements performed by several authors have shown that abrasive particle velocity dropped with an increase in the abrasive particle size. This trend was verified through experimental results provided by Achtsnick (2005), Fokke (1999), McPhee (2001), McPhee and Ebadian (1999), Neilson and Gilchrist (1968), Pashatskii et al. (1970), Stevenson and Hutchings (1995) and Zinn et al. (2002). Examples are shown in Fig. 3.39 and in Figs. 3.42–3.44. Achtsnick (2005) and Stevenson and Hutchings (1995) applied different nozzle types, and they measured particle velocities of particles in the diameter range between $d_P = 63$ and 500 μm. They derived the following regression function:

$$v_P \propto d_P^{-n_d} \quad (3.49)$$

The power exponent took a value of $n_d = 0.29$ for a cylindrical nozzle (Stevenson and Hutchings, 1995), and it took a value of $n_d = 0.36$ for a Laval nozzle with a square cross-section (Achtsnick, 2005). A solution to (3.31) delivers $n_d = 0.36$. Larger particles offer a larger projection area, which, according to (3.27), allows higher friction forces. However, due to their higher weight, larger particles need a longer acceleration distance to achieve a demanded final velocity according to (3.29). Fokke (1999) as well as Settles and Garg (1995) performed numerical

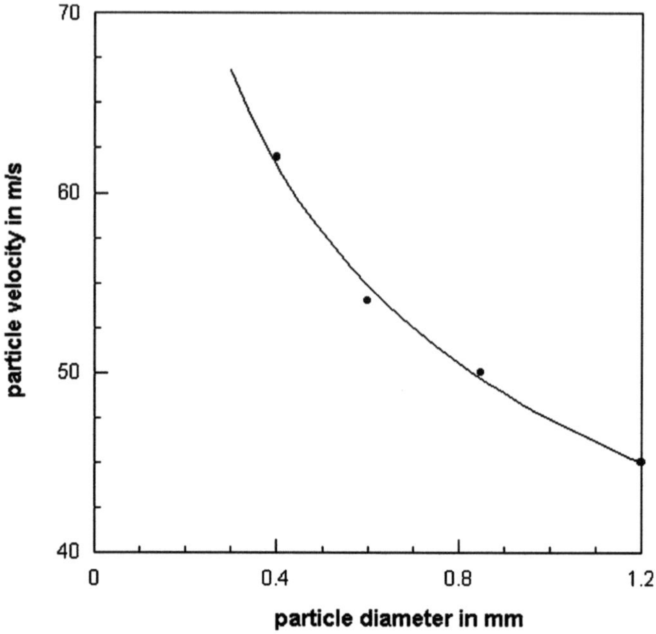

Fig. 3.42 Effect of abrasive particle diameter on particle velocity (Lecoffre et al., 1993)

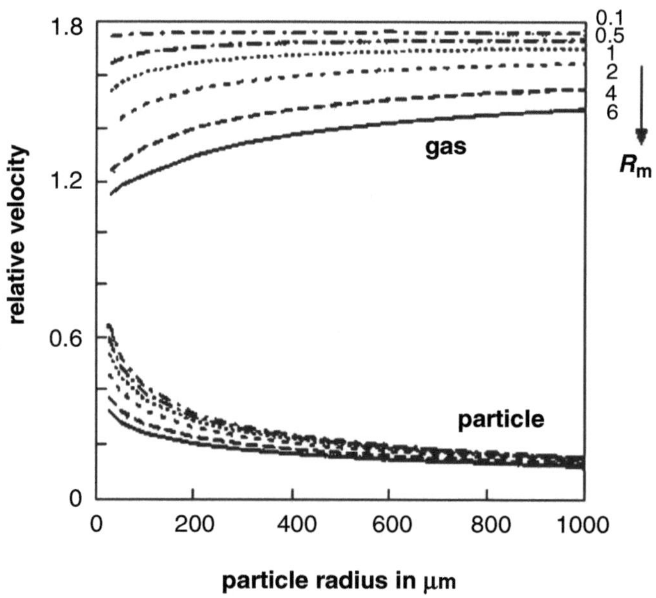

Fig. 3.43 Effects of abrasive particle diameter and mass flow ratio abrasive/air on relative particle velocity and relative air velocity (Fokke, 1999). (Relative velocity is the ratio between actual velocity and velocity of sound.)

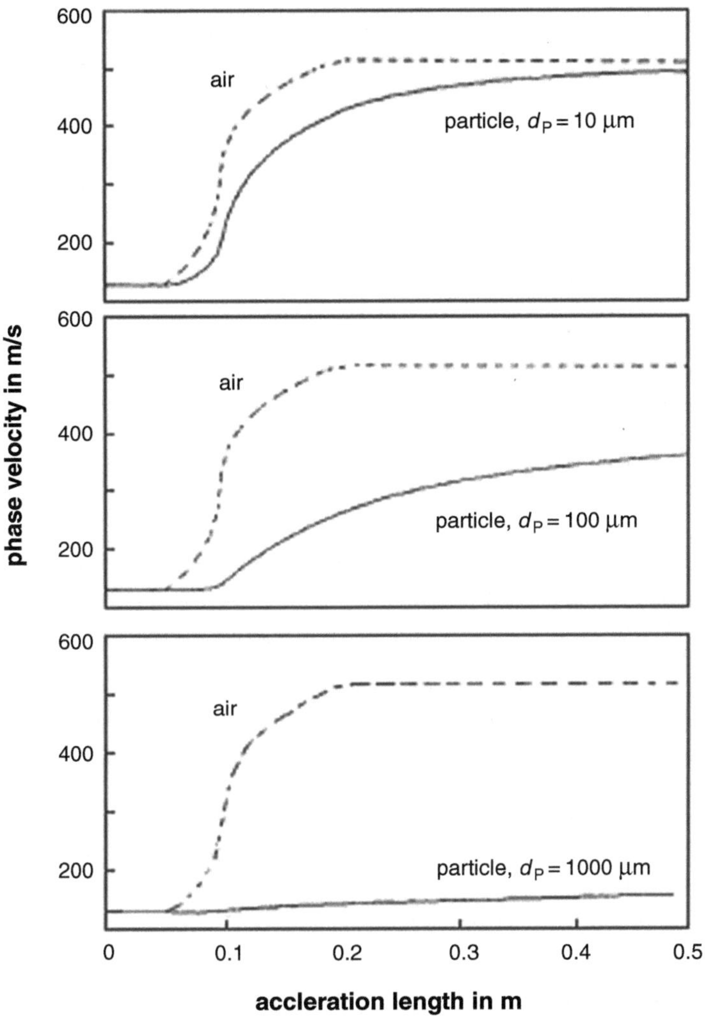

Fig. 3.44 Effect of abrasive particle diameter on particle velocity gradient in a convergent–divergent nozzle (Settles and Garg, 1995)

simulations for Laval-type nozzles, and they could prove that smaller abrasive particles could achieve higher velocities. Results of investigations are shown in Fig. 3.44. A particle with $d_P = 10\ \mu m$ reached a nozzle exit velocity of about $v_P = 500\,m/s$, whereas a particle with a diameter of $d_P = 1{,}000\ \mu m$ reached a velocity of about $v_P = 150\,m/s$ only. The 10 μm particles lagged behind the airflow somewhat, but managed to achieve more than 80% of the air velocity at the nozzle exit. The 100 μm particles lagged more seriously and reached only about half the air velocity at the nozzle exit. The 1,000 μm particles were barely accelerated at all by the air flow in the nozzle. Settles and Garg (1995) performed measurements of the velocities of steel particles (d_P = 50–70 μm) and aluminium particles (d_P = 50–70 μm) accelerated in convergent–divergent nozzles, and they found excellent agreement between the measured velocities and the velocities calculated with their simulation method. The gain in using smaller abrasive particles was especially evident for short nozzles. If longer nozzles were utilised, the influence of the abrasive particle diameter became less important.

3.6.4 Effects of Abrasive Particle Shape on Particle Velocity

A very early statement on the effect of the abrasive particle shape on the particle velocity, based on experimental results, was due to Rosenberger (1939): "*The shape of the abrasive particles also influences the velocity. Spherical particles travel slower than angular particles, other conditions being equal.*"

Shipway and Hutchings (1993a) found experimentally that glass spheres achieved lower final velocities than irregular silica particles for a given air pressure for many nozzle types. They attributed this effect for two reasons. Firstly, the irregularity of the silica shapes means that each particle with a given (sieve) diameter may have less mass than a sphere of this diameter, and may also have a greater drag coefficient. Secondly, the rebound behaviour of spheres and angular particles at the nozzle walls will differ. For a sphere, the rebound angle tended to be equal to or larger than the approach angle. An angular particle can rotate on impact, leading to a rebound angle which can be smaller than the approach angle. This may lead to higher acceleration along the nozzle, and therefore a greater final velocity. Fokke (1999) applied a numerical procedure developed for spherical steel particles and compared the numerical results with experimental results obtained with irregular steel grit particles. He noted a 20% difference between numerical and experimental results. This 20% increase in abrasive particle velocity for grit particles is, however, a very preliminary number, and further research is needed.

3.6.5 Effects of Abrasive Material Density on Particle Velocity

A very early statement on the effect of the abrasive material density on the particle velocity, based on experimental results, was due to Rosenberger (1939): "*The abrasive velocity bears some relation to the specific gravity of the abrasive material, being lowest when the specific gravity is high and vice versa.*"

Results from measurements performed by Stevenson and Hutchings (1995) with a cylindrical nozzle in the abrasive material density range between $\rho_P = 2{,}500\,\mathrm{kg/m^3}$ (glass beads) and $5{,}600\,\mathrm{kg/m^3}$ (zirconia sand), and investigations performed by Neilson and Gilchrist (1968a) and by Remmelts (1969) have shown that particle velocity dropped if particle material density increased. An empirical relationship reads as follows:

$$v_P \propto \rho_P^{-n_\rho} \tag{3.50}$$

Stevenson and Hutchings (1995) estimated a value of $n_\rho = 0.54$. A solution to (3.31) delivers $n_\rho = 0.39$. This inverse relationship is basically due to the larger momentum of the heavier abrasive material, which, for equal particle diameter, requires longer acceleration distances. For longer nozzles, the difference in the terminal velocity will therefore reduce. Remmelts (1969) reported a velocity ratio of 1.45 for the velocities of crushed slag ($\rho_P = 2{,}900\,\text{kg/m}^3$) and cut steel wire ($\rho_P = 7{,}800\,\text{kg/m}^3$), which agrees well with the values plotted in Fig. 3.19.

If (3.50) is combined with (3.49), an *abrasive parameter* could be defined for cylindrical nozzles, which determines the effects of abrasive material parameters on the abrasive particle velocity:

$$v_P \propto \underbrace{d_P^{-n_d} \cdot \rho_P^{-n_\rho}}_{\text{abrasive parameter}} \tag{3.51}$$

Heavier particles (e.g. with higher density and larger diameter) would need a longer acceleration distance compared with lighter particles; the relationship is $a_P \propto (d_P \cdot \rho_P)^{-1}$ from (3.29). For a given acceleration distance, particle speed will, therefore, be lower for a heavy particle. This simple argument can partly explain the effects of particle diameter and particle material density.

3.6.6 Effects of Stand-off Distance on Particle Velocity

Bothen (2000), Fokke (1999), Uferer (1992) and Wolak et al. (1977) performed studies into the effects of the stand-off distance on the velocity of abrasive particles. Results of these studies are displayed in Figs. 3.45–3.47. Figure 3.39 shows the effect of variations in stand-off distance on the relative abrasive particle velocity. It was evident that an optimum stand-off distance existed where abrasive particle velocity had maximum values. Because there is still a velocity slip between particles and accelerating gas if the flow exits the nozzle, the particles will be further accelerated until gas and solid medium flow at equal velocities. This effect, illustrated in Fig. 3.46 for two different nozzle types and two different abrasive materials, was experimentally verified by high-speed photograph inspections performed by Bothen (2000). A velocity balance will occur at a certain critical distance from the nozzle exit. If this stand-off distance is being exceeded, particle velocity will start to drop due to effects of air friction. The graphs in Fig. 3.47 illustrate the effect of mass flow ratio abrasive/air on the abrasive velocity. It can be seen that a stand-off distance effect was rather pronounced for the lowest mass flow ratio (the highest air mass flow value). It also seemed from these results that the optimum stand-off distances shifted to higher values for higher mass flow ratios abrasive/air (lower air mass flow rate).

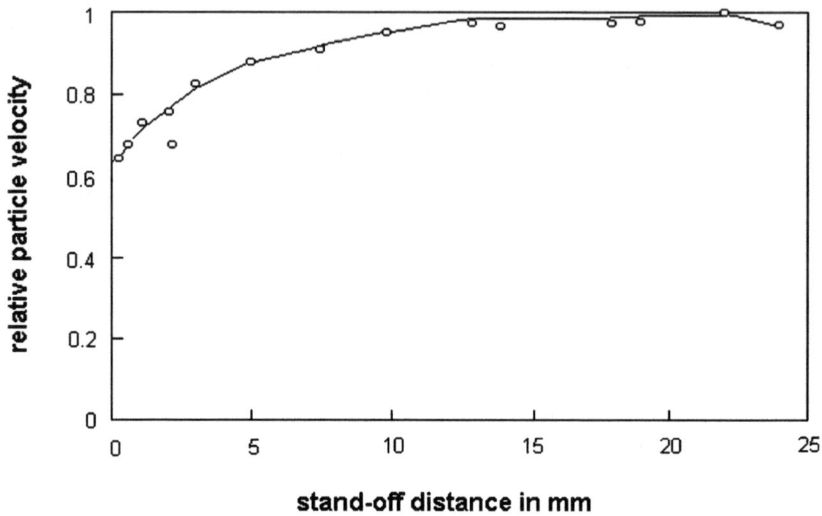

Fig. 3.45 Effect of stand-off distance on relative particle velocity (Bothen, 2000). (Relative velocity is related to the value "1", which characterises the maximum particle velocity.)

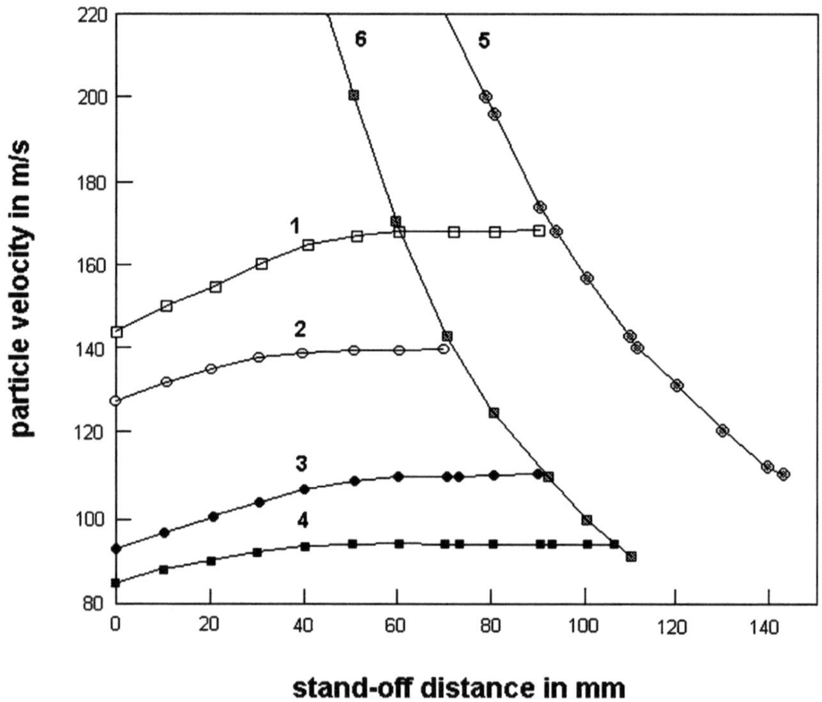

Fig. 3.46 Effect of stand-off distance on particle velocity (Uferer, 1992). "1" – convergent–divergent nozzle (slag); "2" – cylindrical nozzle (slag); "3" – convergent–divergent nozzle (steel cut wire); "4" – cylindrical nozzle (steel cut wire); "5" – convergent–divergent nozzle (air flow only); "6" – cylindrical nozzle (air flow only)

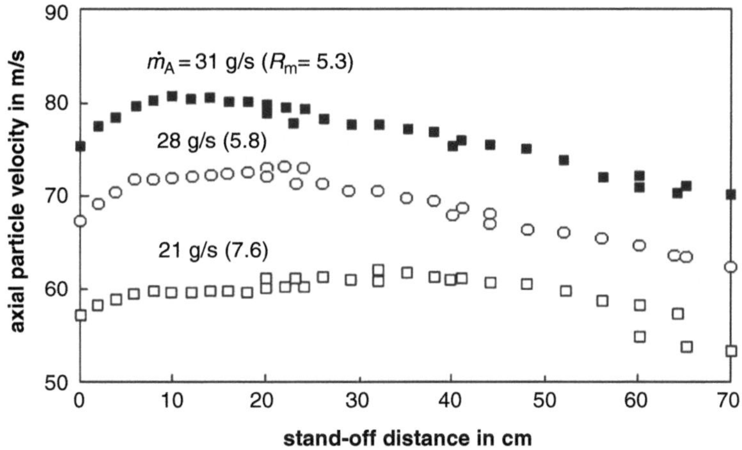

Fig. 3.47 Effects of stand-off distance and air mass flow rate (respectively mass flow ratio abrasive/air) on particle velocity (Fokke, 1999); $d_P = 468$ μm

3.6.7 Effects of Nozzle Length and Nozzle Diameter on Particle Velocity

Results of measurements on the effect of nozzle length on abrasive particle velocity are illustrated in Fig. 3.48. It can be seen that optimum nozzle lengths existed where velocity was highest (Wolak et al., 1977; Stevenson and Hutchings, 1995). This optimum slightly shifted to smaller nozzle length values if nozzle diameter decreased, but it did not seem to depend on the mass flow rate abrasive/air. The nozzle length to give the maximum axial particle velocity, at any given mass flow ratio, was approximately equal to 20 internal diameters of the nozzle for a cylindrical nozzle (Wolak et al., 1977). The dependence of particle velocity on nozzle length, and especially the existence of an optimum nozzle length, may be attributed to several mechanisms. Increased nozzle length increases the time during which the particles are exposed to the acceleration by the air, and consequently the particle velocities increase. However, a longer nozzle imposes proportionally higher friction effects on the air flow, and air velocity and the drag on the particle would decrease resulting in lower particle velocities. Another factor is the friction between particles and nozzle wall, evidenced through the wear of the nozzle walls. This expenditure of particle energy will also reduce particle velocities.

Abrasive particle velocity increased if nozzle diameter increased; this is shown in Figs. 3.41 and 3.48. However, it can be seen from Fig. 3.41 that this effect seemed to vanish for higher values of the mass flow ratio abrasive/air and for short nozzles.

3.6.8 Effects of Nozzle Design on Particle Velocity

Figure 3.49 displays results of abrasive particle measurements performed by Hamann (1987) on blast cleaning nozzles with different layouts. It can be seen that the highest

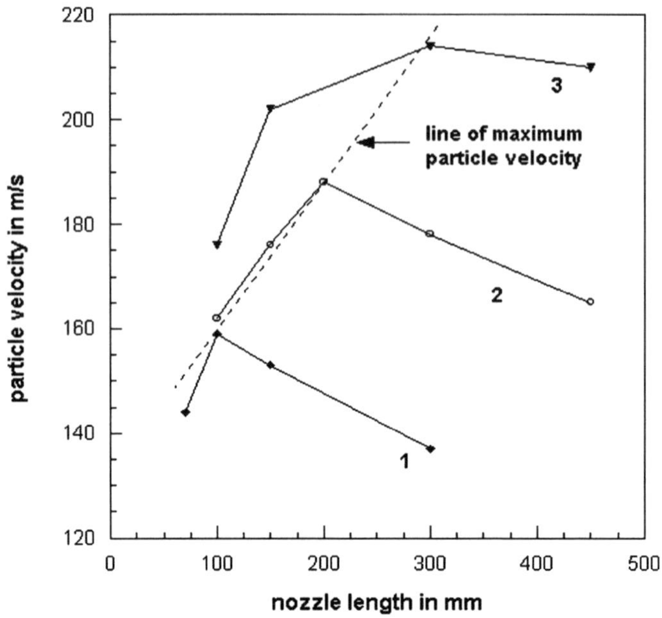

Fig. 3.48 Effects of nozzle length, nozzle diameter and mass flow ratio abrasive/air on particle velocity (Wolak et al., 1977); abrasive type: silicone carbide (mesh 60). "1" – $d_N = 6$ mm, $0.75 < R_m < 1.30$; "2" – $d_N = 9$ mm, $0.88 < R_m < 1.33$; "3" – $d_N = 12$ mm, $0.45 < R_m < 0.71$

abrasive particle velocity could be realised with a divergent–convergent nozzle with a specially designed inlet flow section (nozzle type "4"). The lowest abrasive particle velocity was delivered by a cylindrical nozzle with a bell-shaped inlet section (nozzle type "1"). The differences in abrasive particle velocities were as high as 45% among the tested nozzle layouts. Figure 3.50 shows the effects of the cross-section geometry on the velocity of abrasive particles. It can be recognised that the utilisation of a rectangular cross-section could notably increase the particle velocity compared with the use of a conventional circular cross-section. The effect of the nozzle cross-section on the abrasive particle velocity depended on the nozzle air pressure. The increase in abrasive particle velocity was +67% for a nozzle pressure of $p = 0.45$ MPa, and it was +93% for a nozzle pressure of $p = 0.57$ MPa.

3.6.9 Effects of Nozzle Wall Roughness on Particle Velocity

Shipway and Hutchings (1993a) could prove that the velocities of glass beads accelerated in cylindrical stainless steel nozzles depended on the roughness of the inner nozzle wall. The smoother the wall surface, the higher were the exit velocities of the particles. For a pressure of $p = 0.06$ MPa, for example, the theoretical particle velocity for glass beads ($d_P = 125$–150 µm) was $v_P = 100$ m/s; the particle velocity measured with a smooth nozzle ($R_a = 0.25$ µm) was $v_P = 85$ m/s and the particle

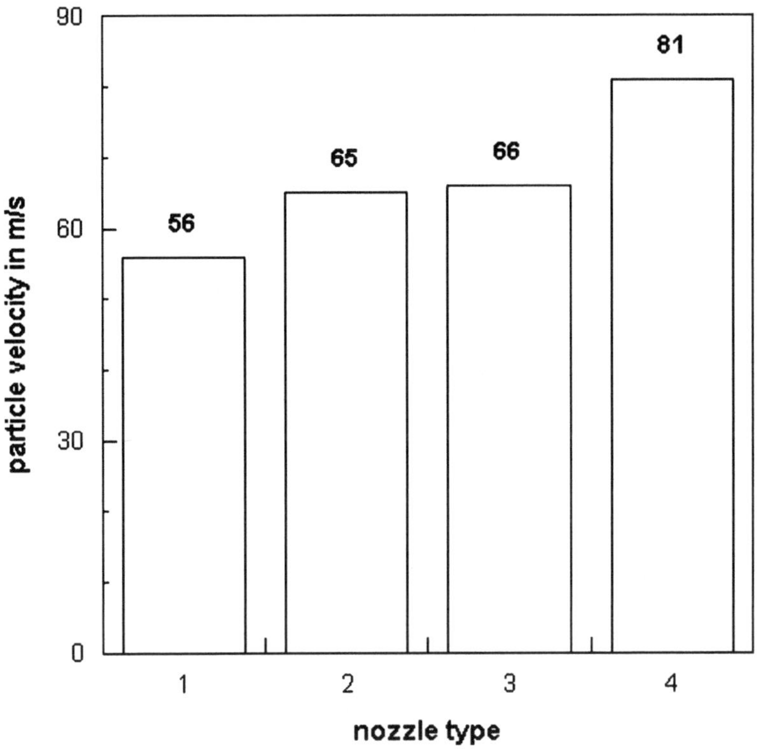

Fig. 3.49 Effects of nozzle type on abrasive particle velocity (Hamann, 1987). Nozzle type: "1" – bell-mouthed + cylinder; "2" – bell-mouthed + convergent; "3" – standard convergent–divergent; "4" – convergent–divergent with specially designed entry section

velocity measured with a rough nozzle ($R_a = 0.94\,\mu$m) was $v_P = 65$ m/s only. It was also shown that the standard deviation for the particle exit velocity increased with an increase in wall roughness. These results were attributed to rebound effects. As the wall roughness increases, the rebound angle tended to increase, leading to a shorter distance between successive impingement points along the nozzle. The impact of abrasive particles with the nozzle wall can be assumed to be a stochastic event, with some particles impacting many times, and others rarely. There will thus be a spread of particle exit velocities, which will tend to increase with wall roughness.

3.6.10 Scaling Laws for Abrasive Particle Velocity

Shipway and Hutchings (1995) performed an extensive experimental study in order to investigate the effect of process parameters on the velocity of abrasive particles accelerated in a cylindrical nozzle. Some results of this study are already presented in Fig. 3.32. Abrasive materials considered in their study included silica sand ($d_P = 90$–$710\,\mu$m; $\rho_P = 2{,}650\,\text{kg/m}^3$), soda lime glass ballotini ($d_P = 125$–$150\,\mu$m;

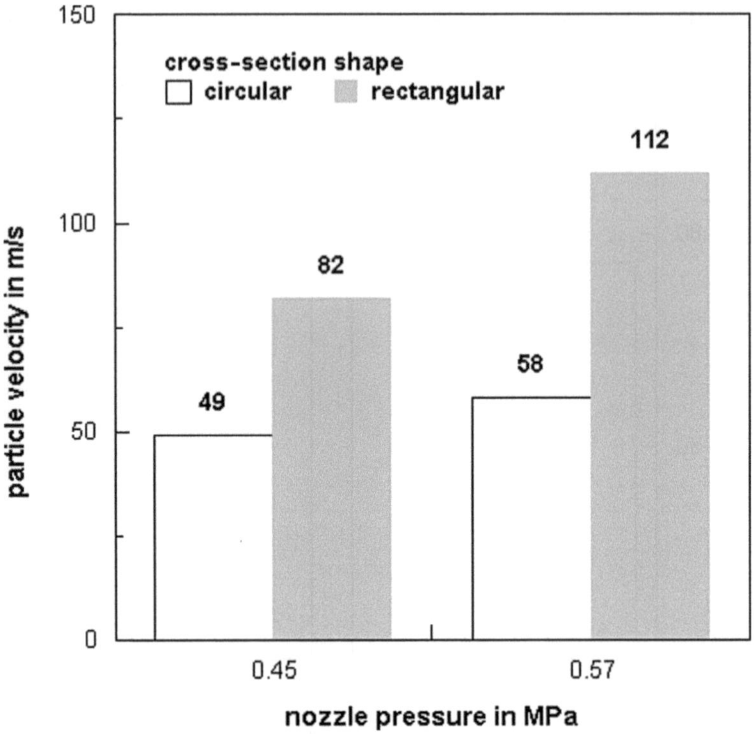

Fig. 3.50 Effects of pressure and nozzle cross-section shape on the velocity of abrasive particles (McPhee et al., 2000)

$\rho_P = 2{,}500\,\text{kg/m}^3$), aluminium oxide ($d_P = 63$–$75\,\mu\text{m}$; $\rho_P = 3{,}950\,\text{kg/m}^3$), silicon carbide ($d_P = 125$–$150\,\mu\text{m}$; $\rho_P = 3{,}160\,\text{kg/m}^3$), steel shot ($d_P = 212$–$300\,\mu\text{m}$; $\rho_P = 7{,}980\,\text{kg/m}^3$) and zirconia sand ($d_P = 125$–$500\,\mu\text{m}$; $\rho_P = 5{,}600\,\text{kg/m}^3$). The authors summarised their results with the following regression equation:

$$v_P \propto \left(\frac{p}{d_P^{0.57} \cdot \rho_P^{1.08}}\right)^{0.5} \tag{3.52}$$

The scaling law for the estimation of the ratio between air velocity and abrasive particle velocity had the following form:

$$\frac{v_P}{v_A} \propto d_P^{-0.285} \cdot \rho_P^{-0.54} \tag{3.53}$$

Both scaling laws are valid for parallel-sided cylindrical nozzles with a nozzle diameter of about $d_N = 5$ mm and for rather low nozzle pressures between $p = 0.005$ and 0.035 MPa.

3.7 Abrasive Stream Energy Flow and Nozzle Efficiency

The energy flow of an abrasive stream exiting a blast cleaning nozzle is given through the following relationship:

$$\dot{E}_P = \frac{1}{2} \cdot \dot{m}_P \cdot v_P^2 \tag{3.54}$$

This relationship is equal to (2.15). The energy flow can be estimated if abrasive particle velocity and abrasive mass flow rate can be measured. Results plotted in Fig. 3.51 illustrate that the abrasive stream energy flow (exit stream power) depended on nozzle design. A convergent–divergent nozzle with a specially designed entry flow section delivered a value of about $\dot{E}_P = 500\,\text{Nm/s}$, whereas a cylindrical nozzle with a bell-mouthed inlet section delivered a value of $\dot{E}_P = 209\,\text{Nm/s}$ only. This is a difference of about 240%. If the abrasive stream energy flow is related to the power of the compressor consumed for the compression of the air (see Sect. 4.2.2), an efficiency parameter can be derived as follows:

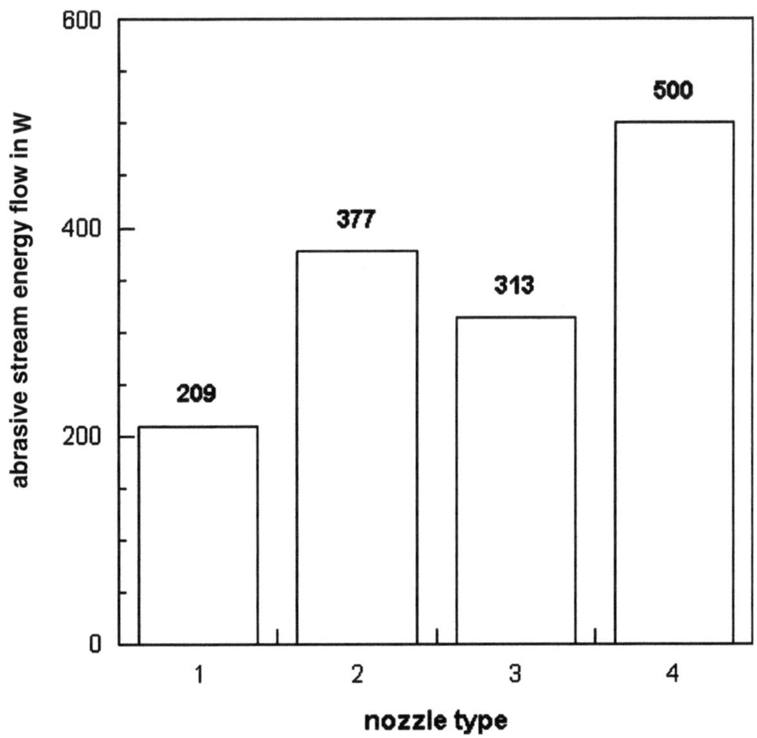

Fig. 3.51 Effects of nozzle type on abrasive stream energy flow (Hamann, 1987). Nozzle type: "1" – bell-mouthed + cylinder; "2" – bell-mouthed + convergent; "3" – standard convergent–divergent; "4" – convergent–divergent with specially designed entry section

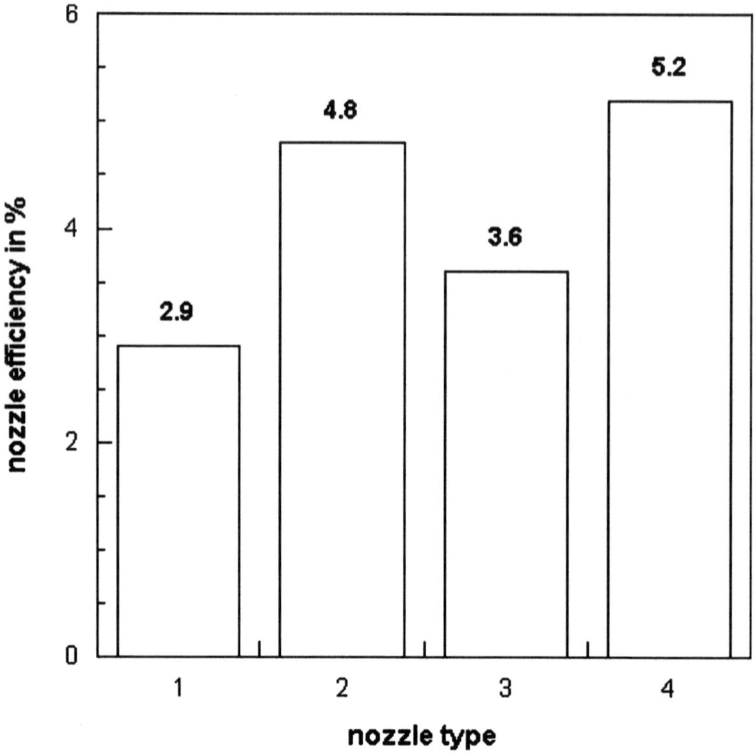

Fig. 3.52 Effects of nozzle type on efficiency (Hamann, 1987). Nozzle type: "1" – bell-mouthed + cylinder; "2" – bell-mouthed + convergent; "3" – standard convergent–divergent; "4" – convergent–divergent with specially designed entry section

$$\eta_N = \frac{\dot{m}_P \cdot v_P^2}{2 \cdot P_H} \tag{3.55}$$

This parameter describes the power transfer between compressed air and abrasive particles. The higher this efficiency parameter, the better is the power transfer. Results of measurements on the effects of varying nozzle types are displayed in Fig. 3.52. The trend is equal to that shown in Fig. 3.51. The certain values are between $\eta_N = 3$ and 5%. Similar results were reported by Uferer (1992). If the compressor power (P_H) in (3.49) is replaced by the power available at the nozzle inlet, (3.55) can characterise the quality of blast cleaning nozzles. According to this criterion, the nozzle with the best quality would be nozzle "4" in Fig. 3.52.

Chapter 4
Blast Cleaning Equipment

4.1 General Structure of Blast Cleaning Systems

The general structure of a pressure blast cleaning system is illustrated in Fig. 4.1. It basically consists of two types of equipment: air suppliers and air consumers. The prime *air supplier* is the compressor. At larger sites, storage pressure vessels accompany a compressor. These vessels serve to store a certain amount of pressurised air, and to allow an unrestricted delivery of a demanded amount of compressed air to the consumers. The prime *air consumer* is the blast cleaning nozzle. However, hoses, whether air hoses or abrasive hoses, are air consumers as well – a fact which is often not considered. Another consumer is the breathing air system. However, it is not uncommon to run separate small compressors for breathing air supply; an example is shown in Fig. 4.1. Further parts of a blast cleaning configuration are control devices, valve arrangements and safety equipment.

4.2 Air Compressors

4.2.1 General Aspects

Compressed air can be generated by several methods as illustrated in Fig. 4.2. For industrial applications, the most frequently type used is the screw compressor. Screw compressors are available in two variants: oil-lubricated and oil-free. Table 4.1 lists technical data of screw compressors routinely used for on-site blast cleaning operations. Screw compressors feature the following advantages:

- no wear because of the frictionless movements of male and female rotors;
- adjustable internal compression;
- high rotational speeds (up to 15,000/min);
- small dimensions.

The fundamental principle for screw compaction was already invented and patented in 1878. It is based on the opposite rotation of two helical rotors with aligned profiles. The two rotors are named as male and female rotors, respectively.

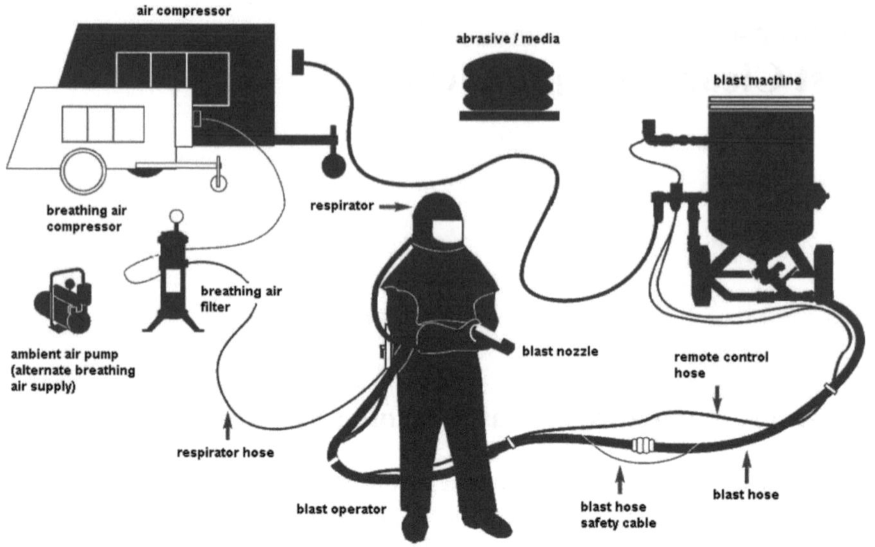

Fig. 4.1 Basic parts of a compressed air system for blast cleaning operations (Clemco Inc., Washington)

The air to be compacted will be sucked into the compressor via an air filter. The air will be compacted in the closed room generated between cylinder wall and the teeth of the two rotors. The sealing between screws and body is due to oil injection. This oil, that also lubricates the bearings and absorbs part of the process heat, will later be removed with the aid of an oil separator. Therefore, oiled screw compressors cause rather low maintenance costs.

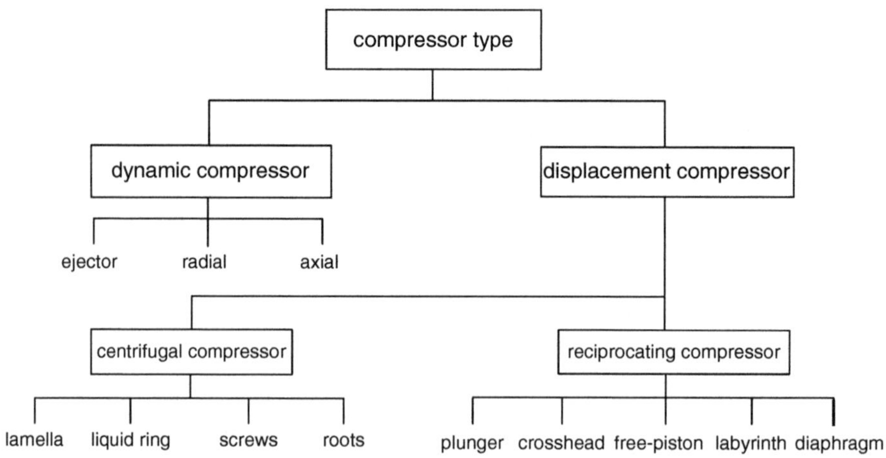

Fig. 4.2 Compressor types for air compression (Ruppelt, 2003)

Table 4.1 Technical data of mobile screw compressors (Atlas Copco GmbH, Essen)

Type	Unit	XAHS 365	XAHS 350	XAS 125
Nominal pressure	MPa	1.2	1.2	0.7
Nominal volumetric flow rate	m^3/min	21.5	20.4	7.5
Power rating in kW	kW	206		
Length total	mm	4,210	4,650	4,177
Width total	mm	1,810	1,840	1,660
Height total	mm	2,369	2,250	1,527
Weight (empty)	kg	3,800		
Weight (ready for operation)	kg	4,300	4,500	1,430
Air exit valves	–	$1 \times 2'' + 1 \times 1''$	$1 \times 1/4'' + 1 \times 3/4''$	$1/4'' + 3 \times 3/4''$
Noise level	dB (A)	74	75	71

The displaced volume per revolution of the male rotor not only depends on diameter and length of the rotor but also on its profile. One revolution of the main helical rotor conveys a unit volume q_0, and the theoretical flow rate for the compressor reads as follows:

$$\dot{Q}_0 = n_C \cdot q_0 \tag{4.1}$$

The actual flow rate, however, is lowered by lost volume; the amount of which depends on the total cross-section of clearances, air density, compression ratio, peripheral speed of rotor and built-in volume ratio. More information is available in standard textbooks (Bendler, 1983; Bloch, 1995; Groth, 1995).

4.2.2 Working Lines

A working line of a compressor is defined as follows:

$$p = f(\dot{Q}_A) \tag{4.2}$$

where p is the pressure delivered by the compressor and $\dot{Q}_A$ is the volumetric air flow rate. The precise shape of (4.2) depends on the compressor type. A working line of a screw compressor is shown in Fig. 4.3 together with the working lines for three nozzles with different nozzle diameters. The working lines for nozzles can be established according to the procedure outlined in Sect. 3.2.1.

It can be seen in Fig. 4.3 that the working line of the compressors and the working lines of two nozzles intersect. The intersection points are called *working points* of the system. This point characterises the parameter combination for the most effective performance of the system. If a compressor type is given, the positions of the individual working points depend on the nozzle to be used. These points are designated "II" for the nozzle "2" with $d_N = 10$ mm and "III" for the nozzle "3" with $d_N = 12$ mm. The horizontal dotted line in Fig. 4.3 characterises the pressure limit for the compressor; and it is at $p = 1.3$ MPa. It can be seen that

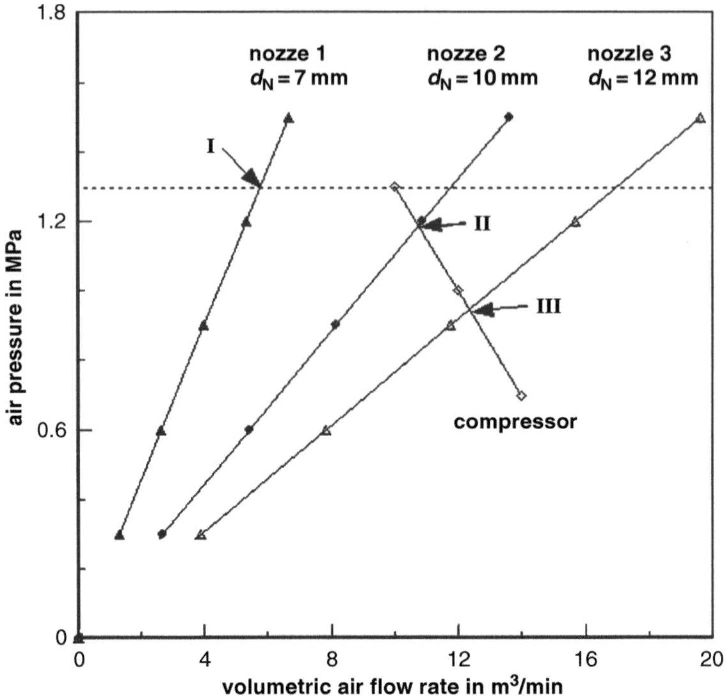

Fig. 4.3 Working lines of a screw compressor and of three blast cleaning nozzles

the working line of the nozzle "1" with $d_N = 7$ mm does not cross the working line of the compressor, but it intersects with the dotted line (point "I"). Because the cross-section of this nozzle is rather small, it requires a high pressure for the transport of a given air volumetric flow rate through the cross-section. This high pressure cannot be provided by the compressor. The dotted line also expresses the volumetric air flow rate capabilities for the other two nozzles. These values can be estimated from the points where working line and dotted line intersect. The critical volumetric flow rate is $\dot{Q}_A = 12\,m^3/min$ for nozzle "2", and it is $\dot{Q}_A = 17\,m^3/min$ for nozzle "3". The compressor cannot deliver these high values; its capacity is limited to $\dot{Q}_A = 10\,m^3/min$ for $p = 1.3$ MPa, which can be read from the working line of the compressor. However, the calculations help to design a buffer vessel, which can deliver the required volumetric air flow rates.

4.2.3 Power Rating

If isentropic compression is assumed (entropy remains constant during the compression), the theoretical power required to lift a given air volume flow rate from a pressure level p_1 up to a pressure level p_2 can be derived from the work done on isentropic compression. This power can be calculated as follows (Bendler, 1983):

$$P_H = \frac{\kappa}{\kappa - 1} \cdot \dot{Q}_A \cdot p_1 \cdot \left[\left(\frac{p_2}{p_1} \right)^{\frac{\kappa-1}{\kappa}} - 1 \right] \tag{4.3}$$

The ratio p_2/p_1 is the ratio between exit pressure (p_2) and inlet pressure (p_1). These pressures are absolute pressures. Results of calculations for a typical site screw compressor are displayed in Fig. 4.4. It can be seen from the plotted lines that the relationship between pressure ratio and power rating has a degressive trend. The relative power consumption is lower at the higher pressure ratios.

The theoretical power of the compressor type XAHS 365 in Table 4.1, estimated with (4.3), has a value of $P_H = 130\,\mathrm{kW}$. In practice, the theoretical power input is just a part of the actual power, transmitted through the compressor coupling. The actual power should include dynamic flow losses and mechanical losses. Therefore, the actual power of a compressor reads as follows:

$$P_K = \eta_{Km} \cdot \eta_{Kd} \cdot P_H \tag{4.4}$$

The mechanical losses, typically amounting to 8–12% ($\eta_{Km} = 0.08$–0.12) of the actual power, refer to viscous or frictional losses due to the bearings, the timing and step-up gears. The dynamic losses typically amount to 10–15% ($\eta_{Kd} = 0.1 - 0.15$)

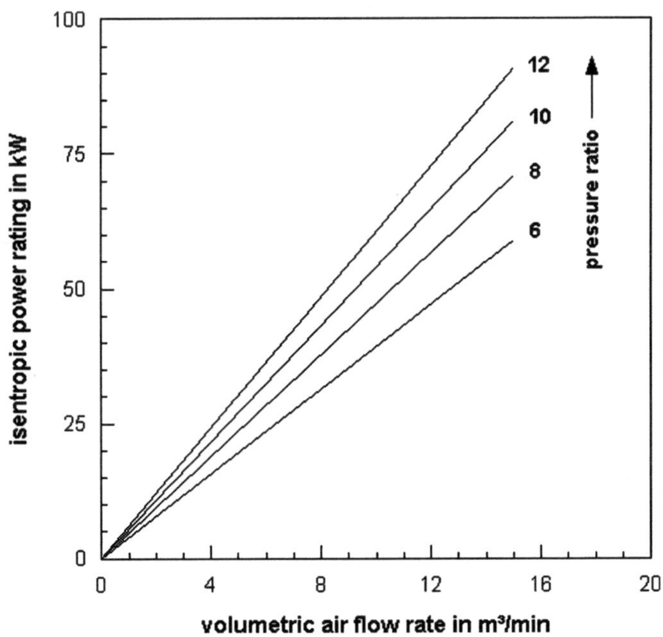

Fig. 4.4 Calculated compression power values, based on (4.3)

of the actual power. More information on these issues can be found in Bloch (1995) and Grabow (2002). The actual power rating of the compressor type XAHS 365 in Table 4.1 is $P_K = 206\,\text{kW}$. If the theoretical power of $P_H = 130\,\text{kW}$, estimated with (4.3), is related to this value, the losses cover about 36%.

Air compressors can be evaluated based on their specific power consumption, which is defined as the ratio between actual power rating and volumetric air flow rate:

$$P_S = \frac{P_K}{\dot{Q}_A} \quad (4.5)$$

For the compressor type XAHS 365 in Table 4.1, the specific power consumption is, for example, $P_S = 9.6\,\text{kW/(m}^3\text{/min)}$. Different types of compressors have different specific power consumptions even if they deliver equal pressure and volumetric air flow rate values. Larger compressors have lower specific power consumption; thus, they perform more efficient. The physical unit of the specific power consumption is that of a specific volumetric energy (kWh/m^3), and it can, therefore, also characterise the energy required for the compression of a given air volume.

Part of the compression energy is consumed by the heating of the gas. Gas temperature increases during the compression process. For an adiabatic compression process, the final gas temperature can be calculated with the following equation (Bendler, 1983):

$$T_K = T_1 \cdot \left(\frac{p_2}{p_1}\right)^{\frac{\kappa-1}{\kappa}} \quad (4.6)$$

Results of calculations are displayed in Fig. 4.5. It can be seen that air temperatures as high as $\vartheta = 300°\text{C}$ can be achieved. Because hot air can carry much more moisture than cold air, there is a high risk of condensation in the blast cleaning system. More detailed information on this issue is presented, among others, by Siegel (1991). This author provides a nomogram where the amount of condensation water can be read for different pressure ratios. A typical calculation example ($p_2 = 0.6\,\text{MPa}$, $\vartheta_1 = 20°\text{C}$, 60% relative humidity) delivers a condensation water rate of 8 g per cubic metre of air. For a volumetric air flow rate of $\dot{Q}_A = 10\,\text{m}^3\text{/h}$, the total amount of condensation water would be about 5 l/h. Therefore, an after cooling process is recommended after the compression process.

4.2.4 Economic Aspects

The technical and economical evaluation of compressors is a complex issue. However, the key performance parameters, pressure (p) and volumetric air flow rate ($\dot{Q}_A$), usually allow a selection of appropriate consumers (e.g. grinders and blast cleaning nozzles). Key roles in the interaction between compressor and air consumers not only play dimension and condition of the consumers, in particular blast cleaning nozzles (see Fig. 4.3); but also the dimensions of connecting devices,

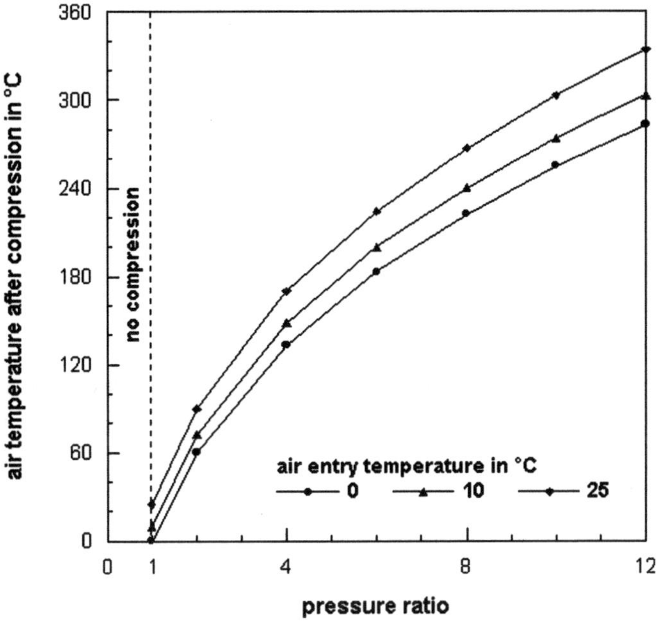

Fig. 4.5 Calculated air exit temperature after adiabatic compression; based on (4.6)

in particular hose lines, valves and fittings. If these parts are insufficiently tuned, efficiency drops and costs increase. These aspects are discussed in the following sections.

Pressure losses in hoses, fittings and armatures as well as leakages must also be taken into account if the size of a compressor needs to be estimated. This aspect is discussed in Sects. 4.4 and 4.5.

Another problem is pressure fluctuation, which affects the volumetric air flow rate. A rule says that even good maintained compressors require a correction factor of 1.05. This means a plus of +5% to the nominal volumetric flow rate requested by the consumer.

The pressure valve located at the outlet of the compressors should be adjusted to the nozzle diameter of the blast cleaning system. Some relationships are listed in Table 4.2. A general recommendation is as follows: $d_{\mathrm{VK}} \geq 4 \cdot d_{\mathrm{N}}$. For a nozzle with a diameter of $d_{\mathrm{N}} = 10\,\mathrm{mm}$, the minimal internal diameter of the compressor outlet valve should be $d_{\mathrm{VK}} = 40\,\mathrm{mm}$. Values for the sizes of air exit valves of three compressors are listed in Table 4.1.

A good maintenance programme is critical to compressor life and performance. A good maintenance programme is one that identifies the need for service based on time intervals and equipment hours. Additional items that also need to be considered when developing a programme are environmental conditions such as dust, ambient temperature and humidity, where filter changes may be required before the recommended intervals. Most equipment manufacturers have developed a preventive

Table 4.2 Adjustment between nozzle diameter and compressor outlet valve diameter (Clemco Inc., Washington)

Nozzle diameter in mm	Valve diameter in mm
5.0	19
6.5	25
8.0	32
9.5	38
11.0	50
12.5	50
16.0	64
19.0	76

maintenance schedule for their equipment, and it must be followed as a minimum. However, manufacturers cannot account for all operational conditions, and a maintenance plan may be developed by the operator of the equipment. Table 4.3 lists some recommendations.

4.2.5 Aspects of Air Quality

Basically, compressed air can be subdivided into the following four groups:

- oil-free air;
- moisture-free air;
- oil-lubricated air;
- breathing air.

Regulatory demands on the quality of pressurised air are prescribed in ISO 8573-1 (2001). The most important criteria are listed in Table 4.4. It can be seen that the standard distinguished between 10 quality classes for compressed air. Major assessment parameters include solid content (respectively dust), moisture content and oil content.

The requirement for oil-free air comes from surface quality arguments. The occupancy of blast cleaned steel surfaces by oil will reduce the adhesion of the coating systems to the substrate, and it will deteriorate the protective performance. These aspects are discussed in Sect. 8.4. In oil-injected compressors, the air usually picks up a certain amount of oil due to its way through the compaction room. This oil can appear as liquid, aerosol, or even as vapour. Even professionally maintained screw compressors ran without oil separators generate rest oil contents as high as 5 ppm (milligram of oil per cubic metre of air). Part of this oil will be intercepted together with condensation water in appropriate cooling devices. However, in order to also separate oil vapour reliably, multiple-step cleaning systems are required. A typical system consists of the following components:

- an after-cooler to cool down the compressed air;
- a high-performance fine filter to intercept aerosols;
- an activated carbon filter to absorb oil vapours.

Table 4.3 Example of a preventive air compressor maintenance programme (Placke, 2005)

	Daily	Weekly	Monthly	Quarterly	Bi-yearly	Yearly
Small size unit				250 h	500 h	1,000 h
Large size unit				500 h	1,000 h	2,000 h
Compressor oil level	C					
Engine oil level	C					
Radiator cooling level	C					
Meters/lamps	C					
Air filter service gauge	C					
Fuel tank (fill at shift end)	C				Empty	
Water/fuel separator empty	C					
Discharger of pre-cleaner of air cleaner		C				
Alternator belts		C				
Battery connections/level		C				
Tire pressure/tread		C				
Wheel bolts			C			
Hoses (oil, air, intake, etc.)			C			
Automatic shutdown system test			C			
Air purificator system, visual			C			
Compressor oil radiator, external			C	Clean		
Engine oil radiator, external			C	Clean		
Clamps				C		
Air purificator elements				W		
Fuel/water separator element					R	
Compressor element				B	A	
Compressor oil					R	
Wheels (bearings, seals, etc.)					C	C
Engine cooler tests					C	R
Shutdown switch lockout test						C
Scavenging orifice and common elements						Clean
Oil separator element						R
Hook Augen bolts	Check before towing					
Lights (drive, brakes, flasher)	Check before towing					
Engine oil change, filters, etc.	Refer to the engine operators manual					

A – Change only to the small size unit; B – Change only to the large size unit; C – Check (adjust or replace as needed); R – Replace; WI – When indicated

Moisture-free compressed air is recommended for blast cleaning operations to avoid moisturisation of abrasive particles. Moist particles tend to agglutinate which could, in turn, clog pressure air lines. Many compressors are equipped with devices that remove condensation water. These devices include the following parts:

- an after-cooler;
- a condensation water precipitator;
- a filter systems to separate water vapour;
- an air heating systems.

There are also anti-icing lubrication agents available that can absorb water and reduce the hazard of ice formation.

Table 4.4 Quality classes for compressed air (ISO 8573-1)

Class	Solids/dust						Moisture Pressure dew point in °C (X_W = water in g/m³)	Total oil content in mg/m³
	Max. number per m³ of particles with given diameter				Size in µm	Content in mg/m³		
	≤ 0.1	0.1 < 0.5	0.5 < 1.0	1.0 < 5.0				
0	According to operator							
1	–	100	1	0	–	–	≤ −70	≤0.01
2	–	100,000	1,000	10	–	–	≤ −40	≤0.1
3	–	–	10,000	500	–	–	≤ −20	≤1.0
4	–	–	–	1,000	–		≤ +3	≤5.0
5	–	–	–	20,000	–	–	≤ +7	–
6	–	–	–	–	≤5	≤5	≤ +10	–
7	–	–	–	–	≤40	≤10	$X_W \leq 0.5$	–
8	–	–	–	–	–	–	$0.5 \leq X_W \leq 5.0$	–
9	–	–	–	–	–	–	$5.0 \leq X_W \leq 10.0$	–

Table 4.5 Limits for breathing air according to DIN 3188

Medium	Limit
Carbon dioxide	<800 mg/m³ air
Carbon monoxide	<30 mg/m³ air
Dust	Max. 0.01 µm
Oil vapour	0.3 mg/m³ (20°C and 0.7 MPa)

The supply of breathing air is especially important for all blast cleaning operations. Critical substances in breathing air include carbon dioxide, carbon monoxide, dust and oil vapour. Regulatory limits for breathing air are listed in Table 4.5. Compressed air without special treatment cannot meet these requirements. Therefore, compressed air needs to be treated in breathing air treatment devices. These devices usually perform in multiple steps, and they include fine filters to intercept water, oil and dust; activated carbon filters to adsorb oil vapour; and catalysts to strip carbon dioxide and carbon monoxide.

4.3 Blast Machine

4.3.1 Basic Parts

The blast machine is a key part of any dry blast cleaning configuration. The major task of the blast machine is the delivery and dosing of the abrasive particles into the air stream. The structure of a typical blast machine is shown in Fig. 4.6. It consists basically of an air inlet line, a pressure sealing system, the actual storage part and an abrasive metering system. Blast machines are available at numerous sizes.

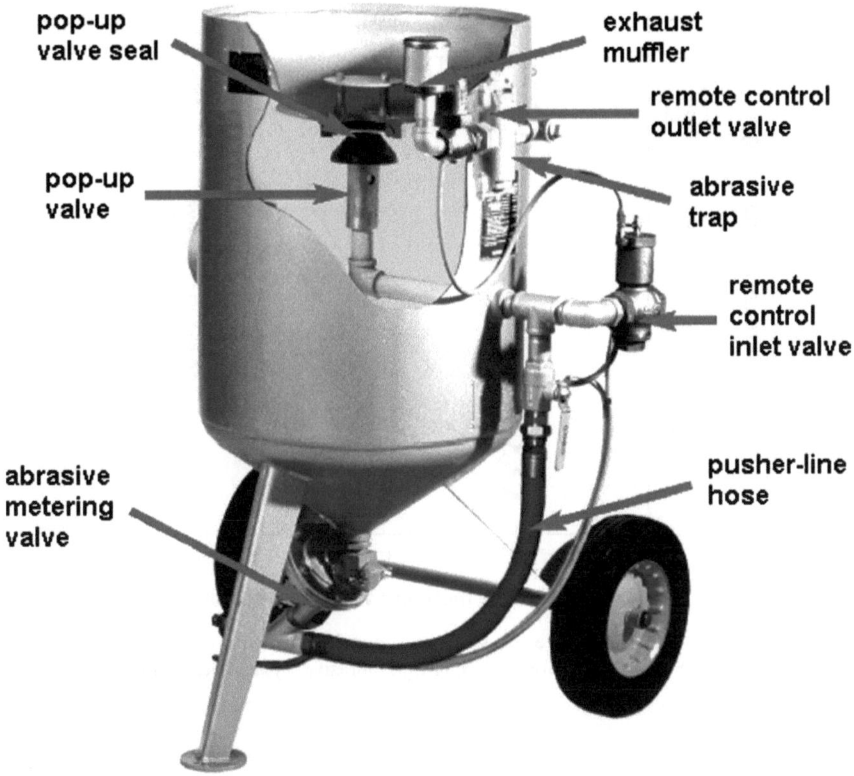

Fig. 4.6 Basic design of a blast pot (Clemco, Inc., Washington)

4.3.2 Abrasive Metering

4.3.2.1 Effects of Process Parameters

The metering of the abrasive particles is a challenging task, and the success of a blast cleaning operation depends to some amount on correct and reliable metering (see Sect. 6.4.1). The mass flow rate of abrasives is regulated simply due to changes in the size of the passage in a metering valve. Plaster's, (1972) review still gives a very good overview on typical pressure vessels and mixing valve designs. More recent information was provided by Nadkarni and Sharma (1996).

The performance of abrasive metering processes was investigated by Bae et al. (2007), Bothen (2000) and Remmelts (1968). The process of abrasive mass flow metering due to valve passage size variations is illustrated in Fig. 4.7, where the abrasive mass flow rate is plotted against the passage size for a given valve system. A power relationship with a power exponent greater unity can be noted between valve opening size and abrasive mass flow rate. The graphs also illustrate the effects of changes in nozzle diameter: the larger the nozzle, the more abrasive material was pushed through the valve passage. Changes in nozzle diameter seemed to affect the

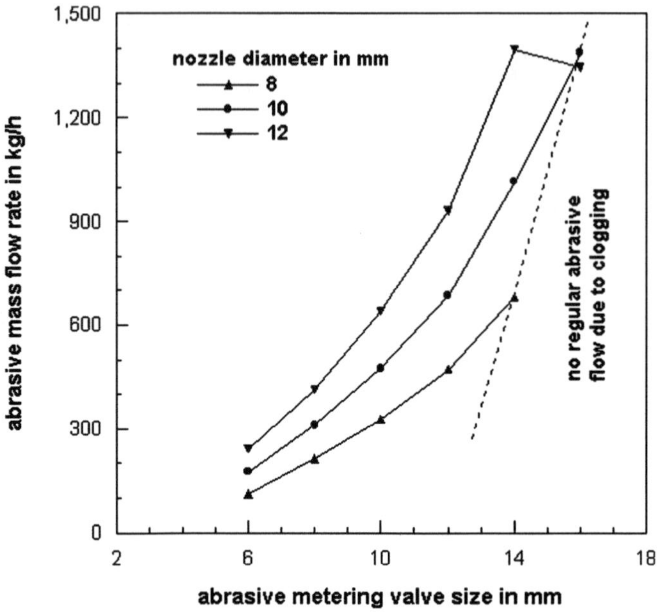

Fig. 4.7 Effects of metering valve passage and nozzle diameter on abrasive mass flow rate (Remmelts, 1968). Air pressure: $p = 0.5$ MPa; abrasive type: Zirconium; abrasive size: $d_p = 100\,\mu m$

abrasive mass flow rate, especially, at the large valve openings. The diameter of the blast cleaning nozzle seemed to influence the power exponents for the individual graphs. The larger the nozzle diameter, the higher was the value for the power exponent. A critical case is illustrated in Fig. 4.7 by the divergent process behaviour for the largest valve opening – here, a clogging of the abrasive material can be noted. The cross-section of the valve opening was too small to maintain the abrasive delivery process if the abrasive mass flow rate exceeded a value of about $\dot{m}_P = 24$ kg/min. Therefore, valve size and nozzle diameter must always be adjusted accordingly.

Effects of air volume flow rate on the abrasive metering process are shown in Figs. 4.8 and 4.9. There is a general trend that abrasive mass flow rate increased if air volume flow rate increased, but the detailed situation is very complex. In the case of the lower air pressure ($p = 0.4$ MPa) in Fig. 4.8, the metering process seemed to become very unstable at high air volume flow rates. It may be considered that the situation shown in Fig. 4.8 applies to micro-blasting processes, which involve very small abrasive particles as well as rather small dimensions for the metering device. A precise abrasive metering process could not be maintained under these special conditions.

Abrasive metering is also sensitive to changes in air pressure. The higher the pressure, the more abrasive material is pushed through the valve passage (Goldman et al., 1990; Mellali et al., 1994; Bothen, 2000; Remmelts, 1968). Examples are shown in Figs. 4.8 and 4.10. Mellali et al. (1994) performed measurements with

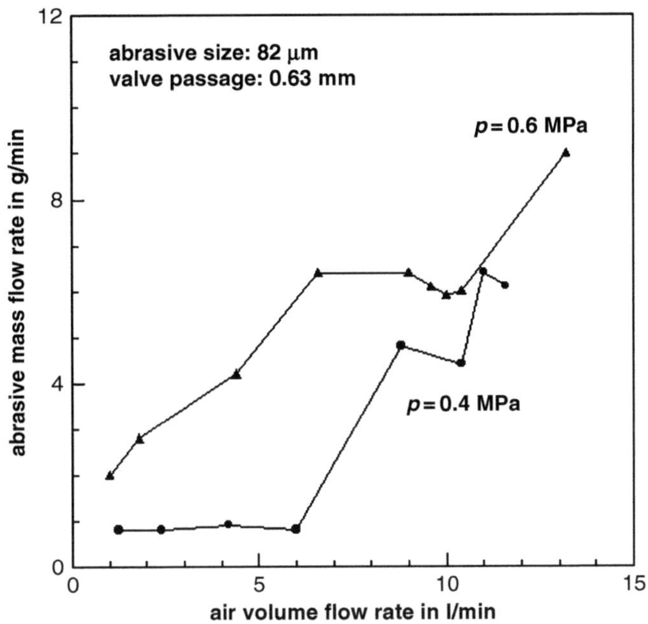

Fig. 4.8 Effects of air volumetric flow rate and pressure on abrasive mass flow rate (Bothen, 2000)

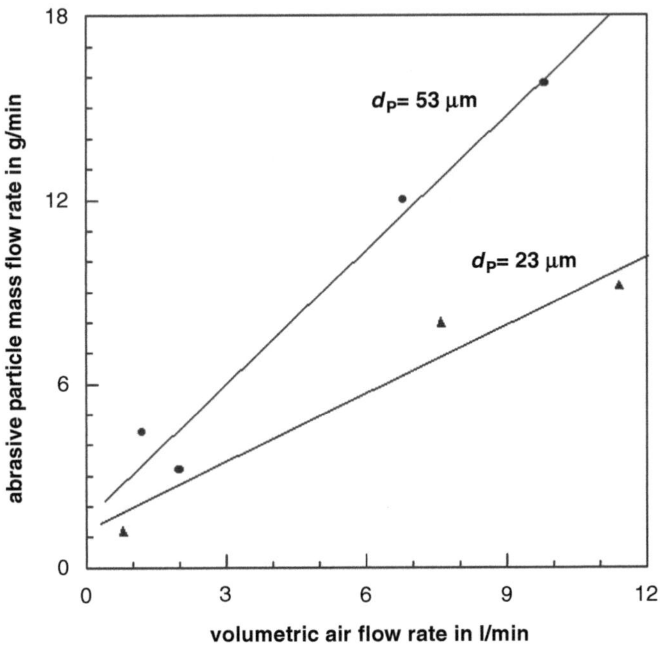

Fig. 4.9 Effects of air volumetric flow rate and abrasive particle size on abrasive mass flow rate for a micro-blasting machine (Bothen, 2000)

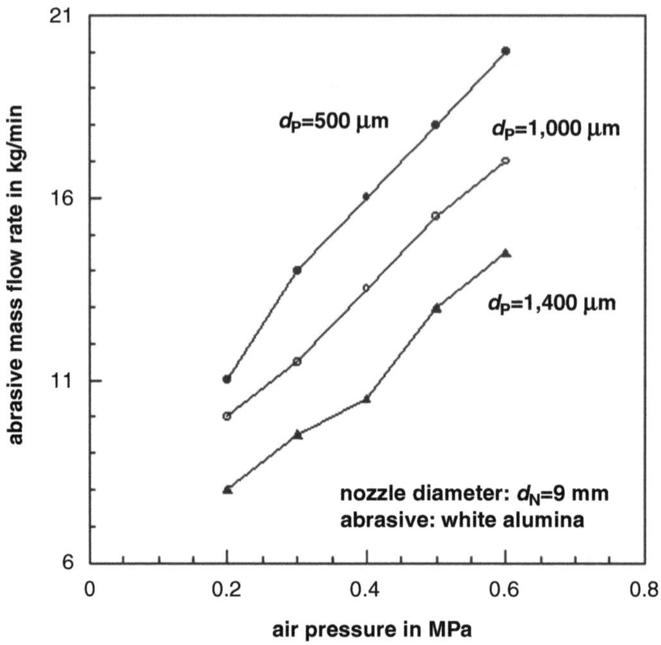

Fig. 4.10 Effects of air pressure and abrasive particle size on abrasive mass flow rate (Mellali et al., 1994)

aluminium oxide abrasives ($d_P = 500$–$1{,}400\,\mu m$), and they found an almost linear relationship between air pressure and abrasive mass flow rate delivered by a laboratory blast pot. Results of their work are provided in Fig. 4.10. It can be seen that the functional relationships between both parameters followed a linear trend and that ascents of the functions depended on the abrasive particle size. The steepest ascent was estimated for the smallest abrasive particle diameter. The difference in abrasive mass flow rate in the parameter range considered in Fig. 4.10 was as high as 300%. Stallmann et al. (1988) measured the abrasive mass flow rate for two slag materials at three different compressor pressure levels, and they noted rather complex relationships as well as abrasive type effects. Whereas abrasive mass flow rate increased with an increase in the compressor pressure for copper slag, it showed maximum values at a moderate compressor pressure for melting chamber slag.

Effects of abrasive particle size variations on the performance of abrasive metering processes were investigated by Bothen (2000), Goldman et al. (1990) and Mellali et al. (1994). It was shown by Mellali et al. (1994) that abrasive mass flow rate delivered by a metering valve arrangement was very sensitive to changes in abrasive particle size. Results are provided in Fig. 4.10. It can be seen that abrasive mass flow rate increased if smaller abrasive particles were added to the system. This trend was also found for the use of glass beads by Goldman et al. (1990), whereby the effect of abrasive size seemed, however, to become insignificant at rather low pressures ($p < 0.2\,\text{MPa}$). For the highest pressure ($p = 0.6\,\text{MPa}$) in Fig. 4.10, the difference in abrasive mass flow rate, caused by changes in the abrasive particle size, was as high as 40%. Another example for the influence of the abrasive particle size on abrasive mass flow rate is depicted in Fig. 4.9. In that particular case, the abrasive mass flow rate delivered by the metering system was larger for the larger abrasive particle diameters at a given valve passage size. This result does not agree with the results delivered by Goldman et al. (1990) and Mellali et al. (1994). A reason could be the very small dimensions for the abrasive materials ($d_{\mathrm{P}} = 23$–$53\ \mu\mathrm{m}$) and the valve ($d_{\mathrm{V}} = 670$–$1{,}000\ \mu\mathrm{m}$) used by Bothen (2000).

Adlassing and Jahn (1961) reported on measurements on the effects of abrasive material density and abrasive bulk density on the abrasive mass flow rate delivered by an abrasive metering device. These authors could prove that the abrasive mass flow rate increased almost linearly with an increase in the abrasive material density. The progress of the linear functions was independent of nozzle pressure ($p = 0.2$–$0.4\,\mathrm{MPa}$). The lowest abrasive mass flow rate was measured for quartz sand ($\rho_{\mathrm{P}} = 2{,}600\,\mathrm{kg/m^3}$; $\rho_{\mathrm{B}} = 1.48\,\mathrm{kg/l}$), and the largest abrasive mass flow rate was measured for steel cut wire ($\rho_{\mathrm{P}} = 7{,}900\,\mathrm{kg/m^3}$; $\rho_{\mathrm{B}} = 4.29\,\mathrm{kg/l}$).

Figure 4.11 illustrates the effects of nozzle layout and number of valve turns on the abrasive metering process. It can be seen that the geometry of the nozzle affected the metering process mainly in the range of high numbers of valve turns. However, the general linear trend between number of valve turns and mass ratio abrasive/air did not seem to be affected by variations in the nozzle geometry. Changes in nozzle geometry have an influence on both air mass flow rate and abrasive mass flow rate. It can be seen that the mass flow ratio abrasive/air took very high values for all numbers of valve turns; it was basically larger than a value of $\dot{m}_{\mathrm{P}}/\dot{m}_{\mathrm{A}} = 2$, which is an upper limit for an efficient blast cleaning process (see Sect. 6.4.1). The increase in the mass flow ratio abrasive/air is not only attributed to a larger amount of abrasive flowing through the larger valve opening, but is also due to a reduction in the volumetric air flow rate. This aspect is illustrated in Fig. 4.12. The higher the number of valve turns, the lower is the volumetric air flow rate measured at the nozzle. Figure 3.11 clarifies the problem from the point of view of abrasive mass flow rate. The trends are equal to those shown in Fig. 4.12. The geometry of the nozzle had a pronounced effect on the absolute values for the volumetric air flow rate, but it did not affect the general trends of the curves. If (3.11) and (3.15) are applied, the volumetric air flow rate at the nozzle can be calculated. For the conditions in Fig. 4.12 (assumed air temperature $\vartheta = 25°\mathrm{C}$), the following values were calculated: nozzle "1" ($d_{\mathrm{N}} = 11.5\,\mathrm{mm}$): $\dot{Q}_{\mathrm{A}} = 8.2\,\mathrm{m^3/min}$; nozzle "2" ($d_{\mathrm{N}} = 11\,\mathrm{mm}$): $\dot{Q}_{\mathrm{A}} = 7.4\,\mathrm{m^3/min}$ and nozzle "3" ($d_{\mathrm{N}} = 12.5\,\mathrm{mm}$): $\dot{Q}_{\mathrm{A}} = 9.6\,\mathrm{m^3/min}$. The amount of displaced air volume depended on number of valve turns, respectively on abrasive mass flow rate; but it could be as high as 50% for the conditions in Fig. 4.12 (for nine valve turns). If, however, the more typical condition of four valve turns is applied, the amount of displaced air volume is between 17% and 25%. These values approve results of measurements performed by other authors (see Sect. 3.2.1).

An increase in the number of valve turns increases the abrasive mass flow rate. An increase in mass flow rate will increase pressure drop in the grit hose, thus reducing the nozzle pressure. This effect is shown in Fig. 4.13. It can be seen that the air

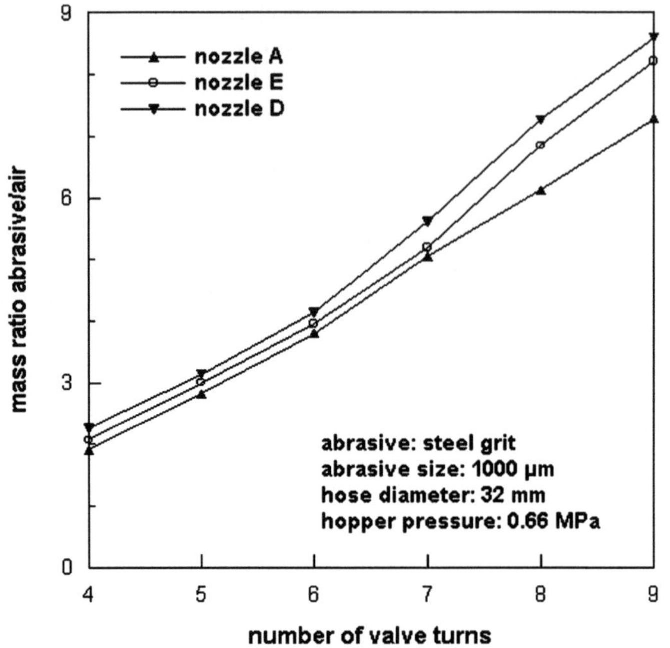

Fig. 4.11 Effects of number of valve turns and nozzle geometry on the mass flow ratio abrasive/air in convergent-divergent nozzles (Bae et al., 2007). Nozzle "A" – nozzle length: 125 mm, throat (nozzle) diameter: 12.5 mm, divergent angle: 7.6°, convergent angle: 3.9°; Nozzle "D" – nozzle length: 185.7 mm, throat (nozzle) diameter: 9.5 mm, divergent angle: 1.2°, convergent angle: 8.5°; Nozzle "E" – nozzle length: 215 mm, throat (nozzle) diameter: 11 mm, divergent angle: 1.3°, convergent angle: 7.9°

pressure at the nozzle dropped if abrasive mass flow rate increased. The pressure drop again depended on the geometry of the nozzle. It was most pronounced for the nozzle "A". For a typical value of $\dot{m}_P = 15$ kg/min, the air pressure dropped from $p = 0.66$ MPa (at the hopper) down to $p = 0.53$ MPa at the nozzle if a grit hose with a diameter of $d_H = 32$ mm was used (hose length was not given). This particular problem will be discussed in more detail in Sect. 4.5.3.

The graphs in Fig. 4.11 illustrate another permanent problem in abrasive metering. The values for the mass ratio abrasive/air were very high if the number of valve turns was high. Mass ratios of $R_m = 1.0$–2.0 are most efficient for an effective blast cleaning (see Sect. 6.4.1). This optimum range was met for the arrangement in Fig. 4.11 for four valve turns only. Any additional valve turn will deteriorate the blast cleaning process although more abrasive mass is being delivered to the cleaning point.

4.3.2.2 Metering Models

The aforementioned relationships can be summarised as follows:

$$\dot{m}_P = f(d_V;\, d_N;\, p;\, d_P;\, \rho_P;\, \rho_B) \tag{4.7}$$

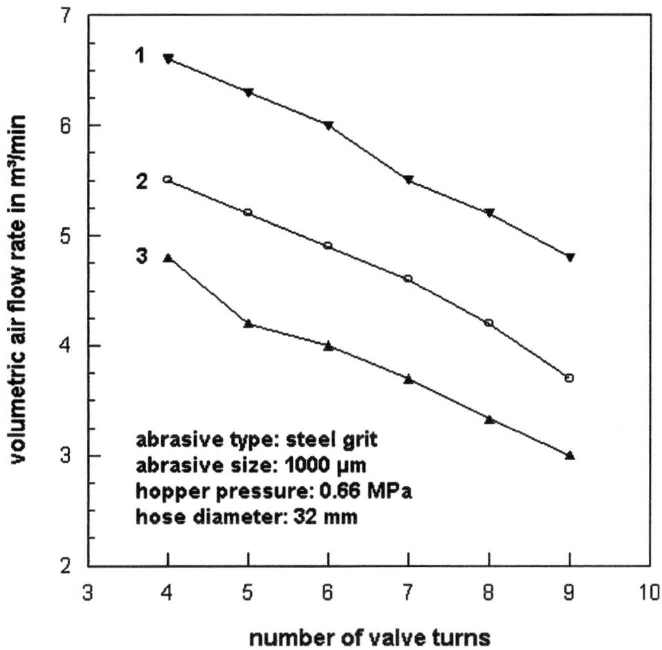

Fig. 4.12 Effects of number of valve turns and nozzle geometry on the volumetric air flow rate in convergent-divergent nozzles (Bae et al., 2007). Nozzle "1" – nozzle length: 150 mm, throat (nozzle) diameter: 9.5 mm, divergent angle: 2.1°, convergent angle: 9.3°; Nozzle "2" – nozzle length: 216 mm, throat (nozzle) diameter: 11.0 mm, divergent angle: 1.3°, convergent angle: 7.9°; Nozzle "3" – nozzle length: 125 mm, throat (nozzle) diameter: 12.5 mm, divergent angle: 7.6°, convergent angle: 3.9°

This complex relationship makes it almost impossible to reliably precalculate a certain desired abrasive mass flow rate.

Brauer (1971) reviewed the results of experimental investigations in the field of bulk material transport, and he suggested the following relationships:

$$\dot{m}_P \propto d_V^{2.5 \text{ to } 2.96} \tag{4.8a}$$

$$\dot{m}_P \propto d_P^{-0.18 \text{ to } -1.0} \tag{4.8b}$$

$$\dot{m}_P \propto \rho_P \tag{4.8c}$$

The qualitative trends between abrasive mass flow rate and valve opening size (Fig. 4.7), particle density and particle size (Fig. 4.10), which were discussed earlier, are properly reflected by these relationships.

Beverloo et al. (1961) developed a model for the approximation of the mass flow rate of particulate solids flowing through the discharge openings of hoppers. The model considers gravity-induced discharge only, and it is valid for particle sizes

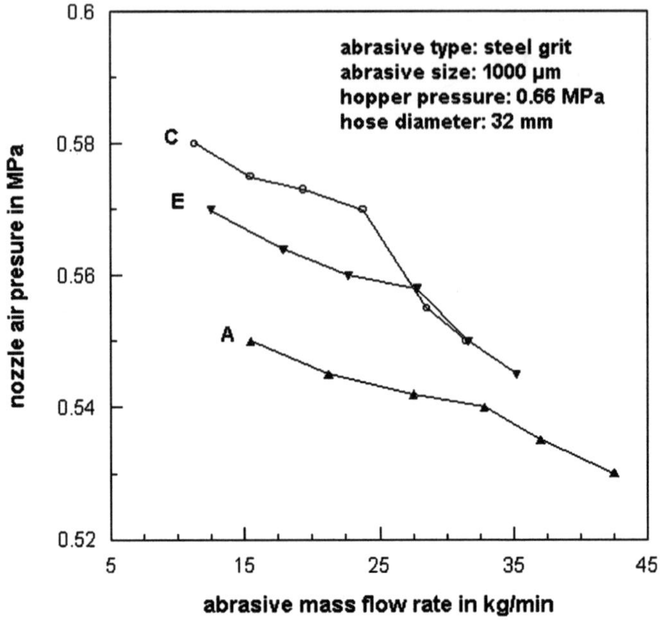

Fig. 4.13 Effects of abrasive mass flow rate and nozzle geometry on the nozzle air pressure (Bae et al., 2007). Nozzle "A" – nozzle length: 150 mm, throat (nozzle) diameter: 11.5 mm, divergent angle: 2.1°, convergent angle: 9.3°; Nozzle "C" – nozzle length: 125 mm, throat (nozzle) diameter: 12.5 mm, divergent angle: 7.6°, convergent angle: 3.9°; Nozzle "E" – nozzle length: 216 mm, throat (nozzle) diameter: 11.0 mm, divergent angle: 1.3°, convergent angle: 7.9°

larger than $d_P = 500\ \mu m$. Another restriction is $d_V/d_P > 6$. The model delivers the following relationship:

$$\dot{m}_P \propto \rho_P \cdot g^{1/2} \cdot (d_V - k_Z \cdot d_P)^{5/2} \quad (4.9)$$

The parameter k_Z characterises the limit for gravity-induced flow. If pressure gradients are involved in the discharge process, a second term must be added, which leads to the following expression (Seville et al., 1997):

$$\dot{m}_P \propto \underbrace{\rho_P \cdot g^{1/2} \cdot (d_V - k_Z \cdot d_P)^{5/2}}_{\text{gravity induced}} \cdot \underbrace{\left(1 + \frac{\Delta p}{\rho_P \cdot g}\right)}_{\text{pressure gradient induced}} \quad (4.10)$$

The power relationship between mass flow rate and valve opening is clearly expressed in this relationship (see Fig. 4.7). The general trend for the effect of variations in particle size is also recorded, at least for standard dimensions of particles and valve opening (see Fig. 4.10). The proposed linear trend between abrasive material density and abrasive mass flow rate is supported by experimental results reported by Adlassing and Jahn (1961).

In practice, however, a working characteristic, similar to the graphs shown in Figs. 4.7 and 4.11, must be installed for any particular valve type for certain air pressures, nozzle diameters and abrasive materials. Such working characteristics are not available from manufacturers, and it must be estimated experimentally.

4.3.2.3 Abrasive Mass Flow Adjustment

In current industry practice, it is often the potman, who does this adjustment manually. How sensitive the entire blast cleaning procedure reacts on such a manual adjustment is illustrated in Fig. 6.20 and Table 4.6. Figure 6.20 shows that the cleaning rate was very sensitive to the number of turns for a metering valve. If the copper slag was being considered, a change from five turns to six turns led to an increase in cleaning rate from about 60 m^2/h to 72 m^2/h (+20%). The results listed in Table 4.6 illustrate the effects of manual fine adjustment on the blast cleaning process. If the number of turns of the metering valve was changed from 2 to 2.5 for garnet, cleaning rate almost tripled, and the specific abrasive consumption dropped up to –30%. For the steel grit, the situation was different. A change in the number of valve turns from 3 to 3.5 did not affect the cleaning rate, but increased the specific abrasive consumption by +30%. These examples highlight the economic potential of a precise abrasive metering.

Table 4.6 Metering valve adjustment test data (Hitzrot, 1997)

Abrasive material	Number of turns	Abrasive mass flow rate in kg/min	Cleaning rate in m^2/h	Specific abrasive consumption in kg/m^2
Fine coal slag	2	7.6	30.4	15.2
	3	9.5	32.4	17.7
	5	12.6	23.0	32.9
Star blast	2	5.5	24.3	13.6
	3	13.9	38.1	22.2
	5	17.5	36	29.3
Aluminium oxide	2	6.4	11.6	32.9
	3	13.0	19.4	40.0
	5	32.1	30.4	62.7
G-50 steel grit	2	5.4	11.3	28.3
	3	13.7	20.0	41.4
	3.5	17.3	19.2	54.1
	4.5	19.7	19.7	59.6
Garnet	2	2.6	6.6	23.8
	2.5	5.6	19.6	17.2
	3	10.1	20.9	28.8
	3.5	10.6	21.1	30.8
	4.5	21.3	23.7	54.1
Glass blast	2.75	7.6	19.3	23.8
	3	10.0	22.5	26.8
	3.5	11.5	29.9	22.7
	4	18.1	29.9	36.4

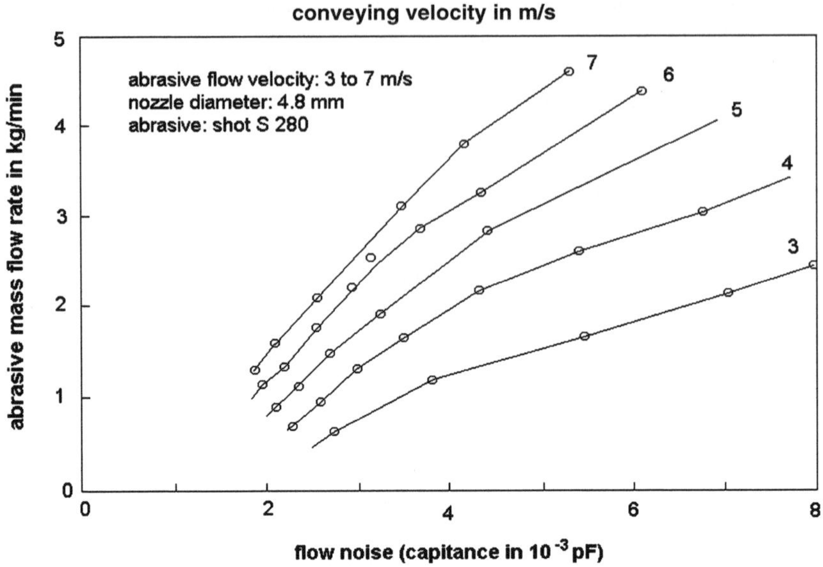

Fig. 4.14 Relationship between abrasive mass flow rate, abrasive conveying velocity in an abrasive hose, and the flow noise (Neelakantan and Green, 1982)

An experienced potman adjusts the abrasive mass flow rate according to the noise developed by the abrasive material if it flows through the hose. An optimum flow pattern causes a typical noise (see Sect. 4.5.1 for flow pattern types). Results plotted in Fig. 4.14 show that this empirical approach has a physical background. The flow noise had distinct relationships with air flow velocity in the hose and abrasive mass flow rate. These relationships offer the opportunity to control and adjust abrasive mass flow rates by acquiring and treating acoustic signals.

4.4 Pressure Air Hose Lines

4.4.1 Materials and Technical Parameters

The transport of the compressed air from the compressor to the blast machine occurs through pressure lines. For on-site applications, these are flexible hose lines. Hose lines are actually flexible hoses operationally connected by suitable hose fittings. Hose fittings are component parts or sub-assemblies of a hose line to functionally connect hoses with a line system or with each other. Pressure air hoses are flexible, tubular semi-finished product designed of one or several layers and inserts. They consist of an outer cover (polyamide, nylon), a pressure support (specially treated high-tensile steel wire) and an inner core (POM, polyamide, nylon). Technical parameters are listed in Table 4.7. It can be recognised from the listed values that the hose diameter is an important handling parameter. An increase in hose diameter is

Table 4.7 Technical parameters for blast cleaning hoses (Phoenix Fluid Handling Industry GmbH, Hamburg)

Internal diameter in mm	Wall thickness in mm	Bend radius in mm	Specific weight in kg/m
19	5.0	95	0.95
25	7.0	125	1.00
32	8.0	200	1.38
38	8.0	240	1.60
42	9.0	330	2.00

accompanied by an increase in bend radius and an increase in specific weight. Thus, larger hoses are more difficult to handle.

4.4.2 Air Hose Diameter Selection

The speed of the air flow through the hose for compressible flow can be calculated based on mass flow conservation, which delivers the following relationship:

$$v_F = \frac{4}{\pi} \cdot \frac{\dot{m}_A}{\rho_A \cdot d_H^2} \tag{4.11}$$

The air density, and therefore the flow velocity, depends on pressure and temperature [see (3.6)]. Typical hose diameters for blast cleaning operations are between $d_H = 19$ mm and 50 mm (see Table 4.7). For a volumetric flow rate of $\dot{Q}_A = 10\,\mathrm{m^3/min}$, delivered at a pressure of $p = 1.0$ MPa, the velocity of the air flow for a hose diameter of $d_H = 40$ mm is $v_F = 13$ m/s. More results of calculations are provided in Fig. 4.15.

An empirical rule for selecting the proper hose diameter is: the flow velocity in the hose should not exceed the value of $v_F = 15$ m/s (Gillessen et al., 1995). Based on (4.11), the corresponding minimum hose diameter is as follows:

$$d_H = 0.29 \cdot \left(\frac{\dot{m}_A}{\rho_A(p, T)}\right)^{1/2} \tag{4.12}$$

In that equation, the air mass flow rate is given in kg/s, and the hose diameter is given in m. If no standard diameter is available for the calculated value, the next larger diameter should be selected. As an example, for an air mass flow rate of $\dot{m}_A = 10$ kg/min, delivered at a pressure of $p = 1.0$ MPa and a temperature of $\vartheta = 20°$C, (4.12) delivers a value of $d_H = 34.5$ mm; the recommended internal hose diameter is $d_H = 38$ mm. The critical hose diameters for the situations displayed in Fig. 4.15 are: $d_H = 45$ mm for $p = 0.7$ MPa; $d_H = 40$ mm for $p = 0.9$ MPa and $d_H = 37$ mm for $p = 1.1$ MPa. The lower the pressure, the higher becomes the selected hose diameter. The reason is the increase in volumetric air flow rate if the air pressure drops [see (3.1)]. For a given air volumetric flow rate, the trend between air pressure and critical hose diameter follows

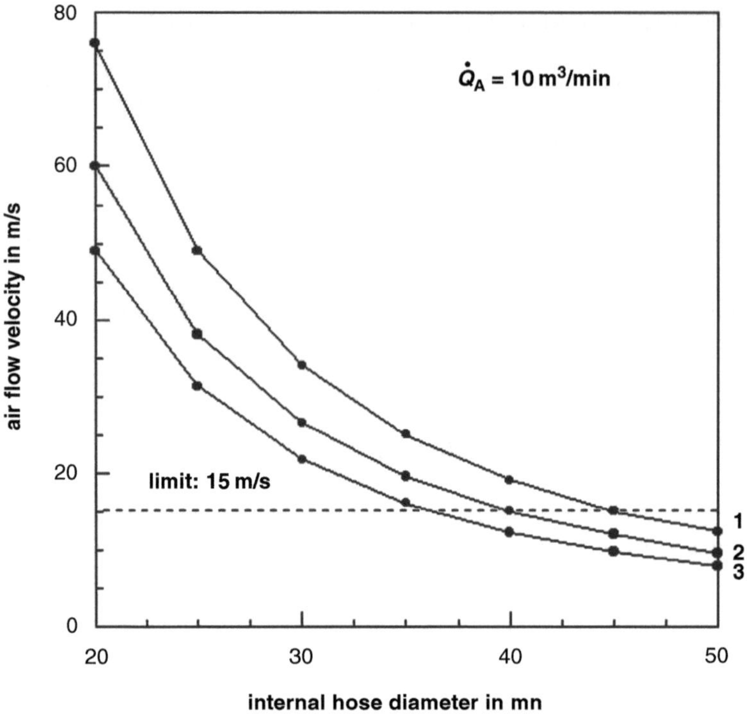

Fig. 4.15 Calculated air flow velocities in blast cleaning air hoses (air flow rate: $\dot{Q}_A = 10\,m^3/min$). Pressure levels: "1" – $p = 0.7$ MPa; "2" – $p = 0.9$ MPa; "3" – $p = 1.1$ MPa

a power relationship with a negative power exponent (for the examples in Fig. 4.15, the power exponent has a value of –0.43).

4.4.3 Pressure Drop in Air Hose Lines

4.4.3.1 General Approach

A permanent problem with air hose lines is the pressure drop in the hose lines. The situation is illustrated in Fig. 4.16. The well-known general approach for estimating the pressure drop for incompressible flow is as follows (Bohl, 1989):

$$\frac{\Delta p_A}{\rho_A} = \underbrace{\sum_i \left(\lambda_{Ai} \cdot \frac{l_H}{d_H} \cdot \frac{v_F^2}{2}\right)}_{\text{straight hose}} + \underbrace{\sum_k \left(\xi_{Ak} \cdot \frac{v_F^2}{2}\right)}_{\text{knees and aramtures}} \tag{4.13}$$

$$\Delta p_A = p_1 - p_2$$

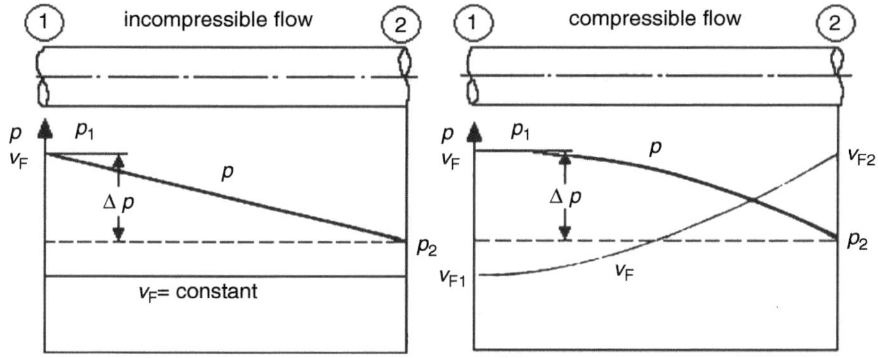

Fig. 4.16 Parameter variation along a hose line for compressible flow conditions (adapted from Wille, 2005)

where, p_1 is the static pressure at the point "1" and p_2 is the static pressure at the point "2" as shown in Fig. 4.16. The parameters λ_A and ξ_A are friction numbers, v_F is the flow velocity, l_H is the hose length, and d_H is the hose diameter.

However, for compressible flow, which should usually be considered for the air flow in blast cleaning hoses, the pressure drop is not linear, and the air flow velocity is not at a constant level over the hose length (see Fig. 4.16, right drawing). Approximations for the calculation of pressure losses for compressible flow can be found in standard monographs on technical fluid dynamics (Glück, 1988; Bohl, 1989; Sigloch, 2004). A feasible approximation is as follows (Bohl, 1989):

$$\frac{p_1^2 - p_2^2}{2 \cdot p_1} = \lambda_A \cdot \frac{l_H}{d_H} \cdot \rho_A \cdot \frac{v_F^2}{2} \cdot \frac{\bar{T}}{T_1} \tag{4.14}$$

Here, the density variation over the hose length (due to changes in pressure and temperature) must be considered. The average temperature can be assumed as follows:

$$\bar{T} \approx \frac{T_1 + T_2}{2} \tag{4.15}$$

The temperature at the end of the hose line can be approximated as follows:

$$T_2 \approx T_1 \cdot \left(\frac{p_2}{p_1}\right)^{\frac{\kappa - 1}{\kappa}} \tag{4.16}$$

If the temperature does not vary notably along the hose length (isotherm flow), the term $\bar{T}/T_1$ in (4.14) can be neglected. For an adiabatic flow, however, the temperature term must be considered.

4.4.3.2 Friction Numbers

The friction number for wall friction depends on the Reynolds number and on the ratio between hose diameter and internal wall roughness. The general relationship is as follows (Bohl, 1989):

$$\lambda_A = f\left(Re_H; \frac{k_H}{d_H}\right) \tag{4.17}$$

The Reynolds number of the air flow through a hose is given as follows:

$$Re_H = \frac{v_F \cdot d_H \cdot \rho_A}{\eta_A} \tag{4.18}$$

It can be seen that Re_H is a function of pressure and temperature, because density and dynamic viscosity of the air are involved in the calculations. In order to consider these effects, (3.6) and (3.7) must be applied. For a pressure of $p = 1.0\,\text{MPa}$, a volumetric flow rate of $\dot{Q}_A = 10\,\text{m}^3/\text{min}$, an air temperature of $\vartheta = 20°\text{C}$ and a hose diameter of $d_H = 35\,\text{mm}$, the Reynolds number is $Re_H = 4.1 \times 10^5$. More results of calculations are provided in Fig. 4.17. It can be seen that changes in temperature have only marginal effects. The Reynolds number decreases if the hose diameter increases. A combination of (4.11) and (4.18) delivers the relationship: $Re_H \propto d_H^{-1}$.

The precise solution to (4.17) is a function of the flow type in the hose and the thickness of the laminar boundary layer at the hose wall. For blast cleaning processes, a turbulent flow ($Re_H > 2{,}300$) is basically assumed. However, even if the flow is turbulent, a thin laminar boundary layer forms at the wall regions of the hoses (Bohl, 1989; Wille, 2005). This laminar layer is illustrated in Fig. 4.18. The thickness of this layer can be calculated as follows (Wille, 2005):

$$\delta_H = \frac{5}{Re_H^{1/2}} \cdot d_H \tag{4.19}$$

Results of (4.19) are displayed in Fig. 4.19. It can be seen that air temperature does not have a notable effect on the thickness of the boundary layer. But the effect of the hose diameter is very pronounced. Combining (4.11), (4.18) and (4.19) delivers the relationship: $\delta_H \propto d_H^{3/2}$.

For $\delta_H > k_H$, the hose surface is considered to be *hydraulically smooth*, and the so-called Blasius equation can be utilised to calculate the friction number for a Reynolds number range between $Re_H = 2.3 \times 10^3$ and 10^5(Bohl, 1989):

$$\lambda_A = 0.3164 \cdot Re_H^{-0.25} \tag{4.20}$$

For higher Reynolds numbers between $Re_H = 10^5$ and 10^6, the so-called Nikuradse equation for hydraulically smooth pipes can be applied (Bohl, 1989):

$$\lambda_A = 0.0032 + 0.221 \cdot Re_H^{-0.237} \tag{4.21}$$

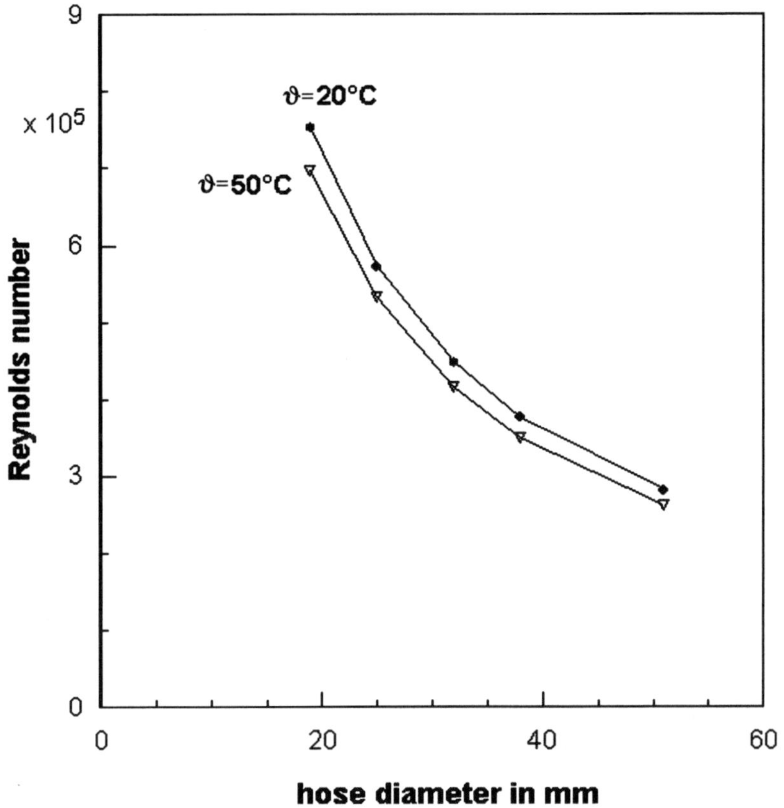

Fig. 4.17 Calculated Reynolds numbers for the flow of air in blast cleaning air hoses for two values of air temperature (air volume flow rate: $\dot{Q}_{\mathrm{A}} = 10\,\mathrm{m}^3/\mathrm{min}$, air pressure: $p = 1.0\,\mathrm{MPa}$)

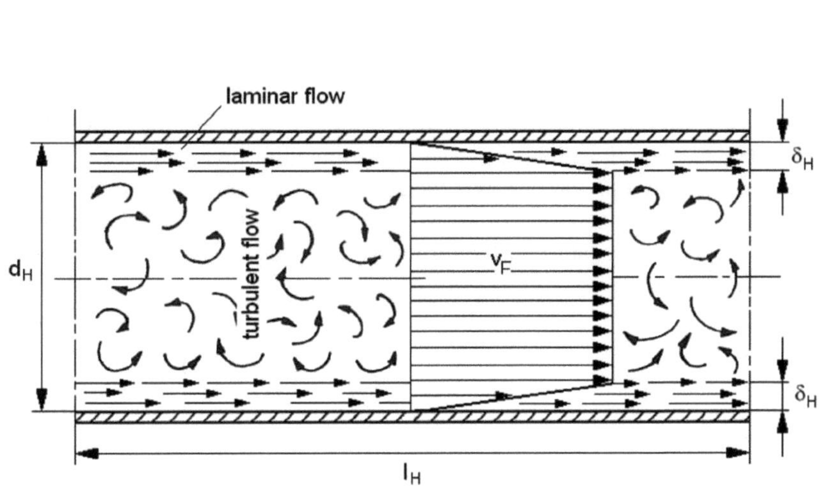

Fig. 4.18 Structure and parameters of a laminar boundary layer on a hose wall (Wagner, 1990)

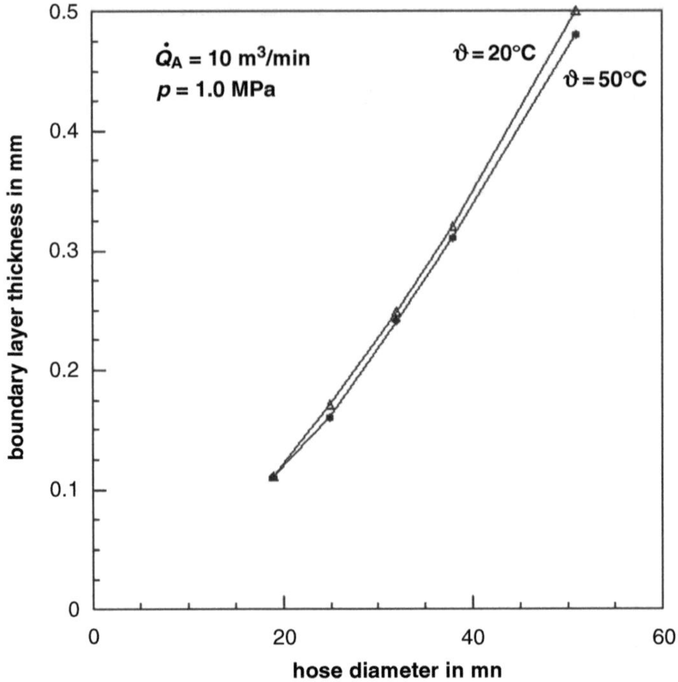

Fig. 4.19 Calculated values for the thickness of laminar boundary layers for the flow of air in blast cleaning hoses for two values of air temperature

In these cases, the friction number is independent of the wall roughness, and it is a function of the Reynolds number only. Equations (4.20) and (4.21) are graphically expressed in Figs. 4.20 and 4.21. Typical values for λ_A can be read from these two graphs.

For $\delta_H < k_H$, the hose surface is considered to be *hydraulically rough*, and the friction number can be estimated from the so-called Prandtl–Colebrook charts, which can be found in standard books on technical fluid mechanics (Oertel, 2001; Wille, 2005). A Prandtl–Colebrook chart is displayed in Fig. 4.22. If the Reynolds number and the ratio d_H/k_H are known, the corresponding value for λ_A can be read at the ordinate. The special case *hydraulically smooth* is also included in that graph. A general empirical relationship for the turbulent flow regime is the Colebrook-White equation (Wille, 2005):

$$\frac{1}{\lambda_A^{1/2}} = -2 \cdot \log \left(\frac{2.51}{\mathrm{Re}_H \cdot \lambda_A^{1/2}} + 0.27 \cdot \frac{k_H}{d_H} \right) \tag{4.22}$$

Equations 4.20–4.22 are illustrated in Figs. 4.20–4.22. For the example mentioned above, the boundary layer thickness is $\delta_H = 0.27$ mm. Rubber hoses, manufactured for blast cleaning applications, have a typical roughness value of about

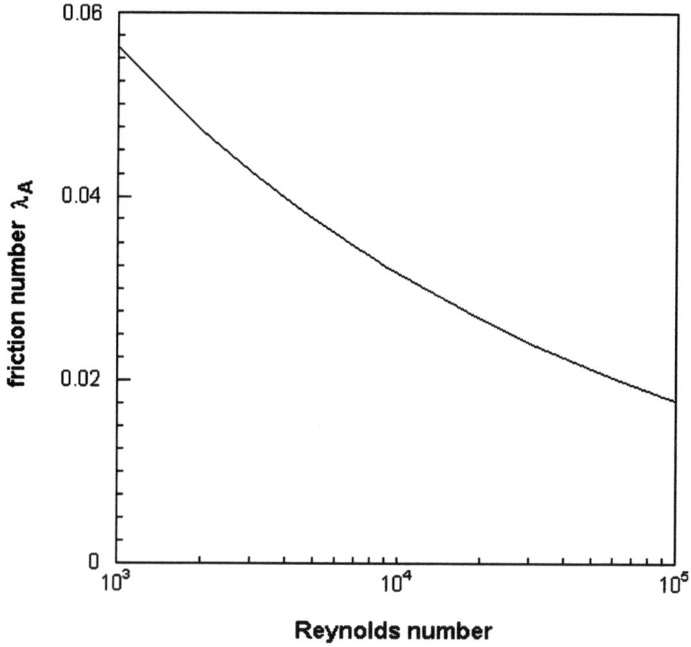

Fig. 4.20 Friction parameter for *hydraulically smooth* flow conditions at high Reynolds numbers: Blasius' solution (4.20)

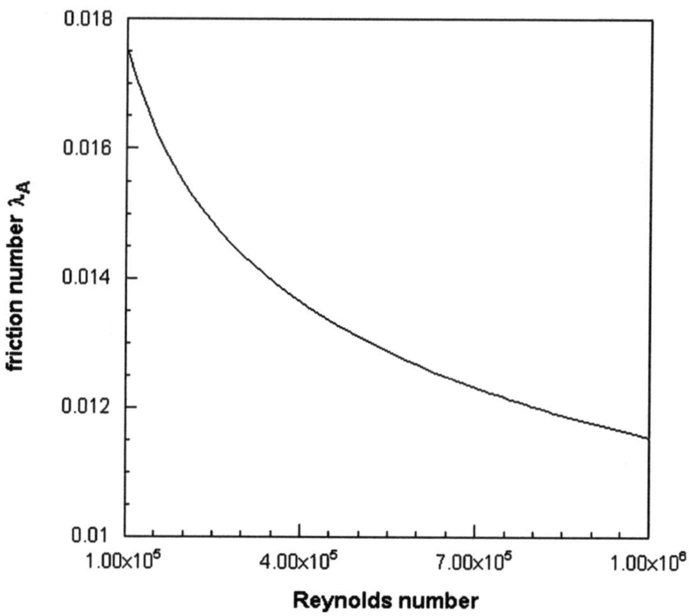

Fig. 4.21 Friction parameter for *hydraulically smooth* flow conditions at very high Reynolds numbers: Nikuradse's solution (4.21)

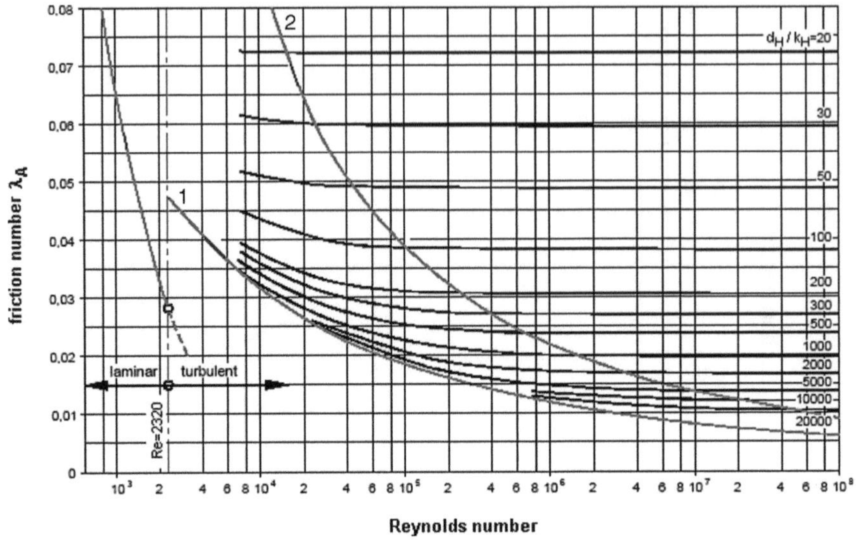

Fig. 4.22 Relationships between Reynolds number, relative roughness and friction parameter (Wille, 2005). 1-hydraulically smooth; 2-hydraulically rough (limit)

$k_H = 0.016\,\text{mm}$ (Bohl, 1989). This value is one order of magnitude lower than the typical values for the thickness of the laminar boundary layer (see Fig. 4.19). The Reynolds numbers for the flow in blast cleaning hoses usually exceed the value $Re_H = 10^5$ (see Fig. 4.17). Therefore, the rather simple (4.21) can be applied for the estimation of the friction number for most blast cleaning applications.

4.4.3.3 Hose Diameter Effects

The equations mentioned above deliver the following relationship between pressure drop and hose diameter:

$$\Delta p_A \propto d_H^{-5} \qquad (4.23)$$

This equation illuminates the overwhelming influence of the hose diameter on the pressure loss. (A precise physical deviation delivers a power exponent value somewhat smaller than 5.) This influence is graphically expressed in Fig. 4.23, which shows results of measurements of the pressure drop in hoses with different diameters. The rapid pressure drop in the hose with the small diameter of $d_H = 19\,\text{mm}$ can be recognised. These experimental results agree very well with results calculated from (4.14). More values, calculated with (4.14), are plotted in Fig. 4.24. The graphs show, among others, that pressure drop reduces at higher air pressures. This phenomenon can be explained with (3.6), which suggests that the air density increases with an increase in pressure. Higher air density means lower air volume, which in turn reduces the air flow velocity in the hose. Equation 4.14 shows that lower air flow velocity leads to less pressure drop. More relationships are displayed in Fig. 4.16. The graphs show the relationship between hose length and air flow velocity in the

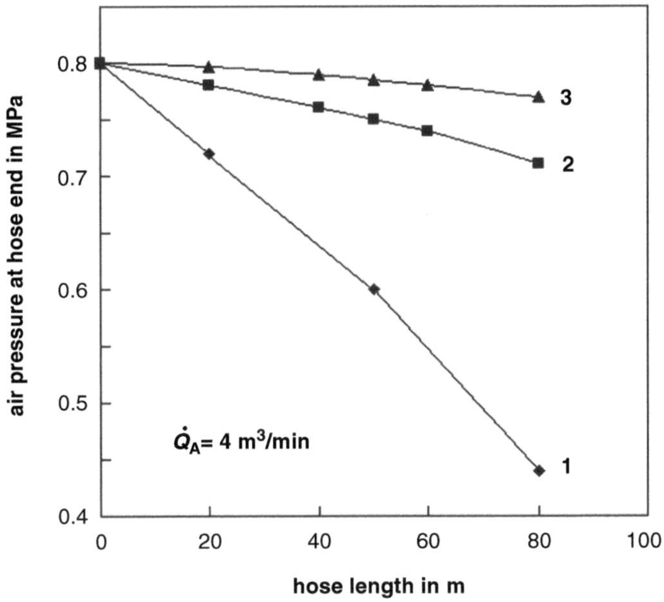

Fig. 4.23 Effect of hose diameter on experimentally estimated pressure loss in air hoses (Neumann, 1985). Air flow rate: $\dot{Q}_A = 4.0\,m^3/min$; hose diameter: "1" – $d_H = 19\,mm$; "2" – $d_H = 25\,mm$; "3" – $d_H = 32\,mm$. Pressure drop is non-linear

hose. It can be seen at the right graph in Fig. 4.16 that the air flow velocity increases with an increase in hose length. The reason is the expansion flow caused by the pressure drop in the hose line. Lower air pressure causes the air density to decrease. The reduction in air density leads to an increase in air volumetric flow rate and, thus, to an increase in flow velocity [see (4.11)]. Another important effect is that of the abrasive material. Although no abrasive material flows through the air hose, it affects the pressure drop. This effect is caused by the reduction in the air volumetric flow rate due to the addition of the abrasive particles [see (3.18) and Fig. 3.11].

4.4.3.4 Pressure Drop in Fittings and Armatures

The precise pressure drop in hose fittings and in armatures, characterised through ξ_A in (4.13), should be measured for any individual fitting. However, such values are not available for an individual accessory in most cases, but pressure loss values for certain groups and types of armatures and valves are published in the technical literature. A large collection of friction numbers for numerous armatures, valves, pipe elements, etc. can be found in Bohl's (1989) and Wagner's (1990) books. Two examples are shown in Figs. 4.25 and 4.26. For most valve constructions, the friction values are almost independent on pipe diameter. It can be seen that friction numbers for armatures are usually one order of magnitude larger than friction numbers for the flow in straight hoses. The valve constructions shown in Figs. 4.25 and 4.26, for example, can have friction numbers between $\xi_A = 1$ and 7.

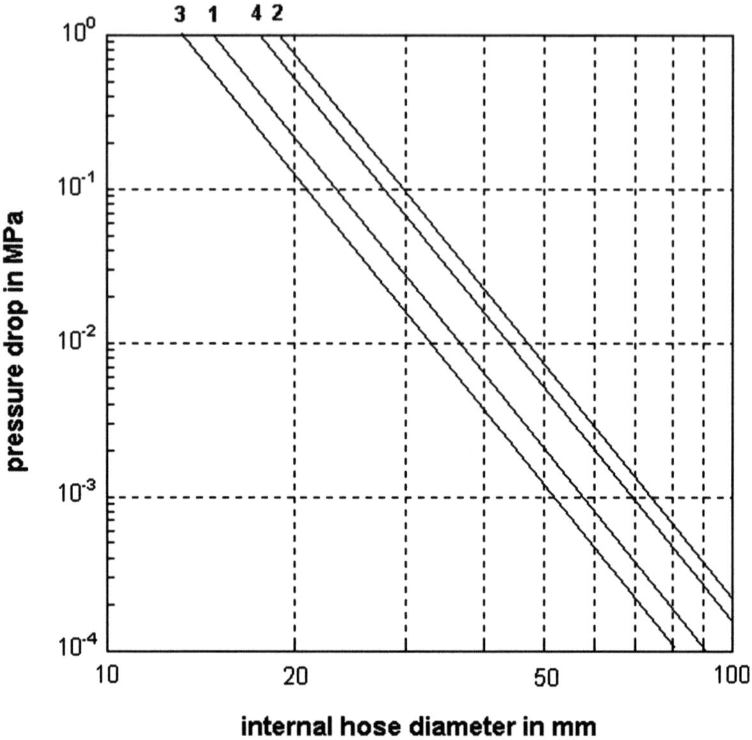

Fig. 4.24 Results of (4.14); hose length: $l_H = 40$ m. Conditions: "1" – $p = 0.7$ MPa, $\dot{Q}_A = 5.0$ m^3/min; "2" – $p = 0.7$ MPa, $\dot{Q}_A = 10$ m^3/min; "3" – $p = 1.0$ MPa, $\dot{Q}_A = 5.0$ m^3/min; "4" – $p = 1.0$ MPa, $\dot{Q}_A = 10$ m^3/min

Another principle for the assessment of pressure drops in armatures is the *equivalent length*. It is assumed that the pressure drop in a certain type of armature corresponds to the pressure drop in a pipe of a certain *equivalent length*. Examples for this procedure are provided in Table 4.8. If, for example, a seat valve with an inlet pipe diameter of 40 mm is considered, the equivalent length is 10 m. These two values must now be inserted into (4.14) in order to calculate the approximate pressure drop for this particular armature ($d_H = 40$ mm, $l_H = 10$ m). More examples can be found in Bohl (1989).

4.5 Abrasive Hose Lines

4.5.1 Conveying Modes in Abrasive Hoses

Abrasive hoses serve to convey the abrasive materials from the blast machine to the blast cleaning nozzle. This process can be considered pneumatic conveying, and

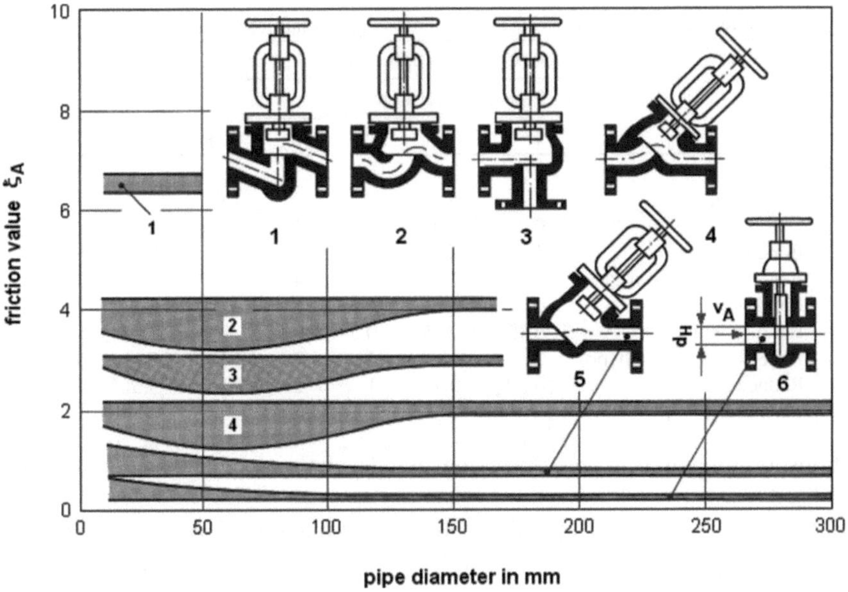

Fig. 4.25 Typical friction values for valve armatures (Wagner, 1990)

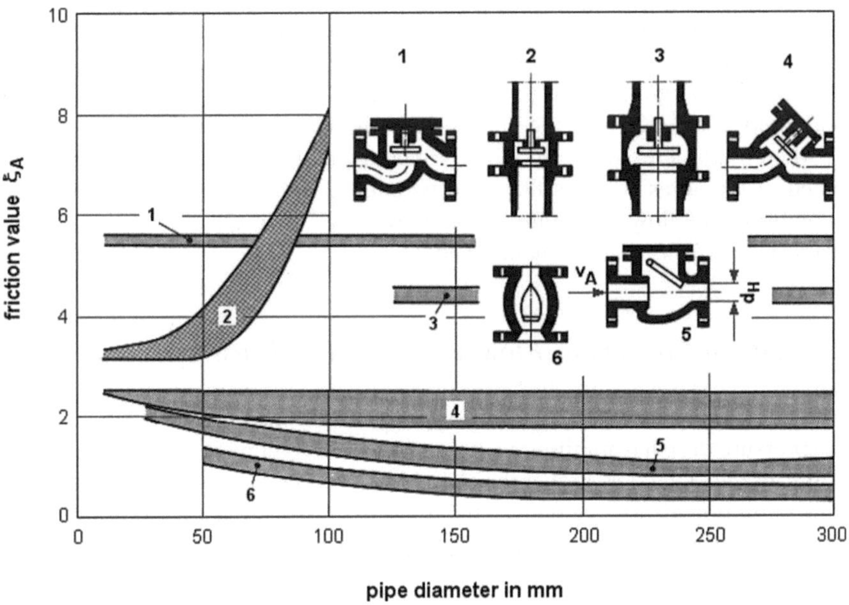

Fig. 4.26 Typical friction values for check valves (Wagner, 1990)

Table 4.8 *Equivalent lengths* for numerous air armatures (Fraenkel, 1954)

Armature	Equivalent length in m						
	Pipe diameter in mm						
	25	40	50	80	100	125	150
Seat valve	6	10	15	25	30	50	60
Streamline valve	3	5	7	10	15	20	25
Gate valve	0.3	0.5	0.7	1	1.5	2	2.5
Bend (peak corner)	1.5	2.5	3.5	5	7	10	15
Bend (smooth corner)	1	2	2.5	4	6	7.5	10
Bend ($r = D$)	0.3	0.5	0.6	1	1.5	2	2.5
Bend ($r = 2D$)	0.15	0.25	0.3	0.5	0.8	1	1.5
Hose coupling (T-shape)	2	3	4	7	10	15	20
Reducer	0.5	0.7	1	2	2.5	3.5	4

relationships known from pneumatic conveying techniques can, to a certain amount, be utilised.

Engineering treatments on pneumatic conveying processes can be found in Buhrke et al. (1989), Marcus et al. (1990), Siegel (1991) and Weber (1974). For fine particles suspended in an air stream, two basic conveying modes can occur: stable flow and unstable flow. Moreover, five different flow patterns can be observed, namely fully suspended (stable), surging (unstable), stationary bed (stable), moving bed (very unstable) and stationary bed (stable). These patterns depend on air conveying velocity and abrasive mass flow rate. Some relationships are illustrated in Figs. 4.27–4.29. Stable conveying conditions are one preposition for an efficient functioning of abrasive hose systems. The graphs plotted in Fig. 4.28 show, in particular, how changes in air flow velocity and abrasive mass flow rate affect the flow regime. An air flow velocity of $v_F = 15$ m/s and an abrasive mass flow rate of $\dot{m}_P = 4$ t/h (67 kg/min) lead to "instable region" flow. If the air flow velocity is increased up to $v_F = 20$ m/s, the process turns into a more effective "hank conveying", whereby the pressure drop slightly increases. "Hunk conveying" can also be obtained, if the abrasive mass flow rate is reduced to $\dot{m}_P = 2$ t/h (33 kg/min). For this condition, the flow turns into "hank conveying", whereby the original air flow velocity ($v_F = 15$ m/s) can be maintained.

4.5.2 Critical Conveying Flow Velocities in Abrasive Hoses

The graphs plotted in Figs. 4.27–4.29 show that a typical air flow velocity exists where pressure drop has minimum values. This flow velocity is denoted "critical air velocity" in Fig. 4.27. The higher the abrasive mass flow rate, the higher is the value for this optimum air flow velocity. This trend is illustrated in Fig. 4.29 by the line designated "optimum". For a typical blast cleaning condition (e.g. $\dot{m}_P = 16$ kg/min), the optimum air flow velocity may be in the range of $v_F = 16$ m/s. If the abrasive mass flow rate is reduced to $\dot{m}_P = 4.2$ kg/min, the optimum flow velocity is about $v_F = 12$ m/s (see Fig. 4.29).

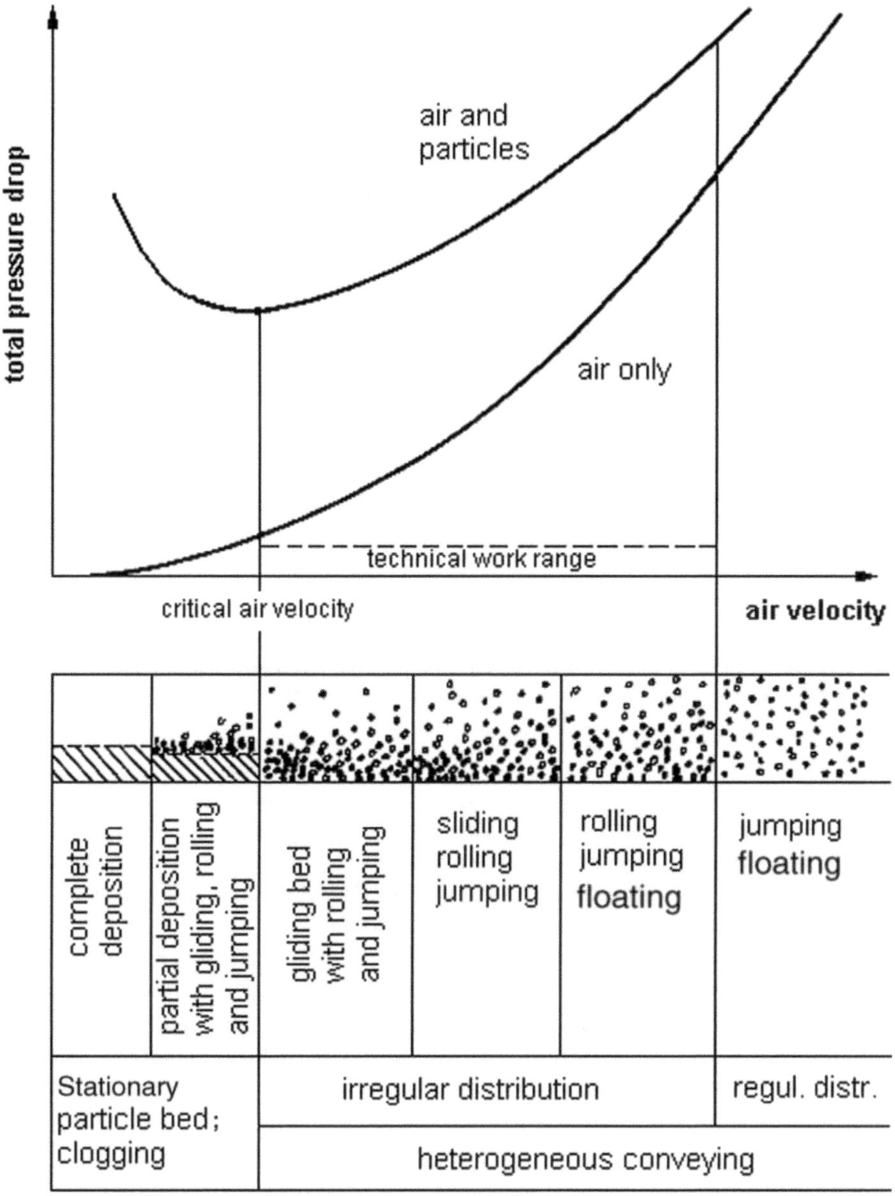

Fig. 4.27 Conveying modes in pneumatic solid particle conveying lines: general relationships (Buhrke et al., 1989)

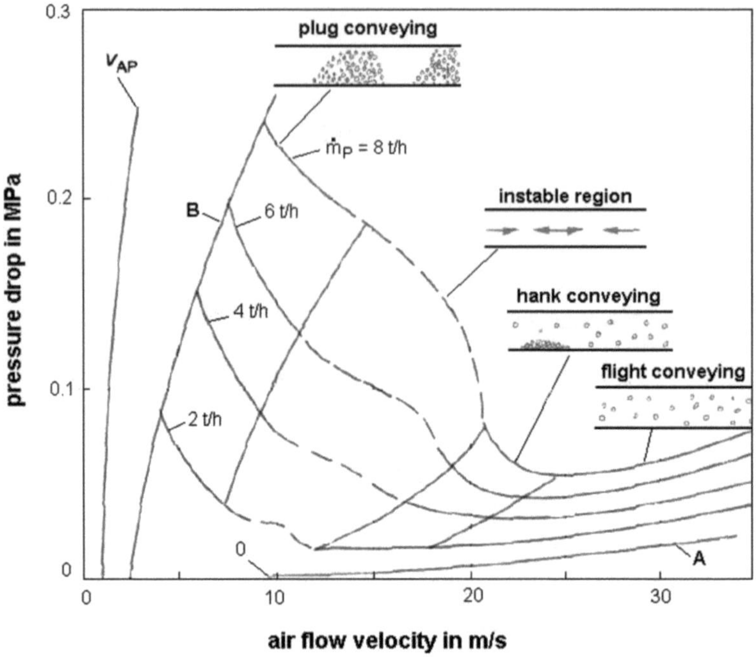

Fig. 4.28 Effect of abrasive mass flow rate on conveying modes in pneumatic solid particle conveying lines (Siegel, 1991); see text for the meanings of "A" and "B"

The line "A" in Fig. 4.28 characterises the plain air flow without any solid particles. The relationship is $\Delta p_A \propto v_F^2$. The line "B" in Fig. 4.28 marks the limits for abrasive conveying for a given abrasive mass flow rate. For $\dot{m}_P = 4$ t/h (67 kg/min), the limiting flow velocity is at about $v_F = 7$ m/s. But the conveying process is still possible for the lower mass flow rate ($\dot{m}_P = 2$ t/h).

The line "v_{AP}" in Fig. 4.28 characterises the general limit for any pneumatic conveying for the given solid material. This critical velocity, called "saltation velocity", is about $v_{AP} = 3$ m/s for the conditions in Fig. 4.28. Each abrasive material requires a saltation velocity, which is the minimum gas flow velocity for horizontal conveying. Certain approaches are known for the analytical estimation of this parameter. A rather simple approach is due to Rizk (1973):

$$\frac{\dot{m}_P}{\dot{m}_A} = \frac{1}{10^{1.44 \cdot d_P + 1.96}} \cdot \left[\frac{v_{AP}}{(g \cdot d_H)^{1/2}}\right]^{1.1 \cdot d_P + 2.5} \tag{4.24}$$

It can be seen from (4.24) that the saltation velocity depends on the mass flow ratio abrasive/air, hose diameter (m) and abrasive particle size (mm). Uferer (1992) adapted a similar model for the use in blast cleaning hoses, and he derived the following relationship:

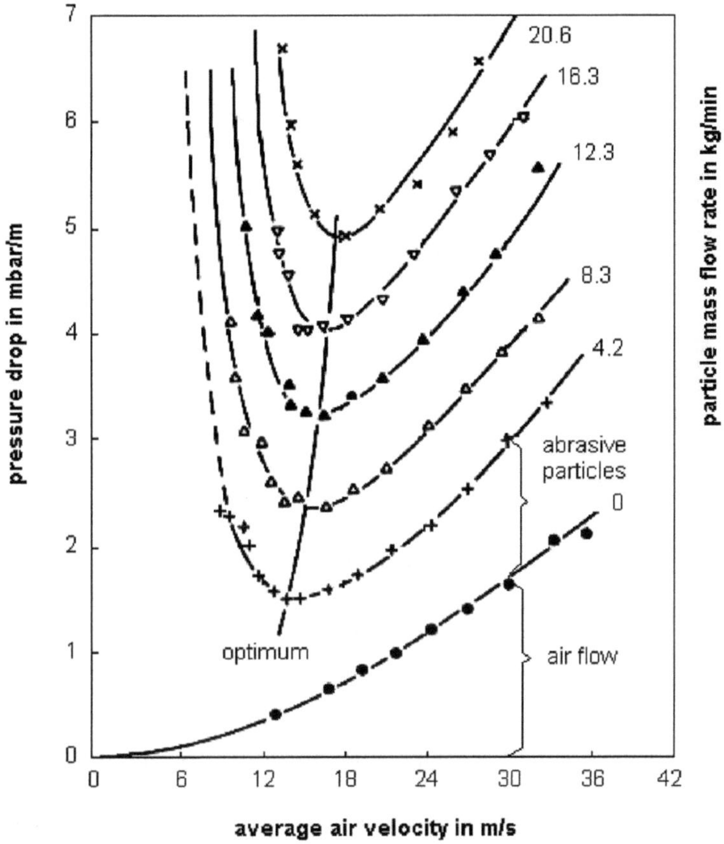

Fig. 4.29 Relationships between air velocity, abrasive mass flow rate, and pressure loss in pneumatic conveying lines (Marcus et al., 1990)

$$v_{AP} = 18.8 \cdot \left(\frac{\dot{m}_P}{\dot{m}_A}\right)^{1/3} \cdot d_H^{1/2} \cdot g^{1/2} \tag{4.25}$$

In this simplified approach, abrasive particle size is excluded. For typical conditions ($\dot{m}_P/\dot{m}_A = 1.5$, $d_H = 35\,\text{mm}$), the critical air conveying velocity is about $v_{AP} = 13\,\text{m/s}$. Further results are plotted in Fig. 4.30. It can be seen that saltation velocities typically between $v_{AP} = 10\,\text{m/s}$ and 15 m/s are required for blast cleaning applications.

The actual demanded air velocity in an abrasive hose can be adjusted through variations in the ratio between abrasive hose diameter and nozzle diameter according to the following approach suggested by Uferer (1992):

$$\left(\frac{d_H}{d_N}\right)^2 = \frac{181}{v_F} \tag{4.26a}$$

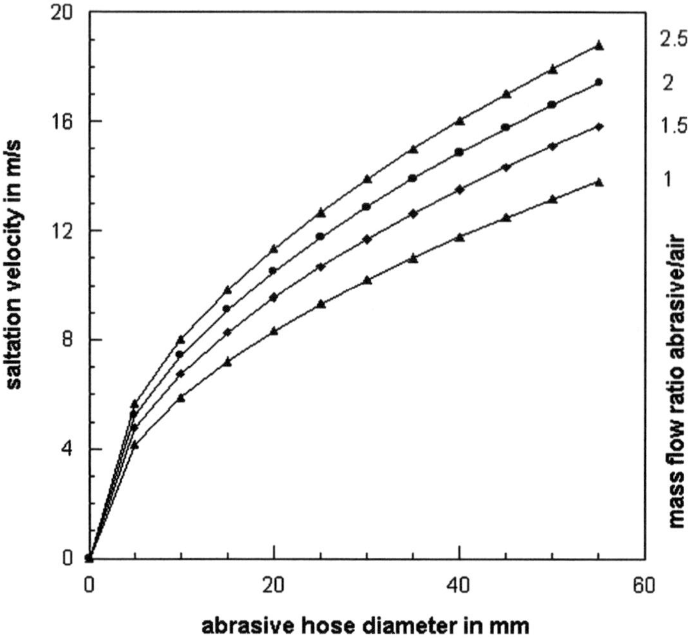

Fig. 4.30 Saltation air flow velocity for particle conveying, based on (4.25)

This relationship holds if air temperature does not vary, and if the air pressure exceeds the value of $p = 0.09\,\text{MPa}$. Results of calculations are plotted in Fig. 4.31. If a value of $v_F = 15\,\text{m/s}$ for the air velocity is being considered (which is just above the saltation velocity), an optimum diameter ratio is at about $d_H/d_N = 3.5$. This result agrees well with recommendations issued by equipment manufacturers, and it verifies the application of methods developed for pneumatic conveying of solids to the condition in blast cleaning hoses. If, for example, a nozzle with a diameter of $d_N = 12\,\text{mm}$ and a mass flow ratio abrasive/air of $R_m = 1.5$ are used, the optimum abrasive hose diameter would be $d_H = 42\,\text{mm}$ according to (4.26a). The next larger standard hose diameter is $d_H = 50\,\text{mm}$, which would deliver a diameter ratio of $50/12 = 4.2$. From (4.26a), the corresponding air flow velocity is about $v_F = 10\,\text{m/s}$, which is lower than the typical saltation velocity plotted in Fig. 4.30 for $d_H = 50\,\text{mm}$ (which is $v_{AP} = 15\,\text{m/s}$). Thus, unsteady abrasive conveying, or even clogging, may occur, which would increase pressure losses in the hose because of air flow through deposited abrasive particle conglomerates (this would apply to the region left from the line marked by "critical air velocity" in Fig. 4.27). The next smaller standard hose diameter is $d_H = 38\,\text{mm}$, which leads to an increase in air flow velocity up to $v_F = 18\,\text{m/s}$. Although the flow is now in the "technical working range" (see Fig. 4.27), this rather high flow velocity would notably increase pressure drop (compare also Fig. 4.29). Equation 4.26a is valid in that particular configuration only for $l_H = 0$ (pressure drop in hoses is not considered). For the case $l_H > 0$, the relationship must be modified as follows (Uferer, 1992):

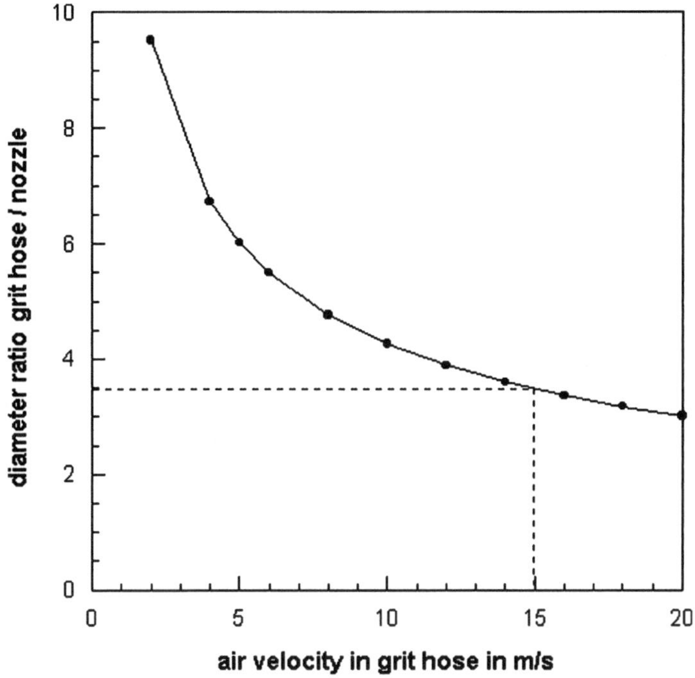

Fig. 4.31 Relationships between air velocity, abrasive hose diameter and nozzle diameter, based on (4.26a)

$$\left(\frac{\mathrm{d_H}}{\mathrm{d_N}}\right)^2 = \frac{181}{\mathrm{v_F}} \cdot \left(\frac{1}{1 + (\Delta \mathrm{p_T}/\mathrm{p})}\right) \tag{4.26b}$$

For $\Delta p_T = 0$, (4.26b) reduces to (4.26a). For an assumed pressure drop of 25% and an air flow velocity $v_F = 15$ m/s, (4.26b) delivers an optimum ratio $d_H/d_N = 3.1$. For the example mentioned earlier ($d_N = 12$ mm), the optimum hose diameter is $d_H = 37.2$ mm. The next commercially available hose diameter is $d_H = 38$ mm, which is very close to the requested value. Because the pressure drop is a function of the hose length, the diameter ratio d_H/d_N depends on hose length. In an optimum blast cleaning system, the parameters d_N, d_H and l_H are well balanced, and if one of the parameters changes value, the other parameters must be adjusted accordingly.

4.5.3 Optimum Flow Velocities in Abrasive Hoses

Pressure drop in abrasive hose lines is due to air flow and abrasive material conveying in these hoses. Experience with pneumatic conveying systems has shown that pressure drop depended on air conveying velocity (respectively, dynamic air pressure and air flow Froude number) and mass flow ratio abrasive/air. One example is shown in Fig. 4.29; more information can be found, among others, in Coulson and

Richardson (1968) and Marcus et al. (1990). It can be recognised from the graph in Fig. 4.29 (as well as from Figs. 4.27 and 4.28) that the pressure drop for a solid-air flow is much higher compared with that for a plain air flow. For an air conveying velocity $v_F = 15$ m/s, the pressure drop is $\Delta p_T = 0.5$ mbar/m for air only, but it is about $\Delta p_T = 2.4$ mbar/m for $\dot{m}_P = 8.3$ kg/min. It can also be noted from Fig. 4.29, that pressure loss has distinct minimum values at certain optimum air conveying velocities. This optimum air flow velocity depends on the Froude number of the particle settling flow. For vertical conveying processes, the optimum air flow velocity can be approximated as follows (Ahland, 1966):

$$v_{opt} = 4.1 \cdot g^{0.2} \cdot d_H^{0.2} \cdot v_S^{0.6} \tag{4.27}$$

This equation is valid for a range of Froude numbers (related to settling speed) between $Fr = 2.5$ and 25. The relationship is graphically expressed in Fig. 4.32 for typical blast cleaning conditions. It is important to note that the optimum air conveying velocity depends on hose diameter, although hose size effects become considerable in the range of rather high settling velocities. The settling velocities of abrasive particles in air must be estimated experimentally. Weber (1974) published an extensive number of experimental results. If particle material density and

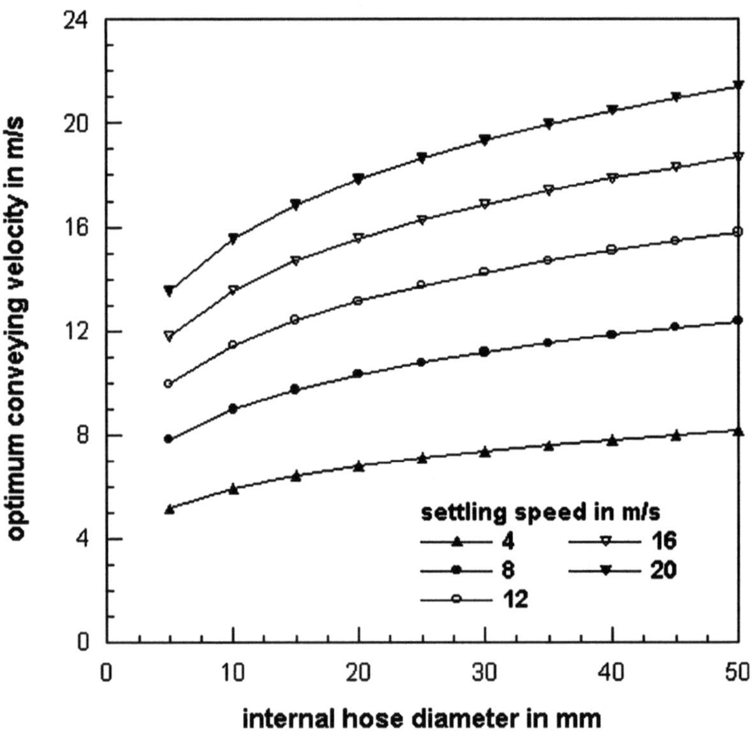

Fig. 4.32 Optimum air velocity for vertical conveying according to (4.26)

particle diameter are known, the settling velocity in air can be read from the corresponding graphs. If only particle properties are considered, and gas properties (mainly density) are excluded, settling velocity drops if particle size and particle material density decrease. A copper slag particle ($\rho_P = 3{,}700\,\text{kg/m}^3$) with a size of $d_P = 1{,}000\,\mu\text{m}$ has a settling speed of about $v_S = 9\,\text{m/s}$, whereas a steel shot particle ($\rho_P = 7{,}000\,\text{kg/m}^3$) of equal size has a settling velocity of about $v_S = 15\,\text{m/s}$. The graphs in Weber's (1974) book are restricted to spherical particles, but a comparison with results of other authors supports the suitability for other particle shapes. Buhrke et al. (1989) published correction factors, which consider effects of particle shape, turbulence degree and particle interactions. More importantly, the graphs plotted in Weber's (1974) book do not consider effects of air density; they apply to atmospheric conditions only, and they may deliver different results if air density variations due to higher air pressures in the hose are taken into account. Some limited measurements of settling velocities of particles in air under different air pressures are reported by Seville et al. (1997). Some of their results are plotted in Fig. 4.33. It can be seen that the air pressure notably affects the settling velocity. For the particles with a diameter of $d_P = 1{,}000\,\mu\text{m}$ suspended in an air temperature of $\vartheta = 27°\text{C}$ ($T = 300\,\text{K}$), the settling velocity is $v_S = 7\,\text{m/s}$ for an air pressure of $p = 0.1\,\text{MPa}$, but it is $v_S = 2.5\,\text{m/s}$ only for an air pressure of $p = 1.0\,\text{MPa}$. This is a reduction of –64%. The effects of air pressure are more pronounced for the larger particle size. A typical average reduction value would be about −50% for the conditions considered in Fig. 4.33. If this reduction factor is applied to (4.27), it can be seen that the optimum air flow velocity changes by a factor of $0.5^{0.6} = 0.66$.

4.5.4 Pressure Drop in Abrasive Hoses

A general formal approach for estimating the pressure drop in an abrasive hose line is as follows:

$$\Delta p_T = \Delta p_A + \Delta p_P \tag{4.28}$$

Here, Δp_A is the pressure drop due to air flow, and Δp_P is the pressure drop caused by abrasive conveying. This relationship is illustrated in Fig. 4.29. In the figure, the lowest line (denoted "0") illustrates the pressure drop due to plain air flow, whereas the next line (denoted "4.2") characterises the total pressure drop due to air flow and abrasive conveying (in that particular case for $\dot{m}_P = 4.2\,\text{kg/min}$). The vertical distance between these two lines, designated "abrasive particles", characterises the pressure drop caused by the abrasive conveying process. The additional pressure loss Δp_P is for two reasons. First, the settling movement of the solid particles in the hose must be balanced; second, the solid particles affect the conditions of the air flow. Based on (4.13) and (4.14), a suitable approach is as follows:

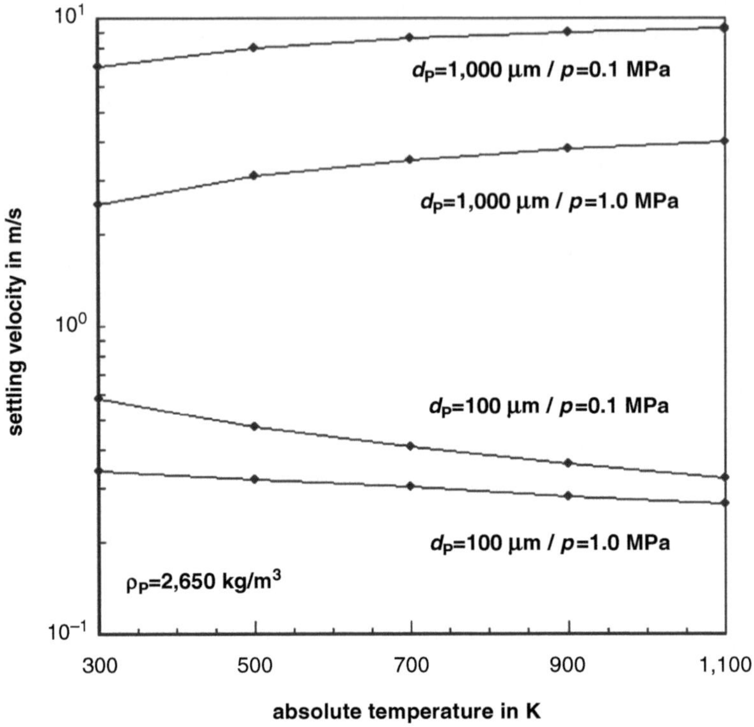

Fig. 4.33 Relationship between air density, particle size and settling velocities for grit particles in air (Seville et al., 1997)

$$\frac{\Delta p_T}{\rho_A} = \underbrace{(\lambda_A + \lambda_P) \cdot \frac{l_H}{d_H} \cdot \frac{v_F^2}{2}}_{\text{straight hose}} + \underbrace{(\xi_A + \xi_P) \cdot \frac{v_F^2}{2}}_{\text{knee or armature}} \tag{4.29}$$

The parameters λ and ξ are friction numbers. The subscript "A" stands for air flow, whereas the subscript "P" stands for abrasive conveying. The friction parameter λ_A can be calculated with (4.21). Corresponding values can be found in Fig. 4.21. The parameter λ_P can be approximated with pneumatic conveying arguments. An approach delivered by Uferer (1992) is as follows:

$$\lambda_P = \frac{C_P}{Fr_P^{\alpha_F}} \tag{4.30}$$

The constant C_P as well as the power exponent α_F depend on abrasive properties. The Froude number is given as follows:

$$Fr_P = \frac{v_F}{(d_P \cdot g)^{1/2}} \tag{4.31}$$

Uferer (1992) performed a number of experiments in order to specify (4.30) for the conditions in blast cleaning hoses. He derived the following semi-empirical relationship:

$$\lambda_P = \frac{C_{TP}}{Fr_P^{0.15}} \cdot \left(\frac{\dot{m}_P}{\dot{m}_A}\right)^{1.8} \tag{4.32}$$

The approach is valid for Froude numbers between $Fr_P = 30$ and 200, and for mass flow ratios abrasive/air between $R_m = 0.5$ and 5.0. The constant C_{TP} is an abrasive material parameter. Typical values for this parameter are listed in Table 4.9. A very rough approximation for slag materials and quartz is as follows (Uferer, 1992):

$$C_{TP} = 0.014 \cdot v_S \tag{4.33}$$

The graphs in Fig. 4.33 can be utilised for the approximation of v_S-values. If an average value of $v_S = 5$ m/s is taken from Fig. 4.33 for $d_P = 1{,}000\ \mu$m in the pressure range between $p = 0.1$ MPa and 1.0 MPa, (4.33) delivers $C_{TP} = 0.07$. This value is in the range for quartz sand and lead-thin slag (see Table 4.9). Results of measurements are compared with results based on (4.32) in Fig. 4.34. Typical values are between $\lambda_P = 0.05$ and 0.2. In certain cases, these values are one order of magnitude larger than friction values for the flow of air only (see Fig. 4.21 for comparative values). This is shown by the dotted line in the lower section of the graph, which characterises a typical friction parameter for the air flow under the given conditions. The lines "1" to "4" in Fig. 4.34 refer to results obtained with the calculation model discussed earlier for two abrasive materials and for different mass flow ratios abrasive/air. These lines follow the relationship $\lambda_P \propto Fr_P^{-0.15}$. The lines "1" (nickel slag, $R_m = 2.0$) and "4" (quartz sand, $R_m = 1.0$) mark typical upper and lower limits for the friction numbers in abrasive hoses. Equations (4.30)–(4.33) can be applied to approximate values for λ_P under different process conditions.

The values for λ_P in Fig. 4.34 are notably higher than values for friction numbers for pneumatic conveying in rigid pipes. Typical examples for friction values for pneumatic conveying in rigid pipes are listed in Table 4.10. More examples are published in Marcus et al. (1990). The reasons for the higher values for the blast cleaning process are that flexible rubber hoses are used for blast cleaning, and that the abrasive particles act as erosive media. Results listed in Table 4.10 very effectively illustrate the effect of material parameters on the friction number. If the hardness of the pipe material drops, friction value increases by a factor of 5

Table 4.9 C_{TP}-values for some abrasive materials (Uferer, 1992)

Abrasive material	C_{TP}-value
Lead–tin slag	0.078
Phosphor slag	0.102
Iron–nickel slag	0.129
Quartz sand	0.07

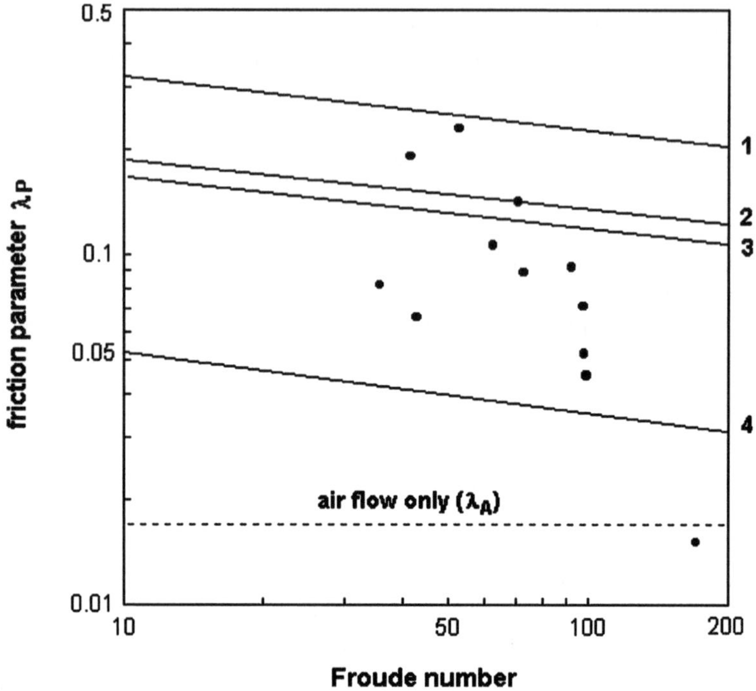

Fig. 4.34 Relationship between Froude number and friction parameter for abrasive-air flow in abrasive hoses (based on results reported by Uferer, 1992). 1 – nickel slag ($R_m = 2.0$); 2 – nickel slag ($R_m = 1.5$); 3 – quartz sand ($R_m = 2.0$); 4 – quartz sand ($R_m = 1.0$)

for quartz. If the abrasive particle material hardness increases (from Mohs 5.5 for glass beads to Mohs 7 for quartz), friction value also increases notably. This latter effect very well demonstrates that hose (with respect to pipe) material erosion has a notable influence on the friction number.

A plainly empirical approach is due to Gasterstädt (1924), who found the following relationship for pressure losses in conveying pipes based on extensive experimental work:

Table 4.10 Effects of material properties on the friction factor in rigid pipes (Weber, 1974)

Abrasive material	Pipe material	Friction factor λ_P	
		Absolute	Relative
Glass beads ($d_P = 4.0$ mm)	Steel (hardened)	0.0025	1.00
	Steel (not hardened)	0.0032	1.28
	Aluminium	0.0051	2.04
	Copper	0.0053	2.12
Quartz ($d_p = 3.0$–5.0 mm)	Steel (hardened)	0.0060	2.40
	Steel (not hardened)	0.0072	2.88
	Aluminium	0.0184	7.36
	Copper	0.0310	12.40

$$\frac{\Delta p_T}{\Delta p_A} = 1 + C_\lambda \cdot \frac{\dot{m}_P}{\dot{m}_A} \tag{4.34}$$

For the case $\dot{m}_P/\dot{m}_A = 0$, (4.34) delivers $\Delta p_T = \Delta p_A$. The empirical constant C_λ characterises the effects of abrasive and pipe wall material; it takes typical values for certain material combinations. Values for this parameter must be estimated by experiments. It can be concluded from the discussion in the previous section that C_λ has high values for hard, irregularly shaped solid particles. An exploitation of experimental results reported by Uferer (1992) for mass flow ratios abrasive/air between $R_m = 1.0$ and 2.0 delivers typical values of $C_\lambda = 1$–4 for slag materials as well as for quartz sand conveyed in blast cleaning hoses. An analysis of the reported results depicted that the C_λ-values showed a relationship to the hose diameter. The larger the hose diameter, the higher were the values for C_λ. Equation (4.34) is graphically expressed in Fig. 4.35 for different C_λ-values. It can be seen that the pressure drop ratio can become as high as $\Delta p_T/\Delta p_A = 10$ for typical mass flow ratios abrasive/air. Although Gasterstädt's (1924) relation helps to find pressure loss values from a restricted number of measurement, its physical relevance is controversial. This approach cannot be used for the estimation of the individual pressure drop caused by abrasive addition. Another critical issue is that $\dot{m}_p$ and $\dot{m}_A$ cannot be varied independently on each other if nozzle flow is considered.

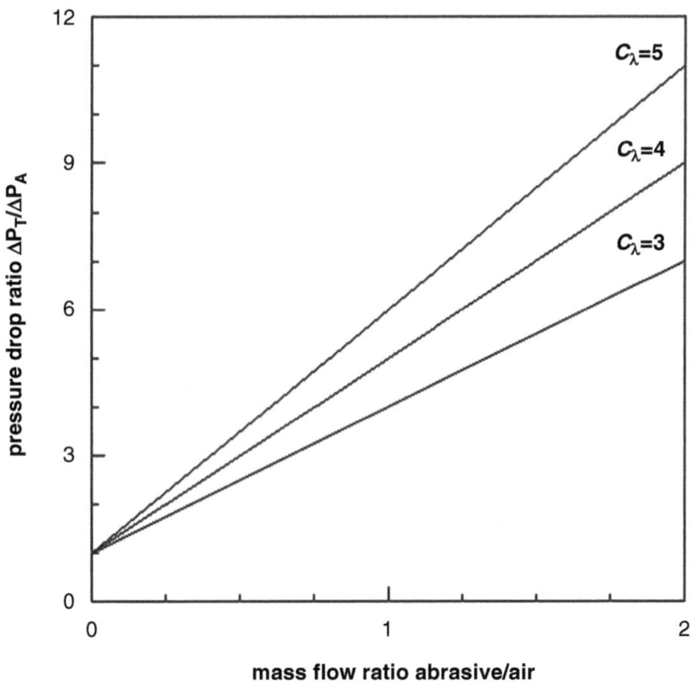

Fig. 4.35 Graphical expression of Gasterstädt's relation for different C_λ-values

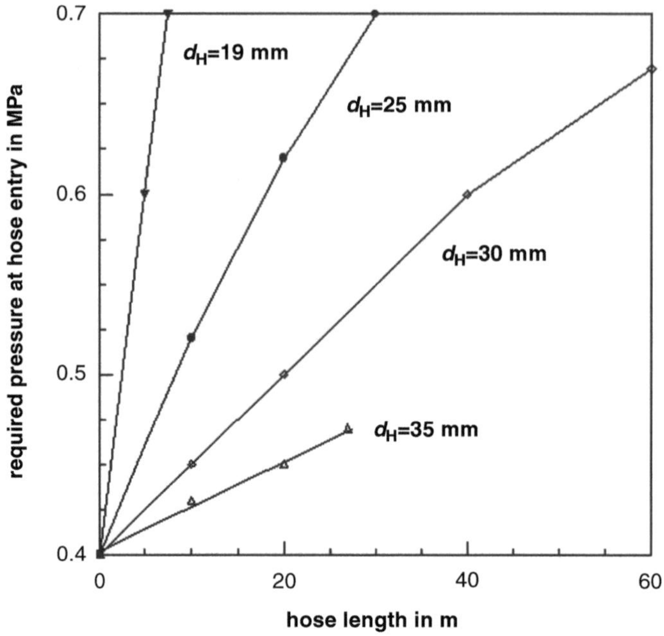

Fig. 4.36 Experimentally estimated pressure drop values in abrasive hoses (Uferer, 1992)

Uferer (1992) performed systematic measurements of pressure drops in blast cleaning abrasive hoses. Results of his work are provided in Fig. 4.36. The graphs not only illuminate the dominating effect of the hose diameter, but also verify that pressure loss is more severe in abrasive hose lines compared with plain air hose lines (compare Fig. 4.24). If a hose with a diameter of $d_{\mathrm{H}} = 25$ mm is in operation, the pressure drop reaches a value of $\Delta p_{\mathrm{T}} = 0.45$ MPa after a distance of $l_{\mathrm{H}} = 3$ m. If the operator can choose either a long air hose line or a long abrasive hose to be utilised, abrasive hose line must be as short as possible.

Results of numerical simulations performed by Tashiro and Tomita (2004) for the calculation of pressure drops in pipes for horizontal pneumatic transport depicted notable effects of abrasive material density, air flow velocity and mass flow ratio abrasive/air on the additional pressure drop caused due to abrasive addition. The additional pressure drop caused by the addition of abrasive particle to the air flow was very pronounced for abrasive materials with rather low densities. If particles with a density of $\rho_{\mathrm{P}} = 2{,}000\,\mathrm{kg/m^3}$ were added into an air stream with a flow velocity of about $v_{\mathrm{F}} = 28$ m/s, the additional pressure drop was about $\Delta p_{\mathrm{P}} = 50$ Pa/m for a mass flow ratio of $R_{\mathrm{m}} = 2$. If particles with a density of $\rho_{\mathrm{P}} = 1{,}000\,\mathrm{kg/m^3}$ were added, the additional pressure drop increased to a value as high as $\Delta p_{\mathrm{P}} = 200$ Pa/m. If the air flow velocity was reduced down to $v_{\mathrm{F}} = 19$ m/s, the values for the additional pressure drop were reduced down to $\Delta p_{\mathrm{P}} = 7$ Pa/m ($\rho_{\mathrm{P}} = 2{,}000\,\mathrm{kg/m^3}$, $R_{\mathrm{m}} = 2$), respectively to $\Delta p_P = 25$ Pa/m ($\rho_P = 1{,}000\,\text{kg/m}^3$, $R_m = 2$). Distinguished effects of air compressibility on the additional pressure drop could not be estimated by Tashiro and Tomita (2004).

Results of measurements on pressure drop in grit hose performed by Bae et al. (2007) were already shown in Fig. 4.13. The lines illustrate the effects of abrasive mass flow rate and nozzle design on the pressure drop. The curves can be fitted with a simple linear law according to the following equation:

$$\Delta p_T = C_1 \cdot \dot{m}_P + C_2 \tag{4.35}$$

The pressure drop is given in MPa, and the abrasive mass flow rate in given in kg/min. The precise values for the regression parameters C_1 and C_2 depend on the geometry of the nozzle. The regression is valid for rather high abrasive mass flow rates between $\dot{m}_P = 11$ kg/min and 40 kg/min. It can only be applied to determine trends, because the hose length was not given in Bae et al. (2007) work. Comparative pressure drop measurements were performed by Bosshard and Fritchman (1992). The authors used steel shot (S110) and deployed moderate air pressures (p = 0.12–0.45 MPa) and moderate abrasive mass flow rates ($\dot{m}_P$ = 0.8–5.0 kg/min). The ratio between hose diameter and nozzle diameter was $d_H/d_N = 2.5$. The authors found that the pressure drop in abrasive hoses increased linearly with an increase in abrasive mass flow rate. The pressure drop ratio between plain air flow ($\dot{m}_P = 0$) and flow with abrasive material was between $\Delta p_P/\Delta p_A$ = 1.5 to 3, and this ratio depended on the abrasive mass flow rate.

The graphs presented in Figs. 4.13 and 4.36 demonstrate that the working line of a nozzle, as plotted in Fig. 4.3, is a function of the pressure drop in the blast cleaning system. An ideally performing system would permanently cross-check the actual nozzle working line with the compressor working line, and it would take corrective action.

Figure 4.37 illustrates the effect of the abrasive hose dimensions on the relative cleaning rate. The graphs are based on measurements performed by Uferer (1992). If pressure drop is not considered ($l_H = 0$), the systems with the nozzle diameter $d_N = 8$ perform at a relative cleaning rate of 100%. If the nozzle diameter increases up to $d_N = 10$ mm (e.g. due to nozzle wear), and no buffer vessel is placed between compressor and nozzle, the efficiency notably drops down to 64%. However, the situation changes if abrasive hoses are considered. It can be seen that the efficiency notably drops for the system with the smaller hose diameter ($d_H = 25$ mm). This effect is due to the severe pressure drop in the narrow hose. If a hose length as short as $l_H = 20$ m is exceeded, this system performs worse than the system with the larger nozzle diameter. At a hose length of $l_H = 50$ m, this system delivers only 40% of the original cleaning rate. For very long hoses ($l_H > 70$ m), the two systems with the larger hose diameter ($d_H = 32$ mm) perform almost equally good. This discussion very well illustrates the complex relationships behind any blast cleaning optimisation procedure.

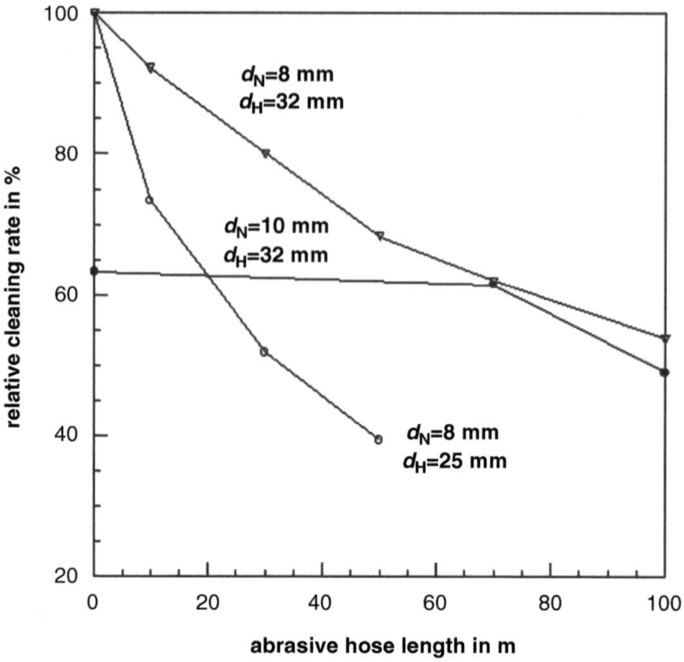

Fig. 4.37 Relationship between nozzle diameter, abrasive hose diameter, abrasive hose length and relative cleaning rate (based on measurements reported by Uferer, 1992)

4.6 Nozzles

4.6.1 Nozzle Types

For blast cleaning operations, the following two prime nozzle types can be distinguished:

- cylindrical nozzles with convergent inlet sections;
- nozzles with a convergent–divergent shape (Laval nozzles).

The performance characteristics of both nozzle types are described in Chap. 3.

For convergent–divergent nozzles, Settles and Geppert (1997) issued the following optimisation design rules:

- The convergent section should be minimised to bring the Mach number between air and abrasive particles to unity ($Ma = 1$) as soon as possible.
- The throat section should not be longer than necessary to avoid its wearing.
- The divergent nozzle section should be contoured rapidly until the Mach number between air and abrasive particles reaches a value of about $Ma = 1.4$ (see Fig. 3.18).
- The divergent contouring should be gradually maintained to maintain the relative Mach number of $Ma = 1.4$.

- The length of the divergent section should be extended as required to achieve the desired abrasive particle velocity at the nozzle exit.
- The ratio between nozzle exit area and nozzle throat area should be chosen for the given exit pressure to be near perfect expansion (see Fig. 3.24).

Each individual blast cleaning nozzle has its particular working line, which is given as follows:

$$p = f(d_N) \cdot \dot{Q}_A \tag{4.36}$$

Three examples for nozzle working lines are plotted in Fig. 4.3. The functions depict a linear relationship between the two parameters (see Sect. 3.2.1). The fundamentals of nozzle flow are discussed in Sect. 3.2.

Blast cleaning nozzles consist of a nozzle body (housing) and an inlet section. Whereas the body is usually made from steel, the inlet sections are made from different materials, including steels, tungsten carbides, ceramics and composite materials.

4.6.2 Nozzle Wear

4.6.2.1 Fundamentals of Nozzle Wear

Nozzle wear is a serious problem with any blast cleaning system. Nozzle wear deteriorates efficiency and often avoids a continuous blast cleaning operation. The basic mechanism is the erosion of the nozzle wall due to impinging abrasive particles. The processes discussed in Chaps. 2 and 5 relate on nozzle wear as well.

Ishii and Kawasaki (1982) performed numerical simulations of the particle streamlines in blast cleaning nozzles. Their results deduced an upper limiting point in the wall region where the particle could impinge, when the impingement of the particles on the nozzle wall occurred in the supersonic section of the nozzle (see Sect. 3.3). The location of this point did not depend on particle size, but on nozzle geometry.

Examples of worn blast cleaning nozzle inlet sections are shown in Fig. 4.38. The images "a" and "c" illustrate the wear of an aluminium oxide nozzle, whereas the images "b" and "d" illustrate the wear of a boron carbide nozzle. It can be seen that the wear did not occur regularly, but rather concentrated in the upper section of the nozzle inlet. Figure 4.39 provides information on the change in the internal nozzle geometry due to wear. It can be seen that the erosion was not regular over the nozzle length; the worn cross-section rather moved towards the nozzle exit over time. But the minimum cross-section, which determines air flow rate and air flow velocity (see Sect. 3.2), was already extended after 6 hours. After an exposure time of $t_B = 20\,\text{h}$, this worn section had reached the nozzle exit. Similar observations were reported by Lukschandel (1973). Observations have shown that the internal geometry of cylindrical nozzles without a convergent inlet section changed over the time; their geometry approached that of convergent–divergent (Laval) nozzle. The same happened with cylindrical nozzles that already contained a convergent

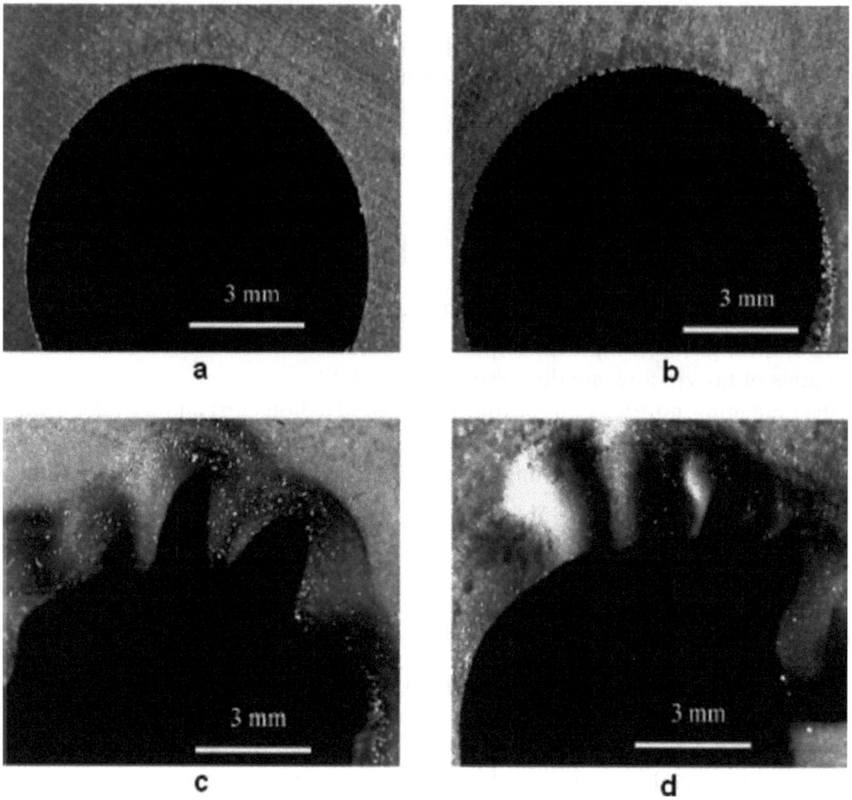

Fig. 4.38 Entry sections of ceramic blast cleaning nozzles (Deng et al., 2003b). (**a**) New aluminium oxide nozzle; (**b**) New boron carbide nozzle; (**c**) Worn aluminium oxide nozzle after $t_B = 4$ h; (**d**) worn boron carbide nozzle after $t_B = 4$ h

inlet section (Pashatskii et al., 1971; Kumar et al. 1983). An example is provided in Fig. 4.40. The dotted line expresses the shape of the worn steel nozzle after an operation period of 25 min. It seemed that the wear, in terms of diameter, increased to approach a saturation value for a given ratio between (eroded) exit diameter and bore diameter; values for this ratio were reported to be between 3 and 5 for conical nozzles (Pashatskii et al. 1971). Sheldon et al. (1977) sectioned an aluminium tube ($d_N = 5$ mm, $l_N = 305$ cm) into individual short tube sections 2.54-cm long. Each individual tube section was carefully weighed, and the tube sections were then re-assembled to form a tube of original length. This tube was eroded with hardened steel shot ($d_P = 270$ μm; $\dot{m}_P = 1.26$ g/s, $p = 0.17$ MPa). After eroding, the tube was disassembled and each section was weighed. It was noted that the erosion rate (kg/kg) was very low at the inlet section of the tube, where the velocity of the particles was rather low, and then rose in a non-linear manner to a maximum value at the exit section of the tube. Deng (2005b) scanned the internal profile of a ceramic nozzle eroded over a period of 50 hours. Results of this study are displayed

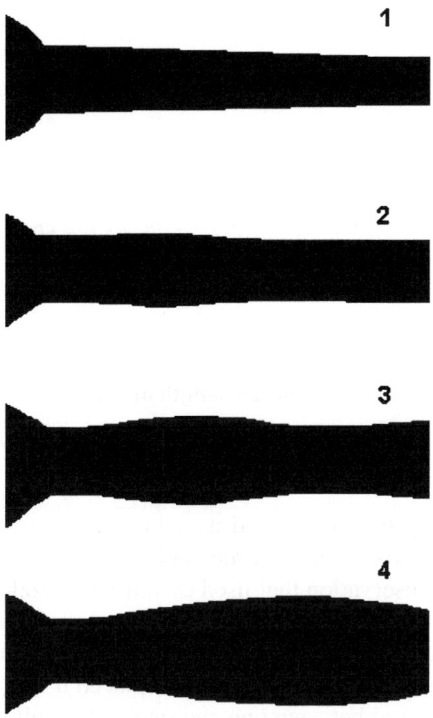

Fig. 4.39 Wear pattern in a blast cleaning nozzle (Gesell, 1969). 1 – new nozzle; 2 – after $t_B = 6\,h$; 3 – after $t_B = 9\,h$; 4 – after $t_B = 20\,h$

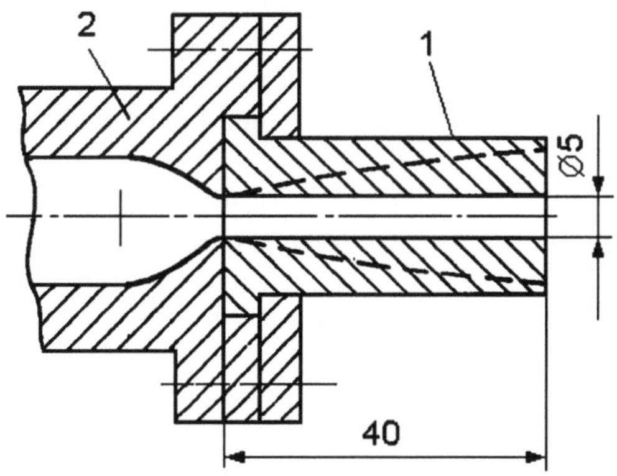

Fig. 4.40 Wear pattern in hardened steel blast cleaning nozzle with convergent entry section (Pashatskii et al., 1971). 1 – wear pattern after $t_B = 25\,min$; 2 – nozzle body. Dimensions in mm

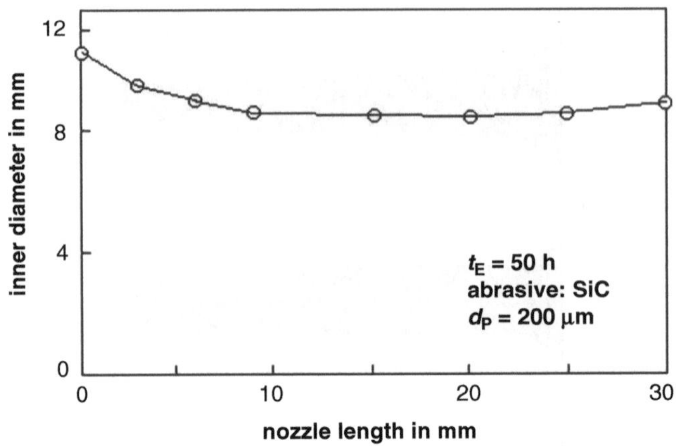

Fig. 4.41 Geometry of a ceramic blast cleaning nozzle after a performance time of 50 h (Deng, 2005b)

in Fig. 4.41. Originally, the nozzle had a cylindrical design, but it changed to a convergent–divergent shape over the time. This change in internal geometry may be one reason for the observation that used cylindrical nozzles sometimes perform better than new, unused cylindrical nozzles.

Worn nozzles should be replaced in time. It is not always easy to define a worn nozzle, but a general rule is: nozzles should be replaced if the (smallest) nozzle bore diameter is being increased between one and one-and-a-half millimetre. Results of quantitative wear measurements on a cylindrical blast cleaning nozzle are displayed in Fig. 4.42. It can be seen that both entry and exit bore diameters of the nozzle increased during the operation. After 9 h, the diameter of the exit bore was increased by about 1 mm; therefore, the value for the minimum diameter in the nozzle, which determines air mass flow rate and air velocity, had changed. The graphs also show a decrease in the wear rate (slopes of the curves) with an increase in operation time. The entry section, in particular, featured a very steep initial wear rate. These curves characterise nozzle wear as a non-stationary process. A quantitative comparison of the wear performance of different nozzles should, therefore, always be performed at operation times long enough to guarantee a stationary wear process. For the example plotted in Fig. 4.42, this critical operation time would be at about 8 h for the exit section.

Equation 3.9 illustrates that an increase in nozzle diameter is accompanied by a decrease in pressure in order to maintain the desired air flow rate. An example of how nozzle wear increased the volumetric air flow rate is shown in Fig. 4.43. The nozzle wear (in terms of diameter increase) shown in Fig. 4.43a followed a square-root relationship:

$$d_N(t_E) \propto t_E^{1/2} \tag{4.37}$$

Such a trend was also found on ceramic nozzles by Bothen (2001) and on steel nozzles by Pashatskii et al. (1971). However, the experimentally estimated increase

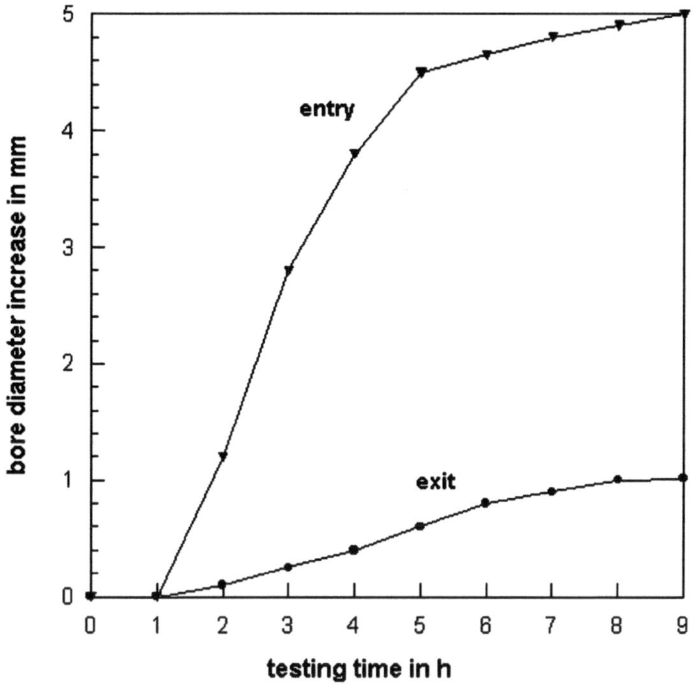

Fig. 4.42 Development of wear of blast cleaning nozzles (Deng et al., 2003a)

in volumetric air flow rate followed a linear relationship as shown in Fig. 4.43b. Because of $\dot{Q}_A \propto d_N^2$, this is not an unexpected result. If the compressor cannot deliver this demanded air flow rate, air pressure drops. According to (3.11), the relationship between nozzle diameter and nozzle air pressure is as follows:

$$\mathrm{d}_\mathrm{N}^2 \propto \mathrm{p}^{-1} \tag{4.38}$$

A combination of $d_N = 12$ mm and $p = 1.0$ MPa delivers a volumetric air flow rate of $\dot{Q}_A = 13.5\,\mathrm{m^3/min}$. If the nozzle diameter increases up to $d_N = 13$ mm, the reduced nozzle pressure is $p = 1.0\,\mathrm{MPa}\cdot(12/13)^2 = 0.85\,\mathrm{MPa}$. To compensate this pressure drop, the compressor must deliver a volumetric air flow rate of $\dot{Q}_A = 15.8\,\mathrm{m^3/min}$ (at $\vartheta = 20°\mathrm{C}$). These calculations show that nozzle wear affects the working line of a nozzle. If the throat diameter of a nozzle is worn from originally $d_N = 10$ mm to 12 mm, the nozzle working line changes notably. This situation is illustrated in Fig. 4.3. The working point for the entire system changes from "II" to "III", and the system must be readjusted. Therefore, wear-resistant nozzles are a basic requirement for stable blast cleaning processes. If the compressor cannot deliver the desired additional volumetric air flow rate, the pressure at the nozzle drops, and the cleaning rate will be reduced. An example is provided in Fig. 4.37. It can be seen that the relative cleaning rate drops from originally 100% for $d_N = 8$ mm down to 64% for $d_N = 10$ mm. This particular example does not consider effects of abrasive hose lines ($l_H = 0$).

(a)

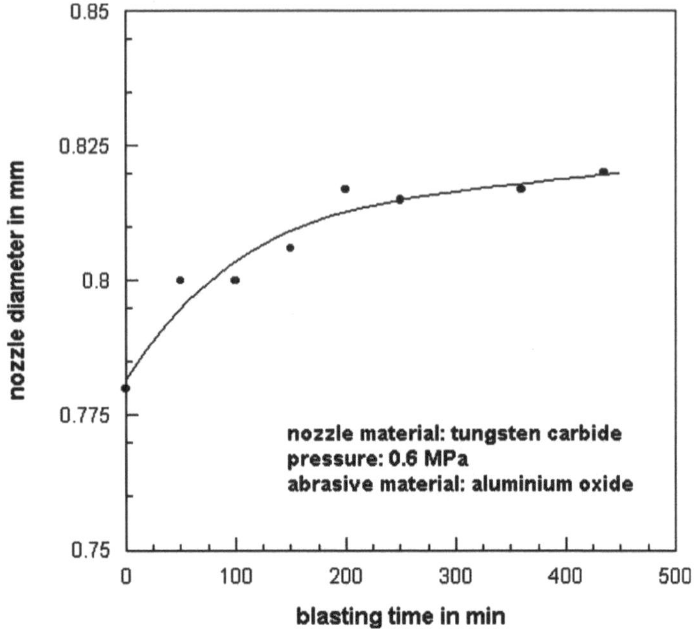

(b)

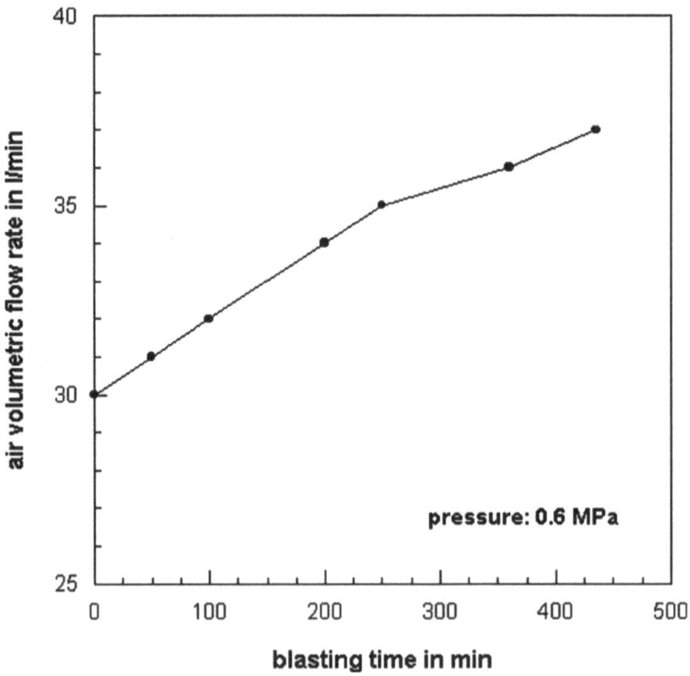

Fig. 4.43 Wear of a Laval nozzle (Bothen, 2000). (**a**) Increase in nozzle diameter; (**b**) Increase in air volume flow rate

4.6.2.2 Parameter Effects on Nozzle Wear

Nozzle wear depends on nozzle and abrasive parameters as well as on process parameters. Investigations into the effects of blast cleaning and material parameters on nozzle wear were performed by many authors.

It is known for more than 40 years (Adlassing and Jahn, 1961) that nozzles made from boron carbide featured the highest wear resistance, and that the use of aluminium oxide as an abrasive accelerated blast cleaning nozzle wear. More recent measurements verified these early results (Grearson et al., 1989). Results from site experience are listed in Table 4.11. The reason for the high wear resistance of boron carbide is its high hardness (see Table 4.12). A typical relationship between the erosion rate of tungsten carbide composites and hardness is as follows (Laugier, 1986):

$$E_R \propto H_N{}^{-3.5} \tag{4.39}$$

Figures 4.38, 4.44 and 4.45 illustrate the effects of nozzle material hardness. Results plotted in Fig. 4.44 show that an increase in nozzle material hardness notably improved the resistance of the nozzle to wear. It can be seen from Fig. 4.45, that the nozzle made from boron carbide experienced a much lower erosion rate compared with the nozzle made from aluminium oxide.

The influence of the abrasive type is illustrated in Table 4.11 and Fig. 4.45. From the materials listed in Table 4.11, corundum (aluminium oxide) abrasives caused the most severe erosion, which may again be due to the high hardness of this material. Figure 4.45 shows, however, that the intensity of nozzle wear is controlled by a combination of the hardness for nozzle material and abrasive material. Although the erosion increased for the alumina nozzle and for the boron carbide nozzle if the abrasive material hardness increased, the alumina nozzle was more sensitive to changes in abrasive material hardness. It will, therefore, basically be the hardness ratio between nozzle material and abrasive material, which determines wear resistance. This ratio is given as follows:

$$R_H = \frac{H_N}{H_P} \tag{4.40}$$

If the hardness ratio is high, wear rate is low and vice versa. These aspects are illustrated in Fig. 4.45, which shows that wear increased if abrasive material hardness

Table 4.11 Nozzle lifetime values (Kennametal, Inc., Charlotte)

Nozzle material	Approximate lifetime in h		
	Abrasive material		
	Steel shot/grit	Quartz sand	Aluminium oxide
Aluminium oxide	20–40	10–30	1–4
Tungsten carbide	500–800	300–400	20–40
Silicon carbide composite	500–800	300–400	50–100
Boron carbide	1,500–2,500	750–1,500	200–1,000

Table 4.12 Mechanical properties nozzle of materials (Deng et al., 2003a)

Nozzle material	Flexural strength in MPa	Hardness in GPa	Fracture toughness in MPa $m^{1/2}$
Boron carbide (B_4C)	350	32.5	2.5
Tungsten carbide (WC/8Co)	1,500	14.8	14.5
Alumina carbide (Al_2O_3/45C)	850	21.5	4.9

increased; but the absolute wear was always less for the boron carbide nozzle. The effect of the nozzle material hardness on nozzle wear is illustrated in Fig. 4.44. Erosion rate notably dropped if a nozzle material with a high hardness was utilised. The performance in terms of reduced wear could be almost doubled if a nozzle material with a hardness of $H_N = 23.8$ GPa [boron carbide composite, B_4C/50 wt.% (W, Ti) C] was replaced by a nozzle material with a hardness of $H_N = 32.5$ GPa (boron carbide, B_4C). Table 4.12 lists mechanical properties of some typical blast cleaning nozzle materials.

Nozzle geometry parameters, namely nozzle diameter and nozzle length, affect the wear performance as well (Adlassing, 1960; Kumar et al., 1983). Results of respective measurements are provided in Fig. 4.46. Nozzle mass loss, which expresses wear, increased if longer and wider nozzles were used. The relationship between bore diameter and nozzle mass loss was of a parabolic shape (Adlassing, 1960). An opposite trend was reported by Kumar et al. (1983) for the wear of very small steel nozzles ($d_N = 0.8$–1.6 mm). These authors found a decrease in wear for larger nozzle diameters. The effects of varying angles of the nozzle entry section on the wear

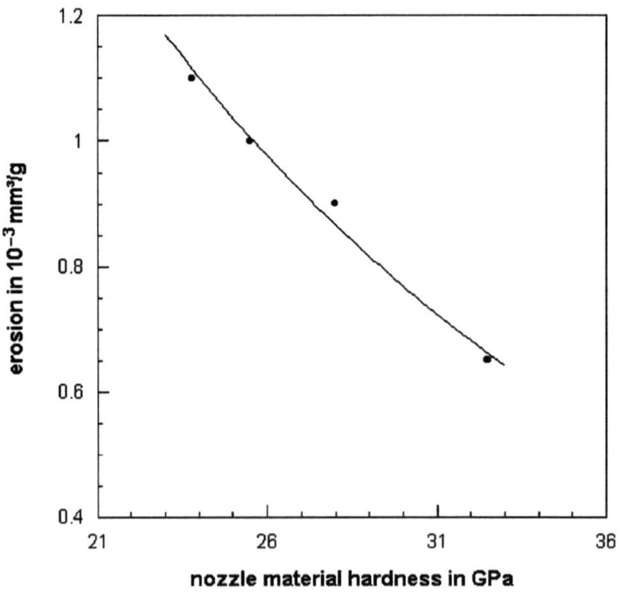

Fig. 4.44 Effect of nozzle material hardness on nozzle wear (Deng, 2005a)

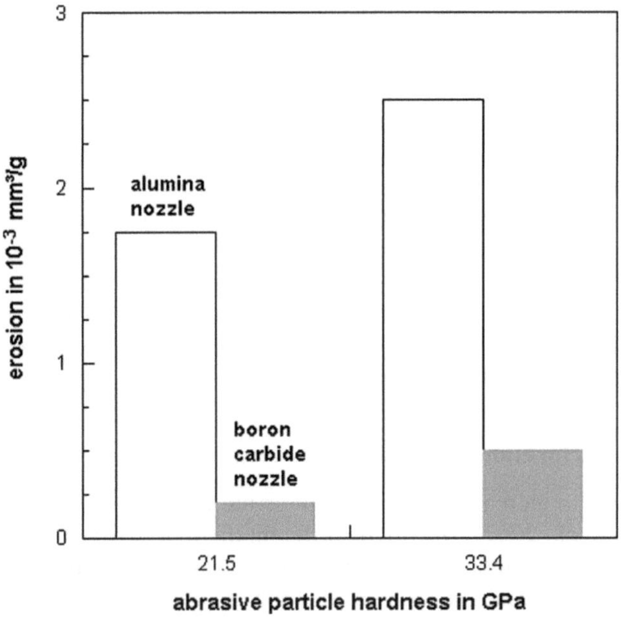

Fig. 4.45 Effect of abrasive material hardness on nozzle wear (Deng et al., 2003b)

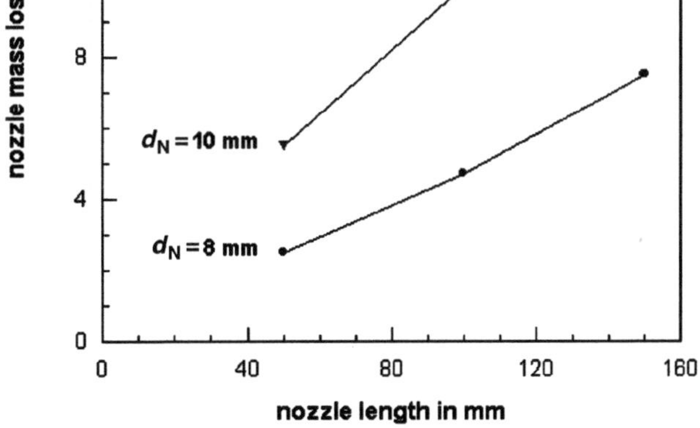

Fig. 4.46 Effects of nozzle length and nozzle diameter on nozzle wear (Adlassing, 1960)

of convergent-cylindrical steel nozzles was also investigated by Kumar et al. (1983), and they could prove that the wear increased for smaller entry angles. This result was contributed to an increase in the length of the convergent section of the nozzle.

Process parameters also affect nozzle wear. It was found by several authors that nozzle wear increased if air pressure rose (Adlassing, 1960; Pashatskii et al., 1971). Nozzle wear was also found to increase linearly if the abrasive particle concentration (Pashatskii et al., 1971) or the mass flow ratio abrasive/air (Kumar et al., 1983) was increased. Kumar et al. (1983) investigated the influence of the abrasive particle size on the wear of steel nozzles. They utilised small aluminium oxide particles ($d_P = 30$ and 38 μm), and they could show that the nozzle wear was more severe for the larger abrasive particles. However, a notable difference between the effects of the two different particle sizes was obvious at rather long exposure times only.

4.6.2.3 Wear Performance of Laminated Ceramic Nozzles

A new approach to increase nozzle lifetime is the utilisation of laminated ceramic nozzles (Deng et al., 2007). Due to the different thermal expansion coefficients and due to shrinkage of the individual layer materials, residual compressive stresses are generated in the laminated sections of the nozzle (entry and exit sections). These compressive stresses may partly balance tensile stresses which form during the erosion process in the nozzle. Figure 4.47 exhibits results of comparative wear tests.

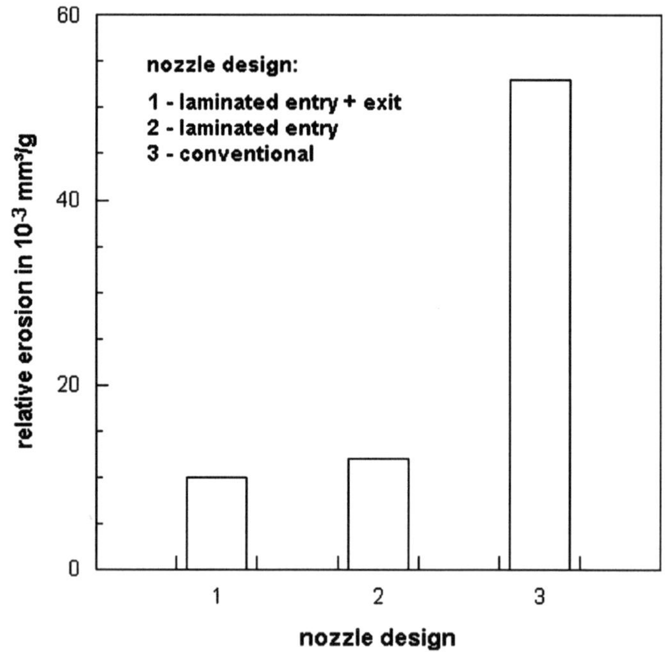

Fig. 4.47 Results of comparative wear measurements on conventional ceramic nozzles and laminated ceramic nozzles (Deng et al., 2007)

The standard nozzle exhibited the most severe wear. The nozzle with a laminated entry section performed better, but the best performance was delivered by the nozzle with laminated entry and exit section. Long-term (540 min) measurements of the entry bore diameter of different nozzles were also made. The entry bore diameter of a conventional nozzle increased up to $\Delta d_{\mathrm{N}} = 7$ mm, whereas the entry bore diameter of a laminated nozzle increased up to $\Delta d_{\mathrm{N}} = 1$ mm only (Deng et al., 2007).

Chapter 5
Substrate and Coating Erosion

5.1 Introduction

The basic process of blast cleaning is the impingement of individual abrasive particles under different conditions on the target material. In the reference literature, this process is often referred to as *solid particle* erosion. The system "coating – interfacial layer – substrate" is illustrated in Fig. 5.1. This complete system responds by the following two mechanisms to the impingement of solid particles:

- erosion of the coating material (cohesive mode);
- debonding of the coating material (adhesive mode).

These mechanisms are illustrated in Fig. 5.2, and they will be discussed in detail in the subsequent sections.

Erosion occurs usually either if the coating is rather thick or if the adhesion of the coating to the substrate is very good. The erosive response of *bulk (coating) materials* can be subdivided into elastic response (brittle) and elastic–plastic response (ductile). These modes of response are illustrated in Fig. 5.3 in terms of scratching images of organic coatings.

Debonding and delamination in the interface between substrate and coating are alternative coating removal mechanisms, and they occur at rather small coating thickness, or if the adhesion is low.

5.2 Mechanical Properties of Oxides and Organic Coatings

5.2.1 Relevant Mechanical Properties

The material to be considered for blast cleaning is rather a material system composed of the three following parts:

- substrate;
- interfacial layer;
- layer (coating, oxide).

Fig. 5.1 System: substrate (aluminium) – interface – coating (epoxy). Photographs: Zhang et al.. (2003). Left: deteriorated adhesion: Right: good adhesion

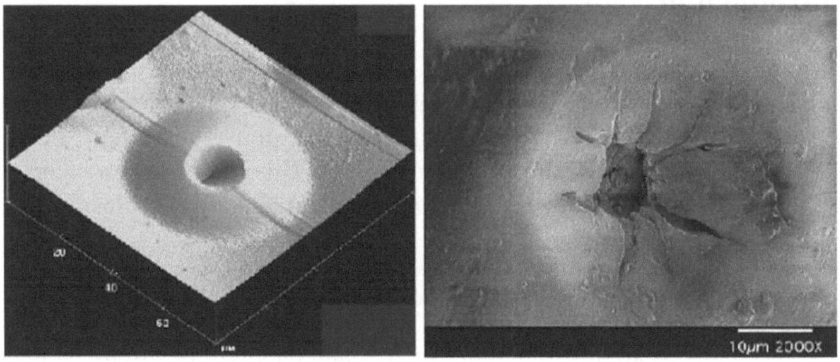

Fig. 5.2 Basic types of coating response to solid particle impingement (Strojny et al., 2000). (**a**) Buckling and debonding; (**b**) Brittle response with bulk material erosion

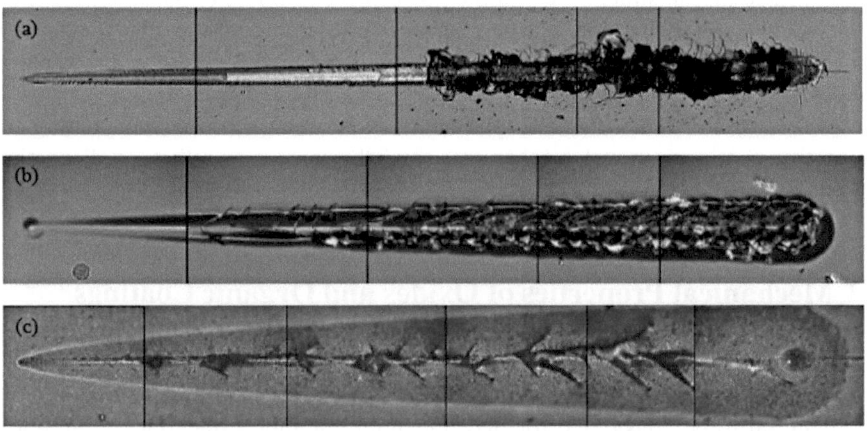

Fig. 5.3 Basic types of organic coating response to scratching (Randall, 2006). (**a**) PVC-based hardcoat finish: elastic response with cracking; (**b**) Silicone finish: elastic-plastic response with permanent deformations; (**c**) Automotive varnish coat: plastic response with some ruptures

Such a system is shown in Fig. 5.1. Whether cohesive mode or adhesive mode dominates depends on the adhesion between coating and substrate and on coating thickness. If both adhesion strength and coating thickness are low, adhesive delamination occurs. For the cohesive mode, the bulk properties are of importance, but it is known that, for coating materials, cohesive properties, e.g. indentation properties, depend on the distance to the substrate (Roche et al., 2003).

Over the years, many erosion studies have been performed on a variation of materials. It was shown that no single material property can determine the resistance of a material against the erosion by impinging solid particles. However, there are some properties which were observed to notably affect the erosion resistance of materials. These *cohesive material properties* include the following:

- hardness;
- Young's modulus;
- strain energy density;
- tensile strength;
- fracture mechanics parameters.

Adhesive system properties, say adhesion strength between substrate and adhering layer (oxide, glue and coating), also affect the behaviour of the system.

An extensive review about parameters and measurements methods for coating materials is provided by Papini and Spelt (2002).

The cohesive properties can be exhibited in a stress–strain diagram of a stressed material volume. Typical stress–strain diagrams for three types of material response are shown in Fig. 5.4. The plot in Fig. 5.4a illustrates the linear-elastic response of a material. This response is characterised by the damage features shown in Fig. 5.3a. The plot in Fig. 5.4b illustrates the elastic–plastic response of a material. This response relates to the damage features shown in Fig. 5.3b. The shapes of stress–strain curves are not general material properties, but depend on the loading conditions. Stress–strain curves of paint materials are, for example, sensitive to the loading rate. This aspect was in detail investigated by Dioh and Williams (1994). The Hardness and Young's modulus represent the deformation response of a material. Hardness is

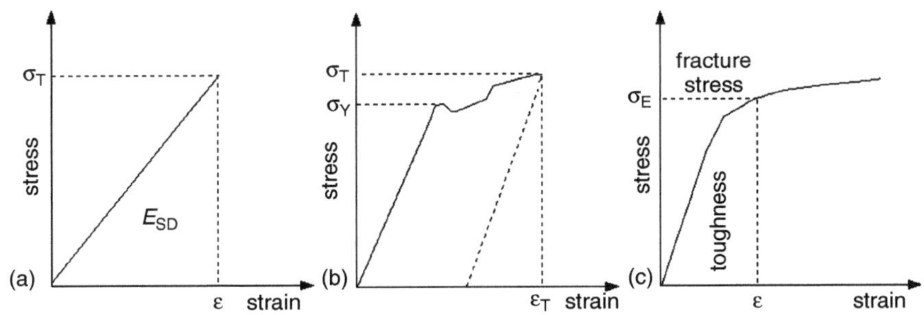

Fig. 5.4 Stress–strain diagrams and deformation parameters. (**a**) Linear-elastic response; (**b**) Elastic-plastic response; (**c**) Dynamic compressive diagram (Levin et al., 1999)

for many materials coupled with the yield strength (Tabor, 1951), and for elastomers it is linearly related to Young's modulus (Li and Hutchings, 1990). *Strain energy density* is the area under the stress–strain curve of a material:

$$E_{SD} = \int_0^{\varepsilon_T} \sigma(\varepsilon)\, d\varepsilon \tag{5.1}$$

It has the unit kJ/m^3 which is that of a specific volumetric energy. For elastically responding materials, elastic strain energy density can be approximated as follows:

$$E_{SD} = \frac{\sigma_T^2}{2 \cdot Y_M} \tag{5.2}$$

The variables are illustrated in Fig. 5.4a. The elastic strain energy density has been applied by several authors as a parameter which can characterise the resistance of a material against solid particle erosion (Bitter, 1963; Kriegel, 1968). The detailed shape of a stress–strain curve can already deliver a rough estimate of the behaviour of the material in question. Some examples are provided in Fig. 5.5. The term "hard" in this graph corresponds to elastic response, whereas the term "soft" points to a rather plastic material response. Levin et al. (1999) extended the stress–strain approach and developed an idea to apply a dynamic (high strain rate) compression stress–

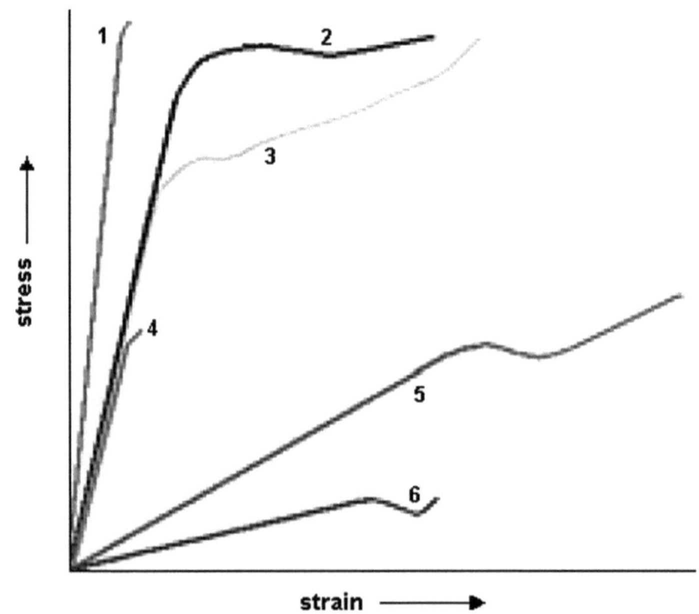

Fig. 5.5 Stress–strain diagrams for different response characteristics (Hare, 1996). Material characteristics: 1 – hard and brittle; 2 – hard and strong; 3 – hard and tough; 4 – weak and brittle; 5 – soft and tough; 6 – soft and weak

strain curve for the assessment of the response of ductile metals to solid particle erosion. This approach is illustrated in Fig. 5.4c. The area under the modified stress–strain curve, denoted "tensile toughness" by the authors, characterises the energy absorbed during the erosion process. The failure stress estimated from such a dynamic stress–strain curve is related to the hardness of the eroded surface as follows:

$$\sigma_E = A_D \cdot H_M \tag{5.3}$$

The constant had values between $A_D = 3.4$ and 4.0 for many metal alloys (Levin et al., 1999).

Mechanical properties depend on a number of physical effects, namely strain rate sensitivity and temperature sensitivity. Solid particle impingement, the basic mechanism for blast cleaning, is associated with high strain rates (see Sect. 5.4.1). Values as high as 10^6 per second can be assumed (Hutchings, 1977a). The response of metals and organic coatings to loading depends on deformation velocity and strain rate. An increase in strain rate may, for example, change the response of organic coatings from plastic deformation to intense chipping, and may cause a two-fold increase in yield stress (Dioh and Williams, 1994). An increase in deformation rate rises tensile strength of organic lacquers (Skowronnek et al., 1991). An increase in strain rate also modifies material properties as shown in Fig. 5.6 for the yield stresses of organic materials (see Fig. 5.4b for the definition of the yield stress). Siviour et al. (2005) found for polymer materials a change in the structures of stress–strain curves if temperature and strain rate were varied.

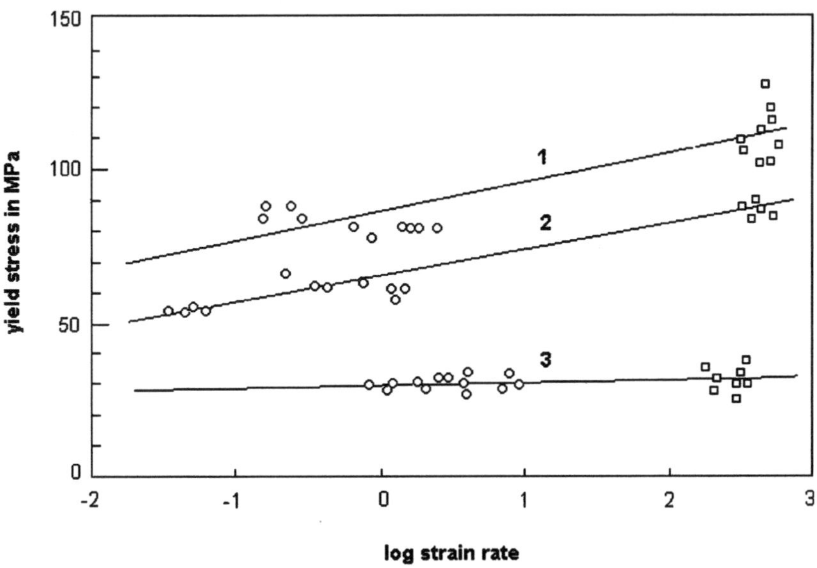

Fig. 5.6 Strain rate effects on yield strength of polymeric materials (Kukoreka and Hutchings, 1984). Materials: 1- polyethersulphone; 2- polycarbonate; 3- high-density polyethylene

Table 5.1 Dynamic hardness values of steel blades and deposits (Raykowski et al., 2001)

Material	Dynamic hardness in GPa
Compressor blade deposit	0.22–0.26
Compressor substrate	0.3–0.43
Turbine blade deposit	6.3

Based on a balance between the kinetic energy of an impinging particle and the work done in plastically deforming the impinged coating material, Tangestanian et al. (2001) derived a *dynamic hardness*:

$$H_d = \frac{m_P \cdot v_P^2}{2 \cdot \pi \cdot \left[\left(d_P^2 - a_{C\,max}^2 \right)^{1/2} \cdot \left(\frac{1}{3} \cdot a_{C\,max}^2 + \frac{2}{3} \cdot d_P^2 \right) - \frac{2}{3} \cdot d_P^3 \right]} \tag{5.4}$$

This parameter is defined as the instantaneous force resisting indentation during a collision divided by the instantaneous contact area. The dynamic hardness is an important property in determining the impact behaviour at high strain rates. Values for this material parameter are listed in Table 5.1.

Temperature variations can be responsible for ductile–brittle (plastic–elastic) transition of coatings under impact conditions (Moore, 2001). At low temperature, brittle fracture will occur with a comparatively low amount of absorbed impact energy. A ductile–brittle transition will occur at some fixed temperature. Other coating properties, namely deformation properties and fracture properties, also depend on temperature; examples are provided in Fig. 5.7 for the variations in fracture toughness and yield strength. Figure 5.8 illustrates the general effect of temperature variations on the behaviour of organic materials.

Fracture mechanics parameters include mainly fracture toughness and energy release rate. Both parameters can be applied to individual materials, but also to

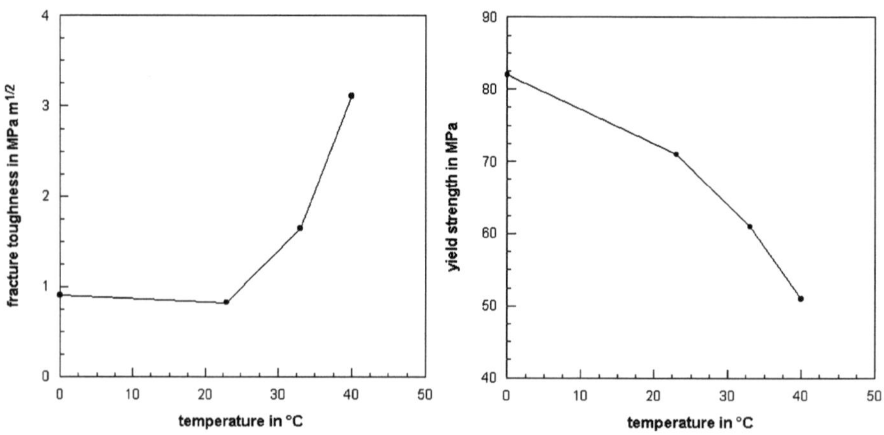

Fig. 5.7 Effect of temperature on mechanical properties of organic coating materials (Moore, 2001). Left: effect on fracture toughness; right: effect on yield strength

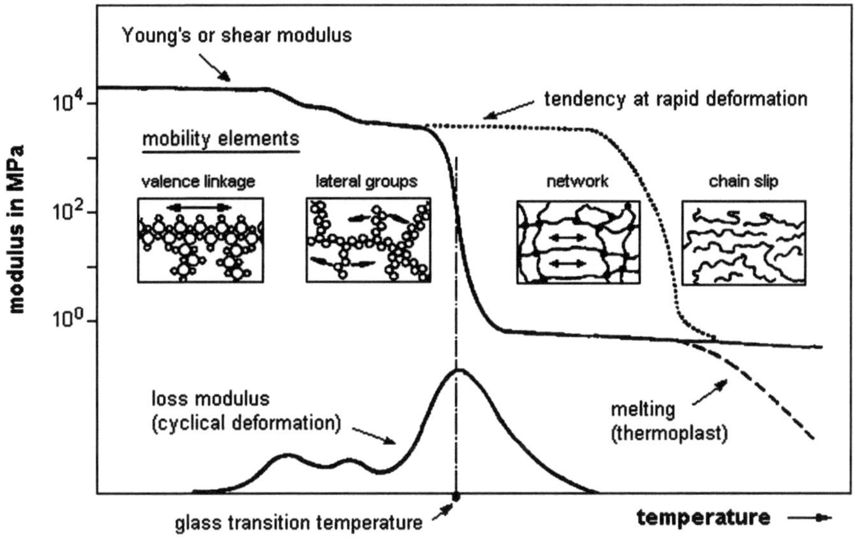

Fig. 5.8 Effects of temperature on the behaviour of organic coating materials (Zorll, 1984)

interfaces between two materials, say coating and substrate, as well as to joints. Principles of fracture mechanics with respect to contact mechanics and erosion are described in Lawn's (1993) book. The fracture toughness characterises a critical value for the stress intensity at the tip of a crack required to extend the crack. It is defined as follows:

$$K_{Ic} = \alpha_C \cdot \sigma_T \cdot (\pi \cdot l_C)^{1/2} \tag{5.5}$$

In that equation, l_C is the crack length, σ_T is the failure tensile stress and α_C is a shape factor. The fracture toughness must be estimated experimentally. Its physical unit is $MN/m^{3/2}$. The critical energy release rate is defined as follows:

$$G_{Ic} = \frac{K_{Ic}^2}{Y_M} \tag{5.6}$$

The critical energy release rate characterises the specific energy required to extend a crack. Its physical unit is J/m^2. The subscript "I" in (5.5) and (5.6) shows that both relationships are valid for a tensile loading mode (mode I) only. A method for the estimation of critical energy release rate for the interfacial zone between steel substrates and adhesives under impact load was developed by Faidi et al. (1990). A typical value for combination steel-epoxy was $G_{Ic} = 0.15\,kJ/m^2$. State-of-the-art measurement methods for the assessment of fracture mechanics parameters for organic coatings as well as for interfaces between organic coatings and substrate materials are described in detail by Papini and Spelt (2002).

5.2.2 Mechanical Properties of Oxides

5.2.2.1 Deformation Parameters

Oxides are basically formed either due to atmospheric effects (corrosion) or due to thermal effects (mill scale). The composition of oxides is complex, and they usually consist of numerous layers with different chemical compositions. Detailed descriptions of mill scale compositions are provided by Wirtz (1962). The mechanical properties of mill scale depend mainly on the formation temperature. The effect of temperature on the Young's modulus of growing mill scale layers was investigated for different metals by Hurst and Hancock (1972) and Tangirala (1998). For high temperatures, Young's modulus reduced. Typical values for Young's modulus of scales were: $Y_M = 2 \times 10^5$ MPa for iron, $Y_M = 3 \times 10^5$ MPa for nickel, and $Y_M = 2.2 \times 10^5$ MPa for an alloyed steel. Table 5.2 lists further elastic parameters for iron oxides at different formation temperatures. For comparison, the elastic parameters of the plain iron are also listed in the table.

5.2.2.2 Hardness

Results of microhardness measurements on oxides of numerous metals were reported by Lepand (1963), Wood and Hodgkiess (1972) and Zieler and Lepand (1964); some results are listed in Table 5.3. It was found that microhardness can basically be related to the crystal structure of the oxides. Oxides with a rhombohedral structure (e.g. Cr_2O_3) featured very high hardness values. When layered structures were formed on pure metals, e.g. FeO, Fe_3O_4 and Fe_2O_3 on iron, the hardness increased from the metal towards the oxide.

5.2.2.3 Adhesion Parameters

Spangenberg (1972) and Engell (1960) performed investigations into the adhesion strength of mill scale to metal substrates. Spangenberg (1972) utilised three steel types as listed in Table 5.4. He derived an empirical relation of the general form:

$$\sigma_M = C_1 + C_2 \cdot h_Z + C_3 \cdot \vartheta_R + C_4 \cdot \varepsilon_M \tag{5.7}$$

Table 5.2 Mechanical properties of iron and iron oxide (Tangirala, 1998)

Parameter	Material	Formation temperature in °C			
		570	674	743	800
Young's modulus in GPa	Iron oxide	182	168	158	151
	Iron	155	150	135	125
Poisson's ratio	Iron oxide	0.34	0.34	0.34	0.34
	Iron	0.34	0.34	0.34	0.34
Fracture stress in MPa	Iron oxide	38	2.4	1.9	4.9

Table 5.3 Microhardness values of metal oxides (Zieler and Lepand, 1964; Wood and Hodgkiess, 1972)

Oxide	Hardness in kg/mm^2
ZnO	184
NiO	600
TiO_2	624
Cu_2O	232
Cr_2O_3	1,820–3,270
FeO	270–390
Fe_2O_3	690
$\alpha-Fe_2O_3$	986–1,219
Fe_3O_4	420–500
$\alpha-Al_2O_3$	2,160

Here, σ_M is the adhesion strength of the mill scale to the substrate (N/cm^2), h_Z is the mill scale layer thickness (µm), ϑ_R is the rolling temperature (°C) and ε_D is the deformation degree (%). The deformation degree is a function of the steel plate thickness before and after the rolling process. Typical values for the adhesion strength as well as the constants C_1 to C_4 are listed in Table 5.4. The effect of the mill scale layer thickness is most important. The effect of the oxidation temperature was investigated in more detail by Engell (1960). This author found that adhesion of oxides to iron is best at moderate temperatures; an example is provided in Fig. 5.9.

5.2.3 Mechanical Properties of Organic Coatings

5.2.3.1 Deformation Parameters

Paul et al. (2004) have shown that numerous organic coating materials (e.g. oxide primer, polyurethane-based enamel) feature a linear stress–strain behaviour according to Fig. 5.4a. The progress of the stress–strain function, thus Young's modulus, depended on coating composition. Figure 5.10 shows the effects of hardener concentration and film thickness on the Young's modulus of organic coatings. It can be noted in the figure that coating dry film thickness affects the mechanical parameter; the higher the film thickness, the higher the values for Young's modulus. Values for

Table 5.4 Adhesion strength values for mill scale (Spangenberg, 1972)

Parameter σ_M in N/cm^2	Steel type Armco iron	St 42	St 70
	200–1,600	100–1,800	200–1,600
C_1	531	1,649	2,019
C_2	11.2	3.5	5.4
C_3	−0.8	−1.8	−1.8
C_4	5.6	9.0	0

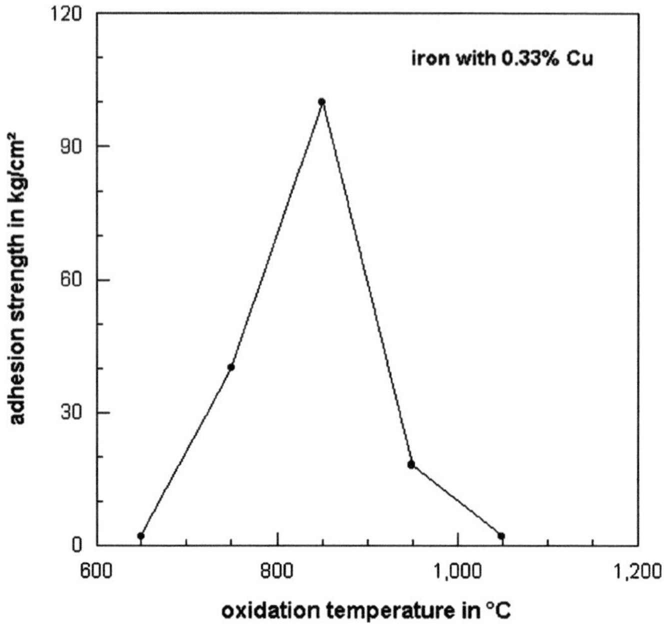

Fig. 5.9 Effect of oxidation temperature on the adhesion of oxides to the metal substrate (Engell, 1960)

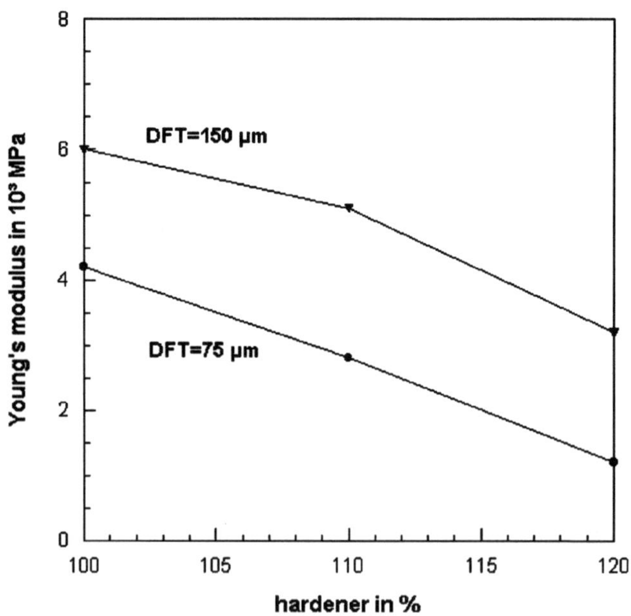

Fig. 5.10 Effects of hardener concentration and coating thickness on Young's modulus (Fokke, 1999)

the strain (relative elongation) of more than 30 epoxy-based organic coatings are listed by Askheim et al. (2001).

Values for fracture toughness and yield strength of an epoxy coating are shown in Fig. 5.7 as functions of temperature.

Impact resistance of coatings is often described in terms of an energy required to penetrate a coating layer of defined thickness. A ranking of different coating materials for a drop weight test is as follows: polyethylene: 30 Nm; polyurethane: 20 Nm; tar epoxy: 5 Nm (Sato et al., 2003). Erosion processes are associated with high strain rates (Hutchings, 1992), which affect materials properties as well as the deformation response of the coating materials. An example is provided in Fig. 5.6 showing a notable increase in yield stress for three polymers for high strain rates. A review on the affects of strain rate variations on mechanical properties of polymer materials was provided by Siviour et al. (2005). The authors also noted significant effects of the temperature on mechanical properties. Storage modulus and peak stress, measured during high strain rate loading, decreased with an increase in temperature. Values for a number of mechanical properties of organic coatings are listed in Tables 5.5 and 5.6.

5.2.3.2 Hardness

Hardness values measured on organic coatings were provided by Fokke (1999), Gnyp et al. (2004), Kotnarowska (1999), Neumaier (1993), Pickles and Hutchings (1997), Rehacek (1982) and Tangestanian et al. (2001). Some results are provided in Tables 5.7 to 5.9. It can be seen that hardness depended on temperature – it usually increased with an increase in temperature. For comparison, a hardness value for steel as a typical substrate material is provided. Vickers hardness of organic coatings is also sensitive to coating material composition and to film thickness. Examples are provided in Figs. 5.11 and 5.12. Vickers hardness increased if volumetric pigment volume and hardener concentration increased, and it dropped if film thickness increased. The latter relationship is of special importance for blast cleaning processes. Neumaier (1993) noted a strong relationship between hardness of organic paint materials and their degree of cross-linkage.

Rehacek (1982) investigated the response of organic coatings to Vickers indentation. He developed a method for the estimation of elastic (reversible) and plastic components of hardness. Results are provided in Table 5.8 and Fig. 5.11. The capability of plastic deformation depended mainly on the resin. It can be seen in

Table 5.5 Mechanical data for polymeric coatings (Rutherford et al., 1997)

Coating	Peak stress in MPa	Strain to break in %	Energy to break in kJ/m^2	Tensile modulus in MPa
R1	29.6	2.1	8.5	1,740
R2	24.4	1.7	5.5	1,680
F1	17.6	22.8	69.9	297
F2	17.5	15.7	50.0	423
L1	26.8	30.7	161.0	1,160
L2	51.6	4.7	39.7	1,870

Table 5.6 Mechanical data for polymeric coatings (Trezona et al., 1997)

Coating	Polymer type	Peak stress in MPa	Failure strain in %	Tensile modulus in MPa	Tensile failure energy in MJ/m^3
F1	Acrylic	17.6	22.8	297	3.04
F2	Acrylic	25.8	35.1	855	5.25
F3	Acrylic	49.1	14.3	1,375	5.10
F4	2C PU	57.7	29.0	1,418	9.19
R1	Acrylic	24.4	1.7	1,680	0.17
R2	Acrylic	29.6	2.1	1,740	0.24
R3	Acrylic	47.1	2.9	1,802	0.65
R4	Acrylic	77.0	4.1	2,617	1.87
R5	2C PU	77.0	5.9	1,990	2.27
R6	2C PU	61.6	8.4	1,614	3.60
L1	2C PU	26.8	30.7	1,160	4.02
H1	2C PU	51.6	4.7	1,870	0.87

Table 5.7 Brinell hardness values for certain organic coatings (Gnyp et al., 2004)

Coating name and composition	Thickness in μm	Treatment temperature in °C	Brinell hardness in MPa
KO-FMI-5	400–450	20	303
		150	277
		170	509
		250	391
Laquer + coal ash + close packing with ultrasound	400–450	20	258
		150	303
		170	407
		250	375
Pompur 804	–	–	143
Ambercoat 2000	–	–	213
Steel substrate	–	–	1,310

Table 5.8 Vickers hardness values for organic coatings (Rehacek, 1982)

Alkyd resin	Vickers hardness in MPa	Amount of plastic deformation in %
Alkyd	82	34 ± 4
Alkyd with low soy bean oil content	66	47 ± 5
Alkyd with moderate linseed oil content	58	42 ± 1
Alkyd with moderate soy bean oil content	17	53 ± 2
Alkyd with high soy bean oil content	5.7	25 ± 8

Table 5.9 Results of deformation measurements on organic paint materials (Neumaier, 1993)

Material	Deformation energy in %		Young's modulus in GPa
	Elastic	Plastic	
Coil coating	19.4	80.6	7.8
Clear lacquer	42.4	57.6	3.2
Filler	29.2	70.8	7.1

Fig. 5.11 that an increase in volumetric pigment concentration led to an increase in hardness. The relative increase in hardness depended on the type of pigment (the addition of iron oxide delivered higher hardness values than the addition of titanium oxide), but not on resin type. The addition of a hardener to the coating material reduced hardness, especially at a higher film thickness. This is verified by the experimental results plotted in Fig. 5.12. Neumaier (1993) found due to comparative hardness measurements on organic paint systems that a spherical indenter promoted an elastic response much more than a pyramid indenter. The energy consumed for permanent deformation in a paint film was about 58% for a pyramid indenter, whereas it was about 10% only for a spherical indenter. Typical elastic and plastic deformation parameters of paint materials, estimated due to indentation tests, are provided in Table 5.9. Therefore, spherical indenters were more suitable for the assessment of the elastic properties of paint films.

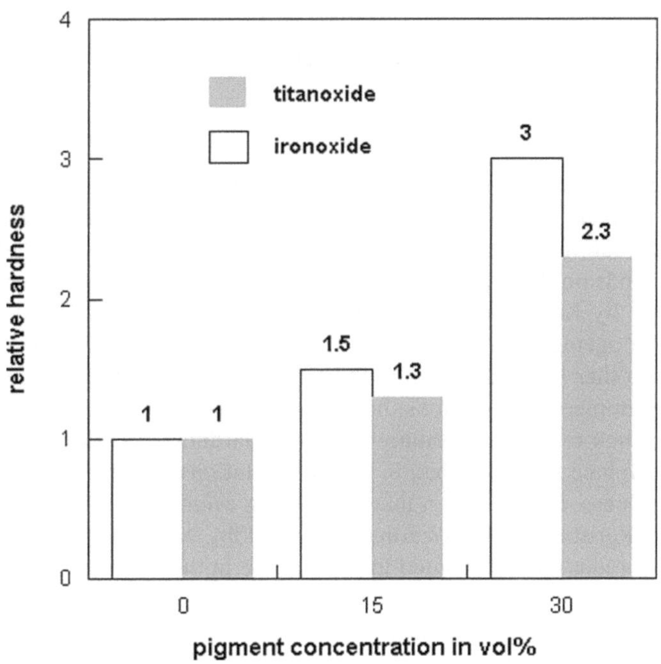

Fig. 5.11 Effects of volumetric pigment concentration and pigment type on Vickers hardness (Rehacek, 1982)

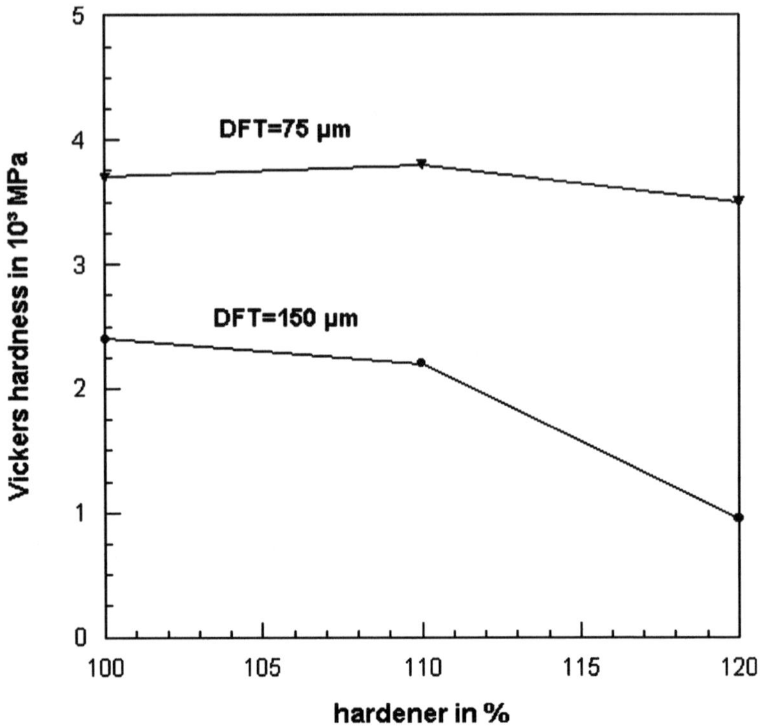

Fig. 5.12 Effects of hardener concentration and coating thickness on Vickers hardness (Fokke, 1999)

The effects of ageing on the hardness of organic coatings are not completely clear. Tangestanian et al. (2001) found a decrease in Vickers hardness of a polyurethane coating if the coating was thermally aged. However, hardness most probably depends on the type of ageing. This was shown through experimental results delivered by Kotnarowska (1999). Hardness (Buchholz hardness) decreased dramatically if ageing occurred due to ultraviolet radiation. Ageing due to thermal shock, on the other hand, did not affect hardness. If ageing took place in salt solutions under immersed conditions, hardness decreased for ageing times of about 600 h, and it then rested on a saturation level. Hardness decrease was more pronounced in sulphate solutions than in chloride solutions. Weathering did not affect Buchholz hardness. It was shown that weathering even can notably increase Vickers hardness (Rehacek, 1982; Trezona et al., 2000b). Neumaier (1993) found that especially UV-radiation contributed to an increase in the hardness of organic paint systems. Figure 5.13 illustrates how coating ageing may affect the deformation behaviour of organic coating materials.

Typical values for the dynamic hardness as defined in (5.4) of an organic coating of different ages are listed in Table 5.10. An interesting conclusion can be made from these results: the elastic property (Young's modulus) remained almost

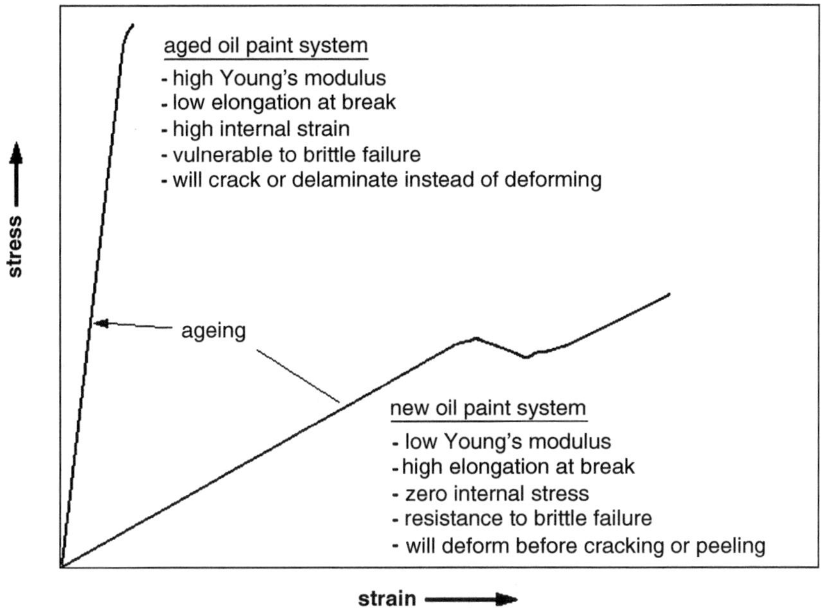

Fig. 5.13 Modification of stress–strain behaviour of coating materials due to ageing (Hare, 1996)

constant, whereas the plastic behaviour (dynamic hardness) was notably affected due to ageing.

During hardness measurements of paint films, the depth of penetration on indenters in the coating should not exceed 10% of the total film thickness in order to exclude any effects of the substrate material (Neumaier, 1993).

5.2.3.3 Fracture Mechanics Parameters

Fracture mechanics parameters include fracture toughness and critical energy release rate (work of fracture). These parameters can be estimated with standard fracture mechanics tests (Ravi-Chandar, 2004), but not much information is available for organic paint films. Some values for the fracture toughness of organic coating materials are listed in Table 5.11. The results show that fracture toughness increased with age. Singh et al. (2004) could show for epoxy resin coatings that the work of fracture depended on the pigment concentration. If pigmented with titanium oxide,

Table 5.10 Mechanical properties of an organic coating system (Tangestanian et al., 2001)

Parameter	Coating age in days				
	fresh	1	2	4	8
Dynamic hardness in GPa	1.43	–	1.64	1.61	1.91
Coefficient of restitution	0.35	–	0.46	–	0.44
Young's modulus in MPa	4,030	4,420	4,160	4,350	4,090

Table 5.11 Fracture toughness values for organic coating materials (Andrews, 2002)

Material	Fracture toughness in $MN/m^{3/2}$	
	New	After 12 months
Acrylated urethane	0.61	1.48
Epoxy	0.87	0.80
Acrylic	0.51	0.73

the work of fracture exhibited maximum values at a pigment concentration of about 15%. Typical values for the work of fracture ranged between 5 and 25 kJ/m^2. Kim and Nairn (2000) published values for the critical energy rate of organic paint films, and they found that the critical energy release rate was a function of the baking time of the coatings. Values ranged between 30 and 200 J/m^2.

Values for the fracture toughness and energy release rate of numerous hybrid sol-gel coatings can be found in Ballard et al. (2001).

5.3 Impact Processes

5.3.1 Impulse and Energy Considerations

If a solid body hits another solid body at high speed, impulse and energy are transferred from the impinging body (particle) to the impinged body (target). The impulse transferred to the target material can be calculated as follows:

$$I_P = \int_0^{t_P} dt = m_P \cdot (v_P - v_{P2}) \tag{5.8}$$

The energy transferred to the target can be calculated as follows:

$$\Delta E_P = \frac{m_P}{2} \cdot (1 - e_R^2) \cdot v_P^2 \tag{5.9}$$

The parameter e_R is known as the coefficient of restitution (sometimes referred to as impact number).

5.3.2 Coefficient of Restitution

The coefficient of restitution characterises the amount of the kinetic energy of an impinging particles which is supplied to the workpiece for deformation and mass removal. Because the loss of energy is mainly due to plastic deformation, the coefficient of restitution can be considered a measure of the deformation capabilities of target and particle. A simple definition for vertical impact, where friction between particle and target surface can be neglected, is as follows:

$$e_R = \frac{v_{P2}}{v_P} = \left(1 - \frac{E_i}{E_P}\right)^{1/2} \tag{5.10}$$

The energy E_i is the energy irreversibly stored in the workpiece. Depending on the material response, this energy will be consumed for plastic deformation, crack formation, stress wave penetration, heat generation, etc. Two limits exist for the coefficient of restitution: for $e_R = 1$ ($E_i = 0$), a completely elastic response occurs, and no energy is transferred into the workpiece; for $e_R = 0$ ($E_i = E_P$), a completely plastic response occurs, and the entire kinetic energy is dissipated into the workpiece. A simple measure for the restitution coefficient is the following, based on changes in the potential energy:

$$e_R = \left(\frac{h_2}{h_1}\right)^{1/2} \tag{5.11}$$

Here, h_1 is the height the particle is located at before the impingement and h_2 is the height of the reflected particle measured after the impingement. Illyes and Brauer (1987) performed a study into the effects of impact parameters on the coefficient of restitution. For the material pair steel–steel, they measured typical values between $e_R = 0.35$ and 0.95. They also noted that this parameter decreased if impingement velocity increased and if impact angle increased. There seemed to exist a critical impact velocity where the coefficient of restitution was independent of impact velocity. This limit was at lower values for shallow impact angles. Tangestanian (1999) investigated the effects of impact velocity on the coefficient of restitution of organic materials. Particles were steel balls with $d_P = 1.5$ mm in diameter. The results of this study indicated a decrease in the coefficient of restitution with an increase in impact velocity. Values for the coefficient of restitution were between $e_R = 0.15$ and 0.43. Ruppel and Brauer (1990) found an inverse power relationship between impact angle and coefficient of restitution:

$$e_R \propto \frac{1}{\varphi^{n_e}} \tag{5.12}$$

The power exponent n_e depended on the target material properties. Hutchings et al. (1981) investigated the rebound behaviour of hard spheres impinging a plastically deformable target material for a wide range of impact velocities and impact angles. They found that rebound velocity was almost linearly related to the impact velocity ($v_{P2} \propto v_P$), whereby the coefficient of proportionality decreased with an increase in impact angle. The rebound angle also showed an almost linear relationship to the particle impact velocity, and the coefficient of proportionality increased if impact angle increased. Sheldon et al. (1977) impinged aluminium with steel balls ($d_P = 3.2$ mm) at velocities between $v_P = 90$ and 200 m/s and noted a power relationship between coefficient of restitution and rebound angle. Values for the coefficient of restitution were rather low and pointed to a high degree of plastic deformation either in the steel balls or in the aluminium targets. The rebound angle was found to depend on the impingement angle in a linear fashion.

For metal alloys, Levin et al. (1999) derived the following relationship between the coefficient of restitution and material parameters:

$$e_R = \frac{1.75 \cdot H_M^{5/8} \cdot k_E^{1/2}}{\rho_P^{1/8} \cdot v_P^{1/4}} \tag{5.13}$$

The variable k_E summarises the elastic properties of the materials:

$$k_E = \frac{1 - v_M^2}{Y_M} + \frac{1 - v_P^2}{Y_P} \tag{5.14}$$

Some conclusions can be drawn from this analysis. For metals with high ratios between hardness and Young's modulus, a larger portion of the incident kinetic particle energy transforms into rebound kinetic energy. Energy used for plastic deformation is lower for hard metals than for soft metals.

Tangestanian et al. (2001) measured the coefficient of restitution for the impingement of steel spheres ($m_P = 14\,\text{mg}$) on at relative low impact velocities ($v_P =$ 30–35 m/s) on polyurethane coatings. Results of these experiments are listed in Table 5.10 as a function of coating age. It can be seen that the parameter was approximately the same for all aged samples, and that the fresh paint had a significantly lower value. This result means that the freshly applied paint would experience greater plastic (permanent) deformation upon impact.

Hutchings et al. (1981) measured rebound parameters of steel balls after the impingement on steel substrates. They found that the rebound velocity increased almost linearly with the incident impact velocity. Rebound velocity also decreased if impingement angle increased, which was also reported by Papini and Spelt (1998a) for the impingement of steel spheres on polyamide/polyurethane coatings. This trend was also observed by Slikkerveer (1999) for the impact of alumina powder particles ($d_P = 29\,\mu\text{m}$, $v_P = 110$–$200\,\text{m/s}$) on glass substrates, but the trend held only up to an impact angle of $\varphi = 75°$. If this angle was exceeded, rebound velocity increased with a further increase in impact angle. Interestingly, this author did not measure the rebound behaviour of individual particles, but the rebound characteristics of a particle flow issued from a blast cleaning nozzle ($d_N = 1.5\,\text{mm}$).

Hutchings et al. (1981) reported that the rebound angle increased if incident impact velocity and impact angle increased. Slikkerveer (1999) could, however, show that the rebound angle of alumina powder particles increased with an increase in impact angle. The relationship was linear, whereby a relationship $\varphi_{\text{rebound}} = 0.5 \cdot \varphi$ could be established. This result was not confirmed for the impact of steel spheres on polyamide/polyurethane coatings, where the rebound angle was more or less independent on incident impact angle (Papini and Spelt, 1998a).

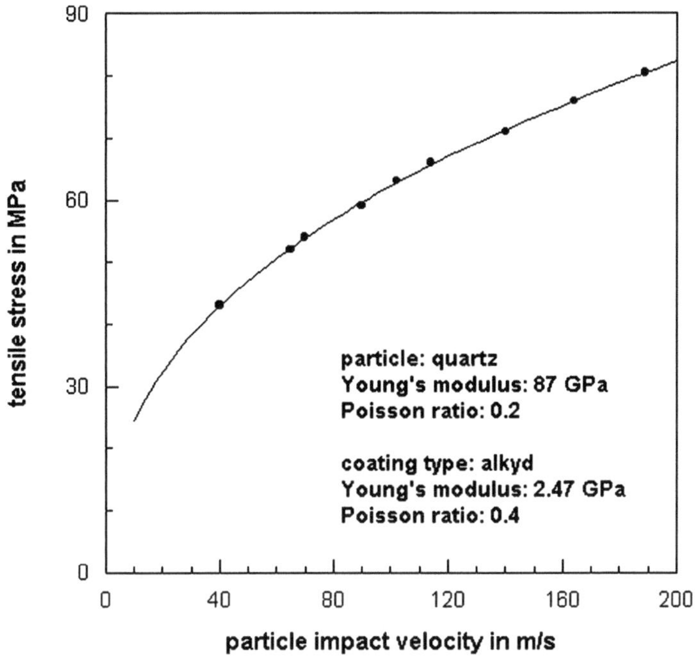

Fig. 5.14 Tensile stresses due to solid particle impingement calculated for a typical substrate-coating arrangement

5.3.3 Energy Absorption

A simple analysis delivers the following subdivision of energy terms:

$$E_P = \frac{m_P}{2} \cdot v_P^2 = \underbrace{\frac{m_P}{2} \cdot v_r^2}_{\text{restitution}} + \underbrace{E_{pp} + E_{ep}}_{\text{particle}} + \underbrace{E_{pm} + E_{em} + E_{0m}}_{\text{target}} + E^* \qquad (5.15)$$

The first subscript "p" stands for plastic deformation, and the first subscript "e" stands for elastic deformation. The second subscript "p" stands for particle, and the second subscript "m" stands for target material. Energy absorption mechanisms related to E^* (surface heating, mechanical activation, light emission) are discussed later in this section.

Figure 5.15 illustrates the situation as expressed by (5.15) and provides a qualitative assessment of the energy situation. The initial kinetic energy of the particle (E_P) is absorbed by both particle (grain) and target material. The energy dissipated by the target is subdivided into elastic deformation energy, plastic deformation energy and the surface energy. The latter parameter is frequently called "fracture energy" and relates to the thermodynamic specific surface energy (see Griffith, 1923). Uetz and Föhl (1978) related this parameter to the erosion rate by assuming $E_R = k_0 \cdot E_{0m}$. It can be seen from Fig. 5.15 that the value for the parameter k_0 depends

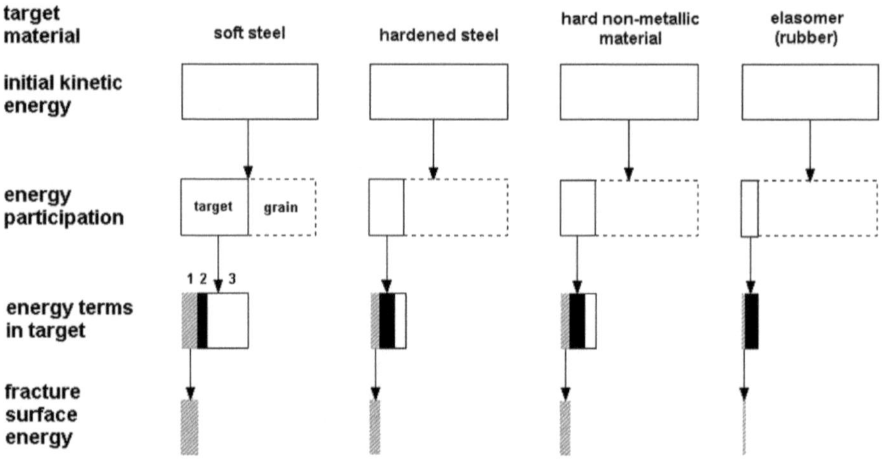

Fig. 5.15 Qualitative proportion of kinetic energy for different target materials during solid particle impinging processes (Uetz and Föhl, 1978). 1 – specific surface energy; 2 – elastic deformation energy; 3 – plastic deformation energy

on the target material. It is rather high for the metals and rather low for the rubber. Figure 5.16 illustrates the situation in a quantitative way for an impinging steel sphere. It can be seen that the concrete energy situation depended on the abrasive materials hardness. The higher this value, the more energy was transferred to the target. For lower abrasive hardness values, a higher amount of energy was transferred to the impinging particle; probably due to permanent plastic deformation of the ball. Hutchings et al. (1976, 1981), Gommel (1967), Uetz and Föhl (1978) and Wellinger and Gommel (1967) performed detailed studies into the energy absorption during abrasive particle impingement.

Hutchings et al. (1981) performed impact experiments with hard steel spheres impinged on soft metals. They found a power relationship between the loss of kinetic energy and particle impact velocity, whereby the power exponent increased if impact angle increased. A model, developed by Hutchings et al. (1976), delivered a power exponent of 2.3 for a steel sphere impinging at an angle of $\varphi = 30°$ on mild steel. These authors also found that the energy loss increased for higher impact angles, whereby the intensity of energy loss was less for higher impact angles.

Gommel (1967b) could show that the energy loss increased if substrate hardness and particle velocity increased. Energy loss was higher for quartz particles compared with steel spheres, which was attributed to the fracture of the brittle pre-damaged quartz. For steel balls, Gommel (1967) found a power-law relationship between the energy loss in the target ($E_{pm} + E_{em}$) and the particle incident impact velocity; with power exponents between 2.4 and 3.3, provided the target material hardness was lower than that of the sphere material.

Illyes and Brauer (1987) defined an abrasive material parameter H_P/Y_M, which was assumed to characterise the type of material response, and found the following relationship between specific energy loss and the material parameter:

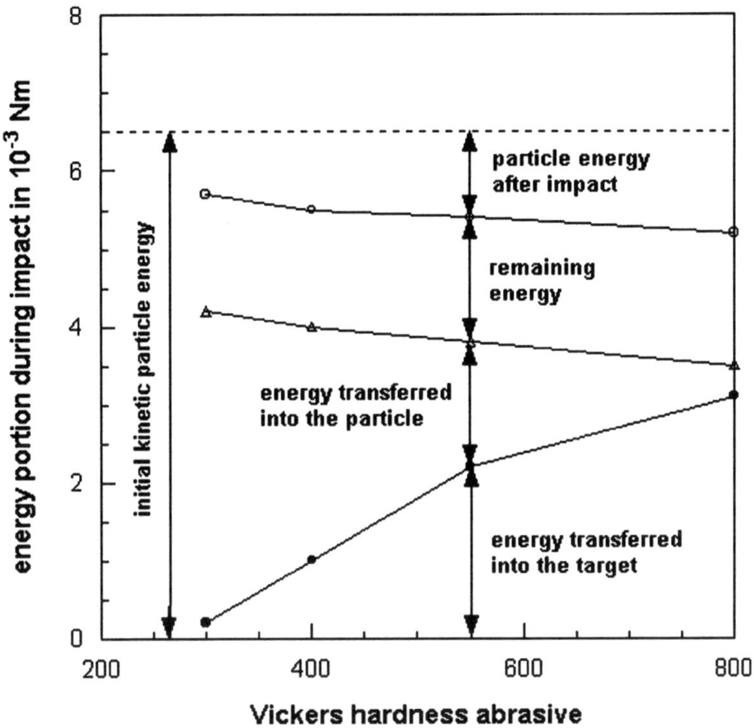

Fig. 5.16 Quantitative proportion of kinetic energy during the impingement of a steel sphere on a steel plate (Uetz and Föhl, 1978)

$$E_I = 1 - 0.125 \cdot \frac{H_P}{Y_M} \tag{5.16}$$

A very similar parameter ratio between hardness and Young's modulus was proposed by Levin et al. (1999).

Uetz and Gommel (1966) performed a study into the temperature increase in the contact zones between steel plates and impinging steel spheres. Results of these investigations are displayed in Fig. 5.17. Temperature values as high as 380°C were measured at the substrate surface. The temperature in the contact zone increased with an increase in impact velocity and a decrease in steel ball diameter. Both heat development and temperature increase are strongly linked to localised plastic deformations in the target material. Gillström and Jarl (2004) impinged steel wires with wheel-driven steel shot ($d_P = 420$–$710\,\mu$m) and measured the temperature rise in the wires as a function of the shot mass flow rate. The authors measured an increase in temperature of up to 75°C, which corresponded to about 33% of the kinetic energy provided by the shot during impact.

Zehnder et al. (1993) performed investigations into the temperature rise in paints during simulated stone impact. Cold rolled steel panels, coated with automobile

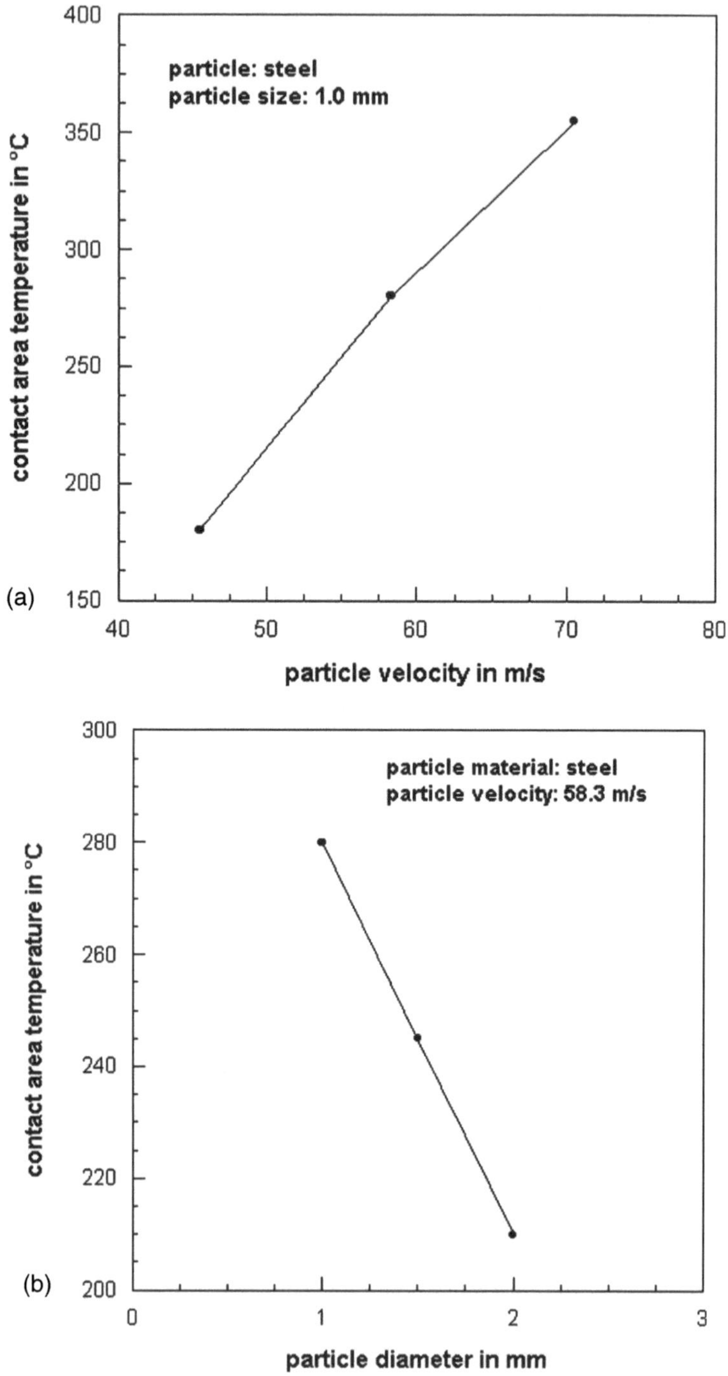

Fig. 5.17 Effects of particle impact parameters on contact temperature (Uetz and Gommel, 1966). (**a**) Effect of particle velocity; (**b**) Effect of particle size

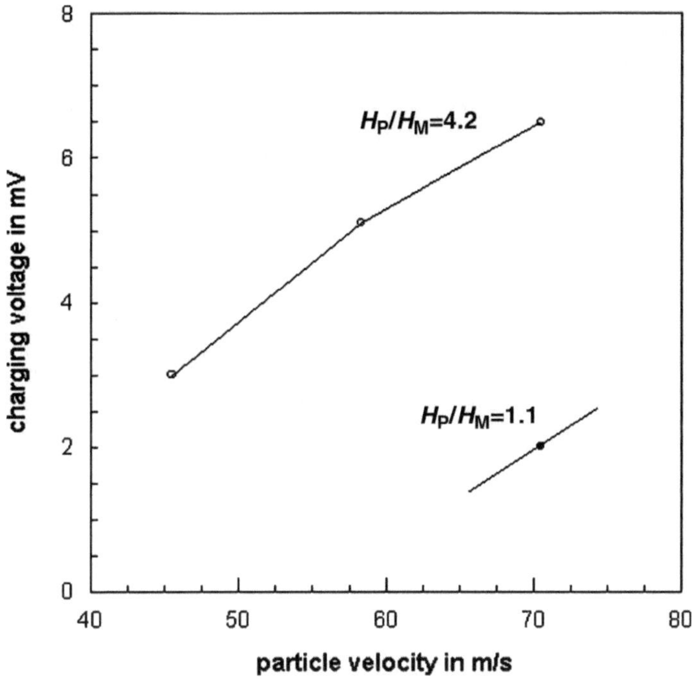

Fig. 5.18 Effects of particle velocity and hardness ratio particle/target on the charging voltage measured during the impingement (Uetz and Gommel, 1966)

paints, were impinged with granite particles at velocities between v_P = 47 and 78 m/s. The temperature rise was as high as 200°C, high enough to put the coatings past their glass transition temperatures.

Uetz and Gommel (1966) measured the mechanical activation of steel plate surfaces during the impingement process. As the results in Fig. 5.18 show, charging voltage increased with an increase in impact speed. The charging process was much more intense if the hardness ratio between impinging particle and impinged plate was high. Spark formation could frequently be observed on more electropositive target materials. Figure 5.19 provides a photograph of sparks produced during the impingement of small sand particles on a titanium alloy surface. The energy absorbed by this process as well as by light emission due to abrasive particle fracture during impingement could not be quantified yet.

5.3.4 Damage Number

Johnson (1972) introduced the following dimensionless number for the assessment of impact processes:

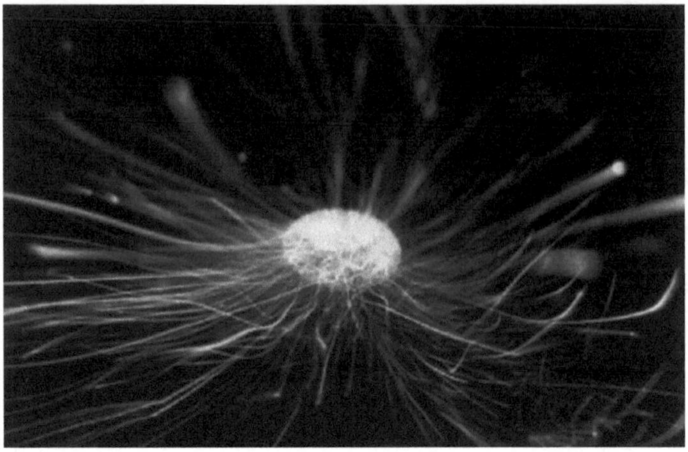

Fig. 5.19 Sparks produced in a titanium alloy impinged by sand particles (Cavendish Laboratory, Cambridge); impact speed: $v_P = 200$ m/s, sand particle diameter: $d_P = 300$–600 µm

$$N_D = \frac{\rho_P \cdot v_P^2}{\sigma_f} \tag{5.17}$$

This *damage number* N_D is a useful guide for assessing the regime of behaviour of metals in impact situations; it can be understood as a measure of the order of strain imposed in the regions were severe plastic deformation occurs. For a typical mild steel, the following regions can be identified: quasi static/elastic regime at $N_D = 10^{-5}$; plastic behaviour starts at $N_D = 10^{-3}$; extensive plastic deformation at $N_D = 10^1$. A weakness attached to the use of the damage number is that no account is taken of projectile nose shape. Walley et al. (1984, 1987) therefore modified this parameter as follows:

$$N_D = \frac{(\chi_G \cdot \rho_P) \cdot v_P^2}{\sigma_f} \tag{5.18}$$

Here, the parameter χ_G is a geometrical factor which can be estimated as follows (Walley et al., 1987):

$$\chi_G = \frac{\text{volume of whole grain}}{\text{volume of part that ploughs the surface}} \tag{5.19}$$

For an irregular quartz particle impinging a polymer surface, the geometrical factor can have a value as high as $\chi_G = 180$ (Walley et al., 1987). If applied to (5.18), this value corresponds to a velocity ratio of about 13. It was in fact noted by Walley et al. (1984, 1987) for polymer materials, that quartz created certain damage features at much lower impact velocities compared with steel balls. This approach, therefore, allows for the scaling of different abrasive materials in terms of failure mapping diagrams (compare Fig. 5.37).

5.3.5 Friction Effects

If a notable horizontal component is involved in the impact process, friction effects between target surface and particle surface become important. The coefficient of friction is the ratio between friction force and normal force. The coefficient of friction for impact conditions can be approximated as follows (Hutchings et al., 1976):

$$\mu_F = \frac{2 \cdot r_P \cdot \omega_P}{5 \cdot (v_P \cdot \sin\varphi + v_{P2} \cdot \sin\varphi_2)} \tag{5.20}$$

This relationship considers the rotation of the impinging particle. A typical value for the pair steel–steel is $\mu_F = 0.04$ (Hutchings et al., 1976).

Ratner and Styller (1981) investigated the effects of impact angle variations on the coefficient of friction. For rather low impact velocities ($v_P = 20\,\text{m/s}$), they found that the coefficient of friction decreased with an increase in impact angle for vulcanised materials. For polymers, in contrast, they found maximum values for the coefficient of friction between $\mu_F = 0.2$ and 0.35 at low impact angles ($\varphi = 30°$ and 40°). The impinging particles were steel beads with a diameter of $d_P = 2\,\text{mm}$.

Friction coefficients for abrasive contact situations for a number of coating materials are listed in Table 5.12. Yabuki and Matsumura (1999) published a number of friction coefficients for particle impingements at low impact velocities. Some of their results are listed in Table 5.13. The authors found that the friction coefficient decreased with an increase in impact velocity, but it rested at a saturation level for velocity values in excess of $v_P = 3\,\text{m/s}$.

Table 5.12 Friction coefficients of organic coating materials (Calabrese and Murray, 1982)

Material	Friction coefficient
Bitumastic	0.03
Epoxy	0.1
Polyethylene	0.05
Polyurethane	0.06
Polyurethane (filled)	0.14
PTFE	0.11
Steel (uncoated)	0.37

Table 5.13 Friction values for particle impingement situations (Yabuki and Matsumura, 1999)

Particle	Particle diameter in μm	Particle velocity in m/s	Target material	Friction coefficient
Steel shot	3,000	0.8	Aluminium	0.22
	3,000	0.9	Brass	0.19
	600	1.4	S45C	0.18
Brass shot	3,000	1.0	Aluminium	0.26
	3,000	1.2	Brass	0.22
	3,000	1.5	S45C	0.17
Steel grit	280	3.0	S45C	0.36
	880	2.1	S45C	0.28
	1,130	1.7	S45C	0.23
Silicone carbide	270	2.7	S45C	0.39
	290	2.3	S45C	0.39
	560	2.3	S45C	0.38
Silica sand	260	2.5	S45C	0.29
	340	2.3	S45C	0.26
	400	2.1	S45C	0.25

5.4 Material Loading Due to Solid Particle Impingement

5.4.1 Loading Parameters

Tensile stresses generated in an elastically responding material by an impinging spherical particle have maximum values at the surface at the edge of contact according to Hertz's (1882) theory for elastic contact:

$$\sigma_T = \frac{(1 - 2 \cdot \nu_M) \cdot F_C}{2 \cdot \pi \cdot a_C^2} \tag{5.21}$$

Here, a_C is the contact radius, and F_C is the contact force. The contact radius is given by:

$$a_C = \left(\frac{3 \cdot k_E \cdot F_C \cdot d_P}{8} \right)^{1/3} \tag{5.22}$$

The contact force generated by an impinging spherical particle can be derived either by applying a force balance (Mintrop, 1941; Timoshenko and Goodier, 1970):

$$m_P \cdot \frac{dv_P}{dt} = -F_C \tag{5.23}$$

or by applying an energy balance (Knight et al. (1977):

$$\frac{2 \cdot \pi \cdot \rho_P \cdot r_P^3}{3} \cdot v_P^2 = \int_0^{z_{max}} F_C(z)\, dz \tag{5.24}$$

A solution to (5.24) is:

$$F_C = \left(\frac{5}{3} \cdot \pi \cdot \rho_P\right)^{3/5} \cdot \left(\frac{3}{4} \cdot k_E\right)^{-2/5} \cdot v_P^{6/5} \cdot \left(\frac{d_P}{2}\right)^2 \quad (5.25)$$

[The relationship $F_C \propto v_P^{6/5}$ was already found by Hertz (1882).] The parameter k_E balances the elastic properties of particle and target material according to (5.14).

A combination of the above-mentioned equations delivers the following relationship between maximum tensile stress and particle velocity:

$$\sigma_T \propto v_P^{2/5} \quad (5.26)$$

Figure 5.14 shows tensile stresses, calculated for typical elastic properties of an organic coating material.

The contact time for an elastic contact was first derived by Hertz (1882) for two spheres with identical properties. Timoshenko and Goodier (1970) offered the following solution (written in a modified form):

$$t_P^E = 2.94 \cdot \left[\frac{5 \cdot \pi \cdot \rho_P}{4} \cdot \left(\frac{1 - \nu_M^2}{Y_M} + \frac{1 - \nu_P^2}{Y_P}\right)\right]^{2/5} \cdot \frac{d_P}{2} \cdot v_P^{-1/5} \quad (5.27)$$

Results of calculations performed with (5.27) are plotted in Fig. 5.20. In reality, however, plastic deformations and fracture processes in particle and target material must be considered. These processes can notably extend the contact time. Thus, a plastic contact time must be added to the elastic contact time. Chaudri and Walley (1978) suggested the following equation for the calculation of the plastic contact time:

$$t_P^{PL} = \frac{\pi}{2} \cdot \left(\frac{m_P}{2 \cdot \pi \cdot r_P \cdot H_{ID}}\right)^{1/2} \quad (5.28)$$

The plastic contact time mainly depends on the dynamic hardness of the target material, and it is independent of the impact velocity. The total contact time is given by:

$$t_P = t_P^E + t_P^{PL} \quad (5.29)$$

An approximation for the strain rates associated with high-speed particle impingement was provided by Hutchings (1977) who derived the following equation:

$$\dot{\varepsilon}_P \cong \frac{2^{3/2}}{2 \cdot \pi} \cdot \frac{v_P^{1/2}}{r_P} \cdot \left(\frac{3 \cdot P_C}{2 \cdot \rho_P}\right)^{1/4} \quad (5.30)$$

The contact pressure in (5.30) can be replaced through the indentation hardness of the target material. The trends for the effects of impact velocity and particle size were experimentally verified by Groß (1988) for aluminium targets. This author

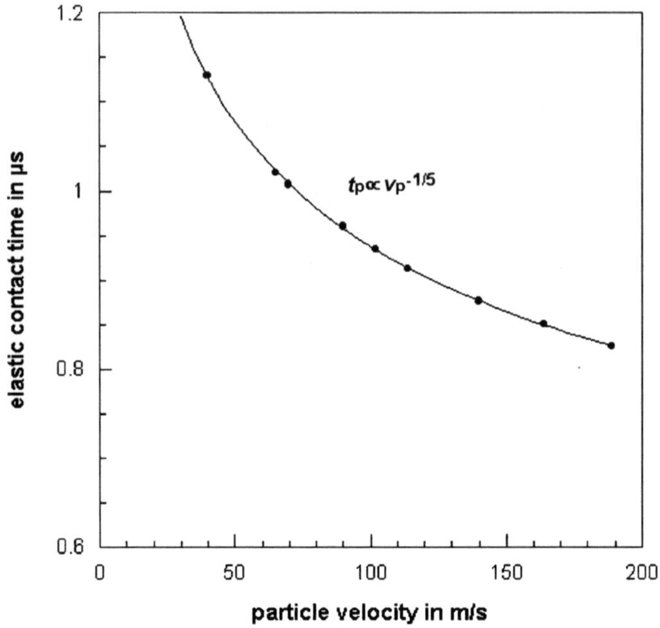

Fig. 5.20 Elastic contact time calculated for a typical substrate-coating arrangement (see Fig. 5.14 for elastic constants)

measured strain rates between $\dot{\varepsilon}_P = 1 \times 10^4$ and 4×10^4 per second for impact velocities up to $\upsilon_P = 130\,\mathrm{m}/s$.

5.4.2 Material Response to Particle Impingement

Depending on the contact situation, materials respond either elastic or plastic to solid particle impingement. Examples are shown in Fig. 5.21. The critical particle velocity for plastic flow during particle impact is (Johnson, 1985):

$$\mathrm{v}_{\mathrm{PL}}^2 = \frac{26 \cdot (\sigma_f/\mathrm{Y_M})^4 \cdot \sigma_f}{\rho_P} \tag{5.31}$$

The threshold particle velocity for Hertzian crack formation can be derived from (5.24) in combination with Auerbach's law ($P_H = A_a \cdot d_P$). This procedure delivers:

$$\mathrm{v_H} = \mathrm{A_a^{5/6}} \cdot \left(\frac{3}{4} \cdot \mathrm{k_E}\right)^{1/3} \cdot \left(\frac{5}{3} \cdot \pi \cdot \rho_P\right)^{-1/2} \cdot \left(\frac{\mathrm{d_P}}{2}\right)^{-5/6} \tag{5.32}$$

Here, A_a is the Auerbach constant. For $\upsilon_H = \upsilon_{PL}$ and $\sigma_f = H_M$, (5.31) and (5.32) deliver the following condition for elastic–plastic transition:

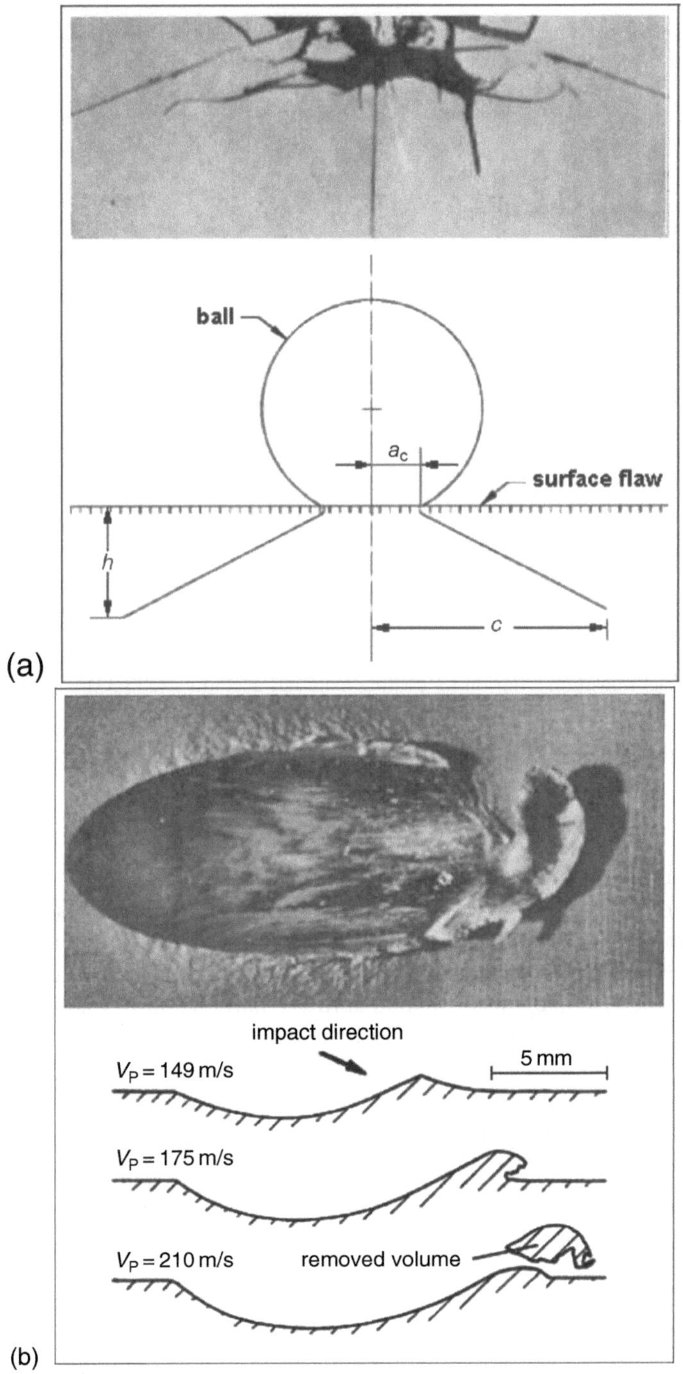

Fig. 5.21 Types of response to solid particle impingement (Aquano and Fontani, 2001). (**a**) Elastic response with cone crack formation; (**b**) Plastic–elastic response at different particle impact velocities ($\varphi = 25°$); the lower drawing is adapted from Winter and Hutchings (1974).

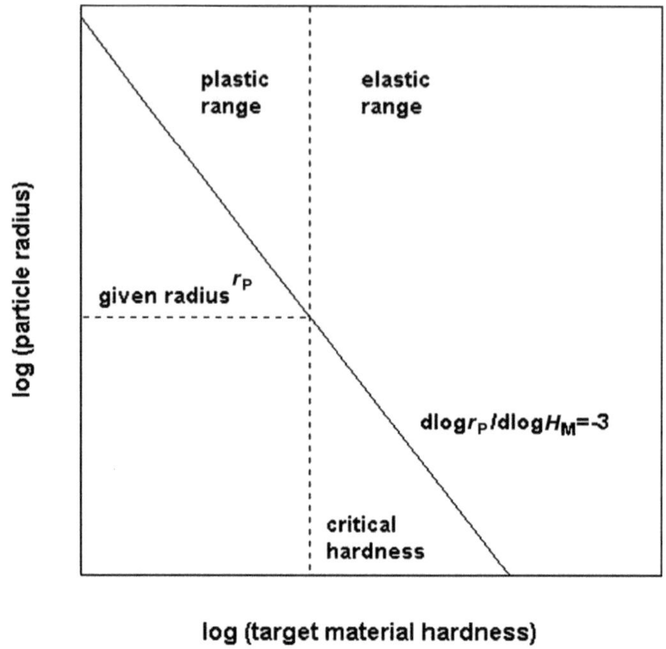

Fig. 5.22 Impact transition criterion for coating materials according to (5.33)

$$\frac{d_{PL}}{2} \propto H_M^{-3} \tag{5.33}$$

This relationship is illustrated in Fig. 5.22. This graph reveals a size and a shape effect for erosion processes. The transition from elastic to plastic response depends on the diameter of the abrasive particles; the smaller the impinging particle, the higher is the probability of plastic response. Also, the higher the curvature of the particle tip (broken, irregularly shaped abrasive particles have high curvature values), the higher is the probability of plastic response.

5.4.3 Formation of Radial and Lateral Cracks

A crack system as shown in Fig. 5.23 forms under certain contact conditions in brittle coatings. *Radial cracks* form in the intermediate surface region of brittle materials if a certain stress level (particle velocity) is exceeded. The formation of a radial crack in a brittle material is illustrated in Fig. 5.24. The figure shows high-speed photographic sequences of the normal impingement of a 1.0-mm diameter glass sphere on a block of soda lime glass. The interframe time was 1 μs. The designation "R" in frame "4" labels the cone and radial cracks formed during the loading. Radial cracks do not lead to material removal, but they reduce strength in

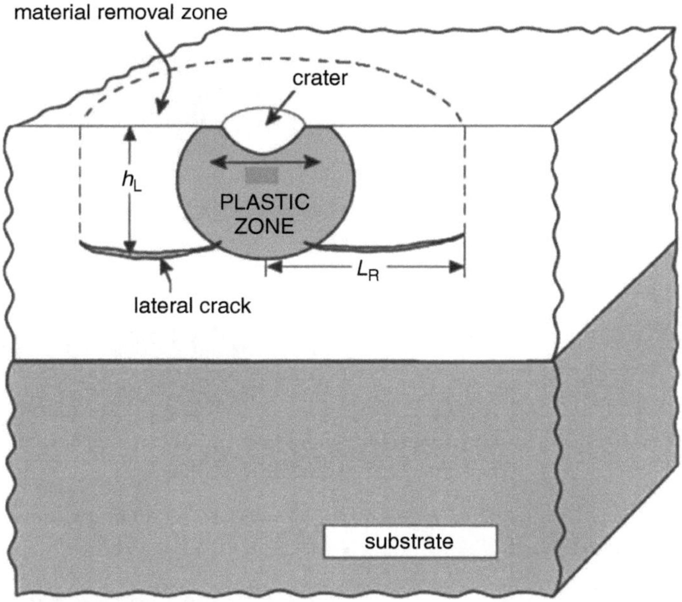

Fig. 5.23 Crack system, formed in the bulk of a brittle coating due to particle impingement (Evans et al., 2006)

the near-surface region. The lengths of these cracks depend on process parameters as follows (Anderson et al., 1993):

$$L_R \propto \frac{d_P^{4/3} \cdot v_P}{K_{Ic}^{2/3}} \tag{5.34}$$

Number and distribution of radial cracks depend on particle velocity, and the relationship between number of cracks and impact velocity is (Kirchner and Gruver, 1978):

$$N_R \propto v_P^{6/5} \tag{5.35}$$

Lateral cracks are critical to material removal processes. They grow from the bottom of the permanent depression during the unloading phase of the contact. They grow into the direction of the surface. If they meet the surface, material is removed. This process is shown in Fig. 5.25. The following two threshold criteria for the formation of lateral cracks were derived by Hutchings (1992). The first criterion reads as:

$$d_P \propto \left(\frac{K_{Ic}}{H_M}\right)^2 \cdot \frac{Y_M^{1/2}}{H_M^{1/4} \cdot \rho_M^{1/4}} \cdot v_P^{-1/2} \tag{5.36a}$$

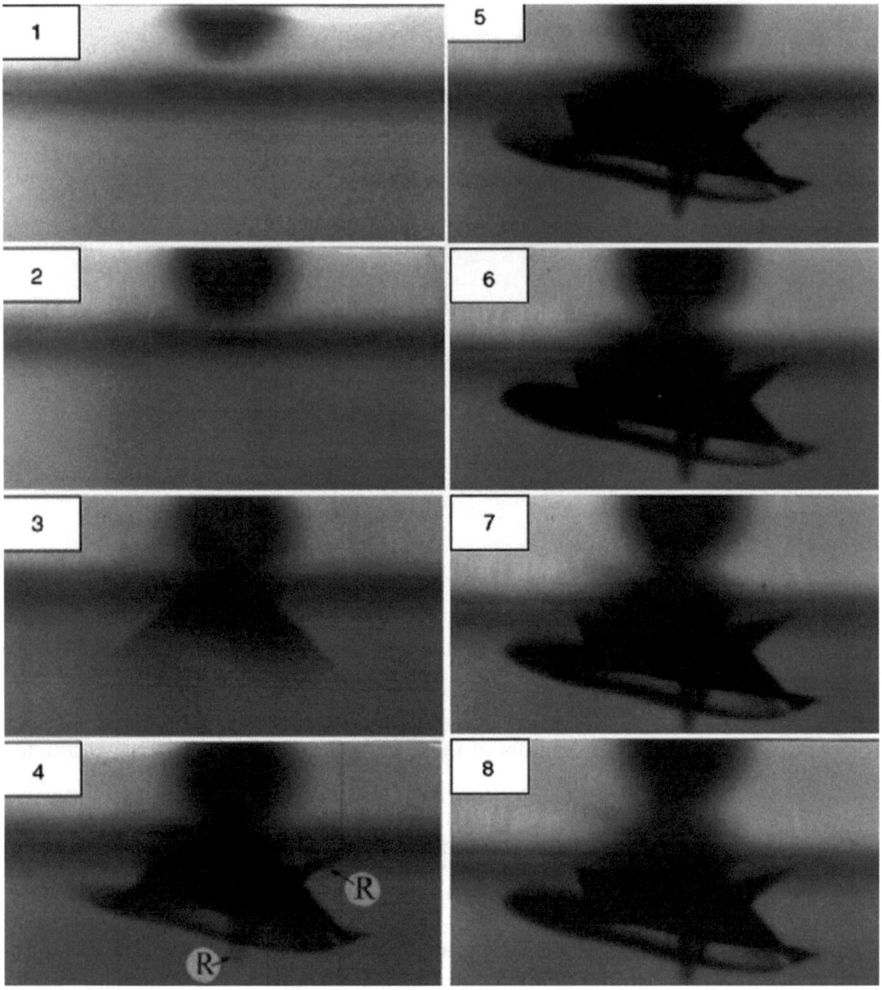

Fig. 5.24 Formation of cone and radial cracks in soda lime glass impinged by a steel sphere at v_P = 140 m/s (Chaudri and Walley, 1978); "R" – cracks

This criterion holds for spherical particles. The second criterion reads as:

$$d_P \propto \left(\frac{K_{Ic}}{H_M}\right)^2 \cdot \frac{Y_M^{1/2}}{H_M^{1/6} \cdot \rho_M^{1/3}} \cdot v_P^{-2/3} \quad (5.36b)$$

This criterion holds for irregular particles. The ratio K_{Ic}/H_M – sometimes referred to as "brittleness" – plays a dominating role. Graphical solutions to (5.36a) and (5.36b) are provided in Fig. 5.26. If the depth, a lateral crack is formed at, is assumed to be equal to the depth of the permanent depression, it can be approximated as follows (Lange and Evans, 1979; Evans et al., 1978):

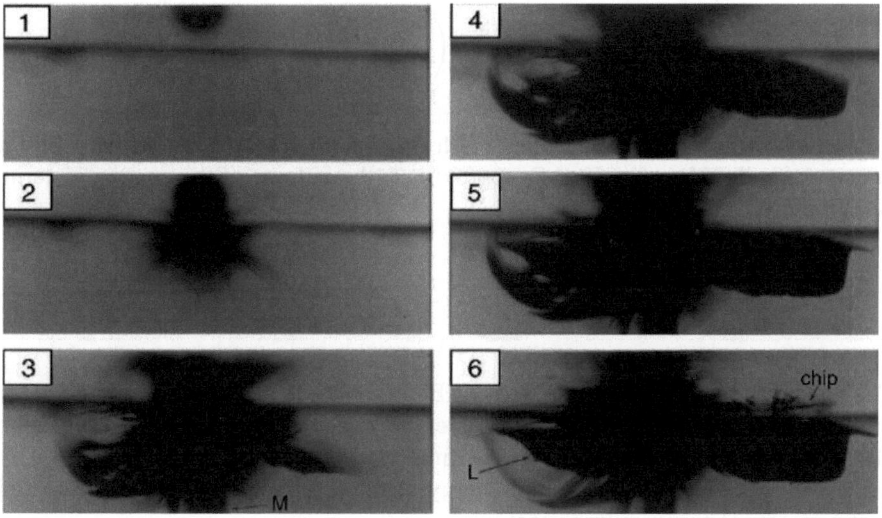

Fig. 5.25 Formation of lateral cracks in soda lime glass impinged by a steel sphere ($d_P = 800\,\mu m$) at $v_P = 300$ m/s (Knight et al., 1977); "L" – lateral crack

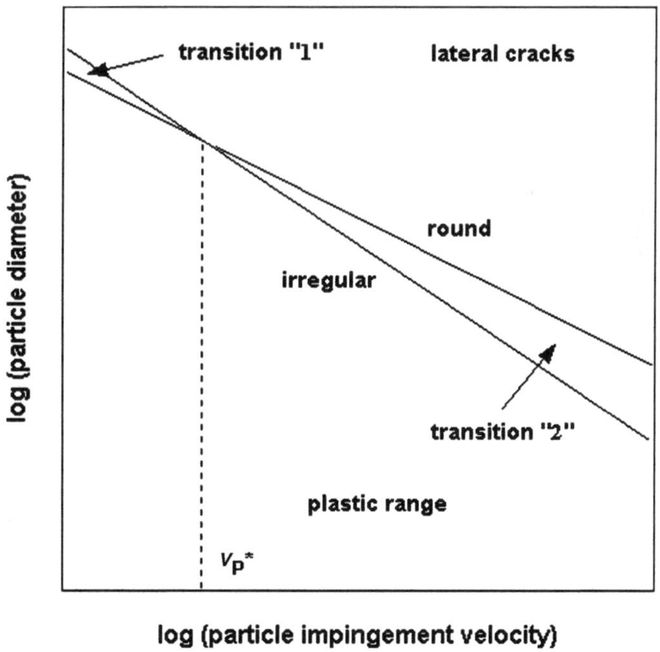

Fig. 5.26 Threshold criteria for lateral crack formation according to (5.36)

$$h_L = \frac{3.5 \cdot d_P}{2} \cdot \left(\frac{\rho_P}{H_M}\right)^{1/4} \cdot v_P^{1/2} \tag{5.37}$$

It can be seen from Fig. 5.23, that length of a radial crack (5.34) and depth of a lateral crack (5.37) can be used to approximate the volume of the coating material being removed from the surface:

$$V_M = \alpha_M \cdot \frac{\pi}{4} \cdot L_R^2 \cdot h_L \tag{5.38}$$

The geometry parameter is $0 < \alpha_M \leq 1$. Equation (5.38) is the basic approach for the modelling of material removal processes due to solid particle impingement in the elastic–plastic response range. More information is provided by Momber (2004a, b). For $h_L = h_C$, the adhesion fracture energy of the interface between substrate and coating material becomes important.

5.5 Material Removal Models

5.5.1 General Aspects of Modelling

The literature about solid-particle erosion is extensive. Adler (1979), Engel (1976) and Preece (1979) presented general reviews about earlier investigations. More recently, Ellermaa (1993) and Meng and Ludema (1995) analysed the state-of-the-art modelling of solid particle erosion. Meng and Ludema (1995) defined four submechanisms by which solid particles separate material from a metal surface. These mechanisms are cutting, fatigue, melting and brittle fracture. Elastic-plastic fracture, as described in Sect. 5.4, must be added as a fifth mechanism. These mechanisms generally do not act separately, but in combination. Their importance for the particular erosion process depends on several factors, such as impact angle, particle kinetic energy, particle shape, target material properties and environmental conditions.

The solid-particle erosion process can generally be characterised by a dimensionless erosion rate:

$$E_R = \frac{m_M}{m_P} \tag{5.39}$$

Thus, the removed volume per solid particle can be defined as follows:

$$V_M = \frac{E_R \cdot m_P}{\rho_M} \tag{5.40}$$

5.5.2 Erosion of Plastically Responding Materials

The material removal process for a plastically responding material is simplified in Fig. 5.27a-c. Examples for a plastic coating response are provided in Fig. 5.3. Magnee (1995) suggested the following generalisation of solid particle erosion models for plastically responding (ductile) materials:

$$V_M \propto \frac{v_P^2 \cdot m_P}{\varepsilon_C} \cdot f\left(\frac{H_P}{H_M}\right) \cdot f(\varphi) \tag{5.41}$$

The effects of the considered abrasive and coating parameters are discussed in Chap. 5.8. An early and often used consideration of the material erosion by micro-cutting is due to Finnie (1958). A typical micro-cutting process is illustrated in Fig. 5.28. The figure shows high-speed photographic sequences of the impingement of a square tool steel plate on a mild steel target at high speed. The interframe time is 19 μm. The plate rotated backwards during impact. Figure 5.29 shows a chip formed during the micro-cutting of low-carbon steel during the impingement with aluminium oxide particles. Finnie (1958) discussed the process by assuming a plastic response character of the material determined by its flow stress. Figure 5.30 shows the basic geometrical and kinematic parameters of this model. After calculating the trajectory

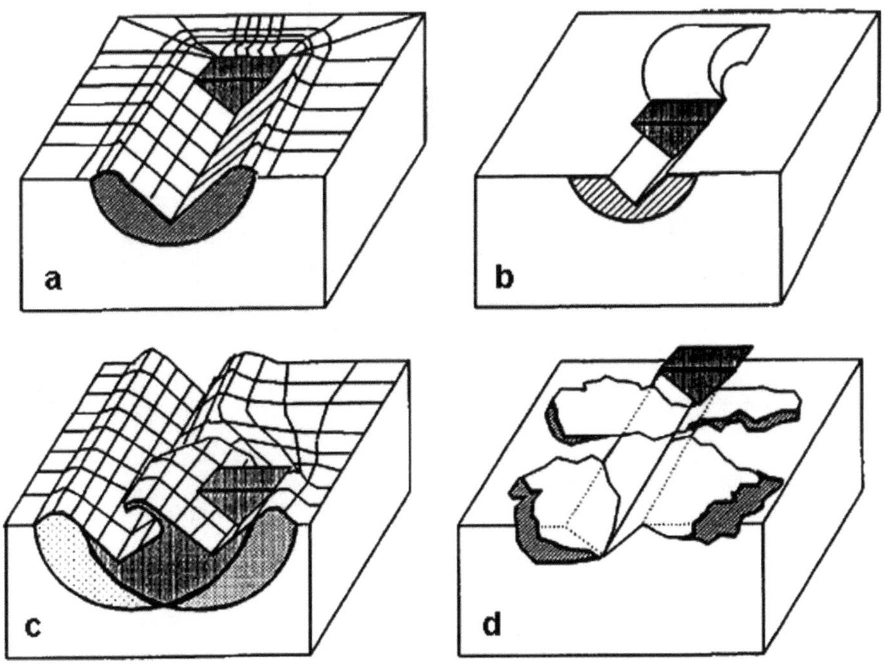

Fig. 5.27 Schematics of material removal in a coating material due to an abrasive particle (adapted from Zum Gahr, 1987). (**a**) Micro-ploughing; (**b**) Micro-cutting; (**c**) Micro-fatigue; (**d**) Micro-fracturing

Fig. 5.28 High-speed photographic images of a micro-cutting process (Hutchings, 1977); v_P = 186 m/s, $\varphi = 30°$.

of a single particle during the removal process, Finnie (1958) derived the following equation for the estimation of the eroded volume:

$$V_M = \frac{m_P \cdot v_P^2}{\sigma_f \cdot K_F \cdot \psi_F} \cdot f(\varphi) \qquad (5.42)$$

$$f(\varphi) = \sin(2 \cdot \varphi) - \frac{6}{K_F} \cdot \sin^2\varphi \left(\text{for } \tan\varphi < \frac{K_F}{6}\right),$$

$$f(\varphi) = \frac{K_F \cdot \cos^2\varphi}{6} \left(\text{for } \tan\varphi > \frac{K_F}{6}\right),$$

$$K_F = \frac{F_Y}{F_X} \cong 2,\ \psi_F \cong 2.$$

Fig. 5.29 Chip formation during the micro-cutting of low-carbon steel (Momber and Wong, 2005b)

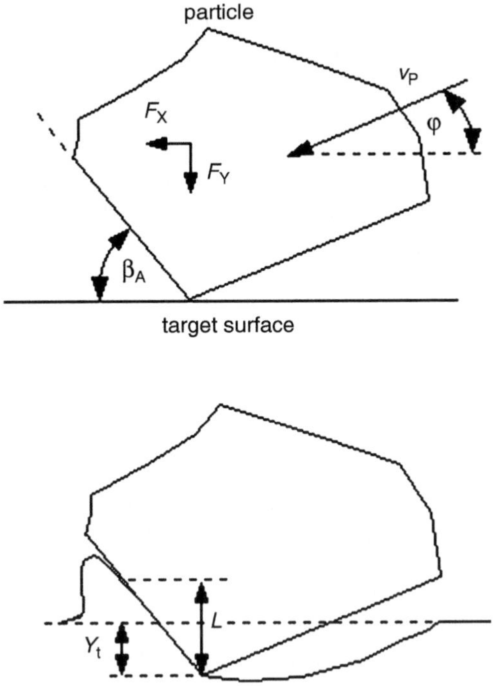

Fig. 5.30 Finnie's (1958) micro-cutting model

Equation (5.42) has the structure of (5.41) when the material's flow stress is replaced by the hardness of the eroded material. The parameter K_F is the ratio of vertical to horizontal force, and $\psi_F = L/y_t$ (Fig. 5.30). Later, Finnie and McFadden (1978) improved the model leading to a particle velocity exponent of about 2.5.

Bitter (1963) developed a more general model. He divided the entire material removal process into two modes, which he called the "cutting wear", that happened at low-impact angles, and "deformation wear", that occurred at high-impact angles. By considering the energies involved in the erosion process, he derived two formulas for both material removal modes. For the "cutting wear" mode, the following relationship was derived:

$$V_{Mcut} = \frac{m_P \cdot [v_P^2 \cdot \cos^2\varphi - C_2 \cdot (v_P \cdot \sin\varphi - v_{EL})^{\frac{3}{2}}]}{2 \cdot \varepsilon_{Ccut}} \qquad (5.43)$$

$$C_2 = f(Y_M, Y_P, \rho_M, \nu_M, \nu_P)$$

For the "deformation wear" mode, the following relationship was derived:

$$V_{Mdef} = \frac{m_P \cdot (v_P \cdot \sin\varphi - v_{EL})^2}{2 \cdot \varepsilon_{Cdef}} \qquad (5.44)$$

The parameter v_{EL} is a threshold impact velocity which must be exceeded to introduce the material removal process. For certain conditions, (5.43) is equal to (5.41). Neilson and Gilchrist (1968b) later simplified this model.

Hutchings (1979b) introduced an alternative discussion of the micro-cutting processes during particle-induced erosion. Based on high-speed photographs and SEM observations, he defined two modes of material removal due to micro-cutting, namely "cutting-deformation" and "ploughing-deformation". The ploughing-deformation mode dominates the material removal by spherical particles, whereas cutting-deformation is significant for sharp-edged, angular particles. Hutchings (1979b) made a further subdivision of the cutting-deformation mode into "type I cutting-deformation" and "type II cutting-deformation", depending on the direction of the particle rotation. For forward rotating particles, "type I" is dominant, and for backward rotation, "type II" is valid (see Fig. 5.21b). Hutchings (1979b) also developed a solid-particle erosion model for normal impact that is based on low-cycle fatigue. Gane and Murray (1979) developed an approach for the transition from a ploughing mode to a cutting mode of erosion. The transition was considered to occur at a critical angle (β_A) between particle face and target surface (see Fig. 5.30). For high values of the face angle, the friction between target material and abrasive face are low, and chip formation is the dominant material removal mode.

The plastic work associated with the deformation of a material around the impact site largely degrades into heat. Hutchings and Levy (1989) gave a review about thermal effects in solid-particle erosion of ductile materials. It appeared from their discussion that thermally determined features of the solid-particle erosion process were not a necessary assumption under all impact conditions. With smaller particles at low impact velocities, for example, thermal effects were not important.

Ellermaa (1993) performed a critical review of solid-particle erosion models developed for the estimation of the materials removal in plastically responding materials. As she has shown, Finnie's model especially exhibited a comparatively high divergence from experimentally estimated values, illustrating that a simple micro-cutting process does not cover the complexity of the material removal process. This result is in agreement with results of erosion debris morphology measurements performed by Momber and Wong (2005b). Based on erosion tests on low carbon steel, the authors found that micro-cutting played a negligible role only, and that about 60% of all acquired debris were of a platelet-type shape as suggested by Bellmann and Levy (1981).

Levin et al. (1999) derived the following relationship for the erosion response of metal alloys:

$$\dot{V}_M \propto \frac{\text{energy used for plastic deformation}}{\text{energy required to cause fracture}} \propto \frac{1 - H_M}{T_D} \tag{5.45}$$

The two material parameters must be estimated from dynamic stress–strain curves (see Fig. 5.4c). In materials with high hardness, the transformation of impact energy into the impinged material is reduced. For high toughness values, more energy is dissipated before the material fractures.

Andrews and Field (1982) discovered and described a certain material removal mode for soft materials (mild steel). Based on high-speed camera images, they showed that single hardened steel spheres could remove material even when they stroke the targets at normal impingement. Material loss occurred by the rapid radial expansion (jetting) of material from under the spheres. This mechanism of erosion is most likely when the deformation is highly localised.

Carter et al. (1991) performed experiments into the effects of reflected abrasive particles on the erosion process for ductile materials. For impact angles larger than $\varphi = 20°$, no observable signs of reflection efficient enough to cause erosion on the receiving erosion plane were detected. The authors did not observe mirror reflection, but rather reflection angles much smaller than the incident angles. The severity of the secondary erosion due to reflected abrasive particles depended on the incident impact angle. Relative to the erosion rate of direct incidence, the secondary erosion was: 50% for $\varphi = 20°$; 15% for $\varphi = 15°$ and 34% for $\varphi = 5$–$10°$. These results were valid for copper targets impinged by corundum particles ($d_P = 30\,\mu m$).

5.5.3 Erosion of Elastically Responding Materials

The material removal process for an elastically responding material is simplified in Fig. 5.27d. An example for the elastic response of an organic coating material is provided in Fig. 5.3a. Erosion models for elastically responding (brittle) materials are well established. The most important material parameters which control the erosion process were identified based mainly on developments in indentation fracture mechanics (Lawn, 1993). The general equation for the material removal in elastically responding materials by an impacting solid particle is given through (5.38).

The erosion model developed by Evans et al. (1978), and the elastic–plastic theory of Wiederhorn and Lawn (1979), related the volume loss to the depth of particle penetration and the maximum size of the lateral cracks which form during impact (Figs. 5.27a and 5.23), whereby it was assumed that the depth of the lateral cracks is proportional to the size of the radial cracks.

Most of the models developed for the erosion by brittle fracture follow the general relation:

$$V_M \propto \left(\frac{d_P}{2}\right)^{C_2} \cdot v_P^{C_3} \cdot H_M^{C_4} \cdot K_{Ic}^{C_5} \cdot Y_M^{C_6} \tag{5.46}$$

Table 5.14 lists the power exponents of the different models related to (5.46).

Table 5.14 Solid particle erosion models for brittle-behaving materials, (5.46)

Model	Reference	c_2	c_3	c_4	c_5	c_6
Elastic model	Sheldon and Finnie (1966)	f(M)[a]	f(M)[a]	–	–	–
Quasi-static lateral crack model	Wiederhorn and Lawn (1979)	3.67	2.45	0.11	−1.33	–
Dynamic lateral crack model	Evans et al. (1978)	3.67	3.17	−0.25	−1.33	–
Modified lateral crack model	Marshall et al. (1982)	3.50	2.33	−1.42	−1.00	1.25

[a] Depends on material structure

5.6 Erosion of Scale

5.6.1 Brittle Erosion Approach

Scale is considered here to be a system of brittle, elastically responding layers that forms on a ductile substrate. In cases, such as for duplex nickel, scale consists of a dense outer and a porous inner layer. The removal of scale is typical of a brittle material. This is verified by Fig. 5.31 which shows partly eroded scale from a low-carbon steel substrate. The formation of crack can be recognised in the untreated scale (upper right region) as well as in the partly eroded scale (lower right region). Levy (1995) noted a mixed response of scale subjected to solid particle impingement, including plastic indentation and the formation of lateral and radial cracks in the outer scale layer, and the formation of Herzian ring cracks in the inner scale layer (see Sect. 5.4). These phenomena are illustrated in Fig. 5.32. Cone cracks form under initial plastically deformed craters. All of this action serves to divide the scale into a mosaic of small, cracked areas that can be removed from the surface by subsequent particle impingement.

From investigations of relatively thick nickel oxide scale, it was determined that scales eroded sequentially down through their thickness by a cracking and chipping mechanism rather than being knocked off the metal in pieces at the scale–metal interface. This incremental erosion process is illustrated in Fig. 5.33 for a thin (20 μm) and thick (100 μm) scale. It can be seen that the scale has a threshold period where the scale is being cracked, but none has been removed. At "E1" for the 100-μm

Fig. 5.31 Scale removal from low-carbon steel; crack formation visible at several locations. (Photo: author)

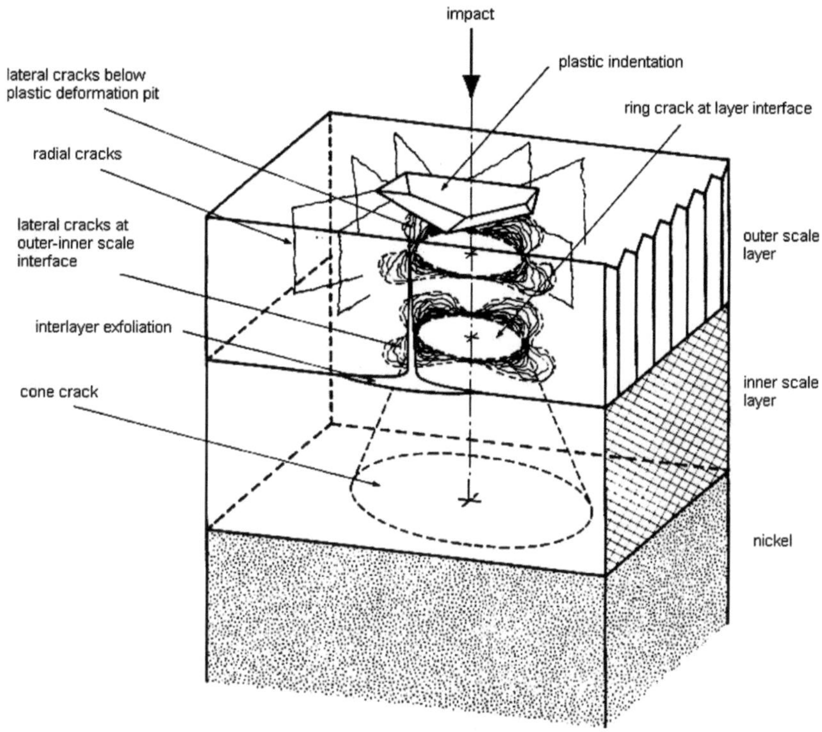

Fig. 5.32 Material removal scheme for scale (Levy, 1995)

scale, weight loss begins to occur. At "E2", the weight loss is primarily that of the dense outer scale layer that occurs at a lower rate than at "E3". At "E3", the particles are eroding the porous inner scale layer, and a maximum erosion rate can be recognised. The 20-μm scale had only the dense outer scale. It reaches its relatively low peak erosion rate nearly compared to the 100-μm scale, and it then fell off rapidly.

The presence of the ductile metal substrate did not appear to have a major effect on the way the brittle scale eroded. However, the ductile substrates had a small effect. The thinner scales could transfer more of the kinetic energy of the impinging particles to the ductile nickel and, hence, they cracked and chipped and eroded at lower rates than the thicker scale. As the thicker scales were removed, their rates of erosion decreased to a rate that became nearly the same for all scale thickness values.

5.6.2 Removal Mechanisms and Modelling

Schmithals (1961) performed a systematic investigation into the removal modes of mill scale during blast cleaning. He derived the following equation for the estimation of rest scale on rolled steel panels as a function of blast cleaning time:

$$m_{SC} = (1 - K_S)^{t_B} \qquad (5.47)$$

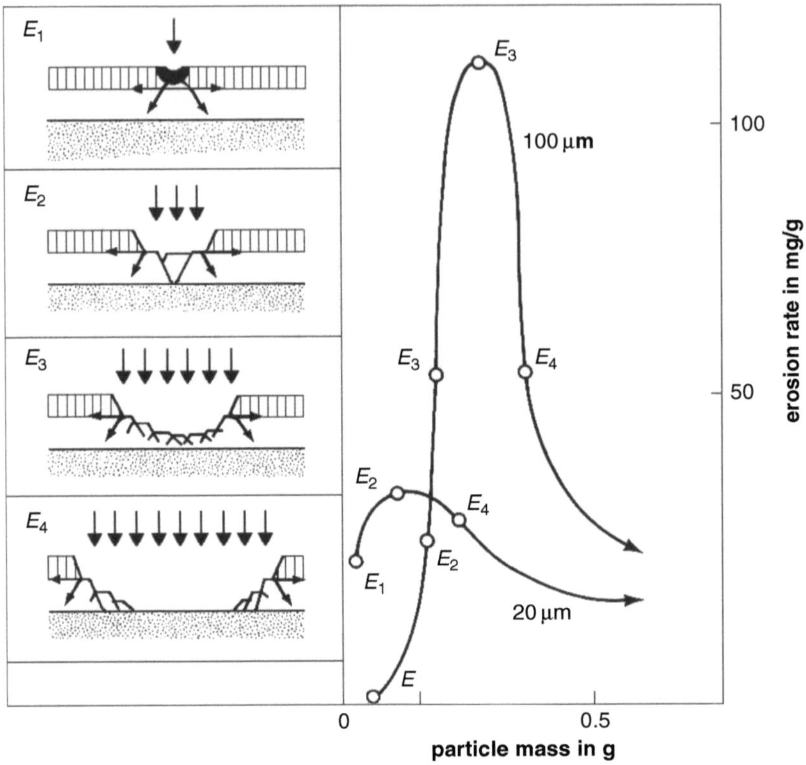

Fig. 5.33 Incremental erosion of nickel oxide scale (Levy, 1995). Impact angle: $\varphi = 90°$

The parameter K_S characterises the resistance of mill scale against blast cleaning. A typical value for this parameter was $K_S = 0.48$. The mass loss of mill scale as a function of abrasive mass follows a typical relationship as shown in Fig. 5.34. The function can be subdivided into two sections: a progressively increasing branch (I) and a linear branch (II). The intersection between these two branches characterises the limit for the complete removal of the mill scale. The linear part of the function is a result of plain steel removal only. The intersection point, characterised by m_E, expresses the mass of abrasive material required to generate a completely mill scale free-steel substrate. Its value depends on the chemical composition of the mill scale. Experimentally estimated results are listed in Table 5.15. In descaling practice, the parameter m_E showed a linear relationship to the specific abrasive mass flow, and an inverse relationship to the traverse speed of the blast cleaning tool required to obtain scale free surfaces (Schmithals, 1961).

Schmithals (1961) distinguished three basic material removal mechanisms for mill scale, which are shown in Fig. 5.35. In case (I), scale is removed at the impinged area, but also on locations further away from the impacted area. In case (II), scale removal is restricted to the impinged area only. In case (III), scale is pressed into the substrate surface, and the pressurised scale band is cracked. In the latter case, the

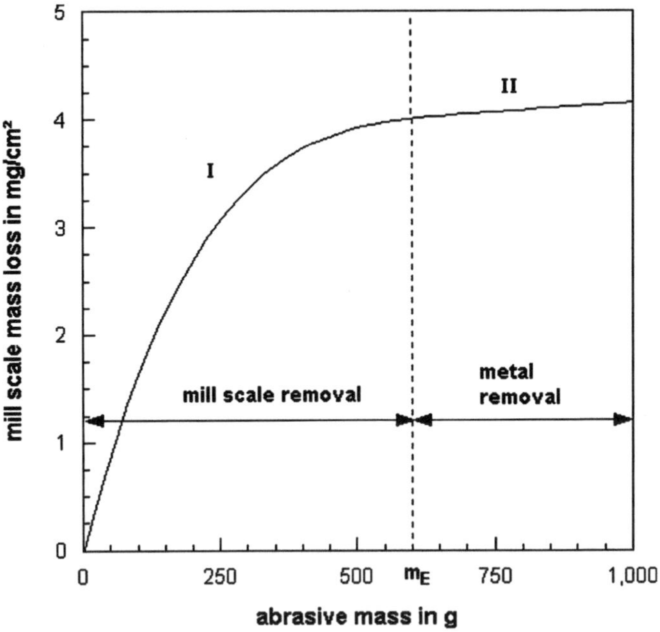

Fig. 5.34 Relation between mill scale mass loss and abrasive mass (Schmithals, 1961)

parameter m_E showed rather high values. If mill scale is being removed according to mechanism (I), the removal process can reliably be modelled with (5.47). If the two other mechanisms were applied, experimental results differed widely from the theoretical results of (5.47).

5.6.3 Removableness of Mill Scale

Rädeker and Wild (1958) performed a study into the removableness of mill scales of different steel types. Surface preparation methods considered in this study included

Table 5.15 Descaling parameter m_E and chemical composition of mill scale (Schmithals, 1961)

Chemical composition of mill scale in %					m_E in g
C	Si	Mn	P	S	
0.05	0.02	0.35	0.018	0.026	605
0.03	0.01	0.31	0.012	0.010	515
0.07	0.01	0.39	0.031	0.014	330
0.08	0.01	0.33	0.013	0.027	370
0.41	0.94	0.97	0.027	0.024	355
1.30	0.24	0.32	0.017	0.010	335
0.05	0.01	0.27	0.040	0.028	515
0.05	0.01	0.36	0.049	0.026	675

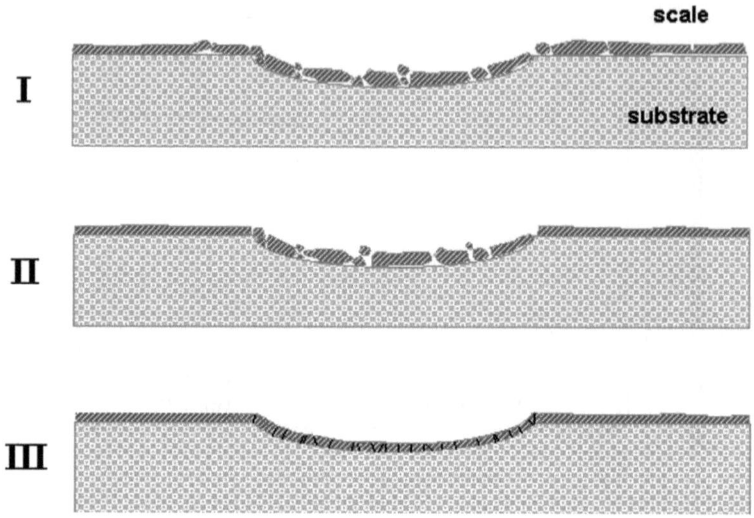

Fig. 5.35 Material removal mechanisms for mill scale during blast cleaning (Schmithals, 1961)

acid pickling, blast cleaning and flame cleaning. For the blast cleaning process, removableness was defined as the number of blast cleaning steps required to completely remove the mill scale. The authors found that the rolling temperature did not affect the removableness in a systematic way. Especially, the scale of unkilled steels did not show any relationship to the rolling temperature. A better correlation was found between the removableness and the adhesion of the mill scale to the core steel (see Fig. 5.9 for typical adhesion strength values). With the exception of some Si–Al-steel, the removableness decreased with an increase in adhesion. Adhesion is, however, not the only criterion for the removableness of mill scale. Manufacturing regime and composition of steel and mill scale affect this parameter as well.

Peltzer (1955) gave some recommendations about the particle size of metallic abrasives for effective removal of mill scale. He found that the optimum blast cleaning abrasive size depended on the plate thickness. For coarse plates (thickness between 2.8 and 6.4 mm), he recommended a particle size of about $d_P = 500\,\mu m$; for moderate plates (thickness between 1.3 and 2.8 mm), he recommended a particle size smaller than $d_P = 200\,\mu m$.

5.7 Erosion of Bulk Polymers and Elastomers

5.7.1 Material Removal Mechanisms for Bulk Polymers

Figure 5.36 illustrates different material removal modes in polymers impinged by solid particles. Zhang et al. (1995) investigated the response of a number of polymers to abrasive erosion and identified different material removal mechanisms,

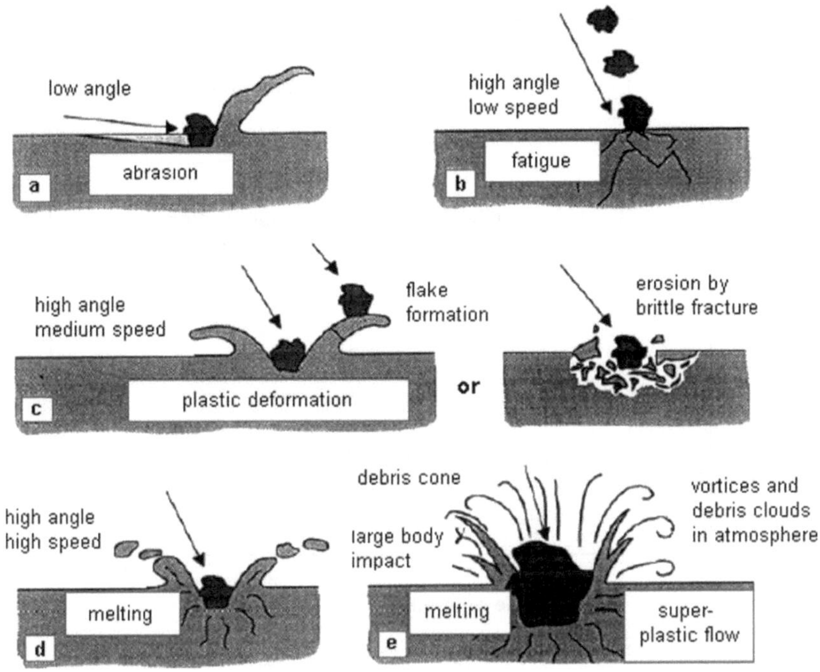

Fig. 5.36 Material removal modes in polymers, impinged by solid particles (Barkoula and Karger-Kocsis, 2002)

namely micro-cutting, micro-delamination and surface peeling. On *polyurethane* surfaces, indentations and scratches were found as results of micro-cutting. The formation of cracks was also noted which nucleated probably from the fracture of intermolecular chains. On *Nylon-6* surfaces, scratches due to micro-cutting, but also some amount of small plastically deformed areas were found. On *polytetraflourethylene* surfaces, material removal occurred due to ploughing and scratch formation, accompanied by plastic deformation.

The erosion of bulk *polyethylene* (PE), *polypropylene* (PP) and *polyetheretherketone* (PEEK) through abrasive particles was in some detail investigated by Walley and Field (1987) and Walley et al. (1984, 1987). They found that PEEK showed less damage in single particle erosion than either PE or PP and explained this observation by the liability of the PEEK to brittle failure. Based on single impact experiment and discussions of crater morphology, the authors identified numerous material removal mechanisms, and they classified these mechanisms as functions of particle impact velocity and angle. Results for PE are illustrated in Fig. 5.37. Smooth craters, which were observed at rather low impact speeds, were defined to be those where very little surface modification has taken place. In a narrow range of shallow impact angles, a regular series of bands of displaced material was observed. As the impact angle raised, the bands became fewer, and most of the displaced material ended up at the end of the crater as a lip. At high impact angles, penetration and, respectively,

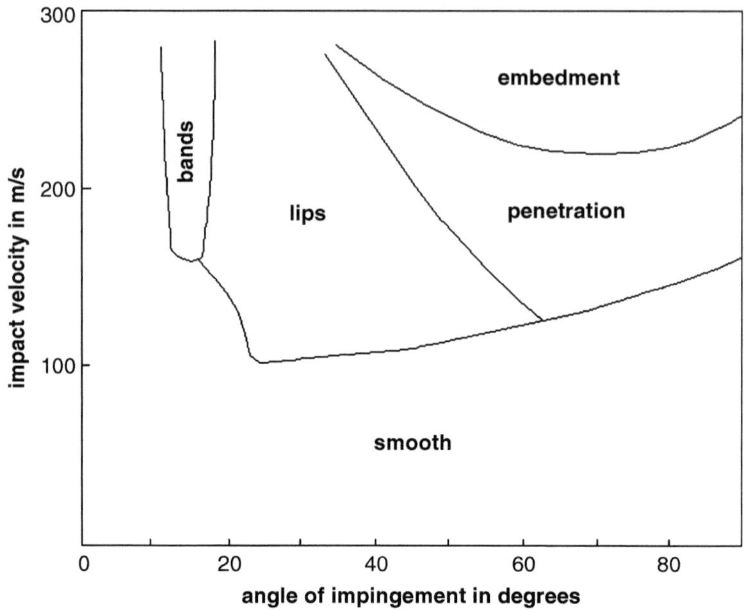

Fig. 5.37 Erosion mechanisms for polymer materials (Walley and Field, 1987)

embedment of spherical abrasives took place. The impact velocity needed to cause the latter two mechanisms to occur had a minimum at an impact angle of about $\varphi = 70°$. Walley et al. (1984, 1987) applied the damage number according to (5.18) for the construction of general damage maps for polymers (see Sect. 5.3.4).

From the geometry point of view, craters could be classified into four types: smooth; ploughed; cut and sharply dented. The frequency of occurrence of the certain geometry depended mainly on impact angle as verified by the results listed in Table 5.16 for PE and PEEK.

For PE, lip volume and crater volume increased with increasing impact velocity according to a power function:

$$V_M \propto v_P^{\alpha_B} \tag{5.48}$$

The power exponent had values $\alpha_B = 2.77$ for the crater volume and $\alpha_B = 2.8$ for the lip volume (Walley and Field, 1987). The specific energy for lip formation as well as for crater formation decreased with increasing impact velocity implying that a greater fraction of the energy dissipated went into permanent material displacement as the velocity rose. For an impact velocity $v_P = 200\,\mathrm{m/s}$, the specific energy values were about $0.4\,\mathrm{J/mm^3}$ for crater formation, and about $1.1\,\mathrm{J/mm^3}$ for lip formation (Walley and Field, 1987). Scratch deformation maps for polymers, very similar to that shown in Fig. 5.37, are issued by Briscoe and Sinha (2003).

Aspects of thermal effects were also investigated by Walley and Field (1987). Based on a heat transfer analysis, they found that a particle impact frequency of

Table 5.16 Percentage of crater types in bulk polymers for various impact angles; see Fig. 5.37 (Walley et al., 1987; Walley and Field, 1987)

Impact angle in °	Percentage of crater type in %							
	Smooth		Ploughed		Cut		Sharply dented	
	PE[a]	PEEK[b]	PE	PEEK	PE	PEEK	PE	PEEK
10	45		30		11		14	
20	28	62	43	21	22	14	7	3
30	42	37	40	32	5	24	13	6
40	62	42	21	47	4	10	13	1
50	68	35	14	46	5	16	13	2
60	80	14	7	59	4	22	9	6
70	90	36	6	46	0	16	4	3
80	86		3		1		10	
90	90	31	5	46	0	21	5	2

[a] Polyethylene
[b] Polyetheretherketone

about 11/s was required to build up enough heat in PE to make thermal effects become significant. This frequency corresponded to a rather high flux rate of about 180 kg/(m^2 s). Measurements delivered real impact frequencies between 0.4 and 1.2 per second; thus one order of magnitude is too low for thermal effects to play a significant role.

5.7.2 Material Removal Mechanisms for Elastomers

Arnold and Hutchings (1992, 1993), Besztercey et al. (1999) and Hutchings et al. (1987) investigated the behaviour of rubber materials during the erosion by impinging abrasive particles. The major mechanism identified by the authors was the propagation of fatigue cracks. The fatigue cracks propagated under the action of tensile stresses generated during particle impact. Crack nucleation could, for example, occur at the interfaces between rubber matrix and filler particles (Besztercey et al., 1999). The individual cracks formed a dense net on the surface as verified by SEM imaging studies (Arnold and Hutchings, 1992, 1993). An example is shown in Fig. 5.38. When individual cracks intersected, material was being detached. The depth of cracked layers in rubber was typically between 10 and 150 μm, and the crack separation distance was typically between 2 and 30 μm. Both parameters depended on abrasive particle diameter; if abrasive size increased, these parameters increased almost linearly (Arnold and Hutchings, 1993).

Hutchings et al. (1987) noted that the concrete material removal modes in rubber depended on the resilience of the materials. High-resilience rubbers formed distinctive surface ridges on erosion at $\varphi = 30°$, similar to features seen on abraded rubber surfaces and possibly indicative of a similar cyclic crack growth mechanism caused by the tangential component of the impact force. Rounded particles of rubber, which

Fig. 5.38 SEM image of an eroded rubber surface, showing fatigue cracks (Arnold and Hutchings, 1992); impact direction from the left, $v_P = 100\,m/s$, $d_P = 120\,\mu m$, $\varphi = 30°$, abrasive: silica

probably provided a source of material loss, formed at the peaks of these ridges. The surfaces of low-resilience rubbers eroded at the same angle, were in contrast much more uniformly roughened, showing evidence of apparently loosely attached angular rubber fragments distributed over the surface, and numerous cracks and fissures. The occurrence of these cracks, which were not seen on the high-resilience rubbers, suggested that erosion may have proceeded by a catastrophic tearing process.

Arnold and Hutchings (1989) found that the flux rate (respectively impact frequency) had strong effects on the erosion regime in rubber, especially if glass beads were used. The strain produced by a single impact was insufficient to cause material removal, and successive impacts were necessary to raise the strain to a sufficient level to cause material removal. The authors also noted an incubation period at low flux rates, within no material was removed, but a darkened area was found on the surfaces of the samples. Infrared spectra delivered evidence for environmental degradation; considerable amounts of oxygen were incorporated into the surface of the elastomers.

5.7.3 Erosion Resistance of Bulk Polymers

Kriegel (1968) derived a material resistance model, which he applied to polymeric materials. An erosion resistance parameter based on this model includes the following parameters:

$$R_E \propto \underbrace{\frac{Y_M}{\rho_P \cdot v_P^2}}_{\text{energy number}} \cdot \underbrace{\frac{v_P}{\dot{N}_P \cdot d_P}}_{\text{frequency number}} \cdot \underbrace{\frac{\sigma_V}{Y_M}}_{\text{strength number}} \tag{5.49}$$

The unit of the erosion resistance is s/mm in (5.49). A similar approach was made by Urbanovich et al. (1995). The strength number in (5.49) balances "erosion strength" (σ_V) and Young's modulus of the target material. The erosion strength is defined as follows:

$$\sigma_V = \frac{\sigma_T - \sigma_{0.1}}{Y_M} \cdot \sigma_T \tag{5.50}$$

In that equation, σ_T is the tensile strength and $\sigma_{0.1}$ is the stress at the elastic limit for a deformation of 0.1%. A combination of (5.49) with (5.50) delivers the following relationship:

$$E_R \propto Y_M^{-1} \tag{5.51}$$

Experimental results displayed in Fig. 5.39 verify this approach: erosion resistance decreased if Young's modulus of the polymeric materials increased. It may be mentioned that this particular trend was observed by Kriegel (1968) and Brauer and Kriegel (1963) for plastics only. For many metals, and especially for brittle materials, an opposite trend was noted.

Cizmas and Slattery (2006) assumed a visco-elastic deformation behaviour and applied a dimensionless analysis to the solid particle erosion of polymers. They introduced a dimensionless modulus of elasticity $[Y_M/(\rho_M \cdot v_P^2)]$ and found that this

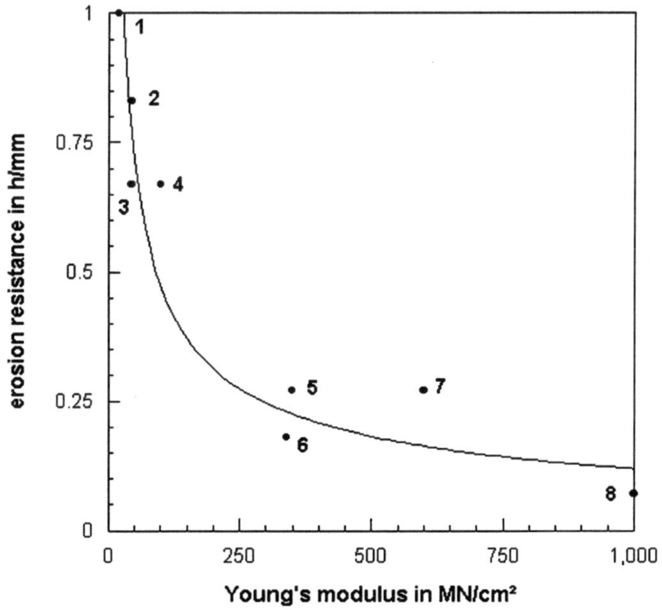

Fig. 5.39 Relationship between Young's modulus of polymeric materials and erosion resistance (Kriegel, 1968). Materials: 1 – soft polyethylene; 2 and 3 – hard polyethylene; 4 – polyamide; 5 – PMMA; 6 – PVC; 7 – phenolic polymer; 8 – epoxy + quartz dust

parameter was proportional to the erosion resistance for a given group of polymers. This approach verifies the "energy number" derived in (5.49).

Böhm et al. (1990) found that the resistance of polymeric materials against abrasion and solid particle erosion reduced if the elongation to tensile fracture increased. Results of their investigation are displayed in Fig. 5.40.

A negative correlation between erosion resistance and hardness was found by Kriegel (1968) for PVC samples, and by Miyazaki (1996) for thermoplastic polyimide resins: erosion resistance decreased if hardness (Shore hardness; Vickers hardness) rose. Results are displayed in Fig. 5.41. Miyazaki (1996) explained this behaviour through the fact that softer polymers could absorb higher amounts of the kinetic energy of the impinging particles prior to fracture. Degree of crystallinity was also important: if the structure changed from an amorphous structure to a crystalline structure, erosion resistance dropped (see Fig. 5.41). This was because hardness increased with a rise in the degree of crystallinity (Miyazaki, 1996).

Friedrich (1986) investigated the resistance of a number of polymers against particle impingement, and he suggested that the ratio H_M/G_{Ic} (denoted "brittleness index" by the author) provides a better indication of erosion resistance than hardness alone. Results of his measurements are provided in Fig. 5.42. It can be seen that the ratio between hardness and fracture energy is a good indication of the erosion resistance of different polymer materials for a wide range of process conditions. The fracture energy of polymers is closely related to the cross-link density

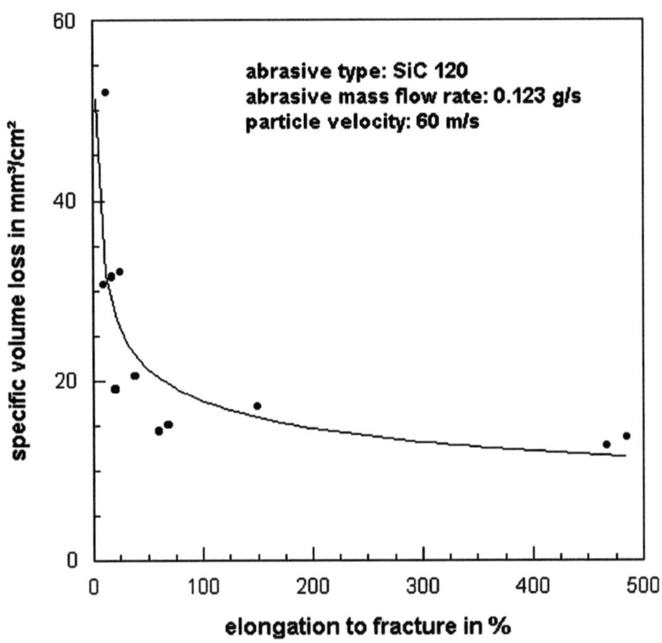

Fig. 5.40 Relationship between elongation to fracture of polymeric materials and erosion resistance (Böhm et al., 1990)

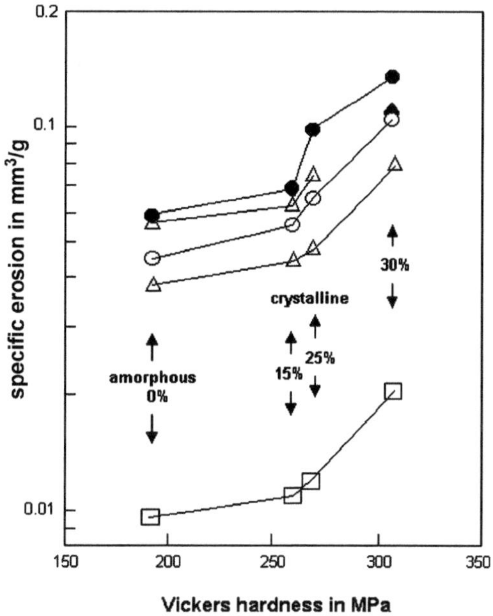

Fig. 5.41 Relationships between erosion rate, Vickers hardness and degree of crystallinity (Miyazaki, 1996).

of cross-linked thermoplastics (Barkoula, 2002). Figure 5.43 shows the effect of cross-link density of polymers on the relative erosion resistance for different impact angles. Erosion resistance initially decreased if cross-link density increased, but rested on a saturation level if cross-link density exceeded a certain threshold. The saturation threshold was lower for shallower impact angles. The resistance of fusion-bonded epoxy powder coatings against slurry erosion was also controlled by the amount of cross-linked bonds (Luo et al., 2003).

Thermal properties, that could play a role in terms of erosion, are thermal conductivity and glass transition temperature. Low thermal conductivity would lead to high temperature increase during plastic deformation. Temperature rise is lower if heat can flow away from the impact site faster than it is being generated. High temperatures may briefly soften polymers; however, as mentioned in Sect. 5.7.1, this becomes critical only at rather high flux rates.

5.7.4 Erosion Resistance of Elastomers

The erosion of rubber was modelled by Arnold and Hutchings (1992, 1993) for oblique and normal impact conditions. The model for normal impact angles delivered the following relationship between erosion rate and material parameters (Arnold and Hutchings, 1993):

$$E_R \propto \frac{\rho_M}{(1 - \nu_M)^{\beta_F}} \qquad (5.52)$$

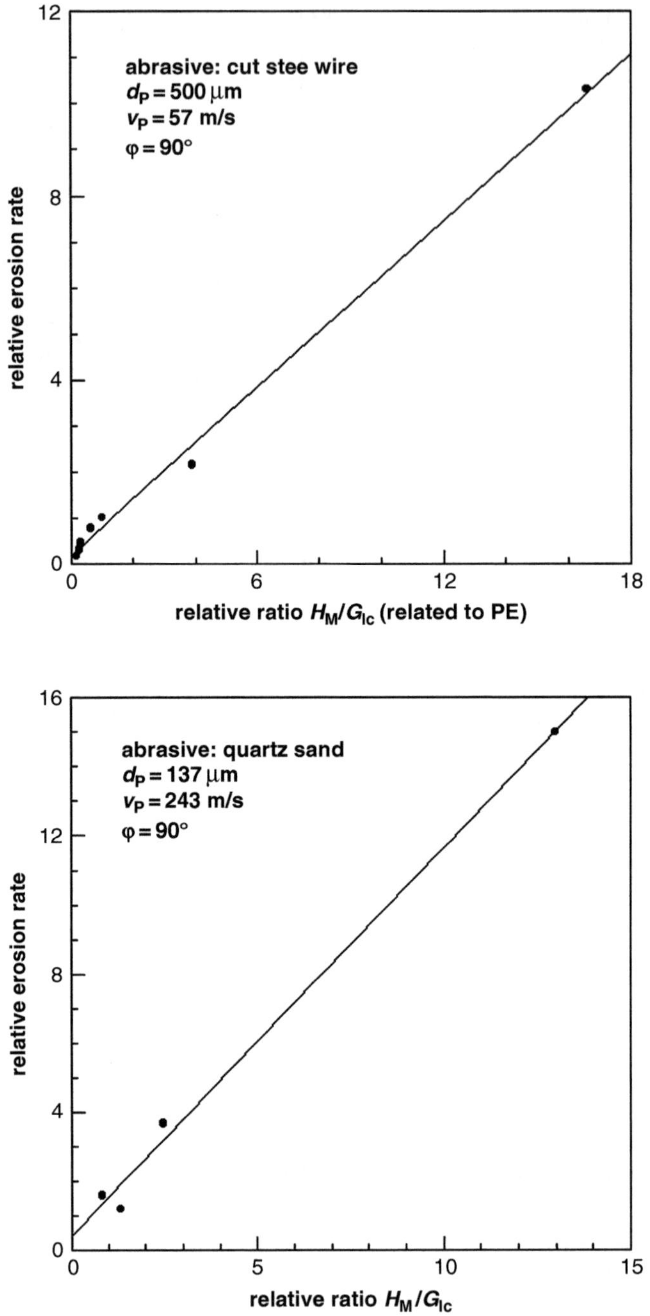

Fig. 5.42 Relationship between "brittleness index" (H_M/G_{Ic}) and erosion resistance of polymer materials (Friedrich, 1986). (**a**) Tests with cut steel wire at low impact velocity; (**b**) Tests with quartz sand at high impact velocity

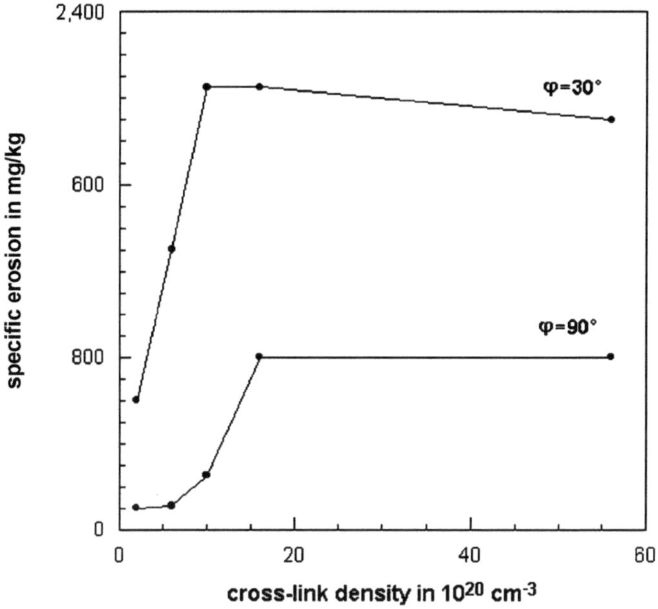

Fig. 5.43 Effect of cross-link density of polymeric materials on specific erosion resistance (Barkoula, 2002)

The model for oblique impact angles delivered the following relationship between erosion rate and material parameters (Arnold and Hutchings, 1992):

$$E_R \propto \rho_M \cdot E_M^{(\beta_F-1)/2} \quad (5.53)$$

From these relationships, erosion resistance decreases if material density increases. Young's modulus has an effect on erosion resistance at oblique impact angles only. Such trends could in fact be observed, if Young's modulus was replaced by material hardness. [Hardness of elastomers has a linear relationship to Young's modulus; Li and Hutchings (1990).] Hardness had an effect on the erosion resistance of rubber mainly at shallow impact angles. For silica particles impinging at an angle of $\varphi = 30°$ and an impact velocity of $v_P = 120\,\text{m/s}$, Arnold and Hutchings (1993) noted an increase in erosion for rubber types with higher hardness values, whereas the erosion rate was not affected by changes in rubber hardness at $\varphi = 90°$. These relationships are illustrated in Fig. 5.44. A general trend between hardness and erosion resistance could neither be observed during tests performed by Hutchings et al. (1987). Samples with moderate hardness values (Shore A) showed the lowest erosion resistance, whereas the resistance was high for samples with low and high hardness values. However, if samples with comparative values for rebound resilience are considered, erosion rate can be related to the hardness of elastomers [Li and Hutchings (1990)]; this is illustrated in Fig. 5.45.

The parameter β_F contained in (5.52) and (5.53) is originally a material fatigue parameter. From tensile fatigue tests, typical values for rubber are between 2.0 and

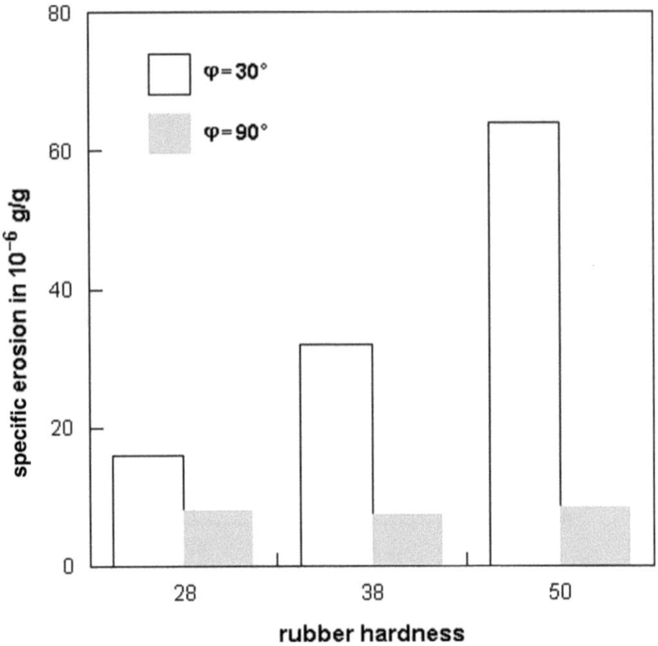

Fig. 5.44 Relationships between target hardness, impact angle and specific erosion of rubber materials (Arnold and Hutchings, 1993)

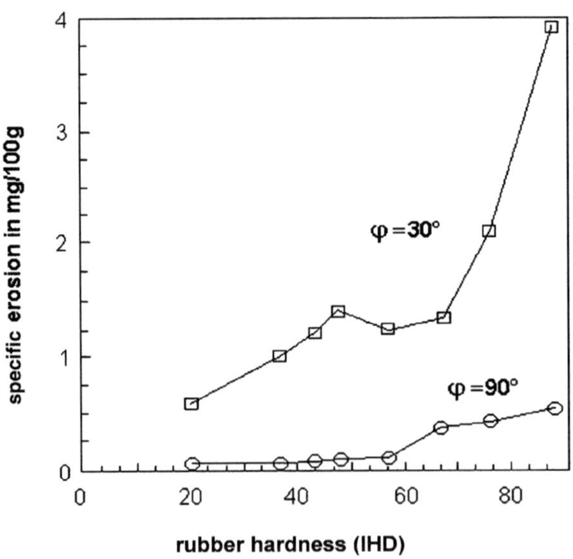

Fig. 5.45 Relationship between target hardness (ASTM D1415) and specific erosion in rubber for almost equal values for rebound resilience (Li and Hutchings, 1990)

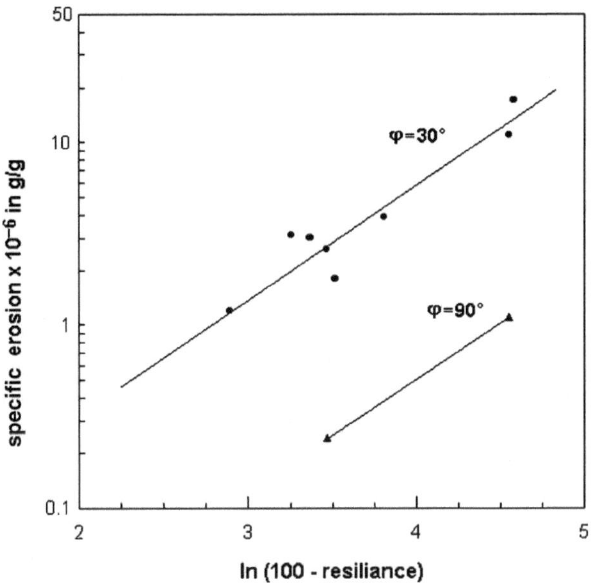

Fig. 5.46 Relationship between rebound resilience and specific erosion of unfilled elastomers (Hutchings et al., 1987)

7.9. Results of erosion tests delivered values between 1.8 and 3.2 for normal impact angles, and values between 2.1 and 4.4 for shallow impact angles (Arnold and Hutchings, 1993).

Figure 5.46 shows the effect of the rebound resilience on the erosion resistance of unfilled elastomers. The quantity "100 – resilience" represents the fraction of the initial energy of the impinging particles which is absorbed by the target material. An inverse relationship can be found in Fig. 5.46 for shallow as well as for perpendicular impact. At constant rebound resilience, a low material hardness correlated with a high erosion resistance for a range of polyurethane elastomers (Li and Hutchings, 1990).

Tensile strength is not a measure of erosion resistance; rubbers with quite different values for tensile strength exhibited similar erosion behaviour. Glass transition temperature also did not show any unique relationship to the erosion resistance of rubbers (Hutchings et al., 1987)

5.8 Erosion of Organic Coatings

5.8.1 Material Removal Mechanisms

Generally, elastic and elastic–plastic response mechanisms may act during coating erosion. The transitions between these two groups depend, among others, on temperature, strain rate and coating thickness. A transition coating thickness can, for example, be assumed for organic coatings. Elastic response (brittle fracture) can be expected in the coating material when the coating thickness is rather large, and when the coating thickness is much larger than the size of the plastic zone around an inherent flaw. This was shown by Moore (2001) for epoxy coatings.

Microscopic inspections of impact sites in epoxy-based organic coatings revealed a large variety of crater topologies. If adhesion strength between substrate and coating was lower than the cohesion strength of the bulk coating material, the damaged surfaces were always several times larger than the area of impact. This phenomenon is described in Sect. 5.5. In organic coating materials, wedge-like craters could be observed, but also lip formation at crater edges (Fokke, 1999). Subsequent impacts near such lips removed more paint material than it would on an undamaged layer. Thus, a simple assumption that each abrasive particle removes a certain amount of paint independently from each other cannot be made. Basically, for rather young epoxy-based organic coatings, a ductile material removal regime with a maximum erosion at an impact angle of $\varphi = 40°$ could be observed (Fokke, 1999). Trezona and Hutchings (2001) measured the size of damage areas in organic coatings formed due to quartz particle impact ($v_P = 58$ m/s), and identified sizes between 15 and 35 μm in diameter. These values were one order of magnitude smaller than the diameters of the corresponding quartz particles ($d_P = 125$–150 μm). Tangestanian et al. (2001) performed surface profilometry on thin organic coatings impinged by steel spheres at rather low velocities ($v_P = 30$–35 m/s), and they found that the impact caused extrusion of the plastically deformed coating into raised edges around the crater.

For enamel coatings as used for pipeline corrosion protection, spalling was identified as the important mechanism during free abrasive wear (Tong et al., 1998). During sliding of abrasive particles against the surface of the coating, circular microcracks were formed under a tangential stress which then propagated on the surface and into the surface layer. Eventually, hemispherical pits were formed. The surfaces inside the pits were rough, which shows that the cracks propagated irregularly into the subsurface layer. Examples are shown in Fig. 5.47. This particular mechanism occurred in coatings with rather low impact toughness (e.g. 2,400 Jm^2).

Luo et al. (2001) proposed a selective material removal mode for the erosion of fusion-bonded epoxy powder coatings, which consist of a soft epoxy resin and a hard filler material. For rather small abrasive particles with low kinetic energies, the mass loss of the coating was determined mainly by the response of the matrix which had a rather low erosion resistance. The matrix was removed, and the filler particles were exposed. If impinged at shallow angles, the filler particle shielded the matrix from direct impacts. For larger abrasive particles with higher kinetic energies, the filler material was destroyed, and the entire material removal was accelerated.

Breinsberger and Koppelmann (1982) performed experiments with impinging steel spheres and cones on organic coating systems. For low impact velocities, they could observe permanent depressions in the coating film only. If, however, a certain threshold velocity was exceeded, crack formation started. Values for this threshold velocity are plotted in Fig. 5.48 for different coating types. It was rather low for the cone-shaped erodent. Ball size did not seem to have a major effect on the threshold velocity. For normal temperatures (0–50°C), the threshold velocity increased if temperature rose,

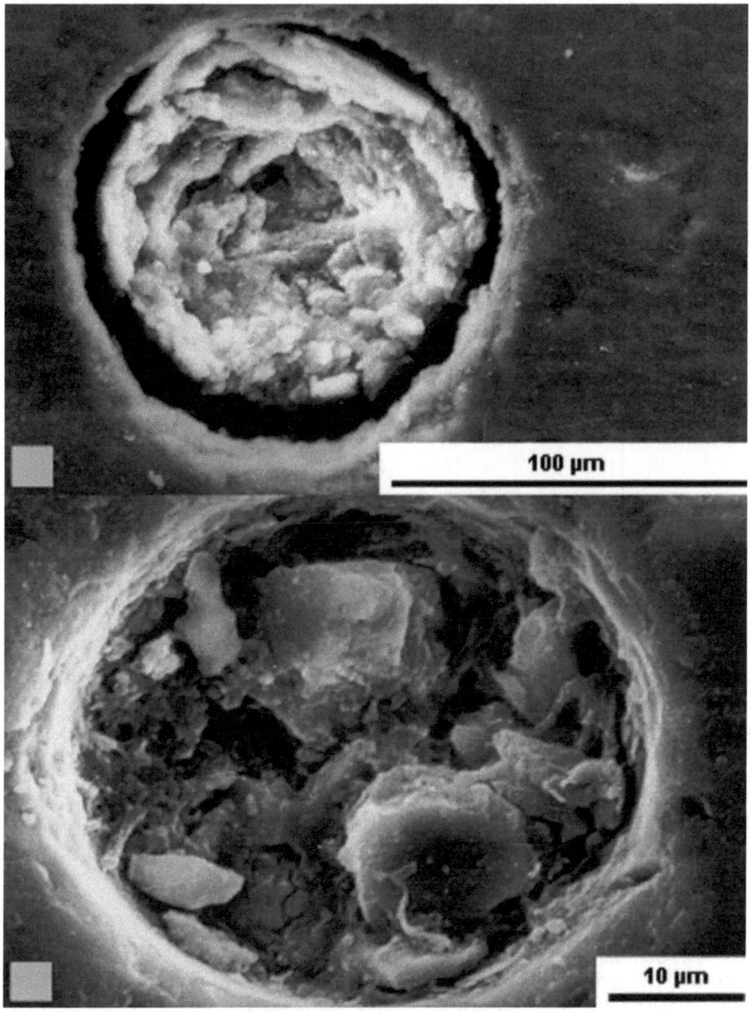

Fig. 5.47 Erosion pits in enamel coatings (Tong et al., 1998)

when steel balls were used. For the cone-shape erodent, the situation was more complex. If the velocity was further increased, the complete coating film was penetrated and the erodents reached the steel substrate surface. If this second threshold velocity was exceeded, any further increase did not lead to a notable rise in the damaged area because the substrate materials absorbed the additional kinetic energy of the erodent.

5.8.2 Erosion Resistance

Relationships to the abrasion resistance of organic automotive clearcoats were tested by Trezona et al. (1997). An example is illustrated in Fig. 5.49. It is clear that

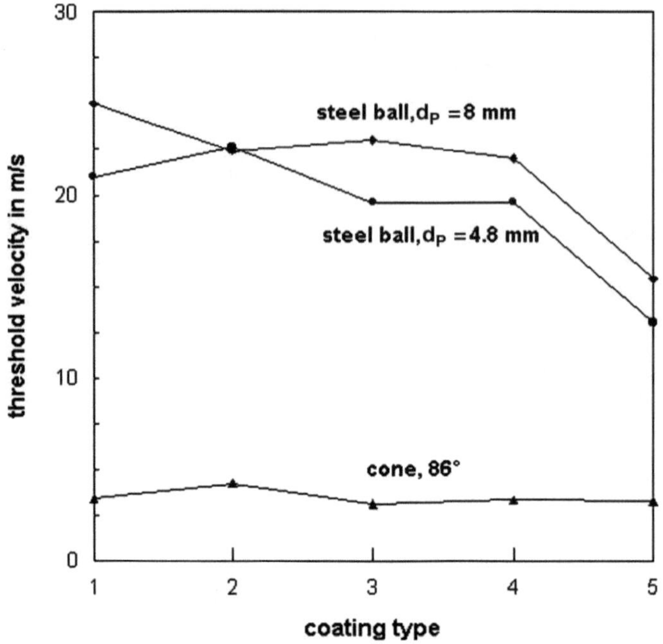

Fig. 5.48 Critical particle impact velocity for crack onset in organic coatings as a function of particle geometry (Breinsberger and Koppelmann, 1982). Notations 1–5: different filler types; coating thickness: DFT = 72–80 μm

although there was a general trend for coatings with higher tensile failure energy to be more durable, there was some scatter especially in the range of moderate energy values.

The energy for failure was taken by Rutherford et al. (1997) as a measure of the resistance of organic coatings against the erosion by solid particle impact. Typical values for the energy for failure are listed in Table 5.6. Results of measurements shown in Fig. 5.50a depict a power relationship. The effect of the failure energy became less pronounced if the energy value increased, and the effect of changes in failure energy was most important for low energy values. The effect of elastic strain energy [see (5.2)], which is a frequently utilised parameter for the assessment of erosion resistance of metals (Bitter, 1963; Kriegel, 1968), on the erosion resistance is shown in Fig. 5.50b. Although there was some trend between both parameters, no valid statement could be made for higher strain energy density values. The Ratner–Lancester parameter, which is frequently utilised to describe the mechanical response of polymers, is plotted against erosion resistance in Fig. 5.50c. There was a unique negative trend between the two parameters with a good reliability:

$$R_E \propto \frac{1}{\sigma_f \cdot \varepsilon_Y} \tag{5.54}$$

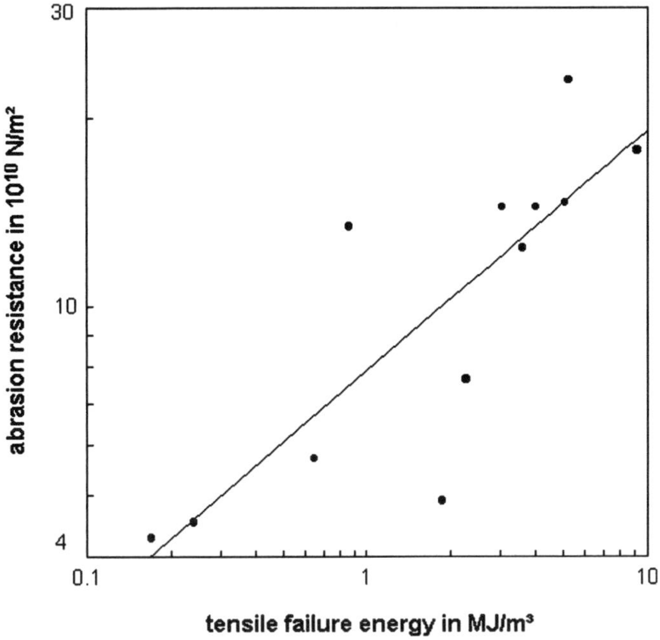

Fig. 5.49 Relationship between tensile failure energy and abrasion resistance of organic paint films (Trezona et al., 1997)

Work on weathered organic coatings indicated a negative correlation between erosion resistance and hardness for automobile clearcoats (Trezona et al., 2000b).

The erosion resistance of organic coating systems was, as experimental results in the temperature range between $\vartheta = 30$ and 65°C (Trezona et al., 2000a) suggested, better at higher temperatures. This is a surprising result because organic coatings are significantly softer at higher temperatures and should absorb more of the energy delivered by the impinging abrasive particles.

Kotnarowska (2003) found a pronounced relationship between erosion intensity (given in μm/kg in her paper) and the dry film thickness of three-layer epoxy coatings. Results are displayed in Fig. 5.51. Erosion resistance basically increased at high film thickness values. For coatings, reinforced with glass micro-spheres, however, erosion resistance had a maximum at moderate values for film thickness (DFT = 120–160 μm) and started to increase for very high film thicknesses. Ramamurthy et al. (1994) referred to effects of water saturation of organic coatings subjected to stone impact. They identified a plastification effect of water in coatings, with a dry coating exhibiting larger damage when compared to one saturated with water vapour.

Luo et al. (2003) investigated the effects of filler materials in fusion-bonded epoxy powder coatings on the resistance against slurry erosion. The authors found that the erosion rate decreased if the content and the size of the filler particles increased. The erosion rate notably decreased with an increase in the fracture

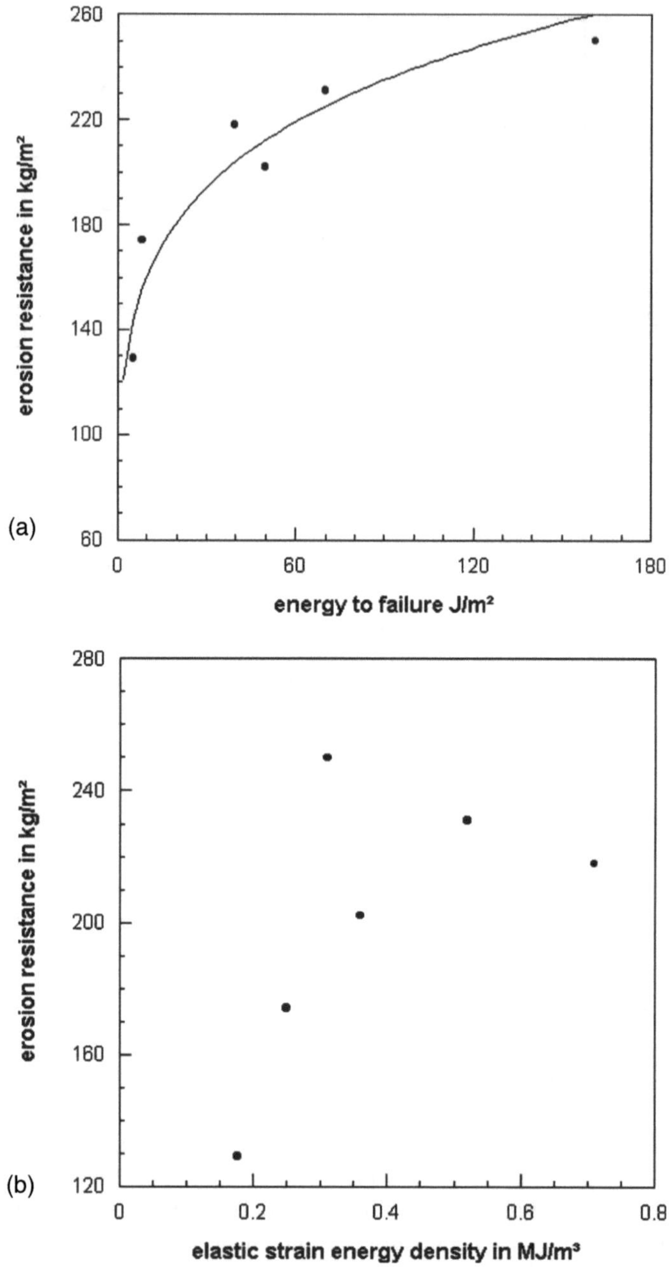

Fig. 5.50 Mechanical material property effects on erosion resistance of polymeric paint films (Rutherford et al., 1997). (**a**) Energy for failure; (**b**) Elastic strain energy density; (**c**) Ratner–Lancaster parameter

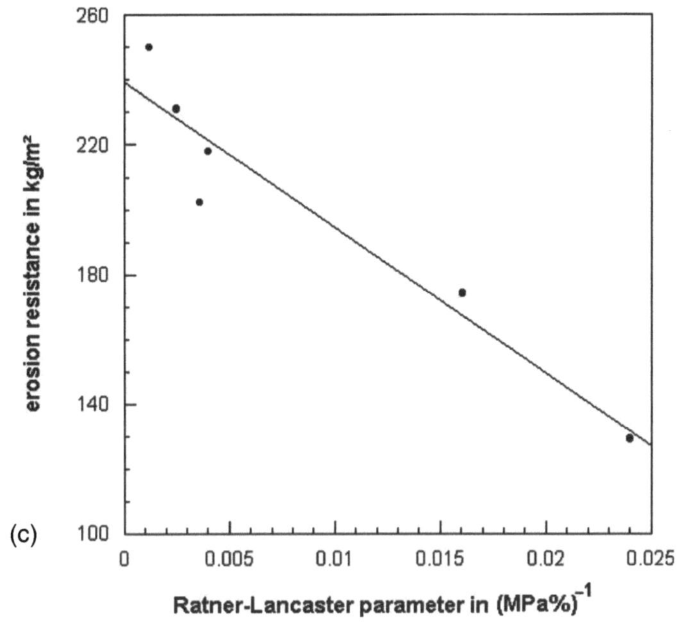

Fig. 5.50 Continued

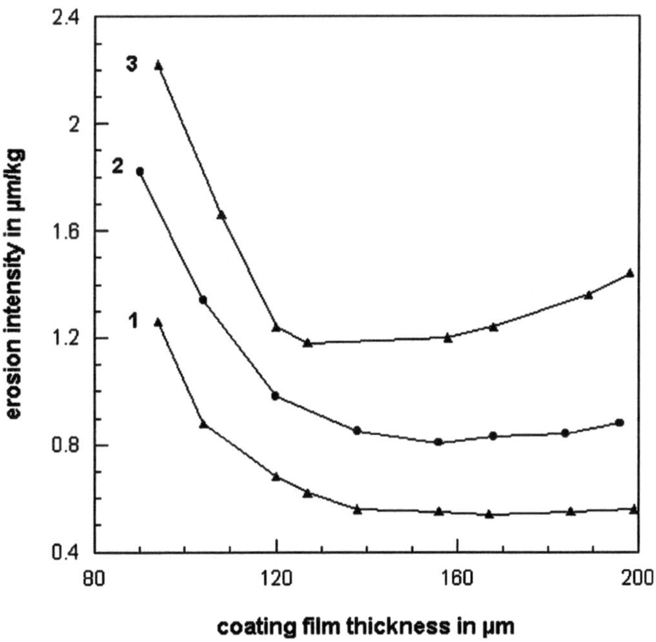

Fig. 5.51 Dry film thickness effects on erosion intensity of organic coatings (Kotnarowska, 2003). 1 – three-layer epoxy coating with composite interlayer; 2 – three-layer epoxy coating; 3 – three-layer epoxy coating modified with glass micro-spheres

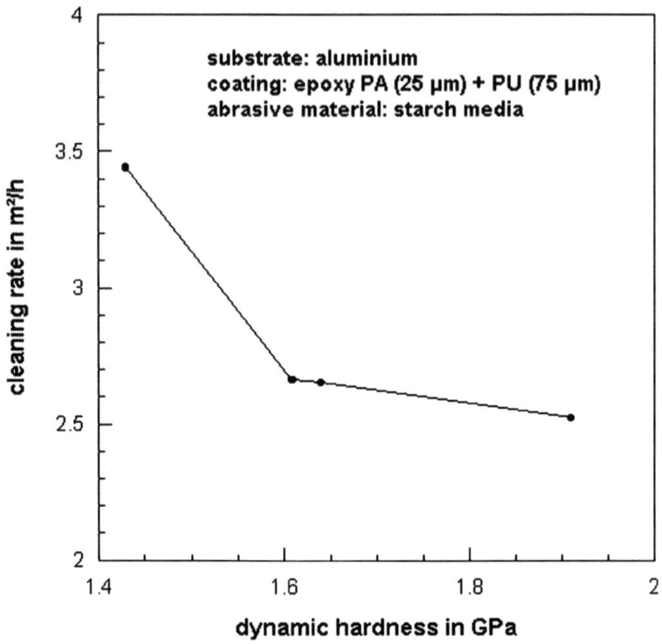

Fig. 5.52 Effect of dynamic hardness on the cleaning rate for an organic coating system (Tangestanian et al., 2001)

toughness of the filler materials. Zorll (1976) could show that the addition of talcum to organic coatings increased the resistance to particle impact.

Branco et al. (2004) performed erosion tests on sprayed ceramic coatings, and they found a significant effect of the porosity on the relative volume loss. The relative volume loss of the coatings increased with high porosity, and this particular result is very important for a sprayed ceramic or metal coating.

Figure 5.52 shows the effect of the dynamic hardness [see (5.4)] of an organic coating system on the cleaning rate. An increase in dynamic hardness notably decreased the cleaning efficiency. The values for the dynamic hardness are listed in Table 5.10.

Fokke (1999) introduced the inverse specific erosion energy with the unit (m^2/J), which could be interpreted as a coating resistance parameter. For epoxy-based organic coatings, values were between 1×10^{-5} and 3×10^{-5} m^2/J, whereas the lower value applied to high impact angles.

5.8.3 Erosion Durability

Rutherford et al. (1997) introduced the parameter *erosion durability* for the resistance of organic coatings to abrasive and erosive wear. This parameter expresses the critical abrasive mass per unit area just required for complete coating removal:

Table 5.17 Values for the erosion durability of organic coatings (Trezona and Hutchings, 2001)

Coating composition	Coating thickness in μm	Erosion durability in kg/m^2	Specific erosion resistance in $kg/m^2/\mu m$
Flexible acrylic/melamine clearcoat	48	260	5.4
	36	130	3.6
Two-component urethane clearcoat	41	240	5.8
	44	205	4.7
Rigid acrylic/melamine clearcoat	37	60	2.0
	35	50	1.4

$$Q_C = \frac{\beta_P^2 \cdot m_P}{2 \cdot \pi \cdot x^2} \cdot \exp\left(-\frac{\beta_P \cdot r_i}{x}\right) \tag{5.55}$$

Its physical unit is kg/m^2. The parameter r_i is the radius of a scar generated at the impinged surface. Typical values for different paint systems are listed in Table 5.17. It was shown that the erosion durability depended on the deformation behaviour of the substrate material. The erosion durability of clear coats, for example, was higher for flexible (polymeric) substrates compared to rigid (steel) substrates (Rutherford et al., 1997; Trezona and Hutchings, 2001). This could be attributed to the much greater elastic modulus of steel which had a significant effect on the magnitude of the forces generated during particle impingement. The effects of other parameters, namely particle velocity, angle of impingement, temperature and particle size, on the erosion durability were investigated by Trezona et al. (2000a). The erosion durability was directly proportional to coating thickness. Therefore, a *specific erosion resistance* may be a more suitable measure of the resistance of coatings to particle impingement. This parameter is defined as follows:

$$Q_t = \frac{Q_C}{h_C} \tag{5.56}$$

The physical unit of this parameter is $kg/(m^2\ \mu m)$. Typical values for the specific erosion resistance are listed in Table 5.17. Based on accurate profile measurements and SEM inspections, Trezona and Hutchings (2001) found that a *critical coating thickness* existed for typical coating materials; if this coating thickness was reached, any individual particle impact led to the total detachment of the remaining coating material from the substrate.

5.9 Debonding of Organic Coatings

5.9.1 Indentation Debonding

The situation of the gradual penetration of an indenter pressed against a thin polymer film adhered to a metal substrate is illustrated in Fig. 5.53. At first, the indenter contacts the coating only. As the force increases, the indenter penetrates to the metal

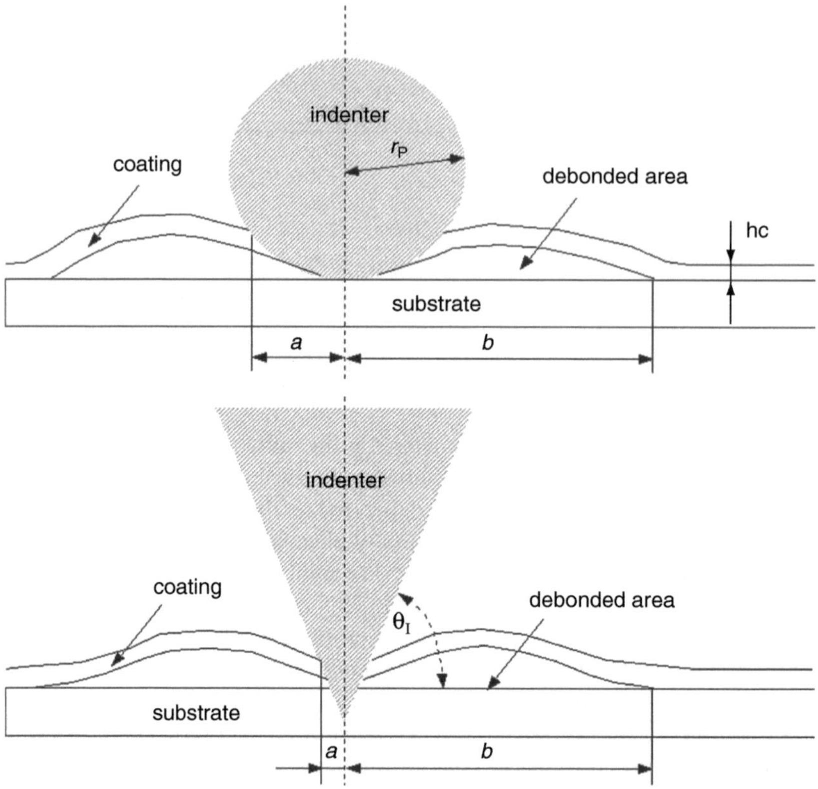

Fig. 5.53 Debonding of a polymer layer from a metal substrate (adapted from Engel and Pedroza, 1983). (**a**) Blunt (spherical) indenter; (**b**) Sharp (conical) indenter

level. A large normal compressive stress is exerted through the polymer film, which is dragged into the contact zone.

Ritter and Rosenfeld (1990) distinguished three basic types of debonding, shown schematically in Fig. 5.54. Type "I" occurs when the deformations in the coating remain elastic up to debonding. In type "II", the coating deformations underneath the indenter are predominantly plastic at debonding, but the substrate is not penetrated. Type "III" occurs when the indenter has penetrated the coating before debonding occurs, so that part of the indentation load is supported directly by the substrate. The failure type for a given system coating/substrate will depend on the properties of the coating, coating thickness, adhesion strength and indenter geometry. Blunt indenters and thick, poorly adhering coatings favour type "I"; whereas sharp indenters and thin, well-adhering coatings favour the types "II" and "III" (Ritter and Rosenfeld, 1990).

Plastic deformations of the substrate metal tend to cause pile-up around the rim of the crater, and further out along the surface a tensile load between film and substrate arises. Separation between coating and steel substrate occurs for the following condition:

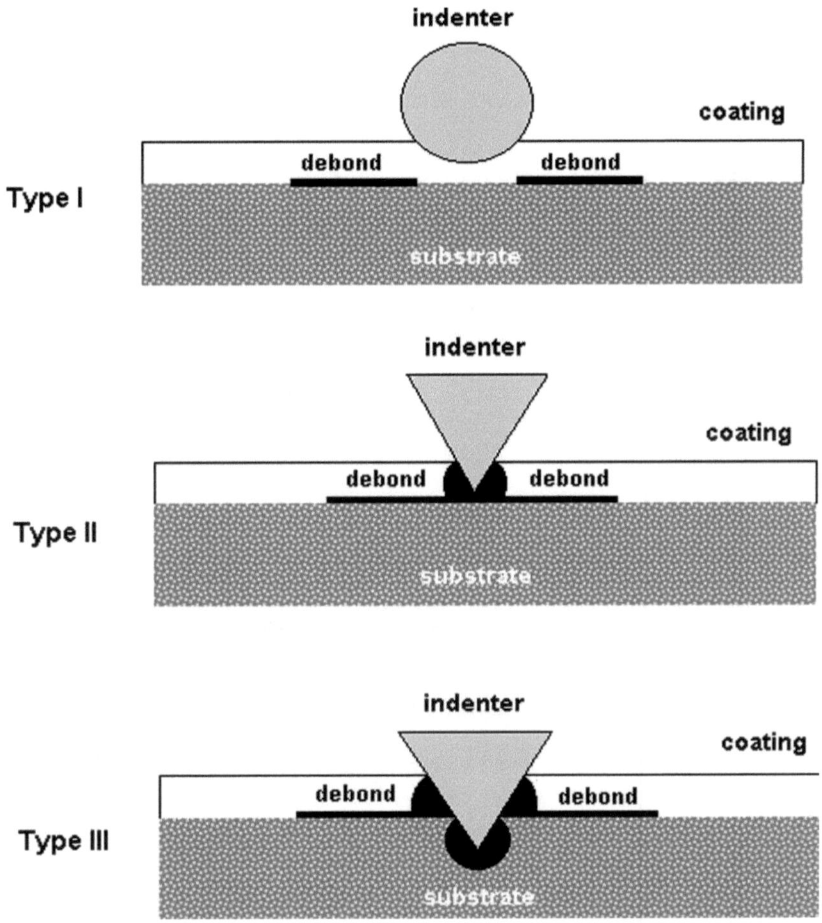

Fig. 5.54 Schematic diagram of three possible types of debonding (adapted from Ritter and Rosenfeld, 1990)

$$\sigma_T > \sigma_B \tag{5.57}$$

The polymer film departed from the substrate along the rim of the indented crater, but it rejoined the substrate beyond an annulus of debonded space, where the tensile stress was insufficient to prevent anchorage. For very sharp indenters, a hole on the bottom of the indentation could be observed frequently (Engel and Pedroza, 1983). Indentation radius ("a" in Fig. 5.53) as well as debonding radius ("b" in Fig. 5.53) had almost linear relationships to the indentation force in the range between 2 and 27 N. Examples are shown in Fig. 5.55. Engel (1985) considered the debonded circular annulus of a polymer coating to be a thin plate which is bent by the applied load. Based on this approach, he derived a maximum radial bending strain. This parameter is denoted as "peel strain", and it is defined as follows:

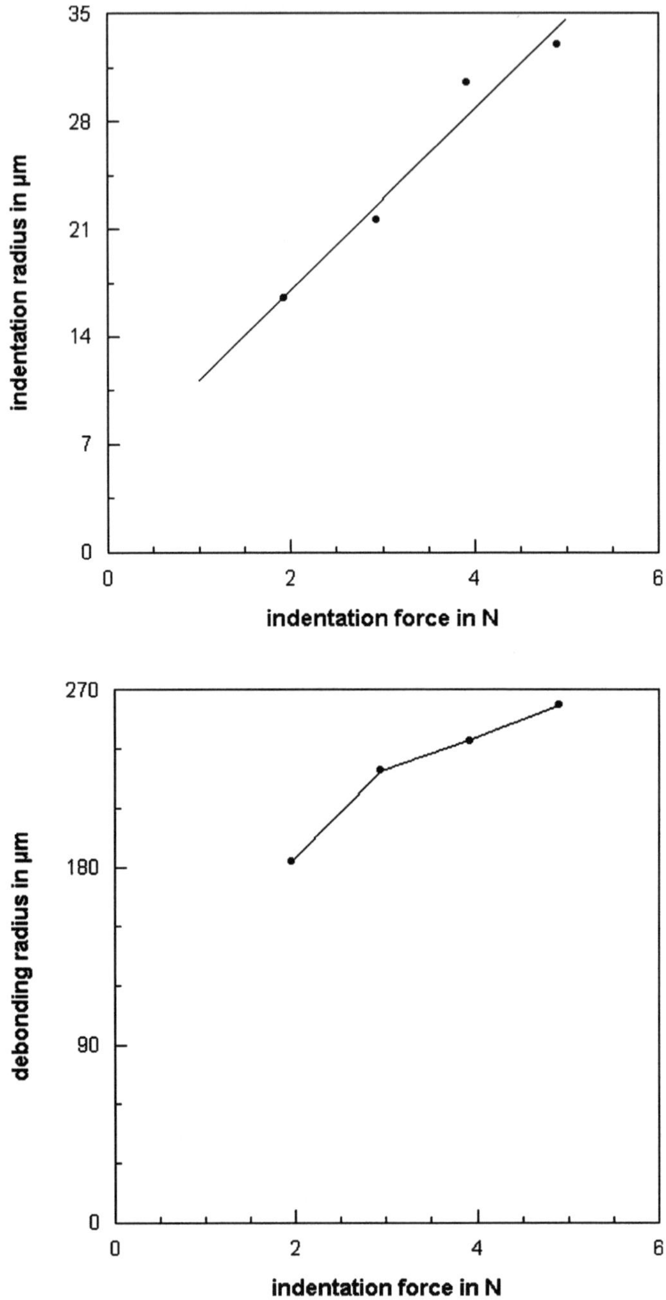

Fig. 5.55 Relationship between indentation force and debonding parameters (results from Engel and Pedroza, 1983). (**a**) Indentation radius; (**b**) Debonding radius

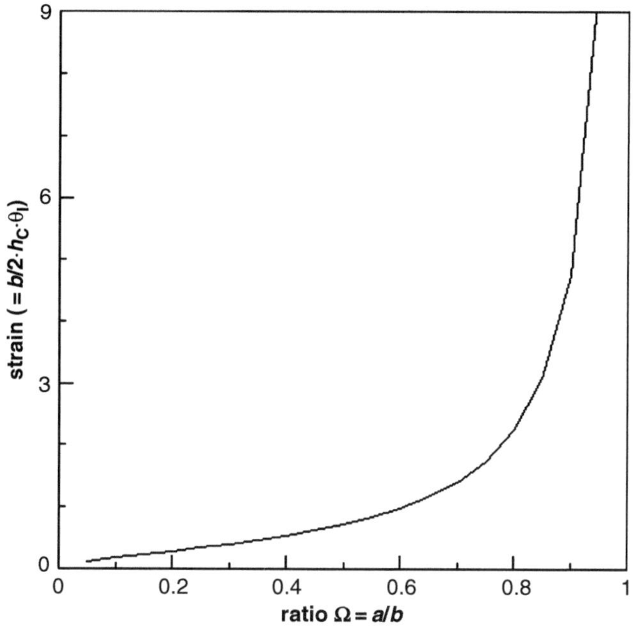

Fig. 5.56 Graphical illustration of (5.59)

$$\varepsilon_0 = \frac{2 \cdot \theta_I \cdot h_C}{b} \cdot \frac{\Omega^2 - \left[1 + \left(1 + \Omega^2\right) \cdot \ln \Omega\right]}{(2 \cdot \Omega \cdot \ln \Omega)^2 - \left(1 - \Omega^2\right)^2} \cdot \Omega$$
$$\Omega = \frac{a}{b} \qquad (5.58)$$

The parameters a, b and θ_I are defined in Fig. 5.53. The peel strain sets the limit of adhesion between a specific combination of substrate and bonded polymer layer. Equation (5.58) is graphically illustrated in Fig. 5.56 For conical indenters with cone angles between $\theta_I = 14.4°$ and $51°$, peel strain was inversely proportional to the indentation force; values for the peel strain were between $\varepsilon_0 = 3\%$ and 7% (Engel and Pedroza, 1983).

5.9.2 Impact Debonding

Impact testing of organic coatings is an event very similar to the erosion of a coating by an impinging abrasive particle. The results of such tests can deliver important information about fundamental mechanisms of coating erosion and debonding. Zosel (1977) and Zorll (1975a) inspected impact marks, formed during impact tests, and noted ring cracks and radial cracks accompanied by wall formation (buckling) around the impact centre. Wall formation (buckling) in organic coatings impinged with a steel ball was proven by Zorll (1975a) due to interference microscopic images. Two examples of such images, illustrating wall formation, are shown in Fig. 5.57. Figure 5.57a illustrates the formation of a single wall in a coating impinged at a low impact velocity. The image shown in Fig. 5.57b is indicative of the formation of multiple walls in a coating impinged at a higher impact velocity. The entire damage area exceeded the contact area by a factor between 100 and 200. These results pointed to the formation and propagation of stress waves in the material. Zorll (1975b) found that only a fraction of the kinetic energy of a steel ball, impinging at low velocity, was dissipated due to the formation of the permanent depression and the wall. The majority of the energy was being distributed in more remote coating locations as well as in the substrate material, but was also absorbed due to elastic rebound. Table 5.18 summarises some results. For higher impact velocities (e.g. $v_P = 50\,m/s$), multiple wall formation (buckling) and first cracks could be observed. A similar transition behaviour of coatings was also detected by Breinsberger and Koppelmann (1982). Zorll (1975a) found finely ground paint particles (size about $3\,\mu m$) under the central damage area and concluded that compressive stresses in the range of 850 MPa were responsible for this special feature. Shear stresses, formed at the interface between coating and substrate, were responsible for coating debonding. Zorll (1983) investigated the effects of substrate topography on the failure mode of coating systems (DFT between 50 and $80\,\mu m$) subjected to impinging steel spheres, and he found that deep, angled profiles promoted cohesive failure; whereas smooth profiles promoted adhesive failure. Therefore, substrate topography may be considered for the modelling of coating removal processes.

It was observed by Zorll (1976) for two-layer coating systems, that the addition of platelet-shaped talcum to the coating reduced the deformation of organic coatings as well as the probability of debonding at higher impact velocities. These results pointed to a reinforcement effect of the talcum platelets. The above-mentioned transition stage between wall formation and cracking did not exist for talcum pigmented coatings, whereas it was registered for iron oxide pigmented coatings. The hardness and pigmentation of the primer determined the response of the entire coating system against impact loading.

Ladstädter (1984) subjected multiple-layered coating systems to high-speed steel bullets and deduced so-called *damage functions*. An example for a damage function is shown in Fig. 5.58. Surprisingly, the author found a reduction in the damaged area for moderate bullet velocities, and he called this effect *softening-effect*. Part of the energy of the impinging particles was dissipated into heat, and it rose coating temperature. A steel ball with a weight of $m_P = 0.5\,g$ and a velocity of about $v_P = 30\,m/s$ may rise the temperature in a deformed coating mass of $m_C = 0.2\,mg$ by a value of 200 K. Mechanical properties of organic materials depend on temperature. Young's modulus of organic coating materials (primer, filler material and top coat), for example, notably decreased if temperature increased (Ladstädter, 1984). For many organic coatings, an increase in 30 K was sufficient to transform the material in the glass-transition stage – the material responded with plastic deformation and could dissipate more energy prior to failure. This aspect is illustrated in Fig. 5.58 for the higher impact velocity. Zosel (1977) could show that complete separation between paint coating and substrate due to delamination occurred only if a certain threshold impact velocity was exceeded.

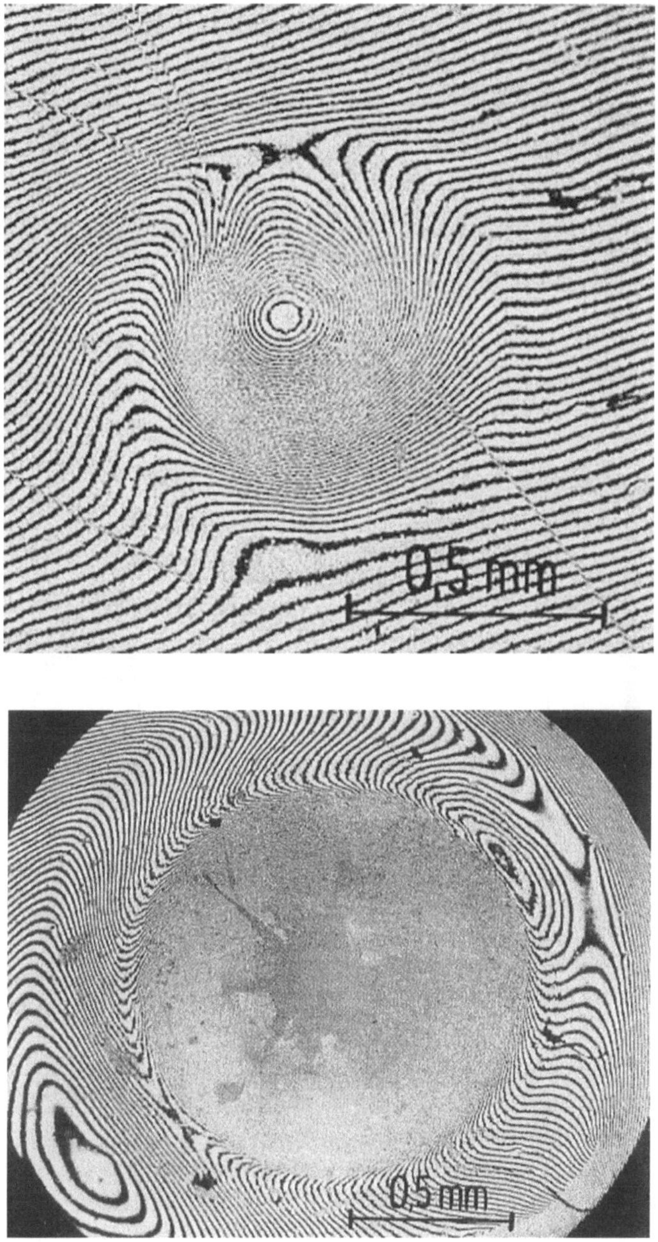

(a)

(b)

Fig. 5.57 Interference microscopic images of organic coatings (polyurethane, DFT = 100 µm) after steel ball impingement (d_P = 3.5 mm); images: Zorll (1975a). (**a**) Lower impingement velocity (v_P = 20 m/s), formation of a single wall; (**b**) Higher impingement velocity (v_P = 50 m/s); formation of multiple walls

Table 5.18 Typical parameters of an impact test for an organic coating (values from Zorll, 1975b); see also Fig. 5.57

Parameter	Value
Ball diameter	3.5 mm
Impact velocity	20 m/s
Ball weight	0.17 g
Kinetic energy ball	34 mJ
Deformed volume (wall)	5.7×10^{-4} mm^3
Deformed volume (depression)	18.1×10^{-4} mm^3
Energy absorbed due to deformation	3×10^{-3} mJ

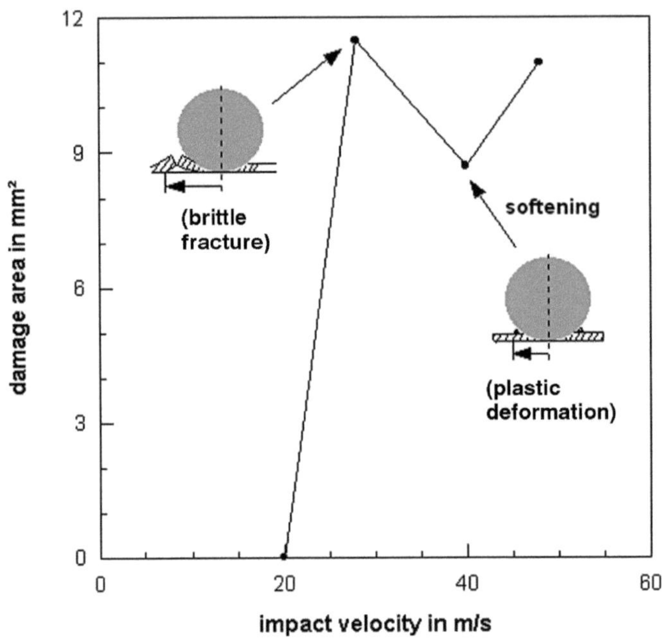

Fig. 5.58 "Damage function" according to Ladstädter (1984)

The value of this critical velocity was dependent of the temperature. It was notable lower for lower temperatures (ϑ = -20°C compared with ϑ = 23°C).

5.10 Coating Removal Models

5.10.1 Ploughing/Delamination Model

A series of papers by Papini and Spelt (1997, 1998a, b) provided some detailed insight in the removal of organic coatings from steel substrate due to spherical abrasive particle impingement. The authors distinguished between ploughing erosion of the bulk coating and coating delamination.

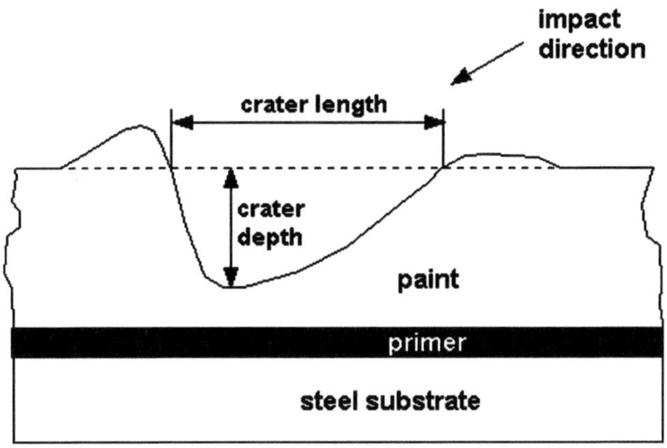

Fig. 5.59 Geometrical situation of ploughing erosion (Papini and Spelt, 1998)

Ploughing erosion occurred at non-rectangular impact. The geometrical situation is illustrated in Fig. 5.59 (see also Fig. 5.21b). At the edge of the impact appeared a certain amount of plastically deformed coating material, which is being knocked off by subsequently impinging particles. The authors modelled this material removal process with an elastic–plastic model, and they obtained good results for crater length, crater depth and rebound parameters (Papini and Spelt, 1998a).

The initiation of the delamination of alkyd paint from steel occurred at a critical shear stress independently on coating thickness. A typical value for an alkyd coating, eroded with impinging glass and steel spheres, was about $\tau_M = 100\,\text{MPa}$ (Papini and Spelt, 1998b). The delamination itself was dominated by a mixed-mode interfacial crack, induced by the buckling of the coating. This situation corresponded to that illustrated in Fig. 5.53a. If the abrasive bead started to penetrate the substrate, coating delamination started, and the coating was going to be removed. A critical impact velocity was needed for this process. For thin coatings (DFT = 20–50 μm), critical velocities were between $v_P = 20$ and 40 m/s (glass beads and steel spheres). Values for critical particle kinetic energies are plotted in Fig. 5.60. It can be seen that the critical particle energy increased linearly with an increase in coating thickness, irrespective of the abrasive type. A range of normal kinetic energies was found where the coating was removed without damaging the steel substrate (Papini and Spelt, 1997). It was also found that coating delamination due to impinging particles had maximum values at normal impact angles (v_P = 55–108 m/s).

5.10.2 Debonding Model

Zouari and Touratier (2000, 2001, 2002) provided a detailed investigation in the removal of a polyurethane coating from an aluminium substrate through impinging spherical particles. They identified the three following failure mechanisms:

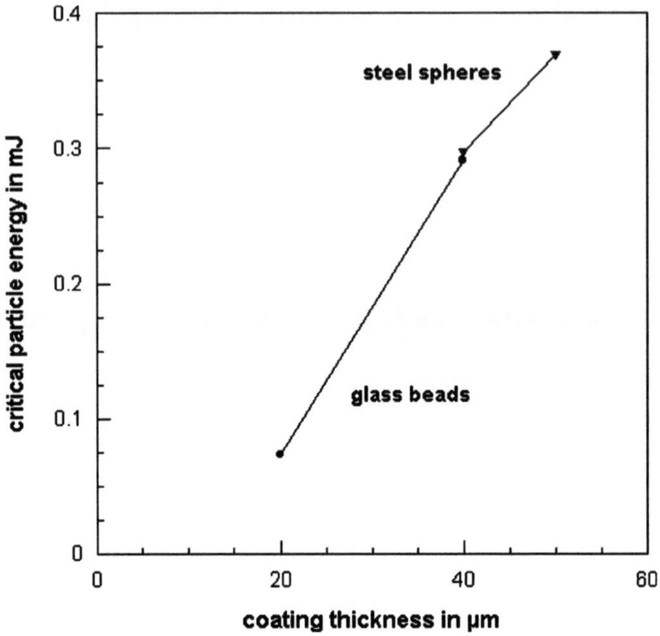

Fig. 5.60 Critical kinetic particle energies for coating delamination (Papini and Spelt, 1998b)

- initiation of delamination due to shear stresses at the interface;
- buckling of the paint film due to compressive stresses originating from particle penetration into the coating;
- delamination of the coating caused by the buckling of the coating film.

This is essentially the mechanism suggested in Sec. 5.10.1. Zouari and Touratier (2002) used a finite element code to numerically model the removal process. Among others, they found that the substrate consumed a high amount of the kinetic energy supplied by the impinging rigid particle (aluminium oxide spheres). The debonding failure criterion assumed by the authors reads as follows:

$$\left(\frac{\sigma_{N}}{\sigma_{NF}}\right)^{2}+\left(\frac{\tau_{N}}{\tau_{M}}\right)^{2} \leq \quad 1 \tag{5.59}$$

Debonding is assumed to occur if the left-hand side of the equation is greater than unity. The coating resistance parameters can be evaluated from pull-off test results; typical values were $\sigma_{NF} = 50\,\text{MPa}$ and $\tau_{M} = 200\,\text{MPa}$ (Zouari and Touratier, 2002). Graphical expressions of the results of the numerical simulations can be found in Zouari and Touratier (2002) paper. The authors found that buckling and coating delamination occurred outside the contact area particle-coating, and they estimated the limits for paint buckling and coating delamination.

5.10.3 *Effects of a Second Phase in the Coating*

Luo et al. (2001) considered the effect of hard fillers in a soft matrix, as found in powder coatings, on the erosion resistance. They developed a simple model for the assessment of the mass loss of a coating subjected to slurry flow. The model reads as follows:

$$\frac{1}{m_C} = \frac{1 - F_f}{m_{matrix}} + \frac{F_f}{m_{filler}} \tag{5.60}$$

Here, m_{matrix} is the mass loss of the matrix material, m_{filler} is the mass loss of the filler material, F_f is the volume fraction of the filler and the quantity "1-F_f" is the volume fraction of the matrix.

Chapter 6
Surface Preparation Process

6.1 Definition of Process and Target Parameters

6.1.1 Process Parameters

Blast cleaning can be considered to be an erosion process. Erosion is a tribological term, and it can be discussed based on a tribological system. The tribological system for solid particle erosion is schematically shown in Fig. 6.1. The tribological system features the loading collective, the wear parameters and the bodies involved in the process. The loading collective characterises the *process parameters*.

The blast cleaning process is characterised by numerous process parameters that determine efficiency, economy and quality of the whole process. Therefore, optimisation of the process is a primary requirement for a successful application. Generally, the process parameters in blast cleaning divide as listed below (see also Fig. 6.2).

(1) Pneumatic parameters:

- air (nozzle) pressure, p;
- nozzle diameter, d_N;

(2) Process parameters:

- stand-off distance, x;
- impact angle, φ;
- exposure time, t_E;
- number of passes, n_S;

(3) Abrasive parameters

- abrasive mass flow rate, $\dot{m}_P$;
- abrasive particle diameter, d_P;
- abrasive particle size distribution, $f(d_P)$;
- abrasive particle shape;
- abrasive particle hardness, H_P;
- abrasive recycling capacity.

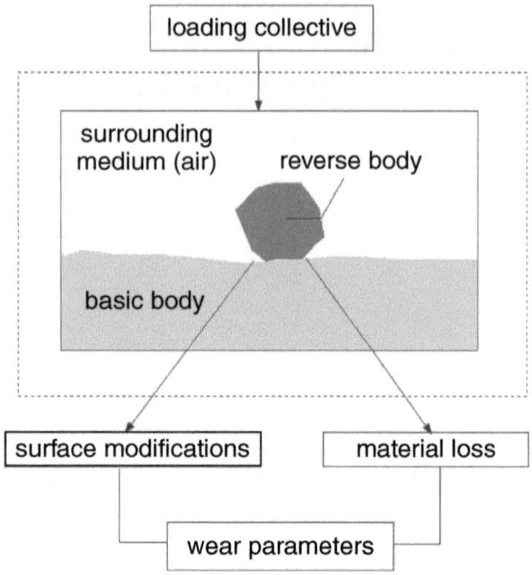

Fig. 6.1 Tribological system for blast cleaning (solid particle erosion)

6.1.2 Target Parameters

The tribological system shown in Fig 6.1 also features wear parameters, which are basically parameters describing material loss and parameters characterising surface modifications. Parameters for the description of surface modifications are discussed in Chap. 7.12.2. Material loss parameters are denoted *target parameters* in this chapter.

Target parameters are illustrated in Fig. 6.2. The most important target parameter in blast cleaning applications is the cleaning rate, which is given as follows:

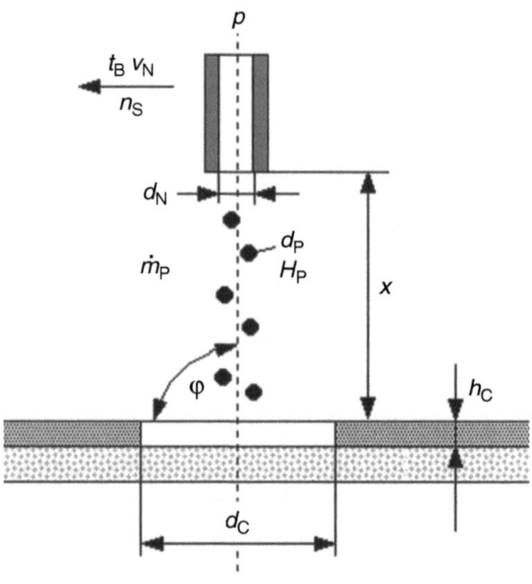

Fig. 6.2 Process parameters and target parameters of blast cleaning processes

$$\dot{A} = \frac{A_M}{t_B} \tag{6.1}$$

In that equation, A_M is the area to be blast cleaned and t_B is the total blast cleaning time. Cleaning rate is usually given in m^2/h. Following an approach of Uferer (1992), the cleaning rate can be expressed in terms of the total kinetic energy of the impinging abrasive particles:

$$\dot{A} = \frac{C_B}{2} \cdot \frac{N_P \cdot m_P}{t_B} \cdot v_P^2 \tag{6.2}$$

The constant C_B is an energy transfer parameter given in s^2/kg. If the thickness of a rust layer or, respectively, a coating system is considered, a volumetric removal rate can be defined as follows:

$$\dot{V}_M = \frac{V_M}{t_B} = \frac{A_M \cdot h_C}{t_B} \tag{6.3}$$

Here, V_M is the removed volume, and h_C is the thickness of the removed material layer. For coatings, h_C equals the dry film thickness. An alternative expression for (6.3) is as follows:

$$\dot{V}_M = A_M \cdot v_N \tag{6.4}$$

Here, v_N is the traverse rate of the nozzle. The unit of the volumetric removal rate is m^3/h.

For optimisation purposes, the consumption of consumable materials need to be considered. The specific abrasive consumption rate, for example, is given as follows:

$$m_S = \frac{\dot{m}_P}{\dot{A}} \tag{6.5}$$

The unit of this parameter is kg/m^2. Similarly, a specific power consumption (kW/m^2) or a specific fuel consumption (l/m^2) could be defined.

6.2 Effects of Pneumatic Parameters

6.2.1 *Effects of Air Pressure*

Tilghman (1870), in his original patent, wrote: "*The greater the pressure of the jet the bigger will be the velocity imparted to the grains of sand, and the more rapid and powerful the cutting effect upon the solid surface.*" In most instances, increasing air pressure increases cleaning rate. A 300% increase in cleaning rate was, for example, reported for the blast cleaning of steel with copper slag if air pressure rose from

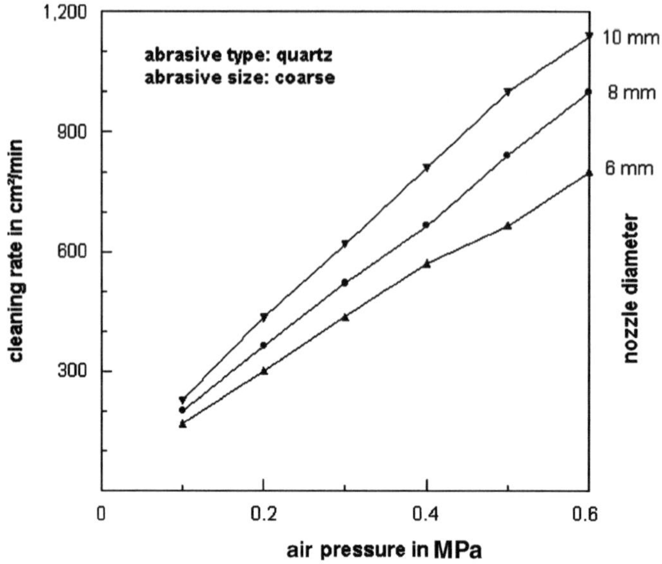

Fig. 6.3 Effects of air pressure and nozzle diameter on cleaning rate (Kalpers, 1949)

$p = 0.53$ to 0.8 MPa (Holt and Austin, 2001). Figures 6.3, 6.4 and 6.9 show general relationships between air pressure and cleaning rate. The higher the nozzle pressure, the more productive is the blast cleaning process in terms of cleaning rate. A linear relationship between air pressure and cleaning rate was also found by Kura (2003) for bar shot, by Kalpers (1949) for grit, and by Seavey (1985) for different non-metallic abrasive materials. A mathematical formulation is:

$$\dot{A} = C_1 \cdot (p - p_C) \tag{6.6}$$

The general structure of this function is the result of complex relationships between pressure and the processes of jet formation, abrasive acceleration and mixing, and material removal. For suction devices, cleaning rate rises according to a square-root relationship with increasing air pressure (Uhlmann et al., 2003). Figure 6.4 provides further insight into the effect of air pressure on cleaning rate. It can be recognised that the pressure influence depended on abrasive material. In the case of copper slag, cleaning rate even dropped at high pressure levels, an effect which can be explained through the friability of this material. At high pressures, this material is fractured in the nozzle and on the substrate surface. Such trends were reported by Gesell (1966) for quartz, copper slag and foundry slag. More information on this issue is delivered in Sect. 2.9. Although (6.6) holds for many cases, the real process can differ from a linear relationship, especially if rather hard target materials are being treated.

The first stage, $p < p_C$, characterises an *incubation stage*. In this pressure range, no material removal takes place, although the removal process is invisibly introduced in the material. The parameter p_C is a threshold value that has to be

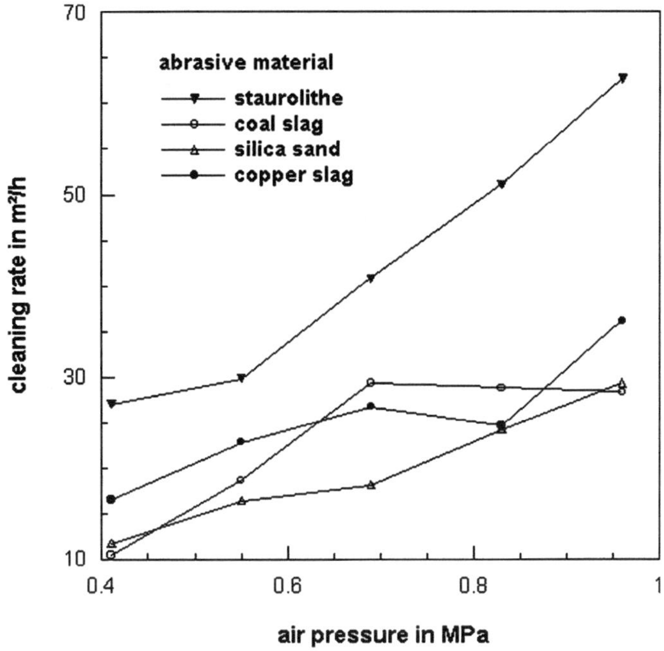

Fig. 6.4 Effects of air pressure and abrasive material on cleaning rate (Seavey, 1985)

exceeded for a measurable material removal. Results of Uferer (1992) deliver a value of $p_C = 0.05$ MPa for the removal of mill scale from steel plates with nickel slag. The threshold pressure could be interpreted as a critical particle impact velocity, which is known from impact testing of organic coatings (Breinsberger and Koppelmann, 1982; Ladstädter, 1984). For elastically responding materials, say mill scale, heavy rust or brittle coatings, a threshold concept developed by Evans et al. (1978) for solid particle erosion can be applied. In this model, the threshold velocity of the particles is given by the following equation:

$$v_C \propto K_{Ic}^2 \cdot c_M^{0.33} \tag{6.7a}$$

In that equation, K_{Ic} is the fracture toughness of the target material, and c_M is the velocity of longitudinal waves in the target material. Values for the fracture toughness of some organic coating materials are listed in Table 5.11. This approach is partly verified by the experimental results presented in Fig. 6.5. For plastically responding materials, say soft coatings and most metal substrates, a rather complex model introduced by Yabuki and Matsumura (1999) can be applied. One basic result of this model is that the threshold velocity, required for micro-cutting, has a linear relationship with the material hardness:

$$v_C \propto H_M \tag{6.7b}$$

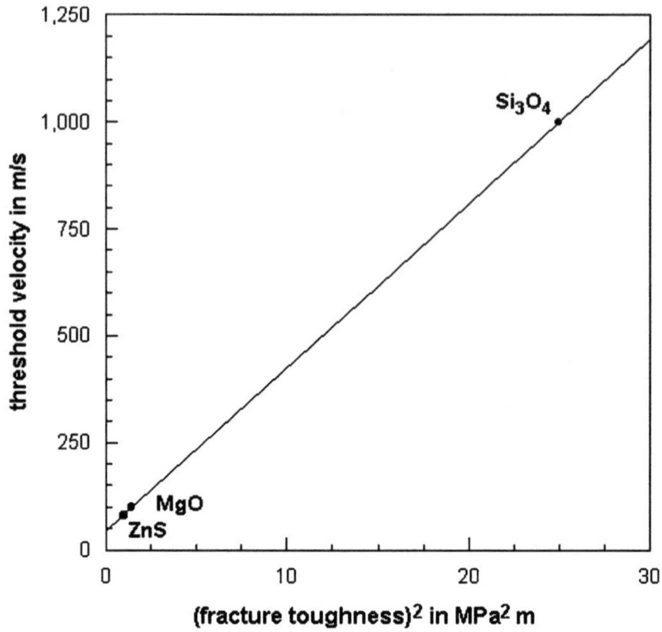

Fig. 6.5 Relationship between threshold particle impact velocity and fracture toughness for brittle target materials (Evans et al., 1978)

Hardness values for some coating materials are listed in Tables 5.1, 5.3 and 5.7–5.10. The threshold values, measured on numerous metals, were too low (between $v_C = 1$ and 3 m/s) that they do not need to be considered in practice (Yabuki et al., 1999). Luo et al. (2001) estimated threshold velocities between $v_C = 6$ and 7 m/s for the slurry erosion of fusion-bonded epoxy powder coatings. Another threshold characteristic is illustrated in Fig. 5.21b, which illustrates the situation for material detachment in a plastically deformable material. It can be seen that a critical particle impact velocity must be exceeded before material removal starts. This value is at about $v_P = 210$ m/s for the situation illustrated in Fig. 5.21b. If this velocity value is not reached, the material only deforms.

Papini and Spelt (1997) provided the idea that coating removal begins only when the coating is fully penetrated for a given coating/substrate/particle system. They derived a critical abrasive impact velocity to cause penetration of the coating to the steel substrate, and they provided a methodology for the calculation of these velocity values. The normal component of the critical penetration velocity increased with larger coating thickness, which was attributed to a relationship between coating thickness and interface shear stress. Typical values for the penetration of alkyd paint layers (DFT = 20–50 μm) were between $v_C = 20$ and 45 m/s. Later, these authors (Papini and Spelt, 1998b) introduced a critical particle energy required for the introduction of coating delamination. This relationship is illustrated in Fig. 5.60, and it can be seen that the threshold energy depended on the coating thickness.

In the second stage, $p > p_C$ – called *linear stage* – cleaning rate increases linearly with an increase in air pressure. Each increase in air pressure leads to a proportional increase in cleaning rate. The factor of proportionality C_1 depends on all the process conditions listed earlier as well as on the properties of the target material. Figure 6.3a reveals a slight effect of the nozzle diameter. For the linear coefficient C_1 exists the following rule of thumb: "*For each 7 kPa increase (in pressure) there is a 1.5 percent increase in productivity.*" (Drisko, 2002). However, results published by Seavey (1985) have shown that C_1 depended on the abrasive material used. Some results of this investigation are plotted in Fig. 6.4. It can be seen that the proportionality factor was rather low for quartz and coal slag, and that it was higher for copper slag and fine-grained staurolite. In some cases, cleaning rate can even drop if pressure is increased. Such phenomena were reported by Seavey (1985) for the use of coal slag. This feature is illustrated in Fig. 6.4. The reason for this behaviour could be the high degree of friability of the slag material. If the pressure, and thus the abrasive particle impact velocity, becomes too high, the slag particles start to fracture during the impact process and do not work efficiently (see Fig. 6.4). Similar is the situation if rather large abrasive particles are being used, as has been observed by Stallmann et al. (1988) for copper slag and melting chamber slag. It is, therefore, a general recommendation to select an air pressure lower than, or close to, the critical pressure for abrasive impact fragmentation. More information on this issue is provided in Sect. 2.9. Results plotted in Fig. 6.9 show that the coefficient C_1 depends also on the nozzle geometry.

Air pressure determines the velocity of the impinging abrasive particles (see Sect. 3.6.1). This fact was considered by Settles and Garg (1995) who calculated the abrasive particle velocities for the cleaning rate examples provided in Fig. 6.4. They computed the following values for the particle velocity ($p = 0.7$ MPa, $d_N = 9.5$ mm; $\dot{m}_P = 9.7$ kg/min): $v_P = 173$ m/s for the silica sand and $v_P = 210$ m/s for the staurolite. From these results, they concluded that the high productivity of the staurolite abrasive is a result of the higher abrasive particle impact velocity.

Abrasive particle velocity has the strongest influence on the erosion durability of organic coatings, if abrasive size, temperature, impact angle and abrasive particle velocity are being considered (Trezona et al., 2000a). For polymeric paint films, a power-law dependency of the erosion resistance (given in kg/m^2) on the abrasive particle velocity can be expected (Rutherford et al., 1997). The following relationship can be assumed:

$$\mathrm{R_E} \propto \frac{1}{\mathrm{v_P^q}} \tag{6.8}$$

Here, q is a velocity exponent. By fitting experimental results obtained with multi-layer organic coating systems applied to galvanised steel substrates, this exponent was found to be $q = 3.5$ (Rutherford et al., 1997), which points to a stronger relationship as for the erosion of bulk polymers ($q = 2.5$).

Particle impact velocity affects the erosion rate according to a power law. A suitable relationship is as follows:

$$\mathrm{E_R} \propto \mathrm{v_P^{\phi}} \tag{6.9}$$

A simple model developed by Rosenberger (1939) for blast cleaning processes delivered a velocity parameter of $\phi = 2.0$.

Power exponents for brittle material removal modes are listed in Table 5.13. Power exponents for polymer coatings (for hydroabrasive erosion) are listed in Table 6.1. For rubber, the power exponent depended on the fatigue-function parameter β_F (see Sect. 5.6.4). Detailed relationships were $\phi = 2 \cdot \beta$ for normal impact angles; and $\phi = \beta_F + 1$ for oblique impact angles (Arnold and Hutchings, 1992, 1993). Slikkerveer (1999) found values between $\phi = 2.87$ and 4.0 for different elastomers, whereby the high value characterised the behaviour of the most "rubber-like" material. For polymers, power exponent values between $\phi = 1.7$ and 2.8 were found (Zhang et al., 1995); and for the slurry erosion of fusion-bonded epoxy powder coatings, power exponents between $\phi = 4.0$ and 5.5 were reported (Luo et al., 2001). A power law with $\phi > 1$ could also describe the influence of the particle velocity on the volume of removed lips during the erosion of polymers (Walley and Field, 1987). Henning and Brauer (1986) found that the power exponent depended on impact angle and abrasive diameter. For PMMA, the exponent was found to vary between $\phi = 2.7$ and 3.2, whereas the latter value was for high impact angles. For rubber, values between $\phi = 2.5$ and 5.0 were found, whereby the precise value depended on the diameter of the impinging particles. Volume loss measurements performed by Tangirala (1998) on brittle iron scale delivered a power exponent slightly larger than unity.

If the Almen intensity was being considered as the target parameter, which is a familiar procedure in shot peening applications, the relationship between shot velocity and Almen intensity was linear (Linnemann et al., 1996).

Rajesh et al. (2004) investigated the effects of impact angle and material type on the particle impact velocity effects. They eroded seven types of polyamides at impact velocities of $v_P = 80$ m/s and, respectively, $v_P = 140$ m/s, which was a velocity increase of +75%. Their results are listed in Table 6.2, and the results witnessed a notable effect of the impact angle on the percentage of increase in the erosion rates. The highest increase of +240% was found for PA11 impinged at an angle of $\varphi = 30°$. For an impact angle of $\varphi = 90°$, however, the increase in erosion rate due to the higher impact velocity was +79% only. For the material PA12, the gain in erosion rate was larger for the high impact angle, which was not found for the other materials.

Fokke (1999) investigated the relationships between the kinetic energy of impinging abrasive particles, the impact area and the volume removed in epoxy-based

Table 6.1 Velocity exponents for polymer coatings (Zolotar, 1973); hydroabrasive erosion, $v_P = 5$–17 m/s

Material	Velocity exponent
Epoxy	3.06
Epoxy-phenol formaldehyde resin	3.20
Methacrylate resin	3.13
Phenol formaldehyde liquid	3.10
Vulcanite	3.02
Phenol formaldehyde powder	3.40

Table 6.2 Percentage increase in erosion rate for an impact velocity increase from $v_P = 80$ m/s to $v_p = 140$ m/s (Rajesh et al., 2004). Variable impact angle

Polyamide	Increase in erosion rate in %	
	30°	90°
PA 6	180	70
PA 11	240	70
PA 12	190	60
PA 12 (L 20)	160	210
PA 66	180	130
PA 66/610	220	30
Aromatic PA	200	50

organic coatings. For the blast cleaned area as the target parameter, the following linear trend was found:

$$A_M = \varepsilon_M \cdot E_P \tag{6.10}$$

The coefficient ε_M is the inverse specific erosion energy (m^2/J), and it depends on impact angle. The inverse specific energy decreased notably if impact angle increased (Fokke, 1999). The volume of removed paint showed a power-law relationship to the impact energy:

$$V_M = 3.1 \cdot 10^{-13} \cdot E_P^{1.5} \tag{6.11}$$

Here, V_M is given in m^3, and the particle impact energy is given in mJ. Results of measurements are presented in Fig. 6.6. The power exponent of 1.5 is right between two exponents estimated by Wood (1999) for the erosion of different metallic and ceramic coatings by a slurry flow. This author found a value of 1.17 for normal impact angles, and a value of 1.98 for an oblique ($\varphi = 30°$) impact angle.

Some results from scale removal experiments (with blast wheels) are provided in Fig. 6.7. The graph shows critical energy conditions for scale removal as functions of impact velocity, abrasive diameter and particle kinetic energy. This graph very well supports the threshold conception mentioned earlier. The removal of the mill scale becomes possible only if a certain impact velocity is exceeded for a given abrasive size. The effect of the impact velocity was pronounced in the range of small abrasive particles. Although these results were obtained with a wheel blast machine, the basic idea will work the same way for air blast machines.

6.2.2 Effects of Nozzle Diameter and Nozzle Length

Figure 6.8 shows typical relationships between cleaning rate and nozzle diameter for two air pressure levels. The cleaning rate almost linearly increases with an increase in the nozzle diameter. A simple expression is:

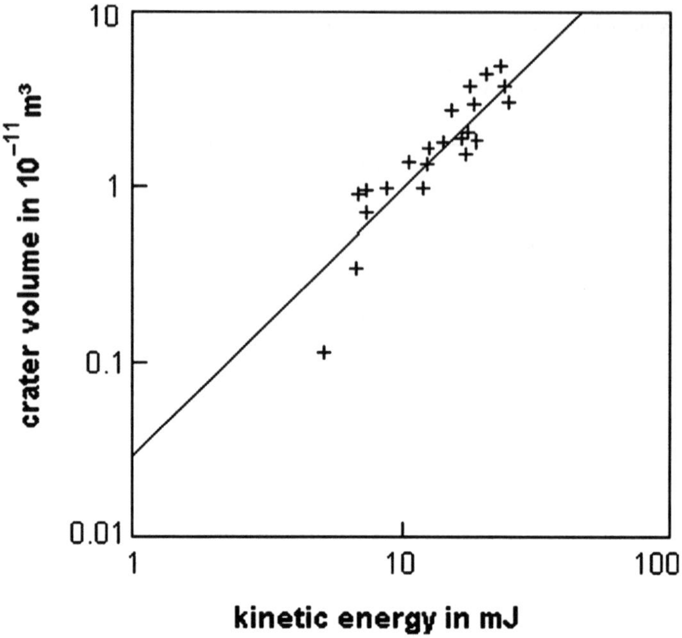

Fig. 6.6 Effect of particle kinetic energy on volume of removed paint (Fokke, 1999)

$$\dot{A} = C_2 \cdot d_N^{\chi_N} \tag{6.12}$$

with $\chi_N < 1$.

The major contribution of the nozzle diameter to the material removal process is the determination of air mass flow rate as well as of abrasive mass flow rate (if a fixed ratio between air mass flow rate and abrasive mass flow rate is desired). Both parameters increase if nozzle diameter rises (see Sects. 3.2 and 4.3.2). Nozzle diameter also affects the size of the blasted area (see Sect. 3.4). A threshold diameter does not seem to exist, although practice shows that a minimum nozzle diameter should not be undercut in order to realise a satisfying performance. The proportionality factor C_2 seems to decrease slightly with an increase in air pressure for the conditions in Fig. 6.8.

It is important to note that a trend as shown in Fig. 6.8 can be realised only if the compressor can deliver a volumetric air flow rate high enough to meet the requirement of a larger nozzle diameter. If the compressor cannot be adjusted to an increasing nozzle diameter, the working lines of compressor and nozzle will not intersect (see Fig. 4.3). The cleaning rate will drop if the nozzle diameter increases. This case is illustrated in Fig. 4.37, where the drop in cleaning rate for the larger nozzle diameter is almost 40%. The reason is the pressure drop in the system which leads to a deteriorated cleaning process. The limit for an increase in nozzle diameter is, therefore, the capacity of the compressor.

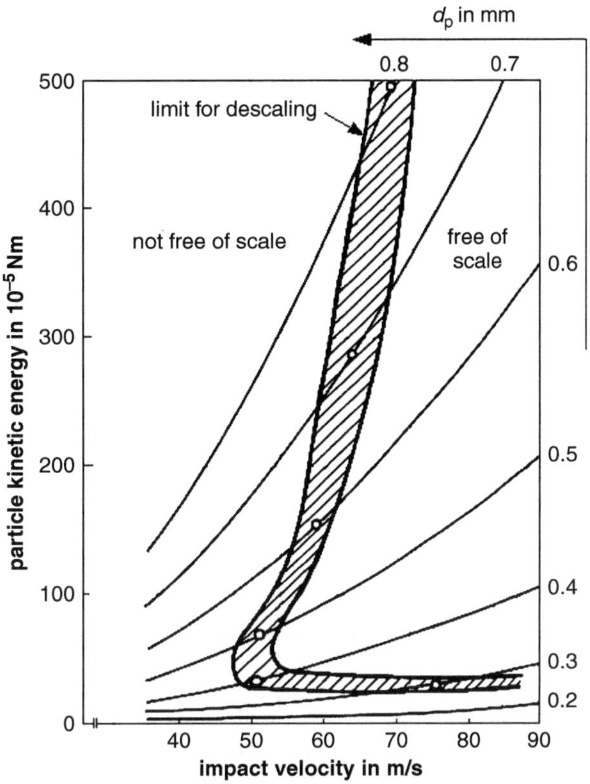

Fig. 6.7 Threshold conditions for mill scale removal from steel substrates (Weidenhaupt, 1970)

Uferer (1992) introduced a nozzle-shape factor, f_N, which depends on nozzle length. Cleaning rate is assumed to rise linearly with an increase in this parameter. For cylindrical nozzles, f_N depends on nozzle length; and for Laval nozzles, f_N depends on air pressure. Table 6.3 lists some typical values. According to these values, Laval nozzles would provide a higher cleaning rate.

6.2.3 *Effects of Nozzle Design*

A number of investigations depicted a notable influence of nozzle design parameters on the efficiency of blast cleaning processes. Djurovic et al. (1999), for example, noted an effect of the nozzle cross-section shape on the removal of organic coatings from aluminium substrates with starch media. The width of the traces formed in the paint layer was 26 mm for a round nozzle exit, but 46 mm for a rectangular nozzle exit; this was an increase of about 180%. It is also known that the energy distribution at the target surface notably depends on the nozzle exit geometry. These relationships are displayed in Figs. 3.33, 3.34 and 3.51.

Further effects of nozzle geometry were investigated by Kline et al. (1988) and Plaster (1972). Results of descaling tests with different nozzle types are summarised

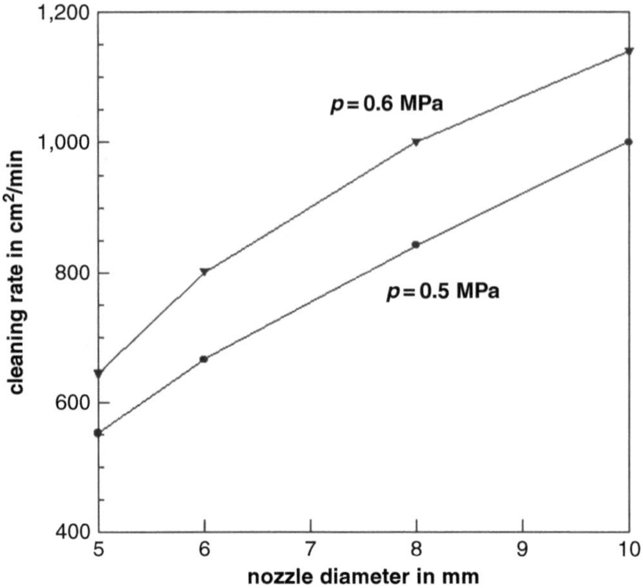

Fig. 6.8 Effect of nozzle diameter on cleaning rate (Kalpers, 1949)

in Fig. 6.9. It can be seen that scale mass loss rate increased with increasing pressure for all nozzle types, which verifies the trends discussed in Sect. 6.2.1. However, the individual trends depended on nozzle geometry. The maximum mass loss was obtained at all pressure levels if a convergent–divergent (Laval) nozzle was utilised. For the highest pressure level, however, this advantage vanished, and a divergent nozzle with a bell-shaped inlet section performed equally.

Kline et al. (1988) performed laboratory and site experiments with a number of different nozzles at higher compressor pressures. The authors cleaned mill scale bearing steel plates to a near-white surface standard, and they tested four different types of nozzles: a standard Laval nozzle, a nozzle with wide throat design, a double Laval

Table 6.3 Blasting nozzle coefficient f_N (Uferer, 1992)

Cylindrical nozzle	
Nozzle length in mm	f_N
50	0.60
80	0.85
100	0.93
120	1.00
150	1.05
Laval nozzle	
Nozzle air pressure in MPa	f_N
<0.3	1.0–1.1
0.3–0.6	1.1–1.3

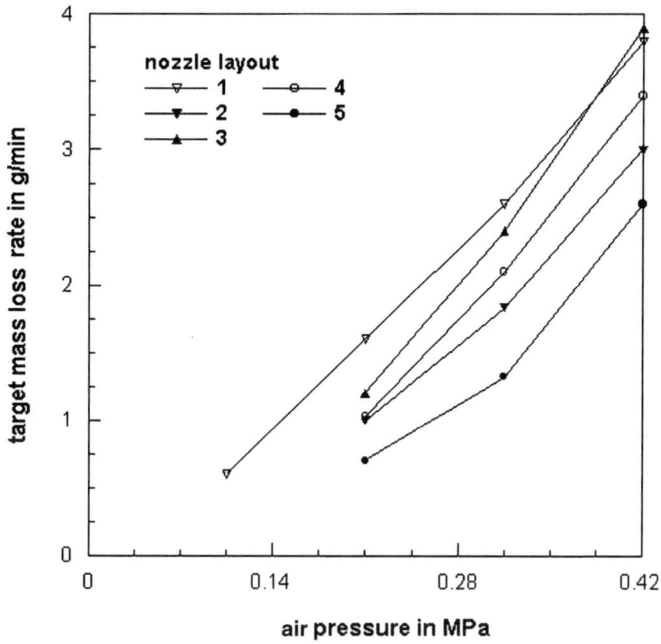

Fig. 6.9 Effects of nozzle design and nozzle pressure on the removal of mill scale (Plaster, 1972). Nozzle layout: 1 – convergent–divergent (Laval) nozzle; 2 – bell-mouthed convergent nozzle; 3 – bell-mouthed divergent nozzle; 4 – bell-mouthed convergent–divergent (Laval) nozzle; 5 – convergent-parallel nozzle (lined with tungsten carbide sections). Abrasive type: crushed chilled cast iron shot; nozzle diameter: $d_N = 9.5$ mm

nozzle and a Laval nozzle with a distinctively large exit end opening. Results of these investigations are plotted in Figs. 6.10 and 6.11. The graph in Fig. 6.10 provides results of laboratory tests. No apparent improvement could be achieved with the wide throat nozzle. This design will benefit only from a larger blast hose that is able to take advantage of the wider throat cross-section (see Sect. 4.5). The double Laval nozzle gave little or no significant improvement compared to the standard Laval design. Productivity could significantly be improved by using the wide exit opening design; the results indicated an improvement of about +50%. The gain was probably due to the larger blast pattern obtained with this nozzle. Measurements of the blast pattern sizes indicated a diameter of 102 mm for the wide exit opening nozzle compared to a diameter of 76 mm for the standard Laval nozzle. Results of field tests are plotted in Fig. 6.11. A laminar flow nozzle was included to these tests, which featured a very smooth transition throat between the convergent and divergent nozzle sections. This design did not deliver a productivity improvement. The double Laval nozzle generated about +10% more productivity improvement over the standard Laval nozzle at all pressure levels. The large exit opening design was significantly more effective than the standard Laval nozzle at the two higher pressure levels. A higher nozzle pressure was beneficial to the cleaning efficiency for all nozzle types, but it was most influencing if the large exit opening design was utilised.

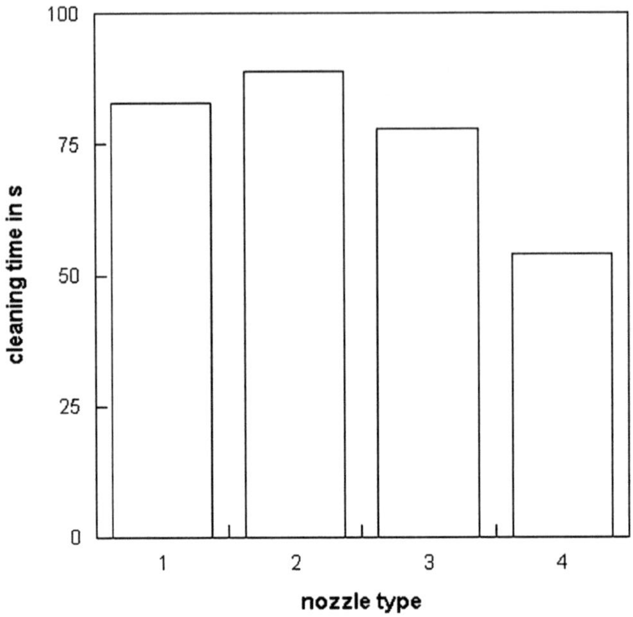

Fig. 6.10 Effects of nozzle design and nozzle pressure on the removal of mill scale (Kline et al., 1988); results of laboratory tests. Nozzle layout: 1 – standard Laval nozzle; 2 – nozzle with wide throat; 3 – double Laval nozzle; 4 – nozzle with distinctively large exit opening

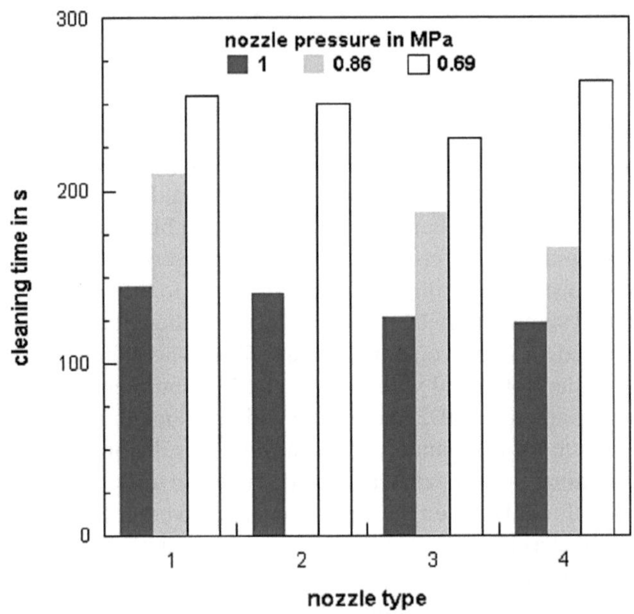

Fig. 6.11 Effects of nozzle design and nozzle pressure on the removal of mill scale (Kline et al., 1988); results of site tests. Nozzle layout: 1 – standard Laval nozzle; 2 – laminar flow nozzle with soft flow transition; 3 – double Laval nozzle; 4 – nozzle with distinctively large exit opening

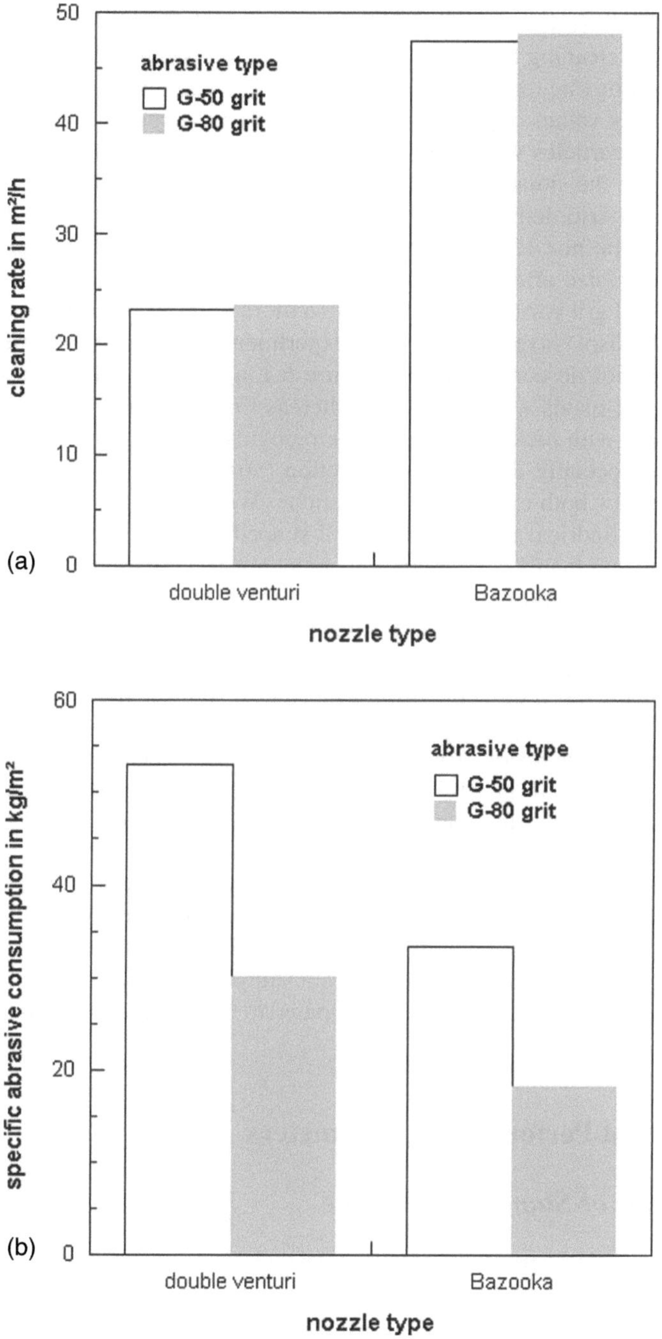

Fig. 6.12 Effects of nozzle design and abrasive type on target parameters (Hitzrot, 1997). "Double venturi" corresponds to nozzle "3" in Figs. 6.10 and 6.11; "Bazooka" corresponds to nozzle "4" in Figs. 6.10 and 6.11. (**a**) Effects on cleaning rate; (**b**) Effects on abrasive consumption

Figure 6.12 illustrates the effects of abrasive particle size on the nozzle design. With respect to cleaning rate, shown in Fig. 6.12a, the size of the abrasives did not affect the cleaning rate for a given nozzle design. The Bazooka nozzle type delivered higher efficiency values compared with the double Laval nozzle, whether small or large steel grit particles were used. If, however, the specific abrasive consumption was considered, the situation changed. This aspect is illustrated in Fig. 6.12b. The double Laval nozzle, fed with smaller steel grit particles, was more efficient than the Bazooka type nozzle, fed with larger steel grit particles. For a given nozzle design, abrasive size affected the specific abrasive consumption notably, whereby the smaller steel grit particles led always to a more efficient performance.

Figure 6.13 displays results of erosion experiments performed by Hamann (1987) with different nozzle configurations. Figure 6.13a applies to the removal of mill scale from steel plates with steel shot, whereas Fig. 6.13b applies to the removal of a PVC plate with nickel slag. It can be recognised that a convergent–divergent nozzle with a specially designed inlet section (nozzle type "4") was the most effective design for both experimental situations. With regard to the removal of the mill scale, a cylindrical nozzle with a bell-shaped inlet section (nozzle type "2") was more efficient than a convergent–divergent nozzle (nozzle type "3"). However, the opposite trend could be found during the treatment of the PVC targets, where the convergent–divergent nozzle performed more effective. It can also be seen that a convergent–divergent nozzle with a short convergent section (nozzle type "2") was very efficient for the removal of mill scale, but it did not show an equally good performance during the treatment of the PVC samples.

A convincing conclusion from the presented results is that an optimum nozzle design does not exist in general. The nozzle design must be adapted to the entire cleaning system, which include abrasive material, process parameters and target material response.

Hutans (1986) placed a pipe between nozzle exit and surface to be blast cleaned in order to reduce the effects of interactions between the abrasive-air flow and the surrounding air. He reported notable improvements in terms of cleaning rate, specific abrasive consumption and specific energy consumption. The savings were larger for blast cleaning in an open environment compared to blast cleaning in a hall.

6.3 Effects of Performance Parameters

6.3.1 Effects of Stand-off Distance

Results of Remmelts (1969) on the effect of variations in stand-off distance on the cleaning rate for mill scale are displayed in Fig. 6.14. Such a trend was also found for the removal of coatings from metal substrates (Uhlmann et al., 2003). Three regions can be distinguished in the graph: an initial region, an optimum region and a decreasing region. The optimum stand-off distance is in the range between $x = 57$ and 67 mm. These values are close to the SSPC Surface Preparation Commentary,

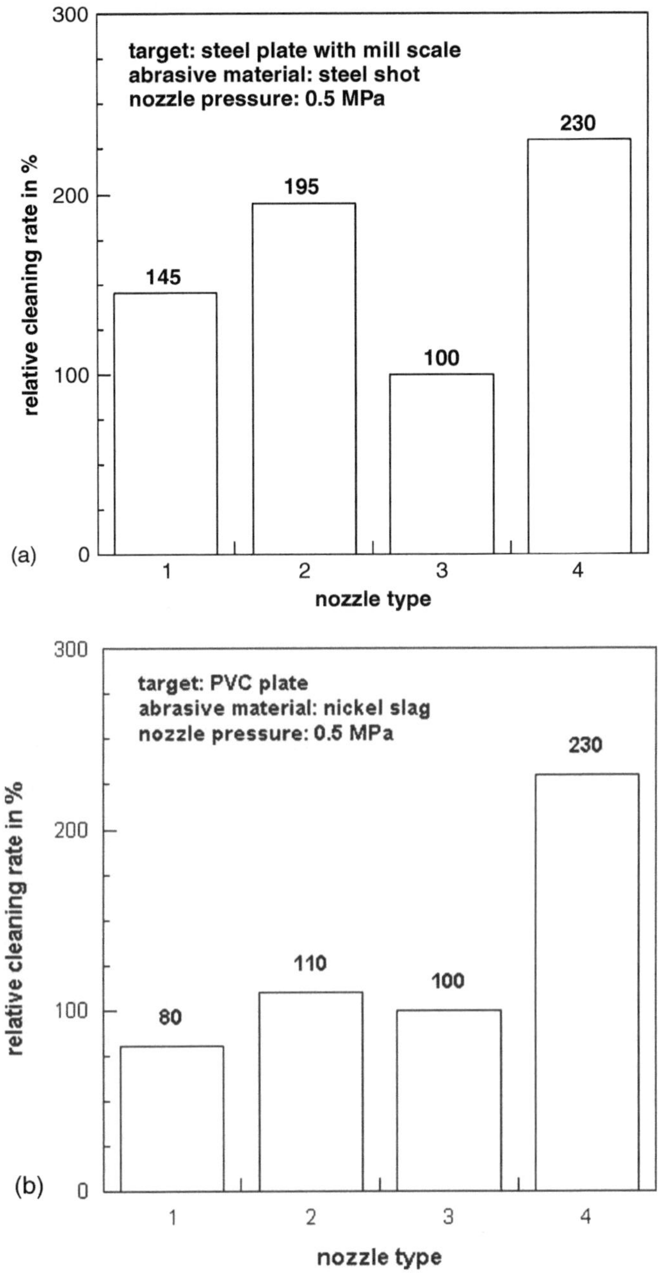

Fig. 6.13 Effects of nozzle design on material removal efficiency (Hamann, 1987). Nozzle layout: 1 – cylindrical nozzle with bell-shaped inlet section; 2 – divergent–convergent nozzle with short divergent section; 3 – standard divergent–convergent nozzle (Laval); 4 – divergent–convergent nozzle with additional inlet flow section. (**a**) Removal of mill scale from steel plates with steel grit; (**b**) Erosion of PVC samples with nickel slag

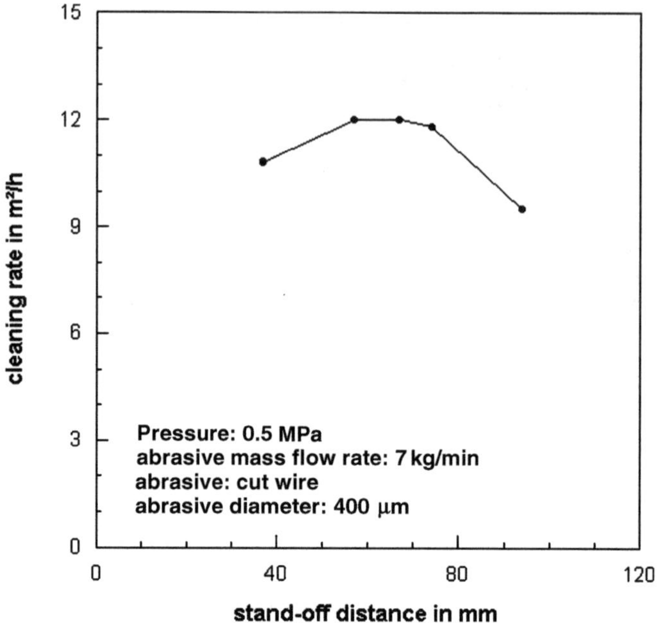

Fig. 6.14 Effect of stand-off distance on cleaning rate for mill scale (Remmelts, 1969)

which states the following: *"For optimum cleaning rate, the nozzle to surface distance is around 46 cm."* This optimum distance can vary depending on the type of substrate, material to be removed and process parameters to be adjusted. An older regulation for the removal of mill scale and rust from ship steels due to blast cleaning recommended optimum stand-off distances between $x = 40$ and 60 cm (STG, 1963).

It was shown in Sect. 3.6.6 that abrasive particle velocity increases further after the particles have exited the nozzle (see Figs. 3.46 and 3.47). This phenomenon explains partly the existence of an optimum stand-off distance for blast cleaning processes. Another aspect is the increase in jet diameter and, thus in the size of the blasted area (see Fig. 3.22). This issue is discussed in Sect. 3.4.

Uferer (1992) introduced a stand-off distance parameter f_X, whose values are listed in Table 6.4 for different abrasive materials. It can be seen that slag and quartzsand are much more sensitive to variations in stand-off distance than steel

Table 6.4 Values for the stand-off distance coefficient f_X for the removal of rust (Uferer, 1992)

Abrasive material	Value for f_X				
	Stand-off distance in mm				
	250	300–400	500	600	750
Steel wire	–	0.90	1.00	1.00	1.00
Slag and quartz	0.95	1.05	1.00	0.85	0.65

wire. This result agrees with the trends shown in Fig. 3.40, where it can be seen that the increase in particle velocity after the nozzle exit was more distinct for the slag material (at least for the convergent–divergent nozzle).

6.3.2 Effects of Relative Particle Distance

The relative distance between particles in the particle stream according to (3.45) affects the erosion of materials. Results cited by Ciampini et al. (2003a) showed a drop in erosion rate from a constant value of unity for low L_P*-values to much lower erosion rates at a L_P* of about 17. This result was attributed to a sudden increase in interference between incidental and rebounding particles at the higher L_P*-numbers.

Balasubramaniyan (1998) has shown that the volume loss of eroded brittle materials was very sensitive to changes in the relative particle distance if $L_P^* < 1$. This would mean that changes in the stream density are critical to the material removal process for $\rho_S^* > \pi/6$.

6.3.3 Effects of Impact Angle

The effect of variations in impact angle on the cleaning rate for mill scale is displayed in Fig. 6.15 for two abrasive mass flow rates. A maximum cleaning rate could be noted at an angle of $\varphi = 45°$ which is rather typical for plastically responding materials. The lowest cleaning rate was found at perpendicular impact for both parameter conditions. These results neither verified the general recommendation in the SSPC Surface Preparation Commentary: "*An 80 to 90 degree angle is best suited for removing mill scale or heavy rust and for cleaning pitted areas*", nor did the scale removal model presented in Sect. 5.6. However, abrasive mass flow rate seemed to play an additional role, as illustrated in Fig. 6.15, and the lower value for the abrasive mass flow rate did not reveal a "ductile" behaviour of the scale. If elastically responding materials, namely heavy rust, heavy mill scale, brittle coatings, need to be removed, a normal impact angle is often the right choice. Averchenko et al. (1970), for example, determined maximum values for the erosion rate of brittle enamel coatings at normal impact angles. For the removal of rust (no platy rust) from steel plates, Uferer (1992) found an increase in cleaning rate if impact angle rose from $\varphi = 45°$ to 90°. Tangirala (1998) noted a maximum volume loss of iron scale if the impact angle was $\varphi = 90°$.

Maximum erosion rates at low impact angles are rather typical for materials being removed by micro-cutting or, respectively, ploughing processes (see Sect. 5.5.2). Such trends were also observed for organic coating materials by Kotnarowska (2003), Zahavi and Schmitt (1981, 1982) and Trezona et al. (2000a); for rubber by Arnold and Hutchings (1992) and Slikkerveer (1999); for enamel coatings by Parslow et al. (1997) and for polyethylene by Walley and Field (1987).

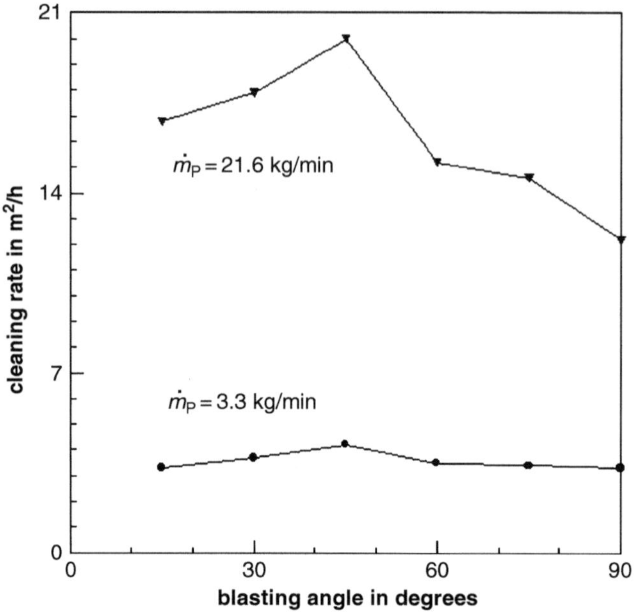

Fig. 6.15 Effects of blasting angle and abrasive mass flow rate on cleaning rate for mill scale (Remmelts, 1969)

An example is provided in Fig. 6.16 which shows that the type of the epoxy coating system did not affect the location of the optimum impact angle. Zahavi and Schmitt (1981, 1982) eroded rather thin organic coatings (DFT between 30 and 75 μm) with quartz sand ($d_P = 210$–297 μm) at a moderate impact speeds ($v_P = 42$ m/s) and investigated the effects of impact angle variations. They found that changes in impact angle were more affective to the erosion of rather hard polyurethane coatings. For elastomeric coating materials, the mass loss due to erosion was almost unaffected if the impact angle exceeded a value of about $\varphi = 45°$.

Optimum impact angles for the erosion of rubber by impinging solid particles were found between $\varphi = 15°$ and $20°$ (Arnold and Hutchings, 1992). Slikkerveer (1999) derived the following relationship between impact angle and erosion rate of rubber materials:

$$E_R = a \cdot (1 + b \cdot \cos^c \varphi) \tag{6.13}$$

The regression parameters had the following values: $a = 0.0072$–0.037; $b = 2.7$–8.7 and $c = 2.2$–8.0. The regression parameter a is the erosion rate at normal impact ($\varphi = 90°$), and the parameter c describes the transition from oblique to normal impact.

Fokke (1999) introduced the inverse specific erosion energy [see (6.10)], and he found a dependence with the impact angle. The inverse specific erosion energy decreased with an increase in impact angle in the impact angle range between $\varphi = 30°$

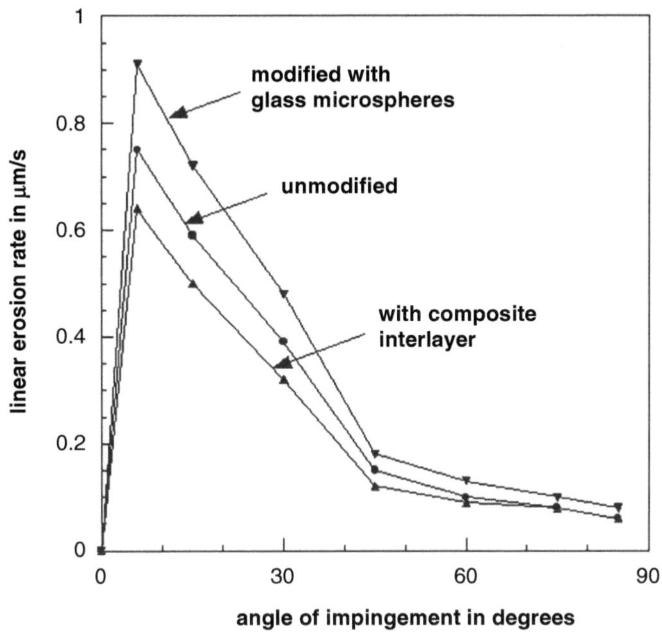

Fig. 6.16 Effect of blasting angle and coating composition on coating removal (Kotnarowska, 2003)

and 45°. For impact angles larger than $\varphi = 45°$, impact angle did not affect the inverse specific erosion energy.

Uferer (1992) introduced an impact angle factor f_ϕ, which has a linear effect on the cleaning rate for the removal of mill scale and rust. Typical values for this parameter are listed in Table 6.5.

6.3.4 Effects of Exposure Time

Removal rate and cleaning rate increase with an increase in exposure time. The respective functional relationship can be described as follows:

$$\dot{A} \propto (t_E - t_I)^{n_t} \tag{6.14}$$

Table 6.5 Values for the blasting angle coefficient f_ϕ (Uferer, 1992)

Blasting angle	Coefficient f_ϕ	
	For mill scale	For rust
30°	1.5	–
45°	1.6	0.6
60°	1.25	–
90°	1.0	0.84

This relationship can be considered a removal kinetics, whereby values for the exponent range between $n_t = 0$ and 1. Therefore, the efficiency of cleaning processes and of material removal processes drops with an increase in exposure time. If the deposit or coating is completely removed from a substrate, $n_t = 0$. It was shown that the precise values for n_t depended, among others, on abrasive type and size (Raykowski et al., 2001). Some relationships are listed in Table 6.6. The parameter t_I is an incubation period which must be exceeded in order to generate a measurable material removal. Equation (6.14) has the same structure as (5.47), which was derived by Schmithals (1961) for the blast cleaning of mill scale.

An alternative exposure parameter is the local exposure time, which is given as follows:

$$t_E = d_J / v_N \tag{6.14a}$$

The jet diameter can sometimes be replaced by the nozzle diameter ($d_J = d_N$). A general plot of local exposure time versus volumetric erosion is shown in Fig. 6.17. It can be seen that the erosion rate (slope of the curve) increased notably at low exposure times. If the local exposure time increases further, efficiency (in terms of the slope of the curve) dropped. From this point of view, short local exposure times (high traverse rates) are recommended. A threshold exposure time (t_I), which separates the incubation period from the erosion period, is also shown in Fig. 6.17. A threshold (incubation) period was found by Friedrich (1986) for the particle erosion of polymers. The actual magnitude of the incubation time depended on the brittleness of the polymers. More brittle polymers did not exhibit a notable incubation period. D'Emanuele et al. (1992) found for copolymer materials that the duration of the incubation period depended on the initial molecular weight of the polymers. These authors characterised the incubation period as a time during which a rapid decrease in polymer molecular weight occurred. Threshold periods are also known from other abrasive jet applications, namely hydroabrasive machining (Momber and Kovacevic, 1998), but also from hydroblasting applications (Momber, 2003, 2005a). The most probable explanation is that erosion of the coating starts after a period of damage accumulation by subsequently impinging abrasive particles (see Fokke, 1999). Threshold limits do not seem to exist for the removal of rather soft coatings. The removal rate should have a maximum at rather short relative exposure times (see Fig. 6.17). After a certain time, a further increase in exposure time reduces the removal rate.

Table 6.6 Removal kinetic power parameter, based on measurements from Raykowski et al. (2001) ($p = 0.35$ MPa, $\varphi = 90°$, $x = 38$ cm)

Abrasive type	Particle diameter in μm	n_t-value
Glass beads	125–177	0.56
	177–250	0.47
	420–590	0.47
Steel shot	90–200	0.51
	90–300	0.60

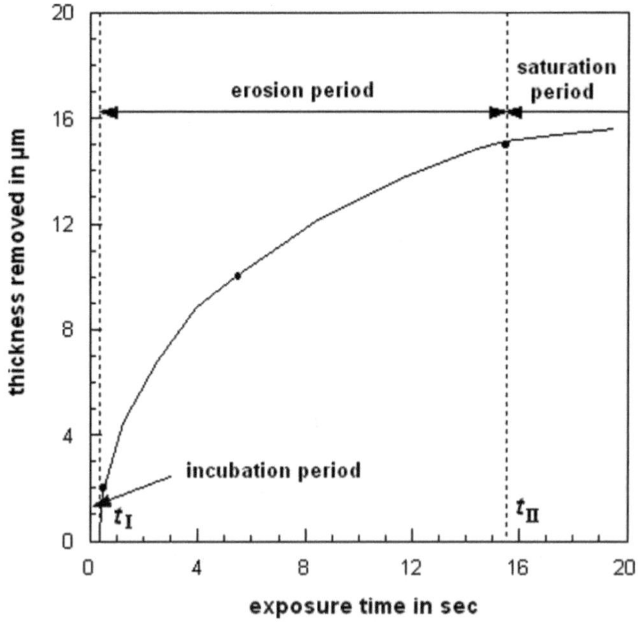

Fig. 6.17 Effect of local exposure time on the removal of a deposit from a turbine blade (based on results of Raykowski et al., 2001)

The qualitative relationship displayed in Fig. 6.17 corresponds well with measurements of area coverage values performed by Tosha and Iida (2001). The authors found an initial increase in the area coverage, which was followed by a saturation level at higher exposure times. Both ranges were separated by a "full coverage time". Coverage time increased if abrasive particle diameter increased, and if abrasive particle velocity decreased (see Sect. 3.5.4). This transition parameter may be close to the exposure time (t_{II}) defined in Fig. 6.17, which separates erosion period and saturation period. This time mark should not be exceeded in order to guarantee effective cleaning conditions. A similar transition parameter – the minimum number of impinging abrasive particles for the complete coverage of an area of 1 m^2 – was defined by Fokke (1999). This particular parameter mainly depended on the kinetic energy of the impinging particles (see Sect. 6.5).

6.3.5 *Effects of Number of Passes*

If the optimum exposure time, t_0, is known, a strategy for multi-pass material removal can be developed. The optimum exposure time can simply be introduced several times into the duration that corresponds to the desired volumetric removal rate. This approach delivers the following relationship:

$$n_S = \frac{\dot{V}_M}{\dot{V}_{M(t_E=t_O)}}; n_S = 1, 2, 3 \ldots \tag{6.15}$$

If, for example, a deposit with a thickness of $h_C = 16\,\mu m$ must be removed from a substrate, a local exposure time of $t_E = 20\,s$ is required. The optimum exposure time for dh_C/dt_E = max shall be $t_O = 2\,s$, which gives $h_C(t_E = t_O) = 6\,\mu m$. The theoretical number of steps calculated from (6.15) is $n_S = 16/6 = 2.67$. In practice, $n_S = 3$. The entire exposure time required to remove the desired coating mass is thus $t_E = 3.2 = 6\,s$ which is about 30% of the time for a one-step removal. The gain in efficiency is, therefore, as high as +70%. This example is based on Fig. 6.17.

6.4 Effects of Abrasive Parameters

6.4.1 Effects of Abrasive Mass Flow Rate

Effects of variations in abrasive mass flow rate on blast cleaning processes were investigated by Bae et al. (2007), Hareux and Riac (1986), Holt and Austin (2001) and Kura (2003). Figures 6.18 and 6.19 show typical relationships between abrasive mass flow rate and cleaning rate. Similar relationships were found for the removal of epoxy coatings from steel plates with steel grit (Bae et al., 2007); and for abrasive erosion of polyurethane and rubber (Zhang et al., 1995). The relationship can be expressed according to a reaction kinetics model (Momber, 1995):

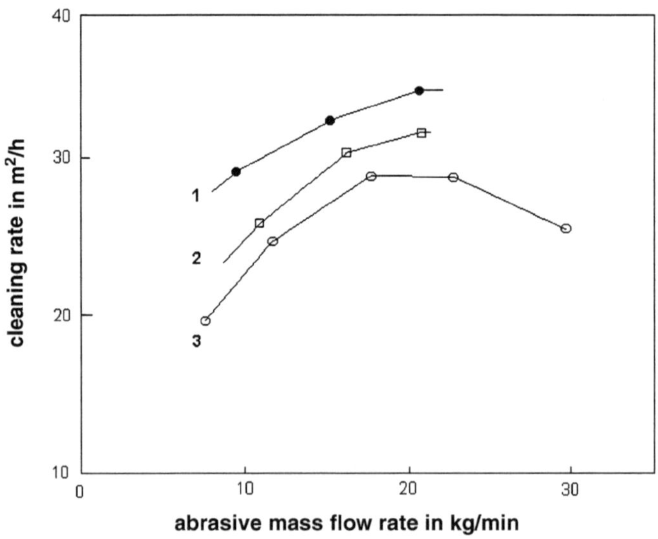

Fig. 6.18 Effect of abrasive mass flow rate on cleaning rate (Hareux and Riac, 1986). Abrasive material: aluminium oxide 700; nozzle types: 1 – long Laval nozzle, $d_N = 9.5$ mm; 2 – short Laval nozzle, $d_N = 9$ mm; 3 – cylindrical nozzle, $d_N = 10$ mm

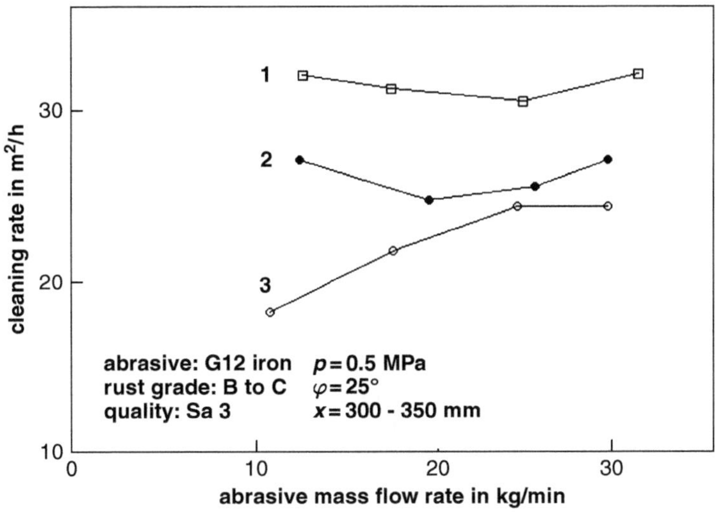

Fig. 6.19 Effect of abrasive mass flow rate on cleaning rate (Hareux and Riac, 1986). Abrasive material: iron shot G12; nozzle type: 1 – long Laval nozzle, $d_N = 9.5\,\text{mm}$; 2 – cylindrical nozzle, $d_N = 10\,\text{mm}$; 3 – short Laval nozzle, $d_N = 9\,\text{mm}$

$$\dot{A} = k \cdot \dot{m}_P^m \tag{6.16}$$

In the equation, the power exponent, m, is a function of the abrasive mass flow rate. For small abrasive mass flow rates, $m = 1$. For the erosion of polymers, values between $m = 0.5$ and 1.0 were estimated (Zhang et al., 1995). For the slurry erosion of fusion-bonded epoxy powders, values between $m = 0.5$ and 0.6 were recorded (Luo et al., 2001). The value for m decreases up to $m = 0$ for optimum abrasive mass flow rates, and it becomes m ¡ 0 for high abrasive mass flow rates. From the point of view of abrasive consumption, the optimum range is at low abrasive mass flow rates and $m = 1$. In this range, each increase in abrasive mass flow rate leads to a proportional rise in the material removal rate. Such effects are known from abrasion tests of organic coatings, where mass loss linearly increases with the number of abrasion cycles (Cambruzzi et al., 2005). Fokke's (1999) erosive cleaning model also leads to a linear relationship between cleaning rate and abrasive mass flow rate (see Sect. 6.5). Results plotted in Figs. 6.18 and 6.19 show that an optimum mass flow rate depends on abrasive type and the nozzle configuration. It seems from the plot in Fig. 6.18, which is valid for aluminium oxide, that the optimum mass flow rate shifted to higher values if convergent–divergent nozzles ("1" and "2") were applied. For this nozzle type, the conditions for maximum cleaning rates were not yet reached. The cylindrical nozzle, however, featured a maximum cleaning rate at an abrasive mass flow rate of $\dot{m}_P = 17\,\text{kg/min}$. For equal abrasive mass flow rates, the convergent–divergent nozzles generated a higher cleaning rate compared with the cylindrical nozzle. The advantage of the convergent–divergent nozzles seems to become even more pronounced at higher abrasive mass flow rates. The situation is different in Fig. 6.19, which is valid for iron grit. In that case, only the curve for the short convergent–divergent nozzle (denoted "3") showed an optimum range for the abrasive mass flow rate. It was at about $\dot{m}_P = 25$ kg/min. The other two nozzle types did not show any optimum range. In particular, the long convergent–divergent nozzle (denoted "1") was rather insensitive to changes in the abrasive mass flow rate. The cylindrical nozzle behaved completely different compared with the situation in Fig. 6.18. Whereas this nozzle exhibited an optimum performance at moderate values for the mass flow rate ($\dot{m}_P = 15$–20 kg/min) in Fig. 6.18, it performed worst in that same abrasive mass flow rate range in Fig. 6.19.

The abrasive mass flow rate determines the number of impinging abrasive particles as well as their kinetic energies. The higher the abrasive mass flow rate, the higher the number of particles involved in the blast cleaning processes. Assuming no interaction between the individual abrasive particles in the course of acceleration, each increase in abrasive mass flow rate leads to a proportional increase in material removal. This holds for relatively low abrasive mass flow rates. It is known from wheel blasting, that a certain abrasive mass exists, which guarantees a complete coverage of a given surface with erosion pits. This critical abrasive mass is typical for a given substrate material, and it depends on abrasive material density and abrasive particle diameter (Safar, 1973). For rather high abrasive mass flow rates, damping mechanisms, particle collision, the generation of debris films and overlap effects may occur. Also, the limited kinetic energy of the air flow distributes over a very high number of particles, which leads to a decrease in the kinetic energy of the individual particles. This effect cancels the positive effect of the higher impact frequency. Figure 2.17 schematically illustrates these relationships. It is also known that an increase in the mass flow ratio abrasive/air reduces the velocity of the particles at the nozzle exit; this is true especially for smaller abrasive particles (see Sect. 3.6.2).

The location of the optimum abrasive mass flow rate depends on the deformation behaviour of the target materials. Whereas materials with the ability of plastic deformation reach the optimum at comparatively high abrasive mass flow rates; elastically responding materials reach the optimum region at lower abrasive mass flow rates. This difference is due to the higher sensitivity of brittle materials to the loading intensity provided by the abrasive particles. In contrast, a material responding with plastic deformation is more sensitive to the frequency of the impacting particles. Therefore, an increase in the abrasive mass flow rate is beneficial for these materials to overcome their plastic-deformation capability.

Experimental investigations have shown that the cleaning rate generally exhibited a maximum at an optimum number of turns on the abrasive metering valve (Holt and Austin, 2001; Kura, 2003; Bae et al., 2007). An example is shown in Fig. 6.20. It can be seen that the different abrasive materials responded differently to changes in the number of valve turns. The copper slag (denoted "1"), in particular, was very sensitive to changes in the number of turns. It can also be seen that the location of the maximum depended on the abrasive type. Each abrasive material is related to a certain number of turns (respectively to a certain cross-section of the valve opening). The optimum number of valve turns is six for the copper slag, and it is four for the

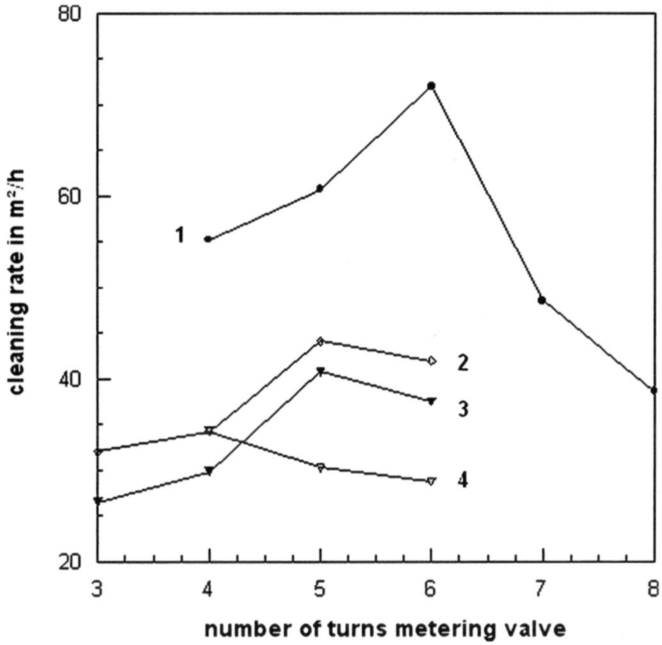

Fig. 6.20 Effect of abrasive metering on cleaning rate (Holt and Austin, 2001). Abrasive material: 1 – copper slag, 2 – hematite, 3 – garnet, 4 – coal slag

coal slag. It is conclusive that the specific abrasive consumption (in kg/m^2) must have a minimum value at that particular number of valve turns. It must, however, be taken into account that abrasive mass flow rate does not always have a linear relationship to the number of turns for all abrasive types. This was shown by Holt and Austin (2001). Therefore, the relationship between cleaning rate and abrasive mass flow rate does not always exhibit an optimum range (especially not for high air pressures), whereas the relationship between cleaning rate and number of valve turns always does.

Bae et al. (2007) published cleaning rates obtained during the removal of epoxy paint from steel substrate, whereby the values for the mass flow ratio abrasive/air were varied. The results depicted that cleaning rate decreased if the value for the mass flow ratio abrasive/air rose. The values for the mass flow ratio considered in this study ($R_m = 4$–4.4) were, however, unusually high.

Papini et al. (2003) defined a critical abrasive mass flow rate for significant inter-particle collision to occur. This critical parameter can be calculated as follows:

$$\dot{m}_C = \frac{4 \cdot \Pi_1 \cdot v_P \cdot \rho_P \cdot \pi \cdot r_P^3}{3 \cdot x} \tag{6.17}$$

The variable Π_1, a dimensionless mass flow rate, is given through the following equation (Papini et al., 2003):

$$\Pi_1 = \frac{\dot{N}_{P1} \cdot x}{v_P} \tag{6.18}$$

Here, the variable $\dot{N}_{P1}$ is a particle frequency at which significant interference (5%) between incident and rebounding particles begins to appear. It was found that this frequency depended, among others, on particle diameter and coefficient of restitution. Papini et al. (2003) performed numerical simulations to estimate values for Π_1 and found that this variable had low values for low x/d_P-ratios. The ratio x/d_P also determined the influence of the coefficient of restitution on Π_1. If the ratio was $x/d_P < 120$, Π_1 was high for high values for the coefficient of restitution; whereas the opposite trend was found for $x/d_P > 120$. Equation (6.17) can also be expressed in terms of the critical particle mass flux, passing through a nozzle:

$$\dot{m}_N = \frac{\dot{m}_C}{\pi \cdot r_N^2} \tag{6.19}$$

Parslow et al. (1997) performed erosion tests on enamel paints with a film thickness of DFT = 50 μm and found a relationship very similar to that plotted in Fig. 6.19. The authors utilised the abrasive concentration (g/m^3) as the evaluation parameter. At high values for the abrasive concentration, the erosion rate approximated a constant value in all cases. The value, where the erosion rate became stable, may be considered a typical parameter for a given paint material.

Walley and Field (1987) introduced an *incubation number* for the erosion of polymers. This number was defined as the number of impacts that have to occur on an impact zone before it contributes to a net mass loss. The incubation numbers were rather large for polymers, suggesting that the amount of deformation needed before material is removed was also large. This parameter had a strong relationship to the impact angle. If impact angle increased, the incubation number increased as well.

Glatzel and Brauer (1978) applied the *collision number* according to (2.12) to erosion processes, and they found that the mass loss decreased with an increase in the collision number according to the following relationship:

$$\Delta m_M \propto e^{-2 \cdot c_K} \tag{6.20}$$

6.4.2 Effects of Abrasive Flux Rate

Abrasive flux rate can be defined as follows:

$$\dot{m}_F = \frac{m_P \cdot \dot{N}_P}{A_C} \tag{6.21}$$

It expresses the mass of abrasive particles impinging a given cross-section during a defined time interval. Its physical unit is kg/(m^2 s). Flux rate, thus, can characterise the impingement frequency. Detailed studies have shown that abrasive flux rate had comparatively little influence on the erosion of brittle materials and metals, but it was a sensitive parameter for the erosion of polymers and elastomers (Walley and Field, 1987; Arnold and Hutchings, 1989). Some results obtained on rubber are displayed in Fig. 6.21. It can be seen that erosion rate decreased as flux rate increased. The effects of varying flux rates were very pronounced in the range of small flux rates. The reasons for this behaviour were attributed to chemical degradation processes in the rubber material, and they were in detail discussed by Arnold and Hutchings (1989). The same trend was noted by Djurovic et al. (1999) for the removal of organic coatings from aluminium substrates with starch media. The authors found that cleaning efficiency dropped if specific abrasive consumption (kg/m^2) increased. Ciampini et al., 2003a) performed a simulation of the flux rate on abrasive particle interactions. They calculated critical values for the flux rate for negligible particle interactions. The critical value depended on the particle diameter. Typical values are listed in Table 6.7.

Henning and Brauer (1986) applied the frequency number according to (2.11), and they found an increase in the erosion rate with an increase in the particle frequency number. The progress of the erosion rate function did not depend on the material type; it had equal values for glass, aluminium, rubber and PMMA.

Hutchings (1981) derived a critical specific abrasive mass (kg/m^2) needed for the incubation of erosion processes in metals. This critical parameter was defined as follows:

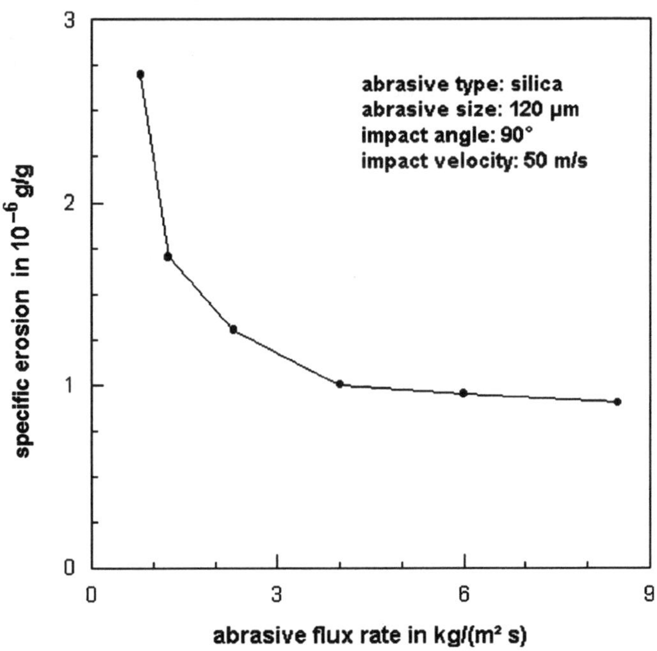

Fig. 6.21 Effect of abrasive flux rate on specific erosion in rubber (Arnold and Hutchings, 1989)

Table 6.7 Critical flux rates for negligible particle interactions (Ciampini et al., 2003a)

Particle diameter in μm	Critical flux rate in $kg/(s \cdot m^2)$
69	0.07
231	0.9
700	8.0

$$\mathrm{m_A} \propto \varepsilon_\mathrm{C} \cdot \frac{\mathrm{d_P}}{\mathrm{v_P^2}} \tag{6.22}$$

The power exponent for the particle velocity corresponded very well with experimentally estimated values (which were between 1.9 and 2.5 for aluminium). The parameter ε_C is a critical strain generated in the target material.

6.4.3 Effects of Abrasive Particle Diameter

Figure 6.22 illustrates a typical relationship between abrasive particle diameter and inverse cleaning rate for descaling. The time required to clean a given area was rather unaffected for small particle sizes. For particle diameters larger than $d_P = 1{,}000$ μm, cleaning time suddenly rose, and the descaling process became very inefficient. The relationship between cleaning rate and abrasive particle diameter can be characterised a follows:

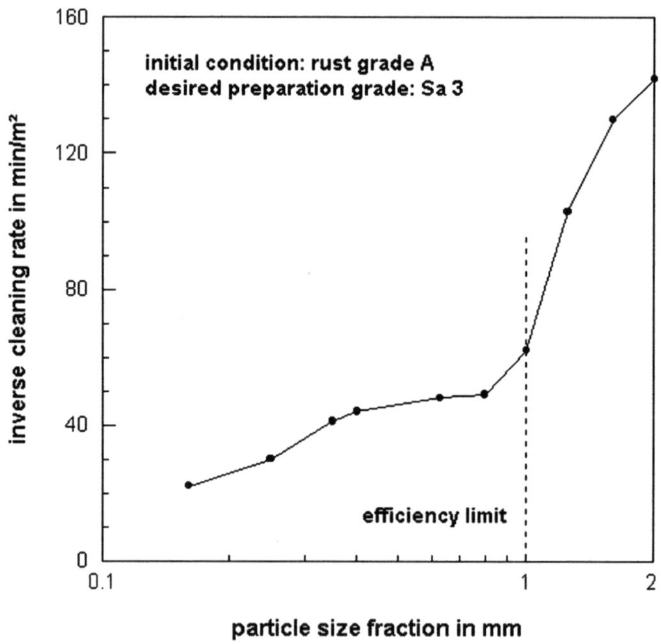

Fig. 6.22 Effect of abrasive particle size on inverse cleaning rate for mill scale (Neumann, 1976)

$$\dot{A} \propto d_P^{\theta_P} \tag{6.23a}$$

with $\theta_P < 0$.

It is important to note that the condition $\theta_P < 0$ holds for the relationship between particle size and cleaning rate as the target parameter. Figure 6.23 shows how a variation in abrasive particle size can be utilised for cleaning rate optimisation if a desired profile roughness must be realised. For a given roughness of $R_Z = 25$ μm, the specific rate varied between 60 min/m^2 (for $d_P = 1.0$ mm) and 130 min/m^2 (for $d_P = 1.6$ mm). This is a tremendous potential for cleaning process optimisation. The results plotted in Fig. 6.24 further verify the positive effect of smaller abrasive particles. For steel descaling, cleaning rate dropped for comparative mass flow rate values if larger abrasives were utilised. This effect is illustrated in Fig. 6.24a. The same trend between cleaning rate and abrasive particle size was reported by Bigos (1959) for the blast cleaning of steel panels with different abrasive materials (iron grit, sand and slag); by Balcar (1986) for the removal of bronze from steel substrates with glass beads; and by Bae et al. (2007) for the removal of epoxy coatings from steel substrates with steel grit. Results of the latter authors are provided in Fig. 6.24b. It can be seen that the relative cleaning rate notably dropped if larger abrasive particles were utilised for the removal of the epoxy primer. Figure 6.25 illustrates the effect of the abrasive size on the specific abrasive consumption. For comparative cleaning rates (about $\dot{A} = 30$ m^2/h), abrasive consumption was lowest for the smallest particle size and the lowest abrasive mass flow rate. Bullett and

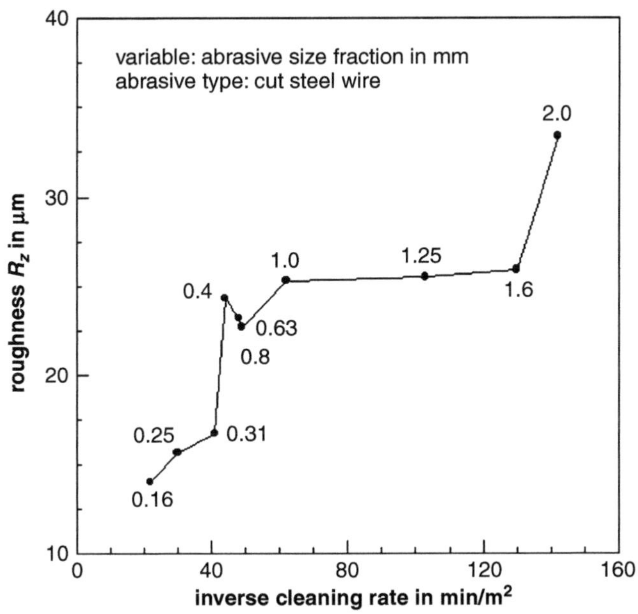

Fig. 6.23 Effects of final substrate roughness and abrasive particle size on inverse cleaning rate for mill scale (Neumann, 1976)

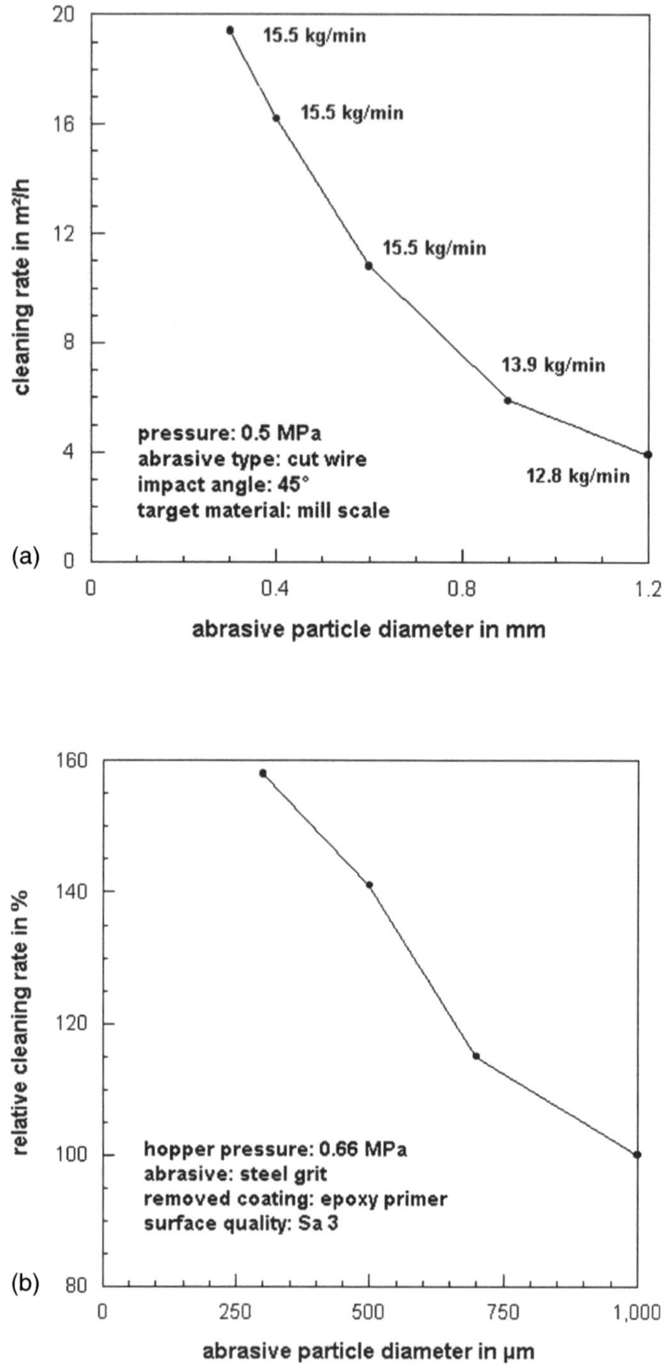

Fig. 6.24 Effect of abrasive particle size on cleaning rate. (**a**) Removal of mill scale (Remmelts, 1969); (**b**) Removal of epoxy primer (Bae et al., 2007)

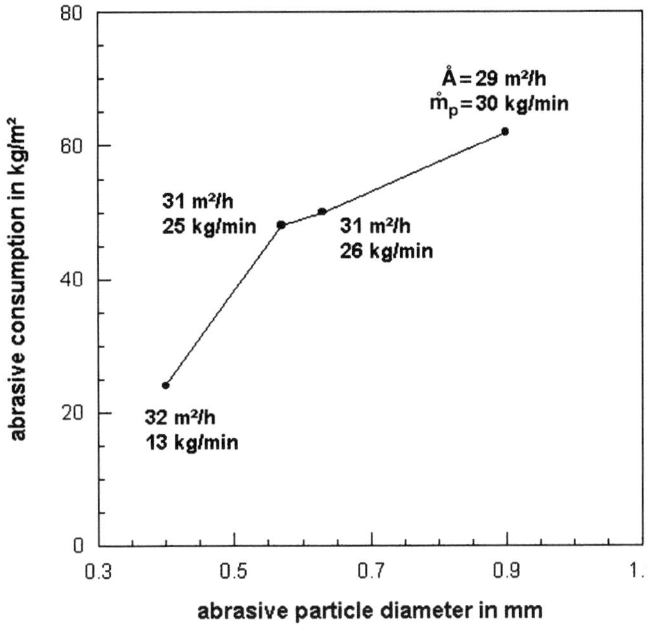

Fig. 6.25 Effects of abrasive particle size on specific abrasive consumption and cleaning rate (Hareux and Riac, 1986)

Dasgupta (1969) investigated the effect of abrasive size variation on the cleaning quality. They doped steel panels with ferrous sulphate and performed blast cleaning tests in order to remove this contaminant. Results of this study are displayed in Fig. 6.26 which reveals that a desired cleanliness (retained ferrous sulphate) could be achieved much earlier if smaller abrasive particles were utilised.

It seems, similar to the discussion in Sect. 6.3.3, that overlap and area coverage effects were important. Tosha and Iida (2001) have shown that the surface density of erosion dents in steel decreased with an increase in abrasive size according to a d_P^{-2}-relationship. Therefore, smaller particles guaranteed a closer coverage of the eroded surface. Smaller abrasive particle diameters also reduce the time where full area coverage starts [see (3.40)]. These findings support the recommendation in the SSPC Surface Preparation Commentary: "*Decreasing abrasive particle size can dramatically increase cleaning rate. The general rule is to use the smallest size abrasive that will do the job.*" Larger abrasive particle size may be beneficial for the removal of heavy coatings and scale.

Results of solid particle erosion tests on polymers and rubber are displayed in Fig. 6.27. Such stationary tests deliver different trends than cleaning tests with moving nozzles, because area coverage and overlap effects are not considered. The curves displayed in Fig. 6.27 can be subdivided into two sections: a linear section and a saturation section, whose locations depended on target material. On polyurethane, for example, the linear section was short, and there was some trend that a further increase in abrasive size would reduce erosion rate, similar to the situations shown in Fig. 6.24.

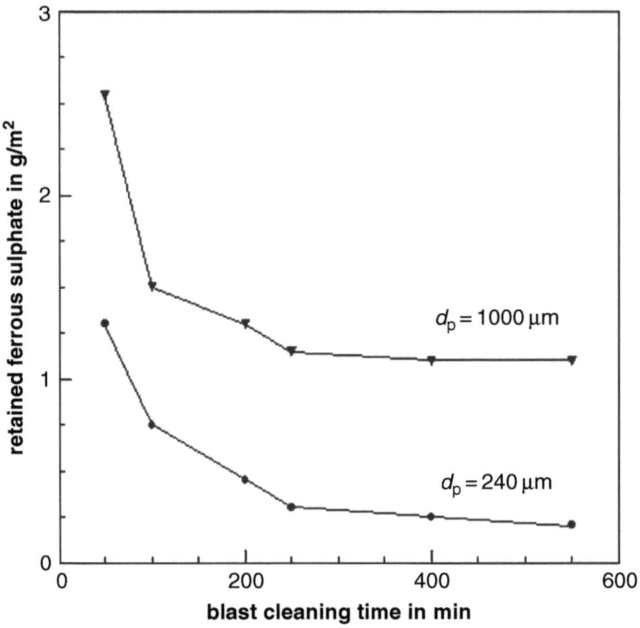

Fig. 6.26 Effect of abrasive particle size on substrate cleanliness (Bullett and Dasgupta, 1969)

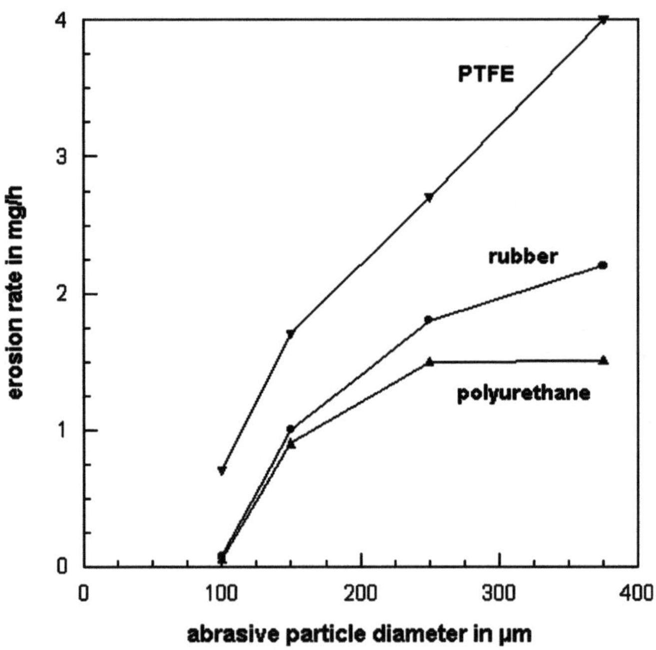

Fig. 6.27 Effect of abrasive particle size on the erosion of organic coatings (Zhang et al., 1995)

For the slurry erosion of fusion-bonded epoxy powder coatings, Luo et al. (2001) recorded two threshold particle diameters, a lower value ($d_P = 80\ \mu m$) and an upper value ($d_P = 410\ \mu m$), which enveloped the linear section. Beyond these two values, any notable particle size effects vanished. In the linear section, erosion rate increased linearly with increasing particle diameter. The reason for this relation was the higher kinetic energy of the larger particles as expressed by $E_P \propto d_P^{2.5}$. (Particle size affects abrasive particle velocity, which leads to a power exponent different from 3.) On the other hand, the number of impinging particles reduces with an increase in the particle diameter (see Sect. 2.6). In addition, abrasive particle velocity decreased if particle diameter increased, especially for low mass flow ratios abrasive/air (see Sect. 3.6.3). These effects became more important in the second range. In this range, the progress of the function dropped because of the reduced impact frequency and the reduced particle velocity. The optimum balance between the kinetic energy of a single abrasive grain and the number of impacting particles was exceeded.

The relationship between erosion rate and abrasive particle diameter can be approximated with a simple power law as:

$$E_R \propto d_P^{\theta_P} \tag{6.23b}$$

with $\theta_P > 0$.

In contrast to (6.23a), the power exponent has values larger than zero. If only the fundamental local material removal process is being considered, θ_P has always positive values. If, however, the cleaning process with a moving nozzle and notable particle interactions is considered, the condition $\theta_P < 0$ holds [see Fig. 6.24 and (6.23a)]. For rubber, the power exponent depends on the fatigue-function parameter: $\theta_P = \beta_F - 1$ (see Sect. 5.7.4 for the fatigue parameter β_F). Depth of both cracked layers and crack separation distance in eroded rubber surfaces increased nearly linearly with increasing particle diameter (Arnold and Hutchings, 1993). For polymers, values for the power exponent in (6.23) were between $\theta_P = 1.0$ and 2.0 (Zhang et al., 1995).

If the complete removal process, including overlap and superposition effects, is considered, values for θ_P may become negative as illustrated in Figs. 6.19a and 6.24 for mill-scale removal and coating removal applications.

Some other aspects that determine the influence of the abrasive particle diameter on the blast cleaning process are the higher impact fracture probability of larger grains (see Sect. 2.2.2) and the relationship between grain size and grain shape (see Sect. 2.3).

Bullett and Dasgupta (1969) investigated the effect of the abrasive particle size on the cleaning intensity. They contaminated rusty steel samples with a layer of ferrous sulphate and blast cleaned the samples with steel grit of two different abrasive sizes: a fine-grained abrasive ($d_P = 240\ \mu m$) and a coarse-grained abrasive ($d_P = 1{,}000\ \mu m$). The cleaning intensity was assessed based on the amount of retained ferrous sulphate after a given cleaning time. The results revealed that the application of the fine-grained abrasive materials led to much lower amounts of

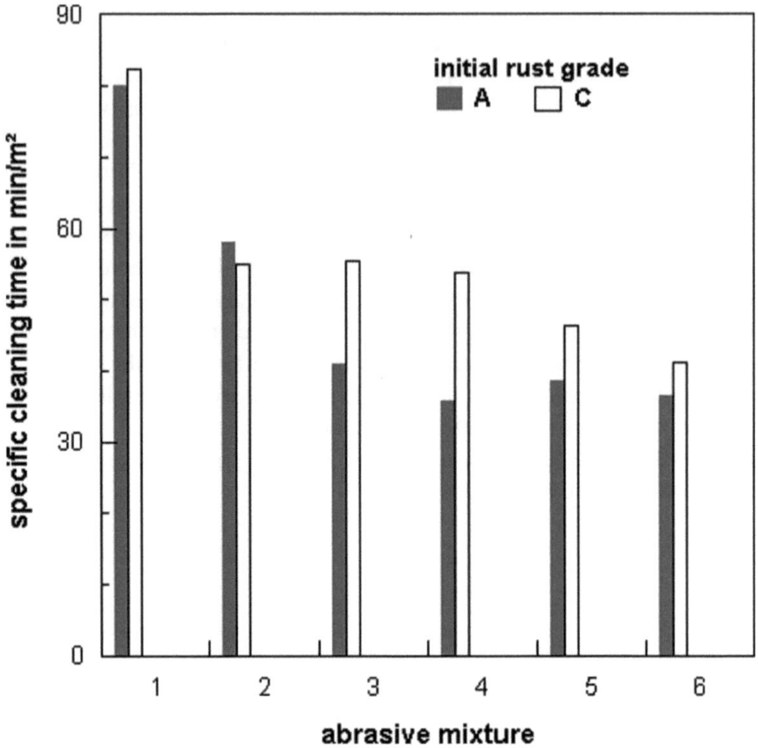

Fig. 6.28 Effects of abrasive mixture and initial cleaning condition on specific cleaning time (Neumann, 1976)

ferrous sulphate at all cleaning time levels. Therefore, an abrasive mixture with a high amount of small particles could guarantee a more thoroughly cleaned substrate.

The effect of abrasive working mixture on the cleaning of steel panels covered with mill scale (grade A), respectively rust (grade C), is illustrated in Fig. 6.28. The mixtures had different particle size class portions. The abrasive mixture "1" (coarse mixture, no grains smaller than $d_P = 315$ µm) could remove mill scale and rust with an equal efficiency, whereas the results for abrasive mixture "4" (medium mixture; no grains larger than $d_P = 1{,}250$ µm, no grains smaller than $d_P = 315$ µm) showed notable differences in the cleaning rates for the two types of oxide.

Safar (1973) defined a critical abrasive mass required for a complete coverage of the surface with erosion pits. For wheel-driven blasting machines, this critical abrasive mass can be approximated with the following relationship:

$$m_G = 2.09 \cdot \rho_P \cdot \left(\frac{d_P}{d_e}\right)^2 \cdot d_P \tag{6.24}$$

This equation should be applied to even surfaces only. It can be seen that the critical mass has a cubic relationship to the abrasive particle size. Table 6.8 lists

Table 6.8 Critical abrasive mass values for complete specimen coverage (Safar, 1973)

Target material	Abrasive diameter in mm			
	1.3	1.8	2.4	3.4
	Critical abrasive mass in kg/m^2			
Cast iron	143	198	265	375
Bronze	113	157	209	296
Carbon steel	107	148	198	281
Alloyed steel	102	141	189	266
Highly alloyed steel	121	167	224	317

experimental results, showing the effects of abrasive particle diameter and target material.

Peltzer (1955) gave some recommendations about the abrasive size for effective removal of mill scale (see Sect. 5.6.3) and cast sand from castings. Some of his recommendations are listed in Table 6.9.

6.4.4 Effects of Abrasive Particle Shape

Figures 6.29–6.31 show the effect of abrasive shape on the removal of organic coatings. Figure 6.29 deals with the removal of baking enamel from different metal substrates. The use of spherical steel particles led to lower cleaning rates compared with the angular grit particles. This effect was most pronounced for the aluminium substrate, where grit particles (angular shape) were much more efficient than shot particles (rounded shape). For a stainless steel substrate, in contrast, particle shape did not affect the coating removal efficiency. Figure 6.30 illustrates some effects of coating composition. All coatings were more sensitive to the impingement of steel balls compared to the impingement of a cone-shaped particle. It can also be seen that the size of the ball played an additional role. Figure 6.31 shows the effects of particle shape and target material hardness. Grit particles were more effective at both target hardness levels, although the differences in specific volume loss were sensitive to the target material hardness. For the lower target hardness value, particle shape had a pronounced influence on the specific volume loss, whereas only a weak effect was found for the higher target hardness value. Irregular particles may, therefore, be recommended for the removal of rather soft materials. For rubber, impinged at

Table 6.9 Particle size recommendations for the removal of cast sand from castings (Peltzer, 1955)

Casting type	Recommended abrasive size	
	Shot	Grit
Iron casting	S 550–S 320	G 16–G 40
Annealed casting	S 550–S 330	G 18–G 40
Steel casting	S 660–S 390	G 14–G 25

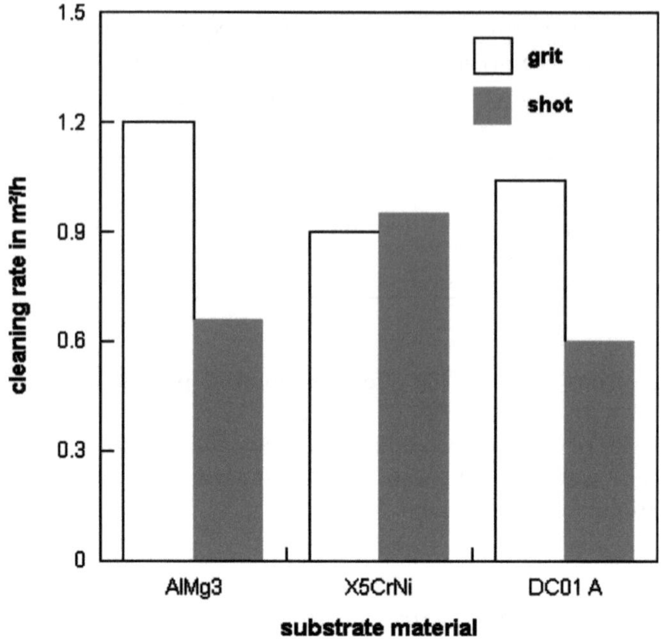

Fig. 6.29 Effect of particle shape on the cleaning rate for baked enamel (Uhlmann et al., 2003)

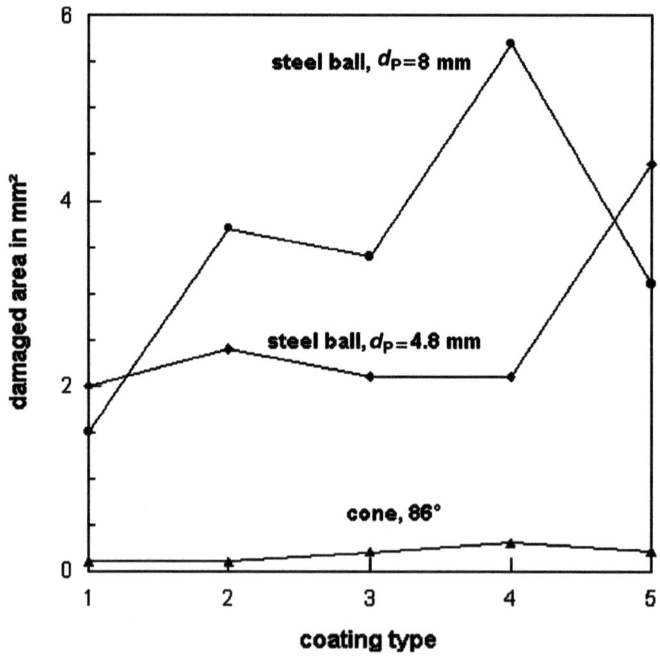

Fig. 6.30 Effect of particle shape on the damage size in different coating types (Breinsberger and Koppelmann, 1982). Coating types: 1-DFT = 72 μm, 150/140 °C; 2-DFT = 77 μm, 120/140 °C; 3-DFT = 78 μm, 160/140 °C; 4-DFT = 78 μm, 160/140 °C; 5-DFT = 80 μm, 160/140 °C

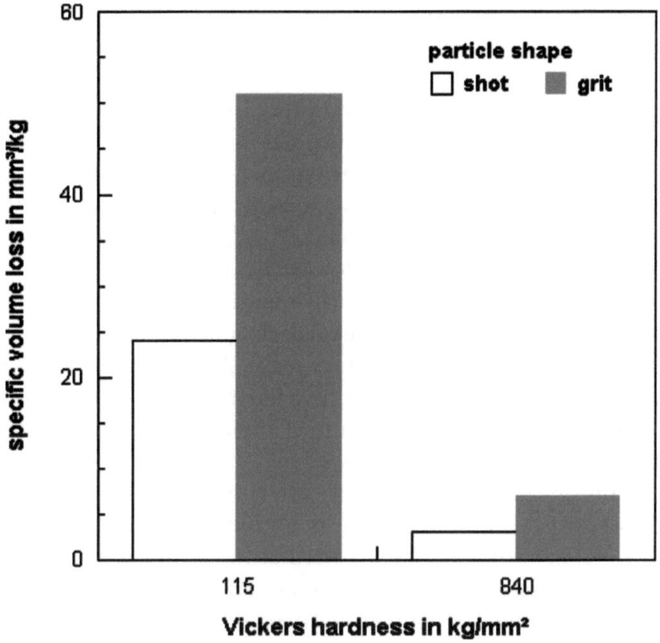

Fig. 6.31 Effects of particle shape and target material hardness on the specific volume loss in steel targets (Wellinger and Uetz, 1955)

oblique impact angles, erosion rate increased substantially for more angular particles (Arnold and Hutchings, 1992).

Basically, these findings support the recommendation given in the SSPC Surface Preparation Commentary: "*Rounded particles are most effective in removing brittle coatings such as mill scale, whereas angular shaped particles are more effective in removing softer coatings such as rust and paint.*"

Systematic studies in the field of solid particle erosion have shown that the abrasive grain shape had an important influence on the material removal regime. Bahadur and Badruddin (1990) related the particle shape influence to the different removal mechanisms, such as micro-cutting for angular particles and micro-ploughing for spherical particles. Cousens and Hutchings (1983) showed that the usually used terms 'ductile' and 'brittle' behaviour are determined by the abrasive grain shape.

Abrasive particle shape also effects the acceleration of the particles in the blast nozzle (see Sect. 3.6.4). Grit particles tend to have higher velocities than shot particles.

6.4.5 Effects of Abrasive Material Hardness

From investigations of abrasion and solid particle erosion is known that a "transition stage" exists at the point of comparable hardness of abrasive material and target material (Wellinger and Uetz, 1955; Uetz, 1986):

$$\frac{H_M}{H_P} \rightarrow 1.0 \text{ to } 1.5 \qquad (6.25)$$

In this region, erosive material removal processes are very sensitive to changes in the relative hardness. Figure 6.32 illustrates these relationships. For the substrate with the high hardness ($H_M = 440\,\text{kg/mm}^2$), the specific mass loss exhibited a high increase if the abrasive hardness exceeded a value of $H_P = 500\,\text{kg/mm}^2$. The corresponding hardness ratio was about $H_M/H_P = 0.9$, which agrees very well with (6.25). For the substrate with the lowest hardness, the progress of the function dropped with an increase in the abrasive material hardness. Beyond a critical hardness ratio between abrasive and target material (at about $H_P/H_M = 2.4$), the progresses of the functions exhibited a steep decrease. Any further increase in the abrasive hardness would not substantially improve the material removal performance. A general rule in the SSPC Surface Preparation Commentary is: "*Select the minimum abrasive hardness that will effectively do the job.*"

Figure 6.33 illustrates the effects of abrasive material hardness on the erosion of rubber. In contrast to Fig. 6.32, there is no unique trend visible in the graph. The maximum specific volume loss occurred at rather low abrasive hardness values ($H_P = 500$–$900\,\text{kg/mm}^2$) and not, as could have been expected, at the highest value for the abrasive material hardness. These relationships were contributed to abrasive particle shape effects. The glass and flint particles were characterised by pronounced edges, and they basically removed material due to micro-cutting. For rubber, as a soft material, this erosion mode contributed to high levels of material

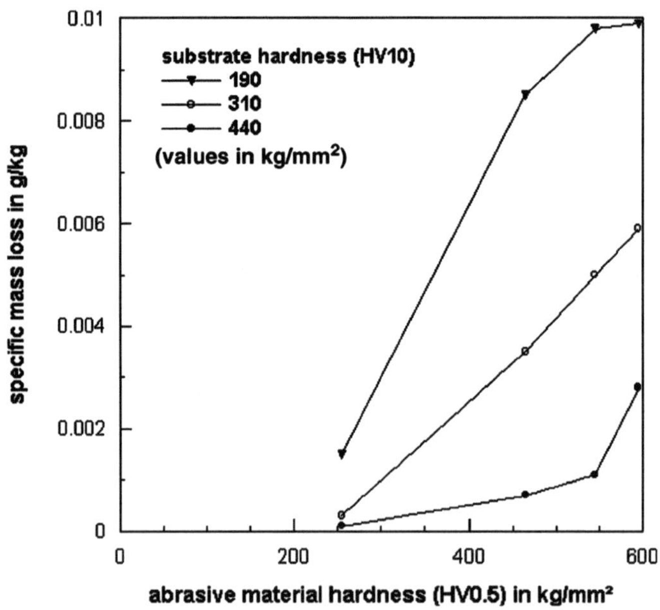

Fig. 6.32 Effect of abrasive material hardness on specific mass removal (Wellinger and Gommel, 1967). Process parameters: abrasive type: cut steel wire; $d_P = 400\,\mu\text{m}$; $v_P = 70\,\text{m/s}$

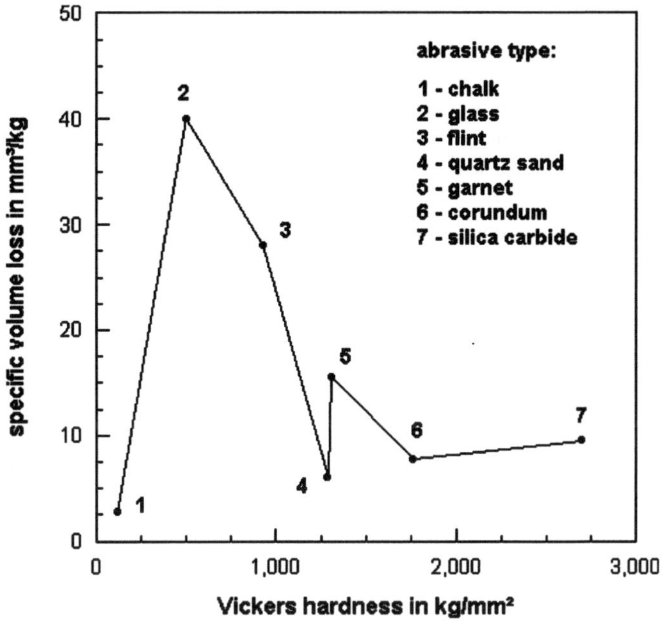

Fig. 6.33 Effect of abrasive material hardness on specific volume loss in rubber (Wellinger and Uetz, 1955)

removal. Particle shape was, therefore, much more important to the rubber material than abrasive material hardness.

Wellinger et al. (1962) investigated the effects of tensile strength of abrasive materials (cut steel wire) on the specific material loss of steel target and found a relationship very similar to that shown in Fig. 6.32. The authors found that the influence of the abrasive material tensile strength vanished for very high values of target material hardness.

6.5 Removal Models

Rosenberger (1939) probably provided the first, simple material removal model for blast cleaning processes whereby the material removal due to the impingement of an individual abrasive particle was considered a machining process.

Fokke (1999) developed a model for the estimation of the cleaning efficiency for the removal of organic coatings from steel substrates due to blast cleaning. The model is based on a geometric description of the coating area removed during the impingement of an individual abrasive particle. Fokke (1999) obtained this area due to precise surveys of impact craters.

For a chosen kinetic energy of a particle (see Sect. 2.6.2 for additional information), a minimum number of particles, which is required to erode an impacted area of 1 m^2, can be computed as follows:

$$N_{P\,min} = \frac{1}{\varepsilon_M \cdot E_P} \tag{6.26}$$

The number is a minimum because its establishment assumes that the impact areas of all particles do not overlap. The physical unit of the minimum number is m^{-2}. The parameter ε_M was experimentally estimated by Fokke (1999); an example is provided in Fig. 6.6. Typical values were between $\varepsilon_M = 2.6 \times 10^{-5}$ and 2.9×10^{-5} m^2/J; they depended on coating hardness and abrasive particle size. A dimensional analysis of the size of craters formed in the coating as a result of particle impingement delivered the following relationship:

$$\frac{V_C}{d_P^3} = \psi_M \cdot \left(\frac{E_P}{H_M \cdot d_P^3}\right)^{1.5} \tag{6.27}$$

The parameter ψ_M is a dimensionless scaling parameter. For a given coating material (given coating hardness), this relationship can be simplified as follows:

$$V_C = \psi_N \cdot E_P^{1.5} \cdot d_P^{1.5} \tag{6.28}$$

The parameter ψ_N is an empirical parameter with the unit ($m^{4.5}/J^{1.5}$). If the abrasive particle size is known, values for ψ_N can be estimated due to linear regressions of experimental results as presented in Fig. 6.6. When a number of particles each remove a volume V_C from $1\,m^2$ of substrate, the coating layer is reduced by an average thickness Δh_C, the total number of impacts required to totally remove the coating down to the substrate, reads as follows:

$$N_P \cdot N_{P\,min} = \frac{n_C}{V_C} \tag{6.29}$$

For a given particle diameter, the number of particles impinging a given area depends on abrasive mass flow rate and traverse speed. The traverse speed can be expressed by the cleaning rate because this parameter is nothing else than an area traversed during a given time period. This reflection leads to the following equation:

$$\dot{A} = \frac{\dot{m}_P}{N_P \cdot N_{P\,min} \cdot V_P \cdot \rho_C} \tag{6.30}$$

The linear relationship between cleaning rate and abrasive mass flow rate corresponds well with the results provided in Sect. 6.4.1 for small and moderate abrasive mass flow rates. The inverse relationship between cleaning rate and abrasive particle size also verifies experimental results obtained on mill scale and soft coatings (see Sect. 6.4.3). It is also conclusive that cleaning rate may reduce for coating materials with higher density values.

Uferer (1992) derived an empirical model for the removal of mill scale and rust from steel substrates. The final equation reads as follows:

Table 6.10 Constants for the model of Kambham et al. (2006)

Constant	*a*	*b*	*c*	*d*	*e*	*f*
Value for rusted panels	−129.40	9,405.97	2,943.53	−235,051.25	−12,593.40	−16,946.26
Value for painted panels	542.45	−67,478.23	−806.87	3,532,289.80	10,379.03	−145,564.76

Table 6.11 Variable range for the model of Kambham et al. (2006)

Variable	Unit	Range
Air pressure	psi	80–120
Abrasive mass flow rate	lbs/min	8–26

$$A_S = \frac{\dot{A}}{\dot{m}_P} = (K_0 \cdot K_1 \cdot \dot{m}_P - a_0 \cdot K_1^2 \cdot \dot{m}_P^2) \cdot f_P \cdot f_N \cdot f_X \cdot f_\phi \tag{6.31}$$

The parameter A_S is the specific cleaning rate in m^2/kg; it is actually the inverse version of (6.5). Values for the parameter constants f_N, f_X and f_ϕ are provided in Tables 6.3–6.5. The constants K_0, K_1 and α_0 must be established due to a standard blast cleaning test. Uferer (1992) recommended the following parameter configuration for such a standard test: $p = 0.25\,\text{MPa}$, $x = 50\,\text{cm}$ and $\varphi = 90°$.

Kambham et al. (2006) issued a model for the removal of rust and coatings from steel substrates due to dry blast cleaning. The model is based on regression statistics. The authors performed numerous blast cleaning trials and applied a standard data-fit method. The final equation reads as follows:

$$\dot{A} = a + \frac{b}{p} + \frac{c}{\dot{m}_P} + \frac{d}{p^2} + \frac{e}{\dot{m}_P^2} + \frac{f}{p \cdot \dot{m}_P} \tag{6.32}$$

The cleaning rate is given in ft^2/h. The regression parameters a to f for the two removal modes "rust" and "coating" are listed in Table 6.10. Table 6.11 lists the parameter ranges for the two process variables. Because the regression coefficients are in the range of about 0.6 only, the use of the model may be restricted to the determination of qualitative trends only. Another limit of the model is its restriction to coal slag as an abrasive material.

6.6 Efficiency of Blast Cleaning

6.6.1 Erosion Efficiency

The efficiency of the erosion process is difficult to evaluate. Following Thiruvengadam's (1967) erosion resistance model (which is, rigorously taken, valid for liquid drop impact), a probable approach involves the strain energy density defined in (5.2). This parameter characterises the amount of energy stored in a stressed volume. If this parameter is being related to the specific material removal energy, the efficiency can be approximated as follows:

$$\Phi_{\mathrm{E}} = \frac{\mathrm{E_{SD}}}{\mathrm{E_{sp}}} \cdot 100 \tag{6.33}$$

The specific energy is given through $E_{\mathrm{P}}/V_{\mathrm{M}}$. From Fig. 6.6, respectively (6.11), one obtains $E_{\mathrm{sp}} \propto E_{\mathrm{P}}^{-1/2}$. A particle with a kinetic energy of 10 mJ removes a paint volume of 10^{-11} m^3 (see Fig. 6.6), which results in a specific energy of $E_{\mathrm{sp}} = 10^3$ $\mathrm{MJ/m^3}$. A typical value for the elastic strain energy density of an organic paint is $E_{\mathrm{SD}} = 5\,\mathrm{MJ/m^3}$ from Table 5.6. For these numbers, (6.33) delivers a material removal efficiency of $\Phi_{\mathrm{E}} = 0.5\%$. If additional energy dissipation due to plastic deformations is assumed, an erosion efficiency of about 1% is an approximate value. This order of magnitude corresponds with results from calculations for hydro-abrasive erosion of steel (Momber et al., 1996). Mineral grinding processes also have a mechanical efficiency in the range of one percent only (Schubert, 1988).

6.6.2 General Aspects of Process Efficiency

Numerous factors affect the efficiency of blast cleaning processes. Experience show that the most important factors are the following:

(1) existing coating type, adhesion and condition;
(2) substrate material properties;
(3) experience and organisation of the working crew;
(4) geometry and accessibility of the objects.

The aspects (1) and (2) are considered for shipyard operations in a benchmarking report (Appleman et al., 1998).

The criterion “existing coatings” is treated in terms of “type of surface” and “coating hardness”, whereas the latter term basically characterises the resistance of the coatings against the action of impinging abrasive particles during blast cleaning. In terms of “type of surface”, four categories are being distinguished:

- Light rust, light mill scale or loose paint: This is a deteriorated surface which requires little effort to clean.
- Tight rust or tight mill scale: This is new structural steel from the mill.
- Thin paint or rusted thin paint: This is previously coated steel plate where the coating thickness is in the range of DFT = 120 to 175 μm.
- Thick paint, heavy mill scale, or heavily pitted rust: This can be steel plate where the coating thickness in the range of, or greater than, DFT = 200 to 250 μm.

  In terms of “coating hardness”, the report distinguished between the following three categories:

- hard coatings: typically chemically cured coatings (epoxy, urethane, zinc-filled coatings);
- soft coatings: typically a more readily deformed surface (alkyd, latex, chlorinated rubber);
- no coating: new mill scale bearing steel.

Numerous remarks on the effects of mechanical properties of coatings on the erosion process are delivered in Chap. 5.8. A further example is shown in Fig. 6.34. The graph illustrates the effect of the target material (e.g. metallic coating) on the specific erosion. It can be seen that specific erosion increased notably in the range of low hardness values. If the hardness was rather high, it did not affect the erosion process. These results correspond to the relationships discussed in Sect. 6.4.5. An additional point of interest, however, is the effect of the air pressure on the erosion of the target material. Pressure effects were very pronounced in the range of low hardness values. However, for higher values of target hardness ($H_M > 700\,kg/mm^2$), the gain of the higher pressure seemed to vanish.

The aspect (3) is illustrated in ISO 12944-4, which states the following: "*Personnel carrying out surface preparation work shall have... sufficient technical knowledge of the processes involved.*" This includes knowledge about the equipment being used, the basic principles of blast cleaning and the effects of major process parameters. Health and safety training is another important issue of personnel qualification. Experience shows that trained blasters can outperform untrained blasters by a factor

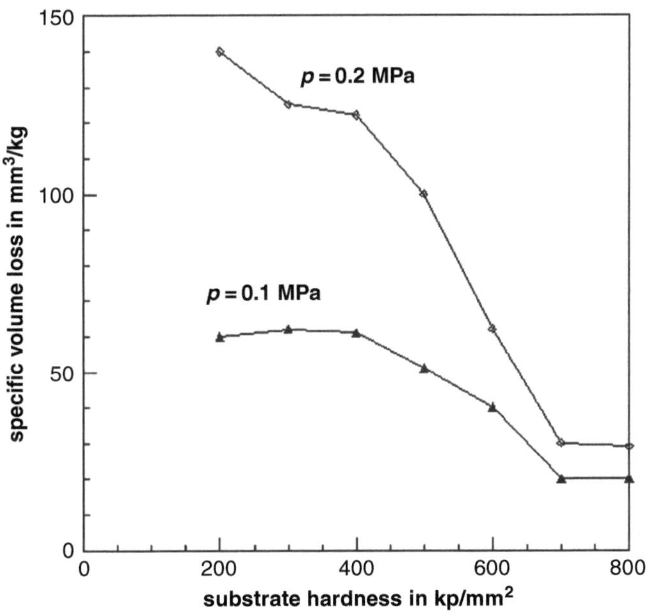

Fig. 6.34 Effect of substrate hardness and air pressure on specific volume loss in metal (Gommel, 1967a)

of about two. Training and qualification counts even more if high-level surface preparation operations are being performed, which would include, among others, the treatment of stainless steel, tank coating surface preparation, or the preparation of substrates for metal-sprayed coatings.

Regarding aspect (4), a detailed investigation has shown that accessibility can dramatically affect efficiency as well as quality of blast cleaning. For steel bridge structures with delicate geometry, only 25–30% of the interior limited access surface could be cleaned by blast cleaning. Also, profile depth was only 85% of the values generated during normal blast cleaning procedures (Bullard et al., 2002). Some results are listed in Table 6.12. Based on the data, blast cleaning inside gap widths of 0.3–0.6 cm on 10-cm-deep back-to-back angles did not reach approximately 50–75% of the total angle depth. That is, only 25–50% of the interior surface was being cleaned. For 5-cm-deep back-to-back angles, 25–50% remained uncleaned, while 50–75% was prepared. Blast cleaning penetration increased when gaps were 1.2 cm and wider, but was also somewhat dependent on angle depth. Cleaning rate also depends on work location. Examples from the ship building industry are listed in Table 6.13. It can be seen that cleaning rate can drop up to 75% for very complex structural shapes.

6.6.3 Aspects of Site Management

Site management has a notable effect on efficiency especially if site environment is not a stable factor in blast cleaning. Here, experience is again an issue. However, other problems are of importance as well, namely the following (related basically to external site applications):

- Work delay occurs while operators are waiting for broken equipment to be repaired.
- Preventive maintenance is being performed during the blast shift and subsequently displaces operators who would be blasting regularly.
- Relocating a compressor or a blast machine is often a timely process. The technician must evaluate the desired location of the unit, search for a suitable power source and obtain the connecting cables before work can continue. Hose lines must also be replaced.

Table 6.12 Abrasive blast penetration at typical difficult-to-access areas (Bullard et al., 2002)

Gap width in cm	Depth cleaned in cm		Area cleaned in %	
	10 cm angle	5 cm angle	10 cm angle	5 cm angle
0.31	2.38	2.40	24	48
0.66	4.60	3.50	46	70
1.25	4.48	5.00	45	100
1.88	9.15	5.00	92	100
2.50	9.63	5.00	96	100

Table 6.13 Cleaning rates modifications due to work location in the ship building industry (NSRP, 1998b)

Location	Relative cleaning rate in %
Hull section; easily reached	100
Complex steel shape; less than 8.25 m elevation	75
Hull section; 8.6–25 m high	75
Complex steel; 8.6–25 m high	75
Hull section; 26–50 m high	50
Complex steel; 26–50 m high	50
Interior tank spaces; little structural steel	50
Interior tank spaces; complex structural shapes	25

- Electrical outages and power supply problems disrupt entire teams during operation. When electrical services on the site are interrupted, qualified technicians must be utilised to restart the units.
- Lack of hose management causes significant delay time, especially if long distances between compressor and blast machine, respectively between blast machine and nozzle, need to be bridged.
- Dressing and inspecting personal protective equipment is a time-consuming function of the manual operator.
- Cranes are often unable to make lifts at night due to poor lighting. Therefore, compressors, abrasive hoppers and other equipment cannot be moved at appropriate speed.

6.6.4 Aspects of Operators' Fatigue

A further aspect that affects efficiency is operator fatigue, especially if the equipment is run manually. Typical problems associated with fatigue can be summarised as follows:

- The grit hoses are supported partly by the operator as he works. Both the weight of the hose and the pull from horizontal friction increase the fatigue. Fatigue increases if hose diameter increases. Wipe hoses are, therefore, frequently used.
- The weight of the nozzle is fatiguing to the operator; this weight is completely supported by the arms and neck of the operator.
- In order to reach surfaces behind obstructions, an operator is forced to position his nozzle in awkward angles. This strain is magnified if the operator stands in a basket on a high-reach.
- While blasting overhead in areas with low clearance, the operator is often forced to a squatting position to blast; this directs forces to the knees.
- Working in overhead areas with tall clearances, the operators are often forced to reach overhead with the nozzle to make contact with the surface. This compounds forces in the elbows and shoulders.
- Operators are often uncomfortable due to dust.

- Operators are often uncomfortable due to cumbersome personal protective equipment.
- Operators often have their vision obstructed by dirty safety glasses.
- Operators often have their vision impaired by poor lighting at night.
- Operators often do not practice sound ergonomic principles as they confirm their duties.
- Operator's efficiency decreases in productivity as their shift progresses. Even after standard breaks, production at the end of the shift is significantly less than at the beginning.

A major conclusion drawn from these observations is the performance of ergonomic training (which may be done by contractors) and the development of ergonomic support devices (which may be done by manufacturers).

Fatigue due to the jet flow reaction force can be approximated as follows:

$$F_R = \dot{m}_A \cdot v_A + \dot{m}_P \cdot v_P \tag{6.34}$$

It can be seen that an efficient nozzle, which delivers high exit velocities for air and abrasive particles, is associated with an increase in fatigue. The same is true for the use of large-diameter nozzles, which allow for high air and abrasive mass flow rates. If typical values from Chap. 2.6 are taken ($\dot{m}_A = 10$ kg/min, $\dot{m}_P = 15$ kg/min, $v_A = 500$ m/s and $v_P = 180$ m/s), a corresponding reaction force of $F_R = 130$ N can be calculated. The reaction forces generated by a blast cleaning nozzle flow were measured by Kline et al. (1988) for different nozzle designs, and values between $F_R = 49$ and 67 N were estimated experimentally. These results are notably lower than the calculated value, which is most probably due to impulse losses during the acceleration process and the flow of the jet through the surrounding air. Therefore, (6.34) delivers rather overestimated values in terms of reaction force assessment. Rosenberg et al. (2006) developed a biomechanical model for the approximation of hand forces and wrist moments. For blast cleaning with steel shot, they reported force values of $F_R = 26$ N at the hand, and moment values of 3 Nm at the wrist.

Critical, respectively permissible, reaction force values do not exist by law for blast cleaning applications. For hydroblasting applications, however, such permissible limits exist, and they may be applied for comparative purposes (Momber, 2003, 2005a). For the operation of hand-held water jet guns, the permissible limit is, for example, at $F_R = 150$ N, which is more than three times higher than the values measured for dry blast cleaning. Another parameter which helps to assess the severity of fatigue due to the jet flow reaction force is the weight of the operator. Experience from water jetting applications shows that a gun can be handled in a safe and efficient way if the reaction force of the jet does not exceed one-third of the weight force of the operator. The weight force of an operator (blaster) is simply:

$$F_W = 9.81 \cdot m_O \tag{6.35}$$

whereby the weight of the operator is given in kg. The fatigue condition is then:

$$\frac{F_W}{3} > F_R \qquad (6.36)$$

The weight force of a 75-kg operator, for example, is $F_W = 735\,N$; one-third of this value is $F_R = 245\,N$, which again is much higher than typical values estimated for blast cleaning.

6.7 Weld Seam Cleaning

Experimental results of weld seam cleaning with different treatment methods were reported by Remmelts (1969) and Blomquist (1997). Some results are summarised in Table 6.14. It can be seen that the proper selection of the abrasive type can have a considerable effect on the cleaning rate. The cleaning rate was high for crystal grit and rather low for steel grit. Vacublast and manual grinding resulted in very low cleaning rates.

Remmelts (1969) investigated the effects of weld type, abrasive size and abrasive mass flow rate in more detail. Results of his study are provided in Table 6.15. The results verify the higher cleaning capability of non-metallic abrasive materials. Cleaning speed was higher and specific abrasive consumption was lower if copper slag was used instead of cut steel wire.

Table 6.14 Cleaning rates for weld seam cleaning (Blomquist, 1997)

Method	Weld seam length in m	Cleaning speed in m/min
Blast cleaning with steel grit	115	1.3
Blast cleaning with aluminium oxide	67	2.1
Blast cleaning with crystal grit	50	2.3
Manual grinding	14	0.03
Vacublast	4	0.93

Table 6.15 Cleaning speeds for weld seam cleaning (Remmelts, 1969). Parameters: $p = 0.5\,MPa$, $d_N = 10\,mm$, $x = 56\,cm$; ship plate (12 mm), arc welding

Type of weld	Abrasive type	Abrasive size in μm	Abrasive mass flow rate in kg/min	Cleaning speed in m/h	Abrasive consumption in kg/m
Butt weld	Cut wire	400	18.7	270	4.2
		900	16.4	135	7.3
	Copper slag	900	5.7	180	1.9
Fillet weld (vertical)	Cut wire	400	18.7	108	10.4
	Copper slag	400	8.9	126	4.3
Fillet weld (flat)	Cut wire	400	18.7	101	11.1
	Copper slag	400	8.9	119	4.5

6.8 Underwater Applications

Blast cleaning can be performed under submerged conditions. Typical applications would include the cleaning of steel piles prior thickness measurements, the cleaning of submerged constructions for inspections and the removal of rust and deteriorated coating systems. However, just a few systematic investigations about the efficiency of submerged blast cleaning applications have been performed. Donker (1985) and Donker and Richter, (1982, 1988) conducted a number of tests at water depths between 10 and 50 m with a special adapter in front of a standard blast cleaning nozzle. This adapter created an air shroud between nozzle exit and target surface. A special bypass-control avoided the penetration of water into the grit hose and kept the abrasive material dry. The experimental conditions are listed in Table 6.16, and results are provided in Table 6.17. The cleaning rate of up to $\dot{A} = 7\,\mathrm{m^2/h}$ was high and comparable to cleaning rates for atmospheric blast cleaning. The authors found, however, that cleaning rate depended on initial surface condition (see Fig. 6.35a). The values for the specific abrasive consumption, provided in Fig. 6.35b, were notably higher than values for atmospheric blast cleaning, and they also depended on the initial condition. Tar epoxy was the most difficult to remove material.

A very special submerged application is "blast zincing" (Groot et al., 1982; Donker and Richter, 1988). In that application, zinc-coated abrasive particles are used as a blasting media, and the particles, either being embedded in the steel substrate or forming a protective layer on the steel surface, are considered to act as sacrificial anodes. The idea is illustrated in Fig. 6.36. Typical performance data for blast zincing is an efficiency of $\dot{A} = 3\,\mathrm{m^2/h}$ and a specific abrasive consumption of $\dot{m}_S = 112\,\mathrm{kg/m^2}$ (Donker and Richter, 1988).

Table 6.16 Experimental conditions for underwater blast cleaning tests for water depths up to 30 m (Donker and Richter, (1982)

Parameter	Value
Nozzle type	Laval nozzle
Nozzle diameter	10 mm
Grit hose diameter	32 mm
Air pressure	0.8 MPa
Air volumetric flow rate	10 m^3/min
Abrasive type	Quartz sand
Abrasive size	1.0–2.0 mm
Abrasive mass flow rate	10 kg/min

Table 6.17 Results of underwater blast cleaning tests (Donker and Richter, 1982)

Parameter	Value
Cleaning rate	2–7 m^2/h
Maximum roughness	40 μm
Preparation grade	Sa 2½ and P Sa 2½

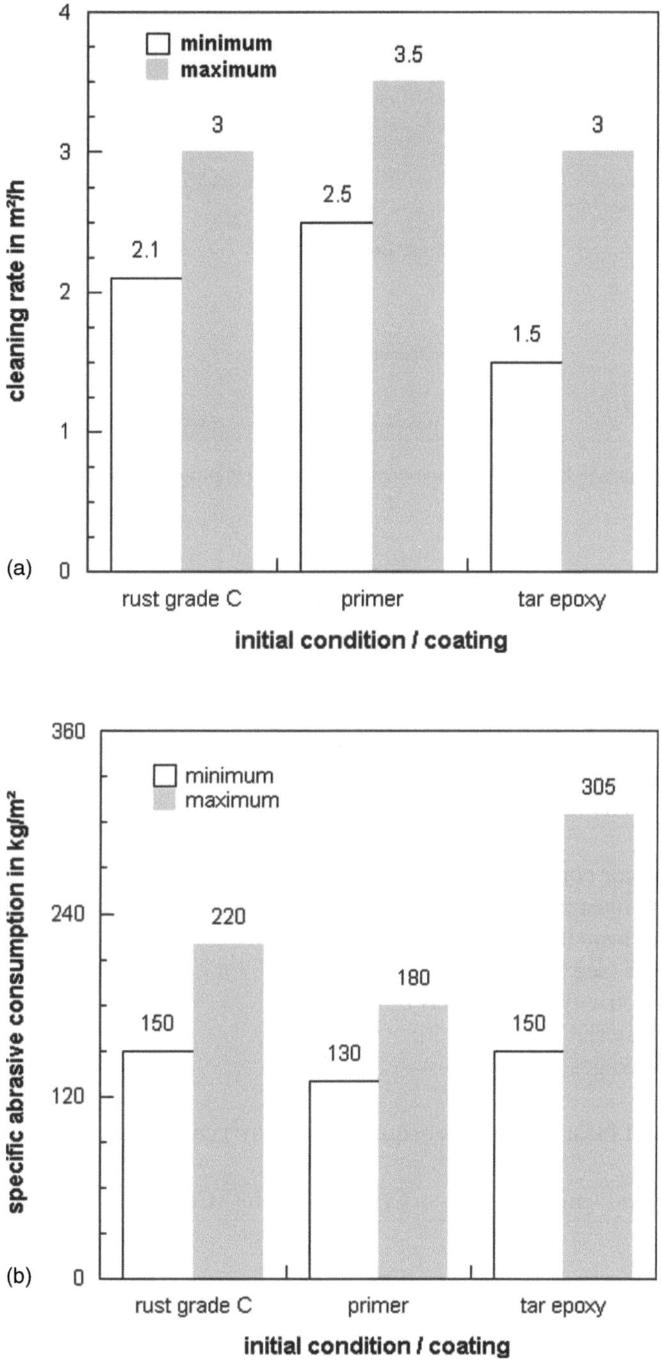

Fig. 6.35 Results of submerged blast cleaning tests (Donker and Richter, 1982); see Table 6.12 for the corresponding operation parameters. (**a**) Cleaning rate; (**b**) Specific abrasive consumption

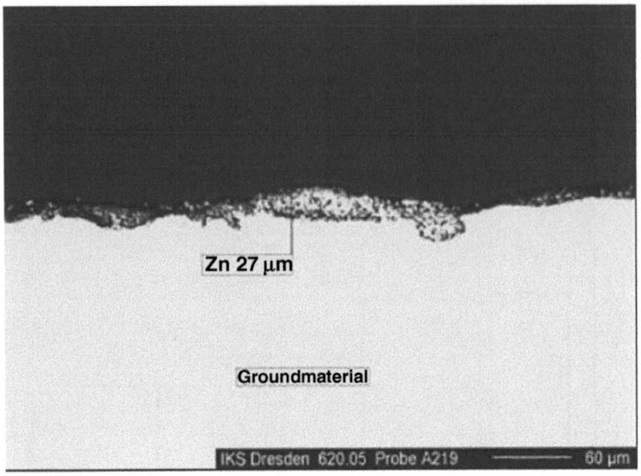

Fig. 6.36 Steel surface blasted with zinc-coated abrasives (Photograph: IKS Dresden)

6.9 Cost Aspects

Dry blast cleaning consumes a notable part of steel refurbishment budgets. A typical value for a 28,400 m^2 project is 42% (Trotter, 2001). For comparison: paint supply cost = 22.1%; painting cost = 20.7% and scaffolding cost = 15.1%. Some cost features for a typical dry blast cleaning system are listed in Table 6.18.

Cost structures for blast cleaning processes are provided in Fig. 6.37. A general cost structure may include the following positions:

- investment air compressor;
- investment blast pot;
- investment hose lines;
- nozzle wear (see Sect. 4.6.2);
- fuel (or electricity, respectively);
- abrasive material (see Chap. 2);
- operators' wages.

The costs of blast cleaning per square metre (m^2) can be calculated as follows:

$$C_{SP} = \frac{(60 \cdot \dot{m}_P \cdot C_P + C_E + C_{LB}) + (60 \cdot \dot{m}_P \cdot C_D + C_{EC} + C_{LC})}{\dot{A}} \quad (6.37)$$

This is a slightly modified version of an equation suggested by Holt and Austin, (2001). Here, the costs types C_E, C_{LB}, C_{EC} and C_{LC} are given in \$/h, whereas the costs types C_P and C_D are given in \$/kg. The abrasive mass flow rate must be given in kg/min. For given costs for labour, disposal, equipment and abrasive material, it is the abrasive mass flow rate makes the difference.

Table 6.18 Cost structures of various preparation methods (Anonymous, 2002)

Direct operating costs[a]	Preparation method	
	Blast cleaning (Sa 2)[b]	Robotic hydroblasting (HB 2)[c]
Labour		
Crew required	20	6
Labour cost per man/hour	20	40
labour cost/hour	400	240
Total in m^2/h	200	200
Hours spent per 10,000 m^2	50	50
Total labour cost	20,000	12,000
Consumables		
Grit cost and disposal coat/h	1,050	32
Fuel cost/h (machine)	117.5	48.80
Fuel cost/h (vacuum)	–	20
Fuel cost/h (filtration)	–	10
Jets cost/h	–	20
Wear cost (seals, nozzles, etc.)	–	10
Misc. filtration expenses cost/h	–	10
Hours spent per 10,000 m^2	50	50
Total consumables cost	58,360	7,444
Equipment use/maintenance		
Diesel engine cost/h	25	10
Smaller engine cost/h	–	7.50
Compressor cost/h	187.50	–
Hours spent per 10,000 m^2	50	50
Total engine maintenance cost	10,625	875
Total cost to clean 10,000 m^2	88,985	20,319
Cost per square metre	8.90	2.03

[a] All cost in US$; grit consumption: 50 kg/m^2
[b] ISO 8501-1
[c] Hydroblasting Standard, International Paint

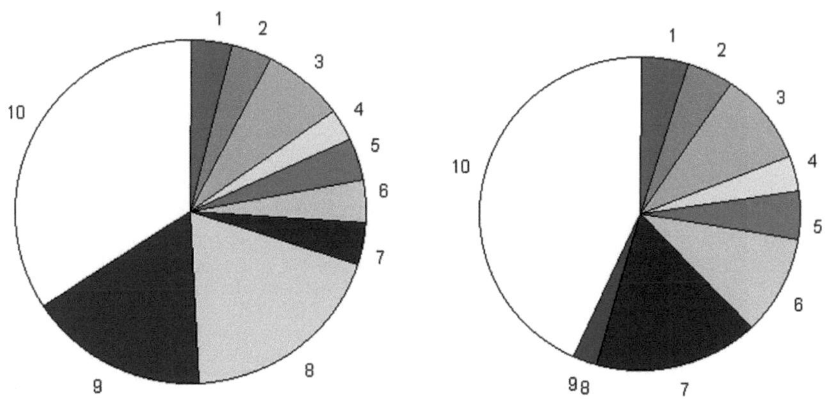

Fig. 6.37 Cost structure of a blast cleaning job (Lyras, 1991). Left: Conventional blast cleaning (1- primer, 2- small equipment, 3- vac truck, 4- compressors, 5- fuel, 6- equipment, 7- abrasive material, 8- disposal, 9- overhead, 10- total labor); Right: recycable blast cleaning (1- primer, 2- small equipment, 3- vac truck, 4- compressors, 5- fuel, 6- equipment, 7- overhead, 8- abrasive material, 9- disposal, 10- total labor)

Table 6.19 Results of comparative cost calculations (Pi and Hoogstrate, 2007)

Parameter	Value	
	Traditional regime	"Optimal" regime
Initial nozzle diameter in mm	3.2	4.4
Nozzle lifetime in hours	300	78
Average cleaning rate in m^2/h	3.8	4.2
Number of used nozzles	1	3.46 (4)
Total working time in hours	300	270
Cost in $/m^2$	42.2	38.8
Total cost in	48,411	44,482

Pi and Hoogstrate (2007) developed an alternative cost calculation model which in particular considered effects of nozzle wear. These authors introduced the concept of an "*optimal exchange nozzle diameter*". This parameter corresponds to the optimum lifetime of a blast cleaning nozzle. Results of calculations are provided in Table 6.19.

Chapter 7
Health, Safety and Environment

7.1 Safety Features of Blast Cleaning

7.1.1 General Safety Aspects

General aspects of health, safety and environment (HSE) for blast cleaning applications are summarised in Fig. 7.1. ISO 12944-4 states the following for surface preparation in general: "*All relevant health and safety regulation shall be observed.*" Blast cleaning owns an injury potential. General sources of danger to blast cleaning operators include the following:

- reactive forces generated by the exiting air-abrasive mixture (see Sect. 6.6.4);
- hose movements;
- uncontrolled escape of pressurised air;
- damaged parts being under pressure;
- dust and aerosol formation;
- sound emitted from equipment and blasting jet;
- impact from rebounding abrasive material and debris from the impact point.

It is generally recommended to carry out a risk assessment of the actual environment where a blast cleaning job will be done before starting the job. This risk assessment may include (French, 1998):

- how access is to be gained?
- is there a need for scaffolding?
- is there confined space?
- what is the surface like where the operators will have to stand?
- the availability of day light or artificial light;
- the presence of electrical supplies/equipment;
- nature of contaminate: Is it toxic? Is it a pathogen? Is it asbestos based? Is it harmful or corrosive?
- general layout that will allow visual contact between the blast cleaning team;
- permit requirements;

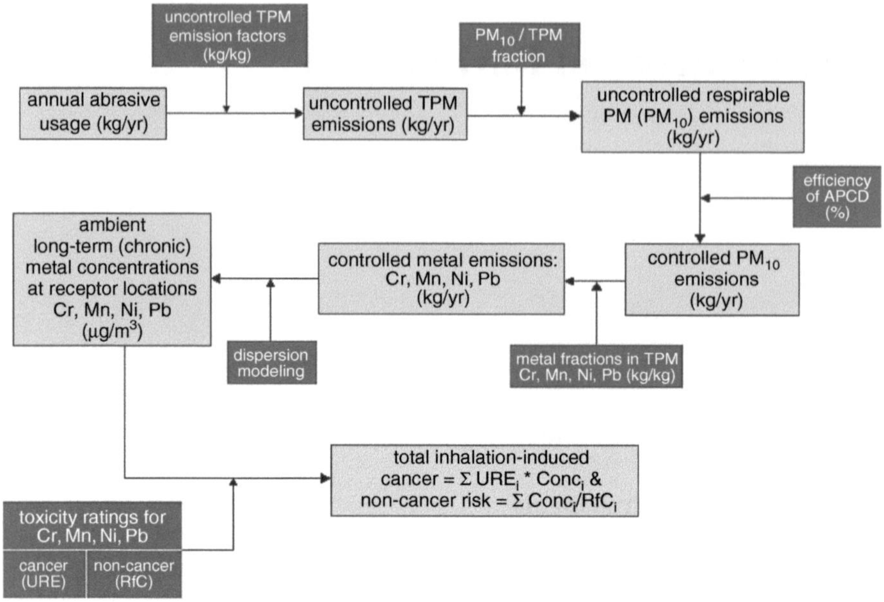

Fig. 7.1 HSE risk analysis for blast cleaning processes (Kura, 2005)

- safety of access (e.g. working on motorways or hazardous areas such as refinery where flameproof equipment and earthing to avoid static electricity may be required);
- who or what will be affected by flying debris?
- is noise a problem?
- will containment be necessary?
- where will the effluent go? (for wet blast cleaning and slurry blast cleaning)

In that context, ISO 12944-4 states the following: "*Personnel carrying out surface preparation work shall have suitable equipment and sufficient technical knowledge of the processes involved.*"

7.1.2 Risk of Explosion

Some source of explosion during blast cleaning can be electric discharge sparks. Safety hazard analyses identified that static electric charges occur in the following three circumstances:

- small particles flowing through piping;
- small particles passing through fine filters or nozzles;
- abrasive particles impinging fixed parts.

Table 7.1 Results of spark measurements during blast cleaning (Stuvex Belgium)

Parameter	Method	
	Dry blast cleaning	Wet blast cleaning
Voltage at the blast cleaned surface in V	500	2–3
Voltage of static electricity at the nozzle in V	5,000–10,000	0

Results of spark measurements performed on oil containers with dry blast and wet blast cleaning techniques are listed in Table 7.1. Dry blast cleaning generated high levels of voltage at the blast cleaned surface as well as at the nozzle. The use of wet blasting equipment helped to keep these levels low. Elbing (2002) reported about measurements of the electrostatic charging of steel during the blast cleaning with carbon dioxide pellets. The author measured values as high as 3,000 V, and he found that the discharge current increased with an increase in air pressure and stand-off distance. The discharge current was rather high for shallow impact angles, but reached a lower saturation level for impact angles $\varphi > 50^\circ$.

The electrostatic discharge in hose lines due to friction between hose wall and flowing abrasive particles can be managed through the use of blast cleaning hoses with low electric resistance. Values for the electrical resistance lower than of 10^3 Ω/m are considered to allow a safe charge elimination (BGR 132, 2003).

The effects of impinging abrasive particles on the ignition of explosive gas mixtures are not well understood. Dittmar (1962) highlighted the fact that sparks must create a certain temperature field in order to ignite gas mixtures. Duration and intensity of the temperature field determine the danger of explosion. The author cited experimental results from machining operations, and he reported that the formation and subsequent combustion of small metal chips generated temperatures up to 2,300°C. These high temperatures were much more critical than the temperatures reached at the tool–chip interface during the material removal process (see Fig. 5.17 for the situation during blast cleaning). Smaller chips generated higher temperatures than larger chips. Dittmar (1962) also reported that rusted steel substrates were much more sensitive to spark generation compared with clean steel substrates.

7.2 Emission of Air Sound

There are four major sources of air sound generated during blast cleaning operations:

- sound emitted from the pressure generating unit (compressor, engine and power transmission);
- sound emitted from the abrasive air jet travelling through the air;
- sound emitted from the erosion site;
- sound emitted from accompanying trades.

Two other items of concern are noise generated by air supply in the helmet and sound attenuation of the helmet.

State-of-the-art air compressors are regularly equipped with sound insolating hoods or even placed in containers. Thus, the air sound emission is limited up to 70–75 dB(A). More critical is the air sound emitted by the jet. This noise is generated due to friction between the high-speed jet and the surrounding air as well as due to turbulences. Thus, the sound level depends on the relative velocity between jet and air, and on the surface exposed to friction. Consequently, air sound level increases as compressor pressure, nozzle diameter and stand-off distance increase. This is verified in Fig. 7.2 where the effect of the nozzle pressure on the noise level is shown. The noise level increased almost linearly with increasing air pressure. Equal trends have been reported for the noise emitted during dry blast cleaning with carbon dioxide pellets (Elbing, 2002).

Fig. 7.3 illustrates results of measurements performed at different blasting sites, where dry blast cleaning, shot blast cleaning and wet blast cleaning were applied. Figure 7.3a includes results from measurements at a dry blast cleaning site. The actual blast cleaning application generated the highest noise levels. Figure 7.3b and d shows results from measurements at wet blast cleaning sites. The noise generated during the actual wet blast cleaning application was lower than the noise level measured for the dry blast cleaning in Fig. 7.3a. Figure 7.3c contains results from measurements at a shot blast cleaning site. The noise level was again lower than the noise level for the dry blast cleaning process mentioned in Fig. 7.3a, which was due to the facts that no air was involved in the mechanically driven shot blast cleaning process, and that the blast cleaning head was sealed. It can be recognised that

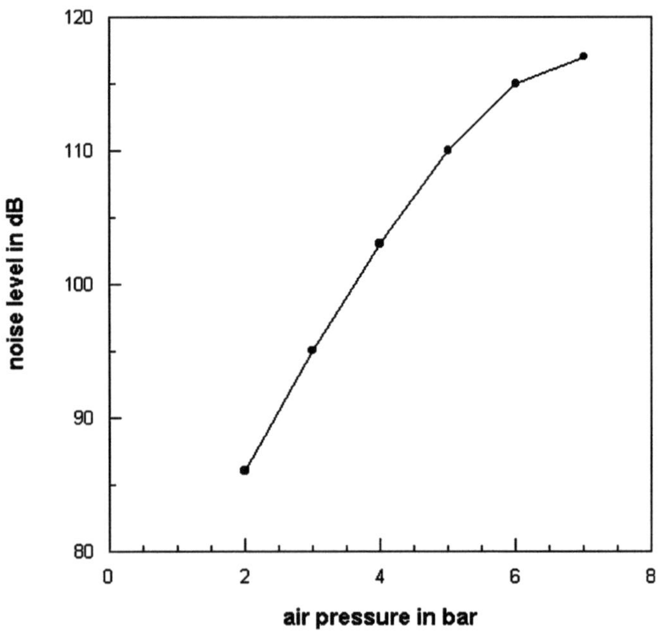

Fig. 7.2 Effect of compressor pressure on noise level (Schaffner, 1997)

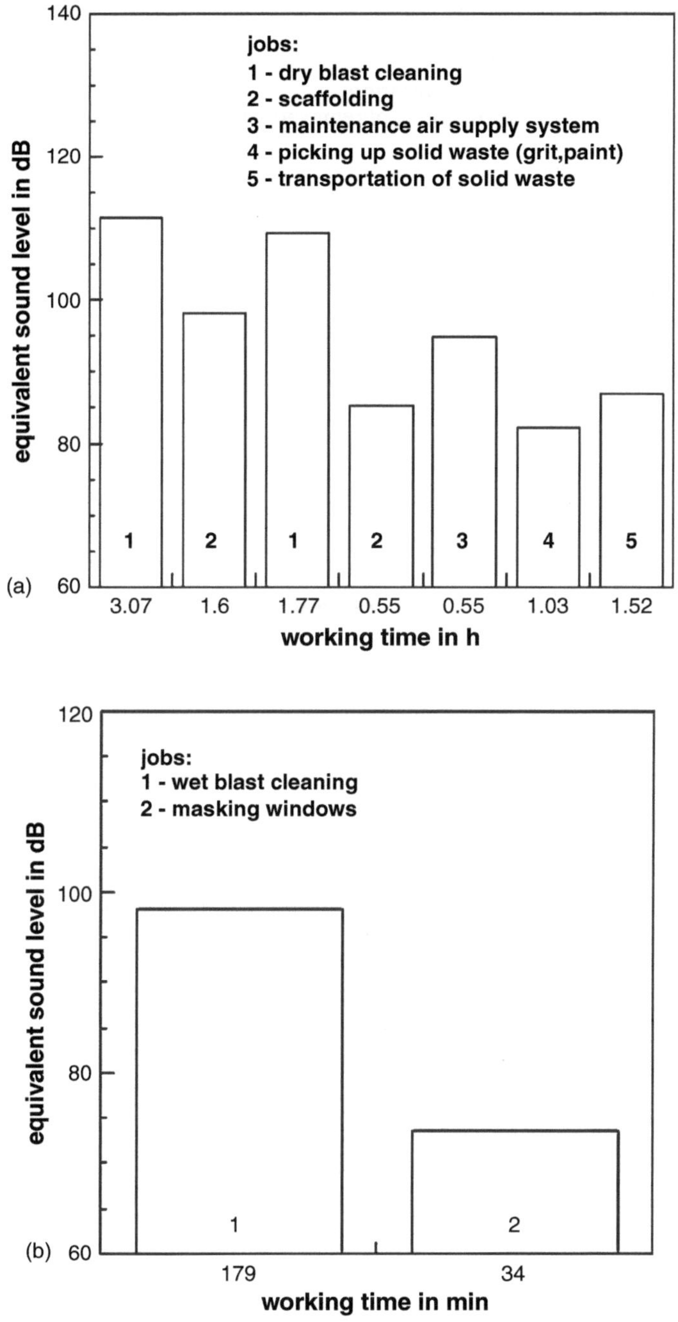

Fig. 7.3 Results from noise-level measurements during steel surface preparation jobs (Knipfer and Funke, 1997). (**a**) Dry blast cleaning; (**b**) Wet blast cleaning; (**c**) Shot blast cleaning; (**d**) Wet blast cleaning

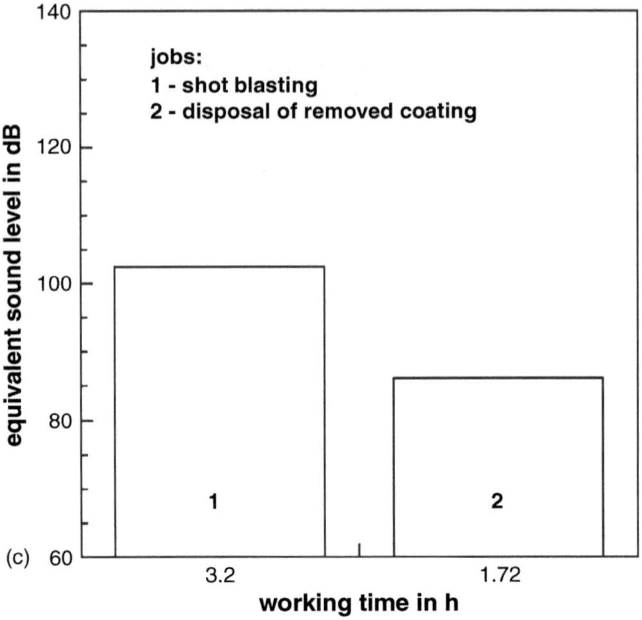

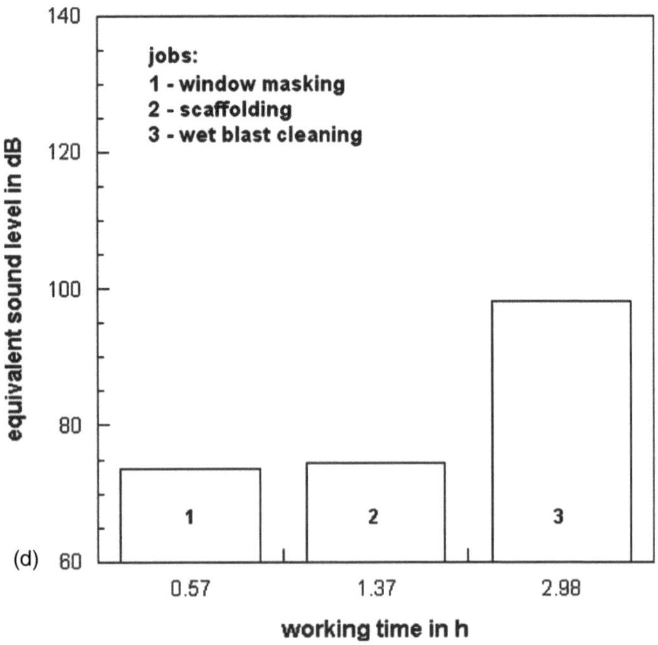

Fig. 7.3 Continued

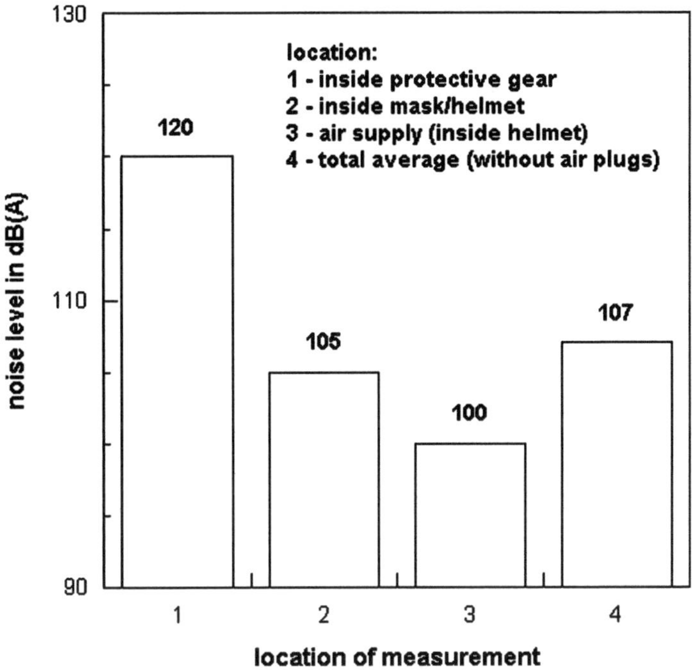

Fig. 7.4 Noise levels at different locations (Ognedal and Harbak, 1998)

the actual blasting operations (dry blast cleaning, shot blast cleaning and wet blast cleaning) generated the highest noise levels among all trades. Shot blast cleaning (which works with shrouded blasting tools) and wet blast cleaning are comparatively silent. Noise emission can notably be reduced if shrouded or sealed tools are used.

Figure 7.4 shows results of air noise measurements performed inside the helmet of blasters. Ognedal and Harbak (1998) concluded from these measurements that blast cleaning may create loss of hearing to the workers, if no additional hearing protection is provided.

The permissible air noise level depends on the exposure time. This is illustrated in Fig. 7.5 based on regularity limits stated in the German standard 'BGV B3 Lärm'. It can be concluded from the graph that ear protection equipment must be worn by any personally involved blasting cleaning operator (see Sect. 7.8).

7.3 Emission of Body Sound

Body sound characterises waves, which carry noise and travel through solid materials. Therefore, even if windows, doors, etc. are properly closed to lock out airborne noise, persons may any way experience certain noise levels. This noise is generated due to vibrations; they occur during the tool impact and depend on the acoustic properties, especially on the sound velocity and the acoustic impedance, of both

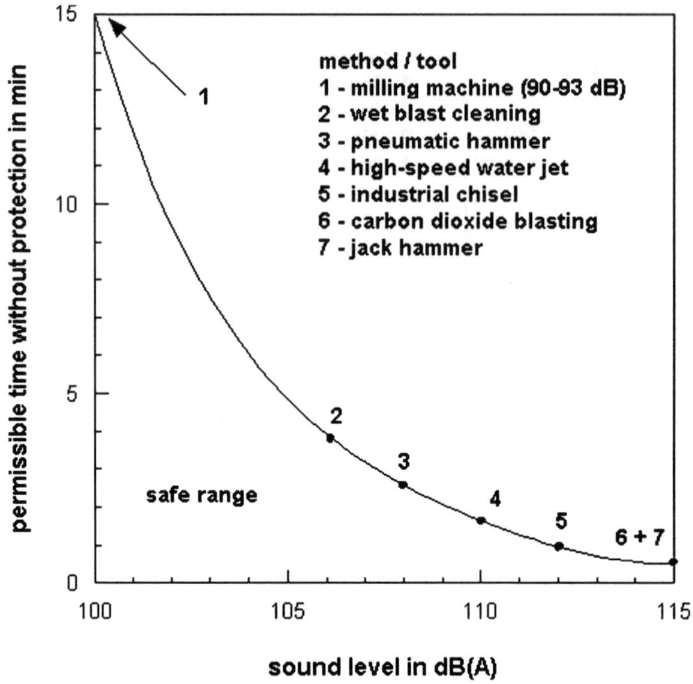

Fig. 7.5 Critical exposure times for different preparation tools (solid line according to BGV B3 Lärm; points from different sources)

the material to be subjected and the preparation tool. The evaluation parameters of the vibration are its amplitude and velocity (frequency). No measurements are available from dry blast cleaning operations. However, there are some measurements available from concrete facades treated with other surface preparation tools. Amplitudes and vibration velocities generated by the tools are plotted in Fig. 7.6. The two mechanical methods generated rather high values for vibration velocities, whereas the application of water jets led to low vibration velocities.

7.4 Emission of Dust

A mist of paint debris and broken abrasive particles is generated during dry blast cleaning in the immediate environment of the operator. An example is shown in Fig. 7.7. A simple model for the evaluation of dust during the blast cleaning of mould casings was introduced by Engelberg (1967).

Unfortunately, the dust is difficult to control. The only way to prevent it is the use of shrouded tools. Another way to protect the operator is the application of mechanically guided tools or robotic machinery. Anyway, both methods fail as it comes to the cleaning of complex structures. A reduction in dust exposure is possible by adding water to the air particle flow (wet blast cleaning and slurry blast

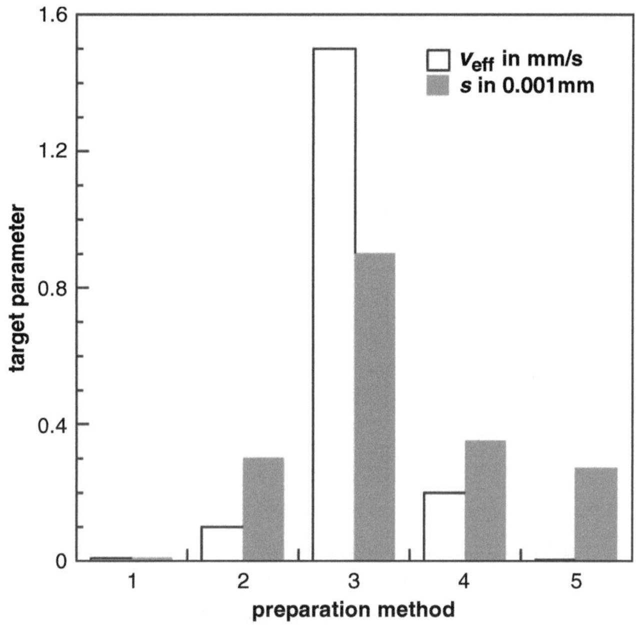

Fig. 7.6 Measurements of body sound emitted from different surface treatment tools (Werner and Kauw, 1991); v_{eff} – effective vibration velocity; s – vibration amplitude. Preparation methods: 1 – water jetting, 2 – hammer and chisel, 3 – jack hammering, 4 – pneumatic hammer, 5 – angle grinder

Fig. 7.7 Dust formation during dry blast cleaning (Photograph: Muehlhan AG, Hamburg)

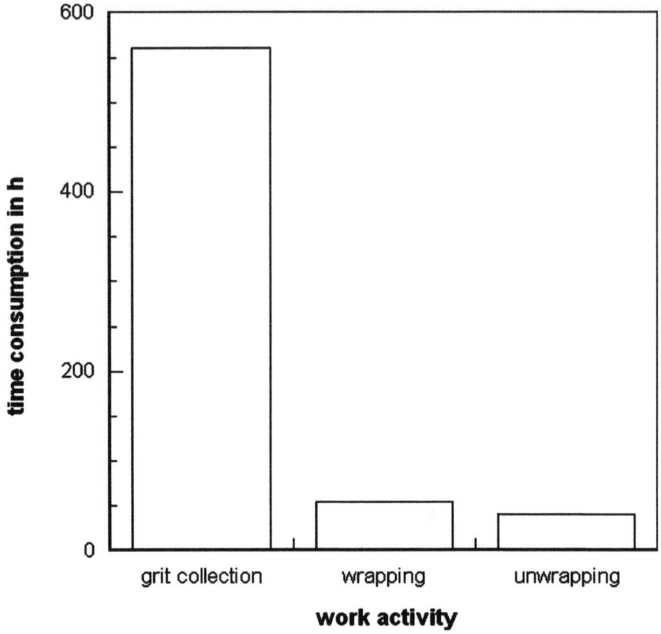

Fig. 7.8 Additional working time in a shipyard due to dust formation (Navy cargo ship in a drydock)

cleaning). Reviews on such methods are provided by Momber and Schulz (2006) and in SSPC (2006).

Some problems associated with dust formation are illustrated in Fig. 7.8. A very high amount of working time is required to wrap and unwrap the object (in the certain case a marine vessel in a drydock) before and after blast cleaning, and to clean up the yard site after the blast cleaning job. Several hundreds of additional working hours were spent in the example shown in Fig. 7.9. For a ship hull of about 8,000 m^2, 5 to 7 days for wrapping up the vessel using an eight-man crew would be required. Unwrapping would require another 4 to 5 days (Nelson, 1996).

Brantley and Reist (1994) investigated the exposure to respirable dust at ten different blast cleaning sites where quartz sand was used. Their results revealed that in general, downwind respirable silica concentration varied as distance raised. The concentration of respirable silica (mg/m^3) reduced with distance from the source (feet) according to the following relationship:

$$m_D \propto x^{-1.17} \quad (7.1)$$

The geometry of the worksite and the position of the workers affected concentrations observed by orders of magnitude. The values measured for respirable dust varied between 0.01 and 10 mg/m^3. Randall et al. (1998) reported on measurements performed during the removal of lead-based paint from a steel bridge with blast

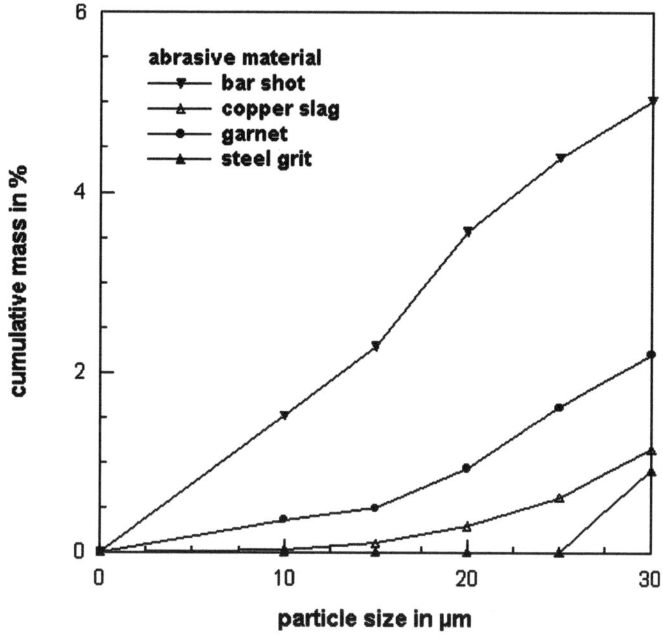

Fig. 7.9 Effects of abrasive type on the particle size distribution functions of dust (Kura, 2005)

cleaning. The authors measured total dust, respirable dust, total lead exposure and the exposure of respirable lead. Results of these measurements are listed in Table 7.2. The values are all above the permissible limits. This situation required the implementation of feasible engineering and work practice controls and the provision of personal protective equipment (PPE) and hygiene facilities supplemented by use of respirators.

Particle size distributions of airborne particles from blast cleaning operations were analysed by Kura (2005) with different methods. Some results are plotted in Fig. 7.9, and it can be seen that the type of abrasive determined the size distribution functions. Steel grit formed rather large dust particles, whereas the dust particles were small for bar shot.

Table 7.2 Air sampling analysis results from the removal of paint from a steel bridge (Randall et al., 1998)

Sampling point	Exposure in μg/m^3			
	Total dust[a]	Respirable dust[b]	Total lead	Respirable lead[c]
Background	300	100	5	*
Blast cleaning area	20,600	6,300	200	100
Blaster 1	4,000	400	50	*
Blaster 2	44,600	6,200	450	120

[a]OSHA PEL: 15,000 μg/m^3
[b]OSHA PEL: 5,000 μg/m^3
[c]OHSA PEL: 50 μg/m^3
*Not detectable

Kura et al. (2006) investigated the effects of nozzle pressure, abrasive feed rate (in terms of number of turns of metering valve) and abrasive mass flow rate on the emission of dust during blast cleaning. Dust emission increased as the nozzle pressure increased if painted panels were blast cleaned. If rusted panels were blast cleaned, dust emission was almost independent of nozzle pressure. The influence of the abrasive feed rate on the emission of particulate matter was sensitive to the nozzle pressure. For low and moderate pressures ($p = 0.55$–0.69 MPa), the emission increased with an increase in the number of valve turns. For higher pressures ($p = 0.83$ MPa), however, the emission showed maximum values at a moderate number of turns. The emissions for rusted panels were almost independent of the abrasive mass flow rate, whereas the emissions for painted panels again showed a complex relationship to abrasive mass flow rate and nozzle pressure. Results reported by Kjernsmo et al. (2003) are presented in Fig. 7.10. The emission of respirable dust increased for higher nozzle pressures. It can also be seen that quartz sand generated more dust than copper sand at equal nozzle pressures ($p = 0.7$ MPa). But this trend turned upside down if water was

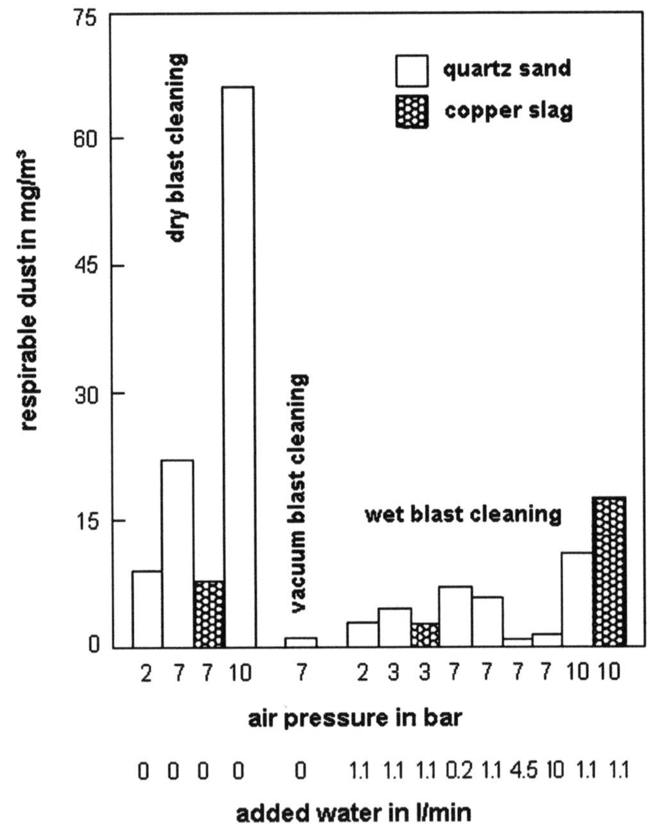

Fig. 7.10 Effects of abrasive type, nozzle pressure and water addition on the formation of respirable dust (Kjernsmo et al., 2003)

added to the nozzle flow; in that case, the dust emission was higher for the copper slag compared with that of quartz sand at equal high nozzle pressure ($p = 1.0\,\text{MPa}$) and equal water flow rate (1.1 l/min). The graphs also illustrate the effect of water addition. The version with the highest amount of added water (4.5 l/min) generated the lowest dust level among all tested configurations.

Greenburg and Winslow (1932) performed an early thorough study into the effects of location, abrasive type and fresh air supply on the concentration of dust during blast cleaning operations. Some results are listed in Table 7.3. It can be seen that the use of a mineral abrasive (sand at that time), even when mixed with a metallic abrasive material, created much higher dust concentrations compared to the use of a metallic abrasive. Kjernsmo et al. (2003) reported on the effects of abrasive type on respirable dust concentration. As shown in Fig. 7.11, quartz sand generated the highest amount of dust (which agreed with the results shown in Fig. 7.10), whereas cast iron generated very low dust levels. Mineral-based abrasive materials are usually more critical to dust formation compared with metallic abrasive materials.

Kura (2003) and Kura et al. (2006) provided the following statistical model for the assessment of parameter effects on dust emission during dry blast cleaning:

$$\mathrm{E_f = a_1 + a_2 \cdot p + a_3 \cdot \dot{m}_p \cdot a_4 \cdot p^2 + a_5 \cdot \dot{m}_P^2 + a_6 \cdot p \cdot \dot{m}_P} \tag{7.2}$$

Here, E_f is a specific dust emission factor, given in g/ft^2. The pressure is given in psi and the abrasive mass flow rate is given in lbs/min. This relationship holds for coal slag and bar shot, and for air pressures between $p = 0.55$ and $0.83\,\text{MPa}$. The constants a_1 to a_6 are regression parameters whose values as listed in Table 7.4.

Plitzko et al. (1998) investigated the effects of abrasive type and water addition on the concentration of respirable dust during the blast cleaning of metal substrates. Some of their results are plotted in Fig. 7.12. It is clear from this graph that even the use of a slurry system (method "5") could not avoid the exposure of impermissibly high dust concentrations. For dry blast cleaning with quartz, the permissible workplace limit was exceeded by a factor of 940. The use of an alternative abrasive material and the addition of water allowed for the reduction of this value, but the permissible limit was still exceeded by a factor of 4.

Katsikaris et al. (2002) noted an effect of the desired substrate surface cleanliness on the concentration of respirable dust. The respirable dust concentration was 399 µg/m^3 for a cleanliness degree of Sa 2 and 525 µg/m^3 for a cleanliness degree of Sa 2½.

Table 7.3 Results of dust measurements for different abrasive materials (Greenburg and Winslow, 1932)

Abrasive material	Dust concentration in 10^6 particles per cubic metre		
	Minimum	Maximum	Average
Sand	6.5	86.9	27.1
Steel	1.4	9.2	4.3
Sand/steel mixture	1.4	66.9	27.8

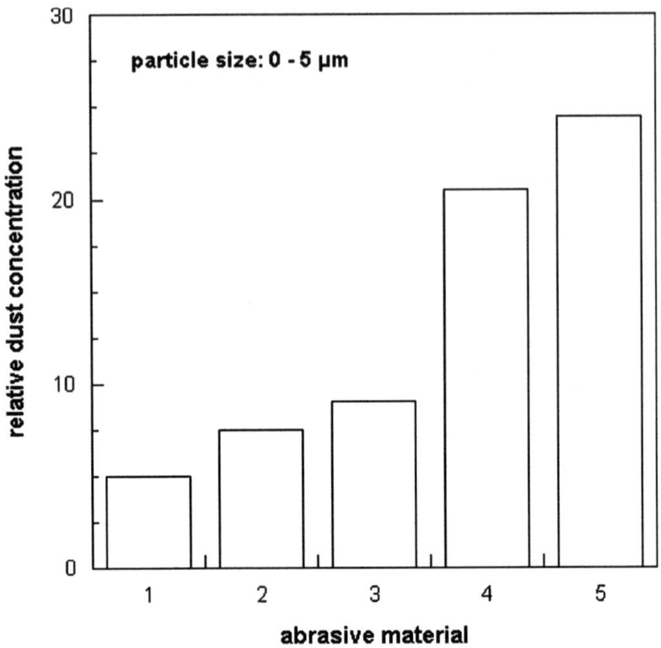

Fig. 7.11 Effects of abrasive material on the formation of dust (Kjernsmo et al., 2003). 1 – cast iron, 2 – aluminium oxide, 3 – aluminium silicate, 4 – olivine, 5 – quartz sand

Dust concentration, especially in confined spaces, can be reduced due to the utilisation of ventilation systems. As shown in Fig. 7.13, ventilation could drop dust concentration to very low values. Critical parameters were ventilation time and system size. The longer the ventilation time, the lower was the dust concentration. It was also shown that small ventilation systems can work very efficiently.

Blast cleaning operators must usually wear respiratory equipment, combined with a separate fresh air supply. It was already shown in an early investigation by Greenburg and Winslow (1932) that the amount of air delivered is of fundamental importance in determining the degree of protection of respiratory devices. Results of their measurements are provided in Fig. 7.14. It can be seen that the dust concentration under the helmet reduced with an increase in air supply. The graphs also illustrate the effects of screens in front of the blaster's eyes. A glass screen notably contributed to a reduction in dust concentration under the helmet.

Table 7.4 Regression coefficients for (7.2)

Target parameter in g/ft^2	Coefficients					
	a_1	a_2	a_3	a_4	a_5	a_6
E_f for painted steel	263.73	2.58	−57.17	−0.03	−0.85	0.71
E_f for rusted steel	−206.40	4.13	8.99	−0.01	1.04	−0.24

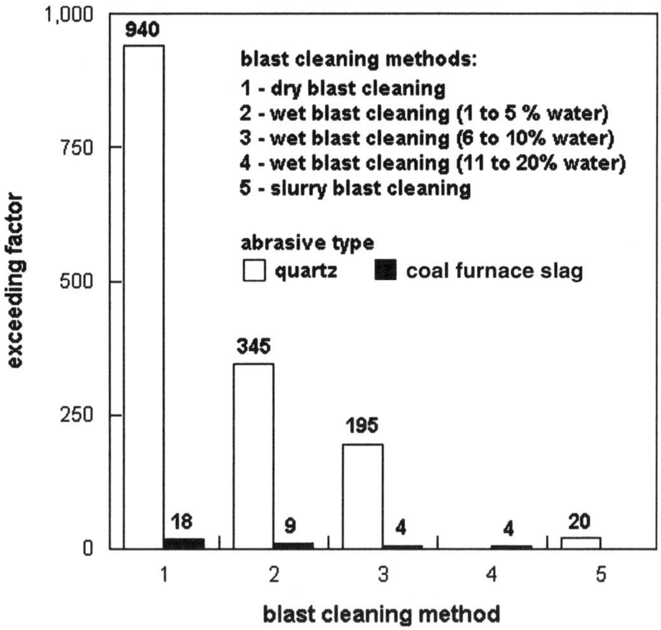

Fig. 7.12 Exceeding of critical dust concentrations for different blast cleaning variations (Plitzko et al., 1998)

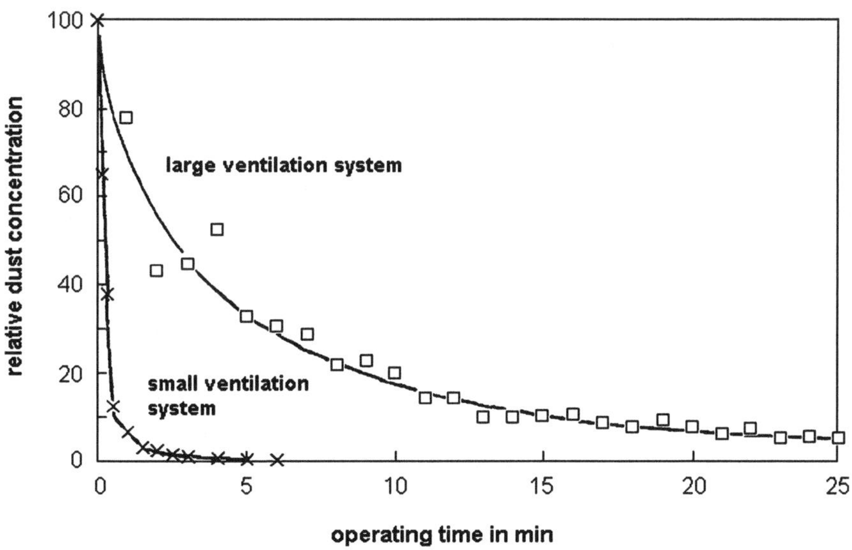

Fig. 7.13 Effects of ventilation on dust concentration (Mickelsen and Johnston, 1995)

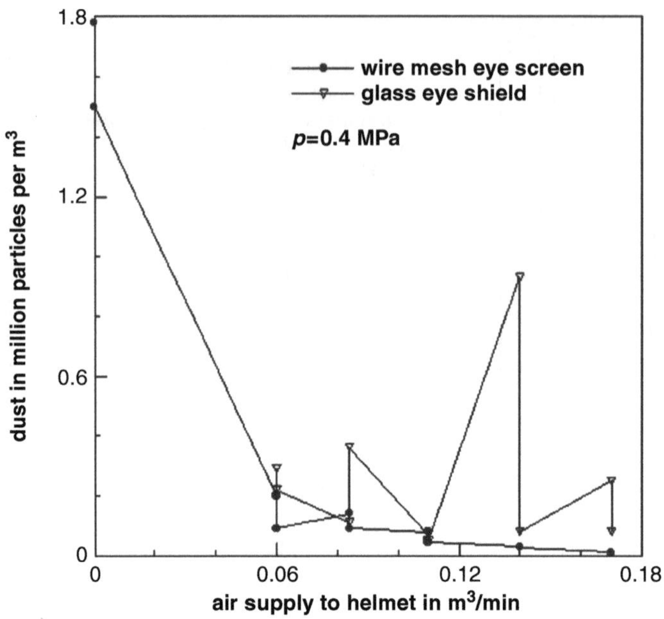

Fig. 7.14 Relationships between air supply to helmet, helmet screen design and dust concentration in helmets (Greenburg and Winslow, 1932)

An extensive database on site measurements of the exposure of workers to total dust, respirable dust, total crystalline silica and respirable crystalline silica can be found in Heitbrink's (1999) report.

7.5 Emission of Airborne Metals

7.5.1 Airborne Lead

Because many old coatings contain lead, there is a critical situation as the lead may enrich the operator's blood due to breathing the aerosol. There are the following two critical levels:

- Action Level (OSHA AL: 30 $\mu g/m^3$): If an operator works in an area at or above that level, the employer must give medical surveillance and training in the hazards of working with lead.
- Permissible Exposure Limit (OSHA PEL: 50 $\mu g/m^3$): This limit is for the average amount of lead in the air over an 8-h day.

Extensive studies have shown that airborne lead concentration does not depend on the main lead concentration in coating systems to be removed (NIOSH, 1997); the correlation between these parameters is very weak (correlation = 0.22). It is, therefore, the surface preparation method that determines airborne lead. Salome

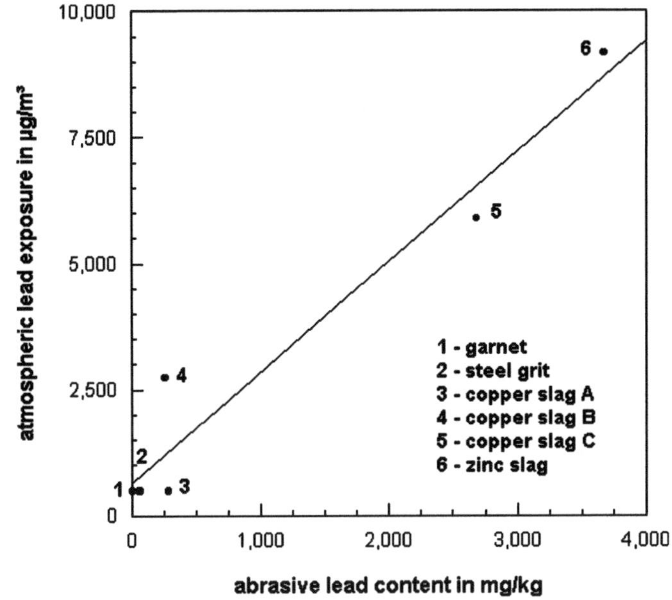

Fig. 7.15 Relationship between lead content in paint and airborne lead exposure for different abrasive materials (Salome and Morris, 1996)

and Morris (1996) have shown that the lead content also affected the amount of atmospheric lead exposure during blast cleaning. Some of their results are plotted in Fig. 7.15. A linear correlation with a correlation coefficient of 0.971 was found.

Blasters and painters are particularly endangered by lead exposure; this was verified by a comprehensive medical surveillance programme designed to prevent load toxicity in bridge workers, including blasters. Some results of these studies are shown in Fig. 7.16, and it can be seen that painters and blasters experienced the highest blood lead levels among all job categories. Cannon et al. (1996) performed a blood lead monitoring during steel bridge rehabilitation work where lead containing paint was blast cleaned. The authors did not find remarkable differences in blood lead levels for blasters, foremen, operators and painters. The only job classification with an average blood lead level greater than a critical level of 20 µg/dl was represented by the foremen. These rather low and evenly distributed blood lead levels were probably due to the fact that the worksite was properly managed with ongoing training, reinforcement of personal protection and hygiene practices, industrial hygiene monitoring and frequent medical surveillance. Conroy et al. (1996) monitored the blood lead levels of bridge workers, including blasters, sweepers, foremen, equipment operators, helpers and supervisors. They estimated blood lead levels were in the range between 26 and 77 µg/dl. Although the certain value depended on the type of work and the work season, they were higher compared to the values reported in the study mentioned earlier. Several reasons accounted for the

Fig. 7.16 Blood lead levels for bridge workers (Maurer et al., 1995)

blood lead elevation: the airborne lead emissions were very high for this project (see Table 7.5), there was lack of water, and the workers did smoke and eat at the construction site. Schulz et al. (2005) also reported on unusually high blood lead levels for workers who were involved in a blast cleaning project, including abrasive collection, machine maintenance and abrasive distribution. Reasons for the high levels were inappropriate air delivery, use of wrong filters and very high air temperatures.

A number of measurements of airborne lead exposure to blast cleaning sites were performed over the years. Some results are displayed in Table 7.6. It can be read from the table that dry blast cleaning generates rather high quantities of lead containing aerosols. Further results of systematic measurements of air samplings in a containment were reported by Jarrett (2003), who found lead concentrations between 400 and 6,000 $\mu g/m^3$ for blasters. Lange (2002) monitored the lead exposure

Table 7.5 Personal exposure to airborne lead by job title and activity (Conroy et al., 1996)

Activity	Airborne lead concentration in $\mu g/m^3$	
	Range	Median
Blasters and sweepers	12–4,401	366
Equipment operators	14–1,400	219
Foremen	26–3,423	160

Table 7.6 Measured airborne lead levels for different preparation methods

Object/condition	Lead level in μg/m³	Reference
Hydroblasting		
Galvanised communication towers	1.5–29	Holle (2000)
Structural steel construction	2–12	Dupuy (2001)
Dock side container crane	2.2[a]	Marshall (2001)
	0.79[a,b]	Marshall (1996)
	<0.99[a,c]	Marshall (1996)
Slurry blast cleaning		
Highway overpass structure	10.4–34.4	Anonymous (1997)
Steel bridge	45.7–305[c]	Frenzel (1997)
	40.1–52.7[d]	Frenzel (1997)
Vacuum blast cleaning		
Steel bridge	27–76[c]	Mickelsen and Johnston (1995)
Dry blast cleaning		
Blast room	1–100,000	Adley and Trimber (1999)
Steel bridge (blaster)	36–4,401	Conroy et al. (1996)
Steel bridge (sweeper)	12–3,548	Conroy et al. (1996)
Steel bridge (foreman)	12–3,423	Conroy et al. (1996)
Steel bridge (equipment operator)	39–1,900	Conroy et al. (1996)
Steel bridge (helper)	22–501	Conroy et al. (1996)
Steel bridge (operator)	50–450[a]	Randall et al. (1998)
Petrochemical tank	3.31[a,c]	Frenzel (1997)
Blast cleaning with pliant media		
Offshore oil platform (blaster)	4,990	Miles (2000)
Offshore oil platform (containment)	980	Miles (2000)
Ice blasting		
Steel bridge	175	Snyder (1999)

[a]TWA 8 h
[b]Downwind
[c]Gun operator
[d]Outside containment

during the removal of lead-based paint from a water tank by blast cleaning, and he noted that the exposure to the blaster on top of the tanks was much higher than the exposure to the blasters working on ground or in a crane.

Tinklenberg and Doezema (1998) constructed a chart where the exposure to operators was plotted against the content of heavy metals in paints, and they suggested a procedure how to read critical heavy metal amounts in paints. For inorganic zinc-rich primers, the following examples were provided. To keep operator exposure to less than a permissible exposure limit (50 μg/m³), the lead concentration in paints should not exceed a value of 280 mg/kg. To keep operator exposure to less than an action level limit (30 μg/m³), the lead concentration in paints should not exceed a value of 170 mg/kg.

Kaufmann and Zielasch (1998) reported about long-term air monitoring during the refurbishment of a steel bridge in Switzerland. The job was started with dry blast cleaning. However, this method was soon replaced by hydroblasting, mainly

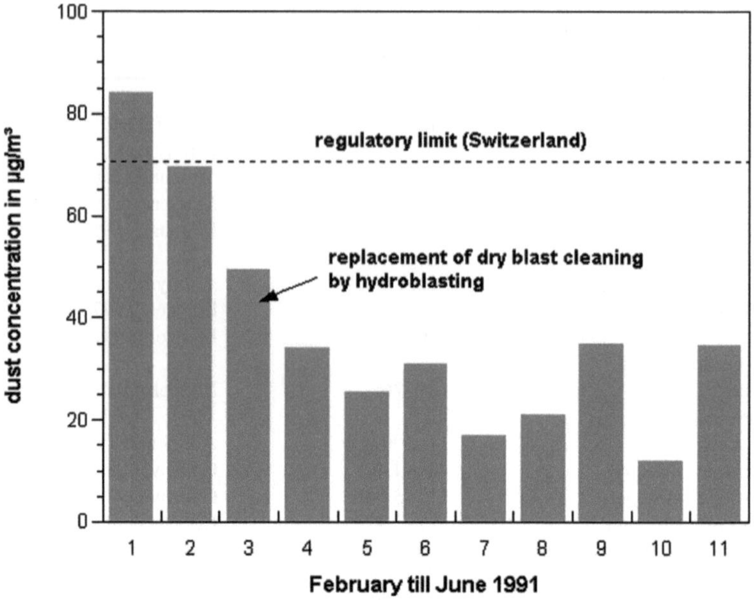

Fig. 7.17 Long-term air monitoring during steel blasting (Kaufmann and Zielasch, 1998)

because of the high dust emission that exceeded regulatory limits. This situation is illustrated in Fig. 7.17. Note that during the introductory phase of the project, where dry blast cleaning was applied, the legal limit of 70 $\mu g/m^3$ was exceeded. After dry blast cleaning was replaced by a hydroblasting method that featured a robotic tool as well as limited gun operations, the regulatory limit could be met during the entire project which lasted over three years (1991–1994).

7.5.2 Other Airborne Metals

A high number of carefully measured data on metal concentrations in airborne particulates emitted during blast cleaning tests were reported by Kura (2005) for a number of abrasive materials.

The exposure of workers to a number of heavy metals during different blast cleaning applications in a ventilated blasting chamber was investigated by Tinklenberg and Doezema (1998). Results of their study are listed in Table 7.7. The data clearly indicated that during blast cleaning, the operators were exposed very well above the permissible exposure limits for lead and cadmium. Even for a paint with a reduced level of cadmium and for cured paint, blast cleaning resulted in exposure above the permissible exposure limits for both lead and cadmium. Tinklenberg and Doezema (1998) designed a chart where the exposure to operators was plotted against the content of heavy metals in paints, and they suggested a procedure how to read critical heavy metal amounts in paints. To keep operator exposure to less than

Table 7.7 Exposure to heavy metals during dry blast cleaning of zinc-rich coatings (Tinklenberg and Doezema, 1998); based on 2 h of sampling

Materials	Metal content in μg/m³					
	Arsenic	Zinc	Lead	Cadmium	Chromium	Copper
Mill scale	*	169 ± 73	11 ± 3	*	24 ± 9	55 ± 20
Blast cleaned steel	*	162 ± 28	9 ± 3	*	24 ± 9	61 ± 13
	*	120,675 ± 41,761	107 ± 26	55 ± 17	23 ± 10	50 ± 23
	*	82,922 ± 28,179	71 ± 17	40 ± 11	17 ± 6	35 ± 19
Primer	*	105,680 ± 13,046	99 ± 15	52 ± 5	17 ± 2	45 ± 7
	*	121,162 ± 45,994	96 ± 19	56 ± 14	16 ± 3	46 ± 10
Topcoat	*	93,637 ± 21,441	71 ± 11	37 ± 6	14 ± 5	30 ± 14
Primer	*	178,266 ± 55,541	106 ± 26	12 ± 3	25 ± 6	50 ± 7

*Results below detectable limits

a permissible exposure limit, the cadmium concentration in an inorganic zinc-rich primer should – as an example – not exceed a value of 12 mg/kg. Airborne cadmium was measured during a bridge blast cleaning project by Conroy et al. (1996). The median concentration inside the bridge containment was 15.7 μg/m³, which exceeded the permissible level (OSHA PEL: 5 μg/m³).

Results of an exhausting study which considered surface condition and wind velocity are provided in Table 7.8. A general trend between wind velocity and metal emission could not be installed based on this data. Iron was the dominating metal in all cases, even where a painted surface was blast cleaned. Permissible exposure times depended very much on the location of the blast cleaning application. Some examples are listed in Table 7.9. It can be seen that the permissible limit for arsenic exposure was reached after 15 min in a blasting room, whereas it was reached after 60 min for an outdoor application.

Table 7.8 Summary of emission factors for metals blast cleaned with silica sand (Kinsey et al., 1994; Anonymous, 1997)

Operation conditions	Emission factor in kg per kg abrasive					
	Cadmium	Chromium	Iron	Manganese	Nickel	Lead
Clean surface						
8 km/h	1.4×10^{-6}	1.5×10^{-6}	1.1×10^{-4}	1.5×10^{-7}	1.1×10^{-6}	1.1×10^{-6}
10 km/h	*	3.3×10^{-6}	2.0×10^{-4}	2.4×10^{-7}	1.6×10^{-6}	1.2×10^{-6}
24 km/h	8.0×10^{-7}	5.4×10^{-6}	1.8×10^{-4}	7.0×10^{-8}	3.0×10^{-6}	3.9×10^{-6}
Painted surface						
8 km/h	2.1×10^{-7}	2.1×10^{-6}	1.0×10^{-4}	2.9×10^{-7}	8.6×10^{-7}	2.8×10^{-6}
10 km/h	*	4.0×10^{-6}	1.6×10^{-4}	1.2×10^{-6}	1.5×10^{-6}	5.6×10^{-6}
24 km/h	7.6×10^{-8}	7.4×10^{-6}	1.5×10^{-4}	1.2×10^{-7}	8.1×10^{-6}	6.3×10^{-6}
Oxidised surface						
8 km/h	3.1×10^{-7}	3.2×10^{-7}	1.4×10^{-4}	4.2×10^{-7}	4.2×10^{-7}	4.5×10^{-6}
10 km/h	*	3.0×10^{-6}	1.9×10^{-4}	2.4×10^{-7}	3.4×10^{-6}	4.9×10^{-6}
24 km/h	3.1×10^{-9}	3.7×10^{-6}	2.2×10^{-4}	8.6×10^{-8}	4.0×10^{-6}	6.6×10^{-6}

*Cadmium was not detected

Table 7.9 Time required to reach OSHA PEL for copper slag (Stephenson et al., 2002)

Contaminant	Time to reach OSHA PEL in min		
	Booth time	Outdoor time	Room time
Total particulate	22	40	15
Arsenic	37	60	15
Lead	37	60	63

7.6 Emission of Minerals and Organic Compounds

7.6.1 Asbestos Fibres

Many old linings contain asbestos. Asbestos fibres are known to be responsible for lung cancer. Results of asbestos emission during the preparation of steel substrates with different methods were reported by Binder (2001), Goergens (2002) and Schröder (2000). Some results are shown in Figs. 7.18 and 7.19. More information is provided in Table 7.10. It can be seen that all preparation methods that contain a liquid phase (wet blast cleaning, water jetting) generate rather low asbestos concentrations.

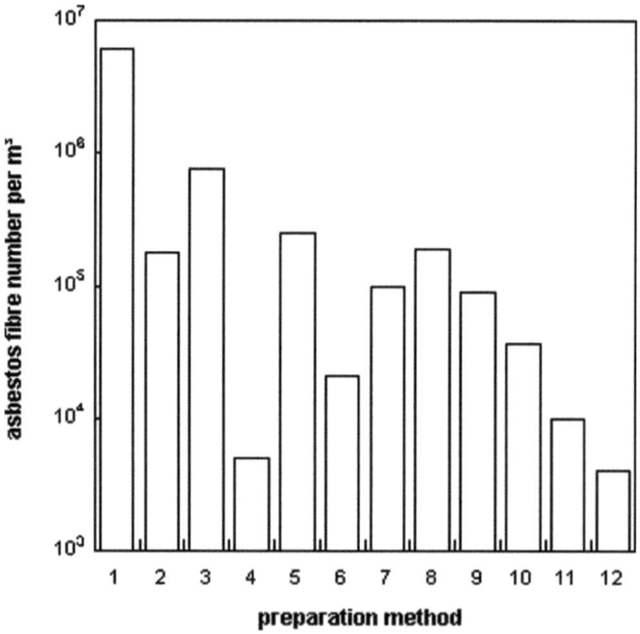

Fig. 7.18 Results of asbestos monitoring (Schröder, 2000). Treatment methods: 1 – dry blast cleaning; 2 – wet blast cleaning; 3 – wet blast cleaning; 4 – abrasive water jetting (85 MPa); 5 – hydroblasting (200 MPa); 6 – abrasive water jetting (120 MPa); 7 – hydroblasting and dry blast cleaning; 8 – wet blast cleaning; 9 – hydroblasting (240 MPa); 10 – wet blast cleaning (copper slag); 11 – water cleaning (13 MPa); 12 – water cleaning (15 MPa)

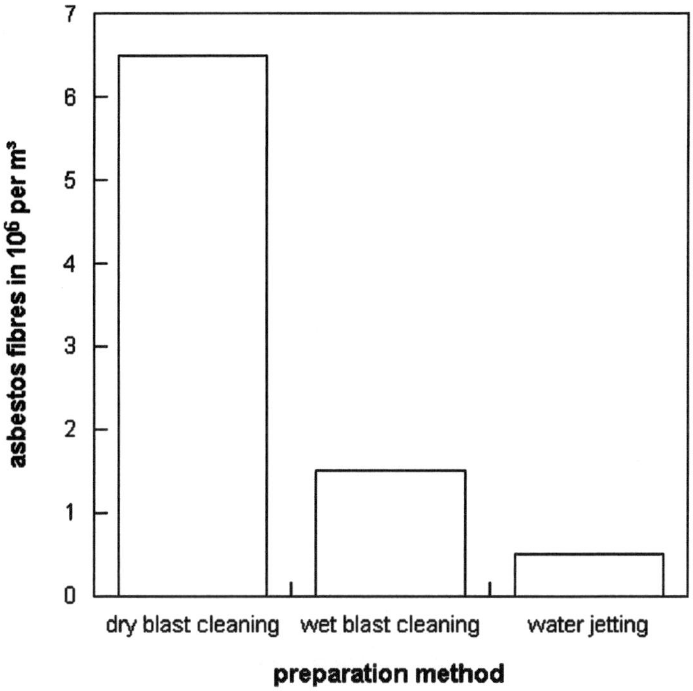

Fig. 7.19 Emission of asbestos fibres for different treatment methods (Goergens, 2002)

7.6.2 Organic Compounds

Tar epoxy coatings contain polycyclic agents, namely polycyclic aromatic hydrocarbons (PAH). Results of measurements of hydrocarbon exposure during paint

Table 7.10 Asbestos and PAH emissions during the coating removal from steel substrates (Schröder, 2000)

Method	Number of measurements	Number of fibres per cubic metre	PAH-value in µg/m^3
Flame cutter	8	881	Regulatory limit[a] exceeded
Needle hammer	1	<5,845	–
	1	14,933	–
	1	281,000	80–130
Burner	7	30,000–165,000	14–48
Hand-held grinder	1	25,000	50–152
Water jet (13 MPa)	1	5,000–10,000	Regulatory limit undercut
Grinding	2	20,000–45,000	–
Scraping	2	<5,000	Regulatory limit undercut
Flame cutter	2	Up to 38,000	Regulatory limit exceeded
Flex sawing (150°C)	1	98,074	–
Water jet	1	<4,045	–
Plane grinding	2	20,000–45,000	Regulatory limit exceeded

PAH Polycyclic Aromatic Hydrocarbons
[a]Limit: 2 µg/m^3

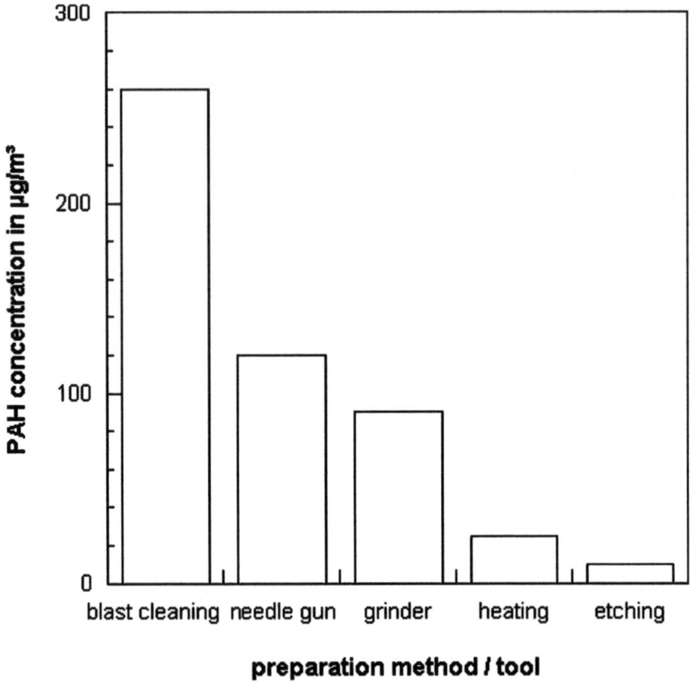

Fig. 7.20 Emissions of PAH for different treatment methods (Goergens, 2002)

removal operation with different treatment methods are reported in Fig. 7.20 and Table 7.10. The Benzo[a]pyren (BaP), mentioned in Fig. 7.20, is a certain type of polycyclic aromatic hydrocarbide. Binder (2001) performed a qualitative assessment of surface preparation methods in terms of emissions. The results of his procedure are listed in Table 7.11. It can be seen that dry blast cleaning has the lowest capability to suppress airborne contaminants. The best data provided high-pressure water jetting with integrated vacuum.

7.7 Vibrations to the Operator

Vibrations generated over a longer period of time in the arms of operators may cause so-called *white fingers*. The vibration generated by the tool is transmitted through the operator's hand where it does some damage to the blood vessels in the fingers (VDI, 1987). Therefore, regulations state minimum working hours depending on the intensity of the vibrations. The intensity is usually given by an acceleration value a_V. Results of measurements obtained from different surface preparation tools are shown in Fig. 7.21. Note from this figure that any point above the solid line is critical to health. Exposure time is the total time vibrations enter the hand per day, whether continuously or intermittently. Requirements for daily

Table 7.11 Assessment scheme for "emission safety" (Binder, 2001)

Method	Achievable limits	
	Asbestos (fibres per cubic metre)	PAH (μg/m³)
Dry blast cleaning	6,000,000	$\gg$2
Vacuum blast cleaning	(>150,000)	(>2)
Wet blast cleaning	>150,000/15,000	>2/±2
High-/ultra-high pressure water jetting	>15,000	±2
Water jetting with vacuuming	(<15,000)	<2
Inductive heating	<15,000	±2
Etching	± 0	±0
Sweeping after Etching	<15,000	>2/±2

Parentheses indicate assumptions

exposure may be summarised as follows (Cooke et al., 2001; see also EC-Machine Guideline):

- $a_V = 1\,m/s^2$ is considered to be potentially hazardous and is the threshold for health risk alert and the need for preventive measures, including workers education.

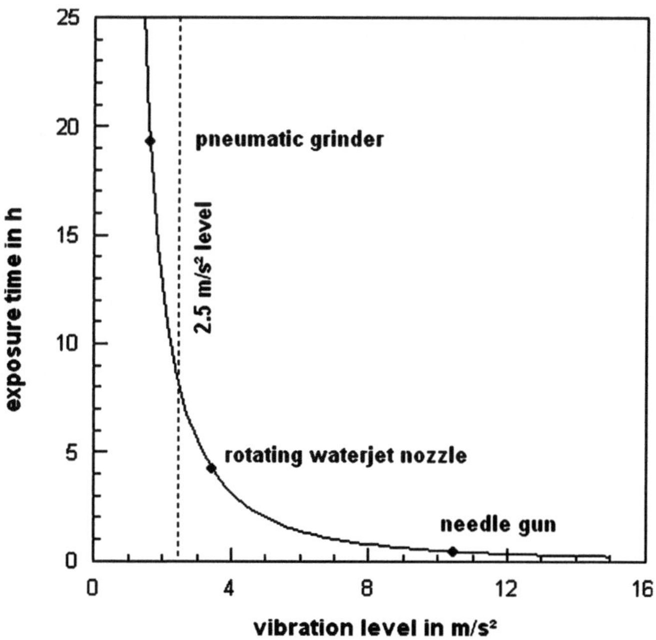

Fig. 7.21 Limits for exposure of the hand per day to vibrations (solid line according to Siebel and Mosher (1984); points from different sources)

Table 7.12 Vibration exposure to blast cleaning operators (Cooke et al., 2001)

Latent interval in years	Hose exposure	Vibration level in m/s^2	
		Highest mean	Highest peak
16	Entirely	2.66	13.0
3	Mostly	3.6	–
22	Mostly	3.6	–

Table 7.13 Vibration measurements on blast cleaning nozzle and hose (Cooke et al., 2001)

Situation	Mean vibration level in m/s^2			
	x-direction	y-direction	z-direction	Total
Right hand on nozzle	1.35	2.66	<1	2.98
	1.91	1.32	<1	2.32
	1.58	1.15	<1	1.95
Left hand on hose	1.00	1.43	<1	1.74
	2.24	1.93	<1	2.96
	1.08	1.36	<1	1.74

Compressor pressure: $p = 0.11$ MPa

- $a_V = 2.5\,m/s^2$ is the threshold for vibration measurement assessment values to be put into the instructions and sales literature and, if the value is less than $2.5\,m/s^2$, that fact shall be stated.
- $a_V = 5\,m/s^2$ is the ceiling level; if the vibration levels cannot be attenuated, exposure time has to be reduced and systematic health surveillance is required if there is daily exposure.
- $a_V = 20\,m/s^2$ is an enhanced risk situation; in addition to the measurements required at $5\,m/s^2$, the offending equipment must be marked.

Cooke et al. (2001) examined a number of working situations in terms of hand-arm vibrations; among them in four cases the blast cleaning equipment was used. Results of their examination are listed in Table 7.12. The critical exposure of $a_V = 1.0\,m/s^2$ was exceeded in all cases over a period of many years. Results of more detailed measurements during a blast cleaning application are reported in Table 7.13. The vibration levels were high in y-direction and negligible in z-direction. The results also showed high fluctuations caused by the unsteady flow of air and abrasive material through hose and nozzle.

7.8 Personal Protective Equipment

Blast cleaning has a certain injury potential to blasters, and PPE must be worn during blast cleaning processes. Required PPE for blast cleaning operators includes the items listed below (BGV D26, 1999).

1. For free blast cleaning:
   - respiratory protection;

- body protection covering shoulder and body;
- protective gloves;
- protective shoes.

2. For free blast cleaning, if poisonous, cancerous, fruit-hurtful or genotype-affecting agents can be exposed:

   - smooth and tear-resistant one-part protective suits (combination suits) in connection with respiratory protection.
     - The combination suits must be ventilated, and they cannot have external pockets;
     - Breathing air supply must be organised in a way that a sufficient and salubrious air supply is guaranteed even if fresh air supply is interrupted.
   - protective gloves;
   - protective shoes.

3. For staying close to blast cleaning machines:

   - eye protection.

4. For cleaning and waste disposal:

   - respiratory protection;
   - protective clothing.

Typical personnel protective clothing and equipment for blast cleaning operators are shown in Figs. 7.22 and 7.23.

Inert substances can cause severe injuries when forcefully injected into the hand. Belsole et al. (1982) described a hand injury subsequent to a pressurised injection of abrasive material. While removing rust from a ship hull, an operator lost control of the grit hose, injuring his left hand. The exact mechanism of injury was unclear, but the hand was struck by the abrasive particle jet and crushed against a steel beam. Roentgenograms could not detect a fracture. However, pinch and grip strengths of the hand were markedly reduced, and diminished sensibility was noted on the fingers of the hand. Only 8 months after the accident, it was found that the radial digital nerve was infiltrated with abrasive material that caused these phenomena. Similar cases were reported by Gelsdorf (1987) and Noetel (1987). A deadman control is, therefore, a mandatory part of any blast cleaning device. This control item must guarantee that no abrasive material leaves the nozzle if the operator loses control over the nozzle or grit hose.

7.9 Confined Spaces

Surface preparation jobs as well as painting jobs are often performed in confined spaces, namely manholes, pipelines, storage vessels, bridge box beams, interior tower cells and ballast tanks. A typical example is shown in Fig. 7.24. Not all

Fig. 7.22 Personnel protective equipment (Photograph: Muehlhan AG, Hamburg)

confined spaces are considered hazardous. However, they must be considered hazardous if they contain or have the potential to contain the following: (Osha, 1993):

- Hazardous atmospheres: This includes (1) lack of oxygen; (2) presence of explosive gases and vapours and (3) presence of toxic dusts, mist and vapours.
- Engulfment hazards: This includes spaces containing materials such as salt, coal, grain and dirt, which can easily shift and trap an operator.
- An internal configuration (slopes or inward configurations) that could trap or asphyxiate: This includes spaces where the bottoms are sloped or curved (e.g. narrow openings at the bottom of a silo) may trap or asphyxiate operators.
- Any other recognised serious hazards: This includes moving parts, power connections, liquid, and anything else that can cause bodily harm. This special situation requires special training because it is reported that operators are still getting hurt in confined spaces. The most important things to understand hazards in confined spaces are as follows (Platek, 2002):
- What hazard will be encountered?
- What equipment or means will offer protection from those hazards?
- How the equipment is used?
- Who can perform the work?
- What happens if something goes wrong?

When a confined space is evaluated, three questions regarding that space should be answered:

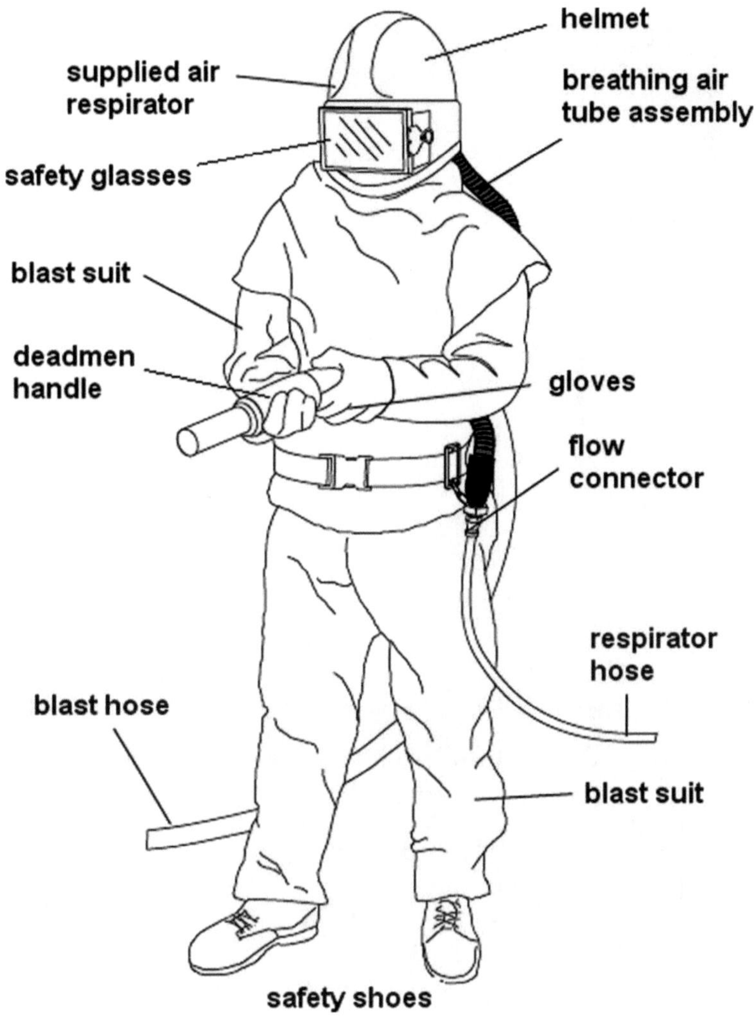

Fig. 7.23 Personnel protective equipment (Clemco Inc., Washington)

- Is the space large enough that the operator can place a part or whole of his body into it?
- Does it have limited entry and exits?
- Is it designed to work continuously?

Training and education are the major methods to reduce risks if work is performed in confined spaces. OSHRA 29 CFR 1910.146 states: "*The employer shall provide training so that all employees whose work is regulated by this section acquire the understanding, knowledge, and skills necessary for the safe performance of the duties assigned under this section.*" Adequate training must be delivered when permit-required confined spaces are encountered and for all of the duties performed

Fig. 7.24 Blast cleaning in a confined space (Photograph: Muehlhan AG, Hamburg)

in and around a confined space. Further information and recommendations can be found in IACS (2003).

7.10 Soil Contamination

Soil contamination due to heavy metals is another health and environmental issue associated with blast cleaning. Lange (2002) performed a systematic investigation into the contamination of soil during the removal of lead-based paint from a steel tank with blast cleaning. The lead concentration in the paint varied between 0.2 and 6.9 wt.%. Soil samples were collected in certain distances from the tank before, during

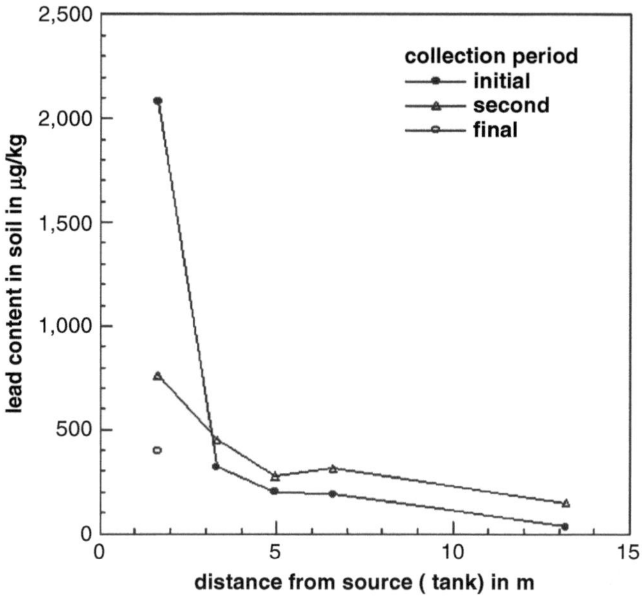

Fig. 7.25 Effect of stand-off distance on lead concentration in soil at a blast cleaning site (Lange, 2002)

and after the blast cleaning operation. Data from this study are plotted in Fig. 7.25. Concentration of lead in the soil generally decreased through distance from the tank. The author also found notable statistical differences among the samples collected during the different periods. The lead content was lowest immediately beneath the tank after the blast cleaning operation. The reasons were machine movements, cleaning operations and the spoilage of sand around the base of the tank.

7.11 Waste Disposal

7.11.1 General Disposal Problems

Waste can result from a variety of activities related to surface preparation and coatings work. Surface preparation, in particular, can produce a considerable amount of waste, mainly spent blasting media and old removed paint or rust products. The problem is illustrated in Fig. 7.26. The image was taken during a ship repair project where copper slag was used in order to remove a deteriorated coating system. The graph plotted in Fig. 7.8 illustrates the high amount of working time to be spent for collecting spent abrasive material in a shipyard.

Especially older paint systems contain hazardous materials such as heavy metals, dioxine, PCBs, etc. A recent report stated that in the USA about 581,000 steel structures contain lead-based coatings, mainly highway bridges, rail bridges and oil

Fig. 7.26 Solid waste to be dealt with after blast cleaning of a ship construction (Photograph: Lightgow Assoc.)

tanks (Randall et al., 1998). Typical examples for hazardous substances contained in paint systems are listed in Table 7.14. Most of these substances are not degradable; their health (and disposal) risk is essential:

- lead is extremely poisonous;
- PCB has chronic toxic effects;
- tar derivatives are carcinogenic;
- chromium-containing dust causes cancer and alters DNA.

These substances can also irritate the skin and cause eczema. A major problem with the removal of these paint types is the contamination of air and soil. Chromium, for example, may affect micro-organisms and prevent the air exchange of the soil. Any blasting medium (solid or liquid) is contaminated with these substances. For spent abrasive materials, for example, the lead contamination level can be as high as 840 mg/kg (Carlson and Townsend, 1998), the zinc contamination level can be as high as 37,000 mg/kg and the cadmium contamination level can be as high as 13 mg/kg. (Table 7.15 provides more data.). Potential concerns with ship maintenance facility abrasive waste are listed in Table 7.16. Concentrations of leachable metals in spent abrasives that are of particular danger to groundwater are listed in Table 7.17. For these reasons, methods that prevent or reduce the uncontrolled formation of dry dust and do not generate solid waste are superior from the point of view of health and ecology.

A management flow chart for waste abrasive blast cleaning media as recommended by Carlson and Townsend (1998) is provided in Fig. 7.27. This chart fea-

Table 7.14 Hazardous substance analysis of paint systems

Substance	Content in paint (%)	Reference
Cadmium	0.014[a]	Dupuy et al. (2001)
	0.003–0.01	Marshall (2001)
Chromium	0.86[a]	Dupuy et al. (2001)
	1.65	Holle (2000)
	2.99	Holle (2000)
	0.093–0.21	Marshall (2001)
Lead	0.31–13.5	Dupuy et al. (2001)
	0.132–0.710	Marshall (2001)
	6.14	Holle (2000)
	11.11	Holle (2000)
	14–20	Mickelsen and Johnston (1995)
PCB	0.12	Holle (2000)
	0.16	Holle (2000)
Zinc[b]	80–85	Tinklenberg and Doezema (1998)

[a]Maximum values
[b]Zinc rich paint

tures a number of test and recycling cycles. A duty of care that addresses waste generation, control and disposal, which is a statutory duty that applies to producers, holders, carriers of waste and those who treat waste, has four major aims (Abrams, 1999):

- to prevent any other person from depositing, disposing of, or recovering controlled waste (residential, commercial and industrial) without a waste management licence or in a manner likely to cause environmental pollution or harm to health;
- to ensure that waste is safely and securely contained, both in storage and transport, in such a way that it cannot escape;
- to ensure that if waste is transferred then it only goes to an authorised person;
- to ensure that when waste is transferred there is a clear, written description of it so that the person receiving the waste can handle it properly and safely without committing any offence.

Table 7.15 Comparison of metals in virgin and in spent abrasive material (Carlson and Townsend, 1999)

Condition	Metals in mg/kg					
	Arsenic	Chromium	Iron	Lead	Nickel	Zinc
No. of samples	15	15	15	15	15	15
Detection limit	0.05	5.0	5.0	25.0	5.0	5.0
Minimum	<0.05	12.6	827	<25	4.8	24.3
Maximum	0.08	59.1	2,801	99.5	53.1	4,328
Geometric mean	0.05	32.8	1,300	36.6	13.2	211
Geometric standard deviation	0.04	1.6	1.4	2.3	2.2	5.8
Arithmetic mean	0.06	35.6	1,380	47.3	18.1	760
Arithmetic standard deviation	0.04	13.3	523	29.4	16.1	1,173

Table 7.16 Concerns with abrasive waste from ship maintenance (Carlson and Townsend, 1999)

Metal	Direct exposure		Groundwater leaching
	Residential	Industrial	
Arsenic	Yes	Possibly	No
Cadmium	No	No	No
Chromium	No	No	No
Copper	Yes	No	Possibly
Iron	Yes	No	Possibly
Lead	No	No	Possibly
Nickel	No	No	No
Selenium	No	No	No
Zinc	No	No	Yes[a]

[a]Compare with Table 7.17

The following steps are helpful to meet the obligations mentioned above:

- Identification of all types of activity involved in the project (e.g. paint removal; storage of chemicals, fuels and paints; application of paint).
- Identification of all sources of waste in terms of "waste streams" (e.g. dry removed paint, blasting water, abrasive and its packaging, dust, chemicals and their packaging, wet paints, fuel), and the estimation of the quantities of waste from each process step prior to the job start.
- Determination of a means of handling and storing waste in order to control and minimise pollution risks. This could include the following:
  - Minimising the amount of abrasives or contaminated water that can be done by some type of containment with extraction if necessary;
  - Storage of contaminated waste in a properly bonded area;
  - Examination of transfer methods from the storage area to the waste contractor to minimise risk of spillage.

7.11.2 Abrasive Material Disposal

The absolute annual abrasive consumption in North America is listed in Table 7.18. The total consumption, which is about 3.3 million tonnes per year, must be disposed or recycled, respectively. Figure 7.28 shows typical values for solid disposal mea-

Table 7.17 Leachable metals in spent abrasive (Tinklenberg and Doezema, 1998)

Condition	Leachable metals in mg/l					
	Arsenic	Zinc	Lead	Cadmium	Chromium	Copper
Virgin abrasive	<0.2	<0.3	<0.2	<0.03	<0.05	<0.1
After metal cleaning	<0.2	<0.3	<0.2	<0.03	<0.05	<0.1
After zinc-rich paint removal	*	770	0.23	0.01	*	*

*Results below detection limits

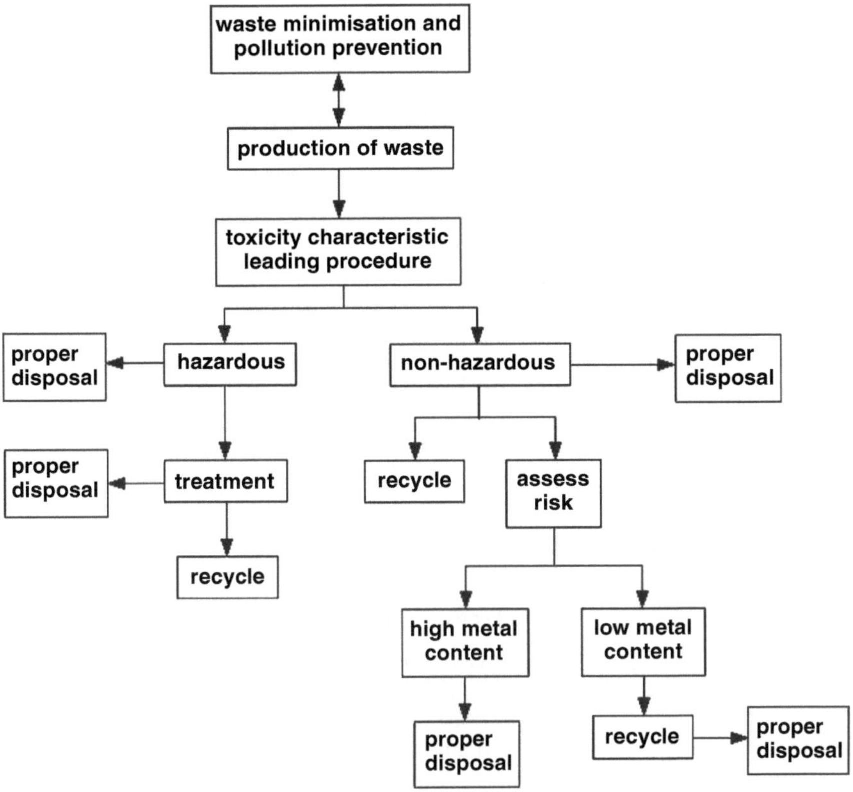

Fig. 7.27 Waste management scheme for blast cleaning processes (Carlson and Townsend, 1998)

sured during the treatment of a ship hull. The specific disposal rate is defined as the ratio between cleaning rate and solid particles collected during the treatment:

$$R_D = \frac{\dot{m}_P + \dot{m}_C}{\dot{A}} \tag{7.3}$$

Therefore, the physical unit is kg/m^2. Grit blasting usually generates a rather

Table 7.18 Annual abrasive consumption in North America (Hansink, 1998)

Abrasive type	Consumption in tonnes per year
Silica sand	2,000,000
Coal slag	750,000
Copper slag	100,000
Steel grit	300,000
Staurolite	70,000
Garnet	30,000
All others	50,000

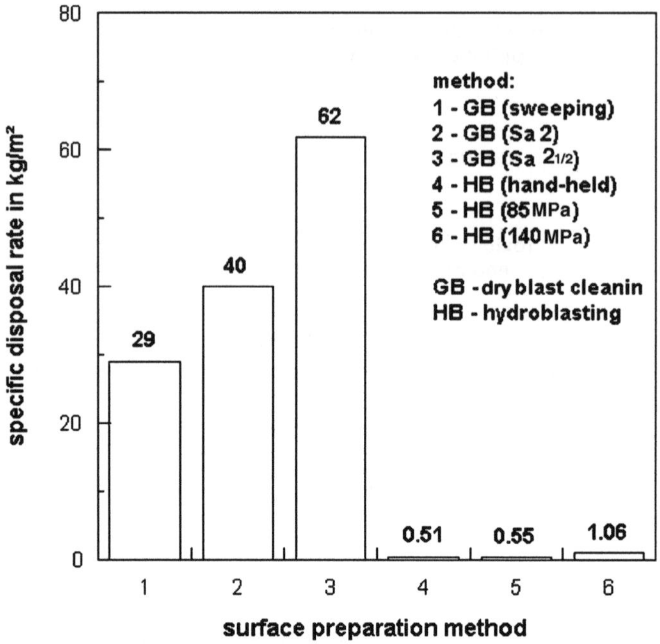

Fig. 7.28 Disposal rates for ship hull treatment (Palm and Platz, 2000)

high amount of solids which is basically due to the abrasive materials spent for the surface preparation. The specific disposal rate increases if the desired surface preparation level increases. It is lowest for simple sweeping jobs and highest for a high-quality surface (Sa 2½). Using average values for blast cleaning, the specific amount of abrasives spent to remove a given mass of paint is about 60 kg/kg. The values plotted in Fig. 7.28 are taken from a ship hull cleaning project. A typical value for steel bridge surface preparation by blast cleaning is $R_D = 42\,\text{kg/m}^2$; in that case, a surface of 120,000 m^2 was blasted with 5 t of abrasive material (Ochs and Maurmann, 1996). Another example is reported by Kaufmann (1998): for a 10,000-m^2 highway steel bridge, a total of 50 t of abrasive material was required; this corresponds to an abrasive disposal rate of $R_D = 50\,\text{kg/m}^2$. More examples are listed in Table 7.19.

A comparative cost calculation for the treatment of railway bridges by blast cleaning and hydroblasting was performed by Meunier and Lambert (1998). Considering an average abrasive consumption of 40 kg/m^2, the following statements could be made:

- supplying abrasives before the blast cleaning stop starts: 350 FrF/t (equivalent to 14 FrF/m^2) $=$ 19%;
- recovery, transport of waste and discharge of abrasives (average distance 100 km): 24 FrF/m^2 $=$ 32%;

Table 7.19 Typical abrasive consumption values for blast cleaning applications

Abrasive type	Abrasive consumption in kg/m^2	Efficiency in m^2/h	Method	Reference
Copper slag	26.2	10.7	Slurry blast cleaning	Da Maia (2000)
Copper slag[a]	25.0	12.2	Slurry blast cleaning	Da Maia (2000)
Sand	22.3	9.2	Slurry blast cleaning	Da Maia (2000)
Bauxite	31.9	–	Dry blast cleaning	Uhlendorf (2000)
Coal slag	50	4	Dry blast cleaning	Cluchague (2001)
Copper slag	40	–	Dry blast cleaning	Beltov and Assersen (2002)
Dolomite	129.6	5.7	Dry blast cleaning	Andronikos and Eleftherakos (2000b)
Garnet	108.6	10.5	Dry blast cleaning	Andronikos and Eleftherakos (2000b)
Nickel slag	91.4	12.0	Dry blast cleaning	Andronikos and Eleftherakos (2000b)
Olivine	105.6	8.7	Dry blast cleaning	Andronikos and Eleftherakos (2000b)
Steel grit	40	–	Dry blast cleaning	Beltov and Assersen (2002)
Coal slag	12	8	Thermo blasting	Cluchague (2001)

[a]Recycled

- right to discharge abrasives according to French Class 1 (tax): 900 FrF/t (equivalent to 36 FrF/m^2) = 49%.

This corresponds to total cost of 74 FrF/m^2 (=100%). It is interesting to note that about 50% of the costs are due to the disposal of the spent abrasive material only.

7.11.3 Contamination of Abrasive Material and Leachable Metals

Because of the intense contact between abrasive material and the material to be removed, abrasive material is usually contaminated. The contaminants may, in particular, include heavy metals and organic compounds. Table 7.20 lists the results of comparative measurements of metal contents in a virgin and a spent mineral abrasive material used for the removal of zinc-based paint. The unused abrasive

Table 7.20 Comparison of metals in virgin and in spent abrasive material (Tinklenberg and Doezema, 1998)

Condition	Metals in mg/kg					
	Arsenic	Zinc	Lead	Cadmium	Chromium	Copper
Virgin	<11.0	<170	<11.0	<1.6	<4.0	<2.5
After steel cleaning	<10.0	<60.0	<10.0	<1.5	<4.0	<5.0
After zinc-rich paint removal	*	37,000	37	13	12	18

*Below detectable limit

Table 7.21 Leachable metals in spent abrasive material (Tinklenberg and Doezema, 1998)

Condition	Metals in mg/l					
	Arsenic	Zinc	Lead	Cadmium	Chromium	Copper
Virgin	<0.2	<0.3	<0.2	<0.03	<0.05	<0.1
After steel cleaning	<0.2	<0.3	<0.2	<0.03	<0.05	<0.1
After zinc-rich paint removal	*	770	0.23[a]	0.099	*	*

*Below detectable limit
[a]One reading

material did not contain heavy metals in high amounts. The blast cleaning of bare steel did not notably change the amounts of heavy metals in the abrasives compared with the unused abrasives. As expected, the abrasive material spent during coating removal contained in particular a very high level of zinc, which may become critical in term of disposal and recycling. Table 7.15 lists the results of measurements from waste samples collected from blast cleaning contractors. Cadmium, copper and selenium were below their respective detection limit for all samples.

Leachable metals are critical to ground water, and their concentration should not exceed certain critical levels. Wastes classified as hazardous must be treated to leachable levels below 0.5 mg/l for lead, 0.11 mg/l for cadmium and 0.60 mg/l for chromium (Drozdz 2000). Wastes that do not exhibit the hazardous characteristics for these metals do not require post-treatment. Some industrial areas use topical stabilisers to prevent spent abrasive material and paint debris from exhibiting the hazardous characteristics for lead. These substances work by reducing the solubility of the lead, thus stabilising it so that it will not leach into the environment when it comes in contact with a liquid. Drozdz (2000) performed a study on the efficiency of four stabilisers and found them very effective at eliminating the hazardous characteristics of lead. However, only one of the stabilisers was capable at eliminating the hazardous characteristics of cadmium, and none for chromium.

Measurements on leachable metals in spent abrasive materials, used for the removal of zinc-rich inorganic primers, were performed by Tinklenberg and Doezema (1998). Results of their measurements are listed in Table 7.21. The results showed that the blast cleaning of a zinc-rich paint could easily produce a waste that will leach zinc above 500 mg/l, which would classify the waste to be hazardous. Other metals were not considered to be critical. Results from leaching tests for abrasive waste collected from shipyards and contractor sites are provided by Carlson and Townsend (1999).

7.11.4 Paint Waste

Typical specific chip disposal rates are between 0.3 and 1 kg/m^2 (see previous section). For the treatment of 3,320 m^2 of a maritime steel construction, 2.7 t of paint were disposed; this is a disposal rate of 0.8 kg/m^2 (Uhlendorf, 2000).

7.12 Recycling of Abrasive Materials

7.12.1 Contamination with Residue

A mobile abrasive material recycling unit for large-scale applications is shown in Fig. 7.29. Table 7.22 lists typical values for the recyclability of numerous abrasive materials.

Spent abrasive material is usually contaminated with residue originating from the material which was blast cleaned. Residue could be metals, soluble substances and organic compounds.

Fig. 7.29 Mobile abrasive recycling unit for large-scale applications (Photograph: Muehlhan AG, Hamburg)

Table 7.22 Workability parameters of abrasive materials (Stieglitz, 1996)

Abrasive material	Number of life cycles	Specific consumption in kg/m^2
Melting chamber slag	1	30–60
Copper slag	1	30–60
Garnet	3–6	10–20
Secondary corundum	10–20	5–15
Fused corundum	10–30	3–10
Sintered bauxite	10–30	3–10
Glass beads	10–30	10
Plastics beads	5–200	1–5
Ceramics	300	1–5
Hard cast	150–500	0.5–0.8
Steel cast (HV 700–900)	800–1,200	0.3
Steel cast (HV 550–750)	1,500–2,500	0.2
Steel cast (HV 400–600)	3,000–5,000	0.1
Cut steel wire	4,000–9,000	0.03

Katsikaris et al. (2001) described a procedure for the recycling of ferrous–nickel slag. Their investigation programme included sieve analysis, electric conductivity, chloride content and organic content. Some results are displayed in Fig. 7.30. Figure 7.30a shows results from electric conductivity readings. The recycled abrasive samples exhibited slightly lower levels compared with the unused sample. Similar is the situation in Fig. 7.30b where the amount of sodium chloride is plotted against the number of cycles. The recycling was, therefore, not critical to soluble substances in the abrasive material. Results of organic content monitoring are listed in Table 7.23. The organic content depended on the abrasive particle sizes; it was high for the large particle fraction ($d_P > 1{,}400\ \mu m$). For the larger particles, an accumulation of organic compounds could be noted.

Katsikaris et al. (2002) investigated the efficiency of recycled ferrous-nickel slag. They found that specific abrasive consumption notably increased if the slag was reused. Whereas for the first usage cycle, the specific abrasive consumption was 99 kg/m^2; it increased to 125 kg/m^2 after three usage cycles.

7.12.2 Use for Construction Materials

The use of paint-contaminated abrasive particles as aggregate material for mortar–cement-based concrete and asphalt concrete was investigated by Madany et al. (1991) and Taha et al. (2001). Madany et al. (1991) used copper slag as a replacement ma-

Table 7.23 Organic content in recycled ferrous nickel slag (Katsikaris et al., 2001)

Grain size in μm	Organic content in wt.%	
	One recycling cycle	Two recycling cycles
<150	1.25	1.61
150–1,400	0.14	0.11
>1,400	6.91	46.14

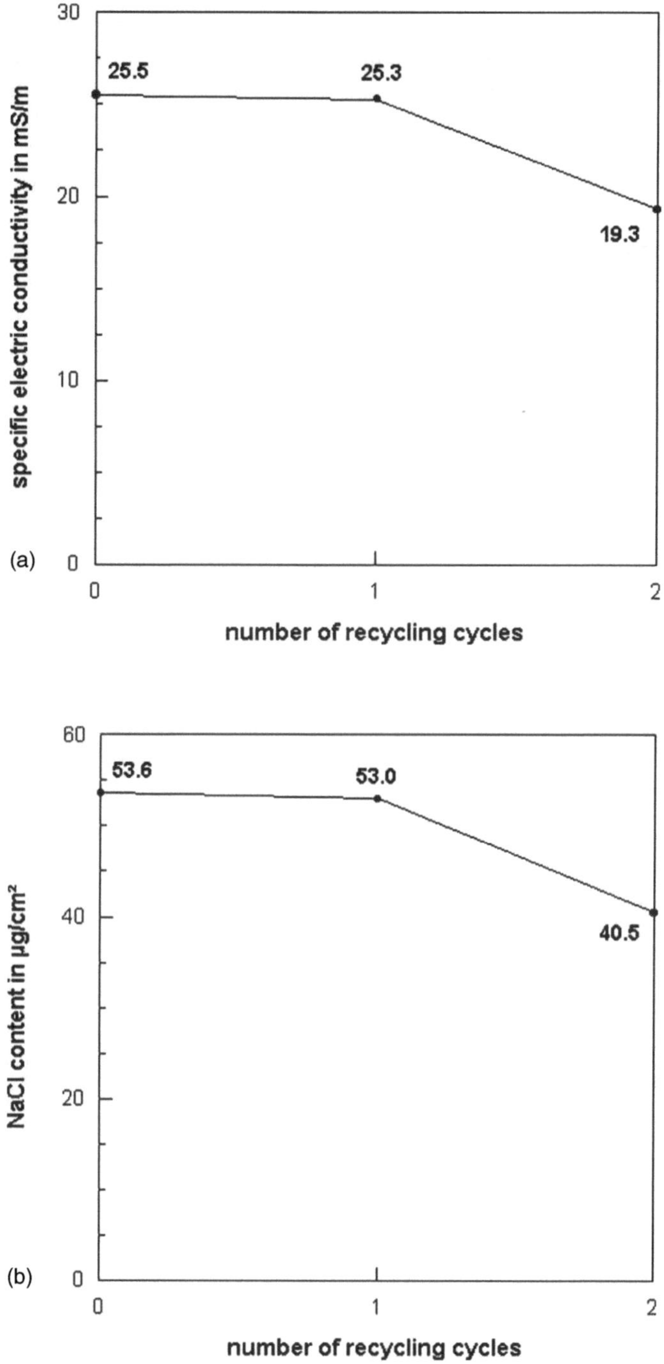

Fig. 7.30 Effects of recycling cycles on soluble substances in abrasive materials (Katsikaris et al., 2001). (**a**) Results of specific electric conductivity readings; (**b**) Results of NaCl readings

terial for sea sand as fine aggregate. They produced mortar samples from ordinary Portland cement and spent abrasive material at weight ratios of 1:1, 1:3 and 1:4. The different mixture ratios, and thus the addition of spent abrasive material, did not deteriorate the 28-day compressive strengths (between 33 and 35 MPa). Concrete samples provided 28-day compressive strengths at 12 MPa. Taha et al. (2001) did not specify the type of abrasive material they used, but mentioned that the waste material contained paint chips and paint particles and other debris generated during the blast cleaning process. Sand was partially and completely replaced by this waste material. The 28-day compressive strengths of cement–mortar specimens were as high as 55 MPa for the specified samples. The authors could also prove that asphalt concretes, modified with abrasive material waste, had high skid resistance values.

Chapter 8
Surface Quality Aspects

8.1 Surface Quality Features

Quality features of substrate surfaces determine the performance and properties of applied coating systems. Related to the performance of corrosion protective coating systems, ISO series 8502 states the following: "The performance of protective coatings of paint and related products applied to steel is significantly affected by the state of the steel surface immediately prior to painting. The principal factors to influence this performance are:

(1) the presence of rust and mill scale;
(2) the presence of surface contaminants, including salts, dust, oil and greases;
(3) the surface profile."

Numerous regulative standards are issued to define these factors, and testing methods are available to quantify them. Blast cleaned surfaces show some distinct features, and extensive experimental studies were performed to address this special point, often in direct comparison to other surface preparation methods.

Figure 8.1 shows a scanning electron microscope image of a steel substrate after blast cleaning. A general distinction can be made between primary and secondary substrate surface features. *Primary surface features* may include those properties which are part of coating specifications. They include the following features:

- visual cleanliness;
- chemical cleanliness;
- physical cleanliness;
- profile properties;
- surface integrity.

Secondary surface features may include properties which are determined by, and depend on, primary features. They may include the following features:

- surface energy;
- wettability;
- adhesion of coating to substrate.

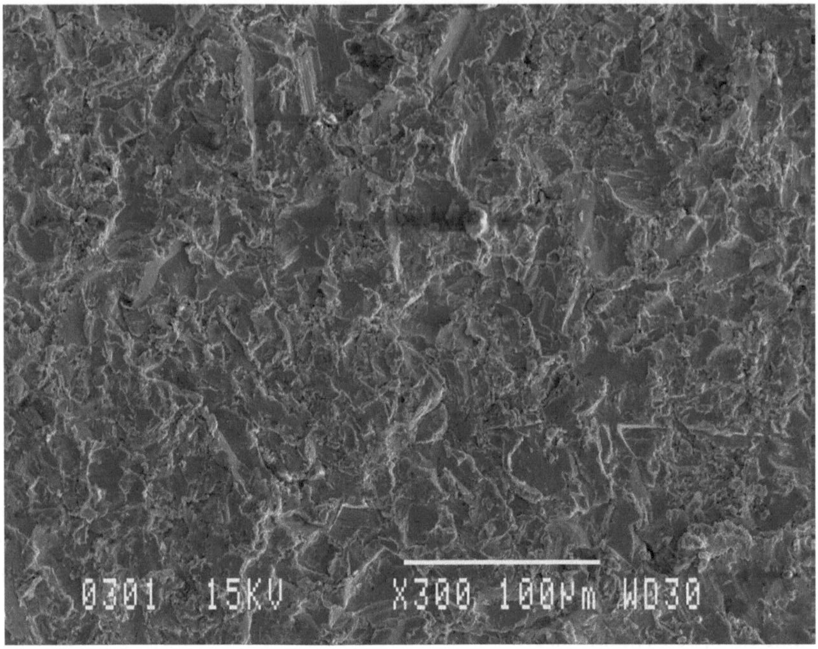

Fig. 8.1 Morphology of a blast cleaned low-carbon steel substrate. Parameters: $p = 0.475$ MPa; $d_N = 8$ mm; $\varphi = 90$; abrasive: aluminium oxide; $\dot{m}_P = 19$ g/s; $d_P = 165$ µm (Photograph: author)

8.2 Visual Cleanliness

8.2.1 Visual Standards

A number of regulatory standards have been developed in order to define and to characterise steel surfaces prepared by blast cleaning. These standards are more or less based on the standard preparation grades given in ISO 8501-1 (uncoated parts of the surface) and ISO 8501-2 (partial surface preparation). Visual blast cleaning standards cover the following two issues:

- initial condition (rusty steel or shop primer);
- visual surface preparation definition (visible contaminants and cleaning degrees).

Table 8.1 provides a general review on current visual surface preparation standards. Visual standards should always be used in conjunction with the written text, and they should not be used as a substitute of a written standard. The standards listed in Table 8.1 are limited to hot-rolled steel surfaces prepared for painting. They are applicable also to steel substrates that show residues of firmly adhering paint or other foreign matter in addition to residual mill scale. Therefore, care must be taken in applying these standards to other substrate materials.

Table 8.1 Contents of visual blast cleaning standards

Standard	Surface reference for			
	Rusty steel	Coating/primer	Flash rust	Cleaning degree
ISO 8501-1	*x*			*x*
ISO 8501-2	*x*	*x*		*x*
International Slurry blasting Standard[a]	*x*		*x*	*x*
SSPC – NACE	*x*		*x*	*x*

[a]Issued by International Paint, Newcastle

8.2.2 Initial Conditions

Initial conditions have a notable effect on the performance of coatings applied to blast cleaned steel substrates. The effects of rust grades and preparation grades on coating lifetime are illustrated in Fig. 8.2. It can be seen that lifetime decreased if rust grade increased and if preparation grade decreased. A high rust grade ("C" or "D") required a higher degree of surface preparation in order to guarantee equal coating lifetimes. The low surface preparation standard Sa 1 was extremely sensitive to changes in the initial conditions. Rust grade "A" (adhering mill scale but little, if any, rust) was least sensitive to changes in surface preparation degree, but

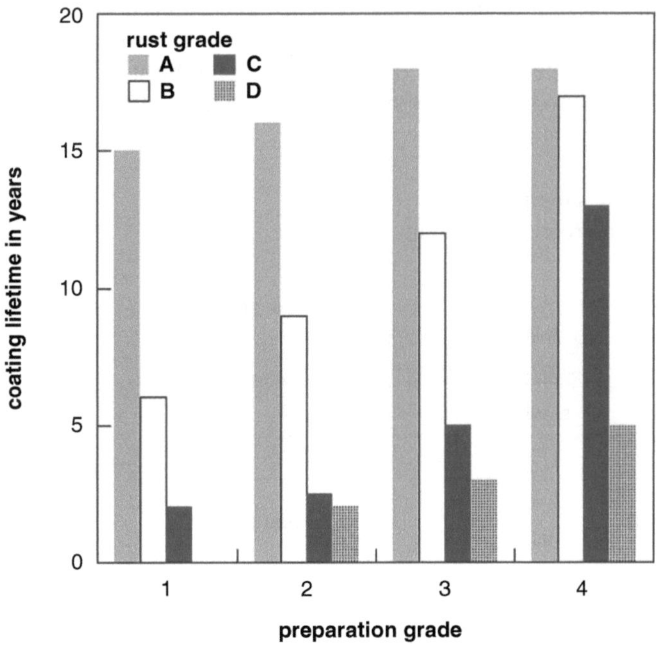

Fig. 8.2 Effects of rust grade and preparation grade on coating lifetime (Bahlmann, 1982). Preparation grades: 1 – brushed; 2 – Sa 1; 3 – Sa 2; 4 – Sa 3 (see Table 8.2 for preparation grades)

if rust grade "C" was present, an increase in the surface preparation grade could substantially extend coating lifetime.

Initial conditions are designated in several visual standards (see Table 8.1). These conditions can be subdivided into two groups:

(1) rusty steel;
(2) primers or coatings.

The initial steel grades apply to uncoated steel surfaces that are deteriorated due to corrosion (either thermal or atmospheric oxidation). Rust grades are illustrated in Fig 8.3. These rust grades are defined as follows:

- Steel grade A: Steel surface largely covered with adhering mill scale but little, if any, rust;
- Steel grade B: Steel surface which has begun to rust and from which the mill scale has begun to flake;
- Steel grade C: Steel surface on which the mill scale has rusted away from which it can be scraped, but with slight pitting visible under normal vision;
- Steel grade D: Steel surface on which the mill scale has rusted away and on which general pitting is visible under normal vision.

Previously coated steel surfaces are designated in ISO 8501-2. There are a large number of possible systems and coating conditions. The cleaning results do not depend only on the intensity of cleaning in these cases, but also essentially on type, thickness and adhesion of the coating systems, and on earlier surface preparation steps. For these reasons, only analogous applications to real cases can usually be derived. The coated steel surfaces considered in visual blast cleaning standards include the following coating/primer systems and conditions:

- coatings:
  - iron oxide shop primer;
  - corrosion protection system;

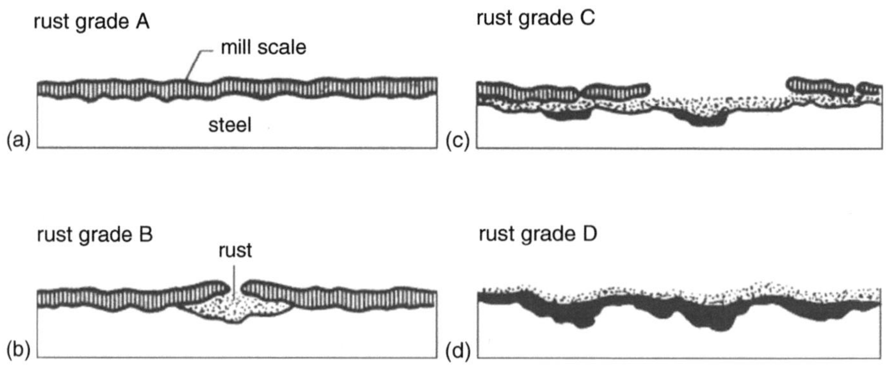

Fig. 8.3 Initial surface conditions according to ISO 8501-1 (adapted from Kjernsmo et al., 2003). (**a**) Rust grade "A"; (**b**) Rust grade "B"; (**c**) Rust grade "C"; (**d**) Rust grade "D"

  - a sound coating;
  - an unsuitable coating;

- conditions:
  - upper side of a hatch cover;
  - upper side of a steel girder;
  - new construction work: tubes in a power station.

Other designations for coated substrate surfaces apply to coating failure schemes, mainly according to the degree of rusting as defined in ISO 4648-3. These particular cases will be discussed in Sect. 9.1.

8.2.3 Preparation Grades

Effects of blast cleaning preparation grades on the performance of a metal-sprayed coating are shown in Fig. 8.4. It can be seen from the graphs that pull-off strength increased if the preparation grade increased. The curves for iron grit and silica sand showed almost equal linear trends, whereas the trend was different if copper slag was used as a blast cleaning medium. One reason for the different trend of copper slag could be the high friability of copper slag. Because the very thorough

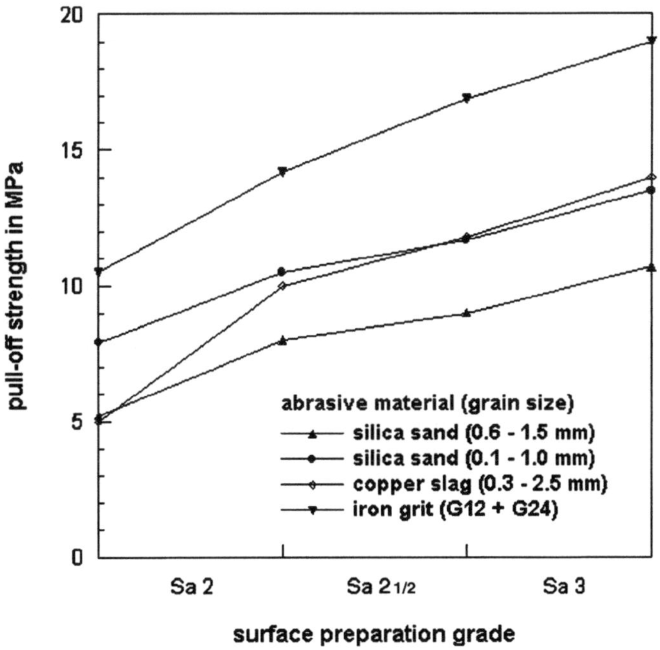

Fig. 8.4 Effects of blast cleaning preparation grades on pull-off strength of arc-sprayed aluminium (Bardal et al., 1973)

preparation grade Sa 3 required a very intense material treatment, slag particles were fractured. The fracture debris did not effectively contribute to the material removal process. The surface texture was changed, leading to a deteriorated bond between substrate and coating, and the initially sharply rising curve started to drop.

Preparation grades as defined in ISO 8501-1 indicate the following two designations:

- method of surface preparation;
- degree of cleaning.

The preparation method dry blast cleaning is designated by the letters "Sa" throughout the standard. Degrees of cleaning range from "1" to "3". These degrees are defined in Table 8.2. The preparation grades are defined by written descriptions of the surface appearance after the blast cleaning operation, which are also provided in Table 8.2, together with representative photographic examples.

Cleaning degrees are defined according to the presence of visible contaminants. These visible contaminants include the following substances:

- rust;
- previously existing coatings;
- mill scale;
- foreign matter.

Table 8.2 Blast cleaning preparation grades and cleaning degrees (ISO 8501-1)

Preparation grade		Designation	Description of surface (when viewed without magnification)
Preparation method	Cleaning degree		
Sa	1	Light blast cleaning	The surface shall be free from visible oil, grease, dirt, dust, and from poorly adhering[a] mill scale, rust, paint coatings and foreign matter.
Sa	2	Thorough blast cleaning	The surface shall be free from visible oil, grease and dirt, and from most of the mill scale, rust paint coatings and foreign matter. Any residual contamination shall be firmly adhering.
Sa	2½	Very thorough blast cleaning	The surface shall be free from visible oil, grease and dirt, and from mill scale, rust, paint coatings and foreign matter. Any remaining traces of contamination shall show only as slight stains in the form of spots or stripes.
Sa	3	Blast cleaning to visually clean steel	The surface shall be free from mill scale, rust, paint coatings and foreign matter. It shall have a uniform metallic colour.

[a]Mill scale, rust or paint coating is considered to be poorly adhering if it can be removed by lifting with a blunt putty knife

Table 8.3 Cleaning degrees for different blast cleaning designations; see also Table 8.2

Standard	Preparation method	Cleaning degree			
ISO 8501-1 (Sa)	Sa	1	2	2½	3
ISO 8501-2 (Sa)	P Sa	–	2	2½	3
SSPC	–	SP 7	SP 6	SP 10	SP 5
NACE	–	4	3	2	1
NACE wet blasting	WAB	–	6	10	–
International Slurry Blasting Standard[a]	SB	–	2	2½	–

[a]Issued by International Paint, Newcastle

The highest cleaning degree always requires that the surface shall be free of all these matters, and it shall have a metal finish. The term "foreign matter" may include larger amount of water-soluble salts and welding residue. Comparative degrees of cleaning as defined for other surface preparation methods than dry blast cleaning are listed in Table 8.3. The achievable preparation grade depends on a number of parameters, namely air pressure, abrasive type and abrasive particle size. Effects of abrasive types were already investigated in an early study conducted by Nieth (1955). This author related the cleanliness to the capability of impinging abrasive particles to deform the substrate. Heavily deformed substrates, which are characterised by folded and bended surface sections, often contained traces of rust and mill scale after blast cleaning. With respect to the abrasive particle size, a comparative investigation of Snyder and Beuthin (1989) has shown that coarse as well as very fine silica sand generated high surface preparation grades (90–95% cleaned to Sa 3; 5–10% cleaned to Sa 2½), whereas medium and fine silica sand generated lower preparation grades (75% cleaned to Sa 3; 25% cleaned to Sa 2½). If copper slag and coal slag were used, the highest preparation grade (Sa 3) could not be achieved. Copper slag delivered 10% cleaned to Sa 2½ and 90% cleaned to Sa 2, whereas coal slag delivered 75% cleaned to Sa 2½ and 25% cleaned to Sa 2.

An early approach to replace the rather imprecise and subjective visual assessment through a physically founded parameter was due to Bullett and Dasgupta (1969). The parameter "reflectivity" of a steel surface, measured with an optical method, was applied for the assessment of the surface cleanliness. Results of reflectivity measurements are shown in Fig. 8.5. Reflectivity increased if treatment time increased, and the progress of the function was very pronounced in the range of short treatment times. A reflectivity value of 360 corresponded to a visually estimated preparation grade Sa 2½. If this preparation grade was achieved, further blast cleaning action delivered a marginal increase in reflectivity only. The value of maximum reflectivity may vary from steel to steel, or with different abrasive materials, but for each combination there is a rapid initial increase with time of blast cleaning towards the asymptotic value. Bullett and Dasgupta (1969) could also show that reflectivity values dropped if a blast cleaned steel was exposed to an open environment. A reflectivity value of 60%, measured immediately after blast cleaning, dropped down to a value of 10% after 24 h of exposure. Apps (1969) applied a reflectance meter for substrate cleanliness assessment, and

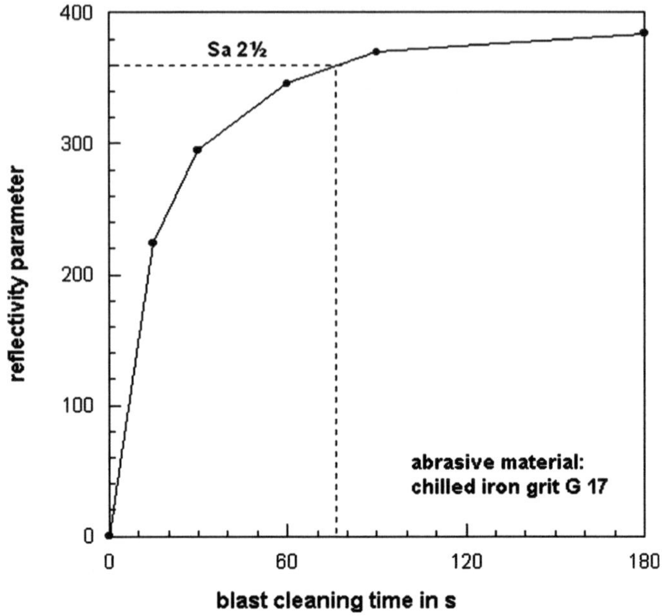

Fig. 8.5 Reflectivity of a blast cleaned steel surface as a function of treatment time (Plaster, 1973)

he investigated the effects of different process parameters on reflectivity. He found that reflectivity dropped with an increase in blasting angle. This author could also show that reflectivity depended on abrasive type and condition. Reflectivity values were high for new and for well-worn chilled iron grit, and they were low for worn, dusty grit. Blasting pressure and stand-off distance did not have any significant effect on reflectivity. Bardal (1973) also made an approach to express visual cleanliness in terms of reflectivity. Reflectivity was defined in his study as the percentage of reflectivity of a base sample, which was a light grey tile. Thus, the unit of reflectivity was percent (%). Some results are displayed in Table 8.4. One striking result is that reflectivity was not a feature of cleanliness standard alone, but also depended on abrasive type. For a cleaning standard of Sa 3, for example, reflectivity was only about 60% for copper slag, but it was about 80% for silica sand. The explanation for this result was the dark colour of the almost black copper slag. Slag debris embedded into the substrate surface

Table 8.4 Effects of surface preparation grade and abrasive type on reflectivity (Bardal, 1973)

Preparation grade	Reflectivity in %	
	Copper slag	Silica sand
Sa 2	40	60
Sa 2$^1/_2$	50	75
Sa 3	60	80

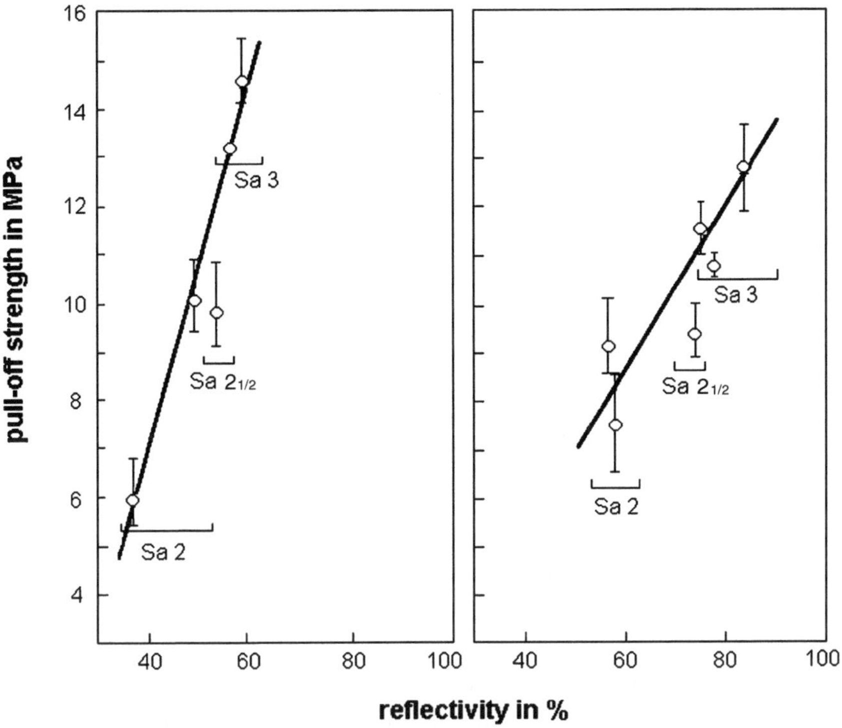

Fig. 8.6 Relationship between reflectivity, abrasive type and pull-off strength for metal-sprayed coatings (Bardal, 1973). Left: Copper slag ($d_P = 300-2,500\,\mu m$); right: Silica sand ($d_P = 600-1,500\,\mu m$)

reduced reflectivity (see Fig. 8.7 and Sect. 8.5) for more information on this issue). It could, however, be shown that reflectivity had a unique relationship to the pull-off strength values for sprayed metal coatings. Results of these investigations are exhibited in Fig. 8.6. The graphs in the figure verify that reflectivity alone is not a sufficient measure of the coating carrying capability of a blast cleaned substrate; abrasive type is another considerable parameter. For equal values of reflectivity of 60%, the substrate prepared with copper slag (left graph) delivered a pull-off strength of about $\sigma_A = 13\,MPa$, whereas the substrate prepared with silica sand (right graph) delivered a pull-off strength of about $\sigma_A = 9\,MPa$ only.

Hochweber (1971) introduced a method for the assessment of surface preparation grades which deployed the differences in the electric resistances between metal substrate and a measurement zone. This parameter, denoted transition resistance, was very low if the substrate featured a high degree of cleanliness. The author found the following relationships between surface preparation grade and transition resistance: Sa 1 = 1.0 Ω; Sa 1 to Sa 2 = 0.5 Ω; Sa 2 = 0.1 Ω; Sa $2^1/_2$ and Sa 3 = 0.05 Ω.

More recently, Terrat and Boissel (1995) developed a method for the assessment of the cleanliness of metal substrates based on the measurements of the electrical surface potential decay. This method proved to be capable to distinguish between clean metal, oxidation products and oil layers.

8.2.4 Special Remarks

The following factors can influence the result of the visual assessment (ISO 8501-1):

- initial state of the steel surface other than any of the standard rust grades A to D;
- colour of the steel itself;
- regions of different roughness;
- surface irregularities, such as dents;
- marks from tools;
- uneven lighting;
- shadowing of the surface profile caused by angled projection of abrasive;
- embedded abrasives.

The latter aspect is considered through a supplement to ISO 8501-1, which illustrates the differences in surface appearance, including colour, which are obtained when the same surface is prepared by blast cleaning with different abrasive materials to the same preparation grade. The situation is shown in Fig. 8.7. This situation is further illustrated by the results of reflectivity measurements as provided in Table 8.4.

For previously coated surfaces, which have been prepared for re-painting, only photographs with rust grades "C" and "D" should be used for visual assessment. The surfaces should be examined either in good diffuse daylight or in equivalent artificial illumination. For rust grades, the worst grade is evident.

Some recent developments revealed the use of vision sensing systems (Carew et al., 2001; Chen and Chang, 2006) and image analysing methods (Gupta et al., 2003; Trujillo and Sadki, 2004; Greverath et al., 2005) for the assessment of blast cleaned steel substrates. Two examples are shown in Figs. 8.8. and 8.9. The graph in Fig. 8.8 shows a pixel histogram for a steel substrate, which was prepared according to a surface preparation grade Sa 3 (bare metal). The dimension for the x-axis was the hue-value of the colour. The rather continuous signal characteristics without a dominating peak, characterised a clean substrate without discolouration. The results shown in Fig. 8.9, where differences in peak location and peak height for two close surface preparation grades in a green-colour histogram could be recognised, showed that colour measurements have promise for detecting subtle differences in blast cleaned surfaces. Software solutions are under development for the automatic detection and quality assessment of blast cleaned substrates (Gupta et al., 2003). An example is provided in Fig. 8.10.

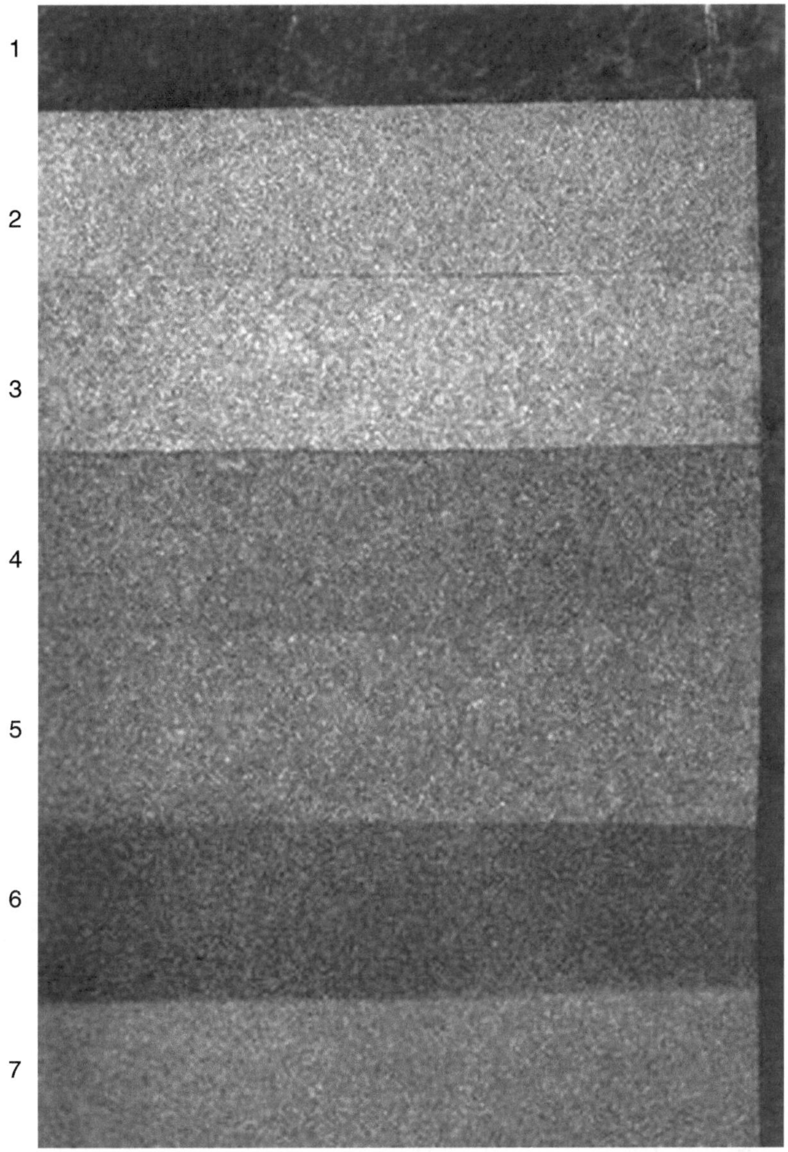

Fig. 8.7 Effects of abrasive materials on visual appearance of blast cleaned steel substrates (ISO 8501-1/1). Substrate condition: 1-Original mild steel plate (rust grade C); 2-blast cleaned to Sa 3 with high-carbon cast steel shot (S 100, Vickers hardness: 390–530 HV); 3-blast cleaned to Sa 3 with steel grit (G 070, Vickers hardness: 390–530 HV); 4-blast cleaned to Sa 3 with steel grit (G 070, Vickers hardness: 700–950 HV); 5-blast cleaned to Sa 3 with chilled iron grit (G 070); 6-blast cleaned to Sa 3 with copper refinery slag; 7-blast cleaned to Sa 3 with coal furnace slag

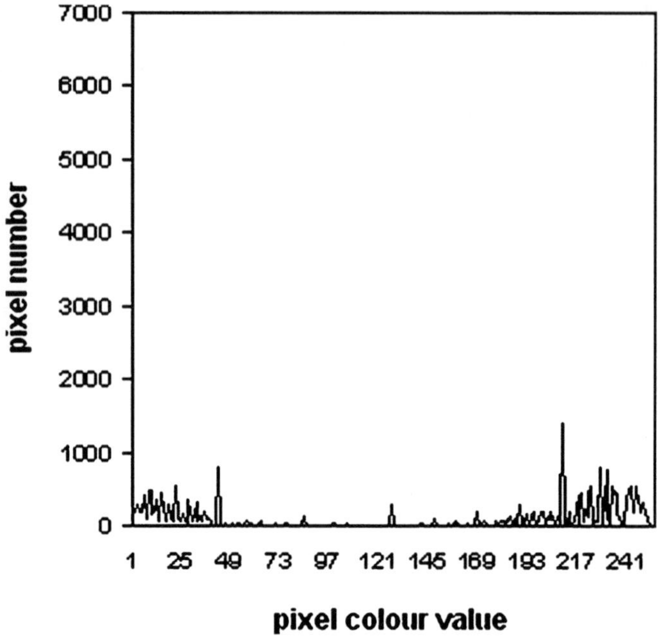

Fig. 8.8 Hue histogram of a blast cleaned stainless steel substrate (Momber, 2005b). Surface preparation grade: Sa 3 (bare metal)

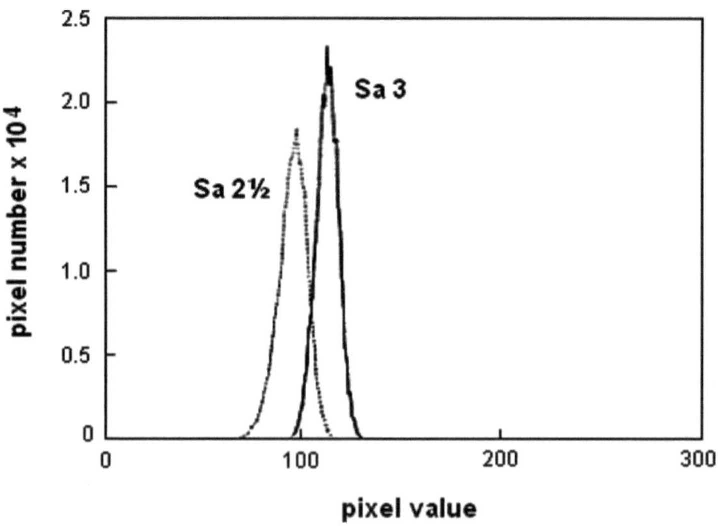

Fig. 8.9 Histogram of the green element in a colour spectrum for two blast cleaning preparation grades (NWU, 1995)

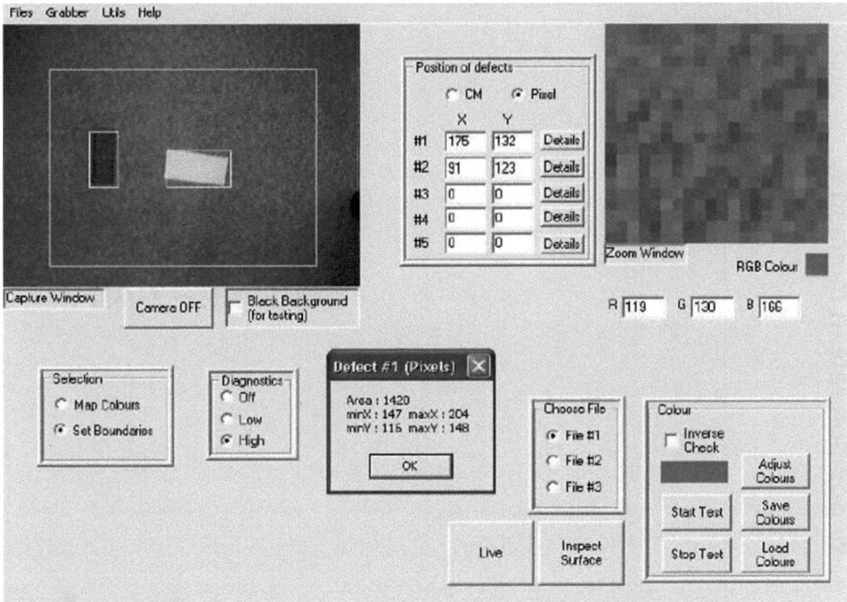

Fig. 8.10 User interface depicting two defects on simulated substrate surfaces (Gupta et al., 2003)

8.3 Dissolved Substances

8.3.1 Definitions and Measurement

Chemical cleanliness mainly considers the presence of dissolved substances on the prepared substrate surface. These substances include dissolved iron and certain salts. Soluble salts, namely chlorides, phosphates, nitrates and sulphates, are very widespread on steel substrates. A major source is sea salt, which affects especially ships, offshore structures and waterfront constructions. However, soluble salts can also arise from chemical processes, cooling towers, agricultural processes and burning of sulphur-containing coal. The detrimental effect of water-soluble contaminants at the steel/paint interface is well known. The amount of salts, especially chlorides, on blasted surfaces is essential for the performance of the applied coating systems. It is often thought that salt contamination is an issue for repair and maintenance of existing structures only. However, new construction work can be affected by salt contamination as well. An example is displayed in Fig. 8.11 showing the contamination of mechanically cleaned steel panels, which were stored on seashore locations, through atmospheric salts. After 12 months of storage, most of the panels displayed high salt contents. Before such panels can go into production, they must be thoroughly cleaned in order to remove salts. Permissible salt levels are specified in accordance to the field of application of the coating system, for example according to atmosphere (air and water) or operation temperature.

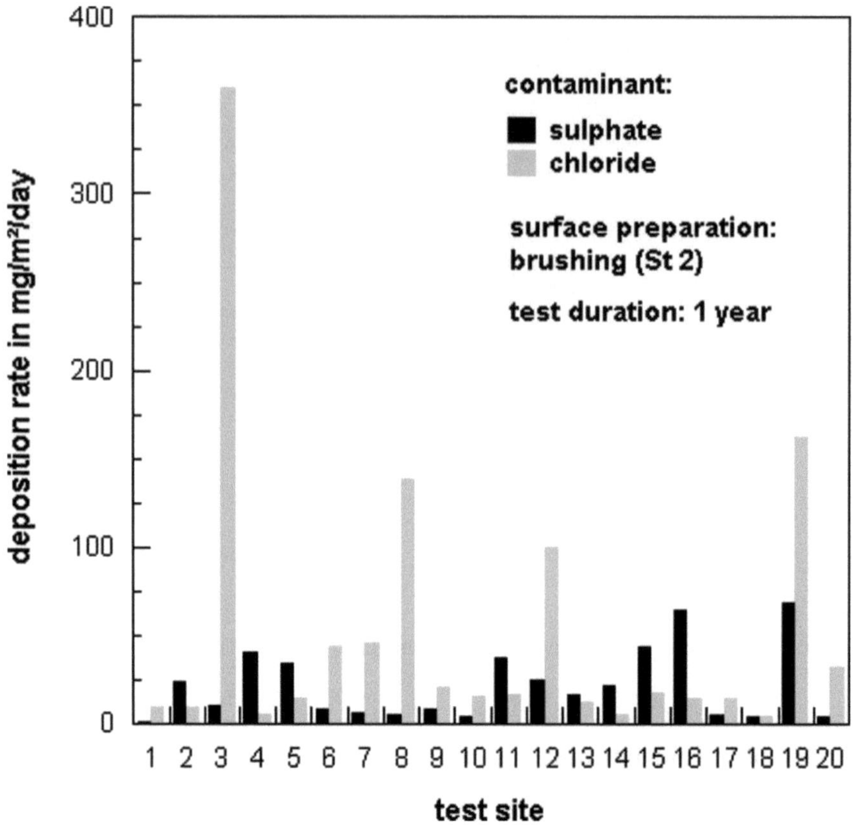

Fig. 8.11 Effects of storage conditions on salt contamination of power tool cleaned steel panels (Flores and Morcillo, 1999). Designations 1–20: locations in Europe and Latin America

Surface contamination by soluble salts has always been an issue for the corrosion protection industry. It was, however, the replacement of lead-based paints (Pb_3O_4) by other paint types due to environmental concerns that caused a different look at salts with respect to coating performance. Salt occupancy applies to non-visible surface contaminants according to SSPC-TU 4. Table 8.5 provides a description of non-visible surface cleanliness definitions. The level of non-visible contaminants that may remain on the surface is usually expressed as mass per unit area, much often in μg/cm^2. The prime salts most commonly encountered are chlorides, sulphates and nitrates. Ferric chlorides, however, tend to be more soluble than other salts of lower formula weight. They, therefore, usually produce rather high osmotic pressures (see Appleman, 2002).

There are several methods used to estimate the salt level on blast cleaned steel substrates, namely:

- Direct salt measurement (swab method or adhesive cell method): salt concentration (ppm or mg/l), cross-section (cm^2) and volume (ml) must be known to estimate salt contamination (μg/cm^2);

Table 8.5 Description of non-visible surface cleanliness definitions (SSPC-SP 12/NACE No. 5)

Term	Description of surface
NV-1	Free of detectable levels of soluble contaminants, as verified by field or laboratory analysis using reliable, reproducible methods.
NV-2	Less than 7 μg/cm² of chloride contaminants, less than 10 μg/cm² of soluble ferrous ion levels, or less than 17 μg/cm² of sulphate contaminants as verified by field or laboratory analysis using reliable, reproducible test methods.
NV-3	Less than 50 μg/cm² of chloride or sulphate contaminants as verified by field or laboratory analysis using reliable, reproducible test methods.

- Measurement of electric conductivity (total soluble substances): usually expressed in μS/cm for liquid solutions;
- Spectrometry: cannot deliver results in terms of salt content per cross-section (μg/cm²).

The latter method cannot only detect a certain salt type, but also its components: in the case of chlorides, its components, such as sodium hypochloride, chlorine oxide, chlorine dioxide or hydrochloric acid, can be detected (Trotter, 2001). Information about the testing of steel substrates for soluble salts and soluble iron corrosion products as well as analysis methods is provided in several parts of ISO 8502.

8.3.2 Effects of Dissolved Substances on Coating Performance

Chloride content on the substrate significantly influences the performance of coating systems. Rust development under the paint film and osmotic blistering are commonly observed at an early stage in organic coatings applied over contaminated steel substrates. This was verified through laboratory and site experiments performed by Mitschke (2001), Morcillo et al. (1989a), Kaiser and Schütz (2001) and Soltz (1991). The investigations of the authors have shown the following:

- chlorides significantly reduced the capability of paint to penetrate and enclose rust (Fig. 8.12);
- time to osmotic blistering decreased if chloride concentration increased (see Table 8.6);
- maximum service temperature of linings decreased if chloride concentration increased (an increase by 1.0 μg/cm² lowers the maximum service temperature by about 6°C);
- number of blisters increased if chloride concentration increased (see Fig. 8.13);
- much higher levels of sulphate contamination (>100–250 μg/cm²) were required to cause coating blistering compared to chloride. Therefore, blistering from seawater sulphate contamination does not appear to be a primary problem.

(a)

(b)

Fig. 8.12 Effects of rust contamination on paint penetration capability. (**a**) Clean rust; (**b**) Sulphate-contaminated rust; (**c**) Chloride-contaminated rust. Magnification: 200 × (Photographs: Institut für Korrosionsschutz GmbH, Dresden)

The very extensive study performed by Soltz (1991) also contains an investigation about the effect of chloride-contaminated abrasives on the coating performance.

However, the major criterion for salt content is the safe or, respectively, permissible salt level that prevents under-rusting or blistering of the applied paint system. There are different values available in the literature; some are summarised

(c)

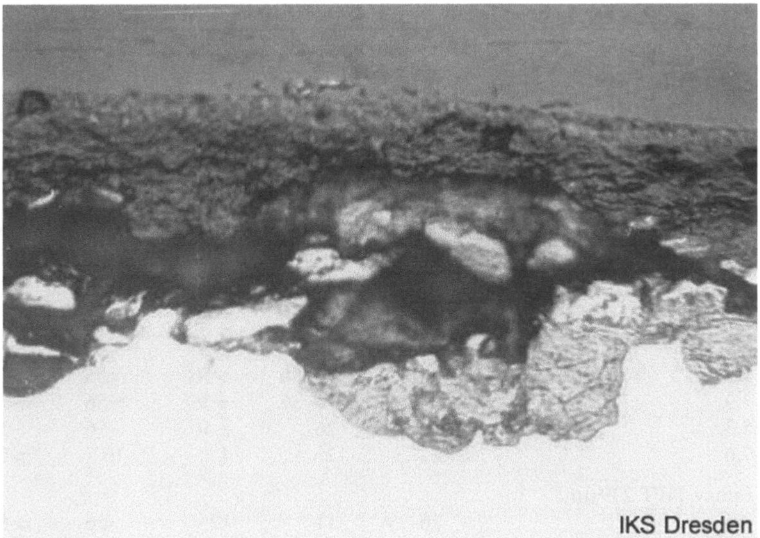

Fig. 8.12 Continued

in Tables 8.7 and 8.8. It must be considered that these global values may be modified for certain applications and coating systems; in such cases, paint manufacturers shall be consulted. Zinc-based systems are far less vulnerable to salt concentration than barrier systems, for example. Thresholds for chlorides and sulphates also depend on DFT of the applied paints; this statement is verified by the values listed in Table 8.8. Further information is provided by Alblas and van London (1997). It is important to realise that each different coating/substrate system is likely to have various parameters, including the chloride levels it can tolerate, that are unique to itself.

It is known that the capability of a primer to penetrate existing rust layers depends on the contamination level (CL) of the rust. The penetration capability is weak if the rust contains salts. This was verified through comparative metallographic studies by Kaiser and Schütz (2001) on clean and contaminated, respectively, steel samples (see Fig. 8.12). The authors defined three levels of salt contamination:

(1) NaCl: $<0.5\,\mu g/cm^2$; Na_2SO_4: $<5\,\mu g/cm^2$;
(2) NaCl: $0.81\,\mu g/cm^2$; Na_2SO_4: $112.6\,\mu g/cm^2$;
(3) NaCl: $87.6\,\mu g/cm^2$; Na_2SO_4: $18.8\,\mu g/cm^2$.

If the samples were almost clean [case (1)], the coating material enclosed and integrated the rust completely. The liquefied coating material penetrated up to the substrate surface, and it was able to wet the substrate. This case is shown in Fig. 8.12a. Penetration capability of the liquefied paint material decreased if the rust contained sulphate [case (2)]; rust particles were not enclosed completely in that case, and flaws occurred between substrate and coating. These flaws are clearly visible in Fig. 8.12b. The worst results, as illustrated in Fig. 8.12c, were obtained with highly chloride-contaminated rust [case (3)]. Large gaps with widths of 30–40 µm appeared between

Table 8.6 Time to failure by blistering for linings (Mitschke, 2001)

Chloride level in μg/cm²	Time to blistering in weeks at various temperatures				
	88 °C	77 °C	66 °C	54 °C	43 °C
Epoxy novolac, DFT 320 μm					
0.6	>56	>56	>56	>56	>56
1.4	>56	>56	>56	>56	>56
3.9	>56	>56	>56	>56	>56
5.3	>56	>56	>56	>56	>56
7.6	>56	36	>56	>56	>56
Epoxy, DFT 193 μm					
0.6	3	26–36	>56	>56	>56
1.4	6	26–36	>56	>56	>56
3.9	6	26–36	>56	>56	>56
5.3	5	26	>56	>56	>56
7.6	2	2	4	10	>56
Epoxy, DFT 239 μm					
0.6	36	11	12	>56	>56
1.4	3	7	12	>56	>56
3.9	1.5	3	7	>56	>56
5.3	1.5	3	7	>56	>56
7.6	1.5	1.5	3	5	3
Epoxy novolac, DFT 262 μm					
0.6	>56	>56	>56	>56	>56
1.4	>56	>56	>56	>56	>56
3.9	>56	>56	>56	>56	>56
5.3	>56	>56	>56	>56	>56
7.6	>56	>56	>56	>56	>56
Epoxy, DFT 252 μm					
0.6	1.5	>56	>56	>56	>56
1.4	1.5	1.5	4	>56	>56
3.9	1.5	1.5	3	>56	>56
5.3	1.5	1.5	10	>56	>56
7.6	1.5	1.5	3	>56	>56
Epoxy, DFT 252 μm					
0.6	36–43	>56	>56	>56	>56
1.4	36–43	43–56	>56	>56	>56
3.9	3	3	>56	>56	>56
5.3	23	23	>56	>56	>56
7.6	3	3	43- 56	>56	>56

coating and substrate. This gaps contained rust particles that were not incorporated into the paint. This caused deteriorated adhesion between steel and paint system.

Tests on contaminated substrates, performed by Allan et al. (1995), showed that the level of dissolved salts not only affected the value of adhesion strength, but also the type of adhesion of coatings to substrates. With zero contaminants, the mode of failure was cohesive within the primer coat. As the salt level increased, progressively

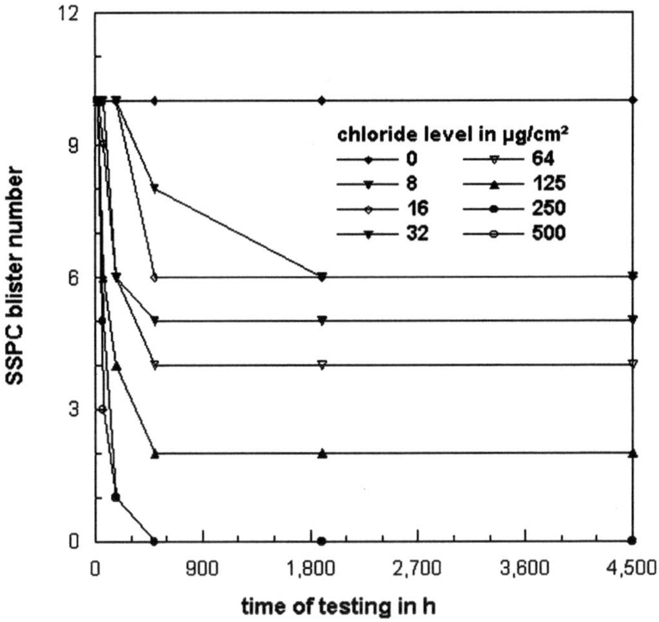

Fig. 8.13 Effects of chloride contamination on blistering intensity (Soltz, 1991)

less primer remained adhered to the steel surface. At higher CL, there was a change from mixed to total adhesive failure of the primer.

Table 8.9 lists further quantitative results. They confirm that with chloride-contaminated steel substrates exhibited the lowest values for adhesion strength, and the highest values for degree of blistering and rusting for all coating systems. These results were caused by the reduced rust penetration capability of the applied paint systems. Thus, rust, in itself, is not a problem; rather it is the contaminants that the rust contains.

Chandler (1966), in an early study on the effects of salts in rust, could show that the presence of sulphates and chlorides in rust increased the corrosion of steel, and this increased with the amount of salts in the rust. Some results of this study are

Table 8.7 Permissible chloride levels on steel substrates

Institution	Permissible chloride content in µg/cm^2
NASA	5
IMO (DE 48/12)	5
SSPC/NACE	7
US Navy (non-immersion service)[a]	5
US Navy (immersion service)[a]	3
Norsok (M-501)	2
Hempel (non-immersion service)[b]	19.5
Hempel (immersion service)[b]	6.9

[a]Cited in Appleman (2002)
[b]Hempel Paints A/S, Longby, Denmark

Table 8.8 Critical salt thresholds that result in early paint deterioration (Morcillo and Simancas, 1997; Appleman, 2002)

Coating system	DFT in μm	Salt thresholds in $\mu g/cm^2$	
		Chloride (Cl)	Sulphate (SO_4)
Unknown	125–225	7–30	70–300
	25–35	>1	–
	7–11	6–25	9–35
	Thin films	7	16
	100–150	–	58.8
	60–190	6–30	100–250
	130–180	5–10	50–100
Epoxy phenolic	One coat	1	–
Epoxy polyamide	Three coats	5	–
Coal tar epoxy	254	50	–
Fusion-bonded epoxy	–	<3	–
Tank lining epoxy	–	10–20	–
Epoxy mastic	Two coats	7	–

displayed in Fig. 8.14. The figure also illustrates that contaminated rust layers were much more sensitive to changes in relative humidity than clean rust or blast cleaned substrates were. Calabrese and Allen (1978) compared the corrosion behaviour of steel plates originally covered with atmospheric (industrial) corrosion products and mill scale. They found that industrially corroded and blast cleaned steel quickly formed new corrosion products, and they attributed this effect to chloride and sulphate trapped in folded substrate regions, which then became active corrosion sites

Table 8.9 Evaluation of coatings for rusted substrates; after one year environmental weathering (Kaiser and Schütz, 2001)

Coating	DFT in μm	Rust contamination	Blistering[a]	Rust[b] degree	Adhesion[c] strength MPa	Failure type
Noverox +	204 ± 22	None	0	Ri 0	1.3 ± 0.6	A/B10, B/C90
HS epoxy	213 ± 17	NaCl	5/2	Ri 0	1.1 ± 0.6	A/B100
	199 ± 20	Na_2SO_4	3/2	Ri 0	1.4 ± 0.2	A/B40, B/C60
Noverox +	213 ± 24	None	0	Ri 0	3.7 ± 1.4	A/B50, C50
DS-mica	221 ± 16	NaCl	5/2	Ri 1	3.2 ± 1.0	A/B70, C30
	208 ± 21	Na_2SO_4	0	Ri 1	4.0 ± 0.8	A/B20, C80
Antitrust +	173 ± 15	None	0	Ri 0	1.0 ± 0.6	B/C100
HS epoxy	192 ± 18	NaCl	5/2	Ri 0	1.9 ± 0.6	A/B100
	182 ± 21	Na_2SO_4	4/2	Ri 0	1.9 ± 0.6	A/B40, B/C60
Antitrust +	181 ± 17	None	0	Ri 0	4.2 ± 1.0	A/B20, C80
DS-mica	178 ± 9	NaCl	5/2	Ri 1	3.6 ± 1.2	A/B80, C20
	169 ± 11	Na_2SO_4	0	Ri 0	4.3 ± 1.5	A/B20, C80
Noxyde	148 ± 15	None	2/2	Ri 0	2.1 ± 0.4	A/B80, B20
	136 ± 11	NaCl	5/2	Ri 2-3	2.0 ± 0.9	A/B80, B20
	151 ± 10	Na_2SO_4	3/2	Ri 0	2.9 ± 0.4	A/B90, B10

[a]ISO 4628-2
[b]ISO 4628-3
[c]ISO 4624

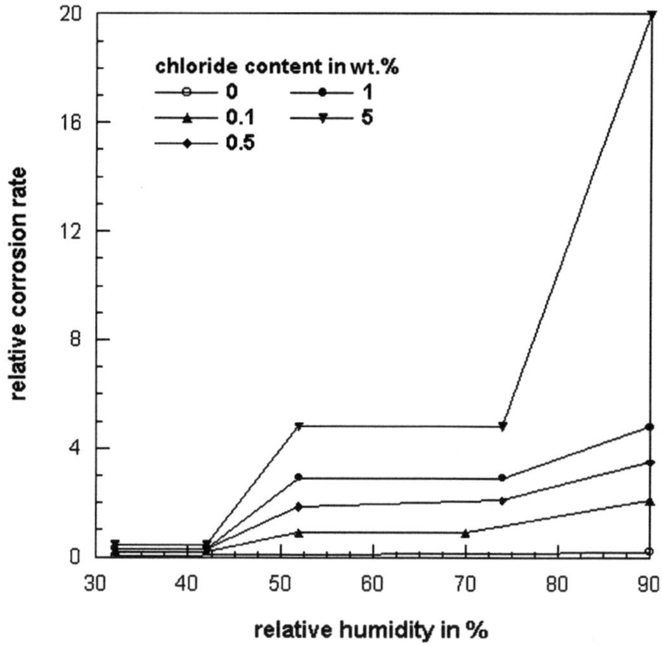

Fig. 8.14 Effects of salt contamination and relative humidity on relative corrosion rate in mild steel (Chandler, 1966)

(see Fig. 8.15). The authors developed a schematic, and suggested an oxidation cycle, which depicted the formation of new surface corrosion products of an industrially corroded, blast cleaned and environmentally tested steel substrate.

8.3.3 Substrate Cleanliness After Blast Cleaning

A number of investigations were performed in order to evaluate the chloride content of steel substrates prepared by different surface preparation methods; this includes the studies of Allen (1997), Brevoort (1988), Dupuy (2001), Forsgren and Applegren (2000), Kuljian and Melhuish (1999), Momber (2003), Momber and Koller (2005), Morris (2000), Trotter (2001), NSRP (1998a) and Van der Kaaden (1994). Some results of these studies are summarised in the Tables 8.10 and 8.11. A notable reduction in chloride level could be noted if wet blast cleaning and hydroblasting were applied. In both these applications, the water flow involved in the preparation process entered pores, pits, pockets, etc., and it swept the salt away. This mechanism was verified by results of SEM inspections of hydroblasted steel substrates (Trotter, 2001). Mechanical methods, such as needle gunning or wire brushing, did not remove soluble salts with the same reliability. Striking features were the high values for soluble iron, potassium and chloride after dry blast cleaning as listed in Table 8.12. Obviously, rust and sea salt could not be removed efficiently by this method. A study that included other salts (sulphates, phosphates and nitrates)

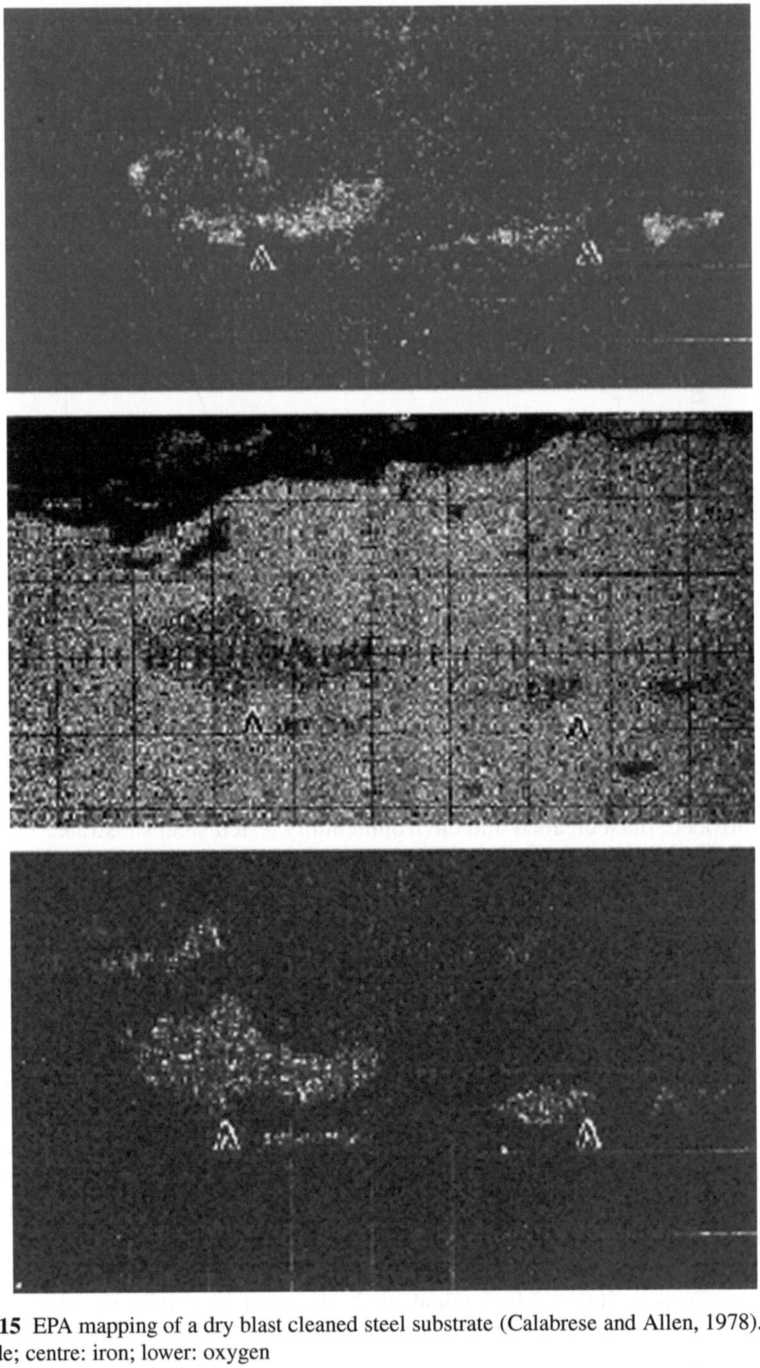

Fig. 8.15 EPA mapping of a dry blast cleaned steel substrate (Calabrese and Allen, 1978). Upper: chloride; centre: iron; lower: oxygen

Table 8.10 Chloride levels measured after different pretreatment methods (Forsgren and Applegren, 2000)

Method	Chloride level in µg/cm^2		
	Bresle (10 min)	SSM (10 s)[a]	SSM (10 min)[a]
No pretreatment	44.8	47.5	61.3
	54.8	72.8	96.3
	15.2	*	*
	24.8	*	*
Wet blast cleaning	1.6	1.4	2.7
	1.6	0.7	2.0
	0	1.7	3.1
	3.2	1.5	4.1
Hydroblasting	1.6	15.2	–
	0.8	1.8	4.2
	0	2.4	4.6
	1.2	0.1	2.1
	2.4	4.8	10.3
	1.2	0	1.0
	0	0	0.8
Wire brush	28.8	63.5	–
	16.0	32.6	58.9
	23.2	15.2	25.0
	17.6	18.1	30.3
Needle gun	27.6	19.9	42.6
	21.2	20.9	35.0
	26.8	41.3	96.1
	29.6	20.6	31.5
Dry blast cleaning	4.4	8.3	14.8
	6.8	10.8	16.5

*No measurements
[a]Surface saltmeter

was performed by Howlett and Dupuy, (1993). This study showed the same trends for these types of salts as for the chlorides. It was further found that blast cleaning did not remove chlorides to safe levels 50% of the time.

Calabrese and Allen (1978) showed through SEM images that dry blast cleaned steel surfaces exhibited layered and cusp surfaces. Folds were formed during the blast cleaning process, and impurities were trapped in these folds. EPA mapping indicated numerous elements present in the traps immediately under the blasted surface, among them are chlorine and oxygen. Examples of these measurements are provided in Fig. 8.15. Calabrese and Allen (1978) showed also that surfaces that had traces of chlorine and sulphur after the blast cleaning process, quickly underwent new corrosion. Neal (1999), also based on SEM imaging, could detect micro-pits, which contained chlorides, directly underneath the surface of dry blast cleaned steel substrates. An example for this situation is provided in Fig. 8.16. Fairfull and Weldon (2001) investigated the influence of different abrasive materials on the

Table 8.11 Surface contaminant results from different preparation methods (Howlett and Dupuy, 1993)

Substrate	Contaminant	Salt level in µg/cm²			
		Surface preparation method			
		Uncleaned	Dry blast cleaned	Hydroblasted	Hydro-abrasive blast cleaned
A-36 steel with mill scale	Sulphates	40	3	0	4
	Phosphates	0	0	0	3
	Chlorides	2	2	1	0
	Nitrates	0	6	0	6
A-285 Grade 3 steel with mill scale	Sulphates	5	5	0	1
	Phosphates	0	1	0	6
	Chlorides	4	3	1	1
	Nitrates	0	11	1	3
Rusted water service pipe	Sulphates	5	2	1	2
	Phosphates	1	2	0	6
	Chlorides	28	32	1	0
	Nitrates	6	1	1	8
Intact coating on water service pipe	Sulphates	8	4	0	0
	Phosphates	0	2	0	3
	Chlorides	6	1	1	0
	Nitrates	4	2	1	5
H_2S scrubber plate	Sulphates	39	7	0	3
	Phosphates	0	0	0	2
	Chlorides	12	8	0	1
	Nitrates	0	1	0	3
Heat exchanger shell	Sulphates	7	4	0	0
	Phosphates	0	0	0	7
	Chlorides	17	31	0	0
	Nitrates	0	3	0	6

Table 8.12 Soluble substances on prepared surfaces (Navy Sea System Comm)

Element	Soluble substance in µg/cm²	
	Hydroblasted	Dry blast cleaned
Nickel	0.006	0.057
Zinc	0.063	1.512
Manganese	0.003	0.031
Magnesium	0.021	0.672
Calcium	0.121	1.989
Copper	0.033	0.250
Aluminium	0.003	0.352
Lead	0.015	0.045
Iron	0.018	9.450
Potassium	0.414	0.513
Sodium	0.855	42.03
Chloride	0.846	62.55
Sulphate	0.211	1.260
Total	2.611 (100%)	120.71 (4623%)

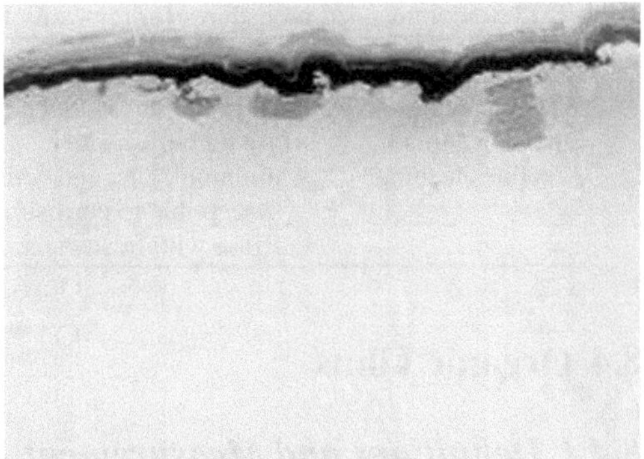

Fig. 8.16 Chloride-filled pits underneath a dry blast cleaned steel surface (Neal, 1999)

contamination of blast cleaned steel substrates. They found that the use of a certain type of coal slag led to a notable contamination of the substrate with sulphates. The sulphate level reached values as high as 9 μg/cm^2, whereas the sulphate level was as low as 1 μg/cm^2 for other abrasive materials (iron oxide, nickel slag, steel grit, olivine, garnet, etc.).

Appleman (2002, 2003) ranked surface preparation methods according to their relative salt removal capability as follows:

- hydroblasting with abrasives: 1.00;
- hydroblasting: 0.95;
- wet blast cleaning: 0.90;
- dry blast cleaning: 0.83–0.90;
- high-pressure water washing: 0.85;
- hand and power tool cleaning: 0.25.

The salt removal capacity of blast cleaning depended on the designated surface preparation degree as follows (Appleman, 2003):

- commercial blast cleaning (Sa 2): 0.83;
- near white blast cleaning (Sa 2½): 0.84;
- white metal blast cleaning (Sa 3): 0.90.

Johnson (1997) introduced an alternative method for the extraction of chlorides from bridge steels. After being dry blast cleaned, the steel may be allowed to set overnight, so chlorides and oxides rise to the surface and dry outside the contaminated pits which could not be cleaned by blast cleaning, and removing the dry, visible blotches by a subsequent blast cleaning step.

Recommended methods for the removal of water-soluble contaminants from steel substrates are listed in Table 8.13.

Table 8.13 Recommended procedures for removal of water soluble contaminants (ISO 12944-4)

Procedure	Remarks
Water cleaning	Fresh water. Pressure (p ¡ 70 MPa) may be used.
Steam cleaning	Rinse with freshwater.
Alkaline cleaning	Aluminium, zinc and certain other types of metal coating may be susceptible to corrosion if strongly alkaline solutions are used. Rinse with freshwater.

8.4 Organic Films

8.4.1 Definitions and Measurement

Organic films, mainly consisting of oil or grease, can come from a variety of sources: diesel fumes, lubrication oils from compressors and power tools, or from contaminated abrasives. They have detrimental effects on the performance of protective coatings. Reasons may be the separation of wet coatings from the substrate material as well as the influence of the wetting behaviour of the surfaces. It may generally be distinguished between hydrophobic and hydrophilic films (see Sect. 8.9 for more details on wettability). Table 8.14 lists some typical examples. Grease, motor oil and silicone lead to a reduction in wettability, whereas NaOH and H_2SO_4 contributed to good wettability. However, contact angle, as a measure of wettability, does not allow a precise indication of grease contamination. This aspect is illustrated in Fig. 8.17. It can be seen that contact angle first rose in a linear fashion if grease contamination increased, but it then started to drop if grease level reached high levels. The utilisation of contact angle measurements requires a smooth surface with a roughness less than $R_Z = 15\,\mu\text{m}$ (Meyer and Schulz, 2001). Piatti et al. (1959) utilised a modified Mettler analysis balance for wettability estimation, and they could show that degreasing improved wettability of austenitic steel by almost +50%.

An accepted standard for the assessment of organic films does not exist. Some recommended procedures are listed in Table 8.15. In practice, the water spray

Table 8.14 Contact angles to contaminated concrete substrates (Gelfant, 1995)

Contaminant	Contact angle in °	Wettability
Laitance	0–20	Hydrophobic
Milk	30–70	Hydrophobic
Vegetable oil	30–60	Hydrophobic
Oleic acid	30–40	Hydrophobic
Silicone	90–100	Hydrophilic
Motor oil	60–80	Hydrophilic
Grease	40–70	Hydrophobic
Hydraulic fluid	20–30	Hydrophobic
Na_2SiO_3	0	Hydrophobic
NaCl	0–20	Hydrophobic
NaOH	0	Hydrophobic
H_2SO_4	0	Hydrophobic

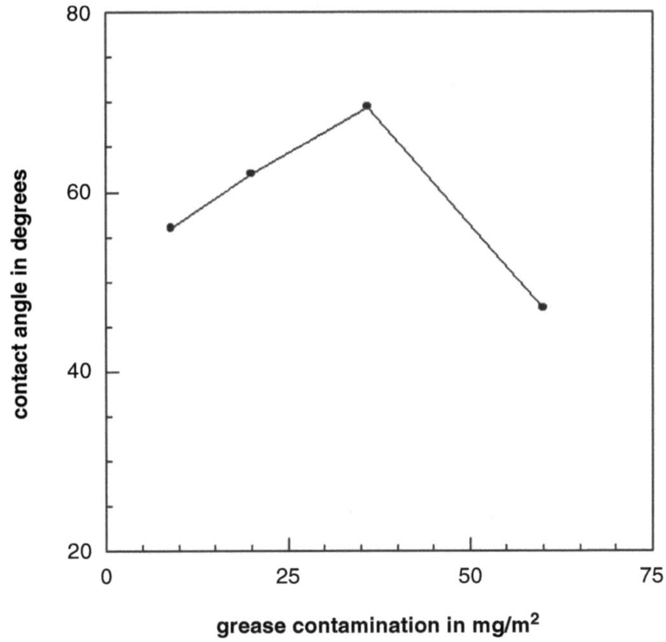

Fig. 8.17 Relationship between grease contamination and contact angle (Meyer and Schulz, 2001). Wetting liquid: water

method as illustrated in Fig. 8.18a is frequently used. If the substrate is greasy or oily, water will not wet these surface sections. It will rather flow besides the contaminated areas. On the hydrophobic greasy and oily sections, the water will not form a film, but will bubble up. Another method, recommended for practice use, is the chalk test as illustrated in Fig. 8.18b. A piece of soft chalk will mark the clean steel surface, but not the contaminated sections. However, this method works for dry grease or oil films only.

8.4.2 Effects of Oil and Grease on Coating Performance

DIN-Fachbericht 28 (2002) defines oil and grease levels to be safe at concentrations lower than 5 μg/cm^2. For values higher than 300 μg/cm^2, the risk of coat-

Table 8.15 Assessment methods for grease and oil (DIN-Fachbericht 28)

Method	Decision
Water rinsing tests	Yes/no
Water spray test	Yes/no
Grease red-test	Yes/no
Fluorescence test	Yes/no
Solvent extraction	Quantitative
Combustion	Quantitative

(a)
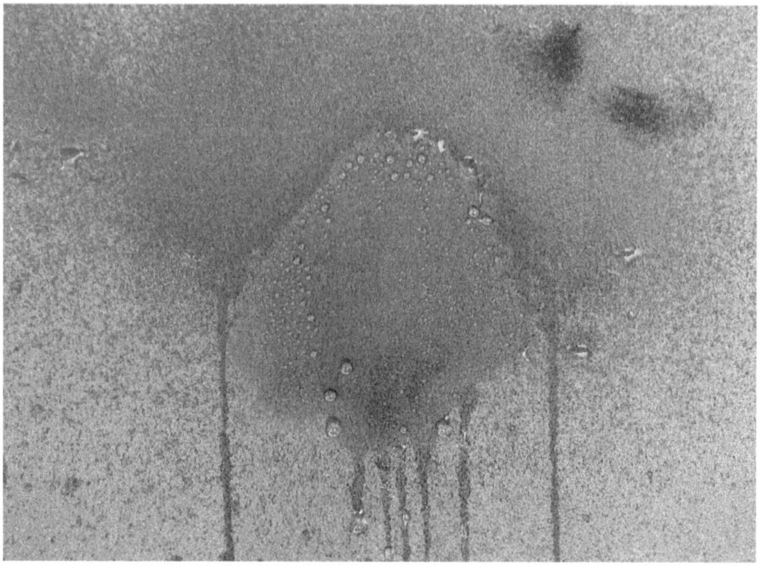

(b)
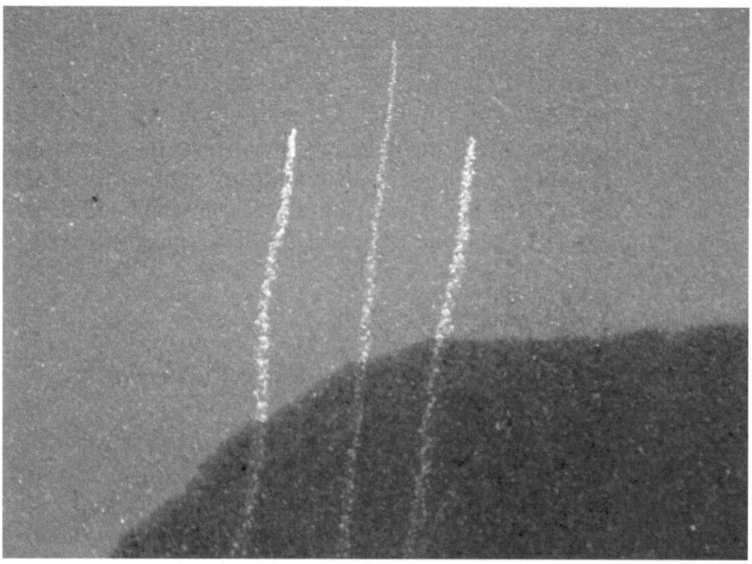

Fig. 8.18 Site methods for grease detection. (**a**) Water spray tests; (**b**) Chalk tests (Photographs: Muehlhan AG, Hamburg)

ing failure is high in general, whereby the probability of coating failure depends on coating type and coating thickness. A study about the effects of organic contaminants on the behaviour of certain organic coatings was performed by Weldon et al. (1987). Results of their measurements are listed in Table 8.16. In terms of adhesion to the substrate, the organic coating systems performed well up to a contamination level of about 600 μg/cm^2. The inorganic zinc-based coating was most sensitive to grease contamination; it failed at a grease level as low as 320 μg/cm^2. Cyclic freeze-thaw-immersion tests of contaminated and subsequently painted panels showed very good results for the organic coating systems, but again a worse performance of the zinc-based coating. An opposite trend was observed for the results of salt fog tests on panels with artificial scribes. In that case, the zinc-based paint performed best. This, however, is a well-known phenomenon. It is the self-healing capability of the zinc that prevents under-rusting and blistering at the scribe (Pietsch et al., 2002; Baumann, 2003; Binder, 2003; Momber and Schulz, 2005). Rider et al. (1999) investigated the effects of organic contaminants on the bond durability of blast cleaned aluminium epoxy joints. After contamination with kerosene, bond durability decreased notably. However, solubility of the liquid organic system into the contaminant material played an additional role. Gause (1989) investigated the effect of a corrosion inhibiting grease (Conoco HD-2) on the peel strength between steel substrates and an insulation rubber bonded with an adhesive. Results of this study are shown in Fig. 8.19, and it can be seen that the grease contamination led to a rapid drop in peel strength. For contamination levels in excess of 2,500 mg/m^2, no direct bond between steel and adhesive could be observed.

Sofyan et al. (2005) reported about the deteriorated bond between HVOF-sprayed WC-Co coatings and steel substrate due to oil on the substrate. Large voids could be observed between coating and substrate, which were signs that the coating did not completely cover the substrate surface.

Table 8.16 Effects of organic contaminants on adhesion of coatings to steel substrates (Weldon et al., 1987)

Contamination level in μg/cm^2	Numeric adhesion rate according to ASTM D3359[a]									
	Light oil		Motor oil				Grease			
	Alkyd	Epoxy	Alkyd	Epoxy	Vinyl	Zinc	Alkyd	Epoxy	Vinyl	Zinc
40	5	5	–	–	–	–	–	–	–	–
80	5	5	5	5	5	5	5	5	5	5
160	5	5	–	–	–	–	–	5	–	–
320	5	5	5	5	5	1	5	5	4	1
600	5	5	–	–	5	0	–	0	4	0
1,200	5	5	4	5	4	0	5	-	0	0
2,400	5	–	–	–	–	–	–	–	–	–

[a]Scale between 0 (very poor) and 5 (very good)

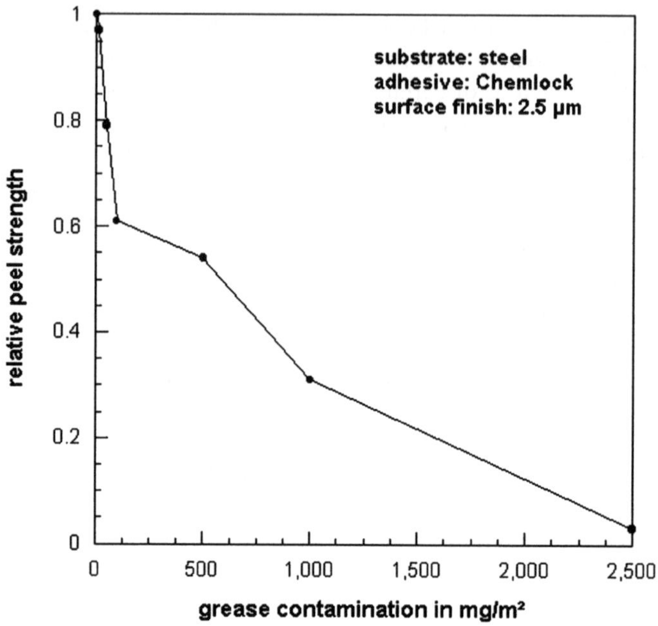

Fig. 8.19 Effects of corrosion-inhibiting grease on peel strength between steel substrate and adherent insulation rubber (Gause, 1989)

8.4.3 Substrate Cleanliness After Blast Cleaning

Blast cleaning is not a suitable method for degreasing. Degreasing must usually be performed before the blast cleaning work starts. However, quantitative demands can usually not be found in data sheets. State-of-the-art methods include steam cleaning, hot-water jetting and chemical degreasing (Van Oojj, 1984). Table 8.17 provides further details.

Table 8.17 Recommended procedures for removal of grease and oil (ISO 12944-4)

Procedure	Remarks
Water cleaning	Fresh water with addition of detergents. Pressure (<70 MPa) may be used. Rinse with fresh water.
Steam cleaning	Fresh water. If detergents are added, rinse with fresh water.
Emulsion cleaning	Rinse with fresh water
Alkaline cleaning	Aluminium, zinc and certain other types of metal coating may be susceptible to corrosion if strongly alkaline solutions are used. Rinse with fresh water.
Organic-solvent cleaning	Many organic solvents are hazardous to health. If the cleaning is performed using rags, they will have to be replaced at frequent intervals as otherwise oily and greasy contaminants will not be removed but will be left as a smeared film after the solvent has evaporated.

8.5 Dust and Embedded Abrasive Particles

8.5.1 Definitions and Measurement

Dust and embedded abrasive debris are common place on blast cleaned surfaces. A collection of examples is provided in Figs. 8.20–8.23. The avoidance of this phenomenon is a critical argument in blast cleaning operations. *Dust* is defined as "*loose particulate matter present on a steel surface prepared for painting, arising from blast-cleaning or other surface preparation processes, or resulting from the action of the environment.*" (ISO 8502-3). *Embedded particles*, in contrast, are tightly anchored in the surface. Dust and embedded particles may act as separators between substrate and coating system. It was shown in a study by Soltz (1991) that this phenomenon applied to larger size grit particles if they were left on surfaces and then painted over. If abrasive particles are notably contaminated with salts they may even cause rusting and blistering (compare Sect. 8.3.2). This can happen even with small amounts of fine dust (Soltz, 1991). Certain studies were performed to investigate dust adherence and particle embedment during blast cleaning operations. The first systematic investigation on this particular issue was probably that of Zaat (1960). The analysis of particulate contaminants on substrates surfaces can be done by applying the following methods:

- optical microscope (Zaat, 1960; Doherty, 1974; Fairfull and Weldon, 2001);
- secondary electron mode of SEM (Fairfull and Weldon, 2001; Momber et al., 2002a, 2004);
- back-scattered mode of SEM (Amada et al., 1999; Momber et al., 2002a, 2004);
- EDXA plots from SEM imaging (Momber and Wong, 2005a; Momber et al., 2002a; Possart et al., 2002).

Two images taken with the secondary electron mode of an SEM are provided in Fig. 8.20. This imaging mode delivers a three-dimensional view on the surface, and it can be seen clearly in Fig. 8.20b how abrasive fragments are just loosely adhere to the steel substrate. An example for the use of the back-scattered mode of an SEM is shown in Fig. 8.21. In that imaging mode, changes in the grey level are indicative of different chemical elements. The white grey sections correspond to steel, whereas the dark grey sections correspond to abrasive material. Two EDXA plots are shown in Fig. 8.22. The plot in Fig. 8.22a was taken from an untreated low-carbon steel sample. The different peaks are all contributed to the chemical composition of the material, whereby the highest peak is for iron (Fe). The plot in Fig. 8.22b was taken after blast cleaning with aluminium oxide. In contrast to the plot for the untreated steel, this plot contains a second dominant peak for aluminium (Al), which is indicative of contamination due to abrasive debris.

Cross cut sections of coated samples were analysed by Momber (2004) and Zaat (1960) in order to directly assess effects on coating adhesion to the substrate. Examples for this type of sample preparation are shown in Fig. 8.23. The images provide interesting information about the substrate structure. A heavily deformed top

(a)

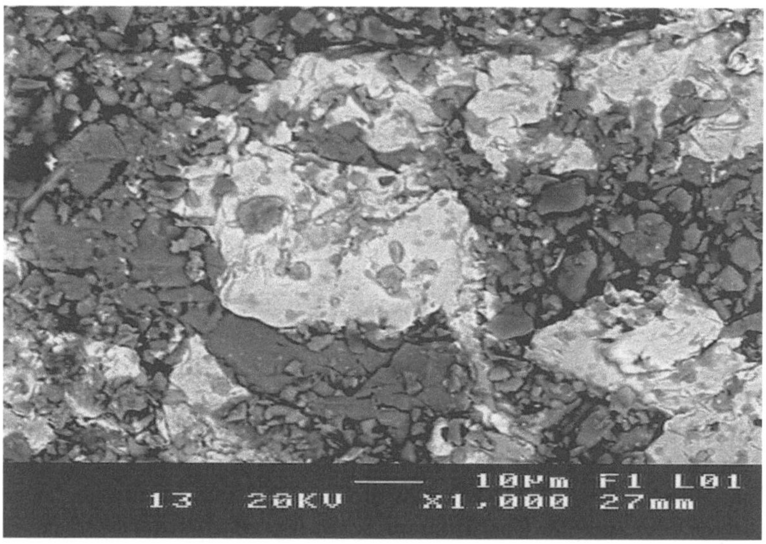

(b)

Fig. 8.20 Dust and embedded debris in carbon steel after blast cleaning. (**a**) Copper slag debris embedment; (**b**) Dust of broken copper slag debris. No fine cleaning was performed (Photographs: Muehlhan AG, Hamburg)

Fig. 8.21 Back-scattered SEM image of embedded aluminium oxide in carbon steel after blast cleaning. No fine cleaning was performed (Photograph: Muehlhan AG, Hamburg)

section can be recognised in Fig. 8.23a, which features lips still attached to the surface. Also visible is the high number of abrasive debris (copper slag) trapped underneath such lips. The image in Fig. 8.23b provides a magnified view on the cross-section of a blast-cleaned steel. A pocket with a length of about 50 µm can be recognised which is completely filled with abrasive (copper slag) fragments. A second, smaller void, also filled with abrasive debris, is situated underneath that pocket.

The modification of metal substrates due to abrasive debris occurs due to two effects. The first effect is the embedment of individual debris in the substrate. This case is illustrated in Fig. 8.20a. A large copper slag fragment can be recognised, which is locked in the steel structure. The second effect is the formation of a loosely adhering dust layer, consisting not only of abrasive debris but also of removed substrate material. An example for this situation is provided in Fig. 8.20b. A large number of copper slag fragments (dark sections), with dimension of some micrometres, which are smeared over the substrate surface, can be seen. The image in Fig. 8.21 covers both effects. In that image, changes in the grey level are indicative of different chemical elements. The very dark grey areas were detected to be copper slag fragments.

Dust grade can be assessed by applying the tape method according to ISO 8502-3. The procedure, together with a typical result of a dust assessment test, is illustrated in Fig. 8.24. Dust can be evaluated according to the size of the particles and the number of the particles. Particle size classes are listed in Table 8.18, whereas particle number classes are displayed in Fig. 8.25. This procedure can, however, be utilised for the detection of debris that are loosely adhering to the substrate. Embedded abrasive fragments cannot be evaluated. Dust classes are rarely specified in data sheets. The demands are rather qualitative. The IMO-resolution for ballast

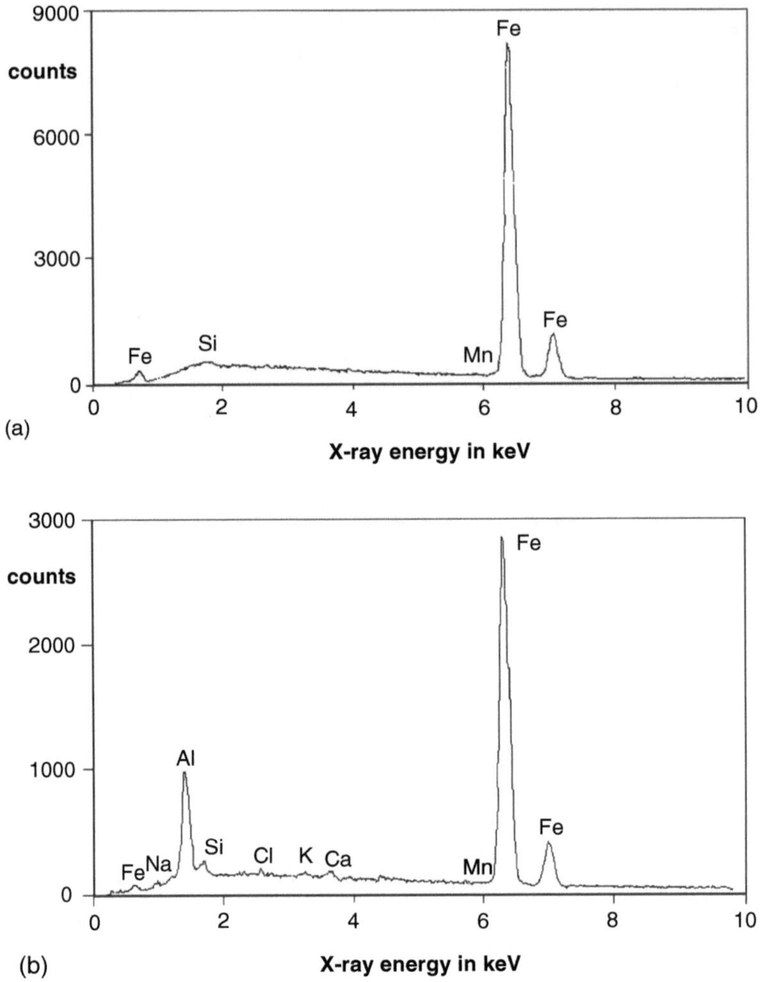

Fig. 8.22 EDXA plots illustrating embedded grit residue (Momber and Wong, 2005a). (**a**) Untreated surface; (**b**) Blast cleaned surface

water tanks in ship building (IMO, 2005) states, for example, that a dust class "1" is the limit for coatings in the ship new construction industry.

8.5.2 Effects of Dust and Particle Embedment on Coating Performance

Embedded particles and loose debris dust deteriorate the adhesion of coatings to the substrate. Figure 8.26 shows results of measurements of the adhesion strength as a function of the amount of embedded grit. The adhesion strength between the sprayed

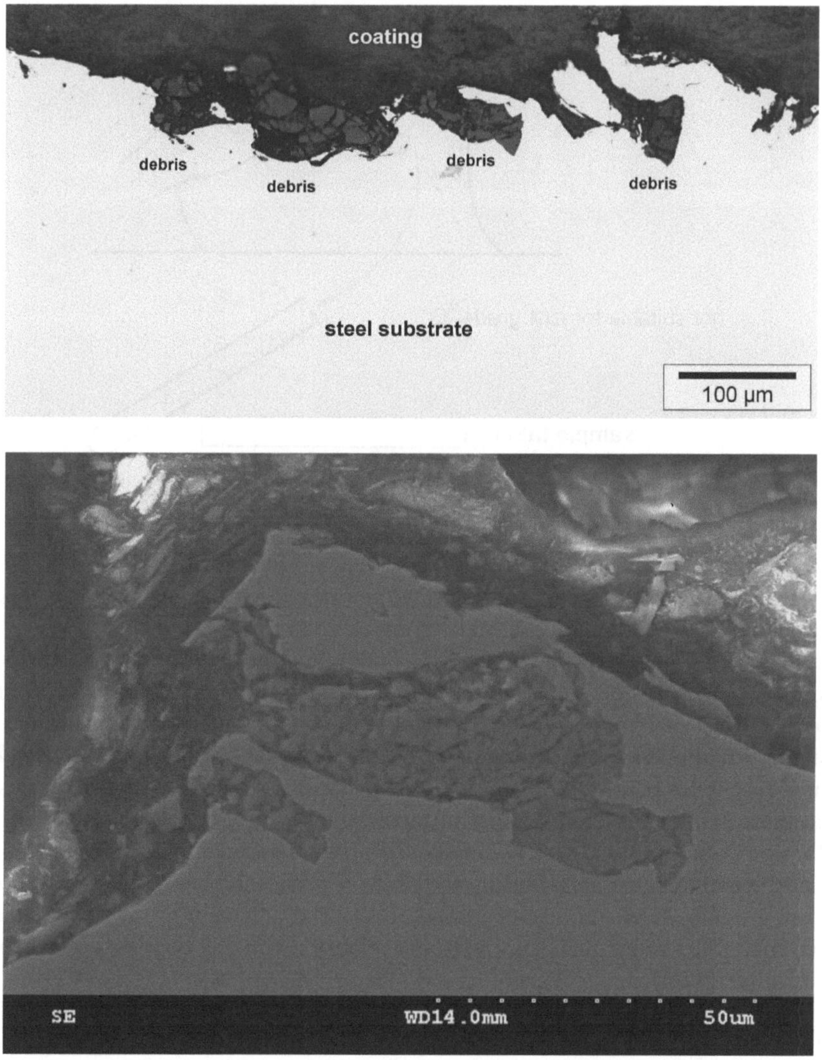

(a)

(b)

Fig. 8.23 SEM images of polished cross-sections of dry blast cleaned and then coated steel substrates. (**a**) General view; (**b**) Closer view. No fine cleaning was performed. Note copper slag debris accumulation in pits (Images: Muehlhan AG, Hamburg)

ceramic coating and the substrate significantly reduced as the substrate surface contained embedded particles. Similar results were reported by Momber et al. (2004) for organic coatings, whereby the authors argued that the rheological properties of the wet paint films played an important role. Maruyama and Kobayashi (2004) have shown that the adhesion of flame-sprayed copper powders to carbon steel substrates improved notably if the substrates were ultrasonically cleaned after blast cleaning. The improvement in adhesion strength was as high as +400%. Other authors,

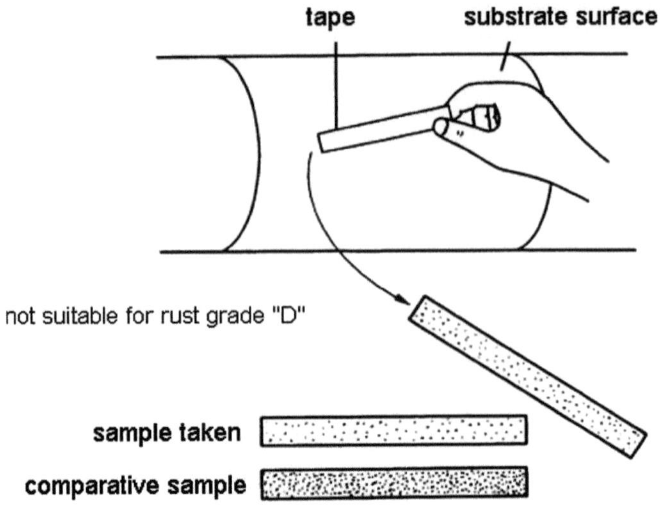

Fig. 8.24 Tape test according to ISO 8502-3 for dust assessment

e.g. Day et al., (2005), found only a random correlation between surface contamination and bond strength of thermally sprayed coatings.

The SEM images displayed in Fig. 8.23 illustrate how abrasive debris form local barriers between substrate and coating. Such images can also be found in Zaat's (1960) early paper. Debris is trapped in cavities generated during the blast cleaning of the substrate. Momber and Koller (2005) and Momber et al. (2004) found that some paint types were extremely sensitive to such dusty substrates, and that these sensitive systems failed in a cohesive fashion at low loads if tested for adhesion with a pull-off tester. Zinc-based primers seemed to be rather insensitive to dust on steel substrates. During the pull-off tests, the coatings failed frequently in the interface between primer and top coat. The adhesion to the dusty substrate was, therefore, better than the inter-coat adhesion for this coating type (Momber and Koller, 2005).

Embedded particles also affect the mechanical behaviour of steel substrates. Kloos et al. (1981) performed a study on the modification of fatigue properties of a high-strength steel (55Cr3) due to embedded non-metallic particles. If the

Table 8.18 Dust size classes (ISO 8502-3)

Class	Description of dust particles
0	Particles not visible under ×10 magnification.
1	Particles visible under ×10 magnification but not with normal or corrected vision (usually particles less than 50 μm in diameter).
2	Particles just visible with normal or corrected vision (usually particles between 50 and 100 μm in diameter).
3	Particles clearly visible with normal or corrected vision (particles up to 0.5 mm in diameter).
4	Particles between 0.5 and 2.5 mm diameter.
5	Particles larger than 2.5 mm in diameter.

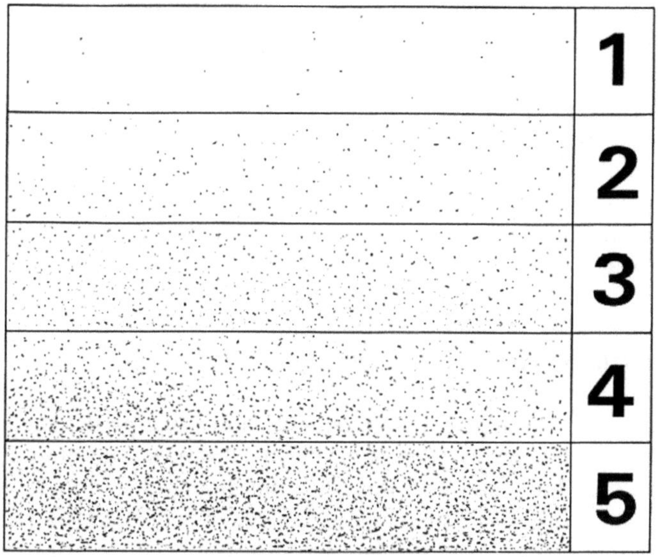

Fig. 8.25 Dust class definitions according to ISO 8502-3

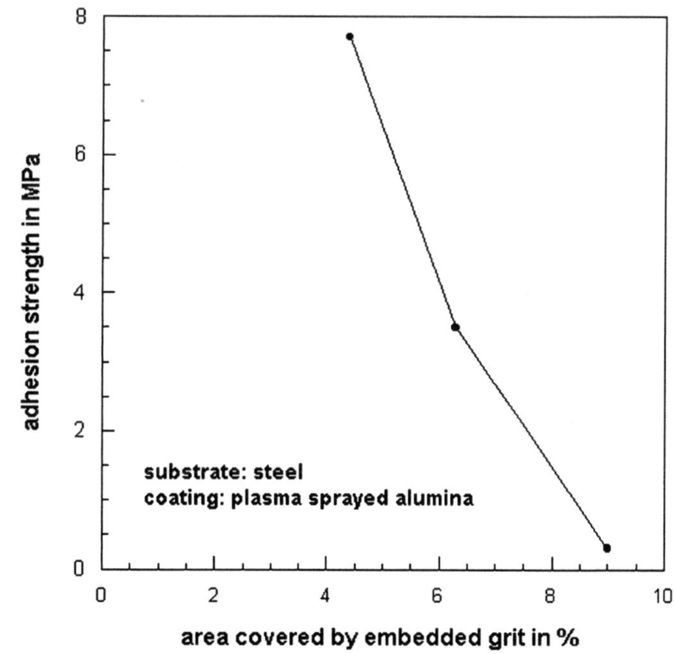

Fig. 8.26 Effects of abrasive debris embedment on pull-off strength of a plasma-sprayed alumina coating on a steel substrate (Griffith et al., 1999)

particle size exceeded a value of 25 μm, they notably reduced the fatigue stress reversals. For particle sizes between 25 and 150 μm, the relationship between inclusion size and fatigue stress reversal followed an inverse power function, whereby the power exponent depended on the stress amplitude. The same trend was found for the relationship between inclusion size and a fatigue strength number (product of fatigue strength and fatigue cycle number to failure). Embedded particles smaller than 25 μm did not affect the fatigue properties systematically.

Dirt contamination also affects surface energy and wettability of the substrates (see Sects. 8.8 and 8.9).

8.5.3 Substrate Cleanliness After Blast Cleaning

Experimental results of different authors have shown that particle embedment in, and contamination by abrasive debris of, metal substrates after blast cleaning can vary between very low values of about 1% and high values of about 50%. The first systematic investigation on abrasive particle embedment after blast cleaning was probably that of Zaat (1960). This author investigated the effects of different abrasive materials, namely zirconium, quartz sand, steel cut wire, aluminium oxide and cast iron. A part of his results is plotted in Table 8.19. The size of the embedded debris was between 10 and 100 μm. The larger debris belonged to the abrasive particles with rather large diameters (cast iron, $d_P = 590\,\mu m$; corundum, $d_P = 750\,\mu m$), whereas the small debris belonged to the zirconium with a small initial grain size ($d_P = 120\,\mu m$). The number of the embedded debris was between 5 and 42 pieces per centimetre. It depended on the blasting direction. The number of embedded debris was usually higher in the direction perpendicular to the blasting direction. The highest numbers were detected after blast cleaning with corundum. The percentage of embedment was highest for the corundum as well. The percentage of the debris contamination layer, which loosely covered the substrate after blast cleaning, also showed the highest value for blast cleaning with corundum. The very different values for the percentage of embedment and the percentage of loose contaminants show how important it is to distinguish between these two types of substrate modification. Substrates blast cleaned with steel cut wire did not show any modification due to debris embedment.

Detailed investigations, performed by Amada et al. (1999), Bahbou et al. (2004), Doherty (1974) and Wigren (1988), have revealed that dust layers as well as particle embedment depended mainly on impact angle and abrasive type. The effect of changes in impact angle is shown in Fig. 8.27. An increase in embedment could be noted as impact angle increased. Maximum embedment occurred at an impact angle of $\varphi = 90°$. These results corresponded to earlier findings of Doherty (1974) who could prove that, after blast cleaning of cold-rolled steel with quartz sand and mineral slag, more abrasive particles were lodged for $\varphi = 60°$ and $90°$ compared with $\varphi = 30°$ and $45°$.

Doherty (1974) conducted investigations into the effects of air pressure and stand-off distance. He found that relationships between these two process parameters

Table 8.19 Abrasive embedment and surface contamination due to abrasive debris for different abrasive materials (Zaat, 1960)

Abrasive type	Abrasive size in µm	Debris size in µm	Number of debris per cm		Embedded surface in %	Contaminated surface in %	Steel chip length in µm
			Parallel[a]	Perpendicular[a]			
Zirconium	120	10	5.5	8	0.004	45	40
Quartz sand	390	20	5.5	9	0.02	50	60
Cast iron	580	60–100	9	13	0.4	55	80
Cut wire	650	–	–	–	0	50	150
Corundum (S)	720	30–50	27	42	1	60	150
Corundum (K)	750	50–100	24	28	2	75	150
Cut wire	970	–	–	–	0	55	200

[a]Related to blasting direction

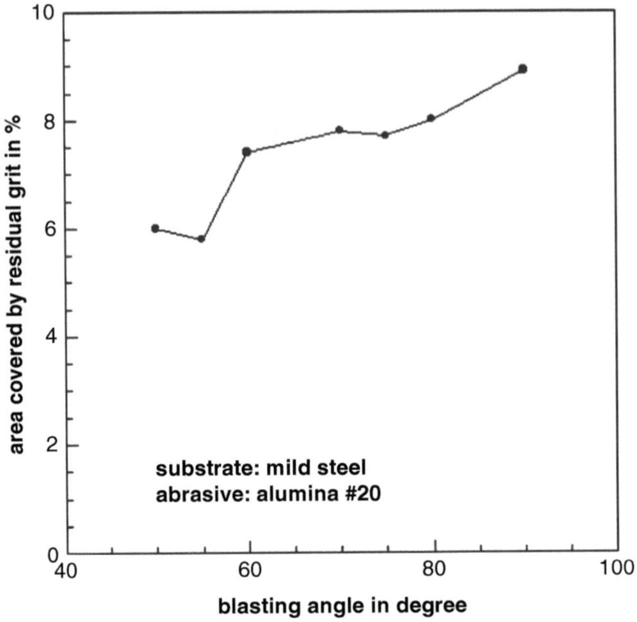

Fig. 8.27 Effects of blasting angle on abrasive debris embedment (Amada et al., 1999)

and the sizes of the particles lodged in the substrate. If pressure decreased and stand-off distance increased, the lodged particles became larger. The size of the embedded particles varied between 80 and 800 μm. Measurements performed by Wigren (1988) have shown that particle embedment decreased with an increase in stand-off distance, whereas an increase in air pressure promoted the embedment of abrasive debris. The latter effect was also noted by Jones and Gardos (1971). An optimisation procedure proposed by Wigren (1988) is shown in Fig. 8.28. According to the proposed procedure, blast cleaning time (t_1–t_3), air pressure and impact angle can be varied in a way that grit embedment has minimum values for a given roughness.

The dependence of particle embedment on abrasive type is illustrated in Tables 8.19 and 8.20. The dramatically different results for the investigated abrasive materials illustrate the effect of grit type and morphology. It seemed from the results listed in Table 8.20 that slag materials (except nickel slag) were rather sensitive to grit embedment. Experiments with copper slag showed that the comminution (breakdown) behaviour of individual particles during the impact at the steel surface seemed to play a notable role. It was apparent that the embedment was not simply due to discrete particles embedded in the substrate, but rather due to extreme breakdown of the slag abrasive into minute particles, or a physical smearing of the grit over the surface (Fairfull and Weldon, 2001). A distinct relationship between hardness of abrasive particles and their embedment in substrate surfaces could not be found. Interestingly, embedment was very intense for abrasive mate-

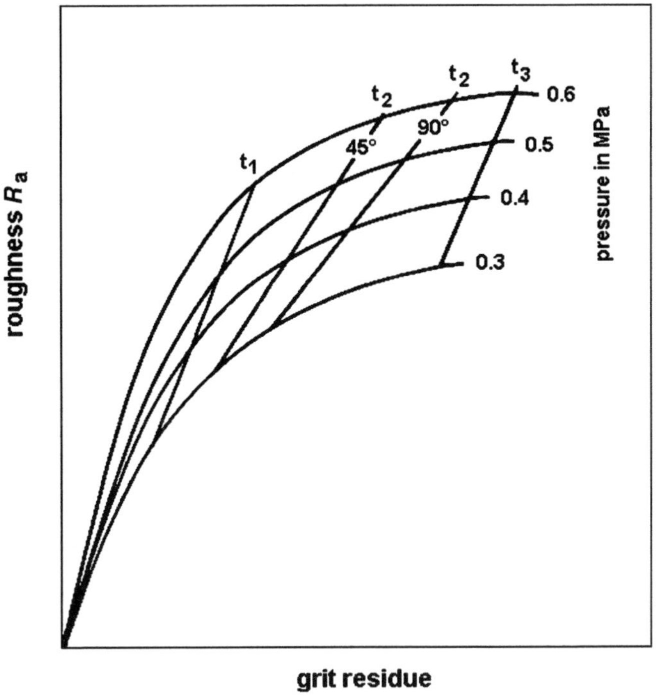

Fig. 8.28 Optimisation procedure for minimising abrasive particle embedment (Wigren, 1988)

rials with moderate hardness values (see Table 8.20). A direct comparison of two abrasive types was performed by Yankee et al. (1991) for the blast cleaning of a titanium substrate, whereas aluminium oxide (high hardness) delivered a contamination level of 12% and silicone carbide delivered a contamination level of only 7%. Day et al. (2005) compared roughness values and abrasive embedment values, and they found that both parameters can be related to each other for given abrasive particle

Table 8.20 Embedment of abrasive debris in a carbon steel (Measurements: Fairfull and Weldon, 2001)

Abrasive type	Embedment (visual) in %	Knoop hardness
Coal slag A	11.1	630
Coal slag B	25.3	669
Copper slag	41.5	523
Garnet A	2.1	1,111
Garnet B	4.7	1,779
Iron oxide	0.7	1,136
Nickel slag	1.2	960
Olivine	15.1	860
Silica sand	2.9	791
Staurolite	0.1	150
Steel grit	4.1	239

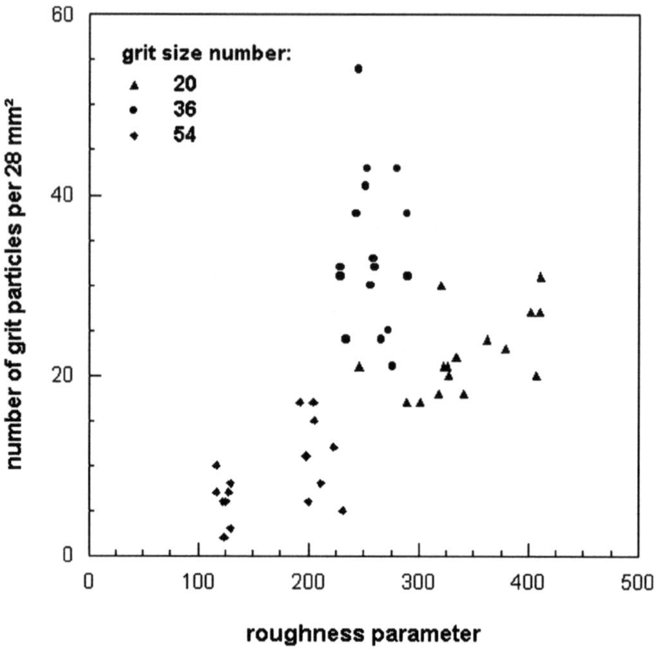

Fig. 8.29 Relationships between substrate roughness, abrasive particle size and abrasive contamination (Day et al., 2005)

sizes. Results of their study are displayed in Fig. 8.29. It can be seen that particle contamination was more severe for a given abrasive particle size if substrate roughness increased. Larger abrasive particles (small grit size number) formed deeper profiles, but also promoted grit embedment.

Neal (1999) found typical grit contamination levels between 10% and 25% on the back side of fusion-bonded epoxy that was applied to a dry blast cleaned pipeline surface. Schuh et al. (2004) detected alumina abrasive debris embedment in blast cleaned titanium substrates, and they found grit contamination levels as high as 42%. Yankee et al. (1991) found grit contamination levels of 12% on titanium substrates blast cleaned with aluminium oxide. Compared to the values for a carbon steel, as listed in Table 8.20, these values are rather high. Obviously, more abrasive material was fragmented during the impingement on the hard titanium surface, and the fragments were smeared across the surface.

A special effect, frequently observed during blast cleaning, is "overblasting" due to multiple blast cleaning steps. This phenomenon applies to the blast cleaning of already blast cleaned surfaces (as usually occurring in blast cleaning of deteriorated coatings). As shown by the results listed in Table 8.21, overblasting increased the grit contamination level due to additional particle embedment. Wigren 1988) found that abrasive embedment quickly increased during short exposure times, but the progress of embedment dropped if a certain critical exposure time (between 2.5 and 3 s) was exceeded. These relationships are illustrated in Fig. 8.28.

Table 8.21 Particle embedment due to overblasting (Momber and Wong, 2005a)

Number of blast cleaning steps	Particle embedment in %
0	0
1	6.7 ± 2
2	7.4 ± 3

Day et al. (2005) performed a statistical analysis on the effect of certain process parameters on the contamination level and derived the following relationship:

$$\mathrm{CL} = -0.33 \cdot \mathrm{G_N} + 0.24 \cdot \mathrm{p} + 0.44 \cdot \mathrm{n_s} + 2.87 \cdot \mathrm{x} + 0.12 \cdot \varphi \tag{8.1}$$

The CL (contamination level) is given as the total number of embedded particles found in an area of 28 mm^2. The grit number (G_N) is given in mesh; p is given in psi; x is given in inch and φ is given in degrees.

8.5.4 Fine Cleaning

Fine cleaning is essential after dry blast cleaning. However, quantitative demands can usually not be found in coating data sheets. For fusion-bonded epoxy, a maximum level for dirt contamination of up to 30% is mentioned to be acceptable (Neal, 1999). Dusty contaminants can be removed by certain methods, including blowing with compressed air (Peters and Meister, 1997), vacuuming, water rinsing and ultrasonic cleaning. In the pipe coating industry, acid washing is frequently used as well. Figure 8.30 illustrates the effect of cleaning on CL and hot cathodic disbonding. Interestingly, although phosphoric acid washing could reduce the degree of contamination, it did not notably improve cathodic bond. One possible reason could be that acid cleaning lowered and smoothed the surface profile. This latter effect is illustrated in Fig. 8.31. Subsequent grinding can also help to eliminate the detrimental effect of embedded grit. This is verified by the results listed in Table 8.22. Wetting force increased if a blast cleaned substrate was subsequently polished with paper. The explanation is that polishing process removed embedded abrasive debris, which improved the wettability of the steel substrate (see Sect. 8.9.3). Yankee et al. (1991) could prove that the efficiency of cleaning methods depended on the abrasive type to be removed. Ultrasonic cleaning was, for example, very efficient for the removal of silicone carbide debris from titanium substrates (cleaning efficiency of 50%), but it was inefficient for the removal of aluminium oxide (cleaning efficiency of 10%). However, for both abrasive types, ultrasonic cleaning was slightly superior over air blasting.

Burgess et al. (2002) investigated the effectivity of several post-blast cleaning methods for stainless steel samples blast cleaned with corundum abrasives ($p = 0.4$ MPa). Before the secondary cleaning, the level of deposited debris was between 7% and 8%. After ultrasonic cleaning, the level could be lowered down to 5.4%, and after a combination of acid etching and ultrasonic cleaning, the level went down to 3%.

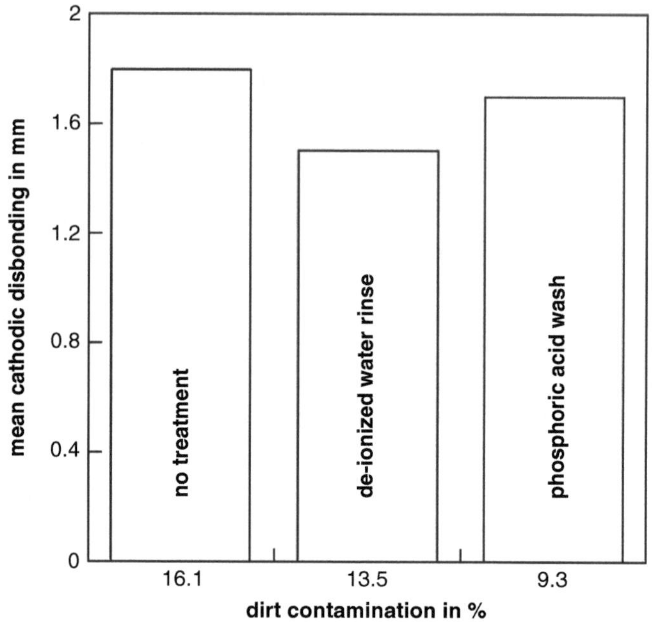

Fig. 8.30 Effects of cleaning methods for debris removal on cathodic disbonding (Neal, 1999)

8.6 Roughness and Profile of Substrates

8.6.1 Definitions and Measurement

Standards for the application of coatings rank the profile of a surface as one of the three major properties that influence coating performance. Substrate roughness is frequently specified by coating manufacturers for coating systems, but not for all. Profile parameters of blast cleaned surfaces can be subdivided into six groups; this includes the following (Griffith et al., 1997; Siegmann and Brown, 1998; Amada and Satoh, 2000):

- height parameters (e.g. average roughness);
- height distribution parameters (e.g. skew and kurtosis);
- bearing parameters;
- angle parameters (e.g. peak slope);
- spacing parameters (e.g. peak spacing);
- fractal dimensions.

Height parameters play an most important role for the assessment of blast cleaned surfaces in practice; they include average statistical roughness (R_a), maximum roughness (R_{max}) and average maximum roughness (R_Z). Angle parameters include e.g. average peak slope (Griffith et al., 1997, 1999). Spacing parameters include, among others, peak count (Roper et al. 2005). Weidenhaupt (1970) provided a

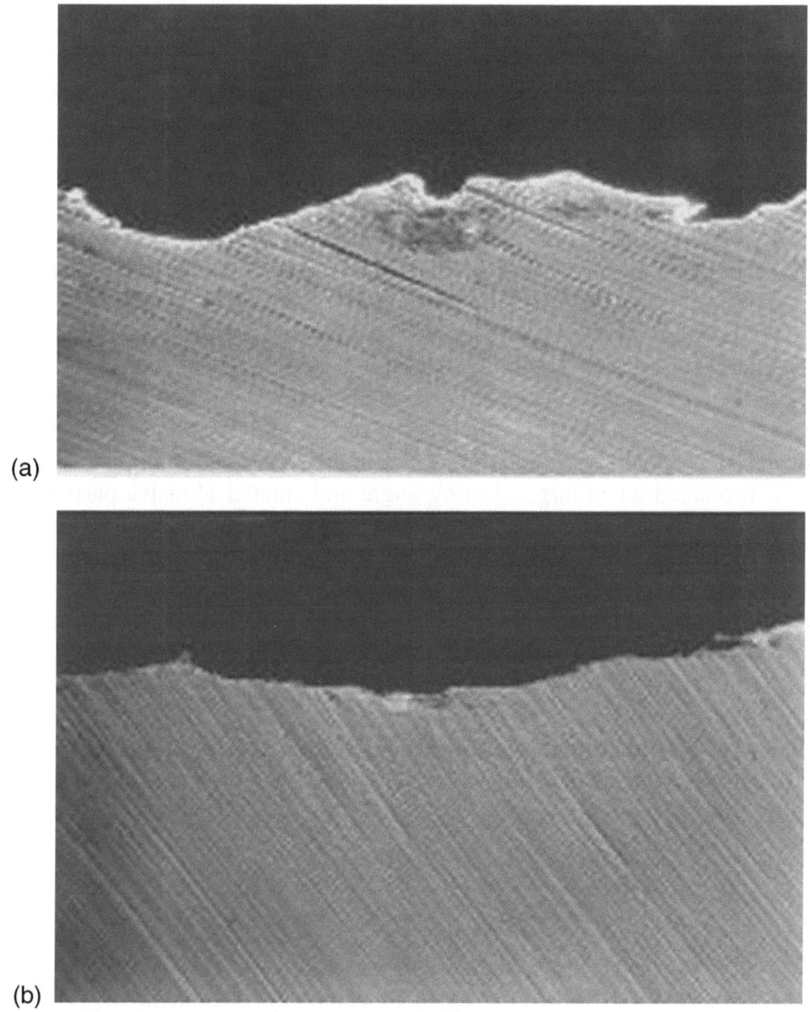

Fig. 8.31 Substrate profile modification due to acid etching (Neal, 1999). (a) Before etching; (b) After etching

number of experimental results for different profile parameters for blast cleaned steel substrates.

The blast cleaning process generates isotropic surfaces, in contrast to grinding and polishing that form anisotropic surfaces. These relationships can be recognised if polar plots of treated surfaces are evaluated. A polar plot of a steel surface treated with different methods is shown in Fig. 8.55. The shape of the plot characterises the surface type. The elliptic shape for the polished surface (inner plot) is typical for an anisotropic surface. The value for the profile parameter (peak spacing) depends on the measurement direction: it is high in 90°-direction. The polar plots for the blast cleaned surfaces, in contrast, are of circular shape. The value of the profile parameter

Table 8.22 Wettability of IN718 after surface treatment; wetting liquid: AMS4777 (Solomon et al., 2003)

Blast cleaning process	Maximum wetting force in N/m
With Al_2O_3	−0.18
	0.09
	0.60
With Al_2O_3 + polishing with paper (400 μm)	0.99

does not depend on the measuring direction. The diameters of the circles express the peak spacing values in the example shown in Fig. 8.55. Doherty (1974) delivered a more detailed study about the effects of blast cleaning parameters on the isotropy of blast cleaned substrates. He found that blast cleaning angle and abrasive material greatly influenced isotropy. This author also distinguished blast cleaned substrates into two types: "normal type" (which is isotropic) and "machine type" (which is anisotropic). "Normal type" areas showed a highly disturbed random surface; this type was produced when large blasting angle and smaller abrasive particles were used. "Machine type" areas, in contrast, had a directionality that varied a little to each side of the blast direction; this type occurred at shallow blasting angle and for larger abrasive particles. For $\varphi = 30°$, all individual cutting marks on the substrate were directed in the blast direction; whereas for $\varphi = 45°$, direction of the cutting marks varied at about 30° to either side of the blast direction. The criteria for generating a "normal type" (isotropic) surface were defined as follows by Doherty (1974): $p > 0.55\,\text{MPa}$, $\varphi > 45°$, $x < 100\,\text{cm}$.

Methods of how to evaluate substrate roughness prior to the application of corrosion protective coatings are outlined in ISO 8503. The following four methods are specified:

- profile comparator (ISO 8503-1, ISO 8503-2);
- microscope (ISO 8503-3);
- stylus instrument (ISO 8503-4);
- replica method (ISO 8503-5).

The comparator method delivers qualitative results only; it distinguishes between "fine", "medium" and "coarse" profiles. Table 8.23 provides a comparison between comparator values and corresponding quantitative roughness values. Profile comparators were basically developed for steel abrasives, in detail for steel shot (comparator profile "S") and steel grit (comparator profile "G"). Despite this limitation,

Table 8.23 Steel substrate profile parameters (ISO 8503-1)

Comparator value	Roughness value (R_{y5})[a] in μm	
	Grit	Shot
Fine	25–60	25–40
Medium	61–100	41–70
Coarse	101–150	71–100

[a] R_{y5} denotes the average of five in-line measurements

Table 8.24 Classification of peak count (Roper et al., 2006)

Classification	Peaks per cm
High	40–60
Medium	30–40
Low	20–30

comparators are used throughout the corrosion protection industry to evaluate profiles formed by other, non-metallic abrasive materials. Roper et al. (2006) performed a classification of peak count as "high", "medium" and "low"; the corresponding quantitative values are listed in Table 8.24.

Many commercial portable stylus instruments read the following profile parameters: R_a, R_Z (R_{y5}) and R_{max}.These parameters are illustrated in Fig. 8.32. However, the arithmetical mean roughness (R_a) is not specified in coating data sheets; however, the two other parameters sometimes are. It is of interest to see how reproducible profile measurements are. This aspect was investigated by Chandler and Shak (1966) and Neal (1999). Some values of Neal (1999) study are provided in Table 8.25. Standard deviations of roughness values measured by four different operators with different levels of experience, who each measured a profile 10 times at a steel pipe, did not exceed a value of 6.3 μm. Chandler and Shak (1966) found that the difference in roughness readings of four different operators varied between 7% and 20%.

Prazak and Eremias (1972) provided an alternative method for estimating a surface roughness factor of metals, which was based on estimating the exchange current of a redox system on a passivated metal surface by measuring the polarisation resistance. This relative roughness factor was defined as follows:

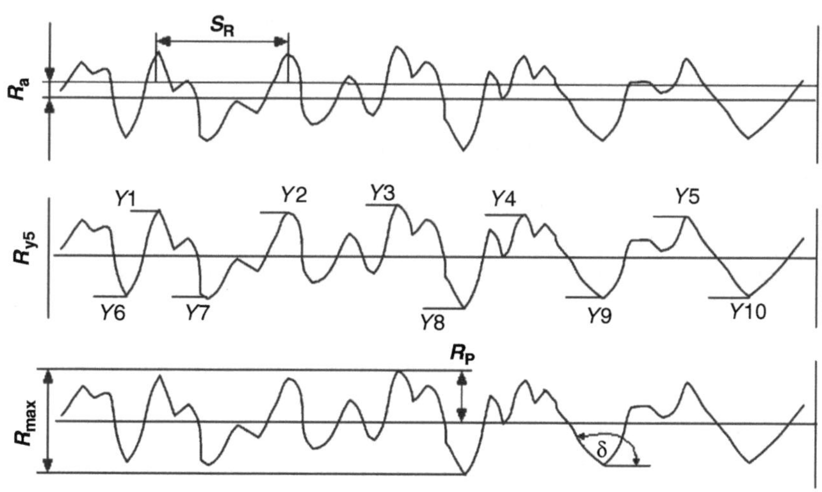

Fig. 8.32 Surface roughness (profile) parameters (Hempel Book of Paints); extended by the author

Table 8.25 Reproducibility of replicate tape profile measurements on dry blast cleaned steel pipes (Neal, 1999)

Parameter	Roughness value in μm				
	Operator				
	1	2	3	4	All
Mean	69.8	70.3	61.2	61.7	65.8
Standard deviation	2.5	4.8	7.4	2.5	6.3
Range	7.6	15.2	25.4	7.6	33.0

$$R_{RF} = \frac{R_{Pst}}{R_P} \tag{8.2}$$

Here, R_{Pst} is the polarisation resistance of an electrode with a standard area, and R_P is the measured polarisation resistance. Because this latter parameter depends on the chemical composition of the metal, the method works only for comparing the surfaces of materials of equal chemical compositions.

8.6.2 *Effects of Roughness on Coating Performance*

Roughness and profile parameters notably affect the adhesion between substrate and coating to be applied. Respective investigations on many coating types can be found in the literature. Griffith et al. (1997) found that adherence of plasma-sprayed aluminium oxide coatings to steel substrates improved if substrate average roughness, average peak slope and peak spacing (Fig. 8.33b) of the profile increased. The effect of the average roughness on the adhesion is shown in Fig. 8.33a, and it can be recognised that adhesion increased in a linear fashion with an increase in roughness. The effect of variations in peak spacing on the adhesion is illustrated in Fig. 8.33b. The adhesion initially steeply increased with an increase in peak spacing, but it dropped if a certain value for the peak spacing (ca. $S_R = 250\,\mu m$) was exceeded. If this case occurred, adhesion between substrate and coating reduced. Therefore, profile parameters must be optimised in order to obtain a maximum adhesion.

Hofinger et al. (2002) performed fracture experiments on interfaces between steel substrates and plasma-sprayed coatings. Their results, listed in Table 8.26, showed that a higher amount of energy was required to separate coating and substrate if substrate roughness increased. Packham (2002) has shown that the adhesion (in terms of the critical energy release rate) of a zinc coating to steel exhibited maximum values at moderate roughness (R_a) values. For high R_a-values, the adhesion deteriorated.

Bergmann (1994) could show that substrate type played an important role. As shown in Fig. 8.34, a higher roughness could deteriorate the adhesion of ceramics coatings plasma sprayed to a certain substrate. Whereas general trends could be established for the zirconium substrate and the aluminium-titanium substrate, the adhesion of the coating applied to the aluminium oxide substrate was very sensitive to changes in substrate roughness. Both facts could be probably explained through

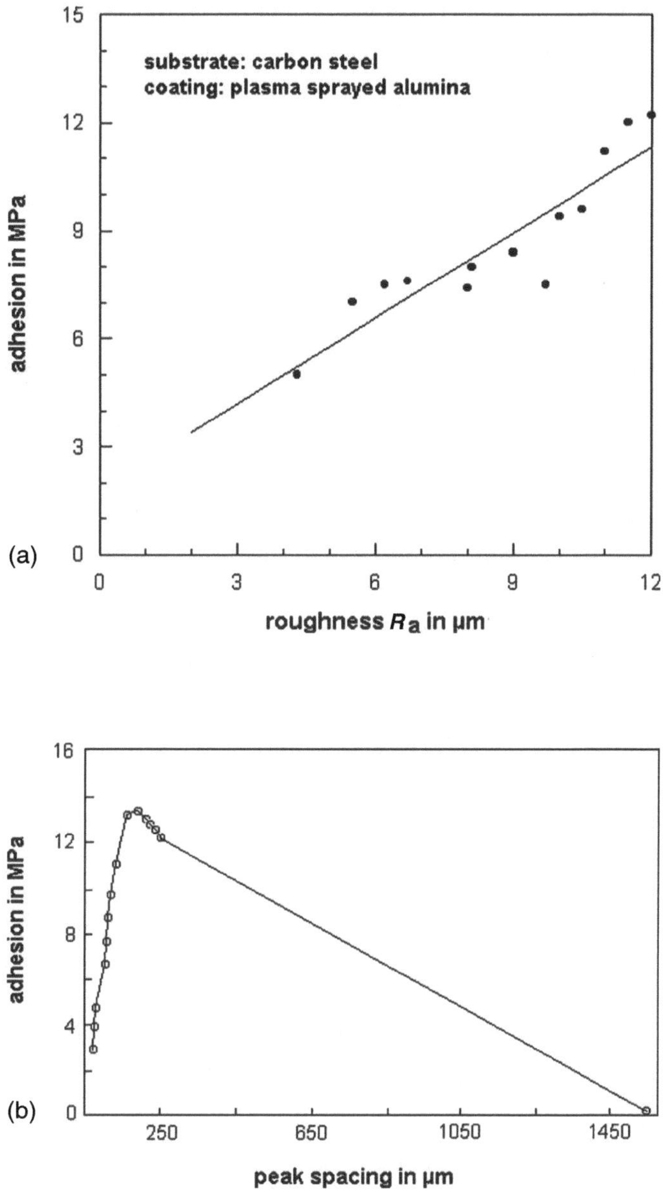

Fig. 8.33 Effects of roughness parameters on the adhesion of plasma-sprayed alumina coatings to a steel substrate (Griffith et al., 1997). (**a**) Effects of average roughness; (**b**) Effects of profile peak spacing

Table 8.26 Roughness effect on interface fracture energy (Hofinger et al., 2002)

Roughness in μm		Interface fracture energy in N/m
R_a	R_Z	
1.3	9.6	500 ± 30
2.2	15.4	530 ± 50
4.8	29.7	580 ± 40

the different thermal residual stresses which depended on the physical properties of both the materials involved in interface formation. It is, therefore, always the combination of substrate and coating material which determines roughness effects. Results displayed in Fig. 8.35, however, show that abrasive grain shape played some role as well. The experimental points marked "1" were for cut steel wire, and only if these points were excluded, roughness had a definitive relationship to adhesion.

Siegmann and Brown (2002) performed systematic tests into the effect of steel substrate profile parameters on the adhesion of metal-sprayed coatings. They found an almost linear relationship between R_a and adhesion strength; however, the relationship was restricted to roughness values $R_a > 3\,\mu m$. The authors also found that the size of the contact area between substrate and coating was of decisive importance. For contact areas larger than $100\,\mu m^2$, a correlation between profile parame-

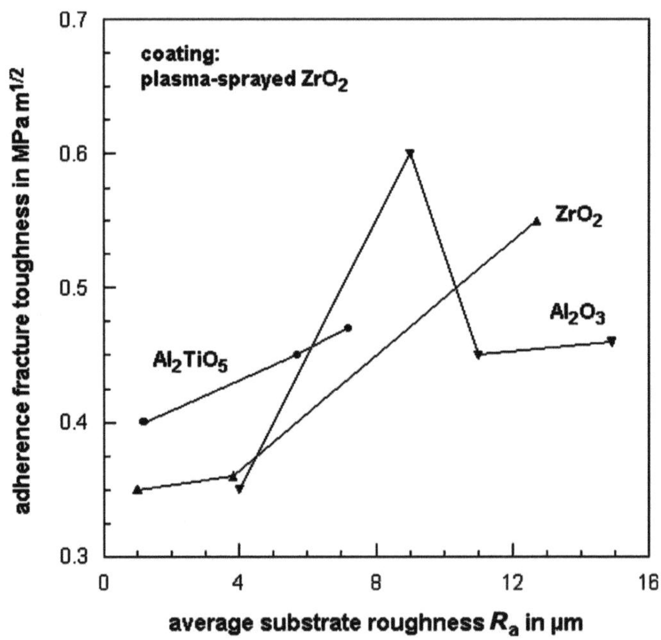

Fig. 8.34 Effects of substrate-coating combination on the roughness influence on the adhesion between ceramic substrates and a plasma-sprayed ceramic coating (Bergmann, 1994)

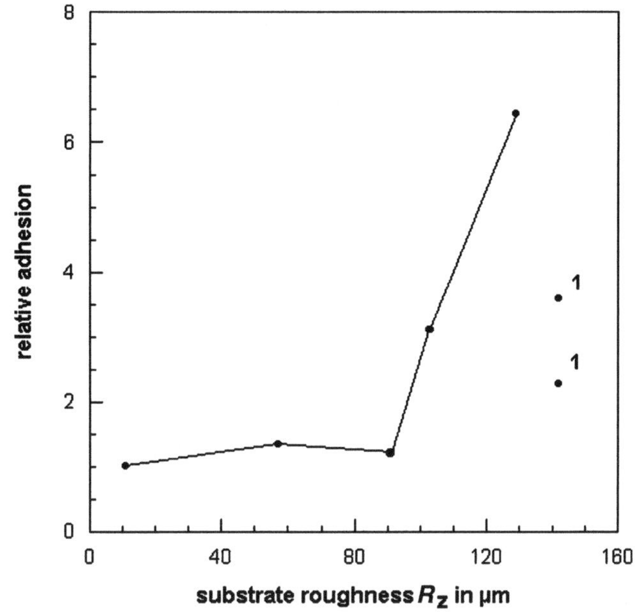

Fig. 8.35 Effects of abrasive particle size and shape on roughness and coating adhesion (Bahlmann, 1982); 1 – cut steel wire

ters and adhesion could be established. Van Tijum and De Hosson (2005) found an almost linear relationship between the relative surface area of a steel substrate and the interface strength between substrate and a polyethylene, but this relationship held only if the increase in surface area was smaller than +150%.

Maruyama and Kobayashi (2004) performed a study about the adhesion of flame-sprayed copper powder to blast cleaned carbon steel substrates. The blast cleaning was carried out with aluminium oxide ($d_P = 116$–$1{,}850\,\mu m$) at an air pressure of $p = 0.55$ MPa. The authors did not find a unique relationship between the maximum roughness (R_{max}) and the adhesion strength. Although the adhesion strength initially increased with an increase in roughness, it dropped at higher roughness values. Thus, an individual roughness parameter could not characterise the quality of the bond between substrate and coating. Maruyama and Kobayashi (2004) introduced a dimensionless "increase ratio of surface area" (see Fig. 8.32). This parameter neither showed any unique relationship to the adhesion strength; best results for the adhesion strength were obtained for moderate values (at about 1.2) for the increase ratio.

Morcillo et al. (1989) investigated the effects of numerous parameters on roughness influence. Some results are displayed in Fig. 8.36. In that example, an organic primer was applied to steel substrates with varying roughness values. It can be seen that rust grade increased (respectively, lifetime of the primer decreased), if the maximum roughness (R_{max}) had high values. The best performance could be realised if the primer was applied over the smoothest profile. It was found that there was a

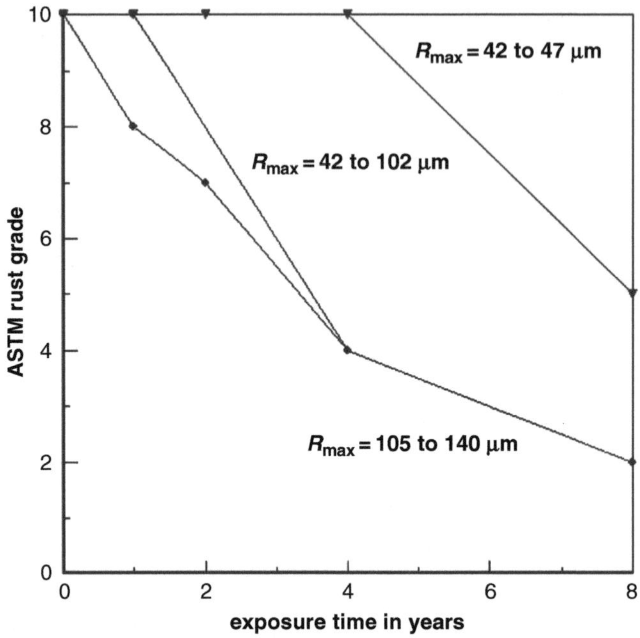

Fig. 8.36 Effects of profile roughness modification and exposure time on the corrosion rate of steel-coated panels (Morcillo et al., 1989)

critical surface profile, the value of which was determined by the environment along with the type and thickness of the coating system. As the coating system increased in thickness, the effect of the surface profile on coating performance diminished. The critical surface profile was found to be a function of the aggressiveness of the environment: a more aggressive environment resulted in a lower critical profile (which corresponded to a higher film thickness over the roughness peak). Bigos (1959) performed investigations into the rusting of organic coatings, and he found that the rusting over roughness peaks was severe for profile values of R_{max} = 100–200 µm, whereas rusting was considerable for profile values of R_{max} = 81–86 µm, and no rusting occurred for profile values of R_{max} = 33–51 µm. Keane et al. (1976) observed similar effects on different coating types. They found that alkyd and vinyl primers performed better over relative small substrate profiles than over very rough profiles in a light industrial environment. The authors concluded that the coating performance seemed to be ordinarily related to the paint thickness over a relative small number of highest peaks out of a total of about 30,000 to 100,000 peaks per 6 cm^2. There were more high peaks and apparently more thin spots of paint films over coarse substrate surfaces. Table 8.27 lists typical values for critical film thicknesses which must be applied over a coarse profile in order to achieve a demanded lifetime for four paint types as functions of the substrate thickness. Truelove (1966) performed detailed measurements of the film thickness of organic paints over peaks and troughs of shot blast cleaned steel substrates, and he could

Table 8.27 Critical film thickness values for coating lifetime (Keane et al., 1976)

Surface profile in μm	Critical film thickness in μm			
	Salt spray test		Mild industrial exposure	
	Alkyd	Vinyl	Alkyd	Vinyl
56	18	23	13	20
61	23	30	23	20
51	30	20	13	20
74	18	20	13	13
127	43	46	25	28

show that the reduction in film thickness (as a fraction of the average film thickness) over peaks had an almost linear relationship to the maximum roughness (R_{max}) of the substrates.

Bardal (1973), and later Roper et al. (2005), introduced an additional surface profile parameter – peak count as illustrated in Fig. 8.32, and they found that this parameter could suitably be related to coating performance, especially for long exposure times. Roper et al. (2005) showed that if profile height was kept constant, peak count could affect the performance of a coating as determined through pull-off adhesion strength, scribe undercut, and in some cases cracking. Some results of this study are shown in Fig. 8.37. Figure 8.37a illustrates the effects of peak count and exposure time on the pull-off strength, whereas Fig. 8.37b illustrates the effects

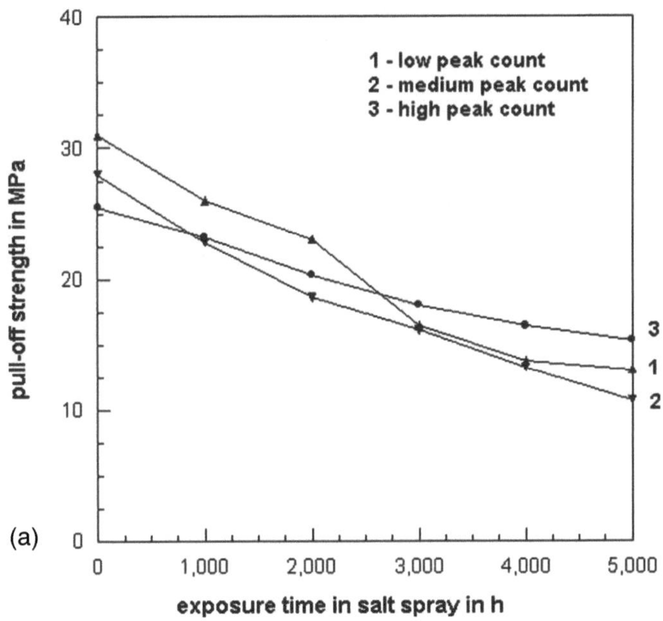

Fig. 8.37 Effects of peak spacing on coating performance (Roper et al., 2005). (**a**) Pull-off strength; (**b**) Delamination after salt spray test

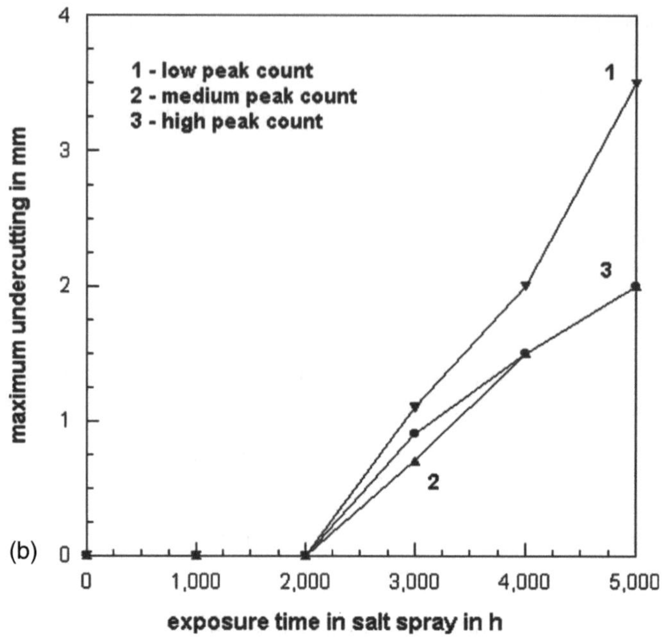

Fig. 8.37 Continued

of both parameters on the delamination at an artificial scribe. High values for the peak count improved the performance of the coating at long exposure times. It was also found that coatings with low wetting capability were less sensitive to changes in peak count. Results of respective measurements are listed in Table 8.28. Feist et al. (1988) investigated the effect of the groove distance of a profile on the adhesion of sprayed zinc and sprayed aluminium to steel substrates. Results of this study are illustrated in Fig. 8.38. Pull-off strength, as a measure of adhesion, dropped notably if a certain critical groove distance was exceeded. In the graph, this critical value was about $S_R = 250\,\mu m$. For substrates with equal values for $R_Z = 500\,\mu m$, pull-off strength of sprayed zinc dropped from $\sigma_A = 10\,MPa$ for $S_R = 200\,\mu m$ down to $\sigma_A = 4\,MPa$ for $S_R = 500\,\mu m$ (Feist et al., 1988).

Roughness and adhesion are not always related to each other in a unique fashion, as shown by the examples in Fig. 8.39 which applies to the adhesion between a steel

Table 8.28 Effects of peak count on coating performance (Roper et al., 2005)

Coating	Exposure time in h	Improvement from low to high peak count in %	
		Pull-off strength	Undercutting
A	5,000	43	43
B	5,000	90	62
C	5,000	100	70
D	5,560	13	83
E	4,222	79	60
F	4,222	−4	57

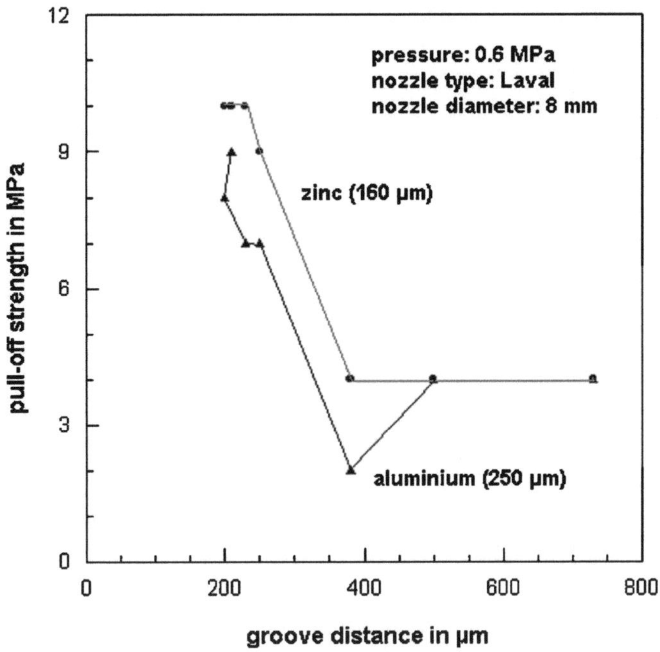

Fig. 8.38 Effects of groove distance on adhesion of metal-sprayed coatings (Feist et al., 1988)

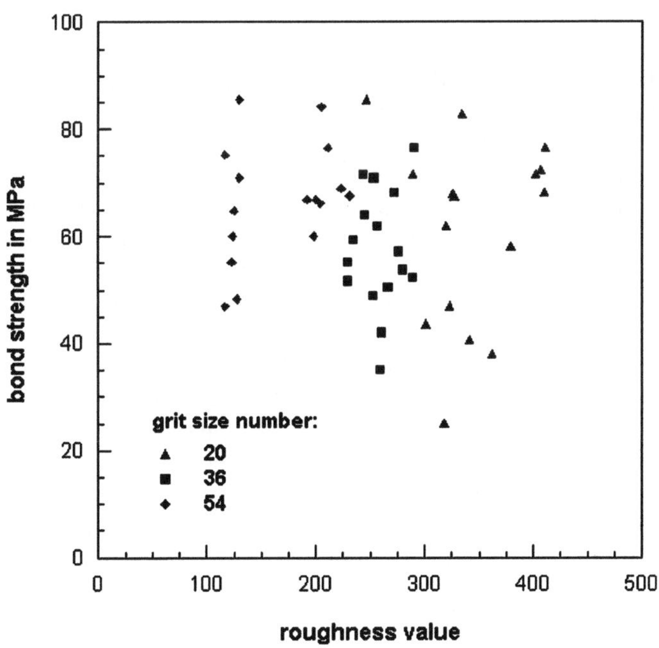

Fig. 8.39 Relationships between substrate roughness, abrasive size number and adhesion (Day et al., 2005)

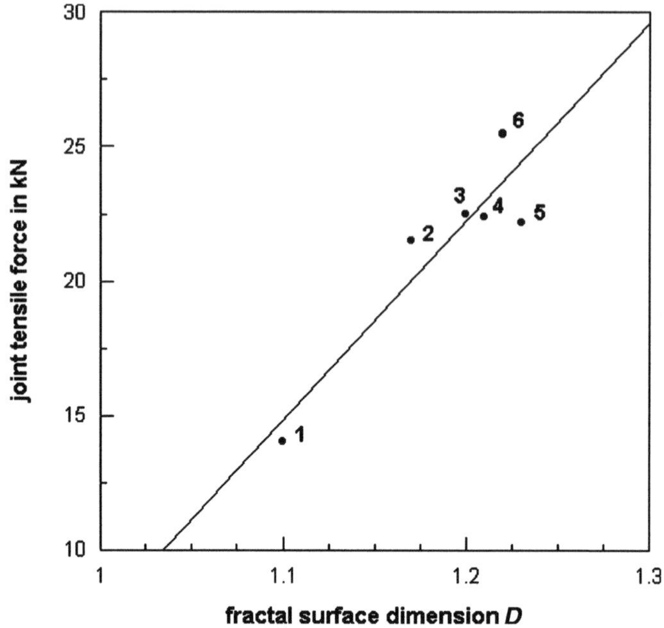

Fig. 8.40 Relationship between fractal surface dimension and the tensile force required to separate a joint (Mannelqvist and Groth, 2001). Surface preparation: 1 – degreased; 2 – blast cleaned with glass beads; 3 – steel brush; 4 – Scotch-Brite pad; 5 – water blasted; 6 – blast cleaned with quartz particles

substrate and a thermally sprayed coating. High roughness values did not necessarily lead to high adhesion. Even if the abrasive particle size is being considered, the relationships did not improve.

Surface profiles can be described by more advanced methods, namely by fractals. Certain authors exploited fractal parameters to characterise blast cleaned surfaces (Mannelqvist and Groth 2001; Siegmann and Brown 2002; Bahbou et al., 2004; Van Tijum and De Hosson 2005), and it was shown that fractal surface parameters could suitably be linked to the bond strength of adhesive joints between two materials. An example is shown in Fig. 8.40. Here, a fractal parameter, denoted "D", showed a satisfying relationship to the tensile strength of a stainless steel joint; no such relationship could be noted for the conventional average roughness (R_a). Van Tijum and De Hosson (2005) introduced a parameter "relative surface area", and they could theoretically show that this profile parameter had a linear relationship to the strength of the interface between steel and polymer if the increase in surface area was less than 150%. The deviation from the linear relationship became important for small values for the Young's modulus of the polymer.

Sancaktar and Gomatam (2001) performed tests on the strengths of single lap joints of rolled steel. The strength was measured with a tensile testing machine at different crosshead speeds. Both failure load and ultimate displacement were estimated. The results depicted an effect of the viscosity of the adhesive materi-

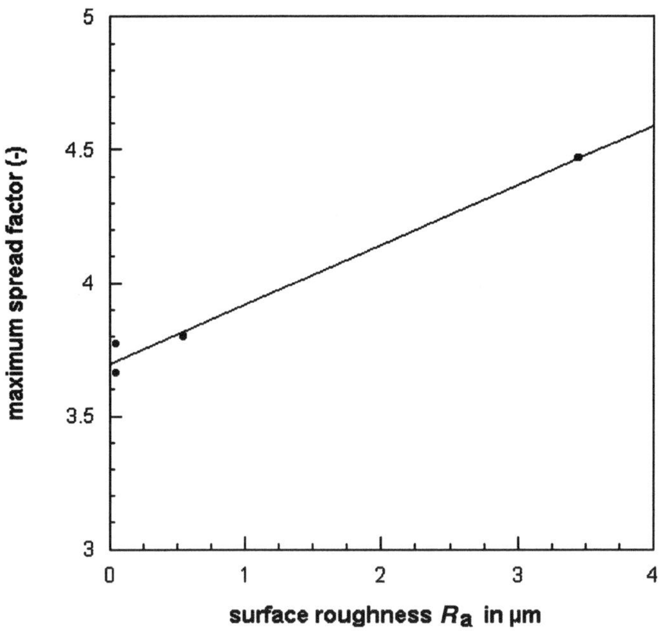

Fig. 8.41 Profile roughness effects on splat formation of liquid paint drops (Siavoshani, 2001)

als. For a low-viscosity adhesive (5–7 Pa s), the two strength parameters increased if the roughness (R_a) of the adherend increased. For a high-viscosity adhesive (170–225 Pa s), no distinctive relationship could be found between roughness of the adherend and strength values of the joint. Surface roughness studies of Rider et al. (1999) established that increasing the adherend roughness from a flat surface to a more profiled roughness, increased the fracture energy of an aluminium-epoxy joint exposed to humid conditions by two orders of magnitude.

Roughness parameters of substrates affect the splat formation of impinging drops of liquefied coating materials. One example is provided in Fig. 8.41. It can be seen that the spread factor increased if average roughness of the substrate increased. Similar results were reported by Sancaktar and Gomatam (2001) for the relationship between substrate roughness (R_a) and adhesive spread parameter. The adhesive (resin) diameter initially increased with an increase in roughness, but started to drop at rather high values for the average roughness. Substrate roughness also affects flattening degree and cooling of plasma-sprayed coatings (see Sect. 9.7). Experimental and numerical results reported by Ivosevic et al. (2006) indicated that an increase in magnitude of the mean roughness promoted splat instability (namely jetting and satellite break-up) and the formation of radial fingers. It was also observed that the increase in surface roughness may result in lower spreading ratio of thermally sprayed polymer particles. Ma et al. (2006) studied the effect of the roughness (R_a) of blast cleaned substrates on the splat formation of HVOF-sprayed tungsten carbide. The results showed that with an increase in roughness, the restriction to flattening was enhanced in a way that the number of spherical to nearly spherical splats reduced, whereas the number of splats with complex morphologies increased. A comprehensive review on these issues is given by Fauchais et al. (2004). Splat morphology can be subdivided into two types: disc-shaped and splash-shaped. The disc-shaped type can be expected for blast cleaned substrates with an isotropic surface. The splash-shaped type will mainly develop on ground or polished substrates with an anisotropic surface. This was verified by SEM inspections performed by Griffith et al. (1997). Splat type notably affects the contact between substrate and first coating layer. Metallurgical sections through interfaces between carbon steel substrates and plasma-sprayed aluminium oxide coatings verified that about 90% of the good contact areas were covered with disc-shaped splats, whereas about 75% of the poor contacts were covered with splash-shaped splats (Griffith et al. (1997).

Detailed investigations of Hansen (1972) revealed that substrate roughness had a notable effect on the appearance of finished organic coating, namely on gloss.

Emrich (2003) performed a detailed investigation on the quality of adhesive bonds in aluminium joints. Based on the results of transmission electron microscopy (TEM) inspections, he argued that the macroscopic profile (roughness in the sense as discussed above) did not have a notable effect on the bond quality. It was rather the microscopic level ($<1\ \mu m$) of the substrate which determined the adhesion between adhesive and substrate. This dimensional level is close to the dimensions of the applied polymers.

8.6.3 Profile Parameters of Blast Cleaned Metal Substrates

8.6.3.1 Introduction

Based on the scenario shown in Fig. 8.42, Chernyavskii (1984) and Knotek and Elsing (1987) developed analytical models for the estimation of the maximum roughness of shot blasted steel substrates. Chernyavskii (1984) solution reads as follows:

$$R_{max} \propto v_p \cdot \sin\varphi \cdot m_p^{1/2} \cdot \sigma_f^{-1/2} \tag{8.3}$$

Knotek and Elsing (1987) derived the following relationship:

$$R_{max} \propto v_p \cdot x \cdot m_p^{1/2} \cdot \sigma_f^{-1/2} \tag{8.4}$$

Both equations provide equal trends for particle velocity, abrasive particle mass and yield strength of the substrate material. The yield strength of the target material is for many metals (Tabor, 1951) and polymers (Pickles and Hutchings, 1997) related to the hardness. It can, therefore, be replaced by the substrate material hardness: $\sigma_f \propto H_M$. This approach has been made by Sorokin et al. (1983). Profile parameters are affected by certain material and process parameters, among them particle

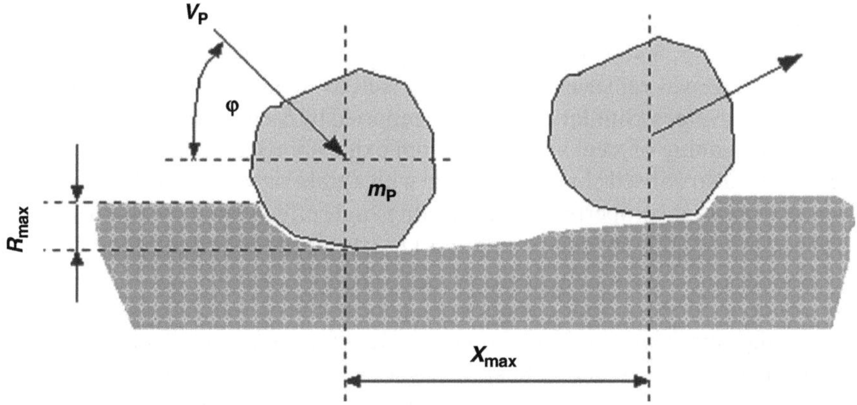

Fig. 8.42 Model for profile formation on a steel substrate due to an impinging abrasive particle (Chernyavskii, 1984)

velocity, blasting angle, blasting time, surface cleaning grade, abrasive hardness, substrate hardness and abrasive working mixture.

8.6.3.2 Effects of Blasting Angle

The effect of the blasting angle on profile values of a carbon steel substrate was investigated by several authors (Keane et al., 1976; Mellali et al., 1994; Ishikawa

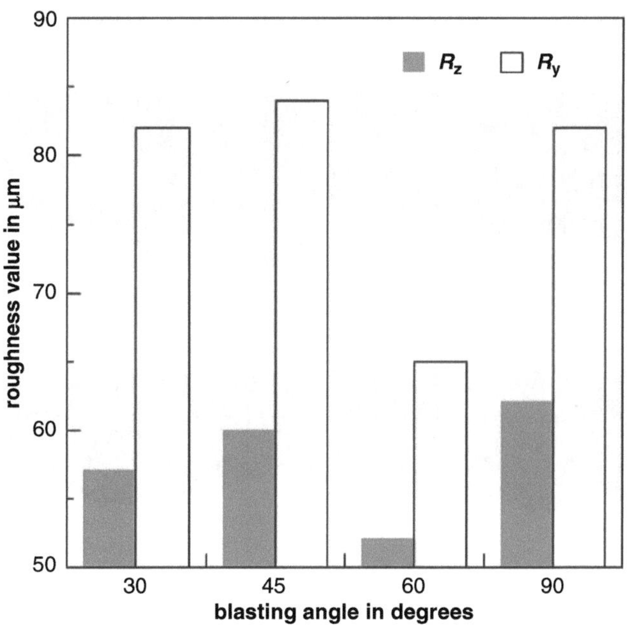

Fig. 8.43 Effects of blasting angle on substrate roughness parameters (Ishikawa and Tobe, 2003)

and Tobe, 2003; Barnett and Burgess, 2007). Results of Ishikawa and Tobe (2003) are provided in Fig. 8.43. There is some range in the neighbourhood of a 60°angle where roughness was rather low. Shallow as well as high blasting angles promoted high roughness values. Similar results were reported by Siegmann and Brown (1998) for the blast cleaning of steel with aluminium oxide abrasives. Mellali et al. (1994), however, who also utilised aluminium oxide with a grain size of $d_P = 1.4$ mm, noted an influence of substrate properties on the blasting angle effect. For rather hard substrate materials ($HV_5 = 200$), average roughness (R_a) dropped only slightly for shallower blasting angles; but for a soft steel, average roughness rapidly felt if the blasting angle was lower than $\varphi = 60°$. Highest roughness values were always obtained at perpendicular impingement. How impact angle affects the appearance of the substrate profile is illustrated in Fig. 8.44. It can be seen that very uneven coarse surface profiles were formed if the blast cleaning was performed at moderate angles.

Bahbou et al. (2004) blast cleaned titanium alloys with aluminium oxide (p = 0.4 MPa, d_P = 160–400 μ m, $\dot{m}_P$ = 1.5 kg/min) and found maximum values for R_a and R_z at perpendicular blasting angles, whereby the parameter R_z was more sensitive to changes in the blasting angle.

8.6.3.3 Effects of Stand-off Distance

The effect of the stand-off distance between nozzle and substrate surface on roughness parameters is not well established. Whereas some authors found that stand-off distance does not seem to affect roughness (Siegmann and Brown 1998; Varacalle et al., 2006), others found a clear, almost linear, increase in roughness (R_Z) for longer stand-off distances (Karpinos et al., 1979). Wigren (1988) found that stand-

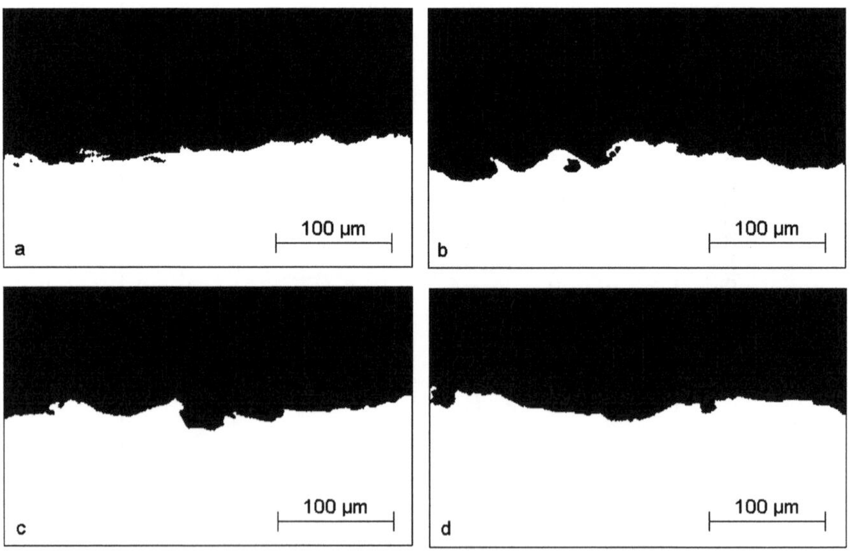

Fig. 8.44 Effects of blasting angle variations on profile shape (Amada and Satoh, 2000); polished cross-sections. **(a)** $\varphi = 45°$; **(b)** $\varphi = 60°$; **(c)** $\varphi = 75°$; **(d)** $\varphi = 90°$

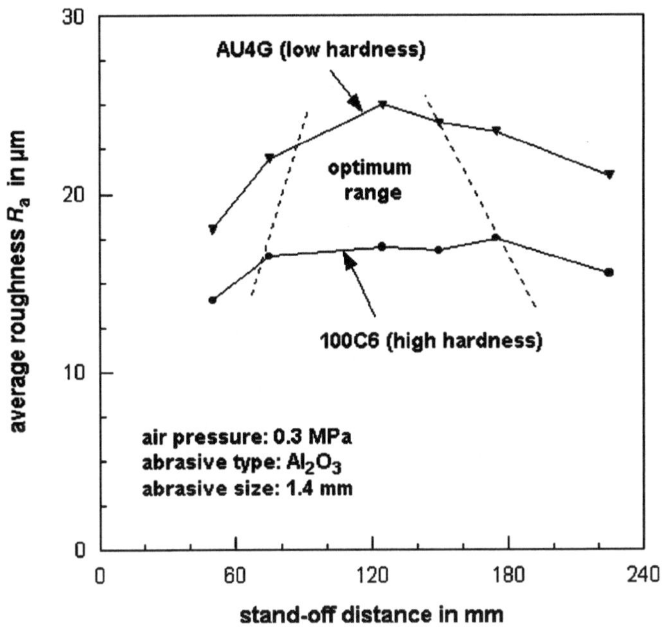

Fig. 8.45 Effects of stand-off distance and substrate material on average roughness (Mellali et al., 1994)

off distance affected roughness if a certain distance was exceeded. Values for this threshold distance depended on air pressure: for $p = 0.4$ MPa, the critical stand-off distance was about $x = 250$ mm. Mellali et al. (1994) noted an optimum range for the stand-off distance where maximum values for the average roughness (R_a) could be achieved. This optimum stand-off distance range depended on substrate hardness. Results of their investigations are displayed in Fig. 8.45. The optimum range was wider for substrate materials with rather high hardness values. With this optimum stand-off distance, rebound effects deteriorate the removal process; for stand-off distances beyond the optimum value, reduced kinetic energy of the impinging particles is assumed to cause the drop in roughness. Effects of substrate materials were also noted by Karpinos et al. (1979), who utilised cast iron shot ($d_P = 400$–$750\,\mu$m) for the treatment of different metals. Whereas the roughness (R_Z) almost linearly increased with longer stand-off distances for carbon steel samples and copper samples, stand-off distance changes did not show a notable effect on the roughness for aluminium samples.

8.6.3.4 Effects of Air Pressure and Abrasive Particle Velocity

It was already Tilghman (1870) who mentioned an effect of air pressure on surface profile: "*The less the pressure of the blast, the finer is the grain of the depolished surface.*" An increase in air pressure usually leads to deeper profiles (Münster and Spähn, 1979; Wigren, 1988; Kniewald, 1993; Varacalle et al., 2006; Barnett and Burgess, 2007). Some authors noted a linear relationship between air pressure and substrate roughness (Wiedenhaupt, 1970; Karpinos et al., 1979; Stallmann et al., 1988; Staia et al., 2000; Minaki et al., 2004; Sofyan et al., 2005). Gesell (1973) cited experimental investigations on the effects of particle impingement velocity on substrate roughness, which can be summarised with the following relationship:

$$R_t = C_R \cdot V_P \cdot d_P \tag{8.5}$$

The constant C_R considers effects of equipment and blast cleaning process. A linear relationship between abrasive impingement velocity and roughness was found by Weidenhaupt (1970) for the descaling of steel with cut steel wire and steel shot, which were accelerated with a wheel blast machine. However, for larger wire particles ($d_P > 700\,\mu m$), the relationship between impingement velocity and roughness tended to a power relationship with a power exponent less than unity. Results of these measurements are provided in Fig. 8.46. Weidenhaupt (1970) theoretically derived a relationship between the roughness and the kinetic energy of the impinging abrasive particles: $R_t \propto E_P{}^{1/2}$. Tosha and Iida (1990) found an almost linear relationship between the impingement velocity of cast steel particles and the maximum roughness of steel and titanium samples, whether steel grit or steel shot was being used.

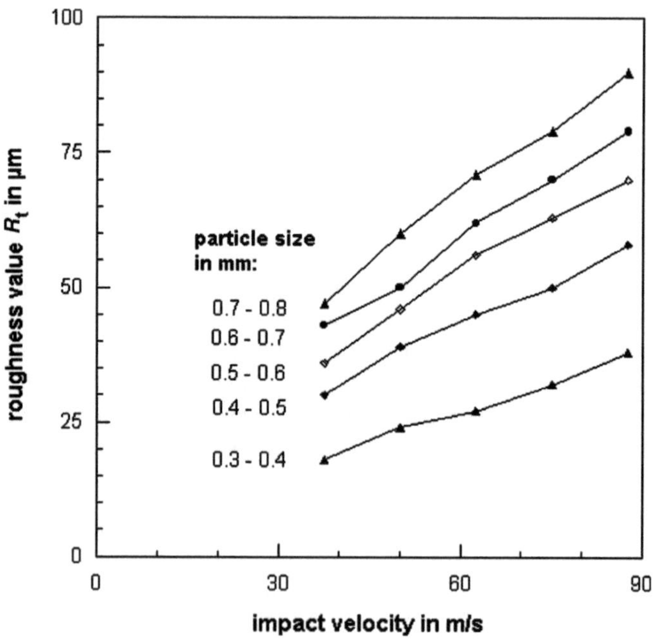

Fig. 8.46 Effects of particle impact velocity and particle size on substrate roughness (Weidenhaupt, 1970)

8.6.3.5 Effects of Abrasive Particle Size and Shape

It was already Tilghman (1870) who mentioned an effect of particle size on surface profile: "*The finer the sand, the finer is the grain of the depolished surface.*" Later, Bigos (1959) reported that the roughness of blast cleaned steel plates increased almost linear with an increase in abrasive particle diameter. The progress of the curve was almost independent of the abrasive type (sand, slag, iron shot and iron grit). A linear relationship between average roughness and abrasive particle diameter was also reported by Bullett and Dasgupta (1969) for the use of chilled iron grit. The authors also noted a linear relationship between abrasive particle diameter and increase in surface area after blast cleaning. Effects of changes in abrasive mixtures on profile parameters are depicted in Fig. 8.47. The average maximum roughness (R_Z) was most sensible to changes in the abrasive mixtures. An interesting detail was the different trends for the conventional roughness parameters (R_Z and R_a) and for the roughness angle (δ_q). Whereas the values for the roughness values increased from condition "1" to "6", the roughness angle had minimum values at for the conditions "1" and "6". The influence of abrasive particle size and shape on the average roughness and maximum roughness is depicted in Fig. 8.48. It can be seen that both roughness values increased in an almost linear fashion with an increase in particle size, irrespectively if shot or grit was used. A linear relationship between abrasive

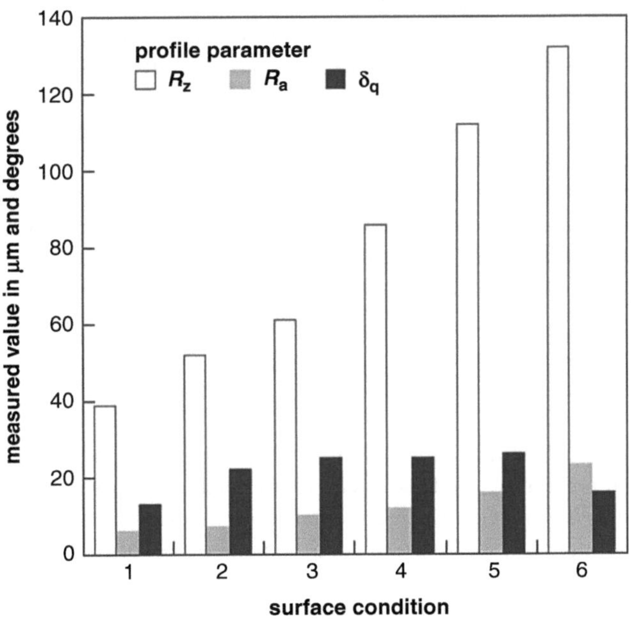

Fig. 8.47 Effects of abrasive mixtures on profile parameters of chromium–nickel steel (Beck and Arndt, 1996). Mixtures: 1 – untreated scale; 2 – garnet (d_P = 250–500 µm, one run; 3 – garnet (d_P = 500–1,000 µm), two runs; 4 – garnet (d_P = 500–1,000 µm), one run; 5 – garnet (new abrasives); 6 – cast steel grit (d_P = 1,000–2,400 µm)

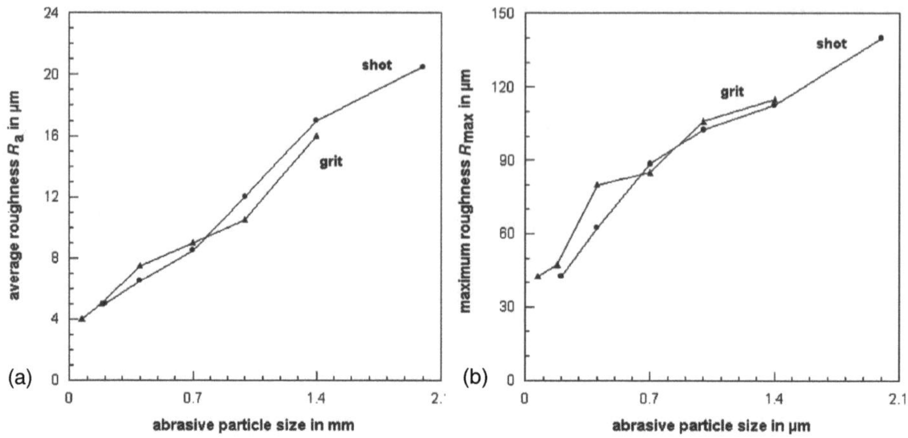

Fig. 8.48 Effects of abrasive particle size and shape on substrate roughness (Morcillo et al., 1989). (**a**) Average roughness, R_a; (**b**) Maximum roughness, R_{max}

particle size and average roughness (R_a) was also found by Mellali et al. (1994) for metal substrates, blast cleaned with aluminium oxide; by Kniewald (1993) for steel and copper, blast cleaned with steel grit; and by Abukawa et al. (2004) for steels, blast cleaned with aluminium oxide. Tosha and Iida (1990) found an almost linear relationship between the diameter of cast steel particles and the maximum roughness of steel and titanium samples, whether steel grit or steel shot was being used. These results verify (8.5). The graphs in Fig. 8.48 also show that particle shape was not of much influence to the profile. Keane et al. (1976) noted a more complex relationship between roughness and abrasive particle size. Although these authors found a linear relationship between roughness and abrasive particle size for some abrasive materials (sand and steel shot), they could also observe a power relationship for other abrasive materials (steel grit and iron grit). A more general expression of (8.5) is, therefore, the following form:

$$R \propto d_P^{n_P} \tag{8.6}$$

In this equation, the parameter n_P characterises the effects of other abrasive and target parameters. For $n_P = 1$, a linear relationship appears, and (8.5) is valid. Weidenhaupt (1970) presented experimental results which verified that the relationship between roughness and particle size depended on substrate hardness. Some results of his work are illustrated in Fig. 8.49. If substrate hardness decreased (respectively abrasive/substrate hardness ratio increased), the relationship was linear ($n_P = 1$) as depicted in Fig. (8.48). For higher substrate hardness values (respectively lower abrasive/substrate hardness ratio), however, power functions with exponents $n_P < 1$ better fitted the relationship. Thus, (8.6) may be modified for this special effect as follows:

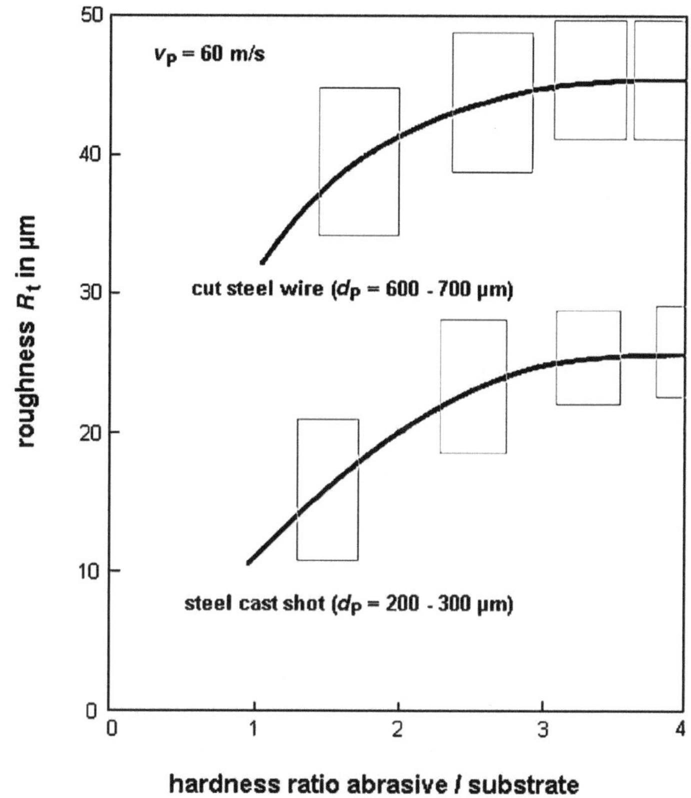

Fig. 8.49 Effects of abrasive type and abrasive hardness on roughness (Weidenhaupt, 1970)

$$R \propto d_P^{f(H_M)} \tag{8.6a}$$
$$n_P = f(H_M)$$

The value of the function f(H_M) increases if substrate hardness decreases. For f(H_M) = 1, the relationship equals (8.5). Wheel blast cleaning results for the descaling of steel, Weidenhaupt (1970) and results from Kniewald (1993) on copper substrates suggested that grit size effects were more pronounced for higher grit impact velocities. Slutzky et al. (1988) performed a statistical study into steel grit size effects on selected roughness parameters; results are listed in Table 8.29. Prazak

Table 8.29 Linear regressions ($y = ax+b$) between abrasive particle size and roughness parameters (Slutzky et al., 1988); abrasive: steel grit, substrate: low-carbon steel, preparation grade: Sa 2½

Roughness value	Correlation equation	Correlation coefficient
R_{max}	$y = 0.041x + 9.512$	0.930
R_Z	$y = 0.031x + 7.581$	0.931
R_a	$y = 0.006x + 1.028$	0.936

and Eremias (1972) performed test in order to investigate abrasive size effects on the relative roughness factor given by (8.2). Their results are listed in Table 8.30. It can be seen that the values for the relative roughness factor increased with an increase in abrasive particle size.

The effect of abrasive particle diameter on the peak count was investigated by Keane et al. (1976). The authors found that the peak count slightly decreased with an increase in abrasive particle diameter, whereas roughness notably increased if larger abrasive particles were used. This example illustrates again the complex relationship between substrate topography features and abrasive particle size.

Weidenhaupt (1970) investigated effects of abrasive particle shape on substrate roughness. If cut steel wire was utilised as a grit material for descaling, cylindrical particles formed deeper profiles than spherical particles at equal impact velocities. Results of this investigation are plotted in Fig. 8.49. Weidenhaupt (1970) also found the following relationship between substrate roughness and abrasive particle kinetic energy: $R_t \propto E_P^{n_E}$. The power exponent was independent of abrasive particle size ($d_P = 300$–$800\,\mu$m), but showed a weak dependence on the abrasive particle shape. For round cut steel wire, $n_E = 0.343$; for cylindrical cut steel wire, $n_E = 0.337$. A theoretical value, derived by Weidenhaupt (1970), is $n_E = 0.5$.

Cross-sections, cut through blast cleaned steel substrates, are shown in Fig. 8.50. The effect of the abrasive types on the profile can be recognised clearly. Corundum and steel grit, for example, produced rather irregular profiles with a pronounced peak-valley structure as illustrated in Fig. 8.50b, whereas glass beads and plastics abrasives formed smooth, regular profiles as illustrated in Fig. 8.50a. Uhlmann et al. (2003) performed a study about the effects of abrasive materials (chilled cast, corundum, plastics and glass beads) on the roughness of different substrate materials. Corundum produced highest roughness values for all substrate materials, but the roughness for an ordinary construction steel was much higher than for a chromium–nickel steel. Martin (1997) compared glass beads, corundum and steel grit for the preparation of pipeline steel, and he found that steel grit formed the deepest profile, followed by corundum and glass beads. Spherical abrasive materials always produced rather shallow profiles.

Yankee et al. (1991) highlighted the influence of the abrasive particle type on the roughness characteristics of blast cleaned profiles. They found notable differences in the roughness characteristics between titanium substrates impinged with silicone carbide and, respectively, aluminium oxide abrasives. Aluminium oxide particles

Table 8.30 Abrasive particle size effects of the relative roughness factor (Prazak and Eremias, 1972)

Abrasive particle diameter in µm	Relative roughness factor
Ground substrate (for comparison)	3.0
300	8.9
600	10.2
900	12.5
1,200	13.7

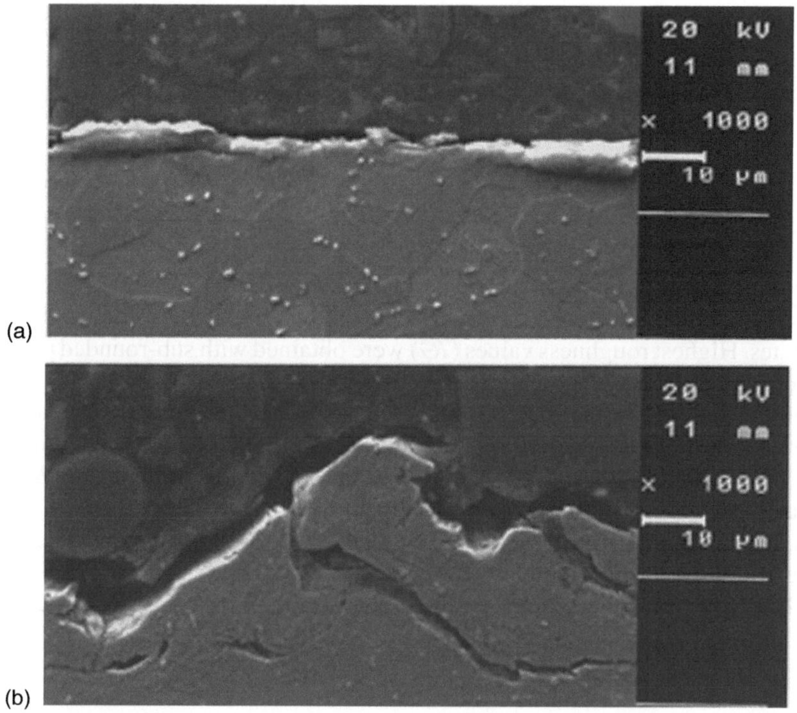

Fig. 8.50 Cross-sections, cut through blasted steel substrates, showing abrasive size effects on substrate profile (Uhlmann et al., 2003); test conditions: $p = 0.6\,\text{MPa}$; $\varphi = 90°$; $v_T = 0.4\,\text{m/min}$; $x = 150\,\text{mm}$; substrate: steel (DC01 A). **(a)** Abrasive material: Plastic pellets "Duroplast" ($d_P = 200$–$600\,\mu\text{m}$); **(b)** Abrasive: steel cast grit ($d_P = 120$–$420\,\mu\text{m}$)

appeared to produce consecutive sharp peaks and deep valleys, while silicone carbide particles produced a series of shallow peaks between deep valleys. To achieve an equal roughness on the substrate for both abrasive types, completely different process parameters needed to be adjusted. This is illustrated by the results listed in Table 8.31. Table 8.32 lists the effects of abrasive type and size on maximum roughness and peak count. It can be seen that the peak count could be notably affected if the abrasive mixture was changed.

Table 8.31 Blast cleaning parameters resulting in equivalent surface roughness R_a (Yankee et al., 1991)

Parameter	Abrasive material	
	Silicone carbide	Aluminium oxide
Air pressure in MPa	0.65	0.34
Stand-off distance in mm	76	127
Blasting angle in °	60	90
Blasting time in s	90	20
Average roughness in μm	3.49	3.50

Table 8.32 Effects of abrasive type and size on profile parameters (Roper et al., 2006)

Abrasive	R_{max} in µm	Peak count in peaks/cm
G-40 steel grit	50–112	48–72
G-25 steel grit	75–137	36–48
G-18 steel grit	100–175	20–30
20/40 flint silica sand	25–87	52–88
20/40 boiler slag	20–75	40–72

Beitelman (2003) applied the shape designations according to Fig. 2.7 to crushed steel grit (G50) and investigated their effects on the roughness of low-carbon steel substrates. Highest roughness values (R_Z) were obtained with sub-rounded particles. Peak density dropped with an increase in particle angularity.

The effects of abrasive material recycling on the profile of blast cleaned steel substrates were investigated by Mellali et al. (1994). The authors used aluminium oxide ($d_P = 500$–$1{,}400\,\mu m$), and they found that the average roughness (R_a) continuously decreased with an increase in the number of recycling cycles (a total of five recycling steps were performed). The intensity in drop of roughness depended on the original abrasive diameter; it was most severe for the largest abrasive particles. This result can be explained by the higher friability of the larger particles (see Sect. 2.9.2).

8.6.3.6 Effects of Abrasive Material Hardness

The hardness of the abrasive material has a moderate effect on the roughness. A metallic abrasive material should be at least four points harder on the Rockwell C scale (HRC) than the substrate. This restriction is due to the deformation of abrasive materials with lower hardness values during impact. A steel grit with a hardness of $H_P = 45$ HRC, for example, is known to quickly round up if used for the blast cleaning of steel substrates (Roper et al. 2006). It is, therefore, not the absolute hardness of the abrasive material, but rather the ratio between abrasive material hardness and target material hardness, which determines the roughness. Illustrative examples are provided in Fig. 8.49. The values for the roughness increased with an increase in the hardness ratio abrasive/substrate. The increase was very pronounced in the range of low values for the hardness ratio, but less intense in the range of higher values. If the hardness ratio had very high values (>3), any further increase in abrasive material hardness did not affect the substrate roughness at all.

8.6.3.7 Effects of Specific Abrasive Rate

Effects of specific abrasive rate (abrasive mass per blast cleaned area) are cited by Gesell (1973). It was shown that roughness had a maximum at moderate values for the specific abrasive rate (between $m_S = 4$ and $8\,g/cm^2$). For lower or higher values of the specific abrasive rate, roughness values dropped. The exact optimum

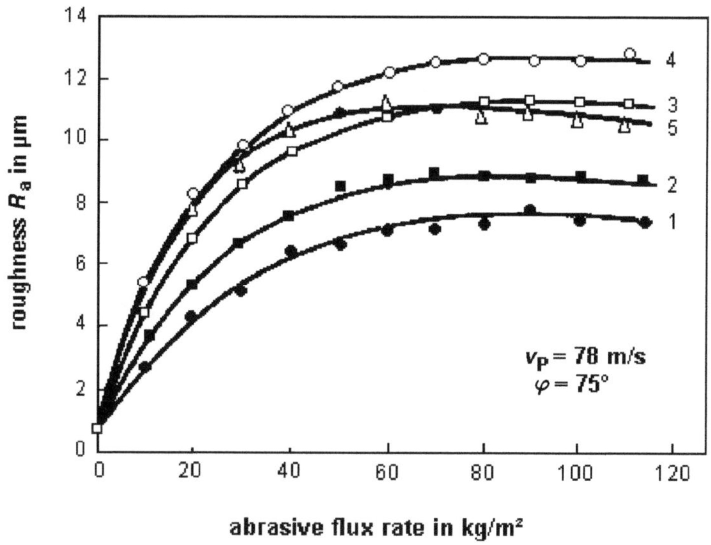

Fig. 8.51 Effects of specific abrasive rate on substrate roughness (Kniewald, 1993). Abrasive material: 1 – steel shot ($d_P = 560\,\mu m$); 2 – steel shot ($d_P = 710\,\mu m$); 3 – steel shot ($d_P = 900\,\mu m$); 4 – steel shot ($d_P = 1{,}120\,\mu m$); 5 – corundum ($d_P = 1{,}120\,\mu m$)

depended on abrasive size. Kniewald (1993) investigated the effect of specific abrasive rates up to $m_S = 120\,kg/m^2$ on the roughness of steel substrates treated with steel grit and aluminium oxide. Results of this study are displayed in Fig. 8.51. Whereas average roughness (R_a) increased rapidly in the range of low specific abrasive rates, it approached a saturation level at higher rates. The point where the saturation started, was the point where the most effective overlap of impact craters occurred. Its location depended on the abrasive type and size. The saturation level was quickly reached for fine-grained steel grit and aluminium oxide. For the aluminium oxide, roughness even seemed to drop for the highest specific abrasive mass values. Values in excess of $m_S = 60\,kg/m^2$ did not lead to any further increase in surface profile.

Minaki et al. (2004) utilised rather small abrasive mass flow rates ($\dot{m}_P =$ 50–300 g/min, aluminium oxide, mesh 700, $p = 0.15$–0.4 MPa, $\varphi = 90\,^\circ$, $d_N =$ 8 mm), and they found that the roughness (R_a) featured maximum values at moderate values for the abrasive mass flow rate (at about $\dot{m}_P = 100$ g/min).

8.6.3.8 Effects of Blasting Time

Wigren (1988) introduced a parameter "blasting time", which he defined as follows:

$$t_B = \frac{3.2 \cdot r_J^2 \cdot n_s}{\pi \cdot V_T \cdot \phi_F} \tag{8.7}$$

In this equation, t_B is the blasting time in s, r_J is the radius of the hit area (jet radius)

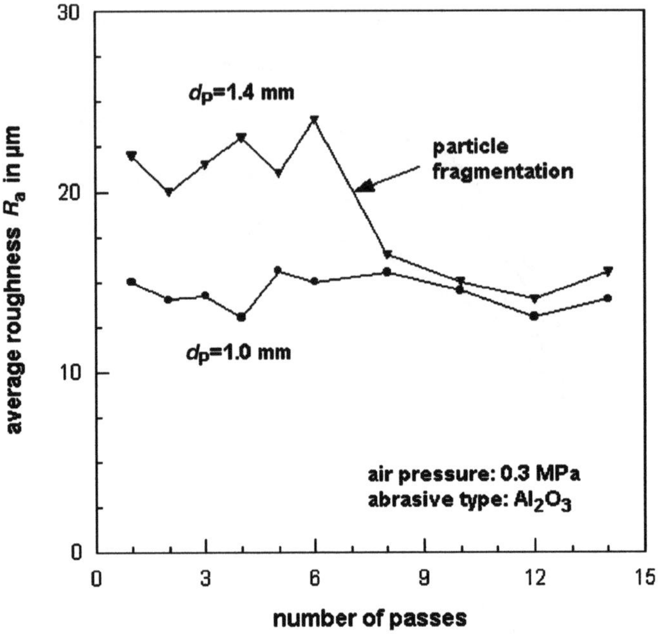

Fig. 8.52 Effects of number of cleaning steps on substrate profile (Mellali et al., 1994)

in mm, n_S is the number of passes, ϕ_F is the diameter of fixture in mm and v_T is the traverse rate in mm/s. Roughness (R_a) increased very quickly for short blasting times between $t_B = 2.5$ and 3.0 s, and it then rested at a certain saturation level, or even slightly dropped. Any further increase in blasting time did not add profile, but only an increase in grit embedment took place (see Sect. 8.6.5). Saturation effects were also reported by Celik et al. (1999) for the blast cleaning of stainless steel with aluminium oxide, and by Jones and Gardos (1971) for the blast cleaning of stainless steel with garnet. Mellali et al. (1994) observed the effect illustrated in Fig. 8.52. Average roughness (R_a) dropped suddenly at a certain number of cleaning passes (corresponds to blasting time), if rather coarse abrasive particles were used. This phenomenon can be explained through particle comminution effects. The coarse particles were crushed during the first blasting passes, and their grain size was reduced (see Sect. 2.9.2). In turn, roughness values dropped if the substrate was impinged by the smaller particles. Mellali et al. (1994) verified this explanation through comparative sieve tests.

8.6.3.9 Effects of Substrate Material

Structure and mechanical properties of the substrate materials affect the topography formation process. Effects of different substrate materials on substrate roughness are depicted in Table 8.33, where it can be seen that hot-rolled steel allowed higher roughness values compared with cold-rolled steel. The differences in roughness led

Table 8.33 Effects of target steel type on roughness (Sancaktar and Gomatam, 2001). Air pressure: 0.55 MPa; abrasive: aluminium oxide #54

Steel type	Roughness value in μm		
	R_a	R_{max}	R_Z
Cold-rolled steel	2.4	23.5	18.9
Hot-rolled steel	3.9	43.8	28.7

to differences in the strength of adhesive joints. Whereas the strength increased up to +51% for joints of cold-rolled steel, it improved up to +100% for joints of hot-rolled steel (Sancaktar and Gomatam, 2001) (values related to untreated substrates).

Uhlmann et al. (2003) investigated the roughness of three metal substrates, blast cleaned with different abrasive materials. The roughness was always highest for an ordinary construction steel, followed by that of an aluminium alloy and a chromium–nickel steel. Wigren (1988) depicted an almost reverse linear relationship between the average roughness of blast cleaned metal substrates and their values for Young's modulus: the higher Young's modulus, the lower the roughness values. This effect was also observed by Mellali et al. (1994), who impinged different metal substrates with aluminium oxide particles, for the relationship between Young's modulus and average roughness (R_a).

Keane et al. (1976) investigated the effects of different material composition of steel plates (caused by different heat treatment regimes) on their influence on the roughness after blast cleaning. They found that small variations in the composition of the steels did not affect the profile height if the substrate quality was high after blast cleaning (Sa 2½, Sa 3). If the substrate quality was lower (Sa 2), even slight deviations in the steel composition did affect the values for the profile height.

Siegmann and Brown (1998) adapted a fractal parameter, called "area-scale fractal complexity" (ASFC), which was found to be linearly related to the arithmetic roughness. The authors could show that this profile parameter decreased according to a reverse linear relationship if hardness of the substrate materials increased. Thus, roughness decreased with rising substrate material hardness. Weidenhaupt (1970) performed blast wheel cleaning tests with cast shot and wire cut, and he noted a certain relationship between the hardness ratio abrasive/substrate and the roughness. If the hardness ratio exceeded a value of $H_p/H_M = 3$, no further increase in substrate roughness occurred (see Fig. 8.49). Abukawa et al. (2004) performed blast cleaning tests on steel samples with aluminium oxide particles, and they found that a lower substrate hardness promoted higher roughness values (R_a). This trend was also observed by Mellali et al. (1994). These results are in agreement with the model of Sorokin et al. (1983) for metals. The authors derived a relationship: $R \propto H_M^{-1/2}$. Abukawa et al. (2004) noted, however, that a certain steel did not follow the above-mentioned trend, and they concluded that other hardness-related factors (morphology, heat treatment regime) should be considered. Jones and Gardos (1971) reported interesting relationships between original substrate roughness, substrate roughness and final substrate roughness. They found that the original roughness affected the roughness after blast cleaning if hard stainless steel was treated. For the treatment of soft stainless steel, not such effects could be determined.

Karpinos et al. (1979), who propelled cast iron shot ($d_P = 400$–$750\,\mu m$) on steel samples, noted an influence of the stand-off distance on the effects of target material variations. Whereas the roughness (R_Z) was higher for aluminium substrates compared with copper substrates for low stand-off distances, the trend was opposite for longer stand-off distances.

Weidenhaupt (1970) noted effects of scale composition on the roughness values of blast cleaned iron metals. The values for the roughness (R_t) were rather low for FeO; moderate for a mixture Fe_3O_4/FeO; rather high for Fe_3O_4. The initial condition of the steel also affects roughness. Heavily weathered or corroded plates, for example, had relatively high surface profiles after blast cleaning.

8.6.3.10 Effects of Surface Preparation Grade

The surface preparation grade characterises the severity of the substrate treatment, and it can be assumed that changes in the surface preparation grade may be related to changes in the profile parameters. Keane et al. (1976) reported some results on the blast cleaning of steel substrates with steel grit, respectively steel shot. They found that the roughness (profile height) very slightly increased if surface preparation degree improved. The values for the roughness were highest for Sa 2 and lowest for Sa 3, either shot or grit has been used, but the trends were statistically insignificant. The peak count of the profile (in number of peaks per unit length) was independent of the surface preparation grade.

8.6.3.11 Effects of Accessibility

Bullard et al. (2002) investigated effects of accessibility to a structure on profile parameters. The roughness of surfaces in gaps with widths between 0.31 and 2.5 cm was about 85% of the values generated during "normal" blast cleaning procedures. The surface profile fell within a typical specification range between 37 and 67 μm. Similarly, the average peak density was approximately 87% of the values generated during "normal" blast cleaning processes.

8.6.3.12 Statistical Assessment Models

Statistically designed experiments were performed by Varacalle et al. (1995, 2006) in order to assess the effects of air pressure, stand-off distance, blasting angle, abrasive material and blasting machine type on the roughness of steel substrates. For SiO_2 as abrasive medium, Varacalle et al. (1995) derived the following regression equation:

$$R_Z = 7.14 - 0.085 \cdot x + 0.61 \cdot p - 0.79 \cdot x \cdot p \tag{8.8}$$

In this equation, R_Z is given in microns; x is given in inch and p is given in ψ. In a subsequent study, the authors derived the following regression equation for the blast cleaning of low-carbon steel with different abrasive materials (Varacalle et al., 2006):

$$R_Z = C_1 + C_2 \cdot x + C_3 \cdot p + C_4 \cdot x^2 + C_5 \cdot p^2 + C_6 \cdot x \cdot p \tag{8.9}$$

In this equation, R_Z is given in 10^{-2} cm; x is given in cm and p is given in kPa. Values for the regression parameters C_1 to C_6 are listed in Table 8.34 for a number of abrasive materials.

Day et al. (2005) performed a statistical analysis on the effect of certain process parameters on the roughness and derived the following relationship:

$$R = -0.33 \cdot G_N + 0.24 \cdot p + 0.44 \cdot n_s + 2.87 \cdot X + 0.12 \cdot \varphi \tag{8.10}$$

In this equation, the grit number (G_N) is given in mesh; p is given in psi; x is given in inch and φ is given in degrees.

8.6.4 Height Distribution Parameters

Height distribution parameters represent the symmetry and sharpness of the profile. Because of the nature of the material removal process, the profiles of blast cleaned surfaces very often feature a Gaussian profile type. Parameters which characterise symmetry and sharpness of a profile include skew and kurtosis. Figure 8.53 shows plots of skew and kurtosis against the average roughness for four different samples. The graph proves that the mean values for skew and kurtosis were closely to the theoretical values for a Gaussian surface type (which are "0" for skew and "3" for kurtosis).

The results plotted in Fig. 8.53 show further that overblasting did not produce a Gaussian surface. Although the skew values remained at about zero, the kurtosis values were higher than 3, which was due to the higher portion of flat areas. A high kurtosis value is, therefore, indicative of overblasting effects.

8.6.5 Profiles of "Overblasted" Steel Substrates

Further interesting aspects associated with blast cleaning are illustrated in Figs. 8.54 and 8.55. Figure 8.54 shows the influence of multiple blast cleaning (overblasting) on roughness values of a steel substrates. The virgin steel is denoted "0", blast cleaned steel is denoted "I" and twice blast cleaned steel is denoted "II". As expected, a single blast cleaning step (as performed during new construction jobs) increased any roughness parameter. The second blast cleaning step (as performed during the stripping of worn coatings or rust), however, again decreased the roughness. This overblasting caused the surface to have a high number of flat regions, a lower peak to valley height and a significant number of laps and tears due to folding and plastic deformation. These phenomena were verified by comparative SEM studies by Momber and Wong (2005a). Other authors (Griffith, 2001) described similar phenomena. An example is provided in Fig. 8.55. The polar plots in this

Table 8.34 Regression parameters for (8.9) (Varacalle et al., 2006)

Abrasive material	Regression parameter					
	C_1	C_2	C_3	C_4	C_5	C_6
HG 16	-7.65×10^{-3}	2.9×10^{-3}	2.29×10^{-4}	-1.88×10^{-4}	-8.76×10^{-7}	1.20×10^{-5}
HG 18	-7.37×10^{-3}	2.29×10^{-3}	2.29×10^{-4}	-1.88×10^{-4}	-8.76×10^{-7}	-1.19×10^{-5}
HG 25	-8.33×10^{-3}	2.49×10^{-3}	2.29×10^{-4}	-1.88×10^{-4}	-8.76×10^{-7}	-1.20×10^{-5}
HG 40	-9.58×10^{-3}	2.44×10^{-3}	2.24×10^{-4}	-1.88×10^{-4}	-8.76×10^{-7}	-1.20×10^{-5}
Copper slag	2.79×10^{-3}	2.21×10^{-4}	1.07×10^{-4}	1.10×10^{-5}	-4.60×10^{-7}	-7.72×10^{-6}
Coal slag	-3.40×10^{-3}	1.02×10^{-3}	1.17×10^{-4}	1.10×10^{-5}	4.60×10^{-7}	-7.72×10^{-6}
Chilled iron	-1.52×10^{-3}	7.37×10^{-4}	1.14×10^{-4}	1.11×10^{-5}	-4.60×10^{-7}	-7.72×10^{-6}

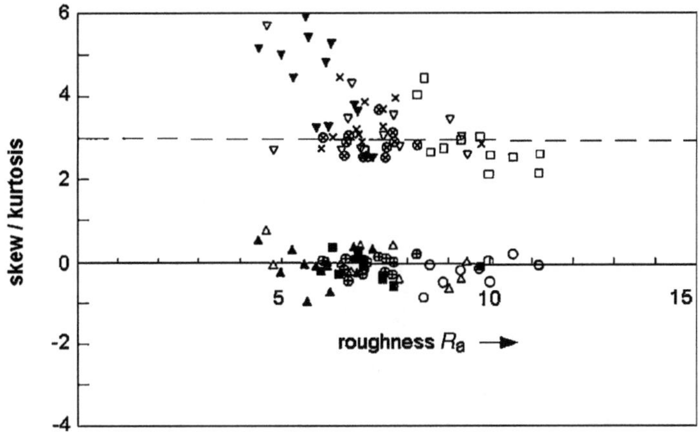

Fig. 8.53 Relationships between blast cleaning conditions, roughness and profile distribution parameters (Griffith et al., 1996). Legend: Δ skew (5.5 µm); ∇ kurtosis (5.5 µm); ○ skew (10 µm); □ kurtosis (10 µm); ■ skew (6.5 µm); x kurtosis (6.5 µm); ⊕ skew (7.5 µm); ⊗ kurtosis (7.5 µm); ▲ skew (overblasted); ▼ kurtosis (overblasted)

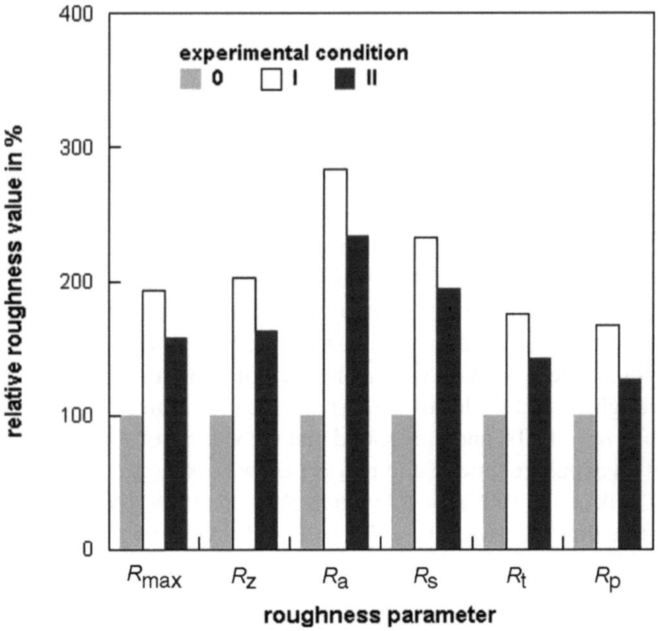

Fig. 8.54 Effects of overblasting on profile roughness parameters (Momber and Wong, 2005a). Experimental condition: 0 – untreated; I – one blast cleaning step; II – two blast cleaning steps; substrate: low-carbon steel

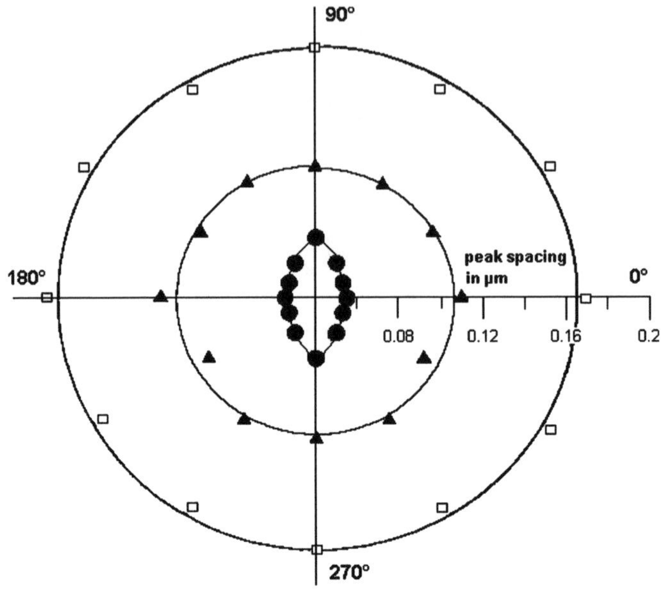

Fig. 8.55 Overblasting effects on peak spacing (Griffith, 2001). Legend: • ground sheet, ▲ overblasted, □ correctly blasted

figure show the effects of blast cleaning steps on the peak spacing. Values for peak spacing were about $S_R = 0.17\,\mu m$ after the first blast cleaning step, but they reduced down to about $S_R = 0.1\,\mu m$ after a second blast cleaning step. Oppermann (1993), who discussed test results obtained on steel samples impinged with steel shot, found that the roughness (R_Z) of the substrate was a function of the area coverage. For an optimum value of the area coverage, the roughness exhibited maximum values.

Siegmann and Brown (1998, 2002) found that roughness increased as a steel substrate was blast cleaned five times compared with a substrate that was blast cleaned once. If, however, the substrate was blast cleaned 10 times, roughness decreased again. Samples of these tests as well as images of generated profiles are shown in Fig. 8.56. Broughton and Lodeiro (2002) blast cleaned aluminium samples at exposure times up to $t_B = 120$ s, and they found that the values for R_a as well as R_q started to decrease if an exposure time of about $t_B = 60$ s was exceeded. Similar results were obtained by Celik et al. (1999) for R_a-values. Wigren (1988) found even much lower critical exposure times, between $t_B = 2.5$ and 3 s. If exposure time increased further, the average roughness of numerous metal alloys started to drop, whereas the levels of grit embedment increased further. There existed a balance between roughness, abrasive embedment and blast cleaning parameters. To achieve high roughness and low percentage of abrasive embedment, higher air pressures and shorter exposure times are preferred over lower air pressures and longer exposure times. Further examples which illustrated these relationships are shown in Figs. 8.28 and 8.29.

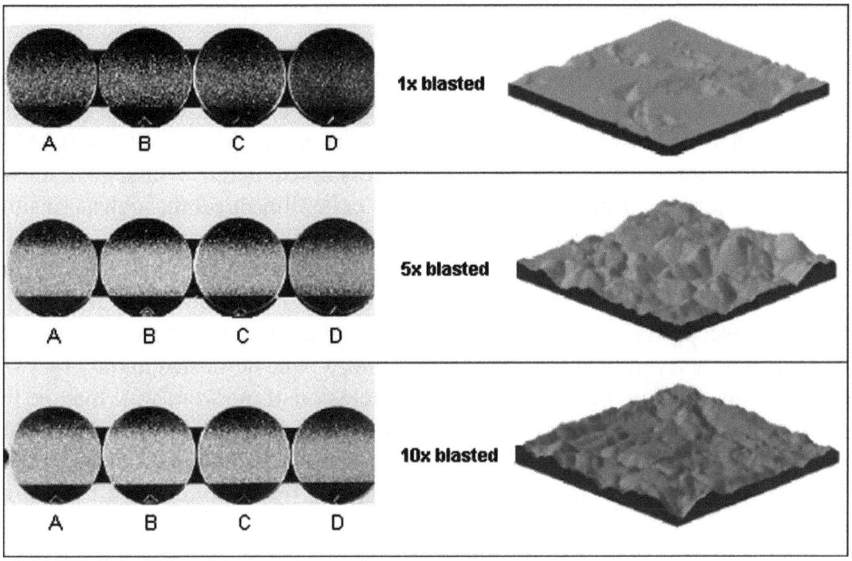

Fig. 8.56 Images of overblasted steel substrates (Siegmann and Brown, 2002)

8.7 Surface Integrity

8.7.1 Introduction

Substrate surface integrity is characterised by near-surface properties of the substrate materials, which may include the following:

- hardness;
- residual stresses;
- fatigue limit;
- stress–strain behaviour;
- metallurgical properties;
- chemical surface state.

Scholtes and Vöhringer (1993) subdivided the consequences of blast cleaning applications on metal surfaces into the following categories:

- changes in dimension;
- changes in topography;
- generation of, and changes in, the number of lattice disturbances (dislocations);
- changes in residual stress;
- changes in phase composition;
- changes in texture condition;
- crack formation;
- changes in density.

The authors also provided a comprehensive review about the effects of blast cleaning applications on these processes.

Guan et al. (2005) performed X-ray diffraction (XRD) and TEM measurements on blast cleaned aluminium samples. The samples were blast cleaned with silica particles with sizes between $d_P = 50$ and 70 µm at an air pressure of p = 0.3 MPa, and they were subsequently annealed. The authors noted a gradual change in the target material grain size from a near-surface nano-crystalline layer through a transition zone to the core of the material samples. Jiang et al. (2006) performed blast cleaning tests on titanium samples with silica grit particles with sizes between $d_p = 200$ and 300 µm at a rather high air pressure of $p = 2.1$ MPa. They applied high-resolution optical microscopy for structure assessment, and they distinguished three separate material zones: a severely deformed surface zone, a zone deformed mainly by twinning and an un-deformed substrate zone. A conclusion of the work was, that the two upper regions were likely responsible for the enhancement of near-surface material properties, namely fatigue, wear resistance and corrosion resistance. Twinning in the near-surface region blast cleaned steel panels was also reported by Klinger et al. (2002).

There is evidence in the engineering literature that the mechanical state of metallic substrates affects the mechanical properties of applied coatings. Results obtained by Osawa et al. (2005), for example, indicated that the delamination resistance of WC-cermet coatings during impact loading depended on hardness and degree of work hardening of substrate materials. Substrates with higher work-hardening coefficients indicated a higher delamination resistance of the coatings.

8.7.2 Substrate Hardness

Modifications in substrate hardness due to blast cleaning were reported by several authors (Remmelts, 1969; Doherty (1974); Leistikow and Kraft, 1974; Bond and Martin, 1984; Tosha and Iida, 1990; Fang and Chuang, 1999; Rhouma et al., 2001; Momber and Wong, 2005a; Jiang et al., 2006). Fang and Chuang (1999) investigated the surface properties of numerous metallic building materials after blast cleaning with angular silicone carbide abrasives. The particle velocity was rather low ($v_P = 30$ m/s). Results of Vickers hardness measurements are shown in Fig. 8.57. It can be seen that surface treatment by blast cleaning altered the hardness. The relative change was highest for the 6063-Al alloy. Interestingly, hardness was almost unaffected after blast cleaning for the weathering steel (ARC-TEN). This material, however, featured an already high initial hardness. Fang and Chuang (1999) also found that the final Vickers hardness depended on blasting angle; it increased if blasting angle rose. It was also found that Vickers hardness of the substrate material increased for higher erosion rates. In a log–log plot, this relationship was reciprocal (Fang and Chuang, 1999). Reasons for hardness modification are mainly plastic deformations of impinged sections, and the embedment of hard abrasive particles in the surface. The latter effect can be excluded during the measurements if cross-sections of blast cleaned samples are inspected.

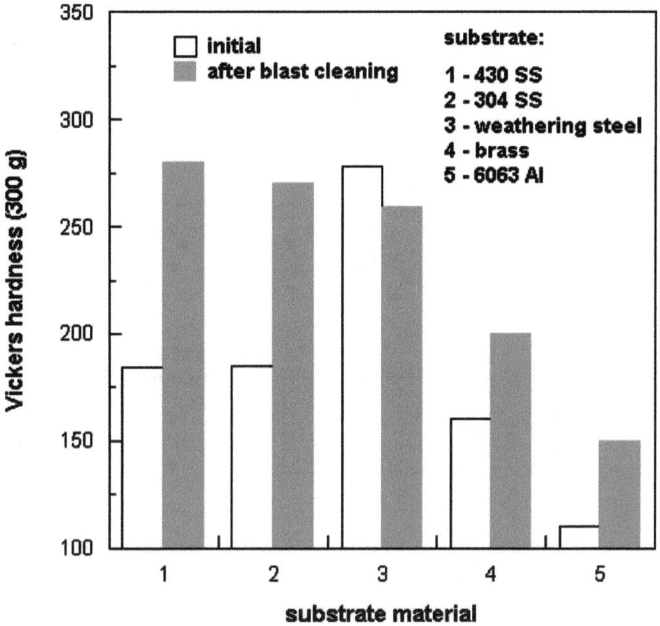

Fig. 8.57 Changes in micro-hardness due to blast cleaning (Fang and Chuang, 1999)

Effects of blast cleaning on the micro-hardness of low-carbon steel were investigated by Momber and Wong (2005a). Results of hardness measurements performed on cross-sections are shown in Fig. 8.58. Average values and standard deviations for the hardness are listed in Table 8.35. It was found that micro-hardness of the near-surface zone increased after blast cleaning. From Fig. 8.58, a depth of the hardened layer of at least 80 μm could be concluded. The increase in hardness was about +20% for one blast cleaning step, and it was about +50% for two blast cleaning steps. Remmelts (1969) published very similar results for blast cleaned steel substrates. He additionally found that larger abrasive particles had a more pronounced effect on surface hardening. The effect of abrasive particle size vanished at distances of about 250 μm. A hardness increase in the near-surface range of steel due to blast cleaning was noted by Bond and Martin (1984), and a hardness increase in the near-surface range of titanium due to blast cleaning was noted by Jiang et al. (2006). The latter authors explained the surface hardening effect by assuming the formation of a nano-crystalline surface layer in course of the blast cleaning process.

Table 8.35 Hardness variation of low-carbon steel due to blast cleaning with alumina abrasives (Momber and Wong, 2005a)

Number of blast cleaning steps	Vickers hardness in kg/mm^2	
	Average	Standard deviation
0	126	8
1	149	13
2	191	17

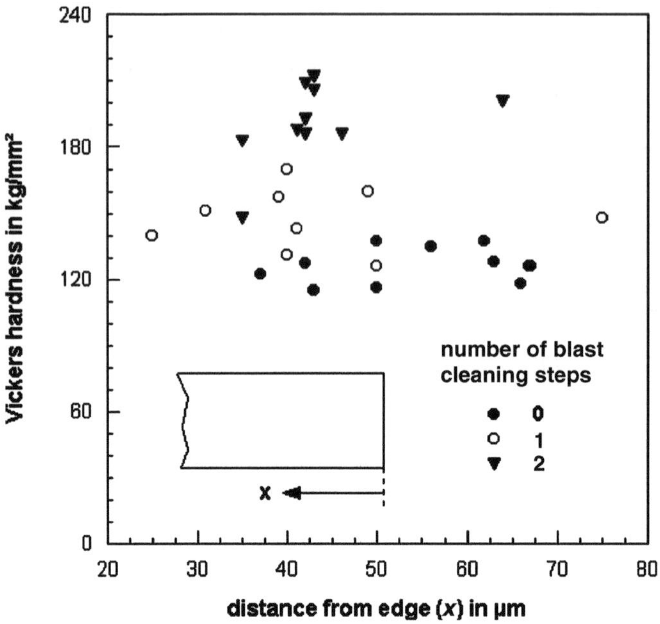

Fig. 8.58 Effects of blast cleaning on near-surface micro-hardness of low-carbon steel (Momber and Wong, 2005a)

Tosha and Iida (1990) investigated effects of abrasive particle shape on hardness modification, and they could show that the surface hardness after blast cleaning was lower than that after shot peening. However, the depths of work-hardening layers produced due to blast cleaning were larger than those produced due to shot peening. The general surface hardness distributions were independent of substrate material (steel, respectively titanium).

The effects of varying abrasive particle sizes on the micro-hardness of near-surface layers of austenitic stainless steel were evaluated by Rhouma et al. (2001). The authors used quartz particles with three different particle size classes ($d_P < 50\,\mu$m; $d_p = 80$–$120\,\mu$m; $d_P = 120$–$200\,\mu$m). Both the depth of the cold worked layer and the level of hardness (HV 50) increased with an increase in the abrasive particle size. The largest particles ($d_p = 200\,\mu$m) provided an increase in hardness up to $H_M = 350$ HV, and they extended the hardened layer to a depth of $350\,\mu$m.

Tosha and Iida (1990) investigated the effects of process parameters on surface hardening. Variations in blasting angles did not notably affect hardness distributions in titanium; an increase in blasting angle only slightly decreased the size of the affected near-surface zone. Maximum hardness as well as thickness of the hardened layers exhibited a pronounced linear relationship to the kinetic energy of an impinging abrasive particle.

8.7.3 Residual Stresses

Peening is known to generate residual stresses in the near-surface region of metals. A very thorough review on the formation of residual stresses during shot peening is given by Herzog et al. (1996).

Blast cleaning can also alter the stress state in the near-surface zone of metal substrates. A Cr–Mo steel, for example, with an initial residual compressive stress value of $\sigma_R = 80\,\text{MPa}$, featured residual stresses between $\sigma_R = 500$ and $600\,\text{MPa}$ after it was blast cleaned with aluminium oxide abrasives (Guilemany et al., 1996). Residual stresses in metals impinged by cast steel particles initially (after 5–10 s blasting time) increased to high values, but dropped at longer blast cleaning times. The temporal location of the residual stress maximum depended on impact angle; it shifted to shorter blasting times for perpendicular impact (Tosha and Iida, 1990). Jiang et al. (2006) measured the depths of zones of residual stresses in thin aluminium samples, blast cleaned with silica oxide ($d_P = 200$–$300\,\mu\text{m}$, $p = 0.3\,\text{MPa}$), and they reported a depth of about $70\,\mu\text{m}$, whereby the maximum residual stress was measured in a depth of about $10\,\mu\text{m}$. Otsubo et al. (2003) noted the formation of compressive residual stresses of $\sigma_R = 600\,\text{MPa}$ at a depth between 50 and $100\,\mu\text{m}$ in austenitic stainless steel. The authors suggested that the formation of a martensite phase in that area was related to this effect. Subsequent annealing released the residual stresses in the blast cleaned specimens.

Effects of blast cleaning parameters on residual surface stresses were investigated by Andziak and Brezezinski (1999), Badawi et al. (1986), Birley and Owens (1979), Da Silva Rocha et al. (2003), Guilemany et al. (1996), Ishikawa and Tobe (2003) and Zinn et al. (2002). Results of investigations of Andziak and Brezezinski (1999) are shown in Fig. 8.59. It can be recognized that the amplitude of the residual stress depended on abrasive material. Spherical abrasives, namely glass beads, generated higher residual stresses compared with irregular aluminium oxide particles. If steel cast particles were utilised, shot particles generated notably higher residual stresses compared with steel grit particles (Tosha and Iida, 1990). Figure 8.60 illustrates the effects of blasting angle variations on residual stresses of a blast cleaned carbon steel substrate. The values for the residual stresses notably changed, and they exhibited a maximum at a blasting angle of $\varphi = 45°$. It was however, shown that the effect of blasting angle additionally depended on blasting time and air pressure (Guilemany et al., 1996).

Tosha and Iida (1990) showed that the magnitudes of the residual stresses depended on abrasive particle size and abrasive velocity. The larger the abrasive particle size was, the smaller were residual stresses, whether shot or grit particles were being used. Badawi et al. (1986) measured longitudinal and transversal residual stresses formed after the blast cleaning of steel substrates with aluminium oxide of different grain sizes. The results displayed in Fig. 8.61 revealed that residual stresses increased if abrasive particle size increased. Rhouma et al. (2001), who blast cleaned austenitic stainless steel with quartz particles ($d_p = 50$–$200\,\mu\text{m}$), could not find a definite effect of abrasive size on stress amplitudes. Effects of particle impact velocity ($v_P = 15$ and $35\,\text{m/s}$) depended on abrasive particle shape. For grit particles,

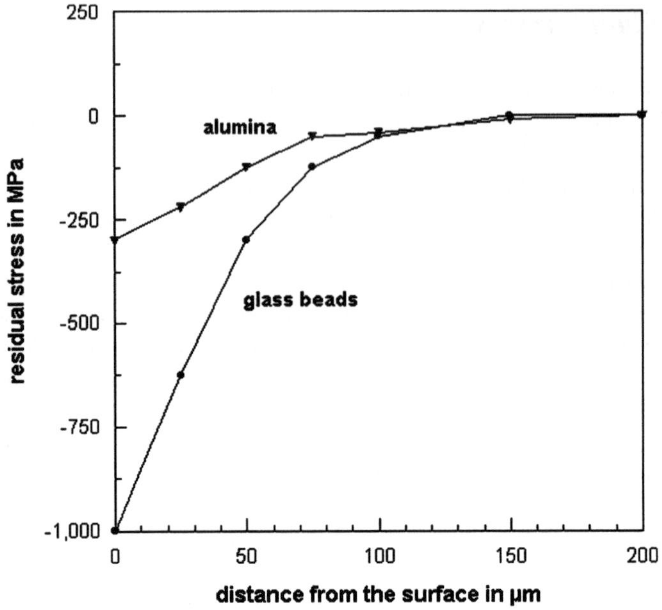

Fig. 8.59 Effects of abrasive type on residual stresses in stainless steel (Andziak and Brezezinski, 1999)

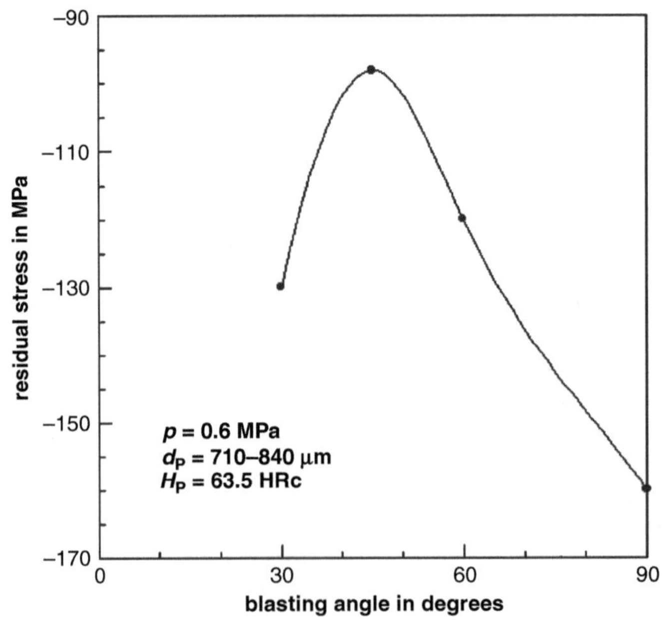

Fig. 8.60 Effects of blasting angle on residual stresses (Ishikawa and Tobe, 2003)

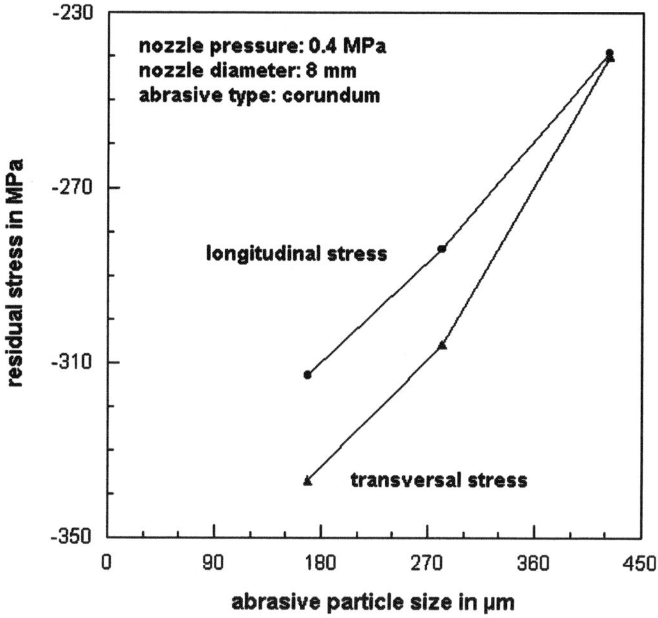

Fig. 8.61 Effects of abrasive size on residual stresses (Badawi et al., 1986)

residual stress decreased if particle velocity increased. For shot particles, the opposite trend occurred, whereas the significance of the velocity effects was rather low. Birley and Owens measured residual stresses after the blast cleaning of an aluminium alloy, and they found that the amplitude of the stresses increased if both air pressure and abrasive particle (aluminium oxide) diameter increased. Changes in impact angle had only marginal effects on the stress amplitude.

The intensities of residual stresses in the near-surface zone of a CrMo-steel, blast cleaned with aluminium oxide, were found to decrease with an increase in blasting time as well as with a decrease in air pressure. An increase in stand-off distance lead to a slight decrease in residual stresses for 45° blasting angles (Guilemany et al., 1996).

Zinn et al. (2002) investigated the residual stress depth distribution of 42CrMo4 steels, blast cleaned with steel shot at moderate impact velocities ($v_p = 25$–45 m/s), and they found that the depth of the stressed layer increased with an increase in impact velocity. Results obtained by Schwarzer et al. (2002) could prove this trend for higher impact velocities ($v_P = 20$–80 m/s). The authors also performed numerical simulations of the peening process, and they showed that the depth of the residual stress zone increased with an increase in shot diameter and dropped for higher impact angles.

Petit-Renaud (2002) performed a statistical analysis for air pressure driven peening processes and derived statistical models. For the estimation of the maximum residual compressive stress generated in a steel after peening, he derived the following model:

$$\sigma_{\mathrm{Rmax}} = C_1 + C_2 \cdot t_B + C_3 \cdot d_N + C_4 \cdot p + C_5 \cdot \varphi + C_6 \cdot \dot{m}_p + C_7 \cdot p^2 + C_8 \cdot t_B \cdot p + C_9 \cdot d_N \cdot \dot{m}_p \quad (8.11)$$

For the estimation of the depth where the maximum residual compressive stress is generated in a steel after peening, Petit-Renaud (2002) derived the following model:

$$h(\sigma_{\mathrm{Rmax}}) = C_1 + C_2 \cdot t_B + C_3 \cdot p + C_4 \cdot x + C_5 \cdot \varphi + C_6 \cdot \dot{m}_p + C_7 \cdot \varphi^2 + C_8 \cdot t_B \cdot p + C_9 \cdot p \cdot \varphi + C_{10} \cdot x \cdot \varphi \quad (8.12)$$

The values for the constants C_1 to C_{10} are listed in Table 8.36. The physical units for the variables are as follows: t_B is given in s, d_N is given in inch, p is given in bar, x is given in mm, φ is given in degrees and $\dot{m}_p$ is given in kg/min.

8.7.4 Substrate Fatigue Strength

Shot peening with steel beads is known to increase fatigue strength of the substrate material by inducing compressive surface stresses. However, it can be expected that blast cleaning also affects the fatigue performance. The relationship between fatigue strength and number of cycles to failure can be expressed as follows:

$$\sigma_F \propto A_F \cdot N_F^{m_F} \quad (8.13)$$

In this equation, A_F represents the fatigue strength coefficient, and m_F represents the fatigue exponent. Both parameters depend on material properties and testing conditions. Values are listed in Table 8.38.

Effects on fatigue parameters of metal as a result of blast cleaning was reported by several authors (Strizhalo et al., 1974; Kloos and Macherauch, 1987; He et al., 1996; Ibrahim and Berndt, 1998; Hernandez et al., 2000; Jiang et al., 2006). Changes in fatigue strengths of metal wires due to blast cleaning with different

Table 8.36 Model constants for (8.11) and for (8.12); Petit-Renaud (2002)

Constant	Target parameter	
	$\sigma_{\mathrm{R\,max}}$ in MPa	$h(\sigma_{\mathrm{R\,max}})$ in µm
C_1	−1, 158	35.8
C_2	58.6	3.11
C_3	9.94	15.3
C_4	−118	−2.14
C_5	−58.3	6.46
C_6	10.2	−5.58
C_7	88.8	−5.34
C_8	17.5	3.83
C_9	26.3	4.33
C_{10}	–	−2.53

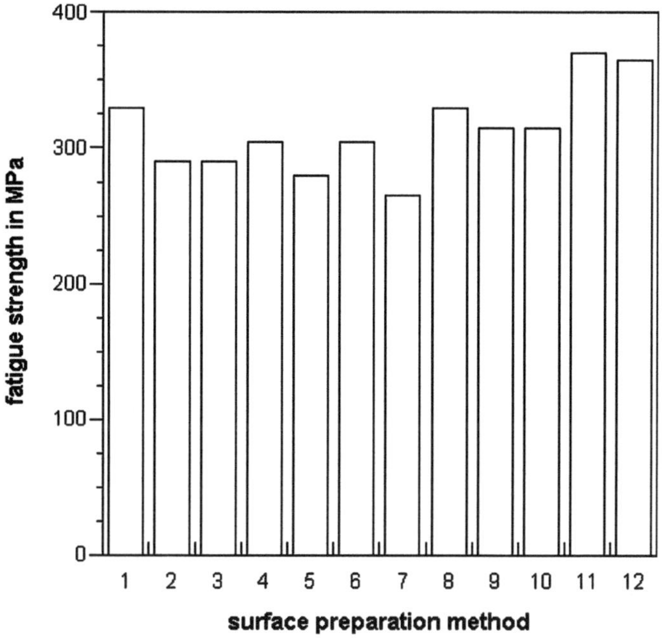

Fig. 8.62 Effects of abrasive types on fatigue strength of steel wires (Kloos and Macherauch, 1987). Surface preparation condition: 1 – as received; 2 – acid pickled; 3 – round sand; 4 – sand dust; 5 – sand dust + carborundum; 6 – sand dust ($p = 0.45$ MPa, $\varphi = 90°$); 7 – sand dust ($p = 0.45$ MPa, $\varphi = 20°$); 8 – steel shot ($d_P = 300\,\mu m$) + steel grit ($d_P = 800\,\mu m$); 9 – steel grit (75%: $d_P = 800\,\mu m$, 25%: $d_P = 300\,\mu m$); 10 – steel grit (25%: $d_P = 800\,\mu m$, 75%: $d_P = 300\,\mu m$); 11 – steel shot ($d_P = 500\,\mu m$); 12 – steel shot ($d_P = 300\,\mu m/500\,\mu m$) + steel grit ($d_P = 800\,\mu m$)

abrasives are illustrated in Fig. 8.62. Fatigue strength increased as steel shot and steel grit, respectively, were used. Blast cleaning with mineral abrasive materials did not enhance fatigue properties. Although the results applied to certain situations and a certain material, they clearly demonstrated effects of blast cleaning on fatigue behaviour of metallic substrate materials. He et al. (1996) showed for metal coatings on steel that interfacial fatigue limit generally increased if the substrates were blast cleaned. Plain blast cleaning (fatigue limit: $\sigma_F = 850\,MN/m^2$) was much more effective than grinding (fatigue limit: $\sigma_F = 450\,MN/m^2$), but a hybrid method consisting of plasma nitriding and subsequent blast cleaning (fatigue limit: $\sigma_F = 1,750$ MN/m^2) had the highest capability of fatigue limit improvement. Table 8.37 lists results of comparative fatigue experiments performed by Ibrahim and Berndt (1998) on steel after different surface preparation procedures. Blast cleaning moderately reduced fatigue life (–6%) compared with polished samples at room temperature, but fatigue life increased (+20%) after blast cleaning at elevated temperatures. For aluminium substrates, fatigue life could always be increased compared with the polished samples, at room temperature

Table 8.37 Statistics of fatigue life of SAER steel (Ibrahim and Berndt, 1998)

Specimen condition	Number of cycles to failure			Standard deviation	Coefficient of variation in %	Relative fatigue life
	Minimum	Mean	Maximum			
Polished (room temperature)	8,200	12,833	18,000	3,120	24	1
Polished (370 C)	7,200	8,366	10,700	1,098	13	0.65
Blast cleaned[a] (room temperature)	9,400	12,088	14,600	1,667	14	0.94
Blast cleaned[a] (370 C)	7,000	10,011	16,400	3,003	30	0.78
Coated WC-Co (room temperature)	248,700	660,688	1,000,100	313,015	47	51.48
Coated WC-Co (370 C)	21,000	35,688	64,800	15,868	44	2.78

[a]Abrasive type: aluminium oxide; abrasive size: grade 24, blasting pressure: 0.5 MPa

(+67%) as well as at elevated temperature (+200%). More details were provided by Ibrahim and Berndt (1998).

Jiang et al. (2006) investigated the fatigue performance of titanium which was blast cleaned with silica grit (d_P = 200–300 µm). They found that blast cleaning increased the fatigue strength of titanium by up to +11%. The fatigue strength was $\sigma_F = 270$ MPa for untreated samples and $\sigma_F = 300$ MPa for blast cleaned samples. Strizhalo et al. (1974) performed low-cycle fatigue tests (2 cycles per minute) on titanium alloy sheet samples. They subdivided a low-fatigue curve into three sections, characterising (1) no rupture, (1) quasi-static rupture and (3) fatigue rupture. The authors showed that blast cleaning ($p = 0.6$ MPa, abrasive: sand, d_p = 25–200 µm) could reduce fatigue strength as well as fatigue life, but it did not change the typical three-section-shape of the low-fatigue curves.

Hernandez et al. (2000) investigated the fatigue behaviour of an AISI 4340 steel which was blast cleaned with aluminium oxide. Some of their results are listed in Table 8.38. The values show that blast cleaning lead to a significant reduction in the fatigue properties of the material. Microscopic inspection of the blast cleaned surfaces indicated that fatigue processes were initiated at abrasive debris retained in the near-surface region of the substrate. The debris acted as nucleation sites for fatigue initiation.

Table 8.38 Fatigue parameters for AISI 4340 steel (Hernandez et al., 2000) See (8.13)

Condition	Fatigue parameter	
	A_F in MPa	m_F
Untreated	1,605	0.075
After blast cleaning[a]	1,245	0.066

[a]Blasting pressure: 0.62 MPa; abrasive type: aluminium oxide; abrasive size: grit 24

8.7.5 Sustrate Deformation Behaviour

Spindler (1958) investigated the effects of blast cleaning on the stress–strain behaviour of unalloyed steel plates, and he noted a thickness effect. For 1.0-mm thick plates, the yield point disappeared after blast cleaning; for 3.0-mm thick plates, the yield point was less dominant after blast cleaning; for 5.0-mm to 8.0-mm thick plates, no effect of the blast cleaning process could be noted.

8.7.6 Substrate Deflection

Abukawa et al. (2004) investigated the deflection (distortion) of steel samples blast cleaned with aluminium oxide particles. They introduced the idea that a stress mismatch, which occurred during blast cleaning, generated a bending moment in the substrate material. They measured deflections with a coordinate measuring machine, and they noted relationships between the intensity of deflection and blast cleaning parameters. Deflection increased if abrasive particle diameter and nozzle air pressure (thus, kinetic energy of the impinging particle) increased. The authors also found a relationship between substrate roughness and deflection.

Jiang et al. (2006) blast cleaned aluminium sheets (thickness 0.8 mm) with silica particles ($d_P = 200$–$300\,\mu m$, $p = 0.3$ MPa), and they observed that the sheet were bent. This effect was explained by the compressive stresses formed at the one side of the sheets.

8.7.7 Tribological Parameters

Guan et al. (2005) performed wear tests on blast cleaned aluminium samples. Among others, they measured adhesive forces and friction coefficients with an atomic force microscope (AFM) under a load of 10 nN. The blast cleaned sample featured the lowest values for both parameters. For higher loading forces (49 mN), when mechanical ploughing dominated the friction force, the results were different. As evidenced in Fig. 8.63a, the coefficient of friction was lower for the blast cleaned sample compared with the value for the annealed sample, but the lowest value was found for the samples which were blast cleaned and subsequently annealed. Values for the wear resistance, as manifested through the volume loss during a micro-scale wear test, are plotted in Fig. 8.63b. Blast cleaning did not improve the wear resistance, but a combination of blast cleaning and subsequent annealing could improve the wear resistance. It was assumed that the formation of a nano-crystalline surface layer was responsible for the higher performance of the substrates treated with blast cleaning and subsequent annealing.

Zhang and Zhou (1997) investigated the effects of blast cleaning on the wear resistance of diamond coatings applied to tungsten carbide substrates. The authors found that the wear rate (g/m) of a diamond coating applied to a ground surface

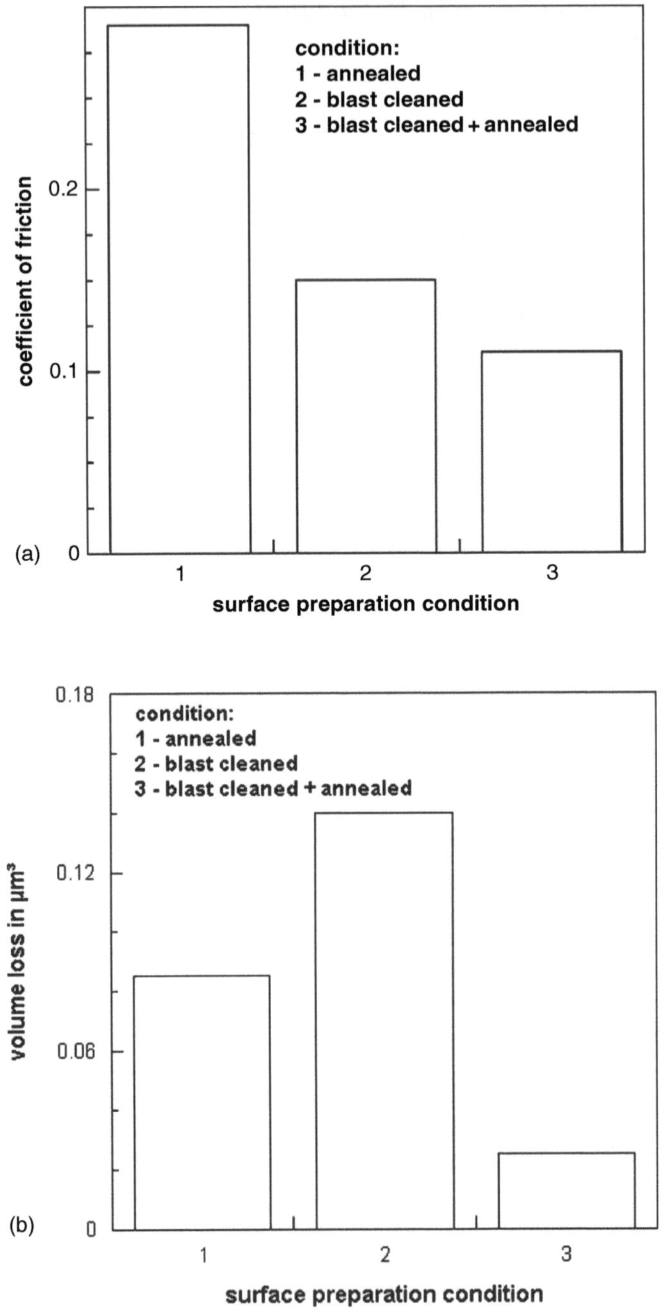

Fig. 8.63 Effects of blast cleaning on tribological properties of aluminium (Guan et al., 2005). Blast cleaning conditions: abrasive material: silica grit; abrasive size: 50–70 µm; air pressure: 0.3 MPa. (**a**) Coefficient of friction (micro-tribometer); (**b**) Volume loss during micro-scale wear test

was between 5 to 14 times higher than those of diamond coatings applied to blast cleaned (aluminium oxide, mesh 120 to 500, $p = 0.3\,\text{MPa}$) surfaces.

Da Silva Rocha et al. (2003) investigated the influence of different surface preparation methods on the performance of tool steel after plasma nitriding. Methods considered included polishing, grinding and blast cleaning (aluminium oxide, $d_P = 700$–$850\,\mu\text{m}$, $p = 0.35\,\text{MPa}$). The authors observed a significant effect of the surface state prior to nitriding concerning the flank wear of drilling tools. Tools which were blast cleaned before nitriding exhibited the best performance, respectively lowest wear. If the nitrogen concentration was high (76 vol-%), the pre-treatment of the steel with blast cleaning notably reduced torque and contact force during drilling. This latter result was attributed to the formation of an interfacial layer with a low coefficient of friction. Further results of interest included the effects of surface preparation on the diffusion of nitrogen and carbon. This issue is in detail described in the original paper.

8.7.8 Weld Seam Morphology

Blast cleaning is one of the several techniques to place oxides in the surface of steel plates to increase weld penetration. Villafuerte and Kerr (1993) performed a systematic study on the effects of blast cleaning on the grain morphology of weld seams formed by gas tungsten arc (GTA) welding. They utilised glass beads, silica and corundum particles ($d_P = 150$–$250\,\mu\text{m}$) at an air pressure of $p = 0.55\,\text{MPa}$. A surface preparation prior to welding was very influential to the solidification grain structure. For untreated steel, the presence of any equiaxed grains was generally limited to the surface of the welds. In steels that underwent a columnar-to-equiaxed transition (CET), blast cleaning not only increased the percentage of equiaxed grains at the weld surface, but also extended the equiaxed region to the interior. This effect, however, was restricted to steels having high amounts of titanium, nitrogen and aluminium, and high amounts of sulphur. The authors constructed maps which allow for the reading of the percentage of equiaxed grains as functions of steel composition and abrasive type.

8.7.9 Near-surface Layer Chemical Composition

Numerous authors found changes in the chemical composition of the near-surface layer of blast cleaned substrate materials (Watts and Dempster, 1992; Jopp, 1995; Martin, 1997; Anagreh and Dorn, 2002; Possart et al., 2002; Emrich, 2003). Changes in chemical surface stages due to blast cleaning (with glass beads and aluminium oxide) were found to influence the curing reactions of epoxy systems (Bockenheimer et al., 2002). An example is provided in Fig. 9.6. Possart et al., (2002) assessed changes in chemical compositions of near-surface layers of aluminium due to the application of different preparation methods. Some results are listed in Table 8.39.

Table 8.39 Mean chemical composition (XPS measurements) of the near-surface layer (10 nm) for treated aluminium samples (Possart et al., 2002)

Method	Element in %						
	Al	O	Mg	Si	Na	Ca	C
Etched	27.6	42.3	<0.1	1.8	<0.1	–	16.6
Glass bead blasted	25.2	39.2	0.4	1.8	12.8	1.0	16.9
Al_2O_3 blasted	44.3	32.8	0.6	0.4	4.2	0.2	16.3

After blast cleaning with glass beads, the surface was completely covered with considerable amounts of sodium (Na) and calcium (Ca), which must have been transferred by the glass beads. An even accumulation of sodium (Na) was also found after blast cleaning with aluminium oxide, even though the blasting medium contained only very little sodium (2.7%). Equal results were obtained by Emrich (2003), who performed blast cleaning experiments on aluminium ($AlMg_3$) samples. Aluminium surfaces under intense mechanical treatment, as due to particle impingement during blast cleaning, seemed to develop some particular affinity for the alkali oxides in the blasting media. There was some general trend that the final state of the exposed surface depended on material removal mode and on material removal capacity of the utilised abrasive materials. If not much material was removed but rather deformed, elements of the abrasive materials were more probably transferred to the substrate surface. If, in contrast, notable amounts of substrate material were removed, bulk properties of the substrate may have determined the state of the newly formed surface. Further evidence is delivered in Fig. 8.64, where the changes in surface chemistry of an ordinary construction steel due to blast cleaning are established based on X-ray photoelectron spectroscopy (XPS) analyses. The use of aluminium oxide, for example, dragged aluminium into the near-surface zone, whereas glass beads added silica to the metal surface. Emrich (2003), who noted element contamination after blast cleaning of aluminium ($AlMg_3$) with corundum and glass beads, concluded that the contaminated layer reduced the shear strength of a subsequently generated adhesion joint, even if the substrate had high roughness values.

Jopp (1995) applied XPS for the analysis of the surface chemistry of a steel substrate (St 37) which was blast cleaned with corundum and, respectively, glass beads. Results of this study are displayed in Fig. 8.65. The designation "unsputtered" corresponds to the very upper layer of the treated steel substrate, whereas the designation "sputtered" is related to surfaces bombarded with argon ions, which allows for the estimation of a depth profile of the surface chemistry. It can be seen that both abrasive materials contributed to a contamination of the steel. The corundum induced aluminium into the surface (Fig. 8.65a), whereas the glass beads induced silica (Fig. 8.65b). Both abrasive materials also induced a certain amount of sodium into the surface. If the upper layers were removed due to argon ion impingement, the ratio between iron and the contaminating elements steadily increased. The ratio Fe to Al, for example, increased from 1.5 (for an unsputtered substrate) to 2.36 (for 2 min sputtering time) up to 3.3 (for 12 min sputtering time). Similar was the trend for the ratio Fe to Si.

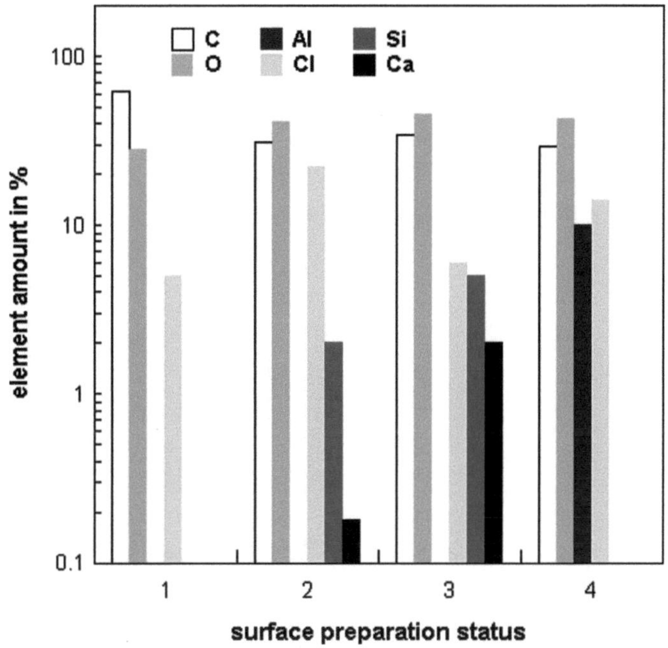

Fig. 8.64 Variations in near-surface chemistry of steel St 37 due to blast cleaning (Martin, 1997). Surface preparation status: 1 – degreasing with acetone; 2 – blast cleaned with steel shot ($d_P = 355$–1,180 μm); 3 – blast cleaned with glass beads ($d_P = 100$–200 μm); 4 – blast cleaned with corundum ($d_P = 150$–210 μm)

Grant et al. (2004) investigated the chemical composition of aluminium alloy surfaces after being treated with different surface preparation methods. The methods used included wiping (with acetone), hand abrading (Scotch Bride) and blast cleaning (with aluminium oxide). The authors deployed X-ray photoelectron spectroscopy (XPS) for the substrate evaluation. After blast cleaning, a large reduction in carbon (C), to a level about one-half of that before blast cleaning was measured. Other important changes included an increase in aluminium (A1) concentration and a decrease in magnesium (Mg) concentration. New elements introduced due to blast cleaning included sodium (Na) and fluorine (F). Measurements of the variations of near-surface chemical composition for aluminium alloys due to blast cleaning with corundum particles and polymer spheres were performed by Anagreh and Dorn (2002a,b).

Tolpygo et al. (2001) performed a systematic study about the effects of blast cleaning (abrasive: aluminium oxide) on the chemical cleanliness of a platinum-modified nickel-aluminide coating prior to the deposition of a thermal barrier coating. The blast cleaning led to contamination by various impurities from the abrasive material, in particular, alkali elements (Li, Na, K, Mg, Ca and Sr) and titanium. During the subsequent high-temperature oxidation, these impurities became incorporated into the growing scale. Their results suggested that impurities introduced by

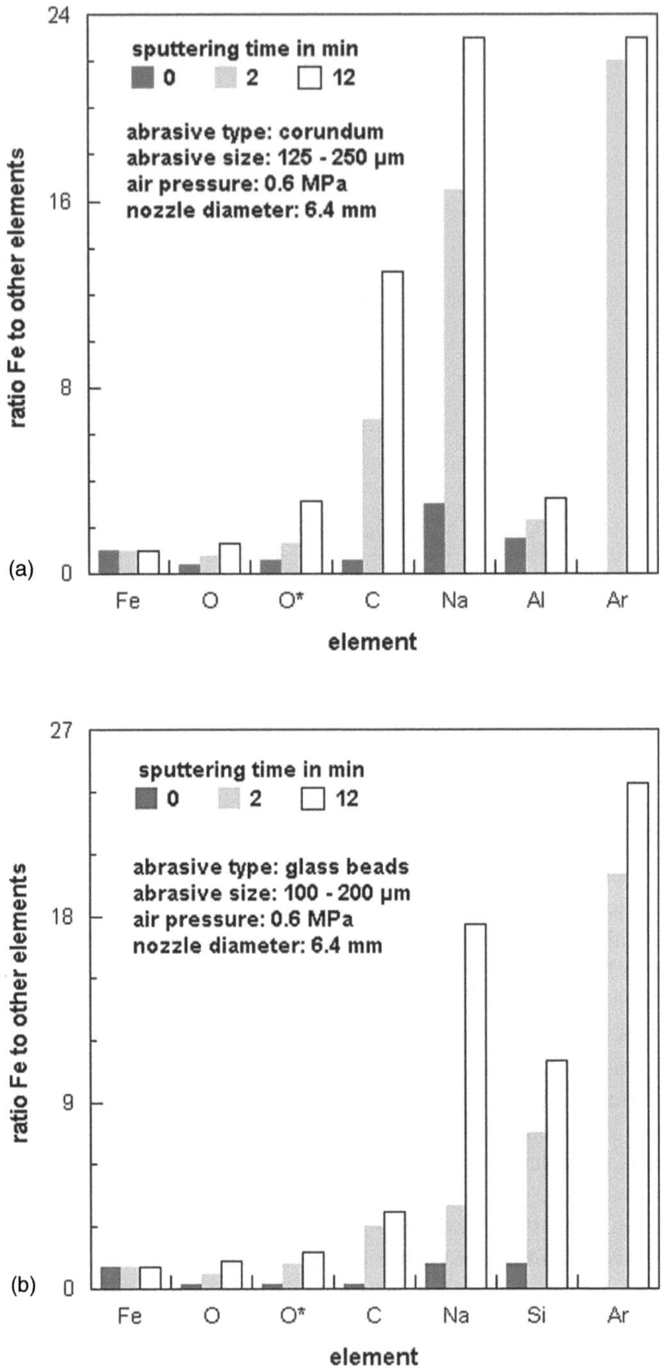

Fig. 8.65 Results of XPS analysis of steel St 37 blast cleaned with different abrasive materials (Jopp, 1995). (**a**) Abrasive material: corundum; (**b**) Abrasive material: glass beads

blast cleaning prior to the thermal barrier coating deposition are expected to have a strong detrimental effect on the coating durability.

8.7.10 Corrosion Resistance

Investigations into the corrosion resistance of steel substrates treated with different surface preparation methods were performed by several authors. Rhouma et al. (2001) estimated the effects of different surface preparation methods on the pitting corrosion and stress corrosion cracking (SCC) of austenitic stainless steel samples. Pitting corrosion was assessed based on potentiodynamic polarisation tests. The resistance to SCC was analysed by immersing the samples in an $MgCl_2$ solution (40 g/l), heated at 140°C, during 48 h. Results of these investigations are listed in Table 8.40. It can be seen that subsequent blast cleaning of ground steel with quartz particles (d_P = 50 to 200 μm) improved the resistance against SCC. This was probably due to the formation of compressive stresses during blast cleaning (see Sect. 8.7.3). If exposed to seawater, blast cleaning also led to better pitting resistance. Pitting potential was 110 mV for the ground samples, 320–360 mV for the blast cleaned samples and 500 mV for wire brushed samples. Similar trends were found by Ladwein and Gümpel (2004) in terms of critical potting potential. It can be seen from the results plotted in Table 8.41 that the critical pitting potential was lowest for ground steel, followed by blast cleaned steel and pickled steel. Jopp (1995) found notable effects of the surface preparation method on the free corrosion potentials of iron samples (Fe 99.5). Free corrosion potentials were highest for degreased surfaces, followed by surfaces blast cleaned with glass beads, and surfaces blast cleaned with corundum. This trend, however, was time dependent. For rather long exposure times (about 40 min) the differences in the corrosion potential vanished, and the corrosion potentials of all prepared surfaces approached a saturation level.

A study about the pitting corrosion of a duplex stainless steel, treated with different surface preparation methods, was performed by Salah-Rousset et al. (1996).

Table 8.40 Influence of surface treatment on the corrosion resistance of AISI316L stainless steel (Rhouma et al., 2001)

Treatment method	Pitting corrosion parameter		
	Pitting corrosion potential in mV/SCE	Repassivation potential in mV/SCE	Stress corrosion cracking
As ground	110	−200	Cracks
Blast cleaned (d_P <50 μm)	320	−110	No cracks
Blast cleaned (d_P = 80–120 μm)	360	−150	No cracks
Blast cleaned (d_P = 120–200 μm)	360	−150	No cracks
Wire brushed (280 rpm)	500	−130	Cracks
Wire brushed (900 rpm)	500	−150	No cracks

Blast cleaning conditions – abrasive type: quartz; air pressure: 0.4 MPa; blasting angle: 45°

Table 8.41 Corrosion resistance and surface energy of duplex stainless steel (steel 1.4301) after surface preparation (Ladwein and Gümpel, 2004)

Preparation method	Critical pitting potential in V	Surface energy in mN/m[a]
Grinding (60 g)	0.18	36
Grinding (120 g)	0.21	38
Blast cleaning ($\varphi = 45°$)	0.30	60
Blast cleaning ($\varphi = 90°$)	0.31	–
Pickling	0.72	51
Electro-polishing	–	47

[a]Sessile drop method

The authors utilized polishing, grinding and blast cleaning for surface treatment and performed electrochemical tests in artificial and natural seawater. It was found that the polished steel with the smoothest surface had the best corrosion resistance in artificial seawater; it showed the highest values for the pitting potential and for the protection potential. The blast cleaned samples performed worst in artificial seawater. It could, however, be shown, that the blast cleaned samples performed best in the natural seawater. The average number of pits with a depth larger than 500 μm in the steel was much lower (one) compared with ground samples (nine). The authors contributed this superior behaviour to the lower susceptibility of the blast cleaned samples to microbiologically influenced corrosion (MIC). The compressive stresses induced during the blast cleaning process made the samples more resistant against stress crack corrosion (SSC), whereas metallurgical changes in the blast cleaned regions helped to resist MIC. Polarization curves conducted under laboratory conditions were unable to duplicate this beneficial role of blast cleaning.

Andronikos et al. (1998) deployed rather unusual abrasive materials (dolomite, marble, olivine) and investigated the effects of these materials on the corrosion rate (in term of weight loss per time) of uncoated and coated (chlorinated rubber) steel specimens. The authors found that the contribution of the abrasive materials depended on the coating condition. Marble performed best for the uncoated steel and garnet performed best for a steel coated with chlorinated rubber with aluminium flakes. For a steel coated with chlorinated rubber with a red mud pigment, all abrasive materials performed equally good after an exposure time of 100 days.

Otsubo et al. (2003) investigated the corrosion resistance of an austenitic stainless steel, and they found that the corrosion resistance deteriorated if the samples were blast cleaned (aluminium oxide 24, $p = 0.6\,\mathrm{MPa}$, $d_N = 8\,\mathrm{mm}$, $\varphi = 75°$). The polarization curves were measured in a H_2SO_4-solution at a temperature of 303 K. The corrosion potentials (V) of the blast cleaned samples were lower than, and the passivation current densities (μA/cm^2) were higher than, those of mechanically ground samples. Immersion tests in a NaCl-solution also revealed a deteriorated performance of the blast cleaned samples. Although the authors noted the formation of a martensite phase at the blast cleaned substrate, they contributed the deteriorated corrosion resistance to the rather coarse profile of the substrate surface.

The effects of surface preparation on the corrosive performance of aluminium samples ($AlMg_3$) was investigated by Emrich (2003). He noted the formation of aluminium hydroxide after the treatment of the original substrate ($AlMg_3$) by blast cleaning, degreasing (acetylene) and acid pickling. The author found further, that blast cleaning with corundum ($p = 0.6$ MPa) led to the shifting of the pitting corrosion potential to higher potential differences (from –0.9 to –0.95 V), which eventually deteriorated the resistance of the material against pitting corrosion. The blast cleaned samples also exhibited rather high values for the free corrosion potential (−1.2 V). After a period of about 130 h, however, the corrosion potential rested on a stable range between –1.1 and –1.12 V versus the reference electrode (Ag/AgCl), irrespectively on the surface preparation method. Emrich (2003) also argued that the cold deformation of the surface during blast cleaning (see Sect. 8.7.3), and the accompanying formation of edge dislocations and helicoidal dislocations, may become the origin of corrosively determined material removal.

Jiang et al. (2006) performed electrochemical tests in order to evaluate the corrosion resistance of titanium substrates. They measured potentiodynamic polarisation curves in a 3.5% sodium chloride solution. The results indicated that blast cleaning delivered a lower corrosion current density (A/cm^2) compared to as-received samples. The lowest corrosion current density, however, was estimated for a combination of blast cleaning and subsequent annealing. The authors contributed this result to the formation of a nano-crystalline layer with a high density of grain boundaries, which in turn were beneficial to the formation of a passive film. Jopp (1995) compared the anodic polarisation curves of surfaces (Fe 99.5) treated with different methods. The highest current (A) values were measured for a surface blast cleaned with corundum, followed by a surface blast cleaned with glass beads and by a degreased surface. This author also estimated the metal loss due to the exchange current and found the following values: 73 μm/a for degreasing, 172 μm/a for corundum and 87 μm/a for glass beads. Thus, blast cleaning deteriorated the corrosion resistance of the material.

Celik et al. (1999) found that the corrosion of a steel substrate, coated with a plasma-sprayed alumina coating, exposed to an H_2SO_4 solution, depended on the roughness of the substrate. The corrosion resistance was lower for the substrates with higher roughness values. For $R_a = 3.37$ μm, the corrosion rate was 0.018 cm/year; whereas for $R_a = 4.02$ μm, the corrosion rate was 0.024 cm/year.

Confente et al. (1995) prepared low-carbon steel rods with different methods and exposed them also to an H_2SO_4-solution. They measured corrosion current densities and corrosion potentials. Results of these measurements are listed in Table 8.42. Mechanically prepared rods (brushed, blast cleaned) behaved much more reactive

Table 8.42 Corrosion resistance of low-carbon steel rods in an H_2SO_4 solution (Confente et al., 1995)

Preparation method	Current density in mA/cm^2	Corrosion potential in mV
Pickling	0.06	−466
Brushing	3.48	−486
Blast cleaning	2.58	−478

than pickled rods in an acid environment, which was attributed to surface hardening effects and to a reviving effect on the surface due to the elimination of any chemisorbed species.

A special problem is the formation of protective oxide layers on stainless steel substrates exposed to boiling water in nuclear power plants (water temperature: 280°C, water pressure: 12 MPa). During growth, these layers incorporate radioactive ^{60}Co in their structures, which is considered a serious health problem. The thicknesses of the oxide layers and the incorporation of ^{60}Co in the oxide layers depended on the surface preparation method being used. Results of an investigation of Rao et al. (1986) on a nuclear grade stainless steel are listed in Tables 8.43 and 8.44. A notable result was the high rate of oxidation after blast cleaning, as evidenced in Table 8.44. The oxide thickness was very large for the blast cleaned steel. This result was explained by the authors through the high level of silica (25%), embedded in the substrate after blast cleaning with the silica sand (indicated in bold in Table 8.44), and through the rather rough topography of the blast cleaned surfaces. Both these factors would contribute to high levels of ^{60}Co buildup. Subsequent electropolishing was, therefore, recommended for this special area of application.

Another corrosion issue is "metal dusting", which is a catastrophic form of carburisation leading to the disintegration of iron-, nickel- and cobalt-base alloys into powdery mixtures of graphite, metal particles, carbides and oxides. Lin et al. (2004) exposed stainless steel samples, which were in the conditions as-ground, blast cleaned and pre-oxidised, to a mixed gas (CO/CO_2) at high temperatures up to 700°C and investigated the resistance of the surfaces to metal dusting. The abrasive material was aluminium oxide ($d_P = 200$–$250\,\mu m$), propelled at an air pressure of $p = 0.7\,MPa$. The authors noted that blast cleaning assisted carbon deposits and filamental carbon formation, and it favoured the formation of a protective chromium-rich oxide on the steel. These processes helped to prevent metal dusting.

Ruttmann and Günther (1965) investigated the effects of blast cleaning on the lifetime of welded steel samples exposed to a boiling $MgCl_2$ solution (140°C). The lifetime criterion was the start of SCC. The authors varied abrasive type, air pressure and exposure time. Some results are displayed in Table 8.45. It can be seen that the untreated samples cracked after 3 h, whereas the blast cleaned samples did not show any cracking even after 9.5 days. The use of steel grit (not listed in Table 8.45) was very effective, but glass beads particles performed excellent as well. The use of

Table 8.43 Effects of surface preparation methods on the buildup of ^{60}Co in oxide layers of stainless steel samples subjected to boiling water in nuclear power reactors (Rao et al., 1986)

Preparation method	Steel grade	^{60}Co buildup in $\mu Ci/cm^2$
Electro-polishing	309	7.0
As received	309	14.1
Blast cleaned (silica sand)	316 NG	12.7
Acid pickled	316 NG	4.5

Table 8.44 Effects of surface preparation methods on the formation of oxide layers in stainless steel (Rao et al., 1986)

Preparation method	Oxide thickness in Å	Oxide layer composition in % (at 50 Å depth)
Cold rolled	~ 100	Fe-27, Cr-7, Ni-4, C-4, O-50
Acid pickled	~ 100	Fe-25, Cr-8, Ni-4, C-15, O-45
Blast cleaned (silica sand)	~ 2, 000	Fe-20, Cr-5, **Si-22**, Ni-3, O-16, C-25
Acid pickled + electropolished	~ 120	Fe-16, Cr-3, Ni-2, O-56 (P, Na < 5)
Blast cleaned + electropolished	~ 70	Fe-30, Cr-16, Ni-3, O-40 (P, Na < 5)

corundum particles delivered good results, but they were not as good as those for the use of glass beads. An increase in air pressure and blast cleaning time improved resistance against SCC. For ferritic steel, exposed to a boiling $Ca(NO_3)_2$ solution (113°C), very similar results could be observed. Blast cleaning extended the time to SCC from 48 h for untreated samples up to 227 h for samples blast cleaned with steel shot and corundum. Münster and Spähn (1979) provided results on the corrosion behaviour of blast cleaned weld seams of Cr–Ni steels. The authors found that blast cleaning with glass beads delivered a cleaning quality comparable to that after acid cleaning. Table 8.46 lists results of the corrosion resistance tests. As can be seen, brushing and grinding led to corrosion as well as SCC. The results for the blast cleaned samples were all good, whether quartz sand, slag or glass beads were being used.

Tolpygo et al. (2001) performed a study into the oxidation of a platinum-modified nickel-aluminide coating after blast cleaning with aluminium oxide. During high-temperature oxidation, impurities originating from the blast cleaning process became incorporated in the growing scale and significantly accelerated the oxide growth.

Leistikow and Kraft (1974) provided a detailed investigation on the hot steam (600 °C, 500 hours) corrosion resistance of an austenitic CrNi-steel. The steel substrate was prepared by electro-polishing, rolling, needle gunning, grinding, turning, sanding and blast cleaning (corundum, $d_P = 250$–$500\,\mu m$, $p = 0.8\,MPa$). The corrosion resistance was measured in terms of specific mass loss. Samples characterised by very smooth surfaces (ground, sanded, turned) experienced the lowest specific mass loss (between 11 and 22 mg/dm^2). Blast cleaned samples performed worse (41 mg/dm^2), but their corrosion resistance was equal to that of the

Table 8.45 Time to SCC of a welded austenitic (X10CrNiTi189) steel (Ruttmann and Günther, 1965)

Method	Abrasive	Pressure in MPa	Time in s	Time to SCC in h
As received	–	–	–	3
Blast cleaned	Glass beads	0.3	30	227
	Glass beads	0.3	60	227
	Corundum	0.3	30	12
	Corundum	0.6	30	60
	Corundum	0.6	60	108

Table 8.46 Results of corrosion and SCC tests on Cr–Ni steel (Münster and Spähn, 1979)

Treatment	Corrosion in water + H_2SO_4	SCC in boiling $MgCl_2$ (35%)
As received	Localised corrosion	SCC
Acid cleaning	No damage	SCC
Brushing	Localised corrosion	SCC
Grinding	No damage	SCC
Blast cleaning[a] (glass beads)	No damage	O.K.
Blast cleaning[a] (quartz sand)	No damage	O.K.
Blast cleaning[a] (slag)	No damage	O.K.

[a]Pressure: $p = 0.6\,\text{MPa}$

needle-gunned substrate (41 mg/dm^2), and it was better compared to samples which were rolled (143 mg/dm^2) and electro-polished (296 mg/dm^2). The authors found a relationship between the degree of surface deformation (surface hardness) and the corrosion resistance. Corrosion resistance was low if degree of deformation was high, and vice versa. A high degree of deformation promoted the formation of thin, almost defect-free, chromate-rich layers with a high corrosion protection potential.

8.8 Surface Energy and Work of Adhesion

8.8.1 Definitions and Measurement

If a liquid drop that rests on a substrate surface is going to be removed, a certain amount of energy will be required. The situation is illustrated in Fig. 8.66. This energy is known as work of adhesion, and it can be calculated as follows:

$$W_A = \gamma_S + \gamma_L - \gamma_{SL} \tag{8.14}$$

Here, γ_S is the specific surface energy of the substrate, γ_L is the surface tension of the liquid and γ_{SL} is the interfacial free energy. These parameters are illustrated in Fig. 8.66a. It can be seen from (8.14) that, for a given coating material, work of adhesion can be increased if specific surface energy of the substrate rises. Surface energy is the sum of contributions from different intermolecular forces, namely dispersion and polar forces. Therefore, the following relationship applies:

$$\gamma = \gamma^d + \gamma^p \tag{8.15}$$

Here, the superscript "d" stands for dispersion and "p" stands for polar. For metal surfaces, the contribution of dispersion forces is usually larger than that of polar forces. Adhesives, in contrast, usually own a high polar component. An alternative expression of (8.14) is:

$$W_A = \gamma_L \cdot (1 + \cos \theta_C) \tag{8.16}$$

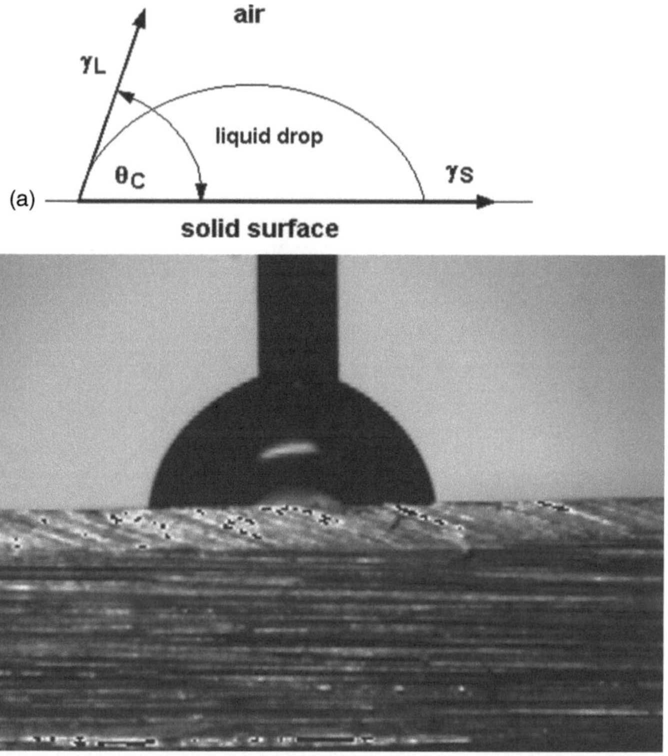

Fig. 8.66 Fundamentals of contact angle estimation. (**a**) Energy balance; (**b**) Contact angle to low-carbon steel (Momber and Wong, 2005a)

Here, θ_C is the contact angle (see Sect. 8.9.1). Whenever the two variables in that equation can be measured experimentally, work of adhesion can be calculated. The relationship between work of adhesion and contact angle as expressed by (8.16) is illustrated in Fig. 8.67. It can be seen that the work of adhesion has a maximum value at a contact angle of $\theta_C = 0°$, which corresponds to complete wetting. Work of adhesion is zero for $\theta_C = 180°$, which counts for complete non-wetting. Values for the work of adhesion between different adhesives and steel as estimated with this relationship are listed in Table 8.47. It can be seen that high values for the work of adhesion promote a high interfacial fracture energy. This relationship is confirmed by experimental results published by Berg (2002). A standard equation for the discussion of wetting effects is the Young equation, which reads as follows:

$$\gamma_{SL} = \gamma_S - \gamma_L \cdot \cos \theta_C \tag{8.17}$$

Based on this equation, a method for the assessment of the paintability of a substrate was developed by Zisman (1972). The method works as follows. For the assessment of the paintability, the contact angles of various liquids to a substrate

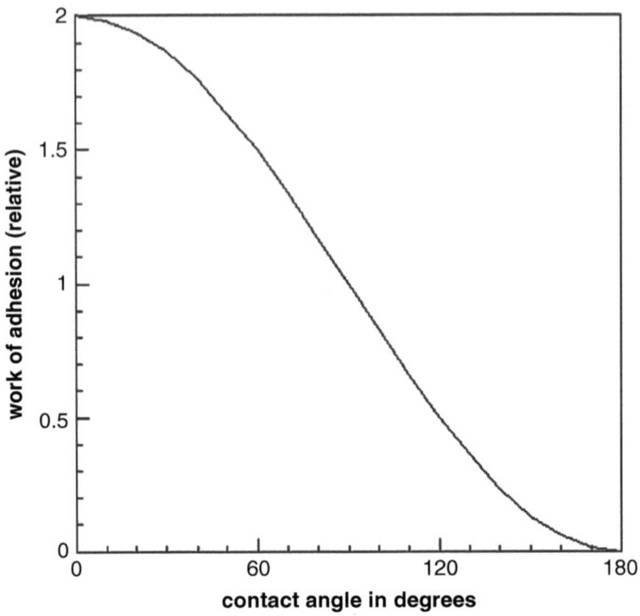

Fig. 8.67 The relationship between work of adhesion and contact angle as expressed by (8.16)

surface are determined, and the cosines of the contact angles are plotted against the surface tension of the liquids (Zisman, 1972). The plot is extrapolated to cos $\theta_C = 1$ ($\theta_C = 0°$), and the intersection point determines the critical surface energy of the substrate. The procedure is illustrated in Fig. 8.68. The critical surface energy in about γ_S= 33 × 10^{-5} N/cm (=33 mJ/m^2) for the example plotted in that figure. More values are listed in Table 8.48. A very similar procedure was suggested by Miller (1973) for the assessment of the critical surface energy of metal substrates. This author could show that a certain minimum amount of substrate surface energy was a requirement to maintain a good adhesion between substrate and applied

Table 8.47 Work of adhesion and interfacial fracture energy for different adhesives and steel (Penn and Defex, 2002)

Adhesive	Work of adhesion in mJ/m^2	Interfacial fracture energy in mJ/m^2
Water (ice), −23 °C	144.4	19,300 ± 3,300
Water (ice), −10 °C	144.4	16,300 ± 3,030
Diiodomethane, −23 °C	101.6	2,490 ± 579
Diiodomethane, −16 °C	101.6	4,710 ± 1,100
Diiodomethane, −6 °C	101.6	[a]
Bromonaphthalene, −23 °C	89.2	1,120 ± 102
Bromonaphthalene, −10 °C	89.2	[a]
Hexadecane, −4 °C	55.4	[a]
Hexadecane, +5 °C	55.4	[a]

[a]Cohesive failure in adhesive

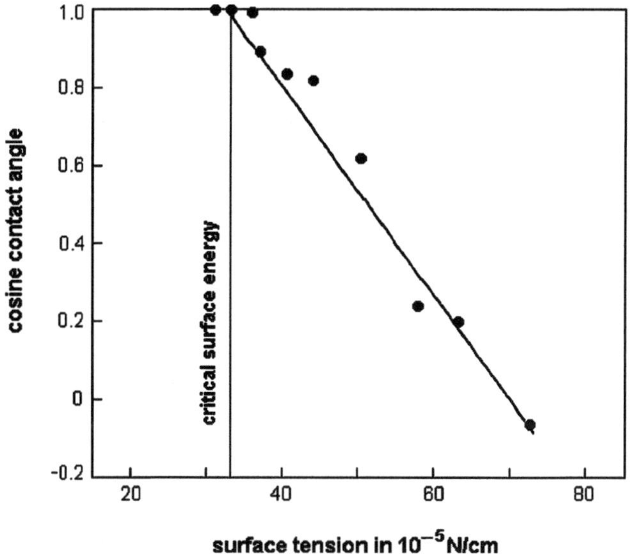

Fig. 8.68 Zisman's plot for wettability assessment (Zisman, 1972)

coating. For an epoxy-polyamide paint, applied to chromated clad aluminium, this critical threshold was about $\gamma_S = 40\,\text{mJ/m}^2$.

It is common in the coating industry to refer to low energy and high energy surfaces. Steel substrates belong to high energy surfaces. Table 8.49 lists surface tension (energy) values for different resins in liquefied state and after hardening. Hardening does not alter the surface energy notably and can, therefore, be utilised for calculations with dry films.

8.8.2 Effects of Substrate Surface Energy on Corrosion and Coating Performance

Ladwein and Gümpel (2004) performed a study into the corrosion resistance of duplex stainless steel as a function of surface preparation. The measure of the corrosion

Table 8.48 Critical surface energies of substrates; data generated according to the procedure shown in Fig. 8.68 (Schoff, 1992)

Substrate	Critical surface energy in mJ/m^2
Zn-phosphated steel	45–56
Fe-phosphated steel	43
Tin-plated steel	35
Treated aluminium extrusions	33–35
Untreated steel	29
SMC polyester	23

Table 8.49 Surface tension values for resins (Chair for Plastics Technology, University of Erlangen)

Resin type	Surface tension in mN/m (mJ/m^2)	
	Liquid state	Hardened
Epoxy/polyamine	40.8	47.7
Polyester (I)	36.1	45.1
Polyester (II)	36.1	47.5
Polyester (III)	36.1	47.7
Alkali-resistant polyester	36.1	46.7
Metacrylate	–	38.4

was the critical pitting potential – the lower the value for this parameter, the lower the corrosion resistance. Results of this study are listed in Table 8.41. It can be seen that ground substrates performed worse and pickled substrates performed best. Blast cleaned surfaces showed a moderate corrosion resistance, whether the surface was blast cleaned at perpendicular or shallow angle. The authors assumed that the surface energies of the substrates after preparation had a determining effect on corrosion resistance, but experimental results did not confirm this approach completely (see Table 8.41).

The adhesion strength between polymeric adhesives and metal substrates and between copolymer films and metal substrates was found to linearly increase with higher metal surface energy (Basin, 1984; Vakula and Pritykin, 1991). However, it is usually not the value for the total surface energy alone that determines adhesion. The polar components of the surface energies play important roles as well. High adhesion between substrate and coating can be expected if the polar components of their surface energies are of equal order, thus $\gamma_S^P = \gamma_L^P$. Examples are shown in Fig. 8.69.

8.8.3 Surface Energies of Blast Cleaned Substrates

As shown in Table 8.41, the surface energies of metal substrates depend on the type of surface preparation. For the condition in Table 8.41, surface energy was high for blast cleaning, and rather low for grinding. Kogan et al. (1993) utilised the surface potential of a surface for the assessment of the activated state, and they found that blast cleaning contributed to an increase in surface potential of a steel substrate compared with mechanical machining. The use of corundum generated a higher surface potential value than the use of shot.

Harris and Beevers (1999) utilised results of contact angle measurements to estimate the surface energies of steel and aluminium substrates blast cleaned with different aluminium oxide abrasives. The effects of the abrasive media on surface energies are listed in Table 8.50. It can be seen that the Pink and White abrasives produced similar surface energy characteristics, but the Brown abrasive delivered a lower total surface energy with higher dispersive and lower polar components

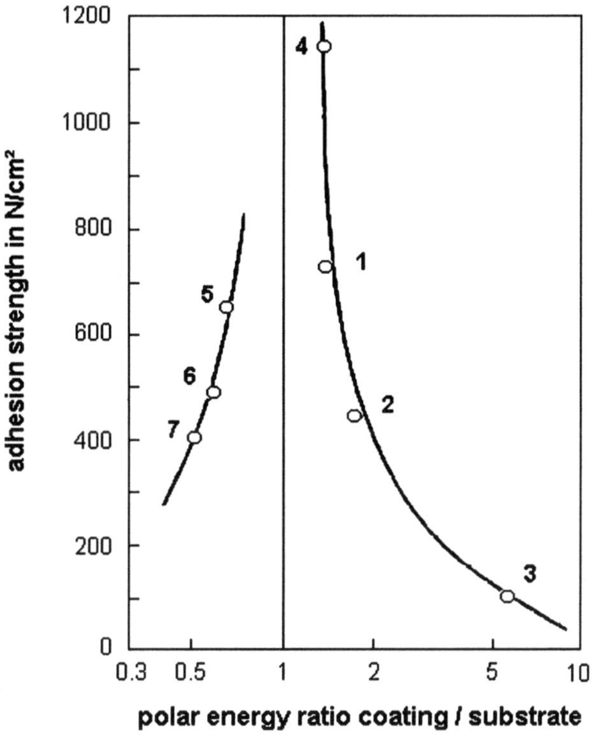

Fig. 8.69 Adhesion strength as a function of the ratio of polar surface energy components of paint and substrate (Potente and Krüger, 1978). Substrates: 1 – post-chlorinated PVC; 2 – styrene-acrylonitrile-copolymer; 3 – polypropylene; 4 – polystyrene; 5 – PVC; 6 – polyamide-6; 7 – PMMA; coating: alkyd-based

than the other abrasive types. The effects of surface roughness and abrasive type on surface energies of blast cleaned substrates are shown in Fig. 8.70. With the Pink and White abrasives, the smoother surfaces exhibited higher surface energy readings than the 60 mesh abrasives, but with the Brown abrasives, surface energy values appeared to be independent of roughness. The changes in surface energy after blast cleaning are associated with chemical changes on the surfaces. These changes in surface composition are due to residues from the abrasive media, and the impurities vary between different abrasive types (see Sect. 8.7.8). Smaller abrasive sizes apparently left a greater percentage of contaminant residues on the surface.

Emrich (2003) measured the specific surface energies of aluminium substrates ($AlMg_3$) prepared with different surface preparation methods. The surface energy after blast cleaning with aluminium oxide ($p = 0.6\,\mathrm{MPa}$) was $\gamma_S = 52\,\mathrm{mJ/m^2}$. This value was higher than those measured after degreasing with acetone, but lower than those estimated after pickling. Emrich (2003) also measured the polar and disperse components of the surface energies. The surface energy of aluminium substrates,

Table 8.50 Contact angle and surface energy data for blast cleaned and solvent wiped substrates (Harris and Beevers, 1999)

Surface treatment	Contact angles in °		Total surface energy in mJ/m^2
	De-ionised water	Diiodomethane	
Mild steel Solvent wiped	68 ± 5	37 ± 7	46 ± 3
Blast cleaned (Brown 180/220)	52 ± 7	18 ± 4	57 ± 3
Blast cleaned (Brown 60)	61 ± 4	21 ± 4	52 ± 2
Blast cleaned (Pink 180/220)	8 ± 3	27 ± 3	74 ± 1
Blast cleaned (Pink 60)	28 ± 4	30 ± 3	68 ± 2
Blast cleaned (White 180/220)	6 ± 2	26 ± 4	74 ± 1
Blast cleaned (White 60)	34 ± 10	25 ± 3	65 ± 5
Aluminium alloy Solvent wiped	54 ± 3	45 ± 3	50 ± 2
Blast cleaned (Brown 180/220)	76 ± 4	33 ± 3	44 ± 1
Blast cleaned (Brown 60)	75 ± 5	30 ± 4	46 ± 2
Blast cleaned (Pink 180/220)	34 ± 3	31 ± 3	64 ± 2
Blast cleaned (Pink 60)	51 ± 3	35 ± 5	54 ± 2
Blast cleaned (White 180/220)	28 ± 6	30 ± 3	68 ± 3
Blast cleaned (White 60)	59 ± 3	28 ± 4	52 ± 2

which were degreased with acetone showed almost no polar component. The surface energy of the substrates blast cleaned with aluminium oxide showed a well-balanced ratio between polar and disperse component, whereby the polar component had a value of $\gamma_{\mathrm{L}}^{\mathrm{P}} = 27\,\mathrm{mJ/m^2}$, and the disperse component had a value of $\gamma_{\mathrm{S}}^{\mathrm{d}} = 25\,\mathrm{mJ/m^2}$. Surface energies of samples which were pickled with acid also showed a good balance between polar and disperse components.

Broughton and Lodeiro (2002) applied the Wilhelmy plate method for the assessment of wettability parameters, and they found an increase in the surface energy of mild steel from $\gamma_S = 34\,\mathrm{mJ/m^2}$ for an untreated substrate to a value of $\gamma_{\mathrm{S}} = 51\,\mathrm{mJ/m^2}$ after blast cleaning with aluminium oxide abrasives. This values corresponds well with that measured by Emrich (2003). Broughton and Lodeiro (2002)

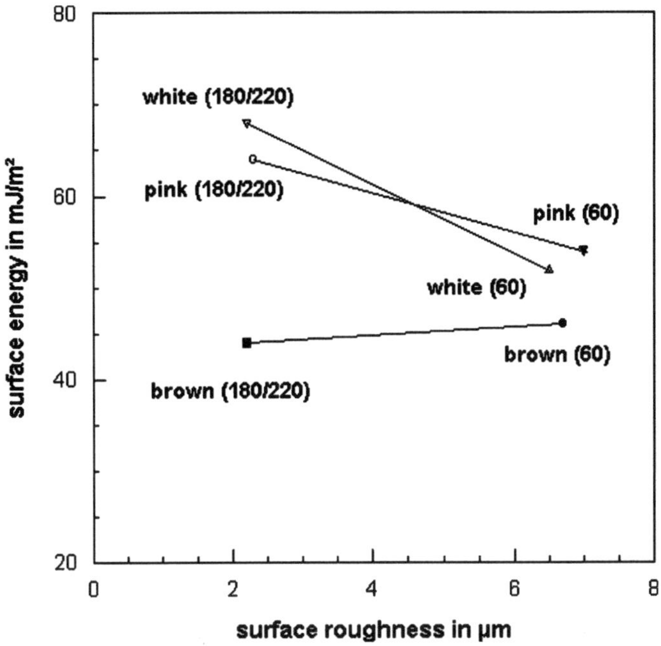

Fig. 8.70 Relationship between surface roughness and surface energy for a blasted aluminium alloy (Harris and Beevers, 1999)

could also show that blast cleaning increased the disperse component of surface energy only (from initially $\gamma_S^d = 32.1$ up to 50.4 mJ/m^2 after blast cleaning) , whereas the polar component of surface energy was reduced due to blast cleaning (from initially $\gamma_S^d = 1.8$ down to 0.5 mJ/m^2 after blast cleaning).

An alternative measure for the reactivity of substrates is the carbon content. The higher the carbon content, the lower the reactivity to the formation of bond forces. Emrich (2003) measured the carbon content on aluminium substrates ($AlMg_3$) treated with different surface preparation methods, and he found that blast cleaning with aluminium oxide ($p = 0.6$ MPa) generated highly reactive, low-carbon (15 atom%) surface. Degreasing with acetone, in contrast, formed a rather low-reactive, high-carbon (33 atom%) surface.

8.9 Wettability of Metal Substrates

8.9.1 Definitions and Measurement

The contact between the liquid coating and the substrate is the result of a wetting procedure. Wettability is often defined through the contact angle of a liquid drop to the substrate. Contact angle is given by the Young equation [see (8.17)]:

$$\gamma_S = \gamma_{SL} + \gamma_L \cdot \cos\theta_C \tag{8.18}$$

The parameters are defined in (8.15) and (8.17). Equation (8.18) is illustrated in Fig. 8.71. For complete wetting, the contact angle has a value of $\theta_C = 0°$; and for no wetting, the contact angle has a value of $\theta_C = 180°$. For low contact angles (usually less than $\theta_C = 90°$), the substrate is considered hydrophilic against the liquid, whereas it is considered hydrophobic for high contact angles. Another parameter which can characterise wettability is the spreading of a liquid over a solid surface. The spreading coefficient is related to the surface tension of the liquid and the contact angle as follows (Crawford and Atkinson, 1996):

$$S_{LS} = \gamma_L \cdot (\cos\theta_C - 1) \tag{8.19}$$

Many factors influence contact angle measurements, the main ones being substrate contamination, substrate roughness and substrate chemical heterogeneity, substrate temperature, but also test duration (Hitchcock et al., 1981; Hazlett, 1993; Shanahan, 1993; Hong et al., 1994; Duncan and Lodeiro, 2004). Examples are illustrated in Figs. 8.72 and 8.73. The effect of changes in surface roughness can be evaluated with Wenzel'a (1936) equation:

$$\begin{aligned} \cos\theta_R &= r_R \cdot \cos\theta_0 \\ r_R &= \frac{A_R}{A_0} \end{aligned} \tag{8.20}$$

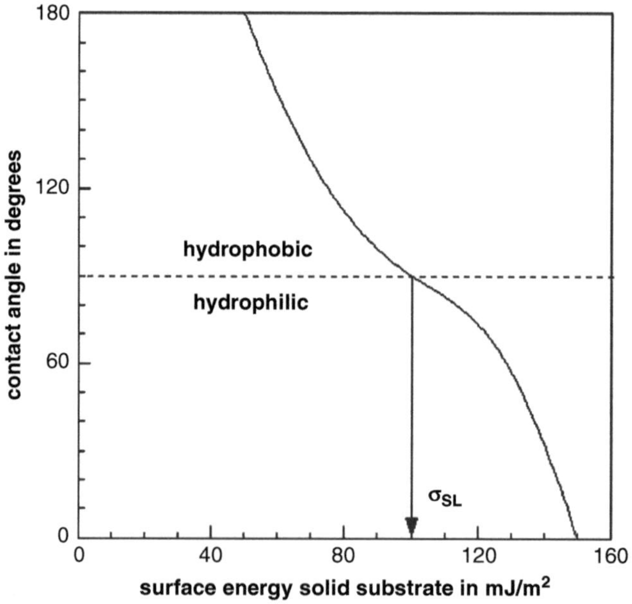

Fig. 8.71 Graphical solution to (8.18)

Fig. 8.72 Effects on contact angle formation (Fraunhofer Society, München). Conditions: left – initial condition; centre – effect of roughness; right – effect of contamination

Here, r_R is a so-called "roughness factor" considering the profile of a rough surface, Θ_R is the contact angle of the rough surface, A_R is the true (rough) surface and A_0 is a perfectly smooth surface. For a completely smooth (untreated) surface, $r_R = 1$ and $\theta_R = \theta_0$. Equation (8.20) is graphically illustrated in Fig. 8.74. It can be seen that the contact angle decreases if roughness increases for $\theta_C < 90°$ (wetting, hydrophilic), and that the contact angle increases if roughness increases for $\theta_C > 90°$ (no wetting, hydrophobic). Experimental work of Hitchcock et al. (1981) has shown that the roughness factor can be linked to the profile roughness. For very smooth substrates ($R_a < 0.1\ \mu m$), the authors derived the following relationship:

$$r_R = 1 + 50 \cdot \left(\frac{R_a}{S_R}\right)^2 \tag{8.21}$$

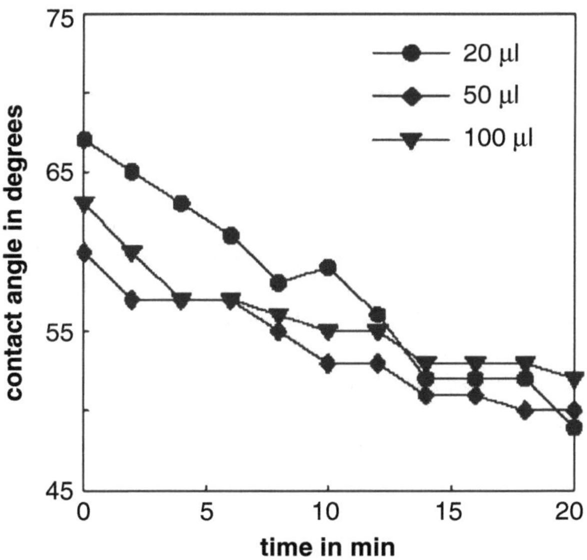

Fig. 8.73 Effects of test duration and drop volume on contact angle to a blasted substrate (Roero, 2005)

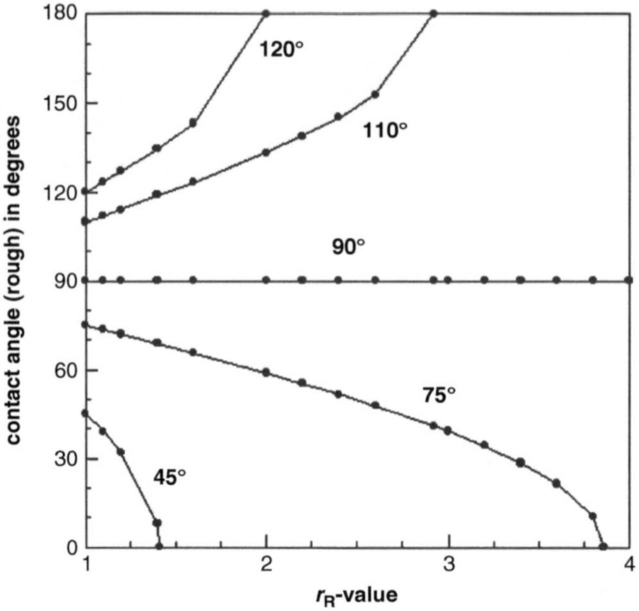

Fig. 8.74 Graphical expression of Wenzel's equation (8.20)

In a more general way, R_a is the average amplitude and S_R the average wavelength of the surface feature (see Fig. 8.32). Minaki et al. (2004) performed measurements of R_a and S_R for different blast cleaning conditions (aluminium oxide, mesh 700, $p = 0.15 - 0.4\,\text{MPa}$, $\check{m}_P = 100\,\text{g/min}$, $t_B = 1 - 10\,\text{s}$, $d_N = 7\,\text{mm}$, $\varphi = 90°$). From the results they reported, typical values for R_a/S_R are between 10^{-3} and 10^{-2}. An example for the roughness effect based on experimentally estimated values is shown in Fig. 8.75 for a hydrophilic surface. As depicted by (8.20), contact angle dropped with an increase in roughness. The same result was reported by Sancaktar and Gomatam (2001) for the contact angles of epoxy adhesives to hydrophobic steel substrates. For very smooth substrates ($R_a < 0.1\,\mu\text{m}$), Hitchcock et al. (1981) found that the contact angle showed a linear relationship with the profile parameter ratio R_a/S_R. Effects of substrate contamination on contact angle to substrate are represented in Table 8.14. Hong et al. (1994) found on aluminium plates that oxidation could significantly reduce the contact angle for distilled water.

The most commonly used method for contact angle measurement is the sessile drop method, whereby θ_C is directly measured for a liquid drop resting on a flat surface of the solid. This procedure is illustrated in Fig. 8.66b. Other methods are outlined by Adamson (1990) and Berg (1993). The sessile drop method delivers three different types of contact angles as illustrated in Fig. 8.76: advancing angle, receding angle and equilibrium angle. The difference between advancing angle and receding angle:

$$H_\theta = \theta_A - \theta_R \tag{8.22}$$

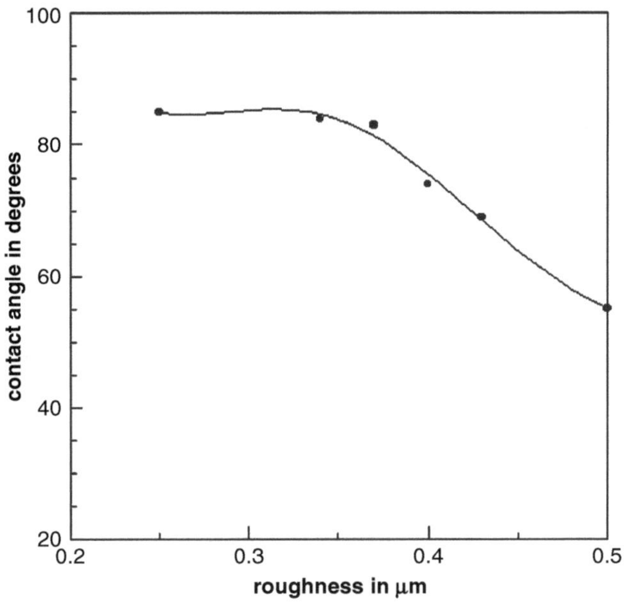

Fig. 8.75 Effects of roughness on contact angles to a hydrophilic aluminium substrate (Duncan and Lodeiro, 2004)

is referred to as contact angle hysteresis, which occurs for a number of reasons. Reasons related to substrate conditions are roughness, surface heterogeneity, diffusion and swelling (Baldan, 2004).

8.9.2 Effects of Wettability on Coating Performance

Mayfarth and Schubert (1989) highlighted the effect of wettability on coating adhesion. They found experimentally for austenitic steel that the best coating performance can be achieved if a maximum wettability can be achieved. It was rather the wettability, and not the roughness, which promoted good adhesion.

Wettability of a substrate influences the process of coating formation, especially the formation of wet films (Vincent, 2001). This was shown, among others, due to investigations of splash morphologies for sprayed coating materials (Griffith et al., 1997; Fauchais et al., 2004). From (8.16) and Fig. 8.67, contact angle affects the work of adhesion between substrate and wet film. If wettability increases (contact angle decreases), work of adhesion rises. However, a definite relationship between wettability and cured coatings is difficult to prove because it is very difficult to exclude other effects. Nevertheless, Fig. 8.77 shows, as an example, how the wettability of a substrate by an adhesive affected the shear strength of an aluminium joint. The better wettability (the lower contact angle) was, the higher was shear strength. The same trend was observed by Minaki et al. (2005) for the adhesion of

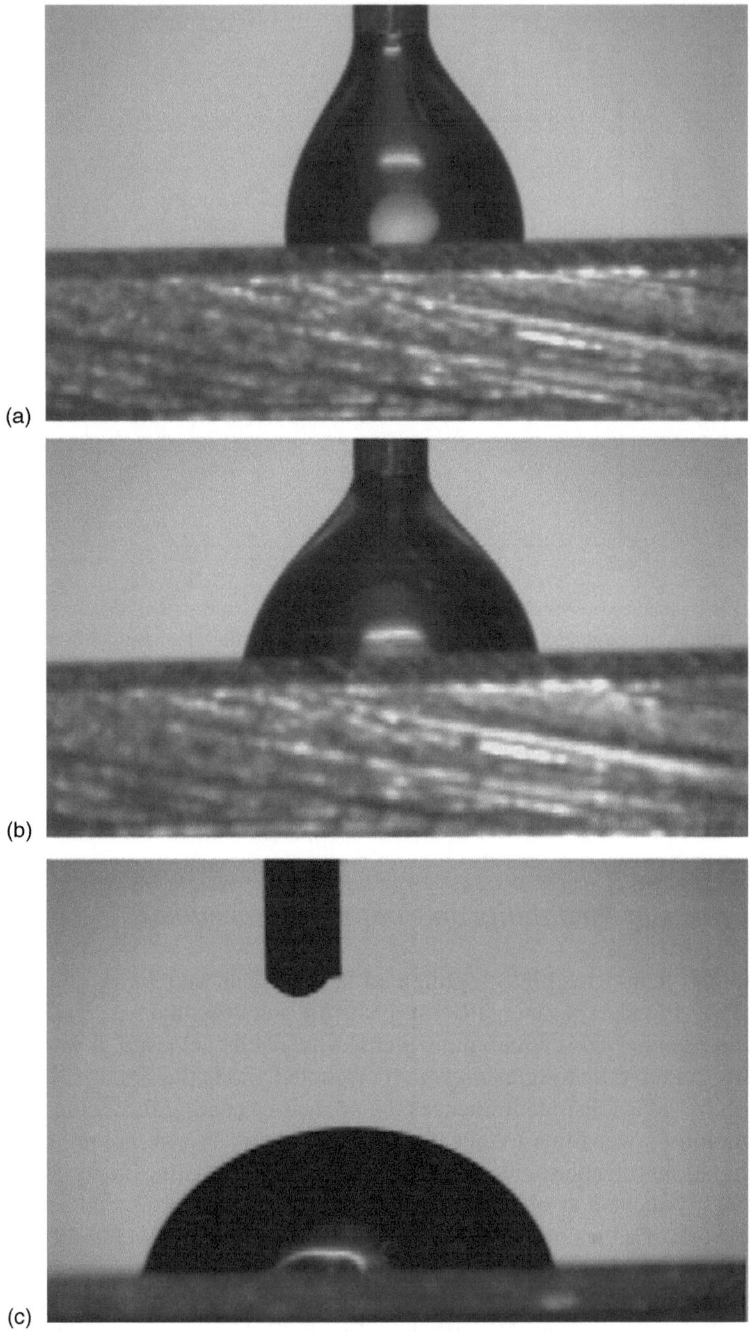

Fig. 8.76 Contact between liquid drop and substrate surface after blast cleaning (Momber and Wong, 2005a). (**a**) Advancing contact angle; (**b**) Receding contact angle; (**c**) Equilibrium contact angle

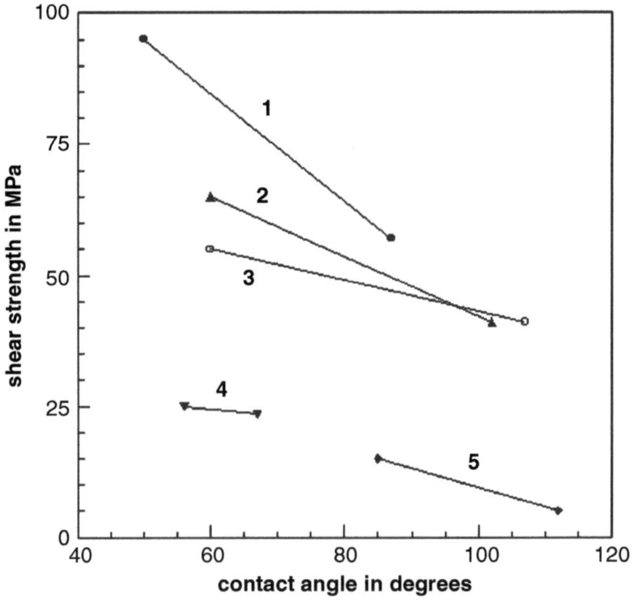

Fig. 8.77 Relationship between contact angle and joint shear strength (Asthana and Sobczak, 2000). Material pairings: 1 – $AlSi_{11}/AlN$; 2 – Al/AlN; 3 – A/lAlN; 4 – $AlTi_6/AlN(1)$; 5 – $AlTi_6/AlN(2)$

plated titanium nitride to blast cleaned stainless steel substrates. Adhesion increased for smaller contact angles.

Tamai and Tanaka (1967) introduced the idea that the advancing contact angles measured on the reverse sides of polymer coatings peeled off from different metal substrates are a measure of the peel strength between the coating and the individual metal. The order of contact angle values for the different substrates was: Au ($\theta_C = 76°$), Fe ($\theta_C = 70°$), Al ($\theta_C = 67°$), Ni ($\theta_C = 62°$) and Cd ($\theta_C = 50°$). The same order was obtained in terms of knife-edge breaking strength between substrate and polymer film.

8.9.3 Wettability of Blast Cleaned Metal Substrates

Solomon et al. (2003) performed wetting experiments on blast cleaned substrates which were later brazed. They found notable effects of blast cleaning media on wettability. Some results are displayed in Table 8.51. Blast cleaning with aluminium oxide yielded surfaces that were most poorly wet. Best wetted surfaces were produced with Ni–Cr–Fe abrasive, and SiC abrasives were intermediate compared to the other two media. Debris embedment into the blast cleaned substrates was the major reason that affected wettability, and this was the reason for the good performance of Ni–Cr–Fe blasted substrates, because this abrasive did not become embedded in the surface. If a substrate, subsequently blast cleaned with aluminium oxide, was

Table 8.51 High-temperature wetting test results on IN718 after surface treatment; wetting liquid: AMS4777 (Solomon et al., 2003)

Blast cleaning process	Maximum wetting force in N/m
With Al_2O_3	−0.18
	0.09
	0.60
With Al_2O_3 + polishing with paper (400 μm)	0.99
Polishing only with paper (400 μm)	1.25
With SiC	1.24
	1.29
	1.07
	0.48
With Ni–Cr–Fe alloy	1.28
	1.25
	0.98

mechanically ground, it improved in terms of wettability. The reason was the removal of the embedded debris (see Table 8.22).

Broughton and Lodeiro (2002) reported about contact angle measurements on blast cleaned mild steel substrates; advancing contact angles only slightly decreased from $\theta_C = 90.5°–86.9°$ after the surface was blast cleaned with aluminium oxide, and receding contact angles only slightly decreased from $\theta_C = 31.1°$ to 30.2° after blast cleaning. Rider et al. (1999) found that the contact angle of water to aluminium substrates was reduced due to blast cleaning. The contact angle of the received sample was $\theta_C = 80°$, and this high value could be lowered down to $\theta_C = 5°$ due to blast cleaning with aluminium oxide powder ($d_P = 50\,\mu m$). Sancaktar and Gomatam (2001) could show that contact angles of a resin to a cold-rolled steel also reduced after blast cleaning with aluminium oxide (from $\theta_C = 42°$ for the untreated substrate to $\theta_C = 15°$ after blast cleaning), and they contributed this result to an increase in roughness due to blast cleaning (compare with Fig. 8.75). Similar results were found by Momber and Wong (2005a) for low-carbon steel substrates, although the reduction was only marginal. More interestingly, the latter authors found that the contact angle increased notably after a second blast cleaning step; this effect could not be explained by geometric arguments and may have been caused by changes in the chemical state of the surface. A similar situation is shown in Fig. 8.78. In contrast to (8.20) as well as to Fig. 8.75, contact angle of the hydrophilic surface increased with an increase in roughness. The explanation is due to changes in the chemical composition of the substrate surface due to abrasive particle impingement (Harris and Beevers, 1999). These results clearly documented the limits to Wenzel's approach, which is a plain geometric approach. Momber and Wong, 2005a) considered contact angle hysteresis according to (8.22), and they found that it was low for an untreated surface ($H_\theta = 7°$) and high for blast cleaned surfaces ($H_\theta = 18–24°$). Kallio et al. (2005) performed abrasion tests on uncoated stainless steel and found that contact angle of water to the substrate decreased as the number of abrasion cycles rose.

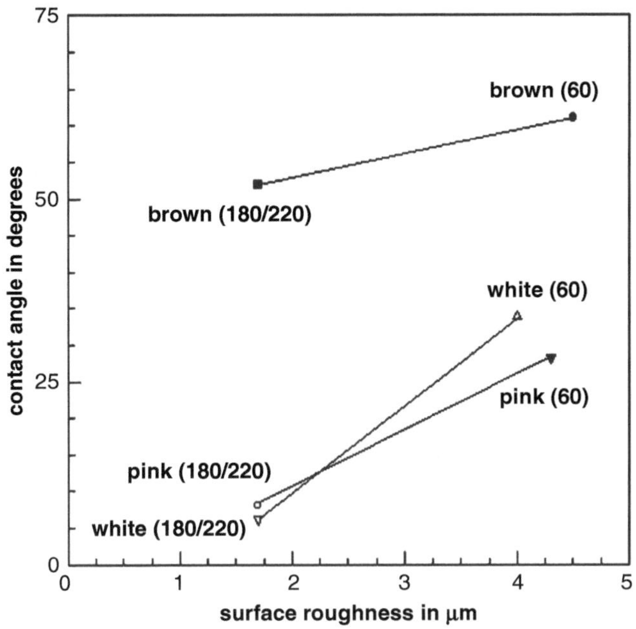

Fig. 8.78 Effects of abrasive type and size on substrate roughness and contact angle (Harris and Beevers, 1999); substrate: steel; wetting liquid: de-ionised water

Minaki et al. (2005) blast cleaned martensite stainless steel with aluminium oxide ($p = 0.2 - 0.4$ MPa, mesh 700, $\dot{m}_P = 50$–300 g/min, $\varphi = 90°$, $d_N = 8$ mm) and performed contact angle measurements with water. The authors found that the contact angle decreased as air pressure and blasting time increased. In general, the substrate surface featured rather high contact angles ($\theta_C = 75$–107°), which pointed to rather hydrophobic surfaces.

Uhlmann et al. (2006) measured contact angles and specific energies of $AlMg_3$ substrates after the treatment with impinging dry ice particles. The estimated contact angles were between $\theta_C = 50°$ and 80°, and the estimated specific surface energies were between $\gamma_S = 10$ and 50 mN/m. Contact angles decreased with an increase in dry ice mass flow rate, whereas the specific energies increased with an increase in dry ice mass flow rates.

A study on the wettability of aluminium substrates ($AlMg_3$) with different wetting liquids (demineralised water, glycerine and diiodmethane) was performed by Emrich (2003), who measured the values of the advancing contact angle. For substrates blast cleaned with aluminium oxide ($p = 0.6$ MPa), he obtained the following results: demineralised water (70% polar): $\theta_C = 30°$; glycerine (40% polar): $\theta_C = 60°$; diazomethane (disperse): $\theta_C = 35°$. These contact angles were lower than those for substrates degreased with acetone, but higher than those obtained for substrate prepared by pickling. These results illustrated the effect of the polar, respectively disperse, components of the testing liquids, although no trend could be established between contact angle and the percentage of polar, respectively disperse, component.

Sancaktar and Gomatam (2001) investigated the effects of different surface preparation methods on the contact angle of an organic adhesive to rolled steel substrates. For cold-rolled steel, the authors found that blast cleaning (aluminium oxide, mesh 54, $p = 0.55$ MPa) generated lower contact angles ($\theta_C = 15°$) compared to etching ($\theta_C = 19°$) and to the untreated substrate ($\theta_C = 41°$). For hot-rolled steel, the substrate formed after etching generated somewhat lower contact angles ($\theta_C = 14°$) than the blast cleaned substrate ($\theta_C = 18°$). The untreated hot-rolled steel featured a high contact angle of $\theta_C = 50°$.

A study into the wettability of liquefied organic coatings to welded metals was performed by Fedko and Tomas (1998); this seems to be the only study which considered organic coating materials as wetting liquid. Some results of this investigation are summarised in Fig. 8.79. It can be seen that "sand" blasting generated very high contact angles compared to grinding. Therefore, the conditions for wetting the weld substrate by the coatings notably deteriorated. Deterioration effects

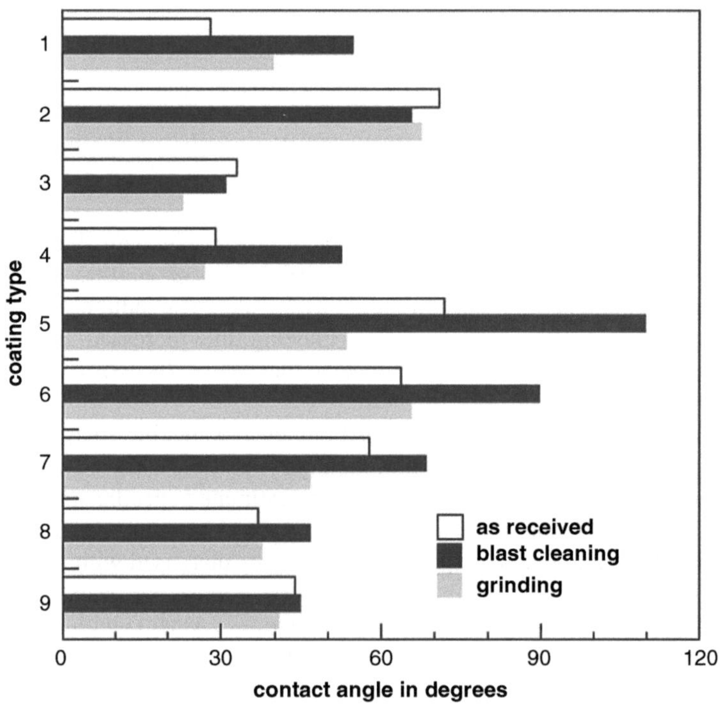

Fig. 8.79 Effects of surface properties on wettability of welded metals by liquefied organic coatings (Fedko and Tomas, 1998). Wetting liquids: 1 – aqueous solution (KBZh); 2 – TsZhS (not specified); 3 – AD (not specified); 4 – aqueous solution of chalk; 5 – MZhS (not specified); 6 – AzhS (not specified); 7 – silicon cream; 8 – emulsion with surface-active agent (P3-1); 9 – emulsion with surface-active agent (P3-2)

occurred namely in case of the aqueous solutions (coatings "4" and "5"), whereas the emulsions (coatings "8" and "9") were less affected. These two latter materials were modified with surface-active agents (soap and calcinated soda), which explains their superior capability to wet even the blast cleaned substrate efficiently.

8.10 Electron Transport Properties

Baer and Wagner (1973) presented measurements of the low-temperature electrical and thermal resistivities of several high-purity tungsten rods. They performed treatments with etching, electropolishing and blast cleaning, and they observed several effects of the surface conditions on the electron transport properties. Both the electrical and thermal resistivities were substantially affected by blast cleaning and etching. Some results for the electrical resistivity are presented in Fig. 8.80. It can be seen that etching and blast cleaning increased the values for the electrical resistivity. The same trend was found for the thermal resistivity. The original paper delivers further information.

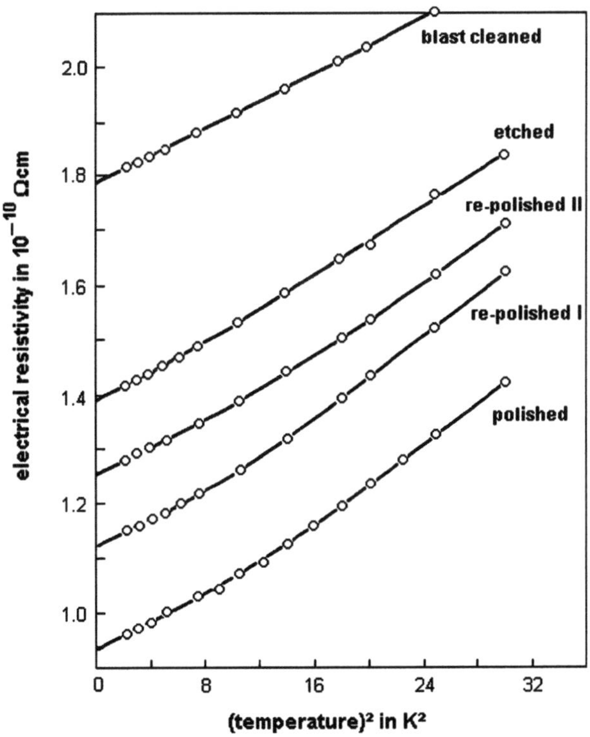

Fig. 8.80 Electrical resistivity as a function of temperature for various surface preparation conditions (Baer and Wagner, 1973)

Gladun et al. (1977) investigated the effects of blast cleaning (corundum, $d_{\mathrm{P}} = 27-31\ \mu\mathrm{m}$) on the low temperature thermal conductivity of a single-crystal niobium specimen. Above a temperature of 2 K, the results of the untreated and the blast cleaned samples were in accord, whereas below 2 K the differences of the sample surfaces, caused by the blast cleaning process, were discernible.

Chapter 9
Coating Performance

9.1 Corrosion Protection Performance of Organic Coatings

9.1.1 Definitions and Methods

There is no single parameter or property that can characterise the corrosion protection capability or performance of coating systems. It is rather a mixture of parameters that must be considered. The same problem applies to testing methods. Standard parameters for the assessment of the behaviour of corrosion protective coatings are summarised in Fig. 9.1. Basically, the performance of undamaged and artificially injured coating systems is evaluated. Examples for the effects of different surface preparation methods on the corrosion at artificial scribes are provided in Fig. 9.2. It can be seen that the performance was worst for the untreated sample and best for the blast cleaned sample. Samples prepared with power tools showed moderate performance.

Failure evaluation of coating systems involves the following three conditions (ISO 4628-1):

- failure size;
- failure distribution;
- failure intensity.

Some authors tried to generalise results of visual inspection methods. Vesga et al. (2000) introduced a *KIV*-value (Constant-Inspection-Visual) for the assessment of primers applied to substrates prepared with different surface preparation methods. The *KIV*-value reads as follows:

$$\text{KIV} = 100 - \sum(\text{corrosion products} + \text{blister size} + \text{blister density}) \qquad (9.1)$$

The criteria for the assessment of the three performance parameters are listed in Table 9.1. The term "corrosion products" corresponds to the degree of rusting according to ISO 4628-2, whereby "blister size" and "blister density" correspond to the degree of blistering according to ISO 4628-3. The higher the *KIV*-value, the better the coating performs. A freshly applied defect-free coating at $t = 0$ has a value

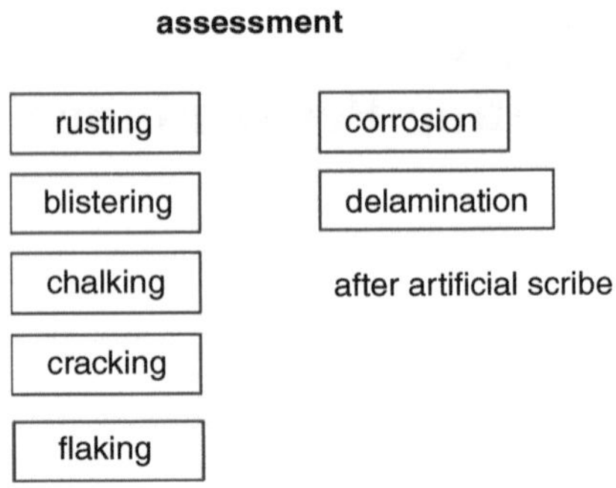

Fig. 9.1 Coating performance assessment parameters according to ISO 4628

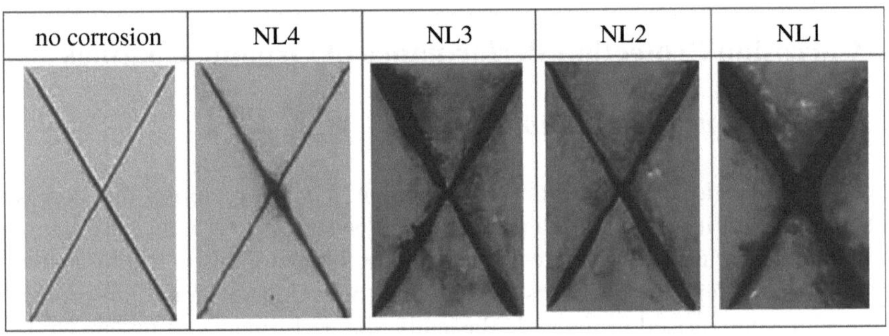

Fig. 9.2 Effects of surface preparation on underscribe corrosion (Kim et al., 2003). NL1 – untreated; NL2 – grinding (light rust removed); NL3 – grinding (rust completely removed); NL4 – dry blast cleaning

of $KIV = 100$. A coating with a value of $KIV = 36$ shows the worst performance. Figure 9.3 illustrates results of this procedure: KIV-values are plotted against the testing duration as functions of different surface preparation methods. The values for KIV decrease, as expected, with an increase in testing time, and they also show a dependence on the surface preparation method, at least for long exposure times.

Artificially injured coatings play a role for laboratory tests, such as for the neutral salt spray tests. In these cases, the artificial scribes simulate mechanical damage to the coating systems. Test duration depends on the corrosivity of the environment the coatings have been designed for. Examples are listed in Table 9.2. For certain

Table 9.1 Criteria for degree of blistering and degree of rusting (ISO 4628-1)

Criterion	Defect quantity	Defect size
0	No (resp. not visible) defects	Not visible at 10 × magnification
1	Very few defects	Visible only at 10 × magnification
2	Few defects	Just visible with unaided eye
3	Moderate number of defects	Clearly visible with unaided eye (up to 0.5 mm)
4	Considerable number of defects	Range between 0.5 and 5.0 mm
5	High number of defects	Larger than 5.0 mm

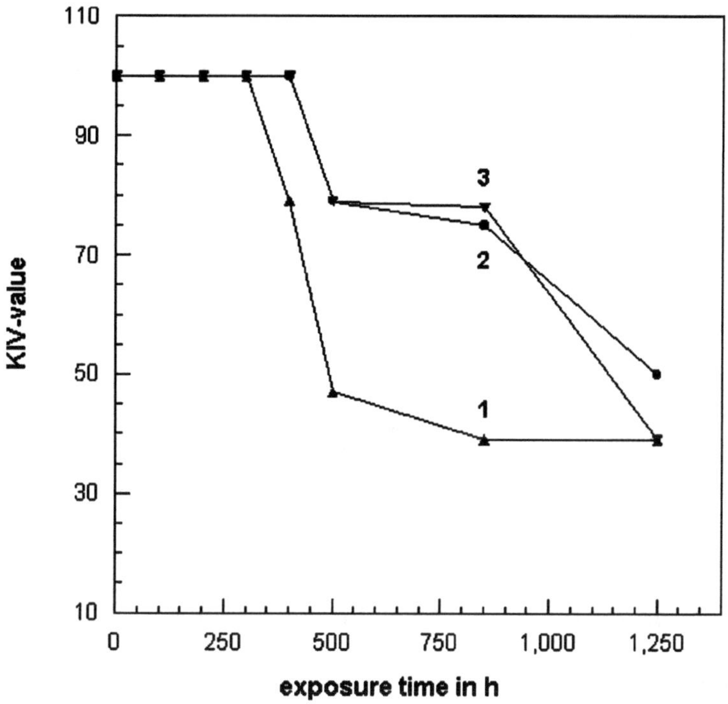

Fig. 9.3 Relationship between KIV and surface preparation methods (Vesga et al., 2000). Preparation methods: 1 – wet blast cleaning; 2 – wet blast cleaning with inhibitor; 3 – dry blast cleaning

application, for example for the use of coatings for offshore structures, special test regimes have been developed. An example is displayed in Fig. 9.4.

The methods for the damage and failure assessment are visually determined, although certain parameters, namely degree of rusting and degree of blistering, can be alternatively assessed by more objective methods, such as computerised image analysis methods (Momber, 2005b). Examples are provided in Fig. 9.5.

Table 9.2 Relationships between corrosivity and test conditions for coatings according to ISO 12944-6 (Projected coating durability: >15 years)

Corrosivity category[a]	Test duration in hours			
	Chemical resistance	Water immersion	Water condensation	Neutral salt spray
C2	–	–	120	–
C3	–	–	240	480
C4	–	–	480	720
C5-I	186	–	720	1,440
C5-M	–	–	720	1,440
Im1	–	3,000	1,440	–
Im2	–	3,000	–	1,440
Im3	–	3,000	–	1,440

[a] Defined in ISO 12944-1

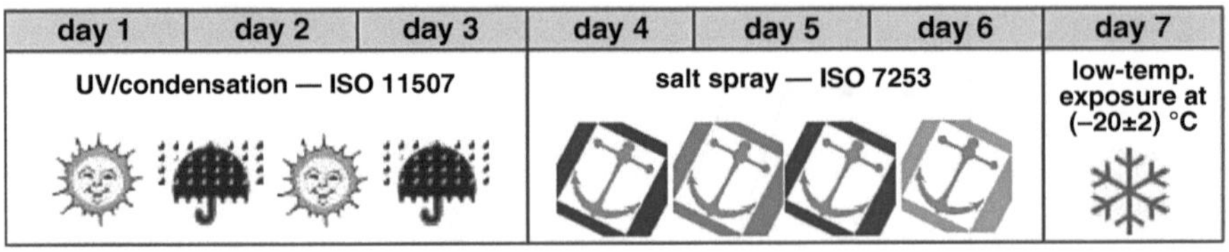

Fig. 9.4 Coating performance testing regime for offshore applications according to ISO 20340

Bockenheimer et al. (2002) performed investigations into the curing reactions of epoxy systems applied to aluminium, and they found different degrees of conversion of epoxy groups on the pretreated surfaces. Results of this study are plotted in Fig. 9.6. It can be seen that blast cleaning notably reduced the final degree of conversion of the epoxy groups. A distinct effect of the abrasive type could also be noted. The authors could further show that blast cleaned surfaces not only influenced the formation of the network structure in the near-interphase region, but also far from substrate.

9.1.2 Coating Performance After Blast Cleaning

9.1.2.1 Introduction

Systematic investigations about the effects of different surface preparation methods on the performance of organic coatings are provided by Allen (1997), Morris (2000), Momber et al. (2004) and Momber and Koller (2005, 2007). The first three authors mainly dealt with the adhesion of organic coatings to steel substrate; their results are presented in Sect. 9.2.

Vesga et al. (2000) utilised the *KIV*-criterion mentioned in Sect. 9.1.1. Results are provided in Fig. 9.3. For comparatively short exposure times ($t < 300$ h) and long exposure times ($t = 1{,}250$ h), this parameter was insensitive to surface preparation methods. At moderate exposure times, primer performance depended notably on surface preparation method. Primers applied over wet blast cleaned substrates deteriorated very quickly after a threshold time level was passed. The decrease in the resistance of primers applied over dry blast cleaned substrates was moderate after the threshold exposure time was exceeded. The addition of an inhibitor to the water for wet blast cleaning did not notably improve the performance of primers for longer exposure times. An inhibitor improved the situation basically for moderate exposure times only. Vesga et al. (2000) found that electrochemical impedance spectroscopy (EIS) can be utilised for the evaluation and assessment of the protective performance of organic coating systems. Pore resistance values measured on primers applied over steel substrates prepared with dry blast cleaning and wet blast cleaning showed the same qualitative trend as the *KIV*-values.

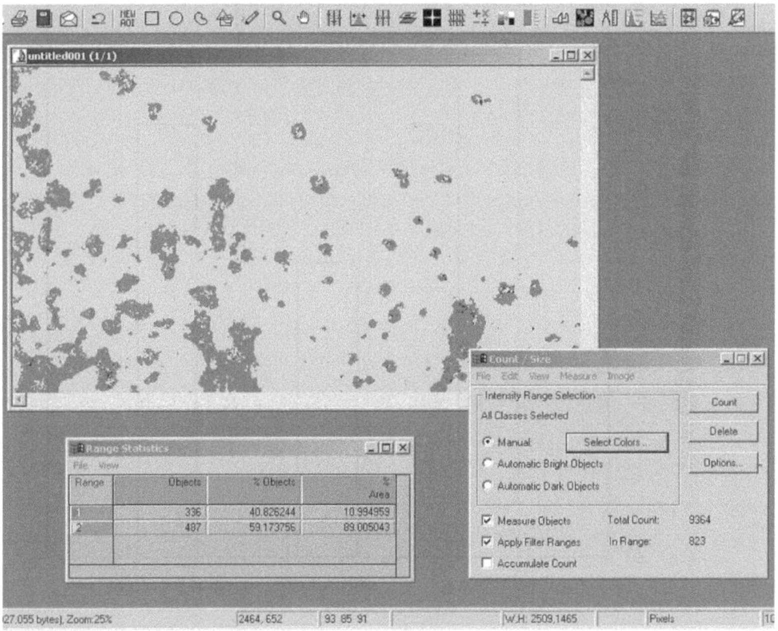

(a)

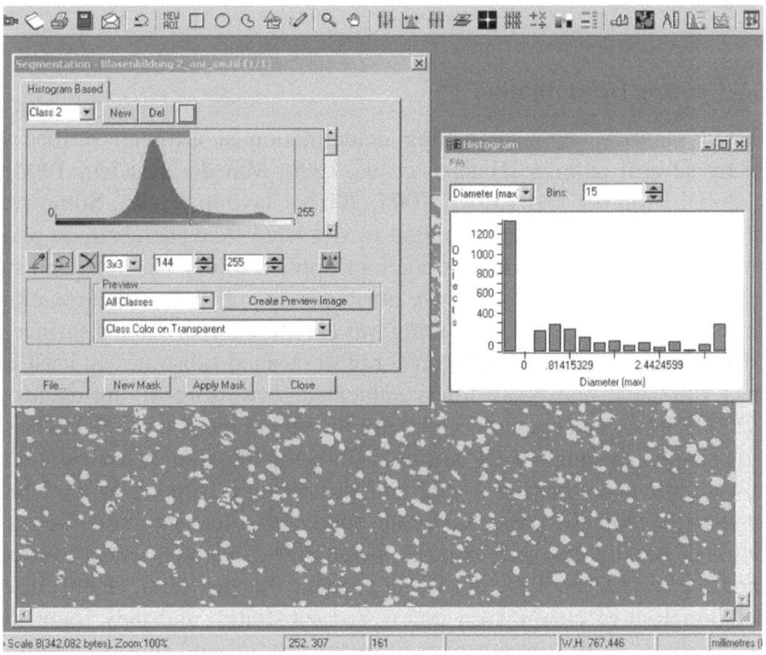

(b)

Fig. 9.5 Assessment of coating damaged based on digital image processing (Images: Muehlhan AG, Hamburg). (**a**) Degree of rusting; (**b**) Degree of blistering

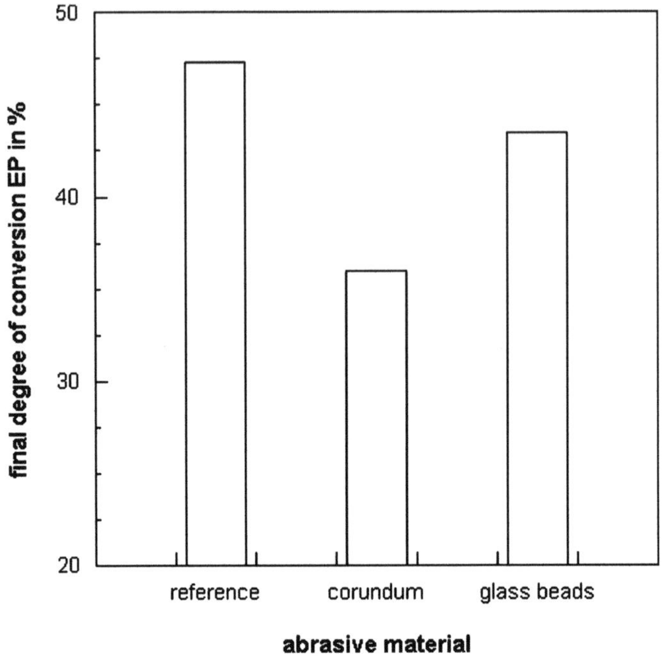

Fig. 9.6 Final degree of conversion of epoxy groups for 2 μm films on aluminium (Bockenheimer et al., 2002)

9.1.2.2 Coating Delamination

Results of measurements of coating delamination at artificial scribes were reported by several authors (Haagen et al., 1990; Van der Kaaden, 1994; Pietsch et al., 2002; Momber and Koller, 2005, 2007; Claydon, 2006). Some results are displayed in Fig. 9.7. Coatings applied to wet blast cleaned substrates showed the lowest delamination rate, whereas coatings applied to dry blast cleaned substrates performed worst. These results were attributed to substrate contamination due to broken abrasive debris. If blast cleaning was compared with manual surface preparation, delamination widths were larger for blast cleaned substrates, at least for epoxy coatings with zinc phosphate fillers subjected to wetting–drying cycles (Pietsch et al., 2002). Results of respective tests are shown in Figs. 9.8 and 9.9. Delamination of zinc phosphate primers at the artificial scribe on blast cleaned substrate occurred due to cathodic delamination. Using zinc dust primers, especially the edges of the scribe were cathodically protected by the anodic dissolution of zinc. Because of the formation of zinc oxides, increasing exposure time can lead to a deactivation of zinc dust and a progression of the corrosion process. Haagen et al. (1990) investigated the delamination of coatings on non-rusted substrates, and they found that blast cleaned surfaces were superior over mechanically ground surfaces. Some of their results are listed in Table 9.3. Figure 9.10 illustrates the effects of abrasive types on coating delamination. The coatings tested showed worse performance over shot

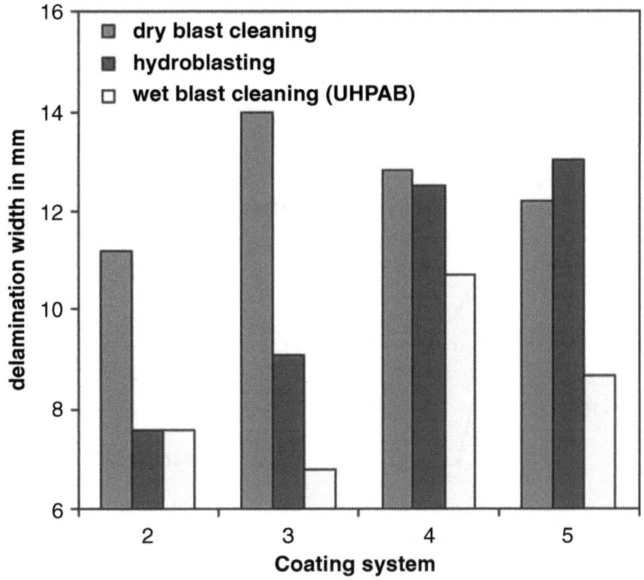

Fig. 9.7 Delamination of organic coatings for different surface preparation methods (Momber and Koller, 2005)

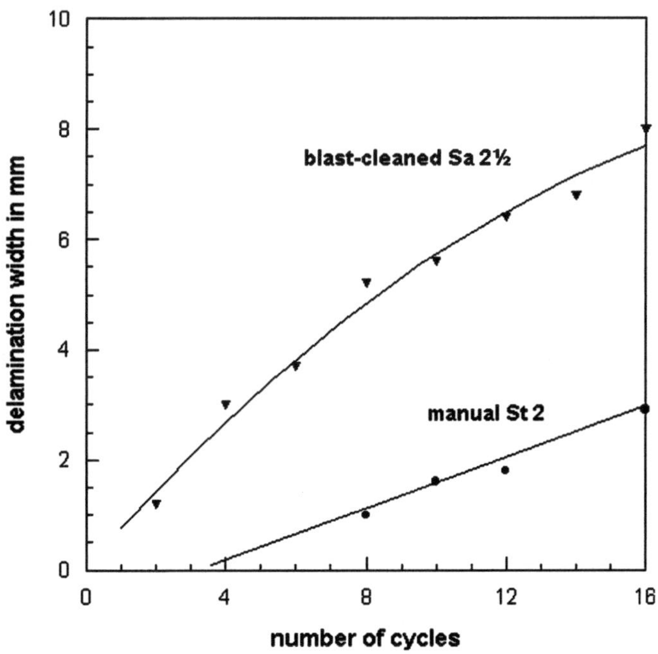

Fig. 9.8 Surface preparation influence on delamination of organic coatings at artificial scribe (Pietsch et al., 2002). Coating: epoxy/polyurethane; Primer: epoxy/zinc-phosphate

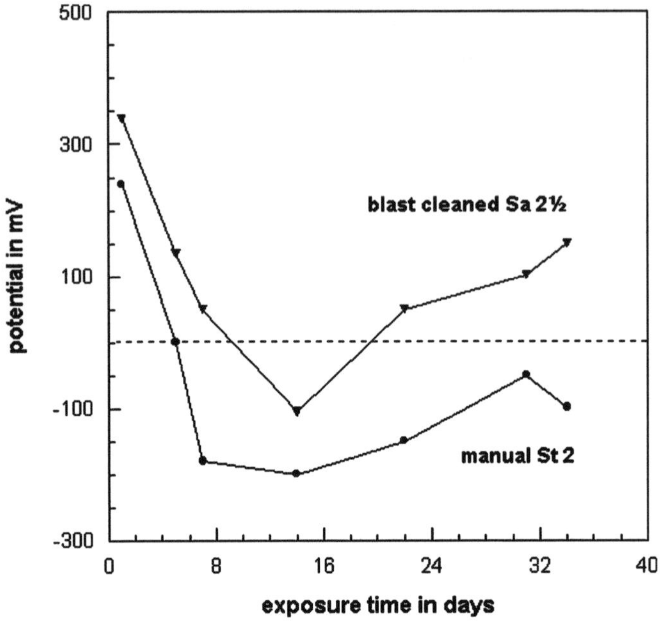

Fig. 9.9 Surface preparation method effects on electric potential below an intact coating (Pietsch et al., 2002). Primer type: zinc dust based primer

blasted steel compared with coatings applied to grit blasted steel during a cyclic corrosion test. If a salt spray test was considered, both abrasive types delivered comparative results. Van der Kaaden (1994) performed a comparative study into the performance of organic coating systems applied to dry blast cleaned and wet blast cleaned steel substrates. The hot-rolled substrates were pre-rusted. Results of this study are listed in Table 9.4. The results reveal the tight relationships between surface preparation method, testing regime, coating type and delamination width. Whereas the wet blasting version with the larger water flow rate (7.0 l/min) showed the best results for the chlorinated rubber in the salt spray test, it performed

Table 9.3 Effects of surface preparation method and test solution on the delamination of coatings after salt spray tests (Haagen et al., 1990), Coating: 2-pack epoxy with micaceous iron ore

Test solution	Delamination in mm	
	Polished	Blast cleaned
NaCl (0.117%)	2–3	2
NaCl (saturated)	4–5	0.5–1
NaCl (5%)	Ca. 11	Ca. 5
NH_4NH_3 (3.2%)	Ca. 1	0
NH_4NH_3 (0.85%)	5–7	2–3
$NH_4Al(SO_4)_2$	2–3	0
NH_4Cl (2.14%)	0.5	0
$CaCl_2$ (2.8%)	1–2	0

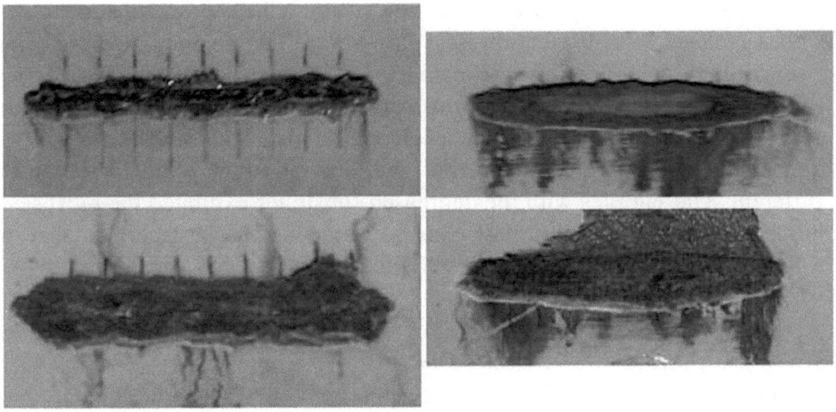

Fig. 9.10 Effects of blast cleaning method on delamination of zinc epoxy primers at an artificial scribe (Claydon, 2006). Upper images: dry blast cleaning with grit; Lower images: dry blast cleaning with shot. Left: after cyclic corrosion test; right: after salt spray test

worst for the high-solid epoxy in the seawater test with cathodic protection. The results for the tests with cathodic protection are of special interest. If the results for chlorinated rubber, obtained during the seawater test, are considered, the preferred surface preparation method would be wet blast cleaning with a low water volume (1.6 l/min). As far as cathodic protection was added, the preferred surface preparation method would be wet blast cleaning with a high volume of water (7.0 l/min). The opposite trend could be recognized if high-solid epoxies were applied to the blast cleaned surfaces.

Emrich (2003) investigated the delamination of adhesive bonds in aluminium ($AlMg_3$) samples. He subjected the samples to a salt spray test over a period of

Table 9.4 Delamination of organic coatings at an artificial scribe (Van der Kaaden, 1994)

Preparation method	Coating system	Delamination in mm			
		Sea water (1 year)	Sea water with cathodic protection (1 year)	Artificial rain water (1 year)	Salt spray test (3,000 h)
Dry blast cleaning	Chlorinated rubber	1.4	814.9	76.1	9.5
	Vinyl/tar	2.5	7.9	55.6	6.0
	Coal tar/epoxy	0.0	0.0	59.1	8.5
	High-solid epoxy	13.3	19.4	65.8	5.5
Wet blast cleaning (1.6 l/min)	Chlorinated rubber	1.2	831.3	77.3	8.0
	Vinyl/tar	0.0	0.0	61.0	6.8
	Coal tar/epoxy	0.0	0.0	46.1	8.3
	High-solid epoxy	13.3	30.0	56.9	4.5
Wet blast cleaning (7.0 l/min)	Chlorinated rubber	8.6	703.8	81.3	6.3
	Vinyl/tar	0.0	0.0	110.1	5.3
	Coal tar/epoxy	0.0	0.0	63.8	8.9
	High-solid epoxy	3.9	43.8	20.3	6.0

2,000 h, and he noted a severe delamination of the adhesive on substrates which were blast cleaned with corundum (p = 0.6 MPa). The delamination was much more severe than delaminations estimated for samples where the substrates were degreased with acetylene. Samples with substrates that were treated by pickling did not show any delamination. If an accelerated corrosion test (6 h in a 5% NaCl solution, subjected to an external current) was applied to the samples, the ranking was different. The samples with the degreased substrates exhibited the most severe delamination, followed by the blast cleaned samples. The best performance was again shown by the samples prepared with pickling.

9.1.2.3 Degree of Rusting

Measurements of the degree of rusting for paints applied to substrates prepared with different surface preparation methods were performed by Grubitsch et al. (1972) and Kogler et al. (1995). Results of the latter authors are displayed in Fig. 1.4. Figure 9.11 shows the effects of different abrasive materials on the degree of rusting of coated (zinc dust) steel panels. There exists the following power relationship between exposure time and degree of rusting:

$$\mathrm{DR} \propto \mathrm{t}_{\mathrm{E}}^{k_{\mathrm{R}}} \tag{9.2}$$

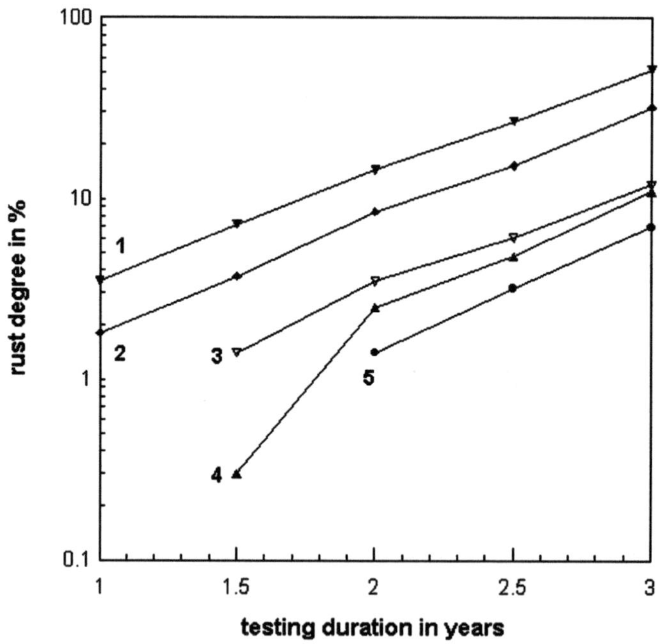

Fig. 9.11 Relationship between ageing kinetics and abrasive materials (Grubitsch et al., 1972). Abrasive materials/method: 1 – slag; 2 – quartz; 3 – aluminium oxide; 4 – steel grit; 5 – etching

Table 9.5 Ageing kinetics parameter in (9.2) for different abrasive materials (Grubitsch et al., 1972)

Abrasive type/method	Grain size in mm	Parameter k_R
Quartz	1.0–2.0	2.6
Corundum	0.8–1.0	–
Slag	1.0–2.0	2.4
Steel grit	0.8–1.0	–
Etching with H_2SO_4	–	–

This relationship could be exploited to describe the kinetics of ageing of a coating system. The power exponent k_R depended on abrasive material type. Values for this parameter are provided in Table 9.5. It can be seen that not only the type of abrasive material determined the ageing kinetics, but also its fineness.

Further results are listed in Table 9.6 where the failure times of two coating systems are listed. The failure time was defined as the time when the first rusting was visible on the coatings. Failure time strongly depended on the abrasive type. For the alkyd paint, for example, failure occurred after 3 months if aluminium oxide was used, but the failure time could be delayed up to 114 months when wet sand was used as an abrasive material. For the acrylic paint, the trend was opposite. Here, the coating applied to the substrate that was blast cleaned with aluminium oxide, showed the best performance.

9.1.2.4 Degree of Blistering

The degree of blistering of organic coatings is sensitive to the type of surface preparation. A systematic study on this issue was undertaken by Kim et al. (2003). Deterioration curves for a coating system, based on the results of long-term blistering tests (251 days) on artificially injured samples, are plotted in Fig. 9.12. Blistering was most severe for the untreated steel and least severe for the blast cleaned substrate. Blast cleaning was more efficient than power tool cleaning. The general relationship

Table 9.6 Effects of abrasive material type on failure times of organic coatings (Boocock, 1992)

Abrasive material	Failure time in months	
	Alkyd paint	Acrylic latex paint
Dry sand	101	114
Wet sand	114	38
Steel shot (S-280)	75	16
Steel grit (G-12)	89	38
Coal slag (coarse)	68	16
Coal slag (fine)	3	–
Staurolite	89	38
Flint	89	94
Copper/coal slag	89	114
Aluminium oxide	3	>126

Surface preparation grade: SP 10 for all samples

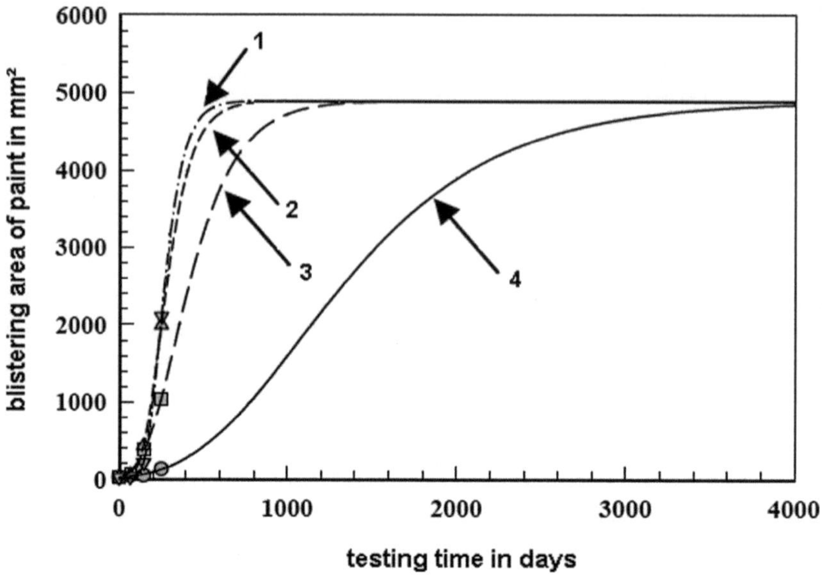

Fig. 9.12 Effects of surface preparation methods on the blister formation kinetics (Kim et al., 2003). Preparation method: 1 – no cleaning; 2 – grinding (light rust removed); 3 – grinding (rust completely removed); 4 – blast cleaning

between exposure time and degree of blistering is essentially equal to (9.2), whereby the power exponent depended on the surface preparation method.

9.2 Adhesion and Adhesion Strength

9.2.1 Definitions and Measurement

9.2.1.1 Definitions

According to Bullett and Prosser (1972) "the ability to adhere to the substrate throughout the desired life of the coatings is one of the basic requirements of a surface coating, second only to the initial need to wet the substrate." Adhesion bases on adhesive forces that operate across the interface between substrate and applied coating to hold the paint film to the substrate. These forces are set up as the paint is applied to the substrate, wets it and dries. The magnitudes of these forces (thus, the adhesion strength) depend on the nature of the surface and the binder of the coating. Five potential mechanisms cause adhesion between the surfaces of two materials (see Fig. 9.13):

- physical adsorption;
- chemical bonding;
- electrostatic forces;

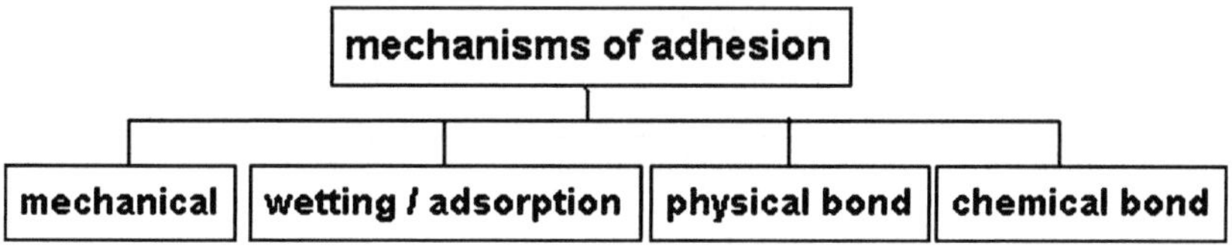

Fig. 9.13 Mechanisms of adhesion

- diffusion;
- mechanical interlocking.

In the mechanical interlocking mechanism, the macroscopic substrate roughness provides mechanical locking and a large surface area for bonding; the paint is mechanically linked with the substrate. Adhesive bonding forces could be categorised as primary and secondary valency forces as listed in Table 9.7. Adhesion depends on numerous factors, including those summarised in Fig. 9.14. It is instructive to note that the adhesion is to a certain amount a “test parameter” depending on test conditions and specifications. Adhesion values get a comparative meaning only if assessed under equal test conditions.

9.2.1.2 Adhesion Measurement

Adhesion between substrate and organic coating can be evaluated on site by different methods, including the following:

- pull-off testing; for coating dry film thickness DFT $> 250\,\mu m$;
- X-cut testing;
- cross-cut testing; for coating dry film thickness DFT $< 250\,\mu m$;
- falling ball impact;
- penknife disbondment.

For adhesive bonds, metallic coatings and ceramic coatings, other, more advanced testing methods (peel tests, indentation debonding tests, scratch tests, beam-bending tests, etc.) are available; a recent extensive review was delivered by Lacombe (2006). Berndt and Lin (1993) and Lin and Berndt (1994) provided a review about methods used to define and measure the adhesion of coatings or deposits formed by thermal spraying; their review included tensile adhesion test, double cantilever beam test, scratch test and bending test.

The pull-off test delivers quantitative information about the strength of the bond (usually given in N/mm^2, respectively MPa), while the picture of the rupture provides information about the weakest part of the system. The adhesion strength (referred to as pull-off strength if measured with the pull-off test) is the relationship between applied force and loaded cross-section:

$$\sigma_A = \frac{F_A}{A_A} \tag{9.3}$$

Table 9.7 Bonding forces and binding energies (Hare, 1996)

Force	Type	Description	Example	Binding energy in kcal/mole
Ionic	Primary valency	Bonding formed by transfer of valency electrons from the outer shell of an electron-donating atom into outer shell of an electron-accepting atom, to produce a stable valency configuration in both.	Metal salts	150–250
Covalent	Primary valency	Bonding formed when one or more pairs of valency electrons are shared between two atoms.	Most organic molecules	15–170
Co-ordinate	Primary valency	Covalent type bond where both of shared pair are derived from one of the two atoms.	Quaternary ammonium compounds	100–200
Metallic	Primary valency	Bonding in bulk phase of metals between positively charged metallic ions and the electron cloud in the lattice points of the structure.	Bulk metals	27–83
Hydrogen bonding	Secondary valency	Forces set up between the unshared electrons on a highly electronegative atom on one molecule and the weak positive charge from the 'exposed' proton of a hydrogen atom.	Water	<12
Dispersion	Secondary valency	Weak forces in all molecules that are associated with temporary fluctuations in electron density caused by the rotation of electrons around atomic nuclei.	Most molecules	<10
Dipole	Secondary valency	Intermolecular forces set up between weak and electronegative charge on one polar molecule and electropositive charge on a second polar molecule.	Polar organics	<5
Induction	Secondary valency	Very weak dipole-like forces between non-polar molecules set up by weak dipoles induced by the proximity of other strongly polar molecules.	Non-polar organics	<0.5

Frequently, adhesion strength is given in kN, which is the unit of a force. Obviously, this information is useful only if the loaded cross-section is known. It can, however, be used as a comparative measure if the loaded cross-section is a constant, exactly defined value.

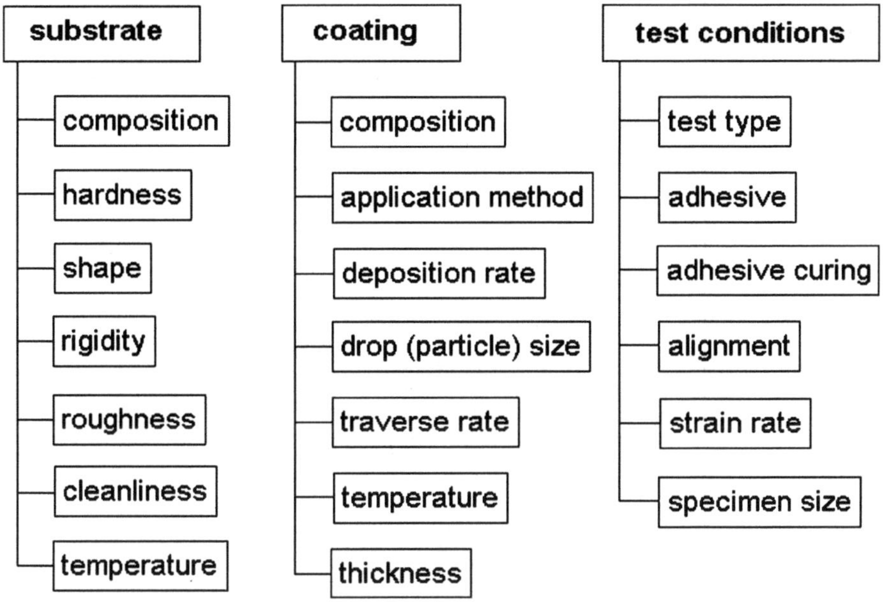

Fig. 9.14 Influence factors on the adhesion of coatings to steel substrates (James, 1984)

Typical failure types to be observed during pull-off tests are either adhesive failure (substrate-coating), cohesive failure (internal coating failure) or mixed adhesive–cohesive failure. More detailed designation is mentioned in Table 9.8. Strictly spoken, a plain adhesion failure will never occur in a coating-substrate system. This restriction is reinforced by XPS (X-ray photoelectron spectroscopy) measurements performed by van den Brand et al. (2004) and Watts and Dempster (1992), who found traces of polymeric material on the substrate surface of a metal–polymer interfacial fracture, which appeared to be a purely adhesive failure from an optical examination.

Time and environmental conditions are important parameters in the experimental estimation of adhesion parameters. Because the hardening of coating materials is a reaction kinetics process, the bond between substrate and coating, respectively adhesive, is a time-domain process. Emrich (2003), for example, measured the shear strength of an aluminium-adhesive joint subjected to a salt spray test. The aluminium substrate ($AlMg_3$) was blast cleaned with corundum ($p = 0.6$ MPa). Prior to the salt spray exposure, the shear strength had a value of 15.5 MPa. After a period of 2,000 h, however, the shear strength had dropped down to a value of 4.5 MPa only. This author could also show that the adhesion of the adhesive was extremely sensitive to ageing when the adhesive was applied to blast cleaned substrates. Other surface preparation methods, namely degreasing with acetylene and pickling, were much less sensitive to ageing effects. Further experimental information on these aspects is available in the literature, and it will be discussed in the following sections.

Desired adhesion depends on the certain case of application. The US Nayy, for example, has defined a general minimum pull-off strength of $\sigma_A = 3.4$ MPa

Table 9.8 Failure modes after pull-off testing of organic coatings (Momber and Koller, 2005)

Method	Failure figure	Failure type[a]
Dry blast cleaning	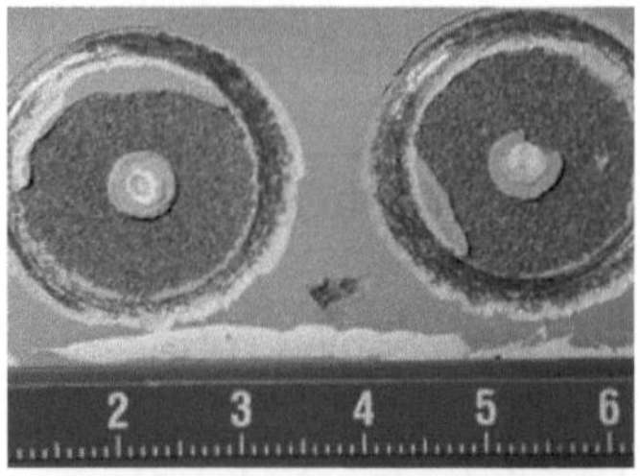	100% A/B
Hydroblasting	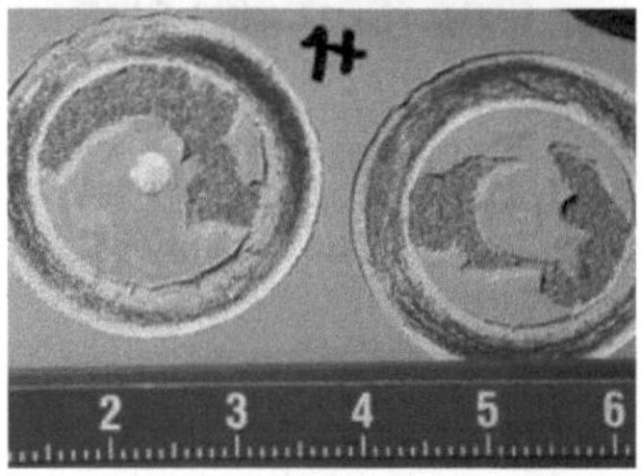	60% B, 40% A/B (left) 70% B, 30% A/B (right)
Wet blast cleaning (Ultra-high pressure abrasive blasting)	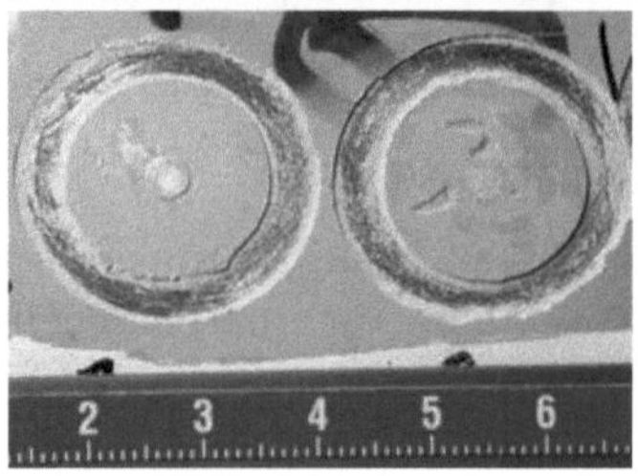	100% B

[a] A/B-adhesive failure coating/substrate
B-cohesive failure coating

measured per ASTM D4541 (Kuljan and Holmes, 1998). Demands for marine constructions are listed in Table 9.9.

9.2.2 Adhesion of Coatings and Adhesives to Metal Substrates

Sobiecki et al. (2003) conducted a study into the effects of surface preparation methods on the structure of the interfacial zone between steel substrate and a tungsten carbide coating. They found that the porosity in the interfacial zone depended on the surface preparation prior to the coating process. The porosity was lowest for grinding and highest for blast cleaning.

Several systematic studies were performed to estimate the adherence of coating systems to steel panels prepared by different methods. Long-term tests in salt water were performed by Allen (1997) and Morris (2000). These studies included hand wire brushing, needle gunning, hydroblasting and blast cleaning. The

Table 9.9 Critical adhesion strength values for some coatings (Norsok, 2004); using equipment according to ISO 4624, and carry out test when coatings are fully cured

Coating type/Application	DFT in μm	Pull-off strength in MPa (absolute minimum)	Failure mode
Thermally sprayed aluminium (or alloys)	200	7.0	–
Thermally sprayed zinc (or alloys of zinc)	100	5.0	Cohesive
Potable water tanks	–	5.0	–
Tanks for crude, diesel and condensate	–	5.0	–
Process vessels (<0.3 MPa, <75°C)	–	5.0	–
Process vessels (<7 MPa, <80°C)	–	5.0	–
Process vessels (<3 MPa, <130°C)	–	5.0	–
Vessels for storage of methanol, etc.	–	5.0	–
Fire protection (cement based)	–	2.0	–
Fire protection (epoxy based)		5.0	–

results, listed in Tables 9.10 and 9.11, illustrated the complex relationships between preparation methods and applied coating systems. Cross-cut, measured after 36 months, was almost independent on the preparation method for many epoxy coatings; exceptions were coal tar epoxy and pure epoxy tank lining, where wire brushing and needle gunning showed worse results compared to hydroblasting and blast cleaning. Penknife disbondment and impact resistance, both measured after 24 months, showed worst results for the mechanical methods (especially for the wire brushing). Impact resistance was more a function of the coating system than of the preparation method; thus, blast cleaned substrates were, on the whole, only slightly superior to manual preparation under the conditions of the impact testing. Regarding the pull-off strength, measured with a commercial adhesion tester, blast cleaning methods were superior to mechanical methods. Some results are shown in Fig. 9.15. There was a certain trend for the blast cleaning methods that pull-off adhesion increased with time. Under simulated ballast tank conditions, coatings applied to blast cleaned surfaces performed far better than coatings applied to mechanically prepared substrates, and equal to those on hydroblasted surfaces. It was observed that paint failure type was often a mixture of cohesive and adhesive failures, and the appearance of the certain mode was denoted in percent (see Table 9.8). However, as shown in Tables 9.10 and 9.11, substrate failure (denoted "S") and coat detachment occurred usually from mechanically prepared surfaces, whereas glue failure (denoted "G") and inter-coat failure (denoted "I") were the principal failure mode on most of the blast cleaned and hydroblasted surfaces.

Björgum et al. (2007) investigated the adhesion of repair coating systems for offshore applications. Pre-rusted steel panels were cleaned with blast cleaning, power tooling and waterjetting. After an accelerated ageing test, the adhesion between coatings and steel substrates was measured with a pull-off device. Although the authors found deviations in the pull-off strength for the different surface preparation methods, these differences were statistically insignificant.

Tests on contaminated substrates showed that the level of dissolved salts affected value and type of adhesion of coatings to substrates. With zero contaminants, the mode of failure was cohesive within the primer coat. As the salt level increased,

Table 9.10 Results of comparative adhesion tests on ballast tank coatings (Allen, 1997)

Method	Adhesion parameter		
	Falling ball impact[a]	Pull-off strength in MPa[b]	Penknife disbondment in mm
Epoxy coating (solvent-less)			
Wire brushing	2	2.8/S	6
Needle gunning	1	2.8/S	5
Hydroblasting (Dw2)	0	6.9/G	0
Hydroblasting (Dw2 FR)	4	3.4/G	0
Hydroblasting (Dw3)	0	3.4/G	0
Hydroblasting (Dw3 FR)	0	4.1/G	0
Blast cleaning (Sa 2½)	1	5.5/G	0
Coal tar epoxy			
Wire brushing	4	2.1/S	10
Needle gunning	3	2.4/S	7
Hydroblasting (Dw2)	0	5.2/I	0
Hydroblasting (Dw2 FR)	2	6.9/I	0
Hydroblasting (Dw3)	0	6.9/I	0
Hydroblasting (Dw3 FR)	2	6.9/I	0
Blast cleaning (Sa 2½)	1	6.6/I	0
Epoxy system			
Wire brushing	2	2.1/S	5
Needle gunning	2	2.8/S	3
Hydroblasting (Dw2)	2	6.9/G	0
Hydroblasting (Dw2 FR)	0	5.5/G	0
Hydroblasting (Dw3)	0	5.2/G	0
Hydroblasting (Dw3 FR)	0	6.9/G	0
Blast cleaning (Sa 2½)	0	5.5/G	0
Glass flake epoxy			
Wire brushing	2	2.8/S	5
Needle gunning	1	4.1/S	3
Hydroblasting (Dw2)	1	6.9/G	0
Hydroblasting (Dw2 FR)	4	5.2/G	0
Hydroblasting (Dw3)	0	3.4/G	0
Hydroblasting (Dw3 FR)	0	5.5/G	0
Blast cleaning (Sa 2½)	0	6.9/G	0

FR flash rust; *Dw* surface cleanliness according to STG 2222
[a]0 = no cracking, no detachment; 1 = slight cracking, no detachment; 2 = slight cracking and detachment; 3 = moderate cracking, no detachment; 4 = moderate cracking, slight detachment
[b]Failure mode: G = glue, I = intercoat, S = substrate

progressively less primer remained adhered to the steel surface. At higher contamination level, there was a change from mixed to totally adhesive failure of the primer (Allan et al., 1995). Baek et al. (2006) reported a notable decrease in pull-off strength if the steel substrate was contaminated with chlorides. The drop in adhesion was very pronounced if a chloride concentration of 7 $\mu g/cm^2$ was exceeded.

Kaiser and Schulz (1987) performed cross-cut adhesion tests on coatings applied to zinc surfaces. If the samples were degreased only, the cross-cut adhesion was very low. The adhesion notably improved if the samples were blast cleaned with coal

Table 9.11 Results of comparative long-term adhesion tests after 12, 24 and 36 months (Morris, 2000)

Method	Cross-cut in mm			Impact resistance[a]			Pull-off strength in MPa[b]		
Time in months →	12	24	36	12	24	36	12	24	36
Solventless epoxy (2 × 125 μm DFT)									
Wire brushing	0	0	0	2	2	3	2.8/S	3.5/S	2.8/S
Needle gunning	0	0	0	1	1	2	2.8/S	5.5/S	5.2/S
Hydroblasting (Dw2)	0	0	0	0	0	1	6.9/S	7.6/I	8.3/G
Hydroblasting (Dw2 FR)	0	0	0	2	3	3	3.5/I	11.0/I	8.6/I
Hydroblasting (Dw3)	0	0	0	0	0	1	3.5/I	11.0/I	10.7/G
Hydroblasting (Dw3 FR)	0	0	0	0	1	1	4.1/I	8.3/I	11.0/I
Blast cleaning (Sa 2½)	0	0	0	1	2	2	5.5/I	12.4/I	10.3/G
Glass flake epoxy (2 × 125 μm DFT)									
Wire brushing	0	0	10	1	1	3	4.1/S	4.1/S	2.1/S
Needle gunning	0	0	2	2	2	3	2.4/S	5.5/S	8.9/S
Hydroblasting (Dw2)	0	0	0	1	1	1	6.9/G	11.0/I	>17.9/G
Hydroblasting (Dw2 FR)	0	0	0	1	2	2	3.4/G	15.2/G	>17.2/G
Hydroblasting (Dw3)	0	0	0	0	0	1	7.6/G	10.3/I	9.7/I
Hydroblasting (Dw3 FR)	0	0	0	1	1	1	6.9/G	16.9/I	>17.2/I
Blast cleaning (Sa 2½)	0	0	0	0	0	1	6.9/G	13.8/G	13.1/G
Low temperature cure glass flake epoxy (2 × 125 μm DFT)									
Wire brushing	0	0	10	1	1	1	2.8/S	4.6/S	7.6/S
Needle gunning	0	0	12	1	1	2	4.1/S	3.4/S	12.1/S
Hydroblasting (Dw2)	0	0	0	2	2	2	6.9/G	17.2/G	16.6/G
Hydroblasting (Dw2 FR)	0	0	0	2	2	2	5.2/G	14.5/I	11.7/G
Hydroblasting (Dw3)	0	0	0	0	0	1	3.4/G	15.2/G	10.3/G
Hydroblasting (Dw3 FR)	0	0	0	0	1	1	5.5/G	16.9/I	13.8/G
Blast cleaning (Sa 2½)	0	0	0	1	1	2	6.9/G	13.8/G	12.4/G
Modified epoxy (2 × 125 μm DFT)									
Wire brushing	0	0	0	1	1	3	4.8/S	5.5/S	2.8/ S
Needle gunning	0	0	0	2	3	3	2.1/S	2.8/S	4.1/ S
Hydroblasting (Dw2)	0	0	0	0	0	0	6.9/I	12.8/I	10.3/ I
Hydroblasting (Dw2 FR)	0	0	0	1	2	2	3.8/I	11.0/I	8.6/ I
Hydroblasting (Dw3)	0	0	0	0	0	1	6.9/I	10.8/I	9.7/ I
Hydroblasting (Dw3 FR)	0	0	0	0	0	0	4.1/I	15.2/I	7.9/ I
Blast cleaning (Sa 2½)	0	0	0	0	0	1	6.9/I	13.1/I	9.7/ G

FR flash rust; *Dw* surface cleanliness according to STG 2222
[a]0 = No cracking; 1 = very slight cracking, no detachment; 2 = slight cracking, no detachment; 3 = moderate cracking, no detachment
[b]Failure mode: S = substrate, I = intercoat, G = glue

furnace slag. However, the authors noted an additional effect of the coating to be applied. Chlorinated polyvinyl chloride (PVC), for example, performed especially good if the zinc substrate was blast cleaned.

Table 9.12 lists results of changes in adherence of two coatings on aluminium and steel after 500 h in a condensing water environment as a function of the metal pretreatment process. Although the values for the adhesion are higher in the case of the blast cleaned surface, the behaviour after exposure to water was similar for the

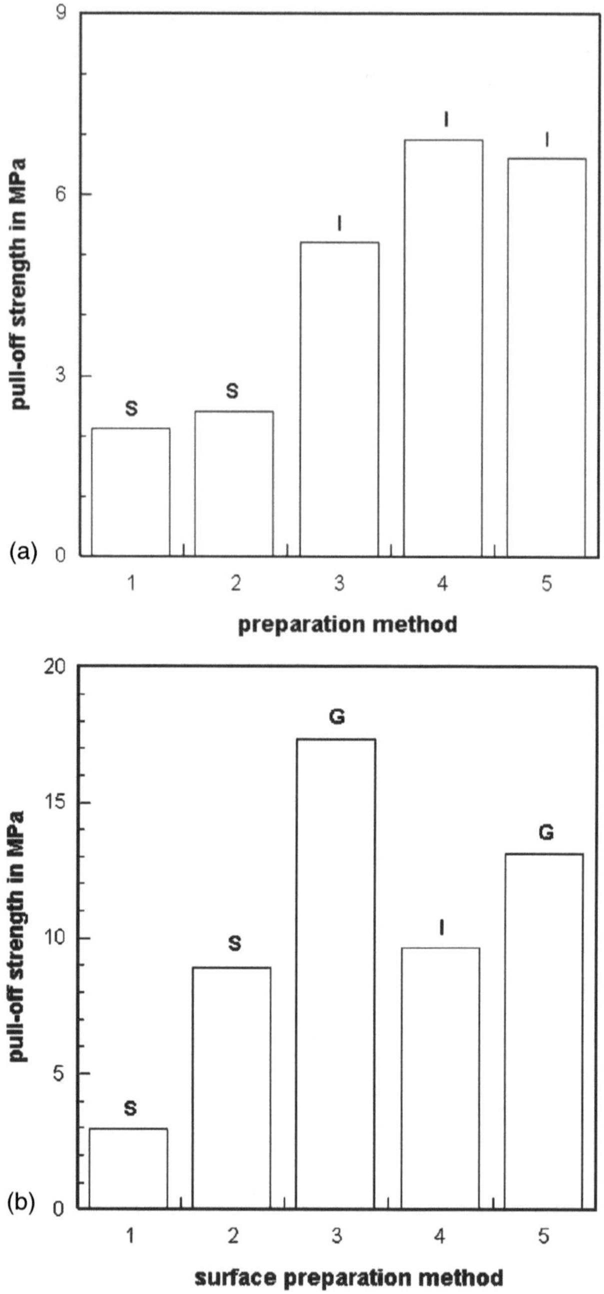

Fig. 9.15 Pull-off strengths after surface preparation-simulated ballast tank conditions. Preparation methods: 1 – hand brush; 2 – needle gunning; 3 – hydroblasting (Dw2); 4 – hydroblasting (Dw3); 5 – dry blast cleaning (Sa 2½); coating thickness: 2 × 125 μm. (**a**) Coal tar epoxy after 24 months (Allen, 1997); (**b**) Glass flake epoxy after 36 months (Morris, 2000). See Table 9.11 for "S", "I" and "G"

Table 9.12 Adherence of coatings after 500 h condensation (Leidheiser and Funke, 1987)

Substrate	Coating	Adhesion before and after water exposure in MPa			
		Degreased		Blast cleaned	
		Before	After	Before	After
Aluminium	Polyurethane	11.4	11.6	27.6	28.2
	Epoxy-polyamide	20.3	22.1	27.6	27.6
Steel	Polyurethane	15.4	3.4	35.9	15.2
	Epoxy-polyamide	19.5	17.4	25.9	21.8

degreased and blast cleaned surfaces. There was very little effect of water exposure for both coatings and for both surface preparation methods in the case of aluminium; both coatings exhibited lower adhesion values after exposure to water for both surface preparation methods in the case of steel.

The effect of cleanliness on the adhesion of thermally sprayed metal coatings to steel substrates is illustrated in Fig. 9.16. Here, substrate cleanliness is characterised through reflectivity. A value of 100% corresponded to the reflectivity of a light grey tile. The higher reflectivity, the higher is surface cleanliness (this relationship holds for a given abrasive material only). It can be seen that high cleanliness promoted high adhesion strength; the relationship was linear for both abrasive types. Another example for the effects of surface cleanliness is illustrated in Fig. 9.17 in terms of surface preparation grade. The relative adhesion of a metal-sprayed coating dropped down to 50%, if the preparation grade was lowered from Sa 3 to Sa 2.

Rider (1987) reported about the bond durability of metals, pretreated with different methods, and adhesives. Wedge style durability tests were conducted, and the durability performance of blast cleaned metallic adherends was compared with standard pretreatments. It was found that blast cleaning at a blasting pressure of $p =$ 0.45 MPa led to a notable reduction in the average length of cracks in the adherend-adhesive system. After a root time of 7 h, for example, the crack length was about $l_C = 107$ mm for abrading with distilled water, but it was $l_C = 60$ mm only for blast cleaning. Watts and Dempster (1992), however, who applied wet blast cleaning with aluminium oxide abrasives to adhesively bonded titanium alloys, found that plain blast cleaning did not perform very well; additional preparation steps (anodising and priming) were required to obtain satisfying results. Wedge splitting tests in a corrosive environment were performed by Emrich (2003) for the assessment of adhesion between aluminium substrates and organic adherends. He found that blast cleaning (corundum and glass beads) and subsequent electropolishing reduced the lengths of the cracks in the interface zones between adhesive and substrate compared to samples which were electropolished only. Regarding the two blast cleaning media, the positive effects were stronger for the samples blast cleaned with corundum compared to samples blast cleaned with glass beads. Opposite trends were observed by Emrich (2003) for samples that were blast cleaned and subsequently pickled. In these cases, the pretreatment with corundum and glass beads deteriorated the resistance of the adhesive joint against crack propagation. The shortest crack lengths were measured for the systems where the substrate was pickled only. After an

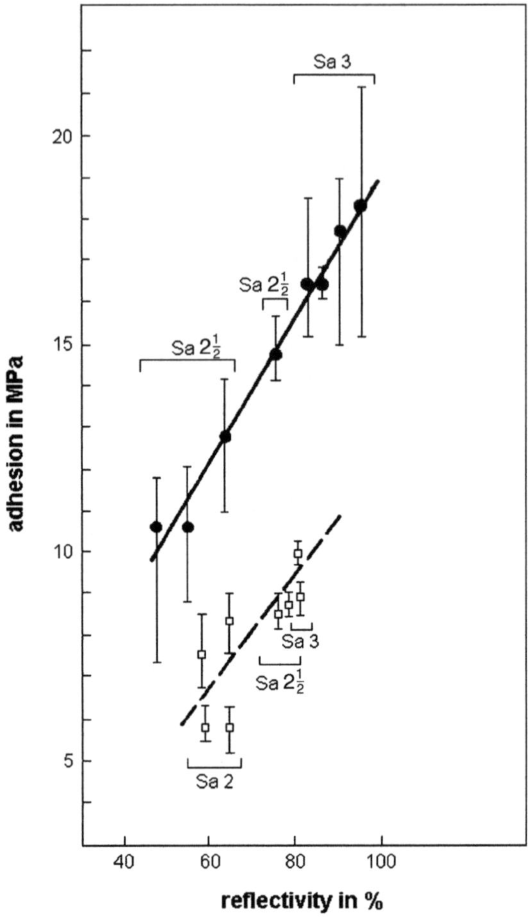

Fig. 9.16 Effect of substrate cleanliness (reflectivity) on adhesion strength of arc-sprayed aluminium (Bardel, 1974). Parameters: $p = 0.4$–0.6 MPa; $d_N =$ 8–12 mm; x = 150–300 mm; $\varphi = 60 - 90°$. Upper curve: iron grit (d_P = 100–900 μm), Lower curve: silica sand (d_P = 600–1,500 μm)

exposure time of about 250 h, however, the influence of the surface preparation methods vanished, and the crack length rested on a stable level of about l_C = 38 mm. The author could also prove that the crack length depended on the surface roughness of the profile. A coarse profile (as achieved after blast cleaning and subsequent pickling) delivered longer cracks than a finer profile (as achieved after blast cleaning and subsequent electropolishing). Emrich (2003) also noted that the deformation behaviour of the adhesive in the wedge splitting test had an additional influence on the results. A rather rigid, less deformable adhesive promoted a quick crack extension.

Bardis and Kedward (2002) performed an investigation into the effects of surface preparation methods on the strength of adhesively bonded composite joints. A double cantilever beam (DCB) test was adapted in order to measure the critical strain energy rates (G_{Ic}) of the bonded systems. Results are displayed in Fig. 9.18. Blast cleaned adherends had higher failure loads and higher G_{Ic}-values than non-blast cleaned ones, though the failure mode did not change. Load displacement curves for the bonded composites also depended on preparation method. Emrich (2003)

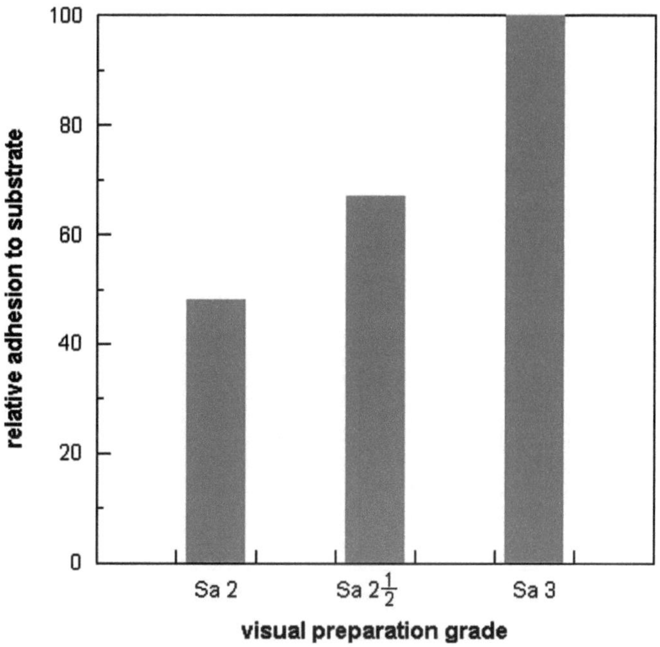

Fig. 9.17 Effects of surface preparation grades on the adhesion strength of metal-sprayed coatings (James, 1984)

estimated the change in the shape of a shear–gliding diagram for adhesive layers. The shear–gliding diagram is comparable with a stress–strain diagram, whereby the stress is replaced by the shear stress, and the strain is replaced by the gliding of the adhesive layer. The results showed that a preparation of the substrate due to blast cleaning (corundum, $p = 0.6\,\mathrm{MPa}$) and degreasing with acetylene led to a notable change in the shape of the shear–gliding diagram. The use of both methods induced a distinctive drop in shear stress after a number of ten loading cycles in a corrosive medium. However, the shear modulus (ratio between shear stress and gliding) did not change after blast cleaning.

Martin (1997) compared the peel resistance characteristics of pipeline coatings as functions of surface preparation procedures. Results of this study are displayed in Fig. 9.19, which shows results of peel resistance measurements after artificial ageing in a salt spray solution. Blast cleaning could notably improve peel strength, but the level of improvement depended on abrasive type and ageing duration. Aluminium oxide and steel grit delivered very good results, whereas glass beads did not contribute to an improvement in the peel strength. The positive effect of blast cleaning seemed to vanish for long ageing duration; after 16 weeks, the adhesion between coating and substrate was completely deteriorated for the degreased and the glass bead blasted samples. Figure 9.20 illustrates the situation after artificial ageing in a hot water immersion chamber. With the exception of the glass bead blasted samples, the peel resistance curves for the different surface preparation methods ran almost

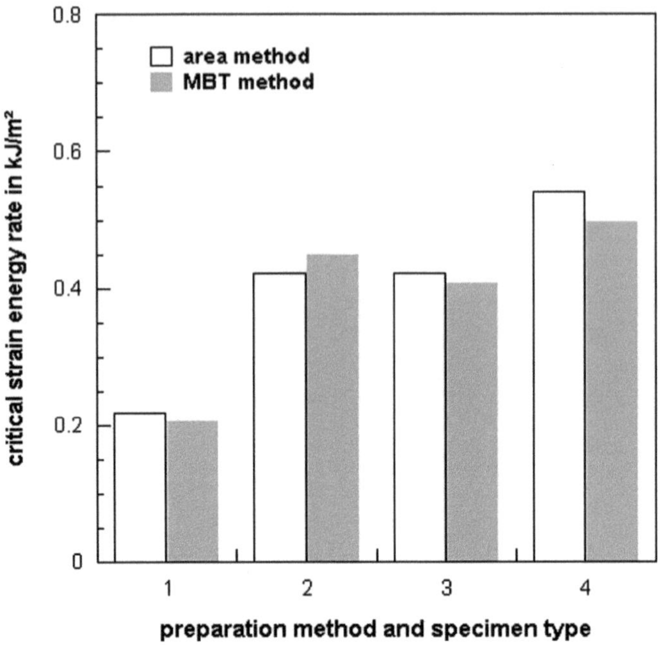

Fig. 9.18 Effect of blast cleaning on the strain energy rate of bonded systems (Bardis and Kedward, 2002). Preparation methods: 1 – RF–RF, no blast cleaning; 2 – RF–RF, blast cleaning; 3 – VB–VB, no blast cleaning; 4 – VB–VB, blast cleaning (RF–RF = release fabric to release fabric orientation; VB–VB = vacuum bag to vacuum bag orientation)

parallel to each other. A gradual reduction in the peel strength with an increase in ageing duration took place. Blast cleaning did not contribute to an improvement in adhesion. However, steel grit showed the best performance among the blast cleaning media in both test situations, and this was contributed to the high roughness at the substrate surface. Substrates with comparative roughness values (glass bead and aluminium oxide) performed quite differently under corrosive environment, and it was concluded that roughness was not the only affecting surface parameter (Martin, 1997). Changes in substrate morphology (contamination) seem to play an important role as well. The worst performance of glass bead can be contributed to the formation of a thin, with Na, Si and Ca, contaminated oxide layer (see Fig. 8.53).

Staia et al. (2000) conducted tests on the adhesion of coatings thermally sprayed on steel substrates. The authors blast cleaned the substrate with aluminium oxide ($d_P = 425$–$850\,\mu$m, $p = 0.34$–0.62 MPa, $\varphi = 75°$) and conducted pull-off tests and interface indentation tests. For the indentation test, they found that critical indentation load, necessary to produce a crack at the interface, as well as the critical length of the crack in the interface between substrate and coating increased if the air pressure increased. Pull-off strength also increased as pressure increased. The authors also found a relationship between air pressure and effects of coating thickness on adhesion. For the rather low air pressure ($p = 0.34$ MPa), critical indentation

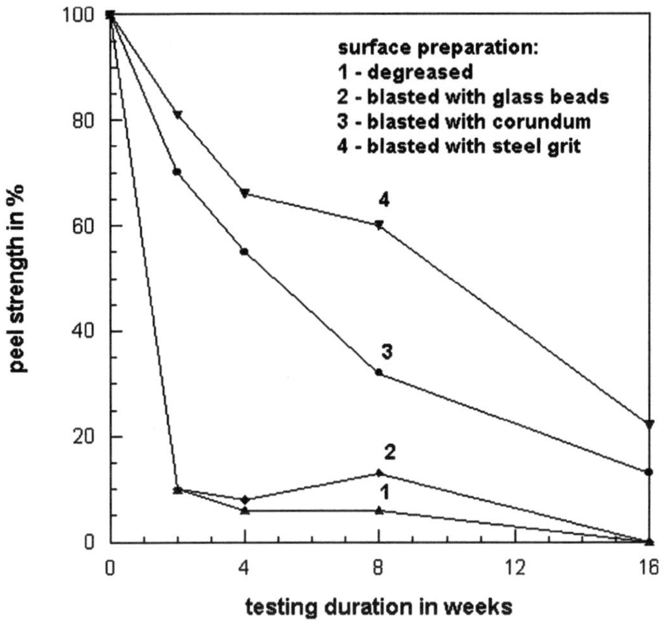

Fig. 9.19 Effects of surface preparation methods on peel resistance of pipeline coatings after salt spray testing (Martin, 1997)

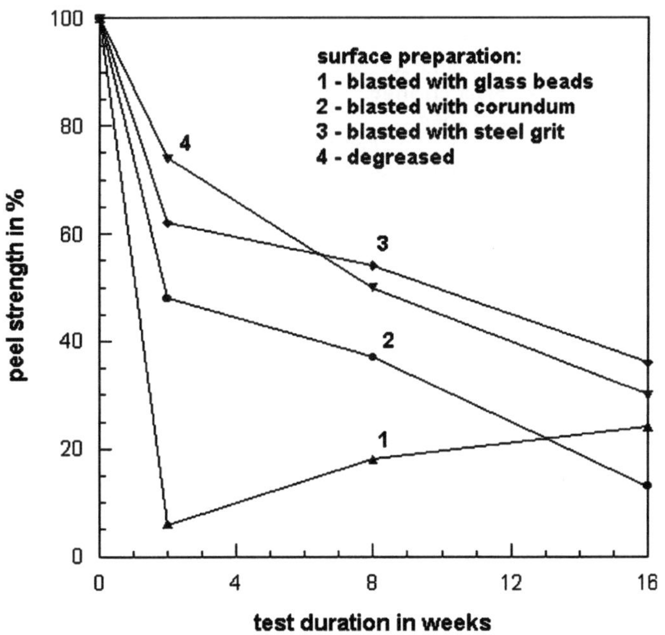

Fig. 9.20 Effects of surface preparation methods on peel resistance of pipeline coatings after immersion tests in 70°C hot water (Martin, 1997)

load depended on coating thickness. This was not the case for the higher air pressures. These results were attributed to the history of residual stress formation in the substrate and the coating material.

Van Rooijen et al. (2005) investigated the effects of chemical and mechanical treatment of steel sheets on the behaviour of fibre–metal laminate (FML). They considered regular steel sheets, molybdenum-enriched steel sheets and aluminium-coated steel sheets. Pretreatment methods were etching and blast cleaning (aluminium oxide, d_P = 149–210 μm, p = 0.2 MPa). Peel tests were performed, and it was shown that blast cleaning delivered the highest values for the peel strength (1.62 MPa). The failure mode was cohesive (in the adhesive material) for the blast cleaned samples, which further proved very good adhesion. Etched samples failed at the interfaces between sheet and adhesive; only after a rather long etching time of 3 min, the failure was partially cohesive. Leahy et al. (2003) performed a study into the bonding of fibre reinforced composites to titanium substrates based on a modified wedge test. They deployed blast cleaning (aliminium oxide, mesh 180/220), anodisation, plasma treatment and silicon sputtering as treatment methods. The joints were subjected to 24-hours cycles (wet/dry, cold/hot) for 12 days. The authors reported that an simple blast cleaning was the least successful treatment. The best bond was achieved for the samples treated wit a combination of anodisation and subsequent blast cleaning.

Figure 9.21 displays results of furnace cyclic tests on the durability of a multi-layer thermal barrier system. Bond coat surface morphology (not substrate surface

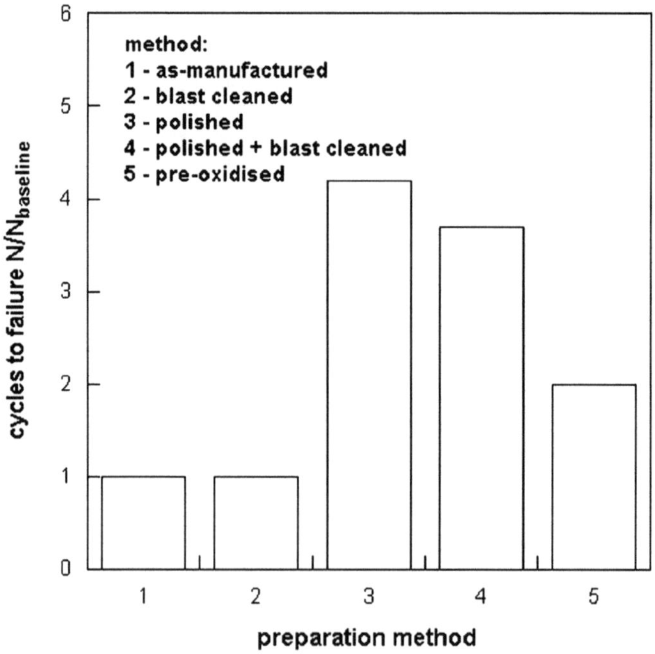

Fig. 9.21 Effects of surface preparation of a bond coat on the failure lifetimes for multi-layer thermal barrier coating systems (Spitsberg et al., 2005). Abrasive type: aluminium oxide

morphology) was varied due to the application of different surface preparation methods, among them combined methods. As the graph clearly shows, the durability was lowest for the systems which were conventionally blast cleaned. Durability could notably be increased if the substrates were treated with a combined method, consisting of polishing and subsequent blast cleaning. Chemical methods also delivered good results. An investigation of the effects of blast cleaning on the durability of thermal barrier coatings (TBS) was also conducted by Xie et a. (2003). The authors blast cleaned a bond coat with aluminium oxide abrasives (grit size 220, $p = 0.2$ MPa, $R_z = 75\,\mu$m) and applied a top coat by means of electron beam physical vapour deposition. The lifetime of the coating and the residual stresses in the thermally grown oxide (TGO) were measured as functions of surface morphology. It was found that the lifetime of the system with the blast cleaned bond coat. The lifetime (thermal spallation cycles) of the systems with blast cleaned bond coats varied over a narrow range of 600 to 750 cycles, whereas the systems with the untreated bond coats featured a wide lifetime range of 190 to 1,917 cycles. This result was attributed to the more consistent surface roughness of the blast cleaned bond coat. Another finding was that the stresses in the thermally grown oxides decreased faster if the bond coat was blast cleaned.

Boue (2005) investigated the effect of surface preparation on the adhesion of coatings to bridge ropes and found that blast sweeping delivered results superior to those measured after simple cleaning. Adhesion strength increased after blast sweeping (e.g. from $\sigma_A = 4.1$ MPa after washing to $\sigma_A = 6.6$ MPa after blast sweeping); percentage of cohesive failure also increased if the ropes were blast sweeped.

Coating type and thickness also determine the effects of surface preparation methods on pull-off strength. Results were provided by Bordeaux et al. (1991). For TiC-coatings, plasma sprayed on inconel substrates, the authors found that pull-off strength was higher for dry blast cleaned substrates (aluminium oxide, $d_P = 7.4\,\mu$m) compared with machined substrates as long as the coating thickness did not exceed a value of 200 µm. Beyond this thickness value, machined substrates provided better adhesion to the coating. It was also found that the microstructure of the coating was modified if the coating was applied to the machined substrate. Lamellae within the coating were folded due to the rather coarse surface relief. Such foldings resulted in oscillation of the laminations within the coating, which were maximum at the surface and vanished further in the coating.

Loh et al. (2002) found that moisture on the surface of steel substrates affected the adhesion of epoxy to the steel. Results of their measurements are provided in Fig. 9.22. Interface fracture energy steadily degraded with increasing moisture content. For a dry substrate interface, for example, fracture energy was 770 J/m^2, whereas it was about 50 J/m^2 only for a moisture content of about 8 wt.%.

For bitumen, pull-off strength depends additionally on temperatures of the substrate and the applied bitumen mass; this was shown by Pawlikowski et al. (1966). Pull-off strength increased if steel substrate temperature rose; pull-off strength was four times higher at a steel temperature of 100°C compared with a steel temperature of 20°C. For a given substrate temperature, pull-off strength only slightly increased with a rise in the temperature of the applied bitumen mass.

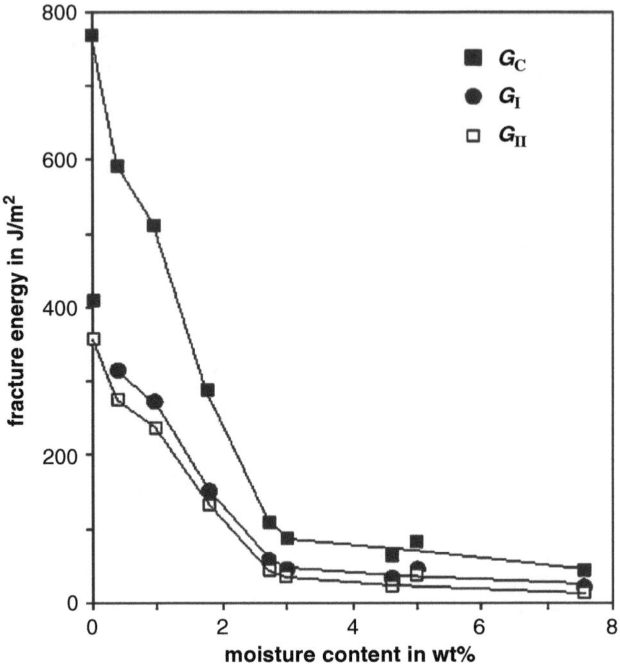

Fig. 9.22 Effect of moisture on the fracture energy of and interface between and epoxy bonded to steel (Loh et al., 2002)

LaBerge et al. (1990) performed tension tests and shear tests to characterise the bond strength of polymer–metal interfaces both for blast cleaned and etched specimens. The Co–Cr substrates were blast cleaned with silica particles (d_P = $600-1{,}000\,\mu m$), ultrasonically cleaned and then coated with high-density polyethylene (HDPE) powder coatings. The bond strengths for the blast cleaned samples were one order of magnitude lower than those for the etched samples, both for the tension and the shear tests. The authors contributed these results to a high amount of pores in the etched substrates, which promoted interlocking effects between substrate and coating.

Aga and Woldesenbet (2007) investigated the effects of surface preparation on the performance of adhesively bonded graphite/epoxy composites subjected to impact. Although their investigation did not deal with metal substrates, it delivered interesting results in terms of adhesion under impact conditions. The authors performed test with a drop-weight impact machine at different energy levels and estimated the debond areas in the adhesive bond after the testing. The substrate was treated with three surface preparation methods, namely abrading with sandpaper, use of a paper peel plied and blast cleaning ($d_P = 22\,\mu m$, $p = 0.55$ MPa). Contact force graphs are shown in Fig. 9.23. The history of the contact forces, but in particular the contact force at the peak of the curves, notably depended on the surface preparation method. The contact force at the peak was highest for the specimen treated with

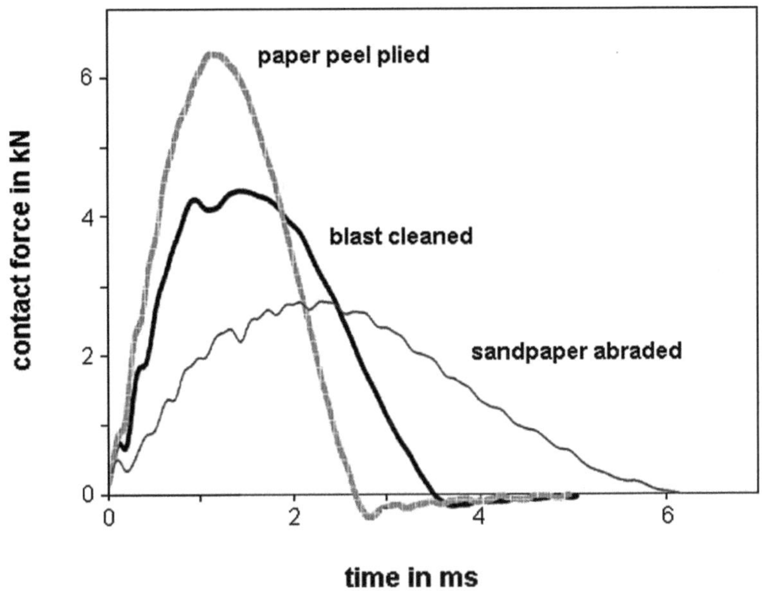

Fig. 9.23 Contact force histories for adhesively bonded graphite/epoxy composite specimens impacted at an energy level of 5.0 J (Aga and Woldesenbet, 2007)

paper peel plied, followed by blast cleaning and treatment with sandpaper. A somewhat different trend was found for the debond areas after the impact tests. Here, blast cleaned samples delivered the largest debond areas, followed by sandpaper treatment and treatment with paper peel plied. The paper-peel ply surface preparation created the most uniform and smoothest surface. The superior performance of the samples treated with that method was contributed to the formation of very low stress concentrations at the uniform, smooth surface.

Sancaktar and Gomatam (2001) performed tests on the strengths of single lap joints of rolled steel. The strength was measured with a tensile testing machine at different crosshead speeds. Both failure load and ultimate displacement were estimated. The results depicted an effect of the viscosity of the adhesive materials. For a low viscosity adhesive (5–7 Pa s), blast cleaning with aluminium oxide ($p = 0.55$ MPa) generated the highest values for the failure load (4,200 N) as well as for the ultimate displacement (0.013 mm). For a high viscosity adhesive (170–225 Pa s), the maximum value for the failure load was measured for etched adherends. The authors also proved that the loading rate affected the strength parameters. Strength values were always higher for a loading rate of 1 mm/min compared with the values for a loading rate of 100 mm/min. It turned out that the blast cleaned samples were least sensitive to changes in the loading rate. Surface roughness studies of Rider et al. (1999) established that the application of blast cleaning (aluminium oxide, $d_P = 50\,\mu$m, $m_S = 1.2$ g/cm^2) increased the fracture energy of an aluminium-epoxy joint exposed to humid conditions by two orders of magnitude. Whereas an ultra-milled aluminium adherend led to a fracture energy of about $G_{Ic} = 5$ kJ/m^2, the blast cleaned aluminium adherend delivered a fracture energy of about $G_{Ic} = 20\,kJ/m^2$ (for a crack velocity of 4 mm/s). Neeb et al. (2000) reported on the performance of adhesive bonds. The substrate was aluminium, and the adhesive was a 2-pack epoxy material. The treatment of the substrate included pickling and blast cleaning ($p = 0.6\,MPa$, $d_N = 3\,mm$, $\varphi = 90°$). Abrasive materials were glass beads ($d_P = 100$–$200\,\mu m$) and corundum ($d_P = 125$–$250\,\mu m$). The adhesion was estimated by means of a wedge test. It was found that the substrate treatment method affected the crack length in the joint. Crack length was highest for the samples blast cleaned with glass beads, and it was lowest for the samples blast cleaned with corundum. The authors contributed these results to the conversion rates of the polymers in the joint. The epoxy applied to the aluminium that was blast cleaned with glass beads showed a high conversion rate and a high final cross-linking density (compare Fig. 9.6). This led to a rather brittle adhesion layer. The epoxy applied to the aluminium that was blast cleaned with corundum, in contrast, showed a low conversion rate (compare Fig. 9.6), and it had a high capability of plastic deformation. Liu et al. (2006) conducted a systematic study into the crack growth in sol-gel treated aluminium/epoxy joints prepared with various methods, namely polishing, etching, sanding and blast cleaning (aluminium oxide, $d_P = 50\,\mu m$, $p = 0.62\,MPa$). Crack growth velocity and strain energy release rate (respectively fracture energy) were assessed by means of a double cantilever beam in a humid environment. The crack growth velocity for a given energy release rate was highest for the polished samples and lowest for the blast cleaned samples. The energy release rate exhibited a strong dependence on the crack growth velocity, which is a known effect for moisture-assisted crack growth. However, the joints formed with the blast cleaned substrates showed the highest values for the energy release rate ($G_{Ic} = 2,615\,J/m^2$), whereas the lowest value was found for the joints formed with the polished substrate ($G_{Ic} = 440\,J/m^2$). Minaki et al. (2007) performed a scratch test in order to assess the adhesion of a plated titanium nitride coat. The substrate was blast cleaned with aluminium oxide ($p = 0.2$–$0.4\,MPa$, mesh 700, $\dot{m}_P = 50$–$300\,g/min$, $\varphi = 90°$, $d_N = 8\,mm$). The authors found that the critical scratch force increased with an increase in air pressure and in blast cleaning time. This result was attributed to the higher values for profile roughness which was believed to promote a better mechanical bond.

Zhang and Zhou (1997) investigated the effects of blast cleaning on the adhesion of diamond coatings applied to tungsten carbide substrates. The adhesion was evaluated through an indentation test. Flaking of the coatings applied to ground substrates was observed at an indentation load of 600 N, whereas the coatings applied to blast cleaned (alumina, mesh 120 to 500, $p = 0.3\,MPa$) substrates did not show any flaking until the indentation load reached a value of 800 N.

The delay time between blast cleaning and spraying, respectively coating, has a definite effect on the pull-off strength of coatings. Results of systematic investigations were reported by Apps (1969) for metal-sprayed coatings and by Bullett and Dasgupta (1969) for organic coatings. The results of the authors revealed that the pull-off strength notably dropped for longer delay times if the substrates were exposed to an open environment. A drop in pull-off strength could be prevented if the blast cleaned substrates were stored in a desiccator (Apps, 1969).

9.2.3 Blast Cleaning Parameters Effects on Adhesion

9.2.3.1 Effects of Blasting Angle

Process parameters also affect adhesion of coatings to substrate. Apps (1969, 1974) and Berndt and Lin (1993) reported about effects of blasting angle and abrasive type on the adhesion of metal-sprayed aluminium coatings. For all situations, optimum values for maximum adhesion could be found at rather high impact angles. In many cases, the optimum blasting angle was at $\varphi = 90°$, but the correct location of the certain optimum angle was affected by the abrasive type. Some results of these investigations are listed in Table 9.13. Amada et al. (1999) found, for aluminium oxide coatings, very low adhesion strengths at low blasting angles, whereas, adhesion was maximum at a blasting angle of $\varphi = 79°$. Ishikawa and Tobe (2003) noted a sensitive relationship between blasting angles and spraying angles. Results of their study are displayed in Fig. 9.24. If both parameters were effectively related to each other, maximum adhesion strength could be achieved. Differences in adhesion strength for different parameter configurations were as high as 300%.

9.2.3.2 Effects of Abrasive Type, Size and Shape

Bahlmann (1982) found that the relative adhesion of organic coatings to steel substrates increased from a value of 1.00 for untreated steel to a value of 1.30 for blast cleaning with round steel grit, and to a value of 6.4 for blast cleaning with irregular chilled casting. Therefore, both hardness and particle shape notably affected adhesion. Similar relationships were reported by James (1984) for thermally sprayed coatings (see Table 9.14). Apps (1974) noted a strong influence of coating thickness on adhesion strength. If, for example, an aluminium coating exceeded a thickness of 200 μm, adhesion to the substrate started to drop. This drop was highly pronounced if copper slag and chilled iron grit were used for blast cleaning, but less important if aluminium oxide abrasive was used.

Varacalle et al. (2006) performed a systematic study into the effects of abrasive types on the pull-off strengths of aluminium, sprayed on a low-carbon steel substrate. Their results, partly listed in Table 9.15, depicted a strong effect. Steel grit delivered the highest adhesion values, whereas chilled iron grit provided the lowest

Table 9.13 Effects of blasting angle and abrasive type on the adhesion of aluminium coatings (Berndt and Lin, 1993); optimum blasting angle designates angles for maximum adhesion strength

Abrasive type	Optimum blasting angle in °
New chilled iron grit	90
Used chilled iron grit	90
Worn chilled iron grit	90
Round shot	20
Alumina grit	60
New copper slag grit	40
Worn copper slag grit	30 and 90

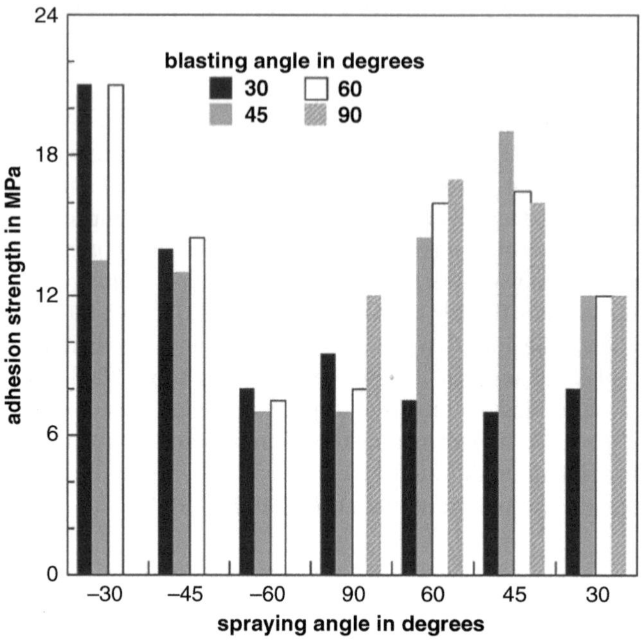

Fig. 9.24 Effects of blast cleaning angle and spraying angle on the adhesion of a metal-spayed coating (Ishikawa and Tobe, 2003)

pull-off strength values. It is obvious from these studies, that the abrasive type must be adjusted to both substrate and coating properties in order to provide maximum adhesion.

Mannelqvist and Groth (2001) reported about the influence of abrasive type on the adhesion of adhesive epoxy joints to stainless steel panels. Results of their study are displayed in Fig. 9.25. Joint tensile strengths of samples blast cleaned with an irregular abrasive (grit) were notably higher than strengths of samples that were blast cleaned with glass beads. Feist et al. (1988) reported about the effects of numerous abrasive materials on the adhesion of sprayed metal coatings to steel; results are plotted in Fig. 9.26. It can be seen that the abrasive type had a notable

Table 9.14 Effect of abrasive type and coating application on relative adhesion of flame-sprayed zinc and aluminium (James, 1984)

Abrasive	Relative adhesion in %			
	Aluminium		Zinc	
	Arc-sprayed	Flame-sprayed	Arc-sprayed	Flame-sprayed
G 12/24	100	33	28	31
Slag	36	31	23	25
Sand (d_P = 0.6–1.5 mm)	72	16	18	17
Sand (d_P = 0.1–1.0 mm)	54	–	22	20

Table 9.15 Effect of abrasive type on the adhesion of sprayed aluminium to blast cleaned low-carbon steel (Varacalle et al., 2006)

Abrasive type	Pull-off strength in MPa
Steel grit HG-16	8.21
Steel grit HG-18	8.07
Steel grit HG-25	7.82
Steel grit HG-40	8.48
Copper slag	6.83
Coal slag	7.07
Chilled iron grit	3.62

influence on the pull-off strength values. Even for equal roughness values (say R_Z = 50 μm), pull-off strength of sprayed aluminium dropped from $\sigma_A = 10$ MPa for basalt or furnish slag to $\sigma_A = 4$ MPa for nickel slag. Similar was the situation for a roughness of $R_Z = 80$ μm. Yankee et al. (1991) could also show that abrasive type can play a decisive role in adhesion. For equivalent roughness values and equal cleaning procedures, it was the profile characteristics (thus, the abrasive shape), that determined the adhesion strength. These effects are illustrated in Fig. 9.27. Blast cleaning with aluminium oxide delivered notably higher adhesion strengths. The distinct profile characteristics generated during the blast cleaning with aluminium

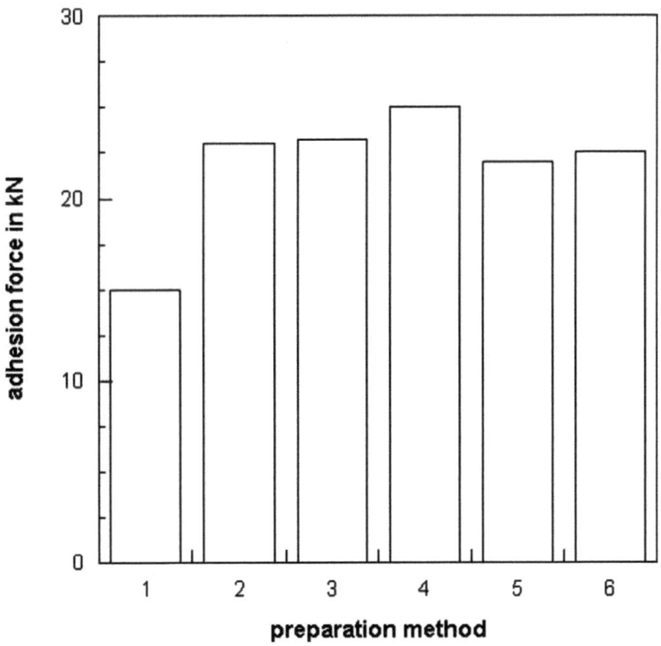

Fig. 9.25 Effects of surface preparation methods on the adhesion of adhesive epoxy joints to steel (Mannelqvist and Groth, 2001). Preparation methods: 1 – degreasing; 2 – Scotch-Brite; 3 – steel brushing; 4 – blast cleaning with grit; 5 – blast cleaning with glass beads; 6 – water blasting

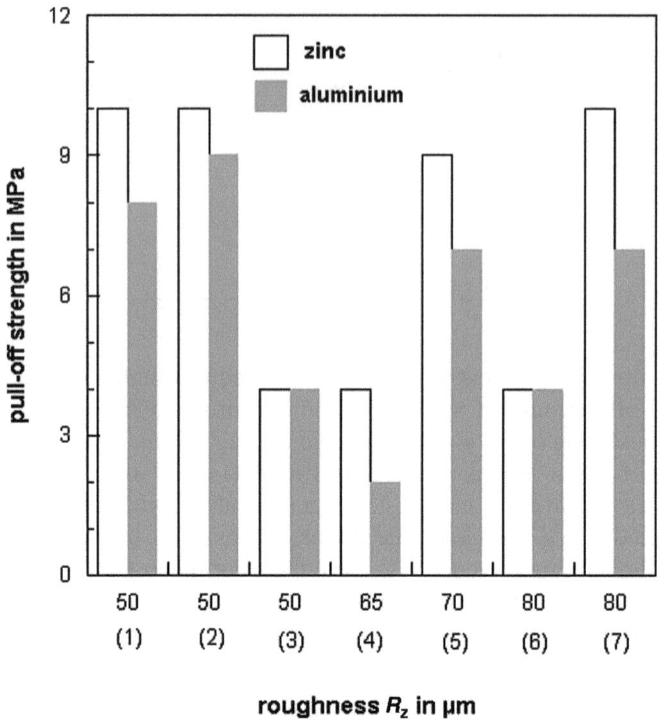

Fig. 9.26 Effects of abrasive materials on the adhesion of metal-sprayed coatings to steel (Feist et al., 1988). Abrasive types: (1) – basalt; (2) – furnace slag; (3) – VV–slag; (4) – electric-furnace slag; (5) – nickel–iron slag; (6) – lead–tin slag. Parameters: $p = 0.6$ MPa; $d_P = 630$–1,250 µm; $d_N = 8$ mm; nozzle type: Laval nozzle

oxide seemed to promote a good bond of the thermally sprayed hydroxylapatite coating to the titanium substrate. However, as also shown in Fig. 9.27, intense post-cleaning of the substrate surfaces with ultrasound reduced the differences in adhesion strength, which pointed to additional contamination effects (see Sect. 8.5.3). Brewis et al. (1999) could prove that the preparation of aluminium substrates with carbon dioxide particles ("dry ice blasting") could notably improve the strength of single-lap shear joints. Joint strength increased from 1,859 N for a degreased surface up to 4,420 N for carbon dioxide blast cleaned surfaces.

Apps (1967) found that the individual influence of the abrasive type to the adhesion of thermally sprayed coatings depended on the blasting angle. Results of his study are plotted in Fig. 9.28. The effect of abrasive deterioration, for example, is much more distinguished if the abrasives were propelled at normal angle. At this angle, even worn steel grit performed better than steel grit that was just used once.

Tests performed on the adhesion of enamel coatings to steel by Sorokin et al. (1977) verified notable effects of particle shape. Steel shot abrasives delivered better bonding conditions than steel grit particles. The coatings were unevenly distributed

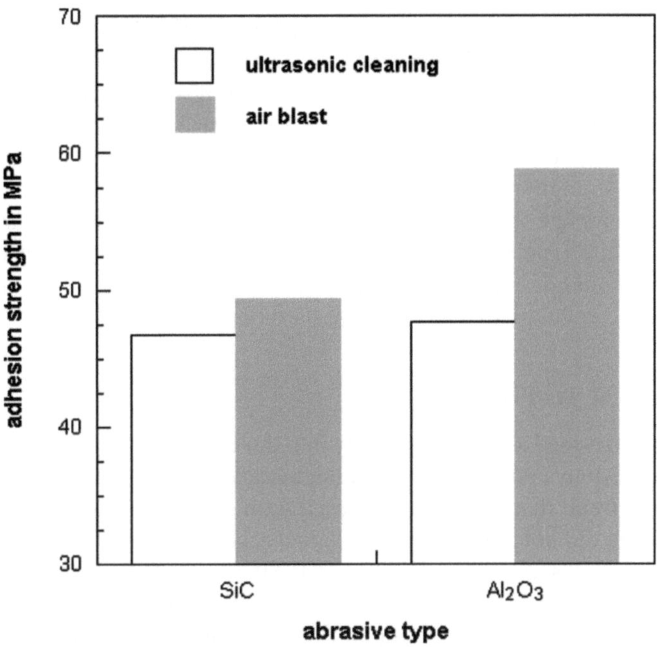

Fig. 9.27 Effects of abrasive type and substrate fine-cleaning on the adhesion of a plasma-sprayed coating to titanium (Yankee et al., 1991)

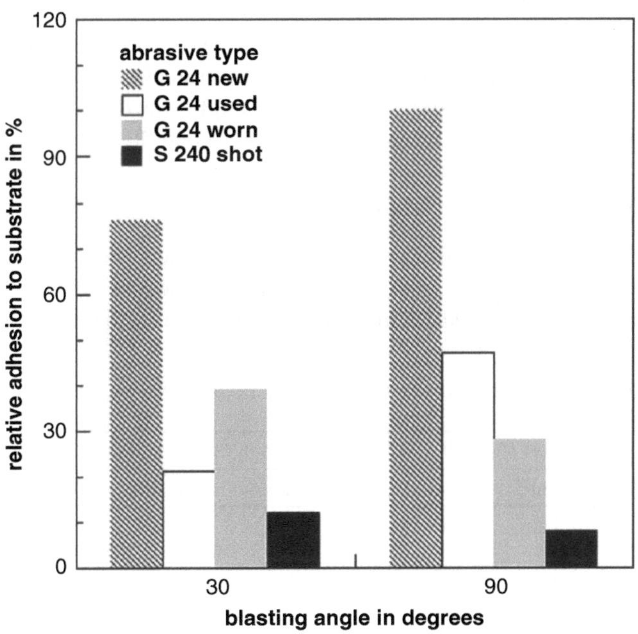

Fig. 9.28 Effects of blasting angle and abrasive quality on the relative adhesion strength of thermally sprayed coatings (Apps, 1967)

over the grit blasted surfaces and peeled during application. Beitelman (2003) applied the abrasive shape designations according to Fig. 2.8 and measured the adhesion performance of organic and metallic coatings to the prepared substrates. Results of this study are provided in Table 9.16. Abrasive particle shape had an influence on the adhesion strength of the metallic coatings, whereas it was insensitive to the adhesion strength of the organic coating. This difference in the coating types was also found for the failure behaviour during the adhesion tests. Particle shape affected the failure type for the metal-sprayed coating, but not that of the organic coating. The amount of cohesion failure of the metal-sprayed coating dropped with a decrease in the angularity of the abrasive particles.

9.2.3.3 Effects of Air Pressure

Apps (1969) performed a systematic study into the effects of blasting pressure variations on the adhesion of metal-sprayed coatings to steel substrates. Although the author noted a certain trend that adhesion increased with an increase in blasting pressure, blasting pressure did not always show a distinct relationship to the adhesion of coatings to steel substrates. An example is illustrated in Fig. 9.29. It seemed that optimum blasting pressure ranges existed which depended on abrasive quality. Worn abrasive materials deteriorated adhesion strength. Sofyan et al. (2005) found an increase in bond between WC-Co coatings and steel if blast cleaning pressure increased.

9.2.3.4 Effects of Stand-off Distance

Apps (1969) performed a systematic study into the effects of changes in stand-off distance on the adhesion of metal-sprayed coatings on steel plates and steel bars, and he did not find any notable trends. The pull-off strength was unaffected by variations in the stand-off distance in the range between $x = 15$ and 90 mm.

9.2.3.5 Statistical Assessment Models

Day et al. (2005) and Varacalle et al. (2006) performed statistical analyses into the effects of numerous process parameters on the adhesion of thermally sprayed coatings to steel substrates. Day et al. (2005) derived the following relationship:

Table 9.16 Abrasive shape effects on the adhesion of coatings to blast cleaned substrates (Beitelman, 2003)

Particle shape[a]	Pull-off strength in MPa		Cohesion failure in %		Adhesion failure in %	
	Organic[b]	Metallic[c]	Organic	Metallic	Organic	Metallic
Very angular	13.3	9.8	100	81	0	19
Angular	13.2	9.4	100	83	0	17
Sub-angular	13.0	9.7	100	86	0	14
Sub-rounded	13.3	8.8	100	45	0	55
Rounded	13.3	8.3	100	44	0	56

[a]Crushed steel grit (G-59); see Fig. 2.9 for shape designations
[b]Zinc-rich organic coating (DFT = 93–130 μm)
[c]Metal-sprayed Zn/Al (DFT = 340–500 μm)

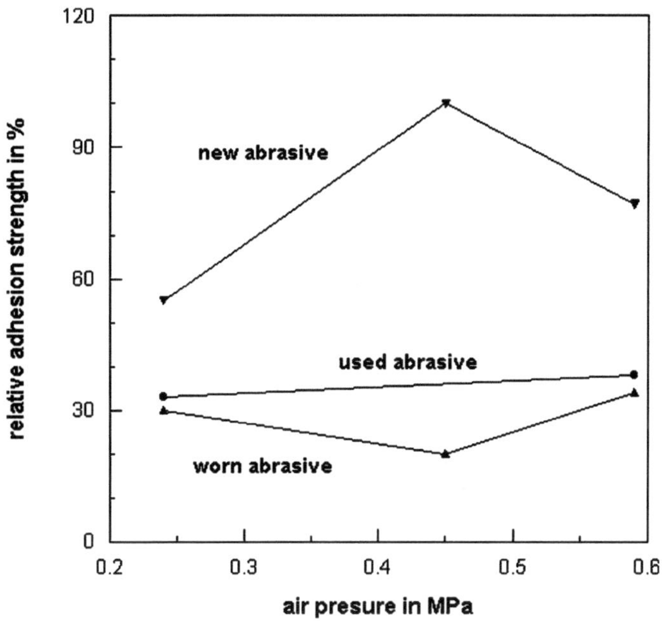

Fig. 9.29 Effects of air pressure and abrasive type on the adhesion of adhesive epoxy joints to steel (Mannelqvist and Groth, 2001)

$$\sigma_A = 38.7 \cdot GN + 76.9 \cdot p + 414.2 \cdot n_S + 182.6 \cdot x + 20.6 \cdot \varphi \quad (9.4)$$

In this equation, the adhesion strength is given in psi, the grit number is given in mesh, the pressure is given in psi, the stand-off distance is given in), and the blasting angle is given in degrees. Varacalle et al. (2006) derived the following relationship for aluminium, sprayed on a low-carbon steel substrate:

$$\sigma_A = 3,518.2 + 457.3 \cdot x + 59.55 \cdot C_G + 8.6 \cdot p_S - 13.78 \cdot x^2 - 0.113 \cdot C_G^2 - 0.012 \cdot {p_S}^2 \quad (9.5)$$

In that equation, the adhesion strength is given in kPa, the stand-off distance is given in cm, the spray pressure is given in kPa, and the spray gun current is given in A. The equation holds for the use of HG 16 steel grit (d_P = 1,000–1,700 µm).

9.3 Mechanical Behaviour of Coatings

Surface preparation methods can affect the mechanical behaviour of coatings, mainly those of sprayed metal or ceramic coatings. Examples are provided in Fig. 9.30. In the two graphs, four sections can be distinguished as functions of coating thickness and power density: (1) fusion of the inconel substrate, (2) segmentation

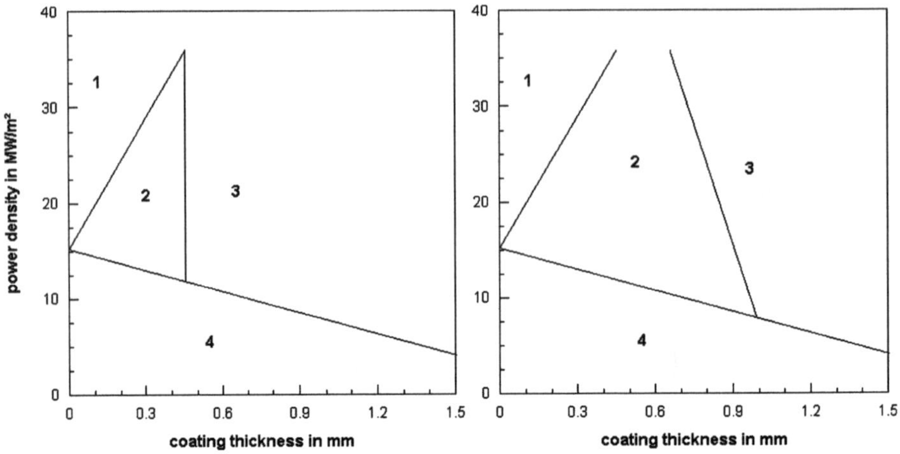

Fig. 9.30 Effects of surface preparation methods on coating failure types during thermal shock tests (Bordeaux et al., 1991). Left: blast cleaning; right: macro-roughening; Failure types: 1 – substrate fusion; 2 – segmentation of coating; 3 – delamination; 4 – no damage

of the coating, (3) delamination and (4) no damage. The no-damage region was not notably affected by the surface preparation method, but the coatings were more sensitive to segmentation if blast cleaning was performed. For blast cleaning, the limit for segmentation was at a coating thickness of about 400 μm, whereas it was at a coating thickness of about 950 μm for the machined substrate. These relationships are of importance for the application of thermal barrier coatings.

Sobiecki et al. (2003) measured the microhardness of tungsten carbide coatings applied to substrates which were prepared with different surface preparation methods, but they did not record any effect.

Bochenin (2005) performed investigation on aluminium coatings deposited by diffusion metallisation on steel substrates. The abrasive material used was iron shot (d_P = 1,000 μm); the air pressure was p = 0.6 MPa. The coated specimens were placed into a furnace, heated to 1,000°C and held for 90 h. The specific weight loss of the coating was defined as a measure for its heat resistance. It was found that heat resistance of the coating could be affected notably due to blast cleaning of the substrate. The heat resistance depended on several blast cleaning parameters. Results are displayed in Fig. 9.31. For the stand-off distance, an optimum value could be detected, whereas heat resistance was highest for a perpendicular blast cleaning angle.

Tolpygo et al. (2001) investigated the behaviour of thermal barrier coatings deposited on (Ni, Pt) Al bond-coat substrates. The samples were cyclically oxidised. Each cycle consisted of 10 h of exposure at 1,150°C, with heating and cooling rates of about 200°C/min. The authors noted that blast cleaning of the substrate with aluminium oxide particles promoted a very high growth rate of the oxide scale. The high oxidation rate was explained by impurities from the blast cleaning

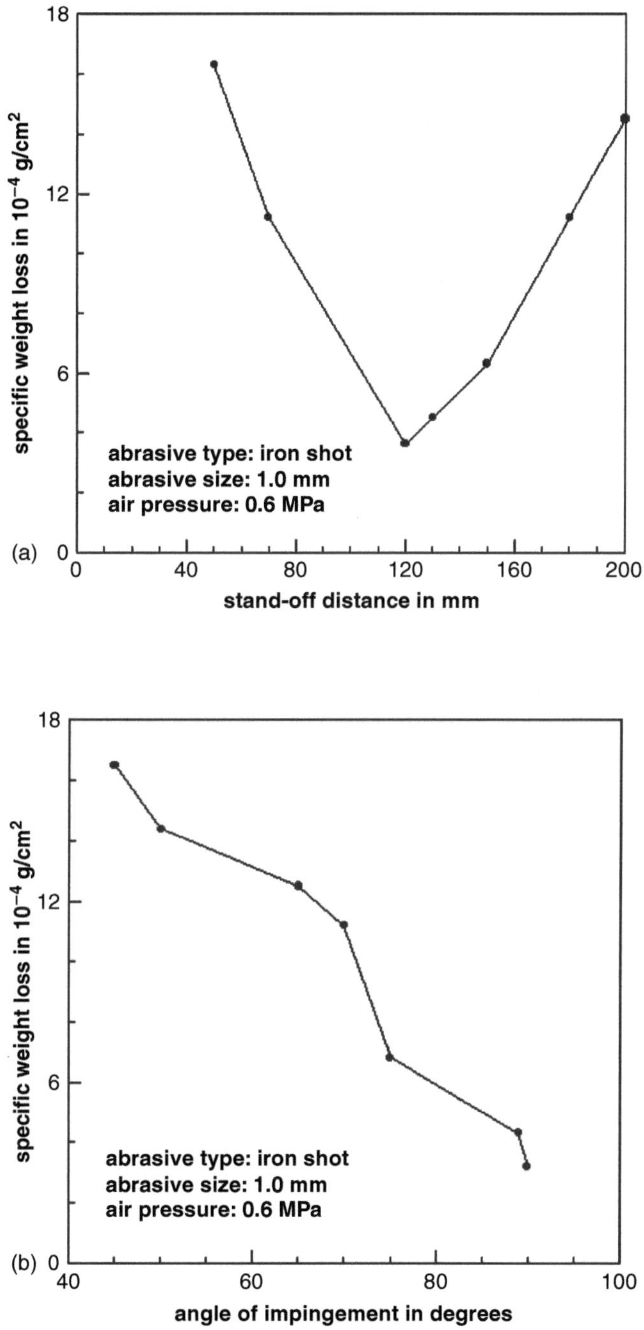

Fig. 9.31 Effects of blast cleaning parameters on the heat resistance of aluminium coatings deposited to a steel substrate (Bochenin, 2005). (**a**) Effect of stand-off distance; (**b**) Effect of blasting angle

process (alkali and titanium), which became incorporated into the growing scale and significantly accelerated the oxide growth. The high grow rate resulted in cracking and spalling of the scale followed by a mass decrease after only 30 ten-hour cycles at 1,150°C. The scale formed on the aluminised surfaces had much lower impurity content and a slower growth rate, and they showed an excellent spalling resistance during cyclic oxidation. Based on these results, blast cleaning is expected to have a detrimental effect on the durability of thermal barrier coatings.

A study into the performance of sol-gel-derived coatings over blast cleaned aluminium alloys was conducted by You et al. (2001). The substrate was blast cleaned with aluminium oxide powder ($d_P = 20$ and $100\,\mu m$). The authors found that the coating layer was more uniform for the sampled blast cleaned with the finer abrasives. These coatings also showed a smaller number of cracks after firing compared with the coatings applied over the substrate blast cleaned with the coarser abrasives. The authors attributed these results to effects of substrate roughness.

9.4 Corrosion Protection Performance of Coatings

The corrosion protection performance of organic coatings can be evaluated by means of electrochemical methods. One method that became notably involved in coating testing during the recent years is EIS. The physical and chemical background is complex and beyond the scope of this book. The reader may refer to Baboian (1986). One assessment parameter, however, is the electrical resistance of a coating. If this parameter has high values, corrosion protection capability of the coating is high as well. Studies where effects of different surface preparation methods on the corrosion protection performance of coatings were investigated by means of EIS were conducted by Lin et al. (1992), Santaga et al. (1998), Vesga et al. (2000) and Elsner et al. (2003). Lin et al. (1992) investigated the effects of surface preparation methods on the electrical resistance of rather thin organic coatings. Results of their study are plotted in Fig. 9.32. It appeared that for the coating systems studied, blast cleaning deteriorated the performance of the coatings. The authors contributed this result to areas of "deficient" coating coverage (e.g. peaks of a rough substrate), which occurred at the blast cleaned surfaces.

Figure 9.33 shows results of EIS measurements performed by Vesga et al. (2000) on organic primers applied to blast cleaned steel substrates. The primer behaviour was subdivided into three stages, denoted "R" (resistive), "CR" (capacitive/resistive) and "C" (capacitive) in Fig. 9.33. The value for the resistance at a given time can indicate the state of the primer degradation. The lower this value, the more severe degradation took place. It can be seen that the resistance had rather low values for the primer applied to the wet blast cleaned steel. The resistance of the primer applied to the dry blast cleaned steel was one order of magnitude higher. It was demonstrated that the pore resistance of the primers showed the same qualitative trend over the

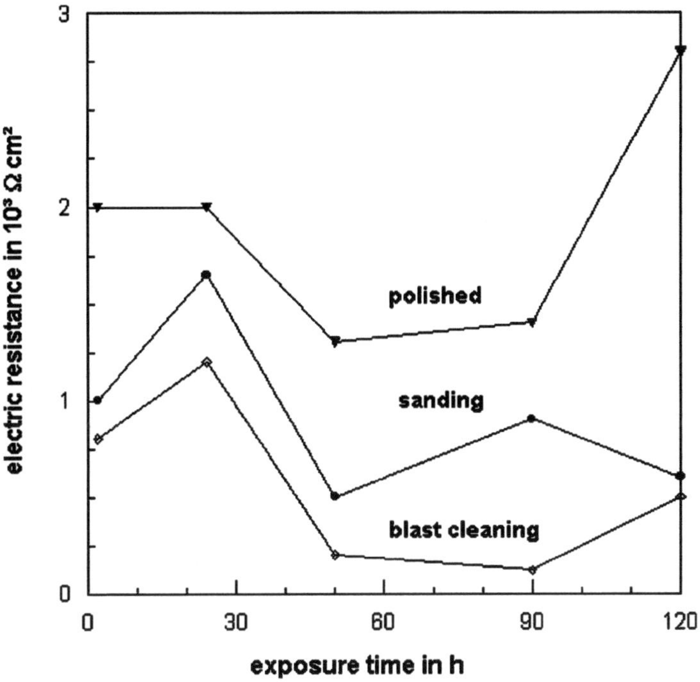

Fig. 9.32 Effects of surface preparation methods on the corrosion protection performance (electric resistance) of thin organic coatings (Lin et al., 1992). Coating: epoxy; substrate: cold-rolled steel; parameters: $p = 0.7$ MPa; $d_P = 150$–$300\,\mu$m; abrasive material: sand

exposure time as the *KIV*-value (see Fig. 9.3). Thus, the resistance seemed to be indicative of the corrosion protective performance of the primer. It can further be seen from the graphs in Fig. 9.33 that the resistive status ("R") was reached after a shorter period of time for the primer applied to the wet blast cleaned steel substrate. In the status "R", the primer may swell excessively and irreversibly, taking up extra water and irons from the electrolyte and may be damaged. Vesga et al. (2000) observed that the primer lost adhesion to the substrate in that stage.

Cambruzzi et al. (2005) utilised EIS for the assessment of abraded coating systems. The background of this study is that paint inspectors sometimes claim that a well-adhering primer coat must not be removed during coating repair applications. If this strategy is being followed, the primer is, if not removed, however abraded by the impinging particles. Cambruzzi et al. (2005) applied a special abrasion test to a polyester powder coating and measured the electric resistance after a variety of abrasion cycles. The results shown in Fig. 9.34 depicted a notable deterioration of the corrosion protection performance of the coating. In less than 300 cycles, almost all samples reached values lower than the protection threshold of $10^6\ \Omega\,\text{cm}^2$. It was observed that the abrasive particle size played an important role in the reduction of the protective properties of the coatings, since the most severe conditions were observed for the coarsest grains.

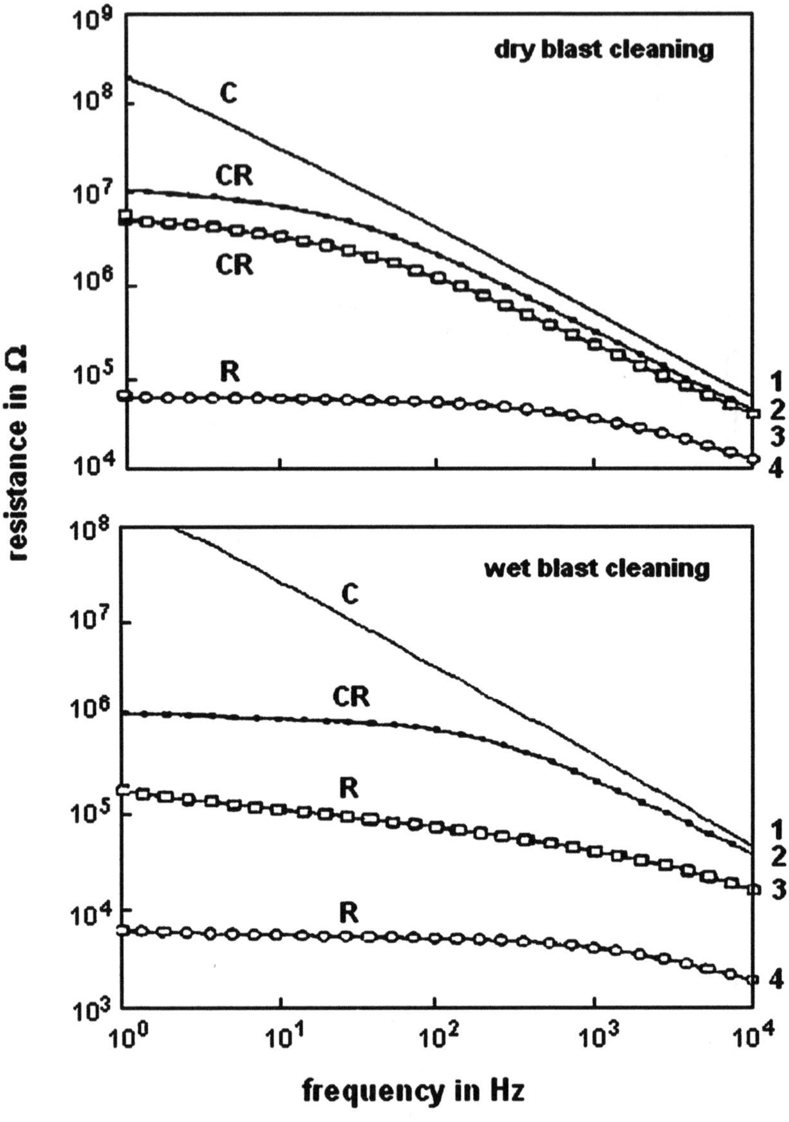

Fig. 9.33 Bode and Nyquist plots for an organic primer applied to blast cleaned steel substrates (Vesga et al., 2000). 1 – initial condition; 2 – after 180 h; 3 – after 360 h; 4 – after 860 h

9.5 Deposition and Transport Phenomena

The deposition rate of a coating is actually not a performance parameter of an already existing coating, but it may affect the behaviour of the final coating. The relationships between deposition rate and blast cleaning processes are not well understood. Heya et al. (2005) performed an investigation in the deposition rate of

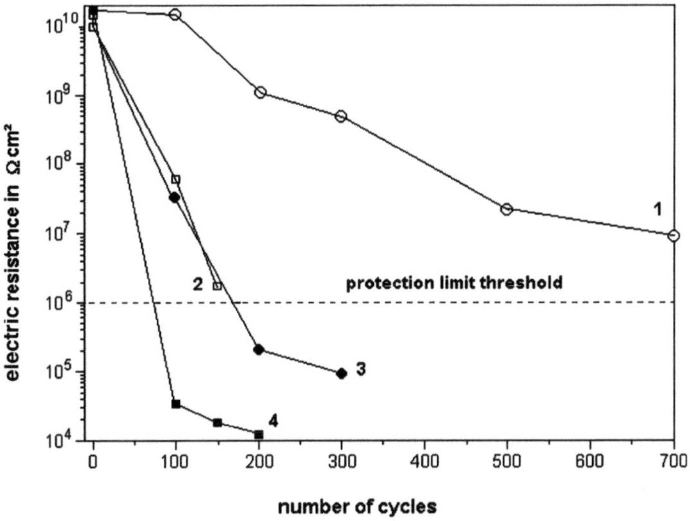

Fig. 9.34 Effects of abrasion damages on the corrosion protection performance (electric resistance) of an organic powder coating (Cambruzzi et al., 2005). Abrasive parameters: 1 – mesh 20–69, 250 g; 2 – mesh 12–20, 250 g; 3 – mesh 20–60, 1000 g; 4 – mesh 12–20, 1000 g)

SiN_X-films on tungsten wires in catalytic chemical vapour deposition (Cat-CVD). If a high deposition rate is required for this process, the temperature is usually increased which is accompanied with a rise in electric power consumption. Heya et al. (2005) blast cleaned the wires with silicon carbide particles with sizes between 10 and 20 μm, and they measured the deposition rates. For a given electric power of 70 kW, the deposition rate increased from about 9 nm/min for untreated wires to 12 nm/min for blast cleaned wires. This result was explained with the higher specific surface of the blast cleaned wires, which was about 35% higher than that of untreated wires.

Another effect worth noting is the influence of profile parameters on the carburisation of turbine blades as witnessed by Locci et al. (2004). Blast cleaning with coarse aluminium oxide provided a more efficient surface condition for carburisation compared with machining and polishing. This effect could directly be contributed to the corresponding surface roughness values. Carbide depth after a 2-hour standard carburisation process was, for example, 33 μm for a roughness of R_a = 0.34 μm, but it increased up to 85 μm for a roughness of R_a = 1.7 μm.

9.6 Wire Embedment in Polymer Matrices

A special case is the treatment of metal wires, which become embedded in a polymer matrix. The performance of such a reinforced structure depends to a great amount on the bond between steel and matrix. Jonnalagadda et al. (1997)

Table 9.17 Effect of surface preparation on the adhesion between metal wires and a polymer matrix (Jonnalagadda et al., 1997)

Surface preparation of the wires	Interfacial bond strength in MPa	Max. wire displacement in μm	Max. shear stress induced in the matrix in MPa
Untreated	10.5	0.14	5.5
Blast cleaned	30.3	0.11	8.9
Hand sanded	9.0	0.31	4.0
Acid etched	8.1	0.32	4.1

performed investigations into the mechanical contact behaviour of nickel–tungsten wire steels (wire diameter: 150 μm) embedded into a commercial polymer material. The authors utilised different methods for the surface preparation of the wires, including acid etching, blast cleaning and sanding. They estimated interfacial bond strength, wire displacement under load and shear stresses induced in the matrix by means of pull-out tests, interferometry and photoelasticity. Results of these studies are listed in Table 9.17. Blast cleaning significantly increased the bond strength, whereas sanding and acid etching actually reduced the interface strength. Blast cleaning resulted in lower wire displacement and higher interfacial stresses.

9.7 Coating Formation Processes

9.7.1 Spreading and Splashing

The formation of splats from impinging liquid metal or ceramic drops can be accompanied by flattening effects. During flattening, molten material flows radially at high speed, while cooling and possibly solidification of the particle/substrate interface takes place. The first sprayed coating particles, which impinge the substrate, hit a profiled surface that considerably affects the flattening process. Flattening can be characterised by a flattening degree, which is the ratio between final splat diameter and initial splat diameter. It is defined as follows (Moreau et al., 1995):

$$\frac{D_S}{D_0} = f_F \cdot \left(\frac{v_D \cdot \rho_C \cdot D_0}{\eta_C} \right)^{0.2} \tag{9.6}$$

In this equation, D_S is the final splat diameter, D_0 is the initial splat diameter, v_D is the velocity of the impinging drop, ρ_C is the coating material density and v_C is the coating material dynamic viscosity. Figure 9.35 illustrates the effects of different surface preparation methods on the flattening degrees of plasma-sprayed molybdenum on a molybdenum substrate. The flattening degree tended to decrease if substrate roughness increased. It seemed that the constant f_F in (9.6) is a function of

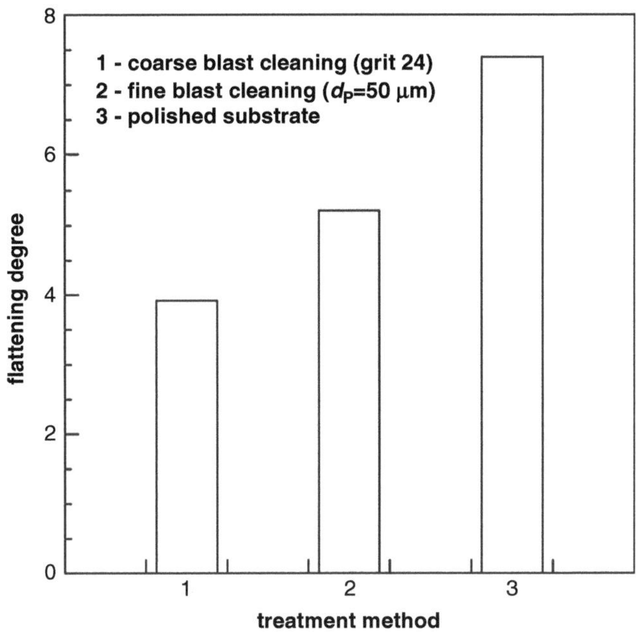

Fig. 9.35 Effects of surface preparation on the flattening degree of plasma-sprayed molybdenum particles (Moreau et al., 1995)

the surface preparation method. It has lower values for the methods which produce rougher surfaces, such as blast cleaning with coarse aluminium oxide particles. Moreau et al. (1995) also found that the surface preparation method affected splat surface and flattening time. The smoother the substrate, the larger the splat surface and the longer the flattening time. The cooling time, in contrast, was found to be longer if the surface was blast cleaned with the coarse aluminium oxide.

Ma et al. (2006) studied the effect of the roughness (R_a) of blast cleaned substrates on the splat formation of HVOF-sprayed tungsten carbide. The results showed that with an increase in roughness, the restriction to flattening was enhanced in a way that the number of spherical to nearly spherical splats reduced, whereas the number of splats with complex morphologies increased.

Liu et al (2006) conducted a study on the spreading kinetics of a wetting liquid for different surface preparation methods, namely polishing, etching, sanding and blast cleaning (aluminium oxide, $d_P = 50\,\mu m$, $p = 0.62\,MPa$). The substrate was aluminium, and the wetting liquid was hexadecane. Results of their investigations are provided in Fig. 9.36. The relationship between spread radius and time followed a power law:

$$\frac{D_S}{\lambda} \propto t^{k_D} \tag{9.7}$$

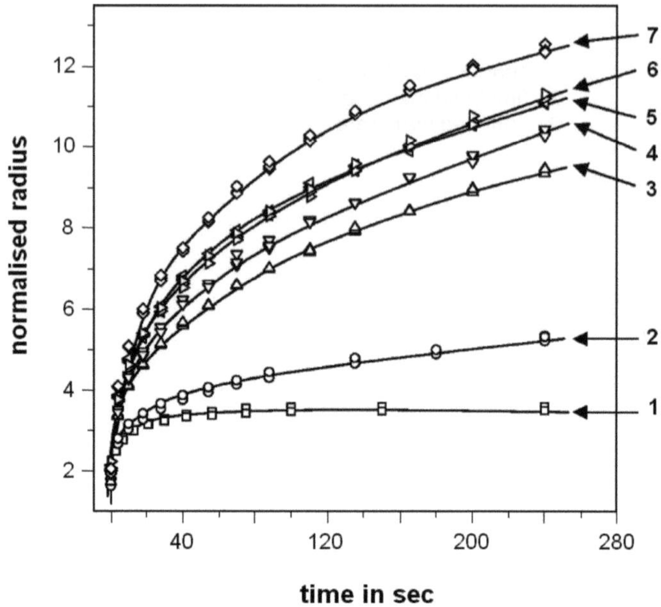

Fig. 9.36 Effects of surface preparation methods on the spreading kinetics of hexadecade on aluminium (Liu et al., 2006). Preparation methods: 1 – polishing; 2 – etching; 3 – sanding (mesh 240); 4 – sanding (mesh 180); 5 - sanding (mesh 120); 6 – blast cleaning; 7 – blast cleaning and subsequent etching. Normalized radius is ratio between spread radius and (drop volume)$^{1/3}$.

The power exponent k_D was a function of the surface preparation methods. Values for the power exponent are listed in Table 9.18. It can be seen that blast cleaning substrates provided the highest values.

9.7.2 Powder Solidification

Sobolev et al. (2000) conducted a study into the solidification of a WC-Co powder during the high-velocity oxygen-fuel spraying on a copper substrate. They generated two roughness levels on the substrate: smooth due to polishing; rough due to blast cleaning. The authors analysed a number of process parameters of the solidification process, namely solidification rate, cooling rate, thermal gradient, crystal size and

Table 9.18 Spreading kinetics power exponent k_D for different surface preparation methods (Liu et al, 2006)

Surface preparation method	k_D-value
Polishing	0.11
Etching	0.16
Sanding (mesh 240 to 120)	0.27
Blast cleaning (aluminium oxide, $d_P = 50\,\mu m$, $p = 0.62\,MPa$)	0.29

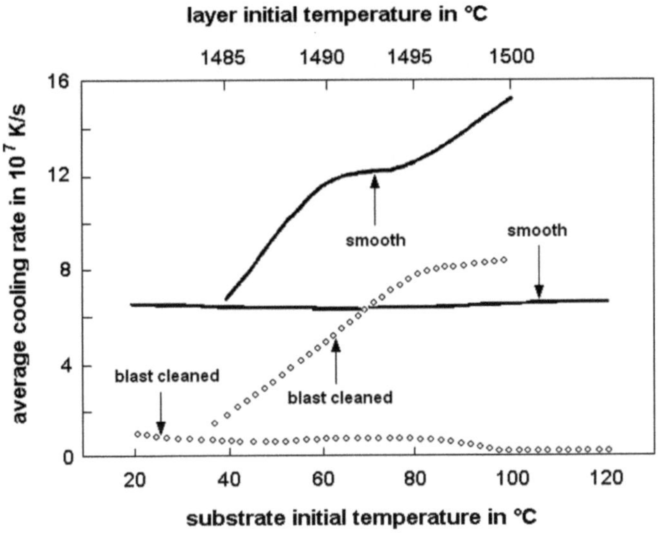

Fig. 9.37 Relationship between solidification rate, initial temperature and surface praparation (Sobolev et al., 2000)

intercrystalline distance. An example is provided in Fig. 9.37. It can be seen that the cooling rate was lower if the powder was sprayed on the blast cleaned substrate. The same trend was found for the thermal gradient and for the solidification rate. The authors also calculated the contact heat transfer coefficient for the substrate-coating interface, and they reported the following values: $6.6 \cdot 10^6$ W/(m^2·K) for the polished substrate and $3.33 \cdot 10^6$ W/(m^2·K) for the blast cleaned substrate. The basic result was that a rough (blast cleaned) substrate allowed more time for forming a good bond to develop a strongly adherent coating. These results are good examples on how blast cleaning can affect the coating formation process in its very early stage.

9.7.3 Nucleation Processes

Zhang and Zhou (1997) found a relationship between the nucleation density of diamond applied to tungsten carbide and the surface preparation method. It was found that blast cleaning provided the highest nucleation density. The authors related this result to the morphology of the blast cleaned substrate (skewness between -1 and -3; compare Fig. 8.53) which provided a suitable contact angle for diamond nucleation.

Machu (1963) discussed the effect of surface treatment on the phosphating process of steel. He pointed out that, from the point of view of electro-chemistry, a high number of activated pits (local anodes) at the steel surface is one preposition for an efficient phosphating process. The number and the energy state of these pits determine number of crystal nuclei, nucleation rate and crystal growth. Such active pits will be created during mechanical pre-treatment, including blast cleaning. As a result, very fine-grained, thin and corrosion protective phosphate layers are being formed on the steel substrate after blast cleaning.

References

Abrams, S., 1999, Handling and disposal of waste. *Protect. Coat. Europe*, Vol. 4, 24–29.

Abukawa, S., Kobayashi, K., Kobayashi, Y. 2004, The relationship of work distortion and surface roughness on grit blasting process. *Proc. Int. Therm. Spray Conf.*, Osaka, 884–889.

Achtsnick, M., 2005, High performance micro abrasive blasting. *PhD Thesis*, Delft University of Technology, Delft, The Netherlands.

Achtsnick, M., Geelhoed, P.F., Hoogstrate, A.M., Karpuschewski, B., 2005, Modelling and evaluation of the micro abrasive blasting process. *Wear*, Vol. 259, 84–94.

Adamson, A.W., 1990, *Physical Chemistry of Surfaces*. 5th edition, John Wiley & Sons, New York.

Adlassing, K., 1960, Einfluß der Düsenform und des Betriebsdruckes auf die Leistung von Druckluftstrahlanlagen. *Giesserei*, Vol. 47, 211–214.

Adlassing, K., Jahn, W., 1961, Die Eigenschaften von Strahlmitteln und Düsenwerkstoffen bei Druckluft-Strahlanlagen. *Giesserei*, Vol. 48, 618–622.

Adler, W.F., 1979, *Erosion: Prevention and Useful Application*. ASTM, New York.

Adley, D., Trimber, K., 1999, Evaluation of substitute materials for silica sand in abrasive blasting. *J. Protect. Coat. Lin.*, Vol. 16, No. 8, 49–71.

Aga, Z.A., Woldesenbet, E., 2007, Surface preparation effect on performance of adhesively-bonded graphite/epoxy composites subjected to impact. *J. Adhes. Sci. Technol.*, Vol. 21, No. 1, 51–65.

Agus, M., Bortolussi, A., Ciccu, R., et al., 1995, Abrasive performance in rock cutting with AWJ and ASJ. *Proc. 8th Am. Water Jet Conf.* (ed. T.J. Labus), Water Jet Technology Association, St. Louis, 31–48.

Ahland, E.O., 1966, Strömungsvorgänge im vertikalen, feststoffbeladenen Förderrohr mit austretendem Freistrahl. *Dissertation*, RWTH Aachen, Germany.

Alblas, B.P., van Londen, A.M., 1997, The effect of chloride contamination on the corrosion of steel surfaces: a literature review. *Protec. Coat. Europe*, Vol. 2, No. 2, 16–25.

Albring, W., 1970, *Angewandte Strömungslehre*. Theodor Steinkopf, Dresden.

Al-Hassani, S.T., 1999, Numerical simulation of multiple shot impact. *Proc. 7th Int. Conf. Shot Peening*, Warsaw, 217–226.

Allan, S.J., May, R., Taylor, M.F., Walters, J., 1995, The effect of salts on steels and protective coatings. *GEC J. of Research*, Vol. 12, 86–92.

Allen, B., 1997, Evaluating UHP waterjetting for ballast tank coating systems. *Protect. Coat. Europe*, Vol. 2, No. 10, 38–64.

Amada, S., Satoh, A., 2000, Fractal analysis of surfaces roughened by grit blasting. *J. Adhes. Sci. Technol.*, Vol. 14, No. 1, 27–41.

Amada, S., Hirose, T., Senda, T., 1999, Quantitative evaluation of residual grits under angled blasting. *Surf. Coat. Technol.*, Vol. 111, 1–9.

Anagreh, N., Dorn, L., 2002a, Klebflächenvorbehandlung von Aluminiumoberflächen mit SIP-Haftvermittler. *Materialwiss. Werkstofftech.*, Vol. 33, 657–666.

Anagreh, N., Dorn, L., 2002b, Einfluss des Strahlmittels auf Oberflächenstruktur und Adhäsionseigenschaften von Aluminiumoberflächen, Teil I+II. *Aluminium*, Vol. 78, 88–94, 194–199.

Anderson, R.M., Adler, T.A., Hawk, J.A., 1993, Scale of microstructure effects on the impact resistance of Al_2O_3. *Wear*, Vol. 162–164, 1073–1080.

Andrews, A.F., 2002, Polysiloxane topcoats—product choice for optimum performance. *SSPC 2002—Technical Presentations*, Tampa, FL, November 2002.

Andrews, D.R., Field, J.E., 1982, The erosion of metals by the normal impingement of hard solid spheres. *J. Phys. D Appl. Phys.*, Vol. 15, 571–578.

Andrews, E.W., Kim, K.S., 1998, Threshold conditions for dynamic fragmentation of ceramic particles. *Mech. Mater.*, Vol. 29, 161–180.

Andrews, E.W., Kim, K.S., 1999, Threshold conditions for dynamic fragmentation of glass particles. *Mech. Mater.*, Vol. 31, 689–703.

Andronikos, G., Valiadis, P., Vassilion, P., 1998, The effect of blasting materials on the corrosion of protected steel in sea water. *Anti-Corr. Meth. Mater.*, Vol. 45, No. 3, 153–157.

Andronikos, G., Eleftherakos, A., 2000a, Alternative surface preparation methods for ship-repairing. *Proc. PCE Conf. Exhib.*, Technology Publications, Pittsburgh, 253–262.

Andronikos, G., Eleftherakos, A., 2000b, Alternatives to slag abrasives for blast cleaning of ships. *Protect. Coat. Europe*, Vol. 5, 54–60.

Andziak, J., Brezezinski, M., 1999, Influence of abrasive blast cleaning and vibrofinishing on surface properties of the stainless steel OH18N9. *Proc. 7th Int. Conf. Shot Blasting*, Warsaw, 60–68.

Anonymous, 1997, Emission factor documentation for AP-42, Section 13.2.6, abrasive blasting. *Final Report*. EPA Contract 68-D2-0159, September 1997.

Anonymous, 2002, Advances in high-production robotic UHP water blasting. *Shiprepair and Conversion Technol.*, 2nd Quarter, 35–40.

Appleman, B.R., 2002, The effect of soluble salts o protective coatings. *SSPC Painting Manual* (ed. R.W. Drisko), Vol. 1, Chapter 2.8, SSPC, Pittsburgh, 119–138.

Appleman, B.R., 2003, Update on soluble salts: progress and critical issues. *National Shipbuilding Research Program*, Panel SP-3, Key West, FL, 26.2–8. February 2003.

Appleman, B.R., Weaver, R.E., Boocock, S.K., 1998, User's guide to selecting abrasives. *J. Protect. Coat. Lin.*, Vol. 15, 89–99.

Apps, R.L., 1967, The effect of grit blasting on the bond strength of flame sprayed aluminium coatings on mild steel. *Proc. 2nd Met. Spray Conf.*, Birmingham, Institute of Welding.

Apps, R.L., 1969, Grit blasting versus bond strength in metal spraying. *Final Report*, The Welding Institute, Cambridge.

Apps, R.L., 1974, The influence of surface preparation on the bond strength of flame-sprayed aluminium coatings on mild steel. *J. Vac. Sci. Technol.*, Vol. 11, 741–746.

Aquaro, D., Fontani, E., 2001, Erosion of ductile and brittle materials. *Meccanica*, Vol. 36, 651–661.

Arnold, J.C., Hutchings, I.M., 1989, Flux rate effects in the erosive wear of elastomers. *J. Mater. Sci.*, Vol. 24, 833–839.

Arnold, J.C., Hutchings, I.M., 1992, A model for the erosive wear of rubber at oblique impact angles. *J. Phys. D: Appl. Phys.*, Vol. 25, A222–A229.

Arnold, J.C., Hutchings, I.M., 1993, Erosive wear of rubber by solid particles at normal incidence. *Wear*, Vol. 161, 213–221.

Askheim, E., Nokleby, J.O., Carlsson, L., Palm, M., 2001, Why do paints crack? *Protect. Coat. Europe*, Vol. 6, No. 3, 49–55.

Asthana, R., Sobczak, N., 2000, Wettability, spreading, and interfacial phenomena in high-temperature coatings. *JOM*, Vol. 52, No. 1, e-supplement.

Averchenko, P.A., Pleskach, V.M., Yurchenko, A.D., Kolesnik, R.I., 1970, Increasing the erosion stability of enamel coatings. *Glass Ceramics*, Vol. 27, No. 10, 342–344.

Baboian, R., 1986, *Electrochemical and Technical Corrosion Engineering*. NACE, Houston.

Badawi, K., Bielle, J., Castex, L., Giraudeau, A., 1986, Influence of sand blasting parameters on the geometrical and mechanical characteristics of 1010 steel sand blasted surfaces. *Advances in Surface Treatments: Technology—Applications—Effects*, Pergamon Press, Oxford, 229–241.

Bae, H.J., Baek, J.J., Lee, C.S., Shin, C.S., Lee, B.H., Shin, S.R., Beak, K.K., Kim, K.S., 2007, Improvement of blasting productivity by optimizing blasting-related operation parameters. *PACE 2007*, Dallas, TX, February 11–14, 2007.

Baek, K.H., Park, C.S., Kim, K.H., Chung, M.K., Park, J.H., 2006, Effect of blasted surface contaminants on coating performance. *Corrosion 06*, San Diego, NACE.

Bahadur, S., Badruddin, R., 1990, Erodent particle characterization and the effect of particle size and shape on erosion. *Wear*, Vol. 138, 189–208.

Bahbou, M.F., Nylen, P., Wigren, J., 2004, Effect of grit blasting and spraying angle on the adhesion strength of a plasma-sprayed coating. *J. Thermal Spray Technol.*, Vol. 13, No. 4, 508–514.

Bahlmann, W., 1978, Das richtige Einwegstrahlmittel für das Freistrahlen von Stahlbauten. *Ind. Lackierbetrieb*, Vol. 46, No. 10, 337–341.

Bailey, A.B., Hiatt, J., 1972, Sphere drag coefficients for a broad range of Mach and Reynolds numbers. *AIAA J.*, Vol. 10, 1436–1440.

Balasubramaniyan, B., 1998, Computational modeling of brittle impact erosion mechanisms. *Master Thesis*, West Virginia University, Morgantown, WV, USA.

Balcar, G.P., 1986, Impact process engineering: a key to success. *Impact Surface Treatment* (ed. S.A. Meguid), Elsevier Appl. Sci. Publ., London, 250–257.

Baldan, A., 2004, Adhesively-bonded bonded joints and repairs in metallic alloys, polymers and composite materials: adhesives, adhesion theories and surface pretreatment. *J. Mater Sci.*, Vol. 39, 1–49.

Ballard, R.L., Sailer, R.A., Larson, B., Soucek, M., 2001, Fracture toughness of inorganic-organic hybrid coatings. *J. Coat. Technol.*, Vol. 73, No. 913, 107–114.

Bandaru, R.K., 2004, Particle breakage in sand blasting due to impact on ductile materials. *MS Thesis*, West Virginia University, Morgantown, WV, USA.

Bardal, E., 1973, The effect of surface preparation on the adhesion of arc- and flame-sprayed aluminium and zinc coatings to mild steel. *Proc. 7th Int. Met. Spraying Conf.*, Welding Institute, Cambridge, 215–223.

Bardal, E., Molde, P., Eggen, T.G., 1973, Arc and flame sprayed aluminium and zinc coatings on mild steel: bond strength, surface roughness, structure and hardness. *Br. Corros. J.*, Vol. 8, 15–19.

Bardis, J.D., Kedward, K.T., 2002, Surface preparation effects on mode I testing of adhesively bonded composite joints. *J. Compos. Technol. Res.*, Vol. 24, 30–37.

Barkoula, N.M., 2002, Solid particle erosion behaviour of polymers and polymeric composites. *IVW-Schriftenreihe*, Band 29, Inst. für Verbundwerkstoffe GmbH, Kaiserslautern, Germany.

Barkoula, N.M., Karger-Kocsis, J., 2002, Processes and influencing parameters of the solid particle erosion of polymers and their composites. *J. Mater. Sci.*, Vol. 37, 3807–3820.

Barnett, K., Burgess, R.A., 2007, Factors influencing anchor profile. *PACE 2007*, Dallas, TX, February 11–14, 2007.

Basin, V.E., 1984, Advances in understanding the adhesion between solid substrates and organic coatings. *Prog. Org. Coat.*, Vol. 12, 213–250.

Bates, R.L., Jackson, J.A., 1980, *Glossary of Geology*. Amer. Geol. Inst., Falls Church.

Baumann, M., 2003, Korrosions- und Beschichtungsschäden an Stahlwasserbauten. *2. Tagung Korrosionsschutz in der maritimen Technik*, German. Lloyd, Hamburg, 124–143.

Baer, D.R., Wagner, D.K., 1973, Effects of surface condition on the transport properties of tungsten. *J. Low Temp. Phys.*, Vol. 13, No. 5/6, 445–469.

Beck, C., Arndt, U., 1996, Tolerierung und Messung der Rauheit gestrahlter Oberflächen. *Strahlmittel und Strahlverfahrenstechnik*, Seminarunterlagen, IKS Dresden, Germany, March 1996.

Beitelman, A., 2003, Recycling steel grit. *Protect. Coat. Europe*, Vol. 19, No. 7, 56–59.

Bellmann, R., Levy, A., 1981, Erosion mechanism in ductile metals. *Wear*, Vol. 70, 1–27.

Belloy, E., Thurre, S., Walckiers, E., Sayad, A., Gijs, M.A., 2000, The introduction of powder blasting for sensor and microsystem applications. *Sens. Actuators*, Vol. 84, 330–337.

Belsole, R.J., Nolan, M., Eichberg, R.D., 1982, Sandblasting injury of the hand. *J. Hand Surg.*, Vol. 7, No. 5, 523–525.

Beltov, S., Assersen, N., 2002, Shipyard blasting and painting facilities. *J. Protect. Coat. Lin.*, Vol. 19, No. 7, 47–48.

Bendler, H., 1983, *Technisches Handbuch Verdichter*. VEB Verlag Technik, Berlin.

Berg, J.C., 1993, *Wettability*. Marcel Dekker, New York.

Berg, J.C., 2002, Semi-empirical strategies for predicting adhesion. *Surfaces, Chemistry and Applications* (eds. M. Chaudhury, A.V. Pocius), Elsevier, Amsterdam, 1–73.

Bergmann, C.P., 1994, Influence of the substrate roughness on the adherence of plasma sprayed coatings. *Proc. 7th Int. Therm. Spray Conf.*, Boston, MS, June 20–24, 683–686.

Berndt, C.C., Lin, C.K., 1993, Measurement of adhesion for thermally sprayed materials. *J. Adhes. Sci. Technol.*, Vol. 7, 1235–1264.

Besztercey, G., Karger-Kocsis, J., Szaplonczay, P., 1999, Solid particle erosion of electrically insulating silicon and EPDM rubber compounds. *Polymer Bull.*, Vol. 42, 717–724.

Beverloo, W.A., Leniger, H.A., van de Velde, J., 1961, The flow of granular solids through orifices. *Chem. Eng. Sci.,* Vol. 15, 260–269.

BGR 132, 2003, Vermeidung von Zündgefahren infolge elektrostatischer Aufladungen. Berufsgenossenschaft, Germany, 2003.

BGV D26, 1999, *BG-Vorschrift Strahlarbeiten*. Steinbruchs-Berufsgenossenschaft, Langenhagen, Germany.

Bigos, J., 1959, Anchor pattern profile and its effect on paint performance. *Corrosion*, Vol. 15, No. 8, 46–50.

Binder, G., 2001, Arbeits- und Umweltschutz bei Korrosionsschutzarbeiten. *Mitt. Bundesanstalt Wasserbau*, No. 83, 73–81.

Binder, G., 2003, Examination of accelerated laboratory tests for corrosion protection. *Protect. Coat. Europe*, Vol. 8, No. 11, 8–16.

Birley, S.S., Owens, A., 1979, Surface stresses induced by grit blasting. *Anti-Corros.*, Vol. 26, No. 7, 5–7.

Bitter, J.G., 1963, A study of erosion phenomena, part I+II. *Wear*, Vol. 9, 5–21 and 169–190.

Björgum, A.J., Knudsen, O.O., Kvernbräten, A.-K., Johnsen, R., 2007, Repair coating systems for bare steel – effect of pre-treatment and conditions during application and curing. *NACE Corrosion Conference*, Houston, Paper 0712.

Bloch, H.P., 1995, *A Practical Guide To Compressor Technology*. McGraw-Hill, New York.

Blomquist, P.A., 1997, Simultaneous three-edge pre-weld cleaning. *J. Ship Production*, Vol. 13, No. 4, 242–257.

Bochenin, V.I., 2005, A radioisotope technique for estimation of heat resistance of aluminium coatings after shot blasting. *Russ. J. Nondestructive Test.*, Vol. 41, No. 12, 775–777.

Bockenheimer, C., Valeske, B., Possart, W., 2002, Network structure in epoxy aluminium bonds after mechanical treatment. *Int. J. Adhes. Adhesives*, Vol. 22, 349–356.

Bohl, W., 1989, *Technische Strömungslehre*. 8. Auflage, Vogel-Verlag, Würzburg.

Böhm, H., Betz, S., Ball, A., 1990, The wear resistance of polymers. *Tribol. Int.*, Vol. 23, No. 6, 399–406.

Bond, F.C., 1953, Work indexes tabulated. *Trans. AIME Mining Eng.*, 315–316.

Bond, F.C., 1961, Crushing and grinding calculations, part I and II. *Br. Chem. Eng.*, Vol. 6, 378–385, 543–548.

Bond, S.D., Martin, J.W., 1984, Surface recrystallization in a single crystal nickel-based superalloy. *J. Mater. Sci.*, Vol. 19, 3867–3872.

Boocock, S.K., 1992, The effect of abrasives on coating performance. *J. Protect. Coat. Lin.*, Vol. 9, No. 9, 52–61.

Boocock, S.K., 1994, SSPC research on performance testing of abrasives and salt retrieval techniques. *J. Protect. Coat. Lin.*, Vol. 11, No. 3, 28–39.

Bordeaux, F., Sait-Jacques, R., Moreau, C., Dallaire, S., Lu, J., 1991, Thermal shock resistance of TiC coatings plasma-sprayed on macroroughened substrates. *Proc. 4th Nat. Therm. Spray Conf.*, Pittsburgh, PA, May 4–10, 127–134.

Bosshard, R.G., Fritchman, T.T., 1992, Definition of blast pressure in air-operated peening machines. *The Shot Peener*, Vol. 6, No. 3, 20–21.

Bothen, M., 2000, *Mikro-Abrasives Druckluftstrahlen*. Verlag Köster, Berlin.

Boue, A., 2005, Eignungsprüfung von Beschichtungssystemen für Brückenseile. *Korrelation von Labortests mit Praxisbedingungen im schweren Korrosionsschutz*, Workshop-Unterlagen, Gesellschaft für Korrosionsschutz e.V., Frankfurt am Main, 98–107.

Bowden, F.P., Tabor, D., 1964, *The Friction and Lubrication of Solids*, Part II, Clarendon Press, Oxford.

Branco, J.R., Gansert, R., Sampath, S., Berndt, C.C., Herman, H., 2004, Solid particle erosion of plasma sprayed ceramic coatings. *Mater. Res.*, Vol. 7, No. 1, 147–253.

Brantley, C.D., Reist, P.C., 1994, Abrasive blasting with quartz sand: factors affecting the potential for incidental exposure to respirable silica. *Am. Ind. Hyg. Assoc. J.*, Vol. 55, 946–952.

Brauer, H., 1971, *Grundlagen der Einphasen- und Mehrphasenströmung*. Sauerländer-Verlag, Aargau.

Brauer, H., Kriegel, E., 1963, Untersuchungen über den Verschleiß von Kunststoffen und Metallen. *Chemie-Ing.-Technik*, Vol. 35, 697–707.

Brauns, E., Determann, H., Kalla, U., 1964, Einfluß der Oberflächenvorbehandlung von Stahl auf das Verhalten con Anstrichen in Seewasser. *Stahl Eisen*, Vol. 84, No. 17, 1082–1087.

Breinsberger, J., Koppelmann, J., 1982, Verhalten von Dreischichtlackierungen im Steinschlagtest. *Farbe Lack*, Vol. 88, 916–920.

Brevoort, G.H., 1988, Abrasive blasting and salt contamination: a case history. *J. Protect. Coat. Lin.*, Vol. 5, No. 5, 24–71.

Brewis, D.M., Critchlow, G.W., Curtis, C.A., 1999, Cryoblasting as a pretreatment to anhance adhesion to aluminium alloys: an initial study. *Adhes. Adhesives*, Vol. 19, 253–256.

Briscoe, B.J., Sinha, S.K., 2003, Scratch resistance and localised damage characteristics of polymer surfaces—a review. *Materialwiss. Werkstofftech.*, Vol. 34, 989–1002.

Broughton, W.R., Lodeiro, M.J., 2002, Review of surface characterisation techniques for adhesive bonding. *NPL Report MATC(A)66*, National Physics Laboratory, Teddington, UK, February 2002.

Broughton, W.R., Lodeiro, M.J., 2003, Assessment of characterisation techniques for evaluating surface treatments for adhesive bonding. *NPL Report MATC(A)140*, National Physics Laboratory, Teddington, UK, June 2003.

Buhlmann, S., 1970, Ein stochastisches Modell der Prallzerkleinerung. *Chemie-Ing.-Techn.*, Vol. 42, No. 5, 277–281.

Buhrke, H., Kecke, H.-J., Richter, H., 1989, *Strömungsförderer*. Vieweg & Sohn, Braunschweig.

Bullard, J., Corbett, W.D., Mozelewski, F.A., 2002, Corrosion protection of limited access areas common to bridge structural steel design. *J. Protect. Coat. Lin.*, Vol. 19, No. 9, 46–50.

Bullett, T.R., Dasgupta, D., 1969, Characterization of blast-cleaned surfaces and its relation to paint performance. *J. Oil Colour Chem. Assoc.*, Vol. 52, 1099–1129.

Bullett, T.R., Prosser, J.L., 1972, Measurement of adhesion. *Prog. Organ. Coat.*, Vol. 1, 45–71.

Burgess, R., Laube, D., Gijs, M.A., 1999 Sidhwa, A., Spinner, C., Zheng, S., Chew, T., Gandy, T., Melosky, S., Vetier, J., 2002, Post blast component cleaning techniques to reduce particle generation in etch and deposit chambers. *Mater. Res. Soc. Symp. Proc.*, Vol. 716, 549–554.

Calabrese, C., Allen, J.R., 1978, Surface characterization of atmospherically corroded and blast cleaned steel. *Corrosion*, Vol. 34, 331–338.

Calabrese, S.J., Murray, S.F., 1982, Methods of evaluating materials for icebreaker hull coatings. *Selection and Use of Wear Tests for Coatings* (ed. R.G. Bayer), ASME, New York, 157–173.

Calboreanu, G., 1991, Influence of target hardness on impact damage of shot. *Wear*, Vol. 150, 315–329.

Cambruzzi, A., Rossi, S., Deflorian, F., 2005, Reduction on protective properties of organic coatings produced by abrasive particles. *Wear*, Vol. 258, 1696–1705.

Cannon, L.J., Maurer, K.F., Woodmansee, J.T., Arena, S.L., McConnell-Meachen, M., 1996, Keeping workers' blood lead levels down on bridge repainting jobs. *J. Protect. Coat. Lin.*, Vol. 12, 64–69.

Carew, T., Ghita, O., Whelan, P.F., 2001, A vision system for detecting paint faults on painted slates. *Int. Conf. Control, Autom. Syst.*, IEEE, New York.

Carlson, J.R., Townsend, T.G., 1998, Management of solid waste from abrasive blasting. *Prac. Period. Hazard., Toxic, Radioact. Waste Manage.*, 72–77.

Carlson, J.R., Townsend, T.G., 1999, Assessment of waste abrasive blasting media from ship maintenance facilities and sandblasting contractor sites. *Proc. CCSE/ASCE Environ. Eng. Conf.*, 651–660.

Carter, G., Bevan, I.J., Katardjiev, I.V., Nobes, M.J., 1991, The erosion of copper by reflected sandblasting grains. *Mater. Sci. Eng. A*, Vol. 132, 231–236.

Celik, E., Demirkiran, A.S., Avci, E., 1999, Effect of grit blasting of substrate on the corrosion behaviouir of plasma-sprayed Al_2O_3 coatings. *Surf. Coat. Technol.*, Vol. 116–119, 1061–1064.

Chandler, K.A., 1966, The influence of salts in rust on the corrosion of the underlying steel. *Br. Corros. J.*, Vol. 1, 264–266.

Chandler, K.A., Shak, B.J., 1966, The assessment of surface profile after blast-cleaning. *Br. Corros. J.*, Vol. 1, No. 9, 307–316.

Chaudri, M.M., Walley, S.M., 1978, A high-speed photographic investigation of the impact damage in sodalime and borosilicate glasses by small glass and steel spheres. *Fracture Mechanics of Ceramics* (eds. R.C. Bradt et al.), Vol. 3, Plenum Press, New York, 349–364.

Chen, P.H., Chang, L.M., 2006, Effectiveness of neuro-fuzy recognition approach in evaluating steel bridge paint conditions. *Can. J. Civil Eng.*, Vol. 33, 103–108.

Chernyavskii, A.N., 1984, Surface roughness after shot blasting. *Chem. Petroleum Eng.*, Vol. 20, No. 1, 29–33.

Ciampini, D., Spelt, J.K., Papini, M., 2003a, Simulation of interference effects in particle streams following impact with a flat surface. Part I: theory and analysis. *Wear*, Vol. 254, 237–249.

Ciampini, D., Spelt, J.K., Papini, M., 2003b, Simulation of interference effects in particle streams following impact with a flat surface. Part II: parametric study and implications for erosion testing and blast cleaning. *Wear*, Vol. 254, 250–264.

Cizmas, P.G., Slattery, J.C., 2007, Dimensionless correlation for sand erosion of families of polymers. *Wear*, Vol. 262, 316–319.

Clausen, R., Stangenberg, J., 2002, Device for the determination of impact velocities in shot peening. *Proc. 8th Int. Conf. Shot Peening*, Garmisch-Partenkirchen, 90–94.

Claydon, D.A., 2006, Performance testing of anti-corrosive coatings. *Proc. PACE Conf.*, Tampa, FL, Conference-CD.

Cleaver, J.A., Ghadiri, M., 1993, Impact attrition of sodium carbonate monohydrate crystals. *Powder Tech.*, Vol. 76: 15–22.

Cluchague, P., 2001, New innovations in surface preparation. *Protect. Coat. Europe*, Vol. 6, No. 11, 13–18.

Confente, M., Geneve, D., Resiak, B., Jallon, M., 1995, Effects of mechanical descaling on the surface of low carbon wire rod for drawing or cold heading. *Wire J. Int.*, No. 2, 238–242.

Conroy, L.M., Menezes-Lindsay, R.M., Sullivan, P.M., Cali, S., Forst, L., 1996, Lead, chromium, and cadmium exposure during abrasive blasting. *Arch. Environ. Health*, Vol. 51, 95–99.

Cooke, R., House, R., Lawson, I.J., Pelmear, P.L., Wills, M., 2001, Hand-arm vibration syndrome from exposure to high-pressure hoses. *Occup. Med.*, Vol. 51, No. 6, 401–409.

Coulson, J.M., Richardson, J.F., 1968, *Chemical Engineering*, Vol. 2, Unit Operations, Pergamon Press, Oxford.

Cousens, A.K., Hutchings, I.M., 1983, Influence of erodent particle shape on the erosion of mild steel. *Proc. 6th Int. Conf. Erosion by Liq. Solid Impact,* (ed. J.E. Field), Cavendish Lab., Cambridge, 41/1–41/7.

Cox, E.P., 1927, A method of assigning numerical and percentage values to the degree of roundness. *J. Paleontol.*, Vol. 1, 179–183.

Crawford, R., Atkinson, D., 1996, *Liquid Surfaces*. Swinburne University, Melbourne.

D'Emanuele, A., Hill , J., Tamada, J.A., Domb, A.J., Langer, R., 1992, Molecular weight changes in polymer erosion. *Pharm. Res.*, Vol. 9, No. 10, 1279–1283.

Da Maia, M.L., 2000, Alternatives to conventional methods and equipment for surface preparation. *Proc. PCE 2000 Conf. Exhib.*, Technology Publication, Pittsburgh, 349–359.

Dahlhoff, B., 1967, Zusammenhang zwischen Zerkleinerungsgeschwindigkeit und Schallgeschwindigkeit. *Chemie-Ing. Techn.*, Vol. 39, 1112–1116.

Da Silva Rocha, A., Strohaecker, T., Hirsch, T., 2003, Einfluss unterschiedlicher Oberflächenzustände vor dem Plasmanitrieren auf Eigenschaften und Zerspanungsverhalten des Schnellarbeitsstahls S 6-5-2. *Materialwiss. und Werkstofftechn.*, Vol. 34, 64–73.

Day, J., Huang, X., Richards, N.L., 2005, Examination of a grit-blasting process for thermal spraying using statistical methods. *J. Therm. Spray Technol.*, Vol. 14, 471–479.

Deng, J.X., 2005a, Sand erosion performance of B_4C/(W,Ti)C ceramic blasting nozzle. *Advances in Appl. Ceram.*, Vol. 104, 59–64.

Deng, J.X., 2005b, Erosion wear of boron carbide ceramic nozzles by abrasive air-jets. *Mater. Sci. Eng. A*, Vol. 408, 227–233.

Deng, J.X., Zheng, Z.C., Ding, Z.L., Wang, J.H., 2003a, Erosion wear of ceramic and cermented carbide nozzles in dry sand blasting process. *Br. Ceram. Trans.*, Vol. 102, 61–65.

Deng, J.X., Feng, Y., Ding, Z., Shi, P., 2003b, Wear behavior of ceramic nozzles in sand blasting treatments. *J. Europ. Ceram. Soc.*, Vol. 23, 323–329.

Deng, J., Liu, L., Ding, M., 2007, Erosion wear behaviours of SiC/(W,Ti)C laminated ceramic nozzles in dry sand blasting processes. *Mater. Sci. Eng. A*, Vol. 444, 120–129.

DIN 1343, 1990, Referenzzustand, Normzustand, Normvolumen—Begriffe und Werte. Deutsches Inst. für Normung, 01-90.

DIN-Fachbericht 28, 2002, Korrosionsschutz von Stahlbauten durch Beschichtungen. Prüfung von Oberflächen auf visuell nicht feststellbare Verunreinigungen vor dem Beschichten. Beuth-Verlag GmbH, Berlin.

Dioh, N.N., Williams, J.G., 1994, The impact behaviour of paints. *J. Mater. Sci.*, Vol. 29, 6091–6096.

Dittmar, P., 1962, Zündgefahren durch Funken aus metallischen Oberflächen. *Jahrb. Oberflächentechnik*, Vol. 18, 56–66.

Djurovic, B., Jean, E., Papini, M., Tangestanian, P., Spelt, J.K., 1999, Coating removal from fibre-composites and aluminium using starch media blasting. *Wear*, Vol. 224, 22–37.

Doherty, C.B., 1974, Surfaces produced by abrasive blasting of steel. *Mater. Perform.*, No. 11, 12–20.

Donker, B., 1985, Underwater sandblasting for surface treatment of submerged steel and concrete structures. *Proc. 1st Int. Conf. Surf. Eng.* (ed. I.A. Bucklow), Vol. III, The Welding Institute, London, 9–14.

Donker, B., Richter, U., 1982, Unterwasser-Sandstrahlen mit Druckluft. *Hansa*, Vol. 119, No. 20, 1365–1367.

Donker, B., Richter, U., 1988, Unterwasser-Konservierung: Erprobungsbericht zum Kooperationsprojekt "Pfahl-Konservierung". *Internal Report GKSS 88/I/9*, GKSS, Geesthacht, Germany.

Drisko, R.W., 2002, *SSPC Painting Manual*, Vol. 1, Surface Preparation Specifications, SSPC, Pittsburgh.

Drozdz, S., Race, T., Tinklenberg, K., 2000, Laboratory evaluation of engineered abrasives and surface treatments for mixed-metal blast media wastes. *J. Protect. Coat. Lin.*, Vol. 18, 41–47.

Duncan, B., Lodeiro, M., 2004, Adhesion durability assessment. *NPL-Report DEPC-MPR*-004, National Physics Laboratory, Teddington, UK, June 2004.

Dupuy, R., 2001, Ultra-high-pressure waterjetting for maintenance coatings applications. *J. Protect. Coat. Lin.*, Vol. 18, No. 8, 68–75.

Dupuy, R., Ashworth, R., Frenzel, L., 2001, Turning a liability into an asset – the story of an old power plant. *Proc. 11th Amer. Water Jet Conf.* (ed. M. Hashish), WJTA, St. Louis, Paper 56.

Elbing, F., 2002, Prozessanalyse und—optimierung des Trockeneinsstrahlens. *1. Treffen Industriearbeitskreis Trockenstrahlen,* Berlin, November, 2002.

Ellermaa, R.R., 1993, Erosion prediction of pure metals and carbon steels. *Wear*, Vol. 162–164, 1114–1122.

Elsner, C.I., Cavlacanti, E., Ferraz, O., Di Sarli, A.R., 2003, Evaluation of the surface treatment effect on the anticorrosive performance of plant systems on steel. *Progr. in Organic Coat.*, Vol. 48, 50–62.

Emrich, S., 2003, Untersuchungen zum Einfluss von Oberflächenchemie und -morphologie auf die Langzeitbeständigkeit geklebter Aluminiumverbunde. *Dissertation*, Universität Kaiserslautern, Germany.

Engel, P.A., 1976, *Impact Wear of Materials*. Elsevier Science Publication Comp., Amsterdam.

Engel, P.A., 1985, Indentation debonding test for polymer coatings adhered to a substrate. *Int. J. Adhes. Adhesives*, Vol. 5, 129–132.

Engel, P.A., Pedroza, G.C., 1983, Indentation-debonding test for adhered thin polymer layers. *Adhesion Aspects of Polymeric Coatings* (ed. K.L. Mittal), Plenum Press, New York, 583–595.

Engelberg, F., 1967, Staubentwicklung in Schleuderradputzräumen und Entstaubung. *Giesserei*, Vol. 54, No. 6, 144–148.

Engell, H.-J., 1960, Die Haftfestigkeit von Oberflächenschichten auf Metallen. *Werkst. Korros.*, Vol. 11, 147–151.

Epprecht, A., 1974, Das mechanische Verhalten von Lackfilmen. *Farbe Lack*, Vol. 80, 505–513.

Evans, A.G., Gulden, M.E., Rosenblatt, M.E., 1978, Impact damage in brittle materials in the elastic-plastic response regime. *Proc. R. Soc. Lond., Ser. A.*, Vol. 361, 343–356.

Evans, A.G., Fleck, N.A., Watanabe, M., Maloney, M., Darolia, R., 2006, Scaling laws governing the erosion and impact resistance of thermal barrier coatings. *Wear*, Vol. 260, 886–894.

Faidi, S.E., Scantlebury, J.D., Young, R.J., 1990, Messung der Haftfestigkeit unter Stoßbelastung. *Farbe Lack*, Vol. 96, No. 11, 853–856.

Fairfull, C.L., Weldon, D.G., 2001, Salt contaminated abrasives and their effect on coating performance. *Proc. SSPC Conf.*, Atlanta, November 11–14, 2001, 30–44.

Fang, C.K., Chuang, T.H., 1999, Surface morphologies and erosion rates of metallic building materials after sandblasting. *Wear*, Vol. 230, 156–164.

Fauchais, P., Fukumoto, M., Vardelle, A., Vardelle, M., 2004, Knowledge concerning splat formation: an invited review. *J. Therm. Spray Technol.*, Vol. 13, 337–360.

Fedko, V.T., Tomas, K.I., 1998, Wetting the surface of welded components by protective coatings. *Welding Int.*, Vol. 12, 47–49.

Feist, K., Schulz, W.-D., Eisengräber, A., 1988, Zur Bedeutung der Rauheitsmaße R_a, R_m, R_z und S_m auf die Haftfestigkeit von Spritzmetallschutzschichten. *Korrosion*, Vol. 19, 307–315.

Finnie, I., 1958, The mechanism of erosion of ductile metals. *Proc. 3rd U.S. Nat. Congr. Appl. Mech.* (eds. R.M. Haythornthwaite, et al.), ASME, New York, 527–532.

Finnie, I., McFadden, A., 1978, On the velocity dependence of the erosion of ductile metals by solid particle at low angle of incidence. *Wear*, Vol. 48, 181–190.

Flavenot, J.F., Lu, J., 1990, Influence of ageing of a cut steel wire shot during shot peening. *Proc. 4th Int. Conf. Shot Peening*, Tokyo, 83–93.

Flores, S., Morcillo, M., 1999, Anticipated levels of soluble salts remaining on rusty steel prior to painting. *Surf. Coat. Int.*, No. 1, 19–24.

Foghelin, M., 1990, The effect of surface preparation on the durability of paint on galvanized steel. *Proc. 11th Int. Conf. Innov. Technol. Trans. Corros. Control*, Vol. 2, Assoiazione Italiana, Milan, 2.283–2.291.

Fokke, M., 1999, *Abrasive Blasting of Metal Surfaces*. Delft University Press, Delft.

Forsgren, A., Applegren, C., 2000, Comparison of chloride levels remaining on the steel surface after various pretreatments. *Proc. PCE Conf. Exhib*, Technology Publication, Pittsburgh, 271–283.

Fraenkel, K.H., 1954, *Manual on Rock Blasting*, Vol. II, Atlas Diesel, Stockholm.

French, M.A., 1998, Safety in high-pressure water jetting. *Water Jet Applications in Construction Engineering* (ed. A.W. Momber), A.A. Balkema, Rotterdam, 387–397.

Frenzel, L.M., 1997, Continuing improvement initiatives of surface preparation with water jetting. *Proc. 9th Am. Water Jet Conf.*, (ed. M. Hashish), WJTA, St. Louis, 697–716.

Friedrich, K., 1986, Erosive wear of polymer surfaces by steel ball blasting. *J. Mater. Sci.*, Vol. 21, 3317–3331.

Gane, N., Murray, M.J., 1979, The transition from ploughing to cutting in erosive wear. *Proc. 5th Int. Conf. Erosion Liq. Solid Impact*, Cavendish Laboratory, 40/1–40/8.

Gasterstädt, J., 1924, Die experimentelle Untersuchung des pneumatischen Fördervorganges. *Forschungsarbeiten auf dem Gebiet des Ingenieurwesens*, Heft 265.

Gause, R.L., 1989, A noncontacting scanning photoelectron emission technique for bonding surface cleanliness inspection. *5th Annual NASA NDE Workshop*, Cocoa Beach, Florida.

Gelfant, F.S., 1995, Contaminated concrete—effect of surface preparation methods on coating peformance. *J. Protect. Coat. Lin.*, Vol. 15, No. 12, 60–72.

Gelsdorf, H., 1987, Sicherheit beim Druckluftstrahlen. *Bau-BG*, No. 1, 24–25.

Gesell, W., 1966, Ersatz von Quarzsand beim Druckluftstrahlen durch nicht Silikose erzeugende mineralische Strahlmittel. *Stahl Eisen*, Vol. 86, No. 14, 906–912.

Gesell, W., 1969, Jahresübersicht Putzverfahren und -einrichtungen. *Giesserei*, Vol. 56, No. 18, 552–557.

Gesell, W., 1973, Strahlmittelfragen—zweite Literatur-Rückschau. *Fachberichte Oberflächentechnik*, Vol. 11, 1–10.

Gesell, W., 1979, Verfahren und Kennwerte der Strahlmittelprüfung. *VDG-Taschenbuch 5*, Gießerei-Verlag GmbH, Düsseldorf.

Gillespie, B., 1996, Image analysis of shot peening media. *Proc. 6th Int. Conf. Shot Peening*, San Francisco, CA, 213–222.

Gillespie, B., Fowler, D.B., 1991, Evaluation of size and shape of shot peening media by image analysis. *SAE Trans.*, Vol. 100, No. 1, 28–39.

Gillessen, R., Lange, H., Schindler, H., 1995, Bemessungen von Stahlrohren. *Stahlrohr-Handbuch* (ed. Hrsg. B. Sommer), Vulkan-Verlag, Essen, 156–281.

Gillström, P., Jarl, M., 2004, Replacement of pickling with shot blasting for wire rod preparation. *Scand. Metall.*, Vol. 33, 178–269.

Gladun, A., Gladun, C., Knorn, M., Vinzelberg, H., 1977, Investigation of the heat conductivity of niobium in the temperature range 0.05–23 K. *J. Low Temp. Phys.*, Vol. 27, 873–886.

Glatzel, W.-D., Brauer, H., 1978, Prallverschleiß. *Chemie Ing.Technik*, Vol. 50, No. 7, 487–497.

Glück, B., 1988, *Hydrodynamische und gasdynamische Rohrströmung—Druckverluste*. VEB Verlag für Bauwesen, Berlin.

Gnyp, L.P., Marukha, M., Heneha, B., Chervatyuk, V., 2004, A device for simultaneous determination of the impact resistance and hardness of insulating coatings of pipelines. *Mater. Sci.*, Vol. 40, No. 2, 291–295.

Goergens, U., 2002, PAK-Problematik im Stahlwasserbau. *BVK-Fachtagung*, Bundesverband Korrosionsschutz, Köln, March 2002.

Goldman, D.B., Sutker, B.J., Schmidt, R.G., Suttmeier, P., 1990, Comparative performance of glass beads in suction and direct pressure shot peening applications. *Proc. 4th Int. Conf. Shot Peening*, Tokyo, 9–18.

Gommel, G., 1967a, Energy, abrasion and comminution in impact processes. *Staub—Reinhaltung—Luft*, Vol. 27, No. 1, 54–61.

Gommel, G., 1967b, Erscheinungen bei stoßender Beanspruchung und ihr Zusammenhang mit Verschleißvorgängen. *Materialprüfung*, Vol. 9, No. 5, 175–178.

Grabow, G., 2002, Optimalbereiche von Fluidenergiemaschinen – Pumpen und Verdichter. *Forschung im Ingenieurwesen*, Vol. 67, 100–106.

Grant, J.T., Smith, J.A., Mazza, J.J., 2004, The characterization of Al alloy surfaces at each stage of preparation for adhesive bonding. *Materiali in Technologije*, Vol. 38, No. 5, 223–231.

Grearson, A.N., Aucote, J., Engström, H., 1989, Wear of ceramics in grit blasting. *Brit. Ceram Trans. J.*, Vol. 88, 213–218.

Green, R.G., Gregory, I.A., Henry, R.M., Hill, E.J., 1981, Measurement of shot velocity at the nozzle of a shot-peening machine. *Proc. Conf. Impact Surf. Treat.*, Elsevier, London, 221–228.

Greenburg, L., Winslow, C., 1932, The dust hazard in air pressure abrasive blasting. *Int. Arch. Occup. Environ. Health*, Vol. 3, No. 4, 577–599.

Greverath, W.-D., Momber, A.W., Opel, H., 2005, Device and method for testing surfaces, in particular steel surfaces, with respect to structure, colour intensity and/or colour distribution. Patent No. WO 2005/057127 A1.

Griffith, A.A., 1921, The phenomena of rupture and flow in solids. *Phil. Trans. Roy. Soc. London*, Ser. A, Vol. 221, 163–198.

Griffith, B., 2001, *Manufacturing Surface Technology*. Penton Press, London.

Griffith, B.J., Gawne, D.T., Dong, G., 1996, The erosion of steel surfaces by brit-blasting as a preparation for plasma spraying. *Wear*, Vol. 194, 95–102.

Griffith, B.J., Gawne, D.T., Dong, G., 1997, The role of grit blasting in the production of high-adhesion plasma sprayed alumina coatings. *Proc. Inst. Mech. Eng., Part B*, Vol. 211, 1–9.

Griffith, B.J., Gawne, D.T., Dong, G., 1999, A definition of the topography of grit-blasted surfaces for plasma sprayed alumina coatings. *Trans. ASME, J. Manuf. Sci. Eng.*, Vol. 121, 49–53.

Groot, R.C., Kik, T.A., van Tongeren, H.P., van Ooij, W.J., 1982, Protection of steel by blasting with zinc-coated abrasives and painting under water or in wet conditions. *Proc. 8th Int. Conf. Org. Coat. Sci. Technol.*, Athens, 395–406.

Groth, K., 1995, *Kompressoren*. Vieweg, Braunschweig.

Groß, K.-J., 1988, Erosion (Strahlverschleiß) als Folge der dynamischen Werkstoffreaktion beim Stoß. *Dissertation*, Universität Stuttgart, Germany.

Grubitsch, H., Sammer, R., Willfurth, L., 1972, Über das Korrosionsverhalten von Stahlblechen, die mit verschiedenen Strahlmittel entrostet und mit Zinkstaubanstrich versehen wurden. *Werkst. Korros.*, Vol. 23, 561–564.

Guan, X.S., Dong, Z.F., Li, D.Y., 2005, Surface nanocrystallization by sandblasting and annealing for improved mechanical and tribological properties. *Nanotechnology*, Vol. 16, 2963–2971.

Guilemany, J.M., Llorca-Isern, N., Szabo, P.J., 1996, Residual stress characterization of grit blasted steel surfaces. *Surf. Eng.*, Vol. 12, 77–79.

Gupta, G., Win, T., Messom, C., Demidenko, S., Mukhopadhyay, S., 2003, Defect analysis of grit-blasted or spray-painted surface using vision sensing techniques. *Image Vision Comput., NZ*, 18–23.

Haagen, H., Konzelmann, R., Kunz, G., 1990, Einfluß atmosphärischer Salze auf den Korrosionsschutz von Beschichtungen. *Farbe Lack*, Vol. 96, No. 4, 255–260.

Hamann, J., 1987, Zur Entwicklung von Strahldüsen für das Druckluft-Freistrahlverfahren hoher Strahlleistung. *Korrosion*, Vol. 18, No. 4, 183–192.

Hamed, A., Mohamed, A., 2001, Simultaneous LDV measurements of gas and particle velocities in two-phase flow. *Proc. 7th Int. Congr. Fluid Dyn. Propul.*, ASME, New York, 1–7.

Hansen, C.M., 1972, Surface roughness profiles and coatings performance. *J. Paint Technol.*, Vol. 44, No. 570, 61–66.

Hansink, J.D., 1998, Economics of abrasive selection for shipyard use. *Protect. Coat. Europe*, Vol. 3, No. 5, 24–27.

Hansink, J.D., 2000, An introduction to abrasives for protective coating removal operations. *J. Protect. Coat. Lin.*, Vol. 17, No. 4, 66–73.

Hare, C.H., 1996, The mechanical properties of coating films and their characterisation. *Protect. Coat. Europe*, Vol. 1, No. 6, 42–57.

Hareux, D., Riac, B., 1986, A comparative study of air blasting using different abrasives—parts 1+2. *Corros. Prot. Mater.*, Vol. 5, No 1, 18–34.

Harris, A.F., Beevers, A., 1999, The effects of grit-blasting on surface properties for adhesion. *Adhes. Adhesives*, Vol. 19, 445–452.

Hauke, W., 1982, Strömungstechnische Untersuchungen an Düsen für das Druckluftstrahlen. *Maschinenbautechnik*, Vol. 31, No. 2, 87–90.

Hazlett, R.D., 1993, On surface roughness effects in wetting phenomena. *Contact Angle, Wettability and Adhesion* (ed. K.L. Mittal), VSP, Utrecht, 73–181.

He, J.W., Hendrix, B.C., Hu, N.S., Xu, K.W., Bell, T., Sun, Y., Mao, K., 1996, Interfacial fatigue limits as measure of cyclic bonding strength of hard coatings. *Surf. Eng.*, Vol. 12, No. 1, 49–54.

Heitbrink, W.A., 1999, Control technology for crystalline silica exposures in construction: wet abrasive blasting. *Report No. ECTB 247-11*, US Department of Health and Human Services, Cincinnati, December 1999.

Henning, R., Brauer, H., 1986, Untersuchung des Prallverschleißes ebener Platten. *VDI Forschungshefte*, No. 636, VDI-Verlag, Düsseldorf.

Hernandez, L., Oliviera, F., Gijs, M.A., 1999 Berrios, J.A., Villalobos, C., Pertuz, A., Cabrera, E., 2000, Fatigue properties of a 4340 steel coated with a Colmonoy 88 deposit applied by high-velocity oxygen fuel. *Surf. Coat. Technol.*, Vol. 133–134, 68–77.

Hertz, H., 1882, Ueber die Berührung fester elastischer Körper. *Journal für die reine und angewandte Mathematik*, Vol. 92, 156–171.

Herzog, R., Zin, W., Scholtes, B., Wohlfahrt, H., 1996, Zur Aussagefähigkeit der Almenintensität als Kennwert bei der gezielten Eigenspannungserzeugung durch Kugelstrahlen, *Materialwiss. Werkstofftech.* Vol. 27, 608–617.

Heya, A., Niki, T., Gijs, M.A., 1999 Takano, M., Doguchi, Y., Yonezawa, Y., Minamikawa, T., Muroi, S., Minami, S., Izumi, A., Masuda, A., Umemoto, H., Matsumura, H., 2005, Improvement of deposition rate by sandblasting of tungsten wire in catalytic chemical vapor deposition. *Jpn. J. Appl. Phys.*, Vol. 44, No. 4A, 1943–1944.

Heywood, H., 1933, Numerical definition of particle size and shape. *Chem. Ind.*, Vol. 32, 149–154.

Hitchcock, S.J., Carroll, N.T., Nicholas, M.G., 1981, Some effects of substrate roughness on wettability. *J. Mater. Sci.*, Vol. 16, 714–732.

Hitzrot, H.W., 1997, Reduced volume of spent abrasive in open air blasting. *NSRP Project No. 3-93-6*, July 1997.

Hochweber, M., 1970, Korrosionsschutz bei Unterwasser- und erdverlegten Stahlkonstruktionen. *Deutsche Farbenzeitschrift*, Vol. 24, 182–186.

Hofinger, I., Raab, K., Möller, J., Bobeth, M., 2002, Effect of substrate roughness on the adherence of NiCrAlY thermal spray coatings. *ASM J. Thermal Spray*, Vol. 11, 387–392.

Holle, D., 2000, Ultra-high pressure waterjetting of hazardous coatings on galvanised communication towers. *J. Prot. Coat. Lin.*, Vol. 17, No. 11, 71–85.

Holt, S., Austin, D.M., 2001, How nozzle pressure and feed rate affect the productivity of dry abrasive blasting. *J. Protect. Coat. Lin.*, Vol. 18, No. 10, 82–104.

Hong, K.T., Imodojemu, H., Webb, R.L., 1994, Effects of oxidation and surface roughness on contact angle. *Exp. Therm. Fluid Sci.*, Vol. 8, 279–285.

Hornauer, K.-P., 1982, Untersuchungen zur Umformung von Bauteilen durch Kugelstrahlen. *Dissertation*, RWTH Aachen, Germany.

Horowitz, I., 1982, *Oberflächenbehandlung mittels Strahlmitteln*. Vulkan-Verlag, Essen.

Howlett, J.J., Dupuy, R., 1993, Ultrahigh-pressure water jetting for deposit removal and surface preparation. *Mater. Perform.*, Vol. 32, 38–43.

Huang, H., Zhu, X.H., Huang, Q.K., 1995, Weibull strength distributions and fracture characteristics of abrasive materials. *Eng. Fracture Mech.*, Vol. 52, 15–24.

Hurst, R.C., Hancock, P., 1972, Measurement of the mechanical properties of growing surface films in oxidising environments. *Werkst. Korros.*, Vol. 23, 773–776.

Hutans, J., 1986, Wirkungsgraderhöhung des Druckluftstrahlens durch Einsatz des Strahlrohres. *Korrosion*, Vol. 17, No. 1, 38–41.

Hutchings, I.M., 1977a, Strain rate effects in microparticle impact. *J. Phys. D Appl. Phys.*, Vol. 10, L179–L184.

Hutchings, I.M., 1977b, Deformation of metal surfaces by the oblique impact of square plates. *Int. J. Mech. Sci.*, Vol. 19, 45–52.

Hutchings, I.M., 1979a, Mechanical and metallurgical aspects of the erosion of metals. *Proc. Corros./Erosion Coal Convers. Syst. Mater. Conf.* (ed. A.V. Levy), NACE., Houston, 393–428.

Hutchings, I.M., 1979b, Some comments on the theoretical treatment of erosive particle impact. *Proc. 5th Int. Conf. Erosion Liq. Solid Impact* (ed. J.E. Field), Cavendish Lab., Cambridge, 36/1–36/6.

Hutchings, I.M., 1981, A model for the erosion of metals by spherical particles at normal incidence. *Wear*, Vol. 70, 269–281.

Hutchings, I.M., 1992 Ductile-brittle transitions and wear maps for the erosion and abrasion of brittle materials. *J. Phys., D: Appl. Phys.*, Vol. 25, A/212–A/221.

Hutchings, I.M., Levy, A.V., 1989, Thermal effects in the erosion of ductile metals. *Wear*, Vol. 131, 105–121.

Hutchings, I.M., Winter, R.E., Field, J.F., 1976, Solid particle erosion of metals: the removal of surface material by spherical projectiles. *Proc. R. Soc. London A*, Vol. 348, 379–392.

Hutchings, I.M., Macmillan, N.H., Rickerby, D.G., 1981, Further studies of the oblique impact of a hard sphere against a ductile solid. *Int. J. Mechan. Sci.*, Vol. 23, No. 11, 639–646.

Hutchings, I.M., Deuchar, D.W., Muhr, A.H., 1987, Erosion of unfilled elastomers by solid particle impact. *J. Mater. Sci.*, Vol. 22, 4071–4076.

IACS, 2003, Confined Space Safe Practice, *Rec. No. 72*, Rev. 1, International Association of Classification Societies, London, October 2003.

Ibrahim, A., Berndt, C.C., 1998, The effect of high-velocity oxygen fuel, thermally sprayed WC-Co coatings on the high-cycle fatigue of aluminium alloy and steel. *J. Mater. Sci.*, Vol. 33, 3095–3100.

Iida, K., 1996, The analysis of the shot velocity thrown from the nozzle and the bladed wheel. *Shot Peener*, Vol. 10, No. 4, 36–38.

Illyes, A., Brauer, H., 1987, Die Energieumwandlung bei ein- oder mehrmaligem Stoß einer Partikel gegen eine feste Wand. *VDI-Forschungshefte*, No. 640, VDI-Verlag, Düsseldorf.

IMO, 2005, Performance Standards for Protective Coatings for Dedicated Seawater Ballast Tanks in all Types of Ships and Double-Side Skin Spaces of Bulk Carriers. International Maritime Organization, London.

Ishii, R., Kawasaki, K., 1982, Limiting particle streamline in the flow of a gas-particle mixture through an axially symmetric nozzle. *Phys. Fluids*, Vol. 25, No. 6, 959–966.

Ishikawa, K., Tobe, S., 2003, The effect of blasting and spraying angles on adhesive strength of aluminium sprayed coating by wire flame spraying. *Nippon Yosha Kyokai Shi*, Vol. 40, No. 3, 107–112.

ISO 1217, 1996, Displacement compressors—acceptance tests. 1996–09, International Organization for Standardization, Geneva.

ISO 12944-4, 1998, Paints and varnishes—corrosion protection of steel structures by protective paint systems—Part 4: types of surfaces and surface preparation. 1998-05-15, International Organization for Standardization, Geneva.

ISO 8502-3, 1992, Preparation of steel substrates before application of paint and related products—tests for the assessment of surface cleanliness—Part 3: assessment of dust on steel surfaces prepared for painting (pressure-sensitive tape method). 1992-10-01, International Organization for Standardization, Geneva.

ISO 8573-1, 2001, Compressed air - Part 1: Contaminants and purity classes. International Organisation for Standardization, Geneva.

Ivosevic, M., Gupta, V., Gijs, M.A., 1999 Cairncross, R.A., Twardowski, T.E., Knight, R., Baldoni, J.A., 2006, Effect of substrate roughness on splatting behaviour of HVOF sprayed polymer particles: modelling and experiments. *Int. Therm. Spray Conf. Exhib.*, Seattle, WA, May 15–17, 2006.

James, D.H., 1984, A review of experimental findings in surface preparation for thermal spraying. *J. Mech. Work. Technol.*, Vol. 10, No. 10, 221–232.

Jarrett, C., 2003, Evaluation of elevated blood lead in a commercial painter. *Appl. Occup. Environ. Hyg.*, Vol. 18, 808–811.

Jiang, X.P., Wang, X.Y., Li, J.X., Li, J.X., Man, C.S., Shepard, M.J., Zhai, T., 2006, Enhancement of fatigue and corrosion properties of pure Ti by sandblasting. *Mater. Sci. Eng. A*, Vol. 429, 30–35.

Johnson, W., 1972, *Impact Strength of Materials*. Chapter 9, Edward Arnold, London.

Johnson, K.L., 1985, *Contact Mechanics*. Cambridge University Press, Cambridge.

Johnson, W.C., 1990, Corrosion failure from water-soluble contaminants on abrasives. *J. Protect. Coat. Lin*, Vol. 7, No. 9, 54–59.

Johnson, W.C., 1997, Cost-effective extraction of chlorides from bridge steel. *J. Protect. Coat. Lin.*, Vol. 14, No. 1, 82–92.

Johnson, K.L., Kendall, K., Roberts, A.D., 1971, Surface energy and the contact of elastic solids. *Proc. R. Soc. London A*, Vol. 324, 301–313.

Johnston, M.H., 1998, Nozzle development for dry media blasting processes. *Abrasive Blast Cleaning News*, Vol. 3, No. 3, 4–7.

Jones, J.R., Gardos, M.N., 1971, An investigation of abrasive cleaning. *J. Am. Soc. Lubr. Eng.*, Vol. 27, No. 11, 393–399.

Jonnalagadda, K., Kline, G.E., Sottos, N.R., 1997, Local displacements and local transfer in shape memory alloy composites. *Exp. Mech.*, Vol. 37, No. 1, 78–86.

Jopp, H., 1995, Ein Beitrag zum besseren Verständnis der Wirkungsweise des Strahlens auf die Festigkeit und Beständigkeit von Metallklebungen. *Dissertation*, Kaiserslautern University, Kaiserslautern, Germany.

Kaiser, W.-D., Schütz, A., 2001, Hochdruckwasserstrahlen und restrostverträglicher Beschichtungsstoff. *Korrosionsschutz durch Beschichtungen und Überzüge auf Metallen*, Vol. 2, Part 9, Chapter 8.5, WEKA Media, Kissing, 1–26.

Kaiser, W.-D., Schulz, W.-D., 1987, Duplexsystem Zink plus Anstrich—Teil 2: Untersuchungen zur Optimierung der Haftfestigkeit in Abhängigkeit von Vorbehandlung und Bindemittel. *Korrosion*, Vol. 18, 211–225.

Kalide, W., 1990, *Einführung in die technische Strömungslehre*. Carl Hanser Verlag, München.

Kallio, M., Mannila, J., Gijs, M.A., 1999 Vesa, A., Mahlberg, R., Ritschkoff, A.C., Ohliogschläger, T., 2005, Modification of surface properties of metals by sol-gel coatings. *PACE 2005*, Las Vegas, T 59.

Kalpers, H., 1949, Wirtschaftlichkeitsfragen im Betrieb von Sandstrahlgebläsen. *Metalloberfläche*, Vol. 3, 67–70.

Kambham, K., Sangameswaran, S., Potana, S., Kura, B., 2006, Productivity and consumption variation in dry abrasive blasting with coal slag. *J. Ship Prod.*, Vol. 22, No. 1, 1–8.

Kamzolov, V.N., Maslov, B.N., Pirumov, U.G., 1971, Investigation of particle trajectories in Laval nozzles. *Fluid Dyn.*, Vol. 6, No. 5, 849–856.

Karpinos, D.M., Zilberberg, V.G., Vyaltsev, A.M., Kud, V.S., 1979, Shot-blasting as a mean of preparing surfaces for plasma deposition. *Powder Metall. Met. Ceram.*, Vol. 17, No. 9, 675–678.

Karuppanam, S., Romero, J.S., Rios, E.R., Rodopoulos, C., Levers, A., 2002, A theoretical and experimental investigation into the development of coverage in shot peening. *Proc. 8th Int. Conf. Shot Peening*, Garmisch-Partenkirchen, 101–107.

Katsikaris, K., Voutsas, E., Gijs, M.A., 1999, Andronikos, G., Stamataki, S., Magoulas, K., 2002, Recyclinmg ferrous-nickel slag in blast cleaning. *Waste Manage. Res.*, Vol. 20, No. 3, 269–278.

Katsikaris, K., Voutsas, E., Stamataki, S., Magoulas, K., 2001, Development of recycling process for used ferrous-nickel slag as abrasive material in sandblasting operations. *Proc. 7th Int. Conf. Environ. Sci. Technol.*, Syros, 187–194.

Kaufmann, B., 1998, Traggrund Stahl: Gibt es Alternativen zum Sandstrahlen? Seminarunterlagen, *Der Traggrund—ein ständiger Konfliktherd*? Schweizerischer Fachverband für Hydrodynamik am Bau, Würenlingen, Switzerland.

Kaufmann, B., Zielasch, A.H., 1998, Renovation of steel constructions by a combined waterjetting—waste recycling method. *Water Jet Applications in Construction Engineering* (ed. A.W. Momber), A.A. Balkema, Rotterdam, 313–323.

Keane, J.D., Bruno, J.A., Weaver, R.E., 1976, *Surface Profile for Anti-Corrosion Paints*. Steel Structures Painting Council, Pittsburgh, PA.

Kelly, E.G., Spottiswood, D.J., 1982, *Introduction to Mineral Processing*. John Wiley & Son, New York, 21–45.

Kendall, M.A., Quinlan, N.J., Thorpe, S.J., Ainsworth, R.W., Bellhouse, B.J., 2004, Measurements of the gas and particle flow within a converging-diverging nozzle for high speed powdered vaccine and drug delivery. *Exp. Fluids*, Vol. 37, 128–136.

Kiesskalt, S., Dahlhoff, B., 1965, Praktische Bedeutung zweier zerkleinerungsphysikalischer Effekte. *Chemie Ing. Technik*, Vol. 37, 277–283.
Kim, S.R., Nairn, J.A., 2000, Fracture mechanics analysis of coating/substrate systems. Part II: experiments in bending. *Eng. Fracture Mech.*, Vol. 65, 595–607.
Kim, I.T., Itoh, Y., Kainuma , S., Kadota, Y., 2003, Accelerated exposure tests of painted steel with different surface preparations of steel substrate. *Proc. 9th East Asia Pacific Conf. Struct. Eng. Construct.*, Bali, Indonesia.
Kinsey, J., Schliesser, S., Murowchick, P., 1994, Development of particular emission factors for uncontrolled abrasive blasting under simulated windy conditions. *Proc. 87th Annual Meeting*, Cincinnati, Air & Waste Management Assoc., Paper 94-WA71.03, 1–12.
Kirchner, H.P., Gruver, R.M., 1978a, Localized impact damage in a viscous medium (glass). *Fracture Mechanics of Ceramics* (eds. R.C. Bradt et al.), Vol. 3, Plenum Press, New York, 365–377.
Kirk, D., 2007, Generation of air-blast shot velocity. *The Shot Peener*, Vol. 21, No. 1, 26–30.
Kirk, D., Abyaneh, M.Y., 1994, Theoretical basis of shot peening coverage control. *Proc. 5th Int. Conf. Shot Peening*, Coventry, 183–190.
Kjernsmo, D., Kleven, K., Scheie, J., 2003, *Corrosion Protection Inspector's Book of Reference*. Hempel A/S, Lyngby, Denmark.
Kline, E., Mort, G., LeCompte, J., 1988, Improved productivity from new blast nozzle geometry. *J. Protect. Coat. Lin.*, Vol. 5, 8–12.
Klinger, C., Kinder, J., Ell, M., Klingbeil, D., 2002, Zwillingsbildung im Schiffbaustahl der M.V. Estonia. *Werkstoffprüfung: Schadensanalyse—Schadensvermeidung* (eds. Hrsg. G. Lange, M. Pohl), Wiley-VCH, Weinheim, 134–154.
Kloos, K.H., Kaiser, B., Schreiber, D., 1981, Einflüsse unterschiedlicher Reinheitsgrade auf die Dauerschwingfestigkeit des Federstahles 55 Cr 3. *Zeitschrift Werkstofftechnik*, Vol. 12, 206–218.
Kloos, K.H., Macherauch, E., 1987, Development of mechanical surface strengthening processes from the beginning until today. *Shot Peening Sci., Technol., Appl.*, Garmisch-Partenkirchen, 3–27.
Kniewald, D., 1993, Vorbehandlung des metallischen und keramischen Substrats durch Strahlen unter keramischen Plasmaspritzüberzügen. *DVS-Berichte*, Band 152, 118–122.
Knight, C.G., Swain, M.V., Chaudri, M.M., 1977, Impact of small steel spheres on glass surfaces. *J. Mater. Sci.*, Vol. 12, 1573–1586.
Knipfer, C., Funke, H.-W., 1997, Lärmbelastung an Baustellenarbeitsplätzen, Teil V. *BIA Report*, Hauptverband der gewerblichen Berufsgenossenschaften, St. Augustin, Germany.
Knotek, O., Elsing, R., 1987, Computer simulation of different surface topographies of metals produced by blasting processes. *Proc. 3rd Int. Conf. Shot Blasting*, Garmisch-Partenkirchen, 361–368.
Kogan, Y.D., Sazonova, Z.S., Boiko, S.V., Aleksandrov, V.D., 1993, Surface preparation for the application of hardening protective coatings. *Met. Sci. Heat Treat.*, Vol. 35, No. 12, 663–666.
Kogler, P.A., Ault, J.P., Farshon, C.L., 1995, Environmental acceptable materials for the corrosion protection of steel bridges. *Final Report*, Ocean City Research Corp.
Komov, G.A., 1966, Investigation of flow of a dust-laden stream in a Laval nozzle. *J. Eng. Phys. Thermodyn.*, Vol. 10, No. 3, 217–219.
Kotnarowska, D., 1999, Influence of ageing on mechanical properties of epoxide coating. *J. Corros. Sci. Eng.*, Vol. 2, Paper 28.
Kotnarowska, D., 2003, Influence of organic coating macrostructure on its resistance to erosive wear. *Corros. Sci. 21st Century*, UMIST, Manchester, July 2003.
Kriegel, E., 1968, Der Strahlverschleiß von Werkstoffen. *Chemie-Ing.-Technik*, Vol. 40, 31–36.
Kuljian, G., Holmes, B.S., 1998, U.S. Navy experience with waterjetting. *Prot. Coat. Europe*, Vol. 3, No. 16–21.
Kuljian, G.G., Melhuish, D.C., 1999, Water-jetting productivity study for the marine industry. *Proc. 10th Amer. Waterjet Conf.* (ed. M. Hashish), WJTA, St. Louis, Paper 42.

Kukera, S.N., Hutchings, I.M., 1984, Yielding of engineering polymers at strain rates of up to 500 s^{-1}. *Int. J. Mech. Sci.*, Vol. 26, 617–623.
Kumar, R., Verma, A.P., Lal, G.K., 1983, Nozzle wear during the flow of a gas-particle mixture. *Wear*, Vol. 91, 33–43.
Kura, B., 2003, Clean technologies for industries: role of emission test facility in emissions modeling and health risk reductions. *Risk Assess. Shipyard Emissions*, February 2003.
Kura, B., 2005, Residual risk from abrasive blasting emissions: particle size and metal speciation. *Final Report No. 2006-317*, University of New Orleans, New Orleans, LA, December 2005.
Kura, B., Kambham, K., Sangameswaran, S., Silvadasan, X., 2006, Particulate emission and emission factors for speciality sand used in dry abrasive blasting. *J. Ship Prod.,* Vol. 22, No. 1, 33–40.
LaBerge, M., Drouin, G., Gelinas, C., Champagne, B., Bobyn, J.D., 1990, Adherence of HDPE powder coating on Co-Cr surfaces: effect of substrate preparation and gas sterilization. *J. Biomed. Mater. Res.*, Vol. 24, 1427–1438.
Lacombe, R., 2006, *Adhesion Measurement Methods—Theory and Practice*. Taylor & Francis, Boca Raton.
Ladstädter, E., 1984, Grundlagen der Steinschlagsimulation "SPLITT". *Farbe Lack*, Vol. 90, 646–653.
Ladwein, T.L., Gümpel, P., 2004, The influence of functional surface properties of stainless steels on corrosion. *Corrosion 2004*, New Orleans, March 2004, 1–6.
Lange, J.H., 2002, Airborne exposure and soil levels associated with lead abatement of a steel tank. *Toxicol. Ind. Health*, Vol. 18, 28–38.
Lange, F.F., Evans, A.G., 1979, Erosive damage depth in ceramics: a study on metastable, tetrogonal zirkonia. *J. Amer. Ceram. Soc.*, Vol. 62, 62–65.
Lange, G., Schimmöller, H., 1967, Beispiel einer statistischen Auswertung von Härtemessungen. *Materialprüfung*, Vol. 9, No. 4, 143–144.
Larsen-Basse, J., 1993, Effect of atmospheric humidity on the dynamic fracture strength of SiC abrasives. *Wear*, Vol. 166, 93–100.
Laugier, M.T., 1986, Effect of hardness on erosion of WC-Co composites. *J. Mater. Sci.*, Vol. 21, 3548–3550.
Lawn, B.R., 1993, *Fracture of Brittle Solids*. 2nd edition, Cambridge University Press, Cambridge.
Leahy, W., Young, T., Buggy, M., Barron, V., 2003, A study of environmentally friendly titanium pretreatments for adhesive bonding to a thermoplastic composite. *Materialwissenschaft und Werkstofftechnik*, Vol. 34, 415–420.
Lecoffe, Y., Bunazzi, X.H., Jouet, F., Huet, D., 1993, Travel—a real time particle velocity measuring system for use in shot peening. *Proc. 5th Int. Conf. Shot Blasting*, Oxford, 61–68.
Leidheiser, H., Funke, W., 1987, Water disbondment and wet adhesion of organic coatings on metals: a review and interpretation. *JOCCA*, No. 5, 121–132.
Leistikow, S., Kraft, R., 1974, Verbesserung der Heißdampf-Korrosionsbeständigkeit von Incoloy Alloy 800-Rohrmaterial durch verformende Oberflächenvorbehandlungen. *Werkstoffe und Korrosion*, Vol. 25, No. 1, 12–25.
Lepand, H., 1963, Neue Erkenntnisse beim Strahlentzundern von Drähten und Stäben. *Stahl Eisen*, Vol. 83, No. 14, 866–870.
Levin, B.F., Vecchio, K.S., DuPont, J.N., Marder, A.R., 1999, Modeling solid-particle erosion of ductile alloys. *Metall. Mater. Trans.*, Vol. 30A, 1763–1774.
Levy, A., 1995, *Solid Particle Erosion and Erosion-Corrosion of Metals*. ASM International, Materials Park.
Li, J., Hutchings, I.M., 1990, Resistance of cast polyurethane elastomers to solid particle erosion. *Wear*, Vol. 135, 293–303.
Li, L., Kim, J.H., Shukor, M.H., 2005, Grit blast assisted laser milling/grooving of metallic alloys. *Ann. CIRP*, Vol. 54, 183–186.
Lin, C.K., Berndt, C.C., 1994, Measurement and analysis of adhesion strength for thermally sprayed coatings. *J. Thermal Spray Technol.*, Vol. 3, No. 1, 75–104.

Lin, C., Tinh, N., McNight, M.E., 1992, Relation between AC impedance data and degradation of coated steel. *Prog. Org. Coat.*, Vol. 20, 169–186.

Lin, C.Y., Chang, C.H., Tsai, W.T., 2004, Morphological and microstructural aspects of metal dusting on 304L stainless steel with different surface treatments. *Oxidation Met.*, Vol. 62, No. 3/4, 153–174.

Linnemann, W., 1997, Method and apparatus for determining a real velocity distribution of solid particles travelling in a gas carrier flow for shot peening. *U.S. Patent* No. 5,691,483, Nov. 25, 1997.

Linnemann, W., Kopp, R., Kittel, S., Wüstenfeld, F., 1996, Shot velocity measurements. *Proc. 6th Int. Conf. Shot Peening*, San Francisco, 118–129.

Liu, J., Berry, D.H., Seebergh, J.E., Osborne, J.H., Blohowiak, K.Y., 2006, Effect of surface morphology on crack growth at a sol-gel reinforced epoxy/aluminium interface. *J. of Adhesion*, Vol. 82, 487–516.

Locci, I.V., MacKay, R.A., Garg, A., Ritzert, F., 2004, Successful surface treatment for reducing instabilities in advanced nickel-base superalloys for turbine blades. *NASA/TM-2004-212920*, March 2004.

Loh, W.K., Crocombe, A.D., Wahab, M.M., Watts, J.F., Ashcroft, I.A., 2002, The effect of moisture on the failure locus and fracture energy of an epoxy-steel interface. *J. Adhes. Sci. Technol.*, Vol. 16, 1407–1429.

Lukschandel, J., 1973, Die Sandstrahldüse—ein Wirtschaftlichkeitsfaktor. *Fachberichte Oberflächentechnik*, Vol. 11, No. 11, 273–275.

Luo, S., Zheng, Y., Li, J., Ke, W., 2001, Slurry erosion resistance of fusion-bonded epoxy powder coating. *Wear*, Vol. 249, 733–738.

Luo, S., Zheng, Y., Li, J., Ke, W., 2003, Effect of curing degree and fillers on slurry erosion behavior of fusion-bonded epoxy powder coatings. *Wear*, Vol. 254, 292–297.

Lyras, L.G., 1991, The cost of lead paint removal: achieving realistic bid prices. *J. Protect. Coat. Lin.*, Vol. 11, 56–63.

Ma, Z., Cao, S., Wang, F., Liu, Y., Xiao, X., 2006, Effect of substrate surface roughness on the splat formation in the HVOF spraying of WC-Co. *Trans. Beijing Inst. Technol.*, Vol. 26, No. 4, 373–376.

Machu, W., 1963, Über den Einfluß einer Vorbehandlung vor dem Phosphatieren auf die Eigenschaften von Phosphatschichten. *Werkstoffe und Korrosion*, Vol. 16, No. 7, 566–574.

Madany, I.M., Al-Sayed, M.H., Raveedran, E., 1991, Utilisation of copper blasting grit waste as a construction material. *Waste Manage.*, Vol. 11, 35–40.

Magnee, A., 1995, Generalized law of erosion: application to various alloys and intermetallics. *Wear*, Vol. 181–183, 500–510.

Mannelqvist, A., Groth, M.R., 2001, Comparison of fractal analyses methods and fractal dimension for pre-treated stainless steel surfaces and the correlation to adhesive joint strength. *Appl. Phys. A*, Vol. 73, 347–355.

Marcus, D.R., Leung, L.S., Klinzing, G.E., Rizk, F., 1990, *Pneumatic Conveying of Solids*. Chapmann and Hall, London.

Marshall, A.K., 1996, Lead removal with waterjetting. *J. Prot. Coat. Lin.*, Vol. 13, No. 2, 47–51.

Marshall, A.K., 2001, Waterjetting and recoating dockside at the port of Houston authority. *J. Prot. Coat. Lin.*, Vol. 18, No. 5, 63–69.

Marshall, D.B., Lawn, B.R., Evans, A.G., 1982, Elastic/plastic indentation damage in ceramics: lateral crack system. *J. Am. Ceram. Soc.*, Vol. 65, 561–566.

Martin, L., 1997, Untersuchungen der Adhäsion und der Beständigkeit von Beschichtungssystemen für Rohrleitungen. *Dissertation*, Universität Kaiserslautern, Kaiserslautern, Germany.

Martinec, P., 1994, A contribution to the characteristics of mineral abrasives for water jet cutting. *Geomechanics 94* (ed. Z. Rakowski), A.A. Balkema, Rotterdam, 361–365.

Maruyama, T., Kobayashi, T., 2004, Influence of substrate surface roughness on adhesive properties of sprayed coating. *Proc. Therm. Spray 2004, Int. Therm. Spray Conf.*, 266–271.

Maurer, K.F., Castler, L.B., Cullen, M.R., 1995, Making lead paint removal safe in Connecticut, *J. Prot. Coat. Lin.*, Vol. 12, No. 2, 68–76.

McPhee, W.S., 2001, High productivity vacuum blasting system. *Research Report*, Contract-No. DE-AR26-98FT40367, LTC Teletrak, Inc., Alexandria, VA, USA.

McPhee, W.S., Ebadian, 1999, High productivity vacuum blasting system. *Proc. Ind. Partnership Environ. Sci. Technol. Conf.*, Washington, US Dept of Energy.

McPhee, W.S., Lin, C.X., Zheng, B., Kang, H.J., Ade, R., Shea, E., Ebadian, M.A., 2000, High productivity blasting system. *Proc. Ind. Partnership Environ. Sci. Technol. Conf.*, Washington, US Dept of Energy.

Meguid, S.A., Rabie, A.M., 1986, Evaluation of potential techniques for computer control of shot-peening coverage. *Impact Surface Treatment* (ed. S.A. Meguid), Elsevier, London, 208–220.

Mellali, M., Grimaud, A., Fauchais, P., 1994, Parameters controlling the sand blasting substrates for plasma spraying. *Proc. 7th Int. Therm. Spray Conf.*, Boston, MS, June 20–24, 227–232.

Meng, H.C., Ludema, K.C., 1995, Wear models and prediction equations: their form and content. *Wear*, Vol. 181–183, 443–457.

Meunier, P., Lambert, P., 1998, The experience of SNCF in preparing previously painted metal surfaces by UHP waterjetting. *Protect. Coat. Europe*, Vol. 15, No. 9, 34–37.

Meyer, D., Schulz, W.-D., 2001, Minimale Verschmutzung bestimmen—Messung kleinster Restfettbelegungen auf Metalloberflächen. *Metalloberfläche*, Vol. 55, No. 6, 13–18.

Mickelsen, R.L., Johnston, O.E., 1995, Lead exposure during removal of lead-based paint using vacuum blasting. *J. Prot. Coat. Lin.*, Vol. 12, No. 2, 78–84.

Miles, D., 2000, Offshore oil platform surface preparation using the pilant media blasting technology. *Proc. Sem. Increasing Value Coat.*, Orlando, Reprint, 1–8.

Miller, R., 1973, Rapid method for determinig the degree of cleanliness of metal surfaces. *Mater. Prot. Perform.*, Vol. 12, No. 5, 31–36.

Minaki, K., Kitajima, K., Minaki, K., Izawa, M., 2004, Improvement of surface texture of stainless steel by utilizing dry blasting. *Proc. 7th Int. Symp. on Advances in Abrasive Technol.*, Bursa, June 2004, 519–524.

Minaki, K., Kitajima, K., Minaki, K., Izawa, M., Tosha, K., 2005, Improvement of surface texture of stainless steel by utilizing dry blasting: effect of blasting conditions on wettability. *Key Engng. Mater.*, Vol. 291–292, 265–270.

Minaki, K., Kitajima, K., Nakahira, Y., Minaki, K., Izawa, M., Tosha, K., 2007, Improvement of surface texture of stainless steel by utilizing dry blasting. *Key Engng. Mater.*, Vol. 329, 533–538.

Mintrop, H., 1941, Untersuchungen über den Stoß einer Kugel gegen eine ebene Platte. *Forschungsgebiete Ingenieurwesen*, Vol. 12., No. 3, 127–136.

Mitschke, H., 2001, Effects of chloride contamination on the performance of tank and vessel linings. *J. Prot. Coat. Lin.*, Vol. 18, No. 3, 49–56.

Miyazaki, N., 1996, Effect of Crystallization of thermoplastic polyimide resin on erosion rate. *J. Mat. Sci-Lett.*, Vol. 15, 1422–1423.

Mohamed, A., Hamed, A., Lehnig, T., 2003, Supersonic rectangular over-expanded jets of single and two-phase flows. *ISABE 2003*, 11–19.

Momber, A.W., 1995, A generalized abrasive water jet cutting model. *Proc. 8th Am. Water Jet Conf.* (ed. T.J. Labus), Vol. 1, Water Jet Technology Association, St. Louis, 359–371.

Momber, A.W., 2003, *Hydroblasting and Coating of Steel Structures*. Elsevier Applied Science, London.

Momber, A.W., 2004a, Eine Übergangsbedingung beim Strahlverschleiß von Gesteinen und Betonen. *Materialwiss. Werkstofftechn.*, Vol. 35, 151–157.

Momber, A.W., 2004b, Damage to rocks and cementitious materials from solid impact. *Rock Mech. Rock Enging.*, Vol. 37, 57–82.

Momber, A.W., 2005a, *Hydrodemolition of Concrete Substrates and Reinforced Concrete Structures*. Elsevier Applied Science, London.

Momber, A.W., 2005b, Digital image analysis for assessing coated and uncoated surfaces. *J. Protect. Coat. Lin.*, Vol. 22, No. 2, 53–56.

Momber, A.W., 2006, Aspects of salt concentration of prepared steel substrates. *J. Protect. Coat. Lin.*, Vol. 23, No., 2, M2–M8.

Momber, A.W., Koller, S., 2005, Zur Korrosionsschutzwirkung von organischen Beschichtungssystemen auf gestrahlten Stahloberflächen. *Stahlbau*, Vol. 74, No. 10, 780–787.

Momber, A.W., Koller, S., 2007, Effects of surface preparation methods on delamination of organic coatings applied to a metal substrate. *J. Protect. Coat. Lin.*, Vol. 24, in print.

Momber, A.W., Kovacevic, R., 1998, *Principles of Abrasive Water Jet Machining*. Springer-Verlag Ltd., London.

Momber, A.W., Schulz, R.R., 2006, *Betonuntergrund: Eigenschaften—Verfahren—Prüfung*. Birkhäuser Verlag, Basel.

Momber, A.W., Wong, Y.C., 2005a, Overblasting effects on surface properties of low-carbon steel. *J. Coat. Technol.*, Vol. 2, 453–461.

Momber, A.W., Wong, Y.C, 2005b, Geometrical features of wear debris, part I: erosion of ductile steel by solid particle impingement. *J. Mater. Sci.*, Vol. 40, 3517–3522.

Momber, A.W., Kovacevic, R., Kwak, S., 1996, Investigations in abrasive water jet erosion based on wear particle analysis. *ASME J. Tribol.*, Vol. 118, 759–766.

Momber, A.W., Wong, Y., Budidharma, E., Tjo, R., 2002a, Profiling of low-carbon steel with supersonic water jets. *Wear*, Vol. 249, 853–859.

Momber, A.W., Wong, Y.C., Budidharma, E., Tjo, R., 2002b, Hydrodynamic profiling and grit blasting of low-carbon steel. *Tribol. Int.*, Vol. 35, 271–281.

Momber, A.W., Koller, S., Dittmers, H.J., 2004, Effects of surface preparation methods on adhesion of organic coatings to steel substrates. *J. Protect. Coat. Lin.*, Vol. 21, No. 2, 44–50.

Moore, D.R., 2001, Adhesion and fracture of polymeric coatings. *Surf. Coat. Int. Part B Coat. Trans.*, Vol. 84, 243–336.

Morcillo, M., Simancas, J., 1997, Effects of soluble salts on coating life in atmospheric services. *J. Prot. Coat. Lin.*, Vol. 14, No. 9, 40–52.

Morcillo, M., Feliu, S., Simancas, J., 1989a, Korrosionsschutzbeschichtungen für rostige Untergründe. *Farbe Lack*, Vol. 95, No. 10, 726–728.

Morcillo, M., Bastidas, J.M., Simancas, J., Galvan, J.C., 1989b, The effect of the abrasive work mix on paint performance over blasted steel. *Anti Corros.* May, 4–8.

Moreau, C., Gougeon, P., Lamontagne, M., 1995, Influence of substrate preparation on the flattening and cooling of plasma-sprayed particles. *J. Therm. Spray Technol.*, Vol. 4, No. 1, 25–33.

Morris, M., 2000, Update: evaluating UHP waterjetting as preparation for ballast tank coating. *Protect. Coat. Europe*, Vol. 5, No. 9, 54–59.

Münster, R., Spähn, H., 1979, Kann das Beizen von Schweißnähten austenitischer CrNi-Stähle durch andere Verfahren ersetzt werden? *Zeitschrift Werkstofftechnik*, Vol. 10, 37–42.

Murugesh, L., Srinivasan, S., Scattergood, R.O., 1991, Models and material properties for erosion of ceramics. *J. Mater. Eng..*, Vol. 13, 55–61.

Myshanov, A.I., Shirokov, N.N., 1981, Flow of a two-phase medium in a Laval nozzle. *Fluid Dyn.*, Vol. 16, No. 1, 83–86.

Nadkarni, V.S., Sharma, M.C., 1996, Some aspects of mass flow control of shots in pneumatic systems. *Shot Peener*, Vol. 10, No. 3, 30–34.

Neal, D., 1999, Good pipe coating starts with properly prepared steel surface. *Corros. Pipe Protect.*, Vol. 82, No. 3.

Neeb, T., Brockmann, W., Possart, W., Valeske, C., Bockenheimer, C., 2000, Surface modification of metals by mechanical pretreatments. *Proc. 23rd Annual Meeting of the Adhesion Soc.*, February 2000, 437–440.

Neelakantan, M.N., Green, R.G., 1982, The measurement and control of impact finishing processes. *J. Phys. E: Sci. Instrum.*, Vol. 15, 1332–1336.

Neilson, J.H., Gilchrist, A., 1968a, An analytical and experimental investigation of the velocity of particles entrained by the gas flow in nozzles. *J. Fluid Mech.*, Vol. 33, 131–149.

Neilson, J.H., Gilchrist, A., 1968b, Erosion by a stream of solid particles. *Wear*, Vol. 11, 111–122.

Nelson, D., 1996, Stripped clean. *Workboat Magaz.*, Jan./Febr., 52–59.

Nettmann, P., 1936, Kraft- und Luftverbrauch von Sandstrahldüsen. *Automobiltechnische Zeitschrift*, Vol. 39, No. 21, 554–555.

Neumaier, P., 1993, Bestimmung mechanisch-physikalischer Eigenschaften dünner Farb- und Lackschichten. *Farbe Lack*, Vol. 99, No. 8, 683–688.

Neumann, G., 1976, Neue Erkenntnisse beim Entrosten und Entzundern durch Strahlen mit Strahldrahtkorn. *Neue Hütte*, Vol. 21, 45–51.
Neumann, G., 1985, Höhere Effektivität des Druckluftstrahlens—die neue ZKS-Richtlinie R 35–84. *Korrosion*, Vol. 16, 160–164.
Nieth, F., 1955, Die Beschaffenheit der Stahloberfläche bei Anwendung verschiedener Entrostungs- und Entzunderungsverfahren. *Metalloberfläche—Teil A*, Vol. 9, No. 10, 174–178.
Ninham, A.J., Hutchings, I.M., 1983, A computer model for particle velocity calculation in erosion testing. *Proc. 6th Int. Conf. Erosion Liq. Solid Impact* (eds. J.E. Field, N.S. Corney), Cavendish-Laboratory, Cambridge, Paper 50.
NIOSH, 1997, Protecting workers exposed to lead-based paint hazards—a report to congress. DHHS (NIOSH) Publication No. 98–112, New York.
Noetel, K.H., 1987, Korrosionsschutzarbeiten – Sicherheitstechnische und arbeitsmedizinische Aspekte. *Bau-BG*, No. 4, 168–172.
Norsok, 2004, Surface preparation and protective coating. *Norsok Standard M*-501, Standards Norway, Lysaker, June 2004.
NSRP, 1998a, Productivity study of hydroblast removal of coatings. *Final Report*. The National Shipbuilding Research Program, NSRP 0520 N3-96-4, US Department of the Navy.
NSRP, 1998b, User's guide to selection of blasting abrasives. *Final Report*. The National Shipbuilding Research Program, NSRP 0511 N3-95-7, US Department of the Navy.
NWU, 1995, *Issues Impacting Bridge Painting*. FHWA/RD/94/098, Chapter 7, Northwestern University, Evanston, IL, USA, August 1995.
Ochs, H.-J., Maurmann, W., 1996, Strahl- und Beschichtungstechnik an der Ruhrtalbrücke. *Bautenschutz Bausanierung*, No. 6, 17–19.
Oertel, M., 2001, *Prandtl-Führer durch die Strömungslehre*. Viehweg, Braunschweig.
Ognedal, T., Harbak, R., 1998, Noise from sandblasting. *J. Acoust. Soc. Am.*, Vol. 103, No 5, 2922.
Ohlsen, J., 1997, Recycling von Feststoffen beim Wasserabrasivstrahlverfahren. *VDI Fortschritt-Berichte*, Reihe 15, No. 175.
Oosthuizen, P.H., Carscallen, W.E., 1997, *Compressible Fluid Flow*. McGraw-Hill Inc., New York.
Oppermann, T., 1993, Beitrag über die Schwingfestigkeitssteigerungen in Wöhler- und Betriebsfestigkeitsversuchen durch Reinigungsstrahlen und Festwalzen von konventionell und vereinfacht wärmebehandelten bauteilähnlichen Stahlproben. *Dissertation*, TH Darmstadt, Germany.
Osawa, S., Itsukaichi, T., Ahmed, R., 2005, Influence of substrate properties on the impact resistance of WC cermet coatings. *J. Therm. Spray Technol.*, Vol. 14, 495–501.
OSHA, 1993, Permit required confined spaces for general industry. *Title 29 CFR 1910.146*, Final Rule, Dept. of Labor, Jan. 14, 1993.
Otsubo, F., Kishitake, K., Akiyama, T., Terasaki, T., 2003, Characterization of blasted austenitic stainless steel and its corrosion resistance. *J. Thermal Spray Technol.*, Vol. 12, No. 4, 555–559.
Packham, D.E., 2002, Surface roughness and adhesion. *Surfaces, Chemistry and Applications* (eds. M. Chaudhury, A.V. Pocius), Elsevier, Amsterdam, 317–349.
Palm, L., Platz, N., 2000, Innovative Technologien zur Entlackung und Farbbeschichtung von Schiffen im Dock. *Forum Thyssen Krupp*, No. 1, 70–73.
Papini, M., Spelt, J.K., 1997, Organic coating removal by particle impact. *Wear*, Vol. 213, 185–199.
Papini, M., Spelt, J.K., 1998a, The plowing erosion of organic coatings by spherical particles. *Wear*, Vol. 222, 38–58.
Papini, M., Spelt, J.K., 1998b, Indentation-induced buckling of organic coatings—part II: measurements with impacting particles. *Int. J. Mech. Sci.*, Vol. 10, 1061–1068.
Papini, M., Spelt, J.K., 2002, The mechanics of coatings. *The Mechanics of Adhesion* (eds. D.A. Dillard, A.V. Pocius), Elsevier, Amsterdam, 303–350.
Papini, M., Ciampini, D., Krajac, T., Spelt, J.K., 2003, Computer modelling of interference effects in erosion testing: effect of plume shape. *Wear*, Vol. 255, 85–97.
Parslow, G.I., Stephenson, D.J., Strutt, J.E., Tetlow, S., 1997, Paint layer erosion resistance behaviour for use in a multilayer paint erosion indication technique. *Wear*, Vol. 212, 103–109.
Pashatskii, N.V., Syromyatnikov, N.I., Kovshov, A.N., 1970, Discharge of a gas with solid particles from nozzles at critical velocities. *J. Eng. Phys. Thermophys.*, Vol. 18, No. 4, 440–443.

Pashatskii, N.V., Syromyatnikov, N.I., Letnitskii, B.A., 1971, Nozzle wear in two-phase flow. *J. Eng. Phys. Thermophys.*, Vol. 21, No. 1, 841–843.

Paul, K.C., Pal, A.K., Gosh, A.K., Chakraborty, N.R., 2004, Measurements of elastic properties of some coating materials. *Surf. Coat. Int. Part B Coat. Trans.*, Vol. 87, No. B1, 47–50.

Pawlikowski, S., Aniol, S., Pollo, I., Respondek, E., 1966, Bestimmung der Adhäsionskraft von Bitumenmassen an Stahl. *Werkst. Korros.*, Vol. 17, 468–470.

Peltzer, O., 1955, Richtige Strahlmittelauswahl bei der mechanischen Entzunderung von Metallen. *Stahl Eisen*, Vol. 75, No. 17, 1115–1117.

Penn, L.S., Defex, E., 2002, Relation between work of adhesion and work of fracture for simple interfaces. *J. Mater. Sci.*, Vol. 37, 505–513.

Peters, F., Meister, D., 1997, Abblasen von Sandkörnern von einer ebenen Fläche. *Chemie-Ing. Technik*, Vol. 69, No. 4, 510–512.

Petit-Renaud, F., 2002, Optimisation of the shot peening parameters. *Proc. 8th Int. Conf. Shot Peening*, Garmisch-Partenkirchen, 119–129.

Pi, V.N., Hoogstrate, A.M., 2007, Cost optimization of abrasive blasting systems: a new and effective way for using blasting nozzles. *Key Engng. Mater.*, Vol. 329, 323–328.

Piatti, L., Küng, A., Kaiser, A., 1959, Die Benetzung der Oberfläche von Werkstoffen. *Werkst. Korros.*, Vol. 10, 239–243.

Pickles, M.J., Hutchings, I.M., 1997, Scratching testing: a means of characterising the in-service performance of automotive polymers. *Proc. Int. Symp. Automot. Technol Autom.* (ed. D. Roller), ISATA, Florence, 391–298.

Pietsch, S., Kaiser, W.-D., Stratmann, M., 2002, Korrosionsschutzwirkung von Beschichtungen am Defekt—Einfluß der Oberflächenvorbereitung und der Pigmentierung der Grundbeschichtung. *Werkst. Korros.*, Vol. 53, 299–305.

Placke, J., 2005, The importance of air compressor maintenance. *Protect. Coat. Europe*, Vol. 10, No. 10, 17–21.

Plaster, H.J., 1972, *Blast Cleaning and Allied Processes*. Vol. 1, Industrial Newspapers Ltd., London.

Plaster, H.J., 1993, A tribute to Benjamin Chew Tilghman. *Proc. 5th Int. Conf. Shot Peening*, Oxford, 2–9.

Platek, M., 2002, Training for confined space entry. *Protect. Coat. Europe*, Vol. 7, 45–52.

Plitzko, S., Gabelmann, J., Gijs, M.A., 1999 Johannknecht, A., Kolmsee, K., Kraus, J., 1998, Staubminderung von Strahlsystemen. *Die BG*, No. 10, 616–620.

Possart, W., Bockenheimer, C., Valeske, B., 2002, The state of metal surfaces after blasting treatment—part I: technical aluminium. *Surf. Interf. Anal.*, Vol. 33, 687–696.

Potente, H., Krüger, R., 1978, Bedeutung polarer und disperser Oberflächenspannungsanteile von Plastomeren und Beschichtungsstoffen für die Haftfestigkeit von Verbundsystemen. *Farbe Lack*, Vol. 84, 72–75.

Prazak, M., Eremias, B., 1972, A method for measuring the surface roughness factor of metals. *Corros. Sci.*, Vol. 12, 463–468.

Preece, C.M., 1979, Erosion. *Treatise on Materials Science and Technology*, Vol. 16, Academic Press, New York.

Rädeker, W., Wild, M., 1958, Die Entfernbarkeit des Zunders von Stahlblechen. *Stahl Eisen*, Vol. 78, No. 2, 100–103.

Rajesh, J.J., Bijwe, J., Venkataraman, B., Tewari, U.S., 2004, Effect of impinging velocity on the erosive behaviour of polyamides. *Tribol. Int.*, Vol. 37, 219–226.

Ramamurthy, A.C., Lorenzen, W.I., Bless, S.J., 1994, Stone impact damage to automotive paint finishes. *Prog. Org. Coat.*, Vol. 25, 43–71.

Randall, N.X., 2006, Characterization of the surface mechanical properties of paints and polymeric surface coatings. *PACE Conf. 2006*, Tampa, FL, Conference-CD.

Randall, P.M., Kranz, P.B., Sonntag, M.L., Stadelmaier, J.E., 1998, Evaluation of needle gun and abrasive blasting technologies in bridge paint removal practices. *J. Air Waste Manage. Ass.*, Vol. 48, 264–270.

Rao, T.V., Vook, R.W., Meyer, W., 1986, Effect of surface treatments on near surface composition of 316 nuclear grade stainless steel. *J. Vac. Sci.Technol.*, Vol. 4, No. 3, 1604–1607.

Ratner, S.B., Styller, E.E., 1981, Characteristics of impact friction and wear of polymeric materials. *Wear*, Vol. 73, 213–234.

Ravi-Chandar, K., 2004, *Dynamic Fracture*. Elsevier, Amsterdam.

Raykowski, A., Hader, M., Maragno, B., Spelt, J.K., 2001, Blast cleaning of gas turbine components: deposit removal and substrate deformation. *Wear*, Vol. 249, 127–132.

Reade, G.W., Kerr, C., Barker , B., Walsh, F.C., 1998, The importance of substrate surface condition in controlling the porosity of electroless nickel deposits. *Trans. Inst. Met. Finishing*, Vol. 76, No. 4, 149–155.

Reams, C.A., 1939, *Modern Blast Cleaning and Ventilation*. Penton Publications, Cleveland.

Rehacek, K., 1982, Exakte Messung der Eindringhärte von Anstrichfilmen mit der Vickers-Pyramide. *Farbe Lack*, Vol. 88, No. 4, 253–263.

Reiners, E., 1960, Die Prallzerkleinerung von spröden Stoffen bei sehr hohen Aufprallgeschwindig-keiten. *Chemie-Ing.-Technik*, Vol. 32, No. 3, 136–142.

Remmelts, J., 1968, Optimum conditions for blast cleaning of steel plate. *Br. Corros. J.*, Vol. 3, 88–98.

Remmelts, J., 1969, Optimum conditions for blast cleaning of steel plate. *Br. Corros. J.*, Vol. 4, 199–206.

Rhouma, A.B., Braham, C., Fitzpatrick, M.E., Sidhom, H., 2001, Effects of surface preparation on pitting resistance, residual stress, and stress corrosion cracking in austenitic stainless steel. *ASM J. Mater. Eng. Perform.*, Vol. 10, No. 5, 507–514.

Rider, A.N., 1987, Bond durability of grit-blast and silane treated metallic adherends bonded with room temperature curing adhesives. *DSTO-TR*-1187, Department of Defence, Washington.

Rider, A.N., Olsson-Jacques, C.L., Arnott, D.R., 1999, Influence of adherend surface preparation on bond durability. *Surf. Interface Anal.*, Vol. 27, 1055–1063.

Ritter, J.E., Rosenfeld, L.G., 1990, Use of indentation technique for studying delamination of polymeric coatings. *J. Adhes. Sci. Technol.*, Vol. 4, No. 7, 551–571.

Rizk, F., 1973, Pneumatische Förderung von Kunststoffgranulaten in horizontalen Rohrleitungen unter Berücksichtigung des Gewichtseinflusses im Zusammenhang mit Gut- und Rohrwerkstoffeigenschaften, insbesondere im optimalen Förderbereich. *Dissertation*, Universität Karlsruhe, Germany.

Roche, S., Pavan, S., Loubet, J.L., Barbeau, P., Magny, B., 2003, Influence of the substrate characteristics on scratch and indentation properties of UV-cured clearcoats. *Prog. Org.. Coat.*, Vol. 47, 37–48.

Roero, C., 2005, Contact angle measurements of sessile drops deformed by a DC electric field. *High Voltage Laboratory Report., Swiss Federal Institute of Technology*, Zurich, Switzerland.

Roper, H.J., Weaver, R.E., Brandon, J.H., 2005, The effect of peak count or surface roughness on coating performance. *J. Protect. Coat. Lin.*, Vol. 22, No. 7, 52–64.

Roper, H.J., Weaver, E.F., Brandon, J.H., 2006, Peak performance from abrasives. *J. Protect. Coat. Lin.*, Vol. 23, No. 6, 24–31.

Rosenberg, B., Yuan, L., Fulmer, S., 2006, Ergonomics of abrasive blasting: a comparison of high pressure water and steel shot. *Appl. Ergon.*, Vol. 37, 659–667.

Rosenberger, W.A., 1939, *Impact Cleaning*. Penton Publ., Cleveland.

Ruff, A.W., Ives, L.K., 1975, Measurement of solid particle velocity in erosive wear. *Wear*, Vol. 35, 195–199.

Rumpf, H., 1965, Die Einzelkornzerkleinerung als Grundlage einer technischen Zerkleinerungswissenschaft. *Chemie-Ing.-Techn.*, Vol. 37, No. 3, 187–202.

Ruppel, P., Brauer, H., 1990, Prallzerkleinerung durch Serienstoß. *VDI-Forschungshefte*, No. 658, VDI-Verlag, Düsseldorf.

Ruppelt, E., 2003, *Druckluft-Handbuch*. 4th edition, Vulkan-Verlag, Essen.

Rutherford, K.L., Trezona, R.I., Ramamurthy, A.C., Hutchings, I.M., 1997, The abrasive and erosive wear of polymeric paint films. *Wear*, Vol. 203–204, 325–334.

Ruttmann, W., Günther, T., 1965, Verhütung von Spannungsrisskorrosion durch Strahlen mit Stahlschrot, Glasperlen und Elektrokorund. *Werkst. Korros.*, No. 2, 104–108.

Safar, K., 1973, Über den Zusammenhang zwischen der Körnung des Strahlmittels und der Oberflächenrauheit von Gußstücken. *Fachberichte Oberflächentechnik*, Vol. 11, No. 4, 105–110.

Sakamura, Y., Matsumoto, M., Suzuki, T., 2005, High frame-rate imaging surface pressure distribution using a porous pressare-sensitive paint. *Meas. Sci. Technol.*, Vol. 16, 759–765.

Salah-Rousset, N.B., Chaouachi, M.A., Chellouf, A., 1996, Role of surface finishing on pitting corrosion of a duplex stainless steel in seawater. *J. Mater. Engng. Perform.*, Vol. 5, No. 2, 225231.

Salman, A.D., Gorham, D.A., 2000, The fracture of glass spheres. *Powder Technol.*, Vol. 107, 179–185.

Salome, F., Morris, H., 1996, Occupational exposures and hazardous wastes from abrasive blast cleaning. *Proc. 13th Int. Corros. Conf. Towards Corros. Prot.*, Melbourne, November 1996.

Sancaktar, E., Gomatam, R., 2001, A study on the effects of surface roughness on the strength of single lap joints. *J. Adhes. Sci. Technol.*, Vol. 15, 97–117.

Santagata, D.M., Sere, P.R., Elsner, C.I., Di Sarli, A.R., 1998, Evaluation of the surface treatment effect on the corrosion performance of painted coated steel. *Prog. in Organic Coat.*, Vol. 33, 44–54.

Sato, H., Kanai, H., Gijs, M.A., 1999 Kawai, Y., Moritaka, H., Ishida, M., Iwami, H., Takahashi, Y., 2003, Development of metallic sheating for protection of offshore steel structures using seawater resistance stainless steel. *Nippon Steel Technical Report*, No. 87, 37–42.

Schaffner, A., 1997, Untersuchung der Lärmbelastung von Arbeitnehmern an Sandstrahlarbeitsplätzen. *Zeitschrift Lärmbekämpfung*, Vol. 44, 150–154.

Schmithals, P.U., 1961, Die Entfernung des Zunders durch Strahlen. *Stahl Eisen*, Vol. 81, No. 25, 1739–1745.

Schoff, C.K., 1992, Wettability phenomena and coatings. *Modern Approaches to Wettability* (eds. M.E. Schrader, G.I. Loeb), Plenum Press, New York, 375–395.

Scholtes, B., Vöhringer, O., 1993, Ursachen, Ermittlung und Bewertung von Randschichtveränderungen durch Kugelstrahlen. *Materialwiss. Werkstofftech.*, Vol. 24, 421–431.

Schröder, H., 2000, Rechtsgrundlagen bei der Entschichtung von asbesthaltigen Altanstrichen. *Sprechtag der Hafenbautechnischen Gesellschaft*, Magdeburg, 5. April 2000.

Schubert, H., 1988, *Aufbereitung fester mineralischer Rohstoffe*. Bd. 1, VEB Deutscher Verlag für Grundstoffindustrie, Leipzig, 21–68.

Schuh, A., Holzwarth, U., Gijs, M.A., 1999 Kachler, W., Göske, J., Zeiler, G., 2004, Oberflächenuntersuchungen an Al_2O_3-rauhgestrahlten Titanplantaten in der Hüftdoprothetik. *Orthopäde*, Vol. 33, 905–910.

Schulz, M., Drach, C., Ihrig, A., Triebig, G., 2005, Zur Frage einer Bleiintoxikation als Berufskrankheit bei Korrosionsschutzarbeiten. *Arbeitsmed. Sozialmed. Umweltmed.*, Vol. 40, No. 1, 4–10.

Schwarzer, J., Schulze, V., Vöhringer, O., 2002, Finite element simulation of shot peening—a method to evaluate the influence of peening parameters on surface characteristics. *Proc. 8th Int. Conf. Shot Peening*, Garmisch-Partenkirchen, 507–515.

Schwate, W., 1986, *Handbuch Drucklufttechnik*. VEB Deutscher Verlag f. Grundstoffindustrie, Leipzig.

Seavey, M., 1985, Abrasive blasting above 100 psi. *J. Protect. Coat. Lin.*, Vol. 2, No. 7, 26–37.

Settles, G.S., Garg, S.T., 1995, A scientific view of the productivity of abrasive blasting nozzles. *J. Protect. Coat. Lin.*, Vol. 12, No. 4, 28–41 and 101–102.

Settles, G.S., Geppert, S.T., 1997, Redesigning blasting nozzles to improve productivity. *Shot Peener*, Vol. 11, No. 2, 8–12.

Seville, J.K., Tüzün, U., Clift, R., 1997, *Processing of Particulate Solids*. Blackie Academic & Professional, London.

SFSA, 1980, Cast steel abrasives. *SFA Designation: 20–66*. Steel Founders Society of America, Rockey River, OH, USA.

Shanahan, M.E., 1993, Effects of surface flaws on the wettability of solids. *Contact Angle, Wettability and Adhesion* (ed. K.L. Mittal), VSP, Utrecht, 159–171.

Sheldon, G.L., Finnie, I., 1966, The mechanism of material removal in the erosive cutting of brittle matrials. *ASME J. Eng. Ind.,* Vol. 88, 363–400.

Sheldon, G.L., Maji, J., Crowe, C.T., 1977, Erosion of a tube by gas-particle flow. *ASME J. Eng.. Mater. Technol.*, No. 4, 138–142.

Shipway, P.H., Hutchings, I.M., 1993a, Influence of nozzle roughness on condition in a gas-blast erosion rig. *Wear*, Vol. 162–164, 148–158.

Shipway, P.H., Hutchings, I.M., 1993b, Attrition of brittle spheres by fracture under compression and impact loading. *Powder Technol.*, Vol. 76, 23–30.

Shipway, P.H., Hutchings, I.M., 1994, A method for optimizing the particle flux in erosion testing with a gas-blast apparatus. *Wear*, Vol. 174, 169–175.

Shipway, P.H., Hutchings, I.M., 1995, Measurement of coating durability by solid particle erosion. *Surf. Coat. Technol.*, Vol. 71, 1–8.

Siavoshani, S.S., 2001, Effect of substrate properties on molten metal droplet impact. *Master Thesis*, University of Toronto, Toronto, Canada.

Siebel, M.K., Mosher, G.E., 1984, Detecting and controlling vibration. *Mod. Casting*, 34–36.

Siegel, W., 1991, *Pneumatische Förderung*. Vogel-Buchverlag, Würzburg.

Siegmann, S., Brown, C.A., 1998, Investigation of substrate roughness in thermal spraying by a scale-sensitive 3-D-fractal analysis method. *Proc. 15th Int. Therm. Spray Conf.*, Nice, 1998, 831–836.

Siegmann, S., Brown, C.A., 2002, Einfluss der Haftgrundvorbereitung auf die entstehende Topographie und Schichthaftung: ein dreidimensionales Fraktalanalyse-Verfahren. *2. GTV-Kolloquium*, Luckenbach, 2002, 1–11.

Sigloch, H., 2004, *Technische Fluidmechanik*, 5th edition, Springer, Heidelberg.

Singh, S.K., Tambe, S.P., Kumar, D., 2004, Effect of pigmentation on fracture toughness of paint films. *J. Mater. Sci.*, Vol. 39, 2629–2632.

Siviour, C.R., Walley, S.M., Proud, W.G., Field, J.E., 2005, The high strain rate compressive behavior of polycarbonate and polyvinylidene diflouride. *Polymer*, Vol. 46, 12546–12555.

Skowronnek, J., Germer, A., Ladstädter, E., 1991, Dehneigenschaften von Autolacken bei schlagartiger Beanspruchung. *Farbe Lack*, Vol. 97, No. 1, 14–17.

Slikkerveer, P.J., 1999, *Mechanical Etching of Glass by Powder Blasting*. Philips Electronics N.V., Eindhoven.

Slutzky, O., Caprapi, J.J., Pessi, P.L., Meda, J.F., 1988, Grit blasting performance on steel surfaces. *Bull. Electrochem.*, Vol. 4, No. 2, 121–130.

Snyder, G., Beuthin, L., 1989, Abrasive selection: performance and considerations. *J. Protect. Coat. Lin.*, Vol. 6, No. 3, 46–53.

Sobiecki, J.R., Ewertowski, J., Babul, T., Wierzchon, T., 2003, The influence of surface preparation on the properties of tungsten carbide coatings produced by gas-detonation method. *Mater. Sci. Forum*, Vol. 426–432, 2587–2592.

Sobolev, V.V., Guilemany, J.M., Calero, J.A., 2000, Development of coating structure and adhesion during high velocity oxygen-fuel spraying of WC-Co powder on a copper substrate. *J. Thermal Spray Technol.*, Vol. 9, No. 1, 100–106.

Sofyan, B.T., Stefano, M., Pardede, J.H., Sofyan, E., 2005, Characteristics of HVOF WC-Co coating used for rocket nozzle application. *Mater. Forum*, Vol. 29, 147–151.

Solomon, H.D., Delair, R.E., Thyssen, J., 2003, The high-temperature wetting balance and the influence of grit blasting on brazing of IN718. *Weld. J.*, 278–287.

Soltz, G.C., 1991, The effects of substrate contaminants on the life of epoxy coatings submerged in sea water. *National Shipbuilding Research Program*, Tasks No. 3-89-2, March 1991, 1–96.

Sorokin, V.M., Shetulov, D.I., Tsvetkov, V.I., Kuznetsov, V.S., Gafiatov, N., 1977, Influence of surface preparation techniques on the quality of vitreous enamel coatings. *Chem. Petroleum Eng.*, Vol. 13, No. 9, 824–826.

Sorokin, G.M., Eroshkin, V.P., Grigorev, S.P., 1983, Calculation of the depth of penetration of an abrasive particle in abrasive-impact wear. *Chem. Petroleum Eng.*, Vol. 19. No. 6, 230–232.

Spangenberg, M., 1972, Zur Haftfestigkeit von Walzzunder auf unlegiertem Stahl. *Werkst. Korros.*, Vol. 23, 880–886.

Sparks, A.J., Hutchings, I.M., 1993, Effects of erodent recycling in solid particle erosion testing. *Wear*, Vol. 162–164, 139–147.

Spindler, H., 1958, Beeinflussung der ausgeprägten Streckgrenze von weichem Stahl durch Sandstrahlen. *Die Naturwissenschaften*, Vol. 45, No. 23, 566–567.

Spitsberg, I.T., Mumm, D.R., Evans, A.G., 2005, On the failure mechanisms of thermal barrier coatings with diffusion aluminide bond coatings. *Mater. Sci. Eng. A*, Vol. 394, 176–191.

SSPC, 2006, Wet abrasive blast cleaning. SSPC-TR2/NACE/6G198SSPC/NACE *Joint Technical Report*, Final Draft, 2006

SSPC-AB 2, 2004, *Abrasive Specification No. 2: Cleanliness of Recycled Ferrous Metallic Abrasives*. Revised version, The Society for Protective Coatings, New York.

Staia, M.H., Ramos, E., Carrasquero, A., Roman, A., Lesage, J., Chicot, D., Mesmacque, G., 2000, Effect of substrate roughness induced by grit blasting upon adhesion of WC-17%Co thermal sprayed coatings. *Thin Solid Films*, Vol. 377–378, 657–664.

Stallmann, K., Sieber, W., Hauser, H., 1988, Strahlentrosten—Optimierung des Strahlmittels und der Strahlbedingungen. *Materialwiss. Werkstofftech.*, Vol. 19, 133–137.

Stephenson, D., Spear, T., Seymor, M., Cashell, L., 2002, Airborne exposure to heavy metals and total particulate during abrasive blasting using copper slag abrasive. *Appl. Occup. Environ. Hyg.*, Vol. 17, No. 6, 437–443.

Stevenson, A.N., Hutchings, I.M., 1995a, Scaling laws for particle velocity in the gas-blast erosion test. *Wear*, Vol. 181–183, 56–62.

Stevenson, A.N., Hutchings, I.M., 1995b, The influence of nozzle length on the divergence of the erodent particle stream in a gas-blast erosion rig. *Wear*, Vol. 189, 66–69.

STG, 1963, Richtlinien für das Reinigungsstrahlen von Schiffsblechen und Formstahl. *STG 4303*, Schiffbautechnische Gesellschaft, Hamburg, Januar 1963.

Stieglitz, U., 1996, Strahlmittelauswahl und Abfallvermeidung. *J. Oberflächentechnik*, Vol. 36, No. 10, 62–67.

Strizhalo, V.A., Zasimchuk, E.E., Morozov, B.S., Bega, N.D., Kuzema, Y.A., Illjin, A.A., 1974, Effect of sand blasting on the low cycle fatigue of titanium alloys. *Strength Mater.*, Vol. 6, No. 9, 1083–1086.

Strojny, A., Moody, N.R., Emerson, J.A., Even, W.R., Gerberich, W.W., 2000, Interfacial fracture of thin polymer films on aluminium. *Mater. Res. Soc. Symp.*, Vol. 629, 5.13.1–5.13.6.

Tabor, D., 1951, *The Hardness of Metals*. Claredon Press, Oxford.

Taha, R., Al-Alawi, D., Al-Nabhani, M., Pillay, A.E., Al-Hamadi, A., 2001, Recycling of paint-contaminated grit. *J. Environ. Monit.*, Vol. 3, 421–424.

Tamai, Y., Tanaka, S., 1967, Contact angle characteristics and breaking strength of paint plastic films. *J. Appl. Polym. Sci.*, Vol. 11, 297–304.

Tangestanian, P., 1999, Starch media blast cleaning: properties and performance of masking tapes and ages paint films. *Master Thesis*, University of Toronto, Toronto, Canada.

Tangestanian, P., Papini, M., Spelt, J.K., 2001, Starch media blast cleaning of artificially aged paint films. *Wear*, Vol. 248, 128–139.

Tangirala, R., 1998, Computional models of particle size effects on brittle oxide scale erosion. *Master Thesis*, West Virginia University, Morgantown.

Tashiro, H., Tomita, Y., 2004, Numerical study of air compressibility during horizontal pneumatic transport. *Particulate Sci. Technol.*, Vol. 22, 139–149.

Terrat, J.-P., Boissel, J., 1995, A new device for checking surface contamination based upon electrical measurement. *Microchim. Acta*, Vol. 120, 183–193.

Thiruvengadam, A., 1967, The concept of erosion strength. *ASTM STP 408*, American Society for Testing of Material, Philadelphia, 22–41.

Tilghman, B.J., 1870, Improvement in cutting and engraving stone, metal, glass, etc. *US States Patent* 108,408, October 18, 1870.

Timoshenko, S.P., Goodier, J.N., 1970, *Theory of Elasticity*. 3rd edition, McGraw-Hill, New York.

Tinklenberg, G.L., Doezema, D.M., 1998, Health concerns for workers using zinc-rich coatings. *J. Protect. Coat. Lin.*, Vol. 15, 36–46.

Tolpygo, V.K., Clarke, D.R., Murphy, K.S., 2001, The effect of grit blasting on the oxidation behavior of a platinum-modified nickel-aluminide coating. *Metall. Mater. Trans.*, Vol. 32A, 1467–1478.

Tong, J., Zhang, M., Jiang, M., Ren, L., 1998, Free-abrasive wear of an enamel coating. *J. Mater. Sci.*, Vol. 17, 523–525.

Tosha, K., Iida, K., 1990, Stock removal and surface residual stress of grit blasted titanium. *Proc. 4th Int. Conf. Shot Peening*, Tokyo, 435–444.

Tosha, K., Iida, K., 2001, On the area coverage of grit blasting. *Proc. Int. Conf. Shot Peening Blast Cleaning* (ed. M.C. Sharma), Bophal, 160–166.

Trezona, R.I., Hutchings, I.M., 2001, Resistance of paint coatings to multiple solid particle impact: effect of coating thickness and substrate material. *Prog. Org. Coat.*, Vol. 41, 85–92.

Trezona, R.I., Hutchings, I.M., Ramamurthy, A.C., 1997, A new technique for determining the micro-scale abrasion resistance of automotive clearcoats. *Proc. Int. Symp. Automot. Technol. Autom.* (ed. D. Roller), Automotive Automation Ltd, Croydon, 913–920.

Trezona, R.I., Pickles, M.J., Hutchings, I.M., 2000a, A full factorial investigation of the durability of automotive clearcoats. *Tribol. Int.*, Vol. 33, 559–571.

Trezona, R.I., Weakley, A.P., Hutchings, I.M., 2000b, Effect of weathering on the mechanical durability of automotive clearcoats. *Surf. Coat. Int.*, Vol. 83, 580–587.

Trotter, L.E., 2001, Comparison of surface preparation using different methods. *Proc. 11th Am. Waterjet Conf.* (ed. M. Hashish), WJTA, St. Louis, 745–763.

Truelove, R.K., 1966, Shotblasted ships plate—the significance of profile and its effect on the performance of protective coatings. *J. Oil Colour Chem. Assoc.*, Vol. 49, No. 1, 57–88.

Trujillo, M., Sadki, M., 2004, Sensitivity analysis for texture models applied to rust steel classification. *Mach. Vis. Appl. Ind. Insp.*, XII (eds. J.R. Price, F. Meriaudeau), Vol. 5303, SPIE Bellingham, 161–169.

Uetz, H., 1986, *Abrasion und Erosion*. Carl Hanser Verlag, München-Wien.

Uetz, H., Föhl, J., 1978, Wear as an energy transformation process. *Wear*, Vol. 49, 253–264.

Uetz, H., Gommel, G., 1966, Temperaturerhöhung und elektrische Aufladung beim Stoss einer Stahlkugel gegen eine Stahlplatte. *Wear*, Vol. 9, 282–296.

Uferer, R., 1992, Optimales Druckluftstrahlen unter variablen Bedingungen. *Dissertation*, Universität Karlsruhe, Germany.

Uferer, R., 1993, Optimales Druckluftstrahlen unter variablen Bedingungen. *J. Oberflächentechnik*, Vol. 33, No. 7, 36–40.

Uhlendorf, H.-J., 2000, Korrosionsschutzmaßnahmen an Hafenanlagen in der Jade. *Hansa*, Vol. 137, No. 8, 75–79.

Uhlmann, E., El Mernissi, A., Dittberger, J., Krieg, M., 2003, Einfluss des Strahlmittels beim Druckluftstrahlen. *J. Oberflächentechnik*, Vol. 43, No. 2, 62–70.

Uhlmann, E., El Mernissi, A., Hollan, R., 2006, Adhäsive Oberflächen-Eigenschaften: Was bringt das Trockeneisstrahlen? *J. Oberflächentechnik*, Vol. 46, No. 2, 44–47.

Urbanovich, L.I., Kramchenkov, E.M., Chunosov, Y.N., 1995, Effect of the parameters of impact action and mechanical and thermal properties of materials on the intensity of their gas-abrasive erosion. *Mater. Sci.*, Vol. 31, No. 2, 263–267.

Vakula, L.V., Pritykin, L.M., 1991, *Polymer Adhesion: Physico-Chemical Principles*. Ellis Horwood, New York.

Van den Brand, J., van Gils, S., Terryn, H., Sivel, V.G., de Witt, J.H., 2004, Changes in epoxy-coated aluminium due to exposure to water. *Progr. Organic Coat.*, Vol. 51, 351–364.

Van der Kaaden, 1994, Wet blasting studied to replace dry blasting in Netherlands shipyards. *J. Protect. Coat. Lin.*, Vol. 11, No. 5, 79–86.

Van Ooij, W.J., 1984, Interfacial interactions between coatings and metals related to adhesion and corrosion protection. *Organic Coatings: Science and Technology* (ed. G.D. Parfitt), Athens, Greece, 1984, 277–289.

Van Rooijen, R.G., Sinke, J., van der Zwaag, S., 2005, Improving the adhesion of thin stainless steel sheets for fibre laminate (FML) applications. *J. Adhes. Sci. Technol.*, Vol. 19, No. 16, 1387–1396.

Van Tijum, R., De Hosson, J.T., 2005, Effects of self-affine surface roughness on the adhesion of metal-polymer interfaces. *J. Mater. Sci.*, Vol. 40, 3503–3508.

Varacalle, D.J., Lundberg, L.B., Hartley, R.S., Walker, J., Riggs, W.L., 1995, Surface preparation via grit-blasting for thermal spraying. *Proc. 8th Natl. Therm. Spray Conf.*, Houston, TX.

Varacalle, D.J., Guillen, D.P., Deason, D.M., Rhodaberger, W., Sampson, E., 2006, Effect of grit-blasting on substrate roughness and coating adhesion. *J. Therm. Spray Technol.*, Vol. 15, No. 3, 348–355.

Vasek, J., Martinec, P., Foldyna, J., 1993, Influence of properties of garnet on AWJ cutting process. *Proc. 7th Am. Water Jet Conf.*, (ed. M. Hashish), Vol. 1, Water Jet Technology Association, St. Louis, 365–387.

VDI, 1987, Einwirkung mechanischer Schwingungen auf den Menschen—Beurteilung, *VDI-Richtlinie 2057/Blatt 3*, Mai 1987.

Verspui, M.A., With G., Dekkers, E.C., 1997, A crusher for single particle testing. *Rev. Sci. Instrum.*, Vol. 63, No. 3, 1553–1556.

Vesga, L.F., Vera, E., Panqueva, J.H., 2000, Use of electrochemical impedance spectroscopy to evaluate the performance of a primer applied under different surface preparation methods. *Prog. Org. Coat.*, Vol. 39, 61–65.

Villafuerte, J.C., Kerr, H.W., 1993, The effect of abrasive cleaning on columnar-to-equiaxed transitions in ferritic stainless steel GTA welds. *International Trends in Welding Science and Technology* (eds. S.A. David, J.M. Vitek), ASM International, Materials Park, 187–191.

Vincent, L.D., 2001, The importance of wetting a substrate. *Mater. Perform.*, No. 2, 40–41.

Wadell, H., 1933, Sphericity and roundness of rock particles. *J. Geol.*, Vol. 41, 316–331.

Wagner, W., 1990, *Strömungstechnik und Druckverlustberechnung*. Vogel Buchverlag, 2nd Ed., Würzburg.

Walley, S.M., Field, J.E., 1987, The erosion and deformation of polyethylene by solid-particle impact. *Philos. Trans. R. Soc. London*, Vol. A321, 277–303.

Walley, S.M., Field, J.E., Yennadhiou, P., 1984, Single solid particle impact erosion damage on polypropylene. *Wear*, Vol. 100, 263–280.

Walley, S.M., Field, J.E., Greenglass, M., 1987, An impact and erosion study of polyetheretherketone. *Wear*, Vol. 114, 59–71.

Watts, J.F., Dempster, B.R., 1992, A comparative study of the influence of surface pretreatment on the failure characteristics of adhesively bonded titanium. *Surf. Interface Anal.*, Vol. 19, 115–120.

Weber, M., 1974, *Strömungs-Fördertechnik*. Krauskopf, Mainz.

Weidenhaupt, W., 1970, Über den Einfluß der Entzunderungs- und Ziehbedingungen auf die Oberflächen-Feingestalt von Stab- und Profilstahl. *Dissertation*, RWTH Aachen, Germany.

Weldon, D.G., Bochan, A., Schleiden, M., 1987, The effect of oil, grease, and salts on coating performance—a laboratory evaluation. *J. Protect. Coat. Lin.*, Vol. 17, No. 6, 46–55.

Wellinger, K., Gommel, G., 1967, Vielfachstoßuntersuchungen Stahlkugel—Stahlplatte im Zusammenhang mit Strahlmittelzertrümmerung und Strahlverschleiß. *Arch. Eisenhüttenwesen*, Vol. 38, No. 5, 355–362.

Wellinger, K., Uetz, H., 1955, Gleitverschleiß, Spülverschleiß, Strahlverschleiß unter der Wirkung von körnigen Stoffen. *VDI-Forschungshefte*, No. 449, 1–40.

Wellinger, K., Uetz, H., Gommel, G., 1962, Gütekennwerte von Strahlmitteln und deren Veränderung während des Strahlvorganges. *Stahl Eisen*, Vol. 82, No. 21, 1436–1445.

Wenzel, R.W., 1936, Resistance of solid surfaces to wetting by water. *Ind. Eng. Chem.*, Vol. 28, 988–994.

Werner, M., Kauw, V., 1991, High pressure water jet system—a new process for cleaning defective mortar joints in historic masonry. *Proc. 9th Int. Brick/Block Masonry Conf.*, Vol. 3, Berlin, 1639–1644.

Wiederhorn, S.M., Lawn, B.R., 1979, Strength degradation of glass impacted with sharp particles. *J. Am. Ceram Soc.*, Vol. 62, 66–70.

Wigren, J., 1988, Grit-blasting as surface preparation before plasma spraying. *Thermal Spray—Advances in Coating Technology* (ed. D.L. Houck), ASM International, Materials Park, 99–104.

Wille, R., 2005, *Strömungslehre*. 8. Auflage, Springer, Berlin.

Winter, R.E., Hutchings, I.M., 1974, Solid particle erosion studies using single angular particles. *Wear*, Vol. 29, 181–194.

Wirtz, H., 1962, *Strahlverfahrenstechnik*. Prost & Meiner-Verlag, Coburg.

Wolak, J., Worm, P., Patterson, I., Bodoia, J., 1977, Parameters affecting the velocity of particles in an abrasive jet. *ASME J. Eng. Mater. Technol.*, Vol. 99, No. 4, 147–152.

Wood, G.C., Hodgkiess, T., 1972, The hardness of oxides at ambient temperatures. *Werkst. Korros.*, Vol. 23, 766–773.

Wood., R.J.K., 1999, The sand erosion performance of coatings. *Mater. Designs*, Vol. 20, 179–191.

Xie, L., Sohn, Y., Jordan, E.H., Gell, M., 2003, The effect of bond coat grit blasting on the durability and thermally grown oxide stress in an electron beam physical vapor deposited thermal barrier coating. *Surface Coat. Technol.*, Vol. 176, 57–66.

Yabuki, A., Matsumura, M., 1999, Theoretical equation of the critical impact velocity in solid particles impact erosion. *Wear*, Vol. 233–235, 476–483.

Yabuki, A.; Matsuwaki, K.; Matsumura, M., 1999, Critical impact velocity in the solid particles erosion of metallic materials. *Wear*, Vol. 233–235, 468–475.

Yankee, S.J., Bletka, B.J., Salsbury, R.L., 1991, Quality control of hydroxylapatite coatings: the surface preparation stage. *Proc. 4th Natl. Therm. Spray Conf.*, Pittsburgh, PA, May 4–10, 475–479.

Yashima. S., Kanda, Y., Sano, S., 1987, Relationships between particle size and fracture energy or impact velocity required to fracture as estimated for single particle crushing. *Powder Technol.*, Vol. 51, 277–282.

You, C., Oh, S., Kim, S., 2001, Influences of heating condition and substrate-surface roughness on the characteristics of sol-gel-derived hydroxyapatite coatings. *J. Sol-Gel Sci. Technol.*, Vol. 21, 49–54.

Zaat, J.H., 1960, Voruntersuchungen über die Strahlreinigung von Stahlkonstruktionen. *Schiff Hafen*, Vol. 12, No. 7, 624–637.

Zahavi, J., Schmitt, G.F., 1981, Solid particle erosion of polymeric coatings. *Wear*, Vol. 71, 191–210.

Zahavi, J., Schmitt, G.F., 1982, Solid particle erosion of coatings on transparent polycarbonate and reinforced composites. *Selection and Use of Wear Tests for Coatings* (ed. R.G. Bayer), ASTM STP 769, New York, 28–70.

Zehnder, A.T., Ramamurthy, A.C., Bless, S.J., Brar, N.S., 1993, Stone impact damage to automotive paint finishes: measurement of temperature rise due to impact. *Int. J. Impact Eng.*, Vol. 13, No. 1, 133–143.

Zhang, B., Zhou, L., 1997, Effect of sandblasting on adhesion strength of diamond coatings. *Thin Solid Films*, Vol. 307, No. 1–2, 21–28.

Zhang, S.W., Wang, D., Yin, W., 1995, Investigation of abrasive erosion of polymers. *J. Mater. Sci.*, Vol. 30, 4561–4566.

Zhang, S., Panat, R., Hsia, K.J., 2003, Influence of surface morphology on the adhesive strength of aluminium/epoxy interfaces. *J. Adhes. Sci. Techn.*, Vol. 17, 1685–1711.

Zieler, W., 1965, Auswahl und Beurteilung von Strahlmitteln unter Berücksichtigung der beim Strahlen erzielbaren Oberflächenbeschaffenheit. *Fachberichte Oberflächentechnik*, Vol. 3, No. 3, 75–84.

Zieler, W.; Lepand, H., 1964, *Strahlen und Strahlmittel*. Carl Hanser Verlag, München.

Zinn, W., Schulz, J., Kopp, R., Scholtes, B., 2002, The influence of the velocity of a peening medium on the almen intensities and residual stress states of shot peened specimens. *Proc. 8th Int. Conf. Shot Peening*, Garmisch-Partenkirchen, 161–166.

Zisman, W.A., 1972, Surface energetics of wetting, spreading, and adhesion. *J. Paint Technol.*, Vol. 44, No. 564, 42–57.

Zolotar, A.I., 1973, Wear of materials under hydroabrasive conditions. *Chem.Petroleum Eng.*, Vol. 9, No. 1, 76–79.

Zorll, U., 1975a, Untersuchungen über Deformation und Rißbildung an Lackschichten bei stoßartiger Belastung. *Farbe Lack*, Vol. 81, 505–509.

Zorll, U., 1975b, Schlagfestigkeitsbestimmung von Blechlackierungen nach dem Kugelstoßversuch. *Metalloberfläche*, Vol. 29, 577–616.

Zorll, U., 1976, Untersuchungen über den Einfluß der Grundbeschichtung auf die Schlagfestigkeit von Zweischichtlackierungen. *Farbe Lack*, Vol. 82, 821–826.

Zorll, U., 1983, Untergrundeinflüsse auf das Verhalten von Korrosionsschutzbeschichtungen bei stoßartiger Belastung. *Werkst. Korros.*, Vol. 34, 514–519.

Zorll, U., 1984, Korrosionsschutz mit Hilfe organischer Schutzschichten und deren Charakterisierung. *Fresnius Z. Anal. Chem.*, Vol. 319, 675–681.

Zosel, A., 1977, Ein Gerät zur Untersuchung der Schlagfestigkeit von Lackfilmen. *Farbe Lack*, Vol. 83, 9–12.

Zouari, B., Touratier, M., 2000, Numerical simulation of aeronautical paint layer decoating. *Finite Elements: Techniques and Developments* (ed. B.H. Topping), Civil-Comp Ltd., Edinburgh, 231–236.

Zouari, B., Touratier, M., 2001, Simulation of decoating of a paint layer by using media blasting. *Proc. 4th Int. ESAFORM Conf. Met. Forming*, University of Liege, 655–657.

Zouari, B., Touratier, M., 2002, Simulation of organic coating removal by particle impact. *Wear*, Vol. 253, 488–497.

Zum Gahr, K.-H., 1987, *Microstructure and Wear of Materials*. Elsevier, Amsterdam.

List of Symbols

$\dot{A}$	Cleaning rate
A_A	Adhesion cross-section
A_a	Auerbach constant
a_C	Contact radius
A_C	Cross-section
A_D	Dynamic stress strain parameter
A_F	Fatigue strength coefficient
A_G	Area of Particle Spread
A_M	Area to be cleaned
A_P	Abrasive particle cross-section
a_P	Particle acceleration
A_R	Rough surface area
A_S	Specific cleaning rate
a_V	Tool acceleration value
A_0	Smooth surface area
c	Speed of sound
C_A	Area coverage
C_B	Energy transfer parameter
C_D	Disposal cost
c_D	Particle drag coefficient
C_E	Equipment cost
C_G	Spray gun current
c_K	Collision number
C_L	Labour cost
c_M	Longitudinal wave velocity
c_P	Isobaric heat capacity
C_P	Abrasive material cost
C_R	Roughness factor
c_R	Particle concentration
C_S	Sutherland parameter
C_{SP}	Specific cost

C_{TP}	Abrasive parameter
c_V	Isochoric heat capacity
C_λ	Friction parameter for abrasive hoses
d^*	Particle size distribution parameter
d_B	Blast pot abrasive outlet valve diameter
d_e	Erosion pit diameter
d_E	LAVAL nozzle exit diameter
d_H	Hose diameter
d_J	Jet diameter
d_N	Nozzle (throat) diameter
d_P	Abrasive particle diameter
d_{PG}	Geometric mean particle diameter
d_{PSt}	Statistical particle diameter
DR	Degree of rusting
D_S	Final splat diameter
d_V	Diameter abrasive metering valve
d_{VK}	Diameter compressor outlet valve
D_0	Initial splat diameter
E_A	Young's modulus abrasive material
E_F	Particle fragmentation energy
E_f	Dust emission factor
E_i	Particle energy stored in workpiece
E_P	Abrasive particle kinetic energy
$\dot{E}_P$	Particle stream energy flow
E_R	Erosion rate
e_R	Coefficient of restitution
E_{SD}	Strain energy density
E_p	Specific energy
E^*	Secondary energy absorption
F_A	Adhesion force
F_C	Contact force
F_D	Drag force
F_f	Volumetric filler fraction
F_P	Abrasive volume fraction
Fr	Froude number
F_R	Jet reaction force
F_W	Weight force
F_X, F_Y	Cutting forces
g	Acceleration
G_N	Grit number
G_{Ic}	Fracture energy (critical energy release rate)
h_A	Enthalpy of air
H_B	Brinell hardness
h_C	Layer thickness
H_d	Dynamic hardness

h_L	Depression depth/lateral crack formation depth
H_M	Target material hardness
H_N	Nozzle material hardness
H_P	Abrasive material hardness
H_v	Vickers hardness
h_Z	Thickness mill scale
H_θ	Contact angle hysteresis
$\dot{I}_A$	Air impulse flow
I_P	Particle impulse
k	Reaction kinetic parameter
k_E	Elastic parameter
K_F	Force ratio
k_H	Internal hose wall roughness
K_R	Mass flow ratio parameter
K_R	Coating ageing parameter
K_S	Mill scale resistance parameter
k_Z	Metering valve flow parameter
K_{Ic}	Fracture toughness
L	Machining geometry parameter
l_C	Crack length
l_H	Hose length
l_N	Nozzle length
L_P	Abrasive particle spacing
L_P*	Relative abrasive particle spacing
L_R	Radial crack length
m	Abrasive mass flow power exponent
M_0	Sieve overflow
Ma	Mach number
$\dot{A}_A$	Air mass flow rate
m_C	Removed coating mass
$\dot{A}_C$	Critical particle mass flow rate
m_D	Dust mass concentration
m_F	Fatigue exponent
m_f	Flow distribution parameter
$\dot{A}_F$	Abrasive flux rate
m_G	Critical abrasive mass
m_M	Removed target mass
$\dot{A}_N$	Abrasive flux rate
m_O	Operator weight
$\dot{m}_P$	Abrasive particle mass
$\dot{m}_P$	Abrasive mass flow rate
m_S	Specific abrasive consumption rate
m_{SC}	Mill scale mass
m_W	Weibull modulus
n_C	Compressor rotor rotational speed

n_d	Particle diameter exponent
n_e	Impact angle exponent
N_F	Fatigue cycle number
n_E	Energy power exponent
n_m	Abrasive mass flow exponent
n_M	Particle size distribution parameter
N_P	Abrasive particle number
n_P	Particle size power exponent
$\dot{N}_P$	Abrasive particle impingement frequency
$\dot{n}_P$	Particle frequency number
N_R	Radial crack number
n_S	Number of passes
n_t	Exposure time power exponent
n_V	Particle velocity exponent
n_ρ	Particle density exponent
p	Static air pressure
$P*$	Power availability
p_0	Atmospheric pressure
p_B	Back pressure
p_C	Threshold air pressure
p_E	Nozzle exit pressure
P_F	Particle fragmentation power
p_G	Gauge pressure
P_H	Theoretical isentropic compressor power
P_K	Actual power rating compressor
P_P	Particle power
p_S	Spray pressure
P_S	Specific power rating compressor
q	Velocity exponent
$\dot{Q}_A$	Air volumetric flow rate
Q_C	Erosion durability
$\dot{Q}_0$	Theoretical compressor air volumetric flow rate
q_0	Unit compressor air volume
Q_t	Specific erosion resistance
R	Mass loss ratio
R_a	Average roughness
R_D	Specific disposal rate
Re	Reynolds number
Re_H	Reynolds number hose flow
R_E	Erosion resistance
R_H	Hardness ratio
r_i	Indent radius
r_i	Scar radius
R_i	Individual gas constant
r_J	Jet radius

R_{max}	Maximum roughness
r_N	Nozzle radius
r_N*	Dimensionless nozzle radius
R_P	Polarization resistance
r_P	Particle radius
r_P*	Dimensionless particle radius
R_{PST}	polarization resistance standard
r_{PL}	Abrasive particle transition radius
r_R	Roughness factor
R_{RF}	Relative roughness factor
R_Y	Average maximum roughness
R_Z	Average maximum roughness
S_{LS}	Spreading coefficient
S_P	Abrasive particle shape parameter
S_R	Peak spacing
S_V	Solid by volume in paint
T	Absolute temperature
t	Time
t_a	Acceleration time
t_B	Blasting time
T_D	Toughness parameter
T_E	Nozzle exit temperature
t_E	Exposure time
t_F	Critical exposure time
t_i	Incubation time
T_K	Absolute temperature after compression
T_N	Normative temperature
t_O	Optimum exposure time
v_A	Air flow velocity
v_{AP}	Saltation velocity
v_C	Abrasive particle threshold velocity
V_C	Crater volume
v_D	Drop velocity
v_{EL}	Threshold particle velocity for elastic response
v_F	Air flow velocity
v_H	Critical abrasive velocity
v_L	Laval velocity
V_M	Removed material volume
$\dot{V}_M$	Volumetric removal rate
v_{min}	Critical conveying velocity
v_N	Nozzle traverse rate
v_{opt}	Optimum air flow velocity
v_P	Particle volume
v_P	Abrasive particle velocity
$\dot{v}_P$	Average abrasive particle velocity

υ_{PL}	Critical abrasive velocity
υ_{Pt}	Threshold abrasive velocity for fragmentation
υ_{rel}	Relative velocity
υ_{S}	Particle settling velocity
υ_{T}	Nozzle traverse rate
W_{A}	Work of adhesion
x	Stand-off distance; dimensional direction
x^*	Dimensionless stand-off distance
x_{w}	Moisture pressure dew point
Y_{M}	Young's modulus target material
Y_{P}	Young's modulus abrasive material
y_{t}	Machining geometry parameter
z	Dimensional direction
α_{B}	Erosion exponent
α_{C}	Crack geometry coefficient
α_{F}	Particle friction exponent
α_{L}	Crack geometry parameter
α_{M}	Contact parameter
α_{N}	Nozzle exit coefficient
α_{P}	Nozzle coefficient
β_{F}	Fatigue parameter
β_{P}	Focus coefficient
χ_{C}	Paint loss correction factor
χ_{G}	Particle geometry parameter
χ_{N}	Nozzle diameter power exponent
χ_{P}	Abrasive assessment parameter
Δh_{C}	Thickness reduction
Δp	Pressure gradient
Δp_{A}	Pressure loss air hose
Δp_{P}	Pressure loss due to abrasive addition
Δp_{T}	Pressure loss abrasive hose
δ_{H}	Thickness laminar boundary layer
δq	Roughness angle
ε	Strain
ε_{0}	Peel strain
ε_{C}	Specific energy parameter
ε_{D}	Mill scale deformation degree
ε_{M}	Inverse specific erosion energy
ε_{Y}	Yield strain
ϕ	Velocity power exponent
ϕ_{D}	Particle disintegration number
ϕ_{F}	Fixture diameter
ϕ_{E}	Erosion efficiency
Φ_{E}	Erosion efficiency
ϕ_{P}	Reduction parameter

γ^{d}	Dispersive specific surface energy
γ_{L}	Specific surface energy – liquid
γ^{P}	Polar specific surface energy
γ_{S}	Specific surface energy – solid
γ_{SL}	Specific surface energy solid–liquid
η_{A}	Dynamic viscosity
η_{C}	Dynamic viscosity of liquefied coating
η_{Kd}	Dynamic losses compressor
η_{Km}	Mechanical losses compressor
η_{N}	Nozzle efficiency
φ	Impact angle
φ_{L}	Laval nozzle coefficient
κ	Isentropic exponent
λ_{A}	Air flow friction parameter
λ_{P}	Abrasive particle flow friction parameter
ν_{A}	Kinematic viscosity
ν_{M}	Poisson ratio target material
ν_{P}	Poisson ratio abrasive material
ω	Nozzle flow parameter
Π_{1}	Dimensionless abrasive mass flow rate
θ_{C}	Contact angle
θ_{J}	Jet expansion angle
θ_{P}	Particle diameter power exponent
ρ_{A}	Gas density
ρ_{B}	Abrasive bulk density
ρ_{C}	Coating material density
ρ_{N}	Normative air density
ρ_{P}	Abrasive material density
ρ_{S}	Particle stream density
σ	Stress
$\sigma*$	Strength parameter
$\sigma_{0.1}$	Elastic deformation limit
σ_{A}	Adhesion strength
σ_{B}	Bond strength
σ_{E}	Failure stress
σ_{f}	Yield stress
σ_{F}	Fatigue strength
σ_{Fr}	Fracture stress
σ_{M}	Adhesion strength mill scale
σ_{N}	Stress normal to interface
σ_{NF}	Normal failure stress
σ_{R}	Residual stress
σ_{Rmax}	Maximum residual stress
σ_{T}	Tensile stress
σ_{V}	Erosion strength

σ_{v_P}	Standard deviation particle velocity
τ_M	Shear failure stress
τ_N	Shear stress
ξ_K	Friction parameter air hose armatures
ξ_P	Friction parameter abrasive hose armatures
ϑ	Celsius temperature
ϑ_R	Rolling temperature
υ_S	Specific gas volume
μ_F	Particle friction parameter
ω_P	Rotational particle speed
Ψ	Outflow function
Ψ_F	Machining parameter
Ψ_M	Dimensionless coefficient
Ψ_N	Empirical coefficient

Index

Erratum

Publisher's Erratum to: Blast Cleaning Technology

Unfortunately, Equation (4.4) of Chapter 4 was printed with errors. The correct Equation (4.4) is given below.

$$P_K = \frac{P_H}{\eta_{Km} \cdot \eta_{Kd}} \quad (4.4)$$

The mechanical losses, typically amounting to 8–12% ($\eta_{Km} = 0.88$–0.92) of the actual power, refer to viscous or frictional losses due to the bearings, the timing and set-up gears. The dynamic losses typically amount to 10–15% ($\eta_{Kd} = 0.85-0.9$)

Page 11. in Table 2.5:
" $*^{a}$" **should read** "σ^{*a}"

Page 408. Line below equation (8.8):
" ψ" **should read** "psi"

MIX
Papier aus verantwortungsvollen Quellen
Paper from responsible sources
FSC® C105338

FSC
www.fsc.org

If you have any concerns about our products,
you can contact us on
ProductSafety@springernature.com

In case Publisher is established outside the EU,
the EU authorized representative is:
Springer Nature Customer Service Center GmbH
Europaplatz 3, 69115 Heidelberg, Germany

Printed by Libri Plureos GmbH
in Hamburg, Germany